Short Story Criticism

Guide to Gale Literary Criticism Series

For criticism on	Consult these Gale series
Authors now living or who died after December 31, 1999	*CONTEMPORARY LITERARY CRITICISM (CLC)*
Authors who died between 1900 and 1999	*TWENTIETH-CENTURY LITERARY CRITICISM (TCLC)*
Authors who died between 1800 and 1899	*NINETEENTH-CENTURY LITERATURE CRITICISM (NCLC)*
Authors who died between 1400 and 1799	*LITERATURE CRITICISM FROM 1400 TO 1800 (LC)* *SHAKESPEAREAN CRITICISM (SC)*
Authors who died before 1400	*CLASSICAL AND MEDIEVAL LITERATURE CRITICISM (CMLC)*
Authors of books for children and young adults	*CHILDREN'S LITERATURE REVIEW (CLR)*
Dramatists	*DRAMA CRITICISM (DC)*
Poets	*POETRY CRITICISM (PC)*
Short story writers	*SHORT STORY CRITICISM (SSC)*
Black writers of the past two hundred years	*BLACK LITERATURE CRITICISM (BLC)* *BLACK LITERATURE CRITICISM SUPPLEMENT (BLCS)*
Hispanic writers of the late nineteenth and twentieth centuries	*HISPANIC LITERATURE CRITICISM (HLC)* *HISPANIC LITERATURE CRITICISM SUPPLEMENT (HLCS)*
Native North American writers and orators of the eighteenth, nineteenth, and twentieth centuries	*NATIVE NORTH AMERICAN LITERATURE (NNAL)*
Major authors from the Renaissance to the present	*WORLD LITERATURE CRITICISM, 1500 TO THE PRESENT (WLC)* *WORLD LITERATURE CRITICISM SUPPLEMENT (WLCS)*

ISSN 0895-9439

Volume 39

Short Story Criticism

Criticism of the Works of Short Fiction Writers

Jenny Cromie
Editor

GALE GROUP
Detroit
New York
San Francisco
London
Boston
Woodbridge, CT

Library of Congress Catalog Card Number 88-641014
ISBN 0-7876-3275-9
ISSN 0895-9439
Printed in the United States of America

10 9 8 7 6 5 4 3 2 1

Contents

Preface

Short Story Criticism (*SSC*) presents significant criticism of the world's greatest short story writers and provides supplementary biographical and bibliographical materials to guide the interested reader to a greater understanding of the authors of short fiction. This series was developed in response to suggestions from librarians serving high school, college, and public library patrons, who had noted a considerable number of requests for critical material on short story writers. Although major short story writers are covered in such Gale series as *Contemporary Literary Criticism* (*CLC*), *Twentieth-Century Literary Criticism* (*TCLC*), *Nineteenth-Century Literature Criticism* (*NCLC*), and *Literature Criticism from 1400 to 1800* (*LC*), librarians perceived the need for a series devoted solely to writers of the short story genre.

Scope of the Series

SSC is designed to serve as an introduction to major short story writers of all eras and nationalities. Since these authors have inspired a great deal of relevant critical material, *SSC* is necessarily selective, and the editors have chosen the most important published criticism to aid readers and students in their research.

Approximately eight to ten authors are included in each volume, and each entry presents a historical survey of the critical response to that author's work. The length of an entry is intended to reflect the amount of critical attention the author has received from critics writing in English and from foreign critics in translation. Every attempt has been made to identify and include the most significant essays on each author's work. In order to provide these important critical pieces, the editors sometimes reprint essays that have appeared elsewhere in Gale's Literary Criticism Series. Such duplication, however, never exceeds twenty percent of an *SSC* volume.

Organization of the Book

An *SSC* entry consists of the following elements:

- The **Author Heading** cites the name under which the author most commonly wrote, followed by birth and death dates. Also located here are any name variations under which an author wrote, including transliterated forms for authors whose native languages use nonroman alphabets. If the author wrote consistently under a pseudonym, the pseudonym will be listed in the author heading and the author's actual name given in parenthesis on the first line of the biographical and critical introduction. Uncertain birth or death dates are indicated by question marks. Single-work entries are preceded by the title of the work and its date of publication.

- The **Introduction** contains background information that introduces the reader to the author and the critical debates surrounding his or her work.

- A **Portrait of the Author** is included when available.

- The list of **Principal Works** is ordered chronologically by date of first publication and lists the most important works by the author. The first section comprises short story collections, novellas, and novella collections. The second section gives information on other major works by the author. For foreign authors, the editors have provided original foreign-language publication information and have selected what are considered the best and most complete English-language editions of their works.

- Reprinted **Criticism** is arranged chronologically in each entry to provide a useful perspective on changes in critical evaluation over time. All short story, novella, and collection titles by the author featured in the entry are printed in boldface type. The critic's name and the date of composition or publication of the critical work are given at the beginning of each piece of criticism. Unsigned criticism is preceded by the title of the source in which it appeared. Footnotes are reprinted at the end of each essay or excerpt. In the case of excerpted criticism, only those footnotes that pertain to the excerpted texts are included.

- Critical essays are prefaced by brief **Annotations** explicating each piece.
- A complete **Bibliographical Citation** of the original essay or book precedes each piece of criticism.
- An annotated bibliography of **Further Reading** appears at the end of each entry and suggests resources for additional study. In some cases, significant essays for which the editors could not obtain reprint rights are included here. Boxed material following the further reading list provides references to other biographical and critical sources on the author in series published by Gale.

Cumulative Indexes

A **Cumulative Author Index** lists all of the authors that appear in a wide variety of reference sources published by the Gale Group, including *SSC*. A complete list of these sources is found facing the first page of the Author Index. The index also includes birth and death dates and cross references between pseudonyms and actual names.

A **Cumulative Nationality Index** lists all authors featured in *SSC* by nationality, followed by the number of the *SSC* volume in which their entry appears.

A **Cumulative Title Index** lists in alphabetical order all short story, novella, and collection titles contained in the *SSC* series. Titles of short story collections, separately published novellas, and novella collections are printed in italics, while titles of individual short stories are printed in roman type with quotation marks. Each title is followed by the author's last name and corresponding volume and page numbers where commentary on the work is located. English-language translations of original foreign-language titles are cross-referenced to the foreign titles so that all references to discussion of a work are combined in one listing.

Citing *Short Story Criticism*

When writing papers, students who quote directly from any volume in the Literature Criticism Series may use the following general format to footnote reprinted criticism. The first example pertains to material drawn from periodicals, the second to material reprinted from books.

Henry James, Jr., "Honoré de Balzac," *The Galaxy* 20 (December 1875), 814-36; reprinted in *Short Story Criticism,* vol. 5, ed. Thomas Votteler (Detroit: The Gale Group), 8-11.

Linda W. Wagner, "The Years of the Locust," *Ellen Glasgow: Beyond Convention* (University of Texas Press, 1982), 50-70; reprinted and excerpted in *Short Story Criticism,* vol. 34, ed. Anna Nesbitt Sheets (Farmington Hills, Mich.: The Gale Group), 80-82.

Suggestions are Welcome

Readers who wish to suggest new features, topics, or authors to appear in future volumes, or who have other suggestions or comments are cordially invited to call, write, or fax the Managing Editor:

Managing Editor, Literary Criticism Series

The Gale Group

27500 Drake Road

Farmington Hills, MI 48331-3535

1-800-347-4253 (GALE)

Fax: 248-699-8054

Acknowledgments

The editors wish to thank the copyright holders of the excerpted criticism included in this volume and the permissions managers of many book and magazine publishing companies for assisting us in securing reproduction rights. We are also grateful to the staffs of the Detroit Public Library, the Library of Congress, the University of Detroit Mercy Library, Wayne State University Purdy/Kresge Library Complex, and the University of Michigan Libraries for making their resources available to us. Following is a list of the copyright holders who have granted us permission to reproduce material in this volume of *SSC*. Every effort has been made to trace copyright, but if omissions have been made, please let us know.

COPYRIGHTED EXCERPTS IN *SSC*, VOLUME 39, WERE REPRODUCED FROM THE FOLLOWING PERIODICALS:

American Literature, v. XXVII, November, 1955; v. 34, May, 1962; v. 46, March, 1974. Copyright © 1955, 1962, 1974, by Duke University Press, Durham, NC. All reproduced by permission.—***American Transcendental Quarterly,*** no. 56, March, 1985. Copyright © 1985 by The University of Rhode Island. Reproduced by permission./ v. 24, 1974. Copyright 1974 by Kenneth Walter Cameron. Reproduced by permission.—***Australian Literary Studies,*** v. 10, May, 1981 for "Proserpina and Pluto, Ariadne and Bacchus: Myth in Patrick White's 'Dead Roses'" by Timothy G.A. Nelson; v. 11, October, 1983, for "'Down at the Dump' And Lacan's *Mirror Stage*" by Veronica Brady. Both reproduced by permission of the respective authors.—***The Australian Quarterly,*** v. XXXVII, 1965.—***Book World-The Washington Post,*** January 28, 1979 for "Fictional Vignettes of Cuba's History" by Dolores M. Martin. © 1979, Washington Post Book World Service/ Washington Post Writers Group. Reproduced by permission of the author.—***Canadian Literature,*** no. 23, Winter, 1965 for "The Enchanted Houses: Leacock's Irony" by D. A. Cameron. Reproduced by permission of the author.—***The CEA Critic,*** v. XXVI, June, 1964; v. 55, Spring/Summer, 1993. Copyright © 1964, 1993 by the College English Association, Inc. Both reproduced by permission.—***Chasqui,*** v. XVII, May, 1988; v. XXI, May, 1992. Both reproduced by permission.—***The Christian Science Monitor,*** v. 56, November 12, 1964 for "Patrick White: The Short Story Pinches" by Robert Kiely. © by Robert Kiely. Reproduced by permission of the author.—***Commonweal,*** v. 81, November 13, 1964. Copyright © 1964 Commonweal Publishing Co., Inc. Reproduced by permission of Commonweal Foundation.—***ESQ: A Journal of the American Renaissance,*** v. 21, 2nd Quarter, 1975. Reproduced by permission.—***The Explicator,*** v. 48, Spring, 1990; v. 50, Spring, 1992; v. 52, Summer, 1994. Copyright © 1990, 1992, 1994 Helen Dwight Reid Educational Foundation. All reproduced with permission of the Helen Dwight Reid Educational Foundation, published by Heldref Publications, 1319 18th Street, NW, Washington, DC 20036-1802.—***Hispania,*** v. 74, December, 1991 for "Language as a Barrier to Communication Between the Classes in Rosario Castellanos's 'La tregua' and Jose Revueltas's 'El lenguaje de nadie'" by Cynthia Duncan. © 1991 The American Association of Teachers of Spanish and Portuguese, Inc. Reproduced by permission of the publisher and the author.—***Humor,*** v. 2, 1989. © 1989. Reproduced by permission of Mouton de Gruyter, a division of Walter de Gruyter & Co.—***Journal of Canadian Fiction,*** no. 19, 1977. Reproduced by permission from Journal of Canadian Fiction, 2050 Mackay St., Montreal, Quebec H3G 2J1, Canada.—***Journal of Canadian Studies/Revue d'études Canadiennes,*** v. 22, Spring, 1987. Reproduced by permission.—***Latin American Literary Review,*** v. VI, Fall-Winter, 1977; v. VII, Spring-Summer, 1979. Both reproduced by permission.—***Letras Femeninas,*** v. XV, Spring, 1989. Reproduced by permission.—***Literature and Medicine,*** v. 7, 1988. © 1988. Reproduced by permission of The Johns Hopkins University Press.—***Literature and Psychology,*** v. XXIV, 1974. © Editor 1974. Reproduced by permission.—***Meanjin Quarterly,*** v. XXIII, 1964.—***Mosaic,*** v. XIV, Spring, 1981. © Mosaic 1981. Acknowledgment of previous publication is herewith made.—***The Nation,*** New York, June 2, 1926; v. 130, June 4, 1930; v. 227, November, 1978. © 1926, 1930, 1978 The Nation magazine/The Nation Company, Inc. All reproduced by permission.—***The National Observer,*** v. 14, January 25, 1975. Reproduced by permission.—***The New England Quarterly,*** v. XLVI, September, 1973 for "Memoranda and Documents: 'The Minster's Black Veil': Shrouded in a Blackness, Ten Times Black" by Robert E. Morsberger. Copyright 1973 by The New England Quarterly. Reproduced by permission of the publisher and the author.—***New Orleans Review,*** v. 12, Spring, 1985. Copyright © 1985 by Loyola University. Reproduced by permission.—***The New Republic,*** v. 172, 1975. © 1975 The New Republic, Inc. Reproduced by permission of The New Republic.—***New York Herald Tribune Books,*** v. 12, December 1, 1929. Copyright © 1929 by The New York Times Company. Reproduced by permission.—***Nineteenth-Century Fiction,*** v. 24, September, 1969, for "'The Minister's Black Veil': Symbol, Meaning, and the Context of Hawthorne's Art" by W. B. Carnochan. Copyright © 1969 by The Regents of the University of California. Reproduced by permission of the publisher and the author.—***Observer Review,*** October 30, 1988. Reproduced by permission.—***Overland,*** March, 1965 for "White's Short Stories" by Andrew Taylor. Reproduced by permission of the publisher and the author.—***Saturday Review,*** v. XLVII, October 31, 1964. © 1964 Saturday Review Magazine, © 1979 General Media International, Inc. Reproduced by permission.—***Semiotica,*** v. 113, 1997. © 1997 by Walter de Gruyter & Co., D-10785 Berlin. Reproduced by permission.—***Southerly,*** v. 24, 1964 for "The Short Stories of Patrick White" by J. F. Burrows. © 1964 by J. F. Burrows. Reproduced by permission of the publisher and the author./v. 24, 1964 for "Writer and Reader" by H. P. Heseltine. © 1964 by H. P. Heseltine. Reproduced by permission of the publisher and the author./ v. 35, 1975 for "Patrick White's 'The Cockatoos,'" by Anthony J. Hassall. © 1975 by Anthony J. Hassall. Reproduced by permission of the publisher and the author.—***Studies in Canadian Literature,*** v. 3, Summer, 1978. Copyright © 1978 Ina Ferris. Reproduced by permission of the editors./ v. 4, Winter, 1979. Copyright © 1979 by T. D. MacLulich. Reproduced by permission of the editors.—***Studies in Short Fiction,*** v. IV, Winter, 1967; v. VII, Spring, 1970; v. 17, Winter, 1980; v. 24, Spring, 1987; v. 25, Winter, 1988; v. 29, Summer, 1992. Copyright 1967, 1970, 1978, 1980, 1984, 1987, 1988, 1992 by Newberry College. All reproduced by permission.—***The Times Literary Supplement,*** October 22, 1964; December 2-8, 1988; January 20, 1989. © The Times Supplements Limited 1964, 1988, 1989. All reproduced from The Times Literary Supplement by permission.—***Westerly,*** v. 40, Autumn, 1995 for "Patrick White's 'Five-Twenty'" by Lee Spinks. Reproduced by permission of the author.—***World Literature Today,*** v. 61, Autumn, 1987. Copyright © 1987 by the University of Oklahoma Press. Reproduced by permission.—***World Literature Written in English,*** v. 14, 1975. © Copyright 1975 WLWE-World Literature Written in English. Reproduced by permission of the publisher.

COPYRIGHTED EXCERPTS IN *SSC*, VOLUME 39, WERE REPRODUCED FROM THE FOLLOWING BOOKS:

Anderson, Helene M. From "Rosario Castellanos and the Structures of Power" in ***Contemporary Women Authors of Latin America.*** Edited by Doris Meyer and Magarite Fernandez Olmos. Brooklyn College Press, 1983. ©1983 by Brooklyn College, The City University of New York. All rights reserved. Reproduced by permission of the editors and the author.—Argyle, Barry. From ***Patrick White.*** Oliver and Boyd LTD, 1975. © Text and Bibliography 1967 Barry Argyle. Reproduced by permission of the author.—Bjorksten, Ingmar. From ***Patrick White: A General Introduction.*** Translated by Stanley Gerson. University of Queensland Press, 1976. English edition © University of Queensland Press, St. Lucia, Queensland, 1976. Reproduced by permission.—Bliss, Carolyn. From "Crusades Against Hoopla and Pain " in ***Critical Essays on Patrick White.*** Edited by Peter Wolfe. G.K. Hall & Co., 1990. Copyright 1990 by Peter Wolfe. All rights reserved. Reproduced with the permission of The Gale Group.—Foster, David William. From ***Studies in the Contemporary Spanish-American Short Story.*** University of Missouri Press, 1979. Copyright © 1979 by The Curators of the University of Missouri. Reproduced by permission.—Friedman, Lenemaja. From ***Shirley Jackson.*** Twayne Publishers, 1975. Copyright © 1975 by G. K. Hall & Co. All rights reserved. Reproduced with the permission of The Gale Group.—Furnival, Chloe. From "Confronting myths of oppression: The short stories of Rosario Castellanos 'Chloe Furnival'" in ***Knives and Angels: Women Writers in Latin America.*** Edited by Susan Bassnett. Zed Books Ltd., 1990. Copyright © Individual contributors, 1990. Editorial copyright © Susan Bassnett. Reproduced by permission.—Hall, Joan Wylie. From ***Shirley Jackson: A Study of the Short Fiction.*** Twayne Publishers, 1993. Copyright 1993 by Twayne Publishers. All rights reserved. Reproduced with the permission of The Gale Group.—Hart, Stephen M. From ***White Ink: Essays on Twentieth-Century Feminine Fiction in Spain and Latin America.*** Tamesis Books Limited, 1993. © Copyright by Tamesis Books Limited, London, 1993. All rights reserved. Reproduced by permission.—Holmes, Charles M. From ***Aldous Huxley and the Way to Reality: From the Early Verse to 'Crome Yellow.'*** Indiana University Press, 1970. Copyright © 1970 by Indiana University Press. Reproduced by permission.—Jackson, Shirley. From "Biography of a Story" in ***Come Along with Me: Part of a Novel, Sixteen Stories, and Three Lectures.*** Edited by Stanley Edgar Hyman. The Viking Press, 1960. Copyright 1948, 1952, © 1960 by Shirley Jackson. Copyright 1944, 1950, © 1962, 1965, 1968 by Stanley Edgar Hyman. All rights reserved. Reproduced by permission of The Viking Press, a division of Penguin Putnam Inc. In the UK by The Linda Allen Literary Agency.—Kempton, Kenneth Payson. From ***Short Stories for Study.*** Harvard University Press, 1953. Copyright 1953 by the President and Fellows of Harvard College. All rights reserved. Reproduced by permission Harvard University Press.—Kiernan, Brian. From ***Patrick White.*** © B. Kiernan 1980. The Macmillan Press, 1980. Reproduced by permission of Macmillan, London and Basingstoke.—Kiernan, Brian. From ***Patrick White.*** © B. Kiernan 1980. The Macmillan Press, 1980. Reproduced by permission of Macmillan, London and Basingstoke.—Myers, David. From the ***Peacocks and the Bourgeoisie.*** Adelaide University Union Press, 1978. Copyright © 1978 by David A. Myers. All rights reserved. Reproduced by permission.—Myers, David. From the ***Peacocks and the Bourgeoisie.*** Adelaide University Union Press, 1978. Copyright © 1978 by David A. Myers. All rights reserved. Reproduced by permission.—Peavler, Terry J. From "Cabrera Infante's Undertow" in ***Structures of Power.*** Edited by Terry J. Peavler and Peter Standish. State University of New York Press, 1996. © 1996 State University of New York. All rights reserved. Reproduced by permission of the State University of New York Press.—Schubert, Maria. From "The Use of Irony in Aldous Huxley's Short Fiction" in ***On Poets and Poetry.*** Edited by Dr. James Hogg. Institut für Anglistik und Amerikanistik, 1984. Reproduced by permission.—Schwartz, Ronald. From ***Nomads, Exiles, & Emigres: The Rebirth of the Latin American Narrative.*** The Scarecrow Press, Inc., 1980. Reproduced by permission.—Shepherd, Ron. From "Narrative Techniques in the Shorter Prose Fiction" in ***Patrick White:***

A Critical Symposium. Edited by R. Shepherd & K. Singh. The Centre for Research in the New Literatures in English, 1978. Copyright © The Centre for Research in the New Literatures in English (CRNLE). Reproduced by permission.—Souza, Raymond D. From ***Guillermo Cabrera Infante: Two Islands, Many Worlds.*** University of Texas Press, 1996. Copyright © 1996 by the University of Texas Press. All rights reserved.—Walsh, William. From ***Patrick White's Fiction.*** Rowman and Littlefield, 1977. © George Allen & Unwin Australia Pty Ltd 1977. Reproduced by permission of HarperCollins Publishers Ltd.—Weigel, John A. From ***Patrick White.*** Twayne Publishers, 1983. Copyright © 1983 by G.K. Hall & Company. All rights reserved. Reproduced with the permission of The Gale Group.—Wilson, R. B. J. From "The Rhetoric of Patrick White's 'Down at the Dump'" in ***Bards, Bohemians, and Bookmen.*** Edited by Leon Cantrell. University of Queensland Press, 1976. © University of Queensland Press, St. Lucia, Queensland, 1976. Reproduced by permission.

PHOTOGRAPHS APPEARING IN *SSC*, VOLUME 39, WERE RECEIVED FROM THE FOLLOWING SOURCES:

Cabera Infante, Guillermo, photograph. AP/Wide World Photos. Reproduced by permission. —Huxley, Aldous, photograph. AP/Wide World Photos. Reproduced by permission.—Jackson, Shirley, photograph. AP/Wide World Photos. Reproduced by permission.—Leacock, Stephen, photograph. AP/Wide World Photos. Reproduced by permission.—White, Patrick, photograph. AP/Wide World Photos. Reproduced by permission.

Guillermo Cabrera Infante
1929–

(Has also written under the pseudonym G. Cain) Cuban-born novelist, short story writer, essayist, critic, scriptwriter, editor, journalist, nonfiction writer, translator, and poet.

INTRODUCTION

Guillermo Cabrera Infante is considered one of Latin America's most original and influential writers. Much of his fiction is set in Havana, where he was raised, and details the repressive and violent social and political climate during the Fulgencio Batista regime prior to the 1959 Cuban Revolution.

BIOGRAPHICAL INFORMATION

Cabrera Infante was born in Gibara, a small city on the northern coast of Cuba. His parents, Guillermo Cabrera and Zoila Infante, founded the local Communist party and were arrested in 1936 because of their political activities. Cabrera Infante was seven years old when his parents were imprisoned under Fulgencio Batista's rule. Following their release from prison, Cabrera Infante's parents continued to suffer political persecution. Blacklisted and unable to find work in Gibara, Cabrera Infante's father decided to move his impoverished family to Havana, where Cabrera Infante later attended the University of Havana. Cabrera Infante developed an interest in literature and left the university in 1948 to pursue a literary career. He edited the journal *Bohemia,* founded the literary magazine *Nueva generación,* and helped establish the Cinemateca de Cuba (Film Library of Cuba). By 1952, Cabrera Infante's writing was censored for its political content, reflecting the author's clandestine activity against the Batista regime. When Fidel Castro seized power in 1959, Cabrera Infante became involved with the new government, serving on the Bureau of Cultural Affairs and as the cultural attaché to Brussels. Following Castro's rise to power, Cabrera Infante also became editor of *Lunes de Revolución,* the literary supplement to the pro-Castro newspaper *Revolución.* In 1961, Castro disbanded *Lunes de Revolución* when its editors protested the censorship of a documentary film directed by Cabrera Infante's brother that depicted Havana's nightlife during the height of Batista's rule. Cabrera Infante published his first short fiction collection, *Así en la paz como en la guerra* (*In Peace as in War*) in 1960. After leaving Cuba in 1965, Cabrera Infante eventually settled in London.

MAJOR WORKS OF SHORT FICTION

Cabrera Infante's short fiction primarily deals with Cuba's political turmoil. The short stories in *Así en la paz como en la guerra* underscore the author's contempt for the Batista dictatorship. "Balada de plomo y yerro" ("Ballad of Lead and Error"), one of the short stories in the collection, takes place in the gangster world of Cuba during the 1950s where political assassination and murders were carried out by the same people the author attempts to provoke in the story. Throughout "Balada de plomo y yerro," a drunken American sings an obscene song in English and, on the grounds that the foul language was an "affront to common decency," Batista's censors jail and fine the author. Cabrera Infante later repudiated *Así en la paz como en la guerra* as overly realistic at the expense of creativity. *Vista del amanecer en el trópico* (1974; *A View of Dawn in the Tropics*), the author's second short fiction collection, has drawn criticism because of its similarity in style and subject matter to *Así en la paz como en la guerra.*

CRITICAL RECEPTION

Both as a novelist and short story writer, Cabrera Infante is praised for his narrative skills, vivid imagery, irreverence, and biting insights. Some critics have compared Cabrera Infante's writing style to that of Ernest Hemingway because the author often intersperses his long, descriptive sentences with short, staccato statements. Other critics have compared Cabrera Infante to Josef Conrad and Vladimir Nabokov because he has written and translated some of his works in English, showing facility with a language other than his own. Cabrera Infante's writing fills the reader "with a heightened awareness of injustice and even evil," said critic Terry J. Peavler.

PRINCIPAL WORKS

Short Fiction

Así en la paz como en la guerra [*In Peace as in War*] 1960

Vista del amanecer en el trópico [*A View of Dawn in the Tropics*] 1974

Other Major Works

Un oficio del siglo XX [as G. Cain] (criticism) 1963

Tres tristes tigres [*Three Trapped Tigers*] (novel) 1967

Wonderwall (screenplay) 1968

Vanishing Point (screenplay) 1970

Under the Volcano (screenplay) 1972

O (essays) 1975

Exorcismos de estilo (essays, poetry, and prose fragments) 1976

Arcadia todas las noches (lectures) 1978

La Habana para un Infante difunto [*Infante's Inferno*] (novel) 1979

Holy Smoke (nonfiction) 1985

CRITICISM

David William Foster (essay date 1977)

SOURCE: "Guillermo Cabrera Infante's 'Vista del amanecer en el tropico' and the Generic Ambiguity of Narrative," in *Studies in the Contemporary Spanish-American Short Story,* University of Missouri Press, 1979, pp. 110-120.

[*In the essay below, which originally appeared in* Caribe *in 1977, Foster explores Cabrera Infante's narrative approach in* View of Dawn in the Tropics.]

> *El general preguntó la hora y un edecán se acercó rápido a musitar: "La que usted quiera, señor Presidente".* (p. 99)[1]

I

While it may be true that ***Vista del amanecer en el trópico*** owes its title as well as many of its narrative segments to material left over from the author's *Tres tristes tigres* (1967), it is undeniable that the distance separating the two works is great and that Cabrera Infante's most recent work of fiction represents a marked change in his writings.[2] The following points constitute basic features of ***Vista*** that any adequate characterization of the work—whether seen as a fragmentary novel or as a loosely connected series of stories[3]—must account for:

1. Narrative texture is the most noteworthy feature. We claim that the texture of a work is the direct manifestation of underlying structures, of its *écriture* as text. Yet, these considerations aside and to focus on only the verbal substance of the text, it is surprising to observe how Cabrera Infante has left behind the norm-breaking linguistic experimentation that distinguishes his *Tres tristes tigres,* José Lezama Lima's *Paradiso,* and Sarduy's *Cobra*—all of which are eminent examples of what Barthes called reader challenging (if not reader defying) *scriptible/writerly* texts. The result is a work that seems to be above all *lectible/writerly,* at least regarding its immediate linguistic expression, which gives the impression of document whose meaning is decidedly transparent. Meaning in the aforementioned novels, of course, is not transparent: whatever meaning that can be purported to underlie the textual *enoncé* is maddeningly elusive. Since the new Latin-American novel is known for its insistence on the nontransparent text whose play of signifiers impedes access to a realm of text-independent meanings, in order to create—to suggest or to insinuate—meanings dependent on the unstable structures of the textual *parole,* Cabrera Infante's shift to a form of pseudo-journalistic expression that seems more document than narrative hopscotch is significant.

2. In ***Vista,*** we encounter a series of fragments whose interrelationship is tenuous. All extensive narratives (save those that suppress any internal division) are made up of fragments, whether the traditional division into chapters or "scenes" or the more experimental division into blocks of narration that are short as such but are tightly interrelated. ***Vista*** follows the pattern of Julio Cortázar's *Rayuela* (1963) rather than that of Augusto Roa Bastos's *Yo el Supremo* (1975), which means a narrative made up of a string of fragments that appear to be autonomous in the sense that, rather than following each other in a continuum, each fragment is isolated graphically to the extent that it begins on a separate page and, if it is especially short, is followed by blank space at the bottom of the page and even by a

blank overleaf. Moreover, each fragment appears in the index with its opening words by way of a title. Since there are 101 fragments in ***Vista,*** the index belongs more to a collection of untitled poems than to a work of fiction. What is particularly significant about this fragmentation—and what sets ***Vista*** off from *Rayuela,* where we can speak of a novel in at least a skeletal fashion, with characters and action-plot trajectory—is that it bespeaks a fundamental ambiguity of genre on Cabrera Infante's part. In other words, it is not clear whether we should speak of an organically structural novel or of a series of short stories, or whether we should speak of fragments that are scenes which, in turn, refer kaleidoscopically to a miscellany of narrative possibilities: an event, an impersonal circumstance, an outstanding individual, even a song or a news item that is spread by word of mouth.

Since the fragments take on the character of autonomous scenes, even when grouped together on the basis of the constant of the *trópico* in the title, the book stands in the end outside the genre of the novel to which *Tres tristes tigres,* when all is said and done, does belong, no matter how hard it may be on occasion to know what is happening in the latter in terms of a unified *fable.* To this extent, ***Vista*** cannot be studied in terms of novel-reading conventions but insists instead on a reading of independent vignettes. Yet, at the same time and due to the organization of the fragments under an umbrella title and our natural desire to seek organic structures where there seems to be only chaos and disorder, the reader discovers common denominators among the fragments in order to bring them together into a homogeneous text, one without gaps on the level of its abstract meaning. By departing from the patterns of easily recognized genres, especially the novel that is based on a trajectory of events and the short story that stands apart from the other stories with which it appears in a collection, the author forces us with unusual emphasis to think about such conventions. We undertake to see how they are applicable to the text at hand, to what extent; and, if they are not applicable, what the conventions are that should be brought to bear in order to achieve a coherent reading of the text.

3. As a result of the foregoing generic ambiguity, ***Vista*** brings into focus the question of extratextual versus intratextual unity.[4] It would be impossible not to notice how the fragments are unified not by the trajectory of persons or events described by the inner action, but by the sweep of Cuban history. This point is made explicitly by the back of the book. But it is also made clear by the internal references of the fragments themselves, where chronological movement and allusions to certain happenings and key figures of Cuba's history are obvious to even the reader who lacks a complete knowledge of the history of the island. It is true that Cabrera Infante can count on a more perfect knowledge on the part of the average reader than would be the case, let us say, if he were dealing with the trajectory of Bolivian history, a country that has not been in the public eye to the same extent as Cuba has been in the last twenty years. It is undeniable that Cabrera Infante's text allows one to read it on various levels, from an approach that what is related is understood as a series of key references to men and events that are part of common knowledge (to which is added "historical fact" in this reading), to a reading where we know that the basis is in history but also that what is narrated is to be taken as history without our having to identify documentarily the points of historical reference. It is probable that an intermediary reading is the most normal or appropriate one, the one that Cabrera Infante counted on implicitly in structuring his stories so as to place emphasis on first what are historically verifiable data and then on what are really fictional elaborations but with a remote and more mythic historical quality.

The end result is a text in which specific extratextual and intratextual knowledge enriches one's reading, but also one in which this knowledge remains more the possibility of concrete historical knowledge and not an obligation imposed on the reader by the author. The effect is at times one of ambiguity or the hint of ambiguity: the reader has the impression that more is going on than he can handle because he has only an imperfect acquaintanceship with Cuban history. Yet, it is an ambiguity that emerges more from the lack of preciseness in the presentation of many of the data, or from a certain obliqueness in the elaboration of the text itself than from the absence of sufficient historical learning on the author's part. One could go so far as to say that such an ambiguity is operant even for the reader who is extensively familiar with Cuban history, since it is an ambiguity that arises functionally from the mode of narration rather than from the formation of the average reader of the text. In this sense, any question concerning Cuban history in ***Vista*** concerns more a trap for an adequate reading of the text and not an inherent feature that necessarily defines as such the nature of that text.

4. The use of the principles of intertextuality—references that are both explicit and oblique to other works of history and literature—as well as the fragmentariness that gives ***Vista*** its particular character contribute to a situation in which the narrative voice, in addition to being multifaceted like that of *Tres tristes tigres,* where we have a text that seems to be self-generating (and self-destructive), depends on the intrinsic nature of each segment, rather than functioning as a "presence" that unites the text as a whole. One could refer to the idea of a pseudo-mythic voice that replaces the perspective of a narrator circumscribed by his limitations as the source of data and opinions (that is, the unreliable narrators of new novel texts that suggest the problem of the inaccessibility of knowledge, such as we have in many of the narrators of Borges's stories). Such a mythic voice insists on a gnosiological primacy based on its being the center whence flow the structures of linguistic expression. It controls expression because it encompasses it as the spokesman of an absolute knowledge as regards the phenomena to be portrayed through the agency of the mythic tale. In primitive, "innocent" contexts, we have myths that lack self-awareness and in which self-contemplation is impossible: they stand as witnesses to an

absolute faith in the expressive power of the word. In the new narrative, the need to achieve distance between the narrator (as the maker of fictions) and the narrative material, as well as to permit the latter to "speak itself," as the cliché goes, or to vanish as a non-meaning that cannot be independent from the narration that articulates it, gives new life to the possibilities of mythic expression whereby the text exists only as the product of *énonciation* by an explicit narrative voice. But, at the same time, in a modern context, where innocence is impossible, where metaliterature—literature that turns in upon itself to engage in self-commentary and self-criticism—becomes an imperative, mythic expression demands dialectics in which the structures of expression embody not only a meaning with an absolute value (the "truth" about something or some experience—in this case, the intrahistorical trajectory of Cuba)—but also an often cutting irony that exposes all of our uncertainties concerning actions, characters, and values that intrahistory represents. In this latter sense, the text can be the expression of a myth while at the same time it bespeaks the strain on myth by modern human ineptness.

Thus, ***Vista*** may be using the anonymity of historical facts and figures to create, on the one hand, a mythic setting in which values are what is most important, but also, on the other, to achieve a demythification of a certain canon of received Cuban history by relating it via a fragmentary narration lacking in one controlling voice as though it were unimportant as a specific story, as if anonymity were a reference to relativity, if not to the cyclical and perennial nature, of the national *gesta.* In this sense, the narration that functions more in terms of the individual fragments than with references to a cohesive voice serves to delineate, rather than a mythic expression that is self-narrating (which is what we associated with epic or mythic texts, characterized by unobtrusive—and, therefore, nonironic—narrators), an ironic and self-challenging text.

II

The foregoing are the features that most distinguish ***Vista***'s *écriture* and that set it off from Cabrera Infante's other writings, despite whatever similarity it may have to them on the basis of the constants that underlie any writer's works. To characterize the fragments' specificity as texts, the following passage will be examined:

> [segmento 4]
>
> Al llegar a una aldea grande, los conquistadores encontraron reunidos en la plaza central a unos dos mil indios, que los esperaban con regalos, mucho pescado y casabe, sentados todos en cuclillas y algunos fumando. Empezaron los indios a repartir la comida cuando un soldado sacó su espada y se lanzó sobre uno de ellos cercenándole la cabeza de un solo tajo. Otros soldados imitaron la acción del primero y sin ninguna provocación empezaron a tirar sablazos a diestra y siniestra. La carnicería se hizo mayor cuando varios soldados entraron en un batey, que era una casa muy grande en la que había reunidos más de quinientos indios, "de los cuales muy pocos tuvieron oportunidad de huir". Cuenta el padre Las Casas: "Iba el arroyo de sangre como si hubieran muerto muchas vacas". Cuando se ordenó una investigación sobre el sangriento incidente, se supo que al ser recibidos los conquistadores con tal amistosidad "pensaron que tanta cortesía era por les matar de seguro".
>
> (p. 17)

In addition to the seemingly cold or detached narrative voice, this segment, which belongs to the first group of texts that deal with the colonization of the island by the Spaniards and the "hosts" of civilization, lends itself to considerations on the point of reference in any code of knowledge and value. In general, ***Vista*** concerns a series of events that satirizes or attacks through satire the official commonplaces of Cuban history (and one will recall that Cabera Infante's political position is both anti-Batista and anti-Castro). Although some of these segments are marked by a truly tragic-pathetic note, Cabrera Infante prefers to focus on his material from a satirical angle where officially propounded pretensions, the kitsch of school texts on Cuban history, and the lachrymose literature of mass taste make up a textual point of reference for the elaboration of his own writing. (For examples of segments of truly tragic-pathetic note, see segment [98], "Primero me quitaron el taller," which deals with the injustices of a social and liberating revolution; and segment [21], "Habian estado jugando," which concerns the Spanish reprisals against independence movements.) What this means is that Cabrera Infante's text degrades another canonical text, either because it forms part of the written elitist tradition or because it is a part of an oral tradition: both cry out for submission into the critical rewriting of iconoclastic literature. Only in this way can the lies, distortions, and mistakes come to surface.

In the segment quoted, we see very well how the process of constructing a text on the degradation of other texts works. On the one hand, we have a story told with all the stylistic flourishes of public-school textbooks: the slightly journalistic tone, made weightier due to more balanced periods. This tone, worthy of an elevated rhetorical standard, is not used to portray the deliberations of a constitutional convention or some other event where such a standard would be an appropriate vehicle of expression, but to report an episode of startling barbarity and military perversion. It is as though this register were being used in a contemporary context to describe police torture, for the values that justify the style or register are in irresolvable conflict with the meaning they convey, and herein lies the deployment of satire for textual degradation. Moreover, this segment contains a reference to Padre de las Casas's chronicle of the Conquest. This reference does not contribute to the neutral journalistic tone, but constitutes rather a rupture with it, to the extent that it is the only sentence in the fragment that establishes the sense most appropriate to the scene in its use of the simile equating the massacre of the Indians with the slaughter of cattle. This play of language is what defines most categorically the essense of the textually elaborated "view" of the tropics put forth by Cabrera Infante's writing.

Another segment that makes a specific issue out of its own textuality is [12], "Dice la historia . . . ," in which there is a hierarchy of references to a slave conspiracy. The segment is made up of four paragraphs. The first one begins with: "Dice la historia . . ." and is followed by a sentence in quotes. The second paragraph opens with "Cuenta la leyenda que . . ." and is followed by the complement introduced by *que,* without quotation marks. The third paragraph, on the other hand, closes the matter with the statement that "En realidad . . ." And the fourth one consists of the single sentence: "Todos los conspiradores fueron ahorcados." In this way, the segment juggles a series of versions, so to speak, on a single matter. History and legend are marked by a single quality that allows them to avoid the central issue: the execution of the conspirators. The proposition of "reality" serves in exchange to put that fact forth, which in the end is the most important one. Thus, it is unquestionable that the text bases its *écriture* on the problematic question of multiple versions of events, versions that disagree with each other, less because truth is relative and unstable, but rather because each version originates in a different understanding of what is important and how it should be presented. The literary text thus defines its own space as a story opposing all other versions and possible texts. See also, in this regard, segment [18], which addresses itself to patriotic poetry: "Los insurrectos lograron tomar. . . ."

One other fragment also suggests the question of fiction and reality in the facts it relates. But here, the text occupies a space in which the distinction is no longer valid or is meaningless:

> [segmento 43]
>
> Los obreros haitianos y jamaiquinos enviaron una delegación a hablar con el hacendado. Decidieron terminar la huelga si recibían el aumento. Todo pareció ir de lo mejor y el hacendado propuso hacer una foto del grupo para conmemorar el acuerdo. Los delegados haitianos y jamaiquinos se colocaron en fila enfrente de la máquina, cubierta con una tela negra. El hacendado salió del grupo para dar una orden a su mayoral. El mayoral destapó la máquina y tranquilamente fusiló con la ametralladora al grupo de delgados. No hubo más quejas de los cortadores de caña en esa zafra y en muchas más por venir.
>
> La historia puede ser real o falsa. Pero los tiempos la hicieron creíble.
>
> (p. 97)

What is most characteristic about this segment is the fact that it discusses in general terms an event of undeniable injustice and moral irresponsibility, this time one that occurred after independence. And one feature that deserves detailed comment is the rhythm of the text between segments that portray the same type of happening but at different moments and in different times in history (the Colonial Period, independence, right-wing dictatorships, socialist government) that are nevertheless homologous in their implications. That is, to say, the segment at hand describes a strike by slaves and Negro workers, and as such is a repetition of an event that is described in segment [12], "Dice la historia . . . ," where the *clases de color* set out to imitate their Haitian counterparts by rising up against Spanish slave owners. This time around it is the Haitian and Jamaican workers who request better working conditions not by demanding a black republic as part of their revolt (an eighteenth-century Enlightenment solution), but a salary increase as part of strike demands (a twentieth-century remedy). The former are hanged, the latter, shot by a machine gun disguised as a camera, which is a brilliant touch and one that symbolizes perfectly the newly dawned age of technology. And, finally, where history, legend, and reality were categorized, in segment [43] we are given a circumstance that is ambivalent as to whether it is fiction or history. What is, thus, at issue is a certain parallelism between the two segments in not only their sociocultural meanings—they are accurate vignettes of an emerging people—but also in their *écriture,* where the tone and essential facts are told as something that is more potentially true than documentarily historic.

This type of segment brings up another question concerning ***Vista***'s *écriture*: how the fragmentation of events and the ambiguity of documentary history result in the participation of figures that are more outlines of a certain form of human conduct than they are independent individuals. It is for this reason that, alongside the ambiguity of historical data, we have the anonymity of historical protagonists. The result is that the personages who appear in Cabrera Infante's stories or texts, many of whom could be easily identified as historical or public names by one type of reader (one certainly in the minority outside of Cuba or a Cuban exile community), do not differ markedly from the sort of character we are accustomed to finding in the *nueva narrativa.*

In a study on how the character-hero of the literature of the last century has given way to the character-*actant* (A. J. Greimas's term) of the contemporary narrative, Jitrik identifies nine key processes. The character-*actant* who exists only to the extent that he intervenes in a fictional text that is not necessarily verisimilar and in a fashion such that we assign him specific structural roles in terms of the overall pattern of the narrative stems from the interest on the part of contemporary fiction in speaking of the world as a structure of circumstances and not as the drama of extravagant personalities. Thus, the character-*actant* is antithetical to the character-hero, who enjoys a well-defined biographical and psychological verisimilitude that gives him the impression of possessing an extratextual autonomy. Undoubtedly, features of this character-*actant,* of this nonexistent cavalier, define the role that Cabrera Infante assigns to the great (but often infamous) figures of Cuban history that parade through his texts:

> 1) *Procedimiento de la "grupalización".* [. . .] un personaje que sea un grupo: es la tentativa de romper la "psicología" radicada en lo individual y proponer una figura más amplia en el interior de la cual se pueden producir desplazamientos—que no se explicitan—y que

> apelan a un nivel más profundo de psiquismo; en el fondo, se trata de volver al momento del mito, más allá del coro que, de todos modos, actuaba como un solo cuerpo aunque de él se desprendieran los personajes. [. . .]: la conjetura se constituye no sólo en cuanto a la "identidad" de los encargados de encarnar la conciencia del grupo, sino en cuanto a la consistencia del grupo mismo, es decir a su posibilidad de ser aprehendido o pensado por lectores acostumbrados a hacer del singular el punto de toda relación con el mundo y del plural una noción que sirve para descripciones de orden general . . .[5]
>
> (p. 82)

There is no doubt that this procedure of categorization (along with those of levelling, metonymy, and disjunction, which is what leads to a kaleidoscopic effect) defines perfectly both the role of individuals and that of events themselves in ***Vista***: participants as well as facts typify metonymically and synecdochically a plural generalness where one has traditionally spoken of a singular trajectory of historically outstanding men and events.

To close this characterization of the texts that make up ***Vista*** and the salient features of their *écriture,* let us examine a segment that exemplifies how Cabrera Infante sees the participation of the character-*actant* within a context shown to be eternal and inalterable. It is in the juxtaposition between the human being as type and his equally paradigmatic circumstance wherein we can see the writer's undeniable humanistic preoccupation, despite his conception of the depersonalized role of the individuals in his texts:

> [segmento 72]
>
> ¿Es cierto que ningún arado se detiene por un moribundo? Los autos pasaron de largo toda la noche mientras el hombre moría a un lado de la carretera. Deben haberlo sacado de la cárcel a medianoche y vinieron y lo mataron aquí. O tal vez ya estaba muerto, torturado, y un carro lo trajo de madrugada y lo dejó junto al laguito. O [tal vez] lo tiraron, al anochecer, de una perseguidora. Le dieron por muerto y el hombre estaba vivo todavía y se estuvo muriendo la noche entera.
>
> Amaneció como siempre. La luna se ocultó temprano y Venus se fue haciendo primero más brillante y después pálida, tenue. Dejó de soplar el viento de tierra, pero había más fresco que al atardecer. Varios gallos cantaron o un solo gallo cantó muchas veces. Los pájaros empezaron a silbar o a piar o a gorjear sin moverse de los árboles. El cielo se hizo azul y luego regresó al violeta, al púrpuro, al rojo, al rosa y más tarde fue naranja y amarillo y blanco al salir el sol. Las nubes llegaron desde la costa. Ahora olía a café. Alguien abrió una cancela. El tráfico se hizo mayor.
>
> El muerto siguió en la cuneta hasta que a media mañana lo levantó el forense.
>
> (p. 163)

Beyond the division of the segment into three parts or "movements," what stands out is the correlation between the first two: the opening paragraph refers to the cruel lot of a political prisoner, while the second alludes to a gorgeous tropical morning. The third paragraph rounds out the juxtaposition with the impersonal journalistic information concerning what happens subsequently to what is now human garbage. What underlies the interfacing of the first two segments is the transition from the personal (the dead man's lot) to the impersonal (the verbal sketch describing the dawn), from an erotesis (the series of rhetorical questions that serve to mark the stages of the first movement) to a lyrical evocation (the use of allusions, a certain type of "emotive" adjective, the references to pleasurable and simple natural phenomena, the use of polysyndeton to reinforce the latter). This rhetorical procedure involving the juxtaposition of two so different verbal subtexts can be identified as the major stylistic feature of segment [72] for inscribing the underlying *écriture,* which in turn concerns the need to structure a portrayal of the violent conflict between the human individual and his socionatural environment.

In the first movement, although there is only one rhetorical question overtly marked with question marks, the subsequent sentences possess an identical interrogative value, as though they were dominated by the abstract clause, "¿Será que . . .?" Thus, we can identify a series of dubitative structures that stress, on the one hand, the ambiguity of this event lost in the night and unknown to the world of the living, while, on the other hand, it calls our attention to how this fact is ambiguous to the extent that it is paradigmatic, typical of this island (not "vale") of tears: "Es cierto . . .?" "Deben [that is, deben de] haberlo sacado . . . ," "O tal vez ya estaba muerto . . . ," "O [tal vez] lo tiraron, al anochecer, de una perseguidora." These four sentences (of the six that make up the paragraph) convey a markedly reserved tone. It is as though it were difficult to establish with any certainty the nature of the events, as though there were too many possible explanations for how a prisoner who has been tortured and is now slowly dying has come to spend the night of his extended agony in a ditch alongside the road.

By way of contrast, the opening sentence of the second movement sets forth, with the authority of a narrator accustomed to executing such verbal portraits, a delightful and eternal scene: "Amaneció como siempre." The extent to which this text is based on an *écriture* of juxtaposition is evident: a movement that dwells on a pathetic and ambiguous human circumstance is correlated with one that places that circumstance within the lush context of a tropical morning. Thus, one could say that, if there is one text in ***Vista*** that synthesizes Cabrera Infante's perspective, his "view" of non-transcendent Cuban history, it is unquestionably this one.

III

Vista is an important collection of texts both for the form adopted for the presentation of Cuba's sociohistorical experience and for its particularly unique *écriture.* This *écriture* is based on a series of principles that substitute for the cohesive novel and the organic collection of autonomous short stories a textuality based on narrative fragments that are neither completely interdependent nor completely autonomous. There are no characters, no "cavaliers," and a documentary precision is lacking that would give the reader facile entrance into extratextual meaning. Thus, he is obliged to maintain his distance and to experience the play of allusions and references as dynamic but nontransparent signifiers. ***Vista*** is, in sum, a collection of texts whose nature is synthesized by a phrase from one of the segments quoted above [43]: "La historia puede ser real o falsa. Pero los tiempos la hicieron creíble".

Notes

1. Guillermo Cabrera Infante, *Vista del amanecer en el trópico* (Barcelona: Editorial Seix Barral, 1974). I know of only two review articles: Eloy González Arguelles, "Guillermo Cabrera Infante: *Vista del amanecer en el trópico,*" *Caribe* 1:2 (1976):121-23; Matías Montes Huidobro, "Review of *Vista del amanecer en el trópico* and *O,*" *Chasqui* 5:2 (1976):81-84.
2. For a representative collection of essays on Cabrera Infante's fiction prior to *Vista,* see Julio Ortega, ed., *Guillermo Cabrera Infante* (Madrid: Ed. Fundamentos, 1974).
3. For what the datum is worth, Editorial Seix Barral published *Vista* in its *Relatos* series.
4. Concerning intertextuality, see Julia Kristeva, *El texto de la novela* (Barcelona: Editorial Lumen, 1974).
5. Noé Jitrik, *El no existente caballero, la idea de personaje y su evolución en la narrative latinoamericana* (Buenos Aires: Ediciones Megápolis, 1975).

Mateo Pardo (review date 1978)

SOURCE: "Bad Art and Good Intentions," in *The Nation,* New York, Vol. 227, No. 15, November 4, 1978, pp. 477-78.

[*In the following review, Pardo faults Cabrera Infante's use of the prose vignette form in* View of Dawn in the Tropics.]

Guillermo Cabrera Infante's new book, ***View of Dawn in the Tropics,*** is a curious example of what can happen when a writer returns to the scenes of his early successes. His admirers will look in vain for the freshness and charm of his first book of short stories or the wild and sometimes exciting verbal experimentation of his first novel. This collection of 101 historical vignettes, printed on 145 largely empty pages, is an attempt, Micheneresque in its audacity and Hemingwayesque in the laconism of its style, to tell the story of Cuba from its geological formation to the present day and for all eternity, but it succeeds only in making one wonder at the immensity of the author's hubris. What, one puzzles, was he thinking of?

The answer lies in Cabrera Infante's earlier work, to which ***View of Dawn in the Tropics*** is related by both title and narrative technique. The title was initially used for an earlier novel which won the Seix Barral prize in Barcelona in 1964. Banned by the Spanish censors because of its prorevolutionary passages, it was expurgated and rewritten by the author and resubmitted with a new title, *Three Trapped Tigers.* It was a great critical success and Cabrera Infante's name was associated by critics with those of Garcia Marquez and Vargas Llosa as another representative of the "boom" in the Latin American novel. The vignette form is also familiar to readers of Cabrera Infante: he used it in his first book, ***Así en la paz como en la guerra,*** published in 1960 and also widely acclaimed by critics.

The fifteen vignettes included in that work recounted some of the heinous crimes committed by the Batista regime against both revolutionaries and nonrevolutionaries. Each was followed by a short story which dealt with Cuban life during the 1950s. The impact of the whole was, at the time, quite powerful. Cabrera Infante was catapulted to fame along with an entire generation of Cuban writers who had turned 30 in 1959. The political and social revolution of the *barbudos* seemed to be bearing its literary fruits. The atmosphere of the period was, as the cliche goes, electric. Nothing seemed impossible because an impossible revolution had triumphed. Cabrera Infante, the editor of the island's newest and most avant garde literary magazine, *Lunes de Revolución,* seemed to be securely placed in the very cockpit of history. But in 1961 the revolutionary government closed *Lunes* down, and Cabrera Infante went to Brussels as a member of the Cuban diplomatic mission. His first novel was not accepted for publication in Cuba and in 1965 he officially defected. He seemed to be exchanging the enviable role of revolutionary writer for the even more enviable one of writer as an anti-Communist exile. Famous and full of promise, he has spent the intervening years apparently producing a mammoth autobiographical novel, *Cuerpos Dirinos,* the prologue of which was published in 1968.

Only a writer of solid talents could have survived the sort of reputation that naturally grew out of such glamorous historical circumstances. Cabrera Infante has not proven to be such a writer. The passage of time has only served to bring out his weaknesses and sap his strengths. The appearance of ***View of Dawn in the Tropics*** in English confirms this. In *Three Trapped Tigers* Cabrera Infante had shown a marvelous ear for colloquial Cuban Spanish and a lively sense of humor that manifested itself in a seemingly unending flow of puns and absurd situations. He sustained a high degree of dramatic tension by the implied contrast between the corrupt night life of Havana and the struggle in the Sierra. But the years have taken their toll and when one reads *Three Trapped Tigers* today one realizes that this implied contrast was at least partially a product of the historical period in which it was first written and one is obliged to lament the amputation to which the work was subjected. Perhaps the passages dealing with the revolutionaries gave it the internally generated equilibrium it sorely lacks today.

Cabrera Infante's early book of short stories has suffered the same fate. The notoriety it gained him seems now to have been largely a product of those exciting early years of the revolution. The vignettes he wrote for it and which contributed so much to his fame seem more than ever to give themselves away for what they are, imitations of Hemingway. And his return to that genre in his new book is a mistake that can be explained only if we assume that he overestimated his own understanding of the vignette form.

Only two great books have been written exclusively in this form, La Bruyere's *Les Caracteres* and Baudelaire's *Le Spleen de Paris.* One is a work of moral and psychological insight while the other is a collection of prose poems. There is no question of linear progression or chronological development in either. Each is composed of parts which seem to bear no necessary relationship to the other. The genre simply doesn't give a writer room to develop any subject that requires characterization or plot. It is meant for quick soundings of the human condition.

Given the above, one can understand why Cabrera Infante was tempted to use this technique. After all, what he has attempted to demonstrate in ***View of Dawn in the Tropics*** is that history is a collection of accidental events, an idiot's tale, and that the true meaning of life lies in the manly stoic virtues that some men and women manifest in their confrontation with it. This is, of course, Papa Hemingway's lesson, and Cabrera Infante is so engrossed by it that he gives us 101 slightly differing versions of it. It is here that one becomes aware of how badly he has miscalculated the possibilities the prose vignette could offer him. He thought that the necessarily accidental relationship between the different vignettes would intensify his basic theme. He goes out of his way to accentuate this effect by eliminating names and dates. But the sequence of the vignettes is chronological. The resulting contradiction destroys the book. On the one hand the reader is expected to derive from a succession of accidentally juxtaposed events the impression that history is absurd while on the other hand he is asked to admire the *macho* and *hembra* heroics of a series of Hemingwayesque souls.

The true essence of man, the reader is asked to believe, is ahistorical. The rub is that in order to make the reader see this, Cabrera Infante has attempted to create the semblance of a historical progression. This false history must be there so that the reader can be led to see its lack of authenticity. The prose vignettes then, must appear to be related in a historical manner. Unfortunately the nature of the prose vignette works against even the appearance of a relationship so that the reader is not at all fooled. He has no need to read the whole book in order to understand what the writer is trying to say because the message is apparent from the first pages and it never changes.

But certainly the road to bad art is paved with good intentions, and one's heart does go out to all those tortured, maimed and killed Cubans who people Cabrera Infante's vignettes. They deserved a better fate in literature as well as in their own lives. They are all quite redundantly exemplary, from the immolated Indian chief who refuses conversion to Christianity because Spaniards can go to heaven, to the mother of the anti-Communist patriot who accuses the present regime of inhumanity and cowardice. They pass before our eyes like shadows in a series of fragmented historical events. Some of these are as well known to those familiar with Cuban history as the Boston Tea Party is to Americans. The burning of the Indian chieftain, or the death of Jose Marti are just two of the many that fall into this category. Even the less familiar events of the Batista period lack freshness here if only because they seem to be variations of those with which the author regaled us in his first book. And two decades of anti-Castro propaganda have familiarized us all with the plight of the Cuban refugee. Cabrera Infante has nothing new to say about their sufferings. What then is one to do with such wisdom as the author deigns to communicate in his final vignette, which I quote in entirety?

> And it will always be there. As someone once said, that long, sad, unfortunate island will be there after the last Indian and after the last Spaniard and after the last of the Cubans, surviving all disasters, eternally washed over by the Gulf Stream: beautiful and green, undying, eternal.

Yes, one is tempted to add, it will even survive ***View of Dawn in the Tropics.***

One parting comment should be made concerning Ms. Levine's translation. On the whole it is quite adequate. In spite of some stylistic awkwardness and a handful of mistranslations (*taller* is a shop and not a theatre, a *mariscal de campo* is a division general not a field marshal, *perseguidoras* are women persecutors not patrol cars and a *turba* is a crowd or rabble not a thug) it does the work no disservice.

Dolores M. Martin (review date 1979)

SOURCE: "Fictional Vignettes of Cuba's History," in *Book World—The Washington Post,* January 28, 1979, p. L4.

[*In the following assessment of* View of Dawn in the Tropics, *Martin considers the vignettes "austere and bitter," adding, "unlike the images of a good film whose overall impact is cohesive and cumulative, the impression left by these sketches is random and sporadic."*]

According to Cuban writer Guillermo Cabrera Infante, he grew up in an atmosphere of "misery, promiscuity and neglect," one of a family of five living in one room and often subsisting on a diet of coffee and milk. How is it, one wonders, that this grandson of a destitute cane-cutter, son of a militant communist worker and product of impeccable proletarian origin, has evolved into one of the most outspoken foes of the Cuban Revolution?

After the fall of Batista in 1959, Cabrera became the editor of *Lunes,* the literary supplement of the daily *Revolución* and possibly the most lively cultural review ever published in Cuba. Its independent policies, however, soon incurred the wrath of orthodox party members, who shut down *Lunes* in 1961 because of the "paper shortage." The incident led to the first open confrontation between the regime and Cuban intellectuals, a confrontation that culminated in 1967 with the widely known censorship of the poet Padilla. The last word, as usual, belonged to Castro, who, in his unique style, laid down the line for Cuban writers: "Art is a weapon of the Revolution" and "Within the Revolution, everything; against the Revolution, nothing." Padilla, who recanted his dissent, remained in Cuba; Cabrera, who flaunted his, went into exile.

Confrontation and censorship notwithstanding, the '60s were prodigious years for the Latin American novel in general and for the Cuban in particular. Among the most astonishing of these novels was Cabrera's *Three Trapped Tigers,* published in 1967 and banned in Cuba. This work is a dazzling assault on Spanish speech by Cuban street-talk, a delightful dissolving of stony, stodgy Castillian prose into something resembling the nonsense of Lewis Carroll, with the bawdiness of Joyce.

View of Dawn in the Tropics was the original title of a much earlier and very different version of *Three Trapped Tigers* which won a Spanish prize but was nonetheless banned by Franco's government in 1964 just as *Tigers* would be banned by Castro's in 1967. Cabrera has since repudiated the 1964 version of ***View of Dawn*** by calling it "a book of absolute socialist realism" and emphasizing that "literature must only have to do with literature," and, presumably, not politics. The question, then, is: Why has Cabrera chosen to write this new version?

Admirers who expect the wonderful exuberance, humor and inventiveness of *Tigers* will be disappointed. The new ***View of Dawn*** is a curiously austere and bitter book, far more reminiscent of the author's early style. His short stories of the '50s (published as ***Asi en la paz como en la guerra*** in Havana in 1960) were separated by 15 historical vignettes which reported with exemplary economy and detachment the atrocities of the Batista regime. ***View of Dawn in the Tropics*** stretches the same form to the limit with more than 100 sketches tracing the history of Cuba from the dawn of man to the dawning of the Revolution. However, the fragile craft of the vignette sinks under so much intention that one wonders if this is the same writer who warned readers of *Tigers* that "any similarity between literature and history is accidental."

The impact of Cabrera's vignettes of the '50s hinged upon the Cuban reader's recognition of the unnamed victims of Batista's atrocities. But what is the non-Cuban reader to make of such cryptic references in ***View of Dawn*** as "the son of a Spanish dancer and a mulatto barber," "the bald little man with the big moustache," or "the big black general?" Even those somewhat familiar with Cuban history may wonder whether one character is Marti and another Maceo or whether the appalling gangster-style killing reported on page 63 is one in which the young Fidel Castro was allegedly involved.

Perhaps Cabrera does not wish his reader to bother with who is who or what is what, but to read on inexorably towards some grim moral about the unchanging venality and brutality in Cuban history. My suspicion is that the fatalism and pessimism of this version of ***View of Dawn*** is the reversal, indeed the mirror image, of the socialist realism and optimism of that earlier version. Instead of the heroic guerillas and liberating progress of 1964, we now have the villainous commissars and despotic regression of 1974.

Nevertheless, some of the sketches (which are very well translated by Jill Levine) have the paradoxical immediacy of good photographs, the illumination of a presence serving to emphasize the shadow of its essence. The vignettes are vivid but, somehow, their ultimate effect is ephemeral. Unlike the images of a good film whose overall impact is cohesive and cumulative, the impression left by these sketches is random and sporadic.

Ronald Schwartz (essay date 1980)

SOURCE: In a review of *View of Dawn in the Tropics*, in *Nomads, Exiles, & Emigres: The Rebirth of the Latin American Narrative,* The Scarecrow Press, Inc., 1980, pp. 65-9.

[*In the following excerpt, Schwartz describes vignettes in* View of Dawn in the Tropics *as imaginative and experimental, and provides an overview of the collection.*]

Cabrera Infante's latest novel, ***View of Dawn in the Tropics,*** is experimental, but is absolutely nothing like his first in style, form, rhythm, size, or characterization. ***View*** is a shorter work, only 141 pages, consisting mainly of a series of small, ironic sketches tracing Cuban history from its earliest times to our own. It contains none of the linguistic pyrotechnics (palindromes, anagrams, etc.), the black (or white) pages, diagrams, drawings, parodies, visual poems, and confusing narrative voices of its predecessor. ***View*** is a somber work, a serious experience, a sobering jolt after *TTT* [*Three Trapped Tigers*]. It contains 103 sections narrated by a single voice (probably Cabrera Infante himself) on history, geography, war, death, and escape. It represents a serious condemnation of Castro's regime.

The series of vignettes contain many cinematic devices. The single unifying pose of the sometimes-elusive narrator is his insistence upon looking at old photographs and interpreting them for us. His reminisences about the wars of 1868, 1898, and 1959 are conceived in cinematic freeze frames that describe a series of usually unidentified protagonists (with one single exception) with the rank of commandant, captain, doctor, or rebel. The length, size, and cinematic style of the sketches are of varying quality, and there are only four literary liaisons or unifying elements between two or three of the 103 vignettes.

The longest entry is a mother's monologue described as a telephone call to the author about the death of her son Pedro Luis Boitel, who died for Cuba under the cruelties of the Castro regime. Cabrera Infante's sketches are, according to the book's dust jacket, "contemporary—vivid and sharp, sometimes cruel and violent, sometimes witty, sometimes sad, frequently deeply ironical, . . . a personal statement of the strategies of history."[1] ***View*** portrays presidents, generals, soldiers, blacks, Spaniards, Americans, rebels, and invaders and reveals the cruelties, hypocrisies, and tragedies that have washed over Cuban soil throughout the centuries. It is Cabrera Infante's sardonic humor, combined with his irresistible, remarkable choice of detail, his ability to pinpoint events without identifying them, that makes his "experimental" ***View*** intriguing, bitterly amusing, and ultimately quite moving as he traverses the centuries of madness of human inhumanity.

One critic viewed the book as the author's attempt "to elevate to myth his central theme, Cuba . . . to stop time and capture the elusive moment and endow it with a certain permanence, creating a new form, the ministory or micronarrative, or perhaps even a poem in prose, counterpointing two realities—the photographic with the real, and saw ***View*** as an exile's condemnation or vindication of his earlier pro-Castro series of short stories ***In Peace as in War.***"[2]

As the book begins, we witness the creation of the island of Cuba at the dawn of time; we go through the exploration, exploitation, and evangelization phases of colonization, aware of the heavy impact of Spain and the dark side of the Spanish character, its injustices, brutalities, and cruelties against the Cuban people. We pass through epochs of slavery (stylized similarly to the television documentary Roots), as rebellion against Spain bloodies the island. Early on, Cabrera Infante is making an anti-war plea, demonstrating with continual heavy-handed irony how even the author of Cuba's National Anthem was put to death, how the poets and artists (much like us) died at the hands of a military that is also perceived as "accidentally" heroic. There are bloodbaths of Haitian and Jamaican workers and gangster massacres, Cuban-style. On two occasions Cabrera describes events that were the plots of major Hollywood films, John Huston's *We Were Strangers* (digging through a cemetery to assassinate a dictator) and Lewis Milestone's *All Quiet on the Western Front* (describing the "lyrical" death of a rebel by stray bullets from a comrade's rifle as he reaches up to pick a mango). Cabrera's cinematic sense never fails him.

Certain vignettes are elevated to allegorical proportions: a man being chased by "Tyranny," how "Death" took the "Others." We witness women losing their entire family, wiping away their tears, and continuing to do their daily wash. Death indeed is a natural part of life in Cuba. We see soldiers machine-gunning mobs of people gathered in front of a national palace by a dictator supposedly to witness his abdication. We view many treacheries and cruelties: young boys single-handedly killing police lieutenants and then handed over to the police by rebel leaders afraid of further retribution; seven men machine-gunned one by one as they leave their cover, giving themselves up to police; the coup de grâce given men after being executed on Christmas Eve. But Cabrera Infante lyrically elevates these last moments of the victims; for example: "Before dying, did the last hostage think he was dreaming?" (p. 70), or "He fell to one side and rolled from the tree down toward the ravine. What was he thinking? Someone once said that we never know what the brave man thinks" (p. 99).

Cabrera Infante graphically describes the ugliness of death, for example, in the comical episode of a homosexual recaught by the police after he had tricked them previously, "found a week later in the gutter. They had cut off his tongue and stuck it in his anus" (p. 78). Or, ". . . the doctor took out a fistful of feces and among them, shining in the sun, six, ten, twelve sharp little gray pieces of schrapnel: a splinter had hit him, splitting up in the intestinal cavity as it entered, forming a shower of swift razors which perforated his intestines and burst his liver" (p. 92).

Cabrera's intent was to write a serious anti-war novel, with occasional seriocomic glimpses into the Cuban character. He documents, for example, attempted assassinations that were successful on paper but disastrous in execution: ironically, "in the beauty of the gesture, destiny had brought together heroism and failure" (p. 87). He repeatedly demonstrates how the spontaneous act (of escape, for example) is more successful than the well-planned plot.

View of Dawn in the Tropics is chock-full of imagery—soldiers lying dead with holes in their necks, bloody faces in a bucolic setting, ironically compared with Renoir's Picnique sur l'Herbe; photographs that reveal "the image of the dead hero when alive" (p. 119); lyrical images of death: ". . . the volley or the single shot wasn't heard but the impact is left and he will fall as long as man exists and they will see him falling when eyes look at him and they will not forget him as long as there is memory" (p. 115); ". . . his gray arm, next to the pale gray chest with the black satin, falling on the black grass, leaning toward the black earth and death forever . . ." (p. 115).

One incredible story, elevated to the level of parable, demonstrates the dark side of the Cuban character. A father, seeking to correct the nocturnal carousing habits of his son asks his friend, the local Chief of Police, to arrest the boy for a single night. However, fate intervenes, and the Police

Chief is killed that evening by a bomb. In retaliation, the police choose ten political prisoners to be killed—and the boy is among them. Although entertaining as a story, Cabrera Infante implies much more about the Cuban mind, its penchant for practical jokes and cruelties, and the tenuous role fate plays in life and death. He also criticizes the Cuban fetish for machismo, having some of his fictional characters liken themselves to bullfighters. The revolution of 1959 was successful in one sense; it changed the Cuban's attitude toward machismo. Ballet dancer Jorge Esquivel recently recalled the time when "people said they'd rather see their sons clean streets than be a ballet dancer. After the Revolution, Fidel went to see Alicia [Alonso], and was so impressed by her that he decided to help her build a ballet company in Cuba."[3] In the main, however, ***View of Dawn in the Tropics*** is an anti-Cuban, anti-Castro work.

In a somewhat autobiographical section, sprinkled with imaginative details, Cabrera Infante recalls how they "took my little theatre away from me" (p. 133); the perils of "nationalization"; his own experiences cutting sugar cane; an infection that led him to be sent home, eventually to flee the country. But his most biting critique of Cuba is his description of the death, after twelve years in prison, of Pedro Luis Boitel, a student leader who "conspired against the powers of the state." Here Cabrera Infante takes pot shots at the ineffectiveness of such international organizations as the Red Cross, the OAS, the Commission on Human Rights, as well as of Cubans themselves: "Not a single voice was raised, nothing was said, nobody said a thing to get them to give him medical care . . . not even the Pope . . . because never has there been a Cuban, the God's honest truth, who has sacrificed himself for this country . . ." (pp. 136-137).

View of Dawn in the Tropics is an ironic book. It describes what is really hidden under the exotic beauty of the Cuban landscape. The dust cover carries the picture of a crocodile ready to bite. ***View*** is a diatribe against war, against all sorts of tyrannies that are antithetical to the natural Cuban way of life. Or is the real Cuban way of life so full of hypocrisy, guile, injustice, political schemes, see-saw skirmishes over the centuries always ending in petty dictatorships and eventual death? People and plots are the real enemies, says Cabrera Infante. The author depicts nature, not nostalgically but as an impersonal entity, immutable, unchanging, a mute spectator:

And it will always be there. As someone once said, that long, sad, unfortunate island will be there after the last Indian and after the last Spaniard and after the last African and after the last American and after the last Cubans, surviving all disasters, eternally washed over by the Gulf stream: beautiful and green, undying and eternal (p. 141).

Certainly, Mario Vargas Llosa would be pleased by Cabrera Infante's latest direction in his pursuit of perpetuating his narrative skill and his imaginative use of storytelling techniques.

Notes

1. G. Cabrera Infante, *View of Dawn in the Tropics*, translated by Suzanne Jill Levine (New York: Harper, 1978), dust jacket.
2. Julio Hernández-Miyares, "Cabrera Infante: A Tiger in the Tropics," Unpublished paper, February 15, 1977.
3. Michael Robertson, "A Cuban Ballet Star Who Cuts Sugar Cane," New York Times (July 15, 1979), pp. 19, 24.

Suzanne Jill Levine (essay date 1987)

SOURCE: "'Vistas of Dawn in the (Tristes) Tropics': History, Fiction, Translation," in *World Literature Today,* Vol. 61, No. 4, Autumn, 1987, pp. 548-53.

[*In the following essay, Levine, who translated* View of Dawn in the Tropics *into English, addresses the collection's origin and major influences, as well as its principal themes.*]

History is a Story

Vista del amanecer en el trópico (1974; Eng. ***View of Dawn in the Tropics,*** 1978) was one of the original titles of the book that became *Tres tristes tigres* (1964; Eng. *Three Trapped Tigers,* (1971), a novel that was going to counterpoint Guillermo Cabrera Infante's *carnevale* to the satyrs and nymphs of Havana nightlife with somber documentary vignettes of history in the making—the revolution against Batista which ended in the victory of Fidel Castro. "Both a chronicle and a Utopian vision of that moment, the original novel was a view of the tropical dawn of Cuba, the dawn of a new historical age," Emir Rodríguez Monegal wrote in a review for *Plural* of the work that finally did become ***Vista del amanecer en el trópico*** in 1974.[1]

However, in 1965 the self-exiled Infante, convinced that the revolutionary government was turning into a repressive regime, particularly after the censorship of the film *P.M.* and after other restrictive measures, disengaged from his work-in-progress the politically engaged vignettes. The documentary *P.M,* filmed by his brother Sabá Cabrera and Orlando Jiménez, was a vivid testimony in black-and-white to the nightlife in Old Havana, though most of the characters were black or mulatto, dancing to hypnotic cha-cha-chas, rumbas, mambos, and boleros, drinking, and occasionally getting into a brawl.

It was not a vision of the "reformed" Cuba that the regime wished to publicize. Also, it was the first time, GCI noted, that an artistic work was censored in Cuba "not for expressing counterrevolutionary ideas, but because of its form as well as content."[2] What his brother Cabrera was not allowed to show in film, Infante would tell in literature.

Literary or esthetic politics, even more than Cuban politics, motivated the transformation of ***Vista*** into *TTT,* however. The original project followed the formula of GCI's first work of fiction, his collection of "lyrical" stories and "epic" vignettes titled ***Así en la paz como en la guerra*** (***In Peace as in War***; 1958); in a similar fashion fiction and history conjoined to form another total or totalitarian Sartrean fiction, a Utopian project proposing a view of history and fiction as a continuum. The text that finally turned into *TTT,* however, recognized no other counterpoint than its own verbal music, making history and politics into a barely audible basso continuo.

Several years later GCI collected the vignettes—which now began with the earliest chronicles of Cuba and ended in the early 1970s, since he had continued to compose new vignettes—and, by means of the cinematic technique of montage, he created out of them a book. Or rather, in making a readerly discovery, he was finally able to write the book, as he explains in his 1986 interview with Danubio Torres Fierro.

> One day, upon reading the new vignettes, which had been published in places as diverse as Mexico and Czechoslovakia, I realized that they had a common denominator: violence. Cuba's history seemed wrought out of a violence which contradicted its peaceful tropical geography. Using these vignettes and others which I wrote on Cuba's most remote and most recent history, plus actual testimonies (for example, in the last part of the book), another ***View of Dawn in the Tropics*** arose, this time turning the exemplary title into an ironic one: History now viewed as a simple story, historical life transformed into mere writing into versions of reality—or rather "reality."
>
> (86)

Completed during somber years for GCI, ***Vista*** was also a less joy(ce)ful book than *TTT.* The vignettes are concise Hemingwayesque glimpses of a moment, an incident, a place, a character, or a text, as William Kennedy observed, "in the tradition of the vignettes of *In Our Time.*"[3] Many of them are descriptions of photographs or engravings—literally moments captured in time in which the still, the visual image, becomes dramatized for an instant, petrifying History in a graphic referent. Some are oral testimonies, transcripts of conversations that actually took place. Inscriptions on photographs, fragments of recorded speeches, national hymns, legends, hearsay, official reports, transcripts—these are the ruins, the textual remains of History which constitute history-as-told in ***Vista.***

The counterpoint between lyricism (Cuba's nature and geography) and the epic (history) had now become a subtle fugue. But Infante—a fanatic subverter of academic or journalistic clichés, even his own—hated the term *vignettes.* First it seemed because he didn't want to appear to be repeating literary strategies, having used vignettes in his collection of stories. There was another reason, though, suggested in a letter early on in our correspondence concerning the book (I translate).

> I promised Prometheus [alluding to a Havana theatre group in the 1950s] not to use that word any more with ***View of Dawn in the Tropics,*** but I don't know what to call these fragments: perhaps *viewgnettes*? And there's a critic in Spain who insists that the book is a novel, with all the generals and the comandantes becoming one captain. What do you think? (4 October 1975)

GCI's main concern here was the *vignettes* spoiled the structural *view* (that is, the reading) of the book as a long poem and not as a series of brief narratives—a serious concern from a pragmatic as well as a more purely literary perspective, if such a distinction is necessary. After the Spanish publisher had mistakenly advertised the work as "una serie de relatos," Cass Canfield Jr. hesitated to publish the book, insisting (correctly) that volumes of stories do not sell well and that ***View*** should come out when GCI's new novel was ready to roll too. The editor finally agreed to publish it when GCI carefully went over the book with him and showed him its undeniable unity. GCI writes in a letter dated 18 September 1976 that "Cass had the idea . . . they were a series of vignettes about Cuba under Batista and not what the book is: a history which denies history and an epic told in lyrical terms about the history imposed upon the geography of that long unhappy island." These last words *long unhappy island* allude to Hemingway's passing description of Cuba in a kind of elegy to the Gulf Stream which appears in his book *Green Hills of Africa.* This elegy, as I'll discuss further, turned out to be the "subtext" of the last vignette of the book.

From Vista To View

Though GCI participated less in this translation than in that of either *TTT* or, later, *Infante's Inferno*—wordplay and excessive elaboration would have upset its delicate balance, the grave contrapuntal effect of its lyricism, understatement, and straightforward violence—he still collaborated significantly. He added some new vignettes which—like one about a black general and another about a failed attack on the presidential palace—underscore an ironic, pathetic view of the "best intentions" of revolution.[4] He also maintained a correspondence with me over a period of four years (1974-78), which dealt with all aspects of the translation, from the most practical issues (getting the book published, pondering over its reception) to answering my many translation questions, discussing the concept of the book, and offering numerous corrections and editorial suggestions.

The subtle variations of style and language in ***View of Dawn in the Tropics,*** and also its demands for documentary authenticity, provided a challenge, whereas its elegant concision made it both pleasurable and more manageable than GCI's more voluminous undertakings. Regarding its deceptive simplicity (in comparison with *TTT*), GCI warned me in a letter of 12 November 1977 (I translate literally):

> ***View,*** despite its apparent easiness, has a lot of tricks to it, of style but also language. In the first pages I use

> many archaic documents mixed into the narration; some of the pages which seem as if they were mine—like that extraordinary graffiti we've already discussed—are really historical documents.

Italo Calvino once said that a real collaboration between author and translator begins with the translator's questions, and that "a translator with no doubts cannot be a good translator."[5] The translator Alastair Reid once pointed out to me an experience I immediately identified with, that of looking up words one already knew—that is, translators have doubts even when they have the answers.

Anyway, my first questions to GCI when I'd already begun to translate ***Vista*** were:

> Dr. Livingston, I presume that on pp. 13-14 of ***Vista*** the quotations from Columbus are from his first voyage, correcto? On p. 17, do you remember from what section of Padre de las Casas' writings comes the quotation? Since both those works are translated, I thought it worthwhile to quote from the translations, if possible. Also, if possible, could you give me a list of the other works you quote from. Most of them probably aren't translated but, if so, I should check into the translations. (My letter, 28 November 1975)

His response, dated 13 December 1975 was prompt, despite protestation to the contrary. (These letters are irresponsibly bilingual, so I've translated most of the Spanish segments.)

> Dear Jill, forgive my delay in answering your letter in turn, but yours had gotten mislaid (in this universe filled with papers that is my *mundo infame* [infamous world], not to be confused please with *mondo cañe* or with *inmundo infante* [filthy Infante, but a pun, hence a better translation would be: Infante's underworld—underwear, get it?] and I couldn't answer yours without having it in view [in sight]: Land! shouted Rodrigo de Triana from the crow's nest—and you're right the quotation is from Columbus's first voyage, but I don't know if it [Columbus's letter] was translated from the Italian or from *hispaniolo antico*. I can't tell you anything about Las Casas—called "Bartolomeo" by C. L. Sulzberger!—I got that quotation (like many of the others [dealing with the Conquest and colonial Cuba]) from Portuondo's history of Cuba. All the quotations come from there, and those that don't come from that history, I've forgotten whence they come since I wrote those vignettes years ago. (For example, the one where the general's mother refuses to recognize him because he surrendered and only accepts him when she finds out that he tried to commit suicide first, and others like that vignette. I don't think there are references to other universal works other than the obvious, Borges and Hemingway, for example, both of whom have written about history and about Cuba; remember the "odious rumba The Peanut Vendor.") [This last quotation is from Borges's *Universal History of Infamy,* translated into English by Norman Thomas Di Giovanni and Borges as "the deplorable rumba"
>
> (*A Universal History,* pp. 19-20).)

At first glance, question and answer seem redundant—that is, that most of the historical quotations came out of Portuondo's book was already known. Still, the author 1) confirms this in detail, a comfort to the ever-doubtful painstaking translator, and 2) he underscores the tentativeness of his originals, or rather his translations' origins, since a) Columbus's letters were translated from the Italian or . . . , and in any case scholars have noted that "Columbus's prose is an imperfect mixture of Italian, Spanish and Portuguese" which, one imagines, the king and queen of Spain—or their secretary—had some difficulty in deciphering.[6] Moreover, to begin with, b) GCI has forgotten—unavoidably or conveniently—the origins of his "quotations"; and finally, c) he alludes to the inevitable mistranslations of History (Sulzberger's version of Las Casas's name, and of course Portuondo's "History of Cuba," an official textbook read by Cuban children in grade school). Infante also mentions in this letter literary quotations: Borges and the pervasive influence of Hemingway, particularly the Hemingway quotation (in the last vignette), which Infante brooded over in a previous letter (27 September 1975).

> Do you think that the vignettes (or whatever they're called) are coming out too Hemingwayan in English? I'm worried about that with some of them, particularly the older ones (like those you're translating now, the one with the two generals), that were written around 1963 or even before. It worries me because of the possible American reader (and especially critic). I know that in others they'll find influences of Borges, though in reality they are homages to the Argentinian—or direct quotations, as you know. But Hemingway is really so dead to me that it would be like performing funeral rites to name him among the influences of the book—although I chose for the end a direct quotation from him, this time consciously, since he is one of the few writers who have written on Cuba, not with the immediacy of the revolution in mind but rather the permanence of the island, which is really the theme of ***View,*** as you well know.

There is more than perhaps meets the eye in this exchange. The real theme of ***View*** turns out to be—via Hemingway—a subversion of the original intention of the heavily Hemingwayesque vignettes: in effect, four centuries of violence are framed by first and last vignettes which speak of the island's permanence. The repeated incidents of violence—though the causes, from conquest to revolution, seem so varied in ideology—also speak of another permanence: the age-old adage, still true, "History repeats itself."

There is, however, another "transgression" which comes into view here. In my letter I ask what amounts to a metatranslational question—that is, am I to respect the original of GCI's "translation" (original, that is) and quote faithfully, by quoting faithfully the (inevitably unfaithful) translation of that original "pretext" already written in English? Or am I, like him (the author), to rewrite the "original," quoting "freely," that is, writing? In his "quotations" of Borges and Hemingway, GCI is really paraphrasing (i.e., rewriting) more than quoting. For example, the phrase "Before dying, did the last hostage think he was dreaming" (*VDT,* 76) alludes to "Did he . . . resume his sleep . . . so that the murderers would be a dream . . .?" from two sentences in Borges's story "La espera" ("The Waiting," from *Labyrinths*), which I've condensed here into one for the purpose of comparison.

GCI was doubtlessly directing me toward the writerly course while at the same time denying (unconscious) influence in favor of (conscious) homage to Borges and Hemingway, two literary Vergils he could not ignore, though he had exorcised at least one of them, Hemingway, through the exorcising (and homaging) device of parody in *TTT:* for example, in the figure of Mr. Campbell, the supposed author of a supposed story that is parodied through translation. Mr. Campbell, apparently a hack writer, is a silly avatar of Hemingway or of a Hemingwayesque character, the hero or antihero now a kvetching, prejudiced American tourist.

Still, not completely exorcised, the "anxiety of influence" lingers on, now multiplied in the dimension of translation. In ***View*** GCI is concerned about the reception of his work in English, the native language of Hemingway. How was GCI to avoid being read as secondary, perpetrating the odious relationship between a mainstream culture and marginal Cuba? He had already been unjustly burned over this issue in John Updike's parochial, prejudiced panning of *TTT* on the grounds that "we" (the English language) did not need a Cuban Joyce.[7]

GCI phrases his concern here, however, not as anxiety but as a parricidal criticism of Hemingway, "because of the bad reputation Hemingway has now" (27 August 1977)—i.e., the fact that Hemingway is passé.

> The particularly vulnerable zones are those written in Brussels. Those written in London are more *mine* [my italics]. What was written in 1963 is too much under the aegis of Borges (aside from the textual quotations), and the form of my vignettes in that period owes a lot to Hemingway.

The distinctions between the "derivative," earlier vignettes and the more "original" later ones (particularly "the originality of paralyzing history in photographs, graphic referents") certainly concern the writer. (Indeed, what GCI defines as his original, final conception of the book, that of "de-signifying history, converting History into stories," could also "derive," in this instance from Borges's "timid games" in *A Universal History of Infamy.*) Perhaps more relevant to the reader, however, is how histories and fictions are transformed into a text whose *originality* lies in its critical dialogue with these urtexts.

I would therefore like to retrace briefly the process of translating the last vignette, GCI's "translation" of Hemingway back into its purloined language, in order to give, if not a view, at least a glimpse of how the translation attempts to continue the dialogue between texts that constitutes the original, at the same time that it marks a critical difference, like all effective translations, parodies, *and* originals.

A Subtext

Let's begin by taking a look at the original's original, not the island of Cuba but Hemingway's now much-prefaced description of the island in the stream. For brevity's sake, I shall transcribe the particular segments of Hemingway's elegy to the Gulf Stream "cited" by Infante, thus unfortunately butchering poor Hemingway, much like the sharks did to the Old Man's big fish. Anyway:

> When, on the sea, you . . . know that this Gulf Stream you are living with . . . has moved, as it moves, since before man, and that it has gone by the shoreline of that long, beautiful, unhappy island since before Columbus sighted it and that . . . those that have always lived in it are permanent and of value because that stream will flow, as it has flowed, after the Indians, after the Spaniards, after the British, after the Americans and after all the Cubans and all the systems of governments, the richness, the poverty, the martyrdom, the sacrifice and the venality and the cruelty are all gone as the high-piled scow of garbage . . . spills off its load into the blue water . . . with no significance against one single, lasting thing—the stream.[8]

Now here is GCI's "translation":

> Y ahí estará. Como dijo alguien, esa triste, infeliz y larga isla estará ahí después del último indio y después del último español y después del último africano y después del último americano y después del último de los cubanos, sobreviviendo a todos los naufragios y eternamente bañada por la corriente del golfo: bella y verde, imperecedera, eterna.
>
> (233)

The "changes" are interesting: 1) Hemingway's "long, beautiful, unhappy" island becomes emphatically more unhappy in GCI's "sad, unhappy and long"; 2) the "after the Indians" series is translated faithfully (GCI's addition of *último* is needed to give the dramatic emphasis that Hemingway's rhetorical repetition makes vivid in English), except GCI omits the British—who perhaps played a more minor role in his view of Cuba's history—and adds the Africans—a principal racial group in Cuba, omitted here by Papa Hemingway, ironically in a book about Africa; 3) GCI condenses all the evils into *naufragios,* literally "shipwrecks," metaphorically to be taken as disasters, all the shipwrecked explorers and refuges signifying, after all, both individual and historical disaster. "Eternally bathed by the Gulf Stream" condenses all that Hemingway is saying about the beauty, power, and permanence of nature, the stream, in opposition to humanity's waste. More significantly, however, the narrator shifts the focus from the stream to the island, which becomes nature, beautiful, green, lasting, eternal, except that *imperecedera* is stronger, more active—more directly associated with the history of violence just told—than the tranquil adjective *lasting.*

GCI is both quoting and paraphrasing Hemingway, thus paying homage but also subtly subverting, switching emphasis, marking a difference by using Hemingway's words to sing not the stream but the island. GCI indicates without saying it that he is not an American adventurer out on his fisherman's yacht, but rather a beached, now-exiled Cuban who has really known this "unhappy" island. Hemingway's nostalgic "long, beautiful, unhappy" becomes more poignant in the words of one who lived it from within.

Here, finally, is the English translation:

> And it will always be there. As someone once said, that long, sad, unfortunate island will be there after the last Indian and after the last African and after the last American and after the last of the Cubans, surviving all disasters, eternally washed over by the Gulf Stream: beautiful and green, undying, eternal.
>
> (141)

Here one can observe a process similar to the original "rewriting." *Always,* like *último,* is added—or intuitively retraced back to the original's original—for the necessary rhetorical emphasis on permanence that the strong formal future tense gives in Spanish, just as the first sentence is turned around so that "always be there" is stressed at the strongest point, the end of the sentence. "Long, sad, unhappy" becomes "long, sad, unfortunate," displacing the simple, original *unhappy,* not only because *unhappy* picks up other connotations in its passage through Spanish—*infeliz* by a contiguity of notions means "mis-" or "unfortunate"—but because, unlike "triste, infeliz," there is no progression between the synonymous *sad* and *unhappy* in English, in either meaning or emotional intensity.

Those of us who translate know that *y* doesn't always translate automatically as "and," since *y* can gracefully disappear between two words, whereas *and* can sometimes stick out like a sore thumb. But here *y,* as GCI (5 December 1977) insisted, "should be 'and,' tying up with the unfinished first vignette"—that is, as the "end" of a long or interrupted sentence, giving the book, again, its "undeniable unity."

On the question of *shipwrecks* versus *disasters* GCI expressed the same doubt as myself: "If we put 'disasters' we lose the connection with the waters and if we put 'shipwrecks' it's too dramatic, metaphoric. Toss a coin, girl, toss a coin." I did toss one, a wooden nickle, and came up with *disasters,* but precisely because *naufragios* serves a metonymic function: i.e., it literally denotes "shipwrecks," but it connotes, in common speech, disasters in general, shipwrecks being one of many possible disasters (and a very common one around Cuba, but not the only one, as *VDT* vividly tells). Again, the general term *disasters* made more sense in this final "eternal" summing up, a summing up which subsumes Hemingway's list of disasters. The word marks a three-way dialogue involving the English translation, the original, and the original's Hemingway an original, just as "after the last" in the American translation marks the subversion of the "subtext" by accepting the "contamination" of the Spanish "translation."

GCI seems to have taken from Hemingway's version both what effective writing in Spanish permitted, and what he interpreted—from his *view*—as the truer version. An act of translation, of criticism, of creation. Hemingway's elegant meditation on nature's truth and human folly is quoted in homage, but the Cuban writer subverts the other's discourse to criticize the "white father's" distanced, estheticized view: the island is finally not a backdrop but very much the foreground. GCI estheticizes too, of course, both in translating and in rewriting Hemingway in his own style. Writing always "falsifies" and/or "magnifies," Borges once whimsically complained.

The American translation of ***Vista*** incorporates, perhaps without intending to, a double vision: Hemingway's original and GCI's interpretation, both by quoting and by misquoting. The linguistic difference—between the original and its urtext—is of course lost in translation, but the critical difference has made its mark.

Hemingway believes he is telling it like it is in his version. GCI's view—critically subsuming Hemingway's—recognizes that all writing is secondary, which may mean that he is closer to telling it like it is. One way to see this view is to look back in laughter at *TTT,* where Hemingway's influence is exorcised in countless ways. The foreword to *Green Hills* was—it would seem, but GCI's the only one who can tell us, if he remembers—the source of one of the satiric epigraphs in *TTT.* Hemingway, taking himself—and realism—quite seriously, writes with humor:

> Unlike many novels, none of the characters or incidents in this book is imaginary. Any one not finding sufficient love interest is at liberty, while reading it, to insert whatever love interest he or she may have at the time. The writer has attempted to write an absolutely true book to see whether the shape of a country and the pattern of a month's action can, if truly presented, compete with a work of the imagination.

The "action" of which the "work of the imagination" falls short, by the way, includes the glorified slaughter of African animals by the stoic, heroic Great White Hunter. Why GCI would wish to bury the American patriarch under numerous parodies would not be difficult to understand. GCI writes a row of nonsequiturs in his *TTT* epigraph.

> The characters, though based on real persons, appear as fictional beings. The proper names mentioned all through the book must be considered pseudonyms. The facts are, at times, taken from reality, but are finally resolved as imaginary. Any similarity between literature and history is accidental.

GCI is pulling everybody's leg—seriously—including Hemingway's. The first sentence is pleonastic play, perhaps making fun of the movie industry's fear of lawsuits. The second sentence is a half-lie, since some of the names are real (like Rine Leal, René Jordan, Jesse Fernández), but a pithy lie, since names (particularly Infante, which means "speechless") are linguistic conventions: even when "real," do they *really* signify? (But let's leave Derrida in peace.) The third sentence makes quite clear that GCI is questioning Hemingway's privileging of the real over the imaginary, and the fourth mocks not only Hemingway's machismo but also Marxist social realism. GCI takes Hemingway's text (and cinematic and sociological clichés) and—as in dream speeches—repeats the words but gives them a different meaning, revealing language's elusiveness despite all intentions to the contrary.

The epigraph "got lost" in translation; neither GCI nor his editor considered it funny enough to clutter up the front of the book, perhaps. Also perhaps, ***View of Dawn in the Tropics*** carries over what GCI is saying (despite language's nonsense) in *TTT,* but this time the joke is dead serious.

Both GCI and I were fairly content—and I suppose relieved—with the translation when it finally came out. Among his comments toward the end of the translation process: "What is coming out very well is the tone, between ironic and factual and often deadpan *écriture*—how do you like the polyglotism?"

Notes

1. Emir Rodríguez Monegal, review of *Vista del amanecer en el trópico,* in *Plural,* Mexico City, May 1975, p. 66. See also *WLT* 50:1 (Winter 1976), p. 123.
2. Danubio Torres Fierro, "Guillermo Cabrera Infante," in *Memoria plural: Entrevistas a escritores latinoamericanos,* Buenos Aires, Sudamericana, 1986, p. 87.
3. William Kennedy, "Island of Luminous Artifact," *Review,* 25-26 (1979), p. 136.
4. Guillermo Cabrera Infante, *View of Dawn in the Tropics,* New York, Harper & Row, 1984, pp. 42, 86. Subsequent references use the abbreviation *VDT.*
5. Italo Calvino, "Statement on Translation," *Translation,* special issue on the Italian book in America, Columbia University, 1986, pp. 109-10.
6. *Noticias secretas y públicas de América,* Emir Rodríguez Monegal, ed., Barcelona, Tusquets, 1984, p. 32.
7. *New Yorker,* 29 January 1972, p. 91.
8. Ernest Hemingway, *The Green Hills of Africa,* New York, Scribner's, 1935.

Nicholas Rankin (review date 1989)

SOURCE: "A scrapbook of oppression," in *Times Literary Supplement,* January 20, 1989, p. 58.

[*Below, Rankin maintains that Cabrera Infante's* View of Dawn in the Tropics *fuses myth and history and is informed by "an exile's perspective."*]

View of Dawn in the Tropics is a brief and poignant history of Cuba, related in 117 sections. These vignettes, fables and snapshot descriptions vary in length from a paragraph to four pages, and their first lines are logged in the index as if they were prose poems. This post-modern technique of making a history from a mosaic of fragments has been employed by the Uruguayan Eduardo Galeano in his epic trilogy *Memory of Fire,* but in G. Cabrera Infante's hands the method is also reminiscent of the *Extraordinary Tales* collated by the Argentines, Borges and Bioy Casares. Here factual history is worn down into fictive myth: the clutter of names and dates and elaborate particularity have been polished away to leave emblematic figures such as "the black general", "the old soldier" and "the comandante", whose violent fates are laconically described.

Key to the book is the first word of the title. As one would expect from this pun-loving writer, "view" has several meanings. In the sense of "opinion", the exiled Cabrera Infante's view of his native land since Fidel Castro took power thirty years ago is clear: Cuba is a tyrannical dictatorship, a black joke far from any "dawn" of progressive enlightenment. Many of the vignettes are distanced by a cool style ("the senator was eating bread when they killed him, and his white linen suit was stained with blood and spilled coffee") which pretends to objectivity. Other sketches are already at one remove, being verbal descriptions of scenes depicted in other media: engravings, a map, photographs, a film. It is an exile's perspective, contemplating the leaves of a scrap-book of oppression and failed revolutions. And in the long view of Cuba's dire history—colonization by great powers, massacre of Indians, enslaving of blacks—the latest régime, with its persecution of dissidents and homosexuals, is regarded as quite consonant with what has gone on before.

The tone of the book does change, however, as chronology brings us up to date. The dead bodies and the gaol-bars become more bitterly personal than ironically picturesque. Three of the last nine vignettes have first-person narrators: a fugitive on a plank-and-tyre raft; a hungry convict in a labour camp; and a "disappeared" prisoner's mother raging with grief. The book is dedicated to one man who was shot by a firing squad and to another who shot himself.

Guillermo Cabrera Infante is perhaps the only naturalized British author who writes in Spanish. ***Vista del amanecer en el tropico,*** originally published in 1974, is here translated by Suzanne Jill Levine, but has been revised by the author. His hand is apparent in the English puns ("a joke is closer to a yoke than you think"), but they are fewer and less laboured than usual; appropriate to a book about a land which appears more sombre than sunny:

> AND IT WILL ALWAYS BE THERE. As someone once said, that long, sad, unfortunate island will be there after the last Indian and after the last Spaniard and after the last African and after the last American and after the last Russian and after the last of the Cubans, surviving all disasters, eternally washed over by the Gulf Stream: beautiful and green, undying, eternal.

Terry J. Peavler (essay date 1996)

SOURCE: "Cabrera Infante's Undertow," in *Structures of Power,* edited by Terry J. Peavler and Peter Standish, State University of New York Press, 1996, pp. 125-40.

[In the following excerpt, Peavler compares Cabrera Infante's short fiction with his more popular works, and asserts that "in Así en la paz como en la guerra *he published some of the finer short stories ever penned by a Spanish American."]*

Guillermo Cabrera Infante's declarations (and declamations) on the subject of politics, particularly vis-à-vis the writer, are perhaps only slightly more extensive than his denials of its importance in his own writings. Scholars, for the most part, follow his suggestions on how to read his works, stressing their apolitical nature, while acknowledging the political content only of ***Así en la paz como en la guerra,*** a book that the author himself has faulted repeatedly for being misguided (nonetheless he recently collaborated in the English translation, *Writes of Passage,* which omits only the highly charged vignettes of the original). Even though the historical sweep of ***Vista del amanecer en el trópico*** is widely recognized and commented upon, it too is generally discussed in aesthetic rather than social or political terms. Nonetheless, if one accepts the idea that even highly aesthetic literature may seek to advance a social agenda, although that agenda may be presented indirectly (e.g., the depiction of a situation that can no longer be endured), then Cabrera Infante is as blameworthy (or praiseworthy) as any author, including in the pages of *Tres tristes tigres* and *La Habana para un Infante difunto.*

Such an affirmation does not contradict Cabrera Infante's insistence that literature can never aspire to be anything other than literature: ". . . la literatura debe exclusivamente tener que ver con la literatura. Cualquier otra preocupación es totalmente extraliteraria y, por tanto, desde mi punto de vista actual, condenada al fracaso" [literature should be exclusively about literature. Any other concern is totally extra-literary and therefore, in my present way of thinking, condemned to failure (Rodríguez Monegal, 64)], nor, for that matter, the Cuban's perception that literature should never seek to be anything other than play: "Literature can *never* be experimental. Literature can and must be a game" ("Cain by Himself," 9). Rather, it acknowledges that while the primary purpose of Cabrera Infante's writings may indeed not be messianic—"No creo que el escritor sea un misionero, ni siquiera creo que el escritor tiene deberes como tal. El único deber, si hay uno del escritor, es escribir lo mejor posible" [I don't believe that the writer is a missionary—I don't even believe that the writer as such has any obligations. The only obligation, if a writer has one, is to write the best he can (Rita Guibert in Ortega, 19)], some of his purportedly most apolitical works offer strong critiques of the societies in which they are set.

Of course the author acknowledges the political intent of some pieces, but apparently only for the purpose of the harshest imaginable repudiation: ***Vista del amanecer en el trópico*** (not the collection of vignettes published in 1974, but the original version, which, once purged of its political demons became *Tres tristes tigres*) "es un libro que yo moralmente repudio" [is a book that I morally repudiate (Rodríguez Monegal, 66)]; "Personalmente lo [***Así en la paz como en la guerra***] considero total y absolutamente fuera de mi canon, que debe comenzar con *Un oficio del siglo XX*" [Personally, I consider it totally and absolutely outside of my canon, which should begin with *Un oficio del siglo XX* ("Viaje verbal," 54)]. The works that the author most values are, in his mind, free from political taint. His masterpiece, *Tres tristes tigres,* is in fact "the most apolitical book ever published by a Spanish American author" ("Cain by himself," 10).

The reader, under such heavy-handed guidance from the author, can easily, too easily perhaps, envision a rather shy, somewhat reclusive Cabrera Infante, living comfortably and contentedly in London, crafting his pyrotechnic puns. The truth of the matter is, or at least seems to be on the basis of each of the author's texts, including *Tres tristes tigres* and his more recent success, *La Habana para un Infante difunto,* that Cabrera Infante suffers deeply. He suffers most certainly from exile, most probably from solitude, perhaps from a sense of grief and guilt at a grand political experiment gone sour, and quite possibly from what seems to be a sort of writer's block: the promised books never seem to materialize. *Cuerpos divinos,* for example, has been promised since 1968, and a book of essays has been underway for several years.

Meanwhile, some of the more interesting writings may well be the overtly political outbursts (most of which have been collected in the very recent *Mea Cuba*) that have appeared from time to time on the pages of *Vanidades,* or *Vuelta,* or *El País.* The "literary" offerings seemed for many years to be filled with the same tired puns—was he capable of mentioning Karl Marx without a Marx brothers pun? True, *La Habana para un Infante difunto* (1979) seems fresher than *O* (1975) or *Exorcismos de esti(l)o* (1976), but its repetitions of its own cleverness also become somewhat wearisome—should the hero not go blind after the first few dozen pages?

Cabrera Infante's meticulously sculpted chronologies ("a la manera de Laurence Sterne"), readily available in a number of books and special issues of journals dedicated to the author, clearly demonstrate his preoccupation with his political past, and with the historical events that shaped his future. More than half of the entries covering the 55 years chronicled in "(C)ave Attemptor!" contain specific references to historical and political events, and clearly reveal his concern with the poverty and injustices of his youth, as well as those events, particularly in Cuba, that have continued to affect him and his Cuban friends.

His successes in literature and in film have brought him financial security and international recognition, which, coupled with his biting sense of humor, have spared him from many of the ravages of exile. Yet he has remained keenly aware of the plight of his countrymen, both at home and abroad, as his preoccupation with the deaths (particularly by suicide) of fellow Cubans attests.[1] One senses the presence—the passion, the frustrations, the anger—of the real Cabrera Infante more in his spirited rebukes of Gabriel García Márquez ("Nuestro prohombre en La Habana") and Hermann Bellinghausen ("El escritor y la aspereza") or in his compassionate portrayal of Nicolás Guillén ("Nicolás Guillén: Poet and Partisan") than one does in his often vacuous word plays.

In a stirring commentary, written some fifty years after the murder of Federico García Lorca, Cabrera Infante, who had had the foresight and the common sense to flee political oppression, chided the Spaniard for his romanticized vision of Havana:

> I could have told him that I've known all kinds of poets in Cuba. Poor poets and sick poets, poets pursued and poets in prison, dying poets and dead poets finally: all dead as the dodo in the end. Poets I've known who were treated not like princes but like scum—called scum, in fact. Called worms also. Poets as pariahs on the island. Poets considered untouchable, poets suffering from political leprosy. But Havana was for Lorca a moving feast, and I don't want to rain on his parade of beauties. I don't want to contaminate his poetry with my experience.
>
> ("Brief Encounter in Havana," 522)

Furthermore, whether Cabrera Infante likes it or not, in ***Así en la paz como en la guerra*** he published some of the finer short stories ever penned by a Spanish American. A few, such as **"Josefina, atiende a los señores," "Abril es el mes más cruel,"** and **"En el gran ecbó,"** are superb. While it is true that **"Resaca,"** which suggested the title for this essay, is coincidentally not only one of the more political but also one of the weaker stories, and that a number of the more heavy-handed vignettes may not be worth saving, their presence hardly justifies throwing out the whole lot. **"Josefina,"** for example, is both one of the best and one of the most political. In fact, it bears a strong odor of "socialist realism," a type of literature that the author would come to abhor, although he admitted that "I am not so much against socialism as I am realism. . . ." ("Talent of 2wo Cities," 18). . . .

Only after Cabrera Infante found refuge in London and turned his energies to writing film scripts did he seem to lose the edge on his humor. His "literary" books (*O,* 1975; *Exorcismos,* 1976) were filled more and more with empty and repetitive puns, while his "political" writings were increasingly devoid of humor.[2] ***Vista del amanecer en el trópico,*** in many ways the most political book yet,[3] provides a sort of watershed between the author who was sometimes angry, sometimes merely frustrated, but always keenly involved in historical and political events, particularly in Cuba, and the creator of verbiage for its own sake that seemingly flows through many pages of *O* and *Exorcismos.*

Vista is a very significant book.[4] It apparently began as a sort of therapy: Cabrera Infante had sunk into a deep depression while working on a film script for *Under the Volcano.* During his recovery, which included shock therapy, he received the devastating news that his old friend, Alberto Mora, had committed suicide in Cuba. The book, dedicated to Mora and to Pinio Prieto (another friend, who had been executed in 1960) is a sort of catharsis, a hymn to Cuba and its violent history. Though absolutely devoid of humor, it is the author's most poetic work, and may someday be judged to be one of his best.

Significantly, ***Vista*** is in many ways a throwback to ***Así en la paz,*** the book Cabrera Infante would like to purge from his canon. While it is even more "committed," it is somewhat cleansed by being made more abstract, more epic. ***Vista*** is devoid of the short stories of its predecessor, which served, frequently, as a respite from the horrors of the vignettes. Instead it offers a series of 100 such horrors, stretching from precolumbian Indian tribes that sought to dominate and destroy each other, to scenes of imprisonment, torture, and murder under Castro.[5] Numbers 99 and 100, which relate the death by hunger of a prisoner of some twelve years and the agony of his mother respectively, are hauntingly reminiscent of vignettes in ***Así en la paz,*** making it perfectly clear that the atrocities commited under Castro are indistinguishable from those under Batista. In fact, the mother's monologue, presented as her half of a telephone conversation that is cut off abruptly (one supposes by Castro's henchmen), is disturbingly like the ravings of the madwoman in *Tres tristes tigres,* or the rambling account of the young girl in **"Un rato de tenmeallá,"** in ***Así en la paz.*** All three reflect a sense of helplessness and despair brought on by constant suffering and repeated abuse by those in positions of authority.[6]

Through the pages of ***Vista*** run Cabrera Infante's old obsessions, including racism and suicide. And for those readers too insensitive to decipher the book's message, the final vignette provides a poetic gloss:

> Y ahí estará. Como dijo alguien, esa triste, infeliz y larga isla estará ahí después del último indio y después del último español y después del último africano y después del último americano y después del último de los cubanos, sobreviviendo a todos los naufragios y eternamente bañada por la corriente del golfo: bella y verde, imperecedera, eterna. [And there it will remain. As someone said, that sad, unhappy and lengthy island will be there after the last Indian and after the last Spaniard and after the last African and after the last American and after the last Cuban, surviving all the shipwrecks and forever bathed by the gulfstream: beautiful and green, imperishable, eternal].
>
> (233)

While ***Vista del amanecer en el trópico*** may never challenge *Tres tristes tigres* for a place atop Cabrera Infante's canon, one cannot but sense in its pages that the author cares and cares deeply about his homeland, his people, and his profession. In that regard it is of a piece with ***Así***

en la paz como en la guerra, *Tres tristes tigres,* and *Un oficio del siglo XX.* His insistence that he wrote it not for political, nor parochial, nor historical, but for aesthetic reasons (Hernández Lima, 141) is also true of the other volumes mentioned, probably including ***Así en la paz*** in its time.

In another ostensibly "nonliterary" piece, his introduction to Carlos Franqui's *Family Portrait With Fidel,* Cabrera Infante is preoccupied with an "official" Cuban photograph, one with two versions. The first shows Castro speaking into a microphone held by an unidentified man, with Carlos Franqui in the background. The second version has the same Castro speaking into the same microphone, held by the same unidentified man—but Franqui has "disappeared," thanks to some anonymous but "official" Cuban censor. The cause of this disappearance was simple: Franqui, like Cabrera Infante before him, not only worked for *Revolución*—in fact he was its founder and editor—but also fled the revolution when he saw it turning sour, and was consequently, in that (ig)noble soviet tradition, "erased." Cabrera Infante's dread of erasure also appears in vignette 85 of ***Vista del amanecer*** in which a photographer dodges away[7] a face in order to make the photograph more compact. The face is that of a comandante who is later "eliminated."

In his introduction to Franqui's book, Cabrera Infante observes that Cubans have managed to create their own unique prose, distinct from Spanish or even South American prose. The authors he mentions, with the single exception of Martí, all wrote after the revolution. Some (Lezama Lima, Carpentier, Piñera) died in an at best uneasy relationship with the government that was forced to recognize them while holding them under great suspicion, if not in outright contempt. Others perished in exile—some by suicide (the ultimate expression of impuissance). All have been "erased" to at least some degree. Their fates have weighed heavily on Cabrera Infante, who has written many articles on suicide, particularly among his countrymen.[8]

Cabrera Infante himself, however, has been incredibly active and visible. In fact, his pen has rarely been still since he left Cuba. In addition to writing numerous screenplays (including "Weekend," "Vanishing Point," "Under the Volcano," etc.) and essays, he has published nine volumes since 1971 (one, *Holy Smoke,* on cigars and cigar smoking) and has collaborated on several translations. Not only is he a prolific writer, he has been vitally important to the advancement of Cuban prose. His irreverence, his humor, and his biting insights have also made him one of the most innovative and significant authors of the "Boom." Unfortunately, he is also a man who seems at times to be drowning in frustration and helplessness, whose bitterness becomes so great that rather than writing, as did Machado de Assis, one of his literary idols, with "a pena da galhofa e a tinta da melancolia" [the pen of mockery and the ink of melancholy (Machado de Assis, 23)], too often he manages to grasp only the same tired language games. When he is at his best, his barbs fill the reader not only with laughter, but with a heightened awareness of injustice and even evil; when his anger exceeds his creative powers, as has been the pattern in recent years, then he seems all the more impotent. He would no doubt argue that his situation and that of his homeland allow room for nothing but bitterness; his devotees might reply that that is all the more reason to distance himself and to treat the issues with a generous dash of humor.

Notes

1. See especially Alvarez-Borland, "Viaje verbal," 56, and "Entre la historia y la nada: notas sobre una ideología del suicidio."
2. See especially Alvarez-Borland, "Viaje verbal," 56, and "Entre la historia y la nada: notas sobre una ideología del suicidio."
3. For a concatenation of the vignettes and their historical antecedents, see Hernández Lima.
4. For a fine analysis of the book's more literary aspects, see David William Foster's "Guillermo Cabrera Infante's *Vista del amanecer en el trópico* and the Generic Ambiguity of Narrative" in Foster, *Studies in the Contemporary Spanish American Short Story.*
5. For a correlation between the vignettes of both books and specific historical events see Hernández Lima, 112-140.
6. "por qué me va a imponer su ley su asquerosa ley" ["why are you trying to sic your law on me your dirty law" (*TTT* 451/487)]; "Ésta es la vida . . . ésta es la libertad en este país" [This is life, this is liberty in this country (*Vista* 227)]; "y el hombre le dice que no la coja con el que no tiene que ver nada y que el hace lo que le mandan y que para eso le pagaban y mama le dijo que estaba bien que ella comprendia todo pero que si no podian esperar un mes mas y el hombre dice que ni un dia y que mañana vendrian a sacar los muebles y que no oponga resistencia porque seria peor porque traerian a la policia y entonces los sacaraian a la fuerza y los meterian en la carcel" [and the man says to her not to get on him about it he doesn't have anything to do with it and he just does what he is told and that is why they were paying him and mama said to him ok that she understood and all but couldn't they way one more month and the man says not a day and tomorrow they were coming to get the furniture and not to put up a fight because it would be worse because they would bring the police and throw them out by force and put them in jail (*Así en la paz,* 14)].
7. Dodging is a darkroom technique by which a photographer removes unwanted material from a photograph. Light rays are blocked after they leave the negative, but before they fall on the print paper. A skilled darkroom technician can effectively

"erase" any portion of a photograph without leaving any evidence that it was ever present on the original negative.

8. The most extensive piece is "Entre la historia y la nada: notas sobre una ideología del suicidio," which was followed by "Más sobre el suicidio en Cuba."

Works Cited

Alvarez-Borland, Isabel. "Readers, Writers, and Interpreters in Cabrera Infante's Texts." *World Literature Today* 61 (1987): 553-58.

Cabrera Infante, Guillermo. *Así en la paz como en la guerra.* Barcelona: Seix Barral, 1971.

———."Brief Encounters in Havana." *World Literature Today* 61 (1987): 519-25.

———. "Cain by Himself: Guillermo Cabrera Infante, Man of Three Islands." *Review: Latin American Literature and Arts* 28 (1981): 8-11.

———. "(C)ave Attemptor! A Chronology (After Laurence Sterne's)." *World Literature Today* 61 (1987): 513-19.

———. "Conversación de *Tres tristes tigres.*" With Rita Guibert. *G. Cabrera Infante.* By Julio Ortega et al. Caracas: Fundamentos, 1974. 19-46.

———. "Entre la historia y la nada: notas sobre una ideología del suicidio." *Vuelta* 74 (1983): 11-22.

———. "Guillermo Cabrera Infante." With Emir Rodríguez Monegal. *El arte de narrar.* By Emir Rodríguez Monegal. Caracas: Monte Avila, 1968.

———. *La Habana para un Infante difunto.* Barcelona: Plaza & Janés, 1986.

———. "The Invisible Exile." *Literature in Exile.* Ed. John Glad. Durham: Duke UP, 1990. 32-40.

———. "Más sobre el suicidio en Cuba." *Vuelta* 79 (1983): 50-51.

———. *Mea Cuba.* Barcelona: Plaza & Janés, 1992.

———. "Nicolás Guillén: Poet and Partisan." *Review: Latin American Literature and Arts* 42 (1990): 31-33.

———. "Nuestro prohombre en La Habana." *Vuelta* 78 May 1983: 51-53.

———. "Portrait of a Tyrant as an Aging Tyro." *Family Portrait with Fidel.* By Carlos Franqui. Trans. Alfred MacAdam. New York: Random House, 1984. vii-xix.

———. *Un oficio del siglo XX.* Barcelona: Seix Barral, 1973.

———. "Talent of 2wo Cities." *Review: Latin American Literature and Arts* 35 (1995): 17-18.

———. *Tres tristes tigres.* Barcelona: Seix Barral, 1970.

———. "Viaje verbal a La Habana, ¡Ah vana!" With Isabel Alvarez-Borland. *Hispamérica: Revista de Literatura* 11 (1982): 51-68.

———. *Vista del amanecer en el trópico.* Barcelona: Seix Barral, 1974.

———. *Writes of Passage.* Trans. John Brookesmith, Peggy Boyars and Guillermo Cabrera Infante. London: Faber and Faber, 1993.

Foster, David William. "Guillermo Cabrera Infante's *Vista del amanecer en el trópico* and the Generic Ambiguity of Narrative." *Studies in the Contemporary Spanish American Short Story.* Columbia: U of Missouri P, 1979. 110-20.

Franqui, Carlos. *Family Portrait with Fidel: A Memoir.* Trans. Alfred MacAdam. New York: Random House, 1984.

Hernández Lima, Dinorah. *Versiones y re-versiones históricas en la obra de Cabrera Infante.* Madrid: Pliegos, 1990.

MacAdam, Alfred. "Seeing Double: Cabrera Infante and Caín." *World Literature Today* 61 (1987): 543-48.

Machado de Assis, *Memórias Pósthumas de Brás Cubas.* 5th ed. São Paulo: Editôra Cultrix, 1968.

Moliner, María. *Diccionario del uso del español,* Vol. 1. Madrid: Gredos, 1966. 2 vols.

Ortega, Julio et al. *G. Cabrera Infante.* Caracas: Fundamentos, 1974.

Pereda, Rosa María. *Cabrera Infante.* Madrid: EDAF, 1979.

Siemens, William L. "Guillermo Cabrera Infante and the Divergence of Revolutions: Political Versus Textual." *Literature and Revolution.* Ed. David Bevan. Amsterdam: Rodopi, 1989. 107-19.

Thomas, Hugh. *Cuba: The Pursuit of Freedom.* New York: Harper & Row, 1971.

Raymond D. Souza (essay date 1996)

SOURCE: "The Apprentice Storyteller," in *Guillermo Cabrera Infante: Two Islands, Many Worlds, University of Texas Press,* 1996, pp. 47-56.

[*In this excerpted chapter from* Guillermo Cabrera Infante: Two Islands, Many Worlds, *the author traces Cabrera Infante's development as a writer, and provides insight into his first book,* Así en la paz como en la guerra.]

Of all Cabrera Infante's activities in the 1950s, creative writing was the least consuming and the most casual. His first story, which was born of an idle boast and a dare, was successfully published and richly compensated for, a fortunate circumstance for such a young writer. Although that initial attainment undoubtedly stimulated his interest and confidence, if for no other reason than for the financial reward he received, it is perfectly human to distrust success when it comes too easily. He was, of course, in the process of finding his own voice by experimenting with different forms and by adapting various narrative styles, and between 1947 and 1960 he composed some twenty stories and submitted several of them to national literary contests. Many of these works appeared in journals like *Bohemia, Carteles, Ciclón,* and *Lunes de Revolución,* but his career as a creative writer at that time was random and unfocused. This was not the case in the film reviews he wrote for *Carteles* during the same period—there the reader finds a more assured and confident voice. In the movie criticism there is a direct relationship between productivity and the evolution of a personal aesthetic sensibility.

Cabrera Infante's first book, ***Así en la paz como en la guerra,*** is a collection of fourteen stories and fifteen vignettes written between 1949 and 1960. Thirty-three years would pass before the English translation, ***Writes of Passage,*** appeared, and when it did the vignettes were expunged from the text. He has repudiated the Spanish edition on several occasions and would prefer that it receive the kind of perfunctory greeting accorded an infrequently seen acquaintance, politely acknowledged and quickly forgotten. Critics who tarry too long with this collection are usually accorded a response similar to that extended to Dr. Frankenstein after his resurrected creature had run amok among his neighbors. Cabrera Infante regards the form of the collection as too consciously artistic and contrived, a position difficult to counter. Several of these works would be only first drafts if he were composing them today.

He has declared ***Así en la paz como en la guerra*** "a book I disown: a Sartrean book. Not the content of the book (a few stories and vignettes) but its form, even if apparently influenced by Hemingway, was inspired, if I may use this verb, by Sartre's tenet on realism. There was more of *Qu'est-ce que la littérature?* than of *In Our Time* in this slim volume of mine." Like Mario Vargas Llosa, he has rejected his early enthusiasm for Sartre. Cabrera Infante's comments on form concern the interweaving of vignettes on the political struggle against Batista with stories about other aspects of existence. Interestingly, this format was used, and in due time abandoned, in the first drafts of *Three Trapped Tigers.* The vignettes in that manuscript eventually provided the basis of another text, ***View of Dawn in the Tropics.*** In the "Prologue to English Readers" of ***Writes of Passage,*** Cabrera Infante declares: "My writing . . . springs up not from life but from reading." This claim, which is reminiscent of Borges, carries more weight without the presence of the vignettes, those intrusions of unsavory realities into the realm of the imaginary.

Cabrera Infante also condemns the social realism that inspired his first book: "As a matter of fact, I am not so much against socialism as I am against realism: the creepy-crawlies on the blank page are symptoms of the delirium tremens suffered after having drunk two pints of the milk of human kindness spiked with a dash of hope, a pinch of faith and a spoonful of charity, stir well while adding some salt of self pity." In these remarks he is expressing an abhorrence of sentimentalism, particularly when combined with political doctrines that provide accurate diagnoses of societal ills, but disastrous and sometimes fatal remedies. Cabrera Infante always has guarded against sentimentality in his works, precisely because he is given to that emotion. His remarks also reveal a strong distrust of committed literature. On another occasion he declared: "The worst thing about the book is the fact that my attitude when I wrote it was very negative. I was completely under the influence of Sartre, because I accepted the premise that a book should be a comprehensive critical act. So not only did I have to include reality, which is an idiotic pretension, but I also had to have criticism of reality and of the work itself."

In spite of the author's reservations, ***Así en la paz como en la guerra*** enjoyed considerable success. By 1964 it was in its fourth printing in Cuba and had appeared in France and Italy in translations published by Editorial Gallimard and Editorial Mondadori. It has done equally well in Seix Barral editions published in Spain. The fifteen vignettes in the collection deal with the brutality and moral corruption of the Batista regime, and most were written in 1958. Surprisingly, he attempted to publish some of them in *Bohemia* and *Carteles,* but the editors had the good sense not to jeopardize their own security and his safety. The vignettes are effectively rendered in a laconic and realistic style. Seymour Menton has commented that "what makes most of the vignettes so effective is the Hemingway-like objective use of the third-person point of view. Sentences are relatively short, the preterit predominates, and there is no editorializing. In fact, the only vignette that clearly violates this last general principle, number 14, is undoubtedly the weakest of all." However, the vignettes in this collection are devoid, for the most part, of the irony and humor found in ***View of Dawn in the Tropics,*** and there is little variety in their content. As soon as the reader becomes attuned to their substance, the reaction is apt to be a resigned shrug as yet another killing appears in the text.

One of the few exceptions is number 10, in which an officer reports to his superior about a successful ambush made possible by an informer. In what is cast as a telephone conversation, a technique that would be used with great success in *Three Trapped Tigers,* the officer finds himself caught between his contempt for the traitor and his general's decision to reward the informer with a major's commission. The officer reveals his true feelings about the betrayer, whom he considers a coward and a homosexual, as well as his abject subservience to his superior. The one-way telephone conversation (we only hear the officer's voice, a technique most likely garnered from film or radio) exposes the distortion of values and the corruption of basic decency that characterized the

Batista dictatorship. Although violence is not the main focus of the vignette, there are enough details of the ambush, including bullets hitting flesh and the informer vomiting after seeing scattered brain tissue, to remind one again of the cruelty of the regime. Many readers are attracted to the vignettes in ***Así en la paz como en la guerra*** because of the historical immediacy they convey—these brief narrations are the product of moral indignation, and their macabre motifs provide ample justification for the revolution. The author's commitment to revolutionary change and his desire to cast off the past also are expressed in the introduction to the collection.

Cabrera Infante's debt to Ernest Hemingway is most apparent in the stylistic rhythm of some of the stories, especially in the mixture of long, descriptive sentences with brief, staccato statements. This influence is most apparent in **"Mar, mar, enemigo" ("The Sea Changes")**, in the stylistic rendering and in the portrayal of the ocean as both an adversary and an ironic symbol of freedom and death. In this work a woman, who had been educated in a convent, awaits the arrival of a man she has been involved with for ten to fifteen years. She is on an island and knows that he is carrying out an illegal activity that he believes will be lucrative. When he never arrives, she reluctantly concludes that he has failed and is most likely dead. Her religious background and his subversive endeavors provide an ethical counterpoint reminiscent of the contradictions in the author's family. The story may articulate, in a vague and indirect manner, a desire to exorcise a negative paternal influence.

In the September 1956 issue of *Ciclón,* a cultural and literary journal, Cabrera Infante published an amusing account of a gala affair held in the gardens of a brewery and sponsored by the producers of Hatuey beer and Bacardí rum to celebrate Hemingway's winning of the Nobel Prize. The commentary reveals his knowledge of Hemingway's works and the sardonic humor that would later characterize his own creative writings. The narration begins with a brief quotation from a terse and factually based newspaper report that conveys little about what really went on. In Cabrera Infante's account, Hemingway is portrayed as gracious but bewildered and harassed by the aggressive antics of his enthusiastic admirers, many of whom have not read his works. They embrace, jostle, and torment him with their excessive attention. Publicity hounds crowd into picture-taking sessions, trying to grasp a moment of fame in the shadow of the celebrity. Everyone seems to want an autograph on the special pamphlets prepared for the ceremony. The gaudy mementos contain a photograph, which Hemingway detests, of the writer in a bathing suit and quotations from his works that mention Hatuey beer. The commercialization of literary fame is conveyed by a pun in the article's title, "El viejo y la marca" ("The Old Man and the Seal"). The playful rendering of the name of Hemingway's novella transforms "sea" into a commercial label.

In a song sung by Amelita Frade, the Nobel laureate is characterized as "a 'tiger' writing," which evokes the title of Cabrera Infante's first novel. Hemingway's announcement that he is going to donate his Nobel Prize medal to Cuba's patron saint leaves some observers nonplussed, wondering about the origins of such sentiments in a writer whose works are anything but religious. Hemingway's disclosure is the ultimate incongruity in the bizarre affair. The portrait of Hemingway and his tormentors brings to mind a laconic observation in Jorge Luis Borges's "Pierre Menard, Author of the Quijote" that "fame is a form of incomprehension, perhaps the worst." In many respects, Cabrera Infante's remarkable account foreshadows, more than the stories of ***Así en la paz como en la guerra*** do, the future course of his work, and it demonstrates that he is at his best when responding to real events and people. Of course, in the process he transforms them into something uniquely his own.

The fourteen stories in ***Así en la paz como en la guerra*** are notable for their variety of techniques and content. Some are elaborate and long, close to being mature works. Others are brief and function as literary jokes, directed either at one of the characters, as in **"Jazz,"** or at the reader, as in **"Cuando se estudia gramática" ("Grammar's for the Birds")**. In the first-mentioned work, a character toys with a friend, offering him some marijuana. When the cigarette is declined, the tempter refuses to acknowledge whether the offer was a subterfuge or not, slyly retreating into an ambiguous play on words. **"Grammar's for the Birds"** relates what happens between a young man and woman during a study session. At one point he asks her to disrobe and she willingly complies with his request. After staring at her for a while, he tells her to put her clothes back on and they resume their studies. An examination of the workings of language turns into a similar inspection of human anatomy—all theory, no practice. Occasionally a story relies excessively on a surprise ending; in **"Abril es el mes más cruel" ("April is the Cruelest Month")**, a young woman unexpectedly jumps to her death during her honeymoon. The dramatic and theatrical ending made it attractive for adaptation to a television program directed by the author, photographed by Orlando Jiménez and featuring Miriam Gómez.

The social panorama of the characters in the collection is extensive and includes, among others, a wealthy businessman, an unfortunate seamstress, a lonely mortuary worker, a callous bordello madam, destitute children, cane field workers, an actress, and a writer. Narrative technique also varies greatly. **"Un rato de tenmeallá" ("Gobegger Foriu Tostay")** consists of a thirteen-page sentence narrated by a six-year-old child who barely understands that the family's impoverishment is compelling an older sister to sell her virginity. The narrative is reminiscent of Joyce's Molly Bloom and Faulkner's Benjy in its portrayal of the flow of consciousness and its ability to combine an aura of innocence and degradation. The introduction to the volume relates this story to the author's personal experience in a room in a tenement, most likely 408 Zulueta, and mentions the small quarters and days without food.

More obvious personal associations appear in **"El día que terminó mi niñez"** (**"The Day My Days as a Child Ended"**), written as a Christmas story for *Carteles.* Many elements in the story parallel the author's life. These circumstances include references to a town by the sea, an absent father looking for work in a distant city, a younger brother, an uncle who expects children to ask for a blessing during a visit, and a mother who gives her oldest son instructions on how to behave in the presence of the aloof relative. However, as in much of Cabrera Infante's autobiographical writing, factual truth is less important than the persuasiveness of the account. A completely different narrative mode, one with several literary connections, is evident in **"La mosca en el vaso de leche"** (**"A Fly in a Glass of Milk"**). This work is a naturalistic portrait of the eroding sanity of a desperate seamstress. Her descent into madness is conveyed by the way her mind fastens on bizarre details in her environment. The portrayal of solitude recalls other characters tormented by estrangement and loneliness in Flaubert's "Un Coeur Simple" ("A Simple Heart"), Faulkner's "A Rose for Emily," and Enrique Labrador Ruiz's "Conejito Ulán" ("Little Bunny Ulán").

The most accomplished pieces in ***Así en la paz como en la guerra*** are **"Josefina, atiende a los señores"** (**"Josefina, Take Good Care of the Señores"**) and **"En el Gran Ecbó"** (**"The Great Ekbo"**), one of the most anthologized stories from the collection. In the first work, which was published in *Ciclón* in May 1955, a woman who runs a brothel talks about her establishment, attempting to pass herself off as a compassionate entrepreneur, devoted to the well-being of her girls and clients. She addresses the presumed listener in a colorful oral language, full of colloquialisms and trite sayings, and in the process she reveals herself as completely insensitive to the sordidness that surrounds her. In fact, she can be accused of being thoroughly alienated from humanity's finer qualities. This becomes distressingly evident when she tells the story of her most popular girl, the one-armed Josephine, who became a prostitute unwillingly through the manipulations of a lover. Josephine's ineffectual attempts to rebel against her situation include an attempted suicide and drug addiction. Her physical deformity is a sign of the emotional damage that is being inflicted on her. Josephine's desperation is only matched by her employer's greed and indifference. What makes the story so successful is the author's ability to use vernacular language effectively. The narrator betrays herself and her occupation with her own words. **"Josefina, Take Good Care of the Señores"** indicates that Cabrera Infante was learning one of the essentials of narrative art, the importance of showing rather than telling.

"The Great Ekbo" is the finest and most sophisticated story in the volume. Two lovers spend part of a rainy day in Havana together, dining and then attending a *lucumí* religious ceremony of African origin (**"Ekbo"** refers to a religious gathering of all the saints). The man tries to be cavalier and ironic in an attempt to resist the melancholy guilt that is seeping into their relationship, but his efforts do little to counter the remorse of his lover, an actress. Her guilt is intensified by photographs of his family, which he carries in his wallet, and by an unknown black woman's admonition at the ceremony that she stop living in sin. There is little action in this story, which depends on fine description and the evocation of mood for its success. In the introduction to the volume, Cabrera Infante remarks that the main character "is an upstart . . . it's as if the Silvestre of 'The Doors' and 'A Nest' had purchased an English sports car."

Although the male protagonist in **"The Great Ekbo"** is unidentified, it is of more than passing interest that he should be associated with other characters named Silvestre. Indeed, that name is used in five of the stories in ***Así en la paz como en la guerra*** and it is, of course, the designation given to the author's alter ego in *Three Trapped Tigers.* The Silvestre in the novel and the main character in **"The Great Ekbo"** share an obsession with time: they both look at events in the present with an eye to how they will be remembered in the future. Although the central character in the story is anonymous, there is a playful reference to his identification in two lines that allude to the origin of his name in Cabrera Infante's experience with popular culture: "Delante, a la izquierda, por entre la lluvia fina, apareció deslumbrante un pequeño cementerio, todo blanco, húmedo, silvestre. Había en él una semetría aséptica que nada tenía que ver con la corrupción y los gusanos y la peste." ("Ahead of them, to the left, a small graveyard shone all white and wild through the rain. Its sterilized symmetry belied any thoughts of maggots and foul corruption").

In the narrator's mind, the cemetery is associated with a denial of death and corruption because he is most likely thinking of "a wry, adult comic book hero," the "back-from-the-dead criminologist Denny Colt," better known as the Spirit. Created on 2 June 1940 by Will Eisner, *The Spirit* was a "weekly seven-page feature, part of a comic book Sunday supplement." The words "cementerio" and "silvestre" in the original version of the short story are oblique references to the Spirit's hideout, Wildwood Cemetery, which appeared in Spanish editions as "Cementerio San Silvestre." This is the fanciful origin of the name of one of the three memorable characters of *Three Trapped Tigers.* The young Cabrera Infante was particularly intrigued with the artistic quality of *The Spirit,* an admiration he maintains to this day, and its incorporation into his narratives is an acknowledgment of a passion from his adolescent years. Silvestre is an illuminating example of Cabrera Infante's utilization of an element from popular culture, one of an abundant number of such references in his works. It also speaks to his playful disposition as well as to the circuitous nature of the creative imagination.

Looking back at the original episodes of *The Spirit,* it is not difficult to see why he was so intrigued with Eisner's work. An episode published in 10 August 1941, for example, begins with a quotation from Michel de Montaigne and concerns a scientist who has successfully condensed time into a liquid element. Through a series of chance occurrences, an unsuspecting individual is able to see the future consequences of his criminal actions. Michael Barrier, in *A Smithsonian Book of Comic-Book Comics,* quotes John Benson, who has commented that "'like Alfred Hitchcock, Eisner *shows* his stories instead of telling them. And Eisner's pictorial sense, like Hitchcock's, is so integral to his sense of narrative that it's often overlooked: the type of story favored by the artist is more likely to be recognized—the "Hitchcock story" or the "Eisner story".'" Benson also points out that Eisner was a master of indirect portrayal and showed the result or reaction to an act rather than the action itself. Cabrera Infante would make ample use of this technique in *Three Trapped Tigers,* especially in the psychiatric sessions of Laura Díaz.

Although Cabrera Infante is not fond of ***Así en la paz como en la guerra,*** the book does indicate some of what was to come. The collection demonstrates, for example, his capacity to employ a variety of narrative styles, ranging from the purely objective to the intimate rendering of a flow of consciousness. His ability to re-create vernacular language as well as his successful assimilation of various influences, like that of Hemingway, also are evident. Even early in his career, it was apparent that he had a natural gift for imitation. A less satisfactory adaptation is the interweaving of highly different narrative modes, particularly the mixture of the stories with the vignettes. That strategy was most likely acquired from Faulkner's *The Wild Palms,* a work whose success is equally debatable. Cabrera Infante's first book attempted to accommodate contradictory tendencies, political commitment and a will to fragmentation, and it is fair to observe that this accounts for the book's deficiencies as well as his dissatisfaction with it.

Several of the characters evoke others who would follow. The actress and her lover in **"The Great Ekbo"** are suggestive of Laura Díaz and Silvestre of *Three Trapped Tigers.* **"Un nido de gorriones en un toldo" ("Nest, Door, Neighbours")** contains a child-woman whose penchant for role-playing leads her and those around her into labyrinths of illusion and deception, much as the formidable Amazon of *Infante's Inferno* and Laura Díaz of *Three Trapped Tigers* do in those novels. The superficial and cynical Solaún of **"Ostras interrogadas" ("Oysters Helping with Their Inquiry")** appears briefly in *Three Trapped Tigers.* These and other elements, such as stories cast in an autobiographical mode, point to the future, but they do not foretell it. It would be a mistake to claim that the major themes and strategies of his artistic maturity can be found in these first works, but it is fair to say that the collection contains experimental variations that enabled Cabrera Infante to explore options during his search for his own voice and that some of these variants would appear again. With the exception of two or three outstanding stories, the volume can be termed a collection of readable works, most likely to interest readers intrigued with historical referents or specifically concerned with Cabrera Infante's career.

Although he is an author who works from fragments, writing segments and eventually expanding them into texts, Cabrera Infante has not produced many short stories, at least in the contemporary understanding of the term. It should be mentioned, however, that many pieces, such as the portrait of Pepe Castro, **"My Unforgettable Character,"** are conceived as stories by Cabrera Infante. He uses such a classification because he feels that once something disappears into a text, it becomes a fiction. For that reason, even works that purport to be historical accounts are fictions, a position that undoubtedly causes some readers difficulty. The fine line between the imaginary and the real is often a problematic distinction in Cabrera Infante's works—what we read is undoubtedly an illusion, but at the level of meaning there is frequently authenticity. Despite the author's misgivings, the stories and vignettes in ***Así en la paz como en la guerra*** are acceptable works, not equal in quality to his later writings, but undeserving of oblivion.

FURTHER READING

Criticism

Alvarez-Borland, Isabel. "Readers, Writers, and Interpreters in Cabrera Infante's Texts." *World Literature Today* 61, No. 4 (Autumn 1987): 553-58.

Describes Cabrera Infante's works published between 1964 and 1974, including *View of Dawn in the Tropics,* as "fictions of interpretation."

Additional coverage of Cabrera Infante's life and career is contained in the following sources published by the Gale Group: *Contemporary Authors,* Vol. 85-88; *Contemporary Authors New Revision Series,* Vol. 29; *Contemporary Literary Criticism,* Vols. 5, 25, 45; *Dictionary of Literary Biography,* Vol. 113; *DISCovering Authors Modules: Multicultural; Hispanic Literature Criticism; Hispanic Writers;* and *Major 20th-Century Writers.*

Rosario Castellanos
1925–1974

Mexican short story writer, poet, novelist, and essayist.

INTRODUCTION

Castellanos is best known for works that reveal and challenge social hierarchies and systematic discrimination in her native Mexico. Using a tone of ironic humor, with which she mocked social conventions, Castellanos employed historical and religious metaphors to illuminate a cultural tradition of oppression in which women and native people are deprived of individual freedom. Personal concerns with solitude, depression, and mortality also recur throughout Castellanos's works. She is recognized as a forerunner of Mexican feminism and a predecessor to many contemporary feminist literary critics.

BIOGRAPHICAL INFORMATION

Born in Mexico City, Castellanos was raised on her parents' estate in Comitán, Chiapas, Mexico. Shunned by her parents in favor of her brother, Castellanos witnessed her brother's suicide and became a solitary child who retreated into literature. After her family's estate was appropriated by the Mexican government in the 1941 land reform plan, Castellanos began her studies in the College of Philosophy and Letters at the National University of Mexico in 1944. While at the university, she joined an international group of Hispanic writers known as the Generation of 1950. Following her parents' deaths in 1948, Castellanos published her first long poem, "Trayectoria del polvo," on the subject of death. In 1950 she received her master's degree in philosophy, writing a thesis entitled "Sobre cultura femenina," and subsequently serving as the cultural program director of Chiapas. In 1957 she married a university professor and gave birth to their son, Gabriel. Castellanos then worked as the information director of the National University of Mexico from 1960 to 1966. She traveled to the United States in 1967 as a visiting professor of Latin American literature at the universities of Wisconsin, Indiana, and Colorado, and chaired the Comparative Literature Department at the National University of Mexico upon her return home. By then divorced, in 1971 she was named ambassador to Israel by President Luis Echeverría. While in Israel she taught Mexican literature at the Hebrew University in Jerusalem and continued to write poetry, short stories, essays, and a play—all of which dealt with women's issues. Castellanos died accidentally of electrocution in 1974. Her body was returned to Mexico City, where she received a state funeral, and was buried in the Rotunda de los Hombres Illustros—a tomb reserved for Mexico's most respected leaders and heroes.

MAJOR WORKS OF SHORT FICTION

Castellanos became aware of gross social and political inequities while growing up as a member of Mexico's wealthy, land-owning class. On her parents' sugar and coffee plantation, she witnessed widespread and officially sanctioned discrimination against the native people who lived in and around Chiapas. As a woman in a male-dominated society, Castellanos was also faced with widespread misogyny. Consequently, injustices against women and minorities were the primary focus of her writings, including her three short story collections: *Ciudad Real* (*City of Kings,*) *Los convidados de agosto* (*Guests in August,*) and *Album de familia* (*Family Album.*) A related issue for Castellanos was language and the ways in which it is used to oppress and manipulate those outside the power structure. Many of Castellanos's stories feature characters who are kept outside of the mainstream by their lack of communication skills, or who simply do not speak the language of the dominant group. Critics have noted a distinct evolution in Castellanos's short fiction: the stories in *Ciudad Real* are set largely in the rural Mexican countryside, those in *Los convidados de agosto* in provincial towns, and in *Album de familia* most of the stories take place in an urban Mexican setting. Additionally, critics have commented on Castellanos's increasing use of humor, frequently ironic, in her later stories, with characters—usually women—quietly but comically subverting the patriarchal status quo using whatever means are available to them in their proscribed domains.

CRITICAL RECEPTION

Castellanos has received international attention for her literary works. Some scholars note the importance of her difficult early life in fostering her writing career and formulating her literary themes. Others remark that her adept use of humor throughout her works helps to present more effectively the sensitive issues surrounding women's lives and the exploitation of Indians in Mexico. Several commentators have asserted that her commanding use of language deftly leads her readers towards an understanding of how language itself is the key to determining the social stature of people within Mexican society. Following her death, José Emilio Pacheco wrote: "When the commotion passes and people reread [Castellanos's] works, it will become evident that nobody in her time had as clear a consciousness of the twofold condition of being a woman and a Mexican. And no one else has made of that consciousness the subject matter and the central line of a body of literary work. Of course we didn't know how to read her."

PRINCIPAL WORKS

Short Fiction

Ciudad Real [*City of Kings*] 1960
Los convidados de agosto [*The Guests of August*] 1964
Album de familia [*Family Album*] 1971

Other Major Works

Apuntes para una declaración de fe (poetry) 1948
Trayectoria del polvo (poetry) 1948
Dos poemas (poetry) 1950
De la vigilia estéril (poetry) 1950
Sobre cultura femenina (essays) 1950
Presentación en el templo (poetry) 1951
El rescate del mundo (poetry) 1952
Balún Canán [*The Nine Guardians*] (novel) 1957
Poemas (1953–1955) (poetry) 1957
Salomé y Judith: Poemas dramáticos (poetry) 1957
Al pie de la letra: Poemas (poetry) 1959
Lívida luz: Poemas (poetry) 1960
Oficio de tinieblas (novel) 1962
Juicios sumarios: Ensayos (essays) 1966
Materia memorable (poetry) 1969
Poesía no eres tú: Obra poética, 1948–1971 (poetry) 1972
Mujer que sabe latin (criticism) 1973
El uso de la palabra (essays) 1974
El eterno femenino: Farsa (drama) 1975
El mar y sus pescaditos (criticism) 1975
Meditación en el umbral: Antología poética [*Meditation on the Threshold: A Bilingual Anthology of Poetry*] (poetry) 1988
The Selected Poems of Rosario Castellanos (poetry) 1988
Another Way to Be: Selected Works (poetry, essays, short stories) 1990

CRITICISM

Phyllis Rodriguez-Peralta (essay date 1977)

SOURCE: "Images of Women in Rosario Castellanos' Prose," in *Latin American Literary Review,* Vol. VI, No. 11, Fall-Winter, 1977, pp. 68-79.

[*In the following essay, Rodriguez-Peralta explores Castellanos's intention in her fiction to demythify cultural and popular images of women.*]

The trajectory of Rosario Castellanos' prose begins within the indigenist literature of twentieth century Latin America and extends the line marked by Alcides Arguedas, Jorge Icaza, Gregorio López y Fuentes, Ciro Alegría, and more recently, by José María Arguedas. Indeed, from the modified use of selective contemporary narrative techniques, and a subtle exploration of psychological perspectives, Arguedas and Castellanos form a link between the indigenist novel of protest against injustice and the contemporary novel of existential determinism.

Castellanos' prose, however, takes a sharp turn away from indigenism and the flavor of the province and enters the terrain of contemporary Mexican women—or better, of contemporary feminism. Vertically the two stages of her literary work oppose each other in space and in time, but horizontally an underlying unity is maintained by an increasingly insistent awareness of woman and her situation. The spatial content of Castellanos' work moves from the primitive Indian surroundings in the southern state of Chiapas, to the narrow ambiance of provincial towns, to the sophisticated, impersonal life of the capital; at the same time the view of women is focused first from a wide lens encompassing an Indian-white panorama, to a closer proximity of provincial women restricted by traditional mores, and then to a close-up of contemporary women in the city who are emerging into the harsh glare of personal choices and personal responsibilities.

The thrust of Castellanos' indigenous-regional work cuts into social and racial problems of the Chiapas area. Yet the preponderance of women characters, contrasting with other indigenous works peopled only with men (or where the women are so peripheral as to give this impression), creates a different texture and indicates the direction in which her prose will develop. Although two novels and two collections of stories belong to this first period of Castellanos' writing, from 1957 to 1964, all salient points can be found in the powerful novel *Oficio de tinieblas* [*The Tenebrae Service*], 1962. The antipathetic separateness of the white and the Indian worlds maintains the constant tension of the novel; any communication between these worlds is impossible whether they exist in the usual state of indifference and scorn pitted against ignorance and misery, or whether they erupt into violence against each other. Under this bristling exterior lies the stratum of women.

Oficio de tinieblas presents the same number of men and women characters who are structured with an equality of roles in the novel even though their importance in the life situation is not equal. The eleven women characters, representing all social castes, can be placed into three groups, with a subdivision into Indian-white within each group:

Group I

(Principal Roles)

Catalina Díaz Puiljá (Indian)

Julia Acevedo

Group II

(Strong Secondary Roles)

Isabel Zebadúa

Idolina

Teresa (Indian)

Mercedes

Group III

(Ancillary Roles)

Marcela (Indian)

Felipa (Indian)

Benita

Christina

Ifigenia (Indian)

Women's existence is separate from men. They function in the subsoil of events, and in spite of the novelty in an indigenous work of their acting directly in front of the reader (rather than through the eyes of men), only one, the mystic Catalina, has any power to cause or influence events.

In this closed society of the Chiapas region, isolated from the mainstream of Mexican life, all women seem to be marginal figures, alienated from society and from each other. They encompass not only the expected victims of man's brutality, but the brutality of women to women. There are no tender relationships, not even between mothers and daughters. In the white world Isabel easily rejects her small daughter in favor of her new husband, and Idolina in turn so hates her mother that she rejoices when her stepfather humiliates her mother in adultery. With less refined cruelty, Felipa, an Indian mother, treats her daughter like a slave and eventually gives her away. Cruelty governs society's attitude toward old maids whose humiliation causes them to isolate themselves within their homes. Only during preparations against a siege by the Indians do they feel secure enough to come out and mingle with other women, laughing and talking, momentarily without fear of open scorn.

The ability to bear children is of prime importance to every woman. Catalina, at twenty, was already set apart from the rest of the Indians in Chamula because of her barrenness. Her desperate efforts to follow all the native prescriptions for fertility lead her through somber shadows into the role of "ilol," one who can face the mysterious. Other women treat her with care because of her unknown powers. Yet within herself she is plagued with constant anxiety as to when her husband will leave her; a marriage without children is not valid and needs only Pedro's words to repudiate her. As the sexton tells the priest: "She is wicked, Father. She is marked. She has never had children."[1] When a young Indian girl is violated by Leonardo Cifuentes, wealthy landowner and an influential citizen of Ciudad Real, Catalina seizes an opportunity to alleviate her own problems. She brings Marcela under her domination, and then accepts the baby, Domingo, as her own. But when her husband and Domingo eventually grow away from her, she knows that the displeasure and the evasion are punishments for her sterility.

In the person of Catalina Díaz Puiljá, Castellanos explores the mystical, intuitive properties of women (conceded to them by primitive cultures) instead of their lucidity or rationally oriented powers of the intellect. Finding the way to attention and power through the dark paths of magic, Catalina is accorded her place of honor and leadership by both men and women. It is she who discovered the old stone gods in a hidden cave. It is she who must be their voice of interpretation for the collective tribal desires. She becomes a great "ilol," with the Indians dependent upon her for the rituals and liturgies which are necessary. Women constantly serve her with obedient, superstitious respect. The exultation she experiences fills the solitude and erases the sense of failure at her childlessness and her estrangement from her husband. During Holy Week she indicates to the Indians that the cross must have a victim. It will be Domingo. Led by their "ilol," they crucify the boy and drink his blood, and being assured by Catalina that they can no longer suffer death, the Indians begin their attacks upon the whites in the area. In the disastrous results, Catalina, powerless and ignored, slinks around the remains like an inoffensive dog.

Julia, in the world of the *ladinos* [whites], must also win acceptance and a place for herself in Ciudad Real because she is different, an outsider. Caught up in liberal groups during her school days, she had become glibly familiar with the terminology of social justice, agrarian reform, and division of wealth. But like the majority of women seen through Castellanos's eyes, her personality remained undefined until shaped by man. She defied convention by living with Fernando, a student leader, but her subsequent boredom soon flattened the adventure. She has no children because she does not want to submit herself completely to anyone, and her goals come to bear on social prestige. In Ciudad Real she imitates the manners and attitudes of the most important women. At first they keep this outsider at bay, excluding her from their gossip while accepting her hospitality. But little by little their discussions center on a common denominator: man, fascinating and frightening.

Access to the life Julia wishes comes through Leonardo. His pursuit of her is a contest in which his experience triumphs over her vulnerability. After she is his possession, Leonardo is bored by their conjugal and tranquil state and her air of a satisfied matron. He no longer thinks of her as a hawk but as a domestic animal of meek expression, and he compares her to his wife, Isabel, who kept him excited and intrigued for a longer time. For her part, Julia looks around with satisfaction at her kingdom—her home in the approved style of Ciudad Real's taste, her power to order a submissive group of servants, her security, her prestige as wife of a government official (usually absent) and the mistress of a wealthy landowner.

Castellanos structures the distance between men and women with as great a disparity as that between Indians and whites, and indeed similarities exist between the divisions. Leonardo is fond of saying that the Indians are like animals who cannot be taught, and that their "*patron*" [boss] is their divinity. To a lesser degree, women, by implication, fall into the same relationship with a husband or a father. Friendships between equals are impossible. Leonardo believes that serious conversation is not for women, and when he does talk occasionally of this plans to Julia, she only measures what these will mean to her. From the moment of their union, Fernando and Julia had ceased to discuss the socio-political ideas that had brought them together. The years, sudden explosions of anger, and sullen moods to which he has become accustomed are all evidence, in his opinion, of the unpredictable physiological fluctuations and the instability of the feminine soul. Cesar, his assistant, who had always lived in a world where women were either submissive or at least hypocritical, cannot understand how a man like Fernando puts up with a woman who treats him with such little respect. But Fernando tolerates Julia's quirks in a kind of pity toward a weaker being. He does not wish to entertain any doubts of her virtue which would imply the necessity of attention, in turn taking time away from his all-consuming work. Fernando and the Indian Pedro, both dedicated to restoring the land to the Indians, are completely devoted to this goal and indifferent to their relationships with their wives. Pedro is awed by his wife's powers, but he believes that woman is only an unconscious instrument between the gods and man. Although belonging on the lowest rung on society's scale, his experiences with white prostitutes had reduced all women to female clay capable of being molded according to man's desires. Therefore he need not feel inferior to anyone.

Castellanos makes use of many contemporary narrative techniques in presenting her powerful drama of conflicting worlds. Although she adopts the traditional narrative viewpoint during most of the novel, she remains invisible and allows the characters to move about freely within their limited spheres. The density of the novel and the number of characters makes an interior quality difficult to achieve. Nonetheless, on occasion Castellanos approximates short interior monologues, as in Isabel's thoughts about her first marriage. Although Julia's device of escaping from Leonardo's conversation is related in traditional manner, the mental processes hover on the edge of interiorization:

> She closed her eyes and took refuge in absurd thoughts, in hypnotic repetitions: "Pablito nailed a little nail, a little nail did Pablo nail; one, two, three, four, one hundred; Lord Jesus Christ, true God and true man. . . . When oranges, oranges, when lemons, lemons."
>
> (p. 199)

Idolina's thoughts are related from without, with quick touches of interior focus:

> Idolina felt the disdain with which they looked at her because she was a girl. . . . What is that old man talking about? It is clear that he enjoys listening to himself. Within the roundabout conversation Idolina catches the drift of his intention: he is trying to separate her from Julia. Why? He says that Julia is not an appropriate friend. No? Then who?
>
> (p. 201)

Complete interiorization is achieved in the thoughts and feelings of Catalina where the prose often turns to "I . . .":

> When I lean over to fan the fire, the vapor from the pots covers my face and bathes me with the steam. . . . Aye, my eyelids close because I do not want to see the sun. How dark it is here inside! I have to grope my way as in the depths of a cave. Of a cave! The echo resounds on the hollow stone. Lizards are crawling, humid creatures. My feet slip on the cold slab. And this damp darkness penetrates to my bones. It is as if I had died and they had buried me, wrapped in an old mat. . . . I am going to rot here, in the tomb, in the cave.
>
> (p. 191)

Standing outside herself—as in experiences of extreme shock or of psychological trance—Catalina often addresses herself as "tú" [You]. Her visions and revelations reach a surrealistic fluidity which in itself conveys the essence of pre-Columbian perspectives and premordial myths.

The incredible scenes of Domingo's crucifixion are also carried along in a surrealistic flow of jumbled impressions, words, sensations, and actions which both intensifies and mitigates the horror. This collective technique functions in a different manner when Castellanos employs collective conversations in order to reveal women's ideas of men: first the father; then the priest; and the cousin, and the friend of the family, and the serenades, and the enemy; and finally the husband who brings pleasure, children, social position. (But if the husband never arrives, my dear, be resigned to emptiness.) The many unidentified women's voices, all chorusing the central theme of their existence, effectively reveal the pathetic limitations of their lives.

In the structure of the novel, time, in general, moves forward at a regular pace, and its flow in the present includes an active past and a mythical past. The latter is strengthened by the opening poetic prose which metaphorically describes the origins of the Indian village, and by the primordial link with magic which comes through a woman. The separate worlds of Indian and white are taken up in segments which include the corresponding spheres assigned to women. Although some characters are introduced piece by piece, their spaces always intersect at the same level.

In the human structure of the Chiapas region, there is both social determinism and sexual determinism. The secondary women characters in this novel, orbiting around the center space which is occupied by man, leave a variety of images. Isabel, Leonardo's wife, belongs to the provincial aristocracy. Expecting dissimulation, not fidelity, she can tolerate any adventure of her husband with inferiors like the Indians, but not with an equal. With her submissive nature, however, she easily forgives her husband. (Such a forgiving spirit does not extend to other women, nor could she pardon cowardice in her first husband.) Isabel cannot understand why her daughter does not grasp that women are of no value without a husband. The unmarried Benita longs to be important to her priest brother (who thinks it takes great Christian charity to listen to her prattle). Her counterpart Dona Cristina, the bishop's housekeeper, finds a sense of belonging by considering herself as part of the clergy. Doña Mercedes, who procures Indian girls for Leonardo, is assured of his financial protection. Doña Ifigenia, an Indian wife of a German landowner, is completely satisfactory in her role because she has the discretion to remain in the background, not even intruding by giving her color to their children. The Indians Marcela and Teresa are victims: the first, of Leonardo's brutality; the second, of the cruelty of Isabel who forced her to nurse Idolina, leaving her own baby to die. The relationship between Teresa and Idolina—who is isolated from everyone by her psychosomatic paralysis—flourishes in a balance of dependence and fidelity. Soothing Idolina with stories of magic in which she herself finds release, Teresa speaks of a great "ilol" and her son made of stone.

The pessimism of this novel holds out little hope for comprehension either between the races of between the sexes. Differing from other indigenous-regional writers, Castellanos tips the usual assessment of victimizer-victim into a closer balance of mutual responsibility. This becomes particularly apparent in the roles of men and women where all contribute to the general condition of ignorance and cruelty. As disagreeable as their male counterparts, not one woman is even indicative of an ideal. Julia, the only woman with opportunity for wider vision,[2] is among the most shallow and insensitive. With a vigorous, asexual approach not confined to characterizations of women, Castellanos creates three strong masculine portraits: Leonardo, Father Mandujano, and the maverick Fernando. The first two have no redeeming features. The negative attributes of Fernando—the only character with heroic possibilities due to his ideals and dedication to social justice for the Indians—lead to total failure.

Castellanos's other regional works, covering the same territory and the same society, leave an equally disheartening picture of backwardness and insensitive cruelty. Her first novel, *Balún-Canán* [*The Nine Guardians*[3]], 1957, although less effective then *Oficio de tinieblas,* adds facets to the images of women. Again men and women are equally despotic in their separate, well-defined spheres. In the role of mothers the women are non-maternal and ineffective, and it seems as though the children serve only to assure their own social esteem and to keep their positions as honored wives. Rearing of children is assigned to Indian "nanas" with little or no supervision. The young girl who speaks throughout much of this novel seems frightened and bewildered by the forces around her, particularly the magic powers of the Indians, although she loves her "nana" and this love is reciprocated many times over by the faithful Indian servant. (The mystic sense of the Indian which permeates all sectors of the structured society of Chiapas is reminiscent of Arguedas's *Todas las sangres* [*All Lineages*] and the unconscious "Indianization" of the whites living in the isolated Peruvian sierra.[4]) In the aftermath of the Mexican Revolution and in a society dominated by men, only one landowner, a white woman, is able to hold her property in the face of government land reforms. She does so by receding into herself and creating the fame of her magical power, accepted unquestioningly by the Indians, both men and women, who serve her with respect and fear.

In the stories of ***Ciudad Real*** (proper name), 1960, and ***Los convidados de agosto***[5] [***Guests in August***], 1964, a less detached Castellanos focuses on individuals existing in the Chiapas region of her novels. With Ciudad Real at its hub, the majority of stories in the first collection touch the lives of humble, marginal men and women. Their roles are scrupulously divided, as always, but both seem equal victims (of fate, of ignorance, of customs, of inhumanity, as the case may be). The tone and the setting change in the last three stories which deal with regional organizations designed to help the Indians. **"La rueda del hambriento"** [**"The Hunger Wheel"**] reveals the complete misunderstanding between the doctor and his Indian patients, and between the doctor and his nurse (who expects, even wishes to be subordinate to him). In **"El don rechazado"** [**"The Rejected Gift"**] an anthropologist engages in a one-sided dialogue with the reader in order to vent his frustration. With all good intentions he had offered to help an impoverished Indian woman by sending her daughter to be educated for useful work. But when he refused to buy the girl in exchange for the expected carafe of liquor and two measures of corn, the woman returned to her "patrona," precisely the person who had previously thrown her out in the streets.

In ***Los convidados de agosto*** the Indian retreats into his own environment, and the stories now enter the rigid homes of prescribed attitude and custom in a provincial town. Some deal poignantly with the plight of unmarried women excluded from the town's approbation because of their civil state. The light tone of mockery with which Castellanos begins turns slowly to distress as she delves into the measures open to "decent señoritas" in order to attract a husband. (The main thing is not to look ridiculous.) The title story is particularly successful in portraying the gnawing hunger of Emelina, who still believes there is hope for her, and the corresponding backbiting and derision of her sister Ester who has become slavishly attentive to their elderly mother. Sweetness and gentleness do not exist in this or in any family environment. Instead there is envy, pretense, superficiality, and slothfulness.

The image of women's subordination to men, a willing and even an abetted subordination, is consistent throughout Castellanos' first literary period. In the white world, successful women use the weapons of their sex to attain their goals of husband, children, and social position, obviously dependent upon the all-important male. Within the family unit, the woman has her own place, apart from the man:

> From now on Romelia would enter the guild of women who never say "I want" or "I do not want" but who always circle around a man in order to achieve their purposes. And that circle is condensed in a phrase: the "señor" wants . . . the need to consult the "señor" first. . . .
>
> (**"El viudo Román"** [**"The Widower Roman"**], ***Los convidados de agosto,*** p. 140)

Such a woman seems content with her marginal role and particularly respects the man who knows how to command. Those women who do not achieve this desired status live alienated from their society. Completely humorless, Castellanos maintains a dispassionate rather than a crusading tone in her considerations, and even though she comes very close to the *solteronas* [spinsters] of the provincial towns, there is rarely compassion. In the Indian world the division between men and women is presented in vanoramic focus with the single powerful portrait of one woman who goes to the forces of darkness and magic to break out of her isolation.

The second stage of Castellanos' work shifts abruptly in attitude, tone, and narrative viewpoint. No longer an observer, in ***Album de familia,*** [***Family Album***] 1971, Castellanos herself enters the alienated society of today, and she uses sarcasm and caustic wit to assail the bastions of women's worlds. In the first story, **"Lección de cocina"** [**"A Cooking Lesson"**], Castellanos, writer, intellectual, and professional woman, assesses her own situation in the kitchen: "My place is here . . . I went astray in lecture halls, in the streets, in offices, in cafes . . ."[6] Parodying an interior monologue, she comments on her state of newlywed: I lost my own name and I am not accustomed to the new one which isn't mine. I also can consciously withdraw into myself, abandon another, expose him to destruction. I should like to whisper my name into your ear so that you remember who it is you are possessing. She thinks of the equal sunburn they suffered in Acapulco:

> He could give himself the luxury of "conducting himself according to who he is" and recline face down so as not to chafe his sore skin. But I, sacrificing little Mexican woman who was born like the dove for the next, smiled like Cuauhtemoc being tortured. . . . The classic position for making love. And I groaned, from laceration, from pleasure. The classic groan, Myths, myths.
>
> (p. 9)

With no restraints she assesses their physical love: "I prefer to believe that what unites me to him is something as easy to erase as a secretion and not so terrible as a sacrament." (p. 11) She will try to impose the rules of this game. But she thinks: If I assume the other attitude, the sinuous, feminine way of all my female ancestors—*las humildes* [the humble ones] who only opened their mouths to agree—I will be pampered and cherished. Only, it is repugnant to me to act like that. If I insist upon my own internal truth, my own authenticity, my husband will feel uncomfortable in my company. When I married him I was prepared to make his home the peaceful retreat he wanted. But I thought the total renunciation of what I am would come on a Sublime Occasion. Not with insignificant, ridiculous matters facing me in the kitchen. . . .

In other stories the modern trappings of open extramarital affairs, homosexuality, abortion and the like, in sophisticated surroundings, jostle with the prudence of traditional Mexican women who put on their masks of docility and raise querulous, alienated children. Castellanos treats it all with flippancy. Even Mexican women writers are not immune to her biting humor. In **"Album de familia"** the superficial, even stupid conversations among these celebrities give Castellanos ample opportunity for merciless caricature, especially of their idol, a foreign poetess of stoic Indian features, renowned as a teacher, who has just received an international literary prize.[7]

It is not that Castellanos is insensitive toward other women writers but that she expects more from them than mere reflections of a stultified, diminished humanity. In speaking of the influence on her own poetry of Delmira Agustini, Juana de Ibarbourou, and Alfonsina Storni, she says that she admired the sumptuous images of the first and the ironic smile of the third, and the oblique as well as direct suicidal impulses of both. And she adds that she quickly learned that everything about Ibarbourou was contrary to herself.[8] She is particularly annoyed with work written by women where the authoress stands at the center and around her whirl her obedient satellites, the greatly enamored men who represent the deliriums of her subconscious. With thinly veiled scorn she dismisses the narcissistic woman protagonist of Maria Luisa Bombal, summing up her opinion in general by stating that when a Latin American woman takes literature into her hands she does so with the same gesture and the same intention as when she takes up a mirror: to contemplate her own image.[9] Castellanos looks for other considerations in a new consciousness of feminine reality.

Many times in her essays and articles[10] Castellanos advises laughter, not flaming indignation nor tremulous tears, as the best weapon for liberation against whatever oppresses. Brandishing her swords of ridicule and wit, she does battle for the full personhood of women in the farce *El eterno feminino* [*Everlastingly Feminine*], published posthumously in 1975.[11] The setting of a beauty salon, archetypical of a female environment, is essential. Lupita (Guadalupe, of course) is about to sit under the dryer as the final step of the beautification process before her wedding. Unknown to her, the owner is trying out a new device connected to the dryer which will allow a client to touch a button and select a dream. Lupita suffers through two disconcerting dream sequences before a short circuit cuts off the electricity. Frantic because her hair is not yet dry, she accepts the solution of the owner to use a wig. But each wig evokes a different vision paralleling its name. In desperation Lupita destroys the last one available, the owner throws her out of the shop even though her hair is damply limp, and Lupita is faced with the knowledge that she will have to take care of the problem of her hair by herself.

The thin texture of this three-act comedy holds up for laughter what is obsolete or useless in convention and custom. The characters and the situations are easily recognized, and the hilarity relies upon this familiarity. In the first act Lupita, taking part in the dream, is completely traditional. On her honeymoon she provides evidence of her virginity and she becomes indignant at the suggestion that she might have enjoyed the sex act. Later she rigorously follows her mother's orders as to how to make her pregnancy miserable for herself and her husband. The children are brats; her husband is unfaithful; she has to kill him and his mistress; she gives television interview and talks about the movie to be made of her life. In advancing age, she and her daughter, Lupita II, have continuous arguments, particularly about Lupita II entering the university:

> LUPITA II: I am a person.
>
> LUPITA: Neither more nor better than I was.
>
> LUPITA II: I have a right to . . .
>
> LUPITA: Nor more intelligent.
>
> LUPITA II: I want to live my life.
>
> LUPITA: Nor freer.
>
> LUPITA II: I want to be happy!
>
> LUPITA: Nor happier.
>
> COMMENTATOR *(Sighing):* There is nothing comparable to maternal love!
>
> (pp. 61-62)

In the second act (and the second dream), Lupita meets various famous women who go through the salient features of their classic roles. There is Eve, of universal fame, and six Mexican women: Malinche, Sor Juana, Josefa Ortiz de Domínguez, Carlota, Rosario de la Peña, and Adelita. Their adjustments of the traditional versions reflect an intent to view history from other angles of reality. Eve, for example, has the audacity to defy God, vowing to conquer her pain and live life fully, while Adam is cowed by the loss of his secure Paradise. It is the women who are adventuresome and their male counterparts, whether Cortés or the Corregidor, are short-sighted and hackneyed. The flexibility of language in the play contributes to the humor. Lyric poetry mixes with commercials, common refrains with comantic postures, vulgarity with poetic dialogue and Mexican corridos. Shifting techniques of invisible reciting voices, a commentator, and accompanying projections on a large screen produce a collage effect.

In the third act, each wig that Lupita puts on gives her a different role to play in society. The "Spinster's Journey" a severe, stiff wig, covers an empty and sad life remote from the warmth of humanity. In "Mud Flower" Lupita, as prostitute, must learn the rules of the game and remember to make her clients believe that she fell into this life completely against her will. In "Usurper" she is an abandoned mistress; and in "Woman in Action" she is an energetic reporter who interviews three outstanding women (each attributes her success to someone or something other than her own ability). In "At Water's Edge" Lupita becomes a professional woman—but one who is carefully feminine and who would abdicate her independence at the first convenient moment. Directing the discussions of a group of women, this Lupita criticizes a new play, *El eterno femenino,* which ridicules family, religion, and country. And no wonder, since it was written by a resentful, bitter divorcee who wants to challenge a society to which she is no longer worthy to belong! In the melee that follows, some shout for motherhood, some to break with the slavery of the beauty routine, some for the pill, all for keeping the maids.

Castellanos's laughter is real and without bitterness; the sincerity of her assessment is also real. And although the denouement is trite—Lupita must face up to fixing her own hair—the implications are far-reaching. In the hysteria of the last scenes, there are three solutions open to the modern Mexican woman: to defend traditions, modernizing them sufficiently to bring them in line with the times; to break completely with the past; to study the problems and then respond in creating a new reality for herself. Castellanos leaves the choice to the audience.

Throughout her prose, whether dealing solemnly with provincial society or satirically with contemporary life, Castellanos sees a fragile order based on simulation. In this complicity she assigns equal responsibility to men and women because each sex notes only the advantages and satisfactions of his or her respective role. Men wear certain masks of hypocrisy and insist that women wear others. Women accept these masks with passivity, inertia, and lack of perception. Mutual deception results, mutual alienation and inability to communicate.

What does Rosario Castellanos want for women? She should like to take away the false images imposed both by men and women. She seeks to demythify female roles so that the woman is no longer an ideal, not the inspiration for the creative and spiritual life of men, not a goddess of fecundity nor a cosmic force, much less the subservient enemy. She leaves the impression that women feel themselves to be victims, and she agrees that they often are, but with their own acquiescence. "Because being a parasite (which is what we are more than victims) does not lack enchantments."[12] In her emerging concept of a new image of women, Castellanos rejects both abnegation and abrasive conflict.[13]

The sudden death of Castellanos in 1974[14] cut off the continuous unfolding of her ideas. In addition, the very short span of the second stage of her literary work robbed her of sufficient time to sharpen and perfect her new literary tools and to explore artistic routes for transposing her developing philosophy into her creative prose. The pessimism of her indigenist writing which gave way to the ironic wit of her most recent work is still one of hopelessness unless woman herself alters her own image. Castellanos leaves in doubt whether this will be possible.

Notes

1. *Oficio de tinieblas.* México, D.F.: Joaquín Mortiz, 1962. p. 224. All quotations are taken from this edition.
2. Julia's mother had the obsession of giving her daughters an education so they would be capable of sustaining themselves in case, like herself, they were abandoned. Unfortunately the mother had substituted coldness and intransigence in the absence of paternal authority.
3. The original novel (México, D.F.: Fondo de Cultura Económica, 1957) was translated into English by Irene Nicholson (New York: Vanguard, 1959).
4. Although Arguedas moves in the same direction as Castellanos, that is, from isolated regions into contemporary city environments, the women in his work are completely incidental. On the other hand, even though Castellanos accords dignity and worth to the Indians as individuals, there is no respect and love for Indian culture, one of the principal notes in Arguedas's prose.
5. *Ciudad Real.* Xalapa: Universidad Veracruzana, 1960. *Los convidados de agosto.* México, D. F.: Era, 1964.
6. *Album de familia.* México, D.F.: Joaquín Mortiz, 1971. p. 7. All quotations are taken from this editon.
7. In "Una tentativa de autocrítica" ["A Tentative Autocritique"], *Juicios sumarios* [*Brief Judgments*], Castellanos says that this work helped her to become an enemy of all her women colleagues. It was originally written in drama form as "Tablero de damas" ["Checkerboard"].
8. From "Si 'Poesía no eres tú' entonces ¿qué?" ["If 'You are not Poetry' then what?"], *Mujer que sabe latín* [*Woman Who Knows Latin*] (México, D.F: Secretaría de Educación Pública, 1973). p. 204
9. From "María Luisa Bombal y los arquetipos femeninos" ["María Luisa Bombal and the Feminine Archetypes"], *Ibid,* p. 144.
10. Her essays and articles are grouped together in various collections: *Sobre cultura femenina* [*Concerning Feminine Culture*], 1950; *Juicios sumarios,* 1966, *Mujer que sabe latín,* 1973; posthumous, *El uso de la palabra* [*Being Able to Speak*], 1974 *El mar y sus pescaditos* [*The Sea and its Tiny Fish*], 1975.
11. Raúl Ortíz, in his introduction to *El eterno femenino* (México, D.F.: Fondo de Cultura Económica), relates that in the fall of 1970 Castellanos became interested in the possibility of a play based on the problems of being a woman in a world conditioned by men. However, she did not finish the play until April of 1973, in Israel.
12. From "La liberación de la mujer, aquí" ["The Liberation of Woman, Here"], *El uso de la palabra* (México, D.F.: Excelsior, 1974) p. 60.
13. Many of her essays and articles approach the most contemporary and liberal ideas of feminism, particularly her desire to undo the idolatry of motherhood and the myths of virginity, and to remove the paralyzing fear of solitude, and sexual and social frustration, from the unmarried. Her level-headed, non-aggressive assessments are never aimed at man, as enemy, but extend to humanity as a whole.
14. Rosario Castellanos: May 25, 1925–August 7, 1974. Her accidental death occurred while she was the Mexican Ambassador in Israel.

    Many of her articles, simply and without elaboration, give poignant insight into her life: "I remained unmarried until I was thirty three years old. . . . Then I entered into a marriage which was strictly monogamous on my part and totally polygamous on the other side. I had three children but the first two died. I received my divorce . . . in my home in Tel Aviv." "Hora de la verdad" ["Hour of Truth"], *Ibid,* p. 257.

    She often writes about her son Gabriel (who was twelve at the time of her death), but her obvious deep love is held in check by her expressed goals that he be independent and able to choose his own way.

    Although her autobiographical details rarely show emotion, an occasional passage dips into her personal feelings, returning quickly to surface humor: "Nevertheless, there is a moment in which I have to admit that I am a totally incapable creature and in which my eyes fill with tears thinking about the fact that I am an orphan and divorced and that, if they had lived, my children would be older than Gabriel and the girl would be going to parties now and would have boyfriends and would think that I am a monster who does not understand her and who is bringing her up badly." *Ibid,* p. 259.

Beth Miller (essay date 1979)

SOURCE: "Rosario Castellanos' 'Guests in August': Critical Realism and the Provincial Middle Class," in *Latin American Literary Review,* Vol. VII, No. 14, Spring-Summer, 1979, pp. 5-18.

[*In the following essay, Miller discusses Castellanos's use of plot, setting, characterization, and narrative techniques in* Los convidados de agosto *to demonstrate her thoughts on sociopolitical issues.*]

Rosario Castellanos (1925-74) was a remarkable prose fiction writer as well as poet.[1] Her novels, *Balún-Canán* [*The Nine Guardians*] and *Oficio de tinieblas* [*Profession of Darkness*], are distinct and original contributions to the body of literature about the Mexican Revolution and to the *indigenista* novel, respectively.[2] Castellanos published, in addition, three volumes of short stories[3] and a sizeable number of essays, most of which have been collected.[4] This study deals with her volume of short stories of 1964, ***Los convidados de agosto*** [***Guests in August***], referring occasionally to Castellanos' essays in order to probe her method of social criticism and examine aspects of her thought, especially in regard to the ideological concerns implicit in the text and that underlie her choice of a specific temporal and geographical setting, of certain signifying elements of plot and characterization, as well as the use of particular narrative techniques.[5]

In *Juicios sumarios* [*Summary Judgments*] of 1966, Castellanos writes that the Mexican literary tradition has always been "instrument, reflection, or victim of ideology."[6] She defined ideology at that time—pejoratively—as "the set of ideas (political, economic, social, and juridical, etc.) that justify and protect the interests of the dominant class at a given moment in history."[7] This view of ideology informs the four stories in ***Guests in August*** and the descriptions of the lives and social relationships of the conservative, middle-class inhabitants of Comitán, a provincial, colonial town in Chiapas, backdrop for the action of the four stories. Since the beliefs and behavior of the towns-people are a manifestation of an archaic version of the hegemonic values and myths of a nation, the narrator's attitude toward individual characters ranges from sympathy to ridicule to condemnation, depending on whether they are viewed as victims, reflections, or instruments of the dominant ideology. The *petit bourgeois* of the town is criticized for its racist and sexist prejudices as well as for the strict adherence to rigid conceptions of hierarchical differences between social classes and a smug, xenophobic provincialism.[8]

In general, Castellanos' narrative mode—one employed by many Latin American writers in the sixties—may be classified as critical realism. Her social criticism, however, is never so deadly serious as to exclude humor or imaginative detail; nor does the narrative mode prevent ample technical experimentation. By focusing on middle-class characters and exposing their assumptions and values, Castellanos is able to comment on a socio-political system and a specific cultural tradition, that is to say, ideology in the broad sense.[9] In ***Ciudad Real*** she had explored, from a more anthropological perspective, relations between the Indians and *ladino* populace in a poor town in Chiapas; in ***Family Album*** she examines the lives of urban middle-class women in Mexico City. Somewhat in the manner of Benito Pérez Galdós, she develops individual character against a background of social customs and mores and, like Thomas Mann, aspires to a "lucid understanding of reality."[10] To a greater extent than these authors however, Castellanos believed that a writer, perhaps especially a Latin American one, has a responsibility to serve as counter-hegemonic social critic. In ***Guests in August*** she employs a number of techniques to increase and draw attention to the distance between the narrator and the narrative, thereby creating an illusion of semi-autonomous characters who serve as individualized "specimens," and of near-objectivity. This illusion is enhanced in part by the language the characters speak, which seems to spring from the characters' psychology although it derives as well from their social circumstances. It is language carefully distinguished from the writer's own for in order to perform the job of social critic Castellanos maintains a stance of objectivity. As an intellectual and "committed" writer, she is more politically sophisticated than any of the characters in the book, and, as an outsider, more able to discern and conceptualize significant social problems and, of course, to portray them artistically in words.

Guests in August

The action of the title-story, **"Guests in August,"** is confined to a single day of celebration in the small town and centers on a crucial event in the life of an unmarried woman. The plot of this well-told tale of suspense, drama, and pathos begins amid festivities and fireworks. The atmosphere created is one of anxious expectation and timorous defiance of the prevailing order, heightened by ambiguous foreshadowing and a reference to "the suspension of daily prohibitions."[11] Castellanos gradually arouses sympathy for the homely protagonist and establishes at the outset that all women experience suffering because of the restrictions imposed on them ("daily prohibitions"), restrictions which do not apply in the same way to men, since in Comitán the sexes follow different sets of rules and are not permitted the same behavior. The men laugh openly, the women covertly, hiding their mouths behind their shawls. The shawls differ in quality according to the women's social class and income, but the women who wear them share a common characteristic as distinctive as skin color. whether respectable matrons and marriage-seekers or poor street vendors and servants, all are female and have learned to conceal their laughter in a hasty gesture that seems instinctive. This image brings to mind the veiling of Moslem women, and Castellanos indeed suggests that such customs serve as emblems of acquired femininity and sociocultural signs of submission.

Emelina, the main character, is awakened from a dream by church bells and releases the pillow she has been embracing as her phantom lover vanishes. A servant brings morning coffee in Emelina's favorite chocolate cup, which had belonged to the grandmother whose name Emelina bears. Her life does not seem to be much different from what it would have been in her grandmother's time, certainly it is much the same as concerns the "daily prohibitions." Emelina has a strong sense of pride in the superiority of her class and family name; she belongs to a "good" family. Although she feels envious of lower-class girls who can more easily take advantage of the annual saint's day celebration to relieve the "weight of spinsterhood," she reflects that these girls "did not have much honor to lose and no family name to protect" (p. 62). Emelina recalls the stories about the ones who got themselves pregnant with strangers on just such a day as this and the exciting consequences they enjoyed: one girl became a seamstress, another ran away to Mexico City and returned briefly as a female bullfighter.

As she muses about the fates of these women, she becomes sad: "Every day is the same in Comitán and before you realize it, you've already grown old and you don't have anything to show for it, not even a memory, a snapshot." (p. 64) She thinks about her older sister Ester, already an old maid, although scarcely older than their brother Mateo. And Emelina realizes that she too is getting old and this will certainly be the last year she can enjoy the August celebration. She avoids looking at herself in the mirror and succeeds in imagining that her wrinkles are disappearing. She feels still young, vibrant, whole. After all, time has scarcely touched her, since she has been merely waiting all her life, has stayed on the edge of things: "How many times had she envied the others, the women who leaped into the current and let themselves be carried along! She ought to have some reward for her self-denial." (p. 67) Castellanos, then, depicts omnisciently, and with sympathy, the tenor of the character's thought, the texture of her life.

This day is clearly a special one for Emelina. For a start, she refuses to go to Mass with her sister. Then, in a symbolic gesture she is incapable of analyzing, she impulsively opens the door of the canary's cage, but the bird is too frightened to escape. As the woman observes, with anguish, her embittered sister and her senile mother she returns obsessively to her anxiety about aging. She fears becoming a sad old lady without ever having felt the weight of a lover on her chest (p. 75). When her sister Ester tries to dissuade her from attending the festivities, chiding her that she cannot compete with the young girls since she is already thirty-five, Emelina bursts into sobs. But then she bathes luxuriously, dresses carefully, and goes to the bullfight with her girlfriend Concha.

Every year the climax of the celebration is the collapse of the wooden bleachers at the bullring. This time, when the ritual occurs Emelina loses consciousness and awakens in the arms of a stranger, a real man, not a fantasy. He revives her with brandy, and soon she begins to feel intoxicated, less from the alcohol than the man's proximity. He leads her to a kind of tavern. Although at first she is too shy to even look at him, she admires the authority in his voice as he orders an expensive wine and is glad to be seen in public with "a magnificent macho." (p. 88)

Emelina talks on and on to him about her family—the insanity of her mother, the incompetence of her brother—about her friend, Concha, who was becoming a dowdy spinster, even about herself. She drinks more and more wine, and her companion becomes bolder and more seductive. Finally, after having drunk a large quantity of wine, he decides it is time to leave and helps her down the stairs and into a taxicab. At last Emelina will get away! But before the car can start up, Emelina's brother and his friend appear on the scene, stop the couple from leaving, and have it out with the stranger. Emelina is dragged home by her brother's friend Enrique who shouts: "You have brought dishonor upon your family name." (p. 95)

With great narrative distance, that of a traditional storyteller, Castellanos relates that when Emelina finally became aware that her first and last opportunity had vanished, she began to howl "like a madwoman, like an animal." (p. 95) Enrique cannot stand the savage, inconsolable wail and leaves her; then he wanders through the streets until he reaches a bordello.

The lot of a spinster in the provinces is not a happy one, less so even than the situation of other women in "respectable" middle-class families. Castellanos contrasts Emelina's lack of freedom to the liberty enjoyed by Mateo and Enrique, as well as to the relative lack of restrictions imposed on women in the lower social classes. The text reiterates that the restrictions are not self-imposed; in this case it is Emelina's family and small-town society that conspire to keep her in her proper place. She yearns for freedom, although her lack of experience has led her to equate freedom with sexual freedom, the easiest to achieve, although she cannot manage more than a taste of that. In the end, she has nothing to look forward to except a useless, bored, dependent existence.

Throughout her narratives, Castellanos pays special attention to the social phenomenon of spinsterhood and the theme of the marginalization of unmarried women. She published a poem on this subject, "Jornada de la soltera" ["The Spinster's Day"] in *Livid Light* (1960):

> The spinster works hard at her ashen task
> on labors without merit or fruit;
> and when the family gathers
> around the fire to hear a story,
> a howl breaks through the air,
> a woman's cry in an immensity of wilderness
> where every rock, every trunk
> consumed by fire, every twisted
> branch, is a pitiless
> judge or a merciless witness.[12]

In ***Guests in August*** Castellanos presents the spinster's case, and although the story is not a treatise, the prose is persuasive. Emelina has longed to "leap into the current" of life; the author's prose becomes a current that carries her along as she dreamed. Her forced removal from the current is violent, and the story's end is a final seal of injustice upon injustice. The other stories in the volume also portray spinsterhood. In **"The Widower Roman"** a young woman, during her marriage ceremony in the church, thinks to herself about the wonderful change that will take place in her life now that she will cease to be a mere "Miss" and assume the privileges of an enviable "Mrs.":

> Beginning today Romelia would enter the league of women who never say "I want" or "I don't want," but always express themselves in a circumlocution involving a man in order to accomplish their purposes. The evasion is dependent on a simple phrase: The *señor* has resolved . . . the *señor* prefers . . . the *señor* orders . . . we cannot contradict the *señor*'s wishes . . . above all we must accomodate the *señor* . . . I first have to consult with the *señor*. . . . The *señor* who will exalt her to the category of *señora* in the eyes of the public will also, in intimacy, give her the exact image of her body that will finally realize the fullness of its being, of its experience, and achieve the functions for which it was created.
>
> (p. 166)

Since the society is male-centered, women who yearn for a place in it must become a satellite to a husband. A spinster, unemployed, has no social role and generally lives as an embarrassing and unwanted burden on her relatives. Of all the unmarried female characters in this collection of stories, only the intellectual narrator in **"Ephemeral Friendships"** deviates from the norm; her solution is to move away to the city and undertake a career, just as Rosario Castellanos did.

"Ephemeral Friendships"

This is a story told as if it were true, and may be based on biographical events, but the art of the story is in its humor and narrative techniques. Castellanos adopts a perspective from which to consider the totality of events sociologically without sacrificing aesthetic values. Through the first-person narration she presents a portrait of Gertrudis, a girl of a lower social class than the narrator's, but her close friend and confidante during their adolescence. Unlike the narrator, Gertrudis seems to be a simple soul, able to live from day to day without reflecting on her actions, unhampered by the nag of memory or the urgent pull of future projects. Her story is presented with humor and irony since it is told from the point of view of her friend, the sophisticated narrator, more as a comic tale of a farcical shotgun wedding than as anything approaching a tragedy of abduction and rape.

The narrator remembers Gertrudis from the convent school they attended together, to which Gertrudis had been sent by her father Don Estanislao, a widower, because he was leading the sort of life he did not want his children to witness. Gertrudis had little interest in formal studies and did not mind being taken out of school when her father remarried and established his new household in another region of the country. The girl had to leave behind her fiancé, Oscar, who was studying electricity by correspondence, with the agreement that as soon as he finished the course and opened his shop they were to get married. The narrator agrees to write some farewell verses to Oscar from Gertrudis and, later, keeps Gertrudis informed by letter of Oscar's conduct and progress. Oscar's own letters, copied word for word from a manual for lovers, are not newsy. (The narrator now believes that it was, ironically, through writing the letters to Gertrudis that she discovered her literary vocation.)

Oscar never does set up his shop; he leaves town and nothing further is known about him. Gertrudis continues uneventfully to tend her father's store until one day a horseman stops for a beer and invites her to run away with him, which she does, taking along her little sister. They spend the night at a house in a village along the road: "Gertrudis didn't think about Oscar at all. She didn't even think about the stranger who was possessing her body and to whom she abandoned herself without resistance or enthusiasm, with no sensuality and no remorse." (p. 19) In the morning they wake to find Don Estanislao at their bedside, with a posse of *vaqueros* and his lawyer. The father has the lawyer declare the couple man and wife before arresting the groom, Juan Bautista González, for cutting telegraph wires. He had been fleeing from the law when he met Gertrudis and now of course is guilty of other crimes as well. Gertrudis goes to live with Juan Bautista's parents, where she works for her keep and visits her husband in jail twice a week until his release. Shortly after he is free, Juan Bautista tells Gertrudis that he wants to return to his childhood sweetheart who has been faithfully, patiently waiting for him to marry her. Gertrudis admires his loyalty and, left to fend for herself, decides to go to Mexico City where she has a girlfriend, the narrator, who writes her long letters.

The narrator's parents will not permit their daughter to be led astray by Gertrudis' bad example and refuse to take her in, but they help her find work and lodging elsewhere. The young women meet secretly on Sundays. The story ends abruptly after the narrator deserts her friend, who is happily munching popcorn, in a movie theatre. She has suddenly realized that Gertrudis would probably not even have remembered her name had they not come together again. The narrator had suggested they go to a movie to take Gertrudis' mind off the telegram she received that morning informing her that Juan Bautista, as a result of his habit of cutting telegraph lines, had been shot in the back and killed. The narrator goes home and tries to write, wondering whether it is worth the struggle; Gertrudis is free of these anxieties, so might it not be simpler merely "to live"? (p. 29)

In this story Castellanos handles point of view so as to establish aesthetic distance—for the reader—without the loss of subjectivity inherent in an omniscient narrator. The narrator is positioned between the reader and the events so that she can interpret the action and the characters in a way the protagonist, Gertrudis, could not. It is a technique similar to Julio Cortázar's in his famous story, "The Pursuer." Because the narrator has a different personality from Gertrudis', and a different set of values, she does not attempt to portray the character's psychology; rather, she uses her own personality as a foil in characterizing Gertrudis and conveys the suspicion that what is natural behavior for Gertrudis would be outrageous in her own case. She, a writer, is analytic and moralistic; Gertrudis is neither. In addition, the two women experience time differently. Gertrudis is not reflective; she lives entirely in the present, as is suggested by the quotation from an anonymous Nahuatl poet that serves as the story's epigraph: ". . .we come to this earth only to get acquainted, we are only passing through here." Hence Gertrudis does not value friendship in the same way the narrator does, but views it as being no more lasting or important than anything else. In its application to the writer-narrator, however, the title is ironic because the very act of writing the story immortalizes both Gertrudis and her relationship with the narrator, therefore, the friendship was not meaningless, not ephemeral. For although we assume the two will never meet again, the narrator will not easily forget Gertrudis after she has analyzed, and put on paper, the lasting influence of her friend on her own life.

"The Caprice Waltz"

In **"The Caprice Waltz"** Castellanos employs a third-person narration, but frequently shifts to subtle indirect quotation in order to reflect the attitudes of the townspeople or to show how these attitudes, at any moment, are influencing what the characters think and say. In general, the narrator stays on the surface, viewing the incidents from a middle distance and developing the characters from the outside, not from within their minds. The story concerns the efforts of two kindly spinster aunts to transform their wild niece into a proper young lady. Their attempts to socialize and civilize the lonely girl are doomed to failure because the middle-class inhabitants of Comitán refuse to admit the stranger into the pattern of their social life. The adolescent girl's struggle for identity is summarized metaphorically in her problematical name. The one given her by her father is Reinerie, but this French-sounding and exotic appellation is hard for her aunts to pronounce, so one calls her Gladys, the other Claudia; the priest suggests María, after the Virgin Mary; Reinerie herself for a time likes Alicia. But the name that matters most is the nickname she is called behind her back (because of the way her aunts dress her), by everyone in town: "Picture Postcard."

Castellanos interprets the situation sociohistorically, and only secondarily in terms of individual psychology. As in *La princesa del palacio de hierro* [*The Princess From the Palace of Iron*], so here what is most striking is the force of social attitudes and the powerful effects of the milieu on behavior. For a while Reinerie makes progress under her aunts' tutelage, learns to wear shoes and fashionable clothing, to eat with the proper utensils, and even to respond to the coded talk of the local girls of her own age. Eventually she also begins to assume the hierarchical class attitudes and the set of values that correspond to her station. At her belated First Communion, she stands decked with laces and brocade, and suddenly glows as she realizes that she is young, beautiful, and rich: "What more could she ask? Only for her mother to die." (p. 46) Her mother, a *mestiza,* has never lived in the town; her function in the story is to mark Reinerie as part Indian, that is, to serve as transmitter of an obscure Indian culture heritage and distinctive physical features which have a social signification as well: at one point the town mothers refer scornfully to Reinerie as "that dressed-up Indian girl."

It is soon apparent that although Reinerie is handsome and healthy, possesses intelligence, wealth, and an old family name—precisely the attributes associated with success by the mainstream of Mexican society—these cannot gain her entrance to the closed social life in the xenophobic provincial town. Even the Church joins with the matrons in excluding the girl. And no one attends the sumptuous "coming-out party" given in her honor by her father, who has on his daughter's behalf acceeded to the aunts' entreaties to legalize his relationship with Reinerie's mother. The town parents forbid their daughters to frequent the aunts' house lest they learn of taboo matters, for Reinerie had witnessed the actual coupling and birth of animals in the wilds where she grew up.

As a result, Reinerie is left alone with her aunts in the stifling atmosphere of the house. The seamstress aunt has lost her clientele, and the piano-teacher aunt all her pupils. Reinerie's response is increasing withdrawal into herself and a gradual return to her old habits; during a period of apparent epileptic seizures and madness, she seeks solace in her mother's Indian language and lore. Finally, after reading the entrails of a black hen, she steals barefoot from the house under the cover of night, as if escaping to a totally different life, and as if going back to a way of life in some corner of a Macondo about which the reader understands no more than do the respectable citizens of Comitán.

The story is so *vraisemblable* (naturalistic in its effects) that the reader may fail to perceive that the portrayal of the cruelty and pettiness of the intolerant society are quite exaggerated and that several of the elements are used symbolically, not merely to produce a reality effect. In the combination of signifying elements (an anonymous pilot on the local airstrip, Reinerie's outlandish imported hat, the **"Caprice Waltz,"** the black hen) as well as in the seriocomic tone of the storytelling, Castellanos brings to mind certain techniques Gabriel García Márquez was to employ in *One Hundred Years of Solitude* and Vargas Llosa in *Captain Pantoja and the Special Service.* Like García Márquez, Castellanos writes from an ideological position that is well to the left of that of the people about whom she writes; at the same time, she goes further than any of her male contemporaries in her critique of male/female sex roles.

In **"The Caprice Waltz"** the message of the closure (Reinerie's return to what she had been at the beginning of the story and her departure from Comitán) may be interpreted in several contexts. Perhaps the most powerful thematic element is the indictment against white racist society for its treatment of Mexican Indians. A feminist reading would emphasize another message: a nonconforming woman is an outsider and has little chance of surviving in a provincial Mexican town, even if she is willing to pay the price of sacrificing her integrity and freedom. The forced isolation and ostracism of marginal women increases their eccentricity, desperation, and inner alienation as is signified by the three women's weird, ritualistic outings to the airstrip.

The men of the town object to women who acquire masculine skills, as Reinerie had, because any deviation in regard to gender conventions threatens the code of sexual polarity. Females are expected to display deference toward males, and this deference is based on forced dependency, as is illustrated in the priest's reaction when Reinerie defended herself with a pistol from a man who offered merely to help her cross a puddle in the road. Here Castellanos comments, leaving no room for misinterpretation, that women's lack of independence enhances male dominance: "the men counted on women's ignorance of life as the indispensable ingredient in their relationships. It was up to the men to prolong it or destroy it. In the first case they were sure of submission. In the second, of gratitude." (pp. 43-44)

"The Widower Roman"

In its adherence to conventions, especially in terms of the plot line, the short novel **"El viudo Román"** [**"The Widower Roman"**] resembles the nineteenth-century "bourgeois" novel—one thinks of Balzac—and the melodramas of Echegaray and Tamayo y Baus. Thematically this story is a descendant of the seventeenth-century Spanish "honor" play. Within the fairly conventional plot development, there is a psychological study of a man, Don Carlos Román, so obsessed with his honor that he incidentally destroys the life of an innocent young woman in order to carry out his monomaniacal scheme. The essential twist in the narration is that the reader does not know of Don Carlos' motivation and strategy until the end of the *récit*; hence, interpretation is only possible in a retrospective analysis or second reading. In this "second reading," whether actual or mental, the events of the first reading take on dimensions of irony and parody, as in a film by Buñuel.

On one level, the story probes the clichés of the bourgeois and masculine ethic that serves as the source of the tragedies of at least two lives in this story—those of Don Carlos' two wives—or five if we count the suicide of Rafael, the solitary madness of Don Carlos, and the largely unperceived suffering and alienation of his servant, Doña Cástula. The conflict takes place in Comitán, a setting in which, as we have seen in the other stories in ***Guests in August,*** social classes are rigidly differentiated not only along economic lines, but according to cultural and ethical precepts that govern the behavior of the individual members of each class in relation to others of their own class as well as to those who are considered to be socially beneath or above them.

The narrative vehicle for Castellanos' critique is the cruel vengeance of a betrayed husband who seeks to restore, in a perverted way, his honor. His definition of honor is a Spanish cultural legacy, as much so as the language he speaks. After discovering that his wife was not a virgin when he married her, he spends years in solitude planning a strategy by which to restore his damaged honor and obtain retribution from the family of the man responsible for "spoiling" his wife. One could view Don Carlos' complex of attitudes against the background of his social class and within the broader cultural context and code of provincial Mexican society, as well as in relation to literary traditions and generic conventions. One could also analyze Don Carlos' actions politically or ideologically as resulting from an exaggeratedly commercial concept of virginity, that is, in terms of property relations, as merchandise bought and sold.

Castellanos' text provides ample material for these varied and simultaneous interpretations. Don Carlos' behavior and values are seen on a surface level as functions of his social class at the beginning of the novel during his long conversation with Doña Cástula, who expresses a sanguine attitude toward her own loss of virginity, like the T. S. Eliot character who was seduced in a canoe on the Thames, but relates the incident without resentment. Cástula (whose name suggests "chastity"), like Don Carlos' deceased wife Estela, had been seduced and abandoned by a man not her husband. Cástula's commonsensical, working-class interpretation of her own loss of virginity contrasts without paradox to Don Carlos' overblown and obsessive concern with his self-esteem. Cástula comments: "Anger? When would I have had time to feel it? I work from morning until night." (p. 102)

In this regard, the text argues that unmarried middle-class women are more oppressed than poor ones. In "good" families, like Estela's or Romelia's, a girl's virginity is one of the family's most prized possessions, to be protected by all family members, female as well as male, and to be used as barter for the girl's marriage. Marriageable females of the middle and upper classes are compared to consumer items to be sold to the highest bidder. Thus, Romelia's stream-of-consciousness flows over possibilities for a husband until she decides that since she will always be economically and socially dependent, whether on her father or husband, the highest priority is someone who will not only cherish and protect her as one would a child, but make her envied and rich. Romelia is a product of her upbringing within the family, of her inferior and frivolous education, of asphyxiating social circumstances and a false morality. More distantly and abstractly, she is a victim of the cultural tradition of *machismo* and the persistent and insidious effects of the patriarchally-conceived cult to the Virgin Mary, "model for all women."

Behavioral norms, as Emelina perceives wistfully in **"Guests in August,"** vary according to social class. Obsessive honor, as is demonstrated by the *caballeros* in the works of Lope de Vega, requires leisure, and is a luxury for those concerned primarily with survival, with making a living day to day. In a given social context, these contrasting norms of conduct, however, serve to distinguish one class from another. Hence Don Carlos reacts with a smug lack of sympathy to Doña Cástula's life story: "In Don Carlos' eyes the conduct of this woman only went to prove the baseness of her condition." (p. 102) Although there is parody in the manner in which such judgments are expressed, from a more sociological point of view the reaction is naturalistic: hunger is more real to Doña Cástula than honor. Despite the fact that she has been Don Carlos' sole companion for many years, she continues to be his servant, and the sex and class distinctions cause an ineradicable difference between them. Thus when Don Carlos asks Doña Cástula what she would do if she had her seducer in her grasp and were able to punish him and so to avenge herself, she responds: "Sir, I am a woman. Matters of revenge are for men, not for me." (p. 102) Doña Cástula had begun to serve Don Carlos' family as his *cargadora,* a servant child who carries around the baby and acts as companion and watchdog. From that job, she later recalls with pride, she had risen by her own merit to cleaning woman, then cook, and finally housekeeper. Doña Cástula, then, because of her institutionalized place in the family and society, accepts unquestioningly these caste-like social-class distinctions; she cannot escape bourgeois condemnation and economic exploitation.

"The Widower Roman" is more slow-moving than the other three pieces in ***Guests in August,*** in part because of the density of the texts (social, cultural, literary) it offers for interpretation. The narrative proceeds in a traditionally realistic manner so that only in retrospect would it occur to the reader to question the probability of the incidents which, in one way, imitate those found in popular novels by a Corí Tellado, and in another, present the paradox of being based on a real-life happening in Chiapas.[13] As the story opens, Don Carlos, a widower in mourning for years, begins to emerge from his self-imposed solitude and retirement. He buys a horse and each morning goes for a ride around the countryside. Through lengthy and complicated maneuvers, and with the help of the parish priest and his trustworthy housekeeper, Don Carlos becomes the suitor of a beautiful young girl, Romelia. He is everything she ever hoped for: a man who will love and protect her, provide her with wealth and social station. Here Castellanos employs, in the manner of Henry James, a limited point of view. Through Romelia's eyes we see Don Carlos as very much in love and rather paternalistically indulgent with Romelia. He seems to understand her weaknesses and her yearning for a stable, peaceful marriage. Romelia imagines beforehand (things do not turn out as she dreams) every detail of her courtship and married life with Don Carlos. She plans to wear forever the locket she received from her beloved, now-deceased brother Rafael, in the belief that a "cult of death" will give her something in common with Don Carlos who maintains his dead wife's room and belongings intact.

The wedding ceremony is elaborate, the bride radiant, proud, relieved to escape spinsterhood. During the reception, a black butterfly enters the room and is thought by many of the guests to be the soul of Don Carlos' first wife. The reader, with hindsight, comprehends the irony of this parodic and symbolic "foreshadowing" element. All seems to proceed according to custom, as Don Carlos leads Romelia across the threshold of the house which is now to be hers as well as his. However, the next morning she awakes to find that the groom has gone for his habitual horseback ride, and left word for her to be dressed to go out by the time he returns. Romelia is disturbed by the message, also because she thinks her locket is missing, but then Doña Cástula locates it on the dressing table. Her husband arrives to announce that they are going to pay a call at the home of Romelia's parents. Much to everyone's surprise, including the reader's, Don Carlos tells the family he is returning their daughter because she is not worthy of living under his roof. Romelia protests that Don Carlos is lying, of course she was a virgin, her father need only examine the sheets.

The father pays no heed to his daughter, for Don Carlos is a man of honor whose word cannot be questioned without violating the shared masculine code of honor. Male bonding, then, is stronger even than family loyalty. The father apologizes to Don Carlos: "What else can one expect from women, whose nature is weak, hypocritical, and cowardly?" (p. 183) It is only when the priest hears the news and goes to investigate the reason for the broken marriage vows, that the reader learns that Don Carlos, like Borges' Emma Zunz, has been acting out an elaborate scheme of vengeance: his first wife had been so in love with Romelia's brother Rafael that she died soon after her forced marriage to Don Carlos. The *récit,* were it not for the irony and social commentary, would be simply a far-fetched tale; the whole air of the story is novelesque. (Don Carlos had to *marry* Romelia in order to see her brother's handwriting on the scrap of paper inside the locket she wore and thus have proof that Rafael was the man his first wife had been in love with.) Castellanos, both in the tone of the narration and in the parodic title (*roman* is French for novel) asks for the reader's indulgence and complicity. The protagonist's name, then, is a sign of the literary *vraisemblance* of the character, for he is a type more common in literature, one hopes, than in life.

Because of Castellanos' sensitivity and her perception that the language of literature can serve as ideological vehicle, the realism in her fiction does not derive from description and anecdote alone, but is in the very fiber of her writing. In these four stories she employs the mode of critical realism in portraying the provincial middle class in southern Mexico, and in terms of her own writing, "exhausts this vein of archaic and provincial life" as literary material for her fiction.[14] Although she was able to see all of Mexican literature as instrument, reflection, or victim of an ideology, at the time she wrote ***Guests in August*** she also held a view of the role of the artist-intellectual as an *engagé* but marginal observer. In addition, her historical sense and sociological inclination led her to the realization that literature has never been "the most ideally-suited vehicle for the expression of ideology" because of the difficulty inherent in all high art and because of the small number of initiates, especially in developing nations, able to understand and enjoy it.[15] That the four stories studied here may be considered ideological reflection and/or vehicle does not contradict aesthetic ends and achievements. As I hope has been demonstrated, literature can be approached as both artistic creation and ideological discourse. This was also Castellanos' perspective:

> . . . the testimony of the Mexican writer is valid. . . . One does not choose the vocation of writing—which Larra said is, in countries like ours, synonymous with crying—because one hopes to gain prestige, wealth, or popularity. The fundamental motives are necessarily of another order: the urgency to apprehend reality and express it in aesthetic forms can be a very strong motivating force, as is the moral imperative of denunciation; and, perhaps, the desire to survive on a page, surrounded by all that we have loved, by all that we have found to be intolerable and painful, by what has excited us, aroused us to rebellion, brought us peace. Grasping that momentary lightening, we discover in its brief clarity, beauty and order, the laws and meaning of the world and of our own lives.[16]

Notes

1. The major part of her poetry is available in a volume of collected work, *Poesía no eres tú [Poetry is Not You*] (México: Fondo de Cultura Económica, 1972).
2. The term *indigenista* is applied to fiction which deals with the problems of the South and Central American Indians. Although *Balún-Canán* (México: Fondo de Cultura Económica, Col. Letras Mexicanas 36, 1957) was translated into English by Irene Nicholson as *The Nine Guardians* (London: Faber, 1958; New York: Vanguard, 1959), Castellanos' second novel, *Oficio de tinieblas* (México: Joaquín Mortiz, 1962), has not been published in English translation; a third novel, *Rito de iniciación,* [*Rite of Passage*], which Castellanos mentions in some of her autobiographical writings and interviews, was never published.
3. *Ciudad Real* [*Royal City*] (Xalapa: Editorial Veracruzana, Col. Ficción 17, 1960); *Los convidados de agosto* (México: Ediciones Era, 1964); *Album de familia*[*Family Album*] (México: Joaquín Mortiz, 1971).
4. Many of her essays were originally published in a variety of journals, but the bulk of the later ones were written for *Excelsior: Juicios sumarios* (Xalapa: Universidad Veracruzana, Col. Cuadernos de la Facultad de Filosofia, Letras y Ciencias 35, 1966); *Mujer que sabe latín* [*A Woman Who Knows Latin*] (México: Secretaría de Educación Pública, Col. SepSetentas 83, 1973); *El uso de la palabra* [*The Use of the Word*] (México: Ediciones de Excelsior, 1974; *El mar y sus pescaditos* [*The Sea and Its Little Fish*] (México: Secretaría de Educación Pública, Col. SepSetentas 189, 1975).
5. Two of her essays from the seventies are especially useful for understanding her attitudes toward women: "La mujer y su imagen" ["Woman and Her Image"] and "La participación de la mujer mexicana en la educación formal ["The Participation of the Mexican Woman in Formal Education"], in *Mujer que sabe latín,* pp. 7-41. For feminist analyses, see Phyllis Rodríguez-Peralta, "Images of Women in Rosario Castellanos' Prose," *Latin American Literary Review,* Vol. 6, No. 11 (1977); and my essays "El feminismo mexicano de Rosario Castellanos" ["The Mexican Feminism of Rosario Castellanos"] and "Personajes y personas: Castellanos, Fuentes, Poniatowska y Sainz ["Characters and Persons: Castellanos, Fuentes Poniatowska and Sainz"] in Beth Miller, *Mujeres en la literatura*[*Women in Literature*] (México: Fleischer Editora, 1978; available through the USC Trojan Bookstore), pp. 9-19 and 65-75.
6. "Ideología y literatura" ["Ideology and Literature"], in *Juicios sumarios,* p. 82. (All English translations from Castellanos' Spanish are my own.) Castellanos' definition of ideology here quoted in the text is more akin to Gramsci's than to Althusser's; see Mario Monteforte Toledo, "Ideología y literatura," in *Literatura, ideología y lenguaje* [*Literature, Ideology, and Language*] (México: Grijalbo, 1976), pp. 237-268.
7. *Juicios sumarios,* p. 76. Roland Barthes, speaking of the European bourgeoisie in general, says that "the bourgeoisie has obliterated its name in passing from reality to representation, from economic man to mental man. . . . Politically, the hemorrhage of the name "bourgeois" is effected through the idea of *nation.* This was once a progressive idea . . . today, the bourgeoisie merges into the nation . . ." in "Myth Today," in *Mythologies,* tr. Annette Lavers (Frogmore: Paladin. 1973), p. 138. Castellanos' view of class is, of course, of Marxist derivation, see Joseph Sommers, *"Oficio de tinieblas," Nexos*, No. 2 (February 1978), 15-16.
8. Castellanos, following Lukacs, defines "realismo crítico" in "La novela mexicana y su valor testimonial" as "una corriente . . . en la que el escritor se sitúa desde una perspectiva para considerar la totalidad de los hechos y sostiene una ideología que le permite juzgar esos hechos y mostrar su relación con los fines buscados" ["The Mexican Novel and Its Testimonial Value. . . . A current in which writer places herself in such a way that she can consider the totality of happenings and maintain an ideology that permits her to judge those happenings and to show her relationship with the sought-after ends"] (*Juicios sumarios,* p. 118). Also see her discussion of "realismo mágico" and "realismo crítico" in her essay on *Pedro Páramo,* in *El mar y sus pescaditos,* pp. 112-15.
9. In the broadest sense, the definition of ideology takes into account what Althusser calls "the 'lived'

relation between man and the world," in his essay "Marxism and Humanism," in *For Marx,* tr. Ben Brewster (New York: Vintage, 1970), p. 233.

10. *Juicios sumarios,* p. 114.
11. *Los convidados de agosto,* p. 57. Hereafter, page numbers in the text will refer to this volume when no other indication is given.
12. *Poesia no eres tú,* p. 175.
13. I owe this information to Margarita García Flores.
14. "Una tentativa de autocrítica," in *Juicios sumarios,* p. 434.
15. See "Ideología y literatura," in *Juicios sumarios,* p. 82.
16. "La novela mexicana y su valor testimonial," in *Juicios sumarios,* p. 130.

Helene M. Anderson (essay date 1983)

SOURCE: "Rosario Castellanos and the Structures of Power," in *Contemporary Women Authors of Latin America,* edited by Doris Meyer and Margarite Fernandez-Olmos, Brooklyn College Press, 1983, pp. 22-31.

[*In the following essay, Anderson discusses Castellanos's exploration of women and power.*]

In 1950 Rosario Castellanos (1925-1974) presented a thesis on feminine culture which has come to be considered the intellectual point of departure for the women's liberation movement in Mexico.[1] According to Mexican essayist, Carlos Monsiváis, no one up to that time had expressed so clearly what it meant to be both a woman and a Mexican.[2] This became, in effect, the central line of Castellanos' work, but always from a very particular perspective: the relationship of women to their culture within the broader relationship in Mexican society of those with power to those deprived of it.

Although her 1973 book of essays, *Mujer que sabe latín . . .* (*Woman Who Knows Latin . . .*) is considered the first provocative Mexican analysis of the image of women within the framework of Western culture in general and Mexican culture in particular, it is well within a national tradition of polemical literature which has existed since the seventeenth century. In this tradition Castellanos examines the issues of image and reality, and submission and domination from a consistently unique, female perspective.

The feminine ideal of Western culture, according to Castellanos, is that of the strong woman of the Scriptures whose strength is defined in terms of her prenuptial purity, marital fidelity, devotion to her children, dedication to domestic obligations, and her prudent administration of a patrimony which she herself is not permitted to inherit or possess. Her virtues are, therefore, constancy, loyalty, patience, chastity, submission, humility, unobtrusiveness, and above all, self-sacrifice. All of these qualities are even more pronounced within Mexican culture. In fact, Castellanos proposes three female archetypes as typical of the Mexican reflection of woman's image: La Malinche, La Virgen de Guadalupe, and Sor Juana Inés de la Cruz.

La Malinche is an Indian woman who was given to Cortés, after he established contact with the first Indian towns on the coast, to serve as his slave, his interpreter, and ultimately, his concubine. Since she knew both the language of the coastal Maya area and the language of the central valley of Mexico (Nahuatl), she became—with the collaboration of Jerónimo de Aguilar who knew both Spanish and Maya—the key instrument by which Cortés was able to open his way into the Mexican interior. This is very significant because La Malinche and Cortés represent, symbolically, Mexico's "ancestral couple," responsible for the "fall" of the Indian nation and the configuration of the Mexican future. Thus, she is the Mexican counterpart of Eve, and through her knowledge she facilitates the penetration and violation of Mexico. These terms are used with purposeful consciousness of their sexual overtones when talking about La Malinche in Mexican history, for she is, in fact, the "Dark Lady" of sinister sexuality.[3] She not only facilitates the violation of her own people, but also becomes the mother of the violator's child. Interestingly enough, however, she can never be the "legal" mother because, historically, the Spanish crown did not recognize the legality of any relationship between Indian women and Spanish men, nor did it confer legitimacy on offspring resulting from such a relationship without the man's express stipulation. Of even greater significance for the symbolic overtones in the figure of La Malinche, she can never be considered the "legal" mother because true motherhood in the Catholic context implies an "immaculate" conception rather than a carnal one. As concubine to Cortés, she represents sexuality. This already sets up, symbolically, a conflictive tension between womanhood and motherhood. The maternal ideal cannot possibly encompass a figure like La Malinche.

The ideal of motherhood has to be La Virgen de Guadalupe, another Mexican legend. The figure of the Virgen Morena that appeared to an Indian, miraculously, became the emblem and symbol of Mexican nationhood during the struggle for Independence. Therefore, nation—or children as future nation—becomes identified with the emblem of motherhood which is untainted by the sexual implications of the Malinche figure: the maternal ideal as a figure unrelated to sexuality.

The third symbolic image of woman in Mexican culture is Sor Juana Inés de la Cruz, the poet-nun who lived in the seventeenth century and who is seen to embody intellectual activism. She entered the convent because only there could she have access to study, to writing, to the kind of activity for which there was no place within the traditional roles for Mexican women in that era. By confronting choice and its consequences rather than waiting to "be chosen" (as sweetheart or wife), she rejected the accepted norm. Moreover, by embodying intellectuality in the figure of a nun, Sor Juana symbolically conveys an image of intellectuality as a negation of both motherhood and sexuality.

For Castellanos, therefore, the three elements which are a symbolic synthesis of woman's image and reality in Mexican culture are sexuality, or betrayal leading to the fall of (Mexican) man; motherhood, which is chaste and excludes any recognition of sexuality; and intellectuality, which is a negation of both motherhood and sexuality. These elements, whose equivalent counterparts are considered integrative in the male, are thus displaced and fragmented in the image of woman in Mexico.

Rosario Castellanos has stated that, when she wrote *Mujer que sabe latín* . . . , her purpose was to raise consciousness, to awaken the critical spirit, to disseminate it and make it infectious, and not to accept any dogma until one is sure it is capable of "resisting a good joke."[4] The "good joke" is perpetrated by the author in her play *El eterno femenino* (*The Eternal Feminine*), a farce set in modern Mexico which satirizes the typical female roles in Mexican society and visualizes projects of defiance and rebellion against them. Ironically, all of the action takes place in a beauty parlor under a hair dryer.

In *El eterno femenino* there are those female characters who do not wish to challenge the status quo, who have managed to adapt to the "cult of the venerated slave"—that comfortable role of mother, wife, or lover. They play the roles of innocent virgins, analytical, pragmatic wives, and self-sacrificing mothers. The fantasy counterparts of these women are the characters who have rejected all stereotypic and conventional behavior, women who establish either tacitly or overtly the necessity of finding another way of being human and free. These are key words in Castellanos' work; it is precisely because she deals with the question of women within the larger context of questions of freedom and liberation, that there is, in her work, an important synthesis of social issues that goes beyond the female and has to do with the fundamental structures of power and the theme of domination and submission within society.

In the beauty salon that serves as the setting for *El eterno femenino,* a device is being sold by an agent for use by women while under the dryer. This device is guaranteed to avoid what the salesman considers to be the greatest danger to which women are susceptible while doing nothing—that is, thinking. Thought in itself is dangerous and must be avoided at all costs. The little device plugged into the dryer triggers a series of scenes which are, in fact, projections of distorted and surrealistic situations in which women either contemplate wild extrapolations of their own image of their roles as proper wives and mothers, or else they are fantasies which absolutely destroy all traditional roles.

Castellanos uses techniques of the theater of the absurd to project fantasies through the little device in the hair dryer. She also inserts herself into the world of her play by having the characters express a variety of speculations on what the author's purpose is in setting up these absurd situations. One character says:

> Do you realize that our most venerated traditions, our dearest symbols, are right now objects of mockery in a theater in the Capital? Against whom are they speaking out? Against one who is the pillar of our society, the one who transmits the values that sustain all of us to future generations, against the one who is the source of our strength and wholeness—the Mexican woman. . . . The attack is specific: and is against the self-sacrifice of mothers, the chastity of sweethearts, the virtue of wives, that is, against all our proverbial attributes. These are attributes in which our most solid institutions are rooted—family, religion, country![5]

By having a character comment on the dire consequences of allowing a playwright to mock the very pillars of society, Rosario Castellanos takes the question of women out of a limited focus and sets it in a more general perspective: the way in which women are conditioned to uphold the structures of power and how, therefore, within the family unit one finds a symbolic synthesis of the social, economic, and cultural structures of society at large. As in her other essays, novels, and short stories, Castellanos goes beyond the limits of conventional discourse on feminist questions and examines the whole question of social justice and economic exploitation, not unlike the concerns of Simone Weil, a writer she greatly admired.[6] This is precisely the preoccupation that binds together the themes of the woman and the Indian in Castellanos' work.

Neither women nor Indians are given the privilege of choice. As an instrument of repression, the mythification of the traditional role models for Mexican women has glorified the negation of choice as one of the most desirable qualities in a "proper" woman:

> Mexican women do not choose. We wait modestly for a man to cast an eye in our direction and note our marvelous qualities. All that follows goes according to fairly rigorous rules. . . . If we manage to wait long enough, if we are finally chosen, the rest flows with mathematical precision. . . . We manage to be satisfied with someone . . . who accepts marriage as a valid institution which one does not treat lightly and within which the wife has a role and must be given that role. . . . Our cardinal virtue is patience, and if we exercise it, we will be rewarded. . . ."[7]

Mexican literature has perpetuated this legacy of the feminine ideal in a series of archetypal characters, reflecting the fact that Mexican reality seems not to have changed its attitudes toward women since 1839 when the wife of the first Spanish Ambassador wrote that Mexican women were devout nuns, impeccable housewives, docile daughters, and dedicated mothers. But the other side of the coin, she observed, was to be seen in the mental asylums and prisons where most of the cases of madness in women had been brought on by abandonment or amorous deceit, sometimes involving the murder of lovers and spouses. These were women who had reached a *situación límite* (a point of ultimate desperation) at which, according to Castellanos, echoing Sartre, nothing is forbidden because nothing matters anymore.[8]

Castellanos' approach to the vital dilemmas of her characters has been substantially influenced by her reading of Simone de Beauvoir, Agatha Christie, Virginia Woolf, and Doris Lessing. It was in de Beauvoir's work that she first encountered female reality discussed not as biological destiny, but as choices influenced by religious, moral, and intellectual factors behind which were specific economic interests. These interests and the systems of exploitation that express them are encapsuled in the structure of the family, for their efficiency depends to a great degree on the dose of dogmatism that can be inculcated in its dependent members. Castellanos found a similar awareness of the intimate relationship between larger economic and social structures and race or gender relationships in the work of Rhodesian-born Doris Lessing. She saw in Lessing's exploration of black and white in Africa an essential point of contact with her own concern for the relationship between Indian and white in Mexico, not to mention the analagous implications this held for the question of women. Castellanos fully appreciates Lessing's perception of the inextricable knot of humiliation, remorse, and mutual dependency that characterizes the relationships between these groups. Indians, blacks, and women share a common reluctance to break that knot for fear of confronting a cold and impersonal alternative. On the other hand, what interests Castellanos even more is Lessing's subordination of the importance of color to economic motives in explaining the African situation. Any exploitative system depends for its survival on creating and sustaining an "inferior," exploitable sector, and in this sense, Indians, blacks, and women have shared a common fate.

Because Rosario Castellanos sees both women and Indians as occupying a confined space within Mexican society, the small town of Comitán in Chiapas becomes the perfect emblem of this confinement. Castellanos spent a good part of her early life in the southern Mexican region of Chiapas, an area deeply permeated by Indian (Tzotzil) culture. It is alive in the stories, traditions, and legends passed on from generation to generation in the language which is still spoken by a majority of the population there. It has also been rocked by repeated political and economic upheavals due to the confrontation between the landless Indian peasants and the white landed gentry. This area is also extremely provincial in its attitude toward the roles of male and female in society. Thus Comitán becomes the natural setting for Rosario Castellanos' narrative. It is here that the dominant problems of Mexican society intersect in the theme of submission vs. liberation.

The utilization of a restricted space to examine larger, hidden tensions draws Castellanos to the work of another woman author, Agatha Christie. In Christie, she admires the ability to detect beneath the apparent placidity and respectability of small English towns, the stifled ambitions, buried resentments, and skeletons hidden in country closets. Castellanos applies a similar optic to the town of Comitán. Delving into the "lives of the obscure" in this remote town, she writes about people of no great social, political, or economic import. They are those who consider themselves *gente decente* (proper citizens). Basically, they are small voices heard in a minor key. Yet it is precisely this dramatic counterpoint between the obscurity of the voice and the emblematic magnitude of the situation that gives such force to Castellanos' narrative.

In ***Los convidados de agosto*** (***The Guests of August***), a collection of short stories, various female characters in the town of Comitán confront their *situación límite*. These characters, reflecting the archetypes Castellanos discusses in her essays, are, among others, restless adolescents on the threshhold of womanhood, impatient to claim its experience and rewards; or spinsters who, in a desperate attempt to break the structures that enclose them, surrender themselves on summer nights to strange men, "without resistance, without enthusiasm, without sensuality, without remorse," but in some last effort to give meaning to their lives which, "like water, seem to filter through the fingers of the hand." They are women left at life's periphery, abandoned by fathers and lovers, whose role it is to wait, for there is nothing more dishonorable than initiating a thrust into life. Time and again, the female characters in Castellanos' stories wait.

When, as in the case of a story entitled **"Vals capricho"** (**"Waltz Caprice"**), a young girl, Reinerie, invades the lives of two maiden aunts who have made their peace with static marginality, the repercussions are immediate. Reinerie has been sent to her aunts by their brother who has, up to then, cared for his daughter alone in a remote jungle region of Mexico; he now wishes her to be educated and made into a proper young woman by his two maiden sisters. When she erupts into their lives, she is all unselfconsciousness and unbridled movement; her knowledge of nature's ways, her initiative of action, her sensual response to the world, her rebellious attitude are all a threat to the social codes which have been established to contain women. As Castellanos points out, a man generally counts on a woman's ignorance and innocence so that she may depend on him and be grateful to him for revealing life to her. Reinerie, however, needs no masculine interpreter of experience or dispeller of ignorance since she has lived in intimate contact with the physical world in the hinterlands. Thus, her presence causes general consternation not only in the lives of her aunts but in the life of the town as a whole. The center of the story becomes the conflict that arises as the aunts attempt to restrain, condition, and mold this young woman according to traditional female roles. Her very name, Reinerie, upsets the aunts for it bears no relationship to conventional names to which they are accustomed. In the course of the story she is called by a series of names simultaneously—Claudia, Gladys—all of which represent approved possibilities of womanhood for this young, untameable woman. In the end, Reinerie leaves, having reappropriated the same state of natural abandon in which she appeared, but not without suffering the consequences of a painful confrontation with her aunts, who are also wounded in the process.

The *soltera,* or spinster, is a prominent figure in Castellanos' stories because if the duty of woman is to wait passively to be chosen, the ultimate embodiment of waiting is the maiden lady. In the title story of ***Los convidados de agosto,*** Emelina, a spinster of thirty-five, is caught between the possibility of life and the abandonment of hope. In a last, desperate attempt to break out of the structures that have confined her to a sterile waiting, she impulsively decides to attend the fair that is being held in honor of the patron saint of the town. Her solitary flight to freedom and an encounter with a stranger dissolves into public humiliation as her brother takes a very inebriated Emelina home by force. Protesting that the stranger did not do anything to her, that he was just going to teach her how to live, she is berated by her brother who sees her behavior as an ineradicable stain on the honor of his name. One final, composite image in the story—very much in keeping with Castellanos' critical vision—is Emelina howling in the streets with the desperation of an animal, while her brother, after satisfying the affront to his honor, is seen knocking at the door of the town brothel.

For Castellanos, spinsterhood within the confines of a small Mexican town is the constant recollection of time, the constant aspect of time slipping away and death slipping in. (In this aspect her stories are not unlike those of Sherwood Anderson's *Winesburg, Ohio.*) *Soltería* is the absolute opposite of everything that constitutes energy, activity, and affirmation of life. The anguished point in the lives of these characters is the approaching moment when hope and resignation lie in the balance. It is within this moment, with its desperate awareness of being the last chance for a thrust into life, that many of her *solteras* are fixed. These women—the unmarried, the abandoned, the aged—will never be free of the conflict between a potential for life that they still feel, and the social impositions that forever determine the channels of their existence.

Castellanos' novel, *Balún-Canán,* fuses the theme of the Indian and the woman. It is set in Chiapas during the time of the presidency of Lázaro Cárdenas when Mexico undertook a program of land redistribution. It was a time of anticlerical legislation as well as of the division of large expanses of land into smaller parcels to be distributed to the Indians, and was thus a time that threatened all the traditional power structures. This novel deals with the repercussions of these events on both the relationships in Chiapas between Indians and *ladinos* (persons of Indian-Spanish racial origin, or *mestizos,* who identify with the dominant culture), and the relationships between men and women.

An important character is the Indian woman, Catalina Díaz Pantelhó, who suffers the knowledge of her inability to bear children. Within the Indian tradition, her husband would have the right to abandon her. Her anguish is intensified by not knowing when her husband will pronounce the words of repudiation. Ultimately, her attempts to harness all the forces at her disposal—both natural and supernatural—to remedy her condition, invest her with the aura of an *ilol,* a seer or sacred spirit. As she becomes more and more obsessed by the need to find a solution to her barrenness, she also becomes transfigured by it. She seems to undergo a process of "dematerialization" whereby her role of woman as potential mother is gradually replaced by that of woman as sacred spirit, preoccupied with things that transcend the immediate problem of motherhood. Her impassioned commitment to the mythic forces that mold the universe of the Tzotziles eventually leads her to galvanize the Indian community around her and to offer, as a kind of sacrifice to the gods of social justice, the illegitimate child she has raised as her own. Suddenly the initial dilemma of the Indian woman takes a turn in another direction: it is precisely the denial of her maternity which frees her to become the catalytic agent of the Indian insurrection when the local landowners refuse to carry out the mandate of the Cárdenas reform. This is an interesting Castellanos twist on the notion of motherhood, not as liberation, but as imprisonment within an alternative role bequeathed to Catalina. The moment that she finally denies the possibility of motherhood, she becomes the agent of true liberation.

Another female figure in the novel dares to challenge traditional roles. Julia Acevedo, La Alazana, a stranger to Comitán, defies custom and walks through the streets alone, her red hair insolently loosened. She has been raised to support herself by a mother abandoned by her husband, and for fear of becoming enslaved, she wants no children of her own. For yet another character, Idolina, passivity itself becomes an instrument of control. Her paralyzing illness is the mechanism of power she comes to exert over those at whose mercy she has always been.

Another aspect of the structures of power, as they relate to Indians and to women, is brought out in *Balún-Canán* when an Indian nursemaid says to the little girl who is the narrator and the daughter of a well-to-do ladino family: "It is very bad to love those who rule, those who possess."[9] When the child, who worships this woman who raised her, looks at her father dismissing his Indian workers, she thinks of him for the first time as "one who rules, one who possesses." The newly raised consciousness in the child's perception of her father's role is Castellanos' way of pointing to the family structure as a microcosm of society as a whole. The same young narrator, for example, finds a notebook in her father's desk which contains a text, obviously taken from an Indian source, which recounts the conquest and suffering of the Indians under the *caixlanes,* or ladino overlords. The child reads it furtively. When her mother discovers her, she admonishes her for playing with things that are part of her brother's inheritance. In other words, the knowledge of the world around her, as represented by the text, is denied to her. It can only be filtered to her through her male counterpart.

In yet another revealing incident in *Balún-Canán,* a ladino visits his family ranch at Chactajal. The owner of the ranch has "inherited" his Indian laborers as well as his property. He boasts to his visitor of the Indian women at his disposal, the number of children he has had with them and the advantages this entails, since the children stay close to the big house and serve with loyalty. Thus, the Indian woman—akin to La Malinche—becomes a mechanism for perpetuating the servitude of her people and the structures of colonialism. Hers is a double submission—as Indian and as woman.

Castellanos signals the fusion of the Indian and the woman's theme in other ways as well, such as in the selection of quotes from Indian texts to serve as epigraphs to her stories. In *Balún-Canán,* she chooses the following lines from a Mayan text:

> We are only returning. We have fulfilled our task. Our days are finished. Think of us. Do not erase us from memory. Do not forget us.[10]

The Indian vision of life is as part of a continuity of the past in the present; one's life is part of an inherited, collective experience. For non-Indians, life is unique and individual, ending in nothingness, thus heightening the panic felt by the lonely spinster. The Indian woman, on the other hand, is transformed by the consciousness of being part of a process that has preceded her and will survive her. By deriving strength from her ancestors as well as from contemporaries, she is better able to confront her *situación límite.*

Rosario Castellanos' awareness of herself as an articulator of the dilemmas of Mexican culture, as a responsible and committed writer, is summed up by some comments she made about the profession of writing and the nature of language in a collection of articles entitled *El uso de la palabra* (*The Use of Words*). Language, for Castellanos, is an instrument of command over one's self and one's reality. She interprets the literary vocation as being rooted in profound levels of human experience. By virtue of having written the words, tensions are released and a sense of liberation achieved.

Language is also a structure of power. When one of her Indian characters speaks in Spanish to the ticket-taker at the ferris wheel, the ladino comments mockingly: "Just listen to him, this Indian who thinks he's equal! He's speaking Spanish! Who ever gave him the right?" Spanish, says the narrator, is a privilege that belongs to us (the ladinos), and we use it by addressing our superiors as *usted,* our equals as *tú,* and Indians as *vos.* One of Castellanos' Indian characters, as he is learning to read and write, thinks: "What a feeling, to discover the names of things, to pronounce them, to write them, and to take possession of the world!"[11]

It is this consciousness of the significance of language as a key to taking possession of the world that infuses all of Rosario Castellanos' work. It is through her language as an author that Mexican women and Mexican Indians finally break the invisible space to which they have been confined and, by clarmoring to be heard, claim their portion of the world.

Notes

1. This thesis was subsequently incorporated into her book of essays, *Mujer que sabe latín . . .* (Mexico: Sep Setentas, 1973). The title is a reference to the well-known Spanish refrain: "Mujer que sabe latín, ni tiene marido ni buen fin." (The woman who knows Latin will find neither a husband or a happy ending, or perhaps, the woman who knows Latin will never were satin.) All translations are mine.
2. See José Emilio Pacheco's introduction to Rosario Castellanos, *El uso de la palabra* (Mexico: Excelsior, 1974), p. 7.
3. For a detailed analysis of the significance of La Malinche in Mexican culture, see Octavio Paz, *El laberinto de la soledad* (Mexico: Fondo de Cultura Económica, 1959), Chapter IV. Also see Leslie A. Fiedler, *Love and Death in the American Novel* (New York: Dell, 1969) for an interesting discussion of the images of the "Dark Lady" and the "Snow Maiden" in literature.
4. *Mujer que sabe latín . . .*, p. 40.
5. Rosario Castellanos, *El eterno femenino* (Mexico: Fondo de Cultura Económica, 1975), pp. 181-82, 187.
6. *Mujer que sabe latín . . .*, pp. 56-61.
7. *Mujer que sabe latín . . .*, pp. 14-15.
8. *Mujer que sabe latín . . .*, p. 19.
9. Rosario Castellanos, *Balún-Canán* (Mexico: Fondo de Cultura Económica, 1957), p. 67.
10. *Balún-Canán,* p. 8.
11. *Balún-Canán,* p. 189.

Mary Gómez Parham (essay date 1988)

SOURCE: "Moving Toward the Other: New Dimensions in Human Relationships in Rosario Castellanos' 'Album de familia,'" in *Chasqui,* Vol. XVII, No. 1, May, 1988, pp. 3-7.

[*In the following essay, Parham explores Castellanos's focus on alienation and her evolving sense of optimism in the stories in her last work of fiction,* Album de familia.]

In ***Album de familia,*** Rosario Castellanos' final work of fiction, she no longer concerns herself with the difficulties of relationships between races, and the setting has moved from provincial to urban Mexico.[1] As racial strife disappears from the stories, relationships between members of the same sex and of the opposite sex become the principal concern. New elements such as homosexuality and feminism-as-politics appear, and three of the stories explore new ways of dealing with the old problem of alienation, injecting in several instances an optimism largely absent in the writer's previous works.[2] In view of these facts, the purpose of this paper will be twofold: to point out and discuss the continued presence of alienation as a central in this last work by Castellanos, while illuminating the emerging tendency—however oblique at times—to a new optimism on the part of the writer.

The narrator of **"Lección de cocina,"** after having had sexual intercourse with her husband, considers the sleeping man and muses dispassionately:

> Hace un año yo no tenía la menor idea de su existencia y ahora reposo junto a él con los muslos entrelazados, húmedos de sudor y de semen. Podría levantarme sin despertarlo, ir descalza hasta la regadera. ¿Purificarme? No tengo asco. Prefiero creer que lo que me une a él es algo tan fácil de borrar como una secreción y no tan terrible como un sacramento.[3]

The woman's fear of entrapment is symptomatic of an alienation from her husband fueled by a resentment which has several causes. Some are superficial, or perhaps symbolic, such as her anger at the fact that during the honeymoon, when they were both badly sunburned, she was the one who suffered most: "El podía darse el lujo de 'portarse como quien es' y tenderse boca abajo para que no le rozara la piel dolorida" (p. 9). The resentment of such a "lujo" has deeper roots, of course. The narrator feels, for instance, that she is for her husband only a means of sexual gratification and her husband's apparent acceptance of his distance from her increases her own sense of distance from *him*. The wife further resents that she is made to feel continually grateful to him for everything he is and does, and yet is herself only appreciated for her virginity: "¿Y tú? ¿No tienes nada que agradecerme? Lo has puntualizado con una solemnidad que pretendía ser halagadora pero que me resultaba ofensiva: mi virginidad" (p. 13). None of her other contributions to their marriage are of consequence. She feels that she is not compensated for her work as homemaker: "No se me paga ningún sueldo, no se me concede un día libre a la semana, no puedo cambiar de amo" (p. 15). And later in life she will be expected to tolerate in silence her husband's infidelity. Yet any suspicion of infidelity on the part of the young wife is a source of great consternation to her spouse, whom she describes as "mi marido, que me espía, que no me deja ni a sol ni a sombra, que sospecha de todo y de todos . . ." (p. 18). As his wife she feels that she is mere chattel. For his part, besides fearing his wife's infidelity, the husband fears entrapment. The woman's response to this distrust is filled with bitterness.[4]

The narrator of this story is a woman rebelling against stereotyped sex roles, the fulfillment of which necessitates hypocritical behavior and thereby builds barriers between the sexes. Culturally imposed codes of behavior make warfare out of relationships between men and women, and offer the protagonist two choices: to be "seductoramente aturdida, profundamente reservada, hipócrita" (p. 21), or to assume "la otra actitud . . . , la femineidad que solicita indulgencia para sus errores" (p. 21). The assumption of either of these roles would require that the heroine deny her true identity. This she resists:

> Yo no soy el sueño que sueña, que sueña; yo no soy el reflejo de una imagen en un cristal; a mí no me aniquila la cerrazón de una conciencia o de toda conciencia posible. Yo continúo viviendo con una vida densa, viscosa, turbia, aunque el que está a mi lado y el remoto, me ignoren, me olviden, me pospongan, me abandonen, me dasamen.
>
> (p. 10)

The narrator here makes clear her wish to be recognized as an individual. Unfortunately, her husband is not equally interested in authenticity, she believes: "Si insisto en afirmar mi versión de los hechos, mi marido va a mirarme con suspicacia, va a sertirse incómodo en mi compañía y va a vivir en la continua expectativa de que se me declare la locura" (p. 22). The narrator's husband's perceived attitude and the woman's inability to assume either of the two roles available to her are factors that may at first glance appear to preclude any rapprochement between the spouses, seemingly imparting to the story the same aura of despair which pervades Castellanos's earlier works. However, in the context of the entire corpus of Castellanos' work the narrator's immediate marital difficulties here are of interest only insofar as they evidence the writer's sustained preoccupation with the problem of alienation between the sexes. This preoccupation is not new. What is new is that in **"Lección de cocina"** Castellanos finally creates a female character capable of analyzing and understanding her situation, of identifying her options and, it logically follows, of formulating modes of resolving her difficulties with men. Because of this, the woman in this story is no longer the long-suffering victim Castellanos' earlier female characters had been.

In the story **"Domingo,"** Castellanos presents an intertwined group of various types of failed relationships. On a Sunday afternoon the characters meet to complain, tease, boast, gossip, and play verbal games but do not communicate on any deep level. Nevertheless, a careful reading of the text reveals evidence of change and movement toward the adoption of a more positive attitude on the part of Castellanos.

Castellanos' familiar preoccupation with the problem of alienation manifests itself in the characters Edith and her husband Carlos, both of whom have lovers whose existence they pretend to be unaware of. They do so because they find it impossible to separate, although the reasons for this are much more those of convenience and habit than those of the heart: "Edith tuvo que reconocer que no todo el mundo estaba atado por vínculos tan sólidos como Carlos y ella. Los hijos, las propiedades en común, hasta la manera especial de tomar una taza de chocolate antes de dormir. Realmente sería muy difícil, sería imposible romper" (p. 27). Thus Edith and Carlos persist in their mutual alienation, finding passing solace in their lovers.

Unfortunately, Edith's promising relationship with her lover Rafael ends in heartbreak, as does the homosexual relationship of Jorge and Luis. Another troubled relationship is that of Octavio and Elisa. Though she, his wife, has just become pregnant with their first child, Octavio is already complaining that she doesn't understand him, while looking to Edith for more than sisterly understanding. And Edith, though unable to divorce her husband, is quite able to flirt with Octavio.[5]

Yet another character, Vicente, has a lover who becomes pregnant and who claims the child is his, but then has an abortion. Of the situation Vicente exclaims, "'¡Carajo, estoy harto de putas!'" (p. 32). But he adds that any "virgencita que viva entre flores" that he finds turns out to be "una hipócrita, aburrida, chupasangre" (p. 33). Believing that these are the only types of women he can find, Vicente is bound to be alienated from most women. Nevertheless, in this attitude of Vicente's are to be found the germs of change. Here, finally, is a man looking, perhaps unconsciously, for a new woman, a woman neither "puta" nor "virgencita hipócrita." His dissatisfaction with traditional, stereotypical womanhood is a completely new and very important element in Castellanos's work, laying the groundwork as it does for the emergence of male-female relationships no longer characterized by exploitation and dishonesty.

The static despair so predominant in Castellanos' earlier works is relieved not only in Vicente's displeasure with conventional non-relationships between men and women, but also in the solace Edith finds in her work. During the party in her home which is the setting for the story, she observes, detached, the activities of her guests and feels excluded. But she is suddenly rescued from the depression of her aloneness by the memory of "la tela comenzada en su estudio, el roce peculiar del pantalón de pana contra sus piernas; el sweater viejo, tan natural, como una segunda piel" (p. 46). The memory of her painting and its physical setting is enough to lift her spirits. The story is in this regard unique in Castellanos' repertoire, as it presents the quite new notion in her *oeuvre* of the possibility of compensation, if not a cure, for the failure of human relationships.

The short novel ***Album de familia*** is the last work in the collection of that name, and Castellanos' preoccupation with the problem of alienation is again found here, and with its usual preeminence. However, both the character and the setting of the work are unique, and it ends on the emerging note of optimism echoed in the stories I have discussed above.

Album de familia is on one level the story of the relationships which exist in the literary world. At the beginning of the story, a reporter explains to the writer Matilde's secretary Victoria that Matilde's winning of the Premio de las Naciones has been well-accepted by the very contentious male writers who did *not* receive the prize. For them, Matilde was never a real threat. As the reporter quips, "'Una mujer intelectual es una contradicción en los téminos, luego no existe'" (p. 71). Matilde's competitors are actually pleased with her success, she says: "'Entre ellos hay entusiasmo. Cada uno se alegra de que Matilde, que en resumidas cuentas no es sino un mal menor, haya servido de piedra de tropiezo para evitar que el otro, el contrincante real, ganara la pelea'" (pp. 72-3).

The ability of Matilde's male rivals to thus undermine her triumph signals their marked disaffection for female writers, above and beyond that common among male writers. The women of the story are, however, equally alienated from the opposite sex. None of them has a satisfactory relationship with a man, and the divorcee, Elvira, goes so far as to formulate the following cynical opinion of marriage, the institution which supposedly symbolized human triumph over alienation between man and woman: "'El matrimonio es el ayuntamiento de dos bestias carnívoras de especia diferente que de pronto se hallan en la misma jaula'" (p. 132). Marriages only survive, Elvira decides, because one of the spouses gives in—in Mexico, she says, usually the female. Elvira believes that marriage promotes difficulties between the sexes in many ways: "'Yo con mi exmarido no pude sostener un diálogo coherente y ponderado sino hasta después de que se dictó la sentencia de divorcio'" (p. 133).

Strife between male and female is equaled or even exceeded by strife between women in this story. As each woman arrives at the gathering, the other women approach her "para practicar juntas ese ritual—un breve contacto de las mejillas—con que las mujeres pactan entre su deseo de besar y su necesidad de morder" (p. 86). For Castellanos, this greeting symbolizes women's deep-seated alienation from each other, although it is interesting that she observes that women do at least have a "deseo de besar[se]."

For sixty-seven pages, seven women scratch and tear at each other's souls in an encounter later described by one of them as a "'Juicio Final en el que cada una de nosotras fue alternativa o simultáneamente defensor, juez y verdugo, pero siempre reo . . .'" (p. 152). In fact, the reporter's appraisal of relations between literary men could easily have been an appraisal of the relations between the women writers who meet with Matilde. And Elvira's description of the war between the sexes also perfectly characterizes the interaction among the majority of the women in this work, writers and non-writers alike. Thus Castellanos portrays an alienation which is equally operative and severe in three different areas: between women and men, between women and women, and between men and men.

Nevertheless, despite this pervasive hostility among human beings, the author ultimately gives this short novel an optimistic dimension only occasionally glimpsed elsewhere in her works. As the story ends, the women dine together, continuing their conversation: "La discusión se prolongaba, en sordina, durante la sobremesa bostezante. Y tal vez alguna quiso llorar—tal vez porque era la más fuerte—pero la sofrenaba el desvalimiento de las otras. Y las otras se aprestaron en vano a restañar esa herida invisible que nunca abrió los labios" (p. 153). These women are willing—as few of Castellanos' characters are—to open up to each other and express honestly their feelings, however ugly at times. This openness give birth to empathy, and they are thus able to begin, hesitantly perhaps, to reach out to each other. The entire story is, then, a lengthy *prise de conscience* similar to that experienced by the protagonist of **"Lección de cocina."** However, in this case Castellanos allows the painful process to bear fruit on the written page in the few final lines quoted above.

These three stories, in the words of Martha Paley Francescato, "constituyen la apertura de nuevas posibilidades,"[6] as I have demonstrated here. Hostility, alienation, problems are still dominant, clearly. But upon reading ***Album de familia,*** and after having studied all of the earlier works of Rosario Castellanos, one is left with the impression that something was changing for the writer, both attitudinally and aesthetically, at the time she wrote this collection. Unfortunately, any nascent metamorphosis was cut short by Castellanos' accidental death at the age of forty-nine, leaving to speculation the question of how this trend might have evolved.

Notes

1. For some examples of criticism of Castellanos' fictional treatment of the theme of Mexican indigenous culture, see John S. Brushwood, *The Spanish American Novel: A Twentieth Century Survey* (Austin: University of Texas, 1975), pp. 236-37, and his *Mexico in its Novel: A Nation's Search for Identity* (Austin: University of Texas, 1973), p. 166. Another invaluable source is the work of Joseph Sommers, which includes the following: "Changing Views of the Indian in Mexican Literature," *Hispania,* 47 (1964), 47-55; "The Indian-oriented Novel in Latin America: New Spirit, New Forms, New Scope," *Journal of Inter-American Studies,* 6 (1964), 249-265; and "Forma e ideologia en Oficio de Tinieblas de Rosario Castellanos," *Revista de crítica literaria latinoamericana,* Nos. 7-8 (1978), 73-91.
2. The corpus of criticism dealing with feminist themes in Castellanos' works is immense and still growing. A landmark compilation of studies and bibliography in this area is Maureen Ahern's and Mary S. Vásquez' (eds.) *Homenaje a Rosario Castellanos* (Valencia: Estudios de Hispanófila, 1980). Other relevant articles are Naomi Lindstrom, "Women's Expression and Narrative Technique in Rosario Castellano's *In Darkness,*" *Modern Language Studies* (1983), 71-80; Beth Miller, "Rosario Castellano's 'Guests in August': Critical Realism and the Provincial Middle Class," *Latin American Literary Review,* 7, No. 14 (1979), 5-19; and Stacey Schlau, "Conformity and Resistance to Enclosure: Female Voices in Rosario Castellanos' *Oficio de tinieblas,*" *Latin American Literary Review,* 7, No. 24 (1984), 45-57. The last three essays include rather extensive bibliographies, as well as incisive observations concerning the writings of Castellanos.
3. Rosario Castellanos, *Album de familia* (Mexico City: Joaquín Mortiz, 1977), p. 11. All references to this work are to this edition.
4. A delightful treatment of the vicissitudes of traditional Mexican courtship and marriage is to be found in dramatic form in Castellanos' *El eterno femenino* (Mexico: Fondo de Cultura Económica, 1975). Though sometimes considered to be technically flawed, the piece is nonetheless highly entertaining, as well as quite instructive on the issue of male-female relationships in Castellanos' homeland.
5. This story introduces in Castellanos' works the theme of homosexuality. and the writer's decision to treat this topic is consistent with the task of *l'écriture féminine,* which Elaine Showalter describes as that of allying oneself "with everything . . . which is muted, silenced or unrepresented" (*The New Feminist Criticism* [New York: Pantheon Books, 1985], p. 9). It is a task which Castellanos embraced long before its importance for woman writers began to be stressed by French critical theorists.
6. Martha Paley Francescato, "Transgresión y aperturas en los cuentos de Rosario Castellanos," in Ahern and Vásquez, p. 15.

Mary Gómez Parham (essay date 1989)

SOURCE: "Alienation in Rosario Castellanos' 'Ciudad Real,'" in *Letras Femeninas,* Vol. XV, Nos. 1-2, Spring, 1989, pp. 22-7.

[*In the following essay, Parham discusses alienation in* Ciudad Real, *arguing that Castellanos illustrates modes of social interaction common in Mexican culture that serve to both protect the individual and manipulate others.*]

The short stories of Rosario Castellanos' second fictional work, ***Ciudad Real,*** all deal in some way with the problem of alienation, especially between Indian and white, though other forms are sometimes equally or even more important, such as alienation between sexes, classes and age groups and between man and nature. Instruments of this alienation include severe codes of courtesy, *machismo* and other forms of sex-role stereotyping, greed and above all, language barriers.

In **"La muerte del tigre,"** the role of oral communication in perpetuating alienation is examined. Octavio Paz asserts in this regard that in Mexico "las complicaciones rituales de la cortesía" are a manifestation of a "peligrosa inclinación . . . por las fórmulas" (Paz 29). These rituals serve both to protect the individual from others and as a means of manipulation of others. This mode of social interaction is observed in the Indians' meeting with the *enganchador*[1] in **"La muerte del tigre."** The oldest of the Indians asks the *enganchador* for work:

> —¿Acaso tú puedes darnos trabajo?
>
> ¿Acaso eres enganchador?
>
> —Precisamente. Y tengo fama de
>
> equitativo. Me llamo Juvencio Ortiz.
>
> —Ah, sí. Don Juvencio.
>
> (20)

Castellanos remarks that "el comentario era, más que eco de la fama, seña de cortesía" (11). Nevertheless, both the Indian and don Juvencio are satisfied with their interaction, though the latter knows that he has little "fama" of anything anywhere (and least of all of being "equitativo") and that it is most unlikely that the Indians in question, who have just arrived in town, have heard of him in any context. It is easy to understand why both Paz and Castellanos so lament the use of such hypocritical "señas de cortesía," which breed distrust and alienation among those who use them.

Shortly after this meeting with the *enganchador,* the Indians sign up for work. When asked their names, they give their real names, but the tradition of deception and distrust between the races is too great to be overcome by one act of honesty:

> —Pablo Gómez Bolom.
>
> —Daniel Hernández Bolom.
>
> —José Domínguez Bolom.
>
> El socio de don Juvencio taladraba a los indios con una inútil suspicacia. Como de costumbre, estaban tomándole el pelo. Después, cuando se escapaban de las fincas sin satisfacer sus deudas, nadie podía localizarlos porque el paraje al que habían declarado pertenecer no existía y los nombres que dieron como suyos eran falsos.
>
> ¡Pero no, por la Santísima Virgen de la Caridad, ya basta! El socio de don Juvencio dio un manotazo sobre la mesa, dispuesto a reclamar. Sólo que sus conocimientos de la lengua indígena no eran suficientes como para permitirle enzarzarse en una discusión.
>
> Refunfuñando, apuntó:
>
> —¡Bolom! Ya te voy a dar tu bolom para que aprendáis.
>
> (23)

Thus Castellanos reveals the essence of the problem at hand: Indian and white can never begin to dissipate their persistent mutual distrust as long as they haven't even a common language in which they can accuse or defend.

The action of the very short **"La tregua"** also centers around the inability of one race to communicate with the other, as an injured white person is murdered by vengeful Indians who believe him to be a *pukuj*[2] who has taken the form of a white man. Both this story and **"La muerte del tigre"** portray nature as hostile to the characters, who in turn are distrustful of and alienated from it.

In **"Aceite guapo,"** we encounter another form of the social reject: the elderly person. The rejecting society is the Indian, and the victim, Daniel Castellanos Lampoy, cannot escape the facts of his age and of his rejection, for "las miradas torvas de sospecha, rápidas de alarma, pesadas de desaprobación de los demás" (37) make it painfully obvious. The old person in Daniel's culture is believed to bring disaster and is avoided or, if necessary, killed. He or she is not even protected by the family, and much less so Daniel, for he is a widower whose children have long since abandoned him. Thus the old man is alienated from both his people and his family: "Hacía años, los años de la viudez, de la ausencia de los hijos, de la soledad, que no hablaba con nadie" (39). His one desire is to find a person with whom he can talk, and through whom he can escape his absolute loneliness. This person becomes the saint of whose statue he is made caretaker, St. Margaret. However, the old man's respite from loneliness is short-lived and the story ends tragically, as again the language barrier between Indian and white destroys the old man's dream world. The sacristan cruelly challenges Daniel one day:

> —Fíjate en la cara de santa Margarita. Es blanca, es ladina, lo mismo que san Juan, que santo Tomás, que todos ellos. Ella habla castilla. ¿Cómo vas a querer que entienda el *tzotzil*?
>
> (p. 46)

For Indian and white the language barrier exists, Castellanos implies, as the most alienating of factors, extending even to relationships with the Divine.

"La suerte de Teodoro Méndez Acubal" is another story of loneliness and despair. The principal alienating agent is money, as the coin found by the old man brings him "una sensación de soledad" and makes of him "un hombre aparte, amordazado por un secreto" (52)—the secret of the coin, which he does not wish to share with his family. In view of this reluctance to share, Teodoro would appear to be, even before he finds the money, a somewhat selfish and alienated individual. The finding of the money, then, only worsens an already existing estrangement.

This is the story, too, of Agustín Velasco, another example of the son spoiled by his mother encountered in Mario and Ernesto of *Balún-Canán.* Like Ernesto, he is very insecure: "Lo atormentaba la sospecha de que era un inútil. . . . Era muy tímido, muy apocado, muy sin iniciativa" (57). Unfortunately, he hasn't the fortitude to admit this fact. Therefore he lives in constant bad faith, alienated from all, including his mother, whose pampering attentions are "su modo de sentir desdén" (p. 57). Finally, in order to disprove his ineptness, Agustín falsely accuses Teodoro of theft.

The heroine of **"Modesta Gómez"** is a poor, probably *mestiza* woman given to a rich white family as a child. From the outset she is estranged from the family. Here once again Castellanos emphasizes the role of language in the alienation of human beings, as Modesta is forbidden to use the *vos* form of address with the boy of the house, whom she plays with and cares for. "Es tu patrón," the boy's mother warns, "y con los patrones nada de confiancitas" (65). However, Modesta's alienation is suffered not only in relationship to the family, but also to her peers. When brought to the family, the other servants treat her coldly. Later, when the girl is raped by Jorge, son of the rich couple (yet another "único varón," spoiled by his parents), and becomes pregnant, the other servants gossip about her, "con risas maliciosas y guiños obscenos" (67). In her subsequent marriage, too, Modesta finds loneliness with a husband who beats her, "echándole en cara el abuso de Jorgito" (70). Distrust between the sexes and alienation bred by sex-role stereotyping (here the requirement of virginity for the female) is again attacked. When Modesta finally becomes an *atajadora*[3] she continues to be lonely and unhappy, for she finds no companionship among the other *atajadoras* and is forced to have dealings with Indians, whom she despises. Thus even the poorest, most miserable of whites and *mestizos* desire to maintain a barrier between themselves and the Indians.

In **"El advenimiento del águila,"** several of Castellanos' most commonly alienated character types again appear. The typical mother's spoiling of her son here produces the extremely exploitative *macho* figure, Héctor. The misogynist Héctor's one goal is to find a rich wife,

> la esposa que ha de proporcionarle holgura y respeto. . . . Puede ser ésta o la otra. A oscuras todas las hembras son iguales. Héctor cumpliría sus deberes como marido preñándola anualmente. Entre los embarazos y la crianza de los hijos, ella se mantendría tranquila en su rincón.
>
> (79-80)

In Emelina's "pecho árido de solterona" (80), Héctor kindles love, and they marry. However, the marriage of two such persons can only end in tragedy. Emelina's love is of course unrequited, as is to be expected with a man such as Héctor who is incapable of love (as Octavio Paz says the *macho* or *chingón* always is). Castellanos writes that "si Emelina no hubiese estado enamorada de Héctor, acaso habría sido feliz" (81). Thus her portrayal of this relationship constitutes another attack on *machismo* as a divisive force. Also, **"El advenimiento del águila"** is a story of alienation between Indian and white, and language is again a factor. Due to the Indians' lack of knowledge of Spanish, Héctor is able to deceive them and extort money from them which he then uses as the basis for an accumulation of great personal wealth.

A lonely spinster is the central character in **"Cuarta vigilia."** For Nides, her chest of gold coins, even when they are no longer gold, performs the function of Matilde's fantasy lover. Because of her imagined fortune, she proudly declares, "Valgo tanto como cualquiera" (99). This inordinate attachment to money leads to disaster, as it does for Teodoro Méndez Acubal. However, Nides is not even conscious of the tragedy she provokes, for the body she buries with her treasure is "de un indio, no de una gente de razón" (100).

"La rueda del hambriento" and the story that follows it, **"El don rechazado,"** both deal with the problems encountered by workers at the government-administered aid center for the Indians of Chiapas. In the first of these stories, Indian-white relationships are as strained as elsewhere, and as complicated by language barriers. And the alienation and distrust between the Indian woman and her husband in **"La rueda del hambriento"** reminds one of the relationship between Felipe and Juana in *Balún-Canán.* When the young mother is unable to nurse her newborn, her husband and his father size up the situation:

> El marido y el suegro se miraron entre sí con una mirada rápida de entendimiento. Era indudable que esta mujer había sido víctima de algún maleficio. Todas paren con facilidad, todas pueden amamantar a sus crías. ¿Por qué ella no? ¿Acaso era culpable y su desgracia le venía como un castigo?
>
> (131)

This is evidence once more of the distrust between the sexes which Castellanos so often points up in her work.

As for relationships between white men and women, **"La rueda del hambriento"** pits the desperate *soltera* against the typical *macho* character. The woman's efforts to penetrate the latter's protective shell meet with no success. When she congratulates him, a doctor, on saving the life of the pregnant Indian and suggests that he be made *padrino* of the baby, he snaps, "No me hacen falta ahijados" (130). The story is nevertheless unique in that the hardened *macho* ultimately admits, "Yo necesito ver gente, necesito encontrar alguno a quien decirle, a quien explicarle . . ." (136). Furthermore, the two characters do come to a certain understanding concerning the clinic which they administer, allowing the story to end on an unusual optimistic note.

Castellanos in **"El don rechazado"** depicts the extreme difficulty involved in overcoming alienation between the races, once it is established. The young anthropologist writes, at the close of the story, "Lo que quiero que usted me diga es, si yo como profesionista, como hombre, incurrí en alguna falta" (148). And clearly, despite his good will, he does. Lacking a comprehensive knowledge of Indian culture, as well as a knowledge of the Indian language, he is not able to conquer the barrier of distrust between Indian and white.

"Arthur Smith salva sin alma," the last story of ***Ciudad Real,*** portrays the alienation of both "American and Mexican religious groups from the Indian."[4] American Protestant missionaries and Mexican priests ultimately unite for their own self-aggrandizement, with little regard for the good of the Indian whose spiritual well-being is ostensibly their concern. Pastor Williams' wife sounds much like Zoraida of *Balún-Canán* when she indelicately expresses the Americans' opinion of the Indians (though in this case the reference is specifically to the Indian cooks): "Son estúpidas, sucias, tercas, hipócritas . . ." (164). The American children are not encouraged to mix with the Indians or even the local white children, an activity which in any case would be difficult since the Americans speak no Spanish. The situation is worsened by the fact that any words actually learned by the Indians from the Americans are English and are of no use in the removal of language barriers between white and Indian Mexicans who must find a way to coexist successfully.

Arthur, who has some knowledge of the Indian language, is given the task of translating the English gospel. He is given an Indian assistant, Mariano, but the two never overcome their mutual estrangement. The following scene illustrates this fact as well as the complexities of the barriers to be removed before the two cultures can communicate.

> A Mariano se le bañaba la cara y el cuello de sudor y cuando Arthur le pedía la correspondencia precisa de un vocablo, respondía con el primero que se le venía a la mente. Y si el texto decía Espíritu Santo, Mariano interpretaba Sol y principio viril que fecunda y azada que remueva la tierra y dedos que modelan el barro. Y si decía demonio, no pensaba en el mal, no temía ni rechazaba, sino que se inclinaba con sumisión, porque después de todo el demonio era sólo la espalda de la otra potencia y había que rendirle actos propiciatorios y concertar alianzas convenientes. Lo que echaba de menos, porque no se mencionaba jamás, era la gran vagina paridora que opera en las tinieblas y que no descansa nunca.
>
> (168)

This story concludes with one of the few instances of human communication with nature to be found in ***Ciudad Real*** or elsewhere in the works of Rosario Castellanos:

> Arthur caminó entre la sombra fresca, aromática y móvil de los pinos. Luego sobre una planicie breve. Al atardecer se sentó a descansar en una piedra.
>
> ¡Qué hermoso era el paisaje! ¡Y qué libre se sentía él porque nada de lo que estaba contemplando le movía a codicia, nada le despertaba el instinto de posesión!
>
> (198)

Arthur, liberated from evil and sure of his own identity, is now at one with his world. It is an accomplishment which few of Castellanos' characters ever know, as they live out their lives alienated from self, others, and nature.

Notes

1. A middleman who recruits Indians to work on the ranches and plantations.
2. An evil spirit believed to take varying forms in order to harm human beings.
3. A woman who earns a living by stealing from the Indian women the goods they are bringing to market.
4. Castellanos admits elsewhere that *Ciudad Real* exhibits a tendency toward didacticism, a tendency which becomes quite pronounced in "Arthur Smith salva sin alma."

Works Cited

Castellanos, Rosario. *Cuidad Real.* Mexico City: Editorial Novaro, 1974.

Paz, Octavio. *El laberinto de la soledad.* Mexico City: Fondo de Cultura Económica, 1959.

Nina M. Scott (essay date 1989)

SOURCE: "Rosario Castellanos: Demythification through Laughter," in *Humor,* Vol. 2, No. 1, 1989, pp. 19-29.

[*In the following essay, Scott argues that Castellanos uses humor to break down cultural myths about women.*]

Do feminists have a sense of humor? Perhaps one of the most appropriate people to ask would have been the late Rosario Castellanos (1925-1974), noted for both her wit and her outspoken feminism. In her creative writing as well as her journalism, she unleashed the formidable arsenal of her humor to attack the kinds of mind-sets and myths that were keeping Mexican women relegated to traditional roles of selfless wife and mother. For Castellanos the problem began with Genesis. A woman, she reports, is to be satisfied with her place in the world because once upon a time a man gave up one of his ribs to create her. "In the first place," she writes, "no one was asking his consent to carry out this operation. Second, while this operation was being performed he was in a state of unconsciousness so complete that when he woke up he had the surprise of that century and all others when he found at his side the seductive creature that in time would incite him to leave paradise. This creature has never stopped beating her breast in repentance for that sin, but in that same breast, lacerated by *mea culpas,* she harbors the eternal flame of gratitude toward him who gave her her being." As will be seen in the following study, this combination of irony and cliché is a hallmark of Castellanos's feminist style. As she observed in 1970 in one of her editorial columns, "When one reads these pages, one asks oneself with indignation how it is possible that at this date in time, when civilized man is crossing the limits of the cosmos, a woman is still striving to cross the domestic threshold, because only beyond this point can she have access to a particle of autonomy, to a crumb of self-determination and independence, to a shred of dignity." For this iconoclast, humor was a very serious business.

Rosario Castellanos (1925-1974), one of modern Mexico's best writers and most outspoken feminists, is famous for the wit and humor that characterize her multifaceted literary production. Ever since the publication in 1950 of her master's thesis *Sobre cultura femenina* [*On Feminine Culture*], Castellanos used her writing not only to discover her own particular identity as a woman but to foreground the absurd and conflictive customs of Mexican society which prevented women in general from developing their selfhood. Her most openly feminist essays are contained in *Mujer que sabe latin* [*Woman Who Knows Latin*] (1984 [1973]) and *El uso de la palabra* [*The Use of the Word*] (1974), the posthumous collection of her editorials from *Excelsior*;[1] in her fiction she is at her most radical in her late works, the dramatic farce *El eterno femenino* [*The Eternal Feminine*] (1975) and ***Album de familia*** [*Family Album*] (1975 [1971]), particularly in the short story **"Lección de cocina"** [**"The Cooking Lesson"**].[2] The focus of this study will concern itself with these four works, examining first Castellanos's iconoclastic stance *vis à vis* destructive myths about women, with a subsequent look at her use of particular types of humor and the justification thereof within the framework of her feminist philosophy.

During her lifetime, Castellanos's wit and charm were legendary. Fellow writer and friend Elena Poniatowska recalls in an essay that

> Rosario in daily life was a woman who laughed and made others laugh with enormous ease; to be with her was a true pleasure . . . a person who knows how to make others laugh is akin to the one who can make good bread, a giver of gifts. Rosario gave with both hands.[3]
>
> (1985: 51, 52)

Poet José Emilio Pacheco made a similar observation in a preliminary note to one of her books after her tragic death in Tel Aviv in 1974:[4]

> Something of what was the insatiable charm of her conversation is left in many of her articles. But the tone, the gesture, the sparkle in her eyes, the smile—neither page nor film can capture those and they have been irremediably lost.
>
> (Castellanos 1974: 8)

Beneath this lighthearted exterior, however, lay intense seriousness of purpose and constant tension, a tension which stemmed from an inability to reconcile herself to her cultural context and manifested itself in a dialectical opposition between understanding and rebellion (Alarcón 1983: 24). In quasi-melodramatic terms Castellanos delineates both her feminist goals and the function which humor assumes in the realization thereof:

> I would suggest a campaign: not to rush to attack our customs with the flaming sword of indignation nor with the mournful tremolo of tears but by showing up that which makes them ridiculous. I assure you that we have inexhaustible material for laughter. And we need to laugh so badly because laughter is the most immediate form of freeing ourselves from that which oppresses us the most, of distancing ourselves from that which imprisons us!.
>
> (1984 [1973]: 39)

Castellanos uses wit and humor as classic weapons of attack against authority, taking pride in becoming one of the "iconoclasts who apply the 'corrosive acid of laughter' to institutions in order to destroy them because they are absurd, because they are unjust, because they lack foundation and meaning. . . ." Like her model Democritus, she is a revolutionary "who has a good time deconstructing mechanisms, showing their inconsistencies, reducing to ashes with one breath a construction which defied the centuries" (1984 [1973]: 184).

Much of Castellanos's efforts to speak out on behalf of women's issues took place on the editorial pages of *Excelsior.* As I said in a previous study on the interrelationship between Castellanos's journalism and her creative writing, "The editorial page has traditionally provided men with a forum from which to express their opinion; a woman's voice was unusual in this context and Castellanos' overt feminism was controversial enough to both attract and alienate readers" (1986: 370). Aware of this, Castellanos often adopted an attitude of humorous self-deprecation in order to defuse potential reader hostility: "My column is the mirror, mirror on the wall whom I ask every Saturday who is the most marvelous woman on this planet, and just as in the fairy tale, it always tells me that Snow White is" (1974: 219); however, Alarcón is also right in her assessment that "Rosario Castellanos controls and masks her intellectual rage through the self-conscious assumption of inferiority" (1983: 52). The lightness of touch was a useful tactic in that it masked her real intention, that of using humor as a means of liberation, for in her opinion "to laugh at something is the most immediate form of putting yourself out of reach of that something" (1984 [1973]: 173). What Castellanos as iconoclast wished most to destroy were the myths which reduced the existence of the Mexican woman to a living cliché. The use of the verbal cliché is one of the hallmarks of Castellanos' humor, a point to which I shall return later.

The introductory essays of *Mujer que sabe latín* provide the reader with a resumé of Castellanos's feminist credo and are a useful point of departure for the examination of her ideas.[5] Castellanos begins by pointing out the male tendency to reduce woman to myth and thereby to nullify her authentic existence: "The process of mythification . . . impedes the free and direct contemplation of the object, the clear understanding of the being which it has substituted and usurped" (1984) [1973]: 7). She cites three categories of myth—esthetic, ethic, and intellectual—all of which contribute to the psychological and physical deformation of women. Castellanos provides numerous examples to illustrate her thesis, and an examination of several of these will provide a sense of the characteristic forms in which her brand of humor is expressed.

Esthetic myths transform woman into muse, Castellanos noted, "and in order to achieve this one must maintain distance and be silent. And be beautiful" (1984 [1973]: 23). In the process of undermining this myth Castellanos points out that, whereas it is a woman's obligation to be beautiful, standards of beauty and fashion are often dictated by men who ignore factors such as physical comfort or well-being.

> Large, vigorous feet are said to be ugly. But they're good for walking and for maintaining oneself in an upright position. In a man large and vigorous feet are more than acceptable: they are obligatory. But in a woman? Even our most ridiculous local troubadors are smitten by "the foot as dainty as a pincushion". With a foot like that . . . you can't go anywhere. Which is what it was all about, evidently.
>
> (1984 [1973]: 9)

To be considered beautiful a woman must be both slender and impeccably groomed, a dictum which applies with slight variations to all social classes. Among the wealthy,

> the wife's function might be that of a decorative piece of furniture which has the advantage, apart from being able to be shown off to visitors, of being able to be transported and displayed at parties and gatherings. She is expected to avoid anything which might spoil her figure and is permitted to give the rest of her free time to charitable works.
>
> (1974: 27)

A middle-class woman has an even harder time living up to expectations:

> She, too, aspires and is obligated to be a decorative element, only she has fewer means and less time at her disposal because she has to take care of all domestic chores and annually brightens her home with a visit by the stork. It is difficult, between diapers and wails . . . to conserve not only equanimity, but human characteristics. The lady begins to forget . . . even the most elementary principles of civilization; she doesn't comb her hair, for example. And, from his impeccable countenance, her husband surveys a dishevelled spouse on his return from his harsh bureaucratic duties.
>
> (1974: 27-28)

The husband's justified response to such slovenliness, Castellanos concludes ironically, is either to go out and party with his friends or to set up a mistress in another apartment.

But it is not only men who impose absurd esthetic expectations: women, too, participate actively in keeping them alive and well. In *El eterno femenino,* for example, the newly pregnant Lupita has just confessed to her mother that the stork is on its way and is severely reprimanded by her mother for feeling and looking fantastic:

> *Mamá* (near fainting): Jesus, Mary and Joseph! You're expecting? And in those clothes? . . . You need a housecoat. Comfortable. From the beginning you have to let the baby grow the way it wants to. [Does as she says.] There. Don't you feel better? No, no, I see it in your face: you're nauseated, terribly nauseated, right?
>
> *Lupita*: No.
>
> *Mamá*: How dare you contradict me? Who knows about these things, you or I? Of course you're nauseated.
>
> (1975: 40)

Another major culprit is the media, for example the popular women's magazines which project false or conflictive images to their readers and thereby foster guilt feelings in women unable to measure up to these expectations. Castellanos describes the hypothetical case of a sleepless woman whose husband has not yet come home:

> To while away the time, what could be better than reading one of those magazines especially designed for housewives? . . . And there on the cover is a seductive young woman with brilliant eyes, brilliant lips, brilliant teeth, and with her hair done by some of the world's best hairdressers. The wife looks at her the way a condemned man might view the vision of an angel. Between irritation and distraction she leafs through the interior pages. Pastries in living color, and here she, at great cost, has just skipped dinner with the hope of taking off even one centimeter from her waistline!.
>
> (1974: 28-29)

The second type of myth is of an ethic nature and relates to the fact that in Mexican society women are taught that their ultimate fulfillment can only come through being, as Alarcón calls it, "Beloved or Mother" (1983: 13). "Among the institutions which cynical wit is wont to attack," Freud observed, "there is none more important and more completely protected by moral precepts, and yet more inviting of attack, than the institution of marriage" (1938: 704). Castellanos would agree. On the one hand she faults an educational system which fails to educate girls so that they can become independently functioning human beings and on the other a culture which encourages women to remain in a permanent state of passive immobility: "The social apparatus . . . has decreed, once and for all, that the only legitimate attitude for womanhood is that of waiting around" (1984 [1973]: 14). Poets, too, have told a woman that domesticity is her principal function: "As the bard Díaz Mirón's verses said, she was born like the dove for the nest. And as don Melchor Ocampo instructed her . . . her mission is that of being the balsam that soothes the wounds which a man incurs in his daily confrontation with life" (1984 [1973]: 31). As in her discussion of the esthetic myth, here, too, Castellanos avoids Manichean oversimplification by underscoring women's complicity in its perpetuation. She once observed that Mexican women tend to be parasites more than victims (1974: 60) and noted that, in Mexican society, "complicity between the executioner and his victim [is] so long-standing that it is impossible to distinguish who is who" (1984 [1973]: 38). The newlywed protagonist of **"Lección de cocina"** ruefully acknowledges this type of complicity. In an imaginary conversation with her friends about her sex life, she knows that instead of articulating her growing disenchantment therewith she would most likely extol and thereby falsify her husband's prowess in bed: "They would subject me to an interrogation. . . . I would invent acrobatics, sublime swoonings, transports, as they say in *A Thousand and One Nights,* records. If you heard me then you wouldn't recognize yourself, Casanova!" (1975 [1971]: 16).

Within the parameters of this discussion of ethic concerns, Castellanos points out that the myth of the glories of motherhood is one of the most powerful in Hispanic culture and, in her opinion, one of the most insidious. To a great extent she blamed the creation and perpetuation of this myth on the teachings of the Church:

> Motherhood redeems woman from the original sin of being one, [and] confers meaning and justification onto her life (which would otherwise be superfluous). It anoints with holy unguents the sexual drive which, by itself, is considered an unparadonable sin when it is a female being who feels it. It exalts the institution of matrimony to the point of absolute stability, makes the domestic yoke easy and the scourge of responsibilities a delight. It serves as an infallible panacea for the deepest and most wrenching personal frustrations.
>
> (1974: 53)

The unctuous clichés in the above lines are paralleled by the hyperbolic sentimentality of those directed at the venerable mother whose life has consisted of abnegation and sacrifice: "Praise the little gray heads! Eternal glory to 'the one who loved us even before she knew us'! Statues in the parks, days set aside to honor her, etc. etc." (1984 [1973]: 16). On the other hand, Castellanos also reminds her readers that the basest insults the Spanish language has to offer refer to mothers and motherhood, "which is nothing more than the other side of the shining coin of her importance" (1974: 53). She points out that the universal exaltation of motherhood as "the fast lane to sanctification" (1984 [1973]: 40) excludes any element of choice on the part of the woman, for Mexican society rejects women who might prefer to be single, choose not to have children, or aspire to an education and a career. This point leads Castellanos to examine the third kind of myth, that which concerns a woman's intellectual development.

With mock seriousness she cites a number of scientific sources, most of them Germanic, to prove that women are endowed with minuscule brains which render them biologically unfit to think. She again faults both society and the Church for limiting the instruction of many women to purely religious subjects, taught by rote memorization or drill in devotional rituals of whose deeper meanings the students are never apprised. An intellectual woman such as Sor Juana, the brilliant, seventeenth-century Mexican nun, was considered "a devouring monster" (1984 [1973]: 211), and even in modern times an intelligent young woman who aspires to a university education is classified by both men and women as "abnormal, pedantic, impertinent, Miss-know-it-all, a ridiculous stuck-up, etc." (1974: 48-49). Supposing that a woman persists and succeeds in entering the career world? Well, Castellanos asks, would *you* entrust a woman architect with the building of *your* house?

> A house is too much money, too many years of dreams and doing without to let some hysterical woman or some lady who's worrying about where her husband is nights throw it all overboard. Besides which, neither one of them would know how to be boss to the kind of people construction workers are. No, as a last resort better hire a contractor.
>
> (1984 [1973]: 36)

The above barrage of clichés may be humorous, but unfortunately it also echoes the opinion of many a potential client. The effect of such attitudes on a trained professional cannot help but be destructive: "Efficiency depends to a large degree on interior equilibrium. An equilibrium which everything conspires to destroy" (1984 [1973]: 36-37).

The examples cited above show several types of humor characteristic of Castellanos's writing: direct, colloquial dialogue, irony, of course, apparent self-denigration, witty asides, and, most of all, the accumulation *ad absurdum* of the hackneyed cliché. The use of the cliché is so constant in her writing that it becomes necessary to ask why Castellanos had such a predilection for this particular form of expression.

In her perceptive article on Castellanos's language, Regina Harrison Macdonald notes that "Language serves as a codifying system for examining false institutions, antiquated prejudices and iron-clad hierarchies which have been erected in the name of Mexican culture" (1980: 41). Because men tend to reify women it is not surprising that they speak of them in clichés. The fact that many women are not trained to think or speak responsibly contributes not only to their continued cultural passivity but also, on a linguistic plane, to their own affinity for the cliché. For those accustomed to mental passivity the cliché is a useful form of expression, for it can be appropriated without thinking. Because of the anonymity of its origin, the cliché avoids responsibility for the opinion stated, yet by dint of repetition it has acquired universal authority and acceptance. For Castellanos the articulation of concepts into language was far too serious a matter to be relegated to a passive act:

> Just the way that the precision of the stamp on a coin, which is what defines its value, is worn off by constant use, so do words become equivocal, multivalent. After too much handling and being spit upon they must undergo a purifying bath in order to recover their original condition.
>
> (1984 [1973]: 179)

Women, especially, had to be made aware of the importance of the conscious speech act and of "the passion of the word which is flesh, which is deed, which is understanding and which will endure as memory" (1984 [1973]: 44).

Aside from the cliché, Castellanos also calls attention to the way in which women are victimized by the use of the euphemism, which by its nature masks and displaces real meaning. Because of their lack of experience in life and in critical thought, she saw women as especially vulnerable to this kind of linguistic deception, so that what is hailed by society as a young woman's "purity" and "virginity," for example, turn out on closer inspection to mean "ignorance" and "confinement" (1984 [1973]: 13, 14). The protagonist of **"Lección de cocina"** has learned something of this lesson of shifting meanings; musing on her lack of physical coordination she observes, "Now it's called clumsiness; before [we got married] it was called innocence and you loved it" (1975 [1971]: 16).

Language as a tool of domination is a frequent topic in her writing. Castellanos was raised in rural Chiapas, near the Guatemalan border, and knew firsthand that the Spanish language had long been used as a tool to keep the Indian and the mestizo in a state of subjection; in her opinion, it had been utilized equally effectively with respect to the female sector of Mexican society. In her campaign to make women linguistically aware, Castellanos does not limit herself to questions of vocabulary and meaning but also points out the power of structural aspects of language to influence thought patterns and attitudes. The suggestive power of passive grammatical constructions is a good example hereof.[6] The expression "to remain single" (*quedarse soltera*) enraged her particularly:

> Because one does not choose to be single as a way of life; rather, as the expression says, one remains single, that is, one accepts passively a fate that others impose on us. . . . What it means is that one has never gone beyond a way of being that is superfluous and adjectival as opposed to another which is necessary and substantive.[7]
>
> (1984 [1973]: 33)

The character of Eve, as presented in *El eterno femenino,* also rebels against the use of the passive construction. When a worried Adam asks her, "Who put those ideas in your head?," she replies tartly, "Ideas are not put in heads; they come out of heads" (1975: 84). In Castellanos's case the rejection of the passive—in both grammatical and behavioral terms—is much more than a personal linguistic peeve: it is a cornerstone of her feminist ethic. Eve, for example, rejects the role of passive recipient in the Garden of Eden and thereby inverts the concept of the Fall. Rather than transgression, the eating of the apple is for her the first act of human freedom, and when Adam laments the past—"We were so happy . . . we didn't need a thing"—Eve's perspective is entirely different: "We didn't want anything, which is different. And we weren't happy. . . . The human condition is not something which is received; it is fought for" (1975: 84).

The affirmation of an active, conscious role in life, especially for women, is thus inseparably linked to Rosario Castellanos's concept of humor. From her close association with both women and the Indian population of her native Chiapas she understood the pernicious psychological damage to people who are permanently marginalized and silenced. As Freud had observed, wit unleashes immediate psychic energy (1938: 733-735), and Castellanos, too, conceived of humor as "the demand for an immediate physical response" (1984 [1973]: 82). Humor as immediate stimulus is therefore a first stage in combatting physical as well as mental passivity. Longer-term strategies involved making patent to Mexican women the absurdity and injustice of widely accepted cultural beliefs and institutions which continued to imprison them. Castellanos, who often made use of mirror imagery in her writing, also applied it to the function of humor as a means to make these absurdities more evident: "Sometimes it's good to go into the fun house and to see our image reflected in mirrors which distort it" (1974: 62). By establishing distance between herself and the institutions of which she is critical, laughter was for her especially useful for keeping a balanced perspective: "Only that person is able to laugh who has been able to safeguard a lightness of spirit because he [sic] has not been tied to any dogma, who has been able to preserve freedom of judgment . . ." (1974: 52). An indispensable ingredient of Castellanos's humor is irony, precisely because "the grain of salt of irony . . . [is] distrust" (1974: 160) and therefore "irony adds a grain more of freedom" (1984 [1973]: 155). For women to learn to distrust both appearances and verbal messages was essential in the battle to achieve authentic selfhood: "The feat of *becoming who you are* . . . demands . . . above all the rejection of those false images which those false mirrors offer to women in the closed galleries where their lives take place" (1984 [1973]: 20). In Castellanos's opinion laughter is revolutionary because it helps to shatter these mirrors. The protagonist of **"Lección de cocina"** has thus come a long way when she is able to say, "I am not the reflection of an image in a mirror. . . . I, too, am a conscience" (1975 [1971]: 10).

But in the final analysis self-discovery alone is not sufficient: "It is not enough . . . to discover what we are. We have to invent ourselves" (1975: 194). In this process of self-creation, humor is again indispensable: "We are agreed on one point: to form our conscience, to awaken the critical spirit, to defend it, to spread it. Not to accept any dogma until we see if it is able to withstand a good joke" (1984 [1973]: 40).

This brief analysis of the function of humor in some of Rosario Castellanos's works offers convincing evidence that laughter was an indispensable part of her feminist stance precisely because it was an extremely serious matter. And whereas she repeatedly stressed the ability of laughter to provide distance, in her role as narrator Castellanos never adopted a peripheral position with respect to her reader. She consistently shared in the painful process of battling for self-affirmation—at considerble personal cost. Elena Poniatowska's splendid essay on her friend (1985) offers many clarifying insights into Rosario Castellanos's life and character. It is not surprising that irony—the classic form of humor of the underdog—should be so prevalent in her writing for, in spite of literary prizes and important political appointments, Castellanos herself was chronically insecure. While ambassadress to Israel, and on the point of attending an important state dinner, she reflected wryly,

> Once I wrote in one of my unforgettable pages that success is no more than a series of well-managed failures. If I wrote something like that it's because it's true. Well, then you have to act according to the principle.
>
> (1974: 270)

"I always had the feeling," Poniatowska writes, "that Rosario walked among people with a flower in her hand, looking for someone to whom to give it" (1985: 57). Her gift turned out to be her humor, by means of which she probed, questioned, and exposed to view the absurd myths and social inequalities endemic to women's roles in Mexico. In this process she was unafraid to make public testimony of her own fears and foibles, which not only attracted the sympathy and loyalty of her readers but gave other women the encouragement to strive for a sense of self. "What are the constants of Rosario Castellanos' life and work?" Poniatowska queries. "Feeling victimized and rising above this feeling . . . by means of irony, intelligence and creativity . . . Women above all recognize themselves in her and feel vindicated" (1985: 131, 107).

Notes

1. *Excelsior* is Mexico City's leading newspaper.
2. "The Cooking Lesson" was translated into English by Maureen Ahern and appears in Meyer, Doris, and Margarite Fernández Olmos (eds.) (1983), *Contemporary Women Authors of Latin America. New Translations.* Brooklyn, N.Y.: Brooklyn College Press, 158-165.
3. All translations in this article are mine.
4. She was electrocuted in a freak accident while serving as Mexican ambassadress to Israel.
5. It is important to note that the title of this work comes from a popular *refrán*—another type of cliché—which in its entirety reads, "Mujer que sabe latín, ni tiene marido ni tiene buen fin", "The woman who knows Latin has neither a husband nor a good end", in and of itself a telling statement as to the misogyny of Hispanic folk wisdom.
6. Note, for example, the accumulation of passive constructions in the passage referring to the wealthy woman.
7. "Substantive," in this context, not only has its usual meaning but also refers to the grammatical function of denoting a noun—equated in Castellanos's mind with masculine properties—as opposed to the generally adjectival function of the feminine.

Chloe Furnival (essay date 1990)

SOURCE: "Confronting Myths of Oppression: The Short Stories of Rosario Castellanos's 'Chloe Furnival,'" in *Knives and Angels: Women Writers in Latin America,* edited by Susan Bassnett, Zed Books Ltd., 1990, pp. 52-67.

[In the following essay, Furnival discusses the "bourgeois male 'utopia' that emerged from the Mexican Revolution," explored by Castellanos in her short stories.]

Rosario Castellanos (1925-74) was born into a white, wealthy landowning family in Mexico City and grew up on the family's estate in the southern, predominantly Indian-populated state of Chiapas. In 1941, President Cárdenas's land reforms[1] finally reached this traditionally closed-off state, dramatically scaling down the Castellanos family's land-ownership there and causing the family's migration to Mexico City. Rosario Castellanos studied philosophy at the national university in Mexico City, presenting her Masters thesis in 1950 entitled *On Feminine Culture* ['*Sobre cultura femenina*']. Later she returned to Chiapas (1956-57) and worked in San Cristóbal de las Casas for the Instituto Nacional Indigenista (INI) on projects that unashamedly aimed at integrating Indians into the mainstream culture.[2] Elements of these various stages in her life can be detected in much of her prose and poetry. The thematic focus of her first novel, *Balún Canán* (1957)[3]—the lives of Indians and women (both Indian and white/mestiza women) in a provincial town in Chiapas—was one that came to dominate subsequent works, in particular her first two collections of short stories, ***Ciudad Real*** [1960, ***Royal City***] and ***Los convidados de agosto*** [1964, ***Guests in August***], and her second novel, *Oficio de tinieblas [1962, Tenebrae*]. Her final anthology of short stories, ***Album de familia*** [1971, ***Family Album***], narrows the concern down to the position of Mexican women. This brief study sets out to show that her short fiction can be seen to provide a critical insight into the bourgeois male 'utopia' that emerged from the Mexican Revolution; her stories expose the racism, sexism, opportunism and hypocrisy that continued to thrive in Mexico's Revolutionary 'utopia'.

Rosario Castellanos's wholehearted acceptance of INI's ideologically unsound project of working towards the elision of all difference between the races, of asserting 'individual humanity' above all else (Castellanos herself believed that, 'The Indians are human beings who are absolutely equal to whites, only that they live under special and terrible conditions'[4]), has to be seen as symptomatic of her reaction against both the widespread perception of Indians as 'exotic creatures' and against an entrenched and oppressive hierarchical system in which differences—between whites, mestizos and Indians, and between men and women—were *exaggerated* in order to keep an archaic, colonial system of oppression intact, a system of which she had first-hand experience in her childhood. Castellanos arrived at an identification of the woman question with the Indian one, chiefly through her readings of the social theories of the French philosopher Simone Weil. Weil had formulated theories of power and oppression in capitalist, technological societies, one of her main tenets being that power debilitates and dehumanizes those who wield it as much as those who are oppressed by it.[5] Castellanos applied this idea to white-Indian, man-woman relationships in Mexico, in which the roles are forever alternating:

> At first glance, one has the impression that the role of victim corresponds to the Indian, and that of victimizer to the other. But human relations are never so schematic, and social ones even less so. The masks sometimes change, the roles alternate.[6]

As will become evident, the dichotomies present in her *indigenista* stories—between victimizer and victim master and slave, linear, historical time and circular, mythical time—are ones that also underpin her later stories that focus on the lives of Mexican women. In some of her essays, Castellanos discusses the way that in Mexican history, both women and Indians have been perceived as 'communities of interpretation' (Edward Said).[7] Historically, both groups were the subject of theological enquiries, the conclusions of which dictated that both women and Indians needed to be placed under the authority of a superior (male) being, which in the case of the Indian was the *encomendero* (white landowner), and in the woman's case, a husband or father.[8] A situation emerged therefore by which the colonial discourses variously used to describe Indians were permeated with the very same terms that were used to describe women, and vice versa. Because both so-called 'minority' groups occupied a position marginal to the dominant centre, they were seen to constitute the boundary between order and chaos, either being seen as representatives of irrationality and 'chaotic' sensuality (which meant that the Indians were variously labelled 'barbaric' or 'savage', and the women lustful 'whores'), or being elevated to representatives of 'a higher and purer nature than men'[9] (so that in this schema, the Indians are 'noble savages', while women were seen as morally superior to men). In short, the Indian and the Mexican woman have, over the centuries, been made the subjects of a set of reductive, crippling myths denying them choice and an autonomous identity. The word 'myth' here refers to the myth-making that underlies systems of oppression, which justify the denigration and exploitation of certain sectors of society. It is myth, by which 'bourgeois ideology continuously transforms the products of history into essential types',[10] that Barthes exposed in *Mythologies* as the delusive element that pervades the discourses of society. In *The Labyrinth of Solitude,* Octavio Paz analyses some of the myths that pervade Mexican culture, one example being his exposition of how 'the Mexican' (which in his text, always means the Mexican *man*) never opens himself up to the world, always viewing life as combat (*lucha*).[11] Set up against the forever pugnacious 'Mexican' is the Mexican woman, who is an enigmatic and passive being; like all women, the Mexican woman is

> a symbol . . . of the stability and continuity of the race. In addition to her cosmic significance she has an important social role, which is to see to it that law and order, piety and tenderness are predominant in everyday life. . . . Thanks to woman, many of the asperities of 'man-to-man' relationships are softened.[12]

Paz explains that because the Mexican way of life is constructed as a mask designed to hide the most intimate feelings of Mexicans, it would be inconceivable to allow woman to cast aside her symbolic role and express herself as an autonomous being, for this would cause the mask—i.e. the whole Mexican way of life—to crumble.[13] So the pressure on the Mexican woman to conform is a formidable one. It could be said that Paz's self-conscious function as the 'unveiler' of the many myths that structure Mexican culture banishes him to a theoretical realm in which his ability to understand and acknowledge the full weight of the Mexican myths does not contribute to their elimination. Rather, the project of deciphering myths signifies a degree of complicity with them; the very process of demythification restores the object under scrutiny to its mystified state. This, according to Barthes, is the paradox that dogs every mythologist[14] (Barthes uses the word 'mythologist' to describe the person who *studies* the myth, the person who creates it being the 'myth-maker'), and in some respects it is a paradox that can be detected in much of Castellanos's non-fiction that takes as its project the unveiling of the myths that surround the Mexican woman.[15] If Octavio Paz was one of the first to draw attention to the masked nature of the Mexican character, then Castellanos was one of the first to show in her fiction and non-fiction alike that those masks were very suffocating indeed for Mexican women.

Reading of some of the stories of her first (*indigenista*) anthology, ***Ciudad Real*** (1960), demonstrates how Castellanos prepared the ground for her fictional treatment of the myths that impair Mexican women's lives. The stories of this anthology focus on critical points of interaction between white/mestizo culture and Indian culture. Most of the stories focus on the repeated cycles of aggression and exploitation that Indians have suffered at the hands of the whites over the centuries since the Conquest. For example, the first story, **"The Death of the Tiger"**[16] traces the downfall of the once-dominant and belligerent Bolometic tribe, reduced by the white invaders to a defeated, bedraggled group who, after centuries of living timidly on sparse, unyielding land beyond the margins of the white settlers' towns, are finally forced to descend to Ciudad Real in search of a livelihood. The only white prepared to communicate with the Bolometic is the *enganchador* (agent), who sees in them welcome prey for his business of supplying cheap labour to white landowners. The *enganchador* and his assistant are appropriately depicted as grotesque, Dickensian caricatures:

> Don Juvencio drummed his fingers on the curve of his stomach, at the height of the waistcoat button where the watch chain should have hung. Remembering that he did not yet own a watch chain made him dig his spurs into the conversation . . . [p. 213] Don Juvencio's assistant showed his teeth in a wicked little smile.
>
> [p. 214]

These two mercenary whites work from a circular office that contrasts with the geometrical layout of the city's streets, but which reflects on their business of perpetuating time-tested patterns of exploiting Indians. The narrative suggests that the tragic plight of the Bolometic can largely be put down to the Indians' lack of means of communicating with the whites: the *enganchador* is easily able to exploit them because he can speak their dialect. The ominous description 'silence spread upon them like a stain' (p. 213) suggests the immediacy of his domination of them through language, for although he speaks to them in their own dialect, they are still rendered silent and therefore powerless. In other stories, however, the whites are depicted as being intolerant of the existing linguistic diversity, forcing the Indians into the straitjacket of the Spanish language, condemning them to be 'foreigners in their own land'. For example, the Indian protagonist of the story **"Aceite guapo"**, Daniel Castellanos Lampoy, seeks consolation from his loneliness in his new job as *mayordomo* (caretaker) to an alabaster saint, Santa Margarita, in a local Catholic church. For hours each day, Daniel sits pathetically talking to the saint at her altar, but the comfort he derives from these 'chats' is quickly dampened when the white sacristan assures Daniel that his words have 'fallen on deaf ears':

> Look at Saint Margarita's face. She's white, she's *ladina,* the same as Saint Juan, Saint Thomas, the same as all the rest of them. She speaks proper Spanish. How do you think she's going to understand the tzotzil dialect?
>
> [p. 47]

The sacristan assures him that only by purchasing and drinking some expensive 'aceite guapo' (alcohol) from a white settler's chemist (i.e. only by further subjecting himself to the economic system that exploits him), will Daniel miraculously attain instant access to the Spanish language, and therefore to the saint. On following the sacristan's advice, Daniel arrives at the church in a drunken stupor, babbling to the saint in what he pathetically believes to be Spanish. Predictably, he is expelled from the church forever. Clearly, this story amounts to a harsh critique of the Catholic Church and its role in the Indian communities. It points to the way that the perpetuation of a type of folk-Catholicism is only to the Church's advantage, for it ensures the devotion of the mass of the Indians, which leaves them at the mercy of hypocritical Church officials. Daniel's turning to white religion as a source of comfort is therefore a paradoxical choice, for the religion forms an integral part of the social structure that victimizes and degrades him. In other stories in this collection, the author's attack on the Catholic Church's treatment of the Indians is extended to include a harsh critique of Catholic missions (see especially the stories **"Arthur Smith salva sin alma"** [**"Arthur Smith Saves His Soul"**] and **"La rueda del hambriento"** [**"The Wheel of Hunger"**].

In all of the *indigenista* stories, any interaction between whites and Indians is filtered through the various stereotypes that each race has formulated for the other, dictating the nature of the confrontation with one another. The stereotypes of the Indians formulated by the whites of San Cristóbal are all pejorative, but they also reveal the whites' fear of the Indians, who, after all, in a state like Chiapas, are in a majority. This fear is clearly demonstrated in the story **"La suerte de Teodoro Méndez Acubal"** [**"Teodoro Méndez's Luck"**], in which a white jeweller is convinced that the Indian (Teodoro) peering into his shop window is about to rob him, simply because, in the white settlers' parlance, all Indians are thieves:

> The Indians are a race of thieves! . . . the man with the nose pressed against the window of his shop was a thief. There was no doubt about it.
>
> [pp. 58-59]

The paralysing effect of stereotypes grounded in myth also dictates the Indians' perception of the whites, in a way that in Castellanos's stories, more often than not, perpetuates their feelings of inferiority to whites, a phenomenon that arguably has its roots in the Conquest (when the Indians' belief that the *conquistadores* were gods whose arrival had been prophesied, put them at a distinct disadvantage in the subsequent battles).[17] The chaos that sometimes arises from the Indians' synthesis of their own myths and legends with the history of their oppression at the hands of the white settlers is dramatized in the story **"La tregua"** [**"The Truce"**], in which a dying white man who stumbles into an Indian village is identified by the Indians as the dangerous, legendary spirit *el pukuj* who periodically appears 'now in the guise of an animal, now in the dress of the white man' (p. 30), and who is always the harbinger of disaster to the tribe. The now prostrate and weak *pukuj* of the story therefore offers the tribe not only an opportunity to wreak their revenge against this mythical spirit, but also a chance to avenge themselves of all the brutality that they have suffered at the hands of the whites. The narrator describes the bloody murder of the white man:

> Then the fury was unleashed. A stick used to beat, a stone used to crush his skull, a machete used to slice off his limbs. The women shouted from behind the walls of their huts, urging the men on to complete their criminal job.
>
> [p. 35]

The white man becomes the fated scapegoat of the Indians' syncretic myth system. What is perhaps interesting to note here is that, notwithstanding her support for INI's integrationist projects, her belief in the Indians' essential sameness to the whites, Castellanos does not shy away from depicting the Indians engaged in a seemingly spontaneous act of barbaric primitivism.[18] Significantly, the very description of this bloody murder once again points to the inhumanity of white rule, for this act was by no means a spontaneous abberration, but the result of centuries of abuse at the hands of the whites, whose organized system of oppression was no less barbaric.

"Modesta Gómez" is a story which reveals that the same forces have caused both the Indian's and the Mexican woman's oppression. Tracing the life of the lower-class mestiza protagonist, Modesta Gómez, the narrative reveals how in a social system grounded in racism, sexism, opportunism and intolerance, each act of brutality engenders another, and that predictably, it is the Indians who ultimately bear the brunt of all the accumulated cruelty of the system. Having been rejected by her family as a young child—the first harsh act in a long chain of them ('One mouth less to feed was a relief for everyone' [p. 65])—Modesta takes up the position of nanny to Jorgito, the son of an upper-class white family. Modesta and Jorgito are the same age, but Jorgito is taught by his mother on numerous occasions that it is acceptable to punish Modesta physically. The outcome of such indoctrination is that in his adolescent years, Jorgito regularly rapes Modesta, and although aware of the nature of her son's nocturnal antics, Jorgito's mother convinces herself that they are 'natural' for his sex:

> Doña Romelia suspected something of her son's antics. . . . But she decided to play ignorant. When all was said and done, Jorgito was a man, not a saint, he was just the age when men feel the urge.
>
> [p. 68]

(Needless to say, when Modesta is visibly pregnant by her son, Doña Romelia throws her out onto the street rather than acknowledge any responsibility for her son's behaviour.)[19] Years later, after the death of her drunken, violent husband, Modesta is forced to become an *atajadora,* a job which consists of snatching from the Indians the products they bring to sell in the market, paying them a meagre sum that is only a fraction of what the produce will be worth in the market.[20] The graphic description of the *atajadoras* (all mestizas) in action points to the desperation of these women as they are forced to literally scrabble around for a livelihood:

> The *atajadoras* threw themselves wildly at the Indians. They struggled, suffocating shouts, to get hold of any object that wouldn't be damaged. Finally, when a woollen blanket or a bag of vegetables or a clay pot were safely in the hands of the *atajadora,* she would rummage in her blouse for a few coins, then toss them to the ground without counting them, leaving the defeated Indian to snatch them up.
>
> [p. 73]

Modesta over-enthusiastically participates in this degrading ritual, singling out a young Indian girl as her first victim:

> Modesta fought until she was on top of her. She pulled the girl's plaits, she slapped her cheeks, she dug her nails into her ears. . . . Inflamed, panting, Modesta grappled with her victim. She didn't want to let her go even when the girl gave her the woollen blanket that she had hidden. Another *atajadora* had to intervene.
>
> [pp. 73-4]

Looking at her bloodied fingernails, Modesta felt satisfied: 'She looked at her bloodstained fingernails. She didn't know why. But she was happy' (p. 74).

Although the Indians are not introduced until the climax of the narrative, their presence is felt throughout, for their very existence on the margins of Ciudad Real determines the nature of the rigid social hierarchy that is completed at the story's close. Modesta and the other *atajadoras,* all of them, as women, the victims of repeated acts of brutality that the system throws up, can only find consolation by entering into another exploitative relationship that ultimately only further entrenches their acquiescence to the system that degrades them. (The same can be said of Jorgito's mother, who compensates for her lack of self-esteem by cruelly exploiting her servants.) The final horrific image of Modesta's bloodstained fingernails explicitly points to the way that the mechanisms of oppression barbarize the oppressors. Modesta's inability to explain her exhilaration indicates the way that a type of fragmented vision is inscribed into the hierarchical social structure, for the system works to ensure that women like Modesta will never be able to assemble the fragments of their experiences into a whole that would unveil the workings of the system. (Undoubtedly, Modesta's final feeling of satisfaction is the effect of a kind of *unconscious* synthesis of the fragments, for it clearly stems from the fact that she feels that she has avenged herself of all the violence that the system has inflicted upon her.) The importance of this story in the anthology lies in its exposure of the multidimensional nature of the oppression suffered by both Modesta and her Indian victim, for as non-white, working-class women, they are both exploited (in the economic sense), and oppressed (in the sense that their sex and race is constructed as inferior to those of the dominant group).[21] The story shows how women in particular are susceptible to the brutality of the power hierarchy, and because of the nature of the system, the possibility of any form of positive interaction between the women of the different social groups is ruled out.

In some of the essays of *La mujer que sabe latín* [*The Woman Who Knows Latin,* 1973], Castellanos seeks to expose the myths that victimize and impair the Mexican woman. Her project was clearly indebted to her reading of Woolf's essays—particularly *A Room of One's Own*—and of Simone de Beauvoir's *The Second Sex.* Although today, the 'demythification' project is regarded as a well-trodden path, in her time, Castellanos was undoubtedly a pioneer in this area within Mexico. She exposed the sexism intrinsic to the Mexican cultural tradition, which stems largely from the way that women's lives are refracted through the national feminine symbols of La Malinche, the Virgin of Guadalupe, and Sor Juana Inés de la Cruz, so that in Mexican society, a woman is pigeonholed resembling either the supposed treacherous whore or the self-abnegating mother or the socially deviant scholar.[22] Castellanos was what today would be termed a liberal-reformist feminist, a stance that advocates the idea that women need to challenge the distorting stereotypes of conventional femininity, and fight for legislation and reform in order that they might take up their rightful and 'equal' places in the linear (masculine) time of project and history.[23] Such a stance can be criticized for its veiled aspirations for women to be able eventually to act and choose on the same terms as men without actually challenging the patriarchal structure,[24] yet it is important to remember that Castellanos was formulating her feminist ideals at a time when Mexican women had only recently (in 1953) gained national suffrage, so women's insertion into existing public life still seemed to be the priority for Mexican feminists.[25] Castellanos admired the work of the North American liberal-feminist Betty Friedan,[26] and like Friedan she eventually grappled with the phenomenon of why women—in Mexico, educated middle-class women in particular—were prepared to limit their horizons and accept marriage and motherhood as their sole vocation in life. Castellanos was aware of how society weighted the odds against the educated woman, for once trying to practise a profession she found herself in a social no man's land: '. . . in the place where Sor Juana was born: Nepantla, the land of in-between, the place without identity. Up until now, that still small group of professional women has tended to consider itself as mutant creatures.'[27]

Castellanos called for consciousness-raising among women, so that they might begin to redefine themselves beyond the terms of patriarchy: 'construir la imagen propia, autorretratarse' ('construct their own image, depict themselves').[28] Such exhortations to women seem to be informed by an idealism in which her vision of women's emancipation located in change at the level of individual subjective consciousness, with no direct reference to the need for change in the structures of society at large. However, this idealism is modified by the pessimism of many of her narratives, in which women (and Indians) come up against much more formidable barriers even when they do attempt to break out of the treadmill of oppression.

In the stories that focus on the lives of women, the status of the *solterona* (spinster) become paradigmatic for the confined status of women in general. Dismissed as an aberation by patriarchal society because of her status and sex, the *solterona* epitomizes in the extreme the position of all women forced to live by the stringent codes of patriarchy. In Castellanos's stories, the *solteronas*' marginalized position does not endow them with more freedom to challenge the social order simply because they devote much of their energy in attempting to integrate into the hostile society that stigmatizes them. Their ultimate aim is usually integration into the world via the 'respectable' path of marriage. That is, the *solterona*'s entry into society is contingent on a man to act as social mediator. The title story of ***Los convidados de agosto* [*Guests in August*]** focuses on an anomalous day in the life of a middle-aged, upper-class spinster, Emelina—anomalous because it is a day of fiesta in her provincial home town. Elements associated with fiesta in Mexico—life and death, dream and reality, the halt of the flow of time and the abrupt break with routine—therefore become integral to, and in many respects determine, Emelina's experiences on this 'exceptional' day in her dreary life. Emelina is first described as waking from a dream (in which she is passionately embracing her fantasy lover) to the knell of the town's funeral bell. This seems to suggest that the life/death dichotomy is inverted in Emelina's case, with activity—life, passion—being confined to her dream world. Reflecting on the scandals of past *fiestas,* it emerges that Emelina harbours a deep fascination and envy for the daring and so-called 'loose' women who were able to exploit the riotous *fiesta* atmosphere to the full: the *toreras* of the previous year with their brassy outfits and provocatively defiant gestures, the women of the *barrios* who got pregnant by strangers and were forced to live in shame. In Emelina's view, the *fiesta* had given these women the much sought-after opportunity to shed 'the burden of spinsterhood' (p. 62). But Emelina too is weighed down by the restrictions of her class, for unlike her those women 'did not have much honour to lose and no surname to safeguard' (p. 62).

Emelina's spinsterhood keeps her in a state of constant anxiety about the passing of time. Her daily ritual of inspecting her naked body for wrinkles is just one manifestation of this. (Significantly, and in harmony with the timeless atmosphere of *fiesta,* Emelina detects no new wrinkles on this day.) Her dislike for the 'sterile lushness' (*verdor estéril*) of the quequextle plant she glimpses from her window, which thrives in 'shady places' (pp. 67-8), symbolically reflects her discontent both with her own sheltered life as a spinster in wealthy surroundings, and with her still-intact virginity. Yet when she picks a branch of the quequextle and attempts to unwind a tight, new shoot, it ominously reverts to its 'natural' position: 'But it was flexible and vigorous. Hardly was it loose when it sprung back to its natural position' (p. 68). (Again, when she impulsively opens the door of her canary's cage, the bird prefers the safety of the cage to the unstructured space of freedom [p. 68].) Later, at the end of the *fiesta* bullfight, in the pandemonium created by the customary collapsing of the wooden spectators' stadium, Emelina faints and is thrown into the arms of a total stranger, and soon afterwards, defying the scandalized stares of the townsfolk, she proudly enters a *cantina* (bar) with the stranger. She is soon very drunk, and allows the stranger to lead her from the *cantina.* But they are intercepted by Emelina's brother, Mateo, who assaults the stranger while her brother's best friend, Enrique, drags the humiliated Emelina home in front of intrigued spectators, unceremoniously dumping her on her doorstep and shouting accusations at her: 'You have brought shame to your family's name! And with a nobody! With an unscrupulous stranger!' (p. 95). The narrative closes with two resonating images: Emelina howling in the street, 'like a madwoman, like an animal', while Enrique abandons her, to go and hammer on the door of a brothel.

Clearly, what is being exposed in this ending are the double standards of a moral code that has as its priority the preservation of 'gentlemen's honour' (enshrined in the family's name) at all costs. The control of women's supposed boundless sexuality is considered to be the mainstay of the system of preserving male honour; women not already under the tutelage of male authority are considered to be replete with latent desires that are incompatible with the smooth functioning of patriarchal society. (Only within the walls of the brothel can this female sensuality be legitimately unleashed for men's pleasure.) Just as the narrative had opened with the rupture of routine that the *fiesta* celebrations bring, so it closes with another rupture, which is this time the total severance of Emelina's already fragile, spinster's hold on the external world. The fact that she is finally reduced to a 'howling animal' suggests that she has now been banished to the realms of absolute marginality. This final animalistic depiction of Emelina confirms an underlying association between her and the bull of the bullfight, for the bull had leapt over the barriers of the stadium only to be skilfully and quickly killed by the *matadero*. Both the death of the bull and the humiliation of Emelina are needed to ensure that male honour and prowess remain intact; both 'deaths' are approved by the community to ensure that tradition is observed. The collective interest in, and approval of, Emelina's punishment is highlighted in the way that it is deemed to be any man's prerogative—not necessarily a relative of Emelina's—to censure her for her transgression of social protocol. The fact that a man with only a casual connection with her family (her brother's friend) is able to take charge of what amounts to her destiny points to the decisive role that the social *milieu* plays in shaping the parameters of a woman's life. The equation is made explicit in this story: the preservation of male domination in such communities implies the confinement or social death of women.

The stories of Castellanos's final anthology, ***Album de familia*** (1971), move out of the enclosure of the provincial town and into the more impersonal world of Mexico City's suburbia. Castellanos's assessment of the conditions of the lives of urban middle-class women in these stories undermines assumptions about the supposed progressive, liberal values of the city; rigid definitions of femininity are proved not to be limited to Mexico's provincial towns. However, the fragmentary nature of life in the metropolis mystifies the mechanisms of power and oppression; the city—like patriarchy—is not a seamless, monolithic structure. The complex web of power relations that constitute patriarchal systems coincides with the fragmented incoherency of urban life, and so the fact that the success of the patriarchal economy is still contingent on confining women to certain roles can be more effectively masked. The first story of the anthology, **"Lección de cocina" ["The Cooking Lesson"]**,[29] analyses the way in which the asymmetrical relations between the sexes in patriarchal societies are sustained by the process of naturalization—the discourse of common sense. Underpinning the entire narrative is the discord between the vitality of the woman's concrete existence (symbolized in the text by a piece of meat) and the rigidity of abstract and stereotypical social prescriptions of femininity (symbolized by the recipe). The narrative is structured around the interior monologue of a newly-wed woman as she prepares a piece of meat for supper. The opening lines describe the kitchen in which the 'action' of the narrative takes place:

> The kitchen is shining white. It's a shame to have to get it dirty. . . . Looking closely, this spotlessness, this pulchritude lacks the glaring excess that causes chills in hospitals.
>
> [p. 158]

The narrator's very denials that the kitchen's sterile ambience recalls the deathlike atmosphere of a hospital ironically establishes the association between the kitchen and death. At the very least, the kitchen's almost blinding whiteness indicates a nullification of all that has preceded it—poignant when combined with the new wife's realization that her assumption of the role of wife has effectively invalidated her active past as an independent woman. The skills she acquired then are now secondary to the new, 'wifely' ones: 'For example, choosing the menu' (p. 158).

As the narrator follows a recipe to prepare a piece of meat, a pattern emerges by which the discrepancy between the reality of an inexperienced and incompetent (by patriarchal society's standards) wife cooking the meat and the ideal, finished product that the recipe promises is a discrepancy which is paralleled by the discrepancy existing between the woman's expectations of marriage and domesticity (expectations themselves constructed by various social discourses) and the reality of the situation: rather than find herself in the domestic bliss that society promises of marriage, she is confined to an orderly, impersonal kitchen, performing chores presumed to be the wife's vocation. Part of her dilemma arises from her awareness that she has *already* complied with the myth-making that surrounds marriage: for example, her sexual relations with her husband fall far short of the myths surrounding marital sex, yet she masochistically assists in their perpetuation.

> But I, self-sacrificing little Mexican wife, born like a dove to the nest, smiled like Cuauhtémoc under torture on the rack when he said 'My bed is not made of roses', and fell silent. Face up, I bore not only my own weight but also his on top of me. The classic position for making love. And I moaned, from the tearing and the pleasure. The classic moan. Myths, myths.
>
> [p. 159]

The narrator explicitly draws an analogy between the meat's metamorphosis through the various stages as she prepares it and her own changing condition from woman to wife. Just as the frozen meat was unrecognizable 'under its icy coating' (p. 159), so too was she once anonymous in society's eyes as a 'frigid' spinster. And just as the meat's 'offensive redness' (p. 160) can be toned down by rubbing spices into it, so too the woman's 'dense, viscous and turbid' (p. 160) vitality and individualism can be tempered by the demands of marriage and domesticity. In this way, the shrivelling up and burning of the piece of meat is ominous, foreshadowing the way in which traditional married life will eventually deform her if she is to meet the standards of the socially prescribed 'recipe' for a 'successful' marriage. ('The meat lies there silently, faithful to its deceased state' [p. 163]. Attention is drawn to the artificiality of both marriage and the recipe/text in this repeated juxtaposition of reality and myth; both are exposed as narrative codes that artificially construct worlds in terms of a particular ideology that upholds the status quo. The commonsense, patronizing language of recipes (which Virginia Woolf once referred to as 'a charming directness'!)[30]—like the patriarchal concept of the marriage union—presents the ideology of female submissiveness to (male) authority as natural and eternal. But because the narrator takes offence at the recipe's presumptuous tone, and goes out of her way *not* to identify herself with the unified and knowing subject whom the recipe addresses, its collusive tone is exposed and therefore undermined:

> Well, just who do you think you're talking to? If I knew what tarragon or *ananas* were I wouldn't be consulting this book, because I'd know a lot of other things too. . . . But you all start from the assumption that we're all in on the secret and you limit yourselves to stating it. I, at least, solemnly declare that I am not, and never have been, in on either this or any other secret you share.
>
> [p. 159]

In the narrator's refusal to recognize herself as the obvious, unified, but contradictory subject that the recipe constructs and addresses, lies the possibility for change, which may be detected in her defiance of convention:

> From today on, I'll be whatever I choose to be at the moment. . . . From the very beginning I will impose, just a bit insolently, the rules of the game. My husband will resent the appearance of my dominance.
>
> [p. 164]

This defiance is symbolically paralleled by the way that the meat remains raw 'in a few obstinate places' (p. 163). The narrator discovers that it is this 'obvious' and contradictory stance that she is expected to adopt if she hopes for a (conventionally defined) successful marriage. Although she recognizes that the contradictions in the recipe's terms of address correspond to her own experiences as a woman living by patriarchal codes, the recipe's final closure (which is based on an illusion that has no bearing on the reality of the burnt-up meat) works to smooth over these contradictions. By contrast, the narrator's text remains open-ended (the last line being: 'And yet . . .' [p. 165]. Because of the text's de-familiarizing of the conventional, the ironic tone used throughout is appropriate, highlighting as it does the incongruity and contradictory nature of reality.[31] Finally, although the story draws on the metaphor of the wife's world as a recipe, the story's message is not just a feminist one, for it also points out that reality lived day by day is a constructed reality.[32]

Although the title story of ***Album de familia*** does not read well as a short story (its long, dense monologues bear witness that it was originally intended to be a stage play)[33], it is important, for it explores a theme that was arguably uppermost in Castellanos's mind in the wake of the boom in Latin American literature: the 'problem' of the woman writer. The boom clearly provides the context, for the story also explores the phenomenon of literary superstardom and how this affects the 'exceptional' woman writer who joins the select group of male boom writers. Matilde Casanova, an internationally acclaimed writer, returns to Mexico after just having won the (fictitious) Premio de las Naciones (this detail, along with the description of her Indian appearance and the reference to her past as a schoolteacher suggests that Gabriela Mistral was the model for this character,[34] although Mistral was clearly pre-boom). Her secretary, Victoria, has arranged for her to meet some of her ex-pupils from her university-teaching days, and also two young students. The problem of the glamour that comes with a writer's fame is explored at great length in the first section of the narrative in a conversation between Victoria and a newspaper reporter of the popular press. Most of the population, like the reporter, have not even read Matilde's work, but the reporter unashamedly and cynically declares that the whole nation is bathing in the glory of her literary prize because, in her view, 'The champion disappears behind the halo of glory and the merit/prize is shared amongst all her compatriots' (p. 69). This journalist can be seen as a representative of both the general public's views of Matilde's achievement, and also, more significantly, of the widespread opinion of women's role in Mexican society. Toeing the party line, the journalist predictably dismisses Victoria's feminism as outdated and irrelevant in revolutionary Mexico where, she declares, 'there no longer exists any position that is inaccessible to Mexican women'. She adds that the requirements for women to 'get on' in Mexico are that they be discreet and accommodating ('do not make any display, nor adopt a defiant attitude' [p. 77]). This strategy is dismissed by Victoria as having for centuries been proved ineffective: 'But that position is the one that our grandmothers adopted! Dissimulation, deceit. What originality!' (p. 77).

Matilde's first entry shows her to be a distraught and anxious woman, unfulfilled by her profession, and suffering because she regards her writing as effective only as a palliative and disguise of the 'crime' of her sterility (p. 82). Matilde therefore displays the exaggerated 'symptoms' of the woman writer who, as Mary Eagleton notes, 'finds herself at a point of tension, aware that her writing both challenges the conventional view of what is appropriate for women and encroaches on what some see as a male preserve'.[35] Her anxiety over this conflict of roles surfaces despite the fact that she is a writer for whom the material obstacles to writing have been solved; she is economically independent, has 'a room of her own', and most important, has the invaluable services of Victoria, who in many respects protects Matilde from the world. Through this relationship between the two women, Castellanos examines the important roles that other women can often play in the lives of successful women writers; Victoria is the substitute 'literary wife' who channels her own creativity into the life of a successful writer.[36] Indeed, towards the end of the narrative, Victoria confesses to have sacrificed her own vocation as a writer and the precarious existence that comes with it so that she might hide 'behind a mask that amplifies my voice', a role that she believes endows her with 'absolute liberation' (p. 150). As Beth Miller notes, Matilde suffers from the syndrome Borges alludes to in 'Borges y Yo' [Borges and I]:[37] she feels that she has become trapped in a duplicitous situation in which the public image of herself becomes confused with her private self. But whereas in Borges's case, the legend and the man turn out to be inextricable, in the case of Matilde the existence of social expectations of a woman's 'true' role determines that this tension will never be resolved for her. Through the other characters of the story—three women writers, Matilde's ex-students—Castellanos reveals the different ways in which women of the same class (i.e. upper-middle and middle class) have attempted to resolve this dilemma. One writer, Elvira, has given up her marriage to continue her career; another, Josefa, has compromised her career for her children, and is obliged to write soap-opera scripts and journalistic pieces to make ends meet; and Aminta is a successful, unmarried writer who has prostituted herself to the commercial side of the business in her quest for fame—her public image is more important to her than the quality of her work. Out of these three writers, Josefa is convinced that she is the only one who has successfully resolved the conflict: 'I am the only one of us who has fully assumed her responsibilities as a woman and mother' (p. 124). But, according to Victoria's interpretation of *machista* Mexican ideology, even Josefa is a 'mutilated' woman by dint of the fact that she has chosen to be a writer as well as a mother:

> In Mexico the alternatives and circumstances for a woman are very limited and precise. Any one who wants to be more or less than daughter, wife and mother, can choose between becoming a black sheep or an immoral woman.
>
> [p. 149]

Matilde's notable absence for much of the narrative contributes to the mythologizing of her, but it also points to the extreme isolation and withdrawal from society that a successful writer can often endure, and that unlike her male counterparts, the woman writer's chosen solitude is in this case tainted by visions of what she lacks as a woman in society's eyes. It could be said that the opening description of the sea's waves symbolically condenses the story's pessimistic message, namely, that this conflict between women's powerful, individual urges and social expectations will be an eternal one:

> . . . the waves stopped at the point at which—why?—they gave up their strength and began to pull back, as if regretful of the impetus that had carried them so far, only to regret their hesitation and start again.
>
> [p. 65]

In another essay, Castellanos subscribes to Virginia Woolf's view that out of all the professions, writing is the one that has been considered most suitable for women to follow because 'The family peace was not broken by the scratching of a pen. No demand was made upon the family purse.'[38]

Just after Castellanos's death in 1974, the Mexican author José Emilio Pacheco wrote in *Excelsior*:

> When the shock of her death passed and her books were re-read, one could see that none of us had in our time such a clear understanding of what the double condition of woman and Mexican meant. . . . Naturally we did not know how to read her.[39]

Her tragic and rather bizarre death (she died after accidentally electrocuting herself while serving as Mexico's Ambassador to Israel) undoubtedly inspired a wave of rereading of her fiction, some of which used the texts as a means of arriving at the woman behind the work. For example, **'Cooking Lesson'** has been referred to as a description of the author's own personal experiences as a newly-wed;[40] the torment that the young narrator-protagonist of *Balún Canán* [*The Nine Guardians*] experiences after the death of her brother Mario is invariably discussed as a direct reference to Castellanos's own devastating experience of overhearing her mother lament the fact that her son, Benjamin, had died and not the young Rosario.[41] Perhaps this mythologizing of Castellanos the woman is almost inevitable given her sudden death, but one of the effects of giving primacy to tracing in her fiction elements of the personal events of her life is that the fiction itself is neutralized: confined to the realm of the writer's private life, which has 'traditionally been the only life any "safe" woman may be presumed to lead'.[42] This does not mean that the formidable influence that certain formative events of the author's life brought to bear on her work should be denied (it is impossible to ignore the author's experience of working with Indians, or her childhood in a provincial town, or, indeed, her experience as a woman living under patriarchy), but it needs to be rejected as the central informing factor of the work. Castellanos was not a 'safe' woman; through her writing, she tackled what she considered to be the major social concerns of her time: the systematic denigration and oppression of women and Indians. In the light of more recent feminist literary theory this unproblematical movement from the text to the world beyond it can be criticized for its unquestioning acceptance of the *patriarchal* view of literature as representation, when the unveiling of the myths circumscribing women's lives is seen to be the most pressing need (as was arguably the case with Castellanos), but this type of social realism is often regarded as the most effective style to adopt.[43]

The influence of Rosario Castellanos's work on twentieth-century Mexican feminism was formidable. From the time of her Masters thesis of 1950—a work which the writer Elena Poniatowska regarded as 'the point of departure for the contemporary women's movement in Mexico'[44]—Castellanos kept up a dialogue with the major trends in international feminist thought, filtering them through

Mexican reality to come up with her unique and often satirical critique of contemporary social codes (see especially her play *The Eternal Feminine*).[45] Her advocacy of a type of integrationalist, liberal feminism, her unswaying conviction (conveyed in many of her essays) that women will be 'liberated' once they have access to study, work and sexual freedom, on the same terms as men—on a par with her belief that the Indians should be integrated into mainstream society in order to 'progress'—is a vision that is counterbalanced by the bleaker one that her short stories engender in focusing on the deeply entrenched values of Mexican society, which would clearly require more than social reform to eradicate. Rosario Castellanos used writing not only as a means of apprehending Mexican reality but also as a means of survival; in her own words, the act of writing realizes

> the desire to survive on a page, surrounded by all that we have loved, by all that we have found to be intolerable and painful, by what has excited us, aroused us to rebellion, brought us peace. Grasping that momentary lightning, we discover in its brief clarity, beauty and order, the laws and meaning of the world and of our own lives.[46]

The fact that Castellanos consciously set out to expose the darker side of the patriarchal 'laws and meaning of the world' in her prose and poetry makes all the more ironic the place of her burial: Mexico City's Rotunda of Illustrious Men.[47]

Notes

1. Before the dictator Porfiro Díaz was overthrown in 1910, 1 per cent of the population owned 97 per cent of arable land, and 96 per cent of the population owned 2 per cent of land. During the six years of Cardenas's presidency (1934-40), over 20 million hectares of land were redistributed to 775,000 people. And more land was distributed between 1935-40 than under all previous administrations put together from 1916. Details in B. Braulio Muñoz, *Sons of the Wind: The search for identity in Spanish American Indian literature,* New Jersey: Rutgers University Press, 1982, p. 224.
2. For details of Mexico's 'official *indigenismo*' see David A. Brading, 'Manuel Gamio and Official Indigenismo in Mexico', *Bulletin of Latin American Research,* Vol. 7, no. 1, 1988, p. 86.

   Castellanos was involved in the creation of Teatro Guinol Petul, whose chief aims were to create didactic puppet shows that would educate the Indians into the mores of the dominant culture. Castellanos described the puppet Petul as 'a man of reason . . . open to the news that his white and mestizo friends brought, thanks to whom their intervention always brought the triumph of intelligence over superstitions, of progress over tradition, and of civilization over barbarism'. Quoted in Mary Seale Vásquez, 'Rosario Castellanos, Image and Idea', in Maureen Ahern and Mary Seale Vásquez, (eds.), *Homenaje a Rosario Castellanos,* Valencia: Albatros Hispanofila, 1980, p. 23. Castellanos also said, 'It is necessary that they [i.e. the Indians] understand that . . . they are cells of a society, of a State, of a nation.' Quoted in Perla Shwartz, *Rosario Castellanos: mujer que supo latín,* Mexico: Editorial Katún, 1984, p. 85.
3. *Balún Canán,* translated by Irene Nicholson as *The Nine Guardians,* New York: Vanguard Press, 1970.
4. Amado Mejías Alonso, 'La narrativa de Rosario Castellanos y el indigenismo', *Cuadernos Americanos,* vol. 260, part 3, pp. 205-6.
5. '[Power] weighs as pitilessly on those who command as on those who obey . . . [creating a vicious circle in which] the master produces fear in the slave, by the very fact that he is afraid of him, and vice versa' (Simone Weil). Quoted in Cynthia Steele, 'The fiction of national formation: the *indigenista* novels of James Fenimore Cooper and Rosario Castellanos', in Bell Gayle Chevigny and Gari Laguardia, (eds.), *Reinventing the Americas: Comparative studies of literature of the United States and Spanish America,* Cambridge: Cambridge University Press, 1986, p. 64.
6. Rosario Castellanos, 'La novela mexicana y su valor testimonial', *Juicios sumarios,* Mexico City: Biblioteca Joven, 1984, p. 122.
7. Edward Said, 'Orientalism', *Race and Class* Vol. XXVII, no. 2, autumn 1985, p. 4.
8. Regina Harrison Macdonald, 'Rosario Castellanos: on language', in Seale Vásquez and Ahern, p. 54-5.
9. Toril Moi, 'Language, Femininity, Revolution: Julia Kristeva and Anglo-American Feminist Linguistics', unpublished lecture, 1983, p. 23. Cited in Deborah Cameron, *Feminism and Linguistic Theory,* New York: St Martin's Press, 1985, p. 127.
10. Roland Barthes, 'Myth Today', in *Barthes: Selected Writings,* Oxford: Fontana Paperbacks, 1983, p. 145.
11. Octavio Paz, *The Labyrinth of Solitude,* (translated by Lysander Kemp), New York: Grove Press, 1961, p. 31.
12. *ibid.,* p. 38.
13. *ibid.,* p. 38.
14. Barthes, pp. 147-9.
15. Her long essays 'La participación de la mujer mexicana en la educatión formal' and 'La mujer y su imagen' in *Mujer que sabe latín,* Mexico: Sepsetentas Secretaria de Education Publica, 1973, pp. 21-41 and pp. 7-21 respectively and 'Otra vez Sor Juana', in *Juicios sumarios*, pp. 22-7 deal with the Mexican myths of femininity.
16. A translation of 'La muerte del tigre' ('Death of the Tiger') by Alberto Manguel appears in A. Manguel (ed.), *Other Fires: Stories from the women of Latin*

America, London: Pan Books, 1986, pp. 207-17. All page references in this study refer to this translation.

17. For a good account of the Conquest, see Tzvetan Todorov, *The Conquest of America* (translated by Richard Howard), New York: Harper & Row, 1984.

18. J. Sommers, 'The Indian-Oriented Novel in Latin America', *Journal of Inter-American Studies,* Vol. 6, part 2, 1964, p. 262. In reference to Castellanos's depiction of a brutal Indian rebellion in her novel *Oficio de tinieblas,* Jean Franco criticizes Castellanos because she 'tacitly acquiesces in the view of the literal-mindedness of the indigenous population propagated by positivism' (J. Franco, *Plotting Women,* London: Verso, 1989, p. 141).

19. 'It is common practice for a prudent middle-class mestizo mother of a pubescent boy to hire a young female servant for general housework "and other duties", the latter expression being a euphemism for initiating the boy into adult heterosexual experience', (Evelyn P. Stevens, 'Marianismo: the other face of machismo', in Anne Pescatello (ed.), *Female and Male in Latin America,* Pennsylvania: University of Pittsburgh Press, 1973, p. 97).

20. 'Hay oficios . . . en los que el despojo aparece como una forma lícita de comercio. El oficio de *atajadora,* por exemplo,' ('There are jobs . . . in which plundering appears as a licit form of commerce. The job of *atajadora,* for example.') From 'El idioma en San Cristóbal de las Casas' in R. Castellanos, *Juicios sumarios*, pp. 130-1.

21. '. . . it is possible to parallel racialized and gendered divisions in the sense that the possibilities of amelioration through legislation appear to be equally ineffectual in both cases . . . the construction of such parallels is fruitless and often proves to be little more than an academic exercise. . . . The experience of black women does not enter the parameters of parallelism. The fact that black women are subject to the *simultaneous* oppression of patriarchy, class and "race" is the prime reason for not employing parallels that render their position and experience not only marginal but also invisible' (Hazel Carby, 'Schooling in Babylon', in Centre for Contemporary Cultural Studies, *The Empire Strikes Back,* London: Hutchinson, 1982, pp. 212-13).

22. See Castellanos's essays, 'La participación de la mujer mexicana en la educación formal', 'La mujer y su imagen', and 'Otra vez Sor Juana'.

23. J. Kristeva, 'Women's Time', in T. Moi (ed.), *The Kristeva Reader,* Oxford: Basil Blackwell, 1986, p. 193.

24. For example, see Mary Evans' critique of the outcome of Simone de Beauvoir's *The Second Sex,* in M. Evans, *Simone de Beauvoir,* London: Tavistock Publications, 1985, especially pp. 57-68.

25. Despite the prominent participation of women in the 'public' side of the revolution—as *soldaderas,* doctors, journalists, nurses, campaigners—women didn't get the national vote until 1953. This delay is largely attributed to the conspicuous participation of some conservative middle- and upper-class women in the counter-revolutionary Cristero Revolt (1926-9) led by clerics. Relevant historical articles on Mexican women are as follows: Beth Miller, 'Women and Revolution: the *Brigadas Femeninas* and the Mexican Cristero rebellion, 1926-29', in S. McGee (ed.), *Women and Politics in 20th Century Latin America,* Studies in Third World Societies 8, no. 15, March 1981, pp. 57-64; Anna Macías, 'Women and the Mexican Revolution 1910-20', in *Americas,* 37, no. 1, 1981, p. 53-82; Anna Macías, *Against All Odds: The feminist movement in Mexico to 1940,* London and Westport: Greenwood Press, 1982; Jane Nash, 'The Aztecs and the Ideology of Male Dominance', *Signs* 4, no. 1, winter 1978, pp. 349-58; Frederick Turner, 'Los efectos de la participación femenina en la Revolución de 1910', *Historia Mexicana* 16, nos. 61-4, 1966-7, pp. 603-17.

26. Castellanos includes an essay on Friedan in *Mujer que sabe latín,* pp. 120-5.

27. R. Castellanos, 'La participación', pp. 37-8.

28. Aurora Ocampo, 'Debe haber otro modo de ser humano y libre: Rosario Castellanos', *Cuadernos Americanos,* vol. 250(5), 1983, p. 210.

29. 'Leccion de cocina', translated by Maureen Ahern as 'Cooking Lesson' in Doris Meyer and Margarite Fernández Olmos (eds.), *Contemporary Women Authors of Latin America: New Translations,* New York: Brooklyn College Press, 1983.

30. 'Cookery books are delightful to read. . . . A charming directness stamps them, with their imperative "Take an uncooked fowl and split its skin from end to end" and their massive commonsense which stares frivolity out of countenance' (Virginia Woolf, review entitled "The Cookery Book of Lady Clark of Tillypronie', in the *Times Literary Supplement,* 25 November 1909. In A. McNeillie (ed.), *The Essays of Virginia Woolf, vol. 1: 1904-1912,* London: Hogarth Press, 1986, p. 301).

31. Roger Fowler (ed.), *A Dictionary of Modern Critical Terms,* London, Henley and Boston: Routledge and Kegan Paul, 1973, p. 101.

32. 'In showing us how literary fiction creates its imaginary worlds, metafiction helps us to understand how the reality we live day by day is similarly constructed, similarly "written"' (Patricia Waugh, *Metafiction,* London and New York: Methuen, 1984, p. 18).

33. Kathleen O'Quinn, '"Tablero de damas" and "Album de familia": Farces on Women Writers' in Ahern and Seale Vásquez, p. 100.

34. Beth Miller, 'Female Characterization and Contexts in Rosario Castellanos' *Album de familia, The American Hispanist*, Vol. 4, Jan-Feb 1979, p. 27.

35. Mary Eagleton, Introduction to 'Women and Literary Production', in Mary Eagleton (ed.), *Feminist Literary Theory, A Reader,* Oxford: Basil Blackwell, 1986, p. 40. 'Outwardly, what is simpler than to write books? Outwardly, what obstacles are there for a woman rather than for a man? Inwardly, I think, the case is very different; she has still many ghosts to fight, many prejudices to overcome. Indeed it will be a long time still, I think, before a woman can sit down to write a book without finding a phantom to be slain, a rock to be dashed against. And if this is so in literature, the freest of all professions for women, how is it in the new professions which you are now for the first time entering?' (Virginia Woolf, 'Professions for Women', excerpt quoted in Eagleton, p. 53.)

36. Mary Eagleton discusses the phenomenon of 'literary wives'—in many cases (she cites Dorothy Wordsworth, Zelda Fitzgerald, Alice James as examples), they were 'the power behind the throne' (Eagleton, p. 44). However, the relationship between Matilde and Victoria is more on a par with those discussed in Gillian Hanscombe and Virginia Smyers in *Writing for their Lives,* London: Women's Press, 1987. Their relationship is comparable to, say, the real-life one between Gertrude Stein and Alice B. Tolkas.

37. Beth Miller refers to Borges's essay-fiction when discussing Matilde's dilemma (Miller, 'Female Characterization', p. 28). Borges's essay can be found in English in *Labyrinths: Selected Stories and Other Writings,* London: Penguin, 1982.

38. Virginia Woolf, 'Professions for Women', in *The Death of the Moth and Other Essays,* London: Hogarth Press, 1942, p. 149, quoted by Castellanos in 'Virginia Woolf o la literatura como ejercicio de la libertad', *Juicios sumarios,* p. 126.

39. José Emilio Pacheco, 'Rosario Castellanos o la literatura como ejercicio de la libertad', *Diorama de la cultura,* supplement of *Excelsior,* 11 August 1974, p. 16, quoted in Ahern and Seale Vásquez, p. 16.

40. 'Si en sus poemas Rosario da amarga cuenta de su fracaso matrimonial—en su prosa, no hay más que leer la ironía en torno a su luna de miel en el cuento "Lección de cocina" . . .' In Elena Poniatowska, *¡Ay vida, no me mereces! Carlos Fuentes, Rosario Castellanos, Juan Rulfo, la literatura de la Onda,* México: Editoria Joaquín Mortiz, 1985, p. 63.

    Two other studies that explicitly make their project the life of Castellanos are: Perla Shwartz, *Rosario Castellanos mujer que supo latín,* México: Editorial Katun, 1984; and Estela Franco, *Rosario Castellanos: semblanza psicoanalítica,* México: Plaza y Janes, 1984, in which the author makes clear her belief that through Castellanos's fiction, she would be able to 'conocerla más fondo' (p. 7). Franco also states, '. . . los textos sirvieron para formular y reforzar atisbos de la dinámica de la personalidad de R.C. . . . Se orientó exclusivamente a trazar una semblanza de la escritora sobre lineamientos psicoanalíticos a partir de su obra' (pp. 8 and 11).

41. *ibid.,* p. 91. Castellanos is said to have overheard her mother say '¿Por qué murió el varón y no la mujercita?' ('Why did the boy have to die and not the little girl?')

42. See Kate Fullbrook, *Katherine Mansfield,* Brighton: Harvester Press, 1987, p. 5.

43. Bell Gayle Chevigny, 'Introduction to the Lives and Fictions of American Women', in Bell Gayle Chevigny and Gari Laguardia, p. 152.

44. Elena Poniatowska, quoted in Mary Seale Vásquez, 'Rosario Castellanos', p. 21.

45. *El eterno femenino,* Mexico: Fondo de Cultura Económica, 1975.

46. 'La novela mexicana y su valor testimonial', in *Juicios sumarios,* p. 130. This translation is taken from Beth Miller, 'Rosario Castellanos' *Guests in August*: Critical Realism and the Provincial Middle Class', *Latin American Literary Review,* Vol. VII, Spring-Summer 1979, no. 14, p. 18.

47. Dan Bell also notes this irony in 'A Woman Who Knew Latin', *The Nation,* 26 June 1989, p. 891.

Cynthia Duncan (essay date 1991)

SOURCE: "Language as a Barrier to Communication Between the Classes in Rosario Castellanos's 'La tregua' and José Revueltas's 'El lenguaje de nadie,'" in *Hispania,* Vol. 74, No. 4, December, 1991, pp. 868-75.

[*In the following essay, Duncan examines language used as an instrument of oppression by middle- and upper-class Spanish-speaking Mexicans against native Mexicans in Castellanos's "La tregua" and José Revueltas's "El lenguaje de nadie."*]

Language is normally perceived to be a vehicle that facilitates communication rather than impedes it. Yet, when cultural, social, and economic barriers exist between two or more interlocutors, attempts at communication often fail, and language becomes a useless, empty vessel which neither contains nor carries real meaning. In Mexico, for example, where an unbridgeable gulf separates the working class from the bourgeoisie, an Indian peasant may find that his words do not possess the same significance as those of a wealthy, land-owning white, even when he speaks the same language and uses the same words to convey a specific piece of information.[1] Obviously, much more than words is involved in the act of transmitting and receiving a message. Whether a person holds power or lacks it, whether he is perceived to be trustworthy or deceitful, and whether he has been assigned a dominant or a subordinant role by the superstructure of society are factors which have an impact on the way his words are interpreted by others. As Rosario Castellanos has noted, language in Mexico functions as an "instrumento de dominio," or a method of establishing control.[2] It perpetuates racial prejudices, class discrimination, and social injustice by calling into question the linguistic competence of its speakers. Those who speak only an Indian tongue are judged inferior to those who speak Spanish; those who speak Spanish poorly are judged inferior to those who speak it well. The ruling class sees Spanish as their prerogative and they jealously guard their hold on it, since language is, for them, a useful means of distinguishing master from servant. Attempts by Indian workers to imitate the language of the bourgeoisie are therefore seen as violations of the social code and are generally discouraged.[3] Even when an Indian achieves linguistic competence in the "master language," he may still find a certain unwillingness on the part of his master to understand the meaning of his words, since communication between the classes could potentially weaken the control that the dominant group exercises over the subordinate group. As long as the subordinate group lacks the means and the power to make their message felt, the dominant group can safely ignore them. Language, in this context, clearly acts as a barrier between the classes rather than a unifying element in society.

Working with the language of the bourgeoisie in order to create a fictional world inhabited by Indian peasants is a particular problem for the socially-committed writer in Mexico. How can the workings of an Indian mind be conveyed in the language of his oppressors? Yet, what choice does the writer have if he wishes to communicate his message to a wide audience? To write a short story or a novel in an Indian language would not only limit the field of writers capable of producing such a literary work, but more importantly, would limit the field of readers to a mere handful. Not only would a writer have difficulty finding a publisher for such a work, but he would fail to attract the "right" kind of reader. Readers who need to be educated about the plight of the Indian are not ordinarily Indians themselves, but members of the upper or middle classes. In order to reach these readers and convey to them the need for social change, Spanish must be used, despite the problems inherent in this choice. Regina Harrison MacDonald has observed that "one means of subverting the hierarchic structures of domination is to take the given system—the ordered, nominalized, and imposed system—and re-order it so that an alternative reality emerges which attains meaning compatible with indigenous mental sets" (50). According to MacDonald, language can then function as "a codifying system for examining false institutions, antiquated prejudices, and iron-clad hierarchies which have been erected in the name of Mexican culture" (41).

Two short stories which use language in precisely this way are **"La tregua"** by Rosario Castellanos and "El lenguaje de nadie" by José Revueltas. In 1960, when many Latin American writers were experimenting with language to create complicated and hermetic texts aimed at a sophisticated reading public, Castellanos and Revueltas undertook a different task. Working within the boundaries of traditional realism, they subvert the traditional function of language as an instrument of oppression on several different levels. In the fictive world of the characters, a breakdown in communication between members of the ruling and working classes temporarily destroys the social, economic, and political control the former normally exercises over the latter. For a brief moment, at least, it is not the bourgeoisie who speaks the dominant tongue and determines the meaning of language, but the Indian workers who interpret words in a way that is meaningful to them. As literary texts, then, both stories subvert the power of Spanish, the language of the ruling class, by re-ordering it to express a worldview more in keeping with the mindset of the rural proletariat.[4] Spanish is not used to uphold the power structure of the white landowner or the white government official but, rather, to express the harsh reality of the Indian peasant. Under these circumstances, language ceases to function as an instrument of oppression in the hands of socially committed writers like Castellanos and Revueltas and becomes, instead, a constructive tool with which to build social awareness in the reader. Helene M. Anderson has observed that "it is this consciousness of the significance of language as a key to taking possession of the world that infuses all of Rosario Castellanos' work. It is through her language as an author that . . . the Mexican Indians finally break the invisible space to which they have been confined and, by clamoring to be heard, claim their portion of the world" (31). Revueltas shows a similar awareness of the social, political, and economic nature of language, and of the writer's ability to order and shape the reader's view of reality. As he explains in his discussion of literary realism, the writer's selection of material and his choice of rhetoric determine the worldview which emerges from the text (*Obra literaria,* I, 27-29).[5] Neither Castellanos nor Revueltas treats the reader as a passive receptor of information, however. In **"La tregua"** and in "El lenguaje de nadie," the reader is called upon to witness and reflect on the consequences of the lack of communication between white and Indian characters in the text. Furthermore, he is asked to play an active role in the reconstruction of the breakdown in communication by piecing together two juxtaposed and conflicting points of view. If he is to grasp the overall significance of the story, he must find meaning where the characters have failed to do so. In this way, the reader is encouraged to overstep the linguistic barriers that inhibit the characters in the text, and to question the hierarchic class system enclosed within those barriers. Margara Russotto sees the reader's role as one of fundamental importance in this kind of text, since the meaning of the text "se completa solamente en manos del receptor" (238).

In **"La tregua,"** the reader is confronted with a situation in which signals cross each time characters from one cultural group attempt to communicate with characters from another. Monolingualism is their most obvious handicap, but it becomes apparent early on in the text that language is not the only impediment to communication. Mutual distrust and dislike also play an important role in the process, making the characters unable and unwilling to communicate even through basic gestures and sounds. The principal barrier to communication in the story goes beyond linguistic limitations and resides, instead, in the different ways the characters interpret the world around them. Since language is a reflection of a worldview, the meaning of words and signs may become confused and altered when transferred from one language to another. The fact that the white and Indian characters in the text interpret the same set of events in radically different ways, and that both points of view are presented to the reader, allows two parallel story lines to develop simultaneously in the narrative. The action and events remain the same in both versions, but the connotation is entirely different in each, due to the choice of words used to describe those events. The reader, therefore, is confronted with two similar yet conflicting interpretations of the text. On one hand,he sees that a white man who is lost and injured, dying of thirst, wanders into an Indian village, where he is brutally murdered by the native inhabitants because of their hatred and resentment toward whites. On the other hand, he sees that an evil spirit (disguised as a white man) comes to the village to wreak havoc and cause destruction, but the Indians liberate themselves from his control by overpowering and destroying him. Both readings are explicit in the text and, in both, someone or something is murdered or destroyed by the Indian villagers. But, whether their action was a heinous crime or a heroic show of courage depends on the way the reader looks at it.

Significantly, the reader is not asked to choose between the two interpretations; instead, he is encouraged to close the communication gap that exists in the text by finding a relationship and striking a compromise between the two readings. This balance is made possible by the incorporation of a flashback scene which explains in clear detail why the Indians do not distinguish between the word for evil spirit (*pukuj*) and white man (*caxlán*).[6] Although the two terms originally had different meanings, cultural conditioning has gradually blurred the distinction between them, and they have come to be regarded as synonyms by the inhabitants of the village. The Indians' experience with whites has been very limited in the past, but it has been of such a violent and horrendous nature that it has led them to impute supernatural powers (normally attributed to evil spirits) to the whites (who are thereby elevated above ordinary human status). This power stems from a socioeconomic and political structure that places the Indians outside the law and gives whites the right to kill Indians without fear of punishment.[7] In the minds of the Indians, then, there is little difference between a white man and an evil spirit: "Cualquiera de las dos posibilidades era ineluctable y tratar de evadirla o de aplazarla con un intento de fuga era un esfuerzo malgastado" (34). An old legend, which has been recounted at the beginning of the story, provides the Indians with proof that they can fight against the *pukuj* only under extraordinary circumstances. If they can find the *pukuj* in a weakened or incapacitated condition, it is possible to capture or destroy him. When they see the *pukuj,* "disfrazado de ladino," lying helpless on the ground, they take advantage of this opportunity to kill their oppressor. Whether the Indians actually believe that they are destroying an evil spirit, or whether they know that their victim is a white man, is a moot point since they do not distinguish between the meaning of the two words. Once the reader grasps this fact, it becomes clear why the Indians do not respond to the white man's pleas for help or read his gestures as signs of human distress.

The most notable stylistic feature of **"La tregua"** is the total absence of dialogue, which underlines and draws attention to the fact that the majority of the characters in the text do not speak Spanish, the language in which the story is told. The reader has access to the thoughts and feelings of the Indian characters only through the words of the omniscient narrator, who acts as a sort of translator in the text.[8] Through the use of indirect interior monologue and condensed, abbreviated reportage of speech acts, the words of the Indian characters are transcribed into descriptive passages in Spanish with a minimum of interference by the narrator. In many instances, the narrator's reluctance to alter the tenor or meaning of the Indians' words is reflected in his own language: the rhythm and cadence of his prose, the structure of his sentences, the vocabulary and the type of images he chooses all suggest direct borrowings from an indigenous language. He neither adds nor subtracts information as he translates, and his tone remains carefully neutral. For example, when he describes the evil spirit, known as "el pukuj," he does not stop to question the existence of such things. Instead, he describes it objectively, as the Indian characters perceive it, in words that attempt to capture the essence of their belief:

> El que camina sobre una tierra prestada, ajena; el que respira está robando el aire. Porque las cosas (todas las cosas; las que vemos y también aquellas de que nos servimos), no nos pertenecen. Tienen otro dueño. Y el dueño castiga cuando alguno se apropia de un lugar, de un árbol, hasta de un nombre.
>
> El dueño—nadie sabría cómo invocarlo si los brujos no hubiesen compartido sus revelaciones—, el pukuj, es un espíritu. Invisible, va y viene, escuchando los deseos en el corazón del hombre. Y cuando quiere hacer daño vuelve el corazón de unos contra otros, tuerce las amistades, enciende la guerra. O seca las entrañas de las paridoras, de las que crían. O dice hambre y no hay bocado que no se vuelva ceniza en la boca del hambriento.
>
> (30)

Fragmented structure, repetition, and the constant use of conjunctions such as *o* and *y* to begin sentences reinforce the notion that the narrator is merely transcribing the thoughts of an Indian character into a written form of language that the reader can comprehend. In a sense, this subverts the normal power structure of language by relegating Spanish, usually the dominant tongue, to a secondary position, and by making the Spanish-speaking reader dependent on the narrator's willingness to translate for him. It also makes the reader aware that, although the language of the bourgeoisie is being used to tell the tale, it has been re-ordered to express a vision more in keeping with the Indian worldview.

Occasionally the narrator must act independently of the Indian characters in order to give the reader access to the thoughts and perceptions of the one character in the story who speaks Spanish and not an Indian tongue, the white man with whom the Indians come into contact. The narrator does this almost out of a sense of duty, and with a notable wariness, as if the Indians' reluctance to approach the white man had also infected him. The white man never emerges as a fully developed character, he is shrouded in mystery which is never clarified, and he is referred to only in generic, impersonal terms, as "un hombre," "el extraño," "el intruso," "el caxlán" (white man) and, ultimately, "el pukuj" (evil spirit). Although the reader could presumably understand the words of this character without the help of the narrator, since both speak Spanish, the narrator does not allow the reader any direct contact with him. In this way, he prevents the white man from becoming the protagonist of the story, by distancing him from the reader, despite the linguistic bond they share. When the narrator offers insight into the white man's behavior, it is with the barest possible detail; for example, to explain why the man falls to his knees and drinks water that has been spilled on the earth, the narrator merely states, "Porque tenía sed" (32). Although this explanation seems somewhat obvious and, therefore, unnecessary, it has an important function in the text. It is an interpretation of the white man's behavior that lies outside the Indian's comprehension and stands in opposition to their perception of events. Thus, it draws attention to the total lack of communication between the two social groups for, despite the seeming transparency of the white man's act, the Indian characters do not understand its meaning.

Through the narrator's occasional wandering outside the Indian's point of view, an alternative reading of the text begins to emerge as the two perspectives are juxtaposed. When the white man gestures to a water jug and cries out with "un doloroso estertor" (29), the Indian woman holding the jug merely stares at him in confusion, because she cannot imagine why an evil spirit would be interested in water. It does not occur to her at any time that she is dealing with a human being suffering from thirst; she believes that she is standing before "el pukuj," and reacts accordingly by throwing the jug to the ground in terror and fleeing for her life. Only the reader has access to both points of view and is capable of seeing why communication breaks down in the text. In order for him to understand the final act of violence that occurs in the story, it is necessary for him to go beyond the limited perspective of any individual character and to examine the socio-economic and political system which created the unbridgeable gulf between the classes.

The reader is called on to play a similar role in José Revueltas' short story, "El lenguaje de nadie," which also juxtaposes differing worldviews. Here, the linguistic problems that beset the characters are more complex and subtle, however, since both the Indian character, Carmelo, and the white landowner, doña Aquilina, technically speak the same language, Spanish. As the story unfolds, however, it becomes clear that words do not always have the same meaning for both characters, due to their different social and economic positions. The title of the story gives an important clue as to the different ways in which language can be read. The meaning of the word *nadie* is purposely ambiguous for, although it is normally used to negate existence, it can also be used in an opposite sense, in certain contexts, to affirm the existence of a specific kind of person, one who is regarded as unimportant and insignificant in society. In the dialogues that take place between Carmelo and Aquilina, confusion always surrounds the meaning of this term. Carmelo has been taught to think of himself as "nadie," a being without value or importance, because of his lowly position on the hacienda. As he puts it to the white landowner, "Cuando uno está tan abajísimo que mero ya ni es uno cristiano, sino como los animales, y ni eso, le parece güeno hasta lo más pior" (90). This makes no sense to Aquilina who, because of her privileged position as a member of the ruling class, thinks of herself as "alguien." She responds to Carmelo's remark by exclaiming, "¿Cuándo se ha visto que alguien prefiera lo malo a lo bueno?" (90) Through dialogues of this type, it becomes apparent that the major stumbling block to communication is not simply a question of lexical differences. Aquilina uses language as a means of perpetuating class barriers, by reading irony into every remark Carmelo makes and by refusing to interpret his words at face value. Because of the prejudice she feels against Indians, she automatically assumes that he is lying, and she is suspicious of his every word and gesture.

Whether Carmelo's humility is entirely sincere or partially feigned is open to interpretation. What emerges most clearly in the text is his awareness of the ruling class's desire to maintain strict barriers between landowner and peasant, and to keep the peasant "in his place." Carmelo does not openly express resentment toward this attitude or show any signs of rebellion. Instead, he tries to fit into the mold the whites have imposed on him in hopes that his good behavior will be rewarded in some small way. He realizes that the most threatening gesture an Indian can make is to regard himself as equal to a white man. For this reason, he is constantly seeking to make Aquilina understand that he accepts his position of inferiority and does not challenge it. He even goes so far as to suggest, on one occasion, "¡Sí, que la patrona manda que me den de azotes, y a fe que haría muy bien, pa' no andar yo de igualado!" (95) Although there is nothing in his tone or manner to suggest that he is speaking ironically, Aquilina immediately reads his remark as a criticism of her treatment of the workers on the hacienda, and she responds with a bitter accusation of her own. She shouts in disgust, "¡Indio terco! No dejan que se les haga el bien, aún cuando uno se lo proponga de todo corazón!" (95) This outburst causes Carmelo to read irony into her words, for, as the omniscient narrator explains, "¿Cómo entender que doña Aquilina quisiera hacerle el bien, si no le daba la única tierra posible para él en el mundo, la única que podía hacerlo feliz, porque cualquier otra tierra jamás estaría al alcance de su mano?" (95).

The plot of the story revolves around Carmelo's repeated attempts to communicate with Aquilina and, specifically, to convince her to give him a small piece of barren ground on the hacienda for his own use. Because of an unwillingness on her part to listen, and an inability on his part to make his words felt, nothing comes of Carmelo's plan. Much of the story deals with Carmelo's metalinguistic reflections on the verbal barrier that separates him from the *patrona,* and the frustrations he feels as a result. He shows an accute awareness of the problem, but he is powerless to act on it:

> Carmelo llegó a estar seguro de que lo que él trataba de expresar, se le imaginaba él mismo estar dicho tal como le salía de los labios, pero que esto no era sino una apariencia, una figuración suya y que, en realidad el demonio en persona cambiaba el significado de sus palabras y aquello que doña Aqulina escuchaba era precisamente lo contrario de lo que Carmelo se había propuesto a decir.
>
> (91)

Carmelo realizes that the linguistic problem he experiences with Aquilina is somehow tied to class and race; as he tells Tiliches, another Indian character in the story, "Es que como semos inditos . . . la gente de 'razón' no nos entiende porque a la mejor hablamos de otros asuntos" (94). This truth is brought home by the fact that although Tiliches is a retarded deaf mute, Carmelo communicates with him, through non-verbal signs, better than he communicates with Aquilina through spoken language. The omniscient narrator confirms Carmelo's view of the situation by explaining, "Con el Tiliches sí era posible entenderse, pese a estar sordo y mudo, pero tan sólo porque los dos hablaban el lenguaje de nadie" (98). Through language which calls attention to itself as language, the story presents as its central theme the breakdown of linguistic signs and the impact that the resulting gap in communication has on people's lives.

Misunderstandings about the meaning of words like *nadie* and *alguien* are repeated throughout the text, and teach the reader that the meaning of certain lexical items may vary a great deal within a common language, depending on the class and social position of the speaker. In a sense, these misunderstandings are merely rehearsals for a much more dramatic communication breakdown at the end of the story, which results in the death of Aquilina at the hands of Carmelo. In this instance, the meaning of the words *difunta* and *viva* are called into question. As was the case with *nadie* and *alguien, difunta* and *viva* usually stand in opposition to one another in standard usage of the language; a person is either dead or alive but cannot be both at the same time. In Carmelo's mind, however, the distinction is not so clear-cut as it is in the minds of members of the bourgeoisie. He believes, as many Mexican peasants do, that the dead can interact with the living, if they so choose, and that they can carry out actions as if they were still alive.[9] For him, there is little difference between life and death since, within the context of his world, both lack importance and value.[10] The lack of distinction between the two conditions allows the meaning of the words to overlap at times, erasing the difference between a dying person and a dead person, or between a living person and a ghost. When Aquilina falls victim to typhus and is abandoned by her house servants, Carmelo remains faithfully at her bedside in hopes that he can convince her to give him the land he wants before she dies. Carmelo knows from experience that anyone who contracts the disease will not recover, for his wife, Prudenciana, and his dog, "El Gurrión," were the first victims of the epidemic on the hacienda. Death is, for him and others of his class, "un suceso habitual e intrascendente" (89). He accepts it as something over which he has no control, and he makes no attempt to resist its natural course. What Carmelo fails to take into consideration, however, is that Aquilina has had throughout her life the advantages of better nutrition, better sanitation, more access to doctors and medicine, more leisure, and all of the other comforts to which the ruling class has access. She does not accept death with the same passivity and resignation as her Indian workers. It is important to note that the death of Aquilina is not explicit in the text, but is implied through an ambiguous phrase which simply states that Carmelo was with her "hasta sus últimos momentos" (97). Since the death of Prudenciana has been described in graphic detail in the opening paragraphs of the story, the reader is left to imagine that Aquilina's death took place in the same way. Carmelo and Tiliches bury both women but, just as it seems that death has had at last a leveling effect on society, it becomes clear that Carmelo has committed a serious error by anticipating the death of Aquilina and burying her while still alive. At least, this is the interpretation white authorities give Carmelo's words, although he himself does not look at the situation in quite the same way. According to Carmelo:

> La difuntita doña Aquilina quiso espantarnos, y nomás empezaron los ruidos que hacía dentro del cajón, de verme la cara que hacía, el Tiliches pegó la carrera y hasta yo mismo después. Pero me puse a reflexionar que harta vergüenza era sentir yo miedo, y armándome de valor fui y arrastré el cajón hasta el hoyo, onde lo dejé caír así nomás, y pa pronto tapé el hoyo de tierra hasta los bordes, manque la difunta seguía golpeando dentro del cajón pa' darme espanto, pero bien que me sobrepuse. . . .
>
> (97-98)

The judge, representing Aquilina's family's interests, reinterprets the meaning of Carmelo's words, and tells him, "Lo que pasó, hijo mío . . . , es que enterraste una mujer viva, y eso se le llama homicidio" (98). Thus, the temporary inversion of normal social order is set back to rights, as the ruling class molds the meaning of Carmelo's language to meet their own ends, and places the burden of communication once again entirely on his shoulders. Just as before in his dealings with Aquilina, Carmelo fails to understand why his words are not interpreted in the same sense he imputes to them. At no time does he grasp the significance of the word *viva,* as it is used by the judge, and place it in opposition to his own word, *difunta.* Instead, he is left to ponder on the workings of the judge's mind, and on the accusation that he has somehow murdered a woman who was already dead. He blames the problems, as always, on his failure to communicate with Aquilina, "porque él no tuvo la ocurriencia de pararse a escuchar lo que quiso decirle la difuntita, desde el más allá . . ." (99).

Only the reader, who has access to both points of view in the text, can close the communication gap that separates the characters from one another and find meaning in what appears to be a gratuitious act of violence. As the reader pieces together the various parts of the story, one clear fact begins to emerge: Aquilina, who throughout her lifetime used language as an instrument of domination, finds that the instrument has been turned against her in the moments before death. For perhaps the first time in her life, she is in a dependent position and is desperate to communicate her needs to one who is in control. Not surprisingly, Carmelo misreads her words and gestures, just as she had misread his on previous occasions, and refuses to cross the linguistic barriers which separate his class from hers. As was the case with **"La tregua,"** the reader of "El lenguaje de nadie" is left to examine the flaws in the system which created the breach between the characters in the story he has just read.

In both texts, language acts as a barrier between the classes because whites (representing the bourgeoisie) and Indians (representing the rural proletariat) are unwilling or unable to communicate. The lack of communication leads in each story to murder, when an Indian, or group of Indians, brings about the death of a white person due to a misunderstanding ostensibly based on the meaning of words. Both stories are clearly aimed at white readers, who are called upon to bridge the communication gap between the characters in order to understand the full significance of the story's message. Ultimately, the reader, as a member of the class which is attacked in the texts, is left with a vague feeling of discomfort and unease, bordering on fear, due to the random nature and senselessness of these deaths. The deaths accomplish nothing, for the Indian characters continue to suffer poverty and injustice. The Indians in **"La tregua"** feel a temporary satisfaction when they kill "el pukuj," but the story ends on a pessimistic note. The narrator explains, "La tregua no fue duradera. Nuevos espíritus malignos infestaron el aire. Y las cosechas de Mukenjá fueron ese año tan escasas como antes" (36). Carmelo, in "El lenguaje de nadie," does not even seem aware that he has killed his oppressor. He only knows that he has lost his one chance at owning land, and all hope for a better future. The social problems exposed in both texts are almost overwhelmingly complex, since the linguistic difficulties experienced by the characters are seen as manifestations of profound psychological differences between the classes. There are no clear-cut ways of determining who is right and who is wrong in the stories. The white characters are presented in the worst possible light, as members of a cruel and unjust ruling class. At the same time, the Indians emerge as flesh and blood characters who are also capable of cruelty and injustice (albeit involuntary or unconscious) when they are given a chance to assert themselves. The reader is not encouraged to find heroes and villains in the texts but, rather, to see that the flaws in both groups are the product of a society which encourages one group to discriminate against the other, and which sets up adversarial relationships between individuals on the basis of class. If the reader can be led to question the hierarchic system responsible for the communication breakdown and the problems that ensue in each story, then language can function in a constructive capacity, as a tool with which to build a social consciousness and a social conscience in the reader.

At first glance, **"La tregua"** and "El lenguaje de nadie" seem curiously old-fashioned and out of place in Mexico's exciting literary scene of the 1960s. When compared to the more experimental works of writers like Fuentes, Sainz, Agustín, Pacheco, and others, these two stories appear to fall more into the mold of an earlier generation, when socially committed writing was equated with a traditional, straightforward prose style. Perhaps for this reason, although Castellanos and Revueltas have a strong following in Mexico, they are not as well-known in international circles as some of their more daring contemporaries. Their texts are deceptively simple, and require a more subtle form of reader participation than what is normally associated with literature of the "boom" years. It is easy to miss the point of the stories if one does not stop to ponder the actual process of communication itself. If one is not especially attuned to the innerworkings of language and its symbiotic relationship with culture, the message conveyed in the stories remains murky and unclear. Unlike similar stories from previous decades, these texts explore much more than the class struggle in Mexico; they are metalinguistic studies of the way language functions to support or undermine the system itself. In this way, they far exceed the limits of traditional realistic fiction and point toward a new awareness of the power of language and of its constructive possibilities.

Notes

1. Race is intimately linked to class in Mexico, since a person's "whiteness" is not so much a question of skin color as it is a matter of socio-economic standing in many cases. For this reason, throughout the present study the Indian is identified with the proletariat and the white is identified with the bourgeoisie. Although there are exceptions to this generalization in real life, it is clear in Castellanos's and Revueltas's texts that they view class and race as inseparable items.
2. Two essays in which Castellanos focuses on this issue are "Notas al margen: el lenguaje como

instrumento de dominio" in *Mujer que sabe latín* and "Divagación sobre el idioma" in *El uso de la palabra.*

3. This attitude emerges clearly in Castellanos's novel, *Balún-Canán,* where one white character says to another: "—Ellos [los indios]—son tan rudos que no son capaces de aprender a hablar español. La primera vez que vine a Chactajal quise enseñarle a hablar a la cargadora de la niña. Y ni atrás ni adelante. Nunca pudo pronunciar la f. Y todavía hay quienes digan que son iguales a nosotros" (96).

   On another occasion, a white character says to his companion: "—Oílo vos, este indio igualado. Está hablando castilla. ¿Quién le daría permiso?" (38)

4. I use the terms "worldview," "mindset," and "cosmovision" interchangeably throughout the present study in the standard way that anthropologists use these terms. They refer to a specific way of looking at the world, a set of beliefs and assumptions about the nature of man and the universe, that govern a specific cultural group's behavior, thoughts and attitudes. A people's worldview is shaped by their history and is often intertwined with the concept of ideology. These terms are not power-assuming or judgmental, since no single cosmovision is held up as a model against which others are compared. The point of both stories analysed here, for example, is that neither the white nor the Indian mindest is the "right way" to see the world. Both are shown to be valid models, although they differ greatly one from the other.

5. Revueltas's vision of himself as an artist has sometimes stood in opposition to his commitment to Marxist ideology. Emma Godoy and C. E. Turán have accused him of being a "bourgeoise writer in disguise" because of the existential undertones running through much of his work. Floyd Merrell, however, defends Revueltas by showing how art and ideology are fused together into an integral whole.

6. In an indirect interior monologue, the thoughts of the Secretario Municipal on this subject are presented to the reader: "Imponer multas, como la ley prescribía, le pareció una medida ineficaz. Se estaba tratando con indios, no con gente de razón, y el escarmiento debía ser riguroso. Para que aprendan, dijo" (33). The Secretario then procedes to burn the Indian "offenders" alive and to raze their village.

7. I do not mean to suggest by this remark that the story is an actual translation from an Indian language into Spanish. It is merely a stylistic device used by Castellanos to create a certain effect on the reader.

8. The concept of *almas en pena* is an established part of Mexican folk culture. It is manifested in countless songs and legends, as well as in numerous works of literature. Perhaps the most famous treatment of *almas en pena* in fiction is Juan Rulfo's *Pedro Páramo.* The attitude expressed by Rulfo's characters toward the dead is similar to that voiced by Carmelo in "El lenguaje de nadie."

9. Octavio Paz's essay, "Todos Santos, Día de Muertos," in *El laberinto de la soledad* expresses this thought best: "La indiferencia del mexicano ante la muerte se nutre de su indiferencia ante la vida. El mexicano no solamente postula la intrascendencia del morir, sino la del vivir. Nuestras canciones, refranes, fiestas y reflexiones populares manifiestan de una manera inequívoca que la muerte no nos asusta porque 'la vida nos ha curado de espantos.' Morir es natural y hasta deseable; cuanto más pronto, mejor. Nuestra indiferencia ante la muerte es la otra cara de nuestra indiferencia ante la vida" (52).

10. Revueltas makes it difficult for the reader to believe that Carmelo intentionally murdered Aquilina, since Carmelo's hopes of acquiring land depend entirely on the patrona's continued existence and, with her death, his hopes are dashed. The judge, working in league with the family, pardons Carmelo's "crime" on the condition that the Indian affix his mark to a document relinquishing ownership of the property. This information is made available to the reader, but not to Carmelo, who signs the paper without understanding the meaning of his act.

Works Cited

Anderson, Helene M. "Rosario Castellanos and the Structures of Power." In *Contemporary Women Authors of Latin America,* ed. Doris Meyer and Margarita Fernández Olmos. Brooklyn: Brooklyn College Press, 1983: 22-32.

Castellanos, Rosario. *Balún-Canán.* México: Fondo de Cultura Mexicana, 1957,

———. "La tregua." In *Ciudad Real.* Xalapa: Universidad Veracruzana, 1960. 29-36.

———. *Mujer que sabe latín.* México: SepSetentas, 1973.

———. *El uso de la palabra.* Mexico: Excelsior, 1974. Godoy, Emma. "¿Materialismo espiritualista? Carta a José Revueltas." *Abside* 33:3 (1969): 291-300.

MacDonald, Regina Harrison. "Rosario Castellanos: On Language." In *Homenaje a Rosario Castellanos,* ed. Maureen Ahern and Mary Seale Vásquez. Valencia: Albatros Hispanófila, 1980. 41-64.

Merrell, Floyd. "Man and his Prisons: Evolving Patterns in José Revueltas' Narrative." *Revista de Estudios Hispánicos* 11 (1977): 233-50.

Paz, Octavio. *El laberinto de la soledad.* México: Fondo de Cultura Económica, 1959.

Revueltas. "El lenguaje de nadie." In *Dormir en tierra.* Xalapa: Universidad Veracruzana, 1960. 89-99.

Russotto, Márgara. "Realismo, lenguaje y significado: reflexiones sobre un cuento de Revueltas." *Cuadernos Americanos* 210 (Jan.-April 1977): 233-46.

Turán, C.E. "La Iconoclastia de José Revueltas." *Cuadernos Americanos* 169 (Jan-April 1970): 97-125.

Hanna Geldrich-Leffman (essay date 1992)

SOURCE: "Marriage in the Short Stories of Rosario Castellanos," in *Chasqui,* Vol. XXI, No. 1, May, 1992, pp. 27-35.

[*In the following essay, Geldrich-Leffman discusses the inherent dialogic nature of marriage reflected in Castellanos's short stories.*]

Prominent in Latin American letters and a leading voice in early Mexican feminism, Rosario Castellanos goes beyond the limits of conventional feminist questions to more universal problems that transcend gender and are concerned with society, language, and creativity. Critical inquiry into her work has concentrated primarily on her feminism and the image of woman, mostly in her novels and in the collection ***Album de familia.*** Quite a few of these studies point to the importance and centrality of the image of marriage in her work (Franco 31; Fiscal, *La imagen* 51; Fiscal, "Identidad y lenguaje" 27), without examining it from the point of view of linguistic and literary technique. Since we have only one significant study of her short stories,[1] I propose to treat the topic of marriage in these narratives and in the process analyze the dialogic nature of these works.

In my emphasis on this approach, I have greatly benefitted from M. M. Bakhtin's theories. The notions of the other, of dialogue, and of the fundamental nature of communication, are a part of his general theory of the social and dialogical nature of human existence and literature. As he affirms, "the very being of man (both internal and external) is a *profound communication.* To *be* means to *communicate* . . . I cannot become myself without the other. . . . Life is dialogical by its very nature. To live means to engage in dialogue, to question, to listen, to answer, to agree, etc." (qtd. in Todorov 96-97).[2] In literary texts dialogue takes place between words, between the different levels of discourse, and "between an author, his characters, and his audience, as well as in the dialogue of readers with other characters and their author" (Holquist 69).

By its very nature marriage participates in this dialogical principle. Lévi-Strauss refers to marriage as a communication device between groups, and he identifies women as the language used by men to perpetuate culture.[3] In Bakhtin's terms marriage can be seen as a dialogue of utterances in their intertextual, socio-cultural context. This formulation is most important to the relevant aspects of Rosario Castellanos's writing, to her views on language and the position of women.

Examining Castellanos's short stories from the point of view of Bakhtin's dialogism should provide new insights into her treatment of marriage as a structural element in her texts and as the sign for her search for a meaningful dialogue. In fact, the turning to or away from the other, that is, the possibility or absence of communication, and the exploration of the relationship with the other lie at the heart of her work (Ahern, *Reader* 8, 9; Ocampo 201, 202).[4] The stories will be studied in chronological order to show the marked development of woman's voice as a participant in the textual dialogue and the increasing intertextual dialogic sophistication of her prose. Marriage in these works is a metaphor for a dialogue between the sexes, presented in terms of dialogism, that is, an intertextual web or a dialogue of texts.[5] An actual dialogue, one of understanding, is possible only between equals, but since woman in the early texts is denied a voice and thus identity and equality, true dialogue and communication are seen as impossible. There is, however, a development from an essentially failed dialogue in the early stories, through the slow emergence in the subsequent ones of woman's voice and self-awareness, on to hope and the possibility of a true encounter, a duet, in the late works.[6]

A brief summary of the author's views on women, marriage and language should contribute to a better understanding of her texts. In the patriarchal world[7] she sees woman as a myth, the incarnation of some antagonistic principle, feared and either elevated and adored as a deity or reduced to impotence and domesticity to become, on the ethical plane, the self-abnegating "hada del hogar."[8] She is entrapped in what Julia Kristeva calls a "sacrificial contract" ("Women's Time" 25) and what René Girard sees as a sacrificial status because of her weakness and relatively marginal position (141-142).

In this liminal state, women have no being and no voice outside of marriage; they acquire a name, social standing and property only through their husbands (Franco 135-136; Fiscal, *La imagen* 149; Carretero 53); marriage and motherhood become the ultimate goals to which they aspire.[9] Castellanos calls for a change to this situation not only for the sake of women but also because husbands are after all not "el milagro de San Antonio, ni el monstruo de la laguna negra." They are human beings "a quienes nuestra inferioridad les perjudica tanto o más que a nosotras, para quienes nuestra ignorancia o irresponsabilidad es un lastre que los hunde" ("La participación de la mujer . . ." *Mujer que sabe latín* 40). She suggests as a remedy that we have to learn to practice one of the easiest and at the same time hardest lessons, "la de considerar que el otro no es una presa ni el cobrador de tributos, sino un yo con su propio centro de gravedad." ("El amor en S. de Beauvoir." *Juicios sumarios* 284).

Equality in dialogue, however, is difficult to achieve; for Castellanos language is an instrument of dominance and power.[10] Whenever the dominated are not spoken with but only spoken to, they are reduced to silence and are denied equality and identity. Very much in the sense of Bakhtin, she writes:

> El sentido de la palabra es su destinatario: el otro que escucha, que entiende y que, cuando responde, convierte a su interlocutor en el que escucha y el que entiende, estableciendo así la relación del diálogo que sólo es posible entre quienes se consideran y se tratan como iguales y que sólo es fructífero entre quienes se quieren libres.
>
> ("Notas al margen: el lenguaje como instrumento de dominio." *Mujer que sabe latín* 180.)

Women, being oppressed and dominated, often are silenced or reduced to a "whispering voice."[11] Such women are frequently portrayed by Castellanos. It is precisely to give them a voice, to show them their right to use language that she writes (Fiscal, "Identidad y Lenguaje" 25, 28, 33; Lindstrom, "Women's Expression" 71, 73). What is needed is "formar conciencia, despertar el espíritu crítico, difundirlo, contagiarlo" ("La participación de la mujer . . . ," *Mujer que sabe latín* 40).[12]

The first collection of short stories, ***Ciudad Real*** (1960) centers around the plight of the indios in the town of San Cristóbal de las Casas and presents the theme of marriage only incidentally. Two of the stories, however, give the stereotyped Mexican paternalistic view of the position of women in a marriage. In neither of these stories are the couples shown as speaking to each other; dialogue is not even attempted and would be impossible because of woman's lack of identity and equality. In **"Modesta Gómez"** the heroine is taken into the home of the wealthy Ochoa family to take care of their youngest son, Jorgito; later she is raped by him and bears him an illegitimate child. Disgraced, she is thrown out of the house by his mother and later marries Alberto Gómez. Modesta accepts her husband's drinking and the physical abuse he inflicts on her and the children, because, "Alberto le había dado su nombre y sus hijos legítimos, la había hecho una señora" (70). The overtones of the word "señora" are obvious; not only does it characterize her as a respected married woman, but it also gives the servant girl the status of the mistress of the house. Identity, social standing and fulfillment as a mother are derived from a man.

On the other hand, **"Advenimiento del Aguila"** presents the man's reasons for wanting to get married: "La esposa que ha de proporcionarle holgura y respeto . . . bueno. Puede ser esta o la otra. A oscuras todas las hembras son iguales. Héctor cumpliría sus deberes como marido preñándola anualmente. Entre los embarazos y la crianza de los hijos, ella se mantendría tranquila en su rincón" (71). Quite clearly he sees the woman as an object of convenience, and literally relegates her to obscurity.

In the next collection, ***Los convidados de agosto*** (1964), the author's concern focuses on the plight of women mired in the oppressive traditions and prejudices of a middle class provincial society (Ocampo 205; González 107; Rosas 235). In these stories women speak, but their voices are solitary; they are not heard by men, or, if they are heard, they are not admitted into a dialogue. Thus marriage does not present opportunities for dialogue because it still functions as the traditional mode of two separate discourses playing out a ritualized encounter of social necessity. In **"Las amistades efímeras"** marriage serves to repair a breach in honor. The two main characters, female friends, are contrasted; Gertrudis creates her life through acts that seem unreasoned, born out of instinct and boredom; the other figure, an unnamed narrator, creates herself and her world through words: "No tenía la menor idea de lo que era ni de lo que iba a ser y me urgía organizarme y formularme, antes que con actos, por medio de las palabras" (11).[13] She discovers her vocation by writing Gertrudis long letters about Oscar, thereby using language as an act of creation, describing, "inventing," Oscar as one would a character for a work of fiction. Ironically, Gertrudis, who was planning to marry Oscar, has no major interest in these letters, and her replies are merely short answers. She also corresponds with Oscar but finds the exchange extremely boring, no doubt because they both use a form-book for letters, the *Epistolario de los enamorados,* which allows no spontaneity, no real communication.

The subtext of the story reveals an interesting dialogue between texts, a formalistic exercise pointing to a ritualistic encounter, devoid of real meaning. For both Gertrudis and Oscar, it is a stylized contact that uses language as a mask or a screen behind which the reality of life is hidden. With the inclusion of the *Epistolario,* Castellanos creates an intertextual[14] referent that serves as a sign for the lack of dialogue. This narrative technique will become more and more prominent in her texts, as she provides an increasingly more complex and richer tapestry for the reader to unravel.

In **"Las amistades efímeras"** marriage is the consequence of an impulsive act of Gertrudis. Out of boredom she runs away with a total stranger, who is then forced by her outraged father to marry her so that her honor will be restored. Gertrudis herself has no voice in the decision, a fact she accepts as part of a woman's life. Later she submits just as naturally to the end of the marriage, when the man decides to marry his childhood sweetheart after he is released from prison. Yet she is not a helpless being; she creates her life through her acts. It is the same kind of creation that her friend, the narrator, has to achieve through words, an act she finds most difficult: "Y yo que estaba construyendo mi vida alrededor de la memoria humana y de la eternidad de las palabras. . . . Quise escribir y no pude. Para qué? Es tan difícil! Tal vez, me repetía yo con la cabeza entre las manos, tal vez sea más sencillo vivir" (29). The text remains open ended (Ahern, *Reader* 34) as in many of Castellanos's stories inviting the reader into a dialogue and the creative weaving of this feminine script.

Marriage as a sign of the predominance of the paternalistic world also underlies **"El viudo Román."** Even though it is the desire and aspiration of all the young girls of Comitán, marriage is the exclusive decision of men. When it comes to asking for the hand of the bride, she is excluded from the formality (161). She is made mute, denied a voice, but is an acquiescing victim, who achieves personhood only through this act of sacrifice. Marriage will initiate her into the mysteries of life but at the same time allow her to remain comfortably child-like, hiding behind her husband to avoid responsibility and to assume a mature identity (166). She will see herself only through the eyes of the other, and the ritualized language allowed her assures the supremacy of that other, who conspires to take initiative away from her.

Even the wedding night is composed of ritualized acts, performed by two beings absorbed not in each other but only in themselves and without voice—the contact of the bodies produces no dialogue (172). The next morning, too, there is no verbal communication between the spouses. Romelia is informed by the maid of her husband's wishes that she get ready to go out, and then she is told by him that they are going to her parents' house. Obediently, she silently follows him, without the right to question him, only to find out that she is being returned to her parents' home accused of not having been a virgin. Using the only language available to her, that of her body, she offers irrefutable proof of her innocence: the bloodstain on the sheet.[15] But her language is not accepted, her text is not even looked at. Only the male discourse is heard, carrying the weight of importance and apparent truth: "Don Carlos ha dado su palabra de honor, y es un hombre de honor. Tengo la obligación de creerle" (178). Romelia's discourse is not answered; she is not permitted to participate in the dialogue by husband or father; she is merely issued orders to leave the room to allow the dialogue between the males. Women, as the oppressed, function as "receptors of commands" (MacDonald 58) so that communication is rendered almost impossible (Schlau 47).

Ironically, as the reader finds out at the end of the story, the word of the so-called man of honor turns out to be a vicious falsehood. Through his confession to his friend, Father Evaristo Trejo, it becomes clear that all this was simply a trick to get the locket that Romelia always wore around her neck; it contained a piece of writing of her dead brother, whom don Carlos suspected of having been the lover of his first wife. The deceit was achieved through a total subversion of language, from his conversations with don Evaristo arranging the marriage, to the nuptial vows, and finally to confession, not to obtain absolution but to be able to brag about his deed to somebody who could not reveal what he heard.

The story **"Tres nudos en la red"** (1961) serves as an interesting bridge between the earlier stories of provincial Chiapas and the later ones situated in urban Mexico (Ahern, *Reader* 36; see also Franco 30). It is also a link to the slowly emerging voice of woman in dialogue and her self-realization, seen through the image of marriage.

The three persons caught in a marriage/family web are separated by the traditional set of values that dominated provincial society, as well as by their own inability to transcend their isolation. The net of the text is woven by the omniscient narrator's discourse and the dialogues of the characters, who are "knots" but also weavers of the web that enmeshes the other. The slow tearing apart of the marriage of wealthy Esteban Sanromán and Juliana, who comes from a lower class, is seen through their nightly discussions, which are mainly recurring disputes about the strangeness of their daughter, Agueda, and the alleged unfaithfulness of Sanromán. They poison the girl with feelings of guilt and worthlessness as she listens to them in the next room. The voices that tear at each other are characterized by Agueda in terms of sexual body imagery. Her father's voice, "maciza como su cuerpo, solemne como sus pasos, certera como la aguda punta del bastón de caoba que acertaba siempre con el sitio exacto donde posarse" (6). Her mother's voice, on the contrary, is heard as "una catarata irreflexiva" (6)[16] which soon ends in silence, motivated not by fear or reasonableness but by the terror of reconciliation, that is, the fear of sex. The attempt at dialogue in this marriage is thus based on rancor and hostility. Even during meals the verbal exchanges are nothing but the prescribed rituals of polite discourse filled with sarcasm. Eventually the household falls into silence: "Ninguno tenía nada que compartir con nadie" (8). Each is caught in his/her own psychological landscape of self absorption; the negatives "ninguno," "nada," "nadie" emphasize the total isolation and disregard of the other and parallel the three knots or voices of the text.

Their wealth gone because of the distribution of the land, the family moves to the capital. As all the props of Esteban's power fall away, money becomes the only intrument of dominance. The marital dialogue now reduces itself to a verbal battle of humiliation for Juliana as she is subjected to interrogation about every cent that she needs for the household. The exchanges are those of master and servant; Juliana is clearly reduced to the powerlessness of a domestic. The reader's reaction to these exchanges is expressed by Agueda as, "Avaricia, abyección. Era esto el matrimonio?" (8) As the net of these discourses forms and molds the girl, she tries to escape and renounce any connection with her parents, in turn liberating her mother as well.

The other part of the net still holds Juliana and closes in even more restrictively when Esteban is diagnosed with possible angina. Her solicitude, nevertheless, ends when she discovers that her husband sees all her efforts as his due. His attitude triggers the ultimate liberation of Juliana who begins to go out increasingly more often and finally leaves for what she calls a needed vacation. In their last dialogue, it is her husband who is left totally speechless. The irony of Juliana's flight becomes poignant when the reader discovers that the cab, instead of taking her to a vacation, takes her to the Cancer Institute where she checks into the ward for incurable cases.[17] She has been driven into final silence since she could not confide her illness to either husband or daughter. There is an ironic reversal of roles between the spouses; here the husband is reduced to the unproductiveness, immobility and silence usually assigned to the woman in the home, whereas now it is the woman who takes on the active role and leaves, consciously electing silence. Leaving provides Juliana with the only opportunity to become her own person, albeit only in death, the ultimate metaphor for the lack of dialogue.

The three knots of this text, represented by the three characters, are paralleled by the three locations of Juliana's life: the provincial city, the capital and eventually the cancer ward, and by the three dialogical exchanges between the spouses, characterized by a lack of love and understanding. The three characters caught in the web struggle to disentangle themselves but it is only the women who succeed to a certain extent.

In the final collection of short stories, ***Album de familia*** (1971), marriage is again used to show woman's dependence, powerlessness and lack of identity. Here the author portrays in the main the world of women living in an urban society and uses a style devoid of her earlier "patetismo," filled with humor ("Satisfacción no pedida," *El uso de la palabra* 211). It is stylistically the most interesting and complex collection, in which the metaphor of marriage becomes the leading figure of the author's search for meaningful dialogue.

From the dialogical point of view, there is a structural counterpoint between the four stories that comprise this collection. The first, **"Lección de cocina,"** and the third, **"Cabecita blanca,"** are linked by a reference to cooking recipes. But if in the first the new bride's inability to understand the text of the cookbook she is trying to read[18] is a sign of the dissatisfaction she feels with her marriage and the traditional status quo, in the other, there is only the photograph of a very elaborate dessert that represents the static, paternalistic views of marriage held by the old widow. The second story, **"Domingo"** introduces a sophisticated, modern marriage, in which both partners feel free to go their separate ways. For the woman, however, this marriage is kept for convenience and status, and art seems the only possible escape from it. The art here is painting, as opposed to writing for the narrator in **"Las amistades efímeras,"** and it is equally problematic. The dialogues however show the protagonist and the men that come to her open house on Sundays in conversations between equals. Structurally connected is the fourth story, **"Album de familia,"** in which marriage plays only a tangential role; the text however is composed of conversations between women that in the end produce true dialogues of understanding. This demonstrates a marked progression toward the possibility of more meaningful human relationships.

In **"Lección de cocina"** Castellanos's best example of "an intrinsically feminine discourse" (Ahern, *Reader* 36; see also Fiscal, *La imagen* 69) she explores her feminist concerns through images of life as a text—the cookbook recipe as a sign for the recipe of a successful marriage. Here she uses feminine metaphors and the traditional scene of kitchen and honeymoon to transmit a radical message so that these become signs of "repression, annihilation, ruin" (Ahern, *Reader* 38; see also Lindstrom, "Rosario Castellanos: Pioneer" 72; González 112). The irony of the discourse, the disproportion between the end, the search for authenticity, and the means, the piece of meat, is what produces the humor the author alludes to ("Satisfacción no pedida," *El uso de la palabra* 213). Just as the meat was cooked and burned because of the failure of the inexperienced cook to understand the language of the cooking manual, so the marital relationship is also going to fail because the new bride does not understand and is not willing to accept the prescriptions of society's recipe for a good marriage. The text of the cookbook as the sign of marriage according to old Mexican recipes is here deconstructed through feminist, dialogic, intertextual means.

It is written in the first person, as an apparent interior monologue.[19] Interspersed throughout the text are literary allusions as signposts for the understanding of the sub-text of the narrative, subverting the apparently simple domestic task. The first such allusion appears in the cookbook itself, deconstructing its homely, culinary simplicity and signaling the impossible quest of the narrator: "Abro un libro al azar y leo: 'La cena de don Quijote.' Muy literario pero muy insatisfactorio." (***Album de familia*** 8). The incongruity of this intertextual referent signals the incongruity of the life of the narrator, as a modern, intellectual woman trying to read the text of a traditional Mexican marriage.

The allusions to *Romeo and Juliet* and to "Rapunzel," function as signs of a fated relationship and the failure of the narrator's marriage, whereas the allusion to *The Thousand And One Nights* and to Casanova express the sexual frustrations of this union (16). The failure of dialogue with her husband is also seen in terms of a comparison between his body that covers her during their moments of love and a tombstone covered with inscriptions of strange names (14). It is in fact the reading of texts that constitute the narrator's life: "De soltera leía a escondidas. Sudando de emoción y de vergüenza. Nunca me enteré de nada" (16). She, however, also subverts the text that the reader is decoding: "Ah, no, no voy a caer en esa trampa: la del personaje inventado y el narrador inventado y la anécdota inventada. Además, no es la consecuencia que se deriva lícitamente del episodio de la carne" (20). And it is precisely through her dialogue within this text that insight is gained: "Yo seré, de hoy en adelante, lo que elija en este momento" (21), even though neither of the options that tradition leaves open are acceptable to her.

To these literary allusions is added another intertextual referent, that of a movie script: "Y un día tú y yo seremos una pareja de amantes perfectos y entonces, en la mitad de un abrazo, nos desvaneceremos y aparecerá en la pantalla la palabra 'fin'" (17). The reference to a perfect loving relationship is, of course, only an illusion, and for her "next movie" the narrator would like to be assigned another role.

The final literary allusion, Ludwig Pfandl's characterization of Sor Juana Inés de la Cruz as belonging to the class of "neuróticos cavilosos" (*Die zehnte Muse* 117), which the narrator applies to herself, signals the open ended text which Francescato considers its great merit (117). The intertextual web of cookbook, literary allusions, and the dialogic voice of the narrator allow the reader creative opportunities and mediate the understanding that the final text of the life of a modern Mexican woman has not yet been written.

In the story, **"Domingo"** we have a continuation of this search for authenticity and identity. Marriage here is not an imposed trap but a consciously accepted arrangement; yet it still does not offer a satisfying dialogue. Painting, to which Edith, the protagonist, was introduced by her lover, opened for her a means of self-expression, a meaningful, creative activity, that allows her to authenticate herself. The moments in her little studio, in front of her easel, are the moments she lives for; Sundays, when she has to attend to her traditional role of wife, mother and hostess, are seen as an invasion of her own life.

On the other hand there is also a marked progression from the dialogic point of view. In **"Lección de cocina"** the narrator's is the only voice-texture used; in **"Domingo"** one layer of the text is achieved by a web of dialogues between the various participants. It is the banter of social verbal games in which no other female voice but Edith's is heard and in which she shares as an equal. She is also a fully participating partner in the private dialogues with Octavio and Vicente in which, on a somewhat deeper level, relationships are explored. The linguistic web is loose and unbinding, just as the web that holds the relationships of these people together is slack and mostly unsatisfying. Edith, as the center of this game of social dialogues, exemplifies a new woman. Yet she has not achieved a station outside the home. Her individuality is still linked there; painting, as her means of escape, is perhaps only a temporary hobby.[20] The narrative is again open ended, an unfinished female text: "Los domingos son mortales. Pero luego viene el lunes y . . ." (**"Domingo"** 46).

As a counterpoint to the relative awareness of the women in the two previous stories, **"Cabecita blanca"** presents with biting irony the total ignorance of the Señora Justina. The picture of a fancy dessert which introduces the narrative represents traditional married life (47): a static text signaling the status quo. The ideal married woman practices the virtue of prudence, understood to mean "el silencio, el asentimiento, la sumisión," (53) and, ironically, the ideal married man belongs in his place, that is at work, at the bar, at the house of his lover, or, as Señora Justina says, in the grave (49). We witness a total disfunction of dialogue and of understanding between the sexes. The irony of Señora Justina's image is that she is not aware of her own situation, which would become a hell were she to perceive it (Castellanos, "Satisfacción no pedida." *El uso de la palabra* 215; Francescato 118). The language used here is that of the old text and is the one rejected by the bride looking for a new one.

Elvira, who never had a coherent dialogue with her husband until after their divorce, relates marriage and dialogue in the last story, **"Album de familia,"** with an allusion to Oscar Wilde: "El único que ha creído que el matrimonio es una asociación de ideas o una larga conversación . . . fue Oscar Wilde. Y no" (132). The importance of this parallel is made emphatic by the fact that the narrative is a web of dialogues between women which results in a sense of self-awareness, similar to that experienced by the narrator of **"Lección de cocina"** (Gómez Parham, 7). The open-ended text here signals the hope for meaning and understanding embodied in the loyalties and support found in a sisterhood of women.

Throughout the stories of Rosario Castellanos, there is then a gradual development of self-awareness in the women. The dialogue of marriage becomes the means through which the reader is made cognizant of the emergence of woman's participatory voice. Marriage also becomes a sign for the limitations of language and the difficulty of the different voices in the text to achieve true harmony and communication with the other. This progression reflects no doubt the author's hope for a development in society that would allow more meaningful relationships: ". . . a hacer de las mujeres colaboradoras eficaces de los hombres en la construcción de un mundo nuevo, luminoso, habitable para aquellos en quienes lo mejor de la humanidad se manifiesta; . . ." ("Mujer liberada—Woolf o la literatura como ejercicio de la libertad," *Juicios sumarios,* 346). Dialogism provides a key to the understanding of Castellanos's short stories and marks the increase in their sophistication. A similar methodology could draw significant conclusions from the novels. The readings offered here provide a clearer insight into her preoccupation with language and writing as a means for women's self-actualization. Thus we are able to share her realization that the definitive text of this self-awareness and of the dialogue of mutual understanding still remains to be written.

Notes

1. By Yolanda Rosas. It is beyond the scope of this paper to give a complete bibliography of critical studies on Rosario Castellanos. From the Works Cited, the interested reader might find Ahern, *Homenaje* and *Reader* especially helpful. They provide excellent bibliographies and critical articles; the latter also has an anthology of Castellanos's works in English.
2. For Bakhtin dialogism is the "characteristic epistemological mode of a world dominated by heteroglossia," which is the "base condition governing the operation of meaning in any utterance." ("Glossary," *The Dialogic Imagination* 426, 428)
3. *Elementary Structures* 496. See also his assertion that marriage regulations are a kind of language that establishes communication between groups (*Structural Anthropology* 61).
4. It is related perhaps to her indebtedness to the existentialist philosophies of Sartre and Simone de

Beauvoir and the views of Simone Weil (Gómez Parham, "Intellectual Influences . . ." 36-37, 38).

5. Even though Bakhtin's theory of dialogism is intimately connected with his analysis of the novel, it is my contention that some of the characteristics mentioned by him (*Discourse* 262-263) can be found in Rosario Castellanos's short stories. See also Maranhâo 13.
6. Nahum Megged maintains that there are no dialogues in Castellanos's works (in Gómez Parham 39, note 8); whereas Fiscal asserts that she at least believes in the possibility of a dialogue between the sexes ("La mujer en . . ." 151, 153).
7. Sociological studies have concluded that patriarchal structure traditionally characterized the Latin American family at all levels. Woman's place was in the home, and she had to defer to her husband in all matters not relating to the home (Nash and Ichen Safa 25). In Mexico even though legislation forbidding discrimination has been in effect for most of the century, this has still not eliminated the problem. Women were seen as "an object within the culture of consumption." (González-Salazar 184; see also Palley 42; Fiscal, "La mujer" 152-153) just as in primitive culture, as Lévi-Strauss points out, woman was both object and means of binding society together (*Elementary Structures* 496).
8. The term was borrowed from Virginia Woolf ("Virginia Woolf o la literatura como ejercicio de la libertad." *Juicios sumarios* 341; see also "El amor en Simone de Beauvoir." *Juicios sumarios* 272-273; and "La mujer y su imagen." *Mujer que sabe latín* 7-8).
9. The word *matrimonium* signifies "legal status of the *mater,*" and is the outcome of two different orientations in the male and female. For the man marriage is derived from a verb and is an act, for the woman it derives from a noun and is a destination, a function—reproductive receptivity to the male who gives her and her offspring identity (Kintz 16-17). See also the ironic description of Castellanos's own reasons for marriage and her way to achieve it ("Génesis de una embajadora." *El uso de la palabra* 206; see also "Hora de la verdad." *El uso de la palabra* 241; and in the same collection, "El hombre del destino" 191-194).
10. Spanish used by the conquering Spaniards to reduce the diversity of Indian dialects, constituted a privilege and expressed, like religion and race, rank. It was not however, according to Castellanos, created as a means of communication but as an object of ornament, and so ambiguity and miscommunication were inherent in it ("Divagación sobre el idioma." *El uso de la palabra* 155).
11. Ahern, *Reader* 43, points to Rosario Castellanos's pioneering perception of the "silences in women's experiences," especially in her essay on Sor Juana Inés de la Cruz which is contemporary with Tillie Olsen's classic study. See also the definition of woman as a *tabula rasa,* and woman seen as an art object, experiencing her own body as the only available medium for her creativity (Gubar 74, 78, 79, 89); as well as the comparison between the literary text and the texture of the woven cloth (Kamenszain 77).
12. To name is to change and literature presents the possibility to transform the world, to change the structures of society that are unjust (See also Fiscal, *La imagen* 96; Anderson 31, Ahern, *Reader* 50). Women have to become conscious of their situation, they have to arrive at self-definition and construct their own image, "to write themselves": "Hay que inventarnos" (Castellanos, *El eterno femenino* 194).
13. Here Rosario Castellanos practices woman writing herself, *écriture feminine,* years before the leading French feminists, Cixous, Irigaray and Kristeva published their seminal works (Ahern, *Reader* xv, 51).
14. The term "intertextuality" was introduced by Julia Kristeva in her presentation of Bakhtin and defined in *La Révolution du langage poétique* (Roudiez, Introduction 15). Todorov uses it to refer to Bakhtin's dialogism, and reserves the term dialogical for specific instances of intertextuality, such as an exchange of responses by two speakers (Todorov 60). For the specific purposes of this paper, the definition of Michael Riffaterre will be helpful: "Intertextuality is that form of reference experienced when the reader finds that a text presupposes another and that the latter provides the former with the means of interpreting it and of justifying its formal and semantic peculiarities . . ." (2). Intertextuality seems to be particularly important to women writers and critics at this moment, (Moira Monteith 5; see Ahern, *Reader* 24 for intertextuality in Castellanos).
15. See Gubar 77, 78 and her reference to woman as text and artifact, the use of blood as a metaphor of creativity and "wounding" at the same time. See also Ahern, *Reader* 51 in reference to Castellanos's predilection for female body metaphors and her connection with Hélène Cixous's call "Write your self. Your body must be heard" ("The Laugh of the Medusa" 880).
16. See Palley 38, 39 and his reference to Irigaray and Lacan who relate "fluidity" of speech to woman and solid, phallic elements to man. See also Showalter, "Feminist Criticism" 16, 17 on biological theories of women's writing; Gubar, "The Blank Page" 75-78; and Kitch 3 on differences between male and female style.
17. Elena Poniatowska sees the figure of Juliana based on Rosario Castellanos's mother, who died of stomach cancer (120).

18. Bakhtin considers the image of the fool, of one not understanding, "of *not grasping* the conventions of society . . . almost everywhere an essential ingredient of prose style" (402). For him such incomprehension is a dialogic category and is always implicated in language. And as for the young bride here, it shows, "a polemical failure to understand someone else's discourse, someone else's pathos-charged lie that has appropriated the word and aspires to conceptualize it, a polemical failure to understand generally accepted, canonized, inveterately false languages with their lofty labels for things and events . . ." (403).
19. In Bakhtin's terms there is really no monologue because every discourse is by its very nature "dialogical." A monologue is a solitary conversation with oneself, in which "the self-consciousness of a solitary individual seeks support and more authoritative reading of its fate in its own self, . . ." (Bakhtin, 145). In this story the dialogical nature of the discourse becomes quite apparent in the narrator's emphatic direction toward two other narratees, a female reader whom she addresses with "usted" and her husband, addressed with "tú" (Ahern, *Reader* 37).
20. Whereas Francescato 118, sees her achieving an equilibrium in her process of betterment, Castellanos regards Edith as a frivolous and lazy person who will get bored even by art and who recognizes herself in her unfinished picture ("Satisfacción no pedida." *El uso de la palabra* 214.) Gómez Parham 5-6, discovers a more positive attitude in this story based on the fact that Edith finds her work a compensation for the "failure of human relationships"; and on the views of the character Vicente about women. The allusions to Joyce's *Ulysses* and to the film *The Battleship Potemkin,* both revolutionary works in their different genres and used in connection with Vicente, present his persona as one in whom such progressive possibilites lie.

Works Cited

Abel, Elizabeth, ed. *Writing and Sexual Difference.* Chicago: U of Chicago P, 1982.

Ahern, Maureen and Mary Seale Vásquez, eds. *Homenaje a Rosario Castellanos.* Valencia: Albatros, 1980.

Ahern, Maureen, ed. *A Rosario Castellanos Reader.* Austin, Texas: U of Texas P, 1988.

Anderson, Helene A. "Rosario Castellanos and the Structures of Power." Meyer and Olmos, *Contemporary Women Authors* 22-32.

Bakhtin, M.M. *The Dialogic Imagination. Four Essays.* Ed. Michael Holquist. Trans. Caryl Emerson and Michael Holquist. Austin: U of Texas P, 1983

Bauer, Gerhard. *Zur Poetik des Dialogs. Leistung und Formen der Gesprächsführung in der neueren deutschen Literatur.* Darmstadt: Wissenschaftliche Buchgesellschaft, 1969.

Brown, Cheryl L. and Karen Olson, eds. *Feminist Criticism: Essays on Theory, Poetry and Prose.* Metuchen, N.J. and London: The Scarecrow Press, 1978.

Carretero, Rocío. "El carácter social de la mujer mexicana en la narrativa de Rosario Castellanos." *La palabra y el hombre: Revista de la Universidad Veracruzana* [Veracruz, Mexico] 61 (1987): 49-55.

Castellanos, Rosario. *Album de familia.* México: Joaquín Mortiz, 1990.

———. *Los convidados de agosto.* México: Biblioteca ERA, 1982.

———. *Ciudad Real.* Xalapa, México: U Veracruzana, 1960.

———. *El eterno femenino.* Farsa. México: Fondo de Cultura Económica, 1987.

———. *Juicios sumarios. Ensayos.* Xalapa, Veracruz, México: [Universidad Veracruzana] Cuadernos de la Facultad de Filosofía, Letras y Ciencias, 1966.

———. *El mar y sus pescaditos.* Prol. Emilio Carballido. México: Eds. Mexicanos Unidos, 1987.

———. *Meditación en el umbral. Antología poética.* Compilador Julian Palley. Prólogo Elena Poniatowska. México: Fondo de Cultura Económica, 1985.

———. *Mujer que sabe latín.* México: SEP Diana, 1979.

———. "Tres nudos en la red." *Revista de la Universidad de México* 8 (1961): 6-11.

———. *El uso de la palabra.* México: Eds. Mexicanos Unidos, 1987.

Cixous, Hélène. "The Laugh of the Medusa." Trans. Keith Cohen and Paula Cohen. *Signs* 1.4 (1976): 875-893.

Fiscal, María Rosa. "Identidad y lenguaje en los personajes femeninos de Rosario Castellanos." *Chasqui: Revista de Literatura Latinoamericana* 14.2-3 (1985): 25-35.

———. *La imagen de la mujer en la narrativa de Rosario Castellanos.* México: U Nacional Autónoma de México, 1980.

———. "La mjuer en la narrativa de Rosario Castellanos." *Texto Crítico* [Xalapa, Veracruz, México] 5.15 (1979) 133-153.

Francescato, Martha Paley. "Transgressión y apertura en los cuentos de Rosario Castellanos." Ahern, *Homenaje* 115-120.

Franco, María Estela. *Rosario Castellanos Semblanza Psicoanalítica. Otro modo de ser humano y libre.* México: Plaza y Janes, 1985.

Girard, René. *Violence and the Sacred.* Trans. Patrick Gregory. Baltimore: Johns Hopkins UP, 1977.

Gómez Parham, Mary. "Intellectual Influences on the Works of Rosario Castellanos." *Foro literario: Revista de literatura y lenguaje* [Montevideo, Uruguay] 7.12 (1984): 34-40.

———. "Moving Toward the Other: New Dimensions in Human Relationships in Rosario Castellanos' *Album de familia.*" *Chasqui: Revista de Literatura Latinoamericana* 17.1 (1988): 3-7.

González, Alfonso. "La soledad y los patrones del dominio en la cuentística de Rosario Castellanos." Ahern, *Homenaje* 107-113.

González-Salazar, Gloria. "Participation of Women in the Mexican Labor Force." Nash and Ichen Safa 183-201.

Gubar, Susan. "'The Blank Page' and the Issues of Female Creativity." Abel 73-93.

Holquist, Michael. *Dialogism: Bakhtin and his World.* London: Routledge, 1990.

Kamenszain, Tamara, *El texto silencioso: Tradición y vanguardia en la poesía sudamericana.* México: U Nacional Autónoma de México, 1983.

Kintz, Linda. *The Dramaturgy of the Subject(s): Refining the Deconstruction and Construction of the Subject to Include Gender and Materiality.* Diss. U Oregon, 1986. Ann Arbor: UMI, 1987. 8622508.

Kristeva, Julia. "Women's Time." Trans. Alice Jardine and Harry Blake. *Signs* 7.1 (1981): 13-35.

Lévi-Strauss, Claude. *Structural Anthropology.* Trans. Claire Jacobson and Brooke Grundfest Schoepf. New York: Basic Books, 1963.

———. *The Elementary Structures of Kinship.* Trans. James Harle Bell, John Richard von Sturmer. Ed. Rodney Needham. Boston: Beacon Press, 1969.

Lindstrom, Naomi. "Women's Expression and Narrative Technique in Rosario Castellanos's *In Darkness.*" *Modern Language Studies* 13.3 (1983): 71-80.

———. "Rosario Castellanos: Pioneer of Feminist Criticism." Ahern, *Homenaje* 65-73.

MacDonald, Regina Harrison. "Rosario Castellanos: On Language." Ahern, *Homenaje* 41-64.

Maranhâo, Tullio, ed. *The Interpretation of Dialogue.* Chicago: U of Chicago P, 1990.

Meyer, Doris and Margarite Fernández Olmos, eds. *Contemporary Women Authors of Latin America.* Brooklyn, New York: Brooklyn College P, 1983.

Miller, Beth. "Women and Feminism in the Works of Rosario Castellanos." Brown and Olson, *Feminist Criticism* 198-210.

Monteith, Moira, ed. *Women's Writing. A Challenge to Theory.* New York: St. Martin's P, 1986.

Nash, June and Helen Ichen Safa. *Sex and Class in Latin America. Women's Perspectives on Politics, Economics and the Third World.* South Hadley, Mass. J.F. Bergin, 1980.

Ocampo, Aurora M. "Debe de haber otro modo de ser humano y libre: Rosario Castellanos." *Cuadernos Americanos* 250.5 (1983): 199-212.

Palley, Julian. Introduction. *Meditación en el umbral. Antología poética.* By Rosario Castellanos. México: Fondo de Cultura Económica, 1985.

Pfandl, Ludwig. *Die zehnte Muse von Mexico: Juana Inés de la Cruz. Ihr Leben—Ihre Dichtung—Ihre Psyche.* München: Hermann Rinn, n.d.

Poniatowska, Elena. "Rosario Castellanos. Vida nada te debo!" *Ay vida, no me mereces!* México: Joaquín Martínez. Contrapuntos, 1987. 43-132.

Riffaterre, Michael. "Textuality. W. H. Auden's 'Musée des Beaux Arts.'" *Textual Analysis. Some Readers Reading.* Ed. Mary Ann Caws. New York: MLA, 1986. 1-13.

Rodríguez-Peralta, Phyllis. "Images of Women in Rosario Castellanos' Prose." *Latin American Literary Review* 6.11 (1977): 68-80.

Rosas, Yolanda. "Soledad y visión de mundo en la cuentística de Rosario Castellanos." *Monographic Review/Revista Monográfica,* [Odessa, Texas] 4 (1988): 230-241.

Roudiez, Leon S. Introduction. *Desire in Language: A Semiotic Approach to Literature and Art.* By Julia Kristeva. Trans. Thomas Gora, Alice Jardine and Leon S. Roudiez. Ed. Leon S. Roudiez. New York: Columbia UP, 1980.

Schlau, Stacey. "Conformity and Resistance to Enclosure: Female Voices in Rosario Castellanos' *Oficio de tinieblas* [*The Dark Service*]." *Latin American Literary Review* 12:24 (1984): 45-57.

Showalter, Elaine. "Feminist Criticism in the Wilderness." Abel 9-35.

Todorov, Tzvetan. *Mikhail Bakhtin: The Dialogical Principle.* Trans. Wlad Godzich. Minneapolis: U of Minnesota P, 1984.

Vásquez, Mary Seale. "Rosario Castellanos, Image and Idea." *Homenaje* 15-40.

Zeitz, Eileen M. "Técnica e ideología en un cuento de Rosario Castellanos." Vol. 2 of *Actas del VIII Congreso Internacional de Hispanistas celebrado en Brown University del 22 al 27 de agosto de 1983.* Madrid: Ediciones Istmo, 1986. 765-771.

Stephen M. Hart (essay date 1993)

SOURCE: "Rosario Castellanos: 'Leccion De Cocina,'" in *White Ink: Essays on Twentieth-Century Feminine Fiction in Spain and Latin America,* Tamesis Books Limited, 1993, pp. 45-53.

[*In the following essay, Hart explores what he considers the protagonist's ironic defiance of patriarchal law in "Lección de cocina."*]

In her essay 'Woman and Her Image', Rosario Castellanos (1925-1974: Mexico) employs Simone de Beauvoir's study, *Le Deuxième Sexe,* to analyse the ways in which women have been mythified and therefore dis-abled (either through beauty or angelicness) concluding that 'woman is stripped of her spontaneity of action, forbidden the initiative of decision, taught to obey the commandments of an ethic that is completely alien to her and has no more justification or basis than that of serving the interests, goals, and end of others'.[1] In her essay Castellanos lists the means by which women are incarcerated within the phallocentric code (her most significant test-case is the male's requirement of virginity in his marriage partner), and then points to images of liberated women who range from real life, such as Sor Juana Inés de la Cruz, to the fictional such as Ana Ozores and Anna Karenina: 'Each one in her way and in her own circumstances denies the conventional, making the foundations of the establishment tremble, turning hierarchies upside down, and achieving authenticity' (p. 244). Their denial of the conventional is a knife which cuts both ways, to use Dostoevsky's phrase, for the act of making the foundations of society tremble often leads to their own death. Strangely, however, few of the female characters in Castellanos's fiction ever manage to embody these feminist values; they are often depicted as trapped in a phallocratic prison.[2] An exception to the rule, however, is the narrator of her short story, **'Lección de cocina'.**

'Lección de cocina', the opening short story of ***Album de familia*** (1971), is Castellanos's master text in the feminist mode, having become, in Seymour Menton's words, 'una especie de manifiesto de la mujer intelectual'.[3] It concentrates on the split Castellanos identified within womanhood, and which she defined (in personal terms) as 'the discrepancy between what that role imposed on me in a country like Mexico and what I wanted to and was able to accomplish in life'.[4] As Beth Miller suggests, **'Lección de cocina'** is based in part on a critique of the traditional portrayal of women in ladies' magazines (such as Mexico's *Casa*) and television commercials.[5] The action of this particular short story takes place within the mind of a woman preparing a meal for her husband who will shortly be returning from work, and it enacts a type of self-discovery which has led one critic to compare **'Lección de cocina'** to the work of Virginia Woolf and Simone de Beauvoir.[6] Set in the kitchen it deals specifically with feminine, domestic space; **'Lección de cocina'** is therefore not only a 'cookery lesson' but also a (moralist) lesson about the social and conceptual space allotted to women by patriarchal law.

In the opening pages of the story, irony is specifically directed at the un-named narrator who is presented as an archetypal Mexican woman, inured to suffering and to whom the liberational discourse of feminism is a closed book. On the surface at least, the narrator seems to accept her appointed lot: 'Mi lugar está aquí. Desde el principio de los tiempos ha estado aquí. En el proverbio alemán la mujer es sinónimo de Küche, Kinder, Kirche' (p. 7).[7] On one level, therefore, Castellanos is, as one critic puts it, '*parodying* an interior monologue' (my emphasis).[8] But in another sense the narrator is clearly an alter ego of the narrator since she is, like the writer Rosario Castellanos, more at home with her books and literary quotations than in the kitchen. Like Castellanos, she is a writer; as she notes later on, her finger-tips are not very sensitive 'por el prolongado contacto con las teclas de la máquina de escribir' (p. 9). Thus, she compares the discourse of advertising food in the supermarket ('¿Qué me aconseja usted para la comida de hoy, experimentada ama de casa, inspiración de las madres ausentes y presentes, voz de la tradición, secreto a voces de los supermercados?', pp. 7-8), with a scene from Cervantes's *Don Quijote,* 'La cena de don Quijote'.[9] The narrator compares the discourse of literature with that of the cookery book, and wonders why literature has such a rich metatext, while the cookery book implicitly takes for granted that its readers will immediately understand its contents: 'Si yo supiera lo que es estragón y ananá no estaría consultando este libro porque sabría muchas cosas. Si tuviera usted el mínimo sentido de la realidad debería, usted misma o cualquiera de sus colegas, tomarse el trabajo de escribir un diccionario de términos técnicos, redactar unos prolegómenos, idear una propedéutica para hacer accesible al profano el difícil arte culinario. Pero parten del supuesto que todos estamos en el ajo y se limitan a enumerar' (p. 8). The answer which the text does not provide is that literature, a male-dominated code, therefore has more importance than the female-dominated discourse of the cookery-book. The comparison between the two codes becomes playful; the narrator goes off the idea of preparing a roast because 'no representa la superación de ninguna antinomia ni el planteamiento de ninguna aporia' (p. 9). The meat will only become tasty if, like a piece of prose taken to pieces by a critic immersed in New Criticism, or like the recipes which effortlessly combine contradictory qualities such as 'la esbeltez y la gula, el aspecto vistoso y la economía' (p. 7), it expresses the transcendance of antimony.

The text continues in its playful vein when referring to the redness of the meat which reminds the narrator of the colour her back went during her honeymoon in Acapulco. Despite her sunburnt skin she accepts her husband's advances on the wedding night: 'El podía darse el lujo de "portarse como quien es" y tenderse boca abajo para que no le rozara la piel dolorida. Pero yo, abnegada mujercita mexicana que nació como la paloma para el nido, sonreía a semejanza de Cuahtémoc en el suplicio cuando dijo "mi lecho no es de rosas y se volvió a callar"[*sic*]' (p. 9).[10] The reference to Cuauhtemoc's torture by fire at the hands of Cortés's men during the Spanish Conquest of America gives a grim poignancy to the narrator's experience of her womanly role which she accepts 'like a dove born for the nest'. The allusion to the Aztec King's fate draws a parallel between the conquest of America and the war between the sexes. For the woman, as for the Amerindian population in the sixteenth century, the odds were stacked against the subaltern.

Once her husband falls asleep the narrator initially feels as if she were reduced to exile, the excluded consciousness of womenkind in a patriarchal society. But she rejects exile, and its implication of gendered surrogacy. She is no longer simply the reflection of male consciousness: 'yo no soy el reflejo de una imagen en un cristal; a mí no me aniquila la cerrazón de una conciencia o de toda conciencia posible. Yo continúo viviendo con una vida densa, viscosa, turbia, aunque el que está a mi lado y el remoto, me ignoren, me pospongan, me abondonen, me desamen' (p. 10). This passage is the first sign of the emergence of a liberated consciousness in the narrator. She considers going to the bathroom and wiping her husband's semen away which, in this context, must be taken as a desire to abolish the presence of patriarchy, but, significantly, she does not do so, since she is joined to her husband through an ecclesiastic bond. Her statement—'Prefiero creer que lo que me une a él es algo tan fácil de borrar como una secreción y no tan terrible como un sacramento' (p. 11)—suggests that, despite her personal preference, the bonds of patriarchy are not so easy to release. It is while the narrator is engrossed in these thoughts that the narrative cuts back to the meat which is cooking. The link term between the two levels is the reference to 'la muerte' (the narrator is prepared to retain the privilege of insomnia until death) which leads to the description of the meat as having taken on a grey hue once the pepper was added ('la carne parece haber encanecido'). It is while her thoughts are on death that the most visible sign of patriarchy surfaces in the text; in marriage, the narrator lost her maiden name and acquired a new identity: 'Porque perdí mi antiguo nombre y aún no me acostumbro al nuevo, que tampoco es mío' (p. 11). She finds herself in a limbo realm; the way in which the narrator describes this no-woman's land is intriguing: 'Cuando en el vestíbulo del hotel algún empleado me reclama yo permanezco sorda, con ese vago malestar que es el preludio del reconocimiento' (p. 11). This vague sense of dis-ease, the text suggests, is the 'prelude to recognition', but this recognition is something which the text implicitly rejects since this would imply an acceptance of the alienating discourse of patriarchy. Recognition, as Castellanos's text goes on to suggest, is always misrecognition for womankind, since it is based on acceptance of phallocentric knowledge, itself closely connected with language and its identity-giving property. This insight is echoed later on when the narrator refers to her husband's body on top of her during love-making in necrological terms: 'Cuando dejas caer tu cuerpo sobre el mío siento que me cubre una lápida, llena de inscripciones, de nombres ajenos, de fechas memorables. Gimes inarticuladamente y quisiera susurrarte al oído mi nombre para que recuerdes quien es a la que posees' (p. 14). The reference to the signs of language ('inscripciones', 'nombres', 'fechas') reinforces once more how language is perceived as a discourse which alienates and marginalises the feminine consciousness.

Once more the narrative returns to the roast; she thinks it is too big, and then that it is taking too long to cook. Once more she questions the gender-coded assumption of the cookery book. When the recipe says that the meat doesn't take long to cook, she asks, how long is long? 'Naturalmente, el texto no especifica. Me supone una intuición que, según mi sexo, debo poseer' (p. 13). Her husband expects his wife to be a virgin, but the narrator's gradually questioning attitude towards this patriarchal assumption is suggested by her statement: 'Cuando la descubriste yo me sentí como el último dinosaurio en un planeta del que la especie había desaparecido' (p. 13). The metaphor of a dinosaur is intriguing, since it relegates the system of values underpinning patriarchy to a pre-human epoch. Halfway through the story the narrator begins to express rancour at her fate, since she is caught between being a housewife (for which 'no se me paga ningún sueldo', p. 15) and her professional career.

Having finished cooking the roast, the narrator is overtaken by a burst of enthusiasm; she imagines her husband and herself disappearing into a film idyll of romantic happiness, or she herself living the life of a wealthy, single woman in New York, Paris or London, or being picked up by a rich gentleman in a car. Unfortunately, however, the meat continues to cook and then starts to shrink and turn black ('La carne está encogiendo. [. . .] La estoy viendo muy pequeña [. . .] está empezando a soltar un humo negro y horrible [. . .] se enrosca igual que una charamusca'; pp. 17-18). The narrator's wild fantasies begin to shrink accordingly, and she is soon left with no more than 'un miserable pedazo de carne carbonizada' (p. 19). When recapitulating her experience, she compares the various stages of the roast to her husband's metamorphoses:

> Mi marido también da la impresión de solidez y de realidad cuando estamos juntos, cuando lo toco, cuando lo veo. Seguramente cambia, y cambio yo también, aunque de manera tan lenta, tan morosa que ninguno de los dos lo advierte. Después se va y bruscamente se convierte en recuerdo y. . . . Ah, no, no voy a caer en esa trampa: la del personaje inventado y el narrador inventado y la anécdota inventada. Además, no es la consecuencia que se deriva lícitamente del episodio de la carne.
>
> (p. 20)

The narrator resists the temptation to conclude her narrative in the self-reflexive mode, thereby converting it into simply an exercise in writing fiction. Rather than a metafictional direction, the story takes a feminist turn and suggests how the burnt meat will continue to operate 'en otros niveles. En el de mi conciencia, en el de mi memoria, en el de mi voluntad, modificándome, determinándome, estableciendo la dirección de mi futuro' (p. 21). At this point in the narrative, it is clear that the narrator has gone through a metamorphosis. She is aware of the non-feminist option, which is to declare weakness, and thereby guarantee 'el triunfo por la sinuosa vía que recorrieron mis antepasadas, las humildes, las que no abrían los labios sino para asentir, y lograron la obediencia ajena hasta al mas irracional de sus caprichos' (p. 21). Declaring oneself the weaker sex, thus, can have its advantages. But the narrator rejects this option as hypocritical; she cannot accept an option just because it is sanctioned by common sense. This will lead to conflict with her husband: 'Si insisto en afirmar mi versión de los hechos mi marido va a mirarme con suspicacia, va a sentirse incómodo en mi compañía y va a vivir en la continua expectativa de que se me declare la locura' (p. 22). It is significant that the narrator chooses to describe her act of defiance as 'mi versión de los hechos', which suggests that her agenda is linguistic as well as performative. To accept her new role is to enter the space of madness, to be declared mad by the system of patriarchy. But to sacrifice her own being for the benefit of her marriage is no longer an option. The narrator has been transformed from a cultural subaltern into a woman in control, intellectually and physically, of her destiny.

'Lección de cocina' ends with a recognition that her experience of burning the meat was a trivial event of everyday life: 'es algo muy insignificante, muy ridículo. Y sin embargo . . .' (p. 22). The 'and yet . . .' with which the story ends is an indication that the culinary mishap raises ideological issues which stretch beyond the trivial event itself. There are four literary/historical references in **'Lección de cocina'**, all of which imply how the story relates back to wider ideological issues. Two of these (Cervantes and Cuauhtemoc) have already been mentioned. The other two, Santa Teresa and Sor Juana, because they are women, act as pivotal reference points in **'Lección de cocina'**. Both women appear together in what is Castellanos's perhaps most famous poem 'Meditación en el umbral'. As the poem opens:

> No, no es la solución
> tirarse bajo el tren como la Ana de Tolstoi
> ni apurar el arsénico de Madame Bovary
> ni aguardar en los páramos de Avila la visita
> del ángel con venablo
> antes de liarse el manto a la cabeza
> y comenzar a actuar.
> Ni concluir las leyes geométricas, contando
> las vigas de la celda de castigo
> como lo hizo Sor Juana (. . .).[11]

In her poem Castellanos ultimately rejects the life-option offered by Santa Teresa which involves waiting in the wilderness for 'la visita / del ángel con venablo', as well as Sor Juana's counting the beams in her cell. It is not that she rejects what they did, but rather the patriarchal society in which they lived which barred them from writing and knowledge (most spectacularly so in the case of Sor Juana). In **'Lección de cocina'** Castellanos offers a similar view of these two mother figures. Her allusion to Santa Teresa strives to express the saint's perception in the language of the modern age: 'Yo estuve todo el tiempo pendiente de la carne, fijándome en que le sucedían una serie de cosas rarísimas. Con razón Santa Teresa decía que Dios anda en los pucheros. O la materia que es energía o como se llame ahora' (p. 20). The narrator of **'Lección de cocina'** re-interprets Santa Teresa's reference to God as a reference to energy, or, more probably, electricity. The narrator concurs with Santa Teresa but distances herself from her belief, reinterpreting the saint's perception of God in contemporary terms. The reference in **'Lección de cocina'** to Sor Juana is more pointed: 'De mí se puede decir lo que Pfandl dijo de Sor Juana: que pertenezco a la clase de neuróticos cavilosos. El diagnóstico es muy fácil ¿pero qué consecuencias acarrearía asumirlo?' (p. 22). As an essay Castellanos wrote on Sor Juana clearly shows, she saw the Mexican writer as a model to be followed.[12] Sor Juana, indeed, had used a culinary metaphor in her famous *Respuesta de la poetisa a la muy ilustre Sor Filotea de la Cruz,* in which she referred ironically to the Church authorities' argument that her intellectual energies might be better served if she were to take up cooking. Sor Juana turned this idea around, poking fun at the church dignitaries, by showing how her mind frequently became involved in the solving of intellectual problems during cooking:

> Pues ¿qué os pudiera contar, Señora, de los secretos naturales que he descubierto estando guisando? Veo que un huevo se une y fríe en la manteca o aceite y, por contrario, se despedaza en el almíbar; ver que para que el azúcar se conserve fluida basta echarle una muy mínima parte de agua en que haya estado membrillo u otra fruta agria; ver que la yema y clara de un mismo huevo son tan contrarias, que en los unos, que sirven para el azúcar, sirve cada una de por sí y juntos no. Por no cansaros con tales frialdades, que sólo refiero por daros entera noticia de mi natural y creo que os causará risa; pero, señora, ¿qué podemos saber las mujeres sino filosofías de cocina? Bien dijo Lupercio Leonardo, que bien se puede filosofar y aderezar la cena. Y yo suelo decir viendo estas cosillas: Si Aristóteles hubiera guisado, mucho más hubiera escrito.[13]

The intertextual allusion to this text turns Rosario Castellanos's **'Lección de cocina'** into a barbed attack on patriarchy which confronts twentieth-century woman as it did Sor Juana in the sixteenth century. Like Sor Juana, Castellanos adopts a mock-ignorant stance in order to give more urgency to her critique of the patriarchal institution of marriage. Though few and far between, the intertextual allusions in Castellanos's text help to create a critique of phallocentric knowledge which takes its point of departure from the space which feminism has identified as the source of female oppression, namely, the kitchen. Like Sor Juana's *Respuesta,* **'Lección de cocina'**, in true emperor's-new-clothes mode, is a reply to those forces within society which attempt to control women's lives.

Notes

1. 'Woman and Her Image', *A Rosario Castellanos Reader,* edited by Maureen Ahern (Austin: University of Texas Press, 1988), pp. 236-44 (p. 240).

2. Naomi Lindstrom discusses the ways in which Castellanos's characters are silenced; see 'Rosario Castellanos: Representing Women's Voice', *LF,* 5:2 (1979), 29-47. On the same theme, see also Lucía Fox-Lockert, *Women Novelists in Spain and Spanish*

America, pp. 202-15. Castellanos has also published a number of novels, of which the best known are *Balún Canán* (1957) and *Oficio de tinieblas* (1962), but it is in her short stories that Castellanos's narrative skill achieves its cutting edge. For a discussion of Castellanos's fiction, see Jean Franco, *Plotting Women: Gender and Representation in Mexico.*

3. Seymour Menton, 'Las cuentistas mexicanas en la época femenista, 1970-1988', *Hispania,* 73:2 (1990), 366-70 (p. 367). For further discussion of Castellanos's work, see Beth Miller, *Uma consciência feminista: Rosario Castellanos* (São Paulo: Editora Perspectiva, 1987).

4. Quoted in Oscar Bonifaz, *Remembering Rosario: A Personal Glimpse into the Life and Works of Rosario Castellanos,* translated by Myralyn F. Allgood (Potomac, Maryland: Scripta Humanistica, 1990), p. 43.

5. 'Female Characterization and Contexts in Rosario Castellanos's *Album de familia*', *AmH,* 4:32-33 (1979), 26-30 (p. 26).

6. Kathleen O'Quinn, '*Tablero de damas* and *Album de familia*: Farces on Women Writers', in *Homenjae a Rosario Castellanos,* ed. Maureen Ahern and Mary Seale Vásquez (Valencia: Albatros, 1980), pp. 99-105 (p. 104).

7. All textual references are to 'Lección de cocina', in *Album de familia* (Mexico: Joaquin Moritz, 1985), 2nd impression of 4th edition, pp. 7-22. Raúl Ortiz y Ortiz, a good friend of Rosario Castellanos and the dedicatee of *Album de familia,* pointed out in a lecture given at University College, London in December 1990 that Castellanos was neither an enthusiastic or a very good cook, a problem which was compounded by her clumsiness. The fact that the narrator of 'Lección de cocina' refers to how clumsy she is ('Y yo, soy muy torpe'; p. 16) reinforces the possibility that the narrator is a projection of some of the author's character traits.

8. Phyllis Rodríguez Peralta, 'Images of Women in Rosario Castellanos's Prose', *LALR,* 6:11 (1977), 68-80 (p. 75).

9. Castellanos is here no doubt alluding to the meal during which Don Quijote gives a speech about 'las armas y las letras'; *El Ingenioso Hidalgo Don Quijote de la Mancha,* ed. John Jay Allen (Madrid: Cátedra, 1977), chapter XXXVIII, Vol. I, pp. 447-51. A mock-ironic parallel is thus established between the hype of advertising and Don Quijote's fulsome speech.

10. This is an embellished version of what Cuahtémoc is reputed to have said. According to Gómara's account, he said '¿Estoi yo en algun deleite, ó baño?'; quoted by W. H. Prescott, *The Conquest of Mexico* (New York: Henry Holt and Company, 1922), II, p. 445. Castellanos's source may have been Rubén Darío's poem, 'A Roosevelt', *Cantos de vida y esperanza* (1905), in which the Nicaraguan poet has Cuauhtemoc say 'Yo no estoy en un lecho de rosas'; Rubén Darío, *Poesías completas,* ed. Alfonso Méndez Plancarte (Madrid: Aguilar, 1968), p. 641. Castellanos's text curiously intercalates the expression 'y se volvió a callar', which is commentary rather than speech.

11. Rosario Castellanos, *Meditation on the Threshold* (New York: Bilingual Press, 1988), p. 48.

12. 'Once Again Sor Juana', *A Rosario Castellanos Reader,* edited by Maureen Ahern (Austin: University of Texas Press, 1988), pp. 222-25.

13. 'Respuesta de la poetisa a la muy ilustre Sor Filotea de la Cruz', *Obras completas de Sor Juana Inés de la Cruz* (México: Fondo de Cultura Económica, 1957), vol. IV, pp. 440-75 (pp. 459-60). Sor Juana would seem to be referring here to Aristotle's discussion in *Physics,* 1, i-vi, of the relationship between substance and its attributes. Though Aristotle does not mention eggs in this section, he uses the example of 'whiteness' to illustrate his argument on various occasions, concluding that 'our principles must be contraries'; both of these ideas are echoed—tongue-in-cheek—in Sor Juana's text; see *The Basic Works of Aristotle,* edited and with an introduction by Richard McKeon (New York: Random House, 1941), pp. 213-28. The quotation may be found on p. 228. Sor Juana no doubt also uses the egg because of its feminine connotations. Castellanos's own text continues and expands Sor Juana's feminocentric dialogue with Aristotle's text.

Additional coverage of Castellanos's life and career is contained in the following sources published by the Gale Group: *Contemporary Authors,* Vols. 53-56, 131; *Contemporary Authors New Revision Series,* Vol. 58; *Contemporary Literary Criticism,* Vol. 66; *DISCovering Authors Modules: and Multicultural; Dictionary of Literary Biography,* Vol. 113; *Hispanic Literature Criticism; Hispanic Writers; Major 20th-Century Writers,* Vol. 1.

"The Minister's Black Veil"
Nathaniel Hawthorne

The following entry presents criticism on Hawthorne's short story, "The Minister's Black Veil." For further information on Hawthorne's complete career, see *SSC,* Volumes 3 and 29.

INTRODUCTION

Hawthorne's "The Minister's Black Veil" is regarded as one of the earliest and greatest examples of American short fiction. Like many of Hawthorne's stories and his novel *The Scarlet Letter,* the story is developed around a single symbol: in this case, the black veil that the Reverend Mr. Hooper wears to hide his face from the world. The story's macabre tone and repressive early-colonial New England Puritan setting are familiar elements in Hawthorne's fiction, and they serve to underscore the unsettling behavior of the main character and the work's concern with the nature of secret sin and humans' fallen nature. Hawthorne's intended meaning with the tale has been the subject of considerable debate, with critics seeing it variously as a deprecation of Puritan fanaticism, a study of a misunderstood outsider ostracized by a community's intolerance, and an exploration of the clergyman's guilt after his crime against a young woman. Other readers argue that the tale is purposefully ambiguous because the psychological and religious complexity it seeks to express could not be captured in a straightforward moral tale.

"The Minister's Black Veil" first appeared in an annual anthology, *The Token,* in 1836, and was collected in *Twice Told Tales* the following year. As Hawthorne points out in a footnote to the story, the character of Mr. Hooper has similarities to those of a real-life clergyman who died some eighty years earlier, Joseph Moody of Maine. However, he says, the veil worn by Moody had a different import as that of Mr. Hooper: the former had accidentally killed a friend, and for the rest of his life hid his face from men. Some critics have also suggested that the character of Mr. Hooper was modeled after that of biblical figures—including Christ, Moses, and several Old Testament prophets.

PLOT AND MAJOR CHARACTERS

The story opens on a Sunday morning in a church in the small New England town of Milford. The parishioners are shocked to see the Reverend Mr. Hooper wearing a dark veil that extends from his forehead to his mouth. The minister gives no explanation for this unusual mask, and the congregation begins to speculate: some insist he has gone mad; others claim it is not the Reverend Mr. Hooper at all. Mr. Hooper seems unconcerned with his congregation's agitation and conducts the service as usual. To the audience, however, the veil clearly intensifies the minister's sermon on the subject of secret sin; some with weak nerves must leave the service. Afterward the congregation resumes their speculation on why Mr. Hooper has donned this veil. Some explain away the mystery with suggestions that perhaps the minister's eyes have been weakened by long hours of reading, but no one dares ask Mr. Hooper directly about his behavior. Old Squire Saunders, with whom the minister dines every Sunday, forgets to ask Mr. Hooper to his home that day, and the pastor returns alone to his parsonage.

Mr. Hooper's afternoon sermon proves little different. He appears in his veil, the congregation questions his sanity, and they are moved almost to terror by the power of his words. After the sermon, Mr. Hooper officiates a funeral service for a young woman. He stands over her as she lies in the coffin, his veil hanging in such a way that, if she were alive, she could see his face. An old superstitious woman witnessing this scene believes she sees the corpse's body shudder. The rest of the congregation is moved by Mr. Hooper's elegy, and some believe that during the funeral procession they see the spirits of the minister and the dead woman walking hand in hand.

That evening Mr. Hooper marries the town's most handsome young couple, but what should be a happy occasion is made melancholy by the strange aura given off by the veil. The wedding is full of bad omens: the bride's fingers grow cold; some believe that the recently buried woman has returned to be married; and as Mr. Hooper prepares to toast the couple he sees his image in a mirror, becomes frightened, spills his wine on the floor, and leaves abruptly.

The following day things grow worse when a young boy terrifies his classmates and himself by wearing a handkerchief over his face in imitation of the minister. A group of "busybodies and impertinent people in the parish" decide to form a committee to question Mr. Hooper about the veil, but when they appear before him they grow fainthearted and do not confront him. Only one person, Mr. Hooper's fiancé, Elizabeth, is not fearful of the veil or what lies behind it. Elizabeth meets her betrothed, and seeing that the veil is nothing more than ordinary material, asks him to show her his face. He refuses, and when she presses the issue, he gives a mysterious explanation that he has vowed to wear the veil forever in recognition of the time when we will all cast aside our veils. Elizabeth says that he should remove the veil for no other reason than to dispel the common notion that he is insane or hiding some sinful scandal. When he again refuses, she begins to cry and tremble. She breaks off her engagement to Mr. Hooper when her final appeal for him to show his face just once is not granted.

Thereafter, no one tries to force the minister to remove his veil. The congregation continues to gossip, but few have the nerve to approach him. Children flee when they see him, and parishioners view him with dread, making him a sad, solitary figure who is often seen walking alone near the graveyard. However, the veil has one good effect: that of making Mr. Hooper "a very efficient clergyman." Dying parishioners often call for Mr. Hooper, and he gains regional fame as a stirring preacher. When finally it comes time for Mr. Hooper to die, he lies on his bed, his face still hidden by the veil, attended by the zealous Reverend Mr. Clark and the faithful spinster Elizabeth. Reverend Clark pronounces Mr. Hooper a "blameless" man, and bends down to remove the veil as a sign of his reward. But Mr. Hooper gathers his energy, clutches the veil tightly to his face, and declares that the veil is a symbol of the secret sin that hides the true face of all men from God and humanity. Out of respect for his wishes, Mr. Hooper is buried with his veil unlifted. But even after many years those who knew Mr. Hooper still shudder when they think that in the grave his face turned to dust beneath that black veil.

MAJOR THEMES

On its most straightforward reading, it seems that the central theme of "The Minister's Black Veil" is made explicit in Mr. Hooper's dying words: everyone has a secret sin that is hidden from all others. The veil, he says, is but a symbol of the masks of deceit and sin that separate all individuals from truly facing themselves, their loved ones, and the divine spirit. All individuals wear such a mask, and Mr. Hooper's veil has been only a symbolic reminder of a truth that most are unwilling to admit. Mr. Hooper pays a high price for this lesson: he is feared, misunderstood, and left to live a lonely, solitary life.

Most commentators, however, perceive far greater complexity behind the seemingly simple "parable," as Hawthorne himself called it. Some view the major theme as the psychological power of guilt, and the minister as a mentally and emotionally unstable man who is driven to make visible his guilt for reasons that may or may not be revealed in the story. Edgar Allan Poe, for example, considers that the insinuated meaning is that the Reverend has committed a "crime of dark dye" against the young woman whose funeral he conducts; some critics, taking Poe's lead, see this as a cause for the guilt Mr. Hooper displays. Other critics have proposed that the story explores Hawthorne's favorite theme of the "fortunate fall," as the strange power of Mr. Hooper's secret heart destroys one aspect of his life but enhances his effectiveness as a preacher. On another reading, Mr. Hooper is an antichrist who pushes himself further and further from the very human companionship and love that could act as his salvation. Still another reading sees the tale as Hawthorne's indictment of the Puritan religious fervor and pessimism that is gives rise to the minister's unbalanced behavior. The minister's refusal to tell his congregation why he wears the veil or to remove it for Elizabeth shows that he suffers from the sin of superiority; he believes he is conscious of a truth that everyone else refuses to acknowledge. This spiritual pride results in the minister's estrangement from the community, and he becomes a monster whose symbolic gesture incites negative consequences. Late twentieth-century analyses have concentrated on the story as a complex literary exercise that makes the veil a symbol for literary symbols themselves, a study in how an artist creates an allegorically and symbolically powerful motif.

CRITICAL RECEPTION

From its initial publication, "The Minister's Black Veil" was hailed as a work of originality and power. Poe called the work a "masterly composition" but suggested that only the most sensitive readers would be able to glean the true import of the narrative and see beyond the obvious moral of the story. Other reviewers and noted writers heaped praise on the story, too, although, as with most of Hawthorne's writing, it never achieved popular recognition during his lifetime. Since the early 1950s, the story has garnered enormous attention from scholars because of its ambiguity. Despite the divided opinion on the "true" meaning of the story, critics concur that the tale is a fine example of Hawthorne's art. It reveals his fascination with New England history and daily life; his deep appreciation of the role of religion in the lives of the inhabitants of a small community; his sensitivity to the psychological complexity of human beings and their relationships with others; and his skillful use of language and multilayered symbolism to create a story that can be read over and over to gain fresh insight. The story, as a tale of secret sin, has also been the subject of much interest because it anticipates Hawthorne's treatment of the same theme in his masterpiece, *The Scarlet Letter.*

PRINCIPAL WORKS

Short Fiction

Twice-Told Tales (sketches and short stories) 1837

Twice-Told Tales (second series) (sketches and short stories) 1842

Mosses from an Old Manse (sketches and short stories) 1846

The Snow-Image, and Other Twice-Told Tales 1851

A Wonder-Book for Girls and Boys 1852

Tanglewood Tales, for Girls and Boys: Being a Second Wonder-Book 1853

Other Major Works

Fanshawe: A Tale (novel) 1828

The Scarlet Letter, A Romance (novel) 1850

The House of the Seven Gables, A Romance (novel) 1851

The Blithedale Romance (novel) 1852

Life of Franklin Pierce (biography) 1852

The Marble Faun; or, The Romance of Monte Beni (novel) 1860; published in England as *Transformation; or, The Romance of Monte Beni* 1860

Our Old Home: A Series of English Sketches (essays) 1863

Passages from the American Note-Books of Nathaniel Hawthorne (journal) 1868

Passages from the English Note-Books (journal) 1870

Passages from the French and Italian Note-Books (journal) 1872

Septimus Felton; or, The Elixir of Life (unfinished novel) 1872

The Dolliver Romance and Other Pieces (unfinished novel) 1876

Doctor Grimshawe's Secret: A Romance (unfinished novel) 1883

CRITICISM

Richard Harter Fogle (essay date 1948)

SOURCE: "An Ambiguity of Sin or Sorrow," in *The New England Quarterly,* Vol. XXI, No. 3, September, 1948, pp. 342-49.

[*In the following essay, Fogle contends that the central message of Hawthorne's "The Minister's Black Veil" is intentionally ambiguous, leaving readers to choose among competing interpretations.*]

Hawthorne's characteristic fusion of simplicity on the surface with layers of complexity beneath is perhaps nowhere more fully in evidence than in **"The Minister's Black Veil,"** a brief, highly typical, and thoroughly successful story. It is subtitled "A Parable," and the outer meaning of the parable is abundantly clear. An apparently blameless minister inexplicably dons a black veil, and wears it throughout his life-time, in despite of many well-meant pleas to cast it off. On his deathbed he reveals its secret and its justification.

> What, but the mystery which it obscurely typifies, has made this piece of crape so awful? When the friend shows his inmost heart to his friend; the lover to his best beloved; when man does not vainly shrink from the eye of his Creator, loathsomely treasuring up the secret of his sin; then deem me a monster, for the symbol beneath which I have lived, and die! I look around me, and lo! on every visage a Black Veil!

The moral is impressive, even terrible; but viewed simply as a proposition it is not difficult to grasp, however it may wind and reverberate within the deeps of the imagination. The veil is the visible symbol of secret sin, suggested by Hawthorne's reading in New England history and legend.[1] Its projection into solid actuality has the effect of isolating the minister from human society, in which unhappy result it presumably differs only in degree from the self-isolation of every living soul.[2] The minister is Everyman, bearing his lonely fate in order to demonstrate a great and tragic truth.

The moral is explicit, and unimpeachably orthodox. The explicit statement, however, leads to more than a single possibility. The self-imposed martyrdom of Father Hooper must correspond with some deep necessity of his nature. He who isolates himself in the outward fact must already have performed the deed in spirit. The act has in it something of caprice; it is entirely out of proportion with any apparent necessity or benefit. By it the minister forfeits the affection of his congregation, his chance of human love and marriage, and the sympathy of society—and to what end? No note of final, compensating triumph sounds for him. With remorseless consistency, Hawthorne pursues him even into his grave. "Still veiled, they laid him in his coffin, and a veiled corpse they bore him to the grave. The grass of many years has sprung up and withered on that grave, the burial-stone is moss-grown, and good Mr. Hooper's face is dust; but awful is still the thought that it mouldered beneath the Black Veil!"

One may feel that the veil is less representative of mankind in general than of the single and arbitrary eccentricity of the minister himself, who severs himself from men through perverse pride, or other obscure and tragic compulsion. His preoccupation with sin has blunted his perceptions of the normal and good, which lies as ready to his hand as evil.[3] In rejecting the love of his fiancé Elizabeth he casts away a gift of inestimable value to satisfy a wild obsession.

If we continue with this reading of the story, we shall take Elizabeth to exemplify the normal and well-ordered mind, as Mr. Hooper is the type of the abnormal, who has lost the power of seeing life steadily and whole. The "calm energy" of her character, her "direct simplicity," contrasts with the "gentle, but unconquerable obstinacy" of the minister, whom her good counsel fails to persuade; and with his infatuated love of mystification. Hawthorne inherited the psychology, but not the theology nor the morality of his Puritan forebears; and Elizabeth is far more likely to represent his ideal than is the gloomy and sin-crazed Hooper.

Which, then, of these two interpretations shall we accept? Both, I conceive—they are both in the story. Either presents its difficulties. If we take **"The Minister's Black Veil"** at its face value as a homily on secret sin, we are confronted with the apparent disproportion between the act and its causes. The minister himself is to outward gaze the gentlest and least sinful of men; and we have no vivid sense of that presence of Evil which would necessitate so heroic an object-lesson. But if we wholly accede to the second interpretation, which makes the steady view of life, the *aurea mediocritas,* the highest good, then the tone and emphasis of the story remains to be explained. It is too deeply gloomy, too intense, fully to harmonize with such a moral, which demands for its inculcation a certain dry sparkle and lightness.

The imaginative and emotional realization of this ambivalence of meaning comes to us upon the vehicle of Hawthorne's characteristic "ambiguity device,"[4] or as it has variously been termed, "the device of multiple choice,"[5] and "the formula of alternative possibilities."[6] The purpose of this device is to suggest a meaning while simultaneously casting doubt upon it, or to offer two or more interpretations at once of the same incident. It is an essential element in nearly all of Hawthorne's tales and romances, an inseparable quality of his style; but significantly it occurs with unusual frequency in **"The Minister's Black Veil."** Here its most marked effect is to maintain a balance between subjective and objective in the portrait of the minister, to invite us inside his character while repelling us from any final certainty about it; and, of course, to preserve the objectivity of the narrator, who simultaneously offers and reserves his judgment. Thus, for example, we do not quite know what Mr. Hooper saw through the veil, "which entirely concealed his features, except the mouth and chin, but *probably*[7] did not intercept his sight, further than to give a darkened aspect to all living and inanimate things." The *probably* bars us from certainty on the point. Again, as the minister preaches for the first time from beneath the veil, it "lay heavily on his uplifted countenance. Did he seek to hide it from the dread Being whom he was addressing?" Hawthorne proposes the question, but does not answer it.

Pressed by Elizabeth to expound the meaning of the veil, Mr. Hooper will reply only darkly. "'If it be a sign of mourning,' says he, 'I, perhaps like most other mortals, have sorrows dark enough to be typified by a black veil.'" When she further urges the scandalous whispers in the village, that he hides his face from consciousness of secret sin, he will not deny the imputation. "'If I hide my face for sorrow, there is cause enough,' he merely replied; 'and if I cover it for secret sin, what mortal might not do the same?'" Hawthorne skilfully holds out the suggestion that the veil is a penance for an actual and serious crime, while at the same time permitting no real and solid grounds for it.[8] The vulgar interpret its meaning vulgarly, the complacent complacently, and men of good will regretfully. The calm good sense of Elizabeth forces her to regard it as the emblem of a tragic but unbased obsession. She finds at first that "there is nothing terrible in this piece of crape," but at length yields to its influence: in her case not from a dread of the veil itself, but of what it tells her of her lover's state of mind.

The mystery of the veil is hidden to the end among these artfully contrived ambiguities. As Elizabeth leaves him, "Mr. Hooper smiled to think that only a material emblem had separated him from happiness, though the horrors, which it shadowed forth, must be drawn darkly between the fondest of lovers." It is confusing to have the symbol detached from its meaning in this fashion; and the passage calls up another consideration. If the veil alone has separated the minister from happiness, what are we to do with "the horrors, which it shadowed forth"? Surely it is in the last analysis they which shut him off from earthly good. The effect is at once to assert and to cast doubt upon the reality of that which the veil portrays but also hides. And the smile itself, shining dimly from beneath the black cloth, emphasizes in its self-irony the ambiguity of the minister's character.[9]

The veil has varying effects upon different minds and different levels of society. To those "who claimed a superiority to popular prejudice," it is merely "an eccentric whim." In the multitude it occasions either impertinence or superstitious dread, reactions equally grievous to its unhappy wearer. It is whispered that the veil is the obscure intimation of a horrible crime; and there are hints of supernatural forces.

> Thus, from beneath the black veil, there rolled a cloud into the sunshine, *an ambiguity of sin or sorrow,* which enveloped the poor minister, so that love or sympathy could never reach him. *It was said,* that ghost and fiend

> consorted with him there. With self-shudderings and outward terrors, he walked continually in its shadow, groping darkly within his own soul, or gazing through a medium that saddened the whole world. Even the lawless wind, *it was believed,* respected his dreadful secret, and never blew aside the veil. But still good Mr. Hooper sadly smiled at the pale visages of the worldly throng as he passed by.

In one respect, however, the veil makes Mr. Hooper a more efficient clergyman, for it "enabled him to sympathize with all dark affections." His words are imbued with its gloomy power, and he can bring sinners to the light denied himself. Yet here as well the effects of the veil are ambiguous. His converts regard him with dread, and not with love or joy, even though they owe their redemption to him. "Dying sinners cried aloud for Mr. Hooper, and would not yield their breath till he appeared; though ever, as he stooped to whisper consolation, they shuddered at the veiled face so near their own." Hawthorne as it were summarizes its twofold influence in a kind of climactic ambiguity, which embodies its dualism in a series of antitheses: "In this manner Mr. Hooper spent a long life, irreproachable in outward act, yet shrouded in dismal suspicions; kind and loving, though unloved, and dimly feared; a man apart from men, shunned in their health and joy, but ever summoned to their aid in mortal anguish."

This dubiety persists in the final scene of the deathbed, despite the explicit pronouncement with which it ends. As the minister lies dying, the veil still rests upon his face, stirred lightly by his faint breath. "All through life that piece of crape had hung between him and the world: it had separated him from cheerful brotherhood and woman's love, and kept him in that saddest of all prisons, his own heart; and still it lay upon his face, as if to deepen the gloom of his darksome chamber, and shade him from the sunshine of eternity." If, however, the veil is emblematic of the common plight of man, why should it isolate its wearer with a poignancy unfelt by other men, and leave him lonely and alone? We have no sense in the story that all men feel as does Mr. Hooper; they are portrayed, in fact, as a cohesive band, united if only in dread of the fearful veil. Even the minister's colleague, praying at the end by his bedside, rather cruelly misunderstands its significance.[10] Or, on the other hand, is it possible that we can go further afield and determine that the message of the veil *is* representative and universal: that the failure to recognize it is simply the last and most chilling proof of man's imprisonment within himself? If this latter interpretation is the true one, we must conclude, I presume, that Hawthorne's emphasis upon the problem as embodied in Mr. Hooper has made it impossible for him to deal with it in other characters. To achieve unity of composition his canvas can contain only one important figure. Or in other words, in order to present forcibly the tragic isolation of one man, Hawthorne is obliged to consider society as a solid group arrayed against his hero, ignoring for the time being the fact that this hero is Everyman.

We conclude, then, without arriving at a clear decision as to the meaning of the tale, but with a sense of depths unplumbed, of rich potentialities not fully realized. The discrepancies between the two interpretations which have been outlined here must go unreconciled. Their mutual presence can, I think, be satisfactorily explained in two ways—one psychological, and one aesthetic—separable, and yet related closely. In the first place, they may be said, as it were, to represent the faculties of Hawthorne's own psychology, the Heart and the Head.[11] His heart, his imagination, the inherited bent of his Puritan ancestry—all his instincts, in short—bind him in sympathy with the possessed minister, brooding over the vague and bottomless abyss of Evil. But his head, his intellect, is with the calm and steady-minded Elizabeth, unable to look upon the minister's vow as other than a sad and fatal but groundless whim. The ancestral Hawthorne stands beside the nineteenth-century Hawthorne in **"The Minister's Black Veil,"** and their voices do not wholly harmonize.

Second, Hawthorne is too honest an artist to force a reconciliation which he has not, in Keats's words, "proved upon his pulses." Having chosen the symbol of the black veil, and invented an action for it, he refrains from pushing the reader to a single dogmatic conclusion. The minister himself believes the veil to be an emblem of the secret sin that poisons the souls of all mankind, but we are not compelled to accept his reading of the matter. We may, if we like, consider it rather a veil upon his understanding, whose gloomy shade conceals from the eyes behind it as much as it discloses. As it casts its shadow over the bright and various colors of the material world—colors distinct to every unhandicapped observer—so does it darken the vision of the spiritual eye.

The imagination of Hawthorne, however, playing freely over the theme, will not content itself within the limits of any single meaning. Beneath the explicit statement, the clear and simple outline of the tale, lies the irony of the minister's smile, the ambiguity of almost every incident. In **"The Minister's Black Veil"** the moral constitutes the framework, but it is merely an element, albeit an indispensable element, of the completed structure.

Notes

1. Cf. Hawthorne's note: "Another clergyman in New England, Mr. Joseph Moody, of York, Maine, who died about eighty years since, made himself remarkable by the same eccentricity that is here related of the Reverend Mr. Hooper. In his case, however, the symbol had a different import. In early life he had accidentally killed a beloved friend; and from that day till the hour of his death, he hid his face from men."
2. The isolation theme in Hawthorne is of primary importance, and has elsewhere been discussed valuably and fully. "Other poets of the past have excelled him in giving expression to certain problems of our inner life, and in stirring the depths of our emotional nature; but not in the tragedies of Greece, or the epics of Italy, or the drama of

Shakespeare will you find any presentation of this one truth of the penalty of solitude laid upon the human soul so fully and profoundly worked out as in the romances of Hawthorne" (Paul Elmer More, "The Solitude of Nathaniel Hawthorne," *Shelburne Essays,* 1, [New York and London, 1904], 27). See also Newton Arvin, *Hawthorne* (Boston, 1929), 30-69, 184-206; and F. O. Matthiessen, *American Renaissance* (New York, 1941), 224-229.

3. Thus in that other dark masterpiece of Hawthorne's, "Young Goodman Brown," one may consider that Brown is so overborne by his contact with evil as to be obsessed. Once he finds that evil exists, his vision of life is filled with it. But Hawthorne suggests a more cheerful aspect of things which Brown ignores.
4. See my "Ambiguity and Clarity in Hawthorne's 'Young Goodman Brown,'" *New England Quarterly,* XVIII (December, 1945), 448-465.
5. Matthiessen, *American Renaissance,* 276.
6. Yvor Winters, *Maule's Curse* (Norfolk, Connecticut, 1838), 18.
7. These and all subsequent italics are mine.
8. For example, on the day the minister first wears the veil he conducts the funeral service of a young lady. In describing this event Hawthorne holds out the suggestion of a mysterious relationship between the corpse and Mr. Hooper, but does not permit this suggestion to develop. "The clergyman . . . bent over the coffin, to take a last farewell of his deceased parishioner. As he stooped, the veil hung straight down from his forehead, so that, if her eyelids had not been closed forever, the dead maiden might have seen his face. Could Mr. Hooper be fearful of her glance, that he so hastily caught back the black veil? A person who watched the interview between the dead and living, scrupled not to affirm, that, at the instant when the clergyman's features were disclosed, the corpse had slightly shuddered, rustling the shroud and muslin cap, though the countenance retained the composure of death. A superstitious old woman was the only witness of this prodigy . . ." "'Why do you look back?' said one in the procession to his partner. 'I had a fancy,' replied she, 'that the minister and the maiden's spirit were walking hand in hand.'"
9. The smile is a recurring motif. Thus, when the minister returns to the parsonage after his first appearance in the veil, "A sad smile gleamed faintly from beneath the black veil, and flickered about his mouth, glimmering as he disappeared." Even on his deathbed the smile casts its dubious influence over the gloomy scene. "Father Hooper's breath heaved; it rattled in his throat; but, with a mighty effort, grasping forward with his hands, he caught hold of life, and held it back till he should speak. He even raised himself in bed; and there he sat, shivering with the arms of death around him, while the black veil hung down, awful, at that last moment, in the gathered terrors of a lifetime. And yet the faint, sad smile, so often there, now seemed to glimmer from its obscurity, and linger on Father Hooper's lips."
10. "'Dark old man!' exclaimed the affrighted minister, 'with what horrible crime upon your soul are you now passing to the judgment?'"
11. For full discussion of the Head and the Heart in Hawthorne's fiction see Matthiessen, *American Renaissance,* 344 ff.

William Bysshe Stein (essay date 1955)

SOURCE: "Notes and Queries: The Parable of the Antichrist in 'The Minister's Black Veil,'" in *American Literature,* Vol. XXVII, No. 3, November, 1955, pp. 386-92.

[*In the following essay, Stein claims that Hawthorne's "The Minister's Black Veil" is modeled on II Corinthians.*]

The ambiguity of **"The Minister's Black Veil"** has been unnecessarily exaggerated in modern criticism,[1] though, paradoxically, its critics have not been entirely at fault. In the note to the subtitle of the tale, "A Parable," Hawthorne appears deliberately to sidetrack the impulse of the reader to seek an analogue to the action in the logical source—the New Testament. Instead he cites a historical origin for the symbol of the veil, the artifice of conflict in the plot. But then he alters certain facts concerning Mr. Hooper's prototype, a clergyman named Moody. One alteration is particularly important; the latter wore a handkerchief over his face, not a veil as does Hawthorne's character.[2] Though it may seem pedantic scholarship to labor this point—an attempt to deprive the creative imagination of its dramatic license—this innocuous departure from truth has led critics to extrapolate the parable almost exclusively from Hawthorne's alleged adaptation of the event in the footnote. This emphasis has fostered many ingenious speculations on Mr. Hooper's perverse behavior. But since Hawthorne offers no basis upon which the critic may dogmatize the focus of his sympathies, any judgment passed upon the moral character of the act must therefore be somewhat gratuitous. This interpretive predicament is somewhat alleviated if one turns to the Bible, Hawthorne's *vade mecum.*

A section of Paul's second epistle to the Corinthians especially illuminates the ambivalent moral problem. The subject of **"The Minister's Black Veil,"** the relationship between the minister and the congregation, is treated at length in this epistle, and, of crucial importance, its implications are dramatized through the dominant symbols of the fictional narrative—the veil and the mirror. As does Hawthorne, Paul assumes that the closeness of the laity to God resides in the nature of the relationship between the people and the minister. But whereas Paul vehemently protests the shortcomings of personal ministration, Hawthorne is noncommittal. The apostle places the burden of responsibility upon the minister who is entrusted with the custodianship of the sacred message. Unlike Hawthorne's Mr. Hooper, Paul's minister is called upon to teach the availability of grace to any sinner who will place his faith in Christ. He is also urged to practice forgiveness, lest he lapse into self-righteousness and spiritual arrogance. In short, according to Paul, the minister must teach others to perceive the salvation which awaits them when they possess a true knowledge of Christ:

> Now thanks *be* unto God, which always causeth us to triumph in Christ, and maketh manifest the savor of his knowledge by us in every place. For we are unto God a sweet savor of Christ, in them that are saved, and in them that perish: To the one *we* are the savor of death unto death; and to the other the savor of life unto life. And who is sufficient for these things? For we are not as many, which corrupt the word of God: but as of sincerity, but as of God, in the sight of God speak we of Christ.[3]

Hawthorne, of course, directly affirms no ideal of ministration, thereby imparting ambiguity to his parable. Yet, as he moves Mr. Hooper through the sequence of action, a mode of ecclesiastical practice is illustrated. As it unfolds, each of the apostolic principles is violated, as if Hawthorne contrived a series of events deliberately contradicting Paul's advice. Coincidentally his travesty omits not a single aspect of the scriptural harangue. Not until Mr. Hooper dons the veil does this profanation take place, the significance of which act will be clarified in the analysis of the ensuing chapter in II Corinthians. Once he takes this step, the people are alienated, not only from him but also from the word of God which he preaches: "it [the veil] threw its obscurity between him and the holy page, as he read the Scriptures; and while he prayed the veil *lay heavily on his uplifted countenance*." This scene excites the following rhetorical question from Hawthorne: "Did he seek to hide it from the dread Being whom he was addressing?"[4] Thus an association is immediately engendered with Paul's contrary instructions that the true minister of the gospel ought to speak the word of Christ in the sight of God.[5] In effect, Hawthorne suggests that Mr. Hooper is perverting the sacred text;[6] instead of bringing the congregation closer to God, he incites them into sinful introspection: "Each member of the congregation, the most innocent girl, and the man of hardened breast, felt as if the minister had crept upon them, behind his awful veil, and discovered their hoarded iniquity of deed or thought."[7]

In the two incidents of the funeral service and the marriage Hawthorne extends the profanation of the divine office. The funeral prayer, which ought to leave the listeners with a belief that the deceased has attained the comfort of Christ, instead terrifies them: "The people trembled, though they but darkly understood him when he prayed that they, and himself, and all of mortal race, might be ready, as he trusted this young maiden had been, for the dreadful hour that should snatch the veil from their faces."[8] The corruption of the sacrament of marriage is dramatically communicated through two symbolic details. The union of man and wife, a promise of new life, instead presages death; the veil casts a shroud over the flames which consecrate the happy event: "Such was its immediate effect on the guests that a cloud seemed to have rolled duskily from beneath the black crepe, and dimmed the light of the candles." And to enhance this blasphemy Hawthorne contrives the spilling of the toast to the happiness of the wedded couple. Involving himself in the horror of the veil he wears, the minister is momentarily distraught: "His frame shuddered, his lips grew white, he spilt the untasted wine upon the carpet, and rushed forth into darkness."[9] The wine in this context, with its implicit allusion to the presence of Christ in the sacrament of marriage, is still another shocking overtone of sacrilege.

The final inversion of Paul's message to the Corinthians occurs in the parting between Mr. Hooper and Elizabeth. And here Hawthorne's addiction to name symbolism appears pertinent, since the name Elizabeth in its common biblical association means consecrated to God. This rejection of heavenly light is symbolized by darkness behind the black veil. In response to Elizabeth's exhortation, "'let the sun shine from behind the cloud,'" there is only "unconquerable obstinacy" and recourse to self-righteous piety: "'If I hide my face for sorrow, there is cause . . . and if I cover it forsecret sin, what mortal might not do the same?'"[10] Thus, scene by scene, Hawthorne exhibits Mr. Hooper's apostasy from the teachings of Christ. Not only does he invert the essence of Paul's epistle, but he also introduces various symbolic actions which enhance the degree of blasphemy. And in this dramatic exaggeration it may be said that he enjoins the reader to look askance at the minister's behavior.

This interpretive instruction becomes more insistent in the remainder of the parallel in the Corinthians as the veil and the mirror symbols converge to comment on secret sin and spiritual cowardice. The delineation of Mr. Hooper's inflexible conviction of secret sin seems consciously contrasted with Paul's stress upon the message of redemptive love in the gospels, written "with the Spirit of the living God; not in tables of stone, but in fleshly tables of the heart." Mr. Hooper's stubborn devotion to the equivalent of irredeemable natural depravity reflects "the letter [that] killeth" in scorn of "the spirit [which] giveth life." And when Paul designates the covenant which Moses sealed with God as "the ministration of death,"[11] Hawthorne's invocation of the associations of death instead of immortality and happiness at the funeral and the marriage respectively moves into clearer focus. He urges that darkness and death be taken as correlatives of the veil in contrast with the light and life which are the surrogate images of the Christian idea of salvation.

Paul is especially vehement in arguing this polarity. He reduces Moses' tables of the law to "a ministration of condemnation," not unlike the accusation of secret sin which Mr. Hooper voices. And there seems little doubt that from this point on Hawthorne's adaptation of the Corinthian text is beyond dispute. Parallel follows parallel, and the case against Mr. Hooper's piety develops into an indictment of the betrayal of Christ. Paul, for instance, declares that Moses indirectly acknowledged the transitory glory of the old covenant when he "put a veil over his face, that the children of Israel could not steadfastly look to the end of that which is abolished,"[12] that is, accept with their hearts the belief that they were the chosen people. Hawthorne's apparent adaptation of this act is charged with savage irony. For when Mr. Hooper affects the veil, he symbolically undermines the dispensation of the new covenant of Christ, denying as it were the doctrine of salvation. Inadvertently he commits heresy! And as Paul next ridicules the concealment of Moses as the opposite of the way the followers of Christ receive his message, "written in [their] hearts, known and read of all men," so Hawthorne introduces the same thought into his fictional narrative. Mr. Hooper's equivocations on the authority of his pronouncements of secret sin reflect deadened spiritual perceptions. He is like the doubtful Israelites whose "minds were blinded, for until this day remaineth the same veil untaken away in the reading of the old testament; which *veil* is done away in Christ. But even unto this day, when Moses is read, the veil is upon their heart."[13] Of course, Mr. Hooper's position is even more sacrilegious. In the name of Christianity, he preaches the penal code of Moses, entirely forgetting the message of love in the new covenant. This interpretation is really not extreme when considered in the light of Hawthorne's constant affirmation of the heart as a symbol of redemptive love. Indeed, one is compelled to consider the black veil a satanic mask: a symbol of denial.

This conclusion is strengthened by a Corinthian reference which Hawthorne seems to invert: "But we all, with open face beholding as in a glass the glory of the Lord, are changed into the same image from glory to glory, *even* as by the Spirit of the Lord."[14] On two different occasions he invokes the mirror symbol to illustrate Mr. Hooper's contempt for spiritual candor. Its usage parallels Paul's earlier warning to the Corinthians that they must not pervent the Christian gift of love, "Lest Satan should get an advantage" over them.[15] At the wedding the minister is frightened by the image of his veiled face: ". . . catching a glimpse of his figure in the looking-glass, the black veil involved his own spirit in the horror with which it overwhelmed all others."[16] Blackness here again is opposed to light, and is a symbol of the antichrist: "But if our gospel be hid, it is hid to them that are lost: In whom the god of this world hath blinded the minds of them which believe not, lest the light of the glorious gospel of Christ, who is the image of God, should shine unto them."[17] In Hawthorne's next observation Mr. Hooper's obsessive fear of reflecting surfaces is once more designed to enforce the latter's inability to practice his faith with unbared face in the spirit of Paul's injunction: Mr. Hooper's "antipathy to the veil was known to be so great, that he never willingly passed before a mirror, nor stooped to drink at a still fountain."[18] Ultimately Hawthorne leaves no doubt that he encourages an identification of the black veil with the devil: "It was said that ghost and fiend consorted with him there."[19] He implies that the minister's fear of the black veil is a fear of the devil with whom he refuses to cope. Instead he cowardly skulks behind it, unwittingly conspiring with the devil to authorize the subordination of good to evil. This corruption of his holy office radically contrasts, not only with Paul's message, but also with Hawthorne's various speculations on the psychology of evil, **"Young Goodman Brown"** serving as a notable secular parallel to the predicament of Mr. Hooper.

The final scene of the story, ending with the minister's violent rebuke of the colleague who urges him to "'cast aside this black veil . . .!'"[20] represents Hawthorne's portrayal of a man "walking in craftiness . . . handling the word of God deceitfully."[21] For the sentiment he expresses contradicts the Christian watchword that "where the Spirit of the Lord *is,* there *is* liberty."[22] He indulges only in negative recriminations, lifting his voice in a thundering denial of the love of God: "'When the friend shows his inmost heart to his friend; the lover to his best beloved; when man does not vainly shrink from the eye of his creator, loathesomely treasuring up the secret of his sin; then deem me a monster. . . . I look around me, and, lo, on every visage a Black Veil!'"[23] The irony of this statement is quite apparent. What Mr. Hooper perceives on the faces of the spectators is a shadow of his own veil. The darkness which envelops his heart blinds him to the meaning of Christian love, even though it now attends him in the person of Elizabeth, who as before noted is a symbol of consecration to God. With a distrust of the power of redemptive love, human or divine, man virtually commits himself to the devil.

On this point Hawthorne admits of no compromise. One needs only to recall the selfless spirit of Beatrice in **"Rappaccini's Daughter"** and Georgiana in **"The Birthmark."** They are spiritual guides in the divine-human sense who sacrifice themselves in order to redeem their beloved ones. But perhaps more pertinent to this story is the saving grace of love which Rosina exercises in **"Egotism, or The Bosom Serpent."** Her name in its obvious association with the rose fosters a conventional identification with the Celestial Rose of Christian iconography and Dante's *Paradiso.* Her kiss awakens the hero from an enchantment of evil, and his heart reads the message of love. Not so with Mr. Hooper. Estranged from the woman he loves, from himself, and from the community, he dies with "the veil . . . upon [his] heart."[24]

Thus the parable of the black veil is the story of betrayal, of a man of God turned antichrist. This cannot be denied, for in the resolution of the plot Hawthorne affirms the dedication of his hero to the old covenant of God, the covenant of irresolution, of spiritual cowardice, of *glory* veiled? As this legalistic code of morality is objectified in the actions of Mr. Hooper, it plays havoc with the nobility of man which Hawthorne continually exalts in his conception of the great brotherhood of humanity. For him law is a symbol of the intellect, an attempt to reason man into a state of moral awareness. Love, on the other hand, addresses itself to the heart, forever speaking a parable of light and life—humanly and divinely.

Notes

1. Examples of two different approaches to the story may be contrasted in the two most recent studies of the author, Richard Harter Fogle's *Hawthorne's Fiction* (Norman, Okla., 1952), pp. 117-127, and William Bysshe Stein's *Hawthorne's Faust* (Gainesville, Fla., 1953), pp. 3-4, 80-81.
2. *The Best of Hawthorne,* ed. Mark Van Doren (New York, 1951), p. 421.
3. II Corinthians 2:7-17.
4. *The Complete Works of Nathaniel Hawthorne,* ed. George P. Lathrop, 12 vols. (Boston, 1883), I, 54. Italics are mine. References to Hawthorne's works are to this edition, cited only by volume and page.
5. See II Corinthians 2:17 and 4:6.
6. *Ibid.,* 4:2-4.
7. I, 55.
8. I, 58.
9. I, 59.
10. I, 61-62.
11. II Corinthians 3:3, 6, 7.
12. *Ibid.,* 3:13.
13. *Ibid.,* 3:2, 14-15.
14. *Ibid.,* 3:18.
15. *Ibid.,* 2:10-11.
16. I, 59.
17. II Corinthians 4:3-4.
18. I, 64.
19. I, 65.
20. I, 68.
21. II Corinthians 4:2.
22. *Ibid.,* 3:17.
23. I, 69.
24. II Corinthians 3:15.

Thomas F. Walsh (essay date 1959)

SOURCE: "Hawthorne: Mr. Hooper's 'Affable Weakness,'" in *Modern Language Notes,* Vol. LXXIV, No. 5, May, 1959, pp. 404-06.

[*In the following essay, Walsh maintains that the difficulty readers have in deciding whether Mr. Hooper acts as a positive or negative moral example comes from Hawthorne's careful balance of light and dark imagery.*]

Critics of Hawthorne's **"The Minister's Black Veil"** have been as fascinated by Mr. Hooper's enigmatic piece of crape as were the minister's own congregation, and, like them, have offered conflicting opinions concerning its significance. Some critics are willing to accept Mr. Hooper's own reasons for wearing it as Hawthorne's, while others prefer to find the answer in what they consider the minister's warped personality, although they fail to comprehend all the facets of that personality.[1] Building on the theory of the latter group, this paper will show that **"The Minister's Black Veil"** is a psychological study of a man whose mistaken notions about the nature of evil prompt him to attempt the salvation of his fellow men by a method which seriously endangers his own salvation: the donning of the black veil.

Mr. Hooper's deathbed remarks show that he intended the black veil to symbolize the secret sin which *all* men "loathsomely treasure up" in their hearts.[2] That he intended himself to typify mankind's evil nature is clear enough, but the reason why he thought himself evil not so clear. Nevertheless, it can be found in an examination of his character prior to wearing the veil. We learn that he was always "reckoned a melancholy man" (I, 58) whose temperament was that of "gentle gloom" (I, 55). But, more important, we learn that ". . . he had never lacked advisers, nor shown himself adverse to be guided by their judgment. If he erred at all, it was by so painful a degree of self-distrust, that even the mildest censure would lead him to consider an indifferent action as a crime" (I, 60). This self-distruct, which the author calls an "affable weakness," explains the donning of the veil, for Mr. Hooper is a man who suffers from an affliction not uncommon to men of religious sensibilities: scrupulosity. If this melancholy man can not distinguish between an indifferent action and a crime, it is not surprising that he should eventually consider all his actions crimes and himself intrinsically evil, and then, by extention, all mankind. His donning of the veil is an indication of that conviction and a symptom of his troubled soul. It is interesting to note that the minister communicates his own inability to discriminate between an indifferent action and a crime to his congregation. This is illustrated by the effect of one of his sermons: "Each member of the congregation, the most innocent girl, and the man of hardened breast, felt as if the preacher had crept upon them, behind his awful veil, and discovered their hoarded iniquity of deed and thought" (I, 55). It is one thing that he should make the truly guilty feel their guilt, but quite another to transfer his own neurotic guilt complex to the innocent, making them feel *as if* they were hoarding iniquity of deed and thought in their hearts.

But the wearing of the veil does not indicate that the minister despairs of his own and his congregation's salvation; on the contrary, it is motivated by his hope for peace of mind in the after-life: "'It is but a mortal veil—it is not for eternity!'" he tells Elizabeth, his betrothed (I, 63). In another passage we read of his "tender and heart-dissolving prayer, full of sorrow, yet . . . imbued with celestial hopes" (I, 58). But, ironically, the veil's effect on the minister is almost opposite to that which he intended.

The light-dark imagery of the tale clearly reveals what harm the veil works in Mr. Hooper's soul. For instance, one passage reads:

> Thus, from beneath the black veil, there rolled a cloud into the sunshine, . . . which enveloped the poor minister, so that love or sympathy could never reach him. . . . With self-shuddering and outward terrors, he walked in its shadow, groping darkly within his own soul, or gazing through a medium that saddened the world.
>
> (I, 65)

And another passage:

> All through life that piece of crepe had hung between him and the world: it had separated him from cheerful brotherhood and woman's love . . . and still it lay upon his face, as if to deepen the gloom of his darksome chamber, and shade him from the sunshine of eternity.
>
> (I, 67)

The images of these two passages make explicit the devastating effects of the veil. Sunshine is equated with love and sympathy, cheerful brotherhood and woman's love, and with eternity; the black veil has separated him from the former and threatens to shade him from the latter. (The sunshine image has the same significance in Elizabeth's exhortation to the minister in an earlier passage: "'Come, good sir, let the sun shine behind the cloud'.") But before we can conclude that the minister is altogether doomed, as are other characters in Hawthorne's fiction who sever themselves from the natural affections of mankind, we must take special notice of Mr. Hooper's smile.

The minister's smile is mentioned eight times and is associated with the light image. For instance, "He smiled again—that same sad smile, which always appeared like a faint glimmering of light, proceeding from the obscurity beneath the veil" (I, 62). In four passages it is described as glimmering or gleaming. It is also generally described as faint. From the smile-light association, then, we can conclude that the smile betokens the minister's tenuous ties with his fellow men and his shaky hold on his own sanity. It indicates that he has not been completely enveloped by the terrifying black veil which has multiplied his doubts about his own salvation. This conclusion becomes irresistible when we remember a most important fact about the veil: "it . . . entirely concealed his features, except the mouth and chin" (I, 53).

The veil-dark imagery is balanced against the smile-light imagery throughout the tale, and from it arises the true ambiguity of the tale: we can never be sure of the minister's final destiny because the minister is not sure of it. Hawthorne carries this ambiguity down to the last paragraph, the smile image once again balanced against the veil image: "Father Hooper fell back upon his pillow, a veiled corpse, with a faint smile lingering on the lips . . . but awful is still the thought that his face mouldered beneath the Black Veil!" (I, 69).

Certain parallels can be drawn between the characters of Mr. Hooper and Goodman Brown. Both are essentially good men and both are mistaken in their belief in the all-pervasiveness of evil, but the difference is that the latter is overwhelmed by his diabolic vision whereas the former is perhaps saved by his strong celestial aspirations. Both redound to the credit of Hawthorne's artistry, that he could create two completely distinctive psychological variations on the same theme.

Notes

1. Chester E. Eisinger in his article, "Hawthorne as Champion of the Middle Way," *NEQ,* XXVII (March, 1954), 27-52, finds Hooper's indictment "an expression of what for Hawthorne was the common fate of all men" (p. 28), and Newton Arvin calls it a "terrible truth" (*Hawthorne* [Boston, 1929], p. 60). On the other hand, Randall Stewart speaks of Mr. Hooper's "diseased self-contemplation" (*Nathaniel Hawthorne: A Biography* [New Haven, 1948], p. 256), and Richard Fogle speaks of him as a man "who severs himself from men either through perverse pride or through some tragic compulsion" (*Hawthorne's Fiction: The Light and the Dark* [Norman, Oklahoma, 1952], p. 34).
2. *The Complete Works of Nathaniel Hawthorne,* with Introductory Notes by George Parsons Lathrop (Standard Library Edition, Boston, 1883), I, 69. Subsequent reference to the tale will be made in the text.

E. Earle Stibitz (essay date 1962)

SOURCE: "Ironic Unity in Hawthorne's 'The Minister's Black Veil,'" in *American Literature,* Vol. 34, No. 2, May, 1962, pp. 182-90.

[In the following essay, Stibitz maintains that Hawthorne used irony in his portrayal of the minister's decision to wear the black veil.]

Because Hawthorne is always very much the same and yet also surprisingly varied, one way of understanding **"The Minister's Black Veil,"** as with any Hawthorne tale, is to read it not only as the unique work of art that it is, but as a tale comparable to others by Hawthorne, viewing it in the context of his essentially consistent thought and art as a whole. Such a reading of **"The Minister's Black Veil"** yields an unambiguous meaning. Hawthorne, with his usual assumption of the reality of personal evil, presents on one level his fundamental belief in man's proneness to hide or rationalize his most private thoughts or guilt. This is the "parable" (of the subtitle) that the Reverend Mr. Hooper seeks to preach with his wearing of the veil. On another level, Hawthorne reaffirms his equally constant belief that man is often guilty of pridefully and harmfully exalting one idea, frequently a valid truth in itself, to the status of an absolute. This is the sin Hooper commits by his self-righteous and self-deceptive insistence upon wearing the veil.

The second level grows out of the first and remains dependent upon it, a structural pattern repeated in varying ways in each major division of the story. Furthermore, this organic relationship of the two levels is ironic. Hooper in his stubborn use of the veil parable of one sin is unconsciously guilty of a greater one—that of egotistically warping the total meaning of life. This irony is compounded in that Hooper's sin is a hidden one—hidden not only from his fellows but from himself. He thus unintentionally dramatizes the very sin of secrecy that he intentionally sets out to symbolize. The central symbol of the veil keeps pace with this added irony: in addition to standing for man's concealment or hypocrisy and for Hooper's own sin of pride with its isolating effects, it stands also for the hidden quality of the second sin. All told, **"The Minister's Black Veil"** is less ambiguous and more unified because it is more ironic than has usually been recognized.

The interpretations various critics have made of **"The Minister's Black Veil,"** taken as a whole, offer three basic points of view. First is the interpretation that the veil indicates some specific crime by Mr. Hooper. This is Poe's view and is one concurred in by Leland Schubert and in part by R. H. Fogle, who holds that a crime by the minister remains an ambiguous possibility in the story.[1] A second view, and the one most widely held, rejects the idea of personal wrongdoing and sees the veil simply as a device chosen by the minister to dramatize a common human failing: man's refusal to show to anyone his inner heart with its likely load of private guilt. Among the critics that have subscribed to this view are Newton Arvin, Gilbert Voigt, Randall Stewart, and Mark Van Doren.[2] Some of the critics who hold generally to this view concern themselves, in addition, with the effect of the veil upon the minister.[3] The third view holds that there is something fundamentally wrong in the minister's wearing of the veil. W. B. Stein is a vigorous exponent of this view, arguing that the story is one of a man of God turned antichrist, especially in Hooper's failure to follow Paul's II Corinthians injunction to ministers to let love be the principle of the relationship with their congregations.[4] Mr. Fogle, basically representative of this view, argues for two meanings.[5] There is the explicit meaning of the veil as a symbol of man's secret sin, with Hooper as Everyman bearing his lonely fate in order to demonstrate a tragic truth; and there is the implicit one of human unbalance, with Hooper's action out of all proportion to need or benefit. The story, says Mr. Fogle, remains ambiguous with the discrepancies in meaning unresolved—albeit an effective lack of resolution. A footnote to Mr. Fogle's argument is Mr. Walsh's comment on the minister's dubious smile, a recurrent element in the story.[6] The smile, always linked with light, though consistently faint, stands in opposition to the veil, always linked with darkness, and produces, says Mr. Walsh, a fundamental ambiguity. Both Mr. Stewart and Mr. Van Doren, in general discussions of Hawthorne's tales, imply that Hooper is perhaps guilty of some spiritually wrong attitude.[7]

That Hooper is in some way in the wrong seems an inescapable conclusion from any careful reading of the story, but some qualification is called for in each of the criticisms presenting this third view. Mr. Stein's low estimate of Hooper must in general be accepted, but because of Hawthorne's humanistic emphasis in this story as well as elsewhere it is very difficult to see Hooper as an antichrist; Mr. Stein makes Hawthorne too orthodox. And the argument for the II Corinthians analogue remains speculative. What Mr. Fogle says about the minister's unbalance is valid, but perhaps less so his judgment about the meaning of the tale as a whole. Against his claim of "discrepancies," of a basic ambiguity, must be asserted the essential unity of the tale. The irony is strongly unifying, not only in tone but also in meaning. Hawthorne here is his usually detached self, but this artistic distance is not noncommittalism. In general too much has been made of Hawthorne's ambiguity in theme. Often he employs ambiguity in details and is ambiguous in total philosophy revealed, but only very rarely does ambiguity qualify a specific theme. Finally, Mr. Walsh's assumption, in his point of ambiguity in the smile-light and veil-dark imagery, that Hawthorne uses light to suggest something spiritually positive, is acceptable. But most readers will not find the smile a true smile or the light clearly light, as the faintness of the whole image makes evident; there is a peculiarly mixed quality about the smile itself—indeed something ironic.

The ironic meaning of **"The Minister's Black Veil"** is incorporated in and, in part, is created by its vertical or logical structure. Out of the first level of meaning, the calling of attention to the truth of man's proneness to the sin of concealment, rises the second level, the minister's sin in making his veil demonstration all-important; and this second level, with its irony, absorbs the first, creating a dominant theme.[8] An analysis that seeks to offer evidence of this unity of form and meaning can best be presented by following the horizontal or chronological structure of the tale—the successive divisions of its narrative development. Narrative sequence and timing are very important here and have usually been neglected in the religious and philosophical discussions of the story. There are five divisions: (1) the first appearance of Hooper wearing the veil at the Sunday morning service; (2) Hooper's appearances at the funeral and at the wedding on the same Sunday; (3) the unsuccessful effort of a deputation from the congregation, and of Elizabeth, his financée, to reason with him about the veil; (4) a summary picture of Hooper's life from the time of these efforts to his death; (5) the deathbed scene. In each of these divisions the two levels of meaning are ironically united to produce a singleness of theme.

At the beginning of the first division the minister is revealed as experiencing a twofold alienation—from man and from God. Because of the strange veil the members of the congregation sense the minister's distance, and he, in turn, sees them darkly. Also the veil comes between him and God as he reads the Scripture and as he prays. That Hooper's estrangement is the first point established in the story suggests the central importance of the minister's second-level sin. In Hawthorne, isolation of one kind or another is consistently presented as the result of sin, and at times as being something very close to sin itself, a sin frequently linked with intellectual or spiritual pride. Here Hooper's alienation argues that the wearing of the veil is in some way profoundly wrong. And under this second level of meaning lies the more briefly developed first level, the veil as the symbol of hidden guilt, which is introduced by the sermon with its condemnation of secret sin.

Not only are the two levels thus established but so also is their ironic relationship. While the one sin is consciously preached (through veil parable and sermon), the second sin is unconsciously embodied (through the minister's egotistic assumptions and actions). Emphasis is upon the minister's pride that leads him to make the truth of man's hypocrisy the only Truth and brings him to force his idea upon the consciousness and conscience of his congregation. For example, though the sermon is supposedly praised as one of the most powerful that the minister has preached, the minister himself is described as creeping upon the members of the congregation behind his awful veil and discovering the hoarded iniquity of each one. In this, Hooper is close to Hawthorne's most damning sin—"the human invasion of the sanctity of the human heart," to use Dimmesdale's description of Chillingworth's sin. That Hooper is acting professionally increases rather than lessens the sin, for as a minister he should have been spiritually more sensitive. Indeed he is like a number of other Hawthorne sinners who ". . . in their attempt to assume the role of God . . . naturally give their allegiance to Satan, and subsequently find themselves contributing to that very imperfection which they had originally wished to eliminate."[9] The irony here is heightened in that the spiritual wrongdoing pictured by the minister in his sermon describes precisely what he is soon guilty of—hiding his sin "from his nearest and dearest, and from his own consciousness."

In the second division, two contrasting yet representative events of life, a funeral and a wedding, dramatize the meaning of the veil on both levels with their continuing ironic tension. At the funeral, the veil for the only time in the story is a truly appropriate emblem. Apart from its somberness it is appropriate (if we accept the idea of the minister's prayer) because the truth of human secretiveness is one that human beings most fully realize when they are confronted with death. Yet even now the incidents that Poe believed linked the minister with the dead girl in some specific crime—for example, his fear that she will see his face—indicate that the wearing of the veil is not entirely right. As often, Hawthorne uses such ambiguous details to enrich the meaning and heighten the tone of the narrative rather than to establish its main direction. These details underscore the meaning already revealed by emphasizing the unnaturalness of Hooper's action, and they heighten the tone by pointing up the ironic discrepancy between the supposedly helpful intent of the minister and the actual spiritual result.

The unbalance of Hooper in his isolation from normal life and love is strongly in evidence at the wedding, where his wearing of the veil brings fear and doubt, a markedly different effect from the feeling of quiet cheerfulness and sympathy he formerly evoked on such occasions. Hooper's use of the veil to instruct his parishioners religiously has resulted in their spiritual impoverishment in that human love has been diminished. To Hawthorne this is a loss of something holy, for throughout his writings the acceptance or rejection of human love usually marks the choice of salvation or damnation. Mr. Hooper faces this choice and is damned by choosing to live by an idea rather than by human love. His unrepentant insistence upon his abstracted idea as central to life violates the warm reality of human existence.

The irony of Hooper's action is humorously symbolized by the prank of the village youngster who in imitation of the minister puts a black handkerchief over his face and so frightens his playmates that he creates a panic in his own mind. The presence of this satiric element, comparable to the dog's chasing its tail in **"Ethan Brand,"** indicates that Hawthorne has a definite point of view and does not intend the story to be ultimately ambiguous. The two levels of meaning are not allowed to stand in uncommitted balance; ironic tension unites them, the first being subsumed into the second.[10]

In the third division, the story comes to its climax with the two futile attempts to break through the wall of isolation that the minister has erected, one attempt by members of the congregation, the other by Elizabeth, his fiancée. Although the two-level irony is present in each of these efforts, the first underscores more the validity of the veil symbol as intended by the minister, the second, the fact of his sin in making the veil idea all important. Even though Mr. Hooper, heretofore, has been almost too amenable to congregational advice, a deputation of parishioners fails in its mission to question him about the veil. Feeling its symbolic truth, the visitors sit speechless before him, aware that his glance goes into their guilty hearts. But as before with the sermon the effect is less than good, for the minister's attitude and action are essentially unkind. It is not the parishioners' guilt alone that alienates them, for we are told that the minister's veil hung down over his heart. Hooper has changed from exhibiting too great submissiveness to displaying an opposite unbalance, the stubbornness of an essentially weak person obsessed with an idea.

In the succeeding scene, Hooper's response to Elizabeth's questions about the veil and his resistance to her pleas to lay it aside constitute a rejection of her love. Her patient efforts to draw him from his vow to wear the veil as a "type and symbol" meet his gentle but insurmountable obstinacy. In Hawthorne, as suggested earlier, the way to salvation is most frequently the acceptance of human love. Hooper fails to take this way. And his reaction to Elizabeth's tears reveals the sharp irony of his attitude, for it is not the hidden-sin meaning of the veil that causes her grief and terror, as he egocentrically thinks, but the rejection of her love and the irredeemable alienation demonstrated by his refusal, even for a moment, to lift the veil.

Hawthorne's description of the minister as gentle, melancholy, and sad and the quiet style of the story throughout tend to hide the fact that we are face to face with an unbalanced and unredeemed sinner. Although Hawthorne does not dwell upon the antecedent cause of Hooper's "fall," some elements of causation are evident and help to illuminate his character and clarify the irony of the tale. The minister is shown as an essentially weak man, poorly prepared by his unmarried solitude, his somewhat morbid temperament, and his professional position to deal in a stable way with an absorbing religious idea that harmonizes with his personal and vocational prejudices. He finds false strength in a kind of fanaticism, which strength destroys him as a balanced human being.

The fourth and penultimate division of the story offers chiefly the results of the events and attitudes already presented, with the ironic pattern of the previous divisions repeated. Here on the dominant second level is the minister's continued isolation, with the veil as a sign of his peculiar sin; on the first level is the account of his work as a minister, with the veil as a valid symbol of the general sin of human duplicity.

Hooper continues to stand abnormally alone in the community. The veil so envelops him with a cloud of sin or sorrow that neither love nor sympathy can reach him, and he fumbles obscurely within his own heart. But the veil also has the supposedly good result of making him an effective minister by enabling him to enter into the dark emotions of agonized sinners. Still this ability is a dubious good, and the terms "efficient" and "awful power," used to describe the minister's spiritual work, are not entirely flattering. Nor is it praise when the author speaks of the terror rather than consolation that Hooper brings to sinners who come to him for help. His awareness of the truth of hidden sin and sorrow ought to enable him not just to enter the lives of his parishioners but to enter comfortingly; however, when with evident irony he egocentrically insists upon the mechanics of the veil, he largely destroys this good potentiality.

The final division of the story, the account of Hooper's death, continues the ironic and unifying relationship of the two levels of meaning. Quantitatively the emphasis is again upon the second level, for of about a thousand words all except a hundred or so are used to picture the minister's intractability in wearing the veil on into death. Organically, this is the emphasis, too, for the irony of his action while depending upon the hidden-sin aspect so absorbs it that the story as it comes to a close is unambiguously one. Although various persons, including Elizabeth, attend Hooper's dying moments, he is spiritually alone. Hawthorne leaves little doubt that this loneliness is the result of the minister's unbalanced action; an idea has supplanted life and love: "All through life that piece of crape has hung between him and the world; it has separated him from cheerful brotherhood and woman's love, and kept him in that saddest of all prisons, his own heart; and still it lay upon his face, as to deepen the gloom of the darksome Chamber, and shade him from the sunshine of eternity." In these closing moments of his life, his monomania is so powerful that even amid his convulsive struggles and amid the wanderings of his mind he is desperately careful to keep the veil over his face. And it is still upon his face when he is buried, a token of his final lack of repentance.

Particularly demonstrative of the ironic union of the two levels of meaning is Hooper's delayed defense of his wearing the veil by saying that everyone around him has on his own black veil. The veil is no longer merely a symbol of the fact of hidden sin or sorrow, but it is also, more dominantly, a symbol of Mr. Hooper's prideful adherence to a destructive idea—the sin of a spiritual egotism that enables him to see the mote in another's eye and blinds him to the beam in his own. The irony has become even more complex than this, for things have gone full circle, and added to the double symbolism is the fact that the veil now stands for a new *hidden* sin. Actually, by focusing attention, including the minister's own concern, on the general sin of human concealment the veil has made effective the hiding of the more important personal sin. For the reader of Hawthorne's story, of course, the veil is now the means of communicating the total irony of the minister's action and of establishing the single meaning that the author wishes to convey.

Notes

1. Poe's review of Hawthorne's *Twice-Told Tales, The Complete Works of Edgar Allan Poe,* ed. James A. Harrison (New York, 1902), XI, III; Schubert, *Hawthorne the Artist: Fine Art Devices in Fiction* (Chapel Hill, 1944), p. 165; Fogle, *Hawthorne's Fiction: The Light and the Dark* (Norman, Okla., 1952), p. 36.
2. Arvin, *Hawthorne* (Boston, 1929), p. 60; Stewart, *The American Notebooks by Nathaniel Hawthorne* (New Haven, 1932), p. xlviii; Voigt, "The Meaning of 'The Minister's Black Veil,'" *College English,* XIII, 337-338 (March, 1952); Van Doren, *Nathaniel Hawthorne* (New York, 1949), p. 87.
3. For example, George Edward Woodberry, *Nathaniel Hawthorne* (New York, 1902), p. 145, and R. R. Male, *Hawthorne's Tragic Vision* (Austin, 1957), p. 17, both of whom note the effect of isolation coupled with that of a shared sense of sin.
4. William Bysshe Stein, "The Parable of the Antichrist in 'The Minister's Black Veil,'" *American Literature,* XXVII, 386-392 (Nov., 1955).

5. Fogle, *Hawthorne's Fiction,* Chapter 3.
6. Thomas Walsh, "Hawthorne: Mr. Hooper's 'Affable Weakness,'" *Modern Language Notes,* LXXIV, 404-406 (May, 1959).
7. Stewart, *Nathaniel Hawthorne: A Biography* (New Haven, 1958), pp. 256-258; Van Doren, *The Best of Hawthorne* (New York, 1951), p. 11. The present view of each of these critics represents an alteration of that in an earlier analysis.
8. Robert Stanton points out that Hawthorne in his four major romances used irony almost exclusively to carry a share of the theme ("Dramatic Irony in Hawthorne's Romances," *Modern Language Notes,* LXXI, 420, June, 1956). See also Robert Allen Durr, "Hawthorne's Ironic Mode," *New England Quarterly,* XXX, 486-495 (Dec., 1957); Durr shows, though not in "The Minister's Black Veil," that Hawthorne is most effectively serious when most deliberately ironic.
9. James E. Miller, Jr., "Hawthorne and Melville: The Unpardonable Sin," *PMLA,* LXX, 93 (March, 1955). Miller's catalogue of Hawthorne's unpardonable sinners does not include Hooper.
10. Cf. Chester E. Eisinger's comment: "To unroll a series of antithetical statements and maintain them in balance by the very tension they themselves generate is typical of Hawthorne's complex and suggestive technique" ("Hawthorne as Champion of the Middle Way," *New England Quarterly,* XXVII, 34-35, March, 1954). It is appropriate to mention here that in a brief comment on "The Minister's Black Veil" Mr. Eisinger approaches the idea of the tale as ironic. He states that paradoxically the minister's "idiosyncratic aberration reveals the universal truth" of the ambiguity and the irresistible power of sin (*ibid.,* pp. 28-29).

Nicholas Canaday, Jr. (essay date 1967)

SOURCE: "Hawthorne's Minister and the Veiling Deceptions of Self," in *Studies in Short Fiction,* Vol. IV, No. 2, Winter, 1967, pp. 135-42.

[*In the following essay, Canaday insists that "The Minister's Black Veil" is not about secret sin so much as it is about "the sin of pride with its demoniac pretensions and inhuman results."*]

Critics have treated the sin of the Reverend Mr. Hooper in **"The Minister's Black Veil"** with a kind of tentativeness not observed in the general critical view of many of Hawthorne's other major characters.[1] That the author's severe moral judgment of Mr. Hooper has never been sufficiently emphasized may be owing not alone to the subtlety of the portrait but also to the brevity of the tale and to the limited cast of characters. The result is that Mr. Hooper is seen in less breadth, though not less depth, than, for example, Arthur Dimmesdale. The rich tapestry of *The Scarlet Letter* pictures complexities of the human soul that can only be suggested in the tale.

"The Minister's Black Veil" has a more exclusively theological base than *The Scarlet Letter,* and thus while it gains in profundity, it loses a measure of universality. In this tale, Hawthorne focuses on man's hypocrisy, specifically that extension of hypocrisy that Reinhold Niebuhr terms the "veiling deceptions" of self.[2] The self as deceiver is constantly engaged in a desperate effort to deceive others with a veil of pretension—whether, indeed, a pretension to respectability, goodness, or even holiness—so that the self as deceiver may gain an ally against the self as deceived. Inevitably the ally of public respect can only be a temporary assuagement of anguish, scarcely of use to the self in believing a deception that the self—as author of the deception—cannot itself believe. This veil of pretension is the result of human hypocrisy, and Mr. Hooper has seen this fact of spiritual life in the members of his congregation and within himself before the tale begins. Upon this general theological base rests the allegory of Mr. Hooper's career.[3]

Yet the broad theological assumption is not the focus of Hawthorne's allegory. It is Mr. Hooper's act of donning the veil, with its ethical and theological results, that is of central thematic concern. Mr. Hooper's awareness of the veiling deceptions of all men has put him in a state of tension that he finds unbearable, and Hawthorne is dramatizing the unhappy results that ensue when Mr. Hooper attempts to ease the tension in the wrong way. Having seen the futility of achieving public respect when self-respect is lacking. Mr. Hooper's response is satanic, motivated by despair and pride.[4] Since it is man's fate to wear a veil, he determines that his will be a real one. With diabolical irony, he mocks himself and his God. Mr. Hooper puts on a real veil to represent (to his congregation, ultimately) the veiling deceptions of all humans and to serve notice (to his God) that he both understands and dares to resent his human condition. Pride is the chief motivation for his act. His veil is visible and tangible and thus superior to the veils all men wear. And so that he will remain intellectually superior to others, pride demands that he merely hint at the meaning of the emblem during his lifetime, reveal it as he expires. He correctly anticipates the consternation his act will cause.[5] The act results in an increasing isolation from fellow man and a growing inhumanity, even cruelty, toward others. Viewed theologically, the results are even more disastrous: the veiling is a conscious and willful act that not only strengthens his pride but also, because it gives him what he believes is a new and superior perspective on human life, results in still another self-deception.

The immediate response of Mr. Hooper's congregation on that first Sunday he wears the veil is one of amazement and confusion. The veil is a barrier between them and their pastor, and his isolation begins at this point. As he prays, the minister's new isolation from God is also revealed: "Did he seek to hide it [his countenance] from the dread Being whom he was addressing?"[6] An estrangement begins here and persists throughout Mr. Hooper's life. One notes that the life of Hester Prynne in *The Scarlet Letter* parallels his in this regard. Her spiritual isolation continues to the end of her life, but like Mr. Hooper she is re-integrated into the community life within a relatively brief time. He becomes by the end of his life the revered Father Hooper. What Hawthorne writes about him applies with equal accuracy to Hester: "Mr. Hooper spent a long life, irreproachable in outward act, yet shrouded in dismal suspicions; kind and loving, though unloved, and dimly feared; a man apart from men, shunned in their health and joy, but ever summoned to their aid in mortal anguish" (I, 66). Both characters redeem themselves in the eyes of mankind, though there are similar reservations in each case; and after their early aberration the townspeople give both a special place in the life of the community, the differences arising solely from Mr. Hooper's position as a clergyman, though even here Hester's role as nurse and confidante is parallel. But as with Hester it is the outward act that is irreproachable; inside there is prideful superiority. Hawthorne's comment on the acceptance of Hester by the people also may serve as a gloss on the status of the venerable Father Hooper: "Society was inclined to show its former victim a more benign countenance than she cared to be favored with, or, perchance, than she deserved" (V, 196).

Mr. Hooper's sermon on the Sunday he first wears the black veil takes secret sin as its subject. The choice of the subject matter does not indicate that he has in mind a specific secret sin of his own, but rather reflects his concern on this momentous day with the veils of deception by which men in general hide their sins and keep them secret. Hawthorne describes the sermon in general terms: "The subject had reference to secret sin, and those sad mysteries which we hide from our nearest and dearest, and would fain conceal from our own consciousness, even forgetting that the Omniscient can detect them" (I, 55). The phrase "would fain conceal from our own consciousness" reveals Hawthorne's understanding of the tension between the self as deceiver and the self as deceived, and the "forgetting that the Omniscient can detect" the sins is, of course, only a momentary forgetting. In short, Mr. Hooper's sermon is motivated and informed by an insight that he has had into the nature of all men by the simple device of examining himself. Unfortunately, the import of the sermon is obscured by the black veil. The effect of the sermon is great, but it is due to the veil and not to the words; its effect is emotional and not intellectual. Mr. Hooper has found a new power to move his congregation, but it is made clear throughout the tale that they never understand him. Something "in the sentiment of the discourse itself, or in the imagination of the auditors" (*Ibid.*), now moves his congregation. The black veil affords his sermon a powerful emotional aura but at the same time obscures its essential meaning.

The obscurity is deliberate and effective. As if to re-emphasize the function of the black veil as barrier to effective communication, Hawthrone puts the final comment on Mr. Hooper's appearance in the mouth of the self-confessed "sober-minded" man of the village, typically the physician. This sage observes: "Something must surely be amiss with Mr. Hooper's intellects" (I, 57). The physician is speaking about the minister's act of donning the veil, and that he makes no reference to the sermon itself indicates that even the more intellectual members of the community have responded only emotionally.

When Mr. Hooper disappears into the parsonage at the end of his first veiled appearance in church, "a sad smile gleamed faintly from beneath the black veil" (I, 56). At this point one might take the smile to indicate fondness; it is soon revealed as diabolical. The melancholy smile is referred to seven more times during the course of the tale: once when he receives the delegation of parishioners, three times in the important central scene with Elizabeth, once as he contemplates the rumors that the veil has given him supernatural powers, once on his deathbed just before he pronounces his final moralizing statement about the veils of men in general, and finally as it lingers on his corpse lying in the coffin. The import of this smile, which is condescending and self-satisfied, is crucial as a symbol of his spiritual pride. Roger Chillingworth's smile of self-irony, mentioned twice in the opening scene of *The Scarlet Letter,* and the constant presence of the same smile during his first interview with Hester in Chapter IV are an effective gloss on Mr. Hooper's smile. Hawthorne describes Chillingworth's smile as "a smile of dark and self-relying intelligence" (V, 97). Therefore, I do not agree with the reading of Thomas F. Walsh that Mr. Hooper's smile is ambiguous in the sense that it "betokens the minister's tenuous ties with his fellow men and his shaky hold on his own sanity."[7] Walsh bases his reading on the *smile-light* association, the smile frequently gleaming or glimmering in contrast to the enveloping blackness of the veil. But again we may profitably go to *The Scarlet Letter* in order to understand this imagery. Hawthorne does something very similar when at the end of the novel he describes the meaning of the heraldic device of the tombstone: the "sombre" legend is "relieved by one ever-glowing point of light gloomier than the shadow" (V, 312). Viewed theologically, the scarlet of passion is gloomier than its Puritan environment, just as Mr. Hooper's smile, though a glimmer of light, is gloomier than the black veil. Hawthorne seems fond of this paradox.

At the moments when he smiles, Mr. Hooper is deceiving himself into believing that he has resolved the tension of his warring self. In the first instance he is bidding farewell to his congregation, proudly perceiving the consternation he has wrought. An ambiguity is possible here: it could be sympathy. But in the second instance a delegation of parishioners has assembled "to make the black veil a subject of friendly remonstrance" (I, 60). Yet the black veil itself intimidates them, and Mr. Hooper speaks not a word. In this tense scene some overt word of sympathy from their pastor is what they require, but they perceive only the melancholy smile. This and later references to the smile consistently indicate Mr. Hooper's pride in a new superiority he feels over ordinary human beings because of his black veil. The view from behind the veil gives Mr. Hooper what he believes to be an absolute perspective on life, but central to Hawthorne's allegory is the author's recognition that finite man can never achieve such a view. The act of donning the veil has thus resulted in further sin: the failure of Mr. Hooper to recognize the finiteness in his new perspective, the pride that accompanies this lack of recognition, and the cruelty that accompanies the pride.

Mr. Hooper's first call to pastoral duty after he has donned the black veil occurs that first Sunday afternoon when he must officiate at the funeral service of a young lady. This scene serves to show the increasing isolation of Mr. Hooper from his flock and affords him the opportunity to hint further at the meaning of the black veil. As he bends over the corpse and his features are momentarily disclosed by the swinging veil, did the corpse shudder? Hawthorne points out that only one person, "a superstitious old woman" (I, 58), so testified. This detail simply reinforces the idea of the emotional response that the veil has engendered in the people. And the people are impressed by his prayer: "The people trembled, though they but darkly understood him when he prayed that they, and himself, and all of mortal race, might be ready, as he trusted this young maiden had been, for the dreadful hour that should snatch the veil from their faces" (*Ibid.*). Again the impression the prayer makes is emotional; they tremble, but they understand only darkly. The universal significance of the veil is only hinted, and there is pride in Mr. Hooper's gnostical attitude.

The wedding scene that follows the same night is the last episode of the first day. The funeral had been a time of grief; now there is a time of joy. At the funeral, Mr. Hooper did nothing to assuage the grief of his parishioners, as his pastoral duty would require; and at the wedding he effectively spoils the joy of the occasion. Hawthorne links these two scenes, putting them in close proximity, in order to show Mr. Hooper's inhumanity in the widest possible spectrum of normal relationships to his congregation. The whisper that "the maiden who had been buried a few hours before was come from her grave to be married" (I, 59) reflects once again the emotional impact of the black veil while at the same time showing how the joy of the wedding was dispelled by Mr. Hooper's presence. When the minister catches a glimpse of his own veil in the wine glass, he shudders with horror, spills the wine, and rushes away. From that moment "the black veil involved his own spirit in the horror with which it overwhelmed all others" (*Ibid.*). Essentially this is a moment when Mr. Hooper sees that he has redoubled his own sin, a moment of self-transcendence when he sees both the sinful nature of the act and the results of it.

Once having established the conflict between Mr. Hooper and his congregation resulting from the wearing of the veil, Hawthorne next turns to a more personal and intimate relationship, that between the minister and his intended bride. It is with Elizabeth that Hawthorne shows the black veil to have its most serious consequences: the violation of a human heart. As Elizabeth comes to him, she is the "one person in the village unappalled by the awe with which the black veil has impressed all beside herself" (I, 61). She asks him to put aside his veil and, failing that, to tell her why he wears it. His smile glimmers faintly as he answers: "There is an hour to come . . . when all of us shall cast aside our veils" (*Ibid.*). Such an answer is unintelligible to Elizabeth, although it hints again at the veiling deceptions of all mankind. Mr. Hooper's pride demands that he do no more than hint. That he smiles before he gives the answer warns the reader that he will be deceptive. Elizabeth then asks him to explain his words, and he replies that "this veil is a type and symbol" (I, 62). Even in that explanation he reveals his pride. The veil is typical of the veils that all men wear and (in his mind) superior because it is a conscious, concrete embodiment of this veiling impulse. So it becomes also, in more general terms and unrecognized by Mr. Hooper, a symbol of the pride of the evil will. Elizabeth, misunderstanding because deliberately misled, assumes it to be a symbol of some grievous and secret affliction. "If it be a sign of mourning," Mr. Hooper continues, "I, perhaps, like most other mortals, have sorrows dark enough to be typified by a black veil" (*Ibid.*). The *if* clause deliberately deceives, as does his statement that follows, again preceded by the same smile: "If I hide my face for sorrow, there is cause enough, . . . and if I cover it for secret sin, what mortal might not do the same?" (*Ibid.*). His real reason is contained in none of these speculations.

Elizabeth represents the norm of human wholeness and love in the story. Her love even transcends the human when it becomes self-sacrificing. In character she is the superior of Mr. Hooper: "Though of a firmer character than his own, the tears rolled down her cheeks" (I, 63). Finally, the "terrors" (*Ibid.*) of the black veil overcome her, and she cannot speak. Her response is stronger than that of the others (terror, not horror) because she is closer to this man; and in a flash of insight she sees the veil truly as a symbol of his own weakness and sin, a symptom of a deep spiritual disease. Her response contains understanding as well as strong emotion. She will not speak of this response, though he specifically asks her how she is affected, and the minister momentarily despairs in his loneliness. After this brief moment of self-transcendence, however, he soon smiles again "to think that only a material emblem had separated him from happiness, though the horrors which it shadowed forth, must be drawn darkly between the fondest of lovers" (I, 63-64). Again he is secretly pleased with the effect of the black veil, failing to see in his ignorance that Elizabeth fears for him and that it is his sin, not his emblem, that has in fact separated him from happiness.

Mr. Hooper spends the rest of his life isolated from human love and sympathy, though Elizabeth remains faithful through all of his life and at the end nurses him on his deathbed. His antipathy to mirrors or the reflecting surface of water becomes well known. He is frightened when he himself sees the black veil. And the antipathy "was what gave plausibility to the whispers, that Mr. Hooper's conscience tortured him for some great crime too horrible to be entirely concealed, or otherwise than so obscurely intimated" (I, 64-65). But this reason is founded only on rumor. Mr. Hooper is frightened not because of a secret sin in his past but because the veil, when he can see its reflection, reminds him of the awful sin embodied in the act of donning the veil. Now he becomes a more effective preacher: he has more power. What this means is that he has a new power to evoke an emotional response of horror in his congregation that they in their ignorance mistake for a powerful spirituality. At the end of the tale Hawthorne summarizes the results of Mr. Hooper's act: "All through life that piece of crape had hung between him and the world: it had separated him from cheerful brotherhood and woman's love, and kept him in the saddest of all prisons, his own heart." (I, 67)

At the end of his life Mr. Hooper pridefully reveals his so-called motive for donning the black veil, that it typifies the veiling deceptions of all men. In his famous comment on this story, Poe rightly calls this speech "the moral put into the mouth of the dying minister" and correctly sees that this overt moral is not "the true import of the narrative."[8] Yet the true import escapes Poe. Hawthorne is not stressing secret sin in this tale, especially sexual sin as Poe suggests. Rather he is exploring the sin of pride with its demoniac pretensions and inhuman results. The misguided minister, aware of the finiteness of the human condition, yet daring to resent it, seeks to compensate for it and thus to overcome it. With satanic irony Mr. Hooper dons the veil in order to gain an absolute perspective on life. The final irony is Hawthorne's, for whom the veil must symbolize the imperfect human vision, which, because of the finiteness of the human condition, sees only darkly.

Notes

1. An excellent summary of the criticism of this tale is provided by E. Earle Stibitz, "Ironic Unity in Hawthorne's 'The Minister's Black Veil,'" *American Literature,* XXXIV (May 1962), 183-184. Not included is the reading of Robert W. Cochran, "Hawthorne's Choice: The Veil or the Jaundiced Eye," *College English,* XXIII (February 1962), 342-346, which sees Mr. Hooper as achieving a steady acceptance of life and the ultimate in human knowledge. Cochran's reading, which he correctly describes as at sharp variance with the consensus, is, I believe, mistaken.
2. *The Nature and Destiny of Man* (New York, 1946), p. 207.
3. Mr. Hooper has an awareness, before the beginning of the story, that Arthur Dimmesdale achieves only near the end of *The Scarlet Letter.* Dimmesdale's act of stripping away all veiling deception and revealing his naked self to the people and to God cannot renew a debilitated body, but it restores the spiritual vitality of his soul.
4. William B. Stein, "The Parable of the Antichrist in 'The Minister's Black Veil,'" *American Literature,* XXVII (November 1955), 390, correctly points to the satanic denial of love in the minister's act, but I believe that Mr. Hooper sees more than merely "a shadow of his own veil" (p. 392) on the faces of his people.
5. In the central chapter of *The Scarlet Letter,* "The Minister's Vigil," we observe Arthur Dimmesdale on the scaffold at midnight having a vision of how it would be should he remain there until morning. He too is thinking of the consternation he would create among his parishioners. Each minister is concerned with his public image even as he proclaims his own sin; and because of the element of pride unmistakably present, we know that true repentance is still in the future.
6. *The Complete Works of Nathaniel Hawthorne,* George P. Lathrop, ed. (Boston, 1883), I, 54. All subsequent page references to this edition will be made parenthetically in my text.
7. "Hawthorne: Mr. Hooper's 'Affable Weakness,'" *Modern Language Notes,* LXXIV (May 1959), 406. E. E. Stibitz, with whose previously cited essay I am in general agreement, accepts Walsh's assumption of ambiguity but stresses its ironic element.
8. *The Works of Edgar Allan Poe,* John H. Ingram, ed. (London, 1899), IV, 218.

W. B. Carnochan (essay date 1969)

SOURCE: "'The Minister's Black Veil': Symbol, Meaning, and the Context of Hawthorne's Art," in *Nineteenth-Century Fiction,* Vol. 24, No. 2, September, 1969, pp. 182-92.

[In the following essay, Carnochan contends that "The Minister's Black Veil" is concerned mostly with the literary nature of symbols, and that questions about Mr. Hooper's moral character would be viewed by Hawthorne as comparatively trivial.]

"The Minister's Black Veil," one of Hawthorne's early tales (1836), has a reputation as one of his best. It has had less attention than, say, **"Rappaccini's Daughter"** or **"My Kinsman, Major Molineux,"** no doubt because it is in some ways less problematic and is a less bravura piece than are they. Still the story presents its own kind of difficulties, and there is no critical unanimity among its readers. On one view the Reverend Mr. Hooper is a saintly figure, calling his people to repentance in the manner of an old testament prophet;[1] on another view he is a victim of monomaniac obsession, one of Hawthorne's unpardonable sinners or, even, a type of antichrist.[2] Between these extremes, opinion shades off to a less monochromatic center.[3] But interpretation of the story generally rests on some moral assessment or explanation of the minister's symbolic self-veiling. The mystery is conceived as one to be *solved,* just as Poe conceived it when he argued that the minister had committed a "crime of dark dye" against the "young lady" whose burial is described.[4] What Poe calls a defect—"that to the rabble its exquisite skill will be *caviare*"—he surely thinks a virtue: he is happy in the discovery of concealed evidence, from which he infers a romantic solution more congenial to his taste than the merely generalized didacticism of the "moral" that the minister pronounces at his death. I shall argue, to the contrary, that neither solutions, like Poe's, nor moral estimates, like many a critic's and even the minister's own, are essential.[5] The story, I believe, is concerned above all with the veil as a symbolic object, pointing toward questions that cluster about the notion of a symbol itself. Beside these questions the moral character of the minister who wears the veil is relatively a minor matter.

If so, this early story has a more important place than it is usually given in Hawthorne's canon: like *The Scarlet Letter*—which is *about* the letter of its title, just as this story is about the veil—**"The Minister's Black Veil"** has to do with the materials of Hawthorne's own art in proportion as it has to do with the nature of symbolic meaning. Thinking about this story, we need to remember all the while the abortive history of Hawthorne's last romances and the altogether desolate end of his literary life—where we get, as Hyatt H. Waggoner has said, "no merely technical failure, and no turning to new subjects that he did not know how to handle, but a failure at the very center, a failure of meaning."[6] This failure of meaning is a failure of the symbolic process: the relationship, always for Hawthorne a difficult matter, between symbol and reference breaks down entirely, and the course of his artistic life can be roughly plotted in terms of this disintegration.[7] **"The Minister's Black Veil"** stakes out the ground on which Hawthorne was to struggle with the angel of destruction.

Even to ask the bald question, "What does the veil stand for?" implies the difficulty of giving any answer. Perhaps it is just as well, however, to frame the question in a way that makes the difficulties apparent. In any case, the Hawthornian business of false leads and doubtful clarifications is under way from the very start of the tale. In an introductory note, we hear about "another clergyman in New England, Mr. Joseph Moody, of York, Maine, who died about eighty years since" and who "made himself remarkable by the same eccentricity that is here related of the Reverend Mr. Hooper." Then, still with an air of being helpful and direct, Hawthorne offers what seem to be distinctions: "In his case [Moody's], however, the symbol had a different import. In early life he had accidentally killed a beloved friend; and from that day till the hour of his death, he hid his face from men." But what sort of distinctions are these? And how precisely are Moody and Hooper different cases? The explanation, on a closer look, turns out not to be an explanation at all. Of what is Mr. Moody's veil a "symbol"? Grief, surely; but we do not know the "accidental" means by which he killed his friend, nor do we know except in a general way why he hid his face from men. We are faced with an "ambiguity of sin or sorrow," as much as in Hooper's case. Hawthorne's note—like the veil itself—obscures as much as it reveals. Still, despite the falseness of its reassurance, there is something of the genuine in it, too; it is in keeping, as I want to show, with the whole point of the tale that Hooper's mysterious veil has a counterpart in reality. Here again it is like the scarlet letter with its counterpart that Hawthorne finds in the custom house and is at such pains to be precise about ("By an accurate measurement, each limb proved to be precisely three inches and a quarter in length" [V, 50]). Each fictional symbol is attached to a fact in the real world.

We can try another question, a little less blatant: what does Hooper's veil stand for in its own context? Because the minister's dying speech sounds a dominant note, or seems to, it is easy to go there first of all:

> When the friend shows his inmost heart to his friend; the lover to his best beloved; when man does not vainly shrink from the eye of his Creator, loathsomely treasuring up the secret of his sin; then deem me a monster, for the symbol beneath which I have lived, and die! I look around me, and, lo! on every visage a Black Veil!

Coming as it does at the end, this looks like summary and conclusion. But that is as deceptive as the authoritative air of the opening footnote. If we throw caution aside and take this last pronouncement as conclusive, the story is that parable of hidden guilt which it is usually supposed to be—and also, I think, a less interesting story than it really is. Hooper's final piety, his deathbed utterance with its implied confession, all this needs to be taken dramatically—as a formal setpiece—and with the reservations appropriate to so pat a gesture. It is the end, or almost the end, of the story—but not the whole of it. We need not, in fact cannot, let it go as a drama of clandestine sin. Granted that Hawthorne was concerned, deeply so, with that theme; but here it is concealment and mystery, not guilt, that concerns him most, and that makes the difference.

The very nature of the veil itself is to avert explicit statements of what it stands for, or at least to throw them immediately in doubt. It is not just that "the meaning of the symbol is ambiguous"; that would tell us little we did not always know. Rather the strange quality of the veil is that not only does it conceal what is behind it, it is a sign of that concealment; it both symbolizes and generates what is symbolized, is its own symbol—and, in its self-containment, is in one sense beyond interpretation, i.e., beyond any rendering in referential terms. But to "mean" is a function of the human, to "be" a function of the divine; a symbol, humanly speaking, implies something symbolized that is not only itself. So the veil, creating meaning and simultaneously hiding it, invites speculation and resists it. No one ever dares ask Hooper why he wears the veil.

The deputation from the church, sent to "deal with Mr. Hooper about the mystery"—how obviously inappropriate is the commercial dealing with mystery—never comes to the point: "Were the veil but cast aside, they might speak freely of it, but not till then." Because the meaning of the veil consists only in what is hidden, meaning is lost in the very act of revelation. It is in this that the veil serves as "type" and "symbol" of types and symbols in their general nature. As language gives a meaning to experience but also comes between the subject and any direct perception or re-creation of that experience, so does the veil. "In a Symbol," says Carlyle (as Professor Teufelsdröckh), "there is concealment and yet revelation."[8] Hooper's veil embodies the paradox.

In this setting the common Hawthornian tactic that F. O. Matthiessen calls "the device of multiple choice" and Yvor Winters "the formula of alternative possibilities"[9] works to special advantage. The tactic is uncomplicated: merely that of offering several explanations of events or symbolic circumstances and apparently leaving the reader, according to his own lights, to accept the one that suits him best. "The reader may choose," says Hawthorne, among the several theories proposed to explain the mark (if there was one) "imprinted" in the Reverend Mr. Dimmesdale's flesh (V, 305-306). But the formula is really designed to prevent, not to encourage, speculation. We are intended *not* to choose; it is difficult to suppose that Donatello has furry ears, but it is damaging to suppose that he doesn't. And, by the same token, it is damaging to limit the extensions of the veil to this one or to that. It is not one veil but every veil. It is the glass through which we see darkly; Hooper appears in the pulpit "*face to face* [my emphasis] with his congregation, except for"—a grim irony—"the black veil." Elsewhere it is associated with the darkness of night that obscures the visible world, or with "the veil that shuts in time from eternity." Sometimes it turns Hooper away from the mirrors of self-knowledge: "In truth, his own antipathy to the veil was known to be so great, that he never willingly passed before a mirror, nor stooped to drink at a still fountain, lest, in its peaceful bosom, he should be affrighted by himself." He resists the last knowledge that he is hidden even from himself. But, still elsewhere, the veil itself becomes a magic mirror, reversing the world of normal experience in its transfiguring presence: the funeral of the young woman is transformed to a marriage ("I had a fancy," says one observer—giving Poe the lead he was looking for—"that the minister and the maiden's spirit were walking hand in hand"), and the "cold fingers" and "deathlike paleness" of a bride at her wedding change the ceremony into a dance of death. For the veil all things are possible; its extensions come naturally from its primary character as a symbol of symbols, hence capable of all their protean changes. If we cannot eliminate the human fact of reference, still we need not commit ourselves to other versions of the absolute and insist on singleness of reference; since a single correspondence cannot be finally established, that way lies either delusion or skepticism and despair.

To insist on a single meaning or explanation is in fact to be like the townspeople of the story, who speculate upon the reasons for Mr. Hooper's veil: "A few shook their sagacious heads, intimating that they could penetrate the mystery; while one or two affirmed that there was no mystery at all, but only that Mr. Hooper's eyes were so weakened by the midnight lamp, as to require a shade." In this case we are specifically not asked to choose—the technique has not yet crystallized into a "formula" of alternative possibilities—and we do well to profit from the absence of advice. The alternatives available are each intended to be unacceptable: on one hand, to be identified with the "sagacious" few who think they can penetrate the mystery; on the other, to deny the mystery altogether. Either choice is self-defeating. But "sagacious" readers have not been wanting.

In truth, however, they have better reasons than any we have seen so far. Misguided prying into the mystery by "all the busybodies and impertinent people in the parish" is one thing; the case of Elizabeth, betrothed to Mr. Hooper, looks more doubtful. Her plea that Hooper take off the veil and reveal his secret to her is a sympathetic one; probably it is her presence that accounts for the view of Hooper as a malevolent spirit: "As his plighted wife, it should be her privilege to know what the black veil concealed." The scene that follows between Elizabeth and Hooper is a strange one, however. To her request that he "lift the veil but once," he answers that it cannot be. The feeling aimed at seems to be that the veil in literal fact *cannot* be removed; it is not, we are made to think, a volitional matter. But Elizabeth bids Hooper farewell, and the strangeness is especially in Hooper's response: "But, even amid his grief, Mr. Hooper smiled to think that only a material emblem had separated him from happiness, though the horrors, which it shadowed forth, must be drawn darkly between the fondest of lovers." On one hand it is "only a material emblem," on the other it seems to be everything; but symbol and thing symbolized, however (other than itself) that may be interpreted, are felt as concordant with one another. And there seems to lie the motive for Elizabeth's reappearance to nurse Hooper at his death—"no hired handmaiden of death, but one whose calm affection had endured thus long in secrecy, in solitude, amid the chill of age, and would not perish, even at the dying hour." The long endurance of a "calm affection" comes unexpectedly after Elizabeth's abrupt farewell in the earlier scene; the assertion of fidelity in the presence of mystery is no easy one for Hawthorne to make, and the narrative lacks cohesion at the point of greatest strain. An assertion, nonetheless, there is: to keep faith is to accept the fact of human meaning behind the veil—even though that meaning, in the nature of things, is hidden to the eye.

But the phantom lure of knowing the unknowable is not so easily set aside. Mr. Hooper's veil and the efforts—Elizabeth's well-intentioned ones, the townspeople's vulgar and impertinent ones—to discover what lies behind it anticipate the veils and masks and efforts to "penetrate their mystery" that are so important in Hawthorne's later fiction. They make a large subject, beyond the reach of this paper.[10] Also beyond the reach of this paper are the details of Hawthorne's decline. But this generalization may be risked: it is the possibility of faith—by that I mean a habit of mind more crucial than any specifically religious belief, the failure of which is sometimes supposed to account for Hawthorne's fate as an artist—that is for him ever more in doubt. The vain hope of lifting the veil and the fears of what might be found there (or, really, what might not be found there) become obsessive and, in the long run, paralyzing to the imagination. A brief and very selective glance ahead will throw a last light on Mr. Hooper's story. Elizabeth, in her enduring affection, is an image of what Hawthorne would, but in the event could not, be.

A good place to look first is Zenobia's legend, in *Blithedale,* of the veiled lady—that odd amalgam of folklore and pure Gothic claptrap ("undeniable nonsense," says Coverdale, "but not necessarily the worse for that")—where the situation is identical, in its essentials, with that of **"The Minister's Black Veil."** The outcome has changed, however, and the Gothic terrors are real enough as things, this time, are forced to their conclusion. The prying Theodore refuses to kiss the lady unless he see her face unveiled; she rebukes him for coming "not in holy faith" but in "scornful scepticism and idle curiosity"; he lifts the veil, still fearing lest he kiss "the lips of a dead girl, or the jaws of a skeleton, or the grinning cavity of a monster's mouth," and the lady vanishes. If Hooper's story and Elizabeth's good faith intimate the presence of meanings behind the veil, even diabolic meanings, Zenobia's fable raises another possibility that is more sinister: "But what, in good sooth, had become of the Veiled Lady? Had all her existence been comprehended within that mysterious veil, and was she now annihilated?" (V, 442; 448; 449) The fears that are buried deep and never (unless, we shall see, at the very end) allowed to emerge in **"The Minister's Black Veil"** are explicit here: that existence is comprehended only in veils and masks, liable to annihilation and revealing then the nothingness behind them.

These fears are the stuff of nightmare, and the carnival scene at the end of *The Marble Faun,* where the masks of the revellers are not just veils that conceal but grotesque images that haunt and mock the observer, marks another critical point on the long downward line. Kenyon, waiting information about Hilda, clings desperately to a lamppost lest he be swept away by the crowd (the allegory is plain enough) and searches the faces about him: "He looked at each mask,—harlequin, ape, bulbous-headed monster, or anything that was absurdest,—not knowing but that the messenger might come, even in such fantastic guise. . . . At times, his disquietude took a hopeful aspect; and he fancied that Hilda might come by, her own sweet self, in some shy disguise which the instinct of his love would be sure to penetrate." To observers on a balcony above the crowd, detached epicurean spectators of the chaos, Kenyon's search for the messenger (intelligence and meaning) and for Hilda (love and requital) makes him ludicrous. His behavior looks "unutterably absurd" as he pores "into this whirlpool of nonsense so earnestly, in quest of what was to make his life dark or bright." The moral of the nightmare scene: "Earnest people, who try to get a reality out of human existence, are necessarily absurd in the view of the revellers and masqueraders." They are absurd because perhaps no "reality" is to be "gotten out" of human existence at all. But then comes the extraordinary sequel, in which the strength of doubt is compensated by an extravagance of rhetoric and event, marking a conviction, surely, that it is now a case of all or nothing. A shower of confetti makes Kenyon look upward to the balcony where he sees the priest to whom Hilda has made confession. He fails to associate him with Hilda, looks back to the crowd, and is immediately struck from one side by a cauliflower, from the other by "a single rose-bud, so fresh that it seemed that moment gathered. It flew from the opposite balcony, smote gently on his lips, and fell into his hand. He looked upward, and beheld the face of his lost Hilda!" (VI, 508; 510) The laughing epicurean gods are replaced by Hilda in her white domino; memories of the ridiculous cauliflower, cancelled out by the mystical rose.

Unintentionally funny as the scene may in some ways be, the urgency of it all is underlined by the tortuous and unsatisfying explanation of events that Hawthorne "reluctantly" added to his romance. He has failed, he thinks, "in throwing about this Romance the kind of atmosphere essential to the effect at which he aimed." That is, he has failed to avert questions on the order of: had Donatello furry ears? "As respects all who ask such questions, the book is, to that extent, a failure." But he goes on, even so, to "throw light upon several matters in which some of his readers appear to feel an interest," and he admits that "he was himself troubled with a curiosity similar to that which he has just deprecated on the part of his readers." This is disastrous, for here is poor Hawthorne as an unspiritualized Paul Pry, a meddling and impotent questioner who cries out finally "with intense earnestness," "Did Donatello's ears resemble those of the Faun of Praxiteles?" and gets the only possible answer: "'I know, but may not tell,' replied Kenyon, smiling mysteriously. 'On that point, at all events, there shall be not one word of explanation.'" (VI, 522; 523; 527) Of course the failure to strike a balance between romance and reality might be set down as a failure of craftsmanship, just as Hawthorne seems to prefer, so dark is the alternative. But in fact all relationships have been shattered—between romance and reality, symbol and reference, cause and effect. For one thing Hawthorne has failed to establish adequate connections between events and failed equally to establish conditions in which these connections could be accepted as present, though concealed. Elizabeth's reappearance at the close of **"The Minister's Black Veil,"** though a little startling, is psychologically plausible—and nothing at all like Hilda's miraculous incarnation on the balcony, an assertion of meaning that is felt only as an isolated event, one with no antecedent cause. For another thing Hawthorne has failed to endow Donatello's ears with the symbolic range, the manifold possibilities of reference, that he imparted to Hooper's veil. Even for Hawthorne, it seems, Donatello's ears require somehow to be one thing or another, to be furry or not; indeed the symbol here has dwindled into a thing. And Hawthorne never had much confidence in "mere" things.

The case of Donatello's ears brings us very close to the last, unfinished fragments where the nature of the disease is defined by symbols or things—who is really to say?—that point nowhere. This is Winters' diagnosis: "We have the symbolic footprint, the symbolic spider, the symbolic elixirs and poisons, but we have not that of which they are symbolic."[11] Or to put it another way: Hawthorne has no assurance that symbols are symbolic of something, and that in turn is to say (with Waggoner) that meanings have failed. Perhaps symbols are no more than things; events, perhaps without explanations; the present, without an identifiable past. In Hawthorne's futile search, while he was in England, for the facts of his own ancestry, he had found that the veil separating him from his origins could not be lifted. He would not have missed the typological possibilities of his failure. It was as though (an American neurosis) he had no origins at all.

From this bleak vantage, we can look back to **"The Minister's Black Veil,"** now in a fuller perspective. Despite Elizabeth's fidelity and despite the wan hope in that "faint, sad smile, so often there, [that] seemed to glimmer from its obscurity, and linger on Father Hooper's lips" as he dies, no one is likely to mistake the mood of the tale. Elizabeth's affection, revealed so late, scarcely relieves the gloom, and the last word is still the veil: "The grass of many years has sprung up and withered on that grave, the burial stone is moss-grown, and good Mr. Hooper's face is dust; but awful is still the thought that it mouldered beneath the Black Veil!" The veil survives the changes of time after its meanings have turned to dust. Acceptance was not Hawthorne's lot, nor was the unreflective life, whose matter-of-factness he sometimes catches sight of with a touch of longing and reproduces here in the accents of the village, at the beginning of the tale:

> "Are you sure it is our parson?" inquired Goodman Gray of the sexton.
>
> "Of a certainty it is good Mr. Hooper," replied the sexton. "He was to have exchanged pulpits with Parson Shute, of Westbury; but Parson Shute sent to excuse himself yesterday, being to preach a funeral sermon."

"Certainty" is for the unthoughtful, acceptance for the faithful; for Hawthorne, there will be only the gathering pressure of questions not to be answered and meanings not to be found. In its fine rhetorical adjustment of means to ends, **"The Minister's Black Veil"** is among Hawthorne's best stories; in mood and substance it is grimly prophetic of what was to come.

Notes

1. See Gilbert P. Voigt, "The Meaning of 'The Minister's Black Veil,'" *CE,* XIII (March 1952), 337-338; also Robert W. Cochran, "Hawthorne's Choice: The Veil or the Jaundiced Eye," *CE,* XXIII (Feb. 1962), 342-346. "The Reverend Mr. Hooper," says Cochran, "has been permitted to cross over beyond the veil of mystery to achieve the ultimate in human knowledge" (p. 345).
2. See E. Earle Stibitz, "Ironic Unity in Hawthorne's 'The Minister's Black Veil,'" *AL,* XXXIV (May 1962), 182-190; William Bysshe Stein, "The Parable of the Antichrist in 'The Minister's Black Veil,'" *AL,* XXVII (Nov. 1955), 386-392; also Nicholas Canaday, Jr., "Hawthorne's Minister and the Veiling Deceptions of Self," *SSF,* IV (Winter 1967), 135-142; and Frederick C. Crews, *The Sins of the Fathers: Hawthorne's Psychological Themes* (New York, 1966), pp. 106-111.
3. E.g., R. H. Fogle, "'An Ambiguity of Sin or Sorrow,'" *NEQ,* XXI (Sept. 1948), 342-349.
4. *The Works of Edgar Allan Poe,* ed. John H. Ingram (London, 1901), IV, 218. For "The Minister's Black Veil," see *The Complete Works of Nathaniel Hawthorne,* ed. George Parsons Lathrop (Boston, 1883), I, 52-69. Quotations from Hawthorne's works are identified in the text by volume and page reference to this edition.
5. George Monteiro comes near my sense of the story by emphasizing Hawthorne's recurrent use of the word "mystery"; *Explicator,* XXII (Oct. 1963), no. 9. So does Frederick W. Turner, III, who says that the veil is "to be interpreted as ignorance or that which divides men from the true knowledge of things"; *SSF,* V (Winter 1968), 187.
6. *Hawthorne: A Critical Study* (rev. ed.; Cambridge, Mass., 1963), p. 236.
7. Rudolph von Abele has done so in *The Death of the Artist: A Study of Hawthorne's Disintegration* (The Hague, 1955). His argument in part is this: "My contention here is that so far as Hawthorne failed to work by the method of presenting things as 'lived experience,' he failed completely, which in practice means that he failed almost every time his symbolism was overt and deliberate" (p. 19). He thinks "The Minister's Black Veil" a success, essentially because it is "realistic": "Hawthorne sometimes resorted to symbols that required no rationalization to be seen in a normative naturalist context. The veil worn by Father Hooper in 'The Minister's Black Veil' is a case in point, and an interesting one. The only problem in connection with it is of motivation, but this problem is satisfactorily solved on a number of different levels—Hawthorne's, Hooper's, the reader's. The gesture may be eccentric, but it is not miraculous, and it is not explained away" (p. 29).
8. *Sartor Resartus,* ed. Charles Frederick Harrold (New York, 1937), p. 219.
9. Matthiessen, *American Renaissance* (New York, 1941), p. 276; Winters, *Maule's Curse* (Norfolk, Conn., 1938), p. 18.

10. The subject becomes even more far-reaching as soon as one looks to other writers contemporary with Hawthorne. Robert Edward Goodfriend raises some of the issues in a master's thesis, "Transformation of the Gothic: A Study of the Veil in the Works of Poe, Hawthorne and Melville" (Stanford, 1965).
11. P. 19.

Robert E. Morsberger (essay date 1973)

SOURCE: "Memoranda and Documents: 'The Minister's Black Veil': 'Shrouded in a Blackness, Ten Times Black,'" in *The New England Quarterly* Vol. XLVI, No. 3, September, 1973, pp. 454-63.

[In the following essay, Morsberger maintains that Mr. Hooper's greatest sin is his Calvinist fixation on his own sinful nature and perverse pride in his own isolation and suffering.]

As a chronicler of New England colonial history, Hawthorne can be said to have created in considerable measure the legend of our Puritan past. Yet there are a good many dramatic episodes and individuals that he only touched on obliquely if at all: the Plymouth plantation, the trials and exile of Roger Williams and Anne Hutchinson (his biographical sketch of the latter consists merely of several frozen tableaux), the Pequot War, the actual trials at Salem for witchcraft, and the Great Awakening. Jonathan Edwards, in some ways the greatest Puritan of them all, never appears in any of Hawthorne's fiction, though the "Surprising Conversions," bizarre behavior, and spiritual crises of the Great Awakening in Northhampton could have provided suitably dramatic material for his fiction, as could the expulsion of Edwards from his parish, and his exile as missionary to the Stockbridge Indians. None of this did Hawthorne deal with directly.

Yet, in a way, one of his greatest Puritan tales, **"The Minister's Black Veil,"** presents the sort of spiritual tension seen in much introspective Puritan literature and perhaps best dramatized in the life and work of Edwards. Set during Edwards' lifetime in the first half of the eighteenth century, the story of the Reverend Mr. Hooper of Milford was, superficially, suggested by the case of Joseph Moody, a clergyman of York, Maine, who wore until his death a black veil to symbolize his having accidentally killed a friend. This guilt for a specific if unintentional sinful act resembles **"Roger Malvin's Burial"** more than it does **"The Minister's Black Veil,"** which deals more generally with Puritan melancholy. In **"The Old Manse,"** Hawthorne noted, "a clergyman,—a man not estranged from human life, yet enveloped in the midst of it with a veil woven of intermingled gloom and brightness." In Father Hooper's case, there is no brightness, only the gloomy estrangement caused by the veil.

It is a mistake to concentrate too much on the veil itself. Aside from Mr. Moody, no one wore such a veil, and the possessor of it is merely an eccentric. But as Ahab tells Starbuck, "All visible objects, man, are but as pasteboard masks. . . . If man will strike, strike through the mask!"[1] D. H. Lawrence's statement about Hawthorne, that "You *must* look through the surfaces of American art, and see the inner diabolism of the symbolic meaning. Otherwise it is all mere childishness,"[2] is particularly applicable to **"The Minister's Black Veil."**

If, then, Hawthorne's tale is to have more significance than simply a curiosity piece about a uniquely obsessed clergyman, what broader meaning does it imply?

Father Hooper himself explains that the veil is a symbol of sin but refuses to answer whether it represents a specific act committed or a general awareness of sinful humanity: "If I hide my face for sorrow, there is cause enough . . . and if I cover it for secret sin, what mortal might not do the same." This is practically a paraphrase of the statement in Thomas Shepherd's *The Sincere Convert* (1641), that ". . . no unregenerate man, though he go never so far, let him do never so much, but he lives in some one sin or other, secret or open, little or great."[3] The concept of secret sin could link the tale to Dimmesdale, Reuben Bourne, or to an apprehensive criminal like Raskolnikov. But *The Scarlet Letter* and **"Roger Malvin's Burial"** between them deal quite adequately with the psychological consequences of secret sin; the impact of **"The Minister's Black Veil"** is the suggestion that it may stand more broadly for a profound sense of blighted human nature.

As in **"Young Goodman Brown,"** Hawthorne is critical of the Puritans' excessive preoccupation with sin, a consequence of their doctrine of total depravity, which Hawthorne rejected. Melville wrote that Hawthorne's effects often come from a sense of Original Sin, but original sin is not total and is balanced by a human capacity for goodness and compassion. For most Christians, Christ came "to redeem the sins of the whole world"; whereas rigid Calvinism maintained that all of mankind deserves damnation and most of mankind will obtain it—all but God's few elect, who are chosen for the unearned grace that comes from limited atonement by Christ, so limited that according to Thomas Shepherd, "most of them that live in the church shall perish."[4] It is this kind of monomaniac obsession with sin that is signified by Hooper's black veil.

Hooper need not have committed any specific sin; for the hardened Puritan, his humanity was sinful enough, and he wore it the way a medieval penitent would his hair shirt. Anything less than absolute perfection was absolute corruption. The saintly John Bunyan, who called himself *The Chief of Sinners,* wrote:

> . . . I saw that I wanted a perfect righteousness to present me without fault before God, and this righteousness was nowhere to be found, but in the person of Jesus Christ.
>
> But my original and inward pollution, that, that was my plague and my affliction; that, I say, at a dreadful

rate, always putting forth itself within me; that I had the guilt of, to amazement; by reason of that, I was more loathsome in my own eyes than was a toad; and I thought I was so in God's eyes too; . . . I thought none but the devil himself could equalise me for inward wickedness and pollution of mind. I fell, therefore, at the sight of my own vileness, deeply into despair; for I concluded that this condition that I was in could not stand with a state of grace. Sure, thought I, I am forsaken of God. . . .[5]

Steeped in Bunyan, Hawthorne would no doubt be familiar with this and similar passages, which are symptomatic of what William James called "the sick soul." But Bunyan also recognized forgiveness and "was in hopes that my sin was not unpardonable. . . ."[6] Hooper, on the other hand, leaves out the prospect of Christian forgiveness. Or if God can forgive him (Hooper tells Elizabeth they may be together in heaven), he can meanwhile not forgive himself.

Though the black veil creates an estrangement between himself and the community, it does make him peculiarly effective as a minister, and the first sermon he preaches after wearing the mask has an impact like Jonathan Edwards' "Sinners in the Hands of an Angry God," preached at Enfield during the height of the Great Awakening. Edwards' pulpitry was like that of Hooper, whom Hawthorne describes as "a good preacher, but not an energetic one; he strove to win his people heavenward, by mild, persuasive influences, rather than to drive them thither by the thunders of the Word." But as at Enfield, the members of Hooper's congregation "felt as if the preacher had crept upon them, behind his awful veil, and discovered their hoarded iniquity of deed or thought." In Edwards' sermon, "There is reason to think, that there are many in this congregation now hearing this discourse, that will actually be the subjects of this very misery to all eternity. We know not who they are, or in what seats they sit, or what thoughts they now have. . . . And it would be no wonder if some persons, that now sit here, in some seats of this meeting-house, in health, quiet and secure, should be there before tomorrow morning."[7] As Bunyan found himself "more loathsome . . . than was a toad" in both his eyes and God's, so Edwards proclaimed; "The God that holds you over the pit of hell, much as one holds a spider, or some loathsome insect over the fire, abhors you, and is dreadfully provoked. . . ."[8]

Edwards, even after his conversion, ordination, and sense of "divine things" and "inward sweetness," resembled Hooper in his gloom:

> Often, since I lived in this town, I have had very affecting views of my own sinfulness and vileness; . . . I have had a vastly greater sense of my own wickedness, and the badness of my own heart, than ever I had before my conversion. It has often appeared to me, that if God should mark iniquity against me, I should appear the very worst of all mankind; . . . My wickedness, as I am in myself, has long appeared to me perfectly ineffable, and swallowing up all thought and imagination; like an infinite deluge, or mountains over my head. I know not how to express better what my sins appear to me to be, than by heaping infinite upon infinite, and multiplying infinite by infinite. . . . When I look into my heart, and take a view of my wickedness, it looks like an abyss infinitely deeper than hell. And it appears to me, that were it not for free grace, . . . I should appear sunk down in my sins below hell itself; far beyond the sight of every thing, but the eye of sovereign grace, that can pierce even down to such a depth.[9]

There was no reason for Edwards, Bunyan, or Hooper to feel this way. Far from being depraved criminals, they led exemplary lives; their wallowing in self-accusing guilt is a kind of spiritual masochism. They were not guilty of the catalogue of colonial crimes that the devil discloses to Goodman Brown, let alone of such horrors as the Inquisition, the butchery of the Thirty Years' War, the sanctimonious slaughter carried out by the Covenanters, or the nightmare of the Middle Passage (to confine oneself to history up to Edwards' time), let alone the atrocities of subsequent history. Samuel Sewall and Cotton Mather, partly responsible for the death of twenty innocent people at Salem, had more reason for remorse; but Mather seems never to have felt it, and Sewall, though he made public confession of his error, continued to live affirmatively. But Hooper has vowed never to remove the veil, and Edwards wrote, "I have greatly longed of late, for a broken heart, and to lie low before God; and, when I ask for humility, I cannot bear the thoughts of being no more humble than other Christians. It seems to me, that though their degrees of humility may be suitable for them, yet it would be a vile self-exaltation to me, not to be the lowest in humility of all mankind."[10]

There is an extremism in this unreasonable self-abasement that is a spiritual flagellation and may be an inverted pride. Edwards had no justification to consider himself the worst of mankind. Yet his spiritual state in such passages can be matched by that of other Puritan writers, John Winthrop and Michael Wigglesworth among them, and it is such a state that is signified by the black veil.

It need not indicate any specific crime; for sin is not an act but a condition, exaggerated by the Puritans to the concept of total depravity. Writing of "the dusky, overshadowed conscience of the Puritans," Henry James noted, "This darkening cloud was no essential part of the nature of the individual; it stood fixed in the general moral heaven under which he grew up and looked at life. It projected from above, from outside, a black patch over his spirit, and it was for him to do what he could with the black patch."[11] Bunyan and Edwards freed themselves from the slough of despond and praised the mercy and love of God more than they chronicled their unworthiness and His wrath, but Hooper remains adamant.

In his insistence on publicly dramatizing the symbol of sin, he drags the judgment of God down to the level of village gossip, as does Dimmesdale in *The Scarlet Letter.* God may know all, but that is no reason why the villagers must understand and judge. Secret sin is hidden not from God but from man. Yet such concealment does isolate the sinner, as Dimmesdale and Reuben Bourne discovered to their sorrow, and this is why Hawthorne so strongly admired the Catholic rite of confession and absolution. Yet as Pascal wrote:

> Is it not true that we hate truth and those who tell it us, and that we like them to be deceived in our favor, and prefer to be esteemed by them as being other than what we are in fact? One proof of this makes me shudder. The Catholic religion does not bind us to confess our sins indiscriminately to everybody; it allows them to remain hidden from all other men save one, to whom she bids us reveal the innermost recesses of our heart, and show ourselves as we are. There is only this one man in the world whom she orders us to undeceive, and she binds him to an inviolable secrecy, which makes this knowledge to him as if it were not. Can we imagine anything more charitable and pleasant? And yet the corruption of man is such that he finds even this law harsh; and it is one of the main reasons which has caused a great part of Europe to rebel against the Church.[12]

Hooper, of course, in confessing all confesses nothing specific, with the result that his wearing the veil accuses everyone as much as himself. His presence is a *memento mori,* and therefore his parishioners shun him. His veil does, however, make him "a very efficient clergyman" by enabling him "to sympathize with all dark affections," a consequence confirmed by a French melancholiac who found that "the experience has made me sympathetic with the morbid feelings of others ever since."[13] Those who desperately request Hooper's ministry are those afflicted by an "agony for sin."

Such agony is real enough, and not only during the seventeenth and eighteenth centuries. Despite its period setting, **"The Minister's Black Veil"** is not merely a historical reconstruction but a story of enduring relevance. To concentrate too much on the setting and on the veil itself rather than on the motivating forces behind it is to make it merely a curiosity piece, like the episode of the student at Oregon State University in the mid-1960's, who attended class shrouded in a black bag.

The veil is merely the external emblem of that condition that William James, in *The Varieties of Religious Experience,* labels "The Sick Soul." For victims of such profound melancholia, "evil is no mere relation of the subject to particular outer things, but something more radical and general, a wrongness or vice in his essential nature."[14] As an example that resembles Father Hooper, James quotes Henry Alline, an evangelist of the early nineteenth century, who confessed, "My sins seemed to be laid open; so that I thought that every one I saw knew them . . . yea sometimes it seemed to me as if every one was pointing me out as the most guilty wretch upon earth. I had now so great a sense of the vanity and emptiness of all things here below, that I knew the whole world could not possibly make me happy. . . ."[15] James examines numerous cases of such pathological and private depression, which he labels *anhedonia,* observing, "For this extremity of pessimism to be reached, something more is needed than observation of life and reflection upon death. The individual must in his own person become the prey of a pathological melancholy."[16]

Father Hooper may seem more outwardly subdued than these cases, for the detached narrator does not lead us into his mind; his voice is muted, and his motives remain hidden behind the mask; he has little dialogue, but twice when he speaks, it is in desperation. Pleading with his betrothed Elizabeth to remain with him, he cries, "Oh! you know not how lonely I am, and how frightened, to be alone behind my black veil. Do not leave me in this miserable obscurity for ever!" And on his deathbed, in final agony more of spirit than of body, he lashes out at his parishioners to "Tremble also at each other!" and denounces their sin when "men avoided me, and women [have] shown no pity, and children screamed and fled. . . . I look around me, and, lo! on every visage a Black Veil!"

If so, the fault is largely his own, for the story can also be seen as a case of the contagion of sin. In his morbid obsession with depravity, Father Hooper becomes guilty of something akin to Hawthorne's Unpardonable Sin, except that his preoccupation is more emotional than intellectual, though it is derived from Calvinist ideology. For the sake of it, and in his obsessive insistence on wearing the veil, he is as much guilty of driving away the companionship of his congregation as they are of reacting with ostracism. The isolation is a mutual act, for he admits, "This dismal shade must separate me from the world; even you, Elizabeth, can never come behind it." If therefore she rejects him as a husband, he drives her to it. The veil is a useless gesture—worse, since it corrupts others by its contagious presence.

William James calls excessive preoccupation with evil a disease; "'Repentance, according to . . . healthy-minded Christians, means *getting away from* the sin, not groaning and writhing over its commission," and he quotes Spinoza's statement that "gnawings of conscience" are "deleterious and evil passions" forming "a particular kind of sadness. . . ."[17] What is missing in Father Hooper's flawed Christianity is forgiveness. This is also a factor missing in rigidly predestinarian Calvinism, according to which everyone deserves damnation, most of mankind will experience damnation, and the grace of God through Christ is a limited atonement reserved only for the arbitrarily chosen "elect." Even Jonathan Edwards conceded that as a youth he had "been full of objections against the doctrine of God's sovereignty, in choosing whom He would to eternal life, and rejecting whom He pleased; leaving them eternally to perish, and be everlastingly tormented in hell."[18] Edwards finally brought himself around to accepting this doctrine, "But never could give an account, how, or by what means, I was thus convinced";[19] one of his sermons is entitled "The Justification of God in the Damnation of Sinners." Despite this, Edwards was enough of a Christian to focus primarily on the love and mercy of

Christ; yet all too often, as in Wigglesworth's "The Day of Doom," the Calvinist Christ appears as a hanging judge, God the Father emerges as the sort of tyrannical adversary Captain Ahab defies, and God the Holy Ghost becomes (in Phyllis McGinley's words) "The Holy Terror."

Yet Puritans could also "Confess Jehovah Thankfully"; and some, like Edward Taylor, were rhapsodic over the love God showed man through the Incarnation and Atonement. Hester Prynne says to Dimmesdale, "Heaven would show mercy . . . hadst thou but the strength to take advantage of it."[20] In his inability or refusal to do so, Father Hooper lets his sin become a spiritual pride. He concedes that "I . . . like most other mortals, have sorrows dark enough to be typified by a black veil." If so, why should he single himself out except from perverse pride or a deep disease of spirit. Presumably all Christian ministers recognize sin in themselves, but they do not act as Hooper did. John Bunyan and Jonathan Edwards did not wear a black veil. St. Peter himself is said to have denounced Christ thrice before the crucifixion; yet not only did he not wear a black veil, but he accepted forgiveness and became the chief of the apostles. Ultimately, Hooper seems like Marlowe's Doctor Faustus, who cries that his sins are so great as to be beyond the power of God's redemption.

In his bleak despair, Hooper also resembles the Beatrice Cenci, of whom Hawthorne has Hilda say in *The Marble Faun,* "She knows that her sorrow is so strange and so immense that she ought to be solitary forever . . ."[21] and like Donatello, of whom Kenyon reflects, ". . . he finds it too horrible to be uttered, and fancies himself the only mortal that ever felt the anguish of remorse."[22] Yet Kenyon lectures Donatello, ". . . you do not know what is requisite for your spiritual growth, seeking, as you do, to keep your soul perpetually in the unwholesome region of remorse. It was needful for you to pass through that dark valley, but it is infinitely dangerous to linger there too long; there is poison in the atmosphere, when we sit down and brood in it, instead of girding up our loins to press onward."[23]

Here, Kenyon can be considered the author's spokesman, for Hawthorne's friend Hillard wrote of him, "There was nothing morbid in his character or temperament. He was, indeed, much the reverse of morbid."[24] And in *Fanshawe,* Hawthorne condemned the "joy of grief" in which "a man becomes a haunter of death-beds, a tormentor of afflicted hearts, and a follower of funerals."[25]

In his final words, Father Hooper exclaims, "When the friend shows his inmost heart to his friend; the lover to his best beloved; when man does not vainly shrink from the eye of his Creator, loathsomely treasuring up the secret of his sin; then deem me a monster, for the symbol beneath which I have lived, and die!" Likewise, Pascal confessed: "Human life is . . . only a perpetual illusion; . . . Man is then only disguise, falsehood, and hypocrisy, both in himself and in regard to others. He does not wish any one to tell him the truth; he avoids telling it to others, and all these dispositions, so removed from justice and reason, have a natural root in his heart."[26] To this extent, Father Hooper may be right; yet as Graham Greene says, echoing Scripture, the unpardonable sin is despair.

Notes

1. Herman Melville, *Moby-Dick,* Charles Feidelson, Jr., editor (Indianapolis, 1964), 220.
2. D. H. Lawrence, *Studies in Classic American Literature,* in *The Shock of Recognition,* Edmund Wilson, editor (New York, 1955), 984.
3. Thomas Shepherd, *The Sincere Convert,* in *American Thought and Writing, The Colonial Period,* Russel B. Nye and Norman S. Grabo, editors (Boston, 1965), I, 96.
4. Shepherd, *The Sincere Convert,* 92.
5. John Bunyan, *Grace Abounding and The Life and Death of Mr. Badman* (London and New York, 1956), 28.
6. Bunyan, *Grace Abounding . . .*, 59.
7. Jonathan Edwards, *Representative Selections,* Clarence H. Faust and Thomas H. Johnson, editors (New York, 1935), 169-170.
8. Edwards, *Representative Selections,* 164.
9. Edwards, *Representative Selections,* 69-70.
10. Edwards, *Representative Selections,* 70-71.
11. Henry James, *Hawthorne,* in *The Shock of Recognition,* Edmund Wilson, editor (New York, 1955), 470.
12. Blaise Pascal, *Pensées,* W. F. Trotter, translator (London and New York, 1954), 31-32.
13. William James, *The Varieties of Religious Experience* (New York, n.d.), 158.
14. James, *Varieties of Religious Experience,* 132.
15. James, *Varieties of Religious Experience,* 156.
16. James, *Varieties of Religious Experience,* 142.
17. James, *Varieties of Religious Experience,* 126.
18. Edwards, *Representative Selections,* 58.
19. Edwards, *Representative Selections,* 58.
20. Nathaniel Hawthorne, *The Complete Novels and Selected Tales,* Norman Holmes Pearson, editor (New York, 1937), 201.
21. Hawthorne, *The Complete Novels . . .*, 627.
22. Hawthorne, *The Complete Novels . . .*, 741.
23. Hawthorne, *The Complete Novels . . .*, 747.
24. *The Atlantic Monthly,* XXVI, 257 (Sept., 1870).
25. Hawthorne, *The Complete Novels . . .*, 71.
26. Pascal, *Pensées,* 32-33.

James Quinn and Ross Baldessarini (essay date 1974)

SOURCE: "Literary Technique and Psychological Effect in Hawthorne's 'The Minister's Black Veil,'" in *Literature and Psychology,* Vol. XXIV, No. 3, 1974, pp. 115-23.

[In the following essay, Quinn and Baldessarini claim that Hawthorne never makes clear Mr. Hooper's motives for wearing the black veil because he wants to show that even the minister is unconscious of what the veil is meant to hide.]

Critical appraisal of the ability of Nathaniel Hawthorne to analyze and convey his appreciation of human psychology has varied greatly in the past century. At first, between his death and the turn of the century, Hawthorne achieved an exalted position in the popular imagination partly because of his expression of a traditional New England Protestant morality. The decreasing acceptance of this moral tradition may partially explain his diminished popularity in the early decades of this century. Furthermore, many critics, while admiring aspects of his artistry, considered his use of allegory somewhat "old-fashioned," psychologically naive and too specifically religious—all this during a rising interest in fictional "realism" which continued well into the twentieth century and ran counter to the "romanticism"[1] as well as the moralism represented by Hawthorne. Significant criticisms of Hawthorne's lack of "realism" include essays by Henry James and Anthony Trollope in 1879 and by Yvor Winters in 1938.[2]

Since the rise of the New Criticism in the 1940's, which discovered in Hawthorne's presentation of human psychology a rich vein of subtle meanings, intriguing ironies and ambiguities, Hawthorne has been the focus of considerable reappraisal.[3] An interesting shift in criticism of Hawthorne was prompted by the more "worldly-wise" view of Hawthorne which arose from analysis of Randall Stewart's edition of *The American Notebooks of Nathaniel Hawthorne* published in 1932.[4] This change was characterized by a revision of the earlier view of Hawthorne as a wounded and solitary Puritanical neurotic presented by Newton Arvin and others.[5] A newer and somewhat foolish view, evident since the 1940's, has de-emphasized his neurotic characteristics. Edward Wagenknecht and Hubert Hoeltje, for example, presented Hawthorne as remarkably normal.[6] In contrast, Frederick Crews, in his more recent full-length psychological study, rejected such attempts to normalize Hawthorne and returned to the earlier view and supported it by including numerous psychoanalytic interpretations of Hawthorne's works.[7] While there had been a tradition of general awareness of psychological tension and stress in Hawthorne's fiction, not until Crews' study was the richness and complexity of Hawthorne's psychology adequately analyzed. The achievement of Crews has not been surpassed. On the other hand, there remains a striking dearth of analysis of the literary techniques by which Hawthorne achieves his psychological effects and the present essay attempts to deal with some aspects of the techniques. Hawthorne's **"The Minister's Black Veil"** is a good departure for such a study since it is one of the most psychologically intriguing and artistically compelling of his tales.

One of the extraordinary qualities of this tale as well as others is Hawthorne's convincing presentation of human moods and feelings, his awareness of conflicting desires, largely unconscious, within each man. As well be shown subsequently, some critics fail to observe the psychodynamic complexity of Hawthorne's characters and interrelationships and accept a simplistic logic, an "either-or" dichotomy, when a story could mean "both" or "all." For example, there are few totally diabolical characters in Hawthorne's fiction. The "villains" found are usually psychologically or spiritually ill in a special way, for villainy, Hawthorne clearly saw, can derive from a striving for perfection, a solipsistic withdrawal from life which is not without devastating effects on others. The tyranny of an overly-constricted conscience can be a cause of evil and spiritual destruction. Often, as in the case of the Reverend Mr. Hooper in **"The Minister's Black Veil."** Hawthorne's characters seem to be victims of forces, largely internal, beyond their control. Hawthorne himself does not facilitate a single judgment of the behavior of his protagonists and indeed appears to be aware of the complexity of their motivations as voiced in the observations of the numerous observing characters of the tales and romances.

Whatever the degree and source of Hawthorne's understanding of his characters, their motivations typically remain complex and obscure. Hawthorne reveals enough to allow us to sympathize, but explication of motivation is left incomplete; we get a glimpse of what a character thinks but not his rationale or philosophy. We are never sure what directs a character on his course of action. What we get is implication, and we must draw our inferences from those implications. This paper is an attempt to demonstrate how Hawthorne graphically creates vivid, sometimes lurid, pictures so that mood and atmosphere are believable enough to overcome our disbelief, while at the same time actions are incongruous enough to cause reflection and to provoke an unsatisfied demand for explication. By not revealing motives—one of Hawthorne's most important literary devices—he gives his tales a tantalizing quality, an iridescence or chameleon-like nature, something previous readers often missed when they took an "either-or" approach to his tales. Hawthorne's tales offer the reader a variety of emotional experiences; each story permits many possible interpretations, and each interpretation can represent a valid but partial response to the content. While it is a truism that each reader brings something different to a piece of fiction, in Hawthorne's tales, to a unique and striking degree, the material forces us to see different things. This is largely because the motivation of the characters is not disclosed and the reader must provide it. In this vein, one critic suggested that Hawthorne "is busy making us his protagonists."[8] Whether or not Hawthorne consciously intended each reader to project his own inner psychodynamics, that is the result; the hue which the story takes is determined by the special angle of vision of the individual observer.

There is great diversity of critical interpretation of **"The Minister's Black Veil,"** and this springs partly from the diverse responses to the black veil itself by the parishioners within the tale. From the start Hawthorne prompts curiosity about the source of the effects of the veil. One sunny Sabbath, the Reverend Mr. Hooper appears among his parishioners wearing, inexplicably, a fold of black cloth that hides part of his face: "Swathed about his forehead, and hanging down over his face, so low as to be shaken by his breath, Mr. Hooper had on a black veil."[9] Confronted with the mystery, the parishioners respond to it in a variety of ways. The minister is seen by the physician of the town to be "ghostlike," distant and insubstantial, and says prayers which seem to be "swept by the fingers of the dead" (p. 58) so awesome and mysterious is he. For others the veil conjures up a vague horror or ill-defined anxiety, as "more than one woman of delicate nerves was forced to leave the meeting-house" (p. 54). For still others it betokens madness: "Our parson has gone mad!" (p 53). Clearly a wide range of self-defensive psychological reactions is set in motion as the members of the congregation, after the initial disturbing sermon, rejoin in a circle as if to reassert their individual identities as well as to secure reassurance from others:

> At the close of the services, the people hurried out with indecorous confusion, eager to communicate their pent-up amazement, and conscious of lighter spirits the moment they lost sight of the black veil. Some gathered in little circles, huddled closely together, with their mouths all whispering in the centre; some went homeward alone, wrapt in silent meditation; some talked loudly, and profaned the Sabbath day with ostentatious laughter. A few shook their sagacious heads, intimating that they could penetrate the mystery; while one or two affirmed that there was no mystery at all, but only that Mr. Hooper's eyes were so weakened by the midnight lamp, as to require a shade . . . None, as on former occasions, aspired to the honor of walking by their pastor's side. Old Squire Saunders, doubtless by an accidental lapse of memory, neglected to invite Mr. Hooper to his table.
>
> (pp. 55-56)

Despite widespread disapproval, Parson Hooper persists in wearing the veil, spreading, in the course of one day, gloom at a wedding and casting an ominous spell over a funeral, in striking contrast to his presumed role as minister and representative of Christ. A church committee is sent to plumb the mystery of the veil "before it should grow into scandal" (p 60), but the veil hangs between the minister and the group of men as an overshadowing barrier, the "symbol of a fearful secret between him and them" (p. 60). Pressed by Elizabeth, his fiancée, to expound the mystery, Hooper will only say that "*If* it be a sign of mourning," then "I, *perhaps,* like most other mortals, have sorrows dark enough to be typified by a black veil" (p. 62) [Italics added]. While she blushingly intimates the nature of the rumors, which the veil has occasioned, the minister with "that same sad smile" (p. 62) replies "and *if* I cover it (my fact) for secret sin, what mortal might not do the same?" (p. 62). As she stands staring at "so dark a fantasy," (p. 63) she too is suddenly overwhelmed by the terrors that the veil "shadowed forth," (p. 64) and she turns to leave the room. In a moment of terrible anguish, an intimation of his own pain attendant upon donning the veil, Hooper pleads with Elizabeth not to leave him:

> Do not desert me, though this veil *must be* between us here on earth. Be mine, and hereafter there shall be no veil over my face, no darkness between our souls! It is but a mortal veil—it is not for eternity! O! you know not how lonely I am, and how frightened, to be alone behind my black veil. Do not leave me in this miserable obscurity forever! [Italics added].
>
> (p. 63)

Elizabeth cannot accept the unexplained necessity for his self-imposed martyrdom in this life and the promise of reunion only in the next. Left alone and without close human ties, Parson Hooper goes through life and to his grave wearing his black veil.

One of the most difficult mysteries of the tale is the fact that the Parson too is distressed to see himself wearing the veil in any reflected image. The scene at a wedding celebration reveals for the first time Hooper's pain at the donning of the veil:

> After performing the ceremony, Mr. Hooper raised a glass of wine to his lips, wishing happiness to the new-married couple in a strain of mild pleasantry that ought to have brightened the features of the guests, like a cheerful gleam from the hearth. At that instant, catching a glimpse of his figure in the looking-glass, the black veil involved his own spirit in the horror with which it overwhelmed all others. His frame shuddered, his lips grew white, he spilt the untasted wine upon the carpet, and rushed forth into the darkness.
>
> (p. 59)

Until then Hooper apparently has not been conscious of the full impact of the veil on others; he only feels it himself when he sees his reflection and then he recoils in horror from his own spirit. Moreover, the occurrence of that reaction at the wedding suggests, too, Hooper's deep feelings of separation from the purpose of the wedding, the joyous celebration of sexual union and shared human intimacy. Perhaps he is reminded that he cannot accept the marital state for himself or more generally cannot overcome estrangement from intimate human relationships ("the untasted wine.") His presence at the wedding seems to portend nothing but evil and foreshadows his rejection of Elizabeth as well as indicating vividly his pathetic gloom, his ultimate separation, aloneness, isolation from other human beings.

These feelings may possibly reflect Hawthorne's own emotional state when he wrote the story in 1835 at the age of 32, about the same age at which Mr. Hooper donned his veil. Hawthorne's good friend from college days, Horatio Bridge, wrote to him in October, 1836:

> I have just received your last [letter] and do not like its tone at all. There is a kind of desperate coolness about it that seems dangerous. I fear you are too good a

> subject for suicide, and that some day you will end your mortal woes on your own responsibility.[10]

In a letter written in December of the same year, Bridge wrote, "The bane of your life has been self-distrust,"[11] and Hawthorne says of Hooper that if the minister erred at all, it was "by so painful a degree of self-distrust" (p. 60). Hawthorne understood Hooper's state of mind all too well. In a passage in **"Night Sketches,"** written in 1838, a piece which might serve as a commentary for **"The Minister's Black Veil,"** Hawthorne writes,

> I look upward, and discern no sky, not even an unfathomable void, but only a black, impenetrable nothingness, as though heaven and all its lights were blotted from the system of the universe. It is as if Nature were dead, and the world had put on black, and the clouds were weeping for her.
>
> (p. 479)

That Hooper is so passive, or perhaps disdainfully impassive, never impatient, angry or uneasy with others, seldom revealing any agitation, helps to elicit a wide range of responses. His "coolness" is part of the mystique of the veil. Were the Reverent Hooper blatantly deranged we could more easily dismiss him as unimportant to us, since it can be easy to avoid personal identification with the madmen of fiction and, while feeling badly for them, place them in a safe and even clinical category. Instead, it is clear that Hooper is "irreproachable in outward action"; he is "the Venerable Father Hooper" (p. 67) or at least no worse than a helpless victim of his unconscious mental quirks. This technique of carefully disallowing easy categorization seems a deliberate attempt on Hawthorne's part to provoke a multiplicity of responses, for near the end of the tale, which is introduced as a "parable," there is an almost explicit invitation to discover the mystery of the veil for ourselves: "What, but the mystery which it obscurely typifies, has made this piece of crape so awful?" (p.69). By deliberately making motives obscure as an artistic device, Hawthorne has constructed a richer tale. This approach, of course, is not without its dangers. Pushed beyond the limits of credibility, the reader can only be troubled by confusion.

Although Hawthorne usually omits explicit statements regarding the factors which motivate his characters, he does imply possible explanations; we are given the implications, the channels and guidelines to allow us to guess what Hooper is thinking. In this instance, Hawthorne strongly suggests that Hooper's donning the veil results from his discovery of his own hitherto unsuspected capacity for evil. The occasion of Hooper's sin, or, more likely, his temptation, is suggested at the very opening of the tale. On the afternoon of the first day of his donning the veil, Hooper officiates at the funeral of a young lady. After delivering an unusually stirring funeral prayer, he bends over the girl's coffin, his veil hanging "straight down from his forehead, so that, if her eyelids had not been closed forever, the dead maiden might have seen his face" (p. 57). He anxiously pulls back the black veil, for at the instant when the parson's features were revealed it was rumored the corpse had "slightly shuddered." After the funeral service two members of the congregation sense that in the procession "the minister and the maiden's spirit" were walking "hand in hand" (p. 58). The modern reader wonders if Hooper had been tempted to seduce the girl. Poe, in his review of Hawthorne's ***Twice-Told Tales*** was the first to observe that there seems to be little reason for juxtaposing the account of her funeral with the minister's donning the veil with its connotations of celibacy if the girl had not been involved in some way with Hooper's strange transformation.

There is indeed much implied about Hooper's celibacy and about his careful, restrained, fussy, and possibly feminine nature:

> Mr. Hooper, a gentlemanly person, of about thirty, though still a bachelor, was dressed with due clerical neatness, as if a careful wife had starched his band, and brushed the weekly dust from his Sunday's garb.
>
> (p. 53)

A number of other statements also suggest a feminine, soft, gentle quality in Hooper. Even the phrase "to take the veil" has traditionally meant to become a nun. Hawthorne does, then, provide some evidence of Hooper's confused sexual identity. Crews even argues "that Hooper donned the veil in order to prevent his marriage."[12] This interpretation seems to imply an almost conscious and deliberate element of cruelty on the part of Mr. Hooper toward his fiancée and certainly requires more knowledge of the minister's motivation than the story provides, although the scene between Hooper and Elizabeth comes very close to suggesting overt cruelty on his part. Nevertheless, Hooper is made, even in that scene, to seem a victim of some inner or secret compulsion. Hawthorne never reveals Hooper's motives; he only suggests that Hooper, too, is a victim and shows the consequences of his celibate life.

Regarding the symbol of the veil itself, a significant but often overlooked point is that the veil is not a complete facecover. It is draped loosely from the head and falls skirt-like below the nose but does not cover the mouth.

> On a nearer view it seemed to consist of two folds of crape, which entirely concealed his features, except the mouth and chin, but probably did not intercept his sight, further than to give a darkened aspect to all living and inanimate things.
>
> (p. 53)

While Robert Crie offers the closest examination of the veil and suggests that it represents "psychological conflict due to sexual maladjustment," a symbolic "fig leaf," behind which Hooper probably hides fantasied mutilation or inadequacy, he fails to note what is covered and what is revealed by the veil.[13] It was probably as important to Hawthorne that Hooper's mouth remained uncovered as the fact that Parson Hooper's nose and eyes were covered. The mouth, exposed beneath the veil, is referred to on eight occasions as an "enigmatic smile." Surely the frequency with which Hawthorne uses this device implies his deliberate intention that it contribute to the enigmatic and ambiguous quality of the central image of the tale. Crews, in his full-length study of Hawthorne's psychological themes, blundered by saying that Parson Hooper felt a need to veil it [his mouth] and thus "imparted a repulsive horror to it," although Crews was correct in finding the image of the veiled face "altogether in keeping with his effeminate nature," toward the acceptance of which Hooper seems inclined.[14] The black crepe evokes the image of a very scanty gown, which covers some but not all of the symbolic "genital" apparatus. Since the nose appears in many classic psychoanalytic writings as a phallic symbol, it would seem that masculinity or male sexuality is something for Hooper to hide from public inspection. The overall image of the *partially*-veiled face suggests uncertainty and ambivalent feelings toward sexual identity. While there is the possibility of fantasized mutilation, as Crie suggests, there is undoubtedly shame expressed in hiding of the nose-phallus as well as elements of provocative exhibitionism in revealing the mouth and voyeurism in veiling the eyes. Crews also notes the exhibitionism:

> The general theme of morbid exhibitionism and alienation from humanity throws an interesting light not only on the hidden meaning of Oberon's [Hawthorne's] art, but also on a parallel hero, the Reverend Hooper. Hooper is the degenerate Hawthornian artist par excellence in asserting vicarious control over his fellow men by withdrawing from a woman and making a public but ambiguous display of his fantasies.[15]

Hooper can see out while viewers are not allowed to see in, and he gains power over them through their fear that he can perceive their deepest thoughts. The element of voyeurism is suggested also in the image of sneaking-up on others' secrets during his first sermon with the veil:

> Each member of the congregation, the most innocent girl, and the man of hardened breast, felt as if the preacher had crept upon them, behind his awful veil, and discovered their hoarded iniquity of deed or thought.
>
> (p. 55)

Thus, in summary, there is a good deal in this image to evoke associations that have to do with confusion about sexual identity, marked ambivalence about sexuality, and a tendency toward perverse behavior.

Although critical interpretations of **"The Minister's Black Veil"** differ greatly, Hooper remaining inscrutable not only to his parishioners but to modern readers as well, there is inevitably the suggestion of something awesome about the figure of Hooper. He is an enigma who elicits but then stifles curiosity. There is sufficient ambiguity regarding his motivation, that he can be seen as a helpless victim or martyr. One critic writes:

> It is not improbable, therefore, that he [Hawthorne] conceived of Hooper as a New England counterpart of the ancient spokesmen of Jehovah who were constrained to resort, at the cost of their own happiness, to symbolic acts that would be more effective than words in shocking heedless sinners into repentance.[16]

Another critic points to prideful aspects of the minister's act and behavior and sees the act of wearing a veil leading to separation from his fellow parishioners and the consequent spreading of fear and gloom which are quite inconsistent with his professional calling:

> The minister is cut off from a community not only by the fact, but also by the symbol; he sees only sin, only isolation and he cannot realize the possibility of virtue, or love and marriage.[17]

It is clear that the effects of Hooper's veil on others are profound. They see him as someone special, not quite like one of them, someone powerful and awesome, a symbol of things beyond their full comprehension. The image of the Parson veiled is like that of a totem or icon—a universal religious symbol. He is seen as a not-quite-human, mysterious, awesome image of profoundly important and universal feelings about the relation of man to that upon which he is dependent—father, heroes, gods, God, Christ or even Satan. These archetypal images and the awesome reactions to them by the parishioners evoke in the reader suspicions of prideful and grandiose intentions behind Hooper's behavior.

That this should happen to a man of the "cloth" suggests further that a religious idea is implied by Hawthorne and this can be interpreted on many levels. Hooper can symbolize Christ incarnate, or the Devil or at least a man in league with the Devil. The fact that Hooper becomes a respected but feared helper among his most distressed or dying parishioners further suggests the concept of witch-doctor, faith-healer, warlock, or Devil's disciple. A Puritanical perversion of the Christian concept of "suffer with me and you will be saved" is suggested too:

> By the aid of his mysterious emblem—for there was no other apparent cause—he became a man of awful power over souls that were in agony for sin. His converts always regarded him with a dread peculiar to themselves, affirming, though but figuratively, that, before he brought them to celestial light, they had been with him behind the black veil.
>
> (p. 65)

Also important to the image of the veiled parson is the fact that Hooper is called "father" during the later phase of his life, after the period of initial reactions has passed. While this evokes many Church-like images of priest or monastic-ascetic, the image can also evoke images or a primitive and universal semi-deified father-ideal, or can even be taken to represent Hawthorne's own father, the sea-captain who died of yellow fever in Dutch Guiana when his son was four years old. Jean Normand writes that nobody was ever to take the place for Nathaniel of the vanished father:

> Later, he [Hawthorne] attempted to compensate for the paternal strength and authority he had lacked as a child by turning to the Puritans of the colonial period. So that the father image in his mind always tended to be somewhat confused with the somber silhouette of the Puritan ancestor.[18]

The anxiety engendered in the parishioners and in readers of **"The Minister's Black Veil"** is never fully resolved, although the point is made that a life has been largely wasted. Even the intense and final death-bed scene offers no release to the reader. One experiences only Hooper's more intensified self-righteousness, and we are forced to consider the absurdity of his life. In the final image, the isolation of Hooper is complete in time and place:

> Still veiled, they laid him in his coffin, and a veiled corpse they bore him to the grave. The grass of many years has sprung up and withered on that grave, the burial-stone is moss-grown, and good Mr. Hooper's face is dust; but awful is still the thought that it mouldered beneath the Black Veil!.
>
> (p. 69)

This touch of green and its hint that the power of Nature and of biological life endures is hardly enough to relieve the blackness of the tale, a darkness which is dramatically emphasized by Hawthorne's occasional touches of light in such phrases as "the light of the candles," "the midnight lamp," "a glass of wine," "a cheerful gleam from the hearth," "at sunset," and "shaded candlelight." These spots of warm color enliven and give variety to the sombre tones. More frequent than hints of color are the number of references to pallor: the bride's "deathlike paleness," and "pale-faced congregation," the minister's own lips that "grew white" upon seeing himself in a mirror. As Walter Blain observes, the composition of this story "is one in which repeated patterns of light, then blackness, then whiteness meaningfully occur."[19]

A creator himself of color symbols, Parson Hooper assumes a black veil. Identification of Hawthorne with Hooper is suggested too in the parallel roles which they play. The moral of Hawthorne's "parable" is not necessarily the same as that of Hooper's but the method of their parables is the same: Hawthorne's tales with their concealment of motives are his veil. We never do learn why the Parson donned the black veil or what he hoped to achieve. Mark Van Doren says of the veil that it is "something we see better then we understand, so that we fear it—we do fear it—without enlightenment."[20] Paul Goodman correctly observes, "The explanation of the mystery is a compounding of the mystery, for we ask, what is it that a man hides? He doesn't know, for he hides it from himself."[21] Indeed, **"The Minister's Black Veil"** is a story about symbolism, about the kind of art at which Hawthorne excelled, and the effects of the symbolic method on both artist and audience. It is about a vision of psychological reality, of ambivalent attitudes, largely unconscious, communicated in the only way appropriate to that vision—indirectly and obliquely, through a central symbol, a black veil, which discloses its meaning in the very fact that it hides it.

Notes

1. Hawthorne's most famous definition of Romance occurs in the "Preface" to *The House of the Seven Gables,* eds. William Charvat, Roy Harvey Pearce, and Claude Simpson (Columbus, Ohio, 1965), p. 1: "When a writer calls his work a Romance, it need hardly be observed that he wishes to claim a certain latitude, both as to its fashion and material, which he would not have felt himself entitled to assume, had he professed to be writing a novel. The latter form of composition is presumed to aim at a very minute fidelity, not merely to the possible, but to the probable and ordinary course of man's experience. The former—while, as a work of art, it must rigidly subject itself to the laws, and while it sins unpardonably, so far as it may swerve aside from the truth of the human heart—has fairly a right to present that truth under circumstances, to a great extent, of the writer's own choosing or creation."
2. Henry James, *Hawthorne* (New York, 1879); Anthony Trollope, "The Genius of Nathaniel," *The North American Review,* CXXIX (September 1879), 203-222; Yvor Winters, "Maule's Curse, or Hawthorne and the Problem of Allegory," *In Defense of Reason* (London, 1947), 3-22.
3. See Seymour Gross and Randall Stewart, "The Hawthorne Revival," *Hawthorne Centenary Essays,* ed. Roy Harvey Pearce (Columbus, Ohio, 1964), pp. 335-366.
4. Randall Stewart, *The American Notebooks of Nathaniel Hawthorne* (New Haven, 1932).
5. Newton Arvin, *Hawthorne* (Boston, 1929). See also Philip Rahv, "The Dark Lady of Salem," *Partisan Review,* VIII (1941), 362-381.
6. Edward Wagenknecht, *Nathaniel Hawthorne: Man and Writer* (New York, 1961); Hubert Hoeltje, *Inward Sky: The Mind and Heart of Nathaniel Hawthorne* (Durham, North Carolina, 1962).
7. Frederick Crews, *The Sins of the Fathers: Hawthorne's Psychological Themes* (New York, 1966).
8. Quentin Anderson, "Introduction," Hawthorne's *Twice-Told Tales* (New York, 1960), xi.
9. *The Complete Works of Nathaniel Hawthorne,* ed. George Lathrop (Boston, 1883–. I. 53 All future references will appear in the body of the text.
10. George Woodberry, *Nathaniel Hawthorne* (Boston, 1902), p. 67.
11. *Ibid.,* p. 68.
12. Crews, 108.
13. "'The Minister's Black Veil': Mr. Hooper's Symbolic Fig Leaf," *Literature and Psychology,* XVII (1967), 211-218.
14. Crews, 113.

15. Crews, 161f.
16. Gilbert Voigt, "The Meaning of 'The Minister's Black Veil,'" *College English,* XIII (March 1952), 338. This view is also held by Leon Howard, "Hawthorne's Fiction," *Nineteenth Century Fiction,* VII (March 1953), 239. Terence Martin, too, views Hooper as "something of a martyr to spiritual truth" in Nathaniel Hawthorne (New Haven, 1965), p. 84.
17. W. Stacy Johnson, "Sin and Salvation in Hawthorne," *Hibbert Journal,* L (October 1951), 40. Another critic who agrees with Johnson on this point is William Stein in "The Parable of the Antichrist in 'The Minister's Black Veil,'" *American Literature,* XXVII (November 1955), 392.
18. Jean Normand, *Nathaniel Hawthorne* (London, 1970), 7. The "Puritan ancestor" referred to at the end of the quotation could be either Nathaniel Hawthorne's earliest ancestor, William Hathorne (Nathaniel added the "w" to his name after graduation from Bowdoin College) who rose in rank to major in the Salem militia and speaker in the House of Delegates or William's son John, one of the three judges in the Salem witchcraft trials of 1692. For more information on Hawthorne's ancestors, see Vernon Loggins, *The Hawthornes: The Study of an American Family* (New York, 1951).
19. Walter Blair, "Color, Light and Shadow in Hawthorne's Fiction," *New England Quarterly,* XV (March, 1942), 77.
20. Mark Van Doren, *Nathaniel Hawthorne* (New York, 1949), p. 87.
21. Paul Goodman, "'The Minister's Black Veil': Mystery and Sublimity," *The Structure of Literature* (Chicago, 1954), pp. 256-257.

Glenn C. Altschuler (essay date 1974)

SOURCE: "The Puritan Dilemma in 'The Minister's Black Veil,'" in *American Transcendental Quarterly,* Vol. 24, No. 1, 1974, pp. 25-7.

[*In the following essay, Altschuler contends that "The Minister's Black Veil" represents one of Hawthorne's most explicit condemnations of the spiritual teachings and revivalism that fueled the Great Awakening of the 1730s and 1740s.*]

Much of Hawthorne's "history" involves moral "tendency." He takes doctrines that developed out of Puritanism, like Antinomianism and Separatism in **"The Man of Adamant,"** and carries them to their logical conclusion. They lead to solipsism; the young Roger Williams should have rejected communion with everyone, including his wife. Ann Hutchinson should have had an evening prayer meeting only with herself. But tendency is not always actuality, and despite the numbers of congregational separations following the Great Awakening, Puritanism did not die of the proliferation of Richard Digbys in its "reductive" left wing. **"The Minister's Black Veil,"** for example, illustrates a more complex situation. If **"The Man of Adamant"** is about the road the Antinomian-Separatist might take, **"The Minister's Black Veil"** reveals the response of a thoughtful "main-stream" Puritan, a non-separating Separatist, aware of his responsibilities in the Puritan community, and desiring shared experience, yet conscious of the degree to which he must separate from others. The destiny of a covenanted community is a collective destiny (thus Winthrop's admonition that the Puritans be "knitt together"), but awareness of sin is a personal affair that tends to separate men when it might unite them.

With the exception of a brief footnote in Michael Bell,[1] critics have ignored when the tale takes place. Hooper is clearly a man affected by the tumult of the Great Awakening. He preaches an election sermon during the administration of Governor Belcher, which would place the story between 1730 and 1741. The reader is given ample evidence of the declension of piety rampant in the populace and of the almost stereotyped enthusiastic responses to Awakening ministerial exhortation. Hawthorne's initial description of the congregation makes the need for Awakening abundantly clear. "Spruce bachelors looked sidelong at the pretty maidens, and fancied that the Sabbath sunshine made them prettier than on weekdays."[2] Thus, the Sabbath seemed to heighten carnality rather than sense of sin.

Enter the Reverend Mr. Hooper, who had had "the reputation of a good preacher but not an energetic one; he strove to win his people heavenward by mild, persuasive influences, rather than to drive them thither by the thunders of the Word."[3] Hawthorne may have used the Reverend Mr. Ruggles of Guilford, Connecticut, as his model for the unconverted Mr. Hooper of Milford, Connecticut. Ruggles is described in Trumbull's History of Connecticut (which appears on Kesselring's list of books Hawthorne read) as "a scholar and a wise man; his morals were not impeachable; but he was a dull and unanimating preacher; and had a great talent in hiding his real sentiments, never coming fully out either as to doctrinal or experimental religion"[4] (italics mine). But Hooper is somehow converted. Hawthorne does not describe the nature of his conversion experience precisely because the Puritans never fully solved the dilemma of the verbalization of such an experience. The yet unregenerate could only understand conversion by experience; the regenerate could believe a verbal account of it only to the degree to which it resembled their recollection of their own experience. The sensitive Hooper was aware that not only had he hidden his real sentiments but that everybody did so. The veil was an outward manifestation and reminder of the distance between man and man—to Hooper, an unbridgeable distance.

The response of the congregation can be seen as Hawthorne's critique of the Great Awakening. At the sight of the black veil and in response to Hooper's sermon on secret sin "each member of the congregation, the most innocent girl and the man of hardened breast, felt as if the preacher had crept upon them, behind his awful veil, and discovered their hoarded iniquity of deed or thought. Many spread their clasped hands on their bosoms . . . with every tremor of his melancholy voice, the hearers quaked."[5] The Awakening had an equal effect upon the innocent and the guilty, on those who might have had an evil passing thought and on those who had committed sins. In fact, given the Puritan mentality, the "innocent" might be more sensitive to their depravity than the "guilty." After all, a true sense of sin was the beginning of salvation. Hawthorne carefully added a vitally important postscript to this unmistakable language of enthusiastic response. At the close of the service the people filed out of the church "conscious of lighter spirits the moment they lost sight of the black veil."[6] The awful effects of Hooper's preaching were by no means long-lasting. In fact, none as on former occasions walked by the minister's side. All went their separate ways.

The most significant result of Hooper's conversion experience is the degree of alienation between him and the surrounding community. This was by no means an uncommon occurrence during the unsettling years of the Great Awakening. Hawthorne could scarcely have missed Trumbull's constant references to separatism as a consequence of the Old-Light/New-Light controversy: "Instead of loving and cleaving to the ministers, who had been their spiritual fathers . . . they were strangely alienated from them."[7] No longer did Hooper break bread with Old Squire Saunders. For many, in fact, he could no longer perform the ministerial function. One lady in the congregation declared that she "would not be alone with him for the world."[8] When the parishioners sent a deputation to ask Hooper about the veil, they found it impossible to converse with him. That they in no way understood him is apparent in their proposed solution to the problem. Hooper had stressed the personal nature of conversion and the importance of the realization that sin is a personal matter, but the congregation thought only in terms of larger authoritative units. The deputies pronounced the matter of Hooper's veil "too weighty to be handled, except by a council of churches, if indeed, it might not require a general synod."[9] Such had been the fate of the vaunted congregational system. The ideas of the congregation were anathema to those newly converted by the Awakening and represent the distance between the gloomy minister and his congregation. They moved to embrace institutions even as he separated himself from them.

If the congregation walked away from its minister, Hooper galloped away from them. The veil was one of separation; of that there was no question. But Hooper did not retire to a Digby-like cave; he was not content to dwell in the Tents of Kedar. On the contrary, he remained as minister to his flock, though that flock could no longer understand him. He held to the community although every theological impulse in him told him that he must separate. Man's fate was to be separate because sin was secret and language inadequate to communicate it to another. In **"Young Goodman Brown"** Hawthorne had revealed the awful consequences that attended the doctrine of visible sanctity. In **"The Minister's Black Veil"** he filled in the details with a far more subtle protagonist. Hooper knew that visible sanctity bore no relation to regeneracy. Yet, good Calvinist that he was, he knew that there were the sinners and the saved. Given the impossibility of knowing one another, then, a community of saints could never be found. Could there, then, be any community at all?

Hooper seemed to deny it, but he clumsily resisted. He continued in his ministerial function, attempting to officiate at a wedding, perhaps the most simple and powerful act of community, a sacrament that he had denied himself. Although he tried to be cheerful and even raised his glass in a pleasant toast to the new-married couple, he cast an air of gloom about the proceedings. Significantly, when he tried to drink a glass of wine, symbolic of holy communion, his "frame shuddered, his lips grew white, he spilt . . . [it] upon the carpet, and rushed forth into the darkness."[10] He had consciously attempted, partially at least, to live in the community, but his newly awakened senses had made him separate.

The dramatic climax of his dilemma came in the interview with Elizabeth, his plighted wife. He explained to her why he must wear the veil for all his mortal days. At first "merely sorrowful" she fixed her eyes on the veil when "like a sudden twilight in the air, its terrors fell around her. She arose and stood trembling before him. 'And do you feel it then, at last?' said he mournfully."[11] Had Elizabeth been awakened? Feeling the presence of a kindred soul, brimming with love for Elizabeth, yet still firm in his resolve to continue wearing the veil, Hooper could prevent his impulse to community from surfacing. During the interview he had spoken to his beloved with a remarkable degree of calmness. Now, for the first and only time, he cried passionately: "Have patience with me Elizabeth. . . . O! You know not how lonely I am, and how frightened, to be alone behind my black veil. Do not leave me in this miserable obscurity forever!"[12] (italics mine). These words could not have been uttered by Richard Digby, a rather one-dimensional Puritan, but only by one being pulled apart by the contrary implications of his theology and the simple needs of the human condition. Elizabeth asked him, much as Mary Goffe asked Digby, to lift the veil but once. By this time Hooper's passion having subsided and his impulse having been replaced by one perhaps more Puritan, he responded: "Never! It cannot be!"[13] In spite of the exclamation points, he no longer cried with passion; he merely "replied" and then added a rueful smile which was to appear again and again in the tale. His devotion to his religious beliefs, his stifling of the familial impulse, was in the tradition of the New Light itinerants as related by Trumbull: Gilbert Tennent's itineracy "was a matter of great self-denial, to leave his family and people for so great a length of time."[14] For Hooper that time was eternity.

The rest of the story, though anti-climax, is instructive for a further glimpse into the clergyman's agony. "It grieved him, to the very depth of his kind heart, to observe how the children fled from his approach, breaking up their merriest sports, while his melancholy figure was yet far off. Their instinctive dread caused him to feel more strongly than aught else, that a preternatural horror was interwoven with the threads of the black crape."[15] Unlike Digby, Hooper was aware of the awful price of his self-imposed separation. Although he stubbornly insisted that the veil should never be removed, he maintained a tenuous connection with humanity. "But still Mr. Hooper sadly smiled at the pale visages of the worldly throng as he passed by."[16] Ironically, the congregation called him "Father," but the minister had consciously rejected parenthood by rejecting Elizabeth. He had similarly ceased to be an effective spiritual father to his flock, who seem most interested in him when on their deathbeds.

Finally, when Hooper died, the death scene is Hawthorne's criticism of the most sympathetic Puritan he had been able to devise. Hooper had focused on an undeniable truth—that man cannot know the innermost heart of his fellow man. This realization had compelled him, in spite of himself, toward solipsism. Though several persons sat in his death-chamber, "Natural connections he had none."[17] The simple message is that the man who separates himself from human love and sympathy, who severs his natural connections, is condemned to a life of woe. The attending physician was ironically described as unmoved, though he sought "only to mitigate the last pangs of the patient whom he could not save."[18] The use of theological language reminds us that the minister had not mitigated the pangs of his patients. Had he done only this he would have lived a far more useful life, at least in Hawthorne's terms. His own pains, too, would have been lighter. Hooper's nurse could not be described as unmoved. If the still-faithful Elizabeth did go through a conversion experience she was able to emerge from it without the solipsism that had enveloped her beloved. Hooper's chosen isolation had resulted in her involuntary solitude, but she had found it impossible to suppress her love. She was "one whose calm affection had endured thus long in secrecy, in solitude, amid the chill of age, and would not perish, even at the dying hours."[19]

The truth that Hooper's veil has obscured is that his attribution of collective guilt has precluded individual responsibility. "When the friend shows his innermost heart to his friend; the lover to his beloved . . . then deem me a monster, for the symbol beneath which I lived, and die!"[20] If Hooper thought he would be rewarded in heaven, Hawthorne hints that he was mistaken. The piece of crape still lay upon his face, "as if to deepen the gloom of his darksome chamber, and shade him from the sunshine of eternity."[21] Even after he has died and his face is dust, "awful is still the thought that it mouldered beneath the Black Veil,"[22] still hidden from the sunshine.

Notes

1. Michael Bell, *Hawthorne and the Historical Romance of New England* (Princeton, N.J.: Princeton University Press, 1971), p. 68.
2. Nathaniel Hawthorne, *Works*, Vol. I, (Boston and N.Y.: Houghton Mifflin and Co., 1900), p. 40.
3. Ibid., pp. 43-44.
4. William Trumbull, *History of Connecticut*, Vol. II. (New Haven: Mattby, Goldsmith and Co. and Samuel Wadsworth, 1818), p. 134.
5. Hawthorne, *Works*, op. cit., p. 44.
6. Ibid., p. 45.
7. Trumbull, op. cit., p. 170.
8. Hawthorne, *Works*, op. cit., p. 46.
9. Ibid., p. 51.
10. Ibid., pp. 49-50.
11. Ibid., p. 54.
12. Ibid., pp. 54-55.
13. Ibid., p. 55.
14. Trumbull, op. cit., p. 243.
15. Hawthorne, *Works*, op. cit., p. 56.
16. Ibid., p. 57.
17. Ibid., p. 59.
18. Ibid.
19. Ibid.
20. Ibid., p. 62.
21. Ibid., p. 59.
22. Ibid., p. 63.

James B. Reece (essay date 1975)

SOURCE: "Mr. Hooper's Vow," in *ESQ: A Journal of the American Renaissance,* Vol. 21, No. 2, 2nd Quarter, 1975, pp. 93-102.

[*In the following essay, Reece demonstrates how it is possible to admire Mr. Hooper's vow to wear the veil while condemning the effects of this demonstration of Puritan religiosity.*]

"The Minister's Black Veil" (1836) is, even among the stories of Nathaniel Hawthorne, unusually complex in potentialities for meaning. Its power to suggest numerous and often contradictory interpretations is reflected in the fact that its critics are in wide disagreement concerning so fundamental a matter as whether the Reverend Mr. Hooper's act of donning the veil and his subsequent insistence that it never be removed result from marked personal failings or from unusual merit.[1] Perhaps the most significant critical challenge of the story is presented in the analysis by Richard Harter Fogle, who believes the minister's veil may be seen both as a "symbol of secret sin"—in which case "the Minister is Everyman, bearing his lonely fate in order to demonstrate a tragic truth"—and also as "less representative of mankind than of the eccentricity of the minister himself, who severs himself from men either through perverse pride or through some other obscure and tragic compulsion." But, Fogle observes, neither of these views is wholly satisfactory:

> If we take **"The Minister's Black Veil"** at its face value as a homily on secret sin, we are confronted with the apparent disproportion between the act and its causes. The minister himself is to outward gaze the gentlest and least sinful of men; and we have no vivid sense of that presence of Evil which would necessitate so heroic an object lesson. But if we wholly accede to the second interpretation, which makes the steady view of life, the *aurea mediocritas,* the highest good, then the tone and emphasis of the story remain to be explained. It is too deeply gloomy and intense to harmonize fully with such a moral, which should demand a certain dry sparkle and lightness.[2]

This [essay] will argue that the apparent tonal inconsistencies which Fogle notes in the story grow out of a fundamental ambivalence in Hawthorne's feelings toward Mr. Hooper's conduct: on the one hand, the minister is a generous-spirited, psychologically stable, selflessly motivated man, all of whose actions spring from an ardent wish to serve God by furthering the spiritual welfare of his congregation; on the other hand, Mr. Hooper, who blamelessly has inherited the errors, as well as the truths, of Calvinist dogma, is a tragically deluded man whose moral perception, though not his moral nature, has been distorted through his lifelong exposure to the severities of his creed. To dramatize this ambivalence Hawthorne presents his story in terms of the familiar convention of the irrevocable sacred vow of the Old Testament. This device enables Hawthorne to depict Mr. Hooper as a rational, supremely dedicated man conducting himself entirely within the framework of the Calvinist ministerial tradition of the eighteenth century and at the same time to show that tradition as seriously flawed by its inordinate rigidity, especially in its insufficient recognition of the love and mercy of God in dealing with frail humankind.

So long as one views the conduct of the minister as springing from psychological or moral weakness,[3] the apparent disparities of the story appear irresolvable. Some of these difficulties, however, recede when one accepts fully Mr. Hooper's assertion, in his interview with Elizabeth, that his actions are the result of his having undertaken a *vow.* This vow, the story strongly suggests, is no mere personal commitment subject to alteration or repudiation: Mr. Hooper's seemingly strange conduct, the reactions of the people of Milford to the veil, and the veil's extraordinary ability to augment the power of the minister's sermons are all consistent with the tradition of the Biblical sacred vow, the terms of which are altogether irreversible and inviolable. His vow, apparently, is of the class defined by the *Oxford English Dictionary* as "a solemn promise made to God . . . to perform some act, or make some gift or sacrifice, in return for some special favor."

Some vows of this kind are recorded in the Old Testament in specific terms. Jacob vowed that, if God would provide for him and permit him to return to his father's house in peace, "then shall the Lord be my God: And this stone, which I have set for a pillar, shall be God's house: and of all that thou shalt give me I will surely give the tenth to thee" (Genesis 28:21-22). Jephthah rashly vowed that in return for God's assistance in defeating his enemies he would, upon returning to his home, sacrifice as a burnt offering "whatsoever cometh forth of the doors of my house to meet me" (Judges 11:30-31). Desiring a son, Hannah vowed that if God "wilt give unto thy handmaid a man child, then I will give him unto the Lord all the days of his life, and there shall no razor come upon his head" (1 Samuel 1:11). In each of these instances the petition was granted through divine intervention and the supplicant fulfilled his promise to God.

There is firm insistence in the Old Testament that a vow made to God must be rigidly fulfilled. "When thou vowest a vow unto God," warns the author of Ecclesiastes, "defer not to pay it; for He hath no pleasure in fools: pay that which thou hast vowed" (5:4). In Deuteronomy a similar insistence is voiced: "When thou shalt vow a vow unto the Lord thy God, thou shalt not slack to pay it: for the Lord thy God will surely require it of thee; and it would be a sin in thee" (23:21). So binding is the obligation to perform what one has vowed to God that Jephthah, in intense grief, kept his sacred promise, even though it meant that his daughter would be the sacrifice he had vowed, "for I have opened my mouth unto the Lord, and I cannot go back" (Judges 11:35). Hawthorne, well acquainted with both the Bible and the conditions of life of the early Puritans and their descendants,[4] might fittingly choose such a vow to represent the harshly restrictive influences which he believed the Calvinist faith had imposed upon its adherents in a former age.

Hawthorne provides Mr. Hooper, a man of little personal force, with ample motivation for adopting some powerful means to increase the effectiveness of his ministry, even to the extent of binding himself to a demanding sacred vow. His habitual manner of behavior and speech is undramatic and subdued. Of a calm, gentle temperament, he lacks the intensity necessary to produce a deep and enduring effect upon his hearers. A "meditative" and "abstracted" man, he receives the delegation from his church with "friendly courtesy," and has a "placid cheerfulness" for such occasions as weddings.[5] He suffers from "so painful a degree of self-distrust, that even the mildest censure would lead him to consider an indifferent action as a crime" (I, 60). His smile, consistently sad and faint, is indicative of the generally forceless quality of his address. The result of his good-natured blandness is that, prior to donning the veil, Mr. Hooper "had the reputation of a good preacher, but not an energetic one: he strove to win his people heavenward by mild, persuasive influences, rather than to drive them thither by the thunders of the Word" (I, 55). His sermons strikingly lacked the very quality that is instantly conferred upon them by the veil: "power" (I, 55). Desirous as he was of serving God, Mr. Hooper, before taking his vow, must have felt keenly the discrepancy between the mildness of his temperament and the force of character necessary to the difficult task of winning sinners to salvation. In the tale Hawthorne, as Woodberry notes, "has used the tradition of an old Puritan minister of the past age."[6] Thomas Hooker, one of those early Puritan divines from whom the tradition sprang, asserts that the conversion of sinners is no easy matter:

> A plain and powerful Ministrie, is the only Ordinary Means to Prepare the heart soundly for Christ. . . . The Elect of God are like trees of righteousness, the Word is like the Ax, that must be lifted by a skilful and strong arm of a cunning Minister, who like a Spiritual Artificer must hew and square, and take off the knotty untowardness in the Soul before we can come to touch close and settle upon the Lord Christ as the Cornerstone. . . . A powerful humbling Ministery is like the Plow, to *plow up the fallow ground, the thorny* sensual hearts of sinful men to receive *the immortal seed of the Word of Promise* and the Spirit of Christ thereby.[7]

Such a man as Mr. Hooper, earnest to serve God but lacking the firmness of address demanded for more than moderate success, might well adopt some extraordinary measure to gain the power to move the hearts of his parishioners to the degree sufficient for their salvation.

In his *Personal Narrative* Jonathan Edwards records an event which occurred early in his ministerial career:

> On January 12, 1723, I made a solemn dedication of myself to God, and wrote it down; giving up myself, and all that I had to God; to be for the future, in no respect, my own; to act as one that had no right to himself, in any respect. And solemnly vowed, to take God for my whole portion and felicity; looking on nothing else, as any part of my happiness, nor acting as if it were; and his law for the constant rule of my obedience: engaging to fight, with all my might, against the world, the flesh, and the devil, to the end of my life.[8]

In a similar manner Mr. Hooper, in several ways a fictional counterpart of Edwards, appears to have dedicated himself wholly to God by solemnly vowing that, in return for divine assistance in moving sinners to salvation, he would conceal his face from mortal sight throughout the remainder of his life, knowingly incurring the penalties of isolation that predictably would follow. The assumption, not unwarranted, that Mr. Hooper has bound himself to such a vow provides a perspective from which the various elements of the story appear not inconsistent, but harmonious.

Such a supposition clarifies his conduct in three significant scenes in which he exhibits his firm resolve never to remove the veil nor to permit its removal. At the funeral of the young lady, as Mr. Hooper bends over the coffin, "the veil hung straight down from his forehead, so that, if her eyelids had not been closed forever, the dead maiden might have seen his face. Could Mr. Hooper be fearful of her glance, that he so hastily caught back the black veil?" (I, 57). The minister's instinctive action in quickly concealing his face behind the veil indicates not that he is in some way associated with the young lady through secret sin,[9] but that he experiences a moment of terror that he might inadvertently have broken his holy vow. When he realizes that the veil no longer hangs between his face and that of another human being, the fear that his vow has been broken occurs prior to the reflection that death has precluded that possibility. The report of a superstitious woman that "at the instant when the clergyman's features were disclosed, the corpse had slightly shuddered" (I, 57) reflects, in a more general sense, the dread consequences of breaking, even unwittingly, one's solemn promise to God.

A scene which especially illuminates the nature of Mr. Hooper's vow and its effect on his conduct is his interview with Elizabeth, his betrothed. Sharing the bewilderment of the general community at the minister's unexplained action, and prompted by the privilege granted by their relationship, she makes a double request: "First lay aside your black veil: then tell me why you put it on" (I, 61). Mr. Hooper's reply is worthy of close scrutiny. He pledges to grant her request ". . . *so far as my vow may suffer* me. Know, then, this veil is a type and a symbol, and I am bound to wear it ever, both in light and darkness, in solitude and before the gaze of multitudes, and as with strangers, so with my familiar friends. No mortal eye will see it withdrawn. This dismal shade must separate me from the world: even you, Elizabeth, can never come behind it!" (I, 62, italics mine). The clear implication of Mr. Hooper's words is that he does not consider himself free to reply as he might choose, but that he is speaking under a restraint the limits of which he clearly perceives. His restraint is his vow, which extends beyond himself and involves considerations that make it unalterable. Mr. Hooper reveals to Elizabeth as much as his vow will permit, but he cannot remove the veil, even for her; nor can he explain why he put it on further than to say that he wears it as a "type and a symbol." Since he had earlier made no explanation at all to the delegation from his church, whose concern was for the same matter, it is only his special relationship to Elizabeth which motivates him, in telling her *all* that his vow permits, to approach the very boundary of what he is forbidden to reveal. To her further inquiry concerning whether the veil is worn for sorrow or for secret sin, he can, therefore, reply only in inconclusive terms.

In taking his vow Mr. Hooper appears clearly to have foreseen that the veil would separate him "from the world," but it had been his hope that his isolation from general mankind would be repaid by the companionship and love of Elizabeth in marriage. Without her he understands that he has no hope of avoiding the pain of total confinement "in that saddest of all prisons, his own heart" (I, 67).

Therefore when she at last feels the terrors of the veil and turns to leave, her action signifies to him an inestimable loss. His painful sense of this threat to the only earthly happiness he still hopes for is seen in his rushing forward to detain Elizabeth and in the vehemence of his plea: "'Have patience with me, Elizabeth!' cried he, passionately. 'Do not desert me, though this veil must be between us here on earth. Be mine, and hereafter there shall be no veil over my face, no darkness between our souls! It is but a moral veils—it is not for eternity! O! you know not how lonely I am, and how frightened, to be alone behind my black veil. Do not leave me in this miserable obscurity forever!'" (I, 63).

Nowhere does Hawthorne indicate with greater clarity the special nature of Mr. Hooper's vow and its enormous significance for the minister than in the incident that immediately follows this plea. Elizabeth asks that he "lift the veil but once, and look me in the face" (I, 63), clearly implying that she will be his wife if, in token of that special relationship, he will but lift the veil to her sight a single time. The force of Mr. Hooper's motivation at this point can be estimated only in terms of the invaluable benefit he is conscious of losing if he refuses a request seemingly so simple and reasonable. Having already forfeited the "cheerful brotherhood" of men, he knows that his refusal now will also deprive him of "woman's love" (I, 67). His "Never! It cannot be!" (I, 63) is dictated by a motivation powerful enough to overcome an almost desperate need. His fear of losing woman's love is overridden by his fear of incurring God's wrath by breaking his vow. At a terrible cost he has observed the restrictions of his sacred pledge.

Many years later Mr. Hooper, having, as Hawthorne truly and yet ironically observes, "wrought so late into the evening, and done his work so well" (I, 66), lies upon his deathbed in the "torpor of mental and bodily exhaustion" (I, 67). Even now his solicitude that his face remain veiled until the very end of his life has in no way diminished. The veil had made him "a very efficient clergyman," and by means of the power operating through it he had brought sinners to "celestial light" (I, 65). The work the veil was intended to accomplish has been done and will not now be negated by the veil's removal. The young attending minister, the Reverend Mr. Clark of Westbury, argues, to no avail, that the removal of the veil would benefit Mr. Hooper by lifting a shadow of suspicion from his name. But when Mr. Clark bends forward to lift the veil, Mr. Hooper, "exerting a sudden energy, that made all the beholders stand aghast . . . snatched both his hands from beneath the bedclothes, and pressed them strongly on the black veil, resolute to struggle, if the minister of Westbury would contend with a dying man" (I, 68). Like Mr. Hooper's spontaneous motion to keep his face veiled while bending over the corpse of the young lady, and like his painful refusal to permit Elizabeth to see his face "but once," his determined deathbed struggle to prevent the veil's removal argues that his concern is for the preservation of his vow. After a lifetime of such dedication and sacrifice, to permit the veil to be removed in the final moments of his life would be unthinkable.

The reaction of Mr. Hooper's congregation to the veil also supports the view that the tradition of the sacred vow operates in the story and strongly suggests that the minister's petition for divine assistance in producing a profound impression through his sermons has been granted. The effects of the minister's simple act of wearing the veil are in such striking disproportion to their apparent cause as to point almost inescapably to the conclusion that more than natural forces are at work and that the veil is their medium. The mere sight of the minister's veiled face fills the members of the congregation with "astonishment" (I, 52) and "amazement"; they are "wonder-struck" (I, 53) and regard Mr. Hooper with "strange and bewildered looks" (I, 56). The effect of that "simple piece of crape" is so powerful that "more than one woman of delicate nerves was forced to leave the meeting-house" (I, 54). Some of the Milford congregation clearly perceive that the veil's effect far surpasses anything that could have been anticipated from such a cause. "'How strange,' said a lady, 'that a simple black veil, such as any woman might wear on her bonnet, should become such a terrible thing on Mr. Hooper's face!'" (I, 56-57). Even the man of science, the physician, observes that "the strangest part of the affair is the effect of this vagary, even on a sober-minded man like myself" (I, 57). These parishioners correctly sense that the veil envelops a mystery which lies beyond their rational perception, that they are in the presence of an "unaccountable phenomenon" (I, 54).

The principal effect of the veil, however, is the extraordinary force it imparts to Mr. Hooper's sermons, an effect that begins the moment he appears before his congregation with his face covered. "A subtle power was breathed into his words," making his first delivery while wearing the veil "greatly the most powerful effort" (I, 55) that the congregation had ever heard from their minister. The sermons themselves undergo no significant change, either in content or manner of delivery. But the black veil—"for there was no other apparent cause" (I, 65)—transforms Mr. Hooper, hitherto a clergyman of no more than ordinary abilities, into "a man of awful power over souls that were in agony for sin" (I, 65). His congregation is sensible of some "unwonted attribute in their minister" (I, 55). Many of his hearers now are "made to quake" (I, 65) upon hearing him speak, and the efficacy of his efforts to bring his parishioners to salvation is signally increased. The veil is repeatedly described in terms of the awe, dread, and terror which it excites, and the suggestion is clear that some powerful supernatural force is operating through it.

The effect of the veil is heightened by the fact that its viewers sense that it is a symbol of unusual power. It is no mere symbol of secret sin, although this is clearly among its meanings. It represents, instead, the complex of theological doctrines which, to the Calvinist mind, follows from the fact of Original Sin: man's fallen state, his just liability to God's condemnation and the torments of hell, and his utter dependence upon God as the sole means of his salvation. The terror which the veil strikes to the heart of each viewer is that of full conviction of his desperate spiritual state and of the certainty of his personal damnation unless he is converted through God's grace. The veil transforms into an intense emotional impact the Calvinist doctrines that Mr. Hooper previously, with little effect, had presented to his congregation in terms of the "mild, persuasive influences" (I, 55) of rational discourse.

In a primary sense the veil represents the separation of mankind from God through sin: "Behold, the Lord's hand is not shortened, that it cannot save; neither his ear heavy, that it cannot hear: But your iniquities have separated between you and your God, and your sins have hid his face from you that he will not hear" (Isaiah 59:1-2). Mr. Hooper's converts affirm that "before he brought them to celestial light" they were, in a figurative sense, "with him behind the black veil" (I, 65), that is, separated from God through sin. When Mr. Hooper comforts dying sinners, the "terrors of the black veil" (I, 65)—the fear of God's judgment and condemnation—outweigh their fear of physical death. At the conclusion of his interview with Elizabeth, the minister "smiled to think that only a material emblem had separated him from happiness, though the horrors, which it shadowed forth, must be drawn darkly between the fondest of lovers" (I, 63-64). Even man's highest earthly happiness is sadly marred by his sense of isolation from God through sin and his consequent liability to spiritual death.

Of these meanings of the veil Mr. Hooper is surely aware, but there is also a meaning beyond his perception: the veil represents those austerities of Calvinist thought which, characteristically in Hawthorne's fiction, isolate man and diminish his potentialities for the happiness and comfort that come from shared experience. Mr. Hooper's sermons, aided by the effect of the veil, terrify his hearers by impressing them deeply with the severity of God's punishment of the unconverted. The cast of mind which results from such views, Hawthorne believed, had imposed a rigidity and gloom upon the daily lives of successive generations of Puritans, denying them their rightful share of human happiness. The first generation of Puritans, Hawthorne wrote in **"Main Street"** (1849), though inspired by a genuine religious fervor, was "stern, severe, [and] intolerant," making it "impossible for the succeeding race to grow up, in heaven's freedom, beneath the discipline which their gloomy energy of character had established; nor, it may be, have we even yet thrown off all the unfavorable influences, which, among many good ones, were bequeathed to us by our Puritan forefathers. Let us thank God for having given us such ancestors; and let each successive generation thank Him, not less fervently, for being one step from them in the march of ages" (III, 460). Hawthorne's conviction of the universality of sin was balanced by the hope that God deals with sinful man, not as an inexorable, wrathful judge, but as a loving and merciful Father. In **"Sunday at Home"** (1837) he voices the simple and sincere prayer, "'Lord, look down upon me in mercy!' With that sentiment gushing from my soul, might I not leave all the rest to Him?" (I, 37). In marked contrast is the inflexible God of Mr. Hooper's strict vow, who forgives no failure on man's part to meet fully the demands of prescribed law. Mr. Hooper's joyless human life, fittingly symbolized by his black veil and his rigid vow, is in turn representative of the impoverished temporal lives of the Puritans and their descendants, upon whom a stern creed had left its ineradicable imprint.

As he must if he is effectively to present **"The Minister's Black Veil"** as a parable of the limiting nature of Calvinist rigidity, Hawthorne views Mr. Hooper in terms of the professional norm rather than the anomalous and establishes the story in an authentic historical context. So firmly is Mr. Hooper placed within the tradition of the eighteenth-century New England Calvinist minister that he seems in most respects typical of the genre; his career, in fact, closely parallels that of the generalized portrait of such ministers drawn by Austin Warren in his depiction of "the divines whose spiritual father was the neo-Calvinist Reverend Jonathan Edwards." Mr. Hooper's lengthy service to a single community was the rule, for, Warren writes, "once settled over a parish, the clergyman commonly stayed for life, commonly a very long life. To be ordained at twenty and stay till eighty would almost be the norm." Like Mr. Hooper, who "had one congregation in the church, and a more crowded one in the churchyard" (I, 66), ministers of his class typically "baptized, married, buried as many as three generations of a family" and, again like Hawthorne's minister, they were "called 'Father' as they grew old." The opinion of one parishioner that Mr. Hooper's eyes were "so weakened by the midnight lamp, as to require a shade" (I, 56), reflects the fact that it was not unusual for ministers of his time and place to be "'at their books thirteen, fourteen, fifteen, and sometimes eighteen hours a day.'" Even in so unusual a matter as keeping his face veiled, Mr. Hooper is not outside the tradition, for his historical counterpart was typically individualistic, often an eccentric who "like the university don, and the [Anglican] vicar . . . was not expected—for good or ill—to be like ordinary people."[10] The fact that Hawthorne's note to **"The Minister's Black Veil"** calls attention to the non-fictional Reverend Joseph Moody, who, for another cause, "made himself remarkable by the same eccentricity that is here related of the Reverend Mr. Hooper" (I, 52) appears to be an attempt to lend credibility to Mr. Hooper's unusual action by pointing to an historical parallel.

Mr. Hooper's terror-inciting veil has been seen as a "satanic mask" (Stein, p. 390) and as the agent of the "spiritual impoverishment" of the Milford congregation (Stibitz, p. 187), evaluations which, however extreme, correctly perceive the veil's limiting influences. Yet, to see the veil solely in this light is to lose sight of the pervasive ambivalence of the story and the context of its setting. The effects produced by the veil are clearly within the limits of what, in Calvinist thought, was believed necessary to bring sinners to salvation. With reference to Jonathan Edwards,

Thomas H. Johnson writes: "Since God's decreeing will is clear to all who will read their Bible, the preacher is under obligation to advocate hell-fire and brimstone now and then, in order to remind men forcibly that 'conversion' is a matter of immediate urgency. The minatory sermon, though seldom used by Edwards in fact, is especially associated with the Calvinism he expounded, and was a traditional part of the Puritan ideology." Edwards' sermon *Sinners in the Hands of an Angry God,* Johnson observes, when "removed from its contextual place in the scheme of salvation which Edwards expounded . . . tends to misrepresent him as one who despised men when in fact he loved them as fellow beings sometimes forgetful of the warnings of a compassionate Father."[11] Mr. Hooper is faced with the identical paradox: his terror-arousing veil is the truest evidence of his love for his congregation, for it is the means by which he would win them to salvation. The use of terror as a means of profoundly moving the unconverted was, to the Calvinist mind, justified by the consideration that, as Edwards wrote, "The only opportunity of escaping is in this world; this is the only state of trial wherein we have any offers of mercy, or there is any place for repentance."[12] The failure of Mr. Hooper's congregation to understand his motives and the isolation he consequently suffers are penalties he has foreseen and knowingly incurred in taking his vow. Such selflessness is consistent with the traditional values of eighteenth-century Calvinist ministers, who, Warren writes, "taught the exacting doctrine that our business is to *love God,* not to assure ourselves of His love for us. In Dr. [Samuel] Hopkins' maxim, the test of a true Christian is his willingness to be damned for the Glory of God, one's '*disinterested benevolence.*'"[13] Mr. Hooper's professional motivation may be seen in such a light. His concern is far less for his earthly happiness, or his own salvation, than for the spiritual well-being of those entrusted to his charge.

It is in his personal, not his professional, life that Mr. Hooper is an anomaly. As a result of his wearing the veil, the people of Milford exclude him from the manifold rewards of sharing in the common hopes, sorrows, and affections of mankind. Throughout his long life Mr. Hooper remains "kind and loving" but in return is "unloved, and dimly feared." Though "irreproachable in outward act," he is "shrouded in dismal suspicions" (I, 66). A "man apart from men" (I, 66), he is cut off from "cheerful brotherhood and woman's love" (I, 67). Such separation from so much that gives value to human life is, to Hawthorne, an awful fate, and those who, like Richard Digby, Goodman Brown, or Ethan Brand, isolate themselves through bigotry, suspicion, or obsession do not escape his censure.

But, as **"The Artist of the Beautiful"** (1844) demonstrates, Hawthorne's thought encompasses an isolation that derives from merit as well as that which arises from moral failing. Owen Warland is isolated by his "genius" (II, 505), his "creative eccentricity" (II, 508), the "innate tendency of his soul" (II, 515) to seek expression in artistic creation. The "moral cold" of isolation which Owen experiences, an authorial comment observes, often comes "to persons whose pursuits are insulated from the common business of life—who are either *in advance of mankind* or apart from it" (II, 518; italics mine). The three representatives of ordinary mankind, Peter Hovenden, his daughter Annie, and Robert Danforth, react to the artist with hostility, secret scorn, and incomprehension respectively. When Owen momentarily puts aside his attempt to realize the beautiful and turns ordinary watchmaker, he quickly wins approval and emerges from his isolation. But in neglecting his genius he has "lost the steadfast influence of a great purpose" (II, 519) and has "ceased to be an inhabitant of that better sphere that lies unseen around us" (II, 525). Hawthorne's intention in **"The Artist of the Beautiful,"** writes Fogle, "clearly is to present Owen Warland as the spiritual norm of his tale and to proclaim through him the superior significance and intensity and the greater value of the artist's experience and interpretation of reality" (p. 86).

Mr. Hooper, like Owen Warland, is set apart from the world, not through moral weakness but through a spiritual strength of a high order. Except for his need to give his congregation the greatest benefit that he can offer, he need not have sacrificed his personal happiness; he might easily have lived out his life as the "beloved" (I, 58) minister of Milford he was before he began to wear the veil. He does not desire isolation and he does not reject woman's love in the person of Elizabeth, as has been suggested.[14] His plea to her to "have patience with me" and "do not desert me" is deeply felt and, to him, momentous. In a comparable moment Owen Warland grows "pale as death" (II, 518) at the thought that Annie Hovenden might, through her sympathy and understanding, save him from isolation, not yet realizing that his hope is futile. As Owen is set apart by his townsmen's failure to comprehend the nature or value of his genius, Mr. Hooper is isolated by the consistently negative responses of the citizens of Milford to him as the wearer of the veil. It is Elizabeth who "turned to leave the room" and who "withdrew her arm from his grasp, and slowly departed" (I, 63). The people of Milford abandon their customary practice of "walking by their pastor's side" (I, 56) and unjustly darken his life with their "dismal suspicions." The dramatic cessation of customary expressions of understanding or affection on the part of the townspeople toward their minister is seen in the fact that on the day he first wore the veil "Old Squire Saunders . . . neglected to invite Mr. Hooper to his table, where the good clergyman had been wont to bless the food, almost every Sunday since his settlement" (I, 56). Mr. Hooper suffers isolation by following his highest impulse—his selfless willingness to sacrifice his personal happiness, if necessary, for the spiritual benefit of his congregation.

Many of those in Hawthorne's fiction who live by the Calvinist faith are hardened by it. Its rigidity was such that, as Hawthorne points out in **"Main Street,"** it "could not fail to cause miserable distortions of the moral nature" (III, 459), distortions which affected the Puritan clergy as well as the laity. The extremes to which Hawthorne believed such warping of the moral sense could lead are seen in his depiction of Cotton Mather in **"Alice Doane's**

Appeal" (1835), in which Mather appears in a procession accompanying those condemned in the Salem witchcraft trials to the place of execution. He appears as "a figure on horseback, so darkly conspicuous, so sternly triumphant, that my hearers mistook him for the visible presence of the fiend himself; but it was only his good friend, Cotton Mather, proud of his well-won dignity, as the representative of all the hateful features of his time; the one bloodthirsty man, in whom were concentrated those vices of spirit and errors of opinion that sufficed to madden the whole surrounding multitude" (XII, 294). In **"Sunday at Home"** Hawthorne's portrait of a minister much closer in time to his own era is, if less extreme, still harsh: "Here comes the clergyman, slow and solemn, in severe simplicity, needing no black silk gown to denote his office. His aspect claims my reverence, but cannot win my love. Were I to picture Saint Peter keeping fast the gate of heaven, and frowning, more stern than pitiful, on the wretched applicants, that face should be my study. By middle age, or sooner, the creed has generally wrought upon the heart, or been attempered by it" (I, 36).

But Mr. Hooper, whose heart never ceases to be kind and loving, is not of this class of clergymen. His place is among that contrasting group of Puritan ministers in Hawthorne's fiction who, dedicated though they are to their stern calling, have nevertheless retained their humanity and sensitivity of feeling. Such is the Reverend George Burroughs of **"Main Street,"** who, condemned in the Salem witchcraft delusion, goes to his death "offering comfort to the weak and aged" among those condemned to die with him and in whom can be seen "a radiance brightening on his features as from the other world" (III, 470). In spirit Mr. Hooper is more akin than not to Arthur Dimmesdale, who "kept himself simple and childlike, coming forth, when occasion was, with a freshness, and fragrance, and dewy purity of thought, which, as many people said, affected them like the speech of an angel" (V, 88). Gentle and loving throughout his life, Mr. Hooper has a likeness to Dimmesdale's colleague John Wilson, in whom the rigors of Puritan life could not efface a "kind and genial spirit" (V, 86).

Mr. Hooper is one of those tragic figures in Hawthorne's fiction who, owing to the fineness of their characters, deserve a happier fate than their lot permits. Such is Ilbrahim, a child of extraordinary gentleness and purity of heart, who, a victim of his place and time, is caught between the bigotry of the Puritans and the perverse fanaticism of the Quakers and cannot live. In Edith and Edgar there are finer sensibilities than can find fulfillment in either the forced gaiety of Merry Mount or the "moral gloom" (I, 84) of the Puritan settlement. Owen Warland's genius, in another age or place, might win, instead of reproach and scorn, the understanding and honor it merits. In the unfortunate time-place context in which it is his lot to be placed, Hawthorne suggests, Mr. Hooper's conduct is more than correct: it is highly admirable. But the context itself is blighting in that it denies that measure of "heaven's freedom" necessary to the expression of what is best in such a man. His incomplete life recalls Chillingworth's discerning remark to Hester Prynne: "I pity thee, for the good that has been wasted in thy nature!" (V, 209). In more propitious circumstances Mr. Hooper might have served God wholly without sacrificing the happiness to which his compassionate heart and generous spirit entitle him. By allowance of kinder chance, he need not have lived "so that love or sympathy could never reach him" nor spent his life "gazing through a medium that saddened the whole world" (I, 65).

Notes

1. Among those who view Mr. Hooper's actions as grave error are Randall Stewart, *Nathaniel Hawthorne: A Biography* (New Haven: Yale Univ. Press, 1948), who sees the minister as a victim of "diseased self-contemplation" (p. 256); William Bysshe Stein, "The Parable of the Antichrist in 'The Minister's Black Veil,'" *American Literature,* 27 (1955), 386-392, who finds Mr. Hooper guilty of "apostasy from the teachings of Christ"; E. Earle Stibitz, "Ironic Unity in Hawthorne's 'The Minister's Black Veil,'" *American Literature,* 34 (1962), 182-190, who views Mr. Hooper as unconsciously committing the sin of "egotistically warping the total meaning of life"; and Michael Davitt Bell, *Hawthorne and the Historical Romance of New England* (Princeton: Princeton Univ. Press, 1971), to whom Mr. Hooper is "a sinner, perhaps the greatest sinner of them all" (p. 67). On the other hand, Gilbert P. Voigt, "The Meaning of 'The Minister's Black Veil,'" *College English,* 13 (1952), 337-338, considers Mr. Hooper to be a "godly preacher" who, at the sacrifice of his own happiness, has adopted "the ancient Hebrew prophets' practice of using striking symbolic acts as means of appealing to hardened sinners"; Robert W. Cochran, "Hawthorne's Choice: The Veil or the Jaundiced Eye," *College English,* 23 (1962), 342-346, believes that Mr. Hooper "profits from his vision" and achieves "the ultimate in human knowledge"; in the view of Terence Martin, *Nathaniel Hawthorne* (New York: Twayne, 1965), Mr. Hooper's veil, worn to communicate a spiritual truth of "man's common nature," fails to convey this meaning and has an ironic divisive effect (pp. 81-85); Jac Tharpe, *Nathaniel Hawthorne: Identity and Knowledge* (Carbondale: Southern Illinois Univ. Press, 1967), concludes that the minister's veil symbolizes a wisdom he has achieved or his intuitive perception of significant truth (pp. 78-80); and Neal Frank Doubleday, *Hawthorne's Early Tales, A Critical Study* (Durham, N.C.: Duke Univ. Press, 1972), rejects interpretations of the tale that view the veil as meaning that Mr. Hooper's actions result from either "a sinful act or a psychological quirk" and sees the tale as one of "human need" growing out of each person's essential isolation (pp. 170-178).

2. *Hawthorne's Fiction: The Light and the Dark,* rev. ed. (Norman: Univ. of Oklahoma Press, 1964), pp. 33-35.
3. Stein, p. 386, characterizes Mr. Hooper's conduct as "perverse"; Fogle, p. 34, attributes the donning of the veil to "caprice"; Stibitz, p. 182, believes Mr. Hooper sins by his "self-righteous and self-deceptive insistence upon wearing the veil."
4. Austin Warren, "Hawthorne's Reading," *The New England Quarterly,* 8 (1935), 480-497.
5. Quotations from "The Minister's Black Veil" are from *The Complete Works of Nathaniel Hawthorne,* ed. George Parsons Lathrop, Riverside Edition (Boston: Houghton Mifflin, 1882-1899), I, 52, 53, 60, 58. Other quotations from Hawthorne's fiction are from the same edition, specific citations appearing in the text of this paper.
6. George E. Woodberry, *Nathaniel Hawthorne* (Boston: Houghton Mifflin, 1902), p. 145.
7. "A Plain and Powerful Ministry," in Roy Harvey Pearce, ed., *Colonial American Writing,* 2nd ed. (New York: Holt, Rinchart and Winston, 1969), pp. 78-79.
8. Clarence H. Faust and Thomas H. Johnson, eds., *Jonathan Edwards: Representative Selections* (New York: American Book Co., 1935), p. 64.
9. This view, first proposed by Edgar Allan Poe in his review of *Twice-Told Tales* in 1842, perhaps finds its most extreme expression in H. Alan Wycherley, "Hawthorne's 'The Minister's Black Veil,'" *Explicator,* 23 (1934), item 11, who infers that "Hooper is the agent of the girl's death."
10. Austin Warren, *New England Saints* (Ann Arbor: Univ. of Michigan Press, 1956), pp. 25, 27, 28-29, 31.
11. *Literary History of the United States,* ed. Robert E. Spiller *et al.* (New York: Macmillan Co., 1948), I, 75, 76.
12. "The Eternity of Hell Torments," quoted in James Carse, *Jonathan Edwards and the Visibility of God* (New York: Scribner's, 1967), p. 157.
13. *New England Saints,* p. 34.
14. Stibitz, p. 108; Fogle, p. 34; Bell, p. 66.

Elaine Barry (essay date 1980)

SOURCE: "Beyond the Veil: A Reading of Hawthorne's 'The Minister's Black Veil,'" in *Studies in Short Fiction,* Vol. 17, No. 1, Winter, 1980, pp. 15-20.

[*In the following essay, Barry turns critical attention to the roles of the secondary characters in "The Minister's Black Veil," concluding that Hawthorne's judgment of their actions is as ambiguous and complex as it is of Mr. Hooper himself.*]

The deliberate ambiguity of style and symbol in Hawthorne's tales provides a rich mine for criticism, but it can beguile us into assuming there is only one lode to the mine. Critics of **"The Minister's Black Veil"** have tended to become so preoccupied with the resonance of the most immediate ambiguity—that of the veil itself—that other elements in the story, most notably the handling of the secondary characters, have been neglected.

Certainly the ambiguity of the veil is central; but it has by now been fully explored. The critical debate surrounding it is too well-known to need repetition here.[1] Suffice it to say that the mainstream of the argument has moved, in logical sequence, from one polarity (seeing the veil as an honestly-accepted symbol of human limitations, and Mr. Hooper thus as an Everyman figure, humbly embodying the fate of all of us who must see life through a veil darkly) to the other polarity (seeing the veil as a truth distorted into an absolute, a symbol of spiritual pride and deliberate self-isolation, with Mr. Hooper thus in a Faust role). And the debate has finally come to an equally logical resolution. E. Earle Stibitz,[2] building on R. H. Fogle's idea that the veil in fact embraces both polarities, argued cogently for the ironic interplay of the two levels of meaning; while W. B. Carnochan,[3] in a brilliant essay, analyzed the essentially literary nature of the symbol, its resistance to reduction into explicit "meanings," its paradoxical embodiment of both "concealment" and "revelation." Surely little more can be said about this. Modern readers can take for granted that Hawthorne's best symbols work very much in the manner of Keats' negative capability, preventing the reader from any "irritable reaching after fact and reason." They dramatize not only Hawthorne's distrust of moral certainties, but also his sense of their artistic bankruptcy.

All this is valuable, and central, to an understanding of **"The Minister's Black Veil."** Yet in nearly all the criticism relating to the story the emphasis has remained on Mr. Hooper and the veil. There has been little exploration of how the moral compass extends to other elements in the story, especially to all the non-veiled characters. But Hawthorne, as usual, is hedging more than one bet in this tale. Throughout the deft juxtapositions of structure and style, the ambiguous veil is used as a catalyst by which other moral and perceptual values are examined.[4]

The fact that Hawthorne intended the moral scrutiny of his story to be directed as much toward the attitudes of the other characters as toward Mr. Hooper's is suggested by the very structure of the tale. In the opening tableau the camera pans, as it were, a cross-section of the congregation ("sexton," "old people," "children," "parents," "spruce bachelors," "pretty maidens,") before it focuses on the entry of Mr. Hooper. In the closing scene, Mr. Hooper's attitude is once more established in terms of dramatic contrast—this time with that of the "young and zealous divine," the Reverend Mr. Clark, whose arguments for the removal of the veil encapsulate most of those used by various people throughout the story (simple curiosity, personal uneasiness, the appeal to a sense of clerical propriety, the assumption of a "horrible crime"). In between these two set-pieces, the narrative is carefully modulated between dramatic incidents involving Mr. Hooper's veil and accounts of the reactions of the congregation to it. After the initial paragraph presenting the range of characters involved in this dialectic, the first conversation is centered on their reactions to the yet-unnamed phenomenon. This then is followed by the narrator's filling us in on "the cause of so much amazement," which, he notes, "may appear sufficiently slight." After this explanatory paragraph, the story reverts to the popular reactions. Then the account of the sermon, followed yet once more by an account of the popular reactions. And so on. The reverting to the effect of the veil is more constant than a *leit motif*; it is part of a carefully-controlled juxtaposition that tightens and extends the dramatic ambiguities of the tale.

"The Minister's Black Veil" is an interesting variation on Hawthorne's theme of spiritual isolation. The isolation of Ethan Brand or Goodman Brown is clearly their responsibility, their "unpardonable sin." But if Mr. Hooper is shown as isolated from the members of his congregation, the fault would seem to rest at least as much with them as with him. Throughout the tale, Hawthorne presents a wide range of attitudes in relation to the veil; but what unifies them all is a refusal, or an inability, to accept Mr. Hooper's acceptance of it. Three people, including Elizabeth, speculate that it is a sign of madness; others see it "a confession of dark crimes." Some "sagacious heads" presume to be able to "penetrate the mystery"; others declare there is "no mystery at all." Yet all agree that "he has changed himself into something awful only by hiding his face." Their reactions are ones of "dread" and "horror," and they are all "conscious of lighter spirits the moment they [lose] sight of the black veil." There is nothing in Mr. Hooper's manner or actions ("nodding kindly to . . . his parishioners," full of "friendly courtesy," "kind and loving") to isolate them. What does so is the projection of their own fears and their own imaginative blindness. Their reactions run a gamut from pettiness to positive cruelty: the excessive propriety of "more than one woman of delicate nerves [who] was forced to leave the meetinghouse"; the comic embarrassment of the "deputation;" the viciousness of those who "made it a point of hardihood to throw themselves in his way"; the superstitiousness which claimed that "ghost and fiend consorted with him"; the general lack of charity that kept him "a man apart from men, shunned in their health and joy, but ever summoned to their aid in mortal anguish." Evil indeed is in the eye of the beholder. If the final paragraph of the tale is essentially negative in its language, it is so not only at the expense of Mr. Hooper. He has been very largely the scapegoat for a conventional morality that could not tolerate the existence of a public conscience.

In this connection, Elizabeth, usually seen as the only affirmative figure in the tale, and as thus marking the extent of Hooper's culpable isolation, becomes herself culpable; at least until the end, she is incapable of the ultimate trust or love required to see in the veil the human reality beyond the symbolic one, although as Mr. Hooper's "plighted wife" she is in the best position to do so. That Hawthorne's attitude to her is more ambiguous than has generally been supposed is seen in the language of the crucial scene between the plighted lovers and by the self-contradictions of her own reasoning. Although she is described as being able to discern in the veil "nothing of the dreadful gloom that had so overawed the multitude," and although she had herself declared to him "there is nothing terrible in this piece of crape except that it hides a face which I am always glad to look upon," she nevertheless, with "calm energy," "determines to chase away the strange cloud," with which the black veil had "impressed all beside herself." There is a brisk intractability reflected in the language and the syntax here. ("As his plighted wife, it should be her privilege . . . ;" "At the Minister's first visit, therefore . . ."). The "calm energy" seems an obstinate determination that her will shall prevail, though the stakes, as she herself has acknowledged, are not high. In the face of his refusal to succumb to her persuasions, her arguments change radically. From her initial acceptance of the veil as "but a double fold of crape," she moves quickly through interpreting it as a token of some "grievous affliction," to an imputation of scandal ("there may be whispers that you hide your face under the consciousness of secret sin"), to seeing it as "perhaps a symptom of mental disease," until finally its "terrors" have been transferred to her. Throughout all these attempts to force Mr. Hooper to place a literal meaning on what he had chosen to describe as "a type and a symbol," his replies, couched as they are in terms of deliberate equivocation ("If it be a sign of mourning . . . I, perhaps, like most other mortals, have sorrows dark enough to be typified by a black veil. . . . If I hide my face for sorrow, there is cause enough . . . and if I cover it for secret sin, what mortal man might not do the same?") recall Christ's "render to Caesar" answer when men of bad faith sought to trap him into literalizing a symbol. Finally, though her lover cries "passionately" to her out of his "miserable obscurity" not to desert him in his fear and loneliness, she presents him with an ultimatum, the cold simplicity of which is a measure of her moral imagination at this stage: "'Lift the veil but once and look me in the face,' said she. 'Never! It cannot be!' replied Mr. Hooper. 'Then, farewell!' said Elizabeth."

Throughout the story, then, Hawthorne builds up a composite picture of the parishioners' responses to the veil, which acts as one side of the dialectical tension on which the story is structured. The dialectic is epitomized by the parallelism of syntax in the final summing-up of Mr. Hooper's life: "In this manner, Mr. Hooper spent a long life, irreproachable in outward act, yet shrouded in dismal suspicions; kind and loving, though unloved and dimly feared; a man apart from men, shunned in their health and joy, but ever summoned to their aid in mortal anguish." The contrast is one between moral attitudes (the minister's kindliness and the parishioners' uncharitable suspicions) and, more importantly, between modes of perception (Mr. Hooper's sense of the symbol as too complex to be able to explain, and the parishioners' literal-mindedness).

Yet Hawthorne is not as unequivocal toward the congregation as the above argument might suggest. The writer who refused to see one-dimensionally even the Puritans condemning Hester Prynne does not render this tale melodramatic by over-simplifying either one of his dramatic polarities. Both his moral and his artistic judgment forbade such glibness. The same ambivalence that surrounds Mr. Hooper in the story also encompasses those who oppose him.

Three factors modify our judgment of Mr. Hooper's judges. One is the narrative style used to describe them. Throughout most of the story this remains jocular, detached, fending off serious criticism. With something of the same authorial facetiousness as in the preamble to **"Rappacini's Daughter,"** Hawthorne even manages to incorporate a mention of his own wedding-knell story. The opening paragraph sets the parishioners in stereotyped roles from which little individuality could be expected: the old people are "stooping," the children are "tripping merrily," the "spruce bachelors" are looking sidelong at the "pretty maidens." The insistence on words such as "seem," "appear," "semblance," assumes their angle of vision, and serves to rationalize their morality of appearances. What W. B. Carnochan has called the "Hawthornian business of false leads and doubtful clarifications" operates in their favor: the rhetorical questions ("Could Mr. Hooper be fearful of her glance, that he so hastily caught back the black veil?") promote their point of view, and the explanations of conduct ("Old Squire Saunders, doubtless by an accidental lapse of memory, neglected. . . .") give them the benefit of the doubt. The style reaches a level of comic burlesque in the description of the "deputation" sent to confront Mr. Hooper. For all their scandal-mongering and their imaginative shallowness, then, Hawthorne's style acts as a brake on the reader's judgment of them. Its gentle distancing is a paradigm of the faint smile with which Mr. Hooper acknowledges the limitations of the human imagination in encompassing his own dark world.

Secondly, the wedding scene in which the minister accidentally catches a glimpse of his veiled face in the looking glass, and rushes out horrified into the night, tends to endorse the judgment of the parishioners. If he henceforth "never willingly passed before a mirror, nor stooped to drink at a still fountain, lest in its peaceful bosom he should be affrighted by himself," who can blame his parishioners for their inability to see beyond the external emblem? Once again the detail breaks up any over-simplified division of sympathies. As if to highlight the fact that questions of perception, and of appearance and reality are at the heart of this tale, the mirror image is a recurrent one. The minister avoids the literal reflection of the looking glass. The "imitative little imp" who covered his face with a black handkerchief in mimicry of Mr. Hooper and almost lost his own wits by the panic he created in his playmates carries the mirror image one step further: he is the reflector reflected, two steps removed from reality, caught in the trap of appearances. The faces peering at Mr. Hooper from behind the tombstones form a more surrealistic kind of mirror which encompasses a double reflection: while they are trying simply to mock the minister they are indeed the "stare of the dead people." Finally, on his deathbed, Mr. Hooper conjures up an ideal world, without veils, where appearance and reality are one: "When the friend shows his inmost heart to his friend; the lover to his best beloved; when man does not vainly shrink from the eye of his Creator, loathsomely treasuring up the secret of his sin. . . ."

The third element in the story that works to modify our judgment of those who stand in opposition to Mr. Hooper is that Elizabeth, the character who most represents the limitations of their understanding at the beginning, is redeemed at the end. It is she who, if the veil had fallen on his deathbed, would "with averted eyes" have "covered that aged face." Her "calm affection" has no egotism left in it, and her willingness to accept the minister now on his own terms suggests a growth in both faith and love. She is still, of course, the loser—for this story of human limitations can have no winners. But her position at the end—neither that of the wilful and insistent Mr. Clark, whom she had resembled earlier in the story, nor that of the detached physician "decorously grave though unmoved"—suggests a middle way, an acceptance of all that the veil represents and an ability to grow in spite of this.

The ambiguities of **"The Minister's Black Veil"** thus extend beyond Mr. Hooper and the veil to the other characters in the story, beyond the symbol itself to the perceiving eyes. If the veil manages to incorporate the paradox of Mr. Hooper's role in the story—so that he is simultaneously Everyman and Faust—it also focuses the paradox implied in the outsiders' perspective: the limitations of their judgments, but also the understandable humanness of them. They form a backdrop of ordinary reality against which the symbolic meaning can be most resonantly played. Within the commonsense framework the most affirmative character of the story finds her growth and self-acceptance.

Notes

1. Good accounts of the history of the critical debate on this story are given in E. Earle Stibitz, "Ironic Unity in Hawthorne's 'The Minister's Black Veil,'" *American Literature,* 34 (May, 1962), 182-190, and W. B. Carnochan, "The Minister's Black Veil," *Nineteenth Century Fiction,* 24 (Sept. 1969), 182-192.
2. E. Earle Stibitz.
3. W. B. Carnochan.
4. One excellent article which does explore the role of Mr. Hooper's congregation is that of Raymond Benoit, "Hawthone's Psychology of Death: 'The

Minister's Black Veil,'" *Studies in Short Fiction,* 8 (Fall 1971), 553-560. Benoit was the first to explore in detail Hawthorne's negative attitude to Mr. Hooper's parishioners; the present article is largely an extension of his. But he sees the attitude as wholly negative, and reads the story in existential terms: Mr. Hooper having learned to live life because he has seen and accepted the anguish of death, while the parishioners live only half-lives, unable to accept the realization of death as an individual destiny.

Rosemary Franklin (essay date 1985)

SOURCE: "'The Minister's Black Veil': A Parable," in *The American Transcendental Quarterly: A Journal of New England Writers,* No. 56, March, 1985, pp. 55-63.

[*In the following essay, Franklin concentrates on Hawthorne's designation and subtitle of "The Minister's Black Veil" as a parable, speculating on the moral and esoteric implications this may have played in the author's imagery, symbolism, and thematic concerns.*]

"The Minister's Black Veil" has provoked as wide a range of interpretations as any other fiction by Nathaniel Hawthorne. Some find Hooper a martyr who sacrifices his personal happiness to his calling; others believe him an antichrist who perverts Jesus' teachings of grace.[1] But all seem to acknowledge that the meaning of the tale is uncertain to even the most perceptive and assume that Hawthorne provided the subtitle, "A Parable," as an ironic and misleading gesture to those readers who might want guidance rather than ambiguity. These critics assume, then, that Hawthorne intended the subtitle to convey its usual denotative meaning, synonymous, according to *Webster's Third International Dictionary*, with "allegory": a "short fictitious story that illustrates a moral attitude or a religious principle." W. B. Carnochan's attitude toward "A Parable" seems to be representative. In remarking on the dying words of Hooper, who accuses all men of hiding secret sin, Carnochan says, "If we throw caution aside and take this last pronouncement as conclusive, the story is that parable of hidden guilt which it is usually supposed to be—and also, I think, a less interesting story than it really is" (185). But the subtitle apparently had a particular generic meaning for Hawthorne, for the tale is one of the six of thirty-nine pieces in ***Twice-Told Tales*** with similarly specific labels, such as **"A Fantasy," "A Morality," "An Apologue,"** and **"A Faery Legend."** Hawthorne seems to have been engaged in experimenting with types other than tale, sketch, and romance. Since these other subtitles elucidate the pieces they precede, Hawthorne's intent in choosing "A Parable" as descriptive of **"The Minister's Black Veil"** should be explored thoroughly.

The parables of Jesus would appear to be the models for Hawthorne, though surprisingly only one critic has pointed to them as an influence. George Monteiro, following the premise that the minister's veil is itself the parable, deems "communication of Christian mysteries" the function of New Testament parables, citing the sower parable; and he damns Hooper for making a "secular mystery" of the veil and for caring little to communicate with his parishioners (item 9). But consideration of the whole biblical passage to which Monteiro refers, including the epilogue to the sower parable, clearly shows that Jesus himself did not successfully communicate to all his hearers through parables, nor did he apparently intend to. After telling the story of the sower, Jesus is queried by his disciples:

> Why speakest thou unto them in parables? He answered and said unto them, Because it is given unto you to know the mysteries of the kingdom of heaven, but to them it is not given. For whosoever hath, to him shall be given, and he shall have more abundance: but whosoever hath not, from him shall be taken away even that he hath. Therefore speak I to them in parables: because they seeing see not; and hearing they hear not, neither do they understand. And in them is fulfilled the prophecy of Esaias, which saith, By hearing ye shall hear, and shall not understand; and seeing ye shall see, and shall not perceive: For this people's heart is waxed gross, and their ears are dull of hearing, and their eyes they have closed; lest at any time they should see with their eyes, and hear with their ears, and should understand with their heart, and should be converted, and I should heal them.
>
> (Matthew 13:10-15)

These remarks suggest that Jesus imparts esoteric knowledge of the "kingdom" only to an elect group; the rest, like Hooper's congregation, see and hear but do not "understand" and "perceive." Hawthorne, therefore, was not modelling his minister's parable on the narratives of Jesus but on the notion, suggested in the gospels of Matthew, Mark, and Luke, that parables will be completely or partially misunderstood by most hearers.

Choosing to interpret Hawthorne's subtitle as a reference to the veil itself or, more specifically, to the minister's act of wearing the veil, and then accepting as Hawthorne's intent that a parable may not always communicate, one will find that Hawthorne's New Testament model clarifies the two major and polar lines of interpretation which have emerged in criticism over the last decades. The traditional reading of the tale blames the congregation for the minister's alienation. The first Sunday the mild-mannered Hooper dons the veil, his very appearance perturbs the congregation, "pale-faced" before him. His words, calm but disquieting, "had reference to secret sin, and those sad mysteries which we hide from our nearest and dearest, and would fain conceal from our own consciousness, even forgetting that the Omniscient can detect them."[2] Hooper's motive in wearing the veil seems clear enough to the reader, considering the subject of the minister's sermon—how we hide our sins and our selves from others—but the congregation leave the church in a quandary, obsessed by the black object itself as they ignore the content of the sermon. ("By hearing ye shall hear, and shall not understand," said Jesus.) At the funeral of the young woman, "The people trembled, though they but darkly understood him, when he prayed that they, and himself, and all of mortal race, might be ready . . . for the dreadful hour that should snatch the veil from their faces" (9:42; emphasis mine). The veil becomes such a barrier between the minister and his people, an ironic reversal which Hooper apparently did not intend, according to this line of interpretation, that they fear individually to advise or confront him. Finally, a deputation visits him but is paralyzed into silence by its awe of the veil. Even Hooper's fiancee, Elizabeth, seems strangely incapable of understanding the message of the "emblem." "There is an hour to come," he tells her, "when all of us shall cast aside our veils." But she replies, "Your words are a mystery too" (9:46). The mystery here lies not in Hooper's veil and words but in the fact that Elizabeth and the others, reared in the embrace of the church and the Bible, cannot immediately understand his allusion to the many veil metaphors of the Old and New Testaments, such as those found in Paul: "But their minds [the Israelite's] were blinded: for until this day remaineth the same veil untaken away in the reading of the old testament; which veil is done away in Christ" (2 Corinthians 3:14). Hooper's congregation misunderstand the parable of the veil just as Jesus' hearers misunderstand the parable of the sower. Thus a perversity in the people's souls emerges as one interpretation of this story.

The ironic connection between a "parable" and misunderstanding also assumes a crucial position at the climax of *The Scarlet Letter* right after Dimmesdale confesses his relationship with Hester and Pearl. Most of the spectators offer "various explanations" for the origin of the letter on the minister's chest, all related to the minister's guilt, but "certain persons" refuse to acknowledge any real connection between the minister and Hester. They consider his "confession" a symbolic gesture: "After exhausting life in his efforts for mankind's spiritual good, he had made the manner of his death a parable, in order to impress on his admirers the mighty and mournful lesson, that, in the view of Infinite Purity, we are sinners all alike" (1:259; emphasis mine). In juxtaposition to **"The Minister's Black Veil,"** quite an ironic reversal lies here in The Scarlet Letter. In the tale the people ignore the universal significance of Hooper's action and seek a specific sin the minister has committed; in The Scarlet Letter, on the other hand, the people ignore a confession of specific sin and choose to see Dimmesdale's act as parabolic. The use of the word parable in the romance not only links these two narratives, whose connections other critics have noted,[3] but also reveals Hawthorne's definition of parable: as the omniscient narrator of the romance says, a parable is an act designed "to impress . . . [a] mighty and mournful lesson."

The reading I have been pursuing here, with its focus on the congregation's perverse misunderstanding of the veil, itself suggests two interpretations: psychological and theological. The parishioners subconsciously deny the "veils" between themselves and God, or other human beings, whether these veils represent unconscious "sins" and impulses or the mysteries of their own natures, and in the act of denying they project onto Hooper their own "guilt," making him a scapegoat or "shadow," a role for which his dark veil appropriately fits him. The theological reading implies that Hooper embraces the doctrine of election. The passage from Matthew quoted above, on seeing and hearing but not perceiving lest the people "should be converted," is itself a quotation from the prophet Isaiah.[4]

The book of the prophet, in fact, appears to be a convincing source of the tale. After a condemnation of the sins and hypocrisies of the people of Judah in the first five chapters, Isaiah recounts his vision of the Lord, the purification of his unclean lips by a coal of fire, and his response to the Lord's call, "Here am I; send me." The Lord's charge follows: "Go, and tell this people [Judah], Hear ye indeed, but understand not; and see ye indeed, but perceive not. Make the heart of this people fat, and make their ears heavy, and shut their eyes; lest they see with their eyes, and hear with their ears, and understand with their heart, and convert, and be healed" (6:9-10). Subsequent chapters contain Messianic prophecies and warnings of the Lord's judgment to come. In the apocalypse, Jehovah "will destroy in this mountain the face of the covering cast over all people, and the veil that is spread over all nations" (25:7). "I will make darkness light before them, and crooked things straight. . . . Hear ye deaf; and look, ye blind, that ye may see" (42:16 and 18). "But your iniquities have separated between you and your God, and your sins have hid his face from you, that he will not hear" (59:2).

These passages are a small sample of the numerous references to light (revelation) and dark (sin, spiritual ignorance), seeing, hearing, and misunderstanding throughout the sixty-six chapters of Isaiah. Hooper—and Hawthorne—had plenty of biblical precedent for Hooper's act. Furthermore, God's calling of Isaiah through a vision helps toward understanding the abrupt addition of the veil to Hooper's mild, ministerial demeanor. A man believing himself called directly by God might persist in his conviction through life despite his own personal unhappiness. Hooper may even have assumed the role of the Suffering Servant Isaiah describes: "He is despised and rejected of men; a man of sorrows, and acquainted with grief: and we hid as it were our faces from him; he was despised, and we esteemed him not" (53:3). Hooper literally veils his face, but the people, ironically, respond in kind: "and we hid as it were our faces from him." Hooper, like the Servant, "was oppressed, and he was afflicted, yet he opened not his mouth . . ." (53:7). Though he preaches eloquently, he silently bears years of ostracism and rarely speaks of the veil. The sad smile flickering over Hooper's face may be interpreted from this point of view as a knowledge of his calling by God and a melancholy realization that his parishioners will not, possibly cannot, understand the non-verbal parable of the veil because they do not stand in the company of the Elect.

The far less sanguine interpretation of the minister as parabolist has, however, equal support from the text. In fact, Hooper as "unhinged" and obsessed is currently a far more popular reading than the one sketched above.[5] On the mistaken assumption that he is imitating Christ, Hooper may have decided to live a parable that he believes will be similar in effect to those of Jesus. As Jesus speaks in parables so that the disciples will "know the mysteries of the kingdom of heaven" but the others will not, so Hooper may have reasoned that the purpose of a parable is partially to conceal. Thus, a veil would be a most appropriate object, especially considering its biblical antecedents, and its dark color would also suggest the mystery to be hidden, in this case, our sinful natures. But here Hooper has departed from his imitation of Christ because his veil does not typify the mysteries of the kingdom, which the Messiah's proverbs veiled, but the mysteries of human nature. Hooper's veil, in fact, works against the human communion he cries for at this death:

> 'What, but the mystery which it obscurely typifies, has made this piece of crape so awful? When the friend shows his inmost heart to his friend; the lover to his best-beloved; when man does not vainly shrink from the eye of his Creator . . . then deem me a monster, for the symbol beneath which I have lived, and die!'
>
> (9:52)

But though he intends to wear a parable of the sin he condemns in others, Hooper's act has become the sin itself. The emblem is no longer a sign of the condition; it is the condition itself. Hooper's error may be detected at the onset of his project when he seems intentionally to veil his motives. His sermon has "reference" to secret sin, Hawthorne's aim in this word choice perhaps being to show that the sermon may not assertively present the subject but only darkly hint at the meaning of the veil. When the deputation visits him, Hooper sits silently with a "sad smile" playing about his face, and Elizabeth's entreaties to explain produce a gentle "but unconquerable obstinacy" (9:46).

William Bysshe Stein ventures to suggest that Hooper is an antichrist in perverting St. Paul's exhortation that a minister should "speak the word of Christ in the sight of God," the gospel of love and foregiveness (388). Hooper, however, is following The One he believes to be the highest New Testament authority, Christ, not St. Paul, about the nature of parable. These curious stories of Jesus were part of the scriptural bedrock of the doctrine of election.[6] Hooper's theological soundness is not in question, then, only his motive. He may have thought a non-verbal parable, an object—accompanied, of course, by the words of his sermon—would be an effective shock to his congregation. Here Hooper is again following sound scriptural antecedents, the prophets who engaged in similar symbolic acts: Jeremiah wore a yoke about his neck to demonstrate the burden of sin, and Ezekiel shaved his head to symbolize his approaching death.[7] At the other extreme, Hooper may arrogantly have decided it his calling to test the souls of his parishioners for signs of election, believing the parable the authoritative and, therefore, best manner of eliciting response. If this latter motive is Hooper's real one, however, we may judge him to be heretically assuming God's role. Even Jesus did not deliver his parables with the purpose of separating the Elect from the damned. In eliciting fear rather than love from his people, Hooper seems to be following, as Stein suggests, the punitive law of the Old Testament (390).

Locating the source for Hawthorne's choice of a subtitle in the effect rather than in the structure of Jesus' parables in no way resolves the interpretive controversy over this story. The critic may argue convincingly from the text that the congregation's failure to see and perceive the parable of the veil is a modern version of the biblical situation. Or, if one prefers to focus on the motives of Hooper, he can question Hooper's deliberate choice of the veil as a parabolic tool to test his people. Finding Hawthorne's source in the effect of Jesus' parables, however, does provide a point around which the ambiguities of interpretation may be clarified.

Up until now in this study, I have been commenting under the assumption that Hawthorne's subtitle is really a reference to Hooper's method of communicating, but patently, "A Parable" is Hawthorne's generic designation for this tale. I believe Hawthorne attached this subtitle to the story with the intent of indicating how he expected it to affect his audience. Perhaps he knew a majority would take it as a simple parable of hidden guilt; perhaps, like Poe, they would jump to the conclusion that the minister has some sin of his own, possibly sexual, to hide. As Nina Baym has demonstrated in the first two chapters of her book *The Shape of Hawthorne's Career*, the young writer desired to find and keep an audience and, accordingly, sought to "Normalize" his fiction (15-83; passim). **"The Minister's Black Veil"** is one of the eight "moralized fictions," as Baym calls them, written between 1834 and 1837, and as a part of this group, it celebrates "the common highway of life and deplore[s] all attempts to step aside from it" (55). Overtly, Hawthorne, in subtitling the tale "A Parable," may have wanted to assure his audience of its accessibility and, concomitantly, of the writer's normalcy in warning of the breakdown of human communion that comes from hiding sin. I differ with Baym, however, in that I believe Hawthorne also permitted here an undercurrent of his ironic, darker, and if you will daemonic, self to play a subtle, subtitle game with his audience. He perhaps counted on only a select (Elect) few remembering the effect of Jesus' parables on his hearers and recognized that the tale would be caviar to the general. No doubt, though, Hawthorne was uneasy with this irony and with himself as this kind of parabolist, for he postponed the collecting of two similarly dark tales, **"My Kinsman, Major Molineux"** and **"Young Goodman Brown."** In all three stories the protagonist finds himself alienated from the majority.

As the years went by, Hawthorne continued to ponder the difficult balance between concealing and revealing both his meanings and himself. The persona of **"The Old Manse"** (1846) seems to want the "honored reader" to believe that the author has invited him on an intimate excursion through his home and grounds, but near the close of the preface he denies almost rudely that he has revealed himself:

> I have appealed to no sentiment or sensibilities save such as are diffused among us all. So far as I am a man of really individual attributes I veil my face; nor am I, nor have I ever been, one of those supremely hospitable people who serve us their own hearts, delicately fried, with brain sauce, as a tidbit for their beloved public.
>
> (10:32-3)

Likewise, as he carefully and ironically maneuvers in **"The Custom-House"** (1850) to find "some true relation with his audience," the persona attempts to locate the ground for autobiography "but still keep the inmost Me behind its veil" (1:4). Thus was Hawthorne's constitutional need for privacy always at war with the writer's mission of communication, and this conflict and its attendant anxiety were never better dramatized than in **"The Minister's Black Veil: A Parable."**

Notes

1. For a summary of interpretations, see Lea Newman, 204-208.
2. All parenthetical volume and page citations to Hawthorne's works refer to *The Centenary Edition.*
3. See Newman, 203.
4. Frederick W. Turner, III, mentions in passing the veil imagery in Isaiah.
5. See Newman, 205-207.
6. Twentieth-century exegetes now argue they are not Christ's words at all. C. H. Dodd deduces from textual analysis that this passage is "not a part of the primitive tradition of the words of Jesus, but a piece of apostolic teaching" (3). The language is characteristic of Paul's. Most likely those who could not understand were the Jews who rejected Jesus as Messiah, and the passage explains that their rejection is a part of God's purpose. Dodd says, "that He desired not to be understood by the people in general, and therefore clothed His teaching in unintelligible forms, cannot be made credible on any reasonable reading of the Gospels" (4). Nevertheless, the Hebrew word of parable, *mashal,* denotes a short story with enigmatic meaning (*The New American Bible*, "Dictionary," 340).
7. Mentioned by Gilbert Voight, 337-338.

Works Cited

Baym, Nina. *The Shape of Hawthorne's Career.* Ithaca: Cornell, 1976.

Carnochan, W. B. "'The Minister's Black Veil': Symbol, Meaning, and the Context of Hawthorne's Art." *Nineteenth-Century Fiction* 24 (1969): 182-192.

Dodd, C. H. *The Parables of the Kingdom.* New York: Scribner's, 1961.

Hawthorne, Nathaniel. *The Centenary Edition of the Works of Nathaniel Hawthorne.* Ed. William Charvat, et al. Columbus: Ohio State, 1974.

Monteiro, George. "Hawthorne's 'The Minister's Black Veil.'" *The Explicator*22 (October, 1963): item 9.

Newman, Lea. *A Reader's Guide to the Short Stories of Nathaniel Hawthorne.* Boston: G. K. Hall, 1979.

Stein, William Bysshe. "The Parable of the AntiChrist in 'The Minister's Black Veil.'" *American Literature*27 (1955): 386-392.

Turner, Frederick W., III. "Hawthorne's Black Veil." *Studies in Short Fiction* 5 (1968): 186-187.

Voight, Gilbert. "The Meaning of 'The Minister's Black Veil.'" *College English* 13 (1952): 337-338.

Judy McCarthy (essay date 1987)

SOURCE: "'The Minister's Black Veil': Concealing Moses and the Holy of Holies," in *Studies in Short Fiction,* Vol. 24, No. 2, Spring, 1987, pp. 131-38.

[*In the following essay, McCarthy illustrates how images of veils in the Bible can bring fresh interpretations to the role of Mr. Hooper and the narrator of "The Minister's Black Veil."*]

Reverend Hooper, who mysteriously dons a black veil to the consternation of his congregation, has received unduly punitive treatment at the hands of some critics, while others have elevated him to patriarchal sainthood.[1] Richard Harter Fogle believes that Hooper is guilty of "perverse pride," and is "sin-crazed"; William Bysshe Stein argues that Hooper is an "antichrist"; E. Earle Stibitz asserts that Hooper is "an unbalanced and unredeemed sinner"; and more recently, Michael J. Colacurcio, almost reluctantly, sees Hooper as a "sick-soul," "sacrilegious," "spiritually deranged and humanly out of control"—in short, "doomed." At the opposite end of the spectrum Gilbert P. Voight compares Hooper to the "ancient Hebrew prophet[s]"; and similarly, Robert W. Cochran sees Hooper as "the instrument . . . the very voice of God."[2]

In almost every instance the negative critical commentary derives from the conscious or subliminal acceptance of the narrator's tone. But the discourse of this story is without question ambiguous, the narrator of dubious reliability. It is, therefore, counterproductive to attempt the illumination of Hooper's character on a narrative basis. However, the critical polarity surrounding Hooper may be resolved through a close scrutiny of the veil as a "sign."[3] There is too startling a resemblance between the veiled Hooper and Moses to be ignored. That Hawthorne was deeply aware of the complexity of Moses as an archetypal character (both in the Old and New Testaments) has been amply demonstrated.[4] It is with subtle perception of complex biblical issues that he fuses Moses with Christ, and the covenants of Law and of Grace (which they respectively represent) in the person of the veiled Hooper.

Hawthorne's narrator tells us that Hooper's veil is an "emblem";[5] Hooper tells Elizabeth that the veil is a "type and a symbol" (p. 46), but of what? What does Hooper's veil signify? The author's note confuses more than it elucidates in its provision of a pseudo-precedent. We are told that Joseph M. Moody historically veiled himself after having accidentally killed a friend. His veil is a symbol of regret and shame, one which "hid his face from men" (p. 37). Though the note tempts us to relate Hooper's veil to sin, it also clearly directs us away from such a conjecture, as it directs us away from any grounding historical source:[6] "In Moody's case, however, the symbol had a *different* import," we are told (p. 37, my emphasis).

In addition to the red-herring note, the language of the text resists easy compartmentalization. We are given questions without answers:

> Did he seek to hide [his face] from the dread Being whom he was addressing?
>
> (p. 39)

or else, the language equivocates:

> Yet *perhaps* the pale-faced congregation was *almost* as fearful a sight to the minister, as his black veil to them. (p. 39, my emphasis)

Hawthorne's celebrated ambiguity cries out for an external referent. And he has provided us with one in his allusive use of Moses and biblical veil imagery.

The superficial connection between Hooper and Moses is obvious: both are veiled figures. Moses dons his veil after speaking with God to conceal his shining face, which has frightened the unregenerate Israelites:

> And when Aaron and all the children of Israel saw Moses, behold, the skin of his face shone; and they were afraid to come nigh him. . . .
>
> And till Moses had done speaking with them, he put a vail on his face. (Exodus 34:30, 33; King James Version)[7]

Similarly, Hawthorne's narrator tells us that "[a]sad smile gleamed faintly from beneath the black veil, and flickered about [Hooper's] mouth, glimmering as he disappeared" (p. 41). Hooper's veil, like Moses', conceals a face which "appeared like a faint glimmering of light" (p. 46).

If asserting a relationship between Hooper and Moses is valid, then an exploration of biblical veil imagery is necessary to yield a complete perception of Hooper's veil. Moses' veil—worn because he has spoken with and seen God, thereby alarming the Israelites—is a precursor of the veil that envelops the Holy of Holies: "And thou shalt put therein the ark of the testimony and cover the ark with the vail" (Exodus 40:3). Within this second veil is the ark, containing the law, and the mercy seat where God sits in judgment. No one of blemish can be admitted within the veil. The high priests (Aaron and his offspring) are admitted only on specified occasions, and then, only to bring the blood offering of an unblemished animal as an atonement for sin. The veil in this instance is of no particular value. It is what lies on either side of the veil that is important. The veil separates glory from corruption, life from death, splendor from squalor, the sacred from the profane. It is inviolable on pain of death:

> And the Lord said unto Moses, Speak unto Aaron thy brother, that he come not at all times into the holy place within the vail before the mercy seat, which is upon the ark; that he die not: for I will appear in the cloud upon the mercy seat.
>
> (Leviticus 16:2)

It is a recurring biblical refrain that in the presence of God's holiness, the corruptible cannot endure.

On one level, Hooper embodies the unremitting inflexibility of Old Testament Law. His voice speaks from within the veil of the Holy of Holies—the place of judgment. The paradoxical elements of tender mercy and inflexible judgment are united behind the veil:

> I am bound to wear it ever, both in light and darkness, in solitude and before the gaze of multitudes, and as with strangers, so with my familiar friends. No mortal eye will see it withdrawn. This dismal shade must separate me from the world: even you, Elizabeth, can never come behind it!
>
> (p. 46)

That this speech is addressed to Elizabeth, whose name means "she worships the Lord God," adds to the poignancy of the unnavigable separation between God and man. Hooper, then, becomes the inviolable image of God, glimmering behind the veil, unable to admit blemished mortals.

In addition to the veil of Moses and the veil of the tabernacle, a third veil is spoken of: the metaphoric veil that hangs over the peoples' hearts. The verses of 2 Corinthians—as Stein, in his "The Parable of the Antichrist in **"The Minister's Black Veil,"**" so aptly observes—unite Moses with Christ, the covenant of Law with the covenant of Grace, in what seems to be a contrasting comparison:[8]

> But if the ministration of death, written and engraven in stones, was glorious, so that the children of Israel could not stedfastly behold the face of Moses for the glory of his countenance; which glory was to be done away:
>
> How shall not the ministration of the spirit be rather glorious? . . .
>
> For if that which is done away was glorious, much more that which remaineth is glorious.

> Seeing then that we have such hope, we use great plainness of speech: And not as Moses which put a vail over his face, that the children of Israel could not stedfastly look to the end of that which is abolished:
>
> But their minds were blinded: for until this day remaineth the same vail untaken away in the reading of the old testament; which vail is done away in Christ.
>
> But even unto this day, when Moses is read, the vail is upon their heart.
>
> (2 Corinthians 3:7, 8, 11-15)

This is the veil of which Hooper exclaims, "I look around me, and, lo! on every visage a Black Veil!" This is the veil which cannot be removed, "On Earth, never!" (p. 39). Contrary to Stein's reading of the Pauline verses, it is the continuity not the contrast of the Old and New Testaments that is revealed. The "glorious" message given to Moses was the Law. The ten commandments, graven in stone, meant an end to moral chaos—that is why judgment must be perceived as a mercy and not a cruelty. But the covenant of Law is only fulfilled in Christ, who becomes the final, ultimate object of judgment. This is the glory that causes Moses' face to shine, and which the Israelites are unable to see. Moses' veil symbolically points to the unseen salvation of Christ.

Hooper's veil, like Moses', also implies Christ. The veil that hangs over the heart cannot be lifted other than by God's gracious hand. Christ is the unblemished high priest, the spotless lamb, the interstice between Mankind and the Holy of Holies. He does not do away with the Mosaic Law, but completes it:

> Think not that I am come to destroy the law, or the prophets: I am not come to destroy, but to fulfill.
>
> (Matthew 5:17)

Finally, Christ's body is the torn veil that permits access to God "by a new and living way, which he hath consecrated for us, through the vail, that is to say, his flesh. . . ." (Hebrews 10:20)[9] There are, then, four uses of the veil in the Bible: Moses' veil conceals God's glory, the veil separates man from the Holy of Holies, it metaphorically hangs in the hearts of the unregenerate, and Christ's body is the torn veil. At the moment of his death, the veil of the tabernacle is rent, symbolizing man's access to the Holy of Holies through Christ. Thus to reject Christ is to place the veil in one's heart.

The veil, hanging in the hearts of the people, obscuring Christ from their vision, has become (for Hooper) an "objective correlative" for Christ, which he wears as a garment of righteousness. What seems to be perversity in his not allowing it to be removed becomes an expression of his identity with Christ. Hooper's smile behind the veil, always associated with faint light, recalls Moses' fading splendor which prepares the way for Christ's permanent splendor. The link is even more compelling when one remembers that Hawthorne subtitled **"The Minister's Black Veil"** "A Parable," associating it clearly with the New Testament parables of Christ.

The reading I am suggesting enables us to view the funeral and marriage scenes from an entirely different perspective than the gloom-doom-secret-sin approach that has dominated criticism of **"The Minister's Black Veil."** In the funeral episode we are given the image of the dead girl's corpse shuddering at the disclosure of Hooper's features. Poe, in his review of this story, asserted that Hooper had committed a "crime of dark dye" against the dead girl; most of the critics agree with this reading, if not in letter, in spirit.[10]

> [T]he bell tolled for the funeral of a young lady. The relatives and friends were assembled in the house, and the more distant acquaintances stood about the door, speaking of the good qualities of the deceased, when their talk was interrupted by the appearance of Mr. Hooper . . . The clergyman stepped into the room where the corpse was laid, and bent over the coffin, to take a last farewell of his deceased parishioner. . . . A person who watched the interview between the dead and living, scrupled not to affirm, that, at the instant when the clergyman's features were disclosed, the corpse had slightly shuddered, rustling the shroud and muslin cap.
>
> (p. 42)

The diffident quality of the "mourners," casually discussing the dead girl's "good qualities," recalls the "minstrels and the people making a noise" in the funeral episode of Matthew 9:23-26, which Christ interrupts. In the biblical incident, Christ asserts that the child "is not dead, but sleepeth" (Matthew 9:24). He then takes her by the hand, and she arises. Correspondingly, we are given the image of the minister and the dead girl's spirit "walking hand in hand" (p. 42). This image of life and grace in death tempers the previous shuddering of the dead girl's corpse. It qualifies the scene, transforming the sinister into the mysterious, replete with "the music of a heavenly harp, swept by the fingers of the dead . . . heard among the saddest accents of the minister" (p. 42). The funeral procession becomes an image of new life.

The funeral scene metamorphoses into the marriage scene. Again, our reader expectation is overturned as the marriage feast, ordinarily a joyful occasion, is presented to us in images of death. The dead girl has returned from the grave to be married. Her "cold fingers" and her "death-like paleness" give us a different perception from that of the funeral episode. There we were given a picture of life and release through death. In the companion scene of the wedding we are shown death in life.[11] The appearance of joy is revealed as a grim and anxious nightmare. Hooper, aware of the disparity of life that consists of spiritual death, sees himself "in a glass darkly," as it were, and is unable to participate in the hollow joy of the wedding: "Beholding as in a glass the glory of the Lord" (2 Corinthians 3:18), Hooper flees the room. He is at once the cause and effect of truth:

> [T]he black veil involved his own spirit in the horror with which it overwhelmed all others. His frame shuddered—his lips grew white—he spilt the untasted wine upon the carpet—and rushed forth into the darkness. For the Earth, too, had on her Black Veil.
>
> (pp. 43-4)

Hooper as a Christ figure parallels the Passion of Christ.[12] The language of this episode is imbued with last supper and crucifixion imagery. Hooper's spilt wine alludes to Christ's refusal of galled wine as he hung upon the cross. This occurs following Christ's oath not to taste wine "until [he] drink it anew . . . in [his] Father's kingdom" (Matthew 26:29). The Earth's Black Veil, Hooper's shuddering frame, his white lips, all invoke the tenor of the crucifixion scene, "when there was a darkness over the whole earth" (Luke 23:44).

The "fearful secret" (p. 45) of the veil is that it points to the profound necessity of Christ. This is not to say, precisely, that it is a symbol of sin. Sin is not the truth of which the veil is an outward symbol. The veil is the manifestation of Christ's efficacy over sin, of man's urgent need of that efficacy, and of the perilous future without Christ's efficacy.

Hooper chooses the outward veil, signifying Christ, as opposed to the inward veil of separation from Christ. In choosing to veil his face, he removes the veil from his heart. At his deathbed Hooper is attended by Elizabeth (remember the meaning of her name). She is the only person who understands the significance of the veil and endorses its meaning. Her relationship to Hooper has become redefined: she is "wed" to him in the sense that the believer is the "bride of Christ." And as such, she insures that the veil remains in place (p. 51).

Our final vision of Hooper (Father Hooper) is as a kind of Suffering Servant. Isaiah 53 contains a prophetic messianic image of which Christ claims to be the fulfillment. The Israelites of the Isaiah passage, with their veiled hearts, have despised and rejected the Suffering Servant and "esteemed him not . . . yet he bore the sin of many, and made intercession for the transgressors." How like Father Hooper this sounds:

> Mr. Hooper spent a long life, irreproachable in outward act, yet shrouded in dismal suspicions; kind and loving, though unloved, and dimly feared; a man apart from men, shunned in their health and joy, but ever summoned to their aid in mortal anguish.
>
> (p. 49)

"A man of sorrows and acquainted with grief," one might add. The style of the narration here recalls the Isaiah passage, as does the content—it is one of the few moments when the narrative tone is in sync with the "signs."

But much of the narrative tone is at odds with the symbols of **"The Minister's Black Veil."** The narration is almost the dismal cataloguing of some incidents in which Hooper figures prominently. But what the narrator points to symbolically is precisely that which he himself stands in such desperate need of. Hooper's veil is, as Carnochan has observed, the embodiment of both "concealment" and "revelation."[13] What Hawthorne subtly reveals to the reader, he withholds from the characters that people his story, including the narrator. While keeping the veil firmly in place over the hearts of the parishioners, he removes the veil from our eyes. He forces us to see what the community of **"The Minister's Black Veil"** (for which the narrator speaks) refuses to see: that we are mortal in body, and that the province of our souls is governed, either by God's mercy, or his judgment.[14] The final sentence of **"The Minister's Black Veil"** characteristically reveals to us, in terms of "signs," what it conceals from the narrator and congregation:

> The grass of many years has sprung up and withered on that grave, the burial stone is moss grown, and good Mr. Hooper's face is dust; but awful is still the thought, that it mouldered beneath the black veil!
>
> (pp. 52-3)

The narrator's veiled heart does not understand the import of Hooper's veil; he sees only the physical decay, the mouldering of the body, the turning to dust that death brings. He has no vision, as Hooper certainly had, of life beyond this mortal "veil of tears." Therefore, Hooper's life of sacrifice and alienation is, for the narrator, one of senseless deprivation whose only reward is the horror of death.

Yet, submerged within the image of the withering grass of this last sentence is what might be interpreted as a warning or a promise, depending on which veil one chooses:

> All flesh is grass. . . . The grass withereth, the flower fadeth: but the word of our God shall stand forever.
>
> (Isaiah 40:6-8)

The word of God in the Old Testament is the Law; in the New Testament, Christ is the Word. Though Hooper is gone, the veil—signifying God's covenant—remains.

Millicent Bell in her "The Obliquity of Signs: *The Scarlet Letter*" refers to Hawthorne's "primary preoccupation with the rendering of reality into a system of signs."[15] And Benita Moore's article, "Hawthorne, Heidegger, and the Holy," contends essentially that Hawthorne "says" by not saying, indicating a reluctance to subvert "truth" with the inadequacies of language;[16] and Hawthorne himself in the "Preface" to *The House of Seven Gables* decries a too direct approach to specifying truth as ". . . sticking a pin through a butterfly—thus at once depriving it of life, and causing it to stiffen in an ungainly and unnatural attitude."[17] It is as if Hawthorne sees existence as indeterminate, an already subjectively interpretive narrative effort; and to attain any sort of "truth," he must resort to the transcendent meanings of signs. But the signs are always given through a fallible human voice that, despite its intended objectivity, is necessarily hermeneutical. The greatness of Hawthorne is that he allows/forces us to participate in and expand upon this interpretive effort.

Notes

1. For negative treatment of Hooper and his veil, see Richard Harter Fogle's "An Ambiguity of Sin or Sorrow," in *New England Quarterly,* 12 (1948), 342-349; William Bysshe Stein's "The Parable of the Antichrist in 'The Minister's Black Veil,'" in *American Literature,* 27 (1955), 386-392; E. Earle Stibitz' "Ironic Unity in Hawthorne's 'The Minister's Black Veil,'" in *American Literature,* 34 (1962), 182-190; and Michael J. Colacurcio's "Parson Hooper's Power of Blackness: Sin and Self in 'The Minister's Black Veil'" in *Prospects: An Annual of American Culture Studies,* 5 (1980), 331-411. For a positive view, see Gilbert P. Voight's "The Meaning of 'The Minister's Black Veil,'" in *College English,* 13 (1952), 337-338; and Robert W. Cochran's "Hawthorne's Choice: The Veil or the Jaundiced Eye," in *College English,* 23 (1962), 342-346. Voight's article in which he discusses Jeremiah's yoke, Ezekiel's shaven face, and Hosea's marriage to a prostitute as signs for the Israelites provided the inspiration for my essay, tracing Hooper's resemblance to Moses.

2. Fogle, p. 343; Stein, p. 391; Stibitz, p. 188; Colacurcio, pp. 347, 354, 361, 398; Voight, p. 338; Cochran, p. 345.

3. See W. B. Carnochan's "'The Minister's Black Veil': Symbol, Meaning, and the Context of Hawthorne's Art" in *Nineteenth-Century Fiction,* 24 (1969), 182-192; and Mellicent Bell's "The Obliquity of Signs: *The Scarlet Letter*" in *Massachusetts Review* (Spring 1982), 9-26. These two articles deal (though in a very different manner from that which I intend) with the pre-eminence of signs in a critical scrutiny of Hawthorne's works.

4. See Ely Stock's "History and the Bible in Hawthorne's 'Roger Malvin's Burial,'" in *Essex Institute Historical Collections,* 100 (1964), 279-296; and Burton J. Fishman's "Imagined Redemption in 'Roger Malvin's Burial,'" in *Studies in American Fiction,* 5 (1977), 257-262.

5. "The Minister's Black Veil" text is from *The Centenary Edition of the Works of Nathaniel Hawthorne, Twice Told Tales* (Columbus: Ohio State University Press, 1974), p. 42. [. . .]

6. Michael J. Colacurcio's article "Parson Hooper's Power of Blackness" is an impressive piece of scholarship that takes great pains to place Hooper in an historical-puritan context. Though I greatly admire the detail of this work and find it full of valuable incidental information, I think that his effort to impose an almost scientific vision of historical "fact" on what he admits is an ambiguous discourse is a house divided.

7. All subsequent biblical references are from the King James Version, hereafter included parenthetically in the text.

8. See Stein for a carefully constructed argument that asserts a relationship between Moses and Hooper. Stein, however, assigns a negative value to this relationship. He dichotomizes Law and Grace, identifies Hooper with Moses and the Law, and dismisses him as an "antichrist." Biblically, however, Law and Grace are not mutually exclusive, but continuous. They are united as surely as Hooper and his veil. Stein's article, therefore, is an intriguing, but harsh misreading of "The Minister's Black Veil."

9. For additional verses that demonstrate the continuity of Law and Grace, of Old and New Testaments, see Galations 3:24; Romans 7:7, 12, 13; Romans 10:4; Hebrews 9:11. Stein's argument fails to see 2 Corinthians in the context of these verses. Hawthorne, I think, was more eclectic.

10. See Carnochan's "'The Minister's Black Veil': Symbol, Meaning, and the Context of Hawthorne's Art," p. 183, n. 4. For specific agreement see Stibitz' "Ironic Unity in Hawthorne's 'The Minister's Black Veil,'" p. 183. For articles that stress Hooper in generally negative terms, see my first note. Also, Frederick Crews, *The Sins of the Fathers* (New York: Oxford University Press, 1966) for a psycho-sexual reading. Crews maintains that Hooper dons the black veil so he won't have to marry Elizabeth (p. 108). Also, see John H. Timmerman's "Hawthorne's 'The Minister's Black Veil,'" in *Explicator* 41 (1983), 29-30; Timmerman contends that Hooper is one of Hawthorne's "arch villains," in the tradition of "Chillingsworth" [sic].

11. See Raymond Benoit's "Hawthorne's Psychology of Death: 'The Minister's Black Veil'" in *Studies in Short Fiction,* 8 (1971), 553-560. Benoit suggests that because Hooper has faced death, he can live, his parishioners cannot really live because they refuse to acknowledge death.

12. See Michael J. Colacurcio's "Parson Hooper's Power of Blackness" pp. 353-4 for a diametrically opposed argument that treats Hooper's wedding actions as "sacrilegious."

13. Carnochan, "Symbol, Meaning and the Context of Hawthorne's Art," p. 186.

14. See Colacurcio's thorough exploration of sin. He is particularly good in presenting Hooper as someone who has the quintessential revelation of the breadth, depth, subtlety and complexity of sin.

15. Bell, "The Obliquity of Signs: *The Scarlet Letter,*" p. 9.

16. Benita Moore, "Hawthorne, Heidegger, and the Holy: The Uses of Literature," *Soundings: An Interdisciplinary Journal,* 64 (1981), 170-196.

17. Nathaniel Hawthorne, *The House of Seven Gables,* Vol. 2 of the Centenary Edition of the *Works of*

Nathaniel Hawthorne (Columbus: Ohio State University Press, 1965), p. 2.

Norman German (essay date 1988)

SOURCE: "The Veil of Words in 'The Minister's Black Veil,'" in *Studies in Short Fiction,* Vol. 25, No. 1, Winter, 1988, pp. 41-7.

[*In the following essay, German examines Hawthorne's careful use of puns in "The Minister's Black Veil," which, he claims, underscore Mr. Hooper's alienation from God and man.*]

The anatomical workings of **"The Minister's Black Veil"** have so long been under the incisive explicatory knives of every type of critic that one might think the story, by now, scraped to the bone. The criticism, generally, has been sound. R. H. Fogle, playing the grand arbiter of good sense, asserts that many interpretations are possible when an author consciously works ambiguity as his principal organizational trope.[1] Still, perspicacious critics can have blindspots.

Little has been said, for instance, concerning Hawthorne's penchant for etymological punning, George Monteiro's brief discussion on the "motif-like use of the term *mystery*"[2] being an exception. An argument can be built, however, to show that Hawthorne painstakingly worked out his themes even on the most fundamental linguistic levels. The argument is based, first, on the thematic relevance of the puns and, second, on the proximity of apparently dissimilar words which are related etymologically.[3]

One of the most easily detectable puns occurs in the text when Mr. Hooper's oldest parishioner seems "not fully to partake of the pre*vail*ing wonder"[4] of his minister's eccentricity. Later, "there was one person in the village [Elizabeth], unap*pall*ed by the awe with which the black veil had impressed all beside herself" (45). Although neither pun is etymologically based, neither seems accidental, and both are associated with characters either too wise to be deceived by, or too innocent to notice, such exhibitionistic trickery.

Often, the proximity of words suggests that Hawthorne engages in self-conscious wordplay, as when, at the end of the story, Reverend Clark asks permission to "cast aside this black *veil* from [Hopper's] face" (51). The narrator then states that Clark "bent forward to *reveal* the mystery of so many years" (51). "Reveal" is related to "veil" and means, literally, to "unveil."[5] The pun fits the proximity and thematic tests used in my argument to exhume puns that skeptics may regard as coincidental. The puns on "veil" especially indicate that Hawthorne consciously used words to reinforce a major theme of the story, that appearances often contradict reality, a theme borne out by the fact that variants of the word "appear" recur frequently throughout the story.

Hawthorne's exploitation of the two-fold aspect of words, which, like people, often have facades masking complex interiors, also rhetorically reinforces the fear and trembling that Hooper's veil inspires. Again, the proximity of the words indicates that Hawthorne was consciously playing off of their root meanings. The sexton exclaims in "astonishment" (from *tonare,* to thunder) in paragraph two of the story. The befuddlement of the parishioners is etymologically suggested by words like "amazement" (OE *amasian,* to confuse), "wonder-struck," and "perturbation" (*turbare,* to disturb). Yet, ironically, Hooper strives "to win his people heavenward, by mild persuasive influences, rather than to drive them thither, by the *thunders* of the Word" (39), "persuasive influences" etymologically suggesting a sweet flowing.

Throughout the story, words that overtly denote quaking are juxtaposed with those which covertly, that is, etymologically, buttress and embellish the trembling imagery. In a single sentence, "There was nothing *terrible* [Gk *tremein,* to tremble] in what Mr. Hooper said . . . yet, with every *tremor* [an overt use] of his melancholy voice, the hearers *quaked* [O]" (40).[6] Later, the veil is described by a lady as "'a *terrible* [covert] thing on Mr. Hooper's face!'" (41). In other overt references, the young woman's corpse "*shuddered,*" and "the people *trembled*" at Hooper's funeral sermon (42). At the wedding, he is still wearing the "*horrible*" (covert use of *horrere,* to tremble) veil as "the bride's cold fingers *quivered* [O] in the *tremulous* [O] hand of the bridegroom" (43). When Hooper toasts the couple, he sees his image reflected in the wine and "the black veil involved his own spirit in the *horror* [C] with which it overwhelmed all others. His frame *shuddered* [O] . . ." (43-44).

Interestingly, Elizabeth denies that there is anything "*terrible* [C] in this piece of crape" (45), probably because she is one of the few innocents in the story. Soon, however, the veil's "*terrors* [C] fell around her. She arose, and stood *trembling* [O] before him" (47). As she leaves, she gives Hooper "one long, *shuddering* [O] gaze" (47), and he smiles "to think that only a material emblem had separated him from happiness, though the *horrors* [C] which it shadowed forth, must be drawn darkly between the fondest of lovers" (47).

In the next paragraph, Hooper begins to think that a "preternatural *horror* [C] was interwoven with the threads of the black crape" (48). His congregation thinks he has committed a crime "too *horrible* [C] to be entirely concealed," and "With self-*shudderings* [O] and outward *terrors* [C], he walked continually" (48) in the shadow of the veil. "Dying sinners . . . *shuddered* [O] at the veiled face so near their own. Such were the *terrors* [C] of the black veil, even when Death had bared his visage" (49). Strangers, who come to see Hooper out of curiosity, are "made to *quake* [O] ere they departed" (49).

Hooper's deathbed is convulsed by a crescendo of paroxysm imagery. His "breath *heaved* [O]; it *rattled* [O] in his throat" as he "sat, *shivering* [O] with the arms of death around him, while the black veil hung down . . . in the gathered *terrors* [C] of a life-time" (52). He asks his attendants, "'Why do you *tremble* [O] at me alone? . . . *Tremble* also at each other!'" (52).

Translingual wordplay involving "breath" also occurs at the time of Hooper's death. He is the "*expiring* [L. *spirare,* to breathe; *ex,* out] minister" who lies quietly in the "torpor of mental and bodily *exhaustion*" except when an "irregular *inspiration* [i.e. a breathing in] seemed to prelude the flight of his *spirit*" [based on *spirare*] (50-51).

The strongest evidence that Hawthorne was "joycing around" with words is the symphony of translingual references to "face" and "looking" which he incorporated into his text to reinforce the deception theme. First, it is noteworthy that "face(s)" is used twenty-eight times, with only three references not mentioning the face as being hidden. Some especially revelatory citations are "hiding his face" (38), "covered his face" (44), "hide your face" and "hide my face" (46), and "faces behind the grave-stones" (48). Significantly, the children, in the first use of "face" in the story, have "bright faces," indicating their innocence and lack of deceit. In Elizabeth's conversation with Hooper, she expresses the wish to see him as he is, without intervening facades, by commanding him, "'look me in the face'" (47). The final reference to an uncovered face occurs in the final line of the story when, ironically, "Hooper's face is dust."

The informing scripture to **"The Minister's Black Veil"** is I Corinthians 13:12, "For now we see through a glass, *darkly;* but then *face to face*: now I know in part; but then shall I know even as also I am known." By donning the veil, Hooper pridefully puts on the face of God, Who sees all yet remains unseen: Hooper "showed himself in the pulpit, *face to face* with his congregation, except for the black veil" (39). Moreover, Hawthorne turned the facets of the variant forms and literal and figurative meanings of "darkly" in phrases such as "darkened aspect" (38), "they but darkly understood him" (42), "rushed forth into the darkness" (44), "darken your eyes" (46), "sorrows dark enough" (46), "no darkness between our souls" (47), "groping darkly within his own soul" (48), "all dark affections" (49), "his darksome chamber" (50), and several others.

Adding further thematic resonances to these references to hidden faces and improper or incomplete understanding are words like "dim," "obscurity," "sable," "black," "*melan*choly," "appearance," "shadow," and their variants, as well as "conceal" and its derivational variants, a word whose root, *celare,* means "to hide" and which is related to the Old English *helan,* Hell. These words serve to highlight the hypocrisy evidenced in the Janus-faced people in the story. Like Robin in **"My Kinsman, Major Molineux,"** Hooper speaks in a different manner to different types of people, knowing, as Robin learned, that a man may "'have several voices . . . as well as two complexions.'" Like the apostle Paul, Hooper tries to be "all things to all men that [he] might by all means save some" (I Cor. 9:22): ". . . he *paid due reverence* to the hoary heads, *saluted* the middle-aged with kind dignity, . . . *greeted* the young with mingled authority and love, and *laid his hands on* the little children's heads to bless them" (41) in Christ-like manner (Hooper dons his veil at age thirty). Yet, though he may present many personae to his parishioners, he wears only one face before God and himself, one whose essence horrifies him as he sees it, not darkly but directly, in the various mirrors in the story. His essential self is undivided and undisguised by the "two-fold crape" of projection and interpretation in which Hooper and his parishioners engage.

In the scenes where Hooper is in confrontation with people, Hawthorne carefully injected certain words to emphasize the fact that humans often veil their innermost thoughts and desires while facing others. Invariably and with intended irony, some form of *vis* (from L. *videre,* to see; sometimes implying "face," as in "visage") is used. During the first sermon at which he wears his veil, the audience longs "for a breath of wind to blow aside the veil, almost believing that a stranger's *visage* would be discovered" (an archaic use of and/or pun on "discovered," meaning "uncovered" as well as "found," occurs here and in several other places in the tale). Hooper's parishioners do not directly ask him the cause of his putting on the veil; they would rather speculate. At the close of the first service, they gather "in little circles," "their mouths all whispering in the centre" (40); some meditate on the meaning of the veil; some talk loudly about it; a few wise ones suggest they can penetrate the mystery of the veil; others surmise that Hooper's eyes have merely been "weakened by the midnight lamp" and require a shade (41). The next day, the women "[gossip] at their open windows," the tavern-keeper tells his guests of the oddity, and the children "[babble] of it on their way to school" (44). Significantly, no one asks Hooper, no one wishes to have the veil of ignorance taken from his own eyes, and no one seems to care about Hooper, only about the effect of his aberration.

Ironically, in the midst of this voyeuristic congregation (cf., "Spruce bachelors looked sidelong at the pretty maidens"), Mr. Hooper "had never lacked ad*vis*ers" (44). However, because of his veil, "of all the busy-bodies and impertinent people in the parish, not one ventured to put the plain question to Mr. Hooper, wherefore he did this thing" (44). When the church members finally decide to send a deputation, Hooper leaves "his *vis*iters the whole burthen of introducing their important business" (44). Unable to broach the subject, "they sat a considerable time, speechless, confused, and shrinking uneasily from Mr. Hooper's eye, which they felt to be fixed upon them with an in*vis*ible glance" (45). As Hawthorne intimates in "invisible," Hooper's glance is "un-seen," and he has "no face." He is invisible, also, in that he refuses ordinary participation in the world.

Even Hooper's meeting with Elizabeth is termed a "*vis*it" (45), one at which he ironically "hides [his] face" (45). At the interview, Hawthorne rings many changes on the variants of "face." Included is an ironic use of "respect": Elizabeth declares, "'Beloved and respected as you are, there may be whispers, that you hide your face under the consciousness of secret sin'" (46). A person worthy of "respect" is literally "looked at [from *spectare*] again [re]"; Hooper, conversely, is looked at again and again by his voyeuristic flock only as an oddity, and in fact they never see his "aspect," a synonym for "face" which Hawthorne uses numerous times in the tale. Similar puns (I contend that Hawthorne used these words tropologically, not simply synonymically) occur in other contexts: "Even the lawless wind . . . *respected* his dreadful secret" (48) and "His converts always *regarded* [cf., Fr. *regarder*] him with a dread peculiar to themselves" (49). In an oblique reference, the narrator relates that Hooper spends "a long life, irreproachable in outward act, yet shrouded in dismal *suspicions*" (49), a word whose core, "spic," is changed from "spectare" (to look), and in this case is used to imply unfounded speculations. Though ostracized throughout his life, Hooper sadly smiles "at the pale *vis*ages of the worldly throng as he passed by" (49). This passage could also contain a visual pun on "pale," which is similar in appearance to "pall"; earlier, Hooper's congregation is described as "pale-faced" when they are "almost as fearful a sight to the minister, as his black veil to them" (39). Although "dying sinners" cry for Hooper, they fear his veiled face, "even when Death had bared his [Death's] visage!" (49). This is the only use of *vis* not directly associated with one of Hooper's confrontations. The dying sinners are more terrified of a concealed human face than of an exposed death's-head. A fatal certainty frightens them less than the intentionally disguised unknown.

At Hooper's deathbed, in the most crucial confrontation of his life, "Several persons were *vis*ible by the shaded candlelight, in the death-chamber of the old clergyman" (50). Hooper remains figuratively invisible, without a face, so Mr. Clark asks him to allow the grievers to "be gladdened by [his] triumphant *aspect*" as he goes to his reward. The dying preacher accuses the "circle of pale *spect*ators" (another pun on pall-pale) by charging, "'I look around me, and, lo! on every *vis*age a Black Veil!'" (52). The irony of the vis-à-vis, in which one party's face is not revealed, is stressed in the next line, in which "his *auditors*" shrink from one another. Throughout the story, the lack of profound spiritual perception contrasts the obsessive interest of the congregation in shallow physical perception. At the conclusion, Hawthorne's reference to the people as "auditors" implies that they remain spiritually blind, despite Hooper's renewal of religious symbology.[7] The informing scripture here is, perhaps, the parable of the sowers, after which Jesus says, "Who hath ears to hear, let him hear" and then, "Therefore speak I to them in parables: because they seeing see not; and hearing they hear not, neither do they understand" (Matthew 13:9 & 13). That Hawthorne used this and other scriptures as a thematic basis for his homiletic tale seems probable, since he subtitled it "A Parable."

In another translingual pun, which occurs at the tête-à-tête between Hooper and the dead maiden in her casket, Hawthorne describes the encounter as "an *interview* between the dead and the living" (42), Hawthorne's word choice implying a *view into* the inner-most spiritual being of each viewer. (This reading is suggested by the meaning of the sentence in the context of the story and by the superficial appearance of the word "interview," though not by its etymology.) The reversal of the normal order "the living and the dead" leads the reader to interpret Hooper, not the maiden, as the "dead" one spiritually, while she is the "living" one, now in heaven, where she can see "face to face, and know" even as she is known, the veil between this and the next world now lifted. The idea that Hooper walks among the oxymoronic crew of the living dead is affirmed immediately after his "interview" with the young woman. At her funeral procession, the bearers go forth, the mourners following, "saddening all the street, with the dead *before* them, and Mr. Hooper in his black veil *behind*" (42). Surely, this vignette is parabolic: the maiden, physically dead, and Hooper, spiritually dead, bracket the still-hopeful living. It may be significant, too, that Hooper dons his veil and alienates his fiancée just before he is to marry into the brotherhood of the flesh.[8] His veil, then, functions as a hymenal symbol as well as a symbol of his overbearing pride which says, "I am better than, or different from, the rest of humanity." The two-fold crape acts as a miniature veil preventing anyone from seeing into Hooper's holy of holies, signifying again that he has blasphemously put on the face of God.

To summarize, the proof of Hawthorne's punning lies in two tests: the proximity of the words in question and their thematic significance. A passage in **"Ethan Brand"** further illustrates that Hawthorne incorporated puns artistically and systematically. Before committing suicide, Brand reflects on the fact that his quest originated out of respect for the human heart. "He remembered . . . with what reverence he had then looked into the heart of man, viewing it as a temple originally divine, and, however *desecrated,* still to be held *sacred* by a brother; with what awful fear he had *deprecated* the success of his pursuit, and *prayed* that the Unpardonable Sin might never be revealed to him." These pairs of words satisfy the proximity and thematic tests; Hawthorne obviously set the words in opposition. He engages in a fairly transparent pun in "desecrated" and "sacred," since the etymological relationship of the words is still visible; "desecrated," meaning made unholy or unsacred, is contrasted with "sacred," something holy. The words have thematic import because the story is about the sacred being profaned. The pun on "deprecated/prayed" is not so evident. "Deprecate," in this context, is used in its uncommon meaning of plead/pray against (L. *precari*); thus, it is linked to "pray" semantically and etymologically. A potentially sly pun in **"The Minister's Black Veil,"** one that seems unintended because trite, is the use of "veil" as an acronym for "evil."

Among the many meanings Hooper's two-fold veil suggests, it surely also signifies that Hooper saw only one aspect of God's nature, His Tyger face. Unlike the philosopher in "The Allegory of the Cave," Hooper returns from his dark night of the soul to show, not understanding and compassionate brotherhood, but melancholy, asceticism, and the brotherhood of sin and isolation.

Notes

1. Richard Harter Fogle, "'An Ambiguity of Sin or Sorrow,'" *New England Quarterly,* 21 (1948), 344.
2. George Monteiro, "Hawthorne's 'The Minister's Black Veil,'" *The Explicator,* 22, 2 (October 1963), 9.
3. Hawthorne's intimate acquaintance with Latin and Greek is attested by his biographers. Randall Stewart (*Nathaniel Hawthorne: A Biography* [New Haven: Yale University Press, 1948], pp. 13-14, 16-18) says that candidates for matriculation at Bowdoin were required "to write Latin grammatically, and to be well versed in . . . the Greek Testament." During the freshman year, "weekly translations into Latin and Greek" were prescribed; during the sophomore year, "weekly translations in Latin and Greek, alternately"; and during the junior year, "translations into Latin and Greek alternately every fortnight." Of Hawthorne's performance, Stewart says, "He excelled in Latin and English." Similarly, Mark Van Doren (*Nathaniel Hawthorne,* no city given: William Sloane Associates, Inc., 1948, p. 18) says, "Especially did he like the Latin, which he wrote with great ease and purity."
4. William Charvat, general editor, *The Centenary Edition of the Works of Nathaniel Hawthorne,* Vol. IX, *Twice-Told Tales* (Columbus: Ohio State University Press, 1974), p. 39. Hereafter, references to page numbers are parenthetically incorporated in the text.
5. All etymologies have been checked in the *OED.* The etymology of "terrible" is substantiated in Ernest Klein's *A Comprehensive Etymological Dictionary of the English Language.*
6. Hereafter, an "O" in brackets will stand for "overt"; after the first use of "covert," a "C" will denote "covert."
7. In Gilbert Viogt's article, "The Meaning of 'The Minister's Black Veil,'" *College English,* 13 (March 1952), 338, Voigt says, "Perhaps the godly preacher is simply resorting to the ancient Hebrew prophets' practice of using striking symbolic acts as means of appealing to hardened sinners who had turned a deaf ear to their words. Thus Jeremiah once placed a yoke upon his neck as a sign of the captivity to which the sins of Judah and its neighboring states were dooming themselves. Similarly Ezekiel shaved the hair from his face and his head. . . . And Hosea went so far as to marry a prostitute. . . ."
8. Similarly, Ethan Brand's self-imposed alienation is signified by his not partaking "of the contents of a certain black bottle" which the other villagers share in a communion-like fashion.

William Freedman (essay date 1992)

SOURCE: "The Artist's Symbol and Hawthorne's Veil: 'The Minister's Black Veil' Resartus," in *Studies in Short Fiction,* Vol. 29, No. 3, Summer, 1992, pp. 353-62.

[*In the following essay, Freedman follows the lead of Carnochan's 1969 article and identifies the most important aspect of "The Minister's Black Veil" as Hawthorne's concern with the power of literary symbolism.*]

Decades of discussion of Hawthorne's **"The Minister's Black Veil"** have inevitably brought the question of the author's attitude toward the minister—whether he is a heroic martyr, a virulent anti-Christ, or some hybrid form between—to a point of diminishing critical returns. The tale was happily revitalized, its interpretive possibilities expanded, by W. B. Carnochan in 1969. In his essay, which offers a reading of the veil as a symbol of symbols, a paradoxical emblem of both revelation and concealment inherently resistant to fixed meanings, Carnochan opened a wide door into this parable and into Hawthorne's practice generally. But there have been surprisingly few visitors. A trifle overwhelmed by Carnochan's reading, Elaine Barry concludes her summary of his conclusions with the awed observation that "Surely, little more can be said about this" (Barry 15), and judging from the relative silence of recent criticism, her reticence has found an echo.[1] Carnochan's essay, however, is as valuable as it is largely because it raises to the surface an element of both the veil and the "Veil" about which a great deal more can and should be said. I will try to say some of that here and in a way that addresses both the question of Hawthorne's views of symbolism and the artist and the controversy over the (im)propriety of the minister's act.

In Carnochan's revisionary view, **"The Minister's Black Veil"** is less a parable of hidden guilt than an exercise in the complex employment of the artistic symbol, and, ultimately, a tale about the nature of such symbols. The principal effect of the veil is "to avert explicit statements of what it stands for." Creating meaning and simultaneously hiding it, inviting speculation and resisting it, the veil not only "conceal[s] what is behind it, but is a sign of that concealment." It is, in short, a "symbol of symbols" (Carnochan 185-87):

> Because the meaning of the veil consists only in what is hidden, meaning is lost in the very act of revelation. It is in this that the veil serves as 'type' and 'symbol' of types and symbols in their general nature. As language gives a meaning to experience but also comes between the subject and any direct perception or recreation of that experience, so does the veil.
>
> (Carnochan 186)

These are Carnochan's points about the veil and they are, in my view, extremely well taken. But they are also brief and partial, leaving much to be said, because Carnochan is more interested in the veil as a clue to Hawthorne's ultimate disintegration as a symbolist, hence as a writer, than in the veil-as-artistic-symbol in the tale.[2] His observations must be extended and many others added if we are to grasp not only the full richness of this symbol of symbols, but also its implications for the artist who so isolatingly wears it. My view of the parable is that it carries autobiographical import more for the artist's dubious present than for his declining future, that it speaks of Hawthorne's adoption of the symbolic method (the donning of the veil), of the power of that alteration of his literary "face," and of its price. Appearing first in *The Token* for 1836, **"The Minister's Black Veil—A Parable"** is one of Hawthorne's earliest symbolic tales. It speaks, I think, of the nature of the symbol he had begun to explore after his earlier failure with *Fanshawe* (1828) and other relatively or baldly realistic fictions, and of its effects not only on his real and imagined readers, but on the artist as well.

The veil, like the artistic symbol it represents, invites a round of tentative interpretations, all based inevitably on surmise. But its chief significance lies not in these "readings," surely not in its "ultimate meaning," which may or may not be revealed, but in its power to stimulate such efforts and in the still more potent emotional effects it produces in those who behold it. Some of the townspeople are amazed, others awed; some are fearful or intimidated, others perplexed or defensively wise, while yet others are inspired or made hopeful. For all the emphasis on interpretive hypotheses—and there is much—there is as much or more on the accompanying emotional impact. And both, of course, are characteristic of the symbol, the latter more profoundly than the former. Symbols, as D. H. Lawrence remarks, "don't 'mean something.' They stand for units of human *feeling,* human experience. A complex of emotional experience is a symbol. And the power of the symbol," like the power of the minister's veil, "is to arouse the deep emotional self, and the dynamic self, beyond comprehension" (Lawrence 158). The "strangest part of the affair," remarks a physician, "is the effect of this vagary, even on a sober-minded man like myself" (Hawthorne 41).

The emphasis on this effect, I believe, reflects Hawthorne's larger concern with the literary symbol as he had begun to employ it in this and other short works. He is preoccupied here with the question of interpretation and effect, tantalized, it seems, by the radiant power of his new instrument. Like ideal readers or critics in relation to a story, the townspeople are obsessed with the veil, intrigued by its possible meanings, overwhelmed by its spiritual and emotive power. Like readers cut off from the author or intimidated by him, "not one ventured to put the plain question to Mr. Hooper, wherefore he did this thing" (44). But eventually, like naive readers unable to control their curiosity and simplistically trustful that the author is the final arbiter of his own meanings (a trust, by the way, that, if we share it, finally reduces the rich tale to the shallowness of the minister's own death-bed fulmination), a few approach him. Futilely, of course, for the creator will not reveal his intentions.

The ultimate naive reader, however, is the minister's fiancée. A simple literalist who perceives none of the symbolic import that perplexes and mortifies the others, Elizabeth "could discern nothing of the dreadful gloom that had so overawed the multitude": to her "it was but a double fold of crape . . ." (45). Such a reader would have the author renounce his symbol and return to the realist's simpler perception of the world (which she has never transcended), undarkened and uncomplicated by the veil. Rejecting her entreaty, the minister echoes the sentiment of Carlyle's Professor Teufelsdröckh in *Sartor Resartus,* a work written but two years earlier than **"The Minister's Black Veil,"** and one whose views on symbolism, so close to that of the parable, may suggest an influence. "Small is this which thou tellest me," declares the Professor,

> that the Royal Sceptre is but a piece of gilt-wood; that the Pyx has become a most foolish box, and truly, as Ancient Pistol thought, 'of little price.' A right Conjuror might I name thee, couldst thou conjure back into these wooden tools the divine virtue they once held. (Carlyle 225)[3]

Hawthorne is such a conjurer, of course, as is Hooper. Both conjure back into the simple materials of literature and earth a power beyond. They do so, as Teufelsdröckh recommends, by planting "into the deep infinite faculties of man, his Fantasy and Heart" (Carlyle 225)—Hooper by means of the veil, the artist by means of the symbol the veil represents. And it is here that Elizabeth, experiencing what both the minister and the artist hope for, feels its effects at last, as its terrors fall around her. Only now does she sense what the physician's wife had remarked earlier: the power with which person and context can invest the otherwise barren tools of art's ministry. "How strange," the wife had mused, "that a simple black veil such as any woman might wear on her bonnet, should become such a terrible thing on Mr. Hooper's face!" (41). The observation is crucial, for it suggests that, like the symbol—indeed like all language—the veil has no detachable or intrinsic significance. The meanings it carries and the impact it generates, finally to Elizabeth as well, are dependent on the user, on the context, and on the inferred intentions of its use. It is when the minister rejects the invitation to removal and literal rendering and, offering evocative symbolic hypotheses for her to ponder, returns the burden of feeling and reflection to this "reader," that she becomes aware of these forces and feels the shuddering impact of the symbol.[4]

"In a symbol," remarks Carlyle, "there is concealment and yet revelation." And the veil, both as symbol and as symbol of . . . , is a concealment that is a revelation of concealment. To the minister and the sinners who become his disciples, it is a concealment revelatory of the universal masking of secret sin ("lo! on every Visage a Black Veil!").

For the reader it is a concealment that reveals concealment as the only viable meaning. In this tale, in all of Hawthorne's best symbolic work, perhaps in all fiction and language, the veil as veiling or veiledness is itself the message. The ambiguity and mystery of the concealing veil become themselves the meaning, suggesting the inaccessibility of determinate meaning or truth. The meaning of a (Hawthorne) story is found not behind its signs or symbols, but in the fact and experience of impenetrability, the realization that no interpretation will suffice. The veil again is a symbol of symbols, more broadly a symbol of the symbolistic resonance of signs. "Speech," as Teufelsdröckh affirms, "is great, but not the greatest." For "Speech is of Time, Silence [like the symbol and the veil] is of Eternity" (Carlyle 219). The Professor's point about the silent power of the symbol—that "Thought will not work except in Silence"—is the parable's point about the veil: namely, that speech, the minister's earlier sermons unaccompanied by the veil, is relatively effete as a stimulant of profoundest thought and recognition. In the symbol, on the other hand, "in many a painted Device or simple Seal-emblem, the commonest Truth stands out to us proclaimed with quite new emphasis" (Carlyle 220). As it does for Hooper, whose sermons assume unprecedented power.

What we see in Hawthorne's tale, of course, is that the moral message of the veil, if indeed there is one, is not disclosed until the minister's death, if even then. The power and consequently the point of the veil lies not in its meaning, its "common Truth," for were it so, Hooper would surely have proclaimed it sooner. Rather, by refusing revelation and provoking an endless battery of possible interpretations and responses, the minister carries Hawthorne's message that the only truth that stands affirmed in the veil is the truth of the artistic symbol's boundless resonance and evocative force. The important truth of the veil is not the universality of concealed sin, for that revelation is too long postponed to be of consequence to most of its observers. The veil speaks far more eloquently of what Carlyle calls "The incalculable influences of Concealment" that account for "the wondrous agency of Symbols" (Carlyle 220).

That the meaning of the veil is in the veil itself and not in any hidden referent seems confirmed by the pointlessness of the Reverend Mr. Clark's last-minute effort to raise the veil in search of its meaning. "'Before the veil of eternity be lifted,'" urges Clark at Hooper's bedside, "'let me cast aside this black veil from your face!' . . . And thus speaking [he] . . . bent forward to reveal the mystery of many years" (51). If Elizabeth is the naive literalist who believes at first that the veil is a mere object rather than a sign or symbol, the Reverend Clark is the simple allegorizer who looks for single meanings directly behind the given sign. The effort is futile, of course, not because Hooper resists it, but because the raising of the veil would reveal only a face and nothing of the veil's meaning. The minister clasps the veil to his face not because its removal would reveal the hidden meaning behind it, but because such an act would remove veil and all meaning together.

Hawthorne emphasizes the point in a fine ambiguity that introduces and casts doubt on the minister's death-bed revelation, which has too often been accepted as the "true meaning" of the veil. "What, but the mystery which it obscurely typifies has made this piece of crape so awful?" asks the minister. Readers have assumed—and been led to assume—that the mystery he speaks of is revealed in the ensuing tirade on the loathsome treasuring up of secret sin. But there is another way to read the minister's question, one that seals the concealed meaning of the veil as artist's symbol, hence as essential mystery, as tightly as Hooper's disclosure seems to shut the door on further queries into what this sign signifies. For what has made this piece of crape so aw[e]ful is precisely "the mystery" it obscurely typifies. The veil, in other words, typifies not *a* mystery to be disclosed, but mystery itself, and it does so by typifying obscurely, in a way that perpetually tempts and frustrates the assignation of all meaning beyond itself.

Such a reading of **"The Minister's Black Veil"** raises again the familiar question of Hawthorne's view of the role and power of the artist and, through that, the nearly threadbare controversy over his attitude toward the minister's donning and wearing the veil. For if the veil is the artist's symbol, then Hooper is a kind of symbolizing artist, the author himself perhaps. Like Hawthorne before he discovered the awesome power of the literary symbol, Hooper was a good but "not an energetic" preacher who "strove to win his people . . . by mild persuasive influences, rather than to drive them thither [to heaven], by the thunders of the Word" (39). When he adopts the symbolic method by donning the veil, however, a telling change is felt in his oratory. The sermon he now delivers is marked by "the same characteristics of style and manner," the same unthundering quietness.

> But there was something, either in the sentiment of the discourse itself, or in the imagination of the auditors, which made it greatly the most powerful effort that they had ever heard from their pastor's lips. . . . A subtle power was breathed into his words.
>
> (40)

As it was into Hawthorne's own written words, and it is not too much, I think, to suggest that **"The Minister's Black Veil—A Parable"** is itself the fictive equivalent of the minister's sermon. Its subject too "had reference to secret sin"; it too is "tinged rather more darkly than usual with the gentle gloom" of its author's temperament; and it too, Hawthorne may well have felt, was his most powerful effort to that time.

That **"The Minister's Black Veil"** is, as the full title indicates, "A Parable," places it in the same category with Hooper's sermon on secret sin—a veiled reference to the veil—and with the veil itself as a bearer of veiled messages. Hawthorne and the minister, in other words, are identified as preacher/artists. Both deliver texts whose subject is the veil and whose parabolic meaning is concealed until the deathbed "revelation," which at once retroactively casts at least putative meaning on both the minister's sermon and the tale that contains it. It is only here that we encounter the allegorical message of the veil and recognize the veil as the hidden referent of Hooper's dark sermon. Hawthorne as artist offers the symbol in search of single meaning. Hooper, the double craftsman, presents a similar challenge in his veil while offering in his sermon-as-veiled-parable meaning in search of attachment to the floating symbol of the veil.

By donning the veil, Hooper becomes what Hawthorne would come to feel himself, more and more strongly as he developed and perfected his symbolic art: a removed and judging observer who felt he could penetrate the mystery of other souls while remaining invisible. The veil conceals the minister's face as effectively as a tale, particularly a veiled symbolic tale, conceals its author and his intent. It hangs before his face, covering everything but the mouth and chin, leaving free, in other words, the speaking organ only. It enables him to preach far more effectively than before, and it causes the members of his magnetized congregation to shrink uneasily from his eye, "which they felt to be fixed upon them with an invisible glance" (45). Passing from the uninspired realism of his earlier work to the eerily suggestive power of the symbolic tales, we feel, with Elizabeth and his congregation, the effects of the veil that is a symbol of symbols.

For Hawthorne, we know, there is a price to be paid for the artist's mission and his remotely scrutinizing insight: the price of personal isolation, the punishment as well as the privilege of the seer who sees and remains himself unseen. The minister, of course, pays the artist's price for his power. He has "changed himself into something awful . . . by hiding his face" and peering, like Hawthorne, through his obscure and somber tales, through a veil that gave "a darkened aspect to all living and inanimate things" (38). Like the poet Coverdale in *The Blithedale Romance,* where the veil is again a focal symbol; like the scientific researchers of the soul that darken his fiction; and like Hawthorne's guilty conception of the writer that these figures typify, Hooper is "a man apart from men," separated from the world by his "dismal shade" (49). He is separated too, and as a result, from happiness, lonely and frightened behind his black veil, where he gropes "darkly within his own soul [and gazes] . . . through a medium that saddened the whole world" (48). Like Hawthorne's image of the minister "gazing darkly within his own soul," the Hawthorne given us by critics and biographers experienced "the perpetual turning in of the mind upon itself, the long introspective brooding over human motives" that probed the soul's secret impulses and laid bare its dark workings (Parrington 437). "I have made a captive of myself and put me into a dungeon," he wrote to Longfellow in 1837,

> and now I cannot find the key to let myself out—and if the door were open, I should be almost afraid to come out. . . . [T]here is no fate in this world so horrible as to have no share in either its joys or sorrows. For the last ten years, I have not lived, but only dreamed about living.
>
> ("To Henry Wadsworth Longfellow")

"[W]ithout thy aid," he wrote to his wife Sophia in 1840,

> my best knowledge of myself would have been merely to know my own shadow—to watch it flickering on the wall, and mistake its fantasies for my own real actions. Indeed, we are but shadows—we are not endowed with real life, and all that seems most real about us is but the thinnest substance of a dream—till the heart is touched.
>
> ("To Sophia Peabody Hawthorne")

This closing phrase, if it is more climax than afterthought, seems to support Malcolm Cowley's hypothesis that Hawthorne's work declined in the final years of his life not, as many have argued, because of his claustrophobic preoccupation with the shadows of his imagination, but because the affections of his heart and his emergence into the too bright world blocked his access to the source of his hermetic inspiration. It was, after all, after his heart was touched by Sophia, his time by the demands of wife and family, his insulated privacy by the demands upon a public figure, that his imagination and his art began to fail. But whatever the cause of his artistic decline, there is a poignant connection between the suspected vacuity of the symbol and Hawthorne's anxiety about the vaporous insubstantiality of the isolated self. In a private world where fantasies are mistaken for human actions and where all that seems most real is but the faint immateriality of a dream, symbol and reality merge in their common lack of substance. The self that wants reality is reflected in the symbol devoid of meaning or reference. Both exist in solitude, draped in the shadow that is all the reality they possess.

While I do not wish to venture into the controversy over the tale's implicit judgment of the minister and his art, whether Hooper is a devoted martyr, an inhuman anti-Christ, or some hybrid form between, I will offer an addendum that touches on the question. The veil, as we have traditionally read the minister's deathbed translation, is the symbol not of human sinfulness, but of the refusal of its revelation, the "loathsome . . . treasuring up" that denyingly conceals what should be made manifest. "When the friend shows his inmost heart to his friend; the lover to his best-beloved; when man does not vainly shrink from the eye of his Creator . . . ," declaims the minister, "then deem me a monster . . ." (52). There is more to this denunciatory confession than at first appears; implicit self-accusation stirs beneath the seeming self-exoneration and projection. On one level, "*then* deem me a monster" invites merely nominal condemnation. The minister alone will continue to wear the veil symbolic of sin's furtive concealment when others have opened their sinfulness to divine and human view. Only at this barely imaginable time will he be monstrous, and then but metaphorically, for his veil is but an emblem of the crime it represents. Indeed, by wearing the veil, the minister exalts himself, becomes, it seems, a kind of Just Man by publicizing on his own face the secretiveness others practice but deny. The minister is as yet no monster, not only because others share his defect but, equally paradoxically, because he achieves in his exposure at least partial absolution from the sin he exposes to view.

And yet, as the minister/artist takes on the character of the symbol he employs, in the very act of exposing the souls and hidden sinfulness of others, Hooper, like the artist, also partakes of the infection he perceives. As the artist falls into isolation in the demanding task of its description, becoming the distanced judge of those whose judgmental detachment he condemns, so Hooper, in the obfuscation of his message, becomes tangled in what he would merely emblemize. Like the power of the purloined letter, hidden by a different sort of minister, the power of the symbol, as of the veil, lies not in its use but its concealment. "With the employment [of the letter]," Poe's narrator observes, "the power departs" (Poe 978). And similarly, the conclusive ascription of any given meaning to the veil or symbol drains the potency bonded to its mystery. By withholding until the moment of his death the presumed meaning of his symbol, Hooper maintains his lifelong grip upon his "readers," but at another price. For in concealing from them the secret of his veil, he turns the symbol into the moral reality it allegedly signifies. The minister's act implicates him in the crime of concealment that the veil symbolizes and condemns. The symbol has become its meaning, the artistic or symbolizing act a patch of the moral as well as existential darkness it illumines. It is in this sense among others that "a preternatural horror was interwoven with the threads of the black crape" (48). And it is for this reason that "the black veil involved [the minister's] . . . own spirit in the horror with which it overwhelmed all others" (43-44). The minister's frame, which is also that of the artist and the narrative, shudders when he glimpses his veiled figure in the looking-glass, not merely for its emblematic potency, but because of the enmeshing tangle of doing and being that twines Ahab to the whale. The "Veil" as fiction, which, like the veil, is a parable finally only of its mystery, weaves the artist into the incriminating veil of his own separating mystification.

Notes

1. Lea Bertani Vozar Newman's survey of "Veil" criticism turns up 24 entries between 1969 and 1985, none of which makes even passing use of Carnochan's observation or approach (Newman 5-12). My own survey of criticism since 1985 likewise turned up empty, though readers of other Hawthorne fictions have been more enterprising. For example, Millicent Bell identifies *The Scarlet Letter* as "an essay in semiology. Its theme is the obliquity or indeterminacy of signs" (Bell 9). Bell suggests Hawthorne "may have been at the threshold of . . . our loss of confidence in the sacred grounding of signs" (12). But if so, his approach to the threshold does not begin in *The Scarlet Letter.* Literature does not work by natural selection. Such innovations are not born, fully formed, in major works. This one, I will argue, is richly presaged in "The Minister's Black Veil."
2. Carnochan's point is that Hawthorne's failure of faith in the meaningfulness of the symbol, first exemplified in "The Minister's Black Veil," was the primary cause of his later failure as an artist. "The vain hope of lifting the veil and the fears of what might be found there (or, really, what might not be found there) becomes obsessive and, in the long run, paralyzing to the imagination" (188).
3. Carnochan mentions Carlyle's discussion of symbols, but only briefly in a single context: "'In a Symbol,' says Carlyle (as Professor Teufelsdröckh), 'there is concealment and yet revelation.' Hooper's veil embodies the paradox" (Carnochan 186). Teufelsdröckh, as we will see, has much more that is relevant to say about "The Minister's Black Veil" than this, much that may have influenced it as well.
4. Elizabeth is the only witness who must be informed that "This veil is a type and symbol." She is a naive interpreter indeed.

Works Cited

Barry, Elaine. "Beyond the Veil: A Reading of Hawthorne's 'The Minister's Black Veil.'" *Studies in Short Fiction* 17 (1980): 15-20.

Bell, Millicent. "The Obliquity of Signs: *The Scarlet Letter.*" *The Massachusetts Review* 23 (1982): 9-26.

Carlyle, Thomas. *Sartor Resartus: The Life and Opinions of Herr Teufelsdröckh.* Ed. Charles Frederick Harrold. New York: Odyssey, 1937.

Carnochan, W. B. "The Minister's Black Veil." *Nineteenth-Century Fiction* 24 (1969): 182-92.

Hawthorne, Nathaniel. "The Minister's Black Veil: A Parable." *Twice-Told Tales.* Ed. William Charvat et al. Columbus: Ohio State UP, 1974. 37-53. Vol. 9 of *The Centenary Edition of the Works of Nathaniel Hawthorne.* 20 Vols. 1968-85.

———. "To Henry Wadsworth Longfellow." 4 June 1837. Woodson 251.

———. "To Sophia Peabody Hawthorne." 4 Oct. 1840. Woodson 495.

Lawrence, D. H. Introduction. *The Dragon of the Apocalypse.* By Frederick Carter. [1930]. *D. H. Lawrence: Selected Literary Criticism.* Ed. Anthony Beal. New York: Viking, 1966. 153-66.

Newman, Lea Bertani Vozar. "One-Hundred-and-Fifty Years of Looking At, Into, Through, Behind, Beyond, and Around the Minister's Black Veil." *Nathaniel Hawthorne Review* 13 (1987): 5-12.

Parrington, Vernon. *Main Currents in American Thought, Vol. 2: The Romantic Revolution in America: 1800-1860.* New York: Harcourt, 1927.

Poe, Edgar Allan. "The Purloined Letter." *Collected Works of Edgar Allan Poe.* Ed. Thomas Ollive Mabbott. Cambridge: Belknap Press of Harvard UP, 1978. 3: 972-97.

Woodson, Thomas, L. Neal Smith and Norman Holmes Pearson. *The Letters 1813-1843.* Columbus: Ohio State UP, 1984. Vol 15 of *The Centenary Edition of the Works of Nathaniel Hawthorne.* 20 vols. 1968-85.

Samuel Coale (essay date 1993)

SOURCE: "Hawthorne's Black Veil: From Image to Icon," in *The CEA Critic,* Vol. 55, No. 3, Spring-Summer, 1993, pp. 79-87.

[*In the following essay, Coale views "The Minister's Black Veil" as a work that develops in stages, noting the transformation of a "literal black crepe" to an "allegorical sign" before becoming a blasphemous icon.*]

In a recent issue of the *Nathaniel Hawthorne Review,* LEA Bertani Vozar Newman reviewed almost all the published criticism on Nathaniel Hawthorne's enigmatic **"The Minister's Black Veil"** (1836) and decided that the text of the tale served as a mirror for the reader, that each critic saw his or her own face reflected in the story.[1] What seems to be closer to the facts of the text itself, however, is that the mirror is opaque—that, as J. Hillis Miller has recently concluded, "The story is the unveiling of the possibility of the impossibility of unveiling" (51). Miller acknowledges "that the story is an allegory of the reader's own situation in reading it" (105) but goes on to suggest that "nothing happens except the proffering of an enigmatic sign" (118).

I'd like to suggest that the enigmatic sign of the black veil is precisely the point of the story, that Hawthorne is really aware of the conscious (or unconscious) need of his characters to idolize and worship sacred signs for the very act of idolatry that they inspire. In effect, the tale re-enacts an act of idolatry, the process within which an image or object becomes transformed into an icon or idol that represents, in all its enigmatic potential, the psychological and/or religious compulsions of people in general and of an American puritanical culture in particular. It's as if all the sermons and legalized texts that the Puritans substituted for ritual and aesthetic worship in their revolution against the decadent Catholic church had not fulfilled the needs of their culture and themselves, and older, perhaps more pagan, forms of idolatry had returned to haunt and hound them.

The process begins when Hawthorne offers a literal description of an object as if it existed in the real world. It is physically and publicly visible by all. From this literal image, Hawthorne moves on to describe the object in terms of an allegorical sign, a recognizable mark or token to be "decoded," defined, and explained by the public at large. The sign stands for a specific law, rule, or identifiable crime, such as Hester Prynne's scarlet *A* in Hawthorne's first romance.

But there is a third phase. This occurs when the object is described as an emblematic symbol or icon, the symbol of a mystery or riddle, filled with unintelligible secrets beyond the power of words or language to define and explain. For example, as Frederick Newberry suggests in the progression of the kinds of images Hawthorne uses to describe Hester in *The Scarlet Letter,* "from Madonna, to nun with a cross, to statue, Hester's metamorphosis retains a resemblance to icons, wholly anathema to the Puritan setting" (176). Hers is no literal letter; nor is it an allegorical sign. It has "ascended" to some higher, more mysterious plane, associated with the almost religious sensibility of icons or idols. It has become an icon for Hawthorne's dark vision of guilt, sin, and isolation.

As David Freedberg explains in *The Power of Images,* "By concentrating on physical images, the natural inclination of the mind to wander is kept in check, and we ascend with increasing intensity to the spiritual and emotional essence of that which is represented in material form before our eyes" (162). "What the pagans—and all makers of images—have to come to terms with," Freedberg notes, "is the phenomenon of presence" (78). "Images work *because* they are consecrated, but at the same time they work *before* they are consecrated. . . . In either event, the phenomenon of consecration fully demonstrates the fact of the potentiality of all images" (99). In effect, Hawthorne's kind of romance could be described as the process wherein certain images become consecrated by his characters, as they have been by his own fascination with them before the romance begins. And these images include the scarlet letter, the house of seven gables, the marble faun, Aylmer's birthmark, the veiled lady in *The Blithedale Romance,* and, of course, the minister's black veil. As W. J. T. Mitchell explains, "An idol, technically speaking, is simply an image which has an unwarranted irrational power over somebody; it has become an object of worship" (qtd. in Freedberg 376).

When such an object or image achieves its transformation into this icon-idol, it takes on the qualities of the kind of image that C. Day Lewis has described: "An image is a fact which has suffered . . . emotional significance by steeping it in the medium of the imagination. . . . [T]he poet will interrogate this image, trying to discover what it means and wither it would lead him" (70)—

> The images in a poem are like a series of mirrors set at different angles so that, as the theme moves on, it is reflected in a number of different aspects. But they are magic mirrors: they do not merely reflect the theme, they give life and form; it is in their power to make a spirit visible.
>
> (80)

Such images as icons acquire what Freedberg refers to as an aura, "that which liberates response from the exigencies of convention[,] . . . allowing the emotions . . . a fuller place in our thinking about all imagery" (433). And the Puritans recognized this so completely that like Zwingli they eradicated liturgies and ceremonies from their churches and replaced images, inevitably seen as idols, with scripture and prayer. They and Zwingli knew that "the yearnings of the human heart, the strange gods that possess us, precede and are the basis of images as idols, and both need to be eradicated from our existence" (Dillenberger 67-68).

The transformation and power of the image-become-icon rest also upon "the power of the exchange between the seeing spectator and the object that speaks to those who see, that gazes at those who speak" (Freedberg 419). The fetishizing gaze is as much a part of the iconic experience as is the icon itself. And Hawthorne steers his mysterious course between the gaze and the image, suggesting that each contributes to the total experience of mystery, riddle, and enigma. Why this image? Why this power? Why this reverence in the face of unanswerable possibilities? The image radiates a certain aura, the gaze half-creates that sensation of presence and aura, and together the image-become-icon and the self-projection of the participant-observer create a total experience of awe, uncertainty, and obeisance. Hawthorne becomes both mesmerizer and medium, at once hypnotizing us with, and being himself hypnotized by, the image. And it is the "neutral territory" in between that opens out into the darker, mysterious realm of his vision of romance.

"The Minister's Black Veil" is one of the earliest tales in which this process can be shown to take place. The process involves both Hooper and his congregation, the desire to read the veil as the specific sign of some specific reason for it, and the experience of gazing upon the veil itself, with all the effects that it creates. In the end, the veil itself remains a riddle, creating its own mystery, in much the same way that the people who gaze upon it imbue their explanations and emotions with their own sense of mystery and fear. The tale is finally not about the minister but about the veil, and it re-enacts a way of seeing, a ritual of gazing that lies at the heart of Hawthorne's romance.

The criticism that Newman has explored focuses more on Hooper than on the veil. Hooper has been regarded as sinful, almost demonic, faithless, proud, sacrilegious, preoccupied with evil, a misguided religious zealot, a rigid Calvinist, an arch villain, a man afraid of women, a selfish soul fleeing from the darkness of sexuality, and a living parable who dooms himself to isolation and despair. The veil on the other hand has suggested a symbol for mortal ignorance, a false *signum diaboli,* a demonic object to be overcome, a symbol of the failure to communicate, and an object whose effects on the townspeople are such that its very presence vindicates Hooper's behavior.[2] The medium of the tale, the veil itself, has been granted the status of an also-ran in the critical history of Hawthorne's story.

As for the Reverend Mr. Hooper, he succeeds as a minister but fails as a man. In confusing his role or function with his inner self—he makes that self an object lesson for his people by wearing the veil and in doing so rejects Elizabeth, who loves him—he confuses the symbol of isolation (the black veil) with his choosing to further his own personal isolation (his rejection of Elizabeth). Masquerading as a *symbol* of isolation and sin, he truly sins by rejecting love and sympathy. In the process, he entombs his self within the black veil and in effect kills the self, transforming it into a mysterious, walking parable. This process suggests what Paul Ricoeur has described as an act of demonic possession. Hooper has become "a sinful being in whom the very act of self-enslavement suppresses itself as 'act' and relapses into a 'state'. . . . A 'yielding' *of* myself that is at the same time a 'reign' *over* myself—there is the enigma of the servile will, of the will that makes itself a slave" (154). And that process suggests the Babylonian "representation of demons as the origin of the state of *being bound*" (153).

Still a bachelor of about thirty years, Hooper is neat, mild, and thoughtful but also removed, melancholy, and filled with self-distrust: "If he erred at all, it was by so painful a degree of self-distrust, that even the mildest censure would lead him to consider an indifferent action a crime" (26). His "same sad smile" masks this melancholy state, and his view of the world through his black veil clearly represents his dark way of seeing and mistrusting all things. He refuses to take the veil off for Elizabeth, "his plighted wife," and informs her that he is bound to wear it forever on earth, that it must separate him from the world. Elizabeth, like everyone else, reaches for some explanation and thinks of "mental disease," but in any case she too falls prey to the "terror" the veil imparts. Hooper pleads that she not desert him, bewailing his loneliness at the very moment he clings to it and is selfishly unable to recognize *her* loneliness. He, too, comes to fear "that a preternatural horror was interwoven with the threads of the black crape," and despite the fact that the veil makes him "a very efficient clergyman" and "a man of awful power," he remains separate and isolated to the end of his life, refusing even to shed the veil on his deathbed, referring to it in his dying moments only as "the mystery which it obscurely typifies," suggesting that if all the villagers (indeed, everyone) revealed themselves, then he would truly be a monster. His face becomes dust, "but awful is still the thought that it mouldered beneath the Black Veil!" (33). The veil in effect has outlived him, acquiring an iconic or idolatrous status in the minds of the villagers for all time.

At first, the villagers of Milford see the veil as a sign of a particular problem, as an allegorical emblem to be "decoded." Here is the second stage of the veil's progress from literal black crepe to allegorical sign. People speculate, fantasize, and wonder, all assuming that a specific and definable mystery is concealed by it. In New England Milford, all the speculations are dark and gloomy, revealing the kind of Puritan mind that feeds on such images. These speculations include madness, the fear of God, Hooper's weak eyes, a fearful secret, mental disease, an eccentric whim, and some great and horrible crime. The questions are meant to separate the questioners from the veil itself, reducing them to prosecuting witnesses rather than participants in some darker rite. In every case, more or less, the speculations remain grim, and these grim explanations embody the Puritans' faith in text and word over image and sacrament, in the clarity of explanation over the mystery of image-icons.

The experience of the veil itself, apart from speculation, suggests dread, horror, terror, and fear, something in league with corpses and the burial ground. "He has changed himself into something awful, only by hiding his face," declares an old woman who with others at the beginning of the story flees from the church before the service is over. The sexton and a stranger wonder if Hooper is really under there. Unlike a woman's bonnet, suggests another woman, the veil is a "terrible thing." A doctor thinks it makes Hooper "ghostlike." Even Hooper is terrified of it when he catches a glimpse of himself in the mirror. Everyone imagines that he may be consorting with ghosts and fiends. And now Hooper's mild-mannered sermons create "the most powerful effort" from behind the veil. Brides shudder at weddings, Hooper may be able to communicate with corpses from behind it, and the veil even terrifies "when Death has bared his visage!" Children fear and flee from him, and even the wind can't blow it aside from his face.

The black veil, itself a riddle but radiating its aura of gloom, death, isolation, and a sin-riddled universe, becomes a dark idol for both Hooper and his congregation—an icon representing their most Puritan and personal fears. As Ricoeur makes clear.

> The world of symbols is not a tranquil and reconciled world; every symbol is iconoclastic in comparison with some other symbol, just as every symbol, left to itself, tends to thicken, to become solidified in an idolatry. It is necessary, then, to participate in the struggle, in the dynamics, in which the symbolism itself becomes prey to a spontaneous hermeneutics that seeks to transcend it.
>
> (354)

The veil's blackness suggests mourning, evil, the absence of light, and other demonic icons such as black cats and the Black Man of the Puritan forest. It's as if this single image or object "embod[ies] one single passion only: the passion for images, and the immanence of desire in the image," and, as Jean Baudrillard continues, such images "have that power of instantaneous visual materialization" (57).

Thus, the veil encapsulates and focuses all the darker Puritan fears and traits, serving as the ultimate Puritan icon or fetish object. Such an object goes beyond what Theodore Ziolkowski refers to as "an unquestioned physical presence in the fictional world[,] . . . things with a tangible reality in the context of the literary work" (8), and in effect becomes a kind of "magic image representing the human body and, by extension, the human soul. . . . [T]here exists an intimate connection, both physical and psychological, between the image and the person that calls it to mind" (16-17). That magic image has become a fetish, an object of almost irrational reverence or obsessive devotion, regarded with the superstitious obeisance of idolatry.

Ziolkowski concludes in reference to Hawthorne's use of images in fiction that the author uses "a variety of narrative devices that leave open the possibility of a rational explanation for seemingly supernatural occurrences even though the 'magic' is never explicitly denied" (230). Beyond Hooper's vague explanations and his reaction to the veil and beyond his congregation's more explicit explanations and their reactions to it lie the fact of the veil itself and the rite of the tale in re-enacting the development or process of its growing presence into the dark idol for an entire community. Thus, suggests Hawthorne, do these Puritans really worship, and such is the extent of their belief in darker powers.

Hawthorne himself early on recognized the power of the veil as a literary image. In his *American Notebooks* in 1836, he mentions an "essay on the misery of being always under a mask. A veil may be needful, but never a mask" (23). Both conceal, but a mask suggests pretense and falsehood, the act of disguise. A veil may appear to be more ambiguous, more "needful" than a mask, since it not only conceals but also suggests protection, ornamentation, a headdress, a covering, and various liturgical cloths. Hooper's choice reflects his vision of himself as a minister in Milford, transfiguring himself into the dreaded icon of his congregation's faith, complete with all its aspects of fear, terror, horror, and fright. Is it any wonder that when Hooper turns to dust, the thought of the black veil remains "awful" in the minds and memories of his survivors?

Hawthorne's veil thus progresses from the literal description of the black crepe at the beginning of the story to the allegorical suggestions made throughout—it is an "appropriate emblem" at funerals, for instance, and at night the earth wears its own black veil—and finally achieves icon status with the death of Hooper and in the memories of his parishioners. The process is complete. The Puritans, in denigrating images, have committed a kind of devil-worship by paying obeisance to another image. It's as if such a compulsion can't be eradicated; it will return in different forms. And any allegorical attempt to limit, define, and explain it is bound to fail. The image takes the people's gaze and becomes a fetish; the story is replete with gazing. As Emily Miller Budick has put it, "What, asks the romancer, is an image, any image, whether conjured by the devil, artist, or historian? Do images enhance our knowledge of truth, or do they substitute for truth and make it inaccessible to genuine human knowledge?" (93). And such a process reflects Hawthorne's own "inward sky" in which "it is dangerous to look too minutely at such phenomena. It is apt to create a substance, where at first there was a mere shadow" ("Letter" 462). This, Hooper and the villagers of Milford have done, and the substance of the black veil will not scare.

In his thorough discussion of the black veil, Michael Colacurcio describes Hooper as an evangelical and orthodox Puritan trying to revive the dying Calvinist faith in the 1730s and 1740s during the Great Awakening. He suggests that Hawthorne employs history to reveal the limits of all personal perceptions at a historical moment and that in doing so, through his ironic presentation of events, Hawthorne warns us that we, too, can and will fall into similar errors in mistaking the particular perception for some universal truth. Hooper imprisons himself in the Puritan belief in the sinful self, which he views as more important than the sacraments, and therefore

> the veil itself—which began as a mere symbol and then became the occasional cause of inadvertent behavior in a life of severe, ironic discipline—has now become the sort of *idée fixe* which by itself orders the entire experience of a mind otherwise out of control.
>
> (345)

Thus, "the symbolic veil will always be destructive of available community; it will continuously heighten and feature what cannot be overcome. Better not wear it. Better do what one can" (385).

It would seem, however, that J. Hillis Miller is correct when he suggests that "works of literature do not simply reflect or are not simply caused by their contexts. They have a productive effect in history" (111). In other words, the "new event functions as a re-reading [an 'inadvertent re-enactment'], perhaps as a misreading and distortion, of previous events" (152-53). Hawthorne's story would seem to be just this kind of re-enactment of a kind of psychological process that can take place anywhere and at any time, at least in American culture. He has re-enacted the human compulsion to worship or idolize, no matter how much people wish to avoid or transcend it. As R. G. Collingwood explains in relation to his idea of history as a re-enactment in the present,

> [W]hat is so revived is not a mere echo of the old activity, another of the same kind; it is that same activity taken up again and re-enacted, perhaps in order that, doing it over again under my critical inspection, I may detect in it false steps.
>
> (293)

"Reenactment is not merely a rational mental process; it is also a physical, visual, and experiential process," as Samuel Laeuchli explains. "To accept reenactment is to incorporate subjectivism, even the lack of ultimate consensus" (152-53). The story does function as an indictment of the Puritan outlook, but it also functions as a psychologically repetitive rite that occurs in a Puritan-influenced, American culture. And by analogy, in people everywhere; hence, the dreamlike undertow of the tale and the impossibility of the reader's extricating himself or herself entirely, caught up not only in the mysteries generated by the opaque veil but also in the process of seeing and idolizing it.

On the other hand, Miller persists in assuming that there is some ultimate, however unknowable, truth or text beyond the veil, since he suggests that all readings are inevitably distortions, defacings, disfigurements, and disruptions. Reading can be seen in this way only if there is something that can be distorted, defaced, disfigured, and disrupted. In effect, he seems to be longing for the logos at the same time he denies that it could ever exist. Miller is unwilling to leave the black veil alone, intact, and mysterious in its own iconic form. He explains that "we want certainty" and suggests that "[a]ll critical essays on the story are so many more attempts to put something verifiable behind the veil" (96, 98). But he seems unable or unwilling to allow the veil its own mystery, its own mysterious presence. Miller may be closer to the mark when he describes the veil as "a sign that is at once blankly realistic and at the same time absolutely allegorical, that is, a sign for the failure of allegory" (120). His "absolutely allegorical" veil may in fact be my icon.

Miller recognizes that in the presence of the veil, "language is brought to a stop, rendered powerless" (96). This is precisely my point. And the fact that "the sign does not authorize any single reading" (115) strengthens the presence of the veil that I have been discussing. Despite its resistance to language, the veil remains present, even in the thoughts of the people after Hooper's death. And the thought of it remains "awful." Some things may be incapable of textual verification, and beyond language there may exist this compulsive process of worship, the fetishizing gaze, the image-become-icon, and the very real sense that within all of these there remains "an impenetrable barrier between person and person" (Miller 78). This last concept after all lies close to the heart of Hawthorne's vision. However much he castigated the Puritans for their dark vision and the often rigid simplicity of it as re-enacted in his fiction, Hawthorne's own dark vision, with its more ambiguous speculations, seems to have transcended even theirs.

The process of turning image into icon occurs as well in *The Marble Faun* and *The Scarlet Letter*, but **"The Minister's Black Veil"** remains one of the earliest recognitions of Hawthorne's dark vision. In the re-enactment of the almost fated and necessary process of transforming an image into an icon, he discovered the medium of his vision and the pattern of his version of the American romance. As James Cox has suggested, "The veil thus causes the story, almost as if it were itself the author. . . . The emblem thus precedes and causes experience" (229). It exerts a fatal presence on all who gaze upon or see through it, for in the end so powerful has it become that we can almost agree with Hooper's last cry: "I look around me, and, lo! on every visage a Black Veil!"

Notes

1. Newman's article includes "A Chronology of Criticism" on the story from 1835 to 1985.
2. Newman discusses all of these critical approaches briefly in "A Chronology of Criticism."

Works Cited

Baudrillard, Jean. *America.* London: Verso, 1989.

Budick, Emily Miller. *Fiction and Historical Consciousness: The American Romance Tradition.* New Haven: Yale UP, 1989.

Colacurcio, Michael J. *The Province of Piety.* Cambridge: Harvard UP, 1984.

Collingwood, R. G. *The Idea of History.* London: Oxford UP, 1946.

Cox, James M. "*The Scarlet Letter:* Through the Old Manse and the Custom House." *Romanticism: Critical Essays in American Literature.* Ed. James Barbour and Thomas Quirk. New York: Garland, 1986.

Dillenberger, John. *A Theology of Artistic Sensibilities.* New York: Crossroad, 1986.

Freedberg, David. *The Power of Images.* Chicago: U of Chicago P, 1989.

Hawthorne, Nathaniel. *The American Notebooks.* Ed. Claude M. Simpson. Columbus: Ohio State UP, 1972.

———. "Letter to Sophia." 19 May 1840. *Hawthorne: The Letters, 1813-1843.* Ed. Thomas Woodson, L. Neal Smith, and Norman Holmes Pearson. Columbus: Ohio State UP, 1984.

———. *Selected Short Stories of Nathaniel Hawthorne.* Ed. Alfred Kazin. New York: Fawcett Premier, 1990.

Laeuchli, Samuel. *Religion and Art in Conflict* Philadelphia: Fortress, 1980.

Lewis, C. Day. *The Poetic Image.* London: Cape, 1947.

Miller, J. Hillis. *Hawthorne and History.* Cambridge, MA: Blackwell, 1991.

Mitchell, W. J. T. *Iconology: Image, Text, Ideology.* Chicago: U of Chicago P, 1986.

Newberry, Frederick. *Hawthorne's Divided Loyalties.* Rutherford, NJ: Fairleigh Dickinson UP, 1987.

Newman, Lea Bertani Vozar. "One-Hundred-and-Fifty Years of Looking at, into, Through, Behind, Beyond, and Around 'The Minister's Black Veil.'" *Nathaniel Hawthorne Review* 13.2 (Fall 1987): 5-12.

Ricoeur, Paul. *The Symbolism of Evil.* Boston: Beacon, 1969.

Ziolkowski, Theodore. *Disenchanted Images: A Literary Iconology.* Princeton: Princeton UP, 1977.

David K. Danow (essay date 1997)

SOURCE: "The Semiotic Significance of 'The Minister's Black Veil,'" in *Semiotica,* Vol. 113, No. 3-4, 1997, pp. 337-46.

[*In the following essay, Danow analyzes the "minimalist" world of "The Minister's Black Veil" and the spatial relationships created by the veil symbol.*]

The Russian semiotician and literary theorist, Jurij Lotman, points out that the spatial order of the world in certain texts 'becomes an organizing element around which its non-spatial features are also constructed' (1977: 220). In other words, while time and space are inextricably bound in life and art, the spatial aspect may on occasion appear dominant as the principal organizational or structural element of the artistic work. Despite E. M. Forster's astute remark that time is 'far more fatal than place' (1927: 29), Lotman's view bears investigation.

The Russian theorist argues that 'the structure of the space of a text becomes a model of the structure of the space of the universe . . .' (1977: 217). If that is so, Nathaniel Hawthorne's **'The Minister's Black Veil'** would appear to offer a perspective on the world that is essentially minimalist. Nonetheless, the story is determined by an array of spatial relations that warrants consideration for what those relations might reveal concerning their meaning in the tale and, more importantly, for the peculiar significance surrounding the minister's veil. Hawthorne's story documents the life of a certain Reverend Mr. Hooper, who resolves to don a black veil, which he never again removes from his face. The reason for his 'taking the veil' remains a matter of gloomy speculation on the part of the townfolk of the story desirous of resolving the enigma in one way or another, whether their collective suppositions reflect positively on their 'good' parson (an adjective appearing no less than nine times in the text of a dozen pages) or not. 'To their imagination', the veil represents 'the symbol of a fearful secret' (1989: 27), although what that secret might be they cannot say.

On the day the minister dons his veil, he delivers a sermon, which 'had reference to secret sin, and those sad mysteries which we hide from our nearest and dearest . . .' (1989: 23). In addition, on that same day, he presides at the funeral of 'a young lady' and serves later at a wedding. Concerning the former, it is observed that at 'the interview between the dead and the living . . . when the clergyman's features were disclosed, the corpse had slightly shuddered. . . .' Another gossipy soul later fancies that 'the minister and the maiden's spirit were walking hand in hand'. That evening, at the wedding of 'the handsomest couple in Milford village', the bride's 'deathlike paleness caused a whisper that the maiden who had been buried a few hours before was come from her grave to be married' (1989: 24-26). But married to whom? To the young bridegroom standing at the altar with another? Or, to the Reverend Mr. Hooper, who, perhaps, was not so good (or not so innocent), after all? In any case, all such whispered innuendo clearly derives from the attendant stigma that the minister himself (intentionally?) incurs by his strange sartorial display.

Hawthorne terms the story 'a parable', attaching to this odd designation an unlikely footnote ostensibly intended to support the veracity of the tale. The note (a kind of subtext) claims that another clergyman in New England had also 'made himself remarkable by the same eccentricity that is here related of the Reverend Mr. Hooper'. But it is also explained that this other supposedly historical personage had done so because: 'Early in life he had accidentally killed a beloved friend; and from that day till the hour of his own death, he hid his face from men' (Hawthorne 1989: 21). In marked contrast, however, Hawthorne's extended text (to which the note is but a brief appendage concerning a parallel incident) does not provide a single definitive index as to why the minister burdened himself with that apparent penance in the first place. The reader is therefore left in a quandary analogous to the one in which the story's characters find themselves. Paradoxically rooted in the absence of a convincing explanation, an additional parallel is thus effected in both the reader's and characters' frustrated need to comprehend the minister's eccentric behavior. Yet the absence of a conclusive resolution ultimately discourages the reader's expectation that a unifying, convincing explanation might eventually be forthcoming.

A second significant 'absence' in the tale is likewise derived from a certain tension created by another, similarly closed channel of communication. For in placing the veil over his face, the minister, in effect (paralleling the overall design of the tale—which does not reveal the rationale for his strange conduct), also deprives his fictive counterparts of a crucial level of information: namely, whatever might have been intuited from his now concealed facial expression. If we take human communication (or dialogic interaction) to be effected on two planes, the verbal and gestural, then in this story the latter is significantly reduced, affording a corresponding reduction in the potential for achieving a certain level of mutual comprehension. As the sexton innocently puts it: 'I can't really feel as if good Mr. Hooper's face was behind that piece of crape' (1989: 22)—a sensed absence, of which Mr. Hooper's 'plighted wife' (1989: 27) also becomes cognizant, causing her to end their betrothal and take her 'farewell' in result of his refusal to 'lift the veil but once, and look me in the face' (1989: 29). Thus are Hawthorne's characters, as well as his readers, left to resolve the perplexing dilemma at the center of this metaphysical mystery or purported morality tale.

While the story may well inspire more thought and critical speculation than the potential for actual resolution, a consideration of the semiotic significance of the minister's black veil nonetheless commands our attention. For it is only as a sign (rather than an object) that we can proceed to make sense of the veil (if not conclusively of the tale)—in analogous fashion to the townfolk of the story, engaged in a like, albeit unwitting semiotic endeavor. For the reader (if not the characters), however, the project is enhanced by the author's designating the veil on no less than four occasions a 'symbol'—something, in other words (no matter how else the term might have been meant), to which meaning might legitimately be attached.[1]

Notwithstanding the fact that Hawthorne could have intuited but little, if anything, of what has been refined as current sophisticated semiotic theory, and could have even less likely been cognizant of what has emerged as contemporary understanding of the symbol as a species of sign, what can be argued with reasonable certainty is that Hawthorne conceived of his term as coinciding with what we understand to be a sign. (This 'coincidence' having been accomplished no less in complete, if unwitting, agreement with Peirce, who would later identify the symbol, bearing a relation to its object of 'an imputed character', with what he termed '*general signs*' [*CP* 1.558]). It has long been the case that the symbol, 'one of the most overburdened terms in the field of the humanities', has been taken as a synonym for 'sign'. As Nöth argues: 'Its ubiquity suggests that *symbol* and *symbolic* are often synonyms of *sign* and *semiotic*' (1990: 115). That such is in fact the case in **'The Minister's Black Veil'** is quickly demonstrated.

In that unusually appended footnote, Hawthorne refers to the other clergyman's veil as being a 'symbol' that 'had a different import' (1989: 21). Different from what, we might well ask? And meaning what to whom? To the townfolk of the story 'that piece of crape . . . seemed . . . the symbol of a fearful secret between him and them' (1989: 27). The minister proclaims to his disenchanted intended: 'Know, then, this veil is a type and a symbol . . .' (1989: 28)—bearing, we can assume, a certain meaning. Finally, at the end, the same doomed figure exclaims: 'What, but the mystery which it obscurely typifies, has made this piece of crape so awful? . . . deem me a monster, for the symbol beneath which I have lived, and die!' (1989: 33). Thus, in each instance, the veil is declared implicitly or explicitly to bear its own semiotic 'import'—if that import signify only the presence of a 'fearful secret' or 'mystery'.

Yet beyond such vague suppositions there exists no dearth of additional *possible* referents corresponding to this intentionally indeterminate sign. First among them is the *suggestion* of 'an ambiguity of sin or sorrow' (1989: 30). Intimately related is the notion of the veil signifying that each of us remains separated from all others by private thoughts, reminiscences of perhaps unworthy deeds, as well as by secret wishes and desires. It may then signify that ever receding moment, 'when the friend shows his inmost heart to his friend; the lover to his best beloved . . .' (1989: 33). But 'a mortal veil' (1989: 29), it also signifies that which 'shuts in time from eternity' (1989: 32), and is, in that sense, a sign of the imminent death that everyone must face. Or, as a kind of ornament, it may be perceived as an autotelic sign, a sign of itself, an aesthetic work (like **'The Minister's Black Veil'**), seeking only that we seriously regard it (not that we necessarily admire it), in what Bachelard terms 'the sacred instant of contemplation' (1964: 209). So, the veil remains an ambiguous sign: it may mean any (or all) of these things; it may mean none of them.

Impossible though it is for Hawthorne to have discerned a conception of the symbol coincident with Peirce's sophisticated formulation, the philosopher's understanding of this particular sign may nonetheless serve us well in coming to grips with Hawthorne's story. For Peirce, the defining characteristic of a symbol is its being habitually interpreted in the same way, as a conventional sign. 'Symbols afford the means of thinking about thoughts in ways in which we could not otherwise think of them. They enable us, for example, to create Abstractions, without which we should lack a great engine of discovery' (*CP* 4.531). (Does not Hawthorne exemplify Peirce's theoretical notion with a profound 'Abstraction' of his own, expressed in aesthetic form?) In Peirce's thought, symbols may be understood as 'Signs that represent their Objects essentially because they will be so interpreted' (*CP* 6.471). Yet it is precisely this dependence upon convention, habituation, the (possible) predictability of the interpretant, that Hawthorne undermines in **'The Minister's Black Veil'**. Because, in the minister's eccentric behavior, there can be no sense of habituation for the seeker of meaning to fall back upon, no reliable interpretant to call upon. In effect, the story stymies all such efforts, reducing (in one sense) its hallmark symbol (unlike the scarlet letter) to an essentially uninterpretable sign. So, when Peirce affirms—'A *symbol* is a sign which would lose the character which renders it a sign if there were no interpretant' (*CP* 2.304)—Hawthorne affords an aesthetic proof of Peirce's theoretical position, since, in the course of the tale, the 'symbol' of the veil will indeed 'lose the character which renders it a sign'. That, in fact, is what happens as the reader (and characters) endeavors to make of the veil a sign (in accord with Hawthorne's repeated insistence that it is a sign)—but without success. So (from a certain negative perspective), the veil reverts from being a potential sign to being only an object (all that it is and all that it can be): two folds of black crape designed to conceal, rather than reveal.

In its status as object, the veil is concrete, an actual physical manifestation in the world occupying a certain minimal space. As an indeterminate sign, it bears a figurative dimension, manifested in a verbal domain of metaphysical concerns. Within that realm of metaphysical abstraction, we are told that 'the Earth, too, had on her Black Veil' (Hawthorne 1989: 26), signifying not only the veil's metaphysical but also its universal aspect, from which none is exempt. Following a like principle of 'nonexclusion', the minister's black veil is juxtaposed to the 'veil of eternity' (1989: 32), from which no one will escape. In immediate physical terms, what is concealed behind the veil is simply a single human face. In its figurative dimension, however, the metaphysical depths contained behind the mask are immense. Still, these two seemingly opposed notions may be neatly aligned in the felicitous phrase of Gaston Bachelard, who explores the possibility of an 'intimate immensity' (1964: 193). Within this seemingly paradoxical union is suggested the potential for communicative intimacy, on the one hand, of which Mr. Hooper's interlocutors are nonetheless deprived. On the other, also concealed behind the veil is the untold spaciousness of the human soul, with its vast potential for secret sins and sufferings, the kind of information that Hawthorne implies but never overtly supplies.

The physical dimension converges on a single visage, the metaphysical aspect embraces the depths of the human soul. In one respect, the story encompasses the minimal, virtually immeasurable space contained under the minister's veil. But it also implicitly explores a great metaphysical depth in all its mystery and immensity, as an 'infinity of intimate space'. The story thus poses a set of interrelated questions that seek, in effect, 'a more intimate relationship between small and large' (Bachelard 1964: 190), between the physical and metaphysical, between matter and spirit. What, then, is concealed behind Mr. Hooper's veil? What secrets are contained in the deepest recesses of the minister's being? Ominous in their 'subtextual' message, such queries derive equally from the (etymologically) linked physical and metaphysical domains. As Bachelard observes: 'Here we discover that immensity in the intimate domain is intensity, an intensity of being, the immensity of a being evolving in a vast perspective of intimate immensity' (1964: 193). What better way to describe the plight of Hawthorne's figure immersed in a drama predicated upon an intensity of opposition between a man and a world of horrified others (an 'overawed . . . multitude' [1989: 27]), between the enhancing power of light and a fearful darkness, fleeting time and eternity, ultimately between a man and himself?

In accord with the physical and metaphysical relations upon which the story is predicated, its spatial relations also allow for a series of linked—if diametrically opposed—potentials: on the one hand, there is the possibility of concealment or containment, as essentially static considerations; on the other, there exists the potential for expansion versus contraction, or divergence as opposed to convergence, as related dynamic concerns. The spatial element, in other words, like the veil itself, yields its own reality—a reality that is manifested, first of all, through transformation. Thus, an old woman hobbling into the meeting house proclaims: 'I don't like it. . . . He has changed himself into something awful, only by hiding his face' (1989: 22). Another remarks: 'How strange . . . that a simple black veil, such as any woman might wear on her bonnet should become such a terrible thing on Mr. Hooper's face'. Yet another good soul observes: 'But the strangest part of the affair is [that] the black veil, though it covers only our parson's face, throws its influence over his whole person, and makes him ghostlike from head to foot' (1989: 24). What is significant here is that the veil, which would appear to contract or reduce the parson's features, is claimed instead to expand upon them (in a kind of 'ghostly' transformation), effecting a change that extends over the whole of him—and, by extension, into the speakers' realm as well.

That such an encroachment—from the private sphere of the 'good' Mr. Hooper into the public domain of his more or less well-intentioned flock—does indeed occur is made evident by the following authorial observation: 'But that piece of crape, to their imagination, seemed to hang down before his heart, the symbol of a fearful secret between him and them' (1989: 27). According to our principle of expansion or divergence, rooted in the spatial relations that govern the tale, the veil now appears on the physical plane to extend 'down before his heart'. On the corresponding metaphysical plane, however, that appearance is effected according 'to their imagination'. Not only has the black veil, then, been expanded (in their minds) but the dread that it conveys has likewise been extended, if not to the very heart of the pastor, surely into the hearts of the townspeople. Yet they are not alone in their perceptions. For, in the bride-(not)-to-be, 'in an instant, as it were, a new feeling took the place of sorrow: her eyes were fixed insensibly on the black veil, when, like a sudden twilight in the air, its terrors fell around her'. In that simile, once again the principle of divergence takes precedence over convergence, as the expansion of the veil's suggestive power (as an ambiguous, indeterminate sign) instills fear and terror in those nearby. 'She arose and stood trembling before him' (1989: 28), we read, a gesture which elicits in turn the query: 'And do you feel it then, at last?' said he mournfully. But what is *it* that she must feel? What is the referent here? Where is the antecedent? In Hawthorne's discarded drafts? In the townspeople's energetic collective imagination? Or is the 'object' contained instead in all that has preceded? In the story itself, which has suggested all along that the veil belongs not only within the pastor's private sphere but has reached beyond into everyone's domain. So that *it* refers to the *intensity* of feeling generated (as Bachelard might conceive it), or the '*horror*' (as Conrad would have it), which 'overwhelmed all others' (1989: 26). In any case, clearly the veil is not a private matter; rather, it belongs to all and clings to all. 'Thus', in accord with our governing principle of expansion and divergence, and as the author informs us, 'from beneath the black veil, there rolled a cloud into the sunshine . . .' (1989: 30)—as good a metaphor as any for the encroachment of the private into the public domain.

If we consider that spatial relations establish a sense of boundaries, or operate within the context of certain already established borders, then the minister's black veil serves in the most basic fashion to create a particular boundary: between the minister and his flock, between him and his betrothed, the man and the world outside. That is, a distinction is made at the most fundamental level between inside and outside—a basic opposition that allows for a single individual or an entire culture to set itself apart from all others. This is what the minister accomplishes, in effect, by donning the veil. He establishes a highly restrictive, closed system, whose sign is that piece of black cloth on his face, representing an ill-defined but essentially religious view. What tenets that view might entail are comprehended and adhered to exclusively by its sole proponent—although affecting in its limited sweep an entire collective.

In undertaking this role, the minister has established himself—both literally and figuratively—inside a certain (religious, philosophical) sphere with respect to the rest of the world that remains outside. In result of this singular act of self-condemnation, he remains, in effect, 'a man apart from men' (1989: 30). In semiotic terms, by retaining his secret motivating idea for himself alone, he is condemned to living behind a sign that will forever remain undefined.

Yet that sign might also be conceived as a discrete text, on a certain par with an artistic work, whose sense and meaning also remain ambiguous. For the minister's black veil is subject to a like critical assessment and interpretation within the literary work itself that a given work (such as **'The Minister's Black Veil'**) might occasion outside itself. We can equate the veil with a work of art, because we can say, with Lotman, that 'a work of art is in principle a reflection of the infinite in the finite. . . . It is the reflection of one reality in another . . .' (1977: 210). That, after all, is essentially the point we have been making all along concerning the minister's black veil. Lotman goes on to say: 'In modeling an infinite object (reality) by means of a finite text, a work of art substitutes its own space, not for a part . . . but also for the whole of that reality . . .' (1977: 211). Our point has been that the veil, in its minimal dimensions as a concrete object, models in a maximal sense 'an infinite object', namely the world, in both its physical and metaphysical reality, which, for Hawthorne's hero, are essentially one and the same.

Conceived thus as a discrete text, the minister's black veil gives rise once more to the question as to what renders this text (or sign) indeterminate? Clearly, the answer resides in a certain *felt* absence—namely, of a fixed and well-defined ideology. We read that 'the Earth, too, had on her Black Veil' (1989: 26). At the end, the minister proclaims on his death bed: 'I look around me, and, lo! on every visage a Black Veil!' (1989: 33). Hence the metaphoric proliferation of this sign as bearing a universal quality but no clear ideology. Ambiguity, of course, is a common (positive) feature of the literary text (as opposed to manuals, handbooks, and the like, where it would be deemed negative). Beyond this surface view, however, ambiguity in this literary text—residing as well in the veil as text—represents an inherent evocative element that inspires not only an attendant sense of mystery but also a certain universality: all of us, the earth as well, are shrouded in our own unseen veils, concealing our mysteries, our secrets, our selves. The minister has thus only hypostatized (though, he does not proselytize) and made visible, as well as physical, what exists as invisible and metaphysical.

He accomplishes this by wearing a black veil that serves to frame, and therefore set apart, an essentially undefined internal universe from a far more evident outside world. An integral sign, the veil *as frame* is also an independent text, since, in the story's terms (as well as in semiotic terms), what is most engaging is not the minister's (undoubtedly ordinary) face but the veil that covers that face. Hence the veil, not the visage, is the focus of the tale, in which the semiotic significance of the veil is that it functions in three interrelated respects: as an integral sign that unifies the text, as the frame that distinguishes a peculiar internal world from the external, and, in result of that basic function, as an independent (sub)text, deserving critical examination, within the greater text.

The veil is thus both a screen and a border, separating the seen from the unseen, the known from the unknown, the world of the living from the dead. A small piece of double folded crape that falls from above the minister's eyes to just over his mouth, the veil itself exists within a highly delimited sphere. Conceived as a discrete text or integral sign, however, the black veil is seen to extend beyond the minister's face; thus, 'it seemed to hang down before his heart . . .' (1989: 27), as it 'throws its influence over his whole person . . .' (1989: 24), extending outward, so that 'from beneath the black veil, there rolled a cloud into the sunshine, an ambiguity of sin or sorrow . . .' (1989: 30). An ambiguous sign, and an ambiguous text, the black veil nonetheless serves unambiguously as a frame that establishes a highly delimited border (although none seem to perceive it solely as such) around the parson's face. Juxtaposed to this limited manifestation, however, is the related figurative concept of 'the veil that shuts in time from eternity' (1989: 32), affording the minister's black veil an added dimension, a corresponding sense of an unfathomed metaphysical magnitude, which, paradoxically, all of its fearful beholders appear immediately, almost inevitably, to recognize.

Note

1. What that meaning might be, as argued here, remains ambiguous. Poe's 'The Masque of the Red Death' (also a kind of parable), in contrast, suggests unambiguously by its very title that the mask (an equivalent term, virtually, to Hawthorne's 'veil') worn by an intrusive figure upon a carnivalized scene is a clear and evident sign of the Red Death that threatens the countryside.

   Adding to the ambiguity of our semiotic endeavor is the fact that Hawthorne also refers four times to the minister's black veil as being an 'emblem'. For our purposes, we will treat it as a symbol exclusively, since, as Thomas A. Sebeok points out, an emblem is, in any case, 'a subspecies of symbol' (1985: 121).

Works Cited

Bachelard, Gaston (1964). *The Poetics of Space,* trans. by Maria Jolas. New York: Orion Press.

Forster, E. M. (1927). *Aspects of the Novel.* New York: Harvest Books.

Hawthorne, Nathaniel (1989). "The Minister's Black Veil." In *Selected Short Stories of Nathaniel Hawthorne.* New York: Ballantine Books.

Lotman, Jurij (1977). *The Structure of the Artistic Text* (Michigan Slavic Contributions 7), trans. by Ronald Vroon. Ann Arbor: Department of Slavic Languages and Literature University of Michigan.

Nöth, Winfried (1990). *Handbook of Semiotics.* Bloomington: Indiana University Press.

Peirce, Charles S. (1931-1958). *Collected Papers of Charles Sanders Peirce,* Charles Hartshorne, Paul Weiss, and A. W. Burks (eds.), Vols. 1-8. Cambridge: Harvard University Press. [Reference to Peirce's papers will be designated *CP.*]

Sebeok, Thomas A. (1985). *Contributions to the Doctrine of Signs* (Sources in Semiotics 4), Lanham, MD: University Press of America.

FURTHER READING

Criticism

Poe, Edgar Allan. "Hawthorne's *Twice-Told Tales.*" *Graham's Magazine* 20 (May 1842): 298-300.

Praises "The Minister's Black Veil" for its "masterful composition," but doubts that most readers will be capable of understanding the story's most subtle allusions and themes.

Voight, Gilbert P. "The Meaning of "The Minister's Black Veil." *College English* 13 (1952): 337-38.

Concludes that Mr. Hooper's decision to wear the black veil makes him a biblical prophet in the line of Jeremiah, Ezekiel, and Hosea, men whose own symbolic actions were "more effective than words in shocking heedless sinners into repentence."

Wycherley, H. Alan. "Hawthorne's 'The Minister's Black Veil.'" *Explicator* 23 (1964): Item 11.

Argues that hints in Hawthorne's "The Minister's Black Veil" indicate that Mr. Hooper is somehow implicated in the death of the young woman whose funeral he officiates, a conclusion similar to Poe's original 1842 review.

Additional coverage of Hawthorne's life and career is contained in the following sources published by the Gale Group: *Authors and Artists for Young Adults,* Vol. 18; *Concise Dictionary of American Literary Biography 1640–1865; DISCovering Authors; DISCovering Authors: British; DISCovering Authors: Canadian; DISCovering Authors Modules: and Most-studied Authors, Novelists; Dictionary of Literary Biography,* Vols. 1, 74; *World Literature Criticism; Yesterday's Authors of Books for Children,* Vol. 2.

Aldous Huxley
1894–1963

British-American novelist, short story writer, essayist, poet, and playwright.

INTRODUCTION

Huxley's short stories, all written between 1920 and 1930, cover a relatively short period in his prolific forty-seven-year writing career. The author celebrated for "novels of ideas," in particular the "dystopian" novel *Brave New World*, is little remembered today for his short fiction, but they do reflect in less complex structure many of the concerns he developed in his mature works. These include the search for order in chaos; the fragmentation, decay, and lack of wholeness and values in postwar society; the hostility of a world that thwarts ambition and expectations; and the artist's quest for identity. Most of the stories are witty and satirize modern values, particularly among the upper class, and display a sometimes bitter skepticism at the meaningless of life. While they were received fairly well during his life, later scholars of Huxley's work have generally ignored the stories, as it is agreed that the author's important ideas and concerns are given a far more eloquent voice in his novels. However, the stories continue to be appreciated for their wry humor, brilliant observation, sophisticated literary style, and skeptical view of humanity in post-World War I England.

BIOGRAPHICAL INFORMATION

Huxley was born in 1894 in Surrey, England, to an intellectually prominent family. His father, Leonard, was a respected essayist and editor, and his grandfather, Thomas Henry Huxley, was a leading biologist and proponent of Charles Darwin's theory of evolution. He was also the great-nephew of the poet Matthew Arnold, the grandson of the Reverend Thomas Arnold, and the nephew of the novelist Mrs. Humphrey Ward. Huxley's brother, Julian, would eventually become a noted biologist and his half-brother, Andrew, would win the 1963 Nobel Prize for his work in physiology. The early years in Huxley's life were passed happily in a stimulating, intellectual household. He was known as a sensitive boy and one who showed a mystical bent early on. But a series of tragedies befell Huxley in his teenage years. In 1908 his mother died of cancer, two years later he contracted an eye disease that permanently damaged his sight, and in 1914 his brother Trevenen committed suicide. These events had a profound effect on the concerns and mood of Huxley's writing.

While at Oxford from 1913 to 1916 Huxley started editing literary journals and began writing. In 1916, he published his first volume of poetry. He married a young Belgian refugee, Maria Nys, in 1919, and a year later his son, Matthew, was born. That year he also published his first volume of stories, *Limbo* to mild critical acclaim; two years later he produced another volume, *Mortal Coils*. Huxley gained wider recognition with his novel *Crome Yellow*; by 1923 his reputation was sufficiently secure that Chatto and Windus agreed to publish two of his works of fiction each year for the next three years. In 1923 Huxley and his wife moved to Italy, where they lived for four years. While abroad he wrote and published the novels *Antic Hay* and *Those Barren Leaves* and two volumes of short fiction, *Little Mexican and Other Stories* and *Two or Three Graces and Other Stories*. Huxley's volume of stories, *Brief Candles*, appeared in 1930, two years after the release of his highly acclaimed novel of ideas, *Point Counter Point*, which secured his reputation as one of the important literary figures of his day.

After 1930, Huxley's work began to reflect his increasing concern with humanistic ideas and ideals as well as politics. This is most vividly shown in *Brave New World*, his ironic satire of a utopia, which warns us against the dangers of political manipulation and technological development. In the late 1930s Huxley moved to California, where he became a screenwriter and developed his interest in mysticism, Eastern thought, and mind-altering drugs; he examines his experiences with one of these, mescaline, in *The Doors of Perception*. Huxley's later work clearly disavows some of the bleakness of his earlier outlook, and seeks a positive solution to the problem of an insane world. Perhaps as an antidote to his despairing sentiments in *Brave New World,* in his final novel, *Island*, he depicts a good utopia.

Huxley remained in California for most of the rest of his life. His wife, Maria, died in 1955, and Huxley married Laura Archera a year later. He died on November 22, 1963, the same day that President John F. Kennedy was assassinated.

MAJOR WORKS OF SHORT FICTION

Huxley produced eight volumes of short stories during his career. The first, *Limbo,* is a collection of six satiric tales about English country-house characters. These youthful wartime stories are full of parallels with Huxley's own life: in "Death of Lully" a woman has breast cancer, as did Huxley's own mother; a suicide like that of Huxley's brother occurs in "Eupompus gave Splendour to Art by Numbers." Also, there are numerous allusions to distorted vision; the stories' narrators are often erudite and urbane as Huxley himself was; many of the characters are cerebral persons who neglect their emotional and social aspects. The tone of the stories, for all their witty satire, is one of decay and fragmentation, of hopes and values lost. The 1922 volume *Mortal Coils* continues many of these themes in a postwar setting. In this volume appears Huxley's best known story, "The Gioconda Smile," about a man, Hutton, who fails in his attempt to live a life of reason and restrain his emotional appetites. Also in the volume is "Nuns and Luncheon," a bitterly sad story of Sister Agatha who falls in love with a wounded soldier she has nursed and who leaves the convent only to be abandoned and humiliated by the man she considered her savior. Huxley's next collection, *Little Mexican* contains the long tale "Uncle Spenser" that captures the harsh realities of lives disrupted by war. While in prison camp, Uncle Spenser falls in love with a fellow prisoner, a girl half his age named Emmy Wendle, whom he believes he will marry, but after the war he cannot find her. Another notable story in the collection, "Young Archimedes," about a child musical genius who commits suicide, is another statement of Huxley's common themes of expectations dashed and the difficulty in coming to terms with reality in a disorderly world.

Two or Three Graces contains a novella of that name and several shorter pieces. Kingham, the central character of the novella, has similarities with the novelist D. H. Lawrence, whom Huxley met in 1915 and became friends with in Italy. Kingham is a writer with perverse passions and whose unreason dominates his affair with Grace Peddley, whom he humiliates in order to stimulate his own emotions. The other stories in the volume are about lonely, ostracized persons whose romantic expectations of the world do not square with its harsh reality. Huxley's final collection of short fiction, *Brief Candles,* is filled with emotionally and spiritually impoverished characters, most notably in "The Claxtons," about a family of egocentric personalities. The novella "After the Fireworks," about an aging novelist who has affinities with Lawrence's view, is a satire of Lawrence's philosophy of harmony expressed through sexuality, as the protagonist becomes literally ill after taking a young lover. This was probably the last short piece Huxley wrote and shows his growing concern with the need for spiritually meaningful answers in a disordered and chaotic world.

CRITICAL RECEPTION

Huxley's reputation was built on his novels and nonfiction, and today scholarly interest in his work is generally confined to his writing in those genres. During his lifetime, Huxley's short fiction drew mixed reviews. With the publication of *Limbo,* Huxley was hailed by many as an important new voice that portrayed with delicacy and sophistication the postwar temperament. However, some critics complained about the self-consciously clever tone and lack of depth to the stories. Virginia Woolf, in an early review of *Limbo,* though, called the tales more than amusing, insisting that when Huxley "forgets himself" his stories can be interesting. The feeling of most critics, however, was that Huxley was not a natural short story writer. While admiring their artistic sophistication, fresh sense of irony, and insightful observation, most early reviewers felt that the tales suffered from saying too much and not staying true to the short story form. Contemporary critics also tend to dismiss Huxley's stories as being of little importance in his literary corpus. They contend Huxley needed the fuller range of the novel to fully develop his ideas, and most of his important concerns are reflected in his longer works. Huxley too felt his calling was not as a short story writer, and in a letter to his father explained that "the mere business of telling a story interests me less and less. . . . The only really and permanently absorbing things are attitudes towards life and the relation of man to the world." Huxley's stories are interesting today primarily for the insight they provide into his development as a writer and for his depiction of the social despair of the postwar period.

PRINCIPAL WORKS

Short Fiction

Limbo 1920
Mortal Coils 1922

Little Mexican and Other Stories 1924
Two or Three Graces and Other Stories 1926
Brief Candles 1930
The Gioconda Smile 1938
Twice Seven; Fourteen Selected Stories 1944
Collected Short Stories 1969

Other Major Works

The Burning Wheel (poetry) 1916
Leda and Other Poems (poetry) 1920
Crome Yellow (novel) 1921
Antic Hay (novel) 1923
On the Margin (essays) 1923
Point Counter Point (novel) 1925
Those Barren Leaves (novel) 1925
Brave New World (novel) 1932
Eyeless in Gaza (novel) 1936
After Many a Summer (novel) 1939
Time Must Have a Stop (novel) 1944
The Perennial Philosophy (essay) 1945
The Gioconda Smile (play) 1948
Ape and Essence (novel) 1948
The Doors of Perception (essay) 1954
The Genius and the Goddess (novel) 1955
Heaven and Hell (nonfiction) 1956
Brave New World Revisited (essay) 1958
Island (novel) 1962
Literature and Science (essay) 1963

CRITICISM

Herbert S. Gorman (review date 1920)

SOURCE: In a review of *Limbo,* in *Aldous Huxley: The Critical Heritage,* edited by Donald Watt, 1975, pp. 43-5.

[*In the following review of* Limbo, *originally published in* The New Republic *in 1920, Gorman compares Huxley's work to Max Beerbohm's.*]

Mr. Aldous Huxley, a new and extremely prepossessing English writer, has just been introduced to America with two volumes, ***Limbo,*** a collection of prose sketches written in a vein that is, to say the least, individual, and *Leda and Other Poems,* containing verse that smacks mightily of Mr. T. S. Eliot, and yet has an intriguing appeal quite its own. It was, I believe, in 1916 that Mr. Huxley's first book, *The Burning Wheel,* was published. A slender volume of verse, bound in paper covers and forming a link in Blackwell's Adventurers All Series, it hardly awakened more than a passing curiosity. But there was more in it than dexterous rhyming. The influence of Jules Laforgue was faintly manifesting itself; a precocious sophistication made itself dimly evident. Mr. Huxley has progressed as a poet since those days.

But it is the prose of Mr. Huxley that has suddenly projected him into the English periodicals and induced an American publisher[1] to bring him out over here. The seven pieces that make up the book (not all of them may be defined by the term 'stories') form a delectable ensemble. Mr. Huxley possesses the insolence of youth and a sprightly sophistication that can hardly be called disillusioned, although it approaches cynicism with frequency. It is a fastidious cynicism, though. If he suggests the pessimist at times we may be very sure that it is not the false pessimism of youth. He does not fly to extremes. He has not suddenly discovered that art is short and time is fleeting or that there are more people in the world intent upon bread and cheese than lyrics and lilies. Mr. Huxley is well-bred, without suggesting it. He is debonair without any flamboyant swashbuckling. He is precise in his prose and irresistible with his epigrams. Above all, he is the City. It is the sophistication of Hyde Park that he emanates.

So I come to the one English writer with whom he appears to have a certain kinship. Behind the pages of ***Limbo*** (at least for me) glimmers the nonchalant phantom of Max Beerbohm. The incomparable Max, a trifle weary, yawning a bit obviously, swings a gallant cane behind the **'Farcical History of Richard Greenow'** and **'Happily Ever After.'** He even appears, perhaps, a trifle more poetical than his wont, in **'Cynthia'** and **'The Bookshop.'** This may be doing a grave injustice to both Max Beerbohm and Mr. Huxley, and perhaps it is wise to insist that I am not attempting to postulate that the younger writer is at all aping his elders. It is merely a kinship of mood, a likeness of general attributes. **'The Farcical History of Richard Greenow'** might have fitted into Max Beerbohm's *Seven Men* without disordering that adorable volume in the least, but it is equally native to ***Limbo.*** Both writers are of the City. Both of them draw their characters with smartness and with individuality. Both of them display a sophistication that is beyond their years. Alas, we may not say this of Max now, but when we consider Max Beerbohm collecting his half dozen essays into a slender volume, writing a farewell preface to them, and publishing them as his *Collected Works,* while he was still in his early twenties, we smile and attribute his gesture to the insolence of youth. The same insolence hovers over ***Limbo.*** If anything Mr. Huxley is a bit more poetic. He is urbane but not to the extent of Max Beerbohm. Neither is his gift of humor so magical, so consistent. Mr. Huxley likes to be serious at times. His sophistication does not suggest the playfulness that is evident in Mr. Beerbohm's work.

The two pieces in ***Limbo*** that appear to stand out most startlingly are **'The Farcical History of Richard Greenow'** and **'Happily Ever After.'** Both of them are animated by a worldliness that is more implicit than expressed. Richard Greenow possesses a dual mind. Mentally he is an hermaphrodite. The figure of this man changes rapidly from light comedy to tragic implications.

The crashing down of the war upon England eventually destroys him. When we consider Richard, part of whose time is taken up living the life of a radical editor of a paper opposing the war and the rest of it existing as a lady novelist writing the most obvious patriotic war-mush, we must smile, but behind the incongruous theme is a passionate and heart-rending situation. Even in his death-throes Richard's dual nature is fighting against itself.

'Happily Ever After' is obviously cynical. It is satire handled with a deftness that is admirable. There is a truthfulness about the figure of Marjorie that ought to hurt. Perhaps this story is the best in point of character drawing, for there is a roundness about all the figures that move through its action. They suggest reality in a vivid and startling fashion. If we are to consider Marjorie being comforted in the arms of George when she hears of Guy's death in battle too seriously, we are apt to grow a bit cynical about the durability of love. . . .

While **'Cynthia'** and **'The Bookshop'** and **'Eupompus Gave Splendour to Art by Numbers'** may be merely mentioned as delicious trifles or tours de force, two other sketches in the book must be especially noted. **'Happy Families,'** written in dialogue form, possesses a symbolical significance that sets it a bit apart from the other efforts. By means of certain figures the hidden traits of the two principal personages are presented. Thus a slobbering Negro who keeps interjecting himself into the action personifies the man's primitive instincts.

'The Death of Lully,' which concludes the book, may be suspected of being an old legend or at least having its derivative inspiration in some old story. It is not Raimon Lully, the contemporary of Molière that is meant, but a religiast of the Mediterranean. Here again there is symbolism, and a surprisingly obvious symbolism for Mr. Huxley.

Limbo, taken as a whole, suggests a fine maturity in a writer so young. Mr. Huxley has fulfilled the promise that he intimated in his earlier books to the few who knew him, and demonstrated that he is one of the finest writers of prose in England today. He is finished and fastidious, sophisticated and diverting, an authentic figure of some actual importance and with many potentialities. That he must take a decided place among the younger contemporary writers in England is without doubt.

Note

1. George Doran in New York. Frank Swinnerton called *Limbo* to Doran's attention: '. . . I suggested to Doran that if he wanted to cultivate young talent, as he did, he should take the American rights.' *Figures in the Foreground,* p. 188.

Virginia Woolf (review date 1920)

SOURCE: In a review of *Limbo,* in *Aldous Huxley: The Critical Heritage,* edited by Donald Watt, 1975, pp. 41-2.

[*In the following review of* Limbo, *originally published in* The Times Literary Supplement *in 1920, Woolf calls Huxley's stories clever, amusing, interesting, and well written.*]

We know for ourselves that Mr. Huxley is very clever; and his publisher informs us that he is young. For both these reasons his reviewers may pay him the compliment, and give themselves the pleasure, of taking him seriously. Instead, that is, of saying that there are seven short stories in ***Limbo*** which are all clever, amusing, and well written, and recommending the public to read them, as we can conscientiously do, we are tempted to state, what it is so seldom necessary to state, that short stories can be a great deal more than clever, amusing, and well written. There is another adjective—'interesting'; that is the adjective we should like to bestow upon Mr. Huxley's short stories, for it is the best worth having.

The difficulty is that in order to be interesting, as we define the word, Mr. Huxley would have to forgo, or go beyond, many of the gifts which nature and fortune have put in his way. . . .

We hold no brief for the simple peasant. Yet we cannot help thinking that it is well to leave a mind under a counterpane of moderate ignorance; it grows more slowly, but being more slowly exposed it avoids that excessive surface sensibility which wastes the strength of the precocious. Again, to be aware too soon of sophisticated society makes it tempting for a young writer to use his first darts in attack and derision. If he is as dexterous and as straightforward as Mr. Huxley the attack is an inspiriting spectacle. Humbug seems to collapse, pretension to be pricked. . . .

It is amusing; it is perhaps true; and yet as one reads one cannot help exclaiming that English society is making it impossible to produce English literature. Write about boots, one is inclined to say, about coins, sea anemones, crayfish—but, as you value your life, steer clear of the English upper middle classes. They lie, apparently, so open to attack, they are undoubtedly such an obstacle to vision; but their openness is the openness of the tiger's jaw which ends by swallowing you whole and leaving no trace. **'Happily Ever After'** is but another proof of their rapacity. Mr. Huxley sets out to kill a great many despicable conventions, and to attack a large and disgusting schoolmaster. But having laughed at the conventions and the schoolmaster, they suddenly turn the tables on him. Now, they seem to say, talk about something that you do believe in—and behold, Mr. Huxley can only stammer. Love and death, like damp fireworks, refuse to flare up in such an atmosphere, and as usual the upper middle classes escape unhurt.

But with Mr. Huxley it is only necessary to wait a little longer; and we can wait without anxiety. He is not merely clever, well read, and honest, but when he forgets himself he discovers very charming things. . . .

Emboldened by our pleasure in such good writing as this, we would admonish Mr. Huxley to leave social satire alone, to delete the word 'incredibly' from his pages, and to write about interesting things that he likes. Nobody ever takes advice; even so, we hazard the opinion that Mr. Huxley's next book will be not only clever, amusing, and well written, but interesting into the bargain.

William Jacob Cuppy (review date 1922)

SOURCE: "Huxley as a Serious Writer," in *Aldous Huxley: The Critical Heritage,* edited by Donald Watt, 1975, pp. 74-6.

[*In the review of* Mortal Coils *below, which was originally published in the* New York Sunday Tribune *in 1922, Cuppy rejects earlier assessments of this collection as superficial, insisting that Huxley is a serious writer.*]

In the *Dial* for June Mr. Raymond Mortimer opines that the principal end and aim of Aldous Huxley is to be 'amusing,' and insists to the author of *Crome Yellow* upon the importance of being earnest.

On May 27 Mr. Burton Rascoe, having lunched, allowed in the Doran offices as to how Aldous Huxley, 'undoubtedly the most adroit and amusing' of the clever young Englishmen, 'deals in superficies, but with a gay, satirical touch.'

On June 13 Mr. Ben Ray Redman, having dined, announced at Mr. Louis Untermeyer's that Aldous Huxley 'was like Oscar Wilde in the '90's, the clever young froth writer of his day.'

If this sort of thing goes on I don't want to.

And it's almost sure to go on, for ***Mortal Coils,*** which has just followed *Crome Yellow,* is a book of shorter pieces almost as clever and amusing as the novel. I want to point out, with due respect, that ***Mortal Coils*** is also just as deeply serious, purposeful, holy, flaming and passionately true and wise as is so certainly *Crome Yellow.*

Aldous Huxley deals in both books (with a gay, satirical touch, truly) with the inevitable cruces of this, our mortal, life, with the sickening, blasting ironies of this vale of tears, with the beautiful poisonous snares of this utterly marvellous world, with the mere emotions and ideas, such as they are, of us human creatures; with the resistless desires and shattering half-truths by which we live and die. Are these superficies? Is this froth?

I should hate to see Aldous Huxley tagged as superficial. Nobody is superficial anyway. There is no such thing. (Least of all Huxley, or Wilde either, for that matter). The author of ***Mortal Coils*** is a direct and lineal descendant, a true son and disciple of the authentic and sacred philosophers of the above-mentioned world. Wisdom has bloomed in him as an orchid, not as a cabbage. That is all.

Does Mr. Huxley deal in half-truths? Is that the charge against him? Do I? Does Nietzsche? Are there any whole-truths? Perhaps not. Surely then, I may insist that Aldous Huxley is a serious and an earnest writer, since I but point to the reverse of the medal. And by way of harmonizing my views with those of one critic I may mention that even superficies may seem to be, if rightly considered, as deep as hell itself, and just as true and important.

'The Gioconda Smile,' the first piece in the new book, sets forth in a fantastically ironic framework the expert and authentic anatomy of the libido of a Mr. Hutton, who was either just an old fool or Everyman, and of the fabulous face of Janet Spence, a homicidal virgin of thirty-six who thought she was by Leonardo. (It is Mrs. Hutton who shuffles off.) Poor old Hutton. One shrinks from the picture. 'And actually, really, he was what?—Who knows.' Absolutely true and beautifully done, except for one dubious page where the author jumps out of Mr. Hutton's skin omnisciently, but awkwardly, to administer the arsenic.

'Nuns at Luncheon' is a tale told by a sob-sister, full of sound without the least fury, signifying everything. Two writers jesting hideously over the seduction of Sister Agatha and discussing how to turn it into salable fiction. Out of heartless comments and brutally callous jokes this Huxley fashions something so piteous and so terrible that few will dare reread it. A masterpiece? Perhaps. The art that produced **'Nuns at Luncheon'** is something to admire.

'Green Tunnels' is a mildly interesting thing about a young girl surrounded by some of those middle-aged grubs that Huxley sometimes digs up. **'The Tillotson Banquet'** is an anecdote—more irony. **'Permutations Among the Nightingales'** contains a woman who is steatopygous, whatever that is.

Several things in ***Mortal Coils*** look like studies for *Crome Yellow.* In fact, ***Mortal Coils*** is the stuff from which *Crome Yellow* are made. But froth? Well, why not? And now I placate Mr. Redman. I bethink me of what Lytton Strachey says apropos another work not so dissimilar as some might think, the *Lettres Philosophiques* of Voltaire.

> He offers one an exquisite dish of whipped cream; one swallows down the unsubstantial trifle, and asks impatiently if that is all? At any rate, it is enough. Into that frothy sweetness his subtle hand has insinuated a single drop of some strange liquor—is it a poison or is it an elixir of life?—whose penetrating influence will spread and spread until the remotest fibres of the system have felt its power.

And this mysterious drop, which I cannot bear to have undervalued or misunderstood, is in the case of *Crome Yellow* and ***Mortal Coils*** simply the immortal soul of the artist who wrote those books.

***Times Literary Supplement* (review date 1924)**

SOURCE: "Huxley's Elasticity," in *Aldous Huxley: The Critical Heritage,* edited by Donald Watt, 1975, pp. 104-05.

[*In the following review of* Little Mexican, *originally published in the* Times Literary Supplement *in 1924, the critic praises the "elasticity" in Huxley's work, admiring what others might criticize as disproportionate description and indulgence of literary power.*]

About Mr. Aldous Huxley there is an elasticity that keeps his work interesting and even exciting. His last novel, *Antic Hay,* was as rigidly constructed and tightly compacted as a novel could well be: technically (we are speaking only of technique), a firm piece of carpentry. The book of fiction before that was ***Mortal Coils,*** in which he was so consciously literary that nearly every one of the stories was offered as an exercise in method. Now comes another book of stories, ***Little Mexican,*** in which none of the six displays its method, and only two are at all firmly carpentered. One of these two is **'Hubert and Minnie'**, a common-place of fiction so far as its subject goes, but as well told on its own lines as any story that we know. From the touch about the ferrets to the afternoon light in the mill-garden the story is a little masterpiece of suggestion, contrast, shading-off, so finely contrived that in the first reading one only feels how actual the story is. **'Fard'** is equally well told; but by comparison with **'Hubert and Minnie'** it seems made-up, not real. The contrast between the opulent mistress and her worn-out old servant-woman is a shallow theme that needed either intensifying in incident or studying at one remove in the manner of some of the stories in ***Mortal Coils,*** if it were not to seem bare. To that manner of seeing things at one remove Mr. Huxley returns with great effect in **'The Portrait'**. Told by a fraudulent picture dealer about a sham old master portrait of a woman, this tale of eighteenth-century Venice, master, jewels, elopements, and what not, takes on a double fantasy; but we wish that Mr. Huxley had not underlined the cheat by showing us the 'devil' employed to paint Venetian old masters. He might as well have told us what happened to Minnie after Hubert left her at the mill.

In the other three stories we come upon what is truly exciting in Mr. Huxley's new book. They are longer than the usual short story, and it looks as if he had determined to challenge any rules there may be about compactness, suggestion, and so forth. **'Uncle Spencer'** begins on the first page of the book: we get to the story on page 80, when the war breaks out, and Uncle Spencer, sugar refiner in Longres, is imprisoned in Brussels with Emmy Wendle, a Cockney 'male impersonator' of the music-halls. Every page of the first eighty, telling of Uncle Spencer's nephew's boyhood in the Belgian town, is delightful. In the end every page helps us to know that fascinating mixture of Mr. Shandy and Sir Roger de Coverley which was my Uncle Spencer. But the purists will certainly tell Mr. Huxley that not a word of it, from his most Proustian sentence to his sharpest, was necessary. Let the purists have their say: we would not lose a word of it, nor a word of the descriptions of Italian scenery which lead us, ever so leisurely, into the tragedy of an Italian peasant-boy and a vulgar woman who adopted him. In a less degree Mr. Huxley lays himself open to the same charge of disproportion in the deliciously wicked tale which gives its title to the book (**'Little Mexican'**, by the way, is a hat, not a film heroine): a tale of an Italian nobleman, who is 'old and gay' like the fairies in Mr. Yeats's poem, the prodigal father of a conscientious and very safely married son. In these cases, either Mr. Huxley is not sure of the worth of his story as a story, or he is so sure of it that he is resolved to indulge himself to the top of his bent in the writing. The result is in each case good enough to warrant him in doing what he pleases and us in pleasantly wondering what he is going to do next.

Arnold Bennett (essay date 1924)

SOURCE: "Arnold Bennett on 'Little Mexican,'" in *Aldous Huxley: The Critical Heritage,* edited by Donald Watt, Routledge & Kegan Paul, 1975, pp. 106-07.

[*In the following excerpt from his journals, the noted author and critic Bennett generally approves of the characterization in the tales in* Little Mexican *but says the stories have no proper end and the characters are drawn a little too thoroughly.*]

About **'Uncle Spencer'**. This is the first book of Aldous Huxley's that I have really liked. Character drawing in it, for the first time in his books. Uncle Spencer is *drawn,* emphatically. But technically the story is clumsy. The story nearly ends artistically. Aldous doesn't finish; he ceases. But another perfect page and the end would have been good. He shirks the final difficulty and so there is no end. Same with the next best story **'Little Mexican'**. No end to it. But the character drawing of the N. Count is good. **'Fard'** is a Chekhov story. But the feelings of the maid when the mistress tells her to rouge herself to hide her tiredness are shirked.

More about novel writing and character drawing. You couldn't fill in a whole character except in a book of enormous length. The young ones don't seem to me to 'select'. They shove in pell-mell whatever happens to strike them. They don't construct even a character. Then they think they are truer to life: but they aren't. Description of faces is futile. Waste of time. Give the reader something to hold on to, and then let him fill in for himself.

L. P. Hartley (review date 1926)

SOURCE: "Two or Three Graces," in *Aldous Huxley: The Critical Heritage,* edited by Donald Watt, Routledge & Kegan Paul, 1975, pp. 137-38.

[*In the following review of* Two or Three Graces, *originally published in the* Saturday Review *in 1926, Hartley calls Huxley a "literary acrobat" whose perfect execution of difficult feats sometimes leaves readers disappointed because there is little to glean behind the lucidity of his words.*]

However good Mr. Huxley's work may be one rarely reads it without a small pang of disappointment. To surpass themselves is for many novelists a comparatively easy task; but here is one who has contrived to set his own standard so high that, captivate and divert us as he may, he still seems to fall short of a proposed excellence. The shadow of a commanding talent and a distinguished mind is thrown across each page, but though Mr. Huxley has many altitudes that are visible enough we can never quite descry that single peak which puts so much, even Mr. Huxley's own work, into the shade. Perhaps it is to his disadvantage that he makes his meaning so clear: he is the victim of his own lucidity. He has such a gift for expression that for the imagination to look beyond the written word in search of private overtones seems an impertinence. And the imagination, always eager to contribute its little quota, however futile and irrelevant, resents being warned off in this way, and sulks because it may not co-operate. It complains that Mr. Huxley makes Aunt Sallies of his characters, setting them up simply to bowl them over with a few good shots, and that these figures of unreason are sometimes too near and too flimsy to justify their impressive bombardment by Mr. Huxley's heavy guns. Grace Peddley, for instance, in the first and most important story: is she made substantial enough to carry our interest through her various metamorphoses, her ungraceful, almost disgraceful, antics as one man's wife and two men's mistress? Are we prepared to shed tears, as Mr. Huxley seems to require us to, over such a figure of fun? But the mind delights in the humours of Grace's progress, rejoices in the deft exposure of Peddley, Rodney and Kingham, never withholds its laughter when for the hundredth time Mr. Huxley demonstrates that futility is futile. It is even impatient of the softer note that has lately crept into Mr. Huxley's voice and makes a faint deprecating undertone to the brilliant derisive music with which he plays his characters out of his pages.

'Half-Holiday' is the best story of the collection. The poor young man whose romantic day-dreams have led him, on behalf of two beautiful young ladies, to interpose in a dog-fight and get bitten, cannot restore the creature because of his stammer:

After this delicious bit of comedy it was a pity to give the story a bitter and unhappy ending: it does not quite 'come off'. At his best Mr. Huxley 'comes off' as few living novelists do. And our enjoyment of his work depends upon its successfulness. If there is no 'pop' we know the wine is flat. Mr. Huxley's work has no intermediate quality; it is flat or it is effervescent. He is a literary acrobat, setting out to do a difficult feat perfectly; he makes no attempt to conceal his virtuosity; he calls upon one to hold one's breath. He may take a tumble, but his successes, of which there are many in ***Two or Three Graces,*** are as undeniable and as instantly recognizable as if they were the work of the hand, not of the pen.

Joseph Wood Krutch (review date 1926)

SOURCE: "More Barren Leaves," in *Aldous Huxley: The Critical Heritage,* edited by Donald Watt, Routledge & Kegan Paul, 1975, pp. 139-41.

[*In the following review originally published in the* Nation *in 1926, Krutch calls "Two or Three Graces" a "grotesquely tragic story" that for all its ironical detachment is essentially concerned with moral questions and "the world and its ways."*]

Mr. Aldous Huxley, probably the most intelligent of *les fauves,*[1] exhibits alternately the two moods, the disdainful and the explosive, of his mind. In the first he is an aloof satirist regarding human follies with an air of great detachment and describing them in a style of limpid simplicity; in the second the mask drops from his face and reveals the pain which lies behind it. Tolerant contempt gives way to ferocious hatred, classic irony to raging disgust, and the author descends from his Olympian height to struggle desperately with the problems which he had mocked others for not solving.

This second mood, definitely foreshadowed in the satiric poems which formed the bulk of the volume called *Leda,* received its fullest expression in that hideous masterpiece *Antic Hay.* An obscene farce at the heart of which lay an utter despair, it seemed to reach the uttermost possible limits of hatred for a world in which nothing could be believed and nothing, not even debauchery, could be enjoyed. Beyond it lay nothing except the desperate conversion of a Huysmans, and perhaps for that reason Huxley has never since let himself go completely. In *Those Barren Leaves* as well as in the present volume there are occasional glimpses of the black abyss from which *Antic Hay* was born, but the mask is resumed and confession is checked. The author, turning his eye upon this character or that situation, regards it with an aloof ironical gaze and pretends to have found his own fixed point of peace—though he never reveals to us just where it is—in the midst of the flux which he describes.

The world with which he deals is essentially a world where there are no faiths but only an infinitude of poses. Biology, anthropology, psychoanalysis, and the rest have made it impossible for anybody to be sure of anything. There are people who pretend to believe in art, in science, or even in morality, but at bottom they know that they have only taken up attitudes and they are so used to pretending at faiths and passions that they do not themselves know when they come closest to sincerity. Painters talk glibly of forms, physiologists of glands, and philosophers of complexes, but none of them know where they are or have continued very much to care. At their best they manage, like the painter Rodney in the present volume, to obtain a success by some simple device; his consists of painting provocative green nudes in a distorted setting. At their worst they merely stand, like one of the minor characters, in the midst of a drunken party and bawl: 'We're absolutely modern, we are. Anybody can have my wife so far as I'm concerned. I don't care. She's free. and I'm free. That's what I call modern.' Between them there is not much to choose and they meet on a common ground. One and all they drink and couple, the only real difference being the extent to which they can dramatize their monotonous experiences.

Such is the milieu of the story **'Two or Three Graces,'** which gives its title to the present volume and which constitutes more than two-thirds of its bulk. Its central character is a pleasant, simple, and rather stupid woman who is drawn into the chaos which she understands rather less than those who make it. Somewhat after the manner of Chekhov's 'Darling' she assumes in desperate earnest the tastes and the poses of her lovers. While she lives with the painter she talks of 'drinking life like champagne' and of 'the duty of obeying one's whims'; when she becomes the mistress of the neo-Nietzschean philosopher she tries her best to be the vampire 'possessed by a devil of concupiscence' which it pleases him to pretend that she is; but all the time she cannot help taking the poses more seriously than those do from whom they are imitated. While they pretend to suffer she really does, and we leave her desperate at the end of one of her affairs, yet inevitably destined to do an eternal *da capo.*[2]

It is a grotesquely tragic story, one which might, indeed, have been woven in as one of the many threads of *Antic Hay,* but it differs in that it is written with an air of ironical detachment which conceals the desperate disgust the former book set out clearly to reveal. In it Mr. Huxley no longer shrieks. He pretends almost to be writing again in the mood of mere satiric extravaganza which marked *Crome Yellow* and which caused him to be compared to Peacock. His clear self-possessed sentences are polite and calm, his analyses minute and unexcited. And yet for all the careful impersonality of manner it is the essential seriousness of his mind, his real concern with the world and its ways, which gives to him his strength. He is at heart no aesthete and no mere Olympian satirist. As surely as the most solemn of moral philosophers he is in search of the good life, and it is the bitterness of his disappointment in not having found it that sets his work so far above that of our merely precious sophisticates. Essentially too serious of mind to be content with the cleverness which is so abundantly his, and possessed of a mind too powerfully critical to fall a victim to any sham philosophy, he has wandered unhappily through a life which has so far revealed to him nothing in which he could believe; and if he has described nothing but folly his descriptions have been significant for the very reason that he would so infinitely have preferred any wisdom that he had been able to find.

Notes

1. Literally 'the wild men' or 'beasts'; refers to a group of early twentieth-century artists who splashed brilliant, jarring colors onto their canvasses in rebellion against the sober browns and blacks of Victorian painters.
2. 'Going back to the beginning and repeating.' A familiar musical notation used in Huxley's story.

Henry Hazlitt (review date 1930)

SOURCE: "This Petty Pace," in *The Nation* (New York), Vol. 130, No. 3387, June 4, 1930, p. 654.

[*In the following review of* Brief Candles, *Hazlitt argues that Huxley brings a message to his stories—that if one tries to be superhuman, one becomes subhuman.*]

After half a dozen volumes Aldous Huxley has returned to the short story, but he does not bring his old irresponsibility with him. He has acquired a Message, and he insists that we shall hear it. It is the same message that raised its head in nearly every one of the essays in "Do What You Will," to wit, that if one tries to be superhuman one ends by being subhuman, that the best way of turning a child into a devil is to try to bring it up as an angel. Against the ideal of superhumanness he pleads for the ideal of perfected humanity. Mr. Huxley's, in other words, is just another brand of humanism. But it is at the farthest pole from Babbittean humanism, for instead of moderation Mr. Huxley believes in excess, provided that one excess is counterbalanced by another, and instead of believing in the will to refrain and the middle level he holds (I am here assuming that one of his characters speaks for him) that a human being should "completely and intensely live . . . on every plane of existence."

There is no need here to examine this philosophy in detail. It is enough to say that Mr. Huxley, in talking of subhuman, human, and superhuman levels, is making as dubious a division as the Babbittean humanists when they talk of man living on three "planes," the natural, human, and religious. For every "plane" on which a human being lives is necessarily a human plane, just as every action he takes is at bottom a natural action. It would not occur to our literary philosophers to divide the actions of a dog into subdoggy, doggy, and superdoggy; it is only when we come to our own race that we consider it necessary to have something fancy in the way of metaphysics. The use of the words "human" and "natural" in so many different senses, each sense carrying within itself its peculiar shade of approval or disapproval, is bound to produce murky thinking and silly conclusions. It is much wiser to ask simply whether a given action or ideal is desirable or undesirable, regardless of what "plane" one may think it on.

That three of the present four stories are written at least in part to support a thesis does not in itself make them any the less amusing. Most satire gains its effect through the very fact that it *is* written to support a thesis, or to ridicule someone else's thesis, e.g., "Candide." When Mr. Huxley mars his work he does so not by having a thesis, but by illustrating his thesis too often through explicit statement rather than indirectly through the story itself. In the present volume he has been content sometimes to allow the story to remain secondary. In **"The Claxtons,"** for example, he does little more than deride a certain type of "spirituality" and the products for which it is responsible. How beautifully the Claxtons live, how spiritually! Even the cat is a vegetarian. There is Herbert, "longlegged and knickerbockered, his fair beard like a windy explosion round his face," who carries a Rücksack even in London as though he were just about to ascend Mont Blanc. When the street boys yell or the flappers whoop with laughter, Herbert ignores them, or else smiles through his beard "forgivingly and with a rather studied humorousness." His wife, Martha, is also spiritual; and she too can smile a beautifully Christian—yet superior—smile. **"The Claxtons"** is less a story than a portrait or a travesty of a type, but it is magnificently done, a merciless exposure of the self-consciously uplifted.

In **"The Rest Cure,"** which comes nearest to the orthodox story, a young English woman rents a villa near Florence and enjoys a mild flirtation with a local Italian; her husband, visiting her for a few days, warns her so brutally against the man that in defiance she gives herself to him; he extorts money from her and quickly tires of her, and the story ends ironically when she shoots herself for the wrong reason. The last and most important story, occupying half of the book, **"After the Fireworks,"** describes what begins as a charming but ends as a sordid affair between a novelist of fifty and a girl admirer of twenty-one. By once more making his hero a novelist Mr. Huxley finds free scope for that brilliant talk, those little essays and excursions into philosophy, the wit and brilliant description, as well as the cynicism, that have always distinguished his work; and he writes, too, a story of great psychological penetration. The diary of the girl, however, leans too heavily in its syntax on "Gentlemen Prefer Blondes," while the comments are a little too intelligent to make that style altogether credible.

Kenneth Payson Kempton (essay date 1953)

SOURCE: "Persons," in *Short Stories for Study,* Harvard University Press, 1953, pp. 272-77.

[*In the following study of "Nuns at Luncheon," Kempton offers two interpretations of the satirical story: as a tale within an anecdote which is a fiction that ends as a polemic, and as a straightforward realistic piece that is no less satirical for being objectified and held in control.*]

The story sparkles. Several technical instruments and factors in the management of content contribute to the display. The immediate scene in the restaurant gathers together and unifies for a single effect a number of told immediate scenes and a multitude of details widely separate in space and time. There are two narrators. The more important because more prominent is, of course, Miss Penny; but the function of "I" should not be underrated or misunderstood. "I" describes Miss Penny, contributes suggestions and a long descriptive scene, spurs on the chief teller or reins her in, and is, actually, the motive force behind the story. It was plainly Mr. Huxley's intention for "I" to represent himself: "I" is a writer of fiction; his laconic and noncommittal speech, well calculated to lead on Miss Penny, was shrewdly managed to draw interest and sympathy while acting as contrast to her voluble telling and overbearing manner; his early statement, "but that had been said before," and, rather late in the story, his reply to Miss Penny's urging that he write a story on the material she is giving him, "You may be sure I shall," seal the certainty. We must take Mr. Huxley's word for it; we cannot, in considering this short story, differentiate between the author as a living person and the author as a character. He is there in the story by his own admission and wish, and is to be appraised as a character. Both narrators, we note, are trained writers, observing life as a matter of course and holding decided opinions about living and dying. Both are acutely imaginative. A further advantage is gained, through instinct or design, by the fact that both tellers are ostensibly only playing with story material, pretending, imagining the writing of *a* story while *the* story is being told; so that they may stop, start again, stop again when and where they wish, interpolate their feelings and opinions or, as effectively, be silent without losing the thread of narrative or becoming incoherent. Thus the vehicle of expression works as smoothly and as effortlessly as a precision machine. Small wonder, then, if the extremely ingenious and intricate structure of the story—its back-and-forth movement in time holding suspense when needed, preparing every detail for the accelerated pace and swift ending—remains unseen.

The strongest element is unclassifiable under technique or content. Only the most captious reader will find **"Nuns at Luncheon"** less than highly readable. Once under way, the story induces a snicker or chortle in almost every line. There is release in the laughter produced, possibly a hysterical or near-hysterical sense of pleasure in seeing institutions and customs long held sacred not only torn to shreds but tramped upon. The incongruity is cumulative, the pressure builds up to a long-pent roar of mirth when Sister Agatha, discovered by woodcutters and unable to explain her predicament because her seducer has stolen her false teeth, is quite naturally taken for a fool. The total effect of the story is both authentic and astounding; burst follows burst of incredible fireworks; yet here it all lies quiet, in cold black type.

Obviously, too, the intent of the author was satire. But when one tries to discover the cause and nature of the attack, and particularly its object or objects, no solution appears. Since Juvenal, this form of writing has seemed best justified, promising permanence as art, when one or more of the following attributes is present: a corrective motive indicated by suggested betterment of conditions satirized; impersonality covering the identity of satirist and the satirized by symbolism or allegory; and detachment from local or temporal circumstances that, being soon forgotten, would render the attack meaningless. None of these conditions obtains here. Miss Penny is exhibited, especially at her triumphant exit from the story, as a growing menace to society about whom nobody, least of all the author, need have the slightest misgivings; the satirist not only appears in person but bids for the reader's interest and sympathy, while the individual satirized is drawn with such vigorous acerbity and exactitude of grotesque detail that, though her identity now after thirty years may be forgotten, she must have had a living prototype (she is as certainly factual and as basically unadulterated fact as was Maugham's portrait of Hugh Walpole in *Cakes and Ale*); and the circumstances of time and place are so particularized that already they are hazed over and in another thirty years may require a gloss. And Miss Penny, although the chief object of attack, is by no means the only one. Any attempt to enumerate other butts will fail unless a list is made of persons and beliefs *not* attacked. We cannot call this story satire. We must call it satirical, bitterly and generally satirical, for some reason not yet determined. We are far from all that laughter.

So doubt enters. We must get at the meaning of the story, and the only method possible is through a study of its enactors, one of whom is Mr. Huxley himself. (Or so he has asked us to believe.)

Two interpretations of the story are tenable, depending on our interpretation of "I" and Miss Penny. Neither redounds greatly to the author's credit as catcher and creator of personality, and the consequent ambiguity between the two readings (although it may have afforded him a private joke-of-all-jokes at the reader's expense) seems to constitute a further detraction from what at first appeared a brilliant achievement in this factor of management.

The only fully grasped person here is Miss Penny. Her the author seems to have known so well that he could embroider factual details into the purely fanciful—such as the earrings, the woman journalist's outward scorn of but inward yearning to write fiction, the savage curiosity of an old maid about sex—without making the caricature too outlandish, in a swiftly moving story, to be credible. By this first interpretation, the author uses Miss Penny not so much as a storyteller, rather as a mouthpiece through which he can jeer at a good many activities and customs and institutions that he personally finds ridiculous: spinsters, journalists, American magazines, Roman and Protestant Churches, universities, sexual inhibitions and sexual drives, but especially and above all ideal love—in short, at almost everything and everybody conveniently in sight at the moment, with one exception. Himself. But this very wanton and extensive jeering, plus his ostentation of utterance and choice of material (note his proffered familiarity with French, German, Latin used mock-heroically or mock-romantically) actually reveal himself as something of a joke that he missed, while at the same time undermining the illusion of reality within which a story must operate. In this instance, the story told by Miss Penny, of the authenticity of whose facts we have no assurance and some cause for doubt, becomes more and more a sort of fairy tale within a warped but perhaps basically factual anecdote, creating neither convincing fiction nor credible fact. By this interpretation the piece begins as fiction but ends as polemic.

It seems hardly necessary to add that the distortion of some unknown person into a caricature called Miss Penny is suggestive of the failure to create individual personalities in Kuno and Sister Agatha. The former is at best, just as visually represented, a worn photograph; he never speaks a word in the reader's hearing; he comes to us via the Doctor, Miss Penny, and Mr. Huxley, and probably was guessed at. Sister Agatha's false teeth give her away at once (as did Miss Penny's "corpses hanging in chains" earrings). She again is only a broad type with luridly grotesque touches, a character who can be pushed at the author's humorous whim from seduction into near-sainthood into farce.

By a second interpretation this story is an intensive, rather than extensive, attack. There is no general polemic, the author is not accountable for what Miss Penny rails at, and the story proper occurs only in the restaurant, its only characters being Miss Penny and Mr. Huxley. The story told by Miss Penny within the story is to be taken as nonsense, made up by her out of whole cloth, and is used merely as a lever by which Mr. Huxley, through his modest aloofness and reluctant participation, pries open and reveals the tremendous sexual yearning and the equally strong sexual repression within Miss Penny's unconsciousness. This leverage begins where Miss Penny wonders if she will ever be "exploited." The negative, embarrassing silence that follows compels her to justify herself as person, as professional, and as contented because courted (if not yet won) spinster. The stages of the told story follow the pattern of this attempted justification, as Miss Penny repeatedly tries to lure Mr. Huxley into collaboration, only to snatch the telling from him. At the same time the author allows her, before the reader's eyes, to deny and refute by implication (note the early description of her eyes and ears; note that she, a reporter of facts, is here spinning the wildest species of yarn while at the same time professing disgust at it and extreme boredom; note the ironic application to her of the funeral of Sister Agatha) all three phases of her intended vindication of herself, and in the very words that she believes creates and confirms them.

Yet, if this interpretation is correct, our conclusion must be that Mr. Huxley has drawn a superficially comic but essentially an incredibly stupid person, a monster in chains, far too exaggerated for anyone not momentarily blinded by laughter to believe. Katharine Brush's "Good Wednesday" shows a similar (much simpler) pattern of self-condemnation disguised as justification, the author using stages in the revelation of the protagonist as substitute for movement by motive-obstacle-success or -failure. But there is no ambiguity, the method is straight and clear, the material no less keenly satirical but carefully objectified and held in control; and the result is a story that provides no laughter but knocks the reader all but off his chair by producing a shattering surprise based on thoroughly realized and thoroughly credible characteristics of human nature that might turn up at any time, anywhere.

Here, what meaning, what general truth is present and demonstrated, by either interpretation? All female reporters are like Miss Penny? All aging spinsters have an ungovernable appetite that will out if properly baited? All social, intellectual, or religious institutions are preposterous? Certainly not. Yet something is achieved here that must be taken reluctantly as the meaning of the story. **"Nuns at Luncheon"** emits a derisive blast at both the possession and the loss of virginity; this, by whatever interpretation of material and details, is proved by the title. It is a curious achievement, a childish revolt from faith once celebrated with hymns and prayers and the building of cathedrals in honor of a virgin. It is an act of defiance of and disbelief in the classical-Christian idea and ideal of humanism; and to it the reader may finally react with a loud laugh or a corresponding disbelief of his own in the author's ability to be, in this instance, anything more durable than a showoff or an incompetent cartoonist.

The story seems to sparkle. The question is whether with the spark of life or the duller, iridescent glow of decomposition.

Characterization must show balance, and within balance characters must usually move—like spinning tops, like persons. Something more or something less than a desire to ridicule humanity is needed behind the writing of a short story. **"Nuns at Luncheon,"** readable as it is, provides an illustration in reverse, an anything-else-but, for personality-catchers.

P. H. Newby (review date 1957)

SOURCE: In a review of Aldous Huxley's *Collected Short Stories,* in *London Magazine* Vol. 4 1957, pp. 65-8.

[*In the following review of* Collected Short Stories, *Newby finds Huxley's short stories strained and anti-intellectual, contending that Huxley is not a true short story writer despite the brilliant analysis and observation revealed in some tales.*]

One thinks of Aldous Huxley as an intellectual writer. One associates him with the Twenties, short skirts and chromium plate; and one thinks of him, again, as an historian and pamphleteer, disenchanted with the twentieth century, doubtful whether the past was any better and apprehensive of the future; a pessimist, in short. The ***Collected Short Stories*** do not, however, bear this out. They provide no text for a dissertation on Mr. Huxley's ideas as they might have done had he been the intellectual, the sustained critic or satirist one, rather idly, supposed. Indeed, there is a strain in the stories which might be thought anti-intellectual. The other misconception is of Mr. Huxley in a bright, Twenty-ish world when he is, more obviously, an Edwardian. The period touch is provided not only by the historical details—a character calling at an inn for a glass of port, a comment on the absurdity of trying to find energy in the atom—but by the urbane literariness of the style.

> The owner of the shop was standing in the doorway, a little man, grizzle-bearded and with eyes very active round the corners of the spectacles that bridged his long, sharp nose.
>
> 'Trade is good?' I inquired.
>
> 'Better in my grandfather's day,' he told me, shaking his head sadly.
>
> 'We progressively grow more Philistine,' I suggested.
>
> 'It is our cheap Press. The ephemeral overwhelms the permanent, the classical.'
>
> 'This journalism,' I agreed, 'or call it this piddling quotidianism, is the curse of our age.'

One would have liked all these stories dated. That one, **"The Bookshop,"** is obviously very early. But how early? When was **"Limbo"** published? By looking up the reference books we can discover all this information for ourselves, but a volume of ***Collected Short Stories*** needs documenting if the author happens to be Aldous Huxley. He has roots in the pre-Joycean strata and one wants to follow them upwards into the clear light of Italy. The discovery of Italy seems to have been determinant in his career. There is an unmistakable cordiality in his references to all things Italian. The possession of Italian blood is a sufficient explanation for beauty. 'Ah, that explained it,' his narrator says of someone he had thought German and now discovers to be Italian. 'I had been wondering how Bavaria could have produced this thin-faced creature with the dark eyes, the finely modelled nose and chin, and the fleshy lips so royally and sensually curved.' The best story of them all, **"Little Mexican"**, is about Italy, and so is the worst. And after Italy? Well, one wants to know. One wants to know about Mr. Huxley himself. The stories and sketches in this volume are illustrations in his biography and reading them is an historical rather than a literary pleasure.

Really intelligent characters are almost as great an embarrassment to a writer as really good ones. If they are presented at all convincingly they are also, like Jane Austen's Emma, not really liked; and in less skilful hands than Jane Austen's these intelligent characters are bores into the bargain. They frustrate the possibility of an interesting story because they are so almighty knowing and self-contained and long-suffering. Mr. Huxley has a great many intelligent people in his stories and he solves the difficulty (rather unfairly, I think) by making them absurd. Think of poor Herbert Claxton, for example, with his beard, knickerbockers and Oriental religiosity! Or John Tarwin, who is an expert on tumours, values people according to their knowledge and ideas and accordingly is turned into a cuckold. In **"Happily Ever After"** (a very good story) there is, certainly, a highly intelligent man who is not made fun of, Mr. Jacobsen. If he is looked at closely, however, Jacobsen turns out to be a scholar, not an intellectual and, indeed, he is to be found criticizing a nascent intellectual for presuming to think. 'It was bad for him to think; he wasn't strong enough.' Presumably Jacobsen is strong enough and his strength is to be gauged from his enjoyment of bad sermons; they afford him 'the philosophic amusement of counting the undistributed middles and tabulating historically the exploded fallacies in the parson's discourse.'

Ideally, one suspects, Mr Huxley would have liked a sympathetic intellectual near the centre of a good many of these stories; but he is defeated by the conventional demands of fiction. In **"Young Archimedes,"** where the attempt is seemingly made, the result is an embarrassing dilettante who meditates for whole paragraphs at a time on music, mathematics, and the rise of civilization. Perhaps this is only another way of saying that Mr Huxley is, by temperament, more of an essayist than a short story writer; or that his short stories are most successful when he is being least himself.

When one thinks of their various limitations, these stories ought, after thirty-five years some of them, to seem faded. But time and again they are redeemed by brilliant analysis and observation. **"Little Mexican"** is a delightful account of an Italian family over a period of years; perhaps it succeeds partly because none of its characters is particularly clever. **"The Gioconda Smile"** succeeds very well in its slightly theatrical, Somerset Maugham-ish way. **"Happily Ever After"** is hard and economical and oddly Kiplingesque. Mr Huxley is, too, an irresistible travelling companion and guide. One would have liked him to say even more about the villas on the Brenta, about Tuscany and Florence, even about London on a Saturday afternoon. There is a great wealth of material in this volume to be explored, and if it is not more successful as a collection of stories then it is probably because Mr Huxley is not by nature one of the two types who really can write stories as distinct from novels; the gossip and the teller of folk tales.

V. S. Pritchett (review date 1957)

SOURCE: "Mellifluous Educator," in *The New Statesman* and *Nation,* Vol. LIII, No. 1371, June 22, 1957, p. 814.

[*In the following review of* Collected Short Stories, *Pritchett contends that the short story form was indadequate for Huxley's "great scoldings."*]

The attraction of the early Huxley was—as I recall—that of a young fashionable preacher: he was brilliant, worldly, flashing with culture. He was profane and yet soothing, destructive but—inevitable in the Huxleys—a mellifluous educator. The pleasure of his novels came not very much from his people (who were indeed thin transcripts from educated society between London and the Mediterranean) but from the non-stop talk by which he drove them into exhaustion and nagged them into nothingness. Talk was the cult of the Twenties and he was its exploiter. With him it was not table talk; he talked the clothes and souls off his people, he talked them out of life into limbo and, since he was astute enough to know what he was doing, ***Limbo*** was the title of his first book of short stories. They are the hors d'oeuvre of a prolonged cannibal feast.

It is thirty-four years since the publication of ***Limbo*** and now we have the ***Collected Stories*** of his lifetime. They belong mainly to a period now remote: the last age of rich old hedonists, businessmen (vulgar), intellectuals (incompetent in love), savage hostesses, grumpy artists. The old educated class is seen breaking with Victorian commitment as it loses its sons or its property, and ascending into that captious island of Laputa which floated in sunny detachment above Western Europe between the wars. As a writer Mr. Huxley has always been proficient in every genre he undertook, but it would not be just to judge him by these shorter pieces. He needed space for the great scoldings, for if you hate life it is best to hate it in a big way. He needed more room for the horrors, the savageries; more room for the kinder and learned comedies. In the very short stories—I exclude his *nouvelles*—his intellect turns out people like skinned rabbits. They are either not worth his trouble or one resents that his brain has reduced their worth. In general his stories are not about people and situations; they are talk about people in relation to ideas that appear to have been set up in order to snub them. It's when the people seem equal to the ideas that the good stories emerge; in the bizarre and tragic **"Sir Hercules,"** in the sinister **"Gioconda Smile,"** in a sharp light thing like **"Half Holiday,"** the geniality of **"Little Mexican,"** one of the rare life-loving tales, in **"The Rest Cure,"** a triumph over the talker, and in the pitying tale of **"Young Archimedes."** Here the driving voice abates and the preacher's chastisements are softened. A very good book.

In the other satires one is sooner or later aware of Mr. Huxley's weariness of his own brain. We cannot separate ideas and people; and there is a disagreeable disparity between the cleverness of the commentary and the banality of his realism. No one drops so surprisingly into cliché when describing the ordinary run of feeling. His lovers speak out of the pages of magazines. Mr. Huxley is self-conscious enough to be uncomfortable about the clichés. After all, are not all the valued human feelings clichés and are they the worse for that? The answer surely is that, to the artist, they are not clichés. It looks as though Mr. Huxley was frantic for novelty when he was tired. In the end it has been the accumulation of novel ideas, once so golden, that have now become heavy as lead in these comedies of displeasure.

One excellent story—**"Chawdron"**—stands out as a remarkable example of a writer's ability to use all his powers. It is at once a story of emotional nausea and a story of talking about it. The influence of Lawrence can be felt here. Lawrence was a master of magnetism in the short story. He forced his characters and their situations to a standstill, while he whipped them by repetitive phrases into greater intensity. Without passion or the poetic imagination, the method becomes merely frenzied and that is Mr. Huxley's case; but the genial, broken-down writer who has talked his talents away redeems him. "Hogwash" is his word for the emotions of the tycoon he is describing. Hogwash, hogwash, hogwash, he repeats throughout, in all varieties of scorn known to a clever man. The effect is funny, cruel, devastating, indignant and dismissive. And the fact that the talker himself, who knows all the beauties and delinquencies of talk, is the prisoner of an old housekeeper who comes in and out contemptuously, without saying a word, adds the final macabre commentary. I have mentioned this Jamesian masterpiece also because it is an example of a story which could hardly now be written. The subject is good enough; the financial chimpanzee who at fifty falls in love with a pious baby-bitch who calls him Nunky and is herself called Fairy by him—that is irresistible. By embedding this in a lot of clever theorising, by working in the usual art notes on St. Catherine of Siena, Carlo Dolci, Rowlandson, Podsnap, Othello and Jesus, the characters are properly snubbed and we are skilfully given an intellectual comedy—but not the *comédie humaine.* This is the kind of tale which is now dealt with directly. We write the dialogue, describe the moves; and being up against the characters themselves and not a sexual theory, we find the situation richer and more alarming. We would see Chawdron corrupting the educated writer. We would see Fairy hating him. We would laugh more or be more terrified. We would have lost educated explanation and its clever footpaths along the precipices of life; we would have lost talk and gained the explicit. But there it is: for better or worse, Mr. Huxley has always been the artist-educator, the preaching connoisseur who finds his stern text in our spiritual bric à brac, the illusions and novelties of belief.

Arthur F. Beringause (essay date 1964)

SOURCE: "Debate Between Body and Soul," in *The CEA Critic,* Vol. XXVI, No. 9, June, 1964, pp. 1, 4.

[*In the following essay, Beringause contends that an analysis of "The Gioconda Smile" reveals that Huxley is more than a "negative propagandist who satirizes negative nostrums."*]

Study of Aldous Huxley's well-known and consistently misinterpreted short story **"The Gioconda Smile"** reveals that his application of Freudian theory to art early made him into a much better craftsman than his critics have been willing to admit. This is not to imply that he accepted psychoanalysis and rejected religion.

Using sordid details of a vulgar love affair as a means for spiritual revelation, Huxley in **"The Gioconda Smile"** strategically blends wit, irony and pathos to achieve a deep intensity. Eager like every serious writer to chart his world for the reader, Huxley exercises cunning control of word and allusion until the pattern of life and death he weaves furnishes a revealing counterpoint of insight and knowledge, belief and feeling. Modern man, the reader learns from **"The Gioconda Smile,"** will endure and prevail only if he sets up religious standards of behavior in the never-ending war between body and soul.

Despite his ultra-modernity (**"The Gioconda Smile,"** appearing in the volume ***Mortal Coils*** in 1922, utilizes devices also being exploited by James Joyce and T. S. Eliot), Huxley is old-fashioned enough to express the meaning of life in religious terms.[1] He has continued, as **"The Gioconda Smile"** demonstrates, notwithstanding the twentieth-century tendency toward defaming literary figures renowned in England's past, to admire Milton, Wordsworth, Arnold. Moreover, he manipulates their work so as to integrate their perceptions with his own belief that absorption in self bars man from redemption and salvation.

"The Gioconda Smile" opens innocently enough with the polite announcement of a maid to a visitor that her mistress will be down in a moment. The mood soon changes. Mr. Hutton, the visitor, cannot bear to look at the homely face of the maid. He wanders around the house and inspects the bric-a-brac, deducing that the mistress is a prig and a snob. His annoyance gives way when, passing a mirror, he observes with admiration his own Shakespearean brow. This observation he associates with a line recalled from Matthew Arnold's sonnet on Shakespeare. "Others abide our question," Hutton recites. "Thou art free."

The line reminds Hutton of another part of the poem, "Footsteps in the sea . . ." Striving to go on with the quotation, Hutton can produce only "Majesty" and "Shakespeare, thou shouldst be living at this hour." Hutton suddenly recognizes that the line refers to Milton, not to Shakespeare, and he moves on to a new train of associations. Not so the reader, who perceives that Hutton has unconsciously become aware of something beyond the mere surface meaning of the words quoted.

The line from Arnold begins a sonnet:

> Others abide our question. Thou art free.
> We ask and ask—thou smilest and art still,
> Out-topping knowledge. For the loftiest hill,
> Who to the stars uncrowns his majesty,
> Planting his steadfast footsteps in the sea,
> Making the heaven of heavens his dwelling-place,
> Spares but the cloudy border of his base
> To the foiled searchings of mortality;
> And thou, who didst the stars and sunbeams know,
> Self-schooled, self-scanned, self-honored, self-secure,
> Didst tread on earth unguessed at.—Better so!
> All pains the immortal spirit must endure,
> All weakness which impairs, all griefs

which bow,
Find their sole speech in that victorious
brow.

Even though Hutton cannot consciously recall the entire poem, Arnold's sonnet on Shakespeare, with its association of majesty and soul and sea, triggers another memory in Hutton's unconscious. To the surface pops the reference to Wordsworth's sonnet on Milton. In Hutton's unconscious, however, lies all of Wordsworth's sonnet:

Milton! thou shouldst be living at this
hour:
England hath need of thee: she is a fen
Of stagnant waters: altar, sword, and pen,
Fireside, the heroic wealth of hall and
bower,
Have forfeited their ancient English dower
Of inward happiness. We are selfish men:
Oh! raise us up, return to us again;
And give us manners, virtue, freedom,
power.
Thy soul was like a star and dwelt apart:
Thou hadst a voice whose sound was like
the sea,
Pure as the naked heavens, majestic, free;
So didst thou travel on life's common way
In cheerful godliness; and yet thy heart
The lowliest duties on herself did lay.

But Hutton—self-absorbed, callous, conceited—cannot at this point consciously perceive the import of the poems. Shakespeare, Arnold maintains, sympathized with mankind's grief, pain, weakness. England, asserts Wordsworth, is a morass of evil in which church, army, family, tradition are rotten and men unhappy because they have forgotten how to "travel on life's common way / In cheerful godliness." Both poems apply to Hutton's story. Behind their associations is the theme that Huxley now proceeds to unravel.

Still strutting before the mirror, Hutton remembers that Milton was called the Lady of Christ's College. He, himself, Hutton preens, ought to be called the Christ of Ladies. Suddenly Hutton becomes aware that Janet Spence is in the room and smiling her **"Gioconda Smile,"** as he playfully terms her quizzical expression. He is unaware of what the reader finds out: true to the legend of La Gioconda, Janet Spence conceals behind her smile the torment of unrequited love.

Hutton, leaving Janet, shows off his physical prowess by running down a driveway as if he were still young. Once hidden from Janet's view, he meets Doris, his youthful mistress, in an automobile parked not far away. They spend the evening together. In a moment of remorse Doris thinks that perhaps Hell does exist, and she asks Hutton if they should give up their illicit love. Hutton attempts to reassure her by asserting that she should have sexual relations with him because according to Freud "repressions are the devil." Having calmed Doris, Hutton returns home, where—alone again—he suffers from "appalling boredom." Seeking out his invalid wife, Hutton finds his irritation exacerbated by her weakness. He remembers that as a young man "he had discovered that not only did he not feel sympathy for the poor, the weak, the diseased, and deformed; he actually hated them." That is the case now. He loathes his wife. And yet he is willing to spend some time reading to her in French because, proud of his accent, he enjoys showing off.

The following day Janet Spence visits the Huttons, who in the warmth of the noonday sun assure her that despite their troubles "It's good to be alive." Watching the two women, one an invalid and the other an old maid, Hutton is again annoyed. He sneaks off to visit Doris, but he finds her company unsatisfying. Despite the physical titillation Doris provides, she herself is vapid. Hutton can find no meaning in life, no lasting joy. He peers out the window of his speeding automobile as if the road ahead were a narrow alley of form and color scooped out of an infinite and indifferent universe. Gratification of physical desire has brought him neither Shakespeare's freedom nor Milton's happiness.

Morose, Hutton returns home and learns from the doctor, who "spoke of death as he would speak of a local cricket match," that Mrs. Hutton had expired. The doctor's attitude is typical of the other members of the subsequent funeral party, particularly of General Grego, who complains that Mrs. Hutton's death has prevented his attending the Harrow-Eton cricket match.

The reader thinks of Wordsworth's sonnet. Hutton, too. That night, without quite knowing why, Hutton sits up late and reads a biography of Milton that impels him to ponder long and seriously whether or not there is a quarrel between body and soul. He vows to lead an upright life. This vow, characteristically, he soon breaks by running off with Doris. Later, again characteristically, he casually marries her as if the relationship were of the slightest importance. Hutton feels gloriously irresponsible, happy and free. Even if life has no meaning, he can be as joyful as Milton, as unconfined as Shakespeare.

The newlyweds return home. Hutton visits Janet Spence, who—ignorant of his marriage—confesses her love for him. Vastly annoyed, Hutton disengages himself and humiliates Janet. He persuades his bride to leave with him at once for Italy. But his equilibrium has been disturbed. Once more the dreadful need to show off is upon him. Despite his recent marriage, he callously seduces the Italian maid-servant.

Janet Spence, angered by Hutton's mistreatment, and driven to fury by news of his marriage, tells everyone that he had murdered his first wife. All believe her—even Doris, whom the rumor soon reaches. Recalled to England, Hutton is placed on trial. Learning of Doris' lack of faith in him, Hutton quarrels with her, screaming that he does not love her. Then he runs away.

Deep-rooted feelings take hold of Hutton, and he consciously recalls his religious upbringing. He finds that he can think of his plight only in spiritual terms. He is overwhelmed by the idea that divine justice is being done him for his cruelty and wantonness. Events, as Milton put it, have justified the ways of God to men. "God exists after all," thinks Hutton. He prays. "His mind seemed to soften and dissolve; a great calm descended upon his spirit." This time Shakespeare's freedom and Milton's cheerfulness stay with him. He is drained of emotion.

Returning to ask forgiveness of Doris, Hutton learns that she has attempted suicide. Able at last because of his spiritual regeneration to help a weaker person, he comforts her. Ironically, however, he is a new man too late: the jury brings in a verdict of wilful murder. After the execution, Janet Spence confesses to the doctor that she had poisoned the first Mrs. Hutton. The doctor gives her a sleeping draught, and the story ends.

But the end is not here for the reader, who now understands the full significance of the title of the volume in which **"The Gioconda Smile"** appears: ***Mortal Coils.*** With this phrase from *Hamlet* Huxley warns that fear of punishment in an after-life ought to make man behave properly on earth: "what dreams may come, / When we have shuffled off this mortal coil, / Must give us pause." Huxley would have the reader turn to religion so that, in Wordsworth's words, we "travel on life's common way / In cheerful godliness." Then, and only then, will England and the modern world no longer be a fen of stagnant waters wherein church, army, family, and tradition have been perverted.

Analysis of **"The Gioconda Smile"**does more than merely present one reading of a skillfully written but misunderstood story. Explication of this part of Aldous Huxley's work indicates that he is more than what he has so often been taken for, a negative propagandist who satirizes nugatory nostrums. He, too, as Joyce would have it, is a "priest of the eternal imagination." Huxley knows how to weave a pattern of word and allusion that, making use of the techniques of poetry, permits him to penetrate the unconscious mind. He, too, labors in the workshop of the human heart. Aldous Huxley is a craftsman worthy of his craft.

Note

1. Reworked into a play, "The Gioconda Smile" uses the same devices as the short story from which it is drawn—only not so subtly, because Huxley must spell out for an audience what he can assume the reader of a short story will have time to figure out for himself. See *The Gioconda Smile* (New York, 1948), previously published as *Mortal Coils—A Play* (New York, 1948).

Charles M. Holmes (essay date 1970)

SOURCE: "Struggles with Style and Form: From the Early Verse to 'Crome Yellow,'" in *Aldous Huxley and the Way to Reality,* Indiana University Press, 1970, pp. 1-38.

[In the following excerpt from his full-length study of Huxley's works, Holmes discusses the early story "Eupompus Gave Splendour to Art by Numbers" and notes its autobiographical elements.]

In Aldous Huxley's **"Eupompus Gave Splendour to Art by Numbers,"**[1] an intelligent, stable, normal man tells the story of his odd but brilliant friend named Emberlin. Emberlin, we learn, has been studying Eupompus, the fifth century B.C. painter mentioned by Ben Jonson, who actually did base his splendid canvases on numbers. One pictured a three-eyed, three-armed, three-naveled human being accompanied by thirty-three thousand "distinctly limned" black swans; others grouped people so as to imitate exactly the various constellations. Eupompus' final painting was designed to symbolize Pure Number, in the form of a "design of planes radiating out from a single point of light." Emberlin's interest in these works, however, has passed well beyond mere curiosity. He himself now counts whenever he has the chance—steps, stairs, and the number of tiles in a Holborn public lavatory. Eupompus killed himself before he finished his final masterpiece; Emberlin, we are told triumphantly, will also soon be mad.

There is no better introduction to the work of Aldous Huxley than **"Eupompus,"** first published in an undergraduate review. It has the bizarre appeal of so much of the early work, the esoteric fecundity whereby Huxley could expand an obscure fragment of knowledge into a distinctive, sophisticated tragi-comedy of the mind. Its medium is the lucid urbanity of the early novels, which in a decade were to bring Huxley international fame. But most important and most surprising, like nearly everything he wrote, this weird tale is autobiographical. Under the zany surface of the story of Eupompus and Emberlin we can discern a portrait—or rather two portraits—of Aldous Huxley.

Huxley himself had the qualities his story attributes to Emberlin. He was "immensely erudite"; Arnold Bennett called his knowledge "inconceivable, incredible, and fantastic."[2] His books and essays were always strikingly, sometimes showily allusive, initially to figures (well known or unknown) in French literature, painting and Western philosophy, and ultimately to mysticism, ecology, and the Buddhist Tantra. Like Emberlin he was often "a mine of irrelevant information." Osbsert Sitwell, speaking of Huxley's hospital visits, recalls the strange comments on Octopoi reading Ovid and making love,[3] doubtless gleaned from the *Britannica* Huxley rummaged in on his travels. For years, the record shows, Huxley also followed "Emberlin's way" of putting into practice "the ideas that he finds in books." He was (by his own admission) the Philip Quarles of *Point Counter Point,* whose "choice of moulds" depended largely on the author he happened to be reading: the "mould" for several years was D. H. Lawrence, later replaced by Meister Eckhart and Gerald Heard, before Huxley developed his own remarkable final synthesis. Finally, Huxley regularly succumbed to what he later called the "Higher Life," in **"Eupompus"** the "glassily perfect universe of ideas." The texture of the novels themselves suggests the degree of this surrender—the shimmering intellectual surface of *Crome Yellow* along with the tedious discourse in *After Many a Summer Dies the Swan.* Though Huxley worried publicly about this leaning in *Point Counter Point* and *Eyeless in Gaza,* he half consciously defended it in *The Perennial Philosophy* and illustrated it in composing his final statement, *Island.* Even Emberlin's love of Pure Number reappears, or at least Eupompus' attempt to capture it in paint. The radiating planes of Eupompus' final painting prefigure some of Huxley's later symbols: the twin cones that triumphantly end the novel *Eyeless in Gaza,* the pattern of telegraph poles and wheel tracks Sebastian sees in *Time Must Have a Stop.*

But Huxley also appears in Emberlin's friend, the narrator of the tale, who is not a caricature of the reality to be, but a kind of idealized, wished-for-self. He is a self-critical opposite, not odd like Emberlin but more conventional. He can recognize the danger of Emberlin's mental gyrations, see things in proportion, live in closer relationship to other human beings. He stands at the end of the tale as a champion of a sane humanity. He is the more spontaneous and balanced intellectual Huxley apparently often wished to be, perhaps the man his brother Julian had in mind as "the greatest humanist of our perplexed era."[4] His analog appears only rarely in Huxley's fiction, where shades of Emberlin are the ones we most frequently see; he sounds more like Huxley's hostile critics than like Huxley himself. Yet he too is both a Huxley creation and a Huxley self-projection. **"Eupompus Gave Splendour to Art by Numbers"** is not merely an amusing, exaggerated, and critical self-portrait, but one self-portrait observing and triumphing over another.

Such autobiographical dialectic is the most persistent pattern in Huxley's work, from the poetry of the Oxford youth to the *Island* of the courageous, distinguished, dying man. His large public, his friends and his opponents, usually envisioned a writer addressing the world in a changing series of tones and modes—in satirical fiction or conventional argument, in bitterness or exhortation, in the frustration or excitement of the quest which completed his life. But simultaneously, more than anyone seems to have suspected, Huxley projected, addressed, and debated with himself. The least public of men, until the last years of his career, he was in a curious but intriguing way among the most public of modern writers. He left no journals so frank as Gide's, few poems so obviously personal as those of Yeats. Instead Huxley's books are a kind of Rosetta stone, a complex but decipherable index to a lonely, anguished, but successful mental journey. Much of his work shows him plagued by inner conflict, struggling to explore his identity. In all the genres at which he tried his hand, a divided Huxley is likely to be present, by implication if not as a kind of Emberlin. In the early years the conflict is internal, and the dialectic involves attitudes and values Huxley seems to be testing for himself.[5] But eventually Huxley's dilemma reverberates with meanings and parallels of significance for other men. For a while his conflict provided material for a particular kind of brilliant art, for the fiction which made him the leading ironist of his age. As his struggle became a search for the answer to ultimate questions, he scorned brilliance, ignored the "rules" of form, irritated the critics and lost his popular appeal. But he left behind the record of a spiritual and intellectual odyssey which ended with a total view, a vision of reality both transcendental and pragmatic.

The conflict Huxley, at twenty-two, projected in **"Eupompus"** was doubtless intensified by certain events of adolescence. . . .

"Eupompus Gave Splendour to Art by Numbers," an exhibit of two contrasting Huxley selves, is also almost a diagram of the first years of Huxley's career: Emberlin is a poet; so, at first, was Huxley—to one critic "among the most promising" of the younger poets of the time.[6] Emberlin has composed in various poetic styles; shifts in style are the distinguishing attribute of Huxley's verse. When the narrator prefers Emberlin's earlier "young ecstatic fashion" he has defined a style of Huxley's first collection, *The Burning Wheel*; when Emberlin wants to destroy the volume he has produced, he suggests the Huxley who rejected (temporarily) his own romantic manner. The narrator regrets forgetting the poems of Emberlin in French, so well suited is the language to Emberlin's "peculiar" muse; four of Huxley's poems appear in French in *Jonah.* And Emberlin's "curious" sonnet to the figure of a princess is, verbatim, the *Jonah* "Minoan Porcelain," by Huxley. . . .

During these early years the subjective, self-examining force was too strong for Huxley to find a proper outlet in drama. Fiction, he soon learned, was clearly the ideal mode. He could separate and embody a number of "selves" in fiction, combine and distribute them in any number of ways. But he could also, to a degree impossible in a play, invent a narrator to project himself, to shape his reader's attitude, to give himself the freedom to say what he wished to say. Having already explored these advantages in **"Eupompus,"** he rapidly produced several collections of stories and tested the even more flexible form of the novel.

Of the five new stories in the first collection, ***Limbo,*** the most revealing is probably **"The Farcical History of Richard Greenow."** Whereas in **"Happy Families"** Aston J. Tyrrell is quartered, Richard Greenow is severed only in two. In the daytime Greenow attends first Aesop (probably Eton) College, then eventually Oxford; dislikes the masses but thinks highly of Fulke-Greville; and behaves as a serious, rational person of taste, intellect, and "powers of malicious irony." But when he has gone to bed and thinks he is asleep, he becomes his other personality, "Pearl Bellairs"—an ultra-romantic sentimentalist who spends the night writing highly marketable trash. The split is often amusing, yet also meaningful, since the activities of both can be traced to those of Huxley himself. But Huxley by the way he narrates the tale obscures the split: sometimes he seems to sympathize with Greenow, sometimes he treats Greenow as a convenient critical device. He uses Greenow's experience to take a crack at public schools; he shows Greenow personifying the "Life Theoretic" clash of thought and action; and in a scene where Greenow is "analyzed by a psychotherapist friend," he communicates his lifelong dislike of Sigmund Freud—unaware while he vents such fixations that the form of his tale is being destroyed. The "freedom" of fiction, we recall, Huxley found "formidable" as well as "lovely." He still was faced with the dilemma of the poems—the struggle between sincerity of self-expression on the one hand, and aesthetic control, or "style" on the other. His handling of point of view determined the result. In defining the narrator and the narrator's attitude toward others, Huxley could produce (as in **"Richard Greenow"**) expressive, loosely structured failures or disciplined, less-than-sincere works of art.

The best stories in ***Limbo*** employ as narrators learned, urbane observers of life, much like the narrator-friend of Emberlin—idealized men rather than omniscient, mildly ironical projections. In **"Cynthia,"** for example, one of the most intriguing stories, the narrator tells us a tale of his friend Lykeham. He captures the setting, this time at Oxford's "Swellfoot" College, by noting contrasting sounds, casually describing them with the technical jargon of music. The college bell was "shouting a deep E flat, with a spread of under-and-over-tones," while Lykeham's guitar "gibbered shrilly and hysterically in D-natural." The narrator learns that Lykeham has just held hands with a "frozenly virginal" goddess, a huntress Cynthia or Diana who has convinced him that he too is divine. Learnedly but unsuccessfully, the two men puzzle over the Olympian meaning of Lykeham's name. Two weeks later, appropriately during a moonlit walk, Lykeham spots his goddess on a distant hill. The narrator joins in the wild race to arrest her, turns away from the couple's "unequivocal" embraces, and checks his mythology again in Lemprière. By Lykeham's return he has the puzzle solved, and laughingly whispers "Goatfoot" (or satyr) in his ear.

Huxley projects himself in **"Cynthia"** as interested but uninvolved, as a narrator who shows no sign of inner conflict or discontent. But though he is therefore an abstracted, false version of Huxley the man, he is nevertheless an appealing person, a man of both morality and taste. He is faced, of course, with a version of the problem of sex and lust: Lykeham is a lecher, Cynthia a pick-up. But he does not treat Lykeham as Huxley later treated Gerry Watchett, the vicious, heartless womanhunter of *Eyeless in Gaza.* Sparing us the details of Lykeham's fornication, he regards the act instead with comic irony: "it is not for a mere mortal," he tells us, "to look on at the embracements of the gods," And though he borrows here Lykeham's mythological disguise, he will not allow Lykeham's trite lyricism to stand. He interrupts Lykeham's talk of "swooning away" and the meeting of eyes, of "rapturous" happiness while holding hands in the dark, with a comment on the "awful novelist's expression," and the image from the ironic poem "Frascati's" of the lovers sweating "quietly . . . palm to palm." From the beginning he wins our sympathy by some disarming remarks on himself, and a knowing reference to "our monstrous century." His early comments on music and, later, on letters, mark him as acute, sensitive, and civilized. The problem of sex and the love of erudition are brilliantly modulated through his sensibility into fully successful comic art. . . .

The vacillations, the struggles with point of view in *Antic Hay* are a clear, though tacit sign of the sincerity-talent dilemma. Huxley's concern for sincerity is put somewhat more directly by Lypiatt, the spokesman-theorist of tragedy and farce. The raving painter, so frequently given to ridiculous dramatic posing, has one important moment of apparently complete candidness. He admits that he may have lied to himself, that he may be a charlatan, merely playing a role, insincere in boasting to others and deceiving himself. Though Lypiatt's life, his verses, his paintings are not Huxley's, his concern for the honesty of his attitude is. Lypiatt can accurately and sincerely understand Myra, though his painting of her is simply bluster and not art. Huxley, on the other hand, has the talent for what is called art, but may feel insincere or fraudulent in producing it. The short stories of ***Mortal Coils*** (1922), a year earlier than *Antic Hay,* highlight the dilemma in another way already familiar from the early poems. The more ironic (and self-suppressive) the story, the more brilliant; the more effectively Huxley wrote, the more popular he became—and the more his concern for sincerity appears to have increased.

Huxley's best-known story, **"The Gioconda Smile,"** depends upon clever, sometimes dazzling ironies. The idea for the story, Huxley tells us, came from a poisoning case of the early 1920's, when a solicitor's wife was "carried off, very suddenly, after eating stewed gooseberries and drinking a glass of wine." The neighbors gossiped, an autopsy revealed the presence of arsenic, but the suspected husband was finally acquitted. Besides inventing new circumstances so that the mystery could be solved, Huxley has transformed the ironic style of the most polished early poems into a fully disciplined, total ironic view. Janet Spence, the murderess, as ironically grotesque as the elephants and amphisbaenae, has a snoutish mouth like a penholder through which she talks like a cannon: "Bang! the charge in her soul was ignited, the words whizzed forth at the narrow barrel of her mouth." Mrs. Hutton thinks of herself as really "fond of French," yet she speaks "of the language of Racine as though it were a dish of green peas." Mr. Hutton, the major character, is sometimes another target, sometimes an ironist himself. He strokes his moustache in frank self-admiration but an instant later sees himself as a fool; he resolves one evening to work harder on his book, then succumbs in the morning to his recurrent sensual itch; he makes a graceful "Cinquecento" gesture to Janet, later runs with the "magnificent canter" of a horse. Hutton is almost as much of an enigma as Gumbril, but contributes to the irony by recognizing this fact himself. Almost all the characters have one justifiable identity to themselves, another ironically ridiculous one to us. Dr. Libbard, the only exception, understands the ironic way things work out. Though he knows of Janet's guilt, he is too fatigued by life's ironies to care. In the poems Huxley had shown a romantic tendency, mocked mildly in *Crome Yellow,* grown more complex in *Antic Hay.* In **"The Gioconda Smile"** the romantic is parodied, through Janet and through the cuddly, imperceptive Doris—whose name, Hutton recalls while kissing her, is "the scientific appellation of the sea-mouse." With the help of this protagonist so unlike yet like himself, Huxley maintained a focus, as he could not in *Antic Hay,* and established an unwaveringly consistent ironic view.

It is in **"Nuns at Luncheon"** that the struggle with irony, the cost of it, begin to be evident. The narrative line of this story is painful as well as bizarre: a young, virginal, recently converted nun, who has proved a wonder at converting others, is put in charge of a convalescent criminal. Unaware that he is an expert seducer and convinced she is acting on behalf of his salvation, she is led to steal clothes from her superior's wardrobe, is whisked by him away from the hospital, crudely seduced in a farmer's hut, then abandoned to return to a living death among the sisters—but not before he has robbed her of all of her teeth! So cruel are these ironies that Huxley, instead of narrating the story himself, turns it over to another writer, the less sensitive Miss Penny, an example of grotesque irony herself. Always wearing "massive and improbable jewellery," she has a pair of lengthy earrings which swing and rattle like "corpses hanging in chains," and she has the habit of laughing like a horse. Too obtuse to see her masculinity and too coarse to see any pathos in her tale, she provides an ironic framework for the irony of the virgin's life—the irony of an insensitive person describing pain.

The inhumanity of the story apparently left Huxley with misgivings. In **"The Tillotson Banquet"** he exposes the dangers of esoteric learning, one of the main supports for his ironic art. In **"Green Tunnels"** irony and its esoteric source are challenged again by the sentiments and fancies of a young, romantic girl sympathetically contrasted with her lifeless elders. Nevertheless, the greatest challenge to the irony of **"Nuns at Luncheon"** is, ironically, in **"Nuns at Luncheon"** itself. As Miss Penny gleefully reports the shocking facts, she raises questions about the very story in which she appears—and thereby very briefly exposes Aldous Huxley. She approves his vision of the nun before her conversion, "apocalyptically" perceiving that everything is "sex, sex, sex" and thus "disgusting." When she suggests that he "write pages about Destiny and its ironic quacking" because it is "impressive" and "there's money in every line," his reply is a terse "You may be sure I shall." And when she finally asks him if he seriously believes in literature, he finds the question "luckily . . . quite meaningless." When she reaches the point of the nun's actual seduction, with "the strangled crying, the movements . . . the emotions pulsing about," she sees it as "ready-made literature," good for many pages. With the absence of comment, the question of sincerity is closed, hidden under the mask almost as soon as it is posed. Nevertheless, while displaying his most sophisticated technique, Huxley has questioned the very value of literary art. Such misgivings, displayed while he plays the role of artist, help determine the very quality of most of his later novels and largely account for his fallen stature in the world of letters today.[7]

After the brutal irony of **"Nuns at Luncheon,"** it is a startling experience to read **"Young Archimedes."** Unlike the other stories in ***Little Mexican*** (London: Chatto & Windus, 1924), all of which are detached if not downright inhumane, this narrative of a peasant boy of potential genius is written with a deep, frank sensitivity. Not only are ironies less piercing, less rigorously imposed—again and again potential ironies are ignored. Instead, the occasional moments of genuine feeling shown by Gumbril have become the vital, integrating force. When Huxley dwells lovingly on the black cypresses and darkly rising Apennines, on the Italian landscape with its "humanness and domestication," he sets the tone for his attitude toward Guido. The obvious, spontaneous sincerity turns the story into the most moving piece that Huxley ever wrote.

The young Guido delights the narrator by sharing his—and Huxley's—musical taste. He is enraptured by the slow movement of Bach's D-Minor Concerto and soon prefers Mozart to Wagner, Debussy and Strauss; he likes "music," as he puts it, better than the human voice. But he shows where his prodigious talent really lies by suddenly proving the Pythagorean theorem, in an impromptu sketch drawn with the burnt end of a stick. By helping the boy to devour mathematics the narrator can watch Guido becoming an ideal human being. The watcher's emotions are stirred as the wonder of genius is revealed, his imagination filled with humility. The run of us, he realizes, could never have developed even our most familiar ideas alone, yet Archimedes had no successor for a thousand years or more, and there has been but one Michelangelo, one Buddha, one Jesus, and one Bach. Moved by the notion that men of genius are perhaps "the only true men," the narrator at one point sees himself as a teachable dog, a metaphor applied scornfully only to others in *Antic Hay.* As Guido shows him his crude but homemade dodecahedron, he feels he should have "gone down on all fours, wagged the spiritual outgrowth of his os coccyx, and barked his astonished admiration."

This appealing combination of the urbane and learned with the humble, absent in all the other early Huxley fiction, is developed effectively as the story moves to its close. When he walks to the grave of the young genius with the father, the narrator is wrapt in learned but irrelevant speculations; poised and impressive in his knowledge of art, he barely hints at his interest in "recognizably human things." When they reach the grave, after the explanation of Guido's suicidal fall, feeling colors the narrator's deep reflective mood. Tears come to his eyes as he thinks of the delighted expression which "illumined . . . [Guido's] face when he learned of some new idea that pleased him." His poise, though he retains it, does not serve to check his emotion; unlike the onlooker who narrates **"Nuns at Luncheon,"** this Huxley projection clearly has a heart that can be moved. Though the father is furious at the Signora responsible for Guido's death, the narrator persuades him to "the harder path of grief." The final catharsis, however, is in his own humble mind and heart. The tragic beauty of Guido's life recalls the lyric beginning of the story, and it merges for the narrator into the wonders of Florence itself. In him we still find the sophisticated, cultured Huxley, but the split seems healed, the mask removed, and we seem to have another brief glimpse of Huxley's soul.

During an interview conducted later in the actual villa of the story, Huxley impressed his interrogator with his "great humanity." Told that his books did not really seem to express this quality, Huxley replied that they "express that part of my mind which is the product of a, perhaps, excessively intellectual upbringing. One generally finds that people who have tried to analyze the world in exclusively intellectual terms, end by discovering what everybody knows, almost by instinct, from the beginning."[8] Feeling, in other words, is inhibited by intellect; the active mind can very easily stifle the heart. In **"Young Archimedes"** the two are harmonized only because Guido is unique in his appeal. As a mathematical genius, Guido's potential is in the purest, least personal human endeavor. As a child he has had no chance to disillusion others—to become, for example, a brilliant but infantile adult like Maartens, the physicist, of *The Genius and the Goddess.* Guido is spared Huxley's irony, his satirizing intellect, his theory of tragedy and farce, not because he is a genius but because he has not lived to show his genius fulfilled He evokes feeling as no other Huxley character can because he personifies an uncontaminated vision, a worthy, unsullied cultural ideal. He is thus in a sense another—flawless—self-projection. We never look upon his like again.

Notes

1. *The Palatine Review,* IV (October, 1916), 5-13. Reprinted in *Limbo* (London: Chatto & Windus, 1920) and *Collected Short Stories* (London: Chatto & Windus, 1957).
2. *The Journal of Arnold Bennett* (New York: The Viking Press, 1933), p. 932. The three adjectives were Huxley's own favorites, Bennett writes on February 14, 1927, in one of several entries referring to Huxley and his wife.
3. *Laughter in the Next Room* (Boston: Little, Brown and Company, 1948), p. 45. Sir Osbert sketches a similar portrait in the *Memorial Volume,* p. 33.
4. *Memorial Volume,* p. 25.
5. Some years later Huxley said to an interviewer: "My chief motive in writing has been the desire to express a point of view. Or, rather, the desire to clarify a point of view to myself. I do not write for my readers; in fact I don't like thinking about my readers. . . . I am chiefly interested in making clear a certain outlook on life." Quoted in *The Huxleys,* pp. 215-216.
6. Harold Monro, *Some Contemporary Poets* (London: Leonard Parsons, 1920), p. 124.
7. See Charles M. Holmes, "Aldous Huxley's Struggle with Art," *Western Humanities Review,* XV (Spring, 1961), 149-156.
8. Y. Maraini, "A Talk with Aldous Huxley," *The Bermondsey Book,* III (June, 1926), 76-77.

Donald J. Watt (essay date 1970)

SOURCE: "The Absurdity of the Hedonist in Huxley's 'The Gioconda Smile,'" in *Studies in Short Fiction,* Vol. VII, No. 2, Spring, 1970, pp. 328-30.

[*In the following essay, Watt argues that in his story "The Gioconda Smile," Huxley crystallizes a significant theme that appears in his work as he seeks value and meaning in life—the absurdity of the hedonist.*]

"The Gioconda Smile," perhaps Aldous Huxley's best-known short story, presents in cameo form one of the leading themes of his major fiction.[1] The utter insufficiency of the hedonist's way of life is a recurring idea in Huxley's fiction, an idea that conveys his seminal theme of the essential absurdity of a life without genuine purpose. Henry Hutton's inner conflict in the story reflects the need of the Huxley hero somehow to temper his irresponsible frivolity and to acquire some substantive emotional, moral, or religious values. Like so many of Huxley's vitiated hedonists-in-spite-of-themselves—Gumbril Jr. in *Antic Hay,* Cardan in *Those Barren Leaves,* Beavis in *Eyeless in Gaza,* Farnaby in *Island*—Hutton refuses to take "yes" for an answer, refuses to discover some antidote for his teleological malaise. Hutton is aware of the fundamental preposterousness of his mode of existence, struggles unsuccessfully to adopt a more responsible way of living, and becomes, in the end, a victim of his own commitment to absurdity.

Hutton is, from the outset, vain, priggish, slightly effete. He fondly imagines himself as "the Christ of Ladies," a gift to the other sex and yet supremely superior to it. He invites Janet Spence to lunch with him and his wife, Emily, quipping cynically: "'You'll do us both good. In married life three is often better company than two.'"[2] On another occasion, as he is chauffeured home, he enjoys the youthful unsophistication of his mistress, Doris, in the back seat of his car. But while he is kissing her he allows his mind to wander to sea-cucumbers and aquariums. A typically jaded Huxley male, he responds to an emotional situation with irrelevance and aloofness, calculatedly shunning real passion. For Hutton recognizes clearly the ingrained imbecility of his frolicking hedonism. He reviews the history of his stale love affairs prior to Doris and concludes that it is all "imbecile wantonness" (p. 33). He wonders if he can even consider himself properly a hedonist because there is no reasoned choice in his pursuit of pleasure. In fact, the irrationality of his capitulation to eroticism, its frustrating nullity, is what bothers him most. His life, he sees, is void of any fruitful, sustaining values. And yet he persists in his folly, perhaps illustrating in action Huxley's favorite passage in Ovid: video meliora proboque; deteriora sequor—"I see the better and I approve; but I pursue the worse." (*Metamorphoses,* VII, 19.)

The death of his wife arrests Hutton momentarily and prompts him to reconsider his situation. For a short time he actually succeeds in living more reasonably, more industriously. He spends his mornings supervising agricultural concerns on his land, while he devotes his afternoons and evenings to serious study for a book, *The Effect of Diseases on Civilization.* But, however laudable his intentions, he returns to Doris within a fortnight: "Unreason had triumphed; at the first itch of desire he had given way." (p. 35)

Hutton senses that life is nothing more than a vast joke. Unable to check his irrational behavior, he commits himself entirely to an absurd existence. He decides to marry Doris, convinced that the match would be "the best joke he had ever made in his life" (p. 37). But the joke backfires when Hutton visits Janet Spence. He is confident and gallant with her, jovially excited at the prospect of playing with her emotions: "He had discovered in irresponsibility the secret of gaiety" (p. 40). His bubbling humor, however, dissipates rapidly when Janet makes an ardent confession of her love for him. Thoroughly discomfited, Hutton slips from her worshipful embrace and retreats from the house. He is dismayed to learn that his frivolity has evaporated in a crisis. Rather than respond in dupery to Janet's passion and take advantage of her, Hutton is immobilized by her gravity. He now discovers that the role of the irresponsible hedonist is not simply dissatisfactory; it is embarrassingly unreliable. Yet his only recourse at this point is to continue to indulge, if halfheartedly, in his hedonistic pursuits.

Absurdity, nonetheless, has a final, more devastating joke to play on Hutton. While he and Doris lounge at a villa in Florence, word arrives that Janet has charged Hutton with murdering Emily in order to marry Doris. At first Hutton is merely amused, knowing that he has married Doris on a whim, as a jest. But damning evidence accumulates until he begins to suspect that he is himself the victim of some indefinable, irresponsible joke. He sees, dimly, that absurdity is exacting its only logical retribution on him: "Confusedly he felt that some extraordinary kind of justice was being done. In the past he had been wanton and imbecile and irresponsible. Now Fate was playing as wantonly, as irresponsibly, with him" (p. 58). Shaken and bewildered, Hutton tries to pray as he used to forty years ago. As he recalls from childhood the nightly prayer blessing his parents and relatives, he is struck by the knowledge that all but one are now dead. The recollection seems to have a grim effect on Hutton, for death, he perceives, is his unalterable destiny. That afternoon the coroner's jury indicts him and, some time after his execution, we discover that it was Janet who poisoned Emily.

Hutton appears, at the last, to be only apparently a man. As death approaches, he grows aware of the total emptiness of his life. Like Edward Darley in Huxley's first chapter of a new, unfinished novel, Hutton comprehends that he is "someone who was going to die."[3] Exposed to the uncompromising truth, with all pretence removed, he sees the inevitable fact of death as the purest form of absurdity. He has toyed with other people's lives for his own amusement. He has driven Janet to murder and Doris to attempted suicide by his thoughtlessness. Now he is caught up by his own folly. Evading responsibility and self-control through a lifetime, Hutton has no viable rationale with which he can counter irresponsibility. Shunning emotional, moral, and religious values habitually, he has nothing with which to fill in the void created by the sudden disappearance of his pursuit of sensuous pleasures. That gay absurdity that in its license had seemed so attractive to him now turns inscrutably upon him. At the end, his diminution is complete; he dies a victim of his own abandonment of responsibility.

Huxley was from the start convinced that existence is strange, multifarious, paradoxical. He admired William Blake's lines, "Do what you will, this world's a fiction / And is made up of contradiction." The force of his writing, though, is emphatically toward some definition of meaning in the context of modernity. As C. J. Rolo proposes, "All his work is a quest for values in the face of scepticism battening at the vitals of belief. . . ."[4] Novels such as *Crome Yellow, Antic Hay*and *Point Counter Point* depict at length the unavoidable failure of hedonism as a way of life, and the man who subscribes to it as his way of life is doomed to a teleological limbo. In this sense, then, in **"The Gioconda Smile"** Huxley crystallizes a significant theme in his work—the absurdity of the hedonist.

Notes

1. The story first appeared in the *English Review,* XXXIII (August, 1921), and was the lead item in *Mortal Coils* (1922), Huxley's second volume of short stories. It is reprinted in several collections, *e.g.,* R. B. Heilman's *Modern Short Stories* and the Cerf-Moriarty *Anthology of Famous British Stories.* Huxley created a much enlarged stage version of the story in 1948, and in the same year he collaborated with Universal-International's Zoltan Korda for a motion picture version called *A Woman's Vengeance,* with Charles Boyer in the leading role.
2. *Mortal Coils,* Collected Works (London, 1958), p. 6. Subsequent references in text to "The Gioconda Smile" are from this edition.
3. See Laura Huxley, *This Timeless Moment: A Personal View of Aldous Huxley* (New York, 1968), p. 238.

4. *The World of Aldous Huxley* (New York, 1947), p. xii.

Maria Schubert (essay date 1984)

SOURCE: "The Use of Irony in Aldous Huxley's Short Fiction," in *On Poets and Poetry,* edited by Dr. James Hogg, Institut für Anglistik und Amerikanistik, 1984 pp. 181-214.

[*In the following essay, Schubert maintains Huxley's short fiction is mainly concerned with humans' inescapable predestinatio, and that the predominant stylistic device he uses to express this is irony.*]

Huxley began his literary career in 1916 with a volume of poems called *The Burning Wheel.* Four years later ***Limbo,*** his first volume of short stories was published, followed by his first novel *Crome Yellow* in 1921. During the period from 1920 to 1930 Huxley tried all literary genres: he wrote poems, short stories, novels, essays, dramas and travel books. The predominant genre in the 1920s, however, was short fiction, and ***Limbo*** was followed by four more volumes of short stories, ***Mortal Coils*** (1922), ***Little Mexican*** (1924), ***Two or Three Graces*** (1926) and ***Brief Candles*** (1930). In these stories Huxley is mainly concerned with the 'human condition', with fate and predestination which man cannot escape, however hard he tries. Recurrent is also his use of irony, a stylistic device Huxley employs most successfully and most brilliantly in his short stories and early novels.

> The single unifying feature in Huxley's work is irony. The moral dilemma is sustained in novel after novel by the irony inherent in the dilemma itself: man as a product of his genes and glands; man as a creature of sensitivity and suffering.[1]

Whether Huxley exploits the ironical relationship between the artist and his work in **"The Tillotson Banquet"** (***Mortal Coils***) or whether he uses lyrical irony as in **"Green Tunnels"** or grim and cruel irony as in **"Nuns at Luncheon"** in the same volume, the device may be traced in the five volumes of short stories and all "major novels, with the exception of Island".[2] "Huxley's art depends above all on a dialectic of ideas", Peter Bowering maintains, "a dialectic engendered by the major ironies inherent in the human condition".[3]

The discrepancy between Huxley the human being and Huxley the author of so many satirical pieces seems to be of great interest in this respect. Laura Huxley's book This Timeless Moment and the contributions of Huxley's relatives, friends and acquaintances to the Memorial Volume (*Aldous Huxley, 1894-1963. A Memorial Volume*) edited by his brother Julian two years after Aldous' death convey a very personal view of Huxley. Their intention is not so much to praise his achievements as a writer, but to praise Huxley the human being, his admirable personality and his noble character. John Atkins writes in his study of Aldous Huxley that nearly all of the 27 contributors "seemed at pains to stress that the popular image of Huxley as an immensely intellectual but essentially cold man was entirely false; that the quality that impressed itself most deeply on his friends was his human warmth, his capacity for pity and his abiding charity".[4]

Humphry Osmond was most impressed by the "kindness and tolerance of this man, whose writings led me to suppose that he would be disillusioned, cynical and even savage".[5] This is exactly what is understood by the discrepancy between the attitude of the writer and the character of the person Aldous Huxley.

His cousin Gervas Huxley, who attended the same preparatory school with him for five years cannot remember him ever "losing his self-control or giving way to violent emotion" as most of the other pupils did. "It was impossible to quarrel with him. Any waves of ill-natured spite or temper broke up at once when they met the shore of his integrity and complete unselfishness".[6]

Laura Huxley's view of her husband—she was his second wife—is not only characterized by deep love and admiration for the man Aldous Huxley, but also by a certain awe that is only too easily transferred to the reader. The warmth with which she describes her husband's first marriage, which had been a very happy one, renders her account of Huxley's life honest, sincere and objective (as far as she can be objective in her position), without the slightest feeling of jealousy or rivalry. His second marriage to the much younger Laura, who was Italian, proved to be very happy as well and was ended, like the first, by death, by Aldous's death on the 22nd of November 1963, the day President Kennedy was assassinated. And like his first wife Maria he had faced death with "dignity and courage",[7] like her he died of cancer, and just as he had been sitting day and night at Maria's deathbed, Laura had been sitting at his, assuring him of her love till the very last moment.

Here the question arises: how can a man like Aldous Huxley, who has experienced real happiness in life, who was so gentle, tolerant and noble, who faced life and death with the same dignity, be capable of such bitter cynicism? According to George Woodcock the source of Huxley's cynicism is the "realization that suffering and death exist",[8] thus supporting Peter Bowering's idea of the irony inherent in the human condition. Aldous Huxley had to make this bitter experience very early in his life. His mother Julia, to whom he was very devoted, died in 1908, when he was only fourteen, too young to be able to cope with this terrible shock, this most incisive event in his life. Ironically he should lose his first wife Maria through the same fatal disease that killed his mother and that should also kill himself. Whereas he was prepared for Maria's death and also for his own—he had developed a deep interest in the idea of "ars moriendi"[9]—he was not prepared for his mother's death. This change in his attitude towards death is best revealed in his short novel *The*

Genius and the Goddess, published in 1955, the year of Maria Huxley's death, where the protagonist John Rivers says to his friend, the narrator,

> "Dying's an art, and at our age we ought to be learning it. It helps to have seen someone who really knew how. Helen [River's wife] knew how to die because she knew how to live—to live now and here and for the greater glory of God.
>
> In the process of living as one ought to live, Helen had been dying by daily installments. When the final reckoning came, there was practically nothing to pay."[10]

But there was much 'to pay' at Julia's death, for his mother was too young to die and Huxley was too young to understand fate's ironic ways, so that his reaction was quite naturally a rebellion against the inevitability of death. An interesting parallel to Huxley's attitude may be found in Dylan Thomas's poem about his father's death "Do not Go Gentle into That Good Night",[11] in which the poet "exhorted his dying father 'Rage, rage against the dying of the light'".[12] Premature death struck the Huxley family a second time when Aldous's favourite brother Trevenen committed suicide as a result of an extremely sensitive disposition, depression, failures and an unhappy relationship to a girl.

Huxley's youth and years of adolescence were overshadowed by personal bereavement, but Charles Holmes claims that Huxley's "period of blindness, even more than the family deaths, had left deep marks".[13] Huxley suffered from an inflammation of the cornea which afflicted him at the age of sixteen. This disease of the eyes called keratitis punctata not only destroyed all his hopes of a career as a writer in Aldous Huxley, but made him also isolated and vulnerable, more isolated and more vulnerable than he already was at that age as a result of his extremely sensitive disposition and his mother's death. "And of course I am also to a considerable extent a function of defective eyesight. Keratitis punctata shaped and shapes me . . .",[14] he wrote to his friend Naomi Mitchison. Huxley's eyesight was considerably improved when he practiced seeing according to the method of Bates, who "was never tired of insisting on a fact which is now a commonplace of psychology, namely that vision is at least fifty per cent a mental process".[15]

A further source of Huxley's irony may be found in his attitude towards war, which soon changed from patriotism to fierce hatred of the horrors of war. In a letter to his brother Julian he writes on March 31st, 1916:

> The longer this war goes on, the more one loathes and detests it. At the beginning I shd. have liked very much to fight: but now, if I could (having seen all the results), I think I'd be a conscientious objector, or nearly so.[16]

His poor eyesight prevented him, of course, from taking an active part in the war and in **"The Farcical History of Richard Greenow"** (***Limbo***) he made the protagonist the conscientious objector he would have preferred to be.

Juliette Huxley, his brother's wife, is also well aware of the obvious discrepancy between the writer and the human being Aldous Huxley when she reflects that "curiously the ferocity which was often manifest in his early work was never apparent in his personal relationships, for he was the gentlest companion".[17] Doubtless she sees the reasons for his ironical tone in his short stories and early novels in these shattering experiences. "One cannot help wondering whether his achievement would have taken a different shape had Aldous not been exposed, in his early formative years, to these traumatic experiences".[18]

Huxley's cynicism is directed against society in general and the human condition and its innate contradictions in particular. His eccentric characters, mainly artists and scientists, are the constant targets of his satire. "The great vice of the intellect is its total indifference to everything outside its own area of reference and this has produced the professional one-sidedness which is the prime object of Huxley's satire".[19] Northrop Frye classifies this form as "Menippean satire":[20]

> The Menippean satire deals less with people as such than with mental attitudes. Pedants, bigots, cranks, parvenus, virtuosi, enthusiasts, rapacious and incompetent professional men of all kinds, are handled in terms of their occupational approach to life as distinct from their social behavior.[21]

"The short form of the Menippean satire", Frye explains, "is usually a dialogue or a colloquy, in which the dramatic interest is in a conflict of ideas rather than of character",[22] of which Huxley's short stories are brilliant examples because the dialogues serve almost exclusively the purpose of dealing with intellectual themes and the different opinions on them.

Huxley's geniuses are all characterized by a professional one-sidedness that makes them rather helpless outside their fields of specialisation. The eminent physician Sir Watney Croker in **"The Rest Cure"** (***Brief Candles***) and the famous biologist Lord Tantamount in *Point Counter Point*have remained children at the bottom of their hearts.

> In the depths of his unspecialized, unprofessional being Sir Watney was a bit of a baby himself. Too much preoccupation with the duodenum had prevented this neglected instinctive part of him from fully growing up.[23]

Nevertheless, he seems quite able to organize his life, he has a professional housekeeper, gives dinner parties for a few privileged (specialists and other important people) and spoils his granddaughter Moira, who is living with him as her parents both died young. But through his lack of instinct, of feeling, through his complete ignorance of the most basic principles of educating children, he becomes indirectly also responsible for Moira's tragic death. This discrepancy between the highly developed intellect and the neglected instinctive part becomes even more obvious in Lord Edward Tantamount:

> At forty Lord Edward was in all but intellect a kind of child. In the laboratory, at his desk, he was as old as science itself. But his feelings, his intuitions, his instincts were those of a little boy. Unexercised, the greater part of his spiritual being had never developed.[24]

But like the great physicist Henry Maartens in *The Genius and the Goddess*, Lord Tantamount has a wife without whom he would be completely helpless, who organizes his life outside his laboratory for him. Although the ambitious physician John Tarwin in **"The Rest Cure"** (***Brief Candles***) claims to be a man of universal genius, as proud of his knowledge of cancer tumours as of his knowledge of history and art, his "appreciation of Nature and his poetical love-longings",[25] he also shows the weaknesses of the Huxleyan specialist, lacking intuition in his marriage to Moira to such a degree that he is also to blame, just as her grandfather, for her suicide.

In Stürzl's opinion the reason for Huxley's one-sided portraits of scientists whose intellect is overdeveloped at the expense of the emotional part is to be found in his own family:

> Wenn auch ältere Wissenschaftler Huxleys, wie etwa der Krebsforscher Tarwin in der psychologisch fein durchdachten Novelle "The Rest Cure" keineswegs vorbildhaft erscheinen und selbst in der Zeichnung der ehrwürdig ergrauten Gelehrtengestalten eine gewisse Ironie durchschimmert, so mag das daher rühren, daβ Huxley in seiner Familie in so enger Beziehung mit der Wissenschaft stand und daher die Schwächen ihrer Vertreter gründlich kennenlernen konnte.[26]

Other eccentrics whose egoism contributes considerably to the ironical tone in Huxley's short stories are the writers Kingham in **"Two or Three Graces"** in the volume of the same name, Tilney in **"Chawdron"** and Miles Fanning in **"After the Fireworks"** (***Brief Candles***). But unsurpassed in their eccentricity and egoism, and thus depicted with greater ironic skill than any other characters of his shorter pieces, are Martha and Herbert Claxton, two hypocritical cranks, in **"The Claxtons"** (***Brief Candles***). Huxley's eccentrics suffer not only from one-sidedness as a result of over-specialisation, but also from a split personality. The division of the self, the duality of nature, is the main theme of the opening short story of ***Limbo*** because Huxley

> doubtless recognized in himself, in the combination of fascination and repulsion with which he regarded his world, in the demands of flesh and spirit that warred within him, the divisions that he portrayed with higher lights in his characters.[27]

Dick Greenow, the protagonist of **"The Farcical History of Richard Greenow"** (***Limbo***) is a Dr. Jekyll-and-Mr. Hyde personality with an alter ego, a woman novelist who writes popular fiction during the night. The male part is an intellectual interested in philosophy and science, who is completely unaware of the female part in him. As long as the woman does not disturb him in his studies, he does not care at all; on the contrary, he lives happily on the profits made by her writing. The title itself is full of bitter irony, as Dick's life ends in a very tragic way. Caused by his split personality his sanity breaks down, "the two personalities have worn out the body, comedy has turned sour".[28] When the woman novelist gradually becomes the dominating part and wants the vote, he is taken to a lunatic asylum, where he dies in delirium after a hunger strike. Not even the very last moments lack the irony of his tragic fate: while shouting and moving wildly with his left hand, his right hand writes, as usual, what the female part dictates him, namely that "World will always be hell".[29]

> Some of this consciousness of duality as a tragic condition appears even in his earliest work, and in his novelle it exists as evidence of the absurdity of human destiny. In Huxley's shorter stories, there is naturally less development of character than in the novelle, and the structure tends to be episodic rather than narrative. While the stress is less on the duality of personality than on those other dualities between action and intent, between expectation and reality which are the more usual province of the ironist.[30]

Absurdity of human destiny is the chief target of Huxley's irony in the two longer short stories **"Uncle Spencer"** (***Little Mexican***) and **"Two or Three Graces"** in the volume of the same name. In **"Uncle Spencer"**, the opening story of ***Little Mexican,*** which occupies almost half the volume, the policy of internment at the beginning of the First World War brings people of different nationalities and different social classes together in a temporary internment camp, which the German authorities have established on the top floor of the Ministry of the Interior in Brussels. Among them are Uncle Spencer, a middle-aged Englishman living in Belgium, and Monsieur Alphonse, an Indian and husband of Uncle Spencer's housekeeper's sister. Monsieur Alphonse becomes the victim of a bad joke of a journalist, a fellow-prisoner, who improvised a trial in which Monsieur Alphonse is cross-examined, found innocent and given a sheet of paper with the words 'laissez passer' on it, the journalist's signature and a seal. Convinced in his naiveté that the document will release him, Monsieur Alphonse is so deeply disappointed and shattered in his beliefs when it is made clear to him that everything was just a joke, that he finally dies of despair. Ironically, "on the thick red wax [of the seal] appeared the figure of a shorthorn cow with, round it, the words: 'Pour l'amélioriation de la race bovine'".[31] It used to be an official seal "with which, in happier times, certain agricultural diplomas were stamped".[32] John Atkins's idea of punishment in Huxley's fiction, which "possesses a peculiar irony of its own",[33] proves true in this novella: Monsieur Alphonse must pay with his life for his foolishness to have taken the joke seriously.

The irony of fate does not spare Uncle Spencer either: he falls in love with a fellow-prisoner, the young music-hall star Emmy Wendle. She also likes Uncle Spencer; above all she feels so safe with him "because he was, obviously, such a gentleman, because of the signs of unworldliness and mild idealism stamped all over his face".[34]

Before Monsieur Alphonse dies, he prophesies how long the war will last and what will become of the other prisoners and surprisingly, all prophecies are fulfilled with remarkable exactness except one. Monsieur Alphonse has foretold that Uncle Spencer's relationship with Emmy Wendle, "that would probably be impossible in peacetime",[35] will end in marriage. Uncle Spencer desperately clings to this prophecy and after the war he searches for her together with his nephew, the narrator of the story, all over London without finding a trace of her. ' "And yet the Indian", he murmured, "he was always right. . . ." And perhaps he may still be right in this. Who knows?'[36]

Irony of fate plays also an important role in **"Two or Three Graces"** in the volume of the same name. Dick Wilkes, a music critic and narrator of this novella, finds it necessary to state that he "was never Grace's lover. . . . An ironic fate had reserved me for a less glorious part—the part, not of the lover, but of the introducer of lovers".[37] "Less glorious", because at some time of his relationship with Grace, mother of three children and wife of a most boring solicitor, he probably wanted to be her lover, and secondly, because the two love affairs which he had unconsciously and unwillingly initiated by introducing her to the painter Rodney Clegg, her first lover, and his friend Kingham, her second lover, left her extremely unhappy when these affairs ended. His own marriage, however, turns out to be extremely happy, the only happy marriage—it bears many autobiographical traits—in all of Huxley's short stories. After Grace's affair with Kingham she is so desperate that Wilkes and his wife are worried about her future.

I

> [Wilkes] was wondering what would become of Grace now. Without Rodney, without Kingham, what would she be? The question propounded itself insistently. And then, all at once, the page of printed music before my eyes gave me the oracular reply. Da capo . . . After all, it was obvious. Da capo. John Peddley, the children, the house and almost certainly another love affair.[38]

Everything would start again from the beginning. Grace Peddley, like Henry Hutton in **"The Gioconda Smile"** (***Mortal Coils***) belongs to those characters whom experience does not teach, who make the same mistakes again and again without gaining any insight through them. She is bored with her life, bored with her husband and wants to escape from the dullness of her home by having love affairs. But she does not realize that these affairs will end sooner or later and leave her more frustrated than she has ever been before. John Peddley, her husband, whose "genius for dulness caused him unfailingly to take an interest in the things which interested nobody else" and who "had the power of rendering the most intrinsically fascinating of subjects profoundly dull"[39] must endure his wife's unfaithfulness, which he does not even realize for a long time, as punishment for his insensitiveness.

Other characters who are punished for being "vicious or foolish", "imbeciles or bores",[40] are Henry Hutton in **"The Gioconda Smile"**, the painter Tillotson in **"The Tillotson Banquet"**, Sister Agatha in **"Nuns at Luncheon"** (all three in ***Mortal Coils***) and Moira in **"The Rest Cure"** (***Brief Candles***). In these shorter pieces the source of irony lies, as already mentioned, in the dualities between action and intent, but the paradox of fate plays again an important role.

According to John Atkins Huxley's best known story **"The Gioconda Smile"** "depends upon clever, sometimes dazzling ironies . . . Huxley has transformed the ironic style of the most polished early poems into a fully disciplined, total ironic view".[41] George Woodcock understands **"The Gioconda Smile"** as "a story of crime and its reasons within the human heart, of the irony of motives misunderstood, of the ways in which our own actions doom us".[42]

Janet Spence misunderstands the intentions of the hedonist Henry Hutton, his first wife Emily does not understand the motives of his actions, and Doris, his lover and later his second wife, misunderstands him right from the beginning of their relationship, and Dr. Libbard, their doctor, understands all their motives and actions but does not interfere. The reason for his indifference and fatigue is not a lack of interest in his patients' private lives, but the fact that he "understands the ironic way things work out"[43] in life. George Woodcock regards Dr. Libbard as a "tired cynic",[44] which does not seem quite justified. He is tired, too tired to care, but he is not a cynic. The reader does not know much about this minor character, nothing about any experiences in his life that might have caused this attitude of total indifference, so that he may assume that Dr. Libbard has witnessed a great deal of life's bitter ironies in his patients' lives. In the short episodes in which he makes his appearance, he is revealed as a competent physician who also shows deep psychological insight into the problems of his patients. Erwin Stürzl describes him as "angeblich einfachen Landarzt, der jedoch als allwissender Beobachter den wahren Grund ihres [Janet's] Siechtums längst geahnt hatte".[45] He has a deep understanding for his patients, for all their weaknesses and faults, but he does not show the slightest intention of attempting to reform them. He does not even blame them because he has realized that life will take its course and man cannot do anything about it or at least very little, because everything is predestined. The experience of crime and cruelty, of guilt and despair in his profession has made him indifferent, not willing to fight against this evil. And yet his presence is a great comfort for those who need it, for Emily, Hutton's sick wife, for Janet Spence who has pangs of conscience, and for the young Doris whom he prevents from committing suicide. Huxley's great ironic skill is also revealed at the end of the short story when Dr. Libbard, the detached spectator, says during one of his frequent visits to Janet Spence:

> "By the way", he said in his soft, melancholy voice, "I suppose it was really you who poisoned Mrs. Hutton."
>
> Miss Spence stared at him for two or three seconds with enormous eyes, and then quietly said, "Yes".

> After that she started to cry.
>
> "In the coffee, I suppose."
>
> She seemed to nod assent. Dr. Libbard took out his fountain pen, and in his neat, meticulous calligraphy wrote out a prescription for a sleeping-draught.[46]

Every word is carefully chosen in these lines, the epithets, the adverbs, and the casual tone, as if they were discussing the weather and not a murder, as if this revelation did not matter at all, as if Janet Spence's confirmation of Libbard's suspicion was of no importance, did not make any difference at all. The truth has been revealed, but nothing is going to happen, nothing is going to change, perhaps because Dr. Libbard believes in the punishment by fate just as Henry Hutton feels that

> some extraordinary kind of justice was being done. In the past he had been wanton and imbecile and irresponsible. Now fate was playing as wantonly, as irresponsibly, with him. It was tit for tat, and God existed after all.[47]

Or perhaps the reason is to be found in the nature of the short story itself, in the 'slice of life story' aspect:

> Die Kurzgeschichte im allgemeinen, sicherlich aber **"The Gioconda Smile"**, zeigt nur ein Stück herausgerissenes Leben das hinterläßt das Bewußtsein vom Fragmentarischen alles Menschlichen, von der Fragwürdigkeit aller menschlichen Einrichtungen, deren Vertretern—wie hier den Jüngern der Justitia—die Wahrheitsfindung letzten Endes versagt bleibt.[48]

It is interesting to note that Huxley also wrote a play (*The Gioconda Smile*, published 1948) with the basic situation unchanged. But Dr. Libbard's role is significantly changed as he saves Hutton, in whose innocence he believes. In Woodcock's opinion "the changed role of Libbard and the contrived happy ending rot the piece of its original sombre impressiveness".[49]

The painter Tillotson in **"The Tillotson Banquet"** (***Mortal Coils***) also belongs to those Huxleyan characters who get what they deserve. The short story is mainly concerned with the ironical relationship between the artist and his work. The artist Tillotson belongs to the world of transitoriness, time does not spare him, does not make him immortal, he is subject to decay and death, whereas his work will live on generation after generation, century after century. The idea of the immortality of art as constrasted with the mortality of man is not new in literature, Shakespeare praises the immortality of poetry in his famous sonnet "Shall I Compare Thee to a Summer's Day".[50] By chance the art critic Spode sees a marvellous painting by Tillotson in Lord Badgery's art collection and finds out that the artist must still be alive. When the Lord decides to have a whole room full of Tillotson frescoes, Spode sets out to search for the artist. He succeeds in finding him at last, but realizes immediately that the Lord's wish will remain unfulfilled: Tillotson is 93, almost blind, and lives in a basement full of beetles in a Holloway slum—a most depressing sight for the young art critic. Spode is really moved by the conditions in which the once great man lives and feels morally obliged to do something for him. A banquet is organized with "patrons and patronesses, art critics and dealers and even a few painters"[51]—all people who hate each other so that they will also get some 'fun' as reward for the money they are supposed to donate on behalf of the old painter. Pathos is added to the comic-ironical scene when Tillotson tries to make a speech and tells the sad story of his master Haydon, constantly repeating himself. Spode is well aware of the fact that ironically Tillotson's paintings were much better than his master's. After this "brief embarrassing interlude"[52] the return to his basement in a borrowed evening suit with the "broad green ribbon of some unknown order"[53]—he is taken home in Lord Badgery's second Rolls Royce—is even more grotesque. The 58 pounds he is presented with after the banquet will help him to survive for a short time only, nobody will look after him, and he will be doomed to oblivion again after this short interlude of his re-discovery so that the reader asks unhesitatingly, 'What was it all for?' The answer lies again in the irony of fate which man cannot escape from. The senile painter, "betrayed by time",[54] is deceived by the illusion that his fame will be restored by his re-discovery, that his life will change completely, which turns out to be a mistake the moment he enters his filthy basement again after the banquet. "The story is amusing, but its humour stems from cruelty".[55]

In **"The Portrait"** (***Little Mexican***) the target of Huxley's satire is also the characters' attitude towards art. When Mr. Bigger, an art-dealer, assures an obviously rich but simple-minded customer that an Old Master is a symbol of social prestige, the customer is flattered because the other has expressed exactly what he himself has always believed—at least since he bought a Manor House which now has to be filled with pictures. Mr. Bigger, being a clever business man, pretends to appreciate the opportunity of being able to discuss painting with an expert, feeling delighted that his ironic remarks are taken seriously by the customer. The story ends with the owner of the Manor House buying a portrait of an Italian Lady of the eighteenth century whose life had been told to him by the art dealer to rouse his interest. The trick has worked, the customer pays almost £ 700 for an imitation Mr. Bigger got for £ 25, not without asking the dealer for a typewritten copy of the story to tell his guests at dinner.

In the final dialogue between Mr. Bigger and the young painter who does the imitations for him Huxley's comic and mocking irony gives way to a more serious irony revealing the hard life of young painters and the unscrupulousness of businessmen. Mr. Bigger gives the young man, who is short of money, generously £ five more than they had agreed for this portrait, for which he himself got nearly £ 700, and the painter does not know how to thank the art-dealer for his benevolence.

Cruel and painful irony is also used in **"Nuns at Luncheon"** (***Mortal Coils***), in which the punishment of Sister

Agatha at the end of the story has a macabre note. The title itself is full of irony, as the story of poor Sister Agatha is told to the narrator by Miss Penny, a woman journalist, over lunch in a London restaurant. The fact that Miss Penny, "an example of grotesque irony herself",[56] who is always wearing "massive and improbable jewellery"[57] (e.g. rattling corpses hanging in chains as earrings) provides an ironic frame for the ironies in the nun's life: "the irony of an insensitive person describing pain".[58] It is the pain of a disgraced nun who is observed by Miss Penny, then a patient in the German hospital where the nun is working, performing no longer the duties of a nurse, but those of a hospital charwoman, dressed in an overall, with a handkerchief instead of a winged coif on her shaven head and without teeth. Eager to get the whole story, Miss Penny sets out to interview the girl's family as soon as she is well again.

Sister Agatha, the efficient nurse who has proved extremely successful at converting patients, also looks after criminals who need medical treatment in hospital. So the young Italian thief Kuno is put into her special charge, in the hope that he will be reformed. But Kuno soon sees his chance and escapes together with the naive Sister Agatha in nuns' clothes, which she has stolen for him. Having still only his salvation in mind she follows him to a shepherd's hut, where Kuno seduces her and robs her of her set of golden teeth. Ironically she has not realized that her talent of conversion does not work with him, that it is he who has done the converting. In her zeal to achieve his salvation she even persuades herself that theft is justified, when it helps to save a person's soul, according to the proverb that the end justifies the means. But there are of course moments when she is overcome by doubt and pangs of conscience, conveyed with brilliant irony by Aldous Huxley. George Woodcock regards her as not being "proof against temptation", she had been "sexually assaulted"[59] by her father's old friend, Professor Engelmann, when she was a young girl. And her set of "imperishable teeth, all gold and ivory",[60] of which she is forcibly deprived by the unscrupulous Kuno, provides the story also with a peculiar irony, as she had got the new set of teeth after losing her own through neglect after her Aunt Bertha's death. She believed she had to do penance for her feeling of relief at the death of poor Aunt Bertha, whom she had hated ever since she kept house for her father after her mother had died.

After her seduction she is forced to attend her own burial and walk as a dead person among the living as punishment for her most shameful behaviour. "The picture is ordinary", Laurence Brander says of this short story, "but the frame is glittering".[61] Charles Holmes claims that the inhumanity in **"Nuns at Luncheon"** goes so far that it "apparently left Huxley with misgivings".[62]

Moira in **"The Rest Cure"** (***Brief Candles***) is, like Monsieur Alphonse in **"Uncle Spencer"** (***Little Mexican***), a victim of her own foolishness and of fate's irony: she has to pay with her life for a series of mistakes she makes and others make, Sir Watney Croker, her grandfather, John Tarwin, her husband, and her Italian lover Tonino. Although Sir Watney loves and spoils her, she is not more than a hobby for him, like fly-fishing and metaphysics. Even when she grew up he wanted her to preserve her childishness, for he himself, because of his specialisation, had remained a child and could only love the child in her. Moira marries John Tarwin, the promising research scientist and youngest member of her grandfather's circle of specialists to escape the life with Sir Watney and his veteran geniuses. Travelling round the world with John Tarwin seemed so much preferable to her than the life she was leading. Naive as she was, she thought that all these smaller reasons added together would be the equivalent of the one big reason, the one cògent reason: love. Moira realizes very soon that she ought not to have married him. After a nervous breakdown—the result of her unbearable marriage—she goes to Florence for a rest cure upon her doctor's advice and falls in love with Tonino, a young Italian, who exploits her financially. After a quarrel, caused by Moira's jealousy, her purse, containing a considerable amount of money, has disappeared. Suddenly her husband's verdict of Tonino, whom he called "a black-haired pimp from the slums of Naples",[63] is brought home to her. She suspects Tonino of having stolen her purse and it becomes clear to her that her husband has always been right about Tonino's character. She cannot bear life any longer with this conviction and kills herself in despair. Huxley ends the story with a "last sardonic twist",[64] an effect of surprise:

> The sound of a shot brought them running upstairs. They found her lying face downward across the bed, still faintly breathing. But she was dead before the doctor could come up from the town, On a bed standing, as hers stood, in an alcove, it was difficult to lay out the body. When they moved it out of its recess, there was the sound of a hard, rather metallic fall. Assunta [the maid] bent down to see what had dropped. "It's her purse", she said. "It must have gut stuck between the bed and the wall."[65]

Moira has again been mistaken, but this time the mistake is fatal. She has been trapped by her naiveté, by her folly, and by her desires. **"The Rest Cure"** is one of Huxley's most interesting short stories, as the author's deep psychological insight is brilliantly mingled with his great ironic skill.

In **"Chawdron"** (***Brief Candles***) chance again plays havoc with the characters' lives. "Huxley has always been impressed by the importance of accident in human affairs",[66] John Atkins maintains. Chawdron, a rich business man, has a weakness for young girls whose only concern is to exploit him. The first to profit from this weakness is Charlotte, a cellist, who knows exactly how to treat Chawdron in order to get what she wants. But unfortunately she makes the mistake of going to America for a concert tour for two months and immediately another young girl, Maggie Spindell, takes her place. She is the governess type and "the unlikeliest femme fatale you ever saw", whose "only visible merit was that she was young",[67] says Chawdron's friend Tilney maliciously. Providence had played an important role in their relationship right from the beginning. If both his secretaries had not fallen ill on the same day—"what a fateful thing to happen!"[68]—Chawdron would never have met his little Fairy, as he calls Maggie Spindell. The secretaries had strict orders to deal with all kinds of begging letters summarily, but as Providence had given both private secretaries the flu Chawdron read the letters himself—the third being by the Fairy. What she wrote impressed him so much that he gave her an appointment and she "came, saw, and conquered".[69] From the moment the Fairy lives in Chawdron's house as his librarian—she is always anxious to be regarded as such—she develops an air of hypocritical spirituality that is only surpassed by Martha Claxton's in the next story of the volume. As the Fairy believes that the spirit of love is incompatible with the eating of meat, she tries to eat as little as possible by means of auto-suggestion. The consequence of her asceticism is naturally a constant bad state of health and "touched by her imagination, the headaches became mystic" so that she died "regularly every Tuesday and Friday".[70] Her predecessor's mistake had been the concert tour to the United States already mentioned, the Fairy's mistake is that she "retired to the mystic death bed once too often",[71] as Tilney again maliciously but brilliantly explains to the narrator. Her pretensions have become true at last and she really dies, another victim betrayed by her own nature and fate.

As in **"The Tillotson Banquet"** (***Mortal Coils***), irony is also used to describe the relationship of an artist to his work, in this case of the writer Tilney. Tilney is a friend of Chawdron, but their relationship is a parasitical one, the rich business man Chawdron wants fame, wants his "little niche in the literary histories",[72] and the young writer needs money—so he writes Chawdron's autobiography and the demands of both men are met. But Tilney soon regrets having sold his talent, having betrayed himself:

> "And the absurd, ironical thing", he continued, "is that the one really good piece of work I ever did is another man's autobiography. I could never prove my authorship even if I wanted to. Old Chawdron was very careful to destroy all the evidences of the crime. The business arrangements were all verbal. No documents of any kind. And the manuscript, my manuscript—he bought it off me. It's burnt".[73]

He knows that it is his fault, that nobody else is to blame, because it was a mutual agreement; but the realisation that he has most probably also sold his 'own little niche' with his manuscript is very bitter for him.

Hypocritical spirituality depicted with great ironic skill is also the main theme of the short story **"The Claxtons"** in the same volume. Already the opening statement reveals the main characters' eccentricity with a brilliantly mocking tone:

> In their little house on the common, how beautifully the Claxtons lived, how spiritually. Even the cat was a vegetarian—at any rate officially—even the cat.[74]

But the reader is soon confronted with the problems caused by false spirituality and Huxley is always ready to uncover and attack hypocrisy wherever he finds it. In John Kooistra's opinion

> **"The Claxtons"** is a model of good writing: the key in which it has been conceived is unvariedly sustained throughout its forty pages, the satire never changes its tone. The principles are dealt with devastating continuity, not once relieved by a walloping sledge-hammer blow.[75]

Another interesting source of irony in this short story is the familiar conflict between body and mind. Joseph Bentley maintains that Huxley's "novels are filled with passages in which the anatomical, scientific, or subtly scatological image intrudes into a context of romance, spirituality, or aesthetic high seriousness",[76] a fact that can also be applied to some of his short stories. Like Maggie Spindell in **"Chawdron"**, Herbert Claxton suffers from constipation, and the context in which Huxley mentions this fact is most striking: while Herbert's daughter Sylvia is playing Chopin's Valse in D flat, he is sitting on the stump of a tree doing breathing exercises for his constipation. Bentley calls this method 'semantic gravitation', which he explains as follows:

> The presence of the elements with low connotation creates a gravitational pressure pulling the high elements downward and thereby functions satirically.[77]

This device is also used in the description of Miss Spindell in **"Chawdron"**, whose "spiritual look in her eyes"[78] undoubtedly comes from uncorrected myopia, from headaches and chronic constipation, thus contributing to the ironic mood of the short story.

Irony of a lyrical quality is used in the short story **"Green Tunnels"** in the volume ***Mortal Coils.*** The lyrical element lies in the romantic dreams of a young girl surrounded by old, lifeless and boring people, her parents and Mr. and Mrs. Topes, who are living in Italy as so many Huxleyan characters. The beauty of the landscape is ironically contrasted with the dull and boring atmosphere in the house so that Barbara's only wish is to escape from this life which is only an endless succession of meals and discussions of art which do not interest her at all. She tries to avoid reality by fleeing into a world of fantasy and imagination which her elders have no access to.

In **"Green Tunnels"** Huxley also criticizes the characters' endeavour to preserve their status in a foreign country. "In India we always made a point of being properly and adequately dressed. An Englishwoman must keep up her position with natives, and to all intents and purposes the Italians are natives",[79] says Mrs. Topes. And she decides to take Italian lessons to be able to talk to the servants—apparently for no other reasons—, because "One must never be ridiculous before servants",[80] and give them orders from the writing table without turning round. So it is not surprising that even young Barbara, brought up never to forget her position, doubts the correctness of her manners on the beach:

> Barbara waved her hand, then thought that the gesture had been a little too familiar . . . and added the corrective of a stiff bow.[81]

In George Woodcock's opinion **"Green Tunnels"** is a "masterpiece in its mingling of multiple ironies with a lyrical tenderness rare in Huxley's work".[82]

There is always the hope in Huxley's work that a more desirable way of life can be found, that the search for this better life will not be in vain. "At no stage was Huxley's satire intended to be merely destructive. It was meant as a corrective, or perhaps even more as a way of seeking and showing truth".[83]

Notes

1. Peter Bowering, Aldous Huxley. *A Study of the Major Novels,* London: Athlone Press, 1968, p. 213.
2. Ibid., p. 214.
3. Ibid., p. 230.
4. John Atkins, Aldous Huxley. *A Literary Study*, London: Calder and Boyars, 1956, p. vii.
5. Julian Huxley, ed., *Aldous Huxley 1894-1963. A Memorial Volume*, London: Chatto & Windus, 1965, p. 116.
6. Ibid., p. 57.
7. Ibid., p. 123.
8. George Woodcock, *Dawn and the Darkest Hour. A Study of Aldous Huxley*, London: Faber & Faber, 1972, p. 37.
9. Ibid., p. 40.
10. Aldous Huxley, *The Genius and the Goddess*, London: Chatto & Windus, 1955, pp. 10f.
11. Dylan Thomas, "Do not Go Gentle into That Good Night", in: *Dylan Thomas: The Poems*, ed. by Daniel Jones, London: Dent & Sons, 1974 (first publ. 1971), pp. 207f.
12. George Woodcock, op. cit., p. 40.
13. Charles Holmes, *Aldous Huxley and the Way to Reality*, Bloomington/London: Indiana University Press, 1970, p. 5.
14. Grover Smith, ed., *Letters of Aldous Huxley*, London: Chatto & Windus, 1969, p. 373.
15. Laura Archera Huxley, *This Timeless Moment*, London: Chatto & Windus, 1969, p. 59.
16. Grover Smith, ed., op. cit., p. 97.
17. Julian Huxley, ed., op. cit., p. 42.
18. Julian Huxley, ed., op. cit., p. 42.
19. Peter Bowering, op. cit., p. 10.
20. Northrop Frye, *Anatomy of Criticism, Four Essays*, Princeton: Princeton University Press, 1957, p. 309.
21. Northrop Frye, *Anatomy of Criticism, Four Essays*, Princeton: Princeton University Press, 1957, p. 309.
22. Ibid., p. 310.
23. Aldous Huxley, *Brief Candles*. Stories, London: Chatto & Windus, 1930, p. 62.
24. Aldous Huxley, *Point Counter Point,* London: Chatto & Windus, 1963 (first published 1928), p. 25.
25. Aldous Huxley, *Brief Candles*, p. 65.
26. Erwin Stürzl, "Aldous Huxley. Zeitgebundenheit und Zeitlosigkeit seines Werkes", in: *Stimmen der Zeit, Monatsschrift für das Geistesleben der Gegenwart*, April 1955, Heft 7, Band 156, p. 53.
27. George Woodcock, op. cit., p. 66.
28. Laurence Brander, Aldous Huxley. *A Critical Study*, London: Hart Davis, 1969, p. 45.
29. Aldous Huxley, *Limbo*, London: Chatto & Windus, 1920, p. 110.
30. George Woodcock, op. cit., pp. 67f.
31. Aldous Huxley, *Little Mexican and Other Stories*, London: Chatto & Windus, 1968 (first published 1924), p. 92.
32. Aldous Huxley, *Little Mexican and Other Stories*, London: Chatto & Windus, 1968 (first published 1924), p. 92.
33. John Atkins, op. cit., p. 91.
34. Aldous Huxley, *Little Mexican*, p. 112.
35. George Woodcock, op. cit., p. 112.
36. Aldous Huxley, *Little Mexican*, p. 154.
37. Aldous Huxley, *Two or Three Graces and Other Stories*, New York: George H. Doran Company, 1926, p. 72.
38. Ibid., p. 217.
39. Ibid., p. 32.
40. John Atkins, op. cit., p. 91.
41. Ibid., p. 32.
42. George Woodcock, op. cit., p. 89.
43. Charles Holmes, op. cit., p. 34.
44. George Woodcock, op. cit., p. 89.
45. Erwin Stürzl, "Huxley. The Gioconda Smile", in: *Die englische Kurzgeschichte, hrsg. v. Karlheinz Göller und Gerhard Hoffmann*, Düsseldorf: Bagel, 1973, p. 233.
46. Aldous Huxley, *Mortal Coils and Other Stories*, London: Chatto & Windus, 1971 (first published. 1922), p. 62.
47. Ibid., p. 58.
48. Erwin Stürzl, "Huxley. 'The Gioconda Smile'", p. 234.
49. George Woodcock, op. cit., p. 91.

50. William Shakespeare, "Shall I Compare Thee to a Summer's Day", in: *Shakespeare's Sonnets*, ed. by W. G. Ingram, London: Univ. of London Press, 1964, p. 45.
51. George Woodcock, op. cit., p. 92.
52. Ibid., p. 93.
53. Aldous Huxley, *Mortal Coils*, p. 145.
54. Laurence Brander, op. cit., p. 49.
55. John Atkins, op. cit., p. 91.
56. Charles Holmes, op. cit., p. 35.
57. Aldous Huxley, *Mortal Coils*, p. 201.
58. Charles Holmes, op. cit., p. 35.
59. George Woodcock, op. cit., p. 95.
60. Aldous Huxley, *Mortal Coils*, p. 216.
61. Laurence Brander, op. cit., p. 49.
62. Charles Holmes, op. cit., p. 35.
63. Aldous Huxley, *Brief Candles*, p. 96.
64. George Woodcock, op. cit., p. 165.
65. Aldous Huxley, *Brief Candles*, p. 77.
66. John Atkins, op. cit., p. 92.
67. Aldous Huxley, *Brief Candles*, p. 25.
68. Ibid., p. 26.
69. Ibid., p. 27.
70. Ibid., p. 42.
71. Ibid., p. 57.
72. Ibid., p. 11.
73. Ibid., p. 9.
74. Aldous Huxley, *Brief Candles*, p. 116.
75. J. Kooistra, "Aldous Huxley", in: *English Studies*, Vol. XIII, Oct. 1931, p. 167.
76. Joseph Bentley, "Semantic Gravitation. An Essay on Satiric Reduction", in: *Modern Language Quarterly*, Vol. XXX, 1, March 1969, p. 5.
77. Ibid., p. 7.
78. Aldous Huxley, *Brief Candles*, p. 42.
79. Aldous Huxley, *Mortal Coils*, p. 174.
80. Ibid., p. 187.
81. Ibid., p. 180.
82. George Woodcock, op. cit., p. 95.
83. Ibid., p. 63.

Works Cited

Atkins, John, *Aldous Huxley. A Literary Study*, Calder and Boyars, 1956.

Bentley, Joseph, "Semantic Gravitation. An Essay on Satiric Reduction", in: *Modern Language Quarterly*, Vol. XXX, 1, 1969, p. 3-19.

Bowering, Peter, Aldous Huxley.*A Study of the Major Novels, London*: Athlone Press, 1968.

Brander, Laurence, *Aldous Huxley. A Critical Study*, London: Hart Davis, 1969.

Frye, Northrop, *Anatomy of Criticism. Four Essays*, Princeton: Princeton University Press, 1957.

Holmes, Charles, *Aldous Huxley and the Way to Reality*, Bloomington/London: Indiana University Press, 1970.

Huxley, Aldous, *Limbo*, London: Chatto & Windus, 1920.

———. *Mortal Coils and Other Stories*, London: Chatto & Windus, 1971 (first published 1922).

———. *Little Mexican and Other Stories*, London: Chatto & Windus, 1968 (first published 1924).

———. *Two or Three Graces* and Other Stories, New York: George H. Doran Company, 1926.

———. *Point Counter Point*, London: Chatto & Windus, 1963 (first publlished 1928).

———. *Brief Candles*. Stories, London: Chatto & Windus, 1930.

———. *The Genius and the Goddess*, London: Chatto & Windus, 1955.

Huxley, Julian, ed., *Aldous Huxley 1894-1963. A Memorial Volume*, London: Chatto & Windus, 1965.

Huxley, Laura Archera, *This Timeless Moment*, London: Chatto & Windus, 1969.

Kooistra, J., "Aldous Huxley", in: *English Studies,* Vol. XIII, Oct. 1931, p. 161-175.

Shakespeare, William, "Shall I Compare Thee to a Summer's Day", in: *Shakespeare's Sonnets*, ed. by W. G. Ingram, London: Univ. of London Press, 1964.

Smith, Grover, ed., *Letters of Aldous Huxley*, London: Chatto & Windus, 1969.

Stürzl, Erwin, "Aldous Huxley. Zeitgebundenhe it und Zeitlosigke it seines Werkes", in: *Stimmen der Zeit, Monatsschrift für das Geistesleben der Gegenwart,* April 1955, Heft 7, Band 156, p. 49-59.

———. "Huxley. The Gioconda Smile", in: *Die englische Kurzgeschichte, hrsg. v. Karlheinz Göller und Gerhard Hoffmann*, Düsseldorf: Bagel, 1973, p. 225-234.

Thomas, Dylan, "Do not Gentle into That Good Night", in: *Dylan Thomas: The Poems*, ed. by Daniel Jones, London: Dent & Sons, 1974 (first publ. 1971).

Woodcock, George, *Dawn and the Darkest Hour. A Study of Aldous Huxley,* London: Faber & Faber, 1972.

FURTHER READING

Bibliography

Eschelbach, Claire John and Shober, Joyce Lee. *Aldous*

Huxley: A Bibliography 1916-1959. Berkeley: University of California Press, 1961, 150 p.

Lists all of Huxley's published writings as well as secondary studies of his work until 1959; includes a foreword by Huxley.

Biographies

Bedford, Sybille. *Huxley*. London: Carrol & Graf, 1985, 769 p.

Comprehensive biography detailing Huxley's literary and private life as well as the intellectual and social era in which he was a central figure.

Huxley, Laura Archera. *This Timeless Moment: A Personal View of Aldous Huxley.* New York: Farrar, Straus & Giroux, 1968. 330 p.

Huxley's second wife describes the period in his life from 1948 until his death in 1963.

Additional coverage of Huxley's life and career is contained in the following sources published by the Gale Group: *Contemporary Authors,* Vols. 85-88; *Contemporary Authors New Revision Series,* Vol.44; *Authors and Artists for Young Adults,* Vol. 11; *Concise Dictionary of British Literary Biography 1914-1945; Contemporary Literary Criticism,* Vols. 1, 3, 4, 5, 8, 11, 18, 35, 79; *DISCovering Authors; DISCovering Authors: British; DISCovering Authors: Canadian; DISCovering Authors Modules: Most-studied Authors, Novelists; Dictionary of Literary Biography*, Vols. 36, 100, 162, 195; *Major 20th-Century Writers*, Vols. 1, 2; *Something about the Author*, Vol. 63; *World Literature Criticism.*

"The Lottery"
Shirley Jackson

The following entry presents criticism on Jackson's short story "The Lottery." For information on Jackson's complete career, see *SSC,* Volume 9.

INTRODUCTION

Jackson's fiction is noted for its exploration of incongruities in everyday life. "The Lottery," perhaps her most exemplary work in this respect, examines humanity's capacity for evil within a contemporary American setting. Noting that the story's characters, physical environment, and even its climactic action lack significant individuating detail, most critics view "The Lottery" as a modern-day parable that obliquely addresses a variety of themes, including the dark side of human nature, the danger of ritualized behavior, and the potential for cruelty when the individual is forced to submit to the mass will.

PLOT AND MAJOR CHARACTERS

"The Lottery" concerns an annual summer drawing held in a small unnamed American town. As the townspeople gather and wait for the ceremony to begin, some calmly piling stones together, they discuss everyday matters of work and family, behaving in ways that suggest the ordinariness of their lives and of the impending event. Tessie Hutchinson, arriving late, talks with her friend, Mrs. Delacroix, about the household chores that almost made her miss the lottery. An air of excitement is evident among the townspeople, who appear to look forward to the annual event. But although everyone appears to agree that the lottery is important, no one seems to remember when it began or what its original purpose was. A repeated phrase, however, ("Lottery in June, corn be heavy soon") suggests that it may have originated as a ritual to ensure a good harvest. As Mr. Summers reads off an alphabetical list of names, the heads of each household come forward to select a folded slip of paper from an old black box. Bill Hutchinson draws the paper with a black mark on it, and people immediately begin speculating about which member of the family will "win" the drawing. Each member of Bill's family draws a slip from the box. Tessie selects the paper with the black mark on it, and she vigorously protests that the drawing was unfair, even pleading that her daughter and son-in-law should be included in the drawing to increase her own chances of survival. Refusing to listen to her, the townspeople circle around her and begin pelting her with the stones they had earlier gathered.

MAJOR THEMES

The principal themes of "The Lottery" rely on the incongruous union of apparent decency and underlying evil in human nature. Citing James G. Frazer's anthropological study of primitive societies, *The Golden Bough,* many critics observe that the story reflects humankind's ancient need for a scapegoat, a figure upon which it can project its most undesirable qualities, and which can be destroyed in a ritually absolving sacrifice. Unlike primitive peoples, however, the townspeople of "The Lottery"—insofar as they represent contemporary Western society—should possess social, religious, and moral prohibitions against annual lethal stonings. Commentators variously argue that it is the very ritualization that makes the murder palatable to otherwise decent people; the ritual, and fulfilling its tradition, justifies and masks the brutality. As a modern parable on the dualism of human nature, "The Lottery" has been read as addressing such issues as the public's fascination with salacious and scandalizing journalism, the McCarthyism of the 1950s, and the complicity of the general public in the victimization of minority groups, epitomized by the Holocaust of World War II.

CRITICAL RECEPTION

"The Lottery" was first published in the *New Yorker* on June 26, 1948, and it generated more letters from readers than any other story the magazine had published up to that point. Most readers who wrote were confused as to the story's meaning, and many took it literally, asking where the ritual took place and whether or not they could go to observe it. According to Lenemaja Friedman, three "main characteristics dominated the letters: bewilderment, speculation, and old-fashioned abuse." Since then, critical reception has generally been favorable, and "The Lottery" has been anthologized many times. Those critics who read the story as a traditional narrative tend to fault its surprise ending and lack of character development as unrealistic, unbelievable, and causing difficulty in reader identification. Other commentators, however, view "The Lottery" as a modern-day parable, arguing that the elements of the story that are often disparaged by critics are actually consistent with the style and structure of parables from the Bible. Generally, critics agree only that the story's meaning cannot be determined with exactitude. While most concede that it was Jackson's intention to avoid specific meaning, some cite flatly drawn characters, unrevealing dialogue, and the shocking ending as evidence of literary infertility. The majority of commentators, though, argue that the story's art lies in its provocative nature and that with its lack of specificity Jackson is able to address a variety of timeless issues with contemporary resonance and, thereby, to stir her readers to reflective thought and debate.

PRINCIPAL WORKS

Short Fiction

The Lottery Or, The Adventures of James Harris 1949
The Magic of Shirley Jackson (short stories and novels) 1966
Come Along With Me: Part of a Novel, Sixteen Stories, and Three Lectures (short stories, novel, and lectures) 1968
The Lottery (single story) 1983
One Ordinary Day (single story) 1990
Charles (single story) 1991

Other Major Works

The Road Through the Wall (novel) 1948
Hangsaman (novel) 1951
Life Among the Savages (nonfiction) 1953
The Bird's Nest (novel) 1954
The Witchcraft of Salem Village (juvenile fiction) 1956
Raising Demons (nonfiction) 1957
The Sundial (novel) 1958
The Haunting of Hill House (novel) 1959
The Bad Children: A Play in One Act for Bad Children (drama) 1959
We Have Always Lived in the Castle (novel) 1962
Famous Sally (juvenile) 1966

CRITICISM

Shirley Jackson (lecture date 1960)

SOURCE: "Biography of a Story," in *Come Along with Me: Part of a Novel, Sixteen Stories, and Three Lectures,* edited by Stanley Edgar Hyman, The Viking Press, 1960, pp. 211-25.

[*In the following lecture, Jackson discusses public reaction to the original publication of "The Lottery" in the* New Yorker.]

On the morning of June 28, 1948, I walked down to the post office in our little Vermont town to pick up the mail. I was quite casual about it, as I recall—I opened the box, took out a couple of bills and a letter or two, talked to the postmaster for a few minutes, and left, never supposing that it was the last time for months that I was to pick up the mail without an active feeling of panic. By the next week I had had to change my mailbox to the largest one in the post office, and casual conversation with the postmaster was out of the question, because he wasn't speaking to me. June 28, 1948 was the day *The New Yorker* came out with a story of mine in it. It was not my first published story, nor my last, but I have been assured over and over that if it had been the only story I ever wrote or published, there would be people who would not forget my name.

I had written the story three weeks before, on a bright June morning when summer seemed to have come at last, with blue skies and warm sun and no heavenly signs to warn me that my morning's work was anything but just another story. The idea had come to me while I was pushing my daughter up the hill in her stroller—it was, as I say, a warm morning, and the hill was steep, and beside my daughter the stroller held the day's groceries—and perhaps the effort of that last fifty yards up the hill put an edge to the story; at any rate, I had the idea fairly clearly in my mind when I put my daughter in her playpen and the frozen vegetables in the refrigerator, and, writing the story, I found that it went quickly and easily, moving from beginning to end without pause. As a matter of fact, when I read it over later I decided that except for one or two minor corrections, it needed no changes, and the story I finally typed up and sent off to my agent the next day was almost word for word the original draft. This, as any writer of stories can tell you, is not a usual thing. All I know is that when I came to read the story over I felt strongly that I didn't want to fuss with it. I didn't think it was perfect, but I didn't want to fuss with it. It was, I thought, a serious, straightforward story, and I was pleased and a little surprised at the ease with which it had been written; I was reasonably proud of it, and hoped that my agent would sell it to some magazine and I would have the gratification of seeing it in print.

My agent did not care for the story, but—as she said in her note at the time—her job was to sell it, not to like it. She sent it at once to *The New Yorker,* and about a week after the story had been written I received a telephone call from the fiction editor of *The New Yorker*; it was quite clear that he did not really care for the story, either, but *The New Yorker* was going to buy it. He asked for one change—that the date mentioned in the story be changed to coincide with the date of the issue of the magazine in which the story would appear, and I said of course. He then asked, hesitantly, if I had any particular interpretation of my own for the story; Mr. Harold Ross, then the editor of *The New Yorker,* was not altogether sure that he understood the story, and wondered if I cared to enlarge upon its meaning. I said no. Mr. Ross, he said, thought that the story might be puzzling to some people, and in case anyone telephoned the magazine, as sometimes happened, or wrote in asking about the story, was there anything in particular I wanted them to say? No, I said, nothing in particular; it was just a story I wrote.

I had no more preparation than that. I went on picking up the mail every morning, pushing my daughter up and down the hill in her stroller, anticipating pleasurably the check from *The New Yorker,* and shopping for groceries. The weather stayed nice and it looked as though it was going to be a good summer. Then, on June 28, *The New Yorker* came out with my story.

Things began mildly enough with a note from a friend at *The New Yorker*: "Your story has kicked up quite a fuss around the office," he wrote. I was flattered; it's nice to think that your friends notice what you write. Later that day there was a call from one of the magazine's editors; they had had a couple of people phone in about my story, he said, and was there anything I particularly wanted him to say if there were any more calls? No, I said, nothing particular; anything he chose to say was perfectly all right with me; it was just a story.

I was further puzzled by a cryptic note from another friend: "Heard a man talking about a story of yours on the bus this morning," she wrote. "Very exciting. I wanted to tell him I knew the author, but after I heard what he was saying I decided I'd better not."

One of the most terrifying aspects of publishing stories and books is the realization that they are going to be read, and read by strangers. I had never fully realized this before, although I had of course in my imagination dwelt lovingly upon the thought of the millions and millions of people who were going to be uplifted and enriched and delighted by the stories I wrote. It had simply never occurred to me that these millions and millions of people might be so far from being uplifted that they would sit down and write me letters I was downright scared to open; of the three-hundred-odd letters that I received that summer I can count only thirteen that spoke kindly to me, and they were mostly from friends. Even my mother scolded me: "Dad and I did not care at all for your story in *The New Yorker,*" she wrote sternly; "it does seem, dear, that this gloomy kind of story is what all you young people think about these days. Why don't you write something to cheer people up?"

By mid-July I had begun to perceive that I was very lucky indeed to be safely in Vermont, where no one in our small town had ever heard of *The New Yorker,* much less read my story. Millions of people, and my mother, had taken a pronounced dislike to me.

The magazine kept no track of telephone calls, but all letters addressed to me care of the magazine were forwarded directly to me for answering, and all letters addressed to the magazine—some of them addressed to Harold Ross personally; these were the most vehement—were answered at the magazine and then the letters were sent me in great batches, along with carbons of the answers written at the magazine. I have all the letters still, and if they could be considered to give any accurate cross section of the reading public, or the reading public of *The New Yorker,* or even the reading public of one issue of *The New Yorker,* I would stop writing now.

Judging from these letters, people who read stories are gullible, rude, frequently illiterate, and horribly afraid of being laughed at. Many of the writers were positive that *The New Yorker* was going to ridicule them in print, and the most cautious letters were headed, in capital letters: NOT FOR PUBLICATION or PLEASE DO NOT PRINT THIS LETTER, or, at best, THIS LETTER MAY BE PUBLISHED AT YOUR USUAL RATES OF PAYMENT. Anonymous letters, of which there were a few, were destroyed. *The New Yorker* never published any comment of any kind about the story in the magazine, but did issue one publicity release saying that the story had received more mail than any piece of fiction they had ever published; this was after the newspapers had gotten into the act, in midsummer, with a front-page story in the *San Francisco Chronicle* begging to know what the story meant, and a series of columns in New York and Chicago papers pointing out that *New Yorker* subscriptions were being canceled right and left.

Curiously, there are three main themes which dominate the letters of that first summer—three themes which might be identified as bewilderment, speculation, and plain old-fashioned abuse. In the years since then, during which the story has been anthologized, dramatized, televised, and even—in one completely mystifying transformation—made into a ballet, the tenor of letters I receive has changed. I am addressed more politely, as a rule, and the letters largely confine themselves to questions like what does this story mean? The general tone of the early letters, however, was a kind of wide-eyed, shocked innocence. People at first were not so much concerned with what the story meant; what they wanted to know was where these lotteries were held, and whether they could go there and watch. Listen to these quotations:

> (Kansas) Will you please tell me the locale and the year of the custom?
>
> (Oregon) Where in heaven's name does there exist such barbarity as described in the story?
>
> (New York) Do such tribunal rituals still exist and if so where?
>
> (New York) To a reader who has only a fleeting knowledge of traditional rites in various parts of the country (I presume the plot was laid in the United States) I found the cruelty of the ceremony outrageous, if not unbelievable. It may be just a custom or ritual which I am not familiar with.
>
> (New York) Would you please explain whether such improbable rituals occur in our Middle Western states, and what their origin and purpose are?
>
> (Nevada) Although we recognize the story to be fiction is it possible that it is based on fact?
>
> (Maryland) Please let me know if the custom of which you wrote actually exists.
>
> (New York) To satisfy my curiosity would you please tell me if such rites are still practiced and if so where?
>
> (California) If it is based on fact would you please tell me the date and place of its origin?
>
> (Texas) What I would like to know, if you don't mind enlightening me, is in what part of the United States this organized, apparently legal lynching is practiced? Could it be that in New England or in equally enlightened regions, mass sadism is still part and parcel of the ordinary citizen's life?
>
> (Georgia) I'm hoping you'll find time to give me further details about the bizarre custom the story describes, where it occurs, who practices it, and why.
>
> (Brooklyn, N.Y.) I am interested in learning if there is any particular source or group of sources of fact or legend on which and from which the story is based? This story has caused me to be particularly disturbed by my lack of knowledge of such rites or lotteries in the United States.
>
> (California) If it actually occurred, it should be documented.
>
> (New York) We have not read about it in *In Fact.*
>
> (New York) Is it based on reality? Do these practices still continue in back-country England, the human sacrifice for the rich harvest? It's a frightening thought.
>
> (Ohio) I think your story is based on fact. Am I right? As a psychiatrist I am fascinated by the psychodynamic possibilities suggested by this anachronistic ritual.
>
> (Mississippi) You seem to describe a custom of which I am totally ignorant.
>
> (California) It seems like I remember reading somewhere a long time ago that that was the custom in a certain part of France some time ago. However I have never heard of it being practiced here in the United States. However would you please inform me where you got your information and whether or not anything of this nature has been perpetrated in modern times?
>
> (Pennsylvania) Are you describing a current custom?
>
> (New York) Is there some timeless community existing in New England where human sacrifices are made for the fertility of the crops?
>
> (Boston) Apparently this tale involves an English custom or tradition of which we in this country know nothing.
>
> (Canada) Can the lottery be some barbaric event, a hangover from the Middle Ages perhaps, which is still carried on in the States? In what part of the country does it take place?
>
> (Los Angeles) I have read of some queer cults in my time, but this one bothers me.
>
> (Texas) Was this group of people perhaps a settlement descended from early English colonists? And were they continuing a Druid rite to assure good crops?
>
> (Quebec) Is this a custom which is carried on somewhere in America?
>
> (A London psychologist) I have received requests for elucidation from English friends and patients. They would like to know if the barbarity of stoning still exists in the U.S.A. and in general what the tale is all about and where does the action take place.
>
> (Oregon) Is there a witchcraft hangover somewhere in these United States that we Far Westerners have missed?
>
> (Madras, India) We have been wondering whether the story was based on fact and if so whether the custom described therein of selecting one family by lot jointly to be stoned by the remainder of the villagers still persists anywhere in the United States. *The New Yorker* is read here in our United States information library and while we have had no inquiries about this particular article as yet, it is possible we shall have and I would be glad to be in a position to answer them.
>
> (England) I am sorry that I cannot find out the state in which this piece of annual propitiatory sacrifice takes place. Now I just frankly don't believe that even in the United States such things happen—at least not without being sponsored by Lynching Inc. or the All-American Morticians Group or some such high-powered organization. I was once offered a baby by a primitive tribe in the center of Laos (Indochina) which my interpreter (Chinese) informed me I had to kill so that my blood lust was satiated and I would leave the rest of the tribe alone. But NOT in the United States, PLEASE.

(Connecticut) Other strange old things happen in the Appalachian mountain villages, I'm told.

As I say, if I thought this was a valid cross section of the reading public, I would give up writing. During this time, when I was carrying home some ten or twelve letters a day, and receiving a weekly package from *The New Yorker,* I got one letter which troubled me a good deal. It was from California, short, pleasant, and very informal. The man who wrote it clearly expected that I would recognize his name and his reputation, which I didn't. I puzzled over this letter for a day or two before I answered it, because of course it is always irritating to be on the edge of recognizing a name and have it escape you. I was pretty sure that it was someone who had written a book I had read or a book whose review I had read or a story in a recent magazine or possibly even—since I come originally from California—someone with whom I had gone to high school. Finally, since I had to answer the letter, I decided that something carefully complimentary and noncommittal would be best. One day, after I had mailed him my letter, some friends also from California stopped in and asked—as everyone was asking then—what new letters had come. I showed them the letter from my mysterious not-quite-remembered correspondent. Good heavens, they said, was this really a letter from *him*? Tell me who he is, I said desperately, just tell me who he is. Why, how could anyone forget? It had been all over the California papers for weeks, and in the New York papers, too; he had just been barely acquitted of murdering his wife with an ax. With a kind of awful realization creeping over me I went and looked up the carbon of the letter I had written him, my noncommittal letter. "Thank you very much for your kind letter about my story," I had written. "I admire *your* work, too."

The second major theme which dominates the letters is what I call speculation. These letters were from the people who sat down and figured out a meaning for the story, or a reason for writing it, and wrote in proudly to explain, or else wrote in to explain why they could not possibly believe the story had any meaning at all.

(New Jersey) Surely it is only a bad dream the author had?

(New York) Was it meant to be taken seriously?

(New York) Was the sole purpose just to give the reader a nasty impact?

(California) The main idea which has been evolved is that the author has tried to challenge the logic of our society's releasing its aggressions through the channel of minority prejudice by presenting an equally logical (or possibility more logical) method of selecting a scapegoat. The complete horror of the cold-blooded method of choosing a victim parallels our own culture's devices for handling deep-seated hostilities.

(Virginia) I would list my questions about the story but it would be like trying to talk in an unknown language so far as I am concerned. The only thing that occurs to me is that perhaps the author meant we should not be too hard on our presidential nominees.

(Connecticut) Is *The New Yorker* only maintaining further its policy of intellectual leg-pulling?

(New York) Is it a publicity stunt?

(New Orleans) I wish Mrs. Hutchinson had been queen for a day or something nice like that before they stoned the poor frightened creature.

(New York) Anyone who seeks to communicate with the public should be at least lucid.

(New Jersey) Please tell me if the feeling I have of having dreamed it once is just part of the hypnotic effect of the story.

(Massachusetts) I earnestly grabbed my young nephew's encyclopedia and searched under "stoning" or "punishment" for some key to the mystery; to no avail.

(California) Is it just a story? Why was it published? Is it a parable? Have you received other letters asking for some explanation?

(Illinois) If it is simply a fictitious example of man's innate cruelty, it isn't a very good one. Man, stupid and cruel as he is, has always had sense enough to imagine or invent a charge against the objects of his persecution: the Christian martyrs, the New England witches, the Jews and Negroes. But nobody had anything against Mrs. Hutchinson, and they only wanted to get through quickly so they could go home for lunch.

(California) Is it an allegory?

(California) Please tell us it was all in fun.

(Los Angeles *Daily News*) Was Tessie a witch? No, witches weren't selected by lottery. Anyway, these are present-day people. Is it the post-atomic age, in which there is insufficient food to sustain the population and one person is eliminated each year? Hardly. Is it just an old custom, difficult to break? Probably. But there is also the uncomfortable feeling that maybe the story wasn't supposed to make sense. The magazines have been straining in this direction for some time and *The New Yorker,* which we like very much, seems to have made it.

(Missouri) In this story you show the perversion of democracy.

(California) It seems obscure.

(California) I caught myself dreaming about what I would do if my wife and I were in such a predicament. I think I would back out.

(Illinois) A symbol of how village gossip destroys a victim?

(Puerto Rico) You people print any story you get, just throwing the last paragraph into the wastebasket before it appears in the magazine.

(New York) Were you saying that people will accept any evil as long as it doesn't touch them personally?

(Massachusetts) I am approaching middle age; has senility set in at this rather early age, or is it that I am not so acute mentally as I have had reason to assume?

(Canada) My only comment is what the hell?

(Maine) I suppose that about once every so often a magazine may decide to print something that hasn't any point just to get people talking.

(California) I don't know how there could be any confusion in anyone's mind as to what you were saying; nothing could possibly be clearer.

(Switzerland) What does it mean? Does it hide some subtle allegory?

(Indiana) What happened to the paragraph that tells what the devil is going on?

(California) I missed something here. Perhaps there was some facet of the victim's character which made her unpopular with the other villagers. I expected the people to evince a feeling of dread and terror, or else sadistic pleasure, but perhaps they were laconic, unemotional New Englanders.

(Ohio) A friend darkly suspects you people of having turned a bright editorial red, and that is how he construed the story. Please give me something to go on when I next try to placate my friend, who is now certain that you are tools of Stalin. If you *are* subversive, for goodness sake I don't blame you for not wanting to discuss the matter and of course you have every constitutional right in back of you. But at least please explain that damned story.

(Venezuela) I have read the story twice and from what I can gather all a man gets for his winnings are rocks in his head, which seems rather futile.

(Virginia) The printers left out three lines of type somewhere.

(Missouri) You printed it. Now give with the explanations.

(New York) To several of us there seemed to be a rather sinister symbolism in the cruelty of the people.

(Indiana) When I first read the story in my issue, I felt that there was no moral significance present, that the story was just terrifying, and that was all. However, there has to be a reason why it is so alarming to so many people. I feel that the only solution, the only reason it bothered so many people is that it shows the power of society over the individual. We saw the ease with which society can crush any single one of us. At the same time, we saw that society need have no rational reason for crushing the one, or the few, or sometimes the many.

(Connecticut) I thought that it might have been a small-scale representation of the sort of thing involved in the lottery which started the functioning of the selective-service system at the start of the last war.

Far and away the most emphatic letter writers were those who took this opportunity of indulging themselves in good old-fashioned name-calling. Since I am making no attempt whatsoever to interpret the motives of my correspondents, and would not if I could, I will not try now to say what I think of people who write nasty letters to other people who just write stories. I will only read some of their comments.

(Canada) Tell Miss Jackson to stay out of Canada.

(New York) I expect a personal apology from the author.

(Massachusetts) I think I had better switch to the *Saturday Evening Post.*

(Massachusetts) I will never buy *The New Yorker* again. I resent being tricked into reading perverted stories like **"The Lottery."**

(Connecticut) Who is Shirley Jackson? Cannot decide whether she is a genius or a female and more subtle version of Orson Welles.

(New York) We are fairly well educated and sophisticated people, but we feel that we have lost all faith in the truth of literature.

(Minnesota) Never in the world did I think I'd protest a story in *The New Yorker,* but really, gentlemen, **"The Lottery"** seems to me to be in incredibly bad taste. I read it while soaking in the tub and was tempted to put my head under water and end it all.

(California; this from a world-famous anthropologist) If the author's intent was to symbolize into complete mystification and at the same time be gratuitously disagreeable, she certainly succeeded.

(Georgia) Couldn't the story have been a trifle esoteric, even for *The New Yorker* circulation?

(California) **"The Lottery"** interested some of us and made the rest plain mad.

(Michigan) It certainly is modern.

(California) I am glad that your magazine does not have the popular and foreign-language circulation of the *Reader's Digest.* Such a story might make German, Russian, and Japanese realists feel lily-white in comparison with the American. The old saying about washing dirty linen in public has gone out of fashion with us. At any rate this story has reconciled me to not receiving your magazine next year.

(Illinois) Even to be polite I can't say that I liked **"The Lottery."**

(Missouri) When the author sent in this story, she undoubtedly included some explanation of place or some evidence that such a situation could exist. Then isn't the reader entitled to some such evidence? Otherwise the reader has a right to indict you as editor of willfully misrepresenting the human race. Perhaps you as editor are proud of publishing a story that reached a new low in human viciousness. The burden of proof is up to you when your own preoccupation with evil leads you into such evil ways. A few more such stories and you will alienate your most devoted readers, in which class I—until now—have been included.

(New Hampshire) It was with great disappointment that I read the story **"The Lottery."** Stories such as this belong to *Esquire,* etc., but most assuredly not to *The New Yorker.*

(Massachusetts) The ending of this story came as quite a jolt to my wife and, as a matter of fact, she was very upset by the whole thing for a day or two after.

(New York) I read the story quite thoroughly and confess that I could make neither head nor tail out of it. The story was so horrible and gruesome in its effect that I could hardly see the point of your publishing it.

Now, a complete letter, from Illinois.

> EDITOR:
>
> Never has it been my lot to read so cunningly vicious a story as that published in your last issue for June. I tremble to think of the fate of American letters if that piece indicated the taste of the editors of a magazine I had considered distinguished. It has made me wonder what you had in mind when accepting it for publication. Certainly not the entertainment of the reader and if not entertainment, what? The strokes of genius were of course apparent in the story mentioned, but of a perverted genius whose efforts achieved a terrible malformation. You have betrayed a trust with your readers by giving them such a bestial selection. Unaware, the reader was led into a casual tale of the village folk, becoming conscious only gradually of the rising tension, till the shock of the unwholesome conclusion, skillful though it was wrought, left him with total disgust for the story and with disillusionment in the magazine publishing it.
>
> I speak of my own reaction. If that is not the reaction of the majority of your readers I miss my guess. Ethics and uplift are apparently not in your repertoire, nor are they expected, but as editors it is your responsibility to have a sounder and saner criterion for stories than the one which passed on **"The Lottery."**
>
> Heretofore mine has been almost a stockholder's pride in *The New Yorker.* I shared my copy with my friends as I do the other possessions which I most enjoy. When your latest issue arrived, my new distaste kept me from removing the brown paper wrapping, and into the wastebasket it went. Since I can't conceive that I'll develop interest in it again, save the results of your efforts that indignity every week and cancel my subscription immediately.

Another letter, this one from Indiana.

> SIR:
>
> Thanks for letting us take a look at the nauseating and fiction-less bit of print which appeared in a recent issue. I gather that we read the literal translation.
>
> The process of moving set us back a few weeks, but unfortunately your magazine and Miss Jackson's consistently correct spelling and punctuation caught up with us.
>
> We are pleased to think that perhaps her story recalled happier days for you; days when you were able to hurl flat skipping stones at your aged grandmother. Not for any particular reason, of course, but because the village postmaster good-naturedly placed them in your hands, or because your chubby fingers felt good as they gripped the stone.
>
> Our quarrel is not with Miss Jackson's amazingly clear style or reportorial observation. It is not with the strong motives exhibited by the native stone-throwers, or with the undertones and overtones which apparently we missed along the way.
>
> It is simply that we read the piece before and not after supper. We are hammering together a few paragraphs on running the head of our kindly neighbor through the electric eggbeater, and will mail same when we have untangled her top-piece. This should give your many readers a low chuckle or at least provide the sophisticates with an inner glow. Also it might interest you to know that my wife and I are gathering up the smoothest, roundest stones in our yard and piling them up on the corner in small, neat pyramids. We're sentimentalists that way.

I have frequently wondered if this last letter is a practical joke; it is certainly not impossible, although I hope not, because it is quite my favorite letter of all **"Lottery"** correspondence. It was mailed to *The New Yorker,* from Los Angeles, of course, and written in pencil, on a sheet of lined paper torn from a pad; the spelling is atrocious.

> DEAR SIR:
>
> The June 26 copy of your magazine fell into my hands in the Los Angeles railroad station yesterday. Although I do not read your magazine very often I took this copy home to my folks and they had to agree with me that you speak strait-forward to your readers.
>
> My Aunt Ellise before she became priestess of the Exalted Rollers used to tell us a story just like **"The Lottery"** by Shirley Jackson. I don't know if Miss Jackson is a member of the Exhalted Rollers but with her round stones sure ought to be. There is a few points in her prophecy on which Aunt Ellise and me don't agree.
>
> The Exalted Rollers donnot believe in the ballot box but believe that the true gospel of the redeeming light will become accepted by all when the prophecy comes true. It does seem likely to me that our sins will bring us punishment though a great scouraging war with the devil's toy (the atomic bomb). I don't think we will have to sacrifice humin beings fore atonement.
>
> Our brothers feel that Miss Jackson is a true prophet and disciple of the true gospel of the redeeming light. When will the next revelations be published?
>
> Yours in the spirit.

Of all the questions ever asked me about **"Lottery,"** I feel that there is only one which I can answer fearlessly and honestly, and that is the question which closes this gentleman's letter. When will the next revelations be published, he wants to know, and I answer roundly, never. I am out of the lottery business for good.

Helen E. Nebeker (essay date 1974)

SOURCE: "'The Lottery': Symbolic Tour de Force," in *American Literature,* Vol. 46, No. 1, March, 1974, pp. 100-07.

[In the following essay, Nebeker analyzes the symbolism in "The Lottery."]

Numerous critics have carefully discussed Shirley Jackson's **"The Lottery"** in terms of the scapegoat traditions of anthropology and literature, pointing out its obvious comment on the innate savagery of man lurking beneath his civilized trappings. Most acknowledge the power of the story, admitting that the psychological shock of the ritual murder in an atmosphere of modern, small-town normality cannot be easily forgotten. Nevertheless, beneath the praise of these critics frequently runs a current of uneasiness, a sense of having been defrauded in some way by the development of the story as a whole.

Virgil Scott, for example, writes that ". . . the story leaves one uneasy because of the author's use of incidental symbolism . . . the black box, the forgotten tuneless chant, the ritual salute—indeed the entire reconstruction of the mechanics of the lottery—fail to serve the story as they might have."[1] Robert Heilman discovers similar technical difficulties. While approving the "deadpan narrative style" which screens us from the "horrifying nightmare" to come, he nevertheless believes that the unexpected shock of the ending "crowds out" the impact of Jackson's thematic revelation. He suggests that the "symbolic intention" should be evidenced earlier in the story because, while "to set us immediately on the track of the symbolism" might reduce the shock, it might, on the other hand, "result in a more durable story."[2] Brooks and Warren praise the story for its "web of observations about human nature" and the "all-too-human tendency to seize upon a scapegoat," visiting upon it "cruelties that most of us seem to have dammed up within us." But then they indicate structural weakness by asserting that Jackson has "preferred to give no key to her parable but to leave its meaning to our inference," allowing "a good deal of flexibility in our interpretation,"[3] while yet insisting that "everything in the story has been devised to let us know how we are to 'take' the final events in the story."[4]

Perhaps the critical ambivalence illustrated above stems from failure to perceive that **"The Lottery"** really fuses two stories and themes into one fictional vehicle. The overt, easily discovered story appears in the literal facts, wherein members of a small rural town meet to determine by lot who will be the victim of the yearly savagery. At this level one feels the horror, senses clearly the "dichotomy in all human nature,"[5] the "doubleness of the human spirit,"[6] and recoils in horror. This narrative level produces immediate emotional impact. Only after that initial shock do disturbing questions and nuances begin to assert themselves.

It is at this secondary point that the reader begins to suspect that a second story lies beneath the first and that Miss Jackson's "symbolic intentions" are not "incidental" but, indeed, paramount. Then one discovers that the author's careful structure and consistent symbolism work to present not only a symbolic summary of man's past but a prognosis for his future which is far more devastating than the mere reminder that man has savage potential. Ultimately one finds that the ritual of the lottery, beyond providing a channel to release repressed cruelties, actually serves to *generate* a cruelty not rooted in man's inherent emotional needs at all. Man is not at the mercy of a murky, savage id; he is the victim of unexamined and unchanging traditions which he could easily change if he only realized their implications. Herein is horror.

The symbolic overtones which develop in this second, sub rosa story become evident as early as the fourth word of the story when the date of June 27th alerts us to the season of the summer solstice with all its overtones of ancient ritual. Carefully the scene is set—the date, the air of festivity, release, even license. The children newly freed from school play boisterously, rolling in the dust. But, ominously, Bobby Martin has already stuffed his pockets with stones and Harry Jones and Dickie Delacroix follow his example, eventually making a great pile of stones in the corner which they guard from the raids of other boys. By the end of just two paragraphs, Jackson has carefully indicated the season, time of ancient excess and sacrifice, and the stones, most ancient of sacrificial weapons. She has also hinted at larger meanings through name symbology. "Martin," Bobby's surname, derives from a Middle English word signifying ape or monkey. This, juxtaposed with "Harry Jones" (in all its commonness) and "Dickie Delacroix" (of-the-Cross) urges us to an awareness of the Hairy Ape within us all, veneered by a Christianity as perverted as "Delacroix," vulgarized to "Dellacroy" by the villagers. Horribly, at the end of the story, it will be Mrs. Delacroix, warm and friendly in her natural state, who will select a stone "so large she had to pick it up with both hands" and will encourage her friends to follow suit. Should this name symbology seem strained, superimposed, a little later we shall return to it and discover that every major name in the story has its special significance.

Returning to the chronology of the story, the reader sees the men gather, talking of the planting and rain (the central issues of the ancient propitiatory rites), tractors and taxes (those modern additions to the concerns of man). The men are quieter, more aware, and the patriarchal order (the oldest social group of man) is quickly evidenced as the women join their husbands and call their children to them. When Bobby Martin tries to leave the group and runs laughing to the stones, he is sharply rebuked by his serious father, who knows that this is no game. Clearly this is more than the surface "idyllic" small-town life noted by Heilman;[7] the symbolic undercurrents prepare us to be drawn step by step toward the ultimate horror, where everything will fuse.

In the fourth paragraph, Mr. Summers, who ironically runs the "coal" business, arrives with the postmaster, Mr. Graves, who carries the three-legged stool and the black box. Although critics have tended to see the box as the major symbol, careful reading discloses that, while the box is referred to three times in this paragraph, the stool is emphasized four times and in such strained repetition as to be particularly obvious. Further, in the next two paragraphs it will be stressed that the box rests upon, is supported by, the *three-legged stool*. It would thus seem that the stool is at least as important as the box: in my opinion, it is the symbol which holds the key to Jackson's conclusive theme. In the interest of structure and coherence, this point must be developed later in the article.

Returning to the symbol of the box, its prehistoric origin is revealed in the mention of the "original wood color" showing along one side as well as in the belief that it has been constructed by the first people who settled down to make villages here (man in his original social group). The chips of wood, now discarded for slips of paper, suggest a preliterate origin. The present box has been made from pieces of the original (as though it were salvaged somehow) and is now blackened, faded, and stained (with blood perhaps). In this box[8] symbol, Jackson certainly suggests the body of tradition—once oral but now written—which the dead hand of the past codified in religion, mores, government, and the rest of culture, and passed from generation to generation, letting it grow ever more cumbersome, meaningless, and indefensible.

Jackson does not, however, attack ritual in and of itself. She implies that, as any anthropologist knows, ritual in its origin is integral to man's concept of his universe, that it is rooted in his need to explain, even to control the forces around him. Thus, at one time the ritual, the chant, the dance were executed precisely, with deep symbolic meaning. Those chosen for sacrifice were not victims but saviors who would propitiate the gods, enticing them to bring rebirth, renewal, and thanking them with their blood. This idea explains the significance of Mrs. Delacroix's comment to Mrs. Graves that "'there's no time at all between lotteries any more'" and her reply that "'Time sure goes fast.'" To the ancients, the ritual was a highly significant time marker: summer solstice and winter solstice, light versus dark, life versus death. These modern women only verify the meaninglessness of the present rite. Later, in a similar vein, when one of the girls whispers, "'I hope it's not Nancy,'" Mr. Warner replies, "'People ain't the way they used to be,'" implying that, anciently, honor and envy were accorded those chosen to die for the common welfare. Another neat symbolic touch tied to the meaningful ritualistic slaughter of the past is suggested by the character Clyde Dunbar. He lies at home, unable to participate in this year's lottery because of his broken leg. This reminds us that in every tradition of propitiation the purity and wholeness of the sacrifice was imperative. This "unblemished lamb" concept is epitomized in the sacrifice of Christ. In view of the interweaving of these ideas, it is difficult to see only "incidental symbolism" or to overlook the immediate and consistent "symbolic intention" of the narrative.

From the symbolic development of the box, the story moves swiftly to climax. Tessie Hutchinson hurries in, having almost forgotten the lottery in her round of normal, housewifely duties. She greets Mrs. Delacroix and moves good-humoredly into the crowd. Summers consults his list, discovers that Clyde Dunbar is missing and asks who will draw for him. When Janey Dunbar replies, "'Me, I guess,'" Summers asks, "'Don't you have a grown boy to do it for you Janey?' *although Mr. Summers and everyone else in the village knew the answer perfectly well*" (italics added). In this seemingly innocent exchange the reader is jarred into a suspicion that the mentioned "grown boy" has been a previous victim and that his father cannot face the strain of being present, raising the question whether the breaking of his leg has been accidental or deliberate. At any rate, this loss of a son will explain the unusual encouragement given Janey by the women as she goes to draw her slip of paper, her great anxiety as she awaits results with her remaining two sons—"'I wish they'd hurry. . . . I wish they'd hurry'"—and her sending her older son with the news to her husband who, we may surmise, waits in agony for the outcome.

Significantly, the name Dunbar may in itself suggest that thin gray line which separates those who have been personally marked by the horror of the lottery from those who have not. If this seems to be flagrant symbol hunting, we might remember that it is Mrs. Dunbar who, at the time of the stoning, holds back as Mrs. Delacroix urges her to action. Mrs. Dunbar, with only small stones in her hands, gasping for breath, says, "'I can't run at all. You'll have to go ahead and I'll catch up.'" But we may believe that she will not. Marked by the loss of her son, she may still be a victim but she will not be a perpetrator. Herein lies the only humane hope raised in the story.

Next, because of the sequence of details, we are brought to consider that Jack Watson is another villager touched personally by the lottery. Immediately after querying Mrs. Dunbar and making a note on his list, Mr. Summers asks, "'Watson boy drawing this year?'" Note that the name Watson does not immediately succeed Dunbar; there seems to be a special quality about those whose names are checked previous to the actual lottery when the names will be called from A to Z. When Jack replies, "'Here . . . I'm drawing for m'mother and me,'" blinking nervously and ducking his head, the crowd responds with "'Good fellow, Jack,'" and "'Glad to see your mother's got a man to do it,'" encouraging him excessively as they do Mrs. Dunbar. Later, after the drawing, they will specifically ask, "'Is it the Dunbars?'" "'Is it the Watsons?'" Surely, at least the elder Watson—and maybe others in the family—has been a previous victim of the rite.

Now the symbolic names crowd upon us: "Old Man Warner," prototype of the prophet of doom, voice of the past, foe of change, existing from everlasting to everlasting; Old Man Warner, seventy-seven (ancient magic number of indefiniteness) years old, the oldest of them all, juxtaposed with Jack Watson, the youngest patriarch, both part of the same unchanging horror. "Steve Adams"—Adam the father of the race and Stephen the first Christian martyr. "Baxter"[9] Martin, the eldest brother of Bobby, again suggesting primitive origins changed only superficially by even the best thought of the centuries. Tessie Hutchinson, more subtle in reference but "Hutchinson" reminiscent of early American Puritan heritage, while "Tessie," diminutive for "Theresa," derives from the Greek *theizein* meaning "to reap," or, if the nickname is for "Anastasia" it will translate literally "of the resurrection." What deliberate symbolic irony that Tessie should be the victim, not of hatred or malice, or primitive fear, but of the primitive ritual itself.

Now, as Tessie stands at bay and the crowd is upon her, the symbols coalesce into full revelation. "Tessie Hutchinson," end product of two thousand years of Christian thought and ritual, Catholic and Puritan merged, faces her fellow citizens, all equally victims and persecutors. Mrs. "Of-the-Cross" lifts her heavy stone in response to ritual long forgotten and perverted. "Old Man Warner" fans the coals (not fires) of emotions long sublimated, ritualistically revived once a year. "Mr. Adams," at once progenitor and martyr in the Judeo-Christian myth of man, stands with "Mrs. Graves"—the ultimate refuge or escape of all mankind—in the fore-front of the crowd.

Now we understand the significance of the three-legged stool—as old as the tripod of the Delphic oracle, as new as the Christian trinity. For that which supports the present day box of meaningless and perverted superstition is the body of unexamined tradition of at least six thousand years of man's history. Some of these traditions (one leg of the stool if you like), are as old as the memory of man and are symbolized by the season, the ritual, the original box, the wood chips, the names of Summers, Graves, Martin, Warner (all cultures have their priesthoods!). These original, even justifiable, traditions gave way to or were absorbed by later Hebraic perversions; and the narrative pursues its "scapegoat" theme in terms of the stones, the wooden box,[10] blackened and stained, Warner the Prophet, even the Judaic name of Tessie's son, David. Thus Hebraic tradition becomes a second leg or brace for the box.

Superimposed upon this remote body of tradition is one two thousand years old in its own right. But it may be supposed the most perverted and therefore least defensible of all as a tradition of supposedly enlightened man who has freed himself from the barbarities and superstitions of the past. This Christian tradition becomes the third support for the blood-stained box and all it represents. Most of the symbols of the other periods pertain here with the addition of Delacroix, Hutchinson, Baxter and Steve.

With this last symbolic intention clearly revealed, one may understand the deeper significance of Jackson's second, below-the-surface story. More than developing a theme which "deals with 'scapegoating,' the human tendency to punish 'innocent' and often accidentally chosen victims for our sins"[11] or one which points out "the awful doubleness of the human spirit—a doubleness that expresses itself in blended good neighborliness and cruelty . . . ,"[12] Shirley Jackson has raised these lesser themes to one encompassing a comprehensive, compassionate, and fearful understanding of man trapped in the web spun from his own need to explain and control the incomprehensible universe around him, a need no longer answered by the web of old traditions.

Man, she says, is a victim of his unexamined and hence unchanged traditions which engender in him flames otherwise banked, subdued. Until enough men are touched strongly enough by the horror of their ritualistic, irrational actions to reject the long-perverted ritual, to destroy the box completely—or to make, if necessary, a new one reflective of their own conditions and needs of life—man will never free himself from his primitive nature and is ultimately doomed. Miss Jackson does not offer us much hope—they only talk of giving up the lottery in the north village, the Dunbars and Watsons do not actually resist, and even little Davy Hutchinson holds a few pebbles in his hands.

Notes

1. Virgil Scott, *Studies in the Short Story,* Instructor's Manual (New York, 1968) pp. 21-22.
2. Robert B. Heilman, *Modern Short Stories; A Critical Anthology* (New York, 1959), pp. 384-385.
3. Cleanth Brooks and Robert Warren, *Understanding Fiction,* 2nd ed. (New York, 1959), pp. 74-75.
4. Ibid., p. 76.
5. Scott, p. 21.
6. Brooks and Warren, p. 76.
7. Heilman, p. 384.
8. Etymologically, the closeness of our words "box" and "book" is indicated in the O. E. derivation from words meaning "evergreen tree or shrub" and "beech tree," probably from the habit of carving runic characters on the beech. The Latin words *codex* and *liber* have the same similarities.
9. Richard Baxter was a seventeenth-century English Puritan minister and writer who postulated the doctrine of free grace.
10. The Ark of the Covenant itself is one of the earliest representations of the literal box.
11. Scott, p. 20.
12. Brooks and Warren, p. 76.

Lenemaja Friedman (essay date 1975)

SOURCE: "The Short Stories," in *Shirley Jackson,* Twayne Publishers, 1975, pp. 63-7.

[*In the following essay, Friedman provides an overview of the plot and major themes in "The Lottery."*]

One of the ancient practices that modern man deplores as inhumanly evil is the annual sacrifice of a scapegoat or a god-figure for the benefit of the community. Throughout the ages, from ancient Rome and Greece to the more recent occurrences in African countries, sacrifices in the name of a god of vegetation were usual and necessary, the natives felt, for a fertile crop. Somewhere along the way, the sacrifice of a human for the sins of the people—to drive evil from themselves—became linked with the ritual of the vegetation god. In Mexico, among the Aztecs, the victims impersonated the particular gods for a one-year period before being put to death; death came then by the thrust of a knife into the breast and the immediate extraction of the heart. In Athens, each year in May, at the festival of the Thargelia, two victims, a man and a woman, were led out of the city and stoned to death. Death by stoning was one of the accepted and more popular methods of dispatching ceremonial victims.

But modern man considers such practices barbaric and, therefore, alien to his civilized behavior. For this reason, many persons were puzzled and shocked by **"The Lottery."** After its appearance in the June 28, 1948, issue of *The New Yorker,* a flood of mail—hundreds of letters—deluged both the editorial offices in New York and the post office in Bennington. No *New Yorker* story had ever received such a response. Of the many letters received, as Miss Jackson recalled, only thirteen spoke kindly to her; and those were from friends. Three main characteristics dominated the letters: bewilderment, speculation, and old-fashioned abuse. "The general tone of the early letters was a kind of wide-eyed shocked innocence. People at first were not so much concerned with what the story meant: what they wanted to know was where these lotteries were held, and whether they could go there and watch." Later, after the story had been anthologized, televised, and dramatized, the tone of the letters became more polite; but people still wondered what the story meant.

She had conceived the story idea, she said, on a fine June morning as she was returning from a trip to the grocery store and was pushing uphill the stroller containing her daughter and the day's groceries. Having the idea well in mind, she wrote the story so easily that the finished copy was almost the same word for word as the rough draft. Her agent, she recalls, did not care for the story; nor was the fiction editor of *The New Yorker* particularly impressed; however, the magazine was going to buy it. When Mr. Harold Ross, then editor of the magazine, indicated that the story might be puzzling to some people and asked if she would care to enlarge upon its meaning, she refused. But later, in response to numerous requests, she made the following statement, which appeared in the July 22 issue of the *San Francisco Chronicle*: "Explaining just what I had hoped the story to say is very difficult. I suppose, I hoped, by setting a particularly brutal ancient rite in the present and in my own village to shock the story's readers with a graphic dramatization of the pointless violence and general inhumanity in their own lives."

Several of Miss Jackson's friends had intimated that the village characters were modeled after actual persons in Bennington; but, if so, she took pains to disguise the fact. The names are plain, solid-sounding: Adams, Warner, Dunbar, Martin, Hutchinson, etc. The name Mr. Summers is particularly suitable for sunny, jovial Joe Summers; it emphasizes the surface tone of the piece and underscores the ultimate irony. Mr. Graves—the postmaster and the assistant to Mr. Summers in the administration of the lottery—has a name that might well signify the tragic undercurrent, which does not become meaningful until the end of the story. As in the other stories designating the presence of evil even in the least likely persons, such as in sweet old ladies, the reader discovers the blight in this deceptively pleasant community. In fact, much of the horror stems from the discrepancy between the normal outward appearance of the village life and its people and the heinous act these people commit in the guise of tradition.

The story begins with a fine sunny morning, June 27 (the fiction editor had asked for a change in date, to coincide with this particular edition of *The New Yorker*). At first, the village appears to have holiday atmosphere; and the reader's expectations are that the lottery is a joyous occasion, ending with a happy surprise for some lucky individual. The whole lottery, one is told, takes less than two hours, so that, if it begins at ten o'clock, the villagers will be home in time for noon dinner. Not until the truth of the lottery is revealed can the reader appreciate the chilling callousness of this business-as-usual attitude on the part of the community and the willingness of the people to accept and dismiss torture-death as a common occurrence. The gathering of the stones in one corner of the square is the part of the ceremony performed by the schoolchildren during their "boisterous play." The children, too, are guilty; they show no sensitivity or emotion about the coming event. Miss Jackson's matter-of-fact description is allied to the attitude of the townspeople, and this objectivity sustains the suspense and heightens the shock of the ending.

As the men congregate, they talk of "planting and rain, tractors and taxes." The women exchange bits of gossip. One notices the first bit of tension when the families gather together; the women, standing by their husbands, call to their children. Mr. Martin speaks sharply to Bobby when the boy runs back to the pile of stones, and Bobby comes quickly. As the black box is set down, the villagers keep their distance, leaving a space between themselves and the stool; and there is hesitation at Mr. Summers's call for assistance. But Miss Jackson so skillfully weaves the tension of the present with description of the past and with the history of the black box that the reader is kept carefully unaware of anything more than what, he supposes, is the normal excitement of the occasion.

Jovial Mr. Summers who, it would seem, is the epitome of civic duty, conducts the lotteries, as he also conducts the square dances, the teen-age club, and the Halloween program. The incongruity of the purpose and the seriousness of these four activities is ironic and testifies to the guilt in Mr. Summers's soul, for he is a willing leader and thus a perpetrator of the evil. His conscience is as blank as the—all but one—little slips in the little black box. He does not recognize evil or, perhaps, know right from wrong. He does not question the tradition of the lottery; instead, his token civic improvements call not for elimination of the lottery but for the substitution of slips of paper for chips of wood—for convenience and expediency.

Mr. Summers's cheerful mien belies the seriousness of the occasion When Tessie has been chosen, and the fatal moment has come, it is Mr. Summers who says, "All right, folks. . . . Let's finish quickly." He shows no hesitation and no compassion. Because of his position in the community, he is the one who might successfully repudiate tradition; but he is representative of conservative elements who, though outwardly progressive, are content to retain existing though harmful customs. He is aware of the changing conditions in other villages; for, as Mr. and Mrs. Adams point out, some villages have already "quit lotteries." The Adamses are among the few progressive people who question the tradition and who implicitly suggest action, but their convictions are not strong; worse, they go along with the majority. Indeed, when the mob is upon Tessie, the hypocritical Steve Adams, ready to kill, is at the front of the group.

Old Man Warner, who miraculously has survived seventy-seven lotteries, is a frightening individual because, still completely superstitious, he wholeheartedly believes in the lottery and is convinced that the ritual is necessary for the welfare of the corn crop. He resents the amiable spirit and the jokes of Mr. Summers ("Bad enough to see young Joe Summers up there joking with everybody"), for he senses the seriousness of the occasion and the necessity of preserving the religiosity of the ceremony. It is not the death of the victim that disturbs him but the possible consequences of an irreligious attitude on the part of the participants. To Mr. Adams, he repeats the old saw: "Lottery in June, corn be heavy soon." Then he adds, after the comment on stopping the lottery, "First thing you know, we'd all be eating stewed chickweed and acorns"—if the lottery were to be abandoned, the crops would be destroyed and man would soon be foraging for food as he did in his cave-dwelling days. He does not want to go back to living in a cave, although in terms of civilization and humanity, he has never emerged from one, "There's *always* been a lottery," he says, and that alone, he supposes, is reason enough to continue the practice.

Tessie Hutchinson shows both the evils and the weaknesses of mankind faced with immediate death. Her hypocrisy indicates that she would willingly take part in the stoning; but, when she is the chosen sacrifice, she protests the unfairness of the method; she is not willing to be a good sport about giving up her life. "Be a good sport, Tessie," Mrs. Delacroix calls; and Mrs. Graves says, "All of us took the same chance." Instead, Tessie reacts like a frightened animal; but, unlike the animal-mother, the human mother does not always seek protection for her offspring. In fact, instead of giving her life for her children, Tessie prefers that they take their chances also—and she tries to have her daughter Eva and her husband Don included in the fatal drawing to increase her own chances for survival. The most pathetic figure of all is little Davy Hutchinson who survives the drawing but who is then forced, unknowing, to take part in the ordeal. Someone gives him a few pebbles so that he, too, may share in the collective murder of his mother; and his silence in this terrible moment is much more chilling than any other response Miss Jackson could have chosen for him.

If anything is illogical about the total ritual, it may be the stoicism of the participants and their complete willingness to sacrifice themselves or members of their families. As not all individuals are equally willing and able to endure pain, much less death, it would seem likely that during lottery time whole families might take to the woods or migrate to other villages. Even the Aztec god-figures, celebrated and worshipped until the sacrifice day, had to be guarded against escape. If the victim escaped, the captain of the guards became the substitute. But, since such practices are not literally a part of our culture, one may say that the story proceeds by way of realism to grimly realistic fantasy. As such, the lottery may be symbolic of any of a number of social ills that mankind blindly perpetrates.

Peter Kosenko (essay date 1985)

SOURCE: "A Marxist/Feminist Reading of Shirley Jackson's 'The Lottery,'" in *New Orleans Review,* Vol. 12, No. 1, Spring, 1985, pp. 27-32.

[*In the following essay, Kosenko argues that the tradition of the lottery represents the inequitable stratification of the social order along lines of gender and economic position.*]

In her critical biography of Shirley Jackson, Lenemaja Friedman notes that when Jackson's story **"The Lottery"** was published in the June 28, 1948 issue of the *New Yorker* it received a response that "no *New Yorker* story had ever received": hundreds of letters poured in that were characterized by "bewilderment, speculation, and old-fashioned abuse."[1] It is not hard to account for this response: Jackson's story portrays an "average" New England village with "average" citizens engaged in a deadly rite, the annual selection of a sacrificial victim by means of a public lottery, and does so quite deviously: not until well along in the story do we suspect that the "winner" will be stoned to death by the rest of the villagers. One can imagine the average reader of Jackson's story protesting: but we engage in no such inhuman practices. Why are you accusing us of *this*?

Admittedly, this response was not exactly the one that Jackson had hoped for. In the July 22, 1948 issue of the *San Francisco Chronicle* she broke down and said the following in response to persistent queries from her readers about her intentions: "Explaining just what I had hoped the story to say is very difficult. I suppose, I hoped, by setting a particularly brutal ancient rite in the present and in my own village to shock the story's readers with a graphic dramatization of the pointless violence and general inhumanity in their own lives."[2] Shock them she did, but probably owing to the symbolic complexity of her tale, they responded defensively and were not enlightened.

The first part of Jackson's remark in the *Chronicle,* I suspect, was at once true and *coy.* Jackson's husband, Stanley Edgar Hyman, has written in his introduction to a posthumous anthology of her short stories that "she consistently refused to be interviewed, to explain or promote her work in any fashion, or to take public stands and be the pundit of the Sunday supplements."[3] Jackson did not say in the *Chronicle* that it was impossible for her to explain approximately what her story was about, only that it was "difficult." That she thought it meant something, and something subversive, moreover, she revealed in her response to the Union of South Africa's banning of **"The Lottery"**: "She felt," Hyman says, "that *they* at least understood."[4]

A survey of what little has been written about **"The Lottery"** reveals two general critical attitudes: first, that it is about man's ineradicable primitive aggressivity, or what Cleanth Brooks and Robert Penn Warren call his "all-too-human tendency to seize upon a scapegoat"; second, that it describes man's victimization by, in Helen Nebeker's words, "unexamined and unchanging traditions which he could easily change if he only realized their implications."[5] Missing from both of these approaches, however, is a careful analysis of the abundance of social detail that links the lottery to the ordinary social practices of the village. No mere "irrational" tradition, the lottery is an *ideological mechanism.* It serves to reinforce the village's hierarchical social order by instilling the villagers with an unconscious fear that if they resist this order they might be selected in the next lottery. In the process of creating this fear, it also reproduces the ideology necessary for the smooth functioning of that social order, despite its inherent inequities. What is surprising in the work of an author who has never been identified as a Marxist is that this social order and ideology are essentially capitalist.

I think we need to take seriously Shirley Jackson's suggestion that the world of the lottery is her reader's world, however reduced in scale for the sake of economy. The village in which the lottery takes place has a bank, a post office, a grocery store, a coal business, a school system; its women are housewives rather than field workers or writers; and its men talk of "tractors and taxes."[6] More importantly, however, the village exhibits the same socio-economic stratification that most people take for granted in a modern, capitalist society.

Let me begin by describing the top of the social ladder and save the lower rungs for later. The village's most powerful man, Mr. Summers, owns the village's largest business (a coal concern) and is also its mayor, since he has, Jackson writes, more "time and energy [read money and leisure] to devote to civic activities" than others (p. 292). (Summers' very name suggests that he has become a man of leisure through his wealth.) Next in line in the social hierarchy is Mr. Graves, the village's second most powerful government official—its postmaster. (His name may suggest the gravity of officialism.) And beneath Mr. Graves is Mr. Martin, who has the economically advantageous position of being the grocer in a village of three hundred.

These three most powerful men who control the town, economically as well as politically, also happen to administer the lottery. Mr. Summers is its official, sworn in yearly by Mr. Graves (p. 294). Mr. Graves helps Mr. Summers make up the lottery slips (p. 293). And Mr. Martin steadies the lottery box as the slips are stirred (p. 292). In the off season, the lottery box is stored either at their places of business or their residences: "It had spent one year in Mr. Graves' barn and another year underfoot in the post-office, and sometimes it was set on a shelf in the Martin grocery and left there" (p. 293). Who controls the town, then, also controls the lottery. It is no coincidence that the lottery takes place in the village square "between the post-office and the bank"—two buildings which represent government and finance, the institutions from which Summers, Graves, and Martin derive their power.

However important Mr. Graves and Mr. Martin may be, Mr. Summers is still the most powerful man in town. Here we have to ask a Marxist question: what relationship is there between his interests as the town's wealthiest businessman and his officiating the lottery? That such a relationship does exist is suggested by one of the most revealing lines of the text. When Bill Hutchinson forces his wife, Tessie, to open her lottery slip to the crowd, Jackson writes, "It had a black spot on it, the black spot Mr. Summers had made the night before with [a] heavy pencil in [his] coal-company office" (p. 301). At the very moment when the lottery's victim is revealed, Jackson appends a subordinate clause in which we see the blackness (evil) of Mr. Summers' (coal) business being transferred to the black dot on the lottery slip. At one level at least, evil in Jackson's text is linked to a disorder, promoted by capitalism, in the material organization of modern society. But it still remains to be explained *how* the evil of the lottery is tied to this disorder of capitalist social organization.

Let me sketch the five major points of my answer to this question. First, the lottery's rules of participation reflect and *codify* a rigid social hierarchy based upon an inequitable social division of labor. Second, the fact that everyone participates in the lottery and understands *consciously* that its outcome is pure chance gives it a certain "democratic" aura that obscures its first codifying function. Third, the villagers believe *unconsciously* that their commitment to a work ethic will grant them some magical immunity from selection. Fourth, this work ethic prevents them from understanding that the lottery's actual function is not to encourage work *per se* but to reinforce an inequitable social *division* of labor. Finally, after working through these points, it will be easier to explain how Jackson's choice of Tessie Hutchinson as the lottery's victim/scapegoat reveals the lottery to be an ideological mechanism which serves to defuse the average villager's deep, inarticulate dissatisfaction with the social order in which he lives by channeling it into anger directed at the *victims* of that social order. It is reenacted year after year, then, not because it is a mere "tradition," as Helen Nebeker argues, but because it serves the repressive ideological function of purging the social body of all resistance so that business (capitalism) can go on as usual and the Summers, the Graves and the Martins can remain in power.

Implicit in the first and second points above is a distinction between universal participation in the lottery and what I have called its *rules* of participation. The first of these rules I have already explained, of course: those who control the village economically and politically also administer the lottery. The remaining rules also tell us much about who has and who doesn't have power in the village's social hierarchy. These remaining rules determine who gets to choose slips in the lottery's first, second and third rounds. Before the lottery, lists are "[made] up of heads of families [who choose in the first round], heads of households [who choose in the second round], [and] members of each household in each family [who choose in the last round]" (p. 294). The second round is missing from the story because the family patriarch who selects the dot in the first round—Bill Hutchinson—has no married male offspring. When her family is chosen in the first round, Tessie Hutchinson objects that her daughter and son-in-law didn't "take their chance." Mr. Summers has to remind her, "Daughters draw with their husbands' families" (p. 299). Power in the village, then, is exclusively consolidated into the hands of male heads of families and households. Women are disenfranchised.

Although patriarchy is not a product of capitalism *per se,* patriarchy in the village does have its capitalist dimension. (New social formations adapt old traditions to their own needs.) Women in the village seem to be disenfranchised because male heads of households, as men in the work force, provide the link between the broader economy of the village and the economy of the household. Some consideration of the other single household families in the first round of the lottery—the Dunbars and the Watsons—will help make this relationship between economics and family power clearer. Mr. Dunbar, unable to attend the lottery because he has a broken leg, has to choose by proxy. The rules of lottery participation take this situation into account: "Grown boy[s]" take precedence as proxies over wives (p. 295). Mrs. Dunbar's son Horace, however, is only sixteen, still presumably in school and not working; hence Mrs. Dunbar chooses for Mr. Dunbar. Jack Watson, on the other hand, whose father is dead, is clearly older than Horace and presumably already in the work force. Admittedly, such inferences cannot be supported with hard textual evidence, but they make sense when the text is referred to the norms of the society which it addresses.[7] Within these norms, "heads of households" are not simply the oldest males in their immediate families; they are the oldest *working* males and get their power from their insertion into a larger economy. Women, who have no direct link to the economy as defined by capitalism—the arena of activity in which labor is exchanged for wages and profits are made—choose in the lottery only in the absence of a "grown," working male.[8]

Women, then, have a distinctly subordinate position in the socio-economic hierarchy of the village. They make their first appearance "wearing faded house dresses . . . [and walking] shortly after their menfolk" (p. 292). Their dresses indicate that they do in fact work, but because they work in the home and not within a larger economy in which work is regulated by finance (money), they are treated by men and treat themselves as inferior. When Tessie Hutchinson appears late to the lottery, other men address her husband Bill, "Here comes your Missus, Hutchinson" (p. 295). None of the men, that is to say, thinks of addressing Tessie first, since she "belongs" to Bill. Most women in the village take this patriarchal definition of their role for granted, as Mrs. Dunbar's and Mrs. Delacroix's references to their husbands as their "old [men]" suggest (pp. 295 & 297). Tessie, as we shall see later, is the only one who rebels against male domination, although only unconsciously.

Having sketched some of the power relations within the families of the village, I can now shift my attention to the ways in which what I have called the democratic illusion of the lottery diverts their attention from the capitalist economic relations in which these relations of power are grounded. On its surface, the idea of a lottery in which everyone, as Mrs. Graves says, "[takes] the same chance" seems eminently democratic, even if its effect, the singling out of one person for privilege or attack, is not.

One critic, noting an ambiguity at the story's beginning, has remarked that "the lottery . . . suggests 'election' rather than selection," since "the [villagers] assemble in the center of the place, in the village square."[9] I would like to push the analogy further. In capitalist dominated elections, business supports and promotes candidates who will be more or less attuned to its interests, multiplying its vote through campaign financing, while each individual businessman can continue to claim that he has but one vote. In the lottery, analogously, the village ruling class participates in order to convince others (and perhaps even themselves) that they are not in fact *above* everyone else during the remainder of the year, even though their exclusive control of the lottery suggests that they are. Yet just as the lottery's black (ballot?) box has grown shabby and reveals in places its "original wood color," moments in their official "democratic" conduct of the lottery—especially Mr. Summers' conduct as their representative—reveal the class interest that lies behind it. If Summers wears jeans, in order to convince the villagers that he is just another one of the common people, he also wears a "clean white shirt," a garment more appropriate to *his* class (p. 294). If he leans casually on the black box before the lottery selection begins, as a President, say, might put his feet up on the White House desk, while leaning he "talk[s] interminably to Mr. Graves and the Martins," the other members of his class, and "seem[s] very proper and important" (p. 294). (Jackson has placed these last details in emphatic position at the end of a paragraph.) Finally, however democratic his early appeal for help in conducting the lottery might appear—"some of you fellows want to give me a hand?" (p. 292)—Mr. Martin, who responds, is the third most powerful man in the village. Summers' question is essentially empty and formal, since the villagers seem to understand, probably unconsciously, the unspoken law of class that governs who administers the lottery; it is not just *anyone* who can help Summers.

The lottery's democratic illusion, then, is an ideological effect that prevents the villagers from criticizing the class structure of their society. But this illusion alone does not account for the full force of the lottery over the village. The lottery also reinforces a village work ethic which distracts the villagers' attention from the division of labor that keeps women powerless in their homes and Mr. Summers powerful in his coal company office.

In the story's middle, Old Man Warner emerges as an apologist for this work ethic when he recalls an old village adage, "Lottery in June, corn be heavy soon" (p. 297). At one level, the lottery seems to be a modern version of a planting ritual that might once have prepared the villagers for the collective work necessary to produce a harvest. (Such rituals do not necessarily involve human sacrifice.) As magical as Warner's proverb may seem, it establishes an unconscious (unspoken) connection between the lottery and work that is revealed by the entirety of his response when told that other villages are considering doing away with the lottery:

> "Pack of crazy fools . . . listening to the young folks, nothing's good enough for *them.* Next thing you know, they'll be wanting to go back to living in caves, nobody work any more, live *that* way for a while. Used to be a saying about 'Lottery in June, corn be heavy soon.' First thing you know, we'd all be eating stewed chickweed and acorns. There's *always* been a lottery."
>
> (p. 297)

But Warner does not explain *how* the lottery functions to motivate work. In order to do so, it would have to inspire the villagers with a magical fear that their lack of productivity would make them vulnerable to selection in the next lottery. The village women reveal such an unconscious fear in their ejaculatory questions after the last slip has been drawn in the first round: "Who is it?" "Who's got it?" "Is it the Dunbars?" "Is it the Watsons?" (p. 298). The Dunbars and the Watsons, it so happens, are the least "productive" families in the village: Mr. Dunbar has broken his leg, Mr. Watson is dead. Given this unconscious village fear that lack of productivity determines the lottery's victim, we might guess that Old Man Warner's pride that he is participating in the lottery for the "seventy-seventh time" stems from a magical belief—seventy-seven is a magical number—that his commitment to work and the village work ethic accounts for his survival. Wherever we find "magic," we are in the realm of the unconscious: the realm in which the unspoken of ideology resides.

Old Man Warner's commitment to a work ethic, however appropriate it might be in an egalitarian community trying collectively to carve an economy out of a wilderness, is not entirely innocent in the modern village, since it encourages villagers to work without pointing out to them that part of their labor goes to the support of the leisure and power of a business class. Warner, that is to say, is Summers' ideologist. At the end of his remarks about the lottery, Warner laments Summers' democratic conduct: "Bad enough to see young Joe Summers up there joking with everybody" (p. 297). Yet this criticism obscures the fact that Summers is not about to undermine the lottery, even if he does "modernize" it, since by running the lottery he also encourages a work ethic which serves his interest. Just before the first round drawing, Summers remarks casually, "Well, now . . . guess we better get started, get this over with, so's we can go back to work" (p. 295). The "we" in his remark is deceptive; what he means to say is "so that you can go back to work for me."

The final major point of my reading has to do with Jackson's selection of Tessie Hutchinson as the lottery's victim/scapegoat. She could have chosen Mr. Dunbar, of course, in order to show us the unconscious connection that the villagers draw between the lottery and their work ethic. But to do so would not have revealed that the lottery actually reinforces a *division* of labor. Tessie, after all, is a woman whose role as a house-wife deprives her radically of her freedom by forcing her to submit to a husband who gains his power over her by virtue of his place in the work force. Tessie, however, rebels against her role, and such rebellion is just what the orderly functioning of her society cannot stand. Unfortunately, her rebellion is entirely unconscious.

Tessie's rebellion begins with her late arrival at the lottery, a *faux pas* that reveals her unconscious resistance to everything the lottery stands for. She explains to Mr. Summers that she was doing her dishes and forgot what day it was. The way in which she says this, however, involves her in another *faux pas*: the suggestion that she might have violated the village's work ethic and neglected her specific job within the village's social division of labor: "Wouldn't have me leave m'dishes in the sink, now, would you Joe?" (p. 295). The "soft laughter [that runs] through the crowd" after this remark is a nervous laughter that indicates, even more than the village women's singling out of the Dunbars and the Watsons, the extent of the village's unconscious commitment to its work ethic and power structure (p. 295). When Mr. Summers calls her family's name, Tessie goads her husband, "Get up there, Bill" (p. 297). In doing so, she inverts the power relation that holds in the village between husbands and wives. Again, her remark evokes nervous laughter from the crowd, which senses the taboo that she has violated. Her final *faux pas* is to question the rules of the lottery which relegate women to inferior status as the property of their husbands. When Mr. Summers asks Bill Hutchinson whether his family has any other households, Tessie yells, "There's Don and Eva . . . Make them take their chance" (p. 299). Tessie's daughter Eva, however, *belongs* to Don and is consequently barred from participating with her parents' family.

All of these *faux pas* set Tessie up as the lottery's likeliest victim, even if they do not explicitly challenge the lottery. That Tessie's rebellion is entirely unconscious is revealed by her cry while being stoned, "It isn't fair" (p. 302). Tessie does not object to the lottery *per se,* only to her own selection as its scapegoat. It would have been fine with her if someone else had been selected.

In stoning Tessie, the villagers treat her as a scapegoat onto which they can project and through which they can "purge"—actually, the term *repress*" is better, since the impulse is conserved rather than eliminated—their own temptations to rebel. The only places we can see these rebellious impulses are in Tessie, in Mr. and Mrs. Adams' suggestion, squelched by Warner, that the lottery might be given up, and in the laughter of the crowd. (The crowd's nervous laughter is ambivalent: it expresses uncertainty about the validity of the taboos that Tessie breaks.) But ultimately these rebellious impulses are channeled by the lottery and its attendant ideology away from their proper objects—capitalism and capitalist patriarchs—into anger at the rebellious victims of capitalist social organization. Like Tessie, the villagers cannot articulate their rebellion because the massive force of ideology stands in the way.

The lottery functions, then, to terrorize the village into accepting, in the *name* of work and democracy, the inequitable social division of labor and power on which its social order depends. When Tessie is selected, and before she is stoned, Mr. Summers asks her husband to "show [people] her paper" (p. 301). By holding up the slip, Bill Hutchinson reasserts his dominance over his wayward wife and simultaneously transforms her into a symbol to others of the perils of disobedience.

Here I would like to point out a curious crux in Jackson's treatment of the theme of scapegoating in **"The Lottery"**: the conflict between the lottery's literal arbitrariness and the utter appropriateness of its victim. Admittedly, Tessie is a curious kind of scapegoat, since the village does not literally choose her, single her out. An act of scapegoating that is *unmotivated* is difficult to conceive. This crux disappears, however, once we realize that the lottery is a metaphor for the unconscious ideological mechanisms of scapegoating. In choosing Tessie through the lottery, Jackson has attempted to show us whom the village might have chosen if the lottery had been in fact an election. But by presenting this election as an arbitrary lottery, she gives us an image of the village's blindness to its own motives. Possibly the most depressing thing about **"The Lottery"** is how early Jackson represents this blindness as beginning. Even the village children have been socialized into the ideology that victimizes Tessie. When they are introduced in the second paragraph of the story, they are anxious that summer has let them out of school: "The feeling of liberty sat uneasily on most of them" (p. 291). Like their parents, they have learned that leisure and play are suspect. As if to quell this anxiety, the village boys engage in the play/labor of collecting stones for the lottery. Moreover, they follow the lead of Bobby Martin, the one boy in the story whose father is a member of the village ruling class (Mr. Summers and Mr. Graves have no boys), in hoarding and fighting over these stones as if they were money. While the boys do this, the village girls stand off to the side and watch, just as they will be expected to remain outside of the work force and dependent on their working husbands when they grow up.

As dismal as this picture seems, the one thing we ought not do is make it into proof of the innate depravity of man. The first line of the second paragraph—"The children assembled first, of course" (p. 291)—does not imply that children take a "natural" and primitive joy in stoning people to death.[10] The closer we look at their behavior, the more we realize that they learned it from their parents, whom they imitate in their play. In order to facilitate her reader's grasp of this point, Jackson has included at least one genuinely innocent child in the story—Davy Hutchinson. When he has to choose his lottery ticket, the adults help him while he looks at them "wonderingly" (p. 300). And when Tessie is finally to be stoned, "someone" has to "[give] Davy Hutchinson a few pebbles" (p. 301). The village makes sure that Davy learns what he is supposed to do before he understands why he does it or the consequences. But this does not mean that he could not learn otherwise.

Even the village adults are not entirely hopeless. Before Old Man Warner cuts them off, Mr. and Mrs. Adams, whose last name suggests a humanity that has not been entirely effaced, briefly mention other villages that are either talking of giving up the lottery or have already done so. Probably out of deep-seated fear, they do not suggest that *their* village give it up; but that they hint at the possibility, however furtively, indicates a reservation—a vague, unconscious sense of guilt—about what they are about to do. The Adams's represent the village's best, humane impulses, impulses, however, which the lottery represses.

How do we take such a pessimistic vision of the possibility of social transformation? If anything can be said against **"The Lottery,"** it is probably that it exaggerates the monolithic character of capitalist ideological hegemony. No doubt, capitalism has subtle ways of redirecting the frustrations it engenders away from a critique of capitalism itself. Yet if in order to promote itself it has to make promises of freedom, prosperity and fulfillment on which it cannot deliver, pockets of resistance grow up among the disillusioned. Perhaps it is not Jackson's intention to deny this, but to shock her complacent readers with an exaggerated image of the ideological *modus operandi* of capitalism: accusing those whom it cannot or will not employ of being lazy, promoting "the family" as the essential social unit in order to discourage broader associations and identifications, offering men power over their wives as a consolation for their powerlessness in the labor market, and pitting workers against each other and against the unemployed. It is our fault as readers if our own complacent pessimism makes us *read* Jackson's story pessimistically as a parable of man's innate depravity.

Notes

1. Lenemaja Friedman, *Shirley Jackson* (Boston: Twayne Publishers, 1975), p. 63.
2. Friedman, p. 64.
3. Stanley Edgar Hyman, ed., *The Magic of Shirley Jackson* (New York: Farrar, Straus and Giroux, 1966), p. viii.
4. Hyman, p. ix.
5. Cleanth Brooks and Robert Penn Warren, eds., *Understanding Fiction* (New York: Appleton-Century-Crofts, 1959; 2nd ed.), p. 74; Helen E. Nebeker, "'The Lottery': Symbolic Tour de Force," *American Literature,* 46 (1974), p. 103. Barring book reviews, dissertations and fugitive references in surveys of American writing, the following criticism should also be mentioned: 1) Skyamal Bagchee, "Design of Darkness in Shirley Jackson's 'The Lottery,'" *Notes on Contemporary Literature,* 9, iv, pp. 8-9; 2) Horst Brinkman, "Shirley Jackson, 'The Lottery' (1948)," in *Die Amerikanische Short Story der Gegenwart,* ed. Peter Freese (Berlin: Erich Schmidt, 1976), pp. 101-09; 3) John V. Hogopian, *Insight I. Analyses of American Literature* (Frankfurt: Hirschgraben, 1971; 4th ed.), pp. 128-32; 4) Robert B. Heilman, ed., *Modern Short Stories, A Critical Anthology* (New York: Harcourt, Brace and World, 1950), pp. 384-85; 5) Seymour Lainoff, "Jackson's 'The Lottery,'" *The Explicator,* 12 (Mar. 1954), item 34; 6) Richard Williams, "A Critique of the Sampling Plan Used in Shirley Jackson's 'The Lottery,'" *Journal of Modern Literature,* 7 (1979), pp. 543-44. This bibliography may not be complete.
6. Shirley Jackson, *The Lottery and Other Stories* (New York: Farrar, Straus and Giroux, 1982), p. 291. Further page references will occur in the body of the paper.
7. I propose this reading only as the most *plausible* way of accounting for the distinction between Horace Dunbar's exclusion from the lottery and Jack Watson's participation in it. To account for this distinction on the basis of age alone seems weak to me, given the value that the village places on work.
8. Jackson's representation of women, of course, is exaggerated, even for her own time. But then the entire story is similarly exaggerated in order to highlight a theoretical framework which Jackson feels is necessary before we can even begin to understand the social world to which the story indirectly refers. Most allegory is similarly abstract.
9. Brinkman, p. 103; my translation.
10. My reading makes Jackson's "of course" ironic: a phrase that appeals to her reader's possible assumption that children are innately depraved, an assumption which the story's other detail questions.

James S. Terry and Peter C. Williams (essay date 1988)

SOURCE: "Literature and Bioethics: The Tension in Goals and Styles," in *Literature and Medicine,* Vol. 7, 1988, pp. 1-21.

[*In the following essay, Terry and Williams include "The Lottery" in a discussion of examples of literature that demonstrates lessons in medical ethics.*]

The power of literary representations of illness and medical care has been as apparent to the bioethics community as it has to all others in the medical humanities. Short stories and poems that are evocative, complex, and imaginatively challenging have been used to supplement or supplant the traditional case study as instruments for raising ethical issues. At best, these literary works more vividly present moral questions and even raise some kinds of issues that case studies leave out. Philosophic understanding of a given moral problem can be enriched by a literary account that places issues in a context of the lives and activities of particular characters. At a minimum, the use of literature in discussions of bioethics offers an escape from too often dry analytic discourse. Tales capture medical audiences in ways that philosophical discussions sometimes cannot.[1]

Nonetheless, using works of literature in teaching bioethics has distinct disadvantages—substantive as well as pedagogical—which this paper attempts to explore. Though there are genuine reciprocal benefits from the marriage of literature and bioethics, the form and process of the two disciplines have significant differences. These differences risk two important deleterious consequences. On the one hand, literary presentations of problems in medical ethics may end up subordinating, misdirecting, or obscuring ethical analysis and discussion. On the other hand, the isolation of an ethical issue in a piece of literature may ignore important features of literature as art or distort the pedagogical values inherent in literary study. The aim of this investigation is neither to cast aspersions on traditional bioethics nor to discourage the use of literature therein. Rather, it is to make the choice of materials and methods more informed and to foster a felicitous alliance. The teacher and the student should realize that important (and often less than obvious) value decisions are made when a course or lecture on bioethics is designed. Without such a realization, the bioethicist using literature or the literary expert teaching bioethics may be encouraging an approach to important problems and issues that is bad for both fields.

It is necessary to begin by characterizing the goals that inform the content and methods of bioethics and of literature. After that characterization we shall look at three common topics—the right to refuse medical treatment, euthanasia, and allocation of scarce resources. For each topic, we will compare a well-known and frequently taught work of literature with a typical case study summarized and discussed in *Cases in Bioethics* published by The Hastings Center.[2] By examining the differences between these two kinds of materials, we hope to demonstrate the shortcomings and strengths of each.

Goals and Methods

Both bioethics and literature are more than subject fields; each field involves a methodology as well. Each stipulates *what* counts as a significant problem for the discipline and *how* one looks for a solution. An understanding of the ways in which these fields may augment or conflict with each other must begin with an appreciation of these differences.

The subject matter of bioethics is both contemporary and historically grounded. Although modern medical care is a primary focus of attention, bioethicists raise questions that have long been of concern to moral philosophers. What kinds of actions are morally correct? What kinds of character are morally praiseworthy? What states of affairs are most worthwhile?[3] In addition to such obviously important substantive questions, bioethics typically involves a particular methodology, determined to some extent by the goals of those who teach and practice it. In their report *The Teaching of Bioethics,* several well-known philosophers and theologians listed three major goals for teachers in the field.[4]

The first is to help students *identify moral issues* in biomedical contexts. This begins with the requirement that one learn to distinguish normative or value questions from other kinds of questions, such as scientific or technical ones. More difficult, one must also learn to distinguish kinds of evaluative questions, separating those involving moral values from those involving non-moral (e.g., religious, legal, or aesthetic) values. Sensitivity to and recognition of moral aspects of situations is a starting point for any study of ethics.

A second goal is to *develop strategies for analyzing moral problems* one confronts. To analyze something is to take it apart and to examine or investigate the parts critically. The parts that are of special interest to the bioethicist are those relevant to justify a decision about moral questions: for example, how one should act, how one should advise another about how to act, or how one should judge actions or persons. One must come to understand the relationships between various systems of moral principles and rules and between virtues, rights, duties, and interests. Furthermore, one must be adept at discovering, criticizing, and making moral argument, at identifying assumptions, at defining key terms. In discussing such skills, K. Danner Clouser writes:

> The main skill is that of reasoning—of self-consciously working toward clarity and precision in thinking, and toward exactness of articulation. . . . One becomes sensitized to precision, to possible ambiguities, to the structure of the argument supporting any claim, to finding the weaknesses of and counterexamples to any argument presented.[5]

Students who become adept at philosophical analysis learn intellectual skills that are relevant to critical thought in any field.

The third aim of those who teach bioethics is to train people to *apply moral values and analytic skills to actual clinical decisions.* The ultimate goal is not abstract but practical, and this feature colors the entire enterprise. Success in learning bioethics is marked by greater ability to reach morally good decisions in clinical practice.

Achieving each of these goals requires the teacher to turn to case studies. Moral sensitivity—the ability to identify moral issues—is best learned by examining clear examples and then moving to more subtle problems. Attention to language and argument—skills in analysis of moral problems—is learned through reflection on issues embedded in case studies. Finally, proficiency in practical reasoning can only be learned by practice in real or hypothetical situations.

Bioethics in its predominant Anglo-American form is a reductive discipline. Its aim is to analyze problems, to break them down into component terms, values, and structures of principles. The bioethicist in this regard is like the medical clinician. Indeed, one sometimes hears of a bioethics "workup" or a bioethics "consult" in which variables are isolated for consideration before being reconstituted into arguments about how to manage a given case.[6] Extraneous elements of the case that should not influence the argument or decision are usually isolated, ignored, or removed. Ambiguity is resolved or controlled as much as possible, by collecting all relevant facts, defining important terms, making premises explicit, and proceeding in the analysis carefully, step by step. The outcome should be a reasoned argument about one or more courses of action and their relative moral preferability.

The concern with cases, though hardly unique to bioethics, is characteristic of it. In the academic classroom, abstracts of actual or hypothetical cases are commonplace. It is difficult to find a bioethics textbook that isn't heavily infused with case descriptions. In fact, textbooks are sometimes wholly organized around cases and discussions of them. For those teaching in clinical settings, appropriate cases arise regularly, but even in these situations other case descriptions are introduced to provide counterexamples of the sort Clouser mentions. Moreover, cases are seldom classic for very long; instead, the rapidly changing conditions of medical practice dictate a continual attention to problems as embodied in new and different case examples.

One other striking characteristic of bioethics teaching in classrooms or on hospital floors is the frequency with which the facts of a case under discussion may be altered in order to further discussion. Asking "What if . . ." is a way to focus on crucial concepts, values, and arguments. In teaching moral sensitivity and moral analysis, problem cases are examples to be altered to make points clear. (Even during deliberation about real clinical cases, the introduction of hypotheticals is often pedagogically valuable, though not always welcomed by those pressured to make decisions.) The problem case, although instrumentally central for achieving the goals of bioethics, often has little intrinsic importance and can be changed at will to promote discussion.

The field of literature and medicine as an academic offering in health care education is newer than bioethics, and its goals and methods are less well articulated.[7] Attempts to specify goals are further complicated by confusions among literature itself, literary criticism, and literature as taught in medical contexts. Like moral philosophy, however, literature and its study have a venerable history, so it is possible to suggest at least some comparisons and contrasts with the model of bioethics sketched above. The contrasts, to us, outnumber and outweigh the similarities.

First, literature begins with *entertainment and aesthetic pleasure*—with the emotional and experiential rather than the objective or the reasonal. An author wants to captivate his or her audience, and those who criticize or teach literature are the author's allies in the process, trying to reveal the full power of the poetry or prose. One may analyze the component parts of literary texts, to show how the elements work to achieve the effects of the whole, but the analysis is always a parallel, never a substitute construction of the work and is meant to serve the work itself rather than some principle embodied therein.[8]

Several corollaries follow from this first goal. First, there is an integrity to a work of literature. One cannot in good conscience change the characters or plot at will to suggest variant outcomes or moral points; the story or poem is as it stands. Second, good criticism or teaching in literature should return the student to the work itself, rather than illustrate abstract principles. Third, classic examples in literature lose their power much more slowly than cases in bioethics. Even works that are centuries old may entertain or edify audiences in various ways. Illumination or edification, however, is seldom charged with the need to make practical decisions. Even when a reader feels that something has been learned from a story or poem, learning generally remains subservient to the particular work in which this or that message about the human condition has been framed.

Another goal of literature conjoined with medicine and health care is to *promote sensitivity and empathy.*[9] Reading literature is often an important form of vicarious experience, and those who have never experienced most health events may gain by walking imaginatively in the shoes of others who have. It is not just aesthetic experience that the teacher of literature wishes to encourage, but human experience of illness and treatment.

A variant of the second goal is to *show how literary artists have approached events or experiences,* even if imperfectly. This explains in part why lesser works, so to speak, are often taught in medical settings. If there is only one work of literature about kidney dialysis or the lives of residents or whatever, that work—even if flawed—may be taught as a way of showing rudimentary elements of literary treatment. The goal here is simply to demonstrate what a medical event might look like from a literary point of view and to show how literary techniques work. This goal is not perfectly compatible with the first goal, since the work of literature here is being stretched beyond its value as aesthetic entertainment to achieve both an intrinsic methodological end and an instrumental substantive end.

A final goal of literature generally and of literature and medicine in particular is to *display ambiguity.* Ambiguity is the coin of the realm in many literary texts. The wealth of connotation and the indeterminancy of expression are celebrated features of language and ideation, not obfuscatory and obstructive barriers in the search for meaning (as they might be to ethicists). Motive and character are equally ambiguous in many works of literature, so that reasons for actions are often difficult to abstract. Attention to language in literature amounts to a process of specifying the range of possible meanings (and thus the ruling out of some possible interpretations of the text) but seldom settles on a single definitive meaning. The power of literary accounts of human behavior often resides in the multiple referents and allusions that a given text may suggest. When one speaks of "layers of meaning," the metaphor does not mean to imply that the bottom layer is the true meaning, but rather that all layers offer potentially valid approaches to the work.

Similarly, literature tends to elaborate, not to pare down and simplify, the human problems it treats. An author and his or her appreciative readers can adopt a much wider definition of what elements are central or extraneous to the subject than can a bioethicist. Embellishment is allowed, even expected. On many occasions, the literary treatment of an old theme is the raison d'être of the work, so much so that a simple plot summary not only fails to do justice to the story or poem but misses the point altogether because it does not account for style and form, nuance and detail. Also, allusion to more than is stated is common practice in literature. Many a literary "case" refuses to stay within apprehendible boundaries, so that any reduction of the work to particular characters or events portrayed may be another kind of narrowing of literature's total range of impact.

Both literature and bioethics, then, offer case studies and require careful strategies of analysis for these case studies to be relevant to medical and moral problems. The use of literary works in the service of bioethics is common practice, despite the fact that the two disciplines diverge in many of their goals and intellectual styles. A comparison of frequently used pieces of literature with typical case studies will demonstrate both the differences of the two fields and the benefits and costs of this union.

Problem One: Refusing Treatment or the Recalcitrant Patient

One issue often explored in medical care is the right of the patient to refuse treatment that objectively seems in the patient's best interest. Issues of autonomy and beneficence frequently come into conflict in health care, and the limits to and justifications for paternalism are a common theme in bioethics.

The short story "The Use of Force" by William Carlos Williams has perhaps the best credentials for being dubbed *the* paradigmatic example of literature and bioethics in a close marriage. The story is anthologized in the two major collections in the field of literature and medicine.[10] It is one of the most frequently taught core texts by those in the field of literature and medicine[11] and has made its way into the ethics curriculum at several medical schools.[12] And its attractiveness is enhanced by the fact that the author was also a doctor. But most important, the story is a clear and poignant example of important ethical issues becoming the occasion for a literary work. While other texts refer to or touch upon bioethics or at least serve as departure points for ethical extrapolation, Williams's story would not exist at all without the conflicts it explores: paternalism versus patient's rights; irrationality and sexuality in the physician-patient relationship; and the status, power, reverence, and fear accorded medical professionals.

The central issue in "The Use of Force" is medical paternalism. A young girl has had a fever for three days. Her parents have finally called the doctor, who has never previously seen any of the family members as patients. The doctor feels duty-bound to examine the girl to rule out diphtheria, which would be dangerous both to her and to the community, and he goes about his work in his "best professional manner" to establish some rapport and examine the girl's throat.[13] But the encounter almost immediately goes sour, especially since the girl silently but adamantly refuses to allow her throat to be examined. At one approach she strikes the physician, knocking off his glasses. Other efforts by both parents and physician to force the girl to open her mouth are equally unsuccessful. "In a final unreasoning assault" ("UF," 60) the throat is exposed by the doctor and the dangerous diphtherial membrane discovered.

The important thing about the paternalism in Williams's story is that it is *not* the ultimate motive for the physician's actions, nor are any of the other social or professional duties that might apply to the situation. Moreover, there is no thorough investigation of alternative courses of action, for example, treating the child as if she had diphtheria, thereby obviating the need for the confirmatory throat examination. Still, some ethical reasoning is made explicit, although it is immediately subordinated to another set of issues:

> The damned little brat must be protected against her own idiocy, one says to one's self at such times. Others must be protected against her. It is social necessity. And all these things are true. But a blind fury, a feeling of adult shame, bred of a longing for muscular release are the operatives. One goes on to the end.
>
> ("UF," 59-60)

The feeling and tone of this passage have been carefully prepared by the doctor-narrator's earlier comments about the girl. When he first saw her he found her "unusually attractive" with "magnificent blonde hair, in profusion" ("UF," 56). Later and still more explicitly, the narrator admits he "had already fallen in love with the savage brat" ("UF," 58). These emotions are totally bound up with the physician's anger and frustration, so much so that when he reports, "I tried to hold myself down but I couldn't" ("UF," 59), the meaning is decidedly ambiguous. It is because of these complicated emotions that the final "assault" carries sexual connotations resembling rape, rather than the beneficent motives that require overruling a patient's wishes for the patient's own good.

The context of the encounter in "The Use of Force" deserves a brief additional analysis. The patients are new to the physician. The parents of the girl, particularly the mother, appear ineffectual and even annoying to the physician. The parents' comments—"He won't hurt you" or "If you don't do what the doctor says you'll have to go to the hospital" or "The nice man . . ." ("UF," 57, 58)—become complicating factors, since these comments increase his scorn for the mother and father and his admiration for the attractive girl and her determined resistance. All of this contextual background serves only to highlight behavior by the doctor that is ultimately irrational.[14]

In short, Williams is displaying, or rather illuminating, a situation in which ethical considerations are subordinated to other human factors. Paternalism or refusals of treatment are bound to become muddy issues under such circumstances, the story suggests. No amount of logical analysis can make it otherwise. This is the way paternalism feels in the real world.

But is this an adequate account of paternalism and related issues in bioethics? A case study subtitled "Eavesdropping on a Medical Assault" offers useful comparisons:

> Recently a middle-class suburban housewife accompanied a friend who had broken her ankle in a fall to the emergency room of their local hospital. In the patient area next to them, separated by a curtain, was a teen-age boy in football uniform. The nurse who took

> information about the friend's accident told them the boy had suffered a shoulder separation in practice.
>
> A doctor and nurse were with the boy, who began to scream, "No! No! Stop! Can't you put me out?" Apparently they were attempting to set his shoulder. The remaining curtains around the boy were quickly pulled. The woman heard no response to the boy's question, only more screams of pain. Someone said, "Give him Demerol." The boy said again, "Can't you put me all the way out?" and several times again shouted "No, No!"
>
> After the medical personnel left him the woman could hear him quietly crying. The friend asked him (through the curtain) how old he was. He said, "Sixteen." She asked, "Is no one with you?" He said, "No, no one was home." The woman asked if someone was trying to reach his parents. He said yes. She called his phone number from the phone in the waiting room but there was no answer.
>
> She then told the boy that he could sue for assault if he was treated without his permission, that perhaps they had needed to move his arm while he was awake to be sure they got it in the right place, but in any case they should have explained what they were doing and have obtained his permission.
>
> Soon a nurse took him away. While the woman waited for the results of her friend's x-rays, she saw the boy's football coaches in the lobby. She overheard one say, "He didn't take it very well, did he?" Shortly after the boy's mother arrived.
>
> A day later the woman wondered to herself: "Did I have a responsibility to do something more, or should I have avoided meddling—and, do I still have some moral responsibility to act—to talk to his parents or to attempt to get the hospital administration to investigate emergency room procedures?"[15]

Like the situation in the Williams story, this case involves a minor, although a more mature one than Williams's girl. There is resistance to medical treatment, which is ultimately forced on the patient in a less than gentle manner. There are even some unusual literary touches in the way the case is written—in the dramatic presentation of the boy's screams, for example, or perhaps in the remarks of the football coach, with their implication regarding machismo.

More important are the differences between this "medical assault" and that presented by Williams. For one thing, the motives of the health personnel are not explored. For another, the case lacks the human details crucial to literature: the appearance of the characters; the look and feel of the emergency room setting; a fuller account of the thoughts and feelings of the women bystanders, which are implied to be pity, shock, or concern, but which are not adequately described.

Most important from a bioethical point of view, the case has as its raison d'être the crucial question: when does one have a moral duty or responsibility to intervene? In fact, precisely to focus the analysis, the reader is prompted with a particular question in the last sentence of the case.

The individuals who comment on this case exercise the skills typical to bioethics.[16] Each addresses the question: "What should the bystander do?" To answer that question, each develops an explicit argument to justify the recommended course of action. Each uses analogies, hypothetical situations arguably comparable, to isolate principles—"Suppose . . ." or "If the facts were different . . ." Conceptual analysis is central to the discussion of each. The commentators explore the related concepts of *duty, obligation,* and *responsibility.* Each addresses the difference between someone being free from the obligation to do something and yet feeling that it is morally proper to do it. Rather than being enticed by the ambiguities of the case, the reader is *warned* to be wary of them and counseled to search for determinative information. Did the boy or his parents consent to the treatment or is consent implied by the emergency situation? Not far in the background are questions regarding the constraints of social institutions—the law regarding battery or a relevant hospital policy. Finally, the reader is exhorted to do two things central to ethical decision making: get accurate information and generate good reasons for action.

The commentators' analyses focus attention on the complexity of ethical language and argument. However, breaking down the case into components with a careful refinement of concepts and reasons somehow leaves the boy, his coaches, his caregivers, and the two witnesses behind.

Problem Two: Active Euthanasia

Richard Selzer's "Mercy" is a short but powerful reflection on the subject of active euthanasia and has been used in some bioethics curricula under that rubric. A man who has suffered from pancreatic cancer for several years is in the final stages of his illness. The man has wasted down to eighty pounds and suffers from uncontrollable pain despite large doses of morphine. The wife and the mother of the man beg the physician to end the suffering, to give a lethal dose of narcotic—which he attempts to do. But although the man's respirations slow and his pulse weakens, the three syringes of morphine that should have killed him fail to do so. As the physician watches at the bedside, realizing that death will not occur, he briefly considers strangling the patient, in fact even places his fingers on the man's windpipe. But he cannot bring himself to continue, and he leaves the room, shaken, to tell the two relatives.

This paraphrase captures the plot of Selzer's piece and might easily be rewritten or used as a case study in bioethics. But any paraphrase robs literary prose of some of its power. The active euthanasia in the story is only, as it were, the occasion to explore other literary concerns: the observation of individuals and events during the process of dying; the description of things medical and human, with both factual and metaphorical accuracy; the recreation of emotions, of passing thoughts and passing time, and of visceral sensations over and above objective reasoning. Consider, for example, the following excerpts:

> The face of the old woman is hoof-beaten with intersecting curves of loose skin. Her hair is donkey brown, donkey grey.
>
> . . . . .
>
> How reduced he is, a folded parcel, something chipped away until only its shape and a little breath are left. His impatient bones gleam as though to burst through the papery skin.
>
> . . . . .
>
> It would be so easy to do it. Three minutes of pressure on the larynx. He is still not conscious, wouldn't feel it, wouldn't know. My thumb and fingertips hover, land on his windpipe. My pulse is beating in his neck, his in mine. I look back over my shoulder. No one. Two bare IV poles in a corner, their looped metal eyes witnessing. Do it! Fingers press. Again he swallows. Look back again. How closed the door is.[17]

In many ways such passages are as much the heart of the story as the plot, and they enhance the decisional considerations surrounding the man in the bed with observation, description, and emotion that are extraneous to the issue of active euthanasia as it is usually formulated. In fact, such literary devices as metaphor or short rhythmic clauses are the very things that would be left out of a protocol presenting the bioethical aspects of this case. And they would be left out for good reason, since their rhetorical power tends to color or cloud a reasoned account of what one should do.

Other issues are clouded in "Mercy" that would need to be clarified and separately analyzed in a serious ethical discussion of active euthanasia. The most notable issue is that of consent. Selzer presents a consultation of the doctor with the wife and mother, but in very abbreviated terms.

> "Please," begs his wife, "we cannot go on like this."
>
> "Do it," says the old woman, his mother. "Do it now."
>
> "To give him any more would kill him," I tell her.
>
> "Then do it," she says.
>
> ("M," 72)

Many questions might be raised about this brief discussion. Why does the mother have stronger status as surrogate decision maker for the patient than the patient's wife? Is the mother's decision consonant with what the patient would want if he were competent? Does she have some sort of advance directive from him? The physician later tells the patient, "'I can get rid of the pain,'" and holds up the syringes, to which the man gasps "'Yes'" ("M," 72). Is that adequate consent, since death was not mentioned? Was the man misled? Or has his intense pain rendered him incompetent? Euthanasia is too weighty an issue to leave such matters ambiguous—which is precisely and perhaps intentionally what Selzer has done.

The very title of the piece would bother many bioethicists, since *mercy killing* is not a term they prefer to apply to the issue of euthanasia. Selzer, however, may want to explore the nature of mercy and the nature of killing, to show how intense a situation can be for the person asked to assist in a death. Consider the closing lines:

> In the corridor the women lean against the wall, against each other. They are like a band of angels dispatched here to take possession of his body. It is the only thing that will satisfy them.
>
> "He didn't die," I say. "He won't . . . or can't." They are silent.
>
> "He isn't ready yet," I say.
>
> "He *is* ready," the old woman says. "*You* ain't."
>
> ("M," 74)

For Selzer, this exchange rounds out the description of the physician's agonizing. The old woman recognizes the shock that the physician has earlier seen in his own face in a mirror. While this dramatic point might have ramifications for an ethical discussion of active euthanasia, its literary purpose is not aimed primarily in that direction. Rather, the last line clinches the story even as it chastens the doctor. Analysis of its other meanings must be superadded.

In sum, Selzer's account of active euthanasia achieves both more and less than a bioethical approach to the issue. "Mercy" might complement but could never substitute for a close philosophical analysis of the relevant considerations. Like the Williams story, there is too much context, too much ambiguity, too much personality, and too much literary style injected into the account to facilitate adequate isolation of values or principles, decisional strategies, and other elements crucial to classical bioethics.

By contrast, a case study that offers the possibility of active euthanasia, together with two bioethics commentaries, involves just such isolation of the morally relevant considerations. Of course there are actors or "characters" involved, but their presence in the case is radically different from the presence of characters in Selzer's work:

> Andrea was a nine-year-old girl who had been diagnosed as having cystic fibrosis at the age of thirteen months. Since then she had been hospitalized twelve times, eight times during the last year.
>
> When admitted for the last time she was already receiving an experimental antibiotic, which was being administered in an attempt to control a resistant pneumonia superimposed on severely damaged lungs, a result of her underlying disease. She was at that time a severely ill, emaciated child with moderately labored breathing. She seemed to have no interest in her environment and refused to communicate with anyone but her mother.

> Because of the severity of the child's illness and because the parents had accurately perceived that the experimental antibiotic was a "last ditch" attempt to control her pulmonary infection, the physicians discussed with the parents their perception of "extreme medical measure" and the significance of a "No Code" order. The parents indicated that in the event of a cardiac or respiratory arrest, they did not want their child to be resuscitated and the appropriate "No Code" order was written. The child was not involved in these conversations or subsequent decision making, nor had the mother previously been able to answer her daughter's questions about death and dying.
>
> As the child's condition continued to decline, the parents asked how much longer she would live and how she would die. At one point the father said: "Watching your own child die is worse than dying yourself." This comment led to a discussion of active euthanasia utilizing intravenous potassium chloride or a similar drug. The physicians pointed out that no matter how hopeless a situation or the amount of suffering that the patient and family were enduring, the law prohibits the active taking of a patient's life. They refused to consider this option.
>
> The following day Andrea's heart began to fail. Her condition became progressively worse, and she died approximately 48 hours later. During these last two days her parents were appalled by her grotesque appearance, with "eyes bulged out like a frog," and were in great despair because of her steadily deteriorating condition. They felt helpless and impotent to alleviate their daughter's distress. Medical treatment was continued to the end, and no measures were taken to hasten Andrea's death.
>
> Approximately two months after her death, the mother was asked if she would still have given permission for active euthanasia if she had been offered that option. She replied, "Yes."
>
> Should active euthanasia be permitted to spare the patient and family from suffering when death is inevitable?[18]

Again the situations in the story and the case are similar: both patients are terminal; their process of dying is disfiguring to themselves and emotionally wrenching to their loved ones; and active euthanasia is favored by family members but ultimately is not performed. Again the case contains a few details that seem like literary features: the father's comment, for example, or the description of the girl's eyes. And both story and case present the problem of drawing distinctions between morally permissible actions in the face of impending death—although the case never approaches so vivid a possibility as strangulation.

Interestingly, the commentaries on the case do discuss motive. One accuses physicians of being inconsistent in their motives when they agree to "No Code" orders but reject active euthanasia. The other accuses Andrea's parents of desiring euthanasia more to assuage their own suffering than for hers. But even this attention to motive is distinctively bioethical rather than literary; that is, the argument about the morality of euthanasia turns on careful distinctions that have been teased out of the case description and analyzed in isolation. There is nothing comparable to Selzer's account of being alone in the room with the patient. Indeed, in the case study the physicians' motives for refusing euthanasia are literarily and morally bland; they don't want to break the law. Key bioethical concepts like competence and consent or actions and omissions become part of the analysis, and alternative scenarios and analogical reasoning are used to get down to the bedrock of moral issues. The ethicists, unlike the author, must be concerned with principles that can be generalized; thus, attention is paid to social policy and to the possibility of abuse. How will the reasons for a decision in this case apply in similar cases? This question, central in principled decision making, is of little relevance to the storyteller. Finally, analysis ultimately leaves the particular "characters" behind in ways that "Mercy" does not, a process that helps to clarify an emotionally charged issue by taking out much of the emotional charge, a charge that is crucial to works of literature.

Problem Three: Allocation of Scarce Resources

So far, literary accounts of bioethical conflict appear to be rich in descriptive and evocative power, complex in personal and contextual issues, but incomplete in analytical or decisional components. What happens when one moves away from the fairly explicit literary treatment of ethics to more abstract comparative texts? A good example is provided by Shirley Jackson's eerie and powerful short story **"The Lottery."**[19]

Although written in simple prose about ordinary people, **"The Lottery"** partakes of science fiction. A small town population meets on a June day every year to engage in a ritual lottery, the origins of which are long forgotten. The task of the lottery is to choose which family will have to sacrifice a member and then which member will be stoned. Some have argued that the lottery should be abandoned, but traditionalists insist that there has always been a lottery, that every townsperson takes the same risk, and that the sentence of such fair procedure must be carried out on the unlucky victim.

As in the previous examples, the bare bones of the plot do not do justice to the story's full details and complexity. The author's genius is in the way this plot is gradually, casually revealed. The folksy tone of the proceedings runs counter to the dark progress toward its outcome:

> "Well, now," Mr. Summers said soberly, "guess we better get started, get this over with, so's we can go back to work. Anybody ain't here?"
>
> "Dunbar," several people said. "Dunbar, Dunbar."
>
> Mr. Summers consulted his list. "Clyde Dunbar," he said. "That's right. He's broke his leg, hasn't he? Who's drawing for him?"

"Me, I guess," a woman said, and Mr. Summers turned to look at her. "Wife draws for her husband," Mr. Summers said. "Don't you have a grown boy to do it for you, Janey?"[20]

Against this dialogue is the information that has been casually provided about the components of the ritual: the collection of a pile of stones; the black box from which chances will be drawn; and the small stool on which the victim will be expected to sit. It is only when Bill Hutchinson selects the fatal slip of paper, meaning that someone in his family must die, that his wife Tessie objects. Her complaints, while rejected by the townspeople, express a horror and dread that the reader has already begun to feel but which few of the townspeople seem to share:

People began to look around to see the Hutchinsons. Bill Hutchinson was standing quiet, staring down at the paper in his hand. Suddenly, Tessie Hutchinson shouted to Mr. Summers, "You didn't give him time enough to take any paper he wanted. I saw you. It wasn't fair!"

"Be a good sport, Tessie," Mrs. Delacroix called, and Mrs. Graves said, "All of us took the same chance."

(**"The Lottery,"** 168)

But she continues to protest as the members of her family draw from another group of paper slips to complete the lottery. The final lines of the story finally give full rein to the horror that has been building all along:

Tessie Hutchinson was in the center of a cleared space by now, and she held her hands out desperately as the villagers moved in on her. "It isn't fair," she said. A stone hit her on the side of the head.

Old Man Warner was saying, "Come on, come on, everyone." Steve Adams was in the front of the crowd of villagers, with Mrs. Graves beside him.

"It isn't fair, it isn't right," Mrs. Hutchinson screamed, and then they were upon her.

(**"The Lottery,"** 171)

In a way, the reader of the story has been sucked into its stream of events and carried along with the flow. One has read about Steve Adams or Mr. Summers or Old Man Warner as if having met them, people like oneself; thus, one cannot distance oneself from the stoning or say, "I would not have participated." It is this cleverness in the story's construction that counts for much of its power and emotional, if uncomfortable, verisimilitude.[21]

Many bioethicists would object to **"The Lottery"** being included in a discussion of the allocation of scarce medical resources. As logicians they might insist that the analogy of the village to a community of patients is inapt, because the resource being distributed harms one to the benefit of others, rather than benefitting one to the harm of others, as would be the case in allocating dialysis machines or Intensive Care Unit (ICU) beds or any scarce medical resource. Aptness also fails in the kinds of death that ensue in the story and in medical modes of random selection, which are more akin to what has been called *passive euthanasia* than to the active stoning of someone. Finally, the typically life-and-death choice among patients wanting a scarce resource cannot aptly be compared to the circumstances in Jackson's village, where the reasons for the whole ritual have been forgotten. One should make such agonizing choices only when forced to do so, not casually or for tradition's sake. **"The Lottery"** might be a parable that symbolically depicts the tendency of human society to require scapegoats or the capacity of ordinary citizens for evil, but such a general moral message is not what bioethicists are after when they discuss allocation of scarce resources.

Decisions regarding the allocation of social benefits and burdens (including scarce medical resources) occur on at least two levels. First, there is the question of selecting a policy concerning how to allocate something. In Jackson's story the community uses a lottery. Second, there is an issue of the fairness in the application of that standard. Did Bill Hutchinson in the story have time to pick the paper he wanted? "The Last Bed in the ICU" raises these issues in a health care setting:

At the age of seventy, Mrs. A has been admitted to the hospital for the fifth time in as many years for treatment of respiratory difficulty. The last time she was in the hospital she had nearly died. She has severe emphysema, and when she developed a cold, her deterioration was so rapid that only artificial respiration in the emergency room saved her life. However, it proved very difficult to wean her from the respirator. She spent four weeks in the Intensive Care Unit and required constant care from the medical staff, principally Intern B. After she was discharged, she remained short of breath even while watching television.

Now, five months later, she has contracted another cold, but this time Intern B has managed to treat her without resorting to the ICU and the respirator. During her illnesses, Mrs. A's two sons have been in constant contact with the medical staff. They have been anxious, agitated, and demanding.

It is now 2 a.m. and Intern B is again called to see Mrs. A, who is becoming increasingly lethargic. It is obvious that she is in respiratory failure, and will probably die before morning if she is not given a respirator.

However, hospital policy requires that respirators be used only in the ICU, where the required supporting staff and facilities are available. There is only one bed open in the ICU. The residents like to save one bed for an emergency. As Intern B approaches, Mrs. A's sons are waiting. He knows their questions: What's wrong now? What will you do?

What should the intern do? And on what basis should he make his decision?[22]

Each of the commentators on this case, responding to their assigned questions, challenges the propriety of the hospital's and resident's allocation policies: for the former, respirators only in the ICU; for the latter, the saving of one bed for emergencies. Questions of efficiency and justice are isolated and discussed. In Jackson's story the necessity of someone's death is a given. The appropriateness of the lottery as a means of choosing the victim is a given. To challenge the starting points of village policy would be to leave Jackson's story behind. Yet for the bioethicist, questioning givens—whether facts or values or policies—is central.

Each commentator on the case addresses the application of the policy to Mrs. A, noting that pertinent facts are missing. Is Mrs. A in the process of dying, or is she medically "salvageable"? Would her life be usefully prolonged by a respirator, or would her quality of life subsequently prove to be not worth the effort? Are the solicitous attentions of her family relevant or irrelevant? But of course, to read these facts one way or the other is immediately to enter the realm of value judgments.

Ethical analyses of the case also look at the rights and interests of the various parties in the situation: the hospital; the residents; Intern B; Mrs. A herself; and the two sons. Whose claims have priority, based upon what persuasive ethical norms—autonomy, social utility, institutional efficiency?[23]

Each commentator notes and uses the distinction between the question regarding who should decide and the question regarding what the decision should be. Consistent with frequent practice, each addresses the former question rather than go out on any limbs to answer the latter. One commentator argues that the question could be reduced to one of "medical eligibility" and thus leaves the decision to "the responsible physician's judgment. . . ."[24] (One wonders how to read "responsible physician" here.) The other commentator opts for the preeminence of autonomy and leaves the decision up to Mrs. A. Each reaches his position after teasing out the value elements in apparently medical decisions. Each relies extensively on hypothetical cases and counterfactual suppositions. Each addresses questions of rational decision making.

As careful and as useful as such analysis may be, it is radically different from the dark vision of allocation portrayed in **"The Lottery."** Instead of rational decision making, Jackson presents the irrational and unquestioning side of human society. Instead of concepts and policies, she calls attention to the voices of the participants in an allocative ritual. And instead of freeing readers to consider alternatives, she traps them into an inevitable horror. It is, as they say, the stuff of fiction.

Conclusion

It should be obvious that literature can be fruitfully used to raise questions of bioethics. There are, however, dangers in doing so. The comparison of selected cases provides the opportunity to reiterate tensions noted above in the juxtapositions of differing goals and styles.

First, the use of literature may frustrate the teaching of bioethics. The richness of literary portrayals of normative situations often threatens to capture the reader and impede clear and careful reflection. To over-simplify, good literature biases; good ethics should be unbiased.

Second, use of literature in teaching bioethics is likely to miss or undervalue the intellectual and personal virtues to be gained from the study of literature for its own sake. There is a not-so-subtle pressure in the medical humanities to make the material practical to health professionals. For bioethics, this pressure manifests itself in impatience with abstraction or with analysis of principles not tied to specific cases. For literature the pressure works in two ways. On the one hand, there is a presupposition that literature is *inherently* impractical and is to be valued or ignored for that reason. On the other hand, there is a willingness to bend aesthetics toward practical matters, if not always by teachers of literature, then by their professional and preprofessional audiences in health care settings. The pressure is unlikely to disappear; only awareness of its presence will keep teachers of literature or bioethics from bending too far.

The most useful thing about literature as an approach to bioethics is that the richness of literary portrayals keeps ethics from being merely about concepts or arguments. Applied ethics, in medicine or any other field, is about real people with characters, in contexts, during real time. Case studies miss this; hypotheticals destroy it. As long as the tension in goals and styles is understood, an alliance of literature and bioethics need not be misguided. Instead, such an alliance offers a fuller, more complex understanding of the human condition.

Notes

1. For suggestive comments about the value of literature in the realm of ethical discussion, see E. D. Pellegrino, "To Look Feelingly—the Affinities of Medicine and Literature," Robert Coles, "Why Novels and Poems in Our Medical Schools?," and Larry R. Churchill, "Why Literature and Medicine?," all in *Literature and Medicine* 1 (1982): 18-22, 32-33, 34-35.
2. Carol Levine and Robert M. Veatch, eds., *Cases in Bioethics from "The Hastings Center Report"* (Hastings-on-Hudson, N.Y.: Hastings Center, 1982.)
3. See Robert M. Veatch et al., *The Teaching of Bioethics: Report of the Commission on the Teaching of Bioethics* (Hastings-on-Hudson, N.Y.: Institute of Society, Ethics and the Life Sciences, 1976), 3.
4. Ibid., 6-8. A fourth goal, replication of bioethicists, is not pertinent to the present discussion.
5. K. Danner Clouser, "Philosophy and Medical Education," in *The Role of the Humanities in Medical Education,* ed. Donnie J. Self (Norfolk, Virginia: Teagle & Little, 1978), 27.
6. On the concept of the ethical workup, see David C. Thomasma, "Training in Medical Ethics: An Ethical Workup," *Forum on Medicine* 1 (December 1978): 33-36.

7. Some scholars argue that literature and medicine is only a "protofield" until its theory is more firmly established: "What is lacking in the 'field'—and in a theory of the field—is interactivity, some demonstration of the inextricable nature of the alliance between literature and medicine that will assert its inevitability and value as an intellectual as well as a pedagogical enterprise." Kathryn Montgomery Hunter, "Literature and Medicine: Standards for Applied Literature," in *Applying the Humanities,* ed. Daniel Callahan, Arthur L. Caplan, and Bruce Jennings (New York: Plenum Press, 1985), 290. Others such as G. S. Rousseau believe that there is not any theory separable from practice at this stage in the development of the field; see G. S. Rousseau, "Literature and Medicine: Toward a Simultaneity of Theory and Practice," *Literature and Medicine* 5 (1986): 152-81.
8. Pellegrino describes "the most important service literature performs" for the physician as follows: "It takes him from the grinding reality of the clinic into realms of imagination, lyricism and drama; it provides those moments of delectation without which the soul shrivels." Pellegrino, 21.
9. For a more complete discussion of this goal, see Pellegrino, 19.
10. See Joseph Ceccio, ed., *Medicine in Literature* (New York: Longman, 1978); and Norman Cousins, ed., *The Physician in Literature* (Philadelphia: Saunders, 1982).
11. Joanne Trautmann Banks, "Core Texts in Literature and Medicine," presentation at the annual meeting of the Society for Health and Human Values, Washington, D.C., October 26, 1985.
12. See Harold Y. Vanderpool et al., *The Values and Ethics of Medicine: Course Syllabus, 1985-1986* (Galveston, Texas: Institute for the Medical Humanities, 1985); Larry Churchill et al., "Social and Cultural Issues in Medical Practice" (syllabus) (Chapel Hill: University of North Carolina Medical School, 1985-1986).
13. William Carlos Williams, "The Use of Force," in *The Doctor Stories,* comp. Robert Coles (New York: New Directions, 1984), 57. All subsequent quotations are from this edition and are cited parenthetically in the text as "UF," followed by the page number.
14. For other interpretations of the Williams story, see Barbara Currier Bell, "Williams' 'The Use of Force' and First Principles in Medical Ethics," *Literature and Medicine* 3 (1984): 143-51; and David B. Morris, "Williams's Force," *Literature and Medicine* 5 (1986): 122-40, both of which cite additional analyses. Neither Bell nor Morris pays sufficient attention to contextual issues of the physician-patient encounter in the story.
15. "Eavesdropping on a Medical Assault," in *Cases in Bioethics from "The Hastings Center Report,"* ed. Carol Levine and Robert M. Veatch (Hastings-on-Hudson, N.Y.: Hastings Center, 1982), 26. Reproduced by permission. Copyright © The Hastings Center.
16. James Smith, "Commentary," and Michael D. Bayles, "Commentary," on "Eavesdropping on a Medical Assault," in Levine and Veatch, 26-27.
17. Richard Selzer, "Mercy," from *Letters to a Young Doctor* (New York: Simon & Schuster, 1982), 72, 73, 74. All subsequent quotations are from this edition and are cited parenthetically in the text as "M," followed by the page number.
18. Hunter C. Leake, III, "Active Euthanasia with Parental Consent," in *Cases in Bioethics from "The Hastings Center Report,"* ed. Carol Levine and Robert M. Veatch (Hastings-on-Hudson, N.Y.: Hastings Center, 1982), 48. Reproduced by permission. Copyright © The Hastings Center.
19. The story originally appeared in *The New Yorker* on June 26, 1948, where it generated more letters from readers than anything published in the magazine to that time. It has been extensively anthologized for introductory courses in literature at the secondary school and college levels. See Peter M. Gareffa, "Shirley Jackson," in *Contemporary Authors,* Vol. 4, New Revision Series, ed. Ann Evory (Detroit: Gale Research, 1981), 321-22; and Terry Heller, "Shirley Jackson," in *Critical Survey of Short Fiction,* Vol. 5, ed. Frank N. Magill (Englewood Cliffs, N.J.: Salem Press, 1981), 1668-74.
20. Shirley Jackson, "The Lottery," in *55 Short Stories from the New Yorker* (New York: Simon & Schuster, 1949), 166. All subsequent quotations are from this edition and are cited parenthetically in the text as "L," followed by the page number.
21. For interpretations of the story, see Cleanth Brooks and Robert Penn Warren, *Understanding Fiction,* 2d ed. (New York: Appleton-Century-Crofts, 1959), 72-76; and Helen E. Nebeker, "'The Lottery': Symbolic Tour de Force," *American Literature* 46 (1974): 100-107. Additional critical commentary, including that of a number of anthologists, is cited in *Twentieth-Century Short Story Explication: Interpretations, 1900-1975, of Short Fiction since 1800,* 3d ed., comp. Warren S. Walker (Hamden, Conn.: Shoe String Press, 1977), 346.
22. "The Last Bed in the ICU," in *Cases in Bioethics from "The Hastings Center Report,"* ed. Carol Levine and Robert M. Veatch (Hastings-on Hudson, N.Y.: Hastings Center, 1982), 82. Reproduced by permission. Copyright © The Hastings Center.
23. Benjamin Freedman, "Commentary" on "The Last Bed in the ICU," in Levine and Veatch, 83.
24. R. B. Schiffer, "Commentary" on "The Last Bed in the ICU," in Levine and Veatch, 82.

A. R. Coulthard (essay date 1990)

SOURCE: "Jackson's 'The Lottery,'" in *The Explicator,* Vol. 48, No. 3, Spring, 1990, pp. 226-28.

[*In the following essay, Coulthard contends that "The Lottery" demonstrates Jackson's "nihilistic" view of humanity.*]

Little has been written about **"The Lottery,"** possibly the most widely known American short story. Perhaps that is because the story seems such a transparent attack on blind obedience to tradition that little or no exegesis is necessary, a reading usually encouraged by discussion questions accompanying this much-anthologized story. But **"The Lottery"** is not an assault on mindless, cultural conformity. It is a grim, even nihilistic, parable of the evil inherent in human nature.

It is not that the ancient custom of human sacrifice makes the villagers behave cruelly, but that their thinly veiled cruelty keeps the custom alive. Savagery fuels evil tradition, not vice versa. This is no chicken-egg question, but a fact evident from the text. From the beginning, the people display no genuine human community, no real bond of love. Considering that one of them could die within the hour, a possibility made more likely by the small number of potential victims, Tessie Hutchinson's tapping her friend Mrs. Delacroix "on the arm as a farewell" hardly seems a sign of sisterly concern. A short time later, it is Mrs. Delacroix who "selected a stone so large she had to pick it up with both hands" when her "friend" Tessie has become the scapegoat. In spite of such communal gestures as the crowd's separating "good-humoredly" to let Mrs. Hutchinson through, the villagers are looking forward to the slaughter, overtly so in the case of the children: "Bobby Martin had already stuffed his pockets full of stones, and the other boys soon followed his example, selecting the smoothest and roundest stones," the ones best for accurate throwing.

Old Man Warner is usually taken to be the most allegorically evil devotee of custom, but he is merely the most honest. He is also the only villager who seems to believe in the supposed original purpose of the sacrifice: "Lottery in June, corn be heavy soon," he intones. The others are willing to risk their own lives for the sheer pleasure of an unpunished annual killing. Mr. Adams and his wife mildly oppose the lottery by telling Old Man Warner that some villages are giving it up, but when it comes time for the stoning, "Steve Adams was in the front of the crowd." Such heavy-handed ironic twists imply that there is no such thing as communal love, or even sympathy, in the human heart.

The soullessness of Tessie Hutchinson even denies the myth of family love. When her family is chosen to supply the victim, Jackson pushes Tessie's survival instinct to the most shameful level by having her turn on her own flesh and blood. Tessie desperately tries to improve her odds for survival by defying tradition and adding her married daughter to the killing pool: "'There's Don and Eva,' Mrs. Hutchinson yelled. 'Make *them* take their chance.'" Tessie thinks, "It wasn't *fair,*" only because another family was not selected, and her husband "regretfully" agrees, for he too could be the final choice. Even the children of Tessie's household share this unconcern for the other family members. When they draw their slips, "Nancy and Bill, Jr., opened theirs at the same time, and both beamed and laughed" because neither is chosen to die.

Jackson's cold comment on the sacrifice itself makes it clear that the killing is a pleasurable end in itself, not an onerous duty demanded by tradition: "Although the villagers had forgotten the ritual and lost the original black box, they still remembered to use stones." That "someone gave little Davy Hutchinson a few pebbles" surely isn't required by custom, and the last line of the story, "then they were upon her," suggests enthusiasm rather than reluctance to murder a member of their community.

In a lecture written to introduce her public readings of **"The Lottery,"** Jackson expressed bewilderment at the furor caused by the June 1948 publication of the story in *The New Yorker.* This lecture implies that Jackson did not understand her story on a psychological level, and did not care to. She apparently wrote it more from instinct than calculation. She says, "The idea had come to me while I was pushing my daughter up the hill in her stroller," and that when she wrote the story, as soon as she got home, "it went quickly and easily" (1309), the published version "almost word for word the original draft" (1310). When a *New Yorker* editor asked Jackson what she wanted him to tell complaining callers, she says she informed him that "anything he chose to say was perfectly all right with me; it was just a story" (1310).

Yet because of **"The Lottery,"** Jackson says, "Millions of people, and my mother, had taken a pronounced dislike of me" (1311). There is no doubt some platform exaggeration in that statement, but Jackson's comment that "of the three-hundred-odd letters that I received that summer I can count only thirteen that spoke kindly to me, and they were mostly from friends" (1311) has the literal ring of truth. Surely such outrage was not prompted by a perception of negative treatment of ignorant villagers enslaved by a primitive custom. It can only be explained as the public's visceral revulsion toward Jackson's extremely cynical view of human nature as devoid of any shred of goodness or even decency. In her brief lecture, Jackson does not even entertain this as a possibility. But her concluding remark, which sounds suspicously as though it had been invented for dramatic purposes, reveals the brutal view of *Homo sapiens* that the author reflected in the ordinary people of **"The Lottery"**: "People at first were not so much concerned with what the story meant; what they wanted to know was where these lotteries were held, and whether they could go there and watch" (1312).

"The Lottery" expresses Shirley Jackson's abysmal opinion of her fellow creatures. Her simple villagers are not brainwashed victims but bloodthirsty victimizers. Ironically, it is probably this nihilistic undercurrent, and not the surface attack on subservience to custom, that gives this parable its continued appeal. **"The Lottery"** is not the story of a custom that makes no sense, but of one that fulfills a deep and horrifying need.

Works Cited

Jackson, Shirley. "The Morning of June 28, 1948, and 'The Lottery.'" *The Story and Its Writer.* 2nd ed. Ed. Ann Charters. New York: St. Martin's Press, 1987.

Nathan Cervo (essay date 1992)

SOURCE: "Jackson's 'The Lottery,'" *The Explicator,* Vol. 50, No. 3, Spring, 1992, pp. 183-85.

[*In the following essay, Cervo explains the biblical significance of the name "Delacroix" in "The Lottery."*]

In Shirley Jackson's **"The Lottery,"** the name "Delacroix" plays a key thematic role. We are told that "the villagers pronounced this name 'Dellacroy'." In French, "Delacroix" means "of the Cross." The mispronunciation signals the villagers' botching of the traditional Christian understanding of the Crucifixion. By so doing, they do not give perfect expression to what may be termed the archetypal mandate urged by their collective unconscious. Instead they conflate Hebrew and Egyptian religious ideas and practices to make them stand in place of the bloodless sacrifice of the Mass. The result is a hodgepodge of elements of the lottery by which the Hebrews chose the scapegoat, the punitive measure of stoning offenders to death (from which Jesus saved the woman taken in adultery), and certain echoes of Osiris as fertility god. This potpourri reveals not only the villagers' confusion but the primitivism to which such confusion necessarily translates whenever "tradition" presents itself as a dangerously profound psychological impasse (not to say obduracy).

That Jackson wishes to suggest the specifically Christian parallel or intent of "Delacroix"/"Dellacroy" is supported by the fact that the lottery takes place on June 27. Twenty-seven is three cubed. So what we have is the motif of the Trinity in a total, intensified interplay with itself, rather than the hypostatic interplay of the Three Persons comprising it. The effect is like that of a psychological ingrown toenail. There is also something of projected hostility in the blurring of the Trinity's relationship with itself (as if this were possible), an odium transmitted by way of caricature.

The idea of the scapegoat is a commonplace of the criticism expended on **"The Lottery."** It is fitted within the sociological context of the archetypal fall guy or else raises questions concerning Original Sin and mankind's need to expiate sin either through personal suffering or vicariously. Clearly, the premises of **"The Lottery"** put Rousseau's benign sentimentality to rout; they are closely allied, in effect, with those of Curzio Malaparte's *La Pelle* (*The Skin*) because, when the chips are down, everybody wants just one thing—to save his own skin.

Those are the anti-Romantic premises of the story; but there is another premise, that evinced by the "Delacroix"/"Dellacroy" dialectic. This premise builds upon and refers to the Day of Atonement lottery, most particularly as practiced in the days of Jesus. That lottery involved two goats; namely, the scapegoat (the goat that was not sacrificed) and the goat to be sacrificed to Jehovah as a sin offering. This latter goat was customarily hurled down a rocky precipice (hence, the twin motifs of stoning and the implicit idea, in Jackson's story, of Jehovah *qua* mountain baal—in keeping with Freud's view of Jehovah as expressed in *Moses and Monotheism*). The sacrificed goat "went rolling and falling down, he did not reach half-way down the mountain, before he became separated limb from limb" (*Yomah,* 6.92, cited by James L. Meagher, *How Christ Said the First Mass* [1906; Rockford, Ill.: Tan Books, 1984] 75). Meagher goes on to observe: "Bloody, torn, mangled, smashed on the rocks far below, lay the sinless victim with the sins of Israel on him, a striking image of the bloody body of the dead Christ with the sins of all mankind on Him" (75).

But what is more central to this explication is the following paragraph from Meagher, who cites *Yomah* (3.53-55):

> Now the high priest comes to the front of the altar, and a priest holds out to him the gold box, wherein are the "lots," on one is written: "For Jehovah," on the other "For Azazael." The Segan is on his right, the head of the family of priests serving that week on his left. If that of Jehovah was taken out by his right hand, the Segan says to him: "My Lord the high priest, raise thy right hand." If that of Jehovah was taken out by his left hand, the head of the family says: "My Lord the high priest, raise thy left hand." He placed the lots on the two goats saying: "To Jehovah, a sin offering." "For Azazael the scapegoat." The whole assembly responded with a mighty voice: "Blessed be the name of His Kingdom's glory forever." (67)[1]

In this historical and anthropological light, it is clear that Mrs. Hutchinson, whose "lot" it is to be stoned to death, is not a scapegoat figure. She is a parodic Christ-figure, slain to appease a demonic entity that is the personification of involuted (perhaps even self-consciously elaborated) ignorance masquerading as primitivistic piety. As metonymic extrapolation of her society, she is to be more properly thought of as a scapegrace.

Note

1. Since "Delacroix" has been corrupted to "Dellacroy," the villagers' choice is really between two demonic entities, one of whom demands a sacrifice, the other that each person nefariously desire to save his or her skin. "Azazael" has been

given several interpretations by biblical scholars. One interpretation holds that Azazael is "A personal being: (a) some demon of the wilderness (Stade); (b) a fallen angel who seduces men to evil ((Book of Enoch 6.7; 8.1 et passim), later identified with Sammael; (c) an epithet applied to the devil (Origen, Hengstenberg, Oehler, Kurz, Keil)" (John D. Davis, *A Dictionary of the Bible* [Philadelphia: Westminster, 1903] 62). Davis uses the spelling "Azazel" instead of "Azazael." According to Meagher, "Azazael means 'Almighty Eloi,' the Eternal Father; for Christ, foretold by the scapegoat, offered himself on the cross to his Father, with the sins of mankind on him" (67, 2n). Jehovah and Azazael blend and are appeased by the Crucifixion. Jesus does not escape but remains, with the sins of the people infesting him, to be sacrificed. That is the meaning of "croix" in "The Lottery." Whenever that is denied, ignored, or caricatured, "croy" prevails (a code word consisting of "roy," mimicking "*roi,*" French "king," and a diminished, truncated *c* standing for Christ debased).

Joan Wylie Hall (essay date 1993)

SOURCE: "The Short Fiction," in *Shirley Jackson: A Study of the Short Fiction,* Twayne Publishers, 1993, pp. 3-96.

[*In the following essay, Hall contends that the stories in* The Lottery and Other Stories, *originally published as* The Lottery; or, The Adventures of James Harris, *form a loosely connected larger work whose major theme is the sense in its main characters of being lost and alone.*]

THE MAN IN A BLUE SUIT AND OTHER UNIFYING DEVICES

In ***The Lottery; or, The Adventures of James Harris*** Shirley Jackson organized 25 of her short stories into a five-part book. Although 17 of the stories had already been published in such magazines as *Mademoiselle* and the *New Yorker,* Jackson had probably been writing with a collection in mind for several years. A note on contributors to the 1944 volume *Cross-Section: A Collection of New American Writing* announced she was working on a book of stories to be published early in 1945.[1] The Shirley Jackson Papers in the Library of Congress include undated manuscripts, probably from 1946 or 1947, of title and contents pages for a collection named ***The Intoxicated.*** Among the 40 stories listed are several never published by Jackson; not listed are **"The Lottery"** and nine other stories from ***The Lottery.***[2] When the book finally appeared in 1949, Jackson's title capitalized on the dramatic response to the publication of **"The Lottery"** in the 26 June 1948 *New Yorker.* So closely has her fame been identified with the one story that subsequent paperback editions have modified or eliminated her subtitle, thus obscuring the volume's loose coherence.

The Farrar, Straus & Giroux paperback, which has gone through several printings since 1982, notes the original title on the back of the title page and retains Jackson's division of the contents but is itself entitled ***The Lottery and Other Stories,*** deflecting the reader's attention from the book's many allusions to James Harris. Even more revisionary is a Fawcett Popular Library printing of 1975, whose title page and garish cover refer only to ***The Lottery*** and whose contents page eliminates Jackson's text divisions. Consequently, the stories seem to be chapters of a bizarre novel; this edition's preliminary blurb outlines an action more melodramatic than any created by Jackson: "From the moment you enter a village where age-old rites of evil lead to modern horror, and encounter a lover who enslaves the soul of every woman he touches, you will be gripped by a fascination that will not let you go until the final shocking revelation."[3] From front cover ("The most eerie and haunting work of our time") to back ("A GEM OF SATANIC SHOCK"), the Fawcett edition suggests a singleness of tone and plot that does not accurately represent the short-story format.

Jackson's book is, in fact, neither as disjointed as the first paperback implies nor as tightly composed as the second insists. Although Susan Garland Mann does not mention Jackson in her guide to more than 120 short-story cycles, the format of ***The Lottery; or, The Adventures of James Harris*** is similar to that of James Joyce's *Dubliners,* Sherwood Anderson's *Winesburg, Ohio,* and Ernest Hemingway's *In Our Time.*[4] References to James Harris are the most obvious link between Jackson's stories. Harris is explicitly identified in six stories, and his presence extends to several more.[5] For example, the "tall, graceful man in a blue suit" who makes a one-sentence appearance at the end of **"The Intoxicated,"** the book's first story, demands a second look when we hear James Harris described by his fiancée in the second story, **"The Daemon Lover"**: "He's rather tall, and fair. He wears a blue suit very often."[6]

James Harris's failure to arrive for his own wedding and his lover's conviction that he is hiding from her inevitably influence the reader's response to all further mention of the names "James" and "Harris." When we learn in **"The Renegade"** that the Walpoles' dog has been killing chickens at the Harris place, we are inclined to sympathize with the distraught Mrs. Walpole. The narrator calls attention to the family name by obscuring it when Mrs. Harris phones with the bad news: "The voice—it was a woman—said, 'I'm sorry to bother you, but this is—'and gave an unrecognizable name" (71). Through the three-page conversation, Mrs. Harris is described only as "the voice" and "the other woman," but the voice speaks "with relish" (71), insinuating that "if Mrs. Walpole wanted to fight . . . she had picked just the right people" (73). In the original *Harper's* version of **"The Renegade"** the angry couple is identified later in the story (by Mrs. Walpole's neighbor, Mrs. Nash) as the Kittredges.[7] By changing the name to Harris in ***The Lottery,*** Jackson efficiently adds this rural conflict to Harris's more typically urban "adventures."

Similar revisions in other stories strengthen the interrelatedness of the collection. When **"A Fine Old Firm"** appeared in the *New Yorker,* Mrs. Concord told Mrs. Friedman that her son Charles would join the law firm of Satterthwaite and Ferguson after his military service and thus needed no introduction to Mrs. Friedman's husband's partnership, Grunewald, Friedman, and White.[8] The transformation to "*Satterthwaite & Harris*" in ***The Lottery*** (196) combines with Mrs. Concord's anti-Semitism to produce a tense conclusion to the women's superficially pleasant conversation. A name substitution in **"The Tooth"** is even more ominous. The *Hudson Review* story describes a housewife whose trip to the dentist leads to her running off with Ray, a poetic man in a blue suit whom she meets on the bus.[9] **"The Tooth"** is placed near the end of ***The Lottery,*** and here Ray becomes Jim, evoking the elusive "daemon lover" James Harris of the second story.

The collection's many references to a Mr. Harris and to Jim, Jimmy, Jamie, and James—often paired with the Harris surname—culminate in the epilogue, a seven-quatrain ballad excerpt that constitutes the last of the book's five parts (305-6). The poem depicts a woman who has been lured from her family by a mysterious lover, whose "cloven foot" she discovers only after she has joined him on shipboard. Although he promises to show her "how the lilies grow / On the banks of Italy," he sinks the ship, admitting "the mountain of hell" is their true destination. At the end of the ballad Jackson identifies the work as "James Harris, the Daemon Lover (Child Ballad No. 243)"; her source is the philologist Francis Child's monumental collection, *English and Scottish Ballads* (1883-98). The plot of the ballad relates to several of Jackson's stories, from **"The Daemon Lover"** and **"The Tooth"** to the humorous **"Dorothy and My Grandmother and the Sailors,"** whose narrator describes a visit to a battleship with her nervous mother and grandmother.

Jackson restores to James Harris some of the demonic character that Stanley Edgar Hyman, in an essay on Child's ballads, finds so disappointingly diluted in American renderings of the "Daemon Lover" ballad. "In the American texts," says Hyman, "the wife of a house carpenter elopes with her sailor beau, the ship springs an accidental leak (in one Virginia text nothing happens to it at all), and the wife regrets her impetuosity."[10] In citing Child, Jackson injects the magic and the supernatural elements that "slough off readily" in domesticated versions, "even where they seem to be the ballad's point" (Hyman 1963, 263-64). Moreover, her portrayals of James Harris offset "the toning down of the frank sexuality of the ballads in America" (Hyman 1963, 265).

In a *New York Times* review Donald Barr complained that the recurrences of James Harris's name in widely differing circumstances "give a false unity to the book and confuse the meaning of individual stories."[11] As Barr implies, the several James Harrises do not seem to be a single, consistent character. The diversity of the descriptions, however, may be credited to the devil's own shape-shifting nature, as well as to Jackson's fascination with role playing and complex personalities. One feature many of her Harrises have in common—whether single or married, passive or aggressive, renamed or new to ***The Lottery***—is the profession of writing. Jackson links the James Harris stories to several others in the collection that reflect a diversified literary tradition. These range from **"After You, My Dear Alphonse,"** with its echoes of the comic strip "Alphonse and Gaston," to **"Come Dance with Me in Ireland,"** whose title is clarified by a shabby character who knew Yeats and who quotes the poet's "Come out of charity, come dance with me in Ireland" (225), a poem derived in turn from a medieval ballad. **"Pillar of Salt"** evokes the biblical story of Lot's wife, and **"Seven Types of Ambiguity"** alludes to William Empson's 1930 book, a classic of literary criticism.

Jackson's literary allusions also unite ***The Lottery*** into a short-story cycle. Much as Joyce Carol Oates parodies, counterpoints, and otherwise refers to familiar works of fiction in the short-story collection *Marriages and Infidelities* (1972), Jackson seems intent on emphasizing the literariness of her text. That books and readers appear throughout ***The Lottery*** is not surprising considering Jackson's and Hyman's reading habits. Judy Oppenheimer estimates that their personal library consisted of 30,000 to 40,000 books.[12] Furthermore, books are an important means of characterization in Jackson's novels. In *The Road through the Wall* (1948), for example, she contrasts two young women by describing the stories they read. Marilyn Perlman methodically works her way through Thackeray for the sake of her vocabulary, while the more childish Harriet Merriam prefers Louisa May Alcott. Harriet wonders whether a girl will move into the neighborhood house-for-rent: "they would be like in *Little Women,* and Harriet's friend would be Jo (or just possibly Beth, and they could die together, patiently)."[13] This romantic vision of death is brutally opposed by the murder and suicide of two local children at the end of the story. A book similarly echoes Jackson's plot in *The Sundial* (1958), where old Mr. Halloran reads about Robinson Crusoe's struggles, while his family and their hangers-on stock up the mansion in the expectation the world will soon end. A reference to long-overdue library books at the beginning of *We Have Always Lived in the Castle* (1962) foreshadows the confrontations between the Blackwood sisters and their hostile town, and the narrator's preference for fairy tales prepares the reader for Mary Katherine's creation of a private world "on the moon."

The emphasis on reading in ***The Lottery*** is nevertheless unusual, even among Jackson's works, if only for the number of characters involved in the act, from a teenager who reads Caesar in Latin class in **"The Intoxicated"** to a private secretary who carries *The Charterhouse of Parma* "for effect" in **"The Villager"** (49). This emphasis is especially noticeable when we compare ***The Lottery*** with 14 stories Hyman collected in ***Come Along with Me*** after Jackson's death. Whereas Hyman's selections span a 27-year period, all the ***Lottery*** stories date from the 1940s, and so we can trace Jackson's preoccupation with the written word in the earlier work to her self-consciousness as a novice writer. In her study of Willa Cather's early fiction Sharon O'Brien describes a corresponding abundance of literary allusions, which O'Brien attributes to "the woman writer's need to declare herself a descendent of the male literary tradition to which she fears she does not belong."[14] While Jackson too may have felt the need to provide herself with a legitimate ancestry, she early on revealed as many ties to women authors and to an oral tradition of myth and ballad-making as to the male literary canon. In interviews, she admired Samuel Richardson, André Gide, and E. M. Forster but also Fanny Burney, Jane Austen, Susan Ferrier, the Brontës, Ivy Compton-Burnett, and—in Jackson's opinion, the best contemporary writers in the short-story form—Katherine Anne Porter and Elizabeth Bowen.[15]

To the varied literary allusions and recurring ballad figure James Harris in ***The Lottery*** may be added yet another connective device—the excerpts from a witchcraft treatise that introduce the book's first four parts. Although Donald Barr objects that these epigraphs, like the reappearances of James Harris, produce a "false unity" (Barr, 4), they explicitly order Jackson's diverse material into book form.[16] The four passages from Joseph Glanvill's *Saducismus Triumphatus; or, Full and Plain Evidence Concerning Witches and Apparitions* (1689) divide the volume into groups of six or seven stories. The epigraph to the book's first part anticipates the demonic journey described in the Child ballad of the epilogue: "She saith, That after their Meetings, they all make very low Obeysances to the Devil, who appears in black Cloaths, and a little Band. He bids them Welcome at their coming, and brings Wine or Beer, Cakes, Meat, or the like. He sits at the higher end. . . . They eat, Drink, Dance and have Musick. At their parting they use to say, *Merry meet, merry part.*"[17] The passage colors the reader's perception of the cocktail party in **"The Intoxicated,"** the keynote story. The drink, the music, and especially the preview of global disaster at the kitchen table are unpleasantly reminiscent of the gathering described by an alleged witch in Glanvill's record of confessions.

The Glanvill passages preceding the next three parts hint at the hidden mysteries that motivate human behavior; one passage presents the devil as a sexual partner and even more directly than the "Daemon Lover" ballad does. *Saducismus Triumphatus* also provides names for three characters in the volume's longest story, **"Elizabeth."** The protagonist, not identified in full until the eighth page, has a namesake in Elizabeth Style, whose dealings with the devil are reported at great length in the witchcraft treatise (Glanvill, 345-62). In her loneliness and frustration, Jackson's Miss Style similarly seeks help from Jim Harris, forgetting "his heavy face, his thin voice" (191). The physical torments to which Elizabeth Style subjects the teenage Elizabeth Hill in Glanvill's account parallel Miss Style's sarcastic jibes at Daphne Hill, an awkward young secretary. Finally, Robert Hunt, frequently cited by Glanvill as a reliable witness, provides a name for the old family friend whose invitations Elizabeth insensitively rejects.

Glanvill's editor, Coleman O. Parsons, remarks that Glanvill influenced many later storytellers and incorporated into his own books such narrative techniques as the heightening of suspense (Glanvill, vii-xvii). In drawing on Glanvill, Jackson achieves the same effect Poe does when he cites Glanvill on "the mysteries of the will" three times in the story "Ligeia." Though the passage may be spurious—Poe's editors have not been able to locate it—the epigraph suggests what Parsons describes as Glanvill's "verbal, atmospheric, and technical appeal to Poe" (Glanvill, xvi). A final attraction Glanvill may have held for Poe, the linking of "the rational to the irrational" (Glanvill, xvi), is a major focus of ***The Lottery.***

This conjunction supplies a recurring plot pattern in which Jackson's characters are distanced from the familiar and the reasonable as they become involved in situations that, at worst, recall the demonic encounters of the Child ballad and of *Saducismus Triumphatus.* Although references to James Harris and to Glanvill's witches frame and punctuate the book with the supernatural, most of the collection's unsettling moments are more mundane. Even the most incredible experiences, those of the jilted fiancée in **"The Daemon Lover"** and the runaway housewife in **"The Tooth,"** could be explained in psychological rather than supernatural terms. Jackson herself demythologizes the Salem witchcraft trials in her children's book on the subject by frequently referring to the villagers' gossip and personal motivations. In an afterword to the paperback edition of *The Witchcraft of Salem Village,* she actually questions the existence of the devil and witches and finds more convincing sources for the "epidemic" in group hysteria or a bread fungus.[18] Yet the epilogue to ***The Lottery*** offers no such assurance, and the reader of the ballad is left in a state of shock that replicates the final condition of Jackson's typical protagonist.

In my discussion of the individual stories, I follow Jackson's four-part division of the 25 works. Her arrangement is not chronological by date of composition, nor does she separate previously published stories from new pieces. What unity there is within each group inheres chiefly in the family status of the characters. The first six stories—**"The Intoxicated," "The Daemon Lover," "Like Mother Used to Make," "Trial by Combat," "The Villager,"** and **"My Life with R. H. Macy"**—focus on singles, one of them a woman who lives alone while her husband is serving in the army. The next seven stories—**"The Witch," "The Renegade," "After You, My Dear Alphonse," "Charles," "Afternoon in Linen," "Flower Garden,"** and **"Dorothy and My Grandmother and the Sailors"**—are concerned with children, and in three instances children are portrayed with their domineering grandmothers. The six pieces in the third group—**"Colloquy," "Elizabeth," "A Fine Old Firm," "The Dummy," "Seven Types of Ambiguity,"** and **"Come Dance with Me in Ireland"**—are the least susceptible to generalization, but most of them portray married women (Elizabeth Style of **"Elizabeth"** wishes she were married) who speak about their husbands or children to friends or others outside the family. Aside from **"Elizabeth,"** whose protagonist is in fact involved in a long-term relationship as passionless as most of the marriages in ***The Lottery,*** **"Seven Types of Ambiguity"** is the only story in the group that does not center on married women. Appropriately titled, this story is curious for several reasons, including its portrayal of James Harris as a polite bookseller with no apparent love interest. A married couple does visit the book shop, but their relationship is secondary to the husband's interaction with a fellow customer. The final group of six stories—**"Of Course," "Pillar of Salt," "Men with Their Big Shoes," "The Tooth," "Got a Letter from Jimmy,"** and **"The Lottery"**—depicts a series of couples whose marriages undergo unusual pressures. References to James Harris are most frequent in the first group of stories, but some form of his name appears in at least two stories in each of the sections that follow. This common thread epitomizes the underlying theme of the intrusion of the irrational into the rational, or the unfamiliar into the familiar, a motif of menace that radiates from the James Harris tales to infect most of the relationships in the book.

Group One: Balancing Acts

"The Intoxicated" introduces the tone of menace by describing an uneasy encounter between an unnamed party guest and the teenage daughter of his host and hostess. Although the title applies most obviously to the male visitor, who is uncomfortably aware of his inebriation, it is also relevant to the excited intensity of Eileen, who disturbs his retreat from the noisy living room. Their conversation across the kitchen table is the first of several verbal duels in ***The Lottery,*** a disconcerting dialogue that leaves the visitor irritated and even shocked. Eileen's imagination, articulateness, and reflection relate her to many of the embattled teenagers in Jackson's longer fiction, from Marilyn Perlman in *The Road through the Wall* and Natalie Waite in *Hangsaman* (1951) through Mary Katherine Blackwood in *We Have Always Lived in the Castle,* her last completed novel. Preliminary small talk about the changing times makes the guest nervous; he feels Eileen's "tone had been faintly surprised, as though next he were to declare for an arena with gladiators fighting wild beasts, or the solitary circular waltzing of a madman in a garden" (4-5).

Their conflict, aggravated by differences of age and sex, comes to a climax when Eileen describes a paper she is writing about the future. She foresees the man's death in the rubbish of fallen churches, apartment houses, schools, and office buildings, but she imagines herself among the survivors of an earth-shaking cataclysm: "'Things will be different afterward,' she said. 'Everything that makes the world like it is now will be gone. We'll have new rules and new ways of living'" (7).[19] Since the kitchen provides no real refuge from the pressures of the cocktail party, the guest returns to the living room, where his hostess is talking earnestly with a James Harris look-alike, "a tall, graceful man in a blue suit" (8). When the now sober visitor describes Eileen to his host as an "extraordinary girl," the father "ruefully" shakes his head and concludes, "Kids nowadays" (8).

Earlier versions of **"The Intoxicated"** end on a more clearly threatening note. In what seems to be the earliest of three drafts, Jackson stops not with the host's rueful words, but with the guest's realization that the two men share an unvoiced terror:

> Suddenly in his host's eyes and tightened mouth he found the fear, the insistent nagging, ("When they come, when they come with their songs and their bright new words, with their gaiety and their cruelty, where will we hide? What will preserve us, who will protect us, what can save us then?").
>
> And he said brightly, looking down into his glass, "She's going to be a fine woman, someday."
>
> (SJP, Box 16)

In reworking the conclusion for the published version, Jackson progressively removed all direct allusion to either man's distress. Another important revision is the transformation of a "heavy red-faced man in a grey suit," who speaks with the hostess in all three drafts, to a graceful man in blue, a substitution whose significance becomes apparent only in the next story. This technique of concealing the ugly and the fearful offsets the full horror of Eileen's vision, but the disturbing quality of that vision anticipates the experiences of many characters in ***The Lottery.***

"The Daemon Lover," one of Jackson's most powerful stories, introduces James Harris by name and is in many ways a more representative work than **"The Intoxicated."** Because it had already appeared in print in *Woman's Home Companion* as **"The Phantom Lover,"** she may have decided to grant the lead position in ***The Lottery*** to a previously unpublished story, especially one whose apocalyptic perspective would set the tone for the more personal disasters of successive stories.[20] Because Jackson publicly commented on very little of her writing, her remarks to a *New York Times* interviewer on the genesis of **"The Daemon Lover,"** as illustrative of her compositional method, are noteworthy: "Someone told me an anecdote, just a few sentences. (Sort of like Henry James, you know.) I like thinking about it, turning it around, thinking of ways to use a situation like that in order to get a haunting note. It gets quite real. I think of what other thing it will go with, while I'm washing the dishes. But I do it because it's fun, because I like it" (Breit, 15). The book's epilogue reveals that one thing Jackson found to go with the anecdote was Child Ballad No. 243, a poem that supplied the "haunting note" in the person of James Harris.

Another element of her design may have been Elizabeth Bowen's "The Demon Lover," written in London during World War II and included in the short-story volume *Ivy*

Gripped the Steps (1946). In her preface Bowen states that the stories, though written separately and published first in magazines—as most of Jackson's were—have a "cumulative and collective meaning that no one of them, taken singly, has by itself." The volume, she adds, is "an organic whole: not merely a collection but somehow—for better or worse—a book."[21] The same could be said of the coherence of ***The Lottery; or, The Adventures of James Harris.*** Although the wartime climate that unites Bowen's stories is virtually absent from Jackson's book (except for a few references to soldiers and sailors), both writers were repeatedly drawn toward portrayals of extreme mental states. Thus in her preface Bowen comments on the hallucinations and the claustrophobia experienced by many of her characters. She numbers the "ruthless young soldier lover" who returns to London in 1941 after a 25-year absence in **"The Daemon Lover"** among the "questionable" ghosts in the book, "for are they subjective purely?" (Bowen, xii). It is tempting to explain away the demon lover in Jackson's story as an illusion of the age-conscious, lovesick protagonist (especially in light of the original title, **"The Phantom Lover"**), but Jackson too creates an objective reality for James Harris. The two stories end quite differently: Bowen's demon lover reclaims his one-time fiancée, while Jackson's Jamie Harris deserts his fiancée of one week on the day set for their wedding. Both conclusions are nightmarish. Each woman forfeits her familiar domestic world, and each receives terrifying confirmation of her early sense of a strangeness in the love relationship.

The ending of Jackson's story is foreshadowed in her opening description of the unnamed protagonist: "She had not slept well; from one-thirty, when Jamie left and she went lingeringly to bed, until seven, when she at last allowed herself to get up and make coffee, she had slept fitfully, stirring awake to open her eyes and look into the half-darkness, remembering over and over, slipping again into a feverish dream" (9). The subject of her remembering is unclear. Is she nervous about the coming marriage, or is she perhaps uneasy that she has begun a sexual relationship with Jamie before the wedding? The "sudden horror" she feels when she realizes that she has not changed the bedsheets, and her tactics "to avoid thinking consciously of why she was changing the sheets" (10), could indicate either anxious anticipation or guilt. Still, changing the bathroom towels three times in the course of the morning seems compulsive, and her accidental ripping and prompt mending of her girlish print dress may be sexually suggestive.

The fiancée's uneasiness begins long before Jamie fails to arrive at the scheduled hour of 10. The note she attempts to write to her sister Anne to announce the marriage only increases the woman's anxiety by reminding her of something odd in the courtship. Hesitant in mid-sentence—"I can hardly believe it myself, but when I tell you how it happened, you'll see it's even stranger than that . . ." (9)—she tears up the page, then turns to consider her depressingly limited wardrobe. She hesitates over the clothes as she had hesitated over the letter. Eager to appear soft and feminine, she nevertheless is repelled at the sight of herself in the mirror wearing a dress whose wide skirt "looked irresistibly made for a girl, for someone who would run freely, dance, swing it with her hips when she walked" (11). Angrily, she accuses herself of trying to look prettier than she is. Applying the proper makeup is "another delicate balance between looking as well as possible, and deceiving as little" (12). The woman "cruelly" reminds herself that, though the marriage license says she is 30, her real age is 34.

The reader infers that the fiancée's life is a series of such delicate balancing acts. Like most of Jackson's protagonists, she loses her customary equilibrium when a totally unexpected counterforce destroys the hard-won balance. Jackson, like Poe, is interested in the mental states that influence characters' responses to such forces—the drunkenness of the man in **"The Intoxicated"** and the chronic alcoholism of the narrator in Poe's "The Black Cat," for example. James Harris is a more formidable adversary than the teenage Eileen, but the fiancée's anxiety at his failure to meet her as planned is intensified by a sleepless night, a lack of food, a headache, a surplus of caffeine from her many cups of coffee, and, finally, the trail of snide remarks that follows her urgent search through the city. Like the boy Robin, who desperately seeks the financial and emotional support of an urban cousin in Hawthorne's "My Kinsman Major Molineux," she too seems trapped in a maze of streets that echo with the hostile laughter of tradesmen and local residents. People repeatedly shut their doors on both suppliants.

Each encounter with a stranger thus prepares the fiancée for the end of her journey. Arriving at an apartment to which she has been directed by a sarcastic boy, she thinks "suddenly, with terror, What shall I say if Jamie is there, if he comes to the door?" (27). She now seems as frightened at the possibility of his presence as she is at his absence. The voices she had heard fall silent, and the only sound is "something that might have been laughter far away." Coincidentally, her final recollection of her parting from James Harris the night before is his "laughing down the hallway" (12). When the woman knocks at the other door in the dirty hallway, it swings open on a messy attic. A bright-eyed rat watches her, "its evil face alert" (27). Stumbling, she closes the door on her skirt, tearing for a second time the dress she had mended in preparation for her wedding. In the days that follow, she returns to the apartment frequently and again hears low voices and laughter: "She came on her way to work, in the mornings; in the evenings, on her way to dinner alone, but no matter how often or how firmly she knocked, no one ever came to the door" (28). Earlier, she had dreamed of quitting her job for a "golden house-in-the-country future" when Jamie became an established writer (12). Her dream is destroyed: still a working woman, she moves between her neat apartment and the shabby building where James Harris has shut her out of his life.

The fiancée realizes she should report Jamie to the police as a missing person, but she knows how foolish she would look explaining he had not arrived for the wedding: "She couldn't tell them any more than that, could not say, 'Yes, it looks silly, doesn't it, me all dressed up and trying to find the young man who promised to marry me, but what about all of it you don't know? I have more than this, more than you can see: talent, perhaps, and humor of a sort, and I'm a lady and I have pride and affection and delicacy and a certain clear view of life that might make a man satisfied and productive and happy; there's more than you think when you look at me'" (23). By striking so cruelly at her fragile dignity, James Harris sends his fiancée on a tortured journey as painful as the ship voyage to hell described in the Child ballad. While few characters in ***The Lottery*** suffer equivalent losses, many of Jackson's women—and a couple of her men—find their pride and their very sense of self as delicate a fabric as the fiancée's print dress.

The other four stories in Jackson's first group repeat in a minor scale the notes of shock and dislocation sounded in **"The Intoxicated"** and **"The Daemon Lover."** Less nightmarish than **"The Daemon Lover,"** these works nevertheless resemble in several ways the existentialist novels and absurdist plays of the postwar years. Like the unnamed protagonists of the first two stories, these characters too are thrown off balance and scramble to secure an identity. At times, they can resolve the crisis only by assuming another identity, which introduces an odd sense of doubleness, a sort of doppelgänger effect. The fact that all the central characters in the first group of stories act without the support, or even the presence, of other family members, emphasizes their essential loneliness. Sometimes Jackson, like the absurdist playwrights, turns this situation to comic effect, but her comedy—like that of Samuel Beckett, Eugène Ionesco, and Harold Pinter—invariably contains an element of threat.

James Harris again embodies the threat in the next story, **"Like Mother Used to Make."** In her biography of Jackson, Judy Oppenheimer describes a true-life source for the incident, involving Stanley Edgar Hyman (Oppenheimer, 102). This peculiar sequel to **"The Daemon Lover"** ends with a man, not a woman, shut out of an apartment that harbors the laughing Mr. Harris. Ironically, David Turner is driven from his own neat home, which James Harris, now described as "a very large man" (35), unwittingly invades. Mr. Harris is admitted by his co-worker, David's neighbor and dinner guest, Marcia. From David's apartment, she presses the buzzer that opens the lobby door after Harris, visiting for the first time, rings her doorbell. Invited in for dessert, Harris assumes that the apartment is Marcia's and that she has baked the delicious pie to which the title alludes. Smiling conspiratorially at David, Marcia easily plays the role of hostess, and David withdraws to wash dishes in the kitchen. When he finally returns to the living room, David speaks awkwardly, and Mr. Harris watches him impatiently. Marcia's "Sit down, Davie, won't you?" is delivered in a tone he recognizes as "the one hostesses used when they didn't know what else to say to you, or when you had come too early or stayed too late. It was the tone he had expected to use on Mr. Harris" (38). Accepting the identity of unwelcome guest, David says his farewells "much more genially than he intended" (39). Marcia closes the door on him as he thanks her for the dinner, and he retreats down the hall to her sloppy apartment.

The situation is humorous but almost as incredible as the plight of the jilted fiancée in **"The Daemon Lover,"** and finally almost as disturbing. Sitting on Marcia's unmade bed, David looks around at her scattered laundry and wind-strewn papers: "It was cold, and it was dirty, and as he thought miserably of his own warm home he heard faintly down the hall the sound of laughter and the scrape of a chair being moved" (40). In both stories, James Harris precipitates the protagonist's exclusion, not only from a physical place but also from emotional sustenance. Both the fiancée and David Turner respond mechanically to their losses. While the woman fruitlessly returns to the closed door, David attempts to restore order by attacking the chaos of Marcia's apartment: "Wearily, David leaned over and picked up a paper from the floor, and then he began to gather them up one by one" (40). Jackson's revision of an early draft radically changes the tone of her original conclusion, where David (there named Jamie Turner) giggles down the hall to Marcia's apartment, elated they have together made "a fool out of a big guy like that." The "big guy" is innocently named Harold Lang in this early form, and James Turner whistles as he picks up Marcia's papers, confident "if Lang stays over there even an hour. . . . I can get this place looking pretty good" (SJP, Box 16).

Analogous to the cluttered attic in **"The Daemon Lover,"** Marcia's rooms in the revised version of **"Like Mother Used to Make"** represent the dark side of life that most of Jackson's characters seem fated to confront. David realizes that Marcia's apartment is an upsetting double of his own: "This apartment was not agreeable for him to come into; it was exactly the same as his: foyer, kitchenette, living-room, and it reminded him constantly of his first day in his own apartment, when the thought of the careful homemaking to be done had left him very close to despair" (31). After his long hours of exertion, only one reminder of the original bleakness remains to worry David; the falling plaster in one corner of his living-room ceiling is a "perpetual trouble to him," and "no power on earth could make it less noticeable" (30). With paint, plants, and carefully selected furnishings, he has otherwise created "the most comfortable home he had ever had" (31). He keeps his single door key "safely" in his pocket, where it gives him a false sense of protection, "the only way into his warm fine home."

Marcia and David are as different as the decor of their apartments. Not only does she lack his neatness, but her loud speech contrasts with his quietness. At the same time, the two are similar in exhibiting a blend of gender characteristics. Reversing the usual male-female stereotypes, Jackson shows David's pleasure in domestic matters—he is "tenderly" accumulating a complete set of silverware (32)—and she describes his blush of pleasure at Marcia's praise. Marcia, on the other hand, is portrayed as a working woman (named "Billie" in the draft) who is "always hungry"; she fills her dinner plate "without admiring the serving silver" (34). Although she calls David "honey" in front of James Harris, their relationship does not appear to be a romantic one. In contrast to David, the large Mr. Harris exudes an oppressive masculinity. To Marcia's amusement and David's distress, he "thickly" announces smoke is good for plants as he lights a cigar. Then he "heartily" holds out a hand, which David "limply" shakes as he leaves his apartment to the outsiders (39). In this final twist, David's "urgency to be rid of them both" (37) is relieved, but only at the cost of surrendering his home. Since Marcia clearly tells him goodnight, he may be providing the setting of the latest of "the adventures of James Harris."

Apartments are also strangely invaded in the next two stories, **"Trial by Combat"** and **"The Villager,"** and in both the motif of doubleness recurs. The "combat" of the first work is restricted to the small-scale skirmishes of two women in a New York roominghouse, but the husbands of both have served in the army, and the title expresses the tension that runs through most of the book. Emily Johnson indirectly accuses her downstairs neighbor, Mrs. Allen, of stealing several items from her furnished room and hopes the thefts will stop. The next day, however, a cheap pair of earrings and two packs of cigarettes are missing, and she subsequently enters Mrs. Allen's apartment, where she finds all her stolen possessions in the dresser. When Mrs. Allen suddenly returns, the startled Emily explains that a terrible headache forced her to come looking for aspirin. "Let's not say any more about it," responds Mrs. Allen, either kindly or threateningly. Triumphant in combat, she promises to come up later, "just to see how you feel" (47).

As in **"Like Mother Used to Make,"** the apartments, as well as the persons who live there, are disconcertingly alike and different. Mrs. Allen's room is "directly below her own" (41), and when Emily first pays a call she sees immediately that the apartment is "almost like her own—the same narrow bed with the tan cover, the same maple dresser and armchair; the closet was on the opposite side of the room, but the window was in the same relative position (42). Emily describes the 60-year-old Mrs. Allen as a mathematical doubling of herself: "More than twice as old as I am, Emily thought, while she stood in the doorway, and a lady still" (42). Neither woman has children; their husbands are gone (Mr. Allen dead and Mr. Johnson apparently overseas); both like flowers; and both mask their frustrations with politeness, a common feature of Jackson's women. When Mrs. Allen catches her in the act of spying, Emily wonders what the older woman could be waiting for "with such a ladylike manner," and when Emily speaks, she recognizes the similarity: "My voice is almost ladylike, too, she thought" (47).

The women are also alike in their efforts to make homes of their small apartments, but the task is not easy, and these homes remain as susceptible to assault as those in the preceding stories. Mrs. Allen tells Emily she has repeatedly complained to the landlady that "you can't make people feel at home if you put all the same furniture in the rooms" (42). Emily has bought asters to brighten her room, but she knows they fade quickly. She "pleadingly" expresses her fear that someone has a key to her door, and when Mrs. Allen explains that all the keys in the building open all the old-fashioned locks, Emily insists, "It *has* to stop" (45). Her key provides no more security than David Turner's in **"Like Mother Used to Make."** Emily's final reluctance to confront Mrs. Allen with the evidence of theft may stem from her identification with the older woman. When she enters the widow's room on her spying mission, Emily experiences "a sudden sense of unbearable intimacy with Mrs. Allen" (46). Staring for the third time at a picture of a dignified-looking Mr. Allen in uniform, she reflects, "They must have had such a pleasant life together, and now she has a room like mine, with only two handkerchiefs of her own in the drawer" (46).

Mrs. Allen is pitiful, but she also has a sinister side that relates her more closely to James Harris than to Emily Johnson. An early instance of the several menacing old ladies in Jackson's fiction, she symbolically erodes Emily's sense of self by stealing her initial pin. In taking "one of a set of china dogs" (41), she further attacks the younger woman's wholeness, while also suggesting that she and Emily constitute a set. Emily wrongly assumes that "her losses were trivial" (41); her original certainty that she can deal with the situation logically is thwarted by the illogical attacks of Mrs. Allen.

The trespassers who explore a modest apartment in **"The Villager"** are not thieves, but one of them is a smiling Mr. Harris, come to answer a classified ad for furniture for sale. By chance, he enters shortly after the arrival of the protagonist, Hilda Clarence, who is there on the same mission. (A note on the door from the absent resident invited Miss Clarence, who had made an appointment, to wait in the unlocked flat.) Hilda lets Mr. Harris think she is Nancy Roberts, a dancer who lives in the apartment with her husband, Arthur. Nancy's scattered books remind Hilda that 15 years ago she herself had come to the city with the dream of becoming a dancer, and she is striking a pose when Mr. Harris walks in. Hilda identifies not only with Nancy but with Mr. Harris, an urban newcomer who plans to get a job and practice his writing craft at night, much as she had become a stenographer to support her now-abandoned goal of dancing professionally.

But after she lies to Mr. Harris that she *is* a dancer, he intrusively wanders around the apartment. The discomfort he inflicts is mild compared to his impact in earlier stories, but when he looks into the dirty bathroom Hilda winces, and when he opens the kitchen door she explains she does not cook much. Neither does Mr. Harris, who pleasantly remarks he needs a wife, evoking a shudder in the reader and perhaps regret on Hilda's part that she has so convincingly adopted the persona of Nancy. Miss Clarence heads for home alone, not waiting to confront her double, but the slight exertion of the dance pose leaves its mark, and the story ends, as most of Jackson's do, on a note of pain: "Her shoulders ached" (56).

Hilda Clarence in several ways resembles the unlucky fiancée of **"The Daemon Lover."** Another unmarried working woman, Miss Clarence too is about 35 and conscious of her appearance (49). Her pride in her competence as a well-paid private secretary is reminiscent of the fiancée's confidence in her personal worth. Both women smoke nervously and become increasingly impatient, frequently checking the time as they are kept waiting past a scheduled hour. Jackson strengthened the similarities between the two stories by renaming Mr. Atkins from the *American Mercury* version of **"The Villager"** as Mr. Harris.[22] The Robertses' old wooden building, the dingy hallway, and the shiny maple furniture in their messy living room compare unfavorably with Miss Clarence's beige and off-white furnishings and her modern apartment house, much as the fiancée's neat rooms contrast with the garret of **"The Daemon Lover."** Though Hilda Clarence's quest from her Greenwich Village home is much less anguished than the fiancée's disillusioning journey, they both make trips into darkness.

"My Life with R. H. Macy," on the other hand, is the one really humorous work in this first division of stories. Shirley Jackson's earliest piece in a national publication, it appeared in the *New Republic* during Christmas week of 1941.[23] In contrast to the minor annoyances that characters experience at the start of the typical Jackson story, **"My Life with R. H. Macy"** opens with a shock. The calm third-person narrator of the first five stories is replaced with the distraught voice of a victim who begins in medias res: "And the first thing they did was segregate me. They segregated me from the only person in the place I had even a speaking acquaintance with; that was a girl I had met going down the hall who said to me: 'Are you as scared as I am?'" (57). Close to the ending mood of the preceding stories, the sense of isolation and displacement is undercut immediately after the speaker answers "yes." The rest of the story sounds like a parody of the tone of menace and the themes of doubleness and identity common to the previous pieces and to many of the succeeding ones. Though disconcerting in this context, the shift in tone provides comic relief that Jackson may have considered necessary. One of the few autobiographical sketches incorporated into ***The Lottery,*** **"My Life with R. H. Macy"** reveals her tendency to recognize the absurd in the mundane and also anticipates her outpouring of fictionalized autobiography in the 1950s.

As the title indicates, the narrator's agony results from her employment at the huge New York department store. Early in **"The Villager"** Hilda Clarence is compared to the many other young adults who moved from small towns to Greenwich Village with "plans to work in Macy's or in a bookshop until they had enough money to pursue their art" (49). The speaker in **"My Life with R. H. Macy"** exaggerates that Macy's alone has 11,700 employees, all of them so much depersonalized that each supervisor is named Miss Cooper and the clerks are called by their numbers, 13-3138 in her case. Workers have additional numbers for their locker, time clock, cash box, cash register, cash-register drawer, and cash-register-drawer key. A misfit from the first day, the protagonist reports for training in a red velvet afternoon dress, while the other young women wear tailored suits. She is further alienated by the special language of Macy's: "Comp. keep for ref. cust. d.a. no. or c.t. no. salebook no. salescheck no. clerk no. dept. date M" (58). The store's secular rituals—incongruously performed against a backdrop of the Christmas season—subsume individuals into groups, units, and departments. Told she cannot wear her hat while punching the clock, the nonconforming speaker leaves for another part of the store, "bowing timidly at the time clock and its prophet" (58). She is sent to lunch three times in one day because the counter head in the book department confuses her with 13-6454 and 13-3141. When she finally sells a copy of her assigned book, *The Stage-Struck Seal,* she destroys the "duplicate triplicate" because she does not know how to file it. Confused by a customer's request for a different title, she is stared at by a fellow employee who illogically explains that "philosophy, social sciences and Bertrand Russell were all kept in dictionaries" (60).

Like most of Jackson's frustrated women, this one comes to a moment of crisis, but her response frees her from a routine that threatens to destroy her individuality. Falling downstairs after her second day of work, she tears her stockings, an accident that—unlike the unfortunate ripping of the fiancée's dress in **"The Daemon Lover"**—is comically resolved. The narrator rejects the doorman's detailed instructions for getting a free replacement and reclaims her identity by buying herself a new pair and exiting through the customers' entrance. Her subsequent long letter to her former employer is sarcastically signed with the total of all her Macy's numbers, divided by 11,700. At the story's end she is characteristically bruised but, unique among the protagonists of the first part of ***The Lottery,*** uncharacteristically jubilant. Although Jackson invokes the comic spirit in several stories that follow, no other central character maintains or recovers a comparable state of command. The menace embodied by James Harris and other strangers in the first group of stories spreads through the rest of the book as friends and family members compound such outside threats to the delicately balanced protagonists. Thus opposed, Jackson's characters have no more chance of maintaining their equilibrium than the "stage-struck seals" that the sympathetic Macy's clerk says she "possessively" tends (59).

Group Two: Rebellious Sons and Daughters

In contrast to the loners of ***The Lottery***'s first six stories, the seven stories in the second part focus on women and girls in family settings; husbands are frequently absent or subordinated to background roles. As their titles insinuate, **"The Witch"** and **"The Renegade,"** the first two stories, have affinities with the first part. The frightening experiences of the two mothers in these stories are all the more terrible in light of their children's casual responses. The mothers in the second part's remaining five stories are also confounded by their sons and daughters, but in less startling ways. Much as **"My Life with R. H. Macy"** renders Jackson's usual themes in a comic mode, most of the works in the second part translate her concerns with anxiety and a sense of self into more realistic situations than those depicted in the first set of stories. Accordingly, the element of the bizarre and the incredible diminishes, though a feeling of strangeness and uneasiness remains throughout.

In a break from the claustrophobic rooms and urban settings of the first several stories, **"The Witch"** takes place on a train passing through an attractive landscape. While the introductory lines of each story in the first group portray a lone adult, **"The Witch"** begins with a family tableau: a talkative four-year-old, Johnny; his mother, who is quietly reading; and a baby girl, who occupies herself with toast and a rattle. At the start, the only disquieting detail is the baby's tendency to "slip slowly sideways," but she is "strapped securely," and her mother straightens her whenever she slides halfway down the seat (63). The one time she bangs her head, her brother Johnny pets her feet until she laughs; he is rewarded with a lollipop. The mother herself is initially so secure that she responds with an automatic "fine" to the boy's constant chatter, even to his unusual claim to have sighted a witch outside. But, as often happens in ***The Lottery,*** the initial sense of control is jeopardized by an outsider, in this case a fellow passenger who fascinates the son but so upsets the mother that her original calm is eventually shattered.

The intruder remains unnamed, but as he enters the coach he looks like an aging James Harris. With his "pleasant face" (as in **"The Villager"**), his blue suit (reminiscent of **"The Daemon Lover"**), and his cigar (as in **"Like Mother Used to Make"**), the friendly traveler charms the child as effectively as Mr. Harris intrigued the women in the earlier stories. The man's blue suit is an addition to Jackson's original manuscript (SJP, Box 19). The boy responds to him with ready laughter, as Marcia responded to James Harris in **"Like Mother Used to Make."** Like the exclusive laughter associated with Jamie Harris in **"The Daemon Lover,"** the good humor shuts out the mother. Though anxious when the white-haired stranger sits down by her son, she soon relaxes and returs "peacefully" to her book, not joining in the conversation.

The crisis thus arrives unexpectedly. A memory of his childhood, which the old man introduces in fairy-tale fashion—"Once upon a time"—suddenly becomes an unbelievable account of savagery, worthy of the Brothers Grimm. The man tells Johnny that he had a sister ("just like yours") on whom he lavished gifts before pinching her to death and dismembering her. The mother's smile fades as she helplessly opens and closes her mouth. Before she manages to ask the storyteller to leave, her son "eagerly" draws out the fact that a bear ate the dead girl's head. Boy and man laugh repeatedly at the distressed mother, threatening to chop off her head and the baby's too. After the stranger excuses himself to leave the car, the woman "urgently" tells Johnny he was just teasing, but the boy, settling down with a fresh lollipop, concludes, "Prob'ly he was a witch" (67).

Robert L. Kelly, who calls the story a "Satanic gem," finds a "subtle link of evil" in the correspondence between Johnny's sucker and the outsider's cigar.[24] When Johnny comments that his father smokes cigars too, the man's retort that *all* men do "raises the possibility that this man also has a paternal claim." Kelly's suggestion is especially intriguing in light of the father's absence from the coach and the gradual alignment of the man and the boy against the woman and the baby girl. The several doubles in Jackson's book incline the reader to view Johnny and the visitor as another such pair. Certainly they seem to speak the same language. When the boy asserts he is 26, the man ignores the woman's corrective "Four" and "politely" repeats "Twenty-six" (65). Instead of ignoring Johnny's references to witches, as his mother has previously done, the stranger takes him seriously and asks whether he has found many. Johnny's innocent delight in the man's sadistic tale inspires the boy to project a similar denouement for his mother. When the woman threatens to call the conductor, he anticipates, "The conductor will *eat* my mommy" (67). The child's ignorant cruelty is mirrored in the deliberate brutality of the man, who unfeelingly asks the mother whether he has frightened her. The stranger's story line is an exaggerated version of the many ***Lottery*** plots in which unsuspecting victims, like Johnny's mother, are abruptly confronted and deprived of control, even the control of their own voices. Most of these victims lack any defense equivalent to the strap that saves Johnny's baby sister from serious slips.

"The Renegade" is an especially effective rendering of this basic plot. Again a horrified mother is dumbstruck to see the cruelty of strangers echoed in her children. In **"The Witch"** the nameless mother's maternal role is emphasized by consistent references to "the mother"; she is never "the woman." Similarly identified by her family relationship, the protagonist of **"The Renegade,"** the mother of twins Judy and Jack, is always called "Mrs. Walpole." Mrs. Walpole too is initially portrayed alone with her children, though a self-absorbed Mr. Walpole joins her in the kitchen after the twins leave for school. Like the sliding baby in **"The Witch,"** the "loitering" twins are an initial, though mild, source of concern for their mother, who is irritated that they might miss the bus. She experiences the "wading-through-molasses feeling of trying to hurry children" (69). Also like the preoccupied mother in the preceding story, who at first repeats "fine" to Johnny's most outrageous assertions, Mrs. Walpole "mechanically" calls her children's names.

In contrast to the other woman, however, Mrs. Walpole clearly struggles from the start to maintain her composure. Not only has the alarm clock failed to go off, but the coffee is too slow and the eggs too soft. With no time even to drink her juice, she has to make an effort to greet Mr. Walpole pleasantly and to prepare his breakfast "patiently." Her mind is "full of unfinished sentences that began, 'Don't you think other people ever have any feelings or—'" (70), sentences she never pronounces. But Mrs. Walpole has just brought matters under control when the ring of her telephone, an "unbearable intrusion," announces her downfall just as abruptly as the stranger's entrance in the railroad coach in **"The Witch."**

The phone call clarifies at least one meaning of the story's title. According to an angry neighbor, the ominously named Mrs. Harris, the Walpoles' dog, Lady, has overnight become a violent killer of chickens. The news affects Mrs. Walpole much as the man's ugly story affected Johnny's mother. She is silent so long the caller asks, "Hello?" before Mrs. Walpole can voice her denial: "That's perfectly ridiculous" (71). Mrs. Walpole seems unusually attached to the dog; in her opinion Lady is "quiet, competent, exceedingly tolerant," qualities that seem more descriptive of the woman herself. It pains her to picture Mr. Harris, who luckily forgot to take his shotgun to the chicken yard, chasing the dog with a stick. Mrs. Walpole speaks weakly; bewildered, she is seized with a "sudden unalterable terror" as she faces "an evil situation she had never known before" (72-73). Reminiscent of the fiancée in **"The Daemon Lover,"** Mrs. Walpole then begins a journey through the village that confirms her apprehension. Spread by the Harrises, news of Lady's attack precedes her, and she—like the fiancée—is the object of knowing looks. In both stories, the evil inheres not simply in the original act of betrayal but in the cruelty of townspeople who further distress the woman victim, for Mrs. Walpole is the story's main victim.

Mrs. Walpole's encounters become increasingly grueling as one person after another offers advice. While her neighbor Mrs. Nash merely suggests a sturdy chain, old Mr. White thinks Lady should be killed, the grocer favors tying a "ripe" dead chicken around her neck, and a male customer at the grocery recommends putting the dog in a pen with a protective mother hen who would scratch out her eyes. The worst suggestion is relayed at the end by the Walpole children, who have been talking with Mr. Shepherd, a "genial man" who gives nickels to the twins and takes boys fishing. The children laughingly describe a spiked collar that would strangle Lady as she pulls at a rope when made to chase chickens. Judy and Jack compete to add gruesome details and sound effects. Recalling Johnny in **"The Witch,"** Jack dramatically concludes, "The spikes cut her head off" (83). Mrs. Walpole is sickened as she watches the twins, "with their hard hands and their sunburned faces laughing together, their dog with blood still on her legs laughing with them" (83). She seeks comfort in the doorway view of "cool green hills" and a "peaceful sky," but when she closes her eyes she suddenly feels "the harsh hands [an echo of the children's "hard hands"] pulling her down, the sharp points closing in on her throat" (83).

Mrs. Walpole's final identification with the female dog is shockingly explicit, but it helps to explain why she is "indescribably depressed" after receiving Mrs. Harris's call (74). For Mrs. Walpole, with her outward restraint and inward turmoil is herself a "renegade" of sorts. She strains to sound "pleasant" when Mr. White asks whether Mr. Walpole has a gun to shoot Lady, trying "not to let her hatred show in her face" (77). Her alarm at the "deliberate, malicious pain" Lady has "inflicted" (81) suggests her fearfulness of releasing her own suppressed violence; again the terms in which she thinks of the dog seem more applicable to a person. Disturbed by "the murderous brutality a pretty dog like Lady could keep so well hidden in their home" (81), Mrs. Walpole perhaps recognizes a similar doubleness in herself. As a mother of fraternal twins, she could be especially conscious of the splits in her own life. The identity Mrs. Walpole feels with Lady may be the reason she does not correct the men in the grocery store when they several times refer to the dog as "he" and "him." Mrs. Walpole neither repeats the pronoun nor calls Lady by name, though the avoidance forces her to speak impersonally of "the dog" (79).

Mrs. Walpole can relate to Lady not only as a female whose usual good manners mask her inner tension, but also as an outsider in the community. The family's recent move from the city has entailed many adjustments, especially for Mrs. Walpole. Although she looks to the landscape for relief at the end of the story, she is generally ill at ease in the country setting. Mrs. Walpole realizes they are "still city folk and would probably always be city folk, people who owned a chicken-killing dog, people who washed on Tuesday, people who were not able to fend for themselves against the limited world of earth and food and weather that the country folk took so much for granted" (74). She is reminded daily of her helplessness, driven always to ask others' advice on everything from trash disposal to weatherstripping and baking. Mrs. Walpole contrasts her inadequacy with the efficiency of Mrs. Nash, who dispenses freshly baked doughnuts early in the morning, wearing a "shockingly clean house dress" in her "freshly washed" kitchen (75). To Mrs. Walpole, her neighbor's bright house, sturdy table, and good kitchen smells are "all symbols somehow of Mrs. Nash's safety, her confidence in a way of life and a security that had no traffic with chicken-killing, no city fears" (76). Mrs. Walpole's own insecurity is further emphasized when the sunlight that crosses Mrs. Nash's kitchen doorway is later juxtaposed with the "dark shadow" that crosses the sunlight in the Walpoles' kitchen entrance as Lady returns (81). It is a moment of dark illumination that relates Mrs. Walpole to several of Jackson's earlier protagonists. The dog is spotted with the blood that makes the woman turn "helplessly" to the pantry, where she blindly removes the first cans she touches for the children's lunch.

Mrs. Wilson, the central character in **"After You, My Dear Alphonse,"** at first seems to have more in common with the capable Mrs. Nash than with the hesitant Mrs. Walpole. She bakes gingerbread, serves a nutritious lunch, and hospitably invites her son Johnny's playmate—sight unseen—to join him for the meal. Mrs. Wilson is not burdened with Mrs. Walpole's crippling anxiety, nor does she experience a sudden moment of horror comparable to that of the mother in **"The Witch."** Nevertheless, she is another of Jackson's divided women. Though scrupulously polite and even charitable, Mrs. Wilson conceals deep insecurities that prevent her from treating Johnny's friend as an individual. From the moment Boyd passes through the kitchen doorway and she sees he is black, she is on guard. Most of the story is told in dialogue, and there are no passages similar to the many in **"The Renegade"** where the narrator expresses Mrs. Walpole's suppressed emotions. But Mrs. Wilson's words and her concluding action suggest that she too feels fundamentally threatened.

The story's title, a familiar line from the comic strip "Alphonse and Gaston," is relevant to the exaggerated civility with which Mrs. Wilson addresses Boyd. M. Thomas Inge, who cites Faulkner's reference to the cartoon in *Light in August,* says Alphonse and Gaston "reside more in the popular consciousness and language as representatives of excessive politeness rather than as comic strip characters."[25] Inge explains that the two Frenchmen adhere so strictly to their mannerly phrases and gestures they are "immobilized" when disasters occur. Mrs. Wilson's speech too is automatically polite but paralyzingly unsuitable to the minor crisis of Boyd's appearance at the lunch table. The title has a more obvious connection with Johnny and Boyd. By playfully repeating "After you, my dear Alphonse" to each other at the beginning, middle, and end of the story, the two friends display their fellowship and, at the same time, their impotence against a world where even kind people like Mrs. Wilson can be insensitively cruel. As Carol Cleveland remarks, the story "speaks lightly but tellingly of racial prejudice."[26]

Mrs. Wilson's prejudice is evident chiefly in the stereotypes that underlie her conversation with Johnny and Boyd. Ironically, she seems determined to have Johnny treat Boyd fairly. She assumes her son is casting the black child in a slave's role since Boyd enters the house with an armload of kindling wood. Johnny "mildly" explains the wood is "dead Japanese" and Boyd is carrying the pile because it came from his place (86). The boys continue to disabuse Mrs. Wilson of her misconceptions about Boyd's appetite, his father's job, the number of his siblings, and his plans for the future. On this last subject, Johnny, caught up in his war games, remarks that they will both become tank drivers. While Mrs. Wilson seems intent on finding nonexistent differences between the two children, the boys' innocent responses show how much they have in common. She feels "defeated" when Johnny mentions that Boyd's father is a foreman, and she quickly changes the subject when Johnny wonders why she thinks Boyd's mother has a job; "You don't work," he reasonably points out (87). Unable to abandon her prejudices, Mrs. Wilson takes a "deep breath" as she works up to her final question, but her sentence is left incomplete as Boyd's "puzzled expression" greets her offer of a bundle of second-hand clothes (88).

Thwarted in her repeated efforts to sympathize, she withdraws the one thing that Boyd really needs. Reaching for another piece of gingerbread, he finds the plate lifted from the table by Mrs. Wilson, whose sudden irritation is noticed by the boys. Cuttingly, she observes, "There are many little boys like you, Boyd, who would be very grateful for the clothes someone was kind enough to give them" (89). Mrs. Wilson never sees that Boyd is a virtual double of her own son. In fact, Johnny's table manners and grammar, as revealed in the course of the meal, are somewhat inferior to those of the always polite but finally confused visitor, who stares at Mrs. Wilson's turned back as Johnny pulls him to the door. The boys' final exchange prevents the story from ending on too heavy a note but also puts the mother in her place. Mrs. Wilson overhears the departing Boyd quietly ask Johnny whether she is still mad. Johnny is not sure, but he does know, "She's screwy sometimes." Linking Johnny's white mother with *his* black one, Boyd identifies with his friend one more time: "So's mine" (89).

Despite the humorous tone and the socially sensitive theme, **"After You, My Dear Alphonse"** leaves the reader with a familiar protagonist: a dumbfounded character whose sense of home and security are menaced by the unexpected intrusion of an outsider. Like the other married women thus far in ***The Lottery,*** Mrs. Wilson faces her challenge without the aid of her husband; Johnny describes his father to Boyd as a "little guy" who would not hurt a flea (87). As in **"Trial by Combat"** brief military references place a small-scale conflict in the context of a world at war. But the disturbing laughter of several earlier characters, including the alarming children in **"The Witch"** and **"The Renegade,"** has an innocent, though still exclusionary, parallel in the giggles of Boyd and Johnny. In a more significant variation on her usual pattern, Jackson depicts Boyd as a harmless outsider, and Mrs. Wilson as a protagonist whom it is difficult to pity. Her oven and her tempting gingerbread are uncomfortably reminiscent of the witch in the fairy tale "Hansel and Gretel."[27]

The centerpiece in the largest group of stories, **"Charles"** presents the book's most humorous treatment of the beleaguered mother. First published as fiction in *Mademoiselle,* the semi-autobiographical story was later incorporated into Jackson's family chronicle, ***Life among the Savages.***[28] Next to **"The Lottery" "Charles"** is the most frequently anthologized piece from Jackson's collection, and probably for a similar reason: both end with an unforgettable scene that suddenly forces the reader to reconsider the whole preceding sequence of events. The mild tension of the opening, as the narrator's son Laurie sets off for kindergarten, ending "an era of my life" (91), hardly prepares us for the startling denouement. But, as frequently happens in Jackson's stories, the tension so steadily increases that the central character, Laurie's mother, is finally forced to take action.

"Charles" is the third story in a row to stage the family drama around the kitchen table. This is the center to which the newly independent Laurie returns each noon to report on the latest exploits of his classmate, the Charles of Jackson's title. Like the children in **"The Witch"** and **"The Renegade,"** Laurie relishes reporting acts of violence and cruelty. He is entertained rather than upset when Charles hits the teacher, kicks the teacher's friend, or punches a boy in the stomach. Laurie grins "enormously," jokes with his father, and laughs "insanely" between accounts of the morning's events (92). Unusual for a father in ***The Lottery,*** Laurie's is not only present, but also supportive of his wife, whose questions and reactions are typically more urgent than his own. When she asks her husband whether kindergarten might be too "unsettling" for Laurie, he assures her everything will be all right (92).

Like most of Jackson's women, the unnamed mother tries to contain her fears. She responds "heartily," for example, when Laurie describes Charles's refusal to do exercises. But she also becomes "passionately" intent on meeting Charles's mother, and she goes to the neutral ground of a PTA assembly alone, no husband by her side. Once there, she is restless, "scanning each comfortable matronly face, trying to determine which one hid the secret of Charles. None of them looked to me haggard enough" (96). She resembles the questing women in **"The Daemon Lover"** and **"The Renegade"** as she cautiously approaches Laurie's teacher for help, and her quest too ends in humiliation. Unexpectedly learning that Laurie has had some adjustment problems, the surprised narrator quickly assigns the blame to Charles. The first protagonist in ***The Lottery*** to laugh, she sympathizes with the teacher for having her hands full with Charles in her class, but she laughs alone. With the teacher's closing words, another of Jackson's women is abruptly enlightened, and speechless as a result: "'Charles?' she said. 'We don't have any Charles in the kindergarten'" (96). The narrator had studied every face but her own for signs of the worry she bears as the anxious mother who unknowingly harbors "the secret of Charles."

In the last three stories in the second group, Jackson broadens her focus on families to include a third generation. Grandmothers are powerful forces in each case, and the challenges issued them by their children or grandchildren form a central conflict in all three. In several ways resembling **"Charles," "Afternoon in Linen"** portrays Harriet, a 10-year-old who deceives her grandmother, embarrassing the woman in front of others. The opening sentence depicts a peaceful scene, a cool room with a view of flowering bushes, that in no way prepares for the final moment of humiliation. An allusion later in the paragraph, however, anticipates the reversal. The two women and two children who gather in the formal room all wear linen, a coincidence that quickly leads the precocious Harriet to identify with an episode from *Through the Looking-Glass,* a fantasy based on reversals. Her grandmother, dressed in white, reminds her of Lewis Carroll's gentleman in white paper, and "I'm a gentleman all dressed in pink paper, she thought" (97).

Harriet is also an Alice, ill-at-ease at the tea party held by her grandmother, Mrs. Lennon. To protect herself from Howard Kator's mocking laughter, she tells the boy's mother that Mrs. Lennon has lied about Harriet's ability to write poems. As Mrs. Lennon pressures her granddaughter to recite, the amused Howard, "his mouth open and a great delight growing in his eyes," becomes a Cheshire cat to Harriet's Alice (99). Mrs. Lennon herself finally reads one of Harriet's poems—recalling the many inset poems in the Alice books—only to have the girl announce she copied the piece from a library book. The incredulous grandmother allows Harriet to remove from her "unresisting" hand the sheaf of papers, which the girl protectively holds behind her back, "away from everyone" (102). The most obvious connection between **"Afternoon in Linen"** and the preceding stories in the second group is the confounding of Mrs. Lennon, the gracious hostess who thought she was in control of the situation. But Harriet is of interest too as a youthful version of the several characters in the book whose sense of dignity and security is threatened. Jackson's original ending made the threat more explicit by stating that the girl held her papers "in back of her, safe" (SJP, Box 15). Harriet shares her first name with a similarly distressed child in Jackson's *The Road through the Wall,* the miserable Harriet Merriam, whose mother invades her privacy by looking through the letters, poems, and other private writings in her desk.

"Flower Garden," another treatment of betrayal of self and others, is among Jackson's best stories. Like **"After You, My Dear Alphonse"** it criticizes racism but probes much further into the pressures that cause an otherwise sympathetic character to turn on persons of a different race and social class. One of Jackson's longest stories (at 30 pages), it also develops symbolic settings in more detail than is usual in ***The Lottery.*** Although elements of the absurd and the bizarre are absent, **"Flower Garden"** exhibits most features of a typical Shirley Jackson story: the besieged female protagonist, the initial uneasiness that grows to desperation, the presence of doubles, the impact of the outsider, and the calm, third-person narrative voice. A striking exploration of the family relationships central to the book's second section, the story is also a superior example of the several stories on social issues that Jackson wrote throughout the 1940s.

The flower garden of the title is the major symbol of the story. Planted by Mrs. MacLane, a young widow who moves to a small Vermont town to begin a new life, the garden flourishes under the care of Mr. Jones, a black man. By the end of the summer, however, the grass turns brown and the roses are dying. A violent thunderstorm blows a neighbor's branch onto the garden, and a discouraged Mrs. MacLane tells Mr. Jones to leave it for the next owner; she and her son will return to the city, where, she says, she will never have to see another garden. The fate of her flowers parallels Mrs. MacLane's rejection by the town; after an early period of warm welcome, she is shunned for her friendliness to Mr. Jones and his children.

While the reader's sympathy is directed to the Joneses and the MacLanes, Jackson complicates that response by relating events from the perspective of one of the townspeople, Helen Winning. This perspective marks a major change from an early, much shorter version of **"Flower Garden"** that told the story from the viewpoint of Mrs. Hanson, as Mrs. MacLane was originally named (SJP, Box 15). Mrs. Winning, not Mrs. MacLane, is Jackson's typically divided protagonist, and though she finally sides with the village against the outsiders, it is not without a struggle. In fact, Mrs. Winning's struggle, rather than Mrs. MacLane's fall from favor, is the main interest of the story. Although the action is not related in the townswoman's voice, her initial envy and admiration of Mrs. MacLane are unmistakable, as is her identification with the town and with the Winnings, "the oldest family in town" (103). As the newest family in town, Mrs. MacLane and Davey introduce a color and vitality that Mrs. Winning finds irresistible. She had once hoped to buy their cottage herself, but has grown used to living in the old family house on the hill, where her mother-in-law holds "the position of authority" (104).

The contrast between the cozy, newly refurbished cottage and the large cold house represents Helen Winning's conflict. When Mrs. MacLane shows Mrs. Winning her small green and rose bedrooms, Helen sighs, thinking of the "oddly-matched, austere bedrooms in the big Winning house" (111). Mrs. Winning feels a "quick wonderful relief" when she sees Mrs. MacLane has furnished the small home exactly as she might have "if she were eleven years younger" (109). Mrs. MacLane is about 30, and the slightly graying Mrs. Winning is probably about 40, but 11 years is also the period she has lived in the hereditary house, where she and her mother-in-law have come to look alike, "as women will who live intimately together, and work in the same kitchen and get things done around the house in the same manner" (103). In one brief seasonal span, from late winter to late summer, Helen grows even more like the older Mrs. Winning. But Mrs. MacLane has a temporary liberating impact on Helen, who surprises herself by telling the newcomer about her desire for the little house: "Why did I say that, she wondered; it had been a very long time since young Mrs. Winning had said the first thing that came into her mind" (108). Mrs. Winning also thinks "wistfully" of the garden Mrs. MacLane will create; maple trees are so thick around the Winning house that only a row of nasturtiums will grow there, carefully tended by Helen.

The smiling, hopeful Mrs. MacLane so affects her caller that Helen makes several suggestions for reciprocal visits to the Winning house, "and all without the permission of her mother-in-law" (111). The older Mrs. Winning is irritated when Helen comes home late, driven there by guilt over the meat she bought an hour earlier at the grocery and "dinner for the Winning men" (111). The younger Howard Winning kisses his mother but only nods to his wife on his way to the table with the oldest and the youngest Howard Winning. Surveying three generations of silent, efficient eaters, Helen is struck, "today more poignantly than ever before, that she had at least given them another Howard, with the Winning eyes and mouth, in exchange for her food and her bed" (112).

Helen's inner bitterness and sense of estrangement from the family are in conflict with her exterior politeness and spirit of cooperation, reminiscent of Mrs. Walpole in **"The Renegade."** In **"Flower Garden"** too an unforeseen crisis makes the strain intolerable. At first, Helen's friendship with Mrs. MacLane provides an escape from the tension at home. It blossoms along with the cottage garden, through days that are "miraculously long and warm" (115). But the idyl does not outlast the summer. Mrs. MacLane's angry response when Davey and Howard call young Billy Jones "nigger" suddenly puts Helen on the defensive. From this point on family ties and communal pressure render the bonds of friendship as fragile as the beautiful blue bowl in the center of Mrs. MacLane's living room. After Mr. Jones, Billy's father, comes to work in the MacLanes' garden, Helen is so "incredulous," "indignant," and "embarrassed" that she discontinues her daily visits (123).

On her first shopping trip without Mrs. MacLane, she has a disturbing conversation with Mrs. Harris, an unpleasant woman who laughingly asks about Mr. Jones and ridicules Mrs. MacLane's green and yellow sandals. Helen realizes the bright shoes are "inevitably right" for Mrs. MacLane, but she begins to worry what the town is saying about the MacLanes since Mrs. Harris invariably repeats the local gossip. When she mentions her annoyance with Mrs. Harris to her mother-in-law, the older Mrs. Winning unexpectedly blames Lucy Harris's bad temper on "that man of hers" (125).

The apparent cruelty of this latest Mr. Harris anticipates Helen's very visible cruelty toward the MacLanes. Weeks after the encounter with Mrs. Harris, another villager, Mrs. Burton, asks Helen whether she minds if Davey MacLane is not invited to a children's party. The younger Mrs. Winning feels troubled, but for her own sake, not on the MacLanes' behalf. Injecting the "weight of the old Winning house into her voice," she not only denies she cares but with malice "carefully" adds that Mrs. MacLane is, after all, "like a second mother to Billy" (129). Then, catching sight of Mrs. MacLane, who may have overheard, the two women laugh, recalling the brutal laughter of earlier stories. During a subsequent exchange with Mrs. MacLane, a courteous but evasive Helen enjoys sounding "exactly like Mother Winning" (131).

When an end-of-summer storm hurls Mrs. Burton's tree branch onto Mrs. MacLane's fading flowers, the town's triumph over the small family is almost complete. Mrs. Burton glances at the damage before symbolically shutting her door against Mrs. MacLane. Helen Winning, starting down the hill on her daily trip to the store, turns without responding to the greetings of both MacLanes. She moves "with great dignity, back up the hill toward the old Winning house" (134). In thus identifying with the ironically named Winnings, Helen seems to resolve her sense of separation from the family, but she loses even more than Mrs. MacLane does. With this final retreat to the dark homestead, Shirley Jackson wisely rewrote her original conclusion, in which the Mrs. Winning character (first called Mrs. Worthing) gave a big going-away party for the departing woman, who cheerfully announced that she would have a garden wherever she went.

"Dorothy and My Grandmother and the Sailors" follows anticlimactically on the disheartening last scene of **"Flower Garden."** Like **"My Life with R. H. Macy,"** the story seems deliberately positioned at the end of a section to offset the preceding gloom with a comic reprise of many familiar elements. As in **"Afternoon in Linen"** and **"Flower Garden,"** an authoritarian grandmother expects women of the younger generation to meet her standards. The moments of anxiety and panic common to previous stories recur. So, less menacingly, do the mealtime gatherings frequent in the second group of stories. Every meal in **"Dorothy and My Grandmother and the Sailors"** is at a restaurant and includes ice cream, however—a holiday spirit unusual for ***The Lottery.*** Equally unusual is the shift from the typical domestic setting in the eastern United States to the male world of a battleship anchored in San Francisco Bay. The first-person narrative relates the story to **"My Life with R. H. Macy"** and **"Charles,"** but this "I" is unique for creating an atmosphere of nostalgia. The opening sentence depicts a scene as attractive as Mrs. MacLane's short-lived flower garden or the glimpse through Mrs. Lennon's living-room window: "There used to be a time of year in San Francisco—in late March, I believe—when there was fine long windy weather, and the air all over the city had a touch of salt and the freshness of the sea" (135). Shirley Jackson generally reserved the first-person point of view for her most obviously autobiographical short stories, and the account of the shipboard excursion relates a childhood adventure with her friend Dorothy Ayling.

Despite its origins in fact and its almost vaudevillian humor, **"Dorothy and My Grandmother and the Sailors"** has a special connection with the James Harris ballad that comprises Jackson's epilogue to the book. The grandmother of the title seems to view each sailor as a potential demon lover and her two young charges as likely victims. Thus she rejoices when the narrator, who strays from the rest of the group, is found "in time" (139). In a more typical Jackson story, the protagonist's sudden perception that she has wandered alone into alien territory would be much more terrifying. Even in the context of a sightseeing expedition, it is an uneasy moment when "the lady [whose dress she was following] turned around and I realized that it was not my mother and I was lost" (138-39). Rescue comes in the person of "a tall man in a uniform with lots of braid" (139), a maritime version of the tall blue-suited James Harris of earlier stories. The grandmother grabs the girl from his side and retreats backward with her to join the mother, who nervously shakes her daughter while asking, "Aren't you ashamed?" (139). The episode so alarms both older women that they put an end to the annual springtime tradition of visiting the fleet, but the story does not end with the daughter's shaming. A second adventure on the journey to town involves Dorothy as well as the narrator. Both girls are panic-stricken when two sailors sit beside them at the movie theater. A wailing Dorothy clutches the grandmother, who assures her she will be safe at home with the older women. The story concludes prosaically with a reference to Dot's new gray coat, bought along with a matching one for the narrator, on the long day in the city: "She wore it all that year" (141).

Though the mood is very different, the plot recalls Helen Winning's eventual withdrawal from the possibilities for a freer life represented by Mrs. MacLane and her colorful house in **"Flower Garden."** The 12-year-old girls too are pulled from their predictable lives in suburban Burlingame to the excitement of the city and the ship. All the older women in the story, though, are intent on shielding them. Even Dot's mother "earnestly" tells the two to stay away from sailors; she herself is "never well enough" to go shopping in the city (136). The battleship becomes a metaphor for the broader male realm. It is hostile ground, where the girls and women tread "cautiously" and look about "apprehensively." In contrast, the narrator's Uncle Oliver (Jackson's own "Uncle Clifford" in her original manuscript [SJP, Box 15]), an ex-navy man who escorts them aboard, touches the paint "affectionately" (137). Gathering a small group of men and boys about him to discuss the ship's radio system, he is oblivious to his niece's misadventure. As in most of Jackson's stories, men are either ineffectual or disconcerting. Initiated into this awareness at the age of 12, the two girls do not complain as they retire to their Burlingame homes and to the sheltering warmth of their identical coats.

Group Three: Language Arts

A more heterogeneous group than the first two parts of ***The Lottery,*** the next six stories continue to explore male-female relationships, but children are much less in evidence than they were in the second group. As in the preceding section, the women are married, or at least in a long-term relationship with a man; men are more prominent than they were in most of the earlier stories, and they are often in conflict with women. Although the action is as realistic as it was in the last five stories, the element of the strange or the absurd so characteristic of the first group (and of the first two stories of the second) occasionally recurs, especially in verbal exchanges. Characters frequently manipulate each other in these stories, and words are often their weapons. Communication, a problem for many of Jackson's protagonists, becomes almost impossible at several points, leading to feelings of estrangement and displacement. Moreover, literary allusions and other references to writing are especially prominent in this section, emphasizing the power of the word—sometimes in contrast to the powerlessness of Jackson's characters.

The title of the first story, **"Colloquy,"** alerts the reader to a focus on language and relationships. Jackson's short stories contain a high percentage of conversation, but **"Colloquy"** is an extreme example. The narrator has little to add to Mrs. Arnold's nervous discussion with a physician; moreover, much of the woman's worry seems to derive from the sudden failure of language to express meaning. Two of her comments to the doctor begin, "When I was a little girl," as she contrasts the simple ways and speech of the past with the chaos of the present. She "hysterically" explains that her husband's anger over his inability to buy a copy of the *Times* led to his jumbled outburst on "social planning on the local level and surtax net income and geopolitical concepts and deflationary inflation" (147). When she asks whether everyone is insane, the doctor "severely" advises her to pull herself together: "In a disoriented world like ours today, alienation from reality frequently—" (147). An incredulous Mrs. Arnold echoes his key words—"Disoriented," "Alienation," "Reality"—as she stands and exits.

The physician's jargon relates him to the pompous Mr. Arnold and thus reduces the "competent-looking and respectable" man (145) to an object of satire. Linda Trichter Metcalf remarks that both men utter words "removed from the operational frame of human activity, and drawn from vocabularies that have no roots in the content of the wife's world."[29] But the doctor's interrupted assessment of Mrs. Arnold's problem also summarizes and illustrates the themes of several stories in ***The Lottery.*** Appropriately, **"Colloquy"** is the first story in Jackson's contents page for the projected collection ***The Intoxicated*** (SJP, Box 16). The physician's comments sound surprisingly like Stanley Edgar Hyman's remarks in the preface to *The Magic of Shirley Jackson* (1966), where he describes Jackson's "fierce visions of dissociation and madness, of alienation and withdrawal, of cruelty and terror" as "a sensitive and faithful anatomy of our times, fitting symbols for our distressing world of the concentration camp and the Bomb" (*MSJ,* viii).

The title character in **"Elizabeth"** has a milder communication problem than Mrs. Arnold, but her underlying discontent is just as serious. Far from being intimidated by words, she deals with them daily as a fiction editor (the position Shirley Jackson held on the Syracuse University literary magazine), and she often uses them dishonestly or cruelly. Perfunctorily reading a new client's manuscript, she copies a paragraph into her own notebook to use in a story she is writing. Her letter to the author follows a formula, and she randomly consults the manuscript to praise a character before delivering a sales pitch for professional editing services. More of an aggressor than Jackson's typical women characters, Elizabeth does not even bother to be polite when she fires the new office secretary, Daphne Hill. Envying the young woman's attractiveness, she criticizes her dress and her untidy hair, then lies that Robert Shax, the head of the literary agency, wants Daphne to quit the job. Elizabeth is similarly ruthless when an old family friend calls with a message from her father and an invitation for the evening; she says she has an important dinner appointment and hangs up before the elderly Mr. Hunt finishes talking. Earlier in the day, she had thrown a plaintive letter from her father into the trash. She resents being reminded of the home she willingly left behind: "They hang on to me, she thought; they're holding me back, with their letters and their 'Yrs. afftly.,' and their sending love back and forth" (177).

The home Elizabeth has established for herself in New York is not a real home either; it can assume a "sham appearance of warmth and welcome" when she needs "a place to hide in" (150), but the single armchair in the one-room apartment is hard and the gray paint on the end table is chipped. Her dusty kitchen is as ill-furnished as the kitchen in **"The Villager,"** and her former competence at cooking has dwindled, "with the rest of her daily life," to "a miniature useful only as a novelty on rare occasions" (189). Even her body has shrunken to an unappealing thinness. The narrator sums up Elizabeth as "a rather unhappy and desperate young woman with little or no ability to make things gracious" (188).

In her desperation, Elizabeth especially resembles the fiancée of **"The Daemon Lover,"** and she too is unfortunate in her men. Her employer-boyfriend's most extravagant display of affection is a pat on her head, and when he says, "We get along pretty well, don't we, Liz?," she simply answers, "Fine" (159). The response is as automatic and perhaps as untruthful as the "fine" with which she earlier reacted to the drugstore clerk's announcement that he had sent his newly completed play to a rival agency. Cynical about her relationship with Robbie, Elizabeth studies him coolly during their argument over Daphne: "He thinks I'm awed, she thought, he's a man and he's cowed me" (169). But she still looks to men for an escape from her boring life.

Finally, Elizabeth phones Jim Harris, the firm's one successful client and now an ex-client because of a fight with Robert Shax. Although he sounds as ordinary as the cigar-smoking Mr. Harris in **"Like Mother Used to Make,"** his signed photograph on the office wall is a troubling icon, a constant reminder of the agency's major loss. For Elizabeth, he is the final hope for a better life, and she refuses to be put off by his evasive references to a visiting kid sister when she pressures him to meet her for dinner. She transforms him in her imagination from a heavy-faced man with a "thin voice" to "a stranger, a gallant dark man with knowing eyes who watched her across a room"; she fantasizes that he is "a quiet troubled man" who loves her and who, like Elizabeth, needs "sunlight, a warm garden, green lawns" (191). In identifying Jim Harris with her dream world, Elizabeth makes of him the mysterious lover that he proves to be in **"The Daemon Lover"** and, even more dramatically, in **"The Tooth,"** a story in the final section of ***The Lottery.***

Unfortunately for Elizabeth, Jim is probably no more willing to play the role of romantic rescuer than Jamie was in **"The Daemon Lover." "Elizabeth"** ends the way the other story began, with careful preparations on the woman's part, but no guarantee the eagerly awaited caller will ever arrive. At one time, Jackson had planned to write a novel about Elizabeth. The action was to parallel "the discovery and condemnation of a witch" as Elizabeth, metaphorically in league with the devil (her employer, Robert Shax), progressed to a "figurative destruction": her decision to return to her childhood home to keep house for her father.[30] Interestingly, the production of words provides the livelihood of the devil and his cohorts in **"Elizabeth."**

In **"A Fine Old Firm,"** as in **"Elizabeth,"** cold women symbolically long for the warmth of the sun, but their manipulative ways leave them in the shadows. This next story, with its restrained portrayal of anti-Semitism, has even more in common with **"Flower Garden,"** where Helen Winning yearned for springtime and then rejected the fruitfulness represented by Mrs. MacLane. Like the two generations of Winning women in "Flower Garden," Helen Concord and her mother in the end present a politely cool front to a generous outsider, Mrs. Friedman; the family names of the Winnings and the Concords are equally ironic. **"A Fine Old Firm"** originally appeared in the *New Yorker,* whose typical stories were, and often still are, less concerned with plot development than with the subtleties of situation and character.[31] Jean Stafford's biographer, Charlotte Margolis Goodman, speculates that many of Stafford's stories might have followed this model because of the early encouragement of Katharine White, the *New Yorker*'s fiction editor.[32] White may similarly have influenced Shirley Jackson, whose **"Trial by Combat," "After You, My Dear Alphonse," "Afternoon in Linen," "Colloquy,"** and **"Come Dance with Me in Ireland"**—all first published in the *New Yorker*—de-emphasize action and stress a civilized confrontation of opposing characters. Dialogue conceals and reveals much in these clashes. It is a story type that can be found in Jackson's earliest fiction for journals at Syracuse University in 1938 and as late as **"A Great Voice Stilled,"** published in *Playboy* in 1960.

Reminiscent of **"Trial by Combat"** and **"After You, My Dear Alphonse,"** the quiet battle in the foreground takes place against the backdrop of world war. Bob Friedman and Charles Concord are army friends, stationed "far away" (195). Their friendship leads Mrs. Friedman, dressed in a warm fur coat, to call unexpectedly on Mrs. Concord, whose house is within a few blocks of hers. A more formal woman than Mrs. Friedman, Mrs. Concord does not echo the caller's easy laughter, and she continues to call her son "Charles" while Helen and Mrs. Friedman refer to him as "Charlie." Both Concord women seem to resent the long-distance friendship that has developed between Mrs. Friedman and Charlie. They do not offer refreshments, nor do they suggest a return visit to their cold living room, but their greatest rebuff is Mrs. Concord's politely automatic rejection of Mrs. Friedman's suggestion that her husband might find a place for Charlie in his law firm. Apparently with no thought of consulting her son, she explains that Charles will join Satterthwaite & Harris, a "fine old firm" in which Mr. Concord's grandfather was a partner (197). Like the Winning homestead in **"Flower Garden,"** the old firm carries the weight of a long tradition. In contrast, the friendship of the two young soldiers seems tenuous, as susceptible to family pressure as the boyish brotherhood of Johnny and Boyd in **"After You, My Dear Alphonse"** or the short-lived companionship of Helen Winning and Mrs. MacLane. Destined to bind himself to Mr. Harris, Charles will probably find it expedient to dissociate himself from the Friedmans and the opportunity for personal freedom that their name implies.

Respectability matters so much to Mrs. Concord that it makes her cruel in her refusal of Mrs. Friedman's offer. Decorum in word and action is equally important to Mrs. Wilkins in **"The Dummy,"** though here too decorum masks fear and disgust. Mrs. Wilkins selects a restaurant that is twice described as "respectable" in the opening sentence, and she nostalgically contrasts an ugly ventriloquist in the floor show with a "nice" young singer in the "nice" programs of the past. After dismissing the dummy act as "coarse," she "primly" turns her attention to her ice cream. The aloof Mrs. Wilkins, however, injects herself into a subsequent three-way dispute among the ventriloquist, his dummy, and his girlfriend or wife; slapping the obnoxious mannequin, she spontaneously produces a rather tasteless show of her own. The distorted figure, with its disembodied speech, is an exaggerated version of wooden humans like Mrs. Wilkins.

Although Mrs. Wilkins and her friend Mrs. Straw leave with dignity, like the affronted Helen Winning at the end of **"Flower Garden,"** they seem more lifeless than the dummy Marmaduke in the instant before Mrs. Wilkins attacks. Wordlessly, Mrs. Wilkins's mouth "opened, and shut again," and Mrs. Straw "watched blankly" (207). Distanced by poor seats and their lack of interest, the two women had been able to ignore the comedy routine between the ventriloquist Joey and the "grotesque wooden copy of the man" (203). But they are close enough to the entertainers' table to hear the nasty conversation that follows between Joey and a woman Mrs. Straw belittles as "our friend in the green dress" (204). Schizophrenically, the ventriloquist addresses the woman with increasing crudeness in Marmaduke's voice; his own tones conceal the anger he projects through the dummy. Thus the grinning mannequin loudly insults her after she pleads with Joey to be quiet and to stop drinking: "Just because a man wants to have a good time she has to freeze up like an icebag" (206-7). The ventriloquist responds to this insinuation of frigidity by warning Marmaduke to "talk nicer to your old mother," but the dummy vulgarly recommends that the "old bag" can "get back on the streets" if she is unhappy with Joey's attempt to enjoy himself (207).

Mrs. Wilkins's disdain for the spectacle does not adequately explain the violence of her response. In directing her slap at the dummy, she transfers her anger much as Joey does. The source of this anger may lie in her unexpected identification with the girl in green, Marmaduke's "old mother." Mrs. Wilkins appears to link the dummy with her son Walter, whose name comes up throughout her conversation with Mrs. Straw. "Seems like there's a lot he doesn't tell us," she complains to her friend (201). Perhaps she hears Walter, not Joey, in Marmaduke's derision and momentarily forgets whom she is striking. The illusion that the dummy is real continues even after the two women stiffly leave. The ventriloquist and the girl look together at the "slumped" and finally silent figure, and she reaches over to straighten his head as if he has drunk himself into the stupor she had dreaded to see in Joey.

In his burlesque duplication of Joey, the dummy is a dramatic image of the many other doubles and role players in ***The Lottery,*** from Hilda Clarence's pose as Nancy Roberts in **"The Villager"** to Laurie's creation of a fractious alter ego in **"Charles."** Marmaduke is an especially uncanny counterpart: "where the man was small and ugly, the dummy was smaller and uglier, with the same wide mouth, the same staring eyes, the horrible parody of evening clothes, complete to tiny black shoes" (203). As Cullen Murphy observes in an *Atlantic* essay, there is "something surreal and ghastly" about a dummy; Murphy cites the several cases in which "dark forces" control the figures in television shows like "The Twilight Zone" and "Night Gallery," as well as in a film which preceded Jackson's story by a few years, the 1945 *Dead of Night.*[33] Also disconcerting is the ventriloquist's separation of language from a human source. When a wooden replica of life is endowed with speech, the effect is akin to that in **"Colloquy,"** where men sound like machines.

The split setting of a two-level bookstore introduces another group of disjunctions in **"Seven Types of Ambiguity."** Dennis Welch posits a "possible ruse in the story and a subtle ambiguity based on the ruse and suggested by the story's title."[34] The ruse involves a contradiction between speech and intent, reminiscent of the contrast between Joey's conciliatory words and the anger he projects through Marmaduke. Welch believes the interest a young character expresses in William Empson's *Seven Types of Ambiguity* masks his collusion with the store owner, Mr. Harris, to unload the book on a naive customer. Welch does not mention the other James Harris stories, but his reading would relate the seemingly benign proprietor to the several earlier Harrises, with their devious behavior. An alternative reading, however, could preserve Mr. Harris's culpability and add to it that of the middle-aged shopper, while rendering the young college student, Mr. Clark, innocent of mercenary designs. Instead of questioning the boy's motives in several times mentioning Empson, we might ask why the customer, who benefits from the boy's advice in selecting the books he has come to buy, does not reward him by giving him a work he so obviously wants but cannot afford. Perhaps envying the 18-year-old's superior education, the man asks Mr. Harris to add the single odd volume to all the neatly matched sets of nineteenth-century British novels he has chosen. Instead of discouraging the purchase, Mr. Harris simply glances up and then adds one more figure to his price list.

Welch credits Shirley Jackson with intentional ambiguity and thus does not insist on his interpretation to the exclusion of others. Moreover, his essay, one of the few written on a Jackson story other than **"The Lottery,"** has the virtue of imaginative attention to the text that Stanley Edgar Hyman praises in a chapter on Empson in *The Armed Vision: A Study in the Methods of Modern Literary Criticism.* Published in 1948, the year before ***The Lottery*** collection, *The Armed Vision* says that Empson's book contains "the most elaborate and probably the finest close reading of poetry ever put down, the fantastic, wonderful, and almost endless spinning out of implications and linguistic possibilities."[35] The spiral stairs to the bookstore's basement room become a metaphor for Empson's intricate readings and for Jackson's surprising twists of plot. "Watch the bottom step," warns Mr. Harris. "There's one more than people think" (210).

There is not only one more step, but also one more story to the shop than is obvious from the main level, again suggestive of Jackson's layers of meaning. The "little upstairs bookshop," a "neat small store" attended by a girl, provides entry to Mr. Harris's very different preserve (209). The underground room seems enormous, its rows of tall bookcases, lines of book tables, and piles of books on the floor lit by dirty ceiling lights that customers are to turn off as they "grope" their way back to Mr. Harris's cluttered desk with their purchases. In contrast to the best-sellers and art books on display upstairs, the basement stock is for more serious readers. Mr. Harris acts as if the large cold room is a man's domain. Although the wife of the middle-aged customer enters the basement first and seems more at ease there than her husband, Mr. Harris leads her to his chair near the coal stove, where she remains seated until her husband signals "Ready, Mother?" at the end of the story (216). The man twice says that "we" would like to buy some books, but the woman makes only one request, for *Jane Eyre,* and the husband and Mr. Clark search through the stacks without any further suggestions from her. A male-female opposition is evident too in Mr. Clark's remark that the woman would be pleased with a set of Jane Austen as well as the set of Brontës, while choosing Dickens, Meredith, and Thackeray for the man. Characterized mainly through her soft voice, the wife remains disappointingly silent when her husband and Mr. Harris complete the sale with the last-minute addition of Empson, a book that the buyer, who used to enjoy Dickens and Twain, will probably never read.

Another text, Yeats's "I Am of Ireland," provides the title for **"Come Dance with Me in Ireland,"** which was selected for *The Best American Short Stories, 1944.* John O'Flaherty, the old man who quotes Yeats in the story, gains dignity from his association with the poet and his poetry, despite a humiliating encounter with three women whose concerns are more prosaic. The impoverished Mr. O'Flaherty is ringing Mrs. Archer's doorbell to sell shoelaces when he almost faints. Much as Mrs. Wilson attempts to impose her charity on Boyd in **"After You, My Dear Alphonse,"** Mrs. Archer and her friends force inappropriate help on the elderly beggar. Mrs. Archer and the middle-aged Mrs. Corn, together with the unmarried Kathy Valentine, speak about him in the third person as if he is not present, and many of their comments are insulting. Mrs. Corn is sure he is drunk. Kathy claims that "these people eat things like heaps of fried potatoes and eggs and—" (222), yet Mr. O'Flaherty barely touches the large meal Jean Archer dutifully prepares. The women introduce themselves as Miss or Mrs., reserving their first names, but Kathy Valentine calls Mr. O'Flaherty John. Mrs. Archer worries that her husband, Jim (the worst name a man can have in ***The Lottery***), might not approve of her generosity to the old man. Mrs. Corn protectively removes the Archer baby from his sight.

When Mr. O'Flaherty suddenly announces, "I knew Yeats," Kathy Valentine dimly responds, "Let me see—he was the writer, wasn't he?" (225). He then recites, "'Come out of charity, come dance with me in Ireland,'" a jibe at the awkward charity of the three women.[36] When the departing man tells Mrs. Archer, "We are of two different worlds, Madam" (226), he does not simply mean he is from what Kathy patronizingly calls "the old country" (225). He may be alluding to Yeats's "Sailing to Byzantium," with its contrast between the timeless world of art and the decaying sensual world represented by the useless meal and also by the Archer baby: "Whatever is begotten, born, and dies" (Yeats, l. 6). The materialistic world, says Yeats, is "no country for old men" (l. 1), for there "an aged man is but a paltry thing, / A tattered coat upon a stick" (ll. 9-10). Recalling the poem's scarecrow metaphor, the story twice mentions John O'Flaherty's "long, shabby black overcoat" (219), which no one invites him to remove.

The narrator's several references to the Archer baby boy contrast to the repeated identification of Mr. O'Flaherty as "the old man," evoking not only the image of the life cycle in "Sailing to Byzantium" but also the description of the young mother in Yeats's "Among School Children." The poem's aging narrator wonders whether the woman

> Would think her son, did she but see that shape
> With sixty or more winters on its head,
> A compensation for the pang of his birth,
> Or the uncertainty of his setting forth?
>
> (Yeats, ll. 37-40)

The maternal trio in Jackson's story is powerless to shield the Archer baby from a sad old age. Mr. O'Flaherty symbolically emphasizes his ties with them all by sarcastically leaving his handful of shoelaces on the floor for Mrs. Archer: "For your kindness. Divide them with the other ladies" (225). Before turning to go, he repeats the title passage—"Come dance with me in Ireland" (226)—to imply there can be a more joyful sort of giving than the women's shallow charity.

Insensitive at heart, the three women resemble the Concord women of **"A Fine Old Firm"** and the Winning women of **"Flower Garden,"** along with Mrs. Wilson of **"After You, My Dear Alphonse."** In contrast to Flannery O'Connor's exploration of salvific "moments of grace," Jackson often exposes such moments of gracelessness. Yeats's metaphor of the dance in all three of his poems mentioned above portrays a harmony unattainable by most of Jackson's protagonists, victims and victimizers alike. Their last names and their small sacrifice of eggs and figs for his lunch promise a fertile love that Kathy Valentine, Mrs. Archer (perhaps an allusion to Cupid), and Mrs. Corn cannot fully share with the man who knew Yeats.

Group Four: The Triumph of James Harris

The climactic last group of six stories is the grimmest in ***The Lottery.*** Pressures on the married female protagonists are so relentless and ubiquitous it seems almost inevitable the victim of the lottery in the final story should be one of their number. In contrast to the comic and satiric stories that conclude the first three sections of the book, **"The Lottery"** starkly proclaims the defeat of Jackson's most familiar character: the woman caught off guard. Despite touches of humor in the first and next to last stories in this section, the central characters in the other four stories are as desperate as the fiancée in **"The Daemon Lover"** and Mrs. Walpole in **"The Renegade."** In none of the preceding sections is the experience of losing control as fatal to the welfare of the women as a group.

The opening story, **"Of Course,"** handles the theme lightly by depicting a housewife's unnerving encounter with her new neighbors, Mrs. Harris and James Junior. "*Nice* people, obviously," Mrs. Tylor thinks as she watches the two get out of a taxi (229), but when she learns of James Senior's many odd prohibitions, she eagerly agrees to accompany her young daughter to the movies, even though she has just volunteered to entertain the Harris boy for the afternoon. Mrs. Tylor's staccato repetition of the title phrase echoes several earlier women—Mrs. Walpole and Elizabeth Style, for instance—whose automatic politeness is hardly expressive of their true feelings. In relaying her husband's disapproval of movies, radios, newspapers, and bridge games, Mrs. Harris likewise masks the anxiety that betrays her only once, when she "uncomfortably" laughs: "You'll be thinking my husband is crazy" (232).

In her manuscript, Jackson called the scholarly writer of Elizabethan monographs Mr. Stuart rather than Mr. Harris, and his son was Charles James Stuart, a humorous composite of the names of the post-Elizabethan Stuart kings (SJP, Box 17). The revisions drop the wordplay to suggest that the menacing spirit of James Harris will live on in a new generation. Though this Mr. Harris—eschewing the *New Republic* and the *New York Times*—seems more eccentric than hazardous, his wife's account of him makes Mrs. Tylor feel "the way she felt when she was irrevocably connected with something dangerously out of control" (232), a sensation that recurs many times in the remaining stories.

Among the best portrayals of lost control is **"Pillar of Salt,"** where a New Hampshire housewife becomes so overwhelmed by her perception of a disintegrating New York City that she is immobilized on a crowded street. Jackson emphasized the woman's growing uneasiness by excising from the manuscript a half-page account of a domestic ritual of dusting and cleaning that temporarily allayed Margaret's restlessness and made her "happy and ready for dinner" (SJP, Box 19). Briefer revisions also contribute to the seriousness of the story; for example, Margaret's husband, Brad, accompanies her to New York not simply for a vacation, as he did in the early version, but to view new products for his hardware store. Originally described as leaving the borrowed city apartment to look at farm machinery, he contemplates blowtorches in the final version, an action more in line with Margaret's vision of destruction. The title **"Pillar of Salt"** is another product of revision, a change from a phrase that was crossed out in the manuscript, almost obscuring the Hitchcockian word *vertigo*. Lot's wife, who was transformed to a salt pillar for her rebellion in looking back upon the burning of Sodom, epitomizes the many women in ***The Lottery*** who numbly sense their once solid worlds falling to ashes.[37]

Ironically, the train ride that brings Brad and Margaret to New York begins with "extreme pleasure" (235). At first they smile at occasional signs of breakdown: the repaired Empire State building (recently hit by a plane), the loose door of one taxi and flat tire of another. Margaret's good mood changes at a friend's party in a neighborhood where, according to a man who stands next to her in the noisy room, "someone's always getting killed" (240). A handwritten revision in Jackson's manuscript identifies the fellow guest as "a tall man in a blue suit," as if he has wandered out of the cocktail hour in **"The Intoxicated,"** but the final version inexplicably omits the guarded reference to James Harris. To Margaret's embarrassment, she flees the crowded apartment when people on the street shout "fire"; and though the fire proves to be two buildings away, a "faint feeling of insecurity tagged her the next day" (241). Brad seems unaffected, but Margaret becomes more and more distressed. The toy cash registers, shopping carts, and telephones she notices while shopping for gifts for her children appear to be "hideous little parodies of adult life" (242). She nervously perceives decay everywhere; the very granite of buildings is "eroding unnoticed" (243), and time itself becomes distorted, with "every hour forty-five minutes long, every day nine hours, every year fourteen days" (243). Like the fiancée in **"The Daemon Lover,"** Margaret is reluctant to voice her fears, "afraid to face the knowledge that it was a voluntary neck-breaking speed, a deliberate whirling faster and faster to end in destruction" (244).

A respite on Long Island, at a strangely familiar beach, recalls a vista Margaret has often entered in her imagination. A tune she remembered on the train from home recurs, "the symbol of the golden world she escaped into to avoid the everyday dreariness that drove her into writing depressing stories about the beach" (246). She laughs in recognition but answers "falsely" when Brad asks her to explain the humor in the "Godforsaken landscape." That Margaret is a writer and a woman of imagination comes as a surprise to the reader, but Margaret has no more success than Elizabeth Style or the demon lover's fiancée in bringing her fantasies to life. Instead, the gray and godforsaken landscape prevails. When a human leg washes up on the dunes, her Long Island host nonchalantly connects it with "one of these killings" (247), but the hysterical Margaret is convinced people are starting to come apart. Back in the city, she tries to calm herself, though the symbolic tune is now "nasty," with a "burden of suavity and expensive perfume" (248). Finally, she turns into the "pillar of salt" of the title while attempting to cross a street to her temporary apartment. She knows that, in wondering how people manage to beat the traffic light and reach the building, "she was lost" (252).

A similar doom befalls a younger housewife in **"Men with Their Big Shoes."** The title is Mrs. Anderson's derisive explanation for the dirt brought into the house where she serves as a cleaning woman for the "young Mrs. Hart," as she is twice called in the opening paragraph. Jackson's emphasis on her naïveté and inexperience is reminiscent of Hawthorne's depiction of the innocent protagonist of "Young Goodman Brown," and Mrs. Hart too is led close to despair by an older guide. In contrast to the cynical Mrs. Anderson, who has been unhappily married for 37 years, Mrs. Hart at the outset is very fortunate: it is her "first summer living in the country, and her first year being married and the mistress of a house; she was going to have her first baby soon, and it was the first time she had ever had anyone, or thought of having anyone, who could remotely be described as a maid" (255). She seems to have realized the country-house dream of the demon lover's fiancée. But when Mrs. Anderson insinuates Mr. Hart might be unfaithful, Mrs. Hart's "faint small uneasiness" about the older woman becomes a "sickening conviction" (256). Mrs. Anderson slyly arranges to move into the Harts' spare room (intended for the baby), arguing that a woman "who's older and knows a little more . . . might see a little more, too, maybe" (264). Wordlessly staring at the housekeeper, Mrs. Hart recognizes "with a sudden unalterable conviction that she was lost." This repetition of the "lost" Margaret's feelings in **"Pillar of Salt"** emphasizes the shared anguish of the women in the final section of ***The Lottery.***

While homes were threatened in **"Trial by Combat," "Like Mother Used to Make,"** and other stories, Mrs. Anderson's attack on the Harts' marital relationship is especially devastating. The housekeeper speaks often and bluntly of gender differences and conflicts that were hinted at in **"The Witch," "The Dummy,"** and **"Seven Types of**

Ambiguity." First, she contrasts men, who dirty the floors with their big shoes, to women: "A woman, you watch them, she always puts her feet down quiet" (255). But the offensive footprints are emblems of more serious, moral missteps. Mrs. Anderson believes all men treat their wives shabbily, whether by drinking, gambling, or chasing other women: "There's nothing any woman can do but make sure when she does have to get out she sure has some place to go," she warns Mrs. Hart (261). When she grimly concludes that fewer women would marry if they knew how their husbands would turn out, Mrs. Hart inadequately responds that "a successful marriage is the woman's responsibility" (261). Mrs. Anderson's innuendos capitalize on the younger woman's reticence in discussing sexual matters. For instance, Mrs. Hart quickly heads for the back door when Mrs. Anderson complains Mr. Anderson was at her all night again—"Not a minute's sleep for me" (259)—but she returns to her seat when it becomes clear he was shouting at his wife to get out. Mrs. Hart also seems ambivalent about her pregnancy, "irritably" smoothing her dress and wishing she could get into "decent" clothes again (263). Finally, her desperately cheerful smile yields to Mrs. Anderson's cruelly "knowing smile" (264).

All the anxieties and yearnings of Jackson's women culminate in the experience of Clara Spencer of **"The Tooth."** The original title, "Persephone," echoes in her surname and suggests that Clara's dreamlike journey to New York in the company of a mysterious stranger comprises an underworld descent (SJP, Box 18). If Clara is Persephone, Jim—who intercepts her on her long bus ride to the dentist's office—must be Pluto, god of the dead. Clara seems most full of life, however, when she rejects her past and runs, hand in hand with Jim, simultaneously on a city street and "barefoot through hot sand" (286). She is a Persephone who lacks any desire to return to her distant home and family.

Much as the Greek myth emphasizes the mother-daughter bond, **"The Tooth"** initially stresses the relationship between Clara and the unnamed man who is repeatedly identified as "her husband." Approaching the late-night bus that will take her from their small town to the city, Clara anxiously clings to his arm. Although she has been too rushed to dress herself properly, she has carefully arranged for the husband's meals and the children's care. Mr. Spencer also sounds solicitous, melodramatically stating he could not forgive himself if the painful tooth "turned out to be something serious" and he let Clara go to "this butcher up here" (266). His alarm is less appropriate to the anticipated dental extraction than it is to major surgery, perhaps of a gynecological nature. The sexual symbolism is made more explicit when the husband "accusingly" reminds Clara the tooth has troubled her repeatedly since he has known her and that she even had a toothache on their honeymoon (267). Clara's surprised "Did I?" suggests a powerful repression of the whole episode. The codeine, whiskey, and sleeping pill she has taken to blunt the present pain so far remove her usual inhibitions that her meeting with Jim in the "strange prison" of a bus is the start of a shocking liberation.

Richard Pascal sympathetically describes Clara's journey as a "quest for self-gratification and pure personal freedom," but he believes that, despite the upbeat tone of the ending, "Jim is a fantasy and she may be insane."[38] Pascal's footnoted comment on other appearances of Jim Harris in ***The Lottery*** obscures the significance of this final sighting of the tall man in a blue suit. In the context of the book's epilogue—Child Ballad No. 243—Jim is no fantasy but a charming stranger who lures the drab housewife with his attentiveness and his poetic speech: "'Even farther than Samarkand,' he was saying, 'and the waves ringing on the shore like bells'" (270). Before her tooth is removed, Clara remains on guard against Jim, who is several times identified as "the strange man" (270-71). She goes alone from the bus stop to the dentist's office, where her tooth now seems "the only part of her to have any identity" (276). Under the gas mask, she hallucinates that she is running down a corridor toward a laughing Jim, who awaits her with open arms. The dental surgeon presides over a sacrificial ceremony that metaphorically uproots Clara's past. "God has given me blood to drink," she cries to the nurse after the extraction (281). Still half asleep, she makes her way to the ladies' room, only to discover that in losing the tooth she has indeed lost her old identity. Not only does she fail to recognize her pale and worried face in the mirror, but she throws away her "C" lapel pin that she pulls off "with a feeling of relief" (285). With her hair freed from its clasp and her face clumsily brightened with lipstick and rouge, the refashioned woman walks "purposefully" to the elevator and is joined outside the building by Jim, who transports her to his exotic world as surely as Pluto transported Persephone.

Coming near the end of the book, **"The Tooth"** brings ***The Lottery*** full circle, back to the dowdy thirtyish woman and the laughing seducer who promised her a pastoral life in **"The Daemon Lover."** Given James Harris's history, Clara's departure with Jim is as hopeless a close as the fiancée's cruel rejection by Jamie in the early story. Though she escapes from the dull routine of domesticity, Clara blindly advances into another kind of bondage. Toni Reed describes the victims of the archetypal demon lover as "women who have stepped outside the accepted perimeters of society in some way," as Clara does by abandoning her conventional life. Typically these women are destroyed, physically or psychologically, because of "their own sense of powerlessness."[39]

Although James Harris figures only peripherally in the next to last story and not at all in **"The Lottery,"** these two final pieces violently reinforce the theme of female impotence and male control. "Got a Letter from Jimmy" recalls the equally brief **"Colloquy"** by dramatizing gender differences in a dialogue format with minimal narrative commentary. Judy Oppenheimer identifies the origins of the story in an argument between Jackson and Stanley Edgar Hyman over his refusal to open a letter from an estranged friend, Walter Bernstein (Oppenheimer, 104-5). The Library of Congress manuscript is entitled "Letter from David" (SJP, Box 16), but Jackson insists on a connection between the frustrated housewives of this story and **"The Tooth"** by changing the name of the writer to Jimmy. In both cases Jim somehow alienates the women from their husbands. The unnamed protagonist also recalls Mrs. Anderson of **"Men with Their Big Shoes"** by harshly contrasting the sexes: "Sometimes, she thought, stacking the dishes in the kitchen, sometimes I wonder if men are quite sane, any of them. Maybe they're all crazy and every other woman knows it but me, and my mother never told me and my roommate just didn't mention it and all the other wives think I know" (287). The three-page play of nerves breaks off with the wife's deadpan decision to murder her husband and to bury him in the basement: "Under the cellar steps, she thought, with his head bashed in and his goddam letter under his folded hands, and it's worth it, she thought, oh it's worth it" (289).

The woman's repressed anger jars with the dinnertime activities in which she is engaged. In her ability to mask passionate thoughts with a polite running conversation, she resembles Mrs. Walpole of **"The Renegade,"** but her rage is even greater, though her cause seems much more trivial than Mrs. Walpole's distress over her dog. She several times thinks "My God" and "Oh, God"—expletives she censors from her mild remarks to her husband. She dramatically anticipates he would break her arm if she accepted his challenge to open the letter herself. Although her determination to kill him should be taken no more seriously than her plan to steal the letter and scramble it with his eggs the next morning, the disparity between her silent monologue and her spoken words is characteristic of Jackson's more seriously threatened protagonists, from the demon lover's fiancée and Emily Johnson in the first group of stories to Mrs. Tylor and Margaret in this last section. Moreover, the mental violence of **"Got a Letter from Jimmy"** serves as a prelude to the physical violence of **"The Lottery,"** whose closing scene release the pent-up tensions of the preceding 24 stories.

This most famous of Jackson's works, originally printed in the *New Yorker,* achieves new significance from its position at the end of the volume. Like so many other stories in the book, **"The Lottery"** concludes with the defeat of a woman, in this case a horrible and final defeat, since Tessie Hutchinson is stoned to death by her townspeople when she draws the winning slip in the annual ritual of the lottery. Many critics emphasize the story's mythic elements, especially the rite of the scapegoat, a victim who must suffer for the well-being of the community. Among Jackson's papers at the Library of Congress is a library book check-out card from her college days for James Frazer's *Golden Bough,* a compendium of myth and folklore that Stanley Edgar Hyman discusses at length in *The Tangled Bank: Darwin, Marx, Frazer and Freud as Imaginative Writers.*[40] Jackson credited a Syracuse University instructor with providing the material for **"The Lottery"** in his Introduction to Folklore course (Friedman, 21). In the most detailed treatment of myth in the story, Helen E. Nebeker comments on the date, the characters' names, and the lottery equipment, particularly the three-legged stool that supports the box holding the slips of paper: "as old as the tripod of the Delphic oracle, as new as the Christian trinity."[41]

Shirley Jackson's account of writing **"The Lottery"** in her lecture "Biography of a Story" is more entertaining than illuminating. Most of the speech consists of excerpts from the hundreds of letters the *New Yorker* received in an unprecedented show of reader response. Jackson identifies three "themes" in these letters: "bewilderment, speculation, and plain old-fashioned abuse."[42] But she avoids any discussion of her own theme. When the *New Yorker* asked that she comment on the work, she said it was "just a story I wrote" ("Biography," 212). Hyman, on the other hand, remarks in his preface to *The Magic of Shirley Jackson,* "She was always proud that the Union of South Africa banned **'The Lottery,'** and she felt that *they* at least understood the story" (*MSJ,* viii). His emphasis on the contemporary relevance of her fiction suggests **"The Lottery"** has at least as much in common with **"After You, My Dear Alphonse," "Flower Garden,"** and **"A Fine Old Firm"** as it does with such mythically based stories as **"The Daemon Lover"** and **"The Tooth."**

Recent critical responses have pursued the direction indicated by Hyman. Peter Kosenko's Marxist-feminist reading concludes that the "democratic illusion" produced by the lottery is "an ideological effect that prevents the villagers from criticizing the class structure of their society."[43] Similarly, Joseph Church accuses Mr. Summers, the director of the lottery, of manipulating the "ostensibly democratic event."[44] According to Church, Tessie Hutchinson's cry of complaint is "a critical voice that states the truth about an unjust social arrangement." Fritz Oehlschlaeger adds that women are particular victims of the lottery, whose "real and continuing function" is "the encouraging of fertility within marriage, along with the patriarchal domination that accompanies it."[45] To lessen their own odds of winning the lottery, women produce large families, but their resistance to male authority is "subtly evident," says Oehlschlaeger. He notes, for example, Mrs. Adams's rebellious observation that "some places have already quit lotteries" (297).

Several assumptions of these critics weaken their arguments that the lottery and the social structure are biased against workers and/or women. Kosenko, for example, remarks that the townspeople address Bill Hutchinson rather than his wife when she arrives late, "since she 'belongs' to Bill" (Kosenko, 29). Yet Tessie has a friendly exchange with Mrs. Delacroix before two or three other neighbors assure Bill, who must be nervous at her absence, that she is making her way through the crowd. Kosenko also accuses Mr. Summers of wearing blue jeans "to convince the village that he is just another one of the common people," a pose that is undercut by the white shirt "more appropriate to *his* class" (Kosenko, 30). Perhaps Mr. Summers's clothing, like his greetings to the lottery participants, simply reflects his attempt to combine dignity and informality. Oehlschlaeger too makes statements that are impossible to substantiate. Because Tessie's fourth child, Davy, is noticeably younger than his siblings, he deduces she has had "recent difficulty in conceiving children" and, having passed her prime for childbearing, is "an extremely appropriate victim of a ceremony designed to promote fertility" (Oehlschlaeger, 264).

Such inferences are debatable, but, in focusing on the gender of the lottery's victim, Kosenko and Oehlschlaeger reach a conclusion toward which the whole book has been tending: women are especially prone to losing. Surely men have drawn the marked slip in the past. The deceased Mr. Watson, whose son Jack nervously selects a paper for himself and his mother, may have been a previous lottery winner. But, given the pattern established in most of the preceding stories in ***The Lottery*** collection, a woman is the more likely protagonist in any painful ritual of Jackson's invention, whether it be a broken engagement, a dental operation, or a community stoning.

Coincidentally, Jackson's "Biography of a Story" links the composition of **"The Lottery"** to a familiar woman's rite. According to Jackson, the story occurred to her three weeks before its publication while she was engaged in the maternal routine of pushing her daughter and the day's groceries uphill toward home in a stroller on "a bright June morning when summer seemed to have come at last" ("Biography," 211). She humorously speculates the strain of the final 50 yards could have "put an edge" to **"The Lottery,"** but the act of writing was unusually effortless. Aside from "one or two minor corrections," the version she sent her agent was virtually identical to her original draft, she says. And the *New Yorker* fiction editor asked only that she change the date she had mentioned in the story to coincide with the day the magazine was issued: 27 June (actually 26 June). Since the first four pages of Jackson's preliminary manuscript are missing from the Jackson Papers, we cannot determine her intended date. Nebeker and others have remarked that the date 27 June "alerts us to the season of the summer solstice with all its overtones of ancient ritual" (Nebeker, 102), and perhaps the allusion was originally even more pointed.

"The Lottery" file at the Library of Congress does clarify a few other features of the story's history, however. A marginal comment on the *New Yorker* galley proof contradicts Jackson's account of composition in "Biography of a Stòry" by noting "Eleanor March 16, 1948" and "*New Yorker* April 12, 1948" (SJP, Box 17). Apparently Jackson completed the story several weeks earlier than her lecture suggested, calling into doubt her reference to an inspirational early summer stroll. More important, her revisions were more extensive than she indicated in the speech. Several of the changes are indeed minor. For example, there is no blank space in the manuscript after Mr. Summers completes the roll call with "Zanini" (298). Immediately after adding the space, Jackson changed her transitional "Then" to "After that." But other revisions are more substantive. Occasionally, the changes responded to remarks in the margin of the manuscript, some of them in the form of questions and imperatives. The careless handwriting resembles Jackson's own, but it could be that of Stanley Edgar Hyman, who often discussed her writing with her. (Jackson rarely, if ever, addressed herself as "you" in the margins of her work.) Reacting to a marginal "Better say what they did!," she added the following sentences to Steve Adams's exchange of greetings with Joe Summers: "They grinned at one another humorously and nervously. Then Mr. Adams reached into the black box and took out a folded paper. He held it firmly by one corner as he turned and went hastily back to his place in the crowd, where he stood a little apart from his family, not looking down at his hand" (296).

Three revisions clarify statements in the original manuscript. After Mr. Summers asked Janey Dunbar whether she had a grown boy to draw for her in the absence of her injured husband, a comment in the margin inquired, "Wouldn't he know? Small place." Jackson subsequently explained, "Although Mr. Summers and everyone else in the village knew the answer perfectly well, it was the business of the official of the lottery to ask such questions formally. Mr. Summers waited with an expression of polite interest while Mrs. Dunbar answered" (295). Similarly, Jackson changed "Mr. Summers said" to "Mr. Summers asked formally" (299) when a marginal note remarked, "Here again, he'd know"—in this case, how many children the Hutchinsons have. Both of these emendations emphasize the ceremonial aspect of the lottery. The most important clarification, however, concerns Tessie's distraught shout when her husband draws the marked lottery slip. Originally, Tessie had accused Mr. Summers, "You made him take it." Addressing the margin's query, "Could you make this a little clearer?," Jackson rephrased the charge to remove the possible implication of force on Mr. Summers's part: "You didn't give him time enough to take any paper he wanted" (298). Joseph Church quotes this passage to support his claim that "Summers and company have rigged the lottery so that they'll never be chosen" (Church, 11), but the original wording would have given much stronger support to his argument.

Another major change appears on a separate scrap of paper that does not correspond to any marginal remark in the draft. In a much reworked typed passage, with several cross-outs and handwritten insertions, Jackson added some of the most familiar lines in the story, Old Man Warner's complaint that "next thing you know, they'll be wanting to go back to living in caves, nobody work any more, live *that* way for a while. Used to be a saying about lottery in June, corn be heavy soon. First thing you know, we'd all be eating stewed chickweed and acorns. There's *always* been a lottery,' he added petulantly. 'Bad enough to see Mr. Summers up there joking with everybody.'"[46] The addition underwent minor changes in punctuation and a modified reference to Mr. Summers as "young Joe Summers" in the published version of **"The Lottery"** (297). Barbara Allen's folkloristic reading suggests the fertility proverb "makes it clear that the ceremony is associated with the success of the year's crop and, by implication, with the community's continued existence."[47] Yet, as Nebeker explains, for several of the villagers, the "present rite" differs from the "meaningful ritualistic slaughter of the past" (Nebeker, 104). With its post office, bank, coal business, and grocery store, the village economy may have grown enough beyond its agricultural foundation to weaken an earlier faith in the necessity of fertility ceremonies. The storyteller observes that "in some towns there were so many people that the lottery took two days and had to be started on June 26th" (291).

The large cast of characters and the communal action distinguish **"The Lottery"** from the rest of Jackson's book, and most critics view the story as either an indictment of unthinking adherence to outmoded ways or a critique of an unjust class system. But we should not overlook Tessie Hutchinson's relationship to the many other women who fight losing battles in ***The Lottery*** collection. Like most of Jackson's housewives, she grows increasingly insecure, even in the company of her family. Her late arrival for the drawing in the town square signals her initial uneasiness. Given the nature of the lottery, Tessie's casual "Clean forgot what day it was" (294) is hard to accept, unless she has repressed the memory as Clara Spencer in **"The Tooth"** repressed the painful aspect of her honeymoon. After Tessie charges Mr. Summers with rushing her husband into drawing the marked slip for the Hutchinsons, Bill himself orders her to be quiet. Unlike such housewives as Mrs. Hart (**"Men with Their Big Shoes"**) and Mrs. Walpole (**"The Renegade"**), Tessie is not reduced to polite rejoinders. Frantically, she demands that her married daughter Eva take a chance along with the rest of the family in the second phase of the lottery, even though Mr. Summèrs gently reminds her that daughters draw with their husbands' families. Before Tessie finally reaches into the battered lottery box, she looks around "defiantly" (300), and Bill has to force the paper from her hand to reveal the black spot to the crowd.

Two of her children, Nancy and Bill Jr., are too busy smiling and laughing in relief at their own safety to express any sorrow for their mother, and Tessie reaches out "desperately" as the townspeople, including her youngest child, advance with stones in their hands (301). Her final scream, "It isn't fair, it isn't right" (302), is cut short as the crowd surrounds her. In death, Tessie becomes the last and the most permanently silenced of the large, confounded sisterhood in ***The Lottery; or, The Adventures of James Harris.*** Though she is stirred to a brief resistance that contrasts with the more usual passivity of Jackson's protagonists, she shares with most of them—girl, woman, and the occasional man—the bleak epiphany that she is lost.

Notes

1. *Cross-Section: A Collection of New American Writing,* ed. Edwin Seaver (New York: L. B. Fischer, 1944), 555. Jackson's "Behold the Child among His Newborn Blisses" appears in *Cross-Section,* 292-98.
2. Shirley Jackson Papers, Box 16, Library of Congress, Washington, D.C.; hereafter cited in text as SJP. This essential collection for research on Jackson contains 41 archival boxes of letters, drafts, proofs, sketches, early diaries, and other material. Boxes 15-19 hold the manuscripts of about 190 stories and other short pieces, many unpublished. The preliminary pages for the "Intoxicated" volume are in a Library of Congress folder with drafts of the story "The Intoxicated," first published in *The Lottery.* Several *Lottery* stories not listed in the contents for "The Intoxicated" appeared in magazines in 1948 and 1949.
3. *The Lottery* (New York: Fawcett Popular Library, 1975).
4. See Susan Garland Mann, *The Short Story Cycle: A Genre Companion and Reference Guide* (Westport, Conn.: Greenwood Press, 1989).
5. A Mr. Harris figures importantly in "The Daemon Lover," "Like Mother Used to Make," "The Villager," "Elizabeth," "Seven Types of Ambiguity," and "Of Course." The name Harris is briefly mentioned in "The Renegade," "Flower Garden," and "A Fine Old Firm." A mysterious Jim in "The Tooth" and a letter writer in "Got a Letter from Jimmy" are further variations on the name.
6. *The Lottery and Other Stories* (New York: Farrar, Straus & Giroux, 1982), 8, 15; hereafter cited in text.
7. "The Renegade," *Harper's,* November 1948, 40.
8. "A Fine Old Firm," *New Yorker,* 4 March 1944, 67.
9. "The Tooth," *Hudson Review* 1, no. 4 (1949): 508 and passim.
10. Stanley Edgar Hyman, "The Child Ballad in America: Some Aesthetic Criteria," in *The Promised End: Essays and Reviews 1942-1962* (Cleveland: World Publishing, 1963), 264; hereafter cited in text.
11. Donald Barr, "A Talent for Irony," *New York Times Book Review,* 17 April 1949, 4; hereafter cited in text.
12. Judy Oppenheimer, *Private Demons: The Life of Shirley Jackson* (New York: G. P. Putnam's Sons, 1988), 171; hereafter cited in text.
13. *The Road through the Wall* (New York: Farrar, Straus, 1948), 134-35.
14. Sharon O'Brien, *Willa Cather: The Emerging Voice* (New York: Oxford University Press, 1987), 372.
15. See Harvey Breit, "Talk with Miss Jackson," *New York Times Book Review,* 26 June 1949, 15; hereafter cited in text. Also, "On an Author," *Herald Tribune Book Review,* 5 July 1953, 2.
16. Lenemaja Friedman says the Glanvill references may have been suggested by the publisher to make *The Lottery* look "mysterious and, therefore, salable" (*Shirley Jackson* [Boston: Twayne

Publishers, 1975], 67-68; hereafter cited in text). On the other hand, the Shirley Jackson Papers contains a folder (Box 20) with two pages of material typed by Jackson from the Glanvill book, including the first of the four passages cited in *The Lottery.* There Jackson spells Glanvill as "Glanvil" and the first word of his title as "*Sadducismus,*" misspellings that are incorporated into *The Lottery.*

17. The passage is omitted from the 1982 paperback edition cited in this study, and it does not appear in the first American edition of 1949, but Jackson apparently saw that it was included in the first British edition of 1950. See Joseph Glanvill, *Saducismus Triumphatus; or, Full and Plain Evidence Concerning Witches and Apparitions,* facsimile ed., introduction by Coleman O. Parsons (1689; Gainesville, Fla.: Scholars Facsimiles and Reprints, 1966), 360-61; hereafter cited in text. The other three passages from Glanvill are on pp. 61, 143, and 227 of *The Lottery*; see Glanvill, 88, 466-67, and 90-91.
18. *The Witchcraft of Salem Village* (New York: Random House, 1956), 146.
19. Compare Eileen's vision to Aunt Fanny's prediction in Jackson's *The Sundial* of an imminent catastrophe whose survivors will be "a kind of chosen people" (*The Sundial* [New York: Farrar, Straus & Cudahy, 1958], 43; hereafter cited in text). "Harrison for President," an unpublished story in SJP, Box 16, closely resembles "The Intoxicated" in pitting a college-age daughter against a male friend of the family who frowns at her rude remarks during a Christmas party in her home.
20. See "The Phantom Lover," *Woman's Home Companion,* February 1949, 24-25, 95-98, 100. Friedman contrasts the two versions, arguing that James Harris "appears to be an actual man" in the *Woman's Home Companion* version but is either imaginary or a phantom in "The Daemon Lover" (51-52). Two other critics who think James Harris may be an illusion are Mary Kittredge ("The Other Side of Magic: A Few Remarks about Shirley Jackson," in *Discovering Modern Horror Fiction,* Vol. 1, ed. Darrell Schweitzer [Mercer Island, Wash.: Starmont, 1985], 10) and Steven K. Hoffman ("Individuation and Character Development in the Fiction of Shirley Jackson," *Hartford Studies in Literature* 8 [1976]: 201).
21. Elizabeth Bowen, preface to *Ivy Gripped the Steps and Other Stories* (New York: Knopf, 1946), ix.
22. See "The Villager," *American Mercury,* August 1944, 186-90.
23. "My Life with R. H. Macy," *New Republic,* 22 December 1941, 862.
24. Robert L. Kelly, "Jackson's 'The Witch': A Satanic Gem," *English Journal* 60 (1971): 1204.
25. M. Thomas Inge, *Comics as Culture* (Jackson: University of Mississippi Press, 1990), 97. Frederick Burr Opper, better known for "Happy Hooligan" and "Maude the Mule," drew "Alphonse and Gaston" for Sunday newspapers from 1902 to 1904. Several early silent films were based on the comic strip (Inge, 143). "Alphonse and Gaston" also appeared in newspaper ads for a short period in the 1940s (see Bill Blackbeard, "Alphonse and Gaston," *The World Encyclopedia of Comics,* ed. Maurice Horn [New York: Chelsea House, 1976], 78).
26. Carol Cleveland, "Shirley Jackson," in *And Then There Were Nine. . . . More Women of Mystery,* ed. Jane S. Bakerman (Bowling Green, Ohio: Bowling Green State University Popular Press, 1985), 201; hereafter cited in text.
27. Shirley Jackson wrote an updated version of the fairy tale in her one-act play, *The Bad Children,* music by Allan Jay Friedman (Chicago: Dramatic Publishing, 1959). The musical was Jackson's gift to her children, inspired by her daughter Joanne's need for a school play (Oppenheimer, 222).
28. See "Charles," *Mademoiselle,* July 1948, 87, 114, and *Life among the Savages* in *The Magic of Shirley Jackson,* ed. Stanley Edgar Hyman (New York: Farrar, Straus & Giroux, 1966), 398-403; hereafter cited in text as *MSJ.*
29. Linda Trichter Metcalf, "Shirley Jackson in Her Fiction: A Rhetorical Search for the Implied Author," Ph.D. diss., New York University, 1987, 126.
30. See SJP, Box 29, for Jackson's notes for the novel. The short story "Elizabeth" develops about half of the plot outline for the book-length project. In the short-story manuscript (SJP, Box 15) James Harris is Mr. Vining, a name Jackson borrowed from the same section of *Saducismus Triumphatus* that provided names for Elizabeth Style, Miss Hill, and Robert Hunt (Glanvill, 361). Shax, a devil's name, was also the name of one of Jackson's many cats (Oppenheimer, 116).
31. Scott Elledge (*E. B. White: A Biography* [New York: W. W. Norton, 1984], 182) thus characterizes the "new writing" promoted by Katherine White at the *New Yorker.* White recommended that editor Harold Ross publish Vladimir Nabokov, James Thurber, John Updike, John Cheever, and Mary McCarthy, among many others.
32. Charlotte Margolis Goodman, *Jean Stafford: The Savage Heart* (Austin: University of Texas Press, 1990), 188.
33. Cullen Murphy, "Hey, Let Me Outta Here!," *Atlantic,* August 1989, 66. Murphy's brief history of ventriloquism points out links with magic and the supernatural. He quotes a practicing ventriloquist on "the schizophrenic aspect of ventriloquism, the tension between illusion and reality, that both attracts and repels" (71).

34. Dennis Welch, "Manipulation in Shirley Jackson's 'Seven Types of Ambiguity,'" *Studies in Short Fiction* 18 (Winter 1981): 27.

35. Stanley Edgar Hyman, *The Armed Vision* (New York: Knopf, 1948), 277. In his acknowledgments Hyman particularly thanks Jackson, "who did everything for me that one writer can conceivably do for another and whose patience and kindness in regard to it are worthy of a far better work" (xiv). *The Armed Vision* is dedicated to Jackson as "a critic of critics of critics."

36. See William Butler Yeats, "I Am of Ireland," in *Selected Poems and Three Plays of William Butler Yeats,* ed. M. L. Rosenthal, 3d ed. (New York: Macmillan, 1986), 153; other poems from this collection cited in text.

37. Among the miscellaneous papers in SJP, Box 41, is a typed page on which Jackson copied the account of Abraham's bargaining with God over the fate of Sodom and Gomorrah from Genesis 18:20ff. The transcription ends with the heading "Chapter 19," a reference to the episode in which Lot's wife becomes a pillar of salt.

38. Richard Pascal, "'Farther than Samarkand': The Escape Theme in Shirley Jackson's 'The Tooth,'" *Studies in Short Fiction* 19 (Spring 1982): 139, 138. Metcalf similarly comments on Clara's "psychological collapse" (92).

39. Toni Reed, *Demon-Lovers and Their Victims in British Fiction* (Lexington: University Press of Kentucky, 1988), viii, 113.

40. Stanley Edgar Hyman, *The Tangled Bank* (New York: Atheneum, 1962), esp. 233-69. Jackson's University of Rochester library check-out card for *The Golden Bough* is inserted in a five-year diary for 1933-37 in SJP, Box 1, file 2. An entry in a separate 1935 diary in the same file says Jackson "Got 'Golden Bough'" on 12 November 1935.

41. Helen E. Nebeker, "'The Lottery': Symbolic Tour de Force," *American Literature* 46 (March 1974): 106; hereafter cited in text. An early folkloristic reading of "The Lottery" is Seymour Lainoff's "Jackson's 'The Lottery,'" *Explicator* 12 (March 1954): item 34. James M. Gibson summarizes several critics' responses to "The Lottery" in the introductory paragraphs of "An Old Testament Analogue for 'The Lottery,'" *Journal of Modern Literature* 11 (March 1984): 193.

42. "Biography of a Story," in *Come Along with Me: Part of a Novel, Sixteen Stories, and Three Lectures,* ed. Stanley Edgar Hyman (New York: Viking, 1968), 214; hereafter cited in text as "Biography."

43. Peter Kosenko, "A Marxist/Feminist Reading of Shirley Jackson's 'The Lottery,'" *New Orleans Review* 12, no. 1 (Spring 1985): 30; hereafter cited in text.

44. Joseph Church, "Getting Taken in 'The Lottery,'" *Notes on Contemporary Literature* 18, no. 1 (September 1988): 10; hereafter cited in text.

45. Fritz Oehlschlaeger, "The Stoning of Mistress Hutchinson: Meaning and Context in 'The Lottery,'" *Essays in Literature* 15 (Fall 1988): 259; hereafter cited in text. Gayle Whittier's provocative essay "'The Lottery' as Misogynist Parable" (*Women's Studies* 18, no. 4 [1991]: 353-66) appeared too late for me to incorporate her discussion of "male dominance" (356), which is more detailed than those of Kosenko and Oehlschlaeger.

46. In SJP, Box 17. This scrap, like Jackson's typical typed drafts, is written all in lowercase letters, which I have capitalized where needed. Hyman's second wife, Phoebe Pettingell, told Judy Oppenheimer that Hyman contributed the proverbial rhyme to "The Lottery" (Oppenheimer, 130, and note on this source, 288).

47. Barbara Allen, "A Folkloristic Look at Shirley Jackson's 'The Lottery,'" *Tennessee Folklore Society Bulletin* 46, no. 4 (December 1980): 121.

Jay A. Yarmove (essay date 1994)

SOURCE: "Jackson's 'The Lottery,'" in *The Explicator,* Vol. 52, No. 4, Summer, 1994, pp. 242-245.

[In the following essay, Yarmove analyzes the meanings of names and dates in "The Lottery," concluding that the story is designed to challenge the complacency of readers who believe a holocaust could never happen in contemporary America.]

The underpinnings of Shirley Jackson's famous post-World War II story **"The Lottery"** demonstrate that the work is far greater than the sum of its parts. The date of the lottery, its location, and the symbolic or ironic names of its characters all work to convey a meaning that is even more disturbing than the shock created by its well-known ending, namely, that despite assurances during the late 1940s that "it couldn't happen here," a microcosmal holocaust occurs in this story and, by extension, may happen anyplace in contemporary America. Coming after the revelation of the depths of depravity to which the Nazis sank in their eagerness to destroy other, "lesser" peoples, **"The Lottery"** upsets the reader's sense of complacency.

Jackson lets us know the time of the lottery at the outset of the story. From the description of the men's talk of "tractors and taxes" (211) and the depiction of Mr. Summers wearing a "clean white shirt and blue jeans" (213), we may assume that we are in the twentieth century, making the story's impact more immediate. But why does the author choose June 27 as the date on which the village holds its lottery? The summer solstice, June 21, has already passed, and the Fourth of July is yet to come. The date, if not the century, seems to have been capriciously chosen. Such is not the case, however. June 27 falls halfway between June 21 (the summer solstice) and July 4 (Independence Day). What significance do these two days bear that makes June 27 the perfect compromise between them?

In European societies, Midsummer's Day was celebrated at the summer solstice, not in the middle of summer as its name would suggest. Authors such as Shakespeare, August Strindberg, and William Golding have employed the pagan undertones of that day as a motif in *A Midsummer Night's Dream, Miss Julie,* and *The Spire,* respectively, for indeed Midsummer's Day has a long, heathen, orgiastic tradition behind it. American Independence Day, on the other hand, is redolent of democracy, freedom, and, to a certain degree, justice, because it marks the birth of a nation anchored in the belief that people "are endowed by their Creator with certain unalienable rights." June 27 bisects the two weeks between these dichotomous dates and may well embody the contrast between superstitious paganism and rational democracy, a dynamic that plays a central role in **"The Lottery,"** especially in light of the story's locale.

At no point does the author tell us where the lottery takes place, but we are made aware of several possible indicators. The town has a population of about 300, and farming seems to be the normal way of making a living. Most of the names are Anglo-Saxon in origin. The land yields an abundance of stones. Most important, the lottery is itself a model—albeit perverted—of participatory democracy, the kind that New England settlers made famous. All of these seem to point to New England as the locale of the story. It is also in keeping with New England's history of witch trials and persecutions. (Being pressed to death by heavy stones was not uncommon as a colonial punishment for witchcraft, as may be seen in Arthur Miller's *The Crucible.*)

Not only do time and place bear important clues as to the allegorical meaning of **"The Lottery,"** but the very names of the characters are laden with significance. The prominent names—Summers, Adams, Graves, Warner, Delacroix, and (most obviously) Tessie Hutchinson—have much to tell us. For the season of the lottery is summer, and the larger scope of this work encompasses mankind in general (for instance, "Adam" means "man" in Hebrew). "Graves" sounds a somber, fore-warning note of what will happen to Tessie, and the oldest man in town, Old Man Warner (the others have either died or been killed off) warns us about the primordial function of the lottery, which is to ensure fertility: "Used to be a saying about 'Lottery in June, corn be heavy soon'" (215). Mrs. Delacroix's name alludes to the pseudo-crucifixion of Tessie.

It is the irony that lies behind the protagonist's name, Tessie Hutchinson, that magnifies the allegorical force of this story. Historically, there really was a well-known New England Hutchinson—Anne Hutchinson, who, having been exiled from the Massachusetts Bay Colony in 1638 because of her religious beliefs, emigrated to Rhode Island, where she established her own church. Eventually, she and most of her family died in an Indian massacre outside of what is today New Rochelle, New York. Some might call such a woman a martyr, who was exiled and died for her beliefs. Our protagonist, however, has no strongly held beliefs, except her belief in self-survival. The name "Tessie" parodies the most famous Tess in literature, Tess Durbeyfield, the protagonist of Thomas Hardy's *Tess of the D'Urbervilles,* who in Hardy's portrait of her as the plaything of fate, dies ignominiously, since "the President of the Immortals, in Aeschylean phrase, had ended his sport with Tess" (446). Now we must ask, Is Tessie Hutchinson in our story an ingenue, as Hardy's protagonist clearly is?

Of course not! Tessie "came hurriedly along the path to the square . . . 'Clean forgot what day it was' she said to Mrs. Delacroix . . . and they both laughed softly. . . . 'I remembered it was the twenty-seventh and came a-running'" (213). "Mrs. Hutchinson said, grinning, 'Wouldn't have me leave m'dishes in the sink, now, would you, Joe?'" (214). Good-natured Tessie actually desires to come to the lottery, going so far as to run to it, although the rest of the townspeople are subdued, even nervous: the men's "jokes were quiet and they smiled rather than laughed" (211). Mr. Summers and Mr. Adams "grinned at one another humorlessly and nervously" (215). Young Jack Watson also appears to be nervous: "He blinked his eyes nervously and ducked his head" (214). Later, someone in the crowd says, "'Don't be nervous, Jack'" (216). And not only the men are nervous, of course. "'I wish they'd hurry,' Mrs. Dunbar said to her older son. 'I wish they'd hurry'" (216). However, to Tessie the lottery seems to be one great lark: when her husband, Bill, is called upon to choose his family's lottery ticket, Tessie urges him, "'Get up there, Bill'" (215), although "by now, all through the crowd there were men holding the small folded papers in their large hands, turning them over and over nervously" (215). What a great contrast there is, in short, between the crowd's nervousness and Tessie's nonchalance.

But when Tessie's family is chosen, she becomes a woman transformed. "Suddenly, Tessie Hutchinson shouted to Mr. Summers, 'You didn't give him time enough to take any paper he wanted. I saw you. It wasn't fair!'" (216). Subsequently, she yells, "'There's Don and Eva [the Hutchinsons' son-in-law and daughter]. Make *them* take their chance!'" (216). Putting aside for the moment her perfidy in singling out her married children as possible victims to increase her own chances of survival, we see that she is manifestly not the good-humored, whimsical matron whom we first saw eagerly entering the lottery. Her protests of the unfairness of the process—a thought that only now has occurred to her, since there is every likelihood of her becoming the chosen victim ("'I tell you it wasn't *fair*'" [217])—have a distinctly hollow ring to them, and her defiant glance around the crowd, her lips pursed, as she truculently goes up to the lottery box to pick her ticket, belies her earlier easygoing demeanor. Thus, the irony behind her name has come full circle. Her final assertion ("'It isn't fair, it isn't right'") is neither the cry of an innocent victim (Tessie is definitely not Tess Durbeyfield) nor a martyr's triumphant statement (Tessie is also certainly not Anne Hutchinson). It is the peevish last complaint of a hypocrite who has been hoisted by her own petard.

There were many Americans who, after the end of World War II and the revelations of the early Nuremburg trials in 1945 and 1946, smugly asserted that such atrocities could happen in Nazi Germany but not in the United States. After all, singling out one person, one religion, one race for pejorative treatment—these things just could not happen here. In her post-war novel *Gentleman's Agreement,* Laura Z. Hobson showed that such discrimination was in fact alive and well. Shirley Jackson adds an even more disturbing note in her story, which was initially published in *The New Yorker* in 1948: custom and law, when sanctioned by a selfish, unthinking populace, can bring an otherwise democratic and seemingly just society to the brink of paganism. Thus the date, the location, and the names in Jackson's story help to create the specter of a holocaust in the United States.

In this, **"The Lottery"** is eerily reminiscent of the ending of Hardy's *Tess.* When Angel Claire and Tess Durbeyfield flee to the pagan temple at Stonehenge, they see the "eastward pillars and their architraves [standing] up blackly against the light, and the great flame-shaped Sunstone beyond them: and the Stone of Sacrifice midway" (442-43). This image is an apt metaphor for the plot of **"The Lottery"**: despite modernity, democracy, and American neighborliness, the primitive, selfish, superstitious ghost of paganism has been allowed to rear its ugly head and destroy one of its own.

Works Cited

Hardy, Thomas. *Tess of the D'Urbervilles.* New York: Dodd, Mead, 1960.

Jackson, Shirley. "The Lottery." *The Lottery.* New York: Popular Library, 1949.

FURTHER READING

Bibliography

Herrick, Casey. "Shirley Jackson's 'The Lottery'." *Bulletin of Bibliography* 46, No. 2 (June 1989): 120- 21.

Secondary bibliography compiled as a supplement to Robert S. Phillips's 1966 checklist of Jackson criticism.

Biographies

Oppenheimer, Judy. *Private Demons: The Life of Shirley Jackson.* New York: G. P. Putnam's Sons, 1988, 304 p.

Detailed biography containing numerous photographs and extensive interviews with Jackson's children and friends.

———. "The Haunting of Shirley Jackson." *New York Times Book Review* (3 July 1988): 1, 16-17.

Provides biographical information on Jackson's writing of "The Lottery" and scrutinizes public and critical reaction to the story.

Criticism

Breit, Harvey. "Talk with Miss Jackson." *New York Times Book Review* (26 June 1949): 15.

Interview that followed the publication of "The Lottery" in which Jackson discusses her writing techniques and favorite authors.

Cleveland, Carol. "Shirley Jackson." In *And Then There Were Nine . . . More Women of Mystery,* edited by Jane S. Bakerman, pp. 199-219. Bowling Green, OH: Bowling Green State University Popular Press, 1985.

Provides an overview of the elements of horror and mystery in Jackson's major works, with recurring reference to "The Lottery."

Halsband, Robert. "Sketch Potpourri." *Saturday Review of Literature* XXXII, No. 19 (7 May 1949): 19, 36.

Review of *The Lottery* in which Halsband divides the stories into three categories: prosaic, socially conscious, and fantastic. Under this rubric, Halsband labels "The Lottery" a "failure" as a horror story, though he concedes that the tale "has at least publicized the work of a subtle and literate storyteller."

Stark, Jack. "Shirley Jackson's 'The Lottery'." In *Censored Books: Critical Viewpoints,* edited by Nicholas J. Karolides, Lee Burress, and John M. Kean, pp. 358-62. Metuchen, NJ, and London: The Scarecrow Press, Inc., 1993.

Discusses the banning of "The Lottery" from classroom study and explains what the story has to teach students about violence, law, individuality, chance, historical, political and social horrors.

Additional coverage of Jackson's life and career is contained in the following sources published by the Gale Group: *Authors and Artists for Young Adults,* Vol. 9; *Contemporary Authors,* Vols. 1-4R, 25-28R; *Contemporary Authors New Revision Series,* Vols. 4, 52; *Concise Dictionary of American Literary Biography,* 1941-1968; *Contemporary Literary Criticism,* Vols. 11, 60, 87; *DISCovering Authors; DISCovering Authors Canadian; DISCovering Authors Modules: Most-Studied Authors; Dictionary of Literary Biography,* Vol. 6; *Major 20th-Century Writers,* Vol. 2; *Something about the Author,* Vol. 2; *World Literature Criticism.*

Stephen Leacock
1869–1944

(Full name Stephen Butler Leacock) Canadian humorist, short story writer, essayist, biographer, and political economist.

INTRODUCTION

The author of thirty-five volumes of humor and twenty-seven works on history, biography, criticism, economics, and political science, Leacock is best known for satirical sketches that poke fun at human foibles. Leacock's acknowledged masterpiece, *Sunshine Sketches of a Little Town,* is a collection of related stories that satirize the provinciality and pettiness of the inhabitants of a small Canadian town. It is the best example of his craft, and uses humor to contemplate the incongruities of life as well as human hypocrisy and pretense. The tone of Leacock's other major work, the collection *Arcadian Adventures with the Idle Rich,* is slightly darker but still uses amiable humor to attack corruption, self-interest, and concern with money and power in a big city in North America. Leacock's conservative political stance is reflected in his humorous sketches of individualism, materialism, and worship of technology. Leacock's distinctive comic style, with its combination of British nonsense humor and understatement and American wit and exaggeration, made him the most popular humorist writing in English between 1910 and 1925. However, for many years his literary importance was overlooked by scholars, and some commentators considered his work lacking in seriousness and complexity. Critical reevaluation of his work has shifted this opinion, earning Leacock the reputation of Canada's comic master. Author and critic J. B. Priestly found Leacock's humor to express an essential Canadian quality, and the novelist Robertson Davies has called him "a humorist of distinguished gifts, with a range and brilliance not often equaled."

BIOGRAPHICAL INFORMATION

Leacock was born in 1869 in Hampshire, England. In 1876 he moved with his family to a 100-acre farm a few miles south of Lake Simcoe near the village of Sutton, Ontario. Life on the farm with his ten brothers and sisters was strenuous. Leacock's father's heavy drinking, wanderings, and eventual disappearance compounded the family's financial difficulties. Leacock's mother, however, was determined to give her children a good education, and Leacock attended Upper Canada College in Toronto. Leacock then entered the University of Toronto on scholarship in 1887 to study modern and classical languages and literature. However, his studies were cut short because his mother needed financial assistance to help raise eight siblings. In 1888 Leacock enrolled in a three-month training course to qualify for teaching high school. After his training he taught first at Oxbridge High School then at Upper Canada College—an engagement that allowed him to continue his studies at the University of Toronto—where he completed his B.A. in 1891.

After earning his degree, Leacock began publishing humorous articles in periodicals. His first piece appeared in the Toronto humor magazine *Grip,* in 1894. He continued to publish humorous sketches in Canadian and American magazines throughout the 1890s. Leacock's interest in the writings of Thorsten Veblen led him to pursue graduate studies in political science and economics under Veblen at the University of Chicago in 1899. While a student at Chicago, Leacock married Beatrix Hamilton, an aspiring actress from Toronto. He completed his Ph.D. in 1903 and began lecturing at McGill University in Montreal. He was appointed full professor and chair of the political science and economics department in 1908, a post he held until his retirement in 1936.

In 1910, with the financial assistance of his brother George, Leacock published *Literary Lapses,* a collection of previously published writings. The volume sold extremely well and was followed the next year with *Nonsense Novels,* a compilation of parodies of some of the most popular genres of literature, which established his fame. In 1912 Leacock published *Sunshine Sketches of Little Town,* a work based in part on his summers spent in Orillia and on his own childhood experiences. It was immensely popular in Canada and the United States, and cemented Leacock's reputation as the foremost humorist in Canada. *Arcadian Adventures with the Idle Rich,* published in 1914 was also a major critical and popular success. In 1925, Leacock's wife died of breast cancer, and he thereafter committed himself to fundraising drives for cancer research.

Leacock also enjoyed a distinguished career as an academic, publishing works in political science, history, and economics and lecturing widely in Canada and abroad. He was known as a great lecturer and raconteur. Leacock also wrote two biographies, *Mark Twain,* and *Charles Dickens, His Life and Work.* In 1935, he published *Humour: Its Theory and Technique.* After his retirement from McGill in 1936 Leacock went on a speaking tour in the west of Canada. The notes and speeches made on this month-long journey were published in *My Discovery of the West: A Discussion of East and West in Canada,* for which he won the Governor General's Award. In the following years, Leacock wrote various books about Canada, including *Canada: The Foundations of Its Future, Montreal: Seaport and City,* and *Canada and the Sea.* In late 1943 Leacock began writing his autobiography, but his work was cut short due to failing health. He was diagnosed with throat cancer in late 1943 and died on March 28, 1944.

MAJOR WORKS OF SHORT FICTION

Most of Leacock's collections of stories include pieces that appeared previously in various magazines. The pieces in his first published work, *Literary Lapses,* include stories, anecdotes, monologues, dialogues, parodies of literary works, and reflections on a variety of topics. The volume is full of lighthearted nonsense stories as well as one of Leacock's best-known and more serious pieces, "My Financial Career," about a prototypical "little man" confronted by a an intimidating institution as he opens a bank account. In the story, Leacock treats with characteristic sympathy the honest and decent but powerless victim of an absurd and hostile world. Leacock's second volume, *Nonsense Novels,* a collection of burlesques of the popular fiction of his day, continues in the vein of the first collection. Among its inspired absurdities are the much-anthologized story "Gertrude the Governess; or, Simple Seventeen," in which the hero Lord Ronald is said to have "flung himself upon his horse and rode madly off in all directions."

Leacock's two most important works stand apart from his other books of humor in their artistic unity and seriousness of purpose, as they move from burlesque and absurdity to more ambitious satire. Both are collections of interrelated stories about lives in fictional towns. In *Sunshine Sketches of a Little Town,* Leacock's masterpiece, the narrator sets a tone of genial deprecation and bemusement as he comments on this lives of the inhabitants of Mariposa, with all their self-importance, pretensions, and hypocrisy. He barely conceals his glee at their follies and imperfections, but in the end the manner of the stories is kindly even as it depicts human weakness and imperfection. The most famous piece in the volume is "L'Envoi: The Train to Mariposa," in which former residents, now urbanized, remember their "sunshine town." The story captures Leacock's concern for the passing of human communities and the dangers that accompany the embracing of new technology and materialism. *Arcadian Adventures with the Idle Rich,* Leacock's second important volume, dissects life in an American city with sharper satire, and his portraits of corruption and self-deception have a sharp edge of criticism not found in *Sunshine Sketches.* The two collections together reveal Leacock's nostalgia and regret for the passing of simpler times and his concern for what results when human social ties are undermined by materialism.

Leacock produced hundreds of sketches in more than a dozen volumes of short fiction, but none have enjoyed the popularity or critical acclaim of *Sunshine Sketches* and *Arcadian Adventures.* Some critics have maintained that Leacock's work showed little sign of intellectual or artistic development after these two successes. Many of his later pieces, like those in his first two volumes, are exuberant nonsense, parodies, or light sketches that undermine popular stereotypes, ideas, institutions, and personalities. However, he did continue to produce excellent sketches throughout his career, notably "The Great Detective," which parodies the detective-story genre, and "Boom Times," a fictional story about this uncle, E. P. Leacock.

CRITICAL RECEPTION

Leacock enjoyed enormous popular success with his short stories and sketches. Beginning with the publication of short pieces in magazines, he quickly found a large audience that appreciated his down-to-earth comic sensibility with its elements of silliness and absurdity. After the publication of *Nonsense Novels,* Leacock became North America's most popular humorist. After the publication of this book, Leacock published about one book of humor a year. Reviewers as well as readers appreciated his work, although some complained that his sketches relied too heavily on formula for their comic effect. Scholarly interest in Leacock's stories was minimal in the years following his death, and many who did study his work felt a sense of unfulfilled potential in his work. Some critics argued that because of his impoverished childhood Leacock felt he had to use uncritically the formulas that brought him commercial success. Others speculated that his insistence on using only kindly humor arrested his development as an artist. They suggested that Leacock backed away from the darker and more cynical view of humanity that is latent in *Arcadian Adventures* and returned instead to the lighthearted optimism of his earlier works. His inability to develop his pessimistic vision of humanity in the industrial age, it was argued, served to thwart his full development as an artist. Beginning in the 1960s, critics began to reassess Leacock's place in Canadian literature, and many found his work, particularly the pieces in *Sunshine Sketches* and *Arcadian Adventures,* to be more serious and modern than had been formerly perceived. Critical interest in Leacock's work has tended to concentrate on *Sunshine Sketches,* and scholars have examined the tales to understand, among other things, Leacock's use of satire, the relationship of the narrator to Leacock himself, and the unity of structure among the sketches. Other subjects of interest to critics of Leacock's work have been the persona of the "little man" or "common uncommon man" in his works and his ironic intent.

PRINCIPAL WORKS

Short Fiction

Literary Lapses: A Book of Sketches 1910
Nonsense Novels 1911
Sunshine Sketches of a Little Town 1912
Behind the Beyond, and Other Contributions to Human Knowledge 1913
Arcadian Adventures with the Idle Rich 1914
Further Foolishness: Sketches and Satires on the Follies of the Day 1916
Frenzied Fiction 1918
The Hohenzollerns in America, with the Bolsheviks in Berlin and Other Impossibilities 1919
Winsome Winnie and Other New Nonsense Novels 1920
The Garden of Folly 1924
The Iron Man and the Tin Woman, with Other Such Futurities 1929
Laugh with Leacock: An Anthology 1930
The Dry Pickwick and Other Incongruities 1932
Funny Pieces 1936
Here Are My Lectures and Stories 1937
Model Memoirs and Other Sketches from Simple to Serious 1938
My Remarkable Uncle and Other Sketches 1942
Happy Stories, Just to Laugh 1943

Other Major Works

Elements of Political Science (nonfiction) 1906; revised 1921
Baldwin, Lafontaine, Hincks: Responsible Government (biography) 1907
The Methods of Mr. Sellyer: A Book Store Study 1914
The Dawn of Canadian History 1914
Moonbeams from the Larger Lunacy (novel) 1915
Essays and Other Literary Studies 1916
My Discovery of England (essays) 1922
Economic Prosperity of the British Empire (nonfiction) 1930
Mark Twain (biography) 1932
Charles Dickens, His Life and Work (biography) 1933
Humor: Its Theory and Technique, with Examples and Samples; A Book of Discovery (essays) 1935
Last Leaves (essays) 1935
The Boy I Left Behind Me (autobiography) 1946

CRITICISM

The Spectator (review date 1912)

SOURCE: "Sunshine Sketches of a Little Town," in *The Spectator,* Vol. 109, No. 4391, August 24, 1912, pp. 277-78.

[*In the following review of* Sunshine Sketches of a Little Town, *the critic calls the work an "exhilarating volume" that breaks new ground as Leacock moves away from "irresponsible fantasies and burlesques" to works that show a fresh and familiar look at humanity.*]

Mr. Stephen Leacock, in a delightful autobiographical preface to his new volume, tells us that many of his friends are under the erroneous impression that he writes his humorous nothings in idle moments when the wearied brain is unable to perform the serious labours of the economist. (Mr. Leacock is head of the Department of Economics and Political Science at McGill University, Montreal.) His own experience is exactly the other way. "The writing of solid, instructive stuff, fortified by facts and figures, is easy enough. There is no trouble in writing a scientific treatise on the folk-lore of Central China, or a statistical inquiry into the declining population of Prince Edward's Island. But to write something out of one's own mind, worth reading for its own sake, is an arduous contrivance only to be achieved in fortunate moments, few and far between. Personally I would sooner have written *Alice in Wonderland* than the whole *Encyclop[dj]dia Britannica.*" Such sentiments are entirely reassuring, and afford a convincing earnest of the joys of perusing these jocund pages. At the same time we demur to Mr. Leacock's estimate of the frequency of his "fortunate moments." This is not the first but the third volume in which he has contributed to the gaiety of the Old as well as the New World, and for a professor of two dismal sciences the contribution strikes us as decidedly liberal.

Hitherto Mr. Leacock has devoted his fortunate moments to irresponsible fantasies and burlesques. Here he breaks new ground as a chronicler of the annals of a small Canadian provincial town. But he is careful to tell us that Mariposa, on the shores of Lake Wissanotti, is not a real town: "on the contrary, it is about seventy or eighty of them." Similarly the characters engaged are not portraits but composite photographs: they represent types, not individuals. We are quite content to accept Mr. Leacock's *caveat*: the important thing, from the point of view of the reader, is that they combine certain local characteristics with a great deal of essential humanity—freshness with familiarity. The peculiar attribute of the Mariposans is their youth and hopefulness. He does well to call his chapters *Sunshine Sketches,* for they have a most welcome freedom from the fashionable pessimism of old-world fiction. The Mariposans have their ups and downs, but they have an invincible resilience; an unquenchable belief in their town and its future; an inexhaustible fund of public spirit. They combine ferocious political partisanship with a complete social solidarity. When the Knights of Pythias—a society nominally devoted to the Temperance cause—give their annual picnic everybody joins in:—

> "In Mariposa practically everybody belongs to the Knights of Pythias just as they do to everything else. That's the great thing about the town and that's what makes it so different from the city. Everybody is in everything. You should see them on the seventeenth of March, for example, when everybody wears a green ribbon and they're all laughing and glad,—you know what the Celtic nature is,—and talking about Home Rule. On St. Andrew's Day every man in town wears a thistle and shakes hand with everybody else and you see the fine old Scotch honesty beaming out of their eyes. And on St. George's Day!—well, there's no heartiness like the good old English spirit after all; why shouldn't a man feel glad that he's an Englishman? Then on the Fourth of July there are stars and stripes flying over half the stores in town, and suddenly all the men are seen to smoke cigars, and to know all about Roosevelt and Bryan and the Philippine Islands. Then you learn for the first time that Jeff Thorpe's people came from Massachusetts and that his uncle fought at Bunker Hill (it must have been Bunker Hill—any way Jefferson will swear it was in Dakota all right enough); and you find that George Duff has a married sister in Rochester and that her husband is all right; in fact, George was down there as recently as eight years ago. Oh, it's the most American town imaginable is Mariposa—on the Fourth of July. But wait, just wait, if you feel anxious about the solidity of the British connexion, till the twelfth of the month, when everybody is wearing an orange streamer in his coat and the Orangemen (every man in town) walk in the big procession. Allegiance! Well, perhaps you remember the address they gave to the Prince of Wales on the platform of the Mariposa station as he went through on his tour to the west. I think that pretty well settled that question."

In one sense the Mariposans recall the attitude of the Irishman who said, "I love action, but I hate work." Their social, convivial, and political activities are immense, but they seem to have no regular business hours. The centre of the town is Josh Smith's Hotel, and the central figure of these pages is Josh Smith himself, a man who started life as a cook in the lumber shanties, who could not read, and who looked like an overdressed pirate. His methods were Napoleonic in their unscrupulousness, but underneath a rough exterior he concealed a kind heart. In any emergency Smith took command and inspired universal confidence. He was at once lavish and shrewd: "never drunk, and, as a point of chivalry to his customers, never quite sober"; finally, as a political candidate, he was irresistible, as the following passage sufficiently proves:—

> "I wish that I were able to narrate all the phases and the turns of the great contest from the opening of the campaign till the final polling day. But it would take volumes. First of all, of course, the trade question was hotly discussed in the two newspapers of Mariposa, and the *Newspacket* and the *Times-Herald* literally bristled with statistics. Then came interviews with the candidates and the expression of their convictions in regard to tariff questions. 'Mr. Smith,' said the reporter of the Mariposa *Newspacket* 'we'd like to get your views of the effect of the proposed reduction of the differential duties.' 'By gosh, Pete,' said Mr. Smith, 'you can search me. Have a cigar.' 'What do you think, Mr. Smith, would be the result of lowering the *ad valorem* British preference and admitting American goods at a reciprocal rate?' 'It's a corker, ain't it?' answered Mr. Smith. 'What'll you take, lager or domestic?' And in that short dialogue, Mr. Smith showed that he had instantaneously grasped the whole method of dealing with the Press. The interview in the paper next day said that Mr. Smith, while unwilling to state positively that the principle of tariff discrimination was at variance with sound fiscal science, was firmly of opinion that any reciprocal interchange of tariff preferences with the United States must inevitably lead to a serious *per capita* reduction of the national industry. 'Mr. Smith,' said the chairman of a delegation of the manufacturers of Mariposa, 'what do you propose to do in regard to the tariff if you're elected?' 'Boys,' answered Mr. Smith, 'I'll put her up so darned high they won't never get her down again.' 'Mr. Smith,' said the chairman of another delegation, 'I am an old free trader—' 'Put it there,' said Mr. Smith, 'so'm I. There ain't nothing like it.' 'What do you think about imperial defence?' asked another questioner. 'Which?' said Mr. Smith. 'Imperial defence.' 'Of what?' 'Of everything.' 'Who says it?' said Mr. Smith. 'Everybody is talking of it.' 'What do the Conservative boys at Ottaway think about it?' answered Mr. Smith. 'They're all for it.' 'Well, I'm fer it too,' said Mr. Smith."

Most of the characters in these pages are engaged in trade or business, but there is one charming exception in the person of the Rev. Dean Drone, the incumbent of the Anglican Church, a gentle old scholar, whose only grievance was that his early instructors had never taught him enough mathematics to grapple with the intricacies of church finance. The failure of his various schemes to extricate himself from the burden of debt—the result of an over-lavish expenditure on bricks and mortar—culminating in a "Whirlwind Campaign," exhibits Mr. Leacock in the new light of a humorist who combines a keen sense of the ludicrous with a genuine gift of pathos. Another most engaging character is the local Judge, of whose judicial temper we get many diverting examples:—

"When the Conservatives got in anywhere, Pepperleigh laughed and enjoyed it, simply because it does one good to see a straight, fine, honest fight where the best man wins. When a Liberal got in, it made him mad, and he said so—not, mind you, from any political bias, for his office forbid it—but simply because one can't bear to see the country go absolutely to the devil. I suppose, too, it was partly the effect of sitting in court all day listening to cases. One gets what you might call the judicial temper of mind. Pepperleigh had it so strongly developed that I've seen him kick a hydrangea pot to pieces with his foot because the accursed thing wouldn't flower. He once threw the canary cage clear into the lilac bushes because the 'blasted bird wouldn't stop singing.' It was a straight case of judicial temper. Lots of judges have it, developed in just the same broad, all-round way as with Judge Pepperleigh.

I think it must be passing sentences that does it. Anyway, Pepperleigh had the aptitude for passing sentences so highly perfected that he spent his whole time at it inside of court and out. I've heard him hand out sentences for the Sultan of Turkey and Mrs. Pankhurst and the Emperor of Germany that made one's blood run cold. He would sit there on the piazza of a summer evening reading the paper, with dynamite sparks flying from his spectacles, and he sentenced the Czar of Russia to ten years in the salt mines—and made it fifteen a few minutes afterwards. Pepperleigh always read the foreign news—the news of things that he couldn't alter—as a form of wild and stimulating torment."

The speculations of Jeff Thorpe, the little barber, who made a small fortune in the mining boom and fell a speedy prey to some Cuban flat-catchers; and the romance of Mr. Pupkin, the little bank clerk, who was afraid to tell his sweetheart that his father was a millionaire, afford congenial scope for Mr. Leacock's skill in handling sentiment in a spirit of kindly satire. There is no bitterness in his laughter, and the epilogue, in which he pictures the dream visit of an exiled Mariposan to the Little Town in the Sunshine, closes an exhilarating volume on a note of tender reminiscence rare in a modern humorist.

Will Cuppy (review date 1929)

SOURCE: "Leacock at Large," in *New York Herald Tribune Books,* Vol. 12, No. 6, December 1, 1929, p. 40.

[*In the following review of* The Iron Man and the Tin Woman, With Other Such Futurities, *Cuppy remarks that the tales contain a great deal of satiric intent but that they allow for serious thinking between laughs.*]

Anything by Stephen Leacock has the very considerable advantage to start with of being by Stephen Leacock. Otherwise Mr. Leacock doesn't seem to do very much about it here lately—and why, his legions of fans may well ask, should he? Isn't he the granddaddy of most of the young speed demons whose humorous essays. If faster and more furious, are not really much better, if the truth were known? Which is by no means to say that Mr. Leacock is slow—perish the thought!

Indeed loyal Leacockians are not likely to complain because their favorite author sets a more decorous pace than sometimes of old. These forty-four "little sketches of today and tomorrow" contain a deal of satiric intent which can do with occasional resting spots between laughs—and the fun is that you may take them as purposeful or not, even to the point of doing a little serious thinking in the clinches. If you are worried about the machine age you may accept **"The Iron Man and the Tin Woman"** as an entertaining prophecy of what we are coming to if not, it's just a typically gay hit or miss collection of Leacockisms—moonbeams for the larger lunacy, mental short circuits, astonishing blooms from the garden of folly and so on.

Those who are always a bit miffed because the latest Leacock book is not entitled **"Nonsense Novels"** may well turn first to the section entitled "Futurity in Fiction" and glue themselves to a burlesque mystery tale called **"Long After Bedtime."** Consider the damning facts detailed in the opening paragraphs. We are aware of a sinister house known as No. 4 John Street ("No. 1 stood first, while No. 2 was just above it. No. 3 coming next in order, and No. 4 being the fourth, or last, of the group"). It is occupied by the family of Mr. John Smith, a stock broker's confidential clerk, reputed as rather above the average as a bridge player, but with no ear for music.

On the night in question, to use Mr. Leacock's own words, the entire Smith household seems to have been in bed and asleep well before midnight. The side bedroom on the right is occupied by the two little girls of the family. Flora and Dora, aged respectively eleven and thirteen. The other side bedroom is occupied by Willie Smith, aged respectively twelve—and remember that Willie could imitate a dog barking. The room at the back is occupied by the maid, Frieda Helsenfish, a Finn, though there seems to have been no reason to connect her with the Finnish Revolution. So far so good.

Now note how Mr. Leacock builds up his suspense almost, if not quite, to the breaking point "At 2 a. m. Mr. Smith, who was never a heavy sleeper, seems to have rolled over in bed. There is no reason to suppose, however, that he rolled far or that he was not able to roll back again. Mrs. Smith appears to have waked up for a moment and said. 'What's the matter' Smith answered. 'Nothing, I just rolled over in bed.' Mrs. Smith said, 'Oh,' perhaps 'Ah.' . . . At 3 a. m. the family were still asleep. . . . The milkman did not notice any broken panes of glass. The man, however, was short-sighted, was new to his route and came from Bobcaygeon, Ontario." I forgot to mention that none of the Smith children had ever shown any tendencies towards somnambulism, hysteria or locomotor ataxia.

Lovers of Leacock parody will find much besides to interest them in this hilarious section anent the newer biography, tabloidism, literary scandals and the encyclopedias, the victims being George Washington, Columbus, Bruce and the spider. Adam, Noah, Tut-ankh-Amen and such. That leaves almost a whole book to examine at leisure for pointers on specialization, social regulation, radio, aviation, athletics, astronomy, travel, Mars, Willie Nut, college, golf, billiards and unclassified. Many of the sketches are those "what would happen if" and "what will happen when" affairs, permitting Mr. Leacock to range widely and wildly in time and space. As for his little story about Iron John and Tin Lizzie just folks who fell in love and were married by a Brass Clergyman and a Cast Iron Sexton to the music of a Metal Choir, one can only venture that there is much in what he says.

D. A. Cameron (essay date 1965)

SOURCE: "The Enchanted Houses: Leacock's Irony," in *Canadian Literature,* No. 23, Winter, 1965, pp. 31-44.

[*In the following essay, Cameron examines how Leacock sees the characters and their actions in* Sunshine Sketches.]

Critical discussions of Stephen Leacock's ***Sunshine Sketches of a Little Town*** revolve about two central questions, upon each of which the critics are sharply divided. The first of these deals with the book's distinctive flavour: is it sharply satiric, or is it composed of kind and fundamentally affectionate comedy? The second question is concerned more with characterization and structure, and with the mind and motives of Leacock himself, the issue being whether or not the book is a tentative, exploratory step in the direction of the fully articulated novel, and therefore whether Leacock achieved his full potentialities as a writer.

Obviously, the two questions are logically related. The first turns on Leacock's relation to his material, on the way in which he saw the material and the way in which he intended his reader to see it. So, essentially, does the second: the novelist's concern is with plot and character treated in terms of certain conventions for which Professor Ian Watt has suggested the term "formal realism".[1] Those who feel that Leacock could never have been a novelist commonly maintain that Leacock did not see his characters, or their actions, in terms of formal realism—which is another way of saying that Leacock's approach to his material is incompatible with the novel form. A detailed discussion of Leacock's work in relation to the novel is hardly possible here, but the view of human character and action which we shall see in Leacock's best book does not seem substantially different from that of such a comic novelist as Fielding.

Our concern, then, is with the terms in which Leacock sees both the people who inhabit his book and their actions. We may call this his vision. What is the characteristic quality of this vision?

For Desmond Pacey, the vision of ***Sunshine Sketches*** is fundamentally kindly; in *The Unsolved Riddle of Social Justice* (1920), modern industrial civilization is criticized from the viewpoint of a benevolent eighteenth-century country squire; and

> In his greatest book of humour, ***Sunshine Sketches of a Little Town*** (1912), Leacock uses gentle irony to suggest the same general outlook. Here he creates an idyll of a small community. . . . [2]

A little later in the same essay, Professor Pacey refers to the book's "genial satire", and he concludes, "The satire in ***Sunshine Sketches*** is . . . very mild and gentle."

Robertson Davies, on the other hand, sees the book as "ferocious and mordant". He goes on:

> What it says, if we boil it down, is that the people of Mariposa were a self-important, gullible, only moderately honest collection of provincial folk; they cooked their election, they burned down a church to get the insurance, they exaggerated the most trivial incidents into magnificent feats of bravery; the sunshine in which the little town is bathed seems very often to be the glare of the clinician's lamp, and the author's pen is as sharp as the clinician's scalpel.[3]

A third position is outlined by Malcolm Ross. After reviewing the disagreement between Davies and Pacey, Ross makes the point that their two positions may not be such uneasy bedfellows as it might at first appear. Leacock, he suggests, is not a satirist:

> Because *he loves what he hates.* And he is not *bribed* into loving what he hates. . . . He just can't help it. To attack and defend, to love and hate in one breath, is not the genius of satire but the genius of irony, the subtler art, the deeper wisdom.[4]

For all this difference of opinion about Leacock's vision, no one has so far offered a close examination of specific passages in the book as a useful means of approaching the question. That is the approach I want to take now. What we will find may be clearer if we bear in mind that the satirist must distinguish sharply between himself and his characters, while the writer of pathos, in contrast, asks not that we observe and judge his characters but that we understand them and identify with them. And the ironist feels both things at once. Seeing the character both from within and without, the ironist simultaneously observes and forgives his weaknesses; he combines the viewpoints of satire and pathos.

Moreover, the ironist's view of character implies an awareness of a leading fact about the human condition: man is at once both social and individual. As a social being, he has a relationship with his fellows, and the relationship carries responsibilities. When he fails to live up to those responsibilities, he is a legitimate object of satire. On the other hand, he is an individual; seen in terms of his own makeup and the forces acting upon it, his failings in the social sphere are understandable, and he may even take on a kind of nobility. The ironic view of character provides a means of reflecting in literature the full complexity of this dual condition.

I want to suggest that although Leacock's vision in ***Sunshine Sketches*** appears at first to be satiric, and although a large element of the book is in fact satiric, its overall vision is ironic, and in its best passages we are aware, however imperfectly, that we are in the presence of basic questions about the nature of truth and the nature of man. Leacock usually begins with an external view of his characters and comes gradually to suggest their inner lives as well; we begin in satire, but we end in irony.

To see how this change takes place, we may examine several passages in some detail. In the following passage, Leacock is satirizing the romantic illusions of Zena Pepperleigh:

> With hands clasped she would sit there dreaming all the beautiful day-dreams of girlhood. When you saw that far-away look in her eyes, it meant that she was dreaming that a plumed and armoured knight was rescuing her from the embattled keep of a castle beside the Danube. At other times she was being borne away by an Algerian corsair over the blue waters of the Mediterranean and was reaching out her arms towards France to say farewell to it.[5]

During several more paragraphs of roughly the same kind, Leacock broadens his satire to include the girls of Mariposa in general: ". . . all the girls in Mariposa were just like that." The edge of the satire is sharpened by contrasting the girls' dreams with their actual situation—gently at first (we see them against "a background of maple trees and the green grass of a tennis court") and then more incisively:

> And if you remember, too, that these are cultivated girls who have all been to the Mariposa high school and can do decimal fractions, you will understand that an Algerian corsair would sharpen his scimitar at the very sight of them.
>
> (p. 169)

We are seeing these girls from the outside, and we continue to do so until the last sentence of the next paragraph. Here is the paragraph:

> Don't think either that they are all dying to get married; because they are not. I don't say they wouldn't take an errant knight, or a buccaneer or a Hungarian refugee, but for the ordinary marriages of ordinary people they feel nothing but a pitying disdain. So it is that each one of them in due time marries an enchanted prince and goes to live in one of the little enchanted houses in the lower part of the town.

Something has changed; the illusion has become the reality. Leacock has gone over to the girls' point of view and is looking at the world through their eyes; the world as they find it really is the romantic place they thought it to be, and they are not disappointed in their hopes. When we were laughing at illusion, moreover, we were actually laughing at truth; the laughter now must be at our own expense, since we ourselves seem to have mistaken truth for illusion. To make it even more clear, Leacock continues:

> I don't know whether you know it, but you can rent an enchanted house in Mariposa for eight dollars a month, and some of the most completely enchanted are the cheapest. As for the enchanted princes, they find them in the strangest places, where you never expected to see them, working—under a spell, you understand—in drug-stores and printing offices, and even selling things in shops. But to be able to find them you have first to read ever so many novels about Sir Galahad and the Errant Quest and that sort of thing.
>
> (pp. 169-70)

Clearly, Leacock is giving us an inside view of the girls' world; from their viewpoint, what we have considered to be appearance has become reality. But there is a further twist of the irony here. So far, Leacock has been saying, essentially, that there is no way to say that one view of the girls' dreams is truer than the other; it is a purely subjective question. But we may recall that the passage began by discussing Zena Pepperleigh in particular, and as the story unfolds we discover that her dream of marrying an enchanted prince is *literally* true, if on a limited scale; Pupkin, the man she does eventually marry, is working as a bank clerk more or less *incognito.* His father, one of the wealthiest men in the Maritimes and a former Attorney General, is a financier who "blew companies like bubbles" and who owns Tidal Transportation Company, Fundy Fisheries Corporation and the Paspebiac Pulp and Paper Unlimited. Pupkin, the only son and heir apparent, who has been sent into the world to make his own name and fortune, is in actual fact a merchant prince.[6]

The motif of the enchanted houses reappears as we leave that part of the book which centres around Pupkin and Zena:

> So Pupkin and Zena in due course of time were married, and went to live in one of the enchanted houses on the hillside in the newer part of the town, where you may find them to this day.
>
> You may see Pupkin there at any time cutting enchanted grass on a little lawn in as gaudy a blazer as ever.
>
> But if you step up to speak to him or walk with him into the enchanted house, pray modulate your voice a little—musical though it is—for there is said to be an enchanted baby on the premises whose sleep must not lightly be disturbed.
>
> (p. 211)

It is still funny: Pupkin is still essentially a comic character, and once again the reader himself is partially the object of the fun. But the passage is irradiated with Leacock's feeling for both the outside of the house, which is comic, and the inside, the wonder and joy of marriage and family. The humour is based on a paradox: the lover as seen by other men is absurdly foolish and richly comic, but at the same time he inhabits a world which for him is utterly transformed into something fresh, golden and magnificent. That Leacock did see his lovers this way, is confirmed by a passage in his own voice:

> For you see, it is the illusion that is the real reality. I think that there are only two people who see clearly (at least as to one another), and these are two young lovers, newly fallen in love. They see one another just as they really are, namely, a Knight Errant and a Fairy. But who realizes that that old feller shuffling along in spats is a Knight Errant, too, and that other is a Fairy, that bent old woman knitting in the corner.
>
> This illusion, greater than reality, we grasp easily in the form of what we call art—our books, our plays.[7]

If we were to examine the whole book in detail, we would find that Leacock's development of character often follows the pattern we have seen in Pupkin. Pepperleigh, for instance, seems at first to be a simple caricature of the country judge: he is rabidly Conservative, ill-tempered and pompous, and his judgements are clearly dictated by his private interests—he acquits his son of an assault charge, and he forces the insurance company to pay for the burnt church. Yet when his son is killed in South Africa, Pepperleigh's pain and the support he derives from his wife display a human being within the caricature.

Similarly, Josh Smith makes dramatic changes in his hotel in order to draw people so that his liquor license will be renewed by popular request; we know he is cynically manipulating his fellow citizens, and that he intends to close the Caff and the Rats Cooler as soon as the license is renewed. Yet the kindly, sympathetic side of the man becomes visible when, at the crucial moment, he does not close up, because to do so would be petty and ungrateful. Jeff Thorpe likewise seems to be a selfish, acquisitive little man, but we discover he intends to use his wealth for the poor and the disabled—though Leacock undercuts Jeff's generous spirit by making his arithmetic suspiciously faulty (pp. 58-59). This pattern is not a formula, nor is it invariable—nothing of the kind happens in the election chapters, for instance—but it is pervasive enough to suggest that it represents one of Leacock's chief beliefs about his characters.

Even minor actions in the book often owe their appeal to this ironic vision. When the Mariposa Belle is sinking in less than six feet of water, part of the fun turns on Leacock's awareness of the difference between the way the event looks to an outsider—the reader—and the way it looks if you are on the steamer:

> Safe! Oh, yes! Isn't it strange how safe other people's adventures seem after they happen. But you'd have been scared, too, if you'd been there just before the steamer sank, and seen them bringing up all the women on to the top deck.
>
> (p. 87)

Two paragraphs later the narrator has forgotten what he said in the first flush of excitement, and now *he* scorns the danger too:

> Really, it made one positively laugh! It sounded so queer and, anyway, if a man has a sort of natural courage, danger makes him laugh. Danger? pshaw! fiddlesticks! everybody scouted the idea. Why, it is just the little things like this that give zest to a day on the water.

Reversing his usual movement, Leacock has abandoned his position beside the narrator and is now inviting us to laugh at the latter's inconsistency.

Perhaps the best illustration of Leacock's irony is afforded by the Reverend Rupert Drone, Dean of the Anglican Church. Dean Drone at first appears to be no more than a caricature of the simple country cleric. His name suggests this; so does his first appearance in the book, just after Josh Smith has begun his flamboyant career as proprietor of the old Royal Hotel:

> When the Rev. Dean Drone led off with a sermon on the text "Lord be merciful even unto this publican Matthew Six," it was generally understood as an invitation to strike Mr. Smith dead.
>
> (p. 20)

Through the first four chapters, Dean Drone remains a figure who appears only occasionally, and then for satiric purposes. (He goes on the Marine Excursion of the Knights of Pythias, for instance, with "a trolling line in case of maskinonge, and a landing net in case of pickerel, and with his eldest daughter, Lillian Drone, in case of young men.") In the fourth chapter he becomes somewhat individualized; we discover that he loves to read Greek, though he refuses to translate any; he cannot do mathematics; he is much impressed by such mechanical contrivances as the airplane. And he has had his great dream: the building of a new church.

But now that the new church has been built, Dean Drone finds it difficult to pay for. A series of attempts to raise money all result in comic catastrophe. Some members of the congregation begin to blame Mr. Drone, and we discover that he can be hurt. Leacock records the incident with a sympathy which, though it is flecked with humour, is remarkably unequivocal:

> Once . . . the rector heard some one say: "The Church would be all right if that old mugwump was out of the pulpit." It went to his heart like a barbed thorn, and stayed there.
>
> You know, perhaps, how a remark of that sort can stay and rankle, and make you wish you could hear it again to make sure of it, because perhaps you didn't hear it right, and it was a mistake after all. Perhaps no one said it, anyway. You ought to have written it down at the time. I have seen the Dean take down the encyclopedia in the rectory, and move his finger slowly down the pages of the letter M, looking for mugwump. But it

> wasn't there. I have known him, in his little study upstairs, turn over the pages of the "Animals of Palestine," looking for a mugwump. But there none there. It must have been unknown in the greater days of Judea.
>
> (p. 114)

The Dean's gentleness, his respect for scholarship and his unworldliness all unite to make us feel his pain, and Leacock's direct reference to the reader ("*You* know, perhaps . . .") is an appeal for sympathy. From this point on, Dean Drone is never again the simple figure of fun he once was.

When the term "mugwump" comes up again, its effect is terrible. The climax of the Church's fund-raising efforts is the Whirlwind Campaign, which is another financial failure, and Mullins, the chairman of the Campaign, comes to give the Dean one hundred dollars which Mullins has himself contributed. Mullins later reports that the rector has been very quiet:

> Indeed, the only time when the rector seemed animated and excited in the whole interview was when Mullins said that the campaign had been ruined by a lot of confounded mugwumps. Straight away the Dean asked if those mugwumps had really prejudiced the outcome of the campaign. Mullins said there was no doubt of it, and the Dean enquired if the presence of mugwumps was fatal in matters of endeavour, and Mullins said that it was. Then the rector asked if even one mugwump was, in the Christian sense, deleterious, Mullins said that one mugwump would kill anything. After that the Dean hardly spoke at all.
>
> (p. 134)

The serious discussion of mugwumps is comic, but we are aware that something dreadful is happening to the Dean. Soon he excuses himself on the ground that he has some letters to write, but:

> The fact is that Dean Drone was not trying to write letters, but only one letter. He was writing a letter of resignation. If you have not done that for forty years it is extremely difficult to get the words.
>
> (p. 135)

The flat simplicity and the understatement of those sentences are heartbreaking. They are succeeded by a passage equally heartbreaking, in which Leacock's irony reaches perhaps its peak in the whole book; only the "Envoi" can compare with it. The Dean's efforts to write the letter lead him into some hilarious thickets of syntax and meaning. The sense of the letter keeps changing; each draft contradicts the previous one, and finally the letter looks like this:

> "There are times, gentlemen, in the life of a parish, when it comes to an epoch which bring it to a moment when it reaches a point . . . where the circumstances of the moment make the epoch such as to focus the life of the parish in that time."
>
> (pp. 137-38)

Yet the context in which this comedy occurs is the moment of final defeat for a good old man who has given his whole life to the charge he is now resigning; who has striven to serve both his gentle God and the community of which he is a devoted member; who has tried, in his humble, unworldly, rather bumbling way to leave the world a better place than he found it. Leacock snaps this essentially bitter moment into perspective by showing us that the Dean has met defeat even on the ground of his pride in his use of language. It has always been an ill-founded pride, and it has given us considerable amusement; now the Dean, too, sees the truth:

> Then the Dean saw that he was beaten, and he knew that he not only couldn't manage the parish but couldn't say so in proper English, and of the two the last was the bitterer discovery.
>
> (p. 138)

concludes the scene:

> He raised his head, and looked for a moment through the window at the shadow of the church against the night, so outlined that you could almost fancy that the light of the New Jerusalem was beyond it. Then he wrote, and this time not to the world at large but only to Mullins:
>
> "My dear Harry, I want to resign my charge. Will you come over and help me?"

In that last passage, the irony twists again. First, of course, we notice that the church is seen through the rector's eyes: "the light of the New Jerusalem" is an example of the comically elaborate religious terms and images through which he sees the world. But the deeper irony arises from the fact that there really *is* a light behind the church, though it is not the light of the New Jerusalem. It is the light of flames: the church is burning at the hands of an arsonist who we are later led to believe is Josh Smith. In order to solve its financial problems, the congregation fires its church; and the irony of this act is complex. It defeats the moral, the religious and the unworldly virtues which Dean Drone stands for—and for what? To solve a problem which is financial and worldly: men, Leacock seems to be saying, do not even understand, let alone obey, religious codes of conduct. The fire destroys all the Dean's illusions about the instruction he has given his flock in moral and ethical matters. Not only does the fire destroy the substance of the Dean's achievement, however, a substance which was rooted in his effectiveness as a Christian leader, but also it destroys the physical church which was the symbol of his achievement. By a further irony, the Dean himself has caused the fire, however inadvertently, through his own mismanagement. And, in a final ironic thrust, we discover that the destruction of this church, which is heavily over-insured, will completely finance a new church. The Dean's symbol is retained, but the fire which allows Mariposa to retain it obliterates its meaning and spirit.

It seems the Dean realizes something of what the burning of the church implies—or perhaps his reaction is simply one of shock:

> So stood the Dean, and as the church broke thus into a very beacon kindled upon a hill—sank forward without a sign, his face against the table, stricken.[8]
>
> (p. 139)

The Dean recovers from his stroke, but he is never fully sane again; still a gentle old man, but now remote from the world, he suffers from hallucinations, and Leacock takes leave of him in a passage which, though coloured with humour, is suffused with compassion:

> So you will understand that the Dean's mind, [sic] is, if anything, even keener, and his head even clearer than before. And if you want proof of it, notice him there beneath the plum blossoms reading in the Greek: he has told me that he finds he can read, with the greatest ease, works in the Greek that seemed difficult before. Because his head is so clear now.
>
> And sometimes—when his head is very clear—as he sits there reading beneath the plum blossoms, he can hear them singing beyond, and his wife's voice.
>
> (pp. 147-48)

Once again there is direct reference to the reader, too: "you will understand." Looking back over the passages we have examined, you are struck by the number of such references, and by the fact that there are two extra characters in each scene: the narrator and the reader. As we have seen, neither is exempt from Leacock's humourous scrutiny. In fact, much of the humour of the book is based on the interplay among the inhabitants of Mariposa, the narrator (who is evidently not Leacock), and the reader.

The Narrator is naïve, unsophisticated, baffled by such abstractions as election issues; a Mariposan to the core, he is something of a Booster and he usually seems quite unaware of moral issues. Like Gulliver at the court of Brobdingnag, he often tells a true story which he expects will display the glories of his home, but which instead exposes its hypocrisy, immorality and pettiness. Such a character is an ideal vehicle of satire, and indeed the narrator does quite unconsciously direct a good deal of the book's satiric thrust. But he is balanced by the reader, and possession of the "real" truth constantly passes back and forth between the two.

This reader-narrator interplay begins the book: the narrator, who knows what Mariposa is "really" like, shows the reader around the town, demonstrating that the surface impression is not the actual truth. ("But this quiet is mere appearance. In reality, and to those who know it, the place is a perfect hive of activity.") Is the narrator right in this and in his other comments on Mariposa? Perhaps—and perhaps not. In the first and last chapters, Leacock's equivocating irony is brought to bear on both the city and the little town. Each has virtues which the other cannot share; each has shortcomings to which the other is immune. The wider scope which the city offers is necessarily accompanied by cold impersonality, while the small town, which provides warmth and community, lacks privacy and tends to stifle initiative. The Mariposan view of the city is instructive here. The town usually sees the city as treacherous and malign: for instance, Mullins reflects, after the Whirlwind Campaign has failed, that there are "so many skunks in Mariposa that a man might as well be in the Head Office in the city" (p. 131), and similar remarks are made throughout the book. Yet, as Desmond Pacey has pointed out, Mariposa spends a great deal of energy in trying to become a metropolis, and the narrator's comment that the town is "a hive of activity" is further evidence of this desire. There is irony, then, in Mariposa's view of the city, an irony which reflects the town's simultaneous rejection of, and longing for, city values. The overall effect of ***Sunshine Sketches*** is to leave us with a similarly complex awareness of the way of life symbolized by Mariposa.

To a considerable extent, the relation between reader and narrator is responsible for this awareness. That relation begins the book and it carries the same theme throughout. It emerges most clearly in the last chapter, where once again the difference between the outsider's view (this time of the whole town) and the insider's view forms the basis of an ironic coda which comments on a whole rural way of life.

Here the irony turns, to a considerable extent, on our new knowledge that both the reader and the narrator are, like the rest of the members of the Mausoleum Club, originally from Mariposa, and on their inability really to go back: we leave them, after our "mad career" on the train to Mariposa, sitting in their armchairs in their club in the city. They have accepted sophisticated city values, and they have done well there; the reader owns a "vast palace of sandstone . . . in the costlier part of the city." And they can never fully be part of Mariposa again; they notice such things as Mariposa's out-of-style clothing. Both reader and narrator see the town from the outside.

Yet as the train thunders north through the woods, we come to identify with Mariposa, with the way of life represented by the people on the train. The excitement of homecoming mounts; the train becomes the fastest, finest and most sociable train in the world; and finally we arrive at the station, while brakemen and porters cry "MARIPOSA! MARIPOSA!"

At that climactic moment Leacock ends the book by pulling us back again to our actual positions, outside the town, smiling at it a little, and yet filled with a sense of lost youth and innocence. The reader and the narrator have paid a heavy price for their success. Though Mariposa has more than its share of stupidity and hypocrisy, it also has simplicity and vigour.

And yet life in Mariposa is more complicated, more equivocal than it seems. The narrator has discovered this as he has matured, and the ironic vision rests partly on his recognition both that Mariposa was a good place to be a child and that it would be a bad place to be an adult. He is nostalgic for Mariposa, but he does not leave the Mausoleum Club.

This recognition, however, seems to imply a contradiction in the narrator. Throughout the book, as we have seen, he has appeared to be a naïve, rather unintelligent Mariposan. Yet in the **"Envoi"** he is evidently a city dweller of considerable penetration and insight. Does this indicate a flaw in Leacock's conception of him? Probably not: it is more likely that Leacock conceived of the narrator as an intelligent man feigning simplicity. This would explain a good deal: the speed with which the narrator moves from cowardice to courage when the steamer sinks for instance, is more credible if the narrator is only pretending to be unaware of the inconsistency. Similarly, the intellectual sparks which glow here and there through the book—the sharp quips on college men and education, for instance, or the occasional satire on jargon and on modern business[9]—have indicated all along that the narrator's mind was more sharply honed than he would have us believe. His apparent inconsistency, then, supports the view of Mariposa we have been suggesting: he cannot go back because he cannot quite fit into the Mariposan framework, however hard he tries; he cannot accept Mariposa's people and events at their face value, though he can recognize that he may have been happier when he could. The same recognition made another boy from Mariposa build a summer home back in the small town he remembered with such affection; but the larger part of the year he spent as a professor at McGill.

All this should give us pause. For if the narrator is not as simple as he looks, what of Leacock? Is he suggesting more than he is saying?

I think he is, or more accurately, I think his book is based on a view of the human condition which is profoundly ironic. We value the truth, but we can never know what is true; ***Sunshine Sketches*** is, among other things, a demonstration of the subjective way in which individuals are doomed to see the world. What is the difference between appearance and reality? How may an individual, limited as his vision must be, tell the difference between them? What is truth, said jesting Leacock, and could not supply an answer—because he could see none, or at least no way to recognize one.

Similarly, though we value our fellow men, we can never really know them either: if we are all condemned to see the world through personal, individual spectacles, then we cannot really communicate with each other; isolation is our fate, and we live and die alone. As E. M. Forster puts it, "we cannot understand each other, except in a rough and ready way; we cannot reveal ourselves, even when we want to; what we call intimacy is only a makeshift; perfect knowledge is an illusion." This sense of isolation is common enough in modern literature; Ernest Hemingway and Forster's own fiction come immediately to mind. In ***Sunshine Sketches*** it is mainly evident in the ironic treatment of character and in the demonstration that each man inhabits a private world. It is also visible in a negative way: three responses which attempt to counteract isolation meet in ***Sunshine Sketches*** and, I suspect, account for part of its appeal—laughter, romantic love, and membership in a small community.

Leacock's attitude to his material, then, is ironic in a way that is based on a deep apprehension of what it means to be human, and his humour is both a vehicle for this apprehension and a defence against the pain it necessarily involves. One always hesitates to say that humour is basically a very serious business, and Leacock himself found a good deal of fun in just that concept. Nevertheless, he saw humour as a way of thinking seriously about life; in *Humour: Its Theory and Technique* (1935), he comments:

> . . . humour in its highest meaning and its furthest reach . . . does not depend on verbal incongruities, or on tricks of sight and hearing. It finds its basis in the incongruity of life itself, the contrast between the fretting cares and the petty sorrows of the day and the long mystery of the to-morrow. Here laughter and tears become one, and humour becomes the contemplation and interpretation of our life.[10]

The contemplation and interpretation of our life. At its best, Leacock's irony leads to no less than that.

Notes

1. *The Rise of the Novel* (Berkeley and Los Angeles, 1957), p. 32.
2. "Leacock as a Satirist," *Queen's Quarterly 58* (1951), p. 213.
3. "On Stephen Leacock" in C. T. Bissell, ed., *Our Living Tradition* (First Series) (Toronto, 1957), p. 147.
4. Preface to the New Canadian Library edition of *Sunshine Sketches of a Little Town* (Toronto, 1960), p. xi.
5. Stephen Leacock, *Sunshine Sketches of a Little Town* (John Lane, London, 1912), p. 167. All further references to *Sunshine Sketches* are to this first edition, and subsequent references are inserted in parentheses in the text.
6. A further irony, which I think a little strained: Pupkin has been sent to Mariposa at the suggestion of a friend of his father, a friend who ignores Pupkin in Mariposa. The friend turns out to be Judge Pepperleigh, Pupkin's future father-in-law, who has been a rather terrifying figure to the young man.
7. *Last Leaves* (Toronto, 1945), p. 89.
8. "A very beacon kindled on a hill" is another case in which a metaphor—i.e., an apparent unreality—becomes the literal truth, just as the metaphor of the enchanted prince did.
9. On education, see pp. 18, 42, 58, 79, 123, 126, 232; on jargon, pp. 15, 81, 86, 88; on business, pp. 39, 106.
10. *Humour: Its Theory and Technique,* (New York, 1935), p. 17.

Douglas Mantz (review date 1977)

SOURCE: "The Preposterous and the Profound: A New Look at the Envoi of *Sunshine Sketches,*" in *Journal of Canadian Fiction,* No. 19, 1977, pp. 95-105.

[*In the following essay, Mantz urges us to read Leacock not only for his genial nonsense or bitter satire but for his "ontological awareness"; he then examines the envoi in* Sunshine Sketches of a Little Town *to show how Leacock moves toward the profound by way of the commonplace.*]

"Personally, I would sooner have written *Alice in Wonderland* than the whole *Encyclopedia Britannica*."[1] This remark, in the preface to ***Sunshine Sketches,*** suggests Leacock should be taken seriously as an artist, that his work—or some of it, at any rate—has what E. R. Wassermann used to call the "ontological seriousness" of a work of art.[2] Of course, *Alice in Wonderland* has long since been rehabilitated for intellectual study, and the same dignity might be accorded Leacock's work since he seems to be associating his work with Dodgson's. But as Donald Cameron pointed out, one is compelled to apologize whenever one attempts to take Leacock seriously.[3] It is true that the very passage in which Leacock defends *Alice in Wonderland* contains philistine satire of scholarly research. But this is surely ironic. Leacock spends a large proportion of the preface wittily detailing his academic career. It is part of the joke, and part of the depth, to see the playfulness of Leacock (of all people) as the defender of imaginative writing against mere scholarly research. Intellectual study will not taint our laughter, nor vice versa. To take Leacock seriously is not to fly in the face of Leacock's opinion, but to fly in the face of the essentially Puritan and philistine notion that laughter cannot be profound.

Leacock asserts the "ontological seriousness" of nonsense humour against all comers, but especially against the unimaginative utilitarian urge to value hard facts more than laughter and fantasy. We must try to read Leacock not only as genial nonsense (*i.e.,* merely for the laugh) nor only as bitter satire (*i.e.,* merely for the gossip); we must also read him for his "ontological seriousness". In concentrating upon the serious side of Leacock we may legitimately regard his work as temporarily set apart from humour, or satire, or even from their bastard offspring, irony. Why not? Surely it is not necessary to add a defense of applying the rigors of literary criticism to Leacock's work. Leacock did not despise literary criticism in the preface to ***Sunshine Sketches.*** Everyone, except those who believe that all literary critics are parasites, will know that literary criticism can have imaginative vision and wit (though not sheer fantasy—whatever that might be), and that writing literary criticism, as senior scholars are fond of saying, is not the same as compiling encyclopedia entries—though, thank God, even literary criticism does descend to facts sometimes. (The reader will notice that I do not speak for economics or political science.) If Leacock could assert that it was a greater achievement to write *Alice in Wonderland* than the whole *Encyclopedia Britannica,* it is necessary to take him seriously as someone who could write the preposterous and the profound at one and the same time.

However preposterous it may sound to say so, I believe I have seldom seen anything more profound in topographical literature than Leacock's presentation of Mariposa in the envoi of ***Sunshine Sketches.*** To consider this relatively short passage, is to gain an insight into Leacock's narrative technique at its best. By examining how Leacock presents Mariposa in the envoi, one may clearly recognize that Leacock moves toward the profound not by way of Dodgson's nonsense-fantasy but by way of the commonplace, which he enriches and goes beyond with no less imaginative vision than his Victorian predecessor. Surely no one would expect Leacock to lecture or to preach at the reader in order to enforce a profound insight; but on the other hand we must not be distracted from Leacock's artistry by his humble pose as a nostalgic bumbler who deals in the commonplace. Like Cohen, Leacock presents his most profound thoughts with a sophisticated but disarming laugh at his own naive idealism.

The main substance of the envoi is, as its title indicates, the train journey to Mariposa. But Leacock sets the stage for the journey with a passage on the nature of "home" which is by no means peripheral; in fact, it is so important that it needs to be considered in detail:

> Odd that you never knew, in all these years, that the train was there every afternoon, puffing up steam in the city station, and that you might have boarded it any day and gone home. No, not "home"—of course you couldn't call it "home" now; "home" means that big red sandstone house of yours in the costlier part of the city. "Home" means, in a way, this Mausoleum Club where you sometimes talk with me of the times that you had as a boy in Mariposa.
>
> But of course "home" would hardly be the word you would apply to the little town, unless perhaps, late at night, when you'd been sitting reading in a quiet corner somewhere such a book as the present one.
>
> (p. 148)

Leacock first describes Mariposa as "home", then changes his mind and says, "'home' means that big red sandstone house of yours in the costlier part of the city." But the Mausoleum Club is then promptly introduced as another alternative meaning for "home". Then it's back to Mariposa again. Leacock's narrator apparently is mistaken or uncertain about the referrent for "home"; but surely the narrator is a very purposeful bumbler. Such bumbling raises the question of what "home" really is, and, by suggesting several different answers, produces a highly sophisticated concept of "home". Apparently, "home" is *not* one's present residence (one's city house) or at any rate not exclusively this; nor is it where one now seems most to belong, to feel "at home", relaxed, made welcome, and where many of one's most enjoyable hours are spent (the Mausoleum Club). Leacock comes back to Mariposa, where he lived in the past, where he spent his childhood, as "home". But what does he mean by this?

Leacock rules out any narrowly geographical sense of Mariposa as "home" when he says that "practically every one" of the rich men in the city's Mausoleum Club "came from Mariposa" (p. 149). Unless we are to believe that dozens of wealthy Montrealers grew up in Orillia, then Mariposa and "home" cannot be equated simply with Orillia—nor with any other geographical entity, not even with Mariposa Township, near Lindsay, Ontario, which is not very far from the farm where Leacock lived as a boy.[4] Because "home" can have several alternative locations, the parameters of Mariposa as "home" are defined not by reference to geography *per se,* but by relation to the mind of the person or persons defining "home". It is basically correct to say Leacock thinks of "home" as a state of mind, but he is more specific than such a general phrase implies. The fact that Leacock grew up near Mariposa is an important clue for understanding Leacock's range of meanings for "home". Mariposa as "home" represents a large shaping influence in one's past, an influence or set of influences which could be found in many places different in location, but not necessarily different in kind. Mariposa as "home" represents a concept of the formative psychological influence of the past. It is perhaps best summarized by the phrase "psychic roots" which indicates that Mariposa belongs to the past, but exists in the present and influences the present in a vital way, as nourishment through the inner core of one's psychological being, so to speak.

It is not quite true that Mariposa has no geographical character, however. A physical location of some kind, or a set of physical locations, is presumed by Leacock's conformity to the practice of identifying "home" not by specific emotions or qualities affecting the mind but by tags of place names. Environmental psychologists may correct me, but I suspect Leacock is following common tendency to think of any particular place in terms of a particular time and set of personal circumstances—just as Orilla calls up in my mind a few parts of a few streets in relation to a general area, as it was, let us say, in 1970-72 when I was a certain type of person, at a certain age, with a unique set of circumstances to define my relationship to the people and the physical, geographical reality of Orillia. In other words, the traditional Maritimer's map of Canada, more or less centred on the Bay of Fundy, with Newfoundland where Greenland should be, and anything west of Toronto as very small and rather dim, is psychologically true—whatever cartographers might think of it. (And similarly the Westerner's map, with anything east of Montreal almost non-existent, is absurd but accurate in the same way.) It is this kind of psychological truth about geographical facts which the envoi deals with. Leacock probably would have been among the first to laugh at and to appreciate the touchingly human honesty of medieval maps of the world centred on the mapmaker's hometown, which contain a good deal of conjecture, misinformation, and even more *terra incognita,* because in ***Sunshine Sketches,*** Leacock drew much the same kind of map for Mariposa. Unlike the medieval mapmaker, however, Leacock laughs at his own "common sense" map of "home" and its environs, and moves through the commonplace toward the profound precisely because he is aware of the incongruity between the commonplace viewpoint of the individual in his own limited background and the accumulated rational knowledge of encyclopedic organization.

Leacock's definition of "home" does not stop at one or two paragraphs. The whole envoi is basically one long, continuous definition of "home" in psychological terms. Leacock makes a transition from an introductory consideration of "home" to the train journey by discussing "homesickness", the traumatic shock of one's first experience in the wider framework of life outside one's psychologically vast but geographically small "home". There is no reason to assume Leacock is writing sentimental eyewash simply because his subject is homesickness, or "cultural shock", as it is more fashionable to call it. The psychological reality of cultural shock has been with us at least since the days of Mrs. Moodie, and in a country with an increasing, mobile population, the experience of moving house and home, and the consequent sense of dislocation may be expected to be widespread and not limited to sissies. Leacock actually points out that behind every experience of the disorientation of cultural shock lies the mental conditioning of "home". Thus, the retrospective quality of the narrator's homesickness is only superficial. Homesickness is introduced to provide an example of the importance and the continuity of "psychic roots" from earlier days into the present. The artistic function of the "homesickness" passage is clear: it forges the bonds which unify the envoi by making the train journey an extension of the exploration of what it means to think of Mariposa as "home". The train journey, which forms the bulk of the envoi, should be seen as the process of going toward Mariposa, *i.e.,* as a progressive clarification of a mental picture of what it means to think of Mariposa as "home".

But what a train journey! Nobody could ever have taken the train from Montreal to Orillia in the way that Leacock seems to describe. It might have been possible to go from Toronto to Orillia on such a train—Leacock's description of the train itself does have a basis in historical fact[5] but this would not fit Leacock's personal circumstances: his city was Montreal. Leacock's train journey is not one specific journey he once made. Nor is it likely to be an account of one particular railway route. In the preface to ***Sunshine Sketches,*** Leacock pointed out that as a town Mariposa was "not a real town" (p. xvi) but a typological composite. Could the journey to Mariposa be any more "real" than the place itself? The train journey is a literary journey rather than a "real" one, a mental construct extrapolated and generalized from physical and geographical fact. What does Leacock add to the facts of a "real" train journey?

Leacock has taken some pains at the beginning of the envoi to suggest that the train journey to Mariposa is a journey back into his childhood. In fact, the movement backward in time in his own mind is fundamental to Leacock's train journey, and movement in exterior space is chiefly important as the means by which a journey into the traveller's past is presented. Notice the slightly strange or mysterious details Leacock also adds to distance this journey from an ordinary one. Much of the journey seems to be made "half dreaming" (p. 151); there is almost something arcane about the journey: "very few people know about it", and many are mistaken about it (p. 149). (Leacock calls this a "joke", but it also has profoundly serious implications.) Gradually, the train, like some mythological Protean being, seems to change, to throw off its disguises and become more and more clearly the Mariposa train as older cars and an old engine replace the others. There is a recurring sense of *déjà vu* as the traveller briefly struggles with his memory to recognize the train, the people, their clothes, and Lake Ossawippi. Up to the point at which the traveller recognizes Lake Ossawippi, the journey abounds in *déjà vu* and explanation; Lake Ossawippi is the turning-point in the traveller's reactions; from that point onward he is looking forward, predicting what he will find and having his expectations confirmed instead of accounting for what he has found after he has noticed it. There is a historical and geographical framework to the journey which Leacock does not violate, although he generalizes it so that the journey is typical rather than particular. But there is also another and more important pattern which shapes the journey: the narrative of the traveller's state of mind in response to the scenes both inside the train and outside it. Even the consideration of various meanings for "home" has a special appropriateness in this light. The envoi is unified and given a dimension of "ontological seriousness" by the pattern of a dream-journey to the interior of the traveller's mind.

Leacock's dream-journey to Mariposa is a journey into his own childhood; but it is also a journey "home" in a wider sense. The train and its passengers, as Leacock presents them, seem mysteriously to change during the journey from exemplars associated with modern, urban life to take on a referent increasingly further back in the past; "last year's fashions", then an engine of "forty years ago" (p. 150), and then back to even more primitive surroundings. The train passes through the city, through suburbs, past "farmsteads" (p. 151), semi-cleared areas, and finally, in twilight, "into great stretches of bush" (p. 151) broken by a strangely familiar "great sheet of blackness" (p. 151) which the traveller recognizes as Lake Ossawippi, the lake of his childhood. Both the language and the sequence have a significance beyond either geography or autobiography. Leacock's train journey turns back the clock of history collectively as well as individually, back through the stages of the national past which lies behind the biography of every Canadian. After considering the envoi in this light, one would not be surprised that Leacock wrote a history of Canada.

I have pointed out that the recognition of Lake Ossawippi (whether it be from Massawippi in Quebec's Eastern Townships, or elsewhere) is the turning-point of the traveller's reactions to his journey. At this crucial point in the narration, Leacock envisions the landscape around Mariposa in terms of its two primordial elements: bush and water. W.O. Mitchell has been much acclaimed, and rightly so, for his vision in reducing the prairie landscape to its two primordial elements of land and sky. Leacock, it seems to me, should be similarly acclaimed for doing much the same thing for the Canadian landscape on a national basis. We seem to have heard so much in recent years about the different geographical regions across the country that we may need to be reminded that large areas in every province of the country were at one time bush and water—and many of them still are. Exceptions notwithstanding, the lowest common denominator of the Canadian landscape is bush and water. They are also the lowest common denominator of the landscape in the envoi. Leacock chose to alter the traveller's reactions to the landscape of the journey at the point of recognizing bush and water. (He had taken the landscape back as far as he could go without resorting to Indian lore or to geological pre-history which are different chapters of the story.) It seems wrong-headed to duck the nationalistic implications of this. It is a fact that Leacock wrote ***Sunshine Sketches*** on commission, a commission to write something "for a purely Canadian audience".[6] Much of the envoi is tantamount to proof that he fulfilled his commission; or, to put it another way, a serious, and profound consideration of Canadian nationalism is one of the things which gives the envoi its depth, its ontological seriousness.

This is where Donald Cameron's suggestion that ***Sunshine Sketches*** is an exploration of subjectivism might be somewhat misleading.[7] I have shown that the envoi extends beyond the personal and individually subjective viewpoint. If, however, Cameron means not individual pecadillo or whim, but the collective subjectivity of nationalism, then I would agree with him. Leacock, as his commission indicates, does not present subjectivity in which there are as many acceptable answers as there are people, but dualism, the dualism of "ours" and "theirs" which is at the core of any recognition of nationalism anywhere—and which does not depend upon individual whim. The distinction between subjectivism and dualism is vital to an understanding of the depth of Leacock's nationalism in ***Sunshine Sketches,*** and of Leacock's narrative technique when, as I have shown him to do in the envoi, he speaks for himself, but not for himself alone.

Early in the envoi, Leacock raised questions about the nature of "true reality" (p. 149) when dealing with his house. He insisted that his big, wooden house in Mariposa was "one of the grandest and finest houses that thought could conceive; much finer, in true reality, than that vast palace of sandstone with the porte-cochère and the sweeping conservatories" (p. 149) in the costlier part of the city. This is not crochety primitivism carried to an insane excess. With a back-to-the-land movement coming into full spate today, we should be able to recognize that Leacock is insisting upon something akin to an alternative lifestyle, an alternative which thousands of our contemporaries have in fact found to be preferable to urban standards of grandeur. Leacock later actually did build his dream-house in the country (now the Leacock Memorial Home). For most of his career, he was an "end-of-term track man", *i.e.,* he left Montreal as soon as he could after the end of classes for the summer; Leacock was committed personally to the ideal of a summer house in the country at least as early as 1908.[8] This does not mean that Leacock was an early advocate of the back-to-the-land movement, nor that he was the part-time avatar of an eighteenth-century country squire. But it is important to recognize that in ***Sunshine Sketches,*** and in his own life, Leacock preferred an alternative lifestyle to that of the city.

Such an alternative is hardly new, of course. It raises the old dualism between two traditional *weltanschauungen* which have often appeared with many different relationships between them in earlier literature. These two *weltanschauungen* have been variously labelled the city and the country, epic and pastoral, and even Mars and Venus.[9] But one cannot apply these terms to Leacock without distorting his work. Leacock's dualism can be grasped much better if one re-defines these two *weltanschauungen* as Leacock aligned them. One side of the dualism would be the centripetal metropolitan values of the state which define the individual primarily in terms of his duty to the collectivity, and by his traditionally masculine aggressiveness or leadership and the heroic courage or ratiocinative power upon which this quality may be based, and by his material possessions; the individual's moral probity is measured by his conformity to the pattern established in a Grand Design of some kind. In short, this is Vergil's epic virtues public and imperial, writ large in Seutonian words of marble. I think the best term for this *weltanschauung,* especially considering Leacock's undoubted classical background, would be *virtus,* or to be more precise, *virtus in imperando.* The other side of the dualism would be the centrifugal, contemplative values of the individual, which define the person primarily in terms of the sense of his own spontaneous trustworthiness which he has within himself and transfers to others, and which takes as ideals a traditionally feminine purity or innocence, and a peaceable contentment with little. The individual's moral probity is assumed to be self-evident within his unique personal response to a partly internalized entity, the outward aspect of which is often associated with the divine Book of Nation (whether written in the charactery of prelapsarian Arcadia or post-industrial Helvellen). In short, this *weltanschauung* consists of Horace's contemplative virtues personal and introspective, written on the inside of Rousseau's Shaftesburian heart. One might call this *humanitas,* or, more accurately, *humanitas rustica.* No doubt these two *weltanschauungen* are somewhat amorphous, but they do indicate two different sets of principles, ideals, and values which ***Sunshine Sketches*** expresses in a particular way. When the two *weltanschauungen* are spelled out in some detail it becomes clear that Leacock is not a subjectivist. He is invoking the *virtus-humanitas* dualism and, when he chooses the Mariposan house rather than the city "palace", for instance, he comes down quite solidly on the side of *humanitas rustica*—though, of course, he is no monkish hermit. Leacock's vision of *humanitas rustica* is gregarious, and witty (sometimes at the expense of his own side). To see Leacock's irony in ***Sunshine Sketches*** within the framework of a *humanitas-virtus* dualism is to deepen one's appreciation of Leacock's irony without running upon the dilemma of seeing his satire as a sophisticated sneer stuck into the midst of a commissioned work written, according to its preface, out of an "affection" for "the scenes and the country that it depicts" (p. xvi).

Although the preface may be at times conventional, generalized, and exaggerated, it is not deceitful. In his article "I'll Stay in Canada", Leacock again comes down strongly on the side of *humanitas rustica* and combines it with nationalism. The article, although written much later in Leacock's career, is very useful to illustrate how Leacock constructs an ontological foundation for ***Sunshine Sketches.*** The parallel to Leacock's *chef d'oeuvre* is even closer when one considers the fact that "I'll Stay in Canada" begins with semantic distinctions about "home", as did the envoi. Leacock has been invited, he says, now that he has retired, to "come home" to England.[10] His reply in a nutshell is "Thank you, Mother England, I don't think I'll 'come home'. I'm 'home' now." (p. 206) Leacock insists that Canada is "home" to him, regardless of where he was born, and that he would not feel "at home" in any other way of life than the Canadian. He brings in a dualism similar to that in the envoi when he says he came from England "wise" according to an English point of view, but "ignorant" according to Canadian one (p. 204). Such dualism enables him to be witty without insulting anyone: "We say 'yep!' when we mean 'yep!' and don't try to make out it's 'yes', which is a word we don't use; and if we mean 'four' we say so and don't call it 'faw'. (p. 204) Leacock is not attacking or satirizing either British or Canadian speech; wittily, but without sneering, he explains one side of a dualism to the other.

In "I'll Stay in Canada" Leacock also considers the state of mind shaped by the geographical and historical backgrounds of Canada—very much the same as he did in the envoi of ***Sunshine Sketches.*** It's the great spaces that appeal," he says (p. 206). (At the crucial point in the envoi, Leacock spoke of "that great space that seems to open out . . . why, surely, yes, Lake Ossawippi".) Leacock explains: "What the English feel about the Armada and the Scottish about Bannockburn, the Canadian, consciously or not, feels about the vast geography of Canada . . . To all of us here, the vast unknown country of the North, reaching away to the polar seas, supplies a peculiar mental background." (p. 206) Clearly, Leacock is thinking in terms of psychic roots, the Canadian landscape, autobiography and nationalism. Leacock says loneliness is not a problem amid vast empty stretches of land isolated and cold—if it were that would be the imperial standard-*virtus.* Instead Leacock says he would "feel lonely without" the vast "primeval wilderness" (p. 206)—this is the Canadian standard, and a version of *humanitas rustica.* What is Leacock saying? He says that he is not lost in the wilderness; that, on the contrary, he finds himself partly because he can identify his special relationship to the primeval landscape of the north, which is a pure and uncrowded volume of the divine Book of Nature. This is *humanitas* *rustica* identified with nationalism and a personal sense of "home"—exactly what I have suggested Leacock is dealing with in the envoi of ***Sunshine Sketches.*** In both the article and the envoi, the landscape gives Leacock a sense of his personal identity by helping to define the national and personal parameters of his "home", but what is implicit in the envoi is explicit in "I'll Stay in Canada".

In "I'll Stay in Canada", again Leacock is no hermit. Nor is he in need of the back-to-nature movement. Part of Leacock's consideration of the primeval wilderness of the north is a vision of it in terms of a "progress" ethic, *i.e.,* in terms of the future economic development of the north. In this article, Leacock actually sees the north going through stages of development similar to those of the landscape in southern Canada which he recounted in the envoi. As McLuhan used to say, we look into the future by looking in a rearview mirror. The north appeals to Leacock's imagination and his sense of grandeur; its potential for economic development associates him with a larger human purpose in the foreseeable reach of history implicitly based upon the past history of Canada. It thus gives him spatial, temporal and purposive orientation toward an individual and collective identity. Thus, in both the envoi and the later article, Leacock uses the Canadian landscape to expound the "us" and "them" of nationalism, and of *humanitas rustica* seen in a duality with *virtus.* Of course, there is a paradox between nationalism, especially where the economic expansion of the collectivity is concerned, and *humanitas rustica.* The ethos of "progress" would seem to be virtually inseparable from the imperialistic ethos of *virtus.* Upon this paradox is founded the gap between the ideal and the reality which gives Leacock in *Sunshine Sketches* the width necessary for self-mocking irony and satire within his basic approbation of the *humanitas rustica* ideal.

The wide range open to Leacock within the *humanitas rustica* tradition is demonstrated when he deals with the characteristics of the train. The journey as Leacock presents it for the traveller's reactions has two main threads: the landscape which seems to unroll itself, and the train which literally supplies the forward movement in the narrative. The train is brought to the fore at key junctures in the plot: at the beginning of the journey (when the traveller seems to look about him at the occupants of the train and notices the train instead of the city or suburban landscape), at the rising action (when the train seems to change into a train of forty years before) and just after the turning-point, the recognition of Lake Ossawippi (when Leacock discusses the train's speed, comfort, sociability, etc.). Landscape and train at the end of the envoi are about as closely linked as the narrative will permit. Thus, the train is too important to be merely a device to allow the passage of time in the journey, although that is one of its functions. The dualism central to the envoi is present not only when the landscape is the focus of attention but also in passages devoted to the train.

At the beginning of the journey, the city people think the train is "just a suburban train" (p. 149), but they are wrong. Leacock seems to suggest that the *virtus* judgment does not look closely enough, and that an alternative is proven correct, of course, when the train "changes its character" (p. 150), and becomes identified with the *humanitas rustica* tradition rather than with the latest in modern, urban efficiency. The landscape becomes important only after the train has made a paradoxical transition from an examplar of the *virtus* tradition to the Mariposa train. (This is equivalent to the progressive north in "I'll Stay in Canada".) Leacock then expounds at considerable length the two standards for judging the speed of trains. Comparisons are specifically made to international speed records and to standards of scientific measurement (25 m.p.h.), but Leacock gives them both the lie and roundly asserts, on personal, experiential grounds which "you can prove . . . for yourself" (p. 152) if you want to, that the Mariposa train is the fastest in the world. Whether or not the traveller is correct here is beside the point—although the logic of relativity (as used in the marking schemes of progressive schools, for instance) has supported notions equally at odds with traditionally accepted standards of comparison while paying lip-service to the "human dignity" of "exceptional" (i.e., backward) child. The important point is that in discussing the train's speed, Leacock has set up a dualism and made his traveller take a stand very clearly within the tradition of *humanitas rustica.* The dualism of confrontation he employs in judging speed is one range of possibilities open to Leacock. But after this first stance, he takes different and even opposed stances in successive paragraphs.

The traveller seems to partly repeat himself in taking his next stance: he says the train is "the fastest . . . the best . . . the most comfortable, the most reliable, the most luxurious, and the speediest train that ever turned a wheel." Obviously he is stumbling over himself in his excess here. Leacock is singling out for absurd praise in this sentence those very aspects of Canadian National's service which have sometimes been found to be notoriously lacking. This is not merely "anti-Canadian Nationalism", of course; it is self-mocking satire. Leacock has taken the satiric potential latent in his preceding paragraph, and developed it to the full at the expense of his narrator and the side his narrator identified himself with. I suspect that most readers have not missed the exposé of inane boosterism in this sentence, nor the *reductio ad absurdum* of the narrator's relativity. But one must not take it out of proportion. This sentence has the earmarks of an afterthought to the text. What would the passage be like without it? Solidly *humanitas rustica,* with most of the self-mockery not brought to the surface. The sentence adds a range of satire to what is in fact a celebration of virtues within the *humanitas rustica* tradition.

In the next paragraph, Leacock praises the sociability of the Mariposa train quite straightforwardly, almost to the point of a blushing panegyric. This is the opposite extreme from the preceding sentence—and so close to absolute praise that Leacock may have included an acid afterthought to cut the forthcoming sweetness. If there is any satire involved here, it is smug criticism of the "dull reserve" (p. 152) of the urban passengers. One may sneer at the conventionality of "old familiar topics" (p. 152) but to do so would be to go against the grain of the paragraph and of the passage as a whole. Thus in three successive paragraphs dealing with the train, Leacock sets up the *virtus-humanitas* dualism in confrontation, identifies his narrator again with the *humanitas* side, mocks the excesses of narrow-minded relativity, and strongly praises the very human blessing of sociability on the train—all within a basic approbation of principles of *humanitas rustica* as found on the train.

It is evident that Leacock does not present merely a nostalgic journey into the country. The train journey is a fictionalized spiritual autobiography emphasizing the psychic roots of an individual and of a nation. One part of the train journey is a retrospective panorama of the nation's history presented in terms of landscape symbolism. Out of nationalism symbolism comes an ever wider symbolism which might best be described as archetypal. The wilderness which unfolds before the traveller is in some sense the primeval ancestral home of everyone, the *locus genesis* of every individual and perhaps ultimately of every nation. We all make our way from the wilderness, presumably toward another or better world of some kind. Another comprehensive symbol in the traveller's journey is the goal of the dream-journey, the ideal place beyond the wilderness—in short, Mariposa, which, like heaven, is wisely kept beyond our grasp when the narrative ends at the Pearly Gates of the railway station. When the traveller arrives at Mariposa he symbolically reaches the state of being "at home" in the ideal community which is beloved—however many things may be wrong with its historical emanation because it characterizes an ideal of home with which all men can identify within the *humanitas rustica* tradition.

Why is it fitting that Leacock should have as his final sentence a reference to the Mausoleum Club rather than ending with the shouts of "MARIPOSA! MARIPOSA!" as the train stops at its destination? Leacock ends this way not so much to reinforce nostalgia as to underline once again the essentially metal and symbolic nature of the train journey. The vision of the journey dissolves but is not lost; Mariposa has not disappeared but, as the final phrases suggest, is as much a part of the mental "home" of almost every one of the people in the Mausoleum Club as it was at the beginning of the envoi. Leacock's artistic creation of the dream-journey has reached its conclusion, but the Mariposan view of life, a type of *humanitas rustica,* continues. In the widest sense, every individual journeys over "a great sheet of blackness" identified with the primeval chaos from which he came, and then arrives at Mariposa and at that Mausoleum Club which is, henceforward, his "home"—while others continue their journey toward their Mariposa. In the widest sense, therefore, Mariposa is the past, the future, the ideal, the ultimate wilderness, the town of one's childhood, the city of one's hopes, and the Mausoleum Club of one's death. Such a conclusion should be no surprise to anyone who takes Leacock seriously as both preposterous and symbolically profound at one and the same time.

It has often been observed that ***Sunshine Sketches*** today remains curiously undated—despite the fact that humour often stands the test of time very poorly. A major timeless element, at least in the envoi, is Leacock's skilful use of symbolism to represent elements so central to Canadian life as not to pass away with the change of generations. This has given ***Sunshine Sketches*** some of its continuing appeal, even to readers whose response to symbolism is as unconscious as their response to the great North. And, of course, the general reader (whoever that might be) has responded because the symbolism, though undoubtedly particularly Canadian, is not exclusively Canadian and becomes a type of the universal *humanitas rustica* tradition. Recognition of Leacock's symbolism does not deny his humour. But had Leacock been merely a jester limited to superficial nonsense, his laughter would have died on his lips, even if they were curled in scorn.

Notes

1. Stephen Leacock, *Sunshine Sketches of a Little Town* (Toronto: McCelland and Stewart, 1960), p. xv. All subsequent references are to this edition.
2. See Earl R. Wasserman, *The Subtler Language; Critical Reading of Neoclassic and Romantic Poems* (Baltimore: Johns Hopkins, 1958), p. 10.
3. D. A. Cameron, "The Enchanted Houses: Leacock's Irony" in *The Canadian Novel in the Twentieth Century,* edited by George Woodcock (Toronto: McClelland and Stewart, 1975), p. 13. Previously published in *Canadian Literature* 23 (Winter, 1965), pp. 31-44. (See p. 43.)
4. See David M. Legate, *Stephen Leacock; A Biography* (Toronto: Doubleday, 1970), p. 11. See also Survey and Mapping Branch, Department of Energy, Mines, and Resources, *Lindsay* 31 D/7, *Beaverton* 31 D/6, *Orillia* 31 D/11 and *Sherbrooke* 21 E/5, Edition 3 MCE, Series A751 (Ottawa: Department of Energy, Mines and Resources, 1971).
5. I am indebted for my knowledge of railways in Leacock's time to my discussions with Dr. N. Hesler of Sackville, New Brunswick, who travelled extensively on trains in the early years of this century—sometimes with Leacock.
6. B. K. Sandwell, "How the 'Sketches' started." *Saturday Night* 67 (August 23, 1952), p. 7.
7. Cameron, *op. cit.,* p. 12. *Canadian Literature* 23 (Winter, 1965), pp. 42, 43. This is my only reservation about Cameron's excellent work, on which my own obviously is founded. I do not wish to cut the ground from under my own feet here. My theoretical foundation vis à vis Cameron is this: by concentrating upon a smaller span than Cameron's, I wish to take his work a step further, particularly

toward recognition of the groundwork of Leacock's ostensible subjectivism and his palpable irony.

8. Legate, *op. cit.,* pp. 48, 162.

9. Raymond Williams, *The Country and the City* (London: Chatto and Windus, 1973), pp. 1-3, 46-48, 165, 166, 289-292, 299-301; Harold E. Toliver, *Pastoral Forms and Attitudes* (Berkeley, University of California, 1971), 1-19; Wasserman, *op. cit.,* pp. 53-61. For further theoretical background, see W. J. Keith, *The Rural Tradition; A Study of the Non-Fiction Prose Writers of the English Countryside* (Toronto: University of Toronto, 1974), pp. 3-24; Maynard Mack *The Garden and the City; Retirement and Politics in the Later Poetry of Pope, 1731-1743* (Toronto: University of Toronto, 1969), pp. 193-201, 232-236; W. H. Auden, *The Enchafèd Flood; or The Romantic Iconography of the Sea* (New York: Random House, 1950), pp. 11-35; William Empson, *Some Versions of Pastoral* (London, Chatto and Windus, 1950), pp. 17-23, 119, 120; and John Chalker, *The English Georgic; A study in the development of a form* (London, Routledge and Kegan Paul, 1969), pp. 15, 207-211.

10. Stephen Leacock, *Funny Pieces; A Book of Random Sketches* (New York: Dodd, Mead, 1936), pp. 284-292. This article is most readily available in *Canadian Anthology,* edited by Carl F. Klinck and Reginald E. Watters, rev. ed., (Gage, 1966), pp. 203-206. All references are to the latter text. The article was omitted from the third edition of this anthology published in 1974.

Ina Ferris (essay date 1978)

SOURCE: "The Face in the Window: *Sunshine Sketches* Reconsidered," *Studies in Canadian Literature,* Vol. 3, No. 2, Summer, 1978, pp. 178-85.

[*In the following essay, Ferris argues that* Sunshine Sketches of Little Town *is a more serious and modern work than commentators have perceived and that the power of the work is found in its narrative voice. However, Ferris also points out that Leacock fails to develop the sketches to their full artistic potential.*]

In the final chapter of ***Sunshine Sketches of a Little Town,*** the narrator turns to a "you" who is simultaneously himself and the reader and offers this advice: "No, don't bother to look at the reflection of your face in the window-pane shadowed by the night outside. Nobody could tell you now after all these years. Your face has changed. . . ."[1] This act of self-scrutiny, implicating both narrator and reader, is the central event of ***Sunshine Sketches.*** Through his anonymous but intimate narrator Leacock generalizes less the collective, external experience of small-town life than the individual, internal experience of recognizing and attempting to integrate a self fragmented through time. **"L'Envoi"** redefines the focus of the entire narrative, exposing the internal nature of its ostensibly external journey and firmly establishing the narrator as the locus of concern. Through the ending Leacock builds into his narrative its own reinterpretation by providing the cue to the rereading that must now take place if his imaginative exploration is to be understood fully. And such a rereading demands that we take seriously the interiorization of fiction in the final pages.

Despite being widely read and taught, ***Sunshine Sketches*** remains one of the most underestimated narratives in our literature. A recent biographer of Leacock has dismissed it as "a parochial treatment of parochialism."[2] Certainly, the surface naivete, crudity, and shallowness of the book encourage underestimation, and its light tone discourages critical seriousness. Reinforcing such discouragement is the formidable voice of Robertson Davies declaring that Leacock "would have laughed at a critic who grew too serious about his work."[3] But it is also Davies, we remember, who insists on the deep vein of melancholy in Leacock and who chooses the darkness of **"L'Envoi"** to represent ***Sunshine Sketches*** in his *Feast of Stephen.* Moreover, the hybrid nature of the work itself creates a confusion that muddies discussion and flattens the narrative. The ongoing (and rather tired) debate about its generic status, for instance, continues to invoke a tradition of formal realism inappropriate to Leacock's book.[4] By recognizing that the formative impulse of ***Sunshine Sketches*** is a psychological one, rooted in the narrator's knowledge of his changed face, we can not only uncover a different and deeper coherence than commonly recognized but also locate Leacock's narrative in the mainstream of modern Canadian writing. This is not to say that Leacock is a conscious literary innovator or a significant precursor of more recent fiction. He is not. But ***Sunshine Sketches***—largely unintentionally perhaps—is a more modern and serious work than commonly perceived. By isolating some of its neglected resonances, we can account more satisfactorily for its enduring power.

The memorable final chapter suggests that the source of that power lies in the narrative voice that here assumes centre stage. Through the internalization of landscape and action in **"L'Envoi,"** the narrator stands revealed as the weary, disillusioned inhabitant of the city we had suspected him of being. The imagery surrounding him points to the underlying impetus for the journey into the past that has constituted the main narrative line. Images of night, autumn, and the Mausoleum Club evoke the problems of time and death that haunt the narrator's present, accentuating the psychological urgency of his imaginative return. Time has eroded his sense of a coherent self, and the creation of Mariposa signals an attempt to rediscover a past self lost "in these long years of money-getting in the city." Through memory and imagination, he may be able to reintegrate the self and so make sense of the moments of his existence before death cuts off the possibility of meaning. By referring to himself as "you," he not only draws the reader into this process but underlines the internal split, the self-alienation, that **"L'Envoi"** as a whole dramatizes and accepts finally as irreparable. Between Mariposa and the Mausoleum Club, as the typography itself emphasizes, there can be no permanent bridge. The train connecting past and present cannot forge the final link, and the selves of then and now remain irretrievably separate. Sitting in the Mausoleum Club, the narrator is left with an empty present and a past that is a nostalgic memory rather than a sustaining presence. Unlike Margaret Laurence, whose *A Bird in the House* recalls ***Sunshine Sketches,*** Leacock cannot find a way to affirm a continuity of the self through time. But in focusing on this problem of the continuity of the self and formulating it in terms of an experienced disjunction between past and present, Leacock's work draws on impulses close to those animating not only Laurence's fiction but also that of other contemporary writers as diverse as Robertson Davies, Mordecai Richler, and Margaret Atwood. "You have to go home again," asserts Morag Gunn.[5] Leacock's narrator tries to do so, but, like the speaker in Al Purdy's "The Country North of Belleville," he has lost his way.

The melancholy awareness of time as separation and disintegration that surfaces so dramatically in the final chapter informs the whole narrative structure of ***Sunshine Sketches.*** But in rereading the whole in light of the final interiorization of fiction, the private dimension of this awareness emerges more clearly. Details interpreted previously in terms of social theme assume a psychological significance, generating a new level of narrative coherence. Thus the disposal of Mariposa's small stone church, recorded in the fourth section, becomes emblematic of psychological process in the narrator. Faced with the question of what to do with this symbol of its past, the town initially decides to incorporate the stone into a new structure. When this proves "impracticable," it contemplates refashioning the stone into a wall as a "token." Eventually, the town abandons entirely the idea of retention, selling off the stone to a building contractor, and the old church," like so much else in life, was forgotten" (p. 61). Despite its light, satiric touch, the passage has a peculiar poignancy, an emotional resonance exceeding that required by its social theme. The explanation lies in its personal significance for the narrator as an image of his own relationship to the past. The actions of the Mariposans—their gradual discarding of the past and choice of money in exchange—mirror his own actions and suggest how the changed face of "L'Envoi" came into being. Contemplating his reflection here, the narrator posits a relationship between the self-fragmentation he now recognizes and his repression of his past: "Perhaps if you had come back now and again . . . it [the changed face] wouldn't have been so" (p. 152).

This is not to deny the public, social level of ***Sunshine Sketches*** as a humorous exposure of small-town consciousness, but it is to suggest that ***Sunshine Sketches*** operates simultaneously and skilfully on several levels. The narrator's Mariposan pose, for example, constitutes an essential strategy in rendering both the social theme and the explorative private journey. Its role in shaping the satiric public vision is well-known and need not be discussed explicitly; our concern is with its function in articulating the psychological theme. In his effort to discover an authentic continuity of the self, the narrator forges a complex voice that mingles the perspective of a Mariposan with that of the city-dweller and so endeavours to fuse the two central experiences of his life. By adopting the tone of a Mariposan, he reactivates the perspective of his youth, capturing through language the values of Mariposa and his own youthful sense of the town as the boundary of the universe. This naive and confident voice is overlaid with the sophisticated adult voice of experience as language modulates from the folksy rhythms of "Anyway, they were fair and straight, this Cuban crowd" to the educated cadence of "It seemed to spoil one's idea of Jeff" (pp. 30, 33). The voice that stumbles over "eggnostic" and "Gothey" can also handle "theodolite" with ease and casually slip in a reference to the *Iliad.* But the very transparency of the Mariposan pose as pose suggests that in bringing to bear upon a single image the divergent perspectives of youth and maturity, the narrator has succeeded less in integrating the selves than in reinforcing his sense of their disjunction. This is particularly apparent in his use of mock-heroic techniques where the double perspective operates most strongly. Josh Smith, for instance, prompts a sequence of Napoleonic allusions that serves simultaneously to recreate the view of childhood and to undercut Mariposa's pretentious self-image. Irony is both indulgence and exposure: the narrator participates in the imaginative world of childhood even as his adult self performs the critical act of judgment. But no significant relationship between the two modes of the self emerges. Rather, they remain juxtaposed, thus only underlining the gap between then and now. Such is the typical pattern of the mock-heroic strain in ***Sunshine Sketches.*** Whether it takes the form of a reference to the "colossal thickness" of the telegraph poles or to the "enchanted princes" of Mariposa, irony tests the self as much as the town and exposes the hollowness in both.

There are moments, however, when the technique becomes more problematic, when irony apparently changes direction as the voices of innocence and experience merge briefly. The voice of experience mingles a critical awareness of the limitations of youth and of Mariposa with a deep yearning for its own lost innocence and simplicity of feeling. Such a yearning permeates the evocative description of Lake Wissanotti on the morning of the ill-fated excursion of the Knights of Pythias. Lingering over the "last thin threads of the mist" and the "long call of the loon," the narrator conjures into being "the land of the silent pine and the moving waters" (p. 36). The utter simplicity of scene calls forth a corresponding simplicity of response and implies a lost relationship to landscape now possible only in memory and the imagination. Immediately following the passage, the ironic mask of the cantankerous provincial returns: "Don't talk to me of the Italian lakes, or the Tyrol or the Swiss Alps. Take them away. Move them somewhere else. I don't want them."

Here the mock-heroic does not yield its usual deflation of the Mariposan sensibility. The moment stands as one in which the selves of then and now achieve a temporary fusion of perspective, their values merging as the experienced adult voice meets the ignorant youthful voice in response to Lake Wissanotti. The comic dismissal of the European Sublime is meant seriously. Such moments are rare and rarely unambiguous, marked by a tentativeness apparent even in the above instance where the nervous rhythms of the provincial voice indicate an underlying uneasiness. Uncertainty of tone marks a similar moment when the narrator asserts that the "foyer of the opera in Paris may be a fine sight, but I doubt if it can compare with the inside of Eliot's drug store." Having set up the expected deflation, he disorders the pattern by pausing and adding, "for real gaiety and joy of living" (p. 111). He may well mean what he says. But we cannot be certain. Such passages, with their blurring of the direction of the irony, raise the possibility of achieving a coherent perspective rooted in a coherent self. But they are only transitory moments, constituting glimpses and guesses. More typically, the pattern is one of the separation of past and present, of juxtaposition rather than integration, culminating in the bleak recognition that "Your face has changed."

Reinforcing the psychological implications of the double voice is the way in which the shape of the external world created by the narrator reflects his sense of a dissociated self. His mind is drawn persistently to isolated or split selves as he turns Mariposa into an extension of his own predicament, translating inner anxieties into external forms. He transforms his own sense of isolation into the isolation of his characters, summing up in the memorable image of Dr. Gallagher and Dean Drone delivering unheeded monologues to one another all the isolated selves of Mariposa (p. 45). Furthermore, the town contains a striking number of characters who suffer from a sense of internal disconnection, most commonly in the form of a frustrated or buried self. The narrator points to the assumptions behind his characterization when he generalizes from the case of Dean Drone: "There was a buried author in him just as there was a buried financier in Jefferson Thorpe. In fact, there were many people in Mariposa like that, and for all I know you may yourself have seen such elsewhere" (pp. 79-80). From Dr. Gallagher to Mallory Tompkins to Myra Thorpe to Peter Pupkin, the Mariposans possess a frustrated level of the self released by the narrator through comedy, pathos, romance, or satire. Where his problem is the relationship between successive selves, theirs is typically that between layers of the self, for Mariposa is a static world released from time. The narrator has lifted his characters out of the horizontal plane of linear time in which he himself exists and placed them in a vertical, spatial plane that allows him to focus on and yet evade his problem.

Such evasion is most apparent in the figure of Dean Drone who, since the externalization of self here admits the problem of time, serves as the closest surrogate for the narrator. The very opening of his story introduces the presence of time and death in the contrast between the plum blossom tree and the aged Dean and in the action of leaves fluttering onto the skull on the table. The pastoral mode in which the Dean exists softens the sense of relentless linear movement but does not deny it. As the narrative evolves, it becomes apparent that the intrusion of materialism into the unworldly existence of Dean Drone is merely the final blow to a spirit already undermined by time and an experience of internal disjunction. Like the narrator, he suffers from the sense of a severed past, having forgotten the Greek for which he received a medal fifty-two years ago. Struggling to decipher the Greek texts, he, too, strives to establish a continuity of the self. But between the world of his youth and the world of now there exists a hiatus dramatized by the death of his wife. The formally ordered world of his little Anglican college with its "clipped hedges" has been replaced by the pragmatic order of a Mariposa dominated by the picaresque figure of Josh Smith. Isolated, archaic, Dean Drone endeavours to connect then and now but cannot succeed within the parameters of his current reality. So his dilemma is resolved magically. After his stroke, the Dean experiences a sudden reintegration, finding that he can read Greek "with the greatest ease" and can hear his wife's voice. In the final tableau the Dean, drifting peacefully toward an easeful death, has been lifted out of time and reality into a timeless world where the pastoral vision is possible. He is a wish-fulfilling figure, but the sober implication is that his internal and external alienation can be resolved only through the magic of a fiction.

Dean Drone illuminates the way in which the imagination and its fictions provide the narrator with a liberation from time. ***Sunshine Sketches*** is shaped as much by the urge to escape time as by the attempt to come to terms with its passage; Mariposa dissolves even as it defines the problem of the self. The whole creation of the town deemphasizes temporality and the irreversibility of linear sequence. "There it lies" on a perennial June afternoon, its timelessness reinforced by the extensive use of the habitual present. Closure within the Mariposan context deliberately stills linear time: the stories typically conclude in the present tense, and the endings possess a tableau-like quality which stretches a moment into forever. The Pupkin household is forever young and enchanted; Dean Drone sits perennially under the plum blossom tree. While the Dean may be dying, he never actually dies. In fact, he turns up again in the two chapters immediately following his own story, and his reappearance points to the insistent anti-chronology of the narrative. Continually, Leacock undermines the tendency to translate the linearity of the reading process into a corresponding linearity of fictional time.

Mariposa is a static world rendered in terms of timeless fictional modes, but it is enclosed by a framework of reminiscence, a form which acknowledges the inescapability of time. The collision of Mariposa with the world of time in the final chapter accounts for the curious emotional impact of recognizing the Mariposans on the train. At this moment, as Donald Cameron points out, the narrator seems to have grown older, while the Mariposans "are perfectly unchanged by the passage of time."[6] These final pages force the direct recognition of Mariposa as refuge from a relentless chronicity and clarify its role as a wish-fulfilling dream for both narrator and reader. Drawing together the psychological strains of the narrative, the last chapter generates a powerful impact and thus suggests that the enduring appeal of ***Sunshine Sketches*** has less to do with its social function as collective memory than with its indulgence of the private, subliminal self. This use of fiction as a way out of time contains literary as well as psychological implications, developing not only the theme of the self but also the related theme of fiction. Fiction, Frank Kermode reminds us, endows time with a human shape, provides a meaningful order.[7] The narrator, conscious of himself as a story-teller, is well aware of this function. "I am afraid that this is no way to tell a story," he announces when, in violation of chronological sequence, he reveals the fact of the Mariposa Belle's accident. The revelation, he explains, has been triggered by his pondering "the contrast between the excursion crowd in the morning and the scene at night" (p. 42). Contrast prompts the desire to discover cause, to connect rationally the antithetical moments. Here he identifies the basic impulse of fiction to provide connections and to transform mere successiveness into significant sequence. A story, he implies, is a rational construct of chronological time, imitating and making sense of its linearity.

The tales of the Mariposans imagine different ways of structuring personal time through different literary modes. But whether time appears as the downward curve of disillusionment (as for Jeff Thorpe) or as the rising curve of fulfillment (as for Josh Smith), it possesses a rational shape and coherence. Such sense making, however, as the narrator seems to realize in his comment on his own narration, is a fiction, "a story." Scepticism about the authenticity and adequacy of fiction underlies ***Sunshine Sketches*** and accounts for its obvious literariness that keeps constantly before the reader the conventionality and fictionality of its resolutions. Romance, pastoral, and picaresque provide the patterns of reconciliation and meaning. Even as the patterns are mocked, they are realized—but only in Mariposa. Time here has been turned into timeless literary convention, and Mariposa differentiated sharply from the real world. While narrative stress on the artificiality of the creation signals a recognition of the inadequacy of traditional modes as models for contemporary experience, no new model emerges. The narrator has not found a fiction that will suffice; his time remains unreconciled.

The distrust of literary convention in ***Sunshine Sketches*** goes beyond its traditional function as a strategy of comedy and realism and points to a basic distrust of the imagination itself. Throughout *Sunshine Sketches,* as both theme and shaping force of the narrative, the operation of the imagination is identified with fantasy, retreat, delusion. Within the stories it appears as snare and distortion—Jeff Thorpe dazzled by the imaginative appeal of Cuba, his daughter deluded by visions of an acting career, Zena Pepperleigh falsifying the world through the lens of romance. For the narrator, as we have seen, it functions primarily as retreat from a painful reality. The train of the imagination may be "the fastest train in the whole world," but it can offer no sustaining insight into the narrator's existential condition. Even when ***Sunshine Sketches*** acknowledges the sustaining power of fiction, as in the case of Judge Pepperleigh and his son, it stresses the falsehood involved. Indulging in the freedom and release that the imagination offers, Leacock yet exposes these as illusory. The view of the imagination implicit in ***Sunshine Sketches*** is thus sceptical and limited. Leacock identifies the imagination with fantasy, unable or unwilling to distinguish between the two. The distinction, as Leacock's much admired Dickens well knew, is crucial. Aware as Dickens is of the real dangers of the uncontrolled imagination and of the ease with which it can be debased into fantasy, he nevertheless affirms its genuine creativity and essential truth. But Leacock lacks this confidence. And it is this, finally, that lies at the root of his failure to develop the complex artistic potential tantalizingly present in ***Sunshine Sketches.*** While Davies is doubtless correct in identifying Leacock's social insecurity, his desire to be liked, as contributing to the decline after ***Sunshine Sketches,***[8] this insecurity but masks a deeper, more crippling uncertainty—the distrust of his own imaginative power.

Notes

1. Stephen Leacock, *Sunshine Sketches of a Little Town,* New Canadian Library (Toronto: McClelland & Stewart, 1960), p. 152. Further references will be incorporated in the text.
2. David M. Legate, *Stephen Leacock: A Biography* (Toronto: Doubleday, 1970), p. 63.
3. *Stephen Leacock* (Toronto: McClelland & Stewart, 1970), p. 7.
4. Donald Cameron, for example, leans heavily on Ian Watt's paradigm for the novel in his argument for Leacock's potential as a novelist. See *Faces of Leacock* (Toronto: Ryerson Press, 1967).
5. Margaret Laurence, *The Diviners* (Toronto: Bantam, 1975), p. 302.
6. *Faces of Leacock,* p. 145.
7. *The Sense of an Ending* (London. Oxford Univ. Press, 1967).
8. See *Stephen Leacock,* p. 26.

T. D. MacLulich (essay date 1979)

SOURCE: "Mariposa Revisited," in *Studies in Canadian Literature,* Vol. 4, No. 1, Winter, 1979, pp. 167-76.

[*In the following essay, MacLulich responds to the critic Ina Ferris's assessment of* Sunshine Sketches of Little Town, *arguing that the collection does not show that Leacock lacked faith in his imaginative power as Ferris claims.*]

In her article "The Face in the Window: *Sunshine Sketches* Reconsidered" *(Studies in Canadian Literature,* 3 [Summer 1978], 178-85), Ina Ferris draws a provocative conclusion. She argues that the ending of ***Sunshine Sketches*** shows that Leacock lacked faith in his own imaginative powers:

> Throughout ***Sunshine Sketches*** . . . the operation of the imagination is identified with fantasy, retreat, delusion. . . . The train of the imagination may be "the fastest train in the whole world," but it can offer no sustaining insight into the narrator's existential condition. . . . Indulging in the freedom and release that the imagination offers, Leacock yet exposes these as illusory. The view of the imagination implicit in *Sunshine Sketches* is thus sceptical and limited.
>
> (p. 184)

Ferris makes her case forcefully. Nonetheless, I wish to disagree. In the first place, the town's uses of the imagination are not ridiculed in Leacock's book; they are sympathetically defended. In the second place, Ferris has neglected one of her own central insights. Although she initially stresses that **"L'Envoi"** implicates *both* narrator and reader as collaborators in its imaginative journey, she ends by applying the lesson of **"L'Envoi"** only to the narrator, who has apparently failed in his attempt to return imaginatively to Mariposa. In the third place, Ferris closely identifies the narrator with Leacock himself. On the contrary, I wish to argue that Leacock—the implied author behind ***Sunshine Sketches***—is distinct from the narrator. At the end of ***Sunshine Sketches*** the author has knowingly succeeded in his imaginative endeavour. Leacock's book does not express a distrust of the imagination, but points out the power of fiction to control the emotions of even sophisticated readers.

Sunshine Sketches is Leacock's one deliberate examination of the "fictionality" of fiction. Even so powerful a work as ***Arcadian Adventures with the Idle Rich*** does not have the reflexive dimension which takes ***Sunshine Sketches*** beyond a merely sociological concern with the customs of late nineteenth-century Ontario small towns. In his later career Leacock succumbed, as Robertson Davies has pointed out,[1] to the temptation to give his readers what they wanted: he became a popular entertainer, manipulated by his readers' expectations, rather than a fully autonomous artist. But in ***Sunshine Sketches*** Leacock triumphantly celebrates the power of the imagination. The knowing use of fiction to make readers aware of their own emotional susceptibilities makes ***Sunshine Sketches*** Leacock's most subtle and most successful work.

Throughout the book, as Donald Cameron points out,[2] the narrator plays on the theme of reality versus illusion, illusion being associated with Mariposa and reality with the city. However, the narrator's repeated suggestion is that in Mariposa *illusion is reality.* For example, the love affair of Zena Pepperleigh and Peter Pupkin begins as an absurd parody of a sentimental romance, but in the end the story has become—without losing its satiric tone—also a sympathetic account of the wayward course of human relationships. Most of the stories in ***Sunshine Sketches*** may also be interpreted in two ways, depending on whether they are read by our "city" or our "Mariposa" self. Josh Smith's machination to keep his liquor license may make him either a conniving trickster or a likeable rogue. Jefferson Thorpe's financial naiveté makes him at once a fool and a symbol of innocence and honesty, the victim of corrupt city swindlers. The fire which destroys the Anglican Church is either a criminal plot or a clever turning of the tables on city financiers, depending on your attitude to the large financial institutions of modern society. Likewise, John Smith's election victory is either an example of corrupt electoral practices or a zestful community ritual which strengthens the town's sense of collective identity. There is no doubt that we are meant to render an adverse judgment on the corruption, skullduggery, and stupidity of the townspeople. Yet we are also meant to see that in many ways Mariposa symbolizes a desirable state of affairs. The town takes care of its own; its citizens co-operate to show a common belief that the world is basically a benign and forgiving place. However misplaced their faith may be, the Mariposans are custodians of a perennially attractive human dream.

Mariposa is a child's world, where evil cannot penetrate and no one can really be hurt by a pratfall or a social disaster. When the narrator slips a banana skin under his characters—when Jefferson Thorpe loses his money, when Dean Drone has a stroke—we know that no harm has really been done and that they will rise whole the next day. When the narrator strips away the masks for a moment, and we see a character naked—Josh Smith rigging the election, Peter Pupkin and Zena Pepperleigh showing their vacuous minds—we may feel a childish delight in seeing others made to look foolish, uncompromised by the sympathy that results from an adult's ability to put himself in another's place. But our response is cruel only as a child is sometimes cruel. The child sees things only from his own point of view; he is cruel because he does not believe an event has consequences beyond its instantaneous outcome. For the child, no discomfort or injury is ever thought of as lasting longer than an instant, and is not real anyway since it is not happening to him. Similarly, we do not believe that permanent harm can be done in Mariposa. In fact, at the end of almost every story in ***Sunshine Sketches*** the action is seen to have been a defense of the status quo, a defense of the very "enchanted" nature of Mariposa itself—rather than an abrasive confrontation with reality such as takes place in most conventional novels. The reader becomes aware that, no matter how dubious or ridiculous the conduct of the Mariposans, none of them is ever permanently changed or seriously injured by events.

Mariposa is depicted as almost perfectly self-contained; the outside world is only a confused rumour, in which it is better not to believe, for if you do, you are sure to lose some of your own inviolable idyllic magic, as Jefferson Thorpe does. The town's appeal is to the regressive qualities in our make-up, to our desire for security. Mariposa contains few anxiety-arousing activities or situations; for example, relations between the sexes are highly stylized, with almost all eroticism removed. There is little competition in the town, except when outside influences intrude. Throughout the book, we are invited to participate vicariously in forbidden activities, such as burning a church for the insurance, fixing an election, imbiding innumerable drinks, and engaging in endless gossip. We are presented with characters with whom we can sympathize and even identify, especially when they are doing something pleasurable or irresponsible. In short, Mariposa is a world of adults playing at being children, a world where child-men come to Smith's Hotel just to admire Josh Smith's enormous watch. It is a world which we know we can never repossess and which we know was never really the true world, but which we yearn towards in Leacock's fiction because in our hearts we wish the world could in fact be so.

Sunshine Sketches appeals to a universal nostalgia for childhood, for a time when your immediate surroundings were, without question, the whole world. Leacock knows he is addressing city readers, whose nostalgia has been blunted by the materialism of their daily lives; yet he knows that nostalgia is there, ready to be evoked by the proper stimulus—and that it is all the stronger for its habitual suppression. Leacock tempts his readers to enter a timeless and magical world, where adults can still appear as embodiments of mysterious and powerful forces and dreams can still appear to be capable of coming true. He creates a world where frame houses really are enchanted castles; where time flows in circles, always returning back to its starting point; where there is no death and burial, but only a painless passing on and interment—a world where a little learning is a lot, where incompetence is normal skill, and normal competence is high ability. It is a world presided over by the imposing bulk of Josh Smith, who seems to possess magical powers and is hedged about with an aura of the forbidden. Josh Smith's profession and costume hint at a daring lack of self-restraint, a breaking of all conventions—which never in fact takes place. He is deliciously wicked, but nonetheless quite safe to know. Thus, on virtually every page the book exploits a nostalgia for a simpler and purer world, a child's world. But we as readers are never completely allowed to forget that both the readers and the narrator of the book inhabit the more sophisticated world of the city. We are given a dual perspective on the town, a view of things both as they appear from within Mariposa (the child-townsman's view) and as they appear from a distance (the adult-city dweller's view). We do not necessarily openly acknowledge the nostalgic level of our responses, but it is nonetheless present, qualifying our awareness of Leacock's satiric intentions.

Sunshine Sketches begins by inviting the reader to an apparent feast of nostalgia. In the opening lines the narrator's voice engages the reader in friendly discourse, flatters and ingratiates him by assuming a shared knowledge, and assures him that in Mariposa he will find only the known, the familiar, the well-loved—there will be no unpleasant surprises:

> I don't know whether you know Mariposa. If not, it is of no consequence, for if you know Canada at all, you are probably well acquainted with a dozen towns like it.[3]
>
> (p. 1)

Then the narrator sets about pretending to adjust the reader's perceptions so that Mariposa can be seen in its true colours. First, the local geography is presented. The steamer, tied with ropes the size they use on the *Lusitania,* floats on a lake which in its landlocked splendour is the only lake in the world. The town's chief thoroughfare is known as "Main Street," for is it not the only main street in the world? The reader is introduced to the bustling commercial and social life of Mariposa, a life as busy and gay as that to be found anywhere in the world. The reader may demur at this. But the narrator anticipates his objections: "Of course if you come to the place fresh from New York you are deceived. Your standard of vision is all astray" (p. 3). If you don't see what he sees, the narrator suggests, *you* are at fault. The obvious discrepancy in experience and standards makes the reader pause. But only momentarily. Quickly he realizes what the narrator means: subjectively, Mariposa is the whole world to its inhabitants. So the reader adjusts his vision and looks again. Gradually he is drawn in, his horizon contracted, until Mariposa becomes the world to him, as it already is to the townspeople. If the reader is not persuaded by the narrator's voice, then he is persuaded by the massive and colourfully draped figure of Josh Smith, nearly three hundred pounds of shrewdness, willpower, patience, ingenuity, and determination. Josh Smith is indubitably *there.*

The reader is completely taken in by Leacock's Mariposa—or almost completely. For the narrator's voice also contains overtones of irony, which the reader is (of course) shrewd enough to detect. The Mariposa Belle is not really as big as the *Lusitania*; the bustle of Main Street is not really equal to the bustle of Threadneedle Street or Lower Broadway. A second standard of vision—that of the man from New York or from the city to the south—is always present in the background, telling us that Mariposa, despite its microcosmic quality, is only a small town of five thousand souls, a smallest part of the world. Moreover, we are reminded of the characters' shortcomings often enough to keep our identification tentative, so that we may disown our own forbidden longings when the surrogates who embody them are revealed as childish.

Throughout ***Sunshine Sketches*** Leacock causes the reader to experience the book on two levels simultaneously. On one level we perceive the pettiness of the characters and the selfishness of their actions. We recognize the limitations of a viewpoint that sees Mariposa as the navel of the universe. At the same time, we also recognize that this small-town society forms a seamless whole, within which the townspeople know their places perfectly. The town not only gives its inhabitants a sense of identity, but also closes ranks and defends them from upsetting intrusions originating in the outside world. Jefferson Thorpe falls from financial eminence not into despair but back into the sheltering and secure societal role he had temporarily vacated. The Mariposa court, though at times "a terrible engine of retributive justice" (p. 7), quickly squelches any hint of scandal surrounding the conflagration which rescues the Anglican congregation from bondage to their outsized Ark on the Hill. Thus, we are made to sympathize with, and even envy, the solidarity and security possessed by the citizens of Mariposa, even as we are amused by their idiosyncrasies and follies.

Leacock's principal means of manipulating the reader is his treatment of the narrator, the invisible extra character who actually guides the reader through the streets and byways of the town. The narrator has a disarming manner; he anticipates objections and agrees with them in advance. In this way, Leacock is able to forestall the scorn and ridicule that would come if his readers thought they were being taken for imperceptive fools. Yet the narrator's personality is really quite changeable; sometimes he is a townsman and sometimes an outsider. However, his inconsistency is not immediately obvious to the reader, for it is masked by the uniformly engaging tone of the narrator's speech. The reader, at each moment, identifies himself with the narrator, regardless of whether the narrator is sympathizing with the townspeople or is remarking on their failings. Only a highly critical reader is aware at first reading of the narrator's variability. When the book has been finished and put aside, more readers will begin to question the narrator's consistency. But Leacock has foreseen this questioning and has turned it against the reader. What the reader finally discovers is that the narrator's ambivalent reaction has been matched by the reader's own divided response to Leacock's little town in the sunshine.

Like the narrator, we as readers are also divided in our attitude towards Mariposa and its people. When we perceive the town as attractive, we are forsaking the "reality principle" which rules ordinary life and responding to Leacock's book in an uncritical and unreasoned way; we are approaching the town as children would. For only a child can with full conviction view the world in quite the rosy terms it assumes for the citizens of Mariposa. But this not the whole story. Some remarks by Robertson Davies are pertinent. Basing his analysis of humour on Freudian ideas, Davies has written:

> The humorist seeks to take us back momentarily to the intellectual freedom of childhood, when everything was fresh to us, and freshly apprehended; if something seemed stupid or unimportant to us, we said so without regard for what the adult world thought; so also, if adults thought it trivial or inopportune or possibly disgusting. The humorist does this, and part of the price he pays for his gift is that he is thought childish, or a trifler, when we have been snatched back into the solemnity of the adult's world.[4]

It is easy to see that when we find Mariposa appealing we are reacting in a childish manner. But Davies's comments also imply that when we laugh at the immature antics of the Mariposans, we are indulging in an equally childish but far less kindly fondness for seeing folly exposed and people made ridiculous. Then, when we have finished reading the book, a new reaction may set in. We may become embarrassed or disgusted at the immature level of our responses, and we may reject the book as trivial. Hence, recognition of the nostalgia inherent in ***Sunshine Sketches*** suggests that we must pause and ask ourselves an important question: Is it possible to go beyond the childish elements contained in our nostalgic reaction to the book and to respond to ***Sunshine Sketches*** in a way that is at once "adult" and sympathetic? Or should we feel embarrassed if we find ourselves responding with empathy to the gallery of none-too-bright misfits and know-nothings who inhabit Leacock's town?

Such a devaluing of the humorist's efforts does not in fact happen at the end of ***Sunshine Sketches.*** Paradoxically, the very admission of the power of childhood to overcome adult awareness is in the end the most "adult" theme of Leacock's best book. Instead of asking us to suspend our sense of adult dignity and engage in a bit of childish foolery, what Leacock actually does in ***Sunshine Sketches*** is to expose the childish motivations of much of what ordinarily passes for adult behaviour, including—and this is the last layer of irony—the reader's own reading of this very book. In ***Sunshine Sketches*** the longing for an escape to childhood operates in so unobtrusive a way that the reader is hardly aware of it until in **"L'Envoi"** he is trapped into admitting that the longing for escape has affected him, as well as the narrator of the book. At the end of **"L'Envoi,"** at the moment when the book appears about to dissolve into unqualified sentimentalism, we are abruptly jerked back to reality. We realize that it is we the readers who have most strongly desired to return to Mariposa and that the narrator has found us out. Leacock deliberately catches the reader in the act of longing for an escape to childhood and then points out that the reader has actually been cooperating in his own evasion of reality. At the opening of **"L'Envoi,"** the narrator's voice again lures the reader into complicity:

> It leaves the city every day about five o'clock in the evening, the train for Mariposa.
>
> Strange that you did not know of it, though you come from the little town—or did, long years ago.
>
> (p. 148)

And we nod in agreement, whether we were raised in a small town or not, for we all lived once in childhood's enchanted country not long ago. The narrator addresses us as one man reminiscing to another, gazing backwards down the perspective of the years to a vanished place we can never recover. Home, he says, now means the city, with its sandstone houses and Mausoleum Clubs. And we nod again, recognizing that this is true. Yet before he is done the narrator means to make us call Mariposa "home."

The narrator's plan of attack is brilliantly simple. First he puts us off guard by openly confessing his strategy: he plans to appeal to our nostalgia for childhood and home. He admits this obliquely by appearing to assert the contrary and insisting on the reader's distance from Mariposa:

> But of course "home" would hardly be the word you would apply to the little town, unless perhaps, late at night, when you'd been sitting reading in a quiet corner somewhere such a book as the present one.
>
> (p. 148)

The thing is perfectly done. We recognize ourselves so exactly that we are not offended or embarrassed at being found out, but utterly charmed. As a result, both narrator and reader are ready to conspire to maintain a pleasurable mutual deception. Then the narrator begins to work a transformation, and, as he flourishes his words, we find ourselves dreaming of Mariposa or whenever we were happiest; and we are drawn aboard the five o'clock train, which we, like the narrator, had thought was only the suburban commuter train. As the train passes the city's outskirts and the commuters drop off, we too recognize our friends Dean Drone and Judge Pepperleigh, and we let down our city reserve and bask in the aura of geniality that only a group of small town people can radiate. Meanwhile, at the periphery of our attention, dream transformations are taking place, which in our unalert state we take for reality:

> The electric locomotive that took you through the city tunnels is off now and the old wood engine is hitched in its place. I suppose, very probably, you haven't seen one of these engines since you were a boy forty years ago—the old engine with a wide top like a hat on its funnel, and with sparks enough to light up a suit for damages once in every mile.
>
> Do you see, too, that the trim little cars that came out of the city on the electric suburban express are being discarded now at the way stations, one by one, and in their place is the old familiar car with stuff cushions in red plush (how gorgeous it once seemed!) and with a box stove set up on one end of it?
>
> (p. 150)

When the Conductor calls "Mariposa! MARIPOSA!" we expect a literal return to take place; we are shocked momentarily when the narrator dispels the illusion and we find ourselves still in the Mausoleum Club. Our response to this awakening is itself ambivalent. As we immediately recognize, the dream of return was impossible. But we are not angry at the deception. We have been so taken in that for a moment we are overcome by the sense of something—something precious—which has been lost; and we can only pause and mourn, half-consciously sensing that it is a part of ourselves for which we mourn. We do not throw down the book, or feel angry with the narrator for deceiving us, for Leacock has made it plain that we have co-operated in our own seduction.

Perhaps we are justified in describing much of the work in Leacock's voluminous literary output as "childish" in a pejorative sense. In many of his later books, Leacock may well have played the down or jester, as Davies insists. But in ***Sunshine Sketches*** the joke is ultimately on the reader. Leacock gives us the pleasure of feeling superior to his town and its citizens, but when we are returned to an adult awareness, it is Leacock who exacts a price, not the reader. The price we pay is a consciousness of our own regression. While reading ***Sunshine Sketches,*** we are lured into being children on the level of our responses, and then we are made aware of what we have done. It is not that the reader is consciously taken in. But Leacock has appealed to a pre-existing willingness to believe in the benign world he portrays and has planted the seeds of an unconscious acquiescence, which he later raises to consciousness. At one point in ***Sunshine Sketches*** the narrator remarks: "in Mariposa all really important speeches are addressed to an imaginary audience of boys" (p. 34). This phrase exactly describes the willful suspension of an awareness of the harsher aspects of reality which is a feature both of Leacock's fictional town and of the reader's response to ***Sunshine Sketches.*** By the end of the book the reader discovers that he has been one of the "boys" whom the narrator is addressing. As we finish reading **"L'Envoi,"** we can only admit that we have tried to play truant from reality, that we have tried to escape back to childhood, and that we have been well and truly caught by Leacock, here acting as a schoolmaster of the imagination.

Notes

1. "Introduction" to *Feast of Stephen* (Toronto: McClelland and Stewart, 1970), p. 19. This introduction is a slightly revised form of *Stephen Leacock* (Toronto: McClelland and Stewart, 1970).
2. "The Enchanted Houses: Leacock's Irony," *Canadian Literature,* No. 23 (Winter 1965), p. 32. This article has been reprinted in *The Canadian Novel in the Twentieth Century,* ed. George Woodcock (Toronto: McClelland and Stewart, 1975), pp. 1-14.
3. *Sunshine Sketches of a Little Town,* New Canadian Library (1912; rpt. Toronto: McClelland and Stewart, 1960). All page references are given in parentheses in the text.
4. "Introduction," p. 41.

Beverly Raspovich (essay date 1981)

SOURCE: "The Leacock Persona and the Canadian Character," in *Mosaic,* Vol. XIV, No. 2, Spring, 1981, pp. 77-92.

[*In the following essay, Raspovich examines the "little man" or "uncommon common man" persona in some of Leacock's most important works, including* Sunshine Sketches of a Little Town, Arcadian Adventures with the Idle Rich, *and* Behind the Beyond.]

Because Canada has often been interpreted as a puritan and sober culture—a country where survival has depended on hard work and where celebration has been at a premium—Canadian humor has seemed almost not to exist. In fact, among Canadians, "the myth of the mirthless Canadian" is a well worn phrase. It is, of course, a carefully rehearsed self-deprecating joke, proving not that the typical Canadian is dour but that he is capable of devious disguises and ironic, detached postures. As a matter of history, at least two Canadian humorists have been instrumental in brilliantly shaping the direction of North American humor by partly stepping outside of their own regional or national mythologies. In the nineteenth century, the Nova Scotian Thomas Haliburton created the resonant comic prototype of the enterprising Yankee in Sam Slick, a character who eclipsed the native U.S. version, Seba Smith's Jack Downing. Similarly, Canada's most famed humorist, Stephen Leacock, is applauded by literary critics south of the border as an originator of the twentieth-century comic figure of the "little man," a type who is known in modern American humor in his simplest definition as the inept, average middle-class citizen harassed by bureaucracy, technology and family. Earlier characterized by his sense of responsibility, decency and concern for others, the average bumbler has more recently turned into a perfect neurotic. From his pictorial representation as Charlie Chaplin and Woody Allen in film and Dagwood Bumstead in comic strip, to his literary expression as a voice in Leacock's famous sketch **"My Financial Career,"** the little man is heralded as a comic representative of modern American society.

Not surprisingly, American critics consider Leacock one of their own, celebrating him primarily as a source of the American mainstream of little-man humor. Norris Yates explains that "it is impossible to say just when the bemused householder and white-collar man became really prominent in American humour, but by 1910 Stephen Leacock, Simeon Strunksy and Clarence Day, Jr. were writing pieces in which the disguise of each author was just that."[1] Leacock's American biographer, Ralph Curry, also emphasizes the little-man aspect of the Leacock persona, pointing out quite correctly the Canadian writer's inspirational effect on Robert Benchley and his favorite character, "the little man in an incomprehensible world."[2]

For the Canadian critic R. E. Watters, however, Ralph Curry "wearing his American spectacles," has misread Leacock; the "little man" Curry describes is portrayed by various American humorists but not by Leacock. For Watters, concerned quite rightly with the subtlety of national characteristics and cultural attitudes which shape and direct humor, Leacock's "favorite character was indeed a 'little man,' but he was a Canadian type, not an American."[3] He suggests that, although they are powerless and subordinate, Leacock's little men are in control of themselves. While they wear masks of "calculated diffidence," their comprehension of self is full and ironic. In this pose they are Canadian archetypes, reflective of the inner strength of a small nation which has survived the imperialism of larger powers. The archetype is therefore "radically different in outlook from such a character as Benchley's befuddled little man in an incomprehensible world or Thurber's Walter Mitty, who can live only by escaping into a fantasy of his own making" (p. 31).

The truth about the national identity of Leacock's little man is an important and more complicated issue than previous analyses have implied. In the first instance, Leacock cannot be easily separated from the mainstream development of American literary humor. As his critical book *The Greatest Pages of American Humour* reveals, he was American humor's ardent student, extremely conscious of its trends and absorbed by its milieu. If his comic voice does not compare in existential anxiety to Walter Mitty or to Benchley's urbanites, it does compare in some ways to those of earlier, admired turn-of-the-century humorists like George Ade and John Kendrick Bangs. Yet R. E. Watters is sensitive to that which escapes the American critics—that other steady side of the Leacock persona which may sometimes shift and merge into the little man profile but which remains a deliberate presence and a standard in the humor. In fact, when the narrative persona is examined closely through the broad scope of Leacock's humor, those private, certain values divined by Watters behind the character of the little man sharpen and coalesce into a definite personality—an authoritative *alter ego,* who is as much a striking expression of the Canadian character as Watters' insightful interpretation of the little man himself.

This *alter ego* as the voice of sure values is itself not entirely free from American trends at the turn of the century. The transition figure between the cracker-box philosopher, the comic oracle of nineteenth-century rural America who appeared in many guises in newspapers and magazines, and the absurd little man, the prophet of the twentieth-century metropolis, was an ideal projection of an urban, middle-class narrator. As the controlling voice behind the humor of the popular American humorist and Leacock favorite, George Ade, this transition type was the "uncommon common man," a character type who managed the humor and who symbolized certain values which are also typical of the Leacock persona. Ade's ideal man, one who rises by his own effort from the country to the city, distrusts the culture of the new middle class but has an equal contempt for the masses, opposes the plutocracy of wealth but is simultaneously entrepreneurial,[4] is similar to Leacock's own authorial stance.

The point of view of the "uncommon common man" in Leacock's humor is best illustrated in the chapter **"L'Envoi"** from ***Sunshine Sketches of a Little Town.*** Here the voice of the narrator is that of a successful city sophisticate who makes a retrospective and affectionate comment on the rural small town. The attitude of the persona is comparable to that of the protagonist husband in such a typical Ade story as "Effie Whitlesy" from *Stores of the Street and of the Town* (1896). In Ade's story, the husband, who is a business success in Chicago, discovers that the new domestic his pretentious wife has hired is none other than his childhood friend from his small-town past. Although Ade's character is approaching the comic status of the hen-pecked little man in his relationship with a snobbish, middle-class wife, he is not ultimately reduced by her. Most important, he, like the Leacock narrator, upholds the memory of country community, its humanism and social democracy. The Ade character insists that his city-bred wife respect the "common" position and the maid Effie as well.[5]

Leacock came slightly late to the new, American middle-class comic mythology illustrated as a social ideal by Charles Dana Gibson, who between 1887 and 1890 created "the Gibson man" and "the Gibson girl" for *Life* magazine.[6] The Gibson man represented a decorous, handsome, solid citizen who by now had substituted good English for the rural idiom of previous comic oracles, who illustrated a new city sophistication and grooming, and who evoked humor because he was burdened by a luxury loving and charmingly irresponsible wife. As one might expect, after 1900 the contours of such a solid citizen began to melt into those of the little man. A good example of the Gibson-man effect on Leacock's humor can be seen in the Fish illustrations for the fifth edition of ***Behind the Beyond,*** the book most central in the presentation of the little man persona. In **"The Dentist and the Gas"** and **"My Lost Opportunities,"** the illustrations of the oppressed persona still retain some of the suave and urbane good looks of the Gibson man.

Leacock was not remote from changing popular continental American comic mythology, its comic stereotypes and the values behind them. For example, Ade's uncommon common man who showed signs of shrinking to little-man status in "Effie Whitlesy" has shrunk another degree in Leacock's Mr. Rasselyer-Brown who is totally under the domestic influence of Mrs. Rasselyer-Brown in ***Arcadian Adventures with the Idle Rich.*** Like Ade's male character, though, Rasselyer-Brown has to be respected for his knowledge of his successful coal business and for being a good male provider. In this sense, he is a solid citizen and represents, among the satirized Arcadians, the best of a bad lot. Like early American humorists of suburbia such as Ade and Bangs, then, Leacock in his sketches of the Smiths and Joneses at cottage, club, breakfast, dinner, tennis, in courtship and in marriage, satirizes the rising middle class with their new riches, but in the same breath he affirms the enterprise and solidity of the uncommon common man.

If the Leacock persona at times reflects some of the values projected by the author's American contemporaries such as Ade and Bangs, the quintessential voice, the *alter ego,* remains nonetheless much more admirable, much more sophisticated, much more literate—in a word, much less common than the turn of the century American stereotype of the uncommon common man. Despite the occasional affectation of "averageness" by the Leacock narrator, the *alter ego,* the real voice of the humor is distinctly that of Canadian gentility. Simply speaking, the voice of this character can be identified as that of a conservative, educated and sometimes slightly dyspeptic Protestant gentleman. This is the voice which begs a preservation of the Victorian code of dignified manliness, and a separation of sexual roles, the voice which in the comic sketch,**"The Restoration of Whiskers: A Neglected Factor in the Decline of Knowledge,"** upholds the restoration of whiskers in place of the smooth-shaven face of the modern hero, "hardly," the author says, "to be distinguished from a girl's."[7] In its extreme definition it is an identity removed from conventional domesticity, one which is singularly chauvinistic, even misogynistic. I suspect, too, that it is a definition which has its atavistic roots in pioneer Upper Canada, a masculine definition which hearkens back, not to the feminine sensibilities of Susanna Moodie and Catherine Parr Traill, but rather to the individualistic, sporting and bachelor code of the likes of William "Tiger" Dunlop, the lettered doctor of the Canadian backwoods, memorable for, among other things, his bachelor existence, his literary spirit of burlesque, his drinking and his will, in which he took a comic revenge on women.[8]

Canadians, it seems, are comfortable with this profile of a whiskered bachelor gentleman, for not only does the Leacock persona predict Robertson Davies' brilliant Canadian comic prophet, Samuel Marchbanks, but historically, from the Fathers of Confederation through our political genealogy of bachelor and pseudo-bachelor prime ministers, an authoritative, rather isolated—even lonely—gentleman has been the supreme voice of the nation. Most important to Leacock's humor, this identity often serves as a voice propounding a contrasting genteel standard to that of the larger American one represented by the modern urbanized little man—even if, in some instances, our authoritative gentleman appears to assume or pretends to little man characteristics.

While the *alter ego* is more noticeable in some volumes and sketches than in others, such as in the "Author's Preface" to *Winnowed Wisdom* where "the darned little average man," with "his limited little mind" is the obvious butt of the superior author's joke,[9] he comes to life with clarity as a Canadian presence in Leacock's humor when one considers in particular the persona in relation to the comic presentation of the professor, the persona in the bush landscape, and the persona in relation to women and fashion.

In an essay entitled "The Apology of a Professor: An Essay in Modern Learning," Leacock begins, "I know no more interesting subject of speculation, nor any more calculated to allow of a fair-minded difference of opinion, than the enquiry whether a professor has any right to exist."[10] Despite this introduction of "calculated diffidence," Leacock is sentimental and annoyed about a disappearing educational ideal—of learning as its own reward transmitted through the aworldly, moral and wise professor. For Leacock the "professor" was both a facet of self and the literate ideal of the genteel Anglo-Saxon class of Canadian society to which he belonged; it was an ideal which he upheld in his humor. Indeed, the voice of the educated professor is the prevailing one in the majority of his volumes. While he may sometimes characterize the professor as a little man in the modern world, a comic character who rides on his mule of Padua in competition with the automobile (p. 31), Leacock is not antagonistic toward the professor but toward a machine society which, with its commercial ethic, relegates the genuine professor to an anachronistic position.

Perhaps Leacock's most bluntly demarcated and most highly caricatured version of the little man as professor is that of Gildas in ***Arcadian Adventures with the Idle Rich.*** Fundamentally a sympathetic rendering, the portrait of Gildas is not, however, without satirical ambivalence. In the first place, the little professor is a scientist, who, behind heavy doors, secluded in his laboratory in the faculty of industrial and mechanical science, is blind to the spectrum of human drama outside his narrow interest. Gildas "beating off fragments with his little hammer,"[11] has very little interest in the effect of his gold discovery on the people at the site, the Tomlinsons of Tomlinson's Creek who are the ultimate victims of his initial stupid act. In this observation of the little professor as blinkered scientist, Leacock is the comic fellow of Benchley and other turn-of-the-century American humorists who distrusted theoretical and applied science when it did not meet the tests of common sense and humanity. In the Gildas character there is something of the distrust of the laboratory as an American joke, popularized for the common man and his suspicion of intellect by John Kendrick Bangs, Finley Peter Dunne, Don Marquis, James Thurber and Benchley.[12]

Even so, Gildas is blessedly remote from Arcadian commercial infection. He demands admiration because he is a genuine wizard playing with little blue flames as "in a magician's cavern" (p. 31). Gildas is a member of that old professorial class who, as defined by Leacock in "The Apology of a Professor," "knew, too, something of the more occult, the almost devilish sciences, perilous to tackle, such as why the sun is suspended from falling into the ocean, or that very demonology of symbolism—the AL-GEB of the Arabians—. . . . A man with such knowledge simply *had* to teach it. What to him if he should wear a brown gown of frieze and feed on pulse! This, as beside the bursting force of the expanding steam of his knowledge, counted for nothing" (pp. 23-24). In Donald Cameron's estimation, "Leacock does not want to emulate such men [as Gildas]. He does not want to be a fool, even a holy one. He does want a share of the Arcadian force and vigour."[13] In truth, Leacock was alternately attracted to, and repulsed by, the fruits of commerce. In ***Arcadian Adventures with the Idle Rich,*** however, the creator of Gildas is calculatingly diffident to the American commercial standard, for it is only through plutocratic spectacles that the little man as aworldly professor assumes comic proportion. Gildas is interpreted as a fool in terms of the values of the young laboratory demonstrator, representative of "one of the richest and best families in town," who knows less of geology, more of finance, and who, symbolically, has "one eye half-closed" (p. 46) when he laughs at the little professor. The final voice, the ultimate persona, is one removed from this standard and this interpretation. From Leacock's vantage point, it is a poor society which allows Arcadian control to corrupt the higher aims of education and intellectualism. Ultimately, the foolishness of Gildas resides only in the foolish eyes of his beholder.

Similarly, in the comic sketch, **"The Reading Public: A Book Store Study,"** from *Moonbeams from the Larger Lunacy,* the persona is a professor who *appears* to be a self-deprecating little man. Disguised in a sporting tie with spots as big as nickels and sage-green fedora, he is instantly recognized by the manager of the book store for what he really is—a professor. The persona appears to be a little man when he recognizes his own worthlessness as a potential customer: "And he knew, of course, that, as a professor, I was no good. . . . He knew that I would hang around for two hours, get in everybody's way, and finally buy a cheap reprint of the *Dialogues of Plato,* or the *Prose Works of John Milton* . . . or some trash of that sort. . . . He despised me, of course. But it is a maxim of the book business that a professor standing up in a corner looks well in a store."[14] Leacock here is using his marvellous ironic sense to shatter the illusion that the shrewd Mr. Sellyer and his clientele have the correct standards. It is not the professor who is "no good" and "little" but those who supposedly have "*real* taste in literature—the ability to appreciate at its worth a dollar-fifty novel of last month, in a spring jacket with a tango frontispiece" (p. 24).

The Leacock persona's positive definition as a professor is, in part, Leacock the man but it also suggests the special Canadian perspective of his humor. Unlike, for example, the American humorist, Robert Benchley, who had scholarly interests but literally kept his more erudite books hidden in the closet,[15] Leacock was more committed to the academic way than to the American standard of mass culture which persuaded many humorists like Benchley. The Canadian author felt an obligation to philosophize about humor, to dignify it with theoretical books, while Benchley wrote only the occasional lighthearted essay. Benchley, antagonistic toward an academic analysis of humor, typically defined humor in these zany, unmistakably American lines which were meant to parody Max Eastman's serious psycho-analytical book, *Enjoyment of Laughter*: "laughter is really caused by a small tropical fly carried from Central America to Spain by Columbus's men, 'returning to America, on a visit, in 1667, on a man named George Altschuh'" (Yates, p. 83). While Benchley was known to cover his volume of Proust with a dust jacket from a murder mystery, one can hardly imagine the professorial Leacock so fearful of appearing pretentious in his reading.

Moreover, if Benchley's pose in print, his depiction of the little man as a middle-brow bumbler, was, as Norris Yates argues, a response to the demands of middle-brow America, Leacock's comic anti-hero, the little man as academic, and his larger authorial voice of an educated persona were similarly rooted in Canadian custom. To view the academic as established wit and humorist in Canadian letters is not a profound observation, but it is a significant one. It signifies a stronger and more conservative division between the literary establishment and the mass of the people, between the voices of cultural authority and those of its followers in Canada, than there is between the masses and literary leaders in the United States. It suggests, in effect, the ongoing legacy of the Anglo-Canadian *belles lettres* tradition on the frontier, the cultured sensibilities of such early Canadian writers as Judge Haliburton, Tiger Dunlop, Susanna Moodie, Catherine Parr Traill and the Stricklands. The modern result, so reflected in the writings of Peter McArthur, Stephen Leacock and Robertson Davies, is a stratum of humor in Canada which is sophisticated, pensive, literary and decorous. Perhaps it predicts too—at least it has in the case of Leacock and Davies—the ongoing development of an authoritative, literate, comic voice.

Although the essential Leacock persona is urbane, he nonetheless remains very much an expression of the Upper Canadian frontier and a rural mythology. For most Canadians, in fact, the true Leacock is the gentleman pioneer farmer, a persona dependent not as much on his authorial voice, but as with the fictionalized "Mark Twain," on his country's popular response to the man and the inherent mythology of his work. This is the Leacock of our popular Canadian poster who is conspicuous in his gentility with cuff-links and tie, and who leans genially on his hoe issuing this wise comic maxim: "I am a great believer in luck and I find the harder I work the more I have of it." A symbol of a dominating aspect of our pioneer past, of the British gentry of old Ontario, this image of Leacock is conveyed through his own mythic recollections of his homestead beginnings and his happy playing at such, as the gentleman-farmer of Orillia. It is a face of Leacock which has become a symbol and statement of a national fantasy and which is very apparent in these sketches about nature and fishing where, unlike the modern neurotic little man, the Leacock persona proves to be experienced in the bush. For Robert Benchley, the little man is a suburbanite who experiences nature over his head and in his backyard. Like Benchley himself, who felt heckled by pigeons and who once was unforgettably attacked by terns on Nantucket Beach, his little man is constantly humiliated in his bouts with his non-human environment. In contrast, in Leacock's humor the essential persona knows the bush, wishes, as a gentleman, to avoid its discomforts, and laughs at those urban little people who ignorantly romanticize it.

The piece most like Benchley's work, and one which is not typical of Leacock's nature sketches, is a neurotic modern comedy of the little man in nature entitled **"To Nature and Back Again."** Here the persona is an American urbanite whose plan is to go to New England for his vacation and to spend it naked in the bush: "for one month, cast off all the travail and cares of civilized life and become again the wild man of the woods that Nature made me."[16] The persona and his absurd fantasy are caught and exposed through the author's mastery of comic exaggeration as, naked in the bush, he meets another vacationer:

> "Do you realize that you are the nineteenth man that I've met in the last three days running about naked in the woods? . . ."
>
> "You don't say so!" I gasped.
>
> "Fact. Wherever you go in the bush you find naked men all working out this same blasted old experiment. Why, when you get a little farther in you'll see signs up: NAKED MEN NOT ALLOWED IN THIS BUSH, and NAKED MEN KEEP OFF, and GENTLEMEN WHO ARE NAKED WILL KINDLY KEEP TO THE HIGH ROAD, and a lot of things like that."
>
> (p. 86)

When the persona awakens from this bad dream to discover himself seminude, an erotically suspect sleepwalker, apprehended by the "cops" in Central Park, the author is clearly saying that the romanticization of the bush by the modern city dweller is a mad self-deception and that really a gentleman ought to know better.

The persistent vision behind Leacock's humorous pieces on nature is not that of omnipotent natural forces overwhelming the little man but rather an experienced appraisal of the hardships of nature and the firm conviction that civilized man ought to avoid such primitive conditions whenever he can. We understand the narrator to be stupid in **"To Nature and Back Again"** because, foolish puppet to the real voice of the piece, he thinks civilization a "curse," preferring "boiled grass and fungi cooked in a hollow stone" to dining at home (p. 82). And in the sketch, **"Back to the Bush,"** from the second edition of ***Literary Lapses,*** we understand the self-possessed persona to be superior because we credit him with the knowledge of bush life. Here the persona and the reader are in the company of well-educated men who, all but the narrator, have gone a little silly. Taken in by the idyllic travel brochures written by the narrator himself, these city men flock to the bush with the illusion of happy survival. Here, too, the message is that vastly superior to the reality of bush-flies, moose, bears and skunks is a standard of dignified and comfortable living. The authorial edict is often, moreover, the enjoyment of nature from the comfortable armchair of the private men's club, or with such luxuries as champagne and hotel dinner-dances close at hand, as in "Roughing It in the Bush: My Plans for Moose-Hunting in the Canadian Wilderness" in *Over the Footlights.*

This voice and this posture are not those of the typical urbanized American little man but those of the Ontario pioneer gentry. Even in humor, Leacock can be seen to belong to a frontier Ontario psychology and the *belles lettres* tradition of nature writing initiated by Susanna Moodie, her sister and the nineteenth-century Otonabee school of nature writers. While these writers recognized and knew the coarse realities of living in the bush, they persisted in presenting a literary view of nature which was essentially romantic and which was meant as a genteel escape from the hard facts of the natural world.[17] Leacock carries on this romantic pioneer tradition in his genial and gently humorous sketches where he idealizes pastoral possibility and leisure in nature through the gentlemanly art of angling. Like the famous and influential Canadian nature writer, Roderick Haig-Brown,[18] Leacock explicitly associates himself with the original company of *belles lettres* nature writers, the Izaac Walton school of fishing, in "What Can Izaac Walton Teach Us?" from *Last Leaves.*

Unlike Walton's serious pastoralism, however, Leacock's fishing and nature idylls can also be pointed comic illusions, ironically understood by the Canadian gentleman in the difficult Canadian climate as pastoral fiction, *preferable* even as literary events rather than real ones. In **"Angel Pond, Lure of the North,"** for example, the Leacock persona mocks from a superior distance and with an eastern eye those who inhabit the landscape of Northwestern Ontario and pretend to an easy, rugged frontier ethos. The persona very definitely knows better when Charlie of Angel Pond nonchalantly replies to the question, "Are the flies bad in summer?" with "Oh, the flies are nothing to us . . . you just smear your face thick with any kind of fat, groundhog fat, skunk's fat. . . . They never get you that way."[19] Ultimately for the sly persona, the best and proper way to enjoy fishing is with comfort and elegance, telling stories about it "round a winter fire, with a glass of something warm within easy reach, at a time when statements cannot be checked. . . ."[20]

Quite obviously, then, the Leacock persona is in nature a member of the Eastern gentry, as knowledgeable about the bush and as unwilling to accept its unpleasantries as he is wise and guarded about love and women. It is well understood that the little man as lover is a constant theme of Leacock's humor and that the author is entirely sympathetic to him in his awkward courtships and unrequited affairs. In **"A Transit of Venus,"** the laughter for the little man and inept lover, Lancelot Kitter, is sympathetic, as it is for Joe in **"A Humble Lover"** whose courtship of Miss Carson is a figment of his imagination. Because Leacock kept faith with the Victorian ideal of hearth and home, family solidarity and the sweet helpmate who is revered in the chapter as **"The Little Girl in Green"** in ***Arcadian Adventures with the Idle Rich,*** he does not want to dismiss the romantic quests of the Lancelot Kitters or Peter Pupkins. In the sunshine, he celebrates their enchanted vision.

The dominant persona is not, however, identifiable with the little man as lover, the domestic little rabbit of twentieth-century American humor. Instead, he is the distanced protector of the little lover and husband, the *I* who is "all for Joe's love affair" in the following excerpt from **"A Humble Lover"**: "I asked Joe, a little later in his courtship, if he had spoken yet to Miss Carson about marriage. He said no, but he had discussed it with his mother. His mother was all for it. He was going to wait awhile and then talk to his father. If his father was for it and his mother and if I was for it, that made three."[21] Remaining outside of the domestic situation, he is the gentleman interloper and observer who may be reduced to little man status by the domestic ménage he visits, but who has the ingenuity to escape and to preserve his ego.

This sense of self-preservation is apparent in **"The Sorrows of a Summer Guest,"** where the persona seems to be a little man when he is unable to master the conventions of being a summer guest at the fashionable Beverly-Jones's. When he fails to please these people, his neurotic sense of displacement is magnified in the style of modern psychological little man comedy: "Not that these people are not doing all they can for me. I know that. I admit it. If I *should* meet my end here and if—to put the thing straight out—my lifeless body is found floating on the surface of this pond, I should like there to be documentary evidence of *that* much."[22] Finally, through his overwhelming fear of being a master-of-ceremonies at an evening gathering of parlor-games, he invents an extravagant excuse and leaves post-haste. By so doing, he is able to preserve his certain, private and superior identity as gentleman traveller and respected club man:

> Just these two bags, porter, and there's a dollar for you. What merry, merry fellows these darky porters are, anyway!
>
> And so here I am in the train, safe bound for home and the summer quiet of my club.
>
> (p. 74)

Moreover, unlike the humor of Robert Benchley where the wife of the little man is just a shadow, in Leacock's humor the persona periodically attacks the dominating wife of the milquetoast character with vengeance. In **"The Cave Man as He Is,"** from ***Frenzied Fiction,*** the persona begins by identifying with the modern little man in his inability to woo women in a "fierce primordial way"—the way that the fifteen-cent magazine and the new fiction advise. The persona seems like the little man himself, lazily fantasizing about dragging women off by hiring an express man to carry one: "But would they come? That's the *deuce* of it. Would they come right along, like the cave-woman merely biting off my ear as they came, or are they degenerate enough to bring an action against me, indicting the express company as a party of the second part?" (p. 93). But with the discovery of hidden caves with original cave-men still in them, the persona more clearly becomes an aloof and dignified *alter ego.* Here he unravels the pathetic deceit of the cave-man dream. The cave-man "has lost all appearance of size," is "quite little," and is completely overrun in the modern way by a virago, a "big-boned woman in a suit of skins" (p. 100). In fact, there is some truth in the cave-man's interpretation of the persona as the real man, the "Outside Man" who knows how "to treat your women! By gee! You take no nonsense from them—you fellows are the real primordial primitive men. We've lost it somehow" (p. 99).

This attack against the little man's wife is apparent in those pieces, **"John and I"** from ***Winsome Winnie*** and

"The Intimate Disclosures of a Wronged Woman" from ***The Iron Man and the Tin Woman,*** where the real persona is obviously male but curiously assumes a feminine disguise. The intention of this pose is sharply satirical. Burlesques of the confessional narratives of women's magazines, such pieces nevertheless function as serious social comments which expose the feminine psyche in marriage as deceptive and overbearing. Beneath Minn's facade of sympathetic attention in **"John and I"** is a hard, manipulating will: "I have always felt that every woman should make all that she can of her husband. So I did my best first of all to straighten up John's appearance. I shifted the style of collar he was wearing to a tighter kind that I liked better, and I brushed his hair straight backward instead of forward, which give him a much more alert look. Mother said that John needed waking up, and so we did all we could to wake him up."[23] In **"The Intimate Disclosures of a Wronged Woman"** from ***The Iron Man and the Tin Woman,*** the persona is more absurd and trivial in her observations, her feminine illogic the source of the amusement, but her attitude to men, particularly in the chapter **"Married Life,"** is shrewd, unsympathetic and highly rational. One of the foremost characteristics of the real Leacock voice, then, is his tenacious male patriarchical position. Infinitely preferable to **"The Awful Woman with the Spectacles"**[24] is the Soft Lady, the doll.[25] Infinitely preferable to the modern age of Gibson girls, the suffragettes, the domineering Mrs. Rasselyer-Browns and Beverly-Joneses are the "good old Victorian days, where women were angels, fairies, godmothers and such. . . ."[26]

Although this detachment from the little man as lover and husband, and the accompanying satire of the little man's wife, may not be exclusively Canadian, it does perhaps suggest a Canadian bias. As John D. Robbins suggests in *A Book of Canadian Humour,* Canadian society, in theory at least, is patriarchal. Because the husband is head of the house, there is nothing inherently funny or incongruous about the domineering husband. The henpecked husband is, however, fair game.[27] Perhaps, too, the selection of a feminine persona as a method of satirical attack against women may portend something less conscious and less deliberate than the humorist's method. It may, in effect, reflect a submerged Victorian neurosis. As child of Queen Victoria's reign and Victorian assumptions in Anglo-Saxon Ontario, Leacock's—perhaps even Canada's—authentic psyche may well be that of a bachelor gentleman, hating and rejecting feminine power in order to preserve his masculinity but ambivalently attracted to and respectful of femininity and the mother-code. Certainly, as the recent revelations of Mackenzie King's diaries and the emerging burlesques of them indicate, it is a psychology understood well enough to be fast becoming a national joke. In any case, the voice of this Leacock persona seems to be a patriarchal Canadian one for it accords with that of Samuel Marchbanks who explains with gentlemanly dignity that, "Nobody has to live in the pattern of Dagwood and Blondie or like a creation of Jimmie Hatlo, who does not choose to do so."[28] The Leacock persona, it seems, is in league with Marchbanks. While the pattern of Blondie and Dagwood is traced, the authorial voice is removed from Blondie's authority—and the subordinate position of the little man.

An Anglo-Canadian statement is also made in those Leacock pieces which deal with fashion, particularly those wherein the persona is incongrously transformed by "feminine" dress. In *A Treasury of Canadian Humour,* Robert Thomas Allen points out that in nineteenth-century Canadian humor jokes were often made at the expense of the Americans. In humorous periodicals such as "The Moon," for example, the idea of the civilized American struck the Canadian as hilariously funny.[29] For Britannia's noblest daughter, the American society girl was particularly vulgar. This Canadian aversion to fashion and affectation lingers on in Leacock, directed not so much toward the Americans, but, with stolid Upper Canadian prejudice, toward the French. In ***Literary Lapses,*** the humor of **"Society Chit-Chat"** depends on the affectation of the fine French phrase in contrast to the realities of practical daily life. In ***Behind the Beyond,*** too, the travelling persona approaches French fashion and culture with the same puritan Anglo-Canadian and commonsense standard. The humor results when the persona falls from this standard into *La Mode Parisienne* and makes a fool of himself. Taking the "stuffy black ribbon" from his "Canadian Christie hat," he replaces it with a "single black ostrich feather . . . fashioned with just the plainest silver aigrette. When I had put that on and pinned a piece of old lace to the tail of my coat with just one safety pin, I walked the street with the quiet dignity of a person whose one idea is not to be conspicuous."[30]

In conclusion, while Leacock was an inventive and prophetic humorist who introduced continental America to the comic archetype of the little man, he did so with a Canadian knowledge of his own pioneer roots and ancestral place and with an aversion to a displacement of the past by modernism. Because he represents the consequence of Leacock's avowed enemy, the Machine Age, the milquetoast figure, the inconsequential man of the masses, was largely unacceptable to the real persona of Leacock's humor, that of the educated, Anglo-Saxon gentleman. With his sure values of dignified living, his books, his club, his civilized comforts, he was the author's instructive response to his own quickly developing industrial society and to North American society at large.

Although Leacock's character is recognizably Canadian, a member of that superior class in Canadian society identified by Robertson Davies as "the clerisy,"[31] the tradition of Protestant gentility was not exclusive to Leacock or to Canada. The American intellectual historian Stowe Persons in *The Decline of the American Gentility* has traced the old, colonial tradition of gentility in the United States, which was inherited from eighteenth-century England and modified by the American experience, through to its decline at the beginning of the twentieth century. He cites as an example of moribund gentry culture the American Academy of Arts and Letters organized in 1904 by such academicians as William Dean Howells and Mark Twain. The intention of the Academy was in part to enforce dignity in manners, as well as in literary style, but as Persons explains, the Academy was founded at a time "when the tide of modernism was already beginning to engulf gentry culture."[32] and not all its members could agree about the extent to which the Academy should be accountable to democracy or to common standards. Interestingly, Persons also notes that by 1882 in the United States the gentry as a class were extremely prone to nervous disorders, to insanity and to alcoholism, and that "those prone to such afflictions constituted a definite physiological type; small in size, with a frail, fine constitution, frequently of superior intellect and a strong emotional nature" (p. 287). Moreover, the gentry had not only become physically "little men," they contributed through their nervousness to a distinctive brand of American humor:

> The distinctive American brand of humor was found to have a deep foundation in nervousness. Humor was an inevitable reaction to excessive strain. The peculiarly American humor of exaggeration, the grotesque, and the absurd had been developed not by the coarse, vulgar type of person, but by the gentry type. The humorous lecture of the later nineteenth century had replaced the cause of a deeply felt need for laughter. Laughing aloud had formerly been considered vulgar; but nervous people were now increasingly resorting to laughter because they had discovered its therapeutic value. The American language similarly showed the influence of nervousness in the course of its divergence from the mother tongue. Clipped words, compressed idioms, indistinct articulation, greater rapidity of speech, the high and monotonous sameness of pitch, all testified to the same cause. Even the musical instruments in the United States were said to be pitched higher than in Europe.
>
> (p.289)

The comic archetype of the little man with his nervous humor can be seen to be related, then, to the decline of the gentry—even to have been gentry-inspired. For a humorist like Robert Benchley, born of New England gentry stock, the type-figure of his humor, which many critics claim was an expression of Benchley's own inept and bumbling self, was, it seems, almost a genetic legacy from an earlier generation.

Though it may be that Leacock's little man also emerged from threatened genteel values, it is not possible to identify Leacock in the way that Benchley, James Thurber and Walter Perelman have been identified: as themselves "Perfect Neurotics."[33] While these authors lived in fast-paced urban societies and projected the phobias and neuroses of urban living through their fumbling little men, Leacock himself belonged to the quiet academic society of his University Club and the rural world of Orillia. Leacock's Canada had not yet reached the stage of urban alienation of Benchley's America; thus the Canadian author's intact, confident and distanced *alter ego* could make a special point of rejecting the nervous, mechanized humor of modern America and the shape of its humor to come: "short and snappy, sarcastic—a bark, a snarl, reverting toward the primitive mockery that was cast out long ago."[34]

Stow Persons has also suggested that the nervousness of Americans and their nervous humor were very much related to the extremes of threatening climate and the alternations of heat and cold and that there is actually, geographically, "a nervous belt, extending westward from southern New England and the Middle Atlantic States along the southern shores of the Great Lakes to southern Minnesota and Iowa eastwards through the Ohio Valley." Persons further explains that, curiously, "North of the nervous belt, in Canada . . . nervousness was much less frequently encountered" (p. 292). If this theory is true, then it serves as a partial explanation, at least, for the Canadian certainty behind Leacock's depiction of the little man. It is certainly true that Canadians pride themselves on their ability quietly to survive in an awesome land and a severe climate. By providing an assured alternative to the little man aspect of his humor, Leacock, it seems, was sensitive to this pioneer fortitude Canadians claim as a national characteristic. More obviously, of course, Leacock was a comic mythologist for his own Canadian region. In his superior pose of the educated gentleman he hearkens back to the transplanted bookishness and gentry culture of the privileged settlers of old Ontario. Because this region has traditionally been the center of Canadian political and cultural power, however, the Leacock face of the lettered patriarch is as much a mythic representation of the Canadian character as Sam Slick's is of America's. Although since Leacock's time, the Canadian character has fractionized, has begun "to split into [the] many characters"[35] which interestingly Constance Rourke identifies in her classic study *American Humor* as the *source* and mainspring of the humorous tradition in the United States, the foremost, original face of Canada and its comic character remains the Leacock man.

As a comic oracle of Canadian society, the Leacock gentleman is a figure, too, who significantly is not without an international perspective. And as one might expect, it is in the international arena that he begins to feel somewhat powerless. In an early piece called **"Abdul Azziz Has His: An Adventure in the Yildiz Kiosk,"** the author fantasizes directly about his own nation's impotent role. In this sketch, a Turkish sultan naively trapped in the web of international politics is the "little man" who is overpowered by a Prussianic Field-Marshall; the Canadian, equally powerless, is personified as a male professor, symbolically disguised in the pioneer garb of poke bonnet and a plain black dress. While Leacock deplores with comic melancholy his country's lack of international clout in this early sketch, in a later one called **"This International Stuff"** from ***Funny Pieces,*** he envisions a new role. Here the persona introduces himself as the average man picking peas in his garden but quickly supercedes this status when he describes himself in ideal terms as a Canadian and an internationally minded man. In **"This International Stuff,"** by confidently espousing democratic intercourse and tolerance on a global level, the Leacock persona affirms a new international authority for Canada. His country's prophet, the persona reflects, too, that orthodox Canadian pursuit of peace, interpreted by the rest of the world as feminine and described by the Canadian writer Hugh MacLennan as our "good woman's hatred of quarrels, the good woman's readiness to make endless compromises for the sake of peace."[36] In the last half of the twentieth century, this national fantasy as projected by the Leacock persona, has been constructively realized. Leacock would have been glad to know that after his death Canada gained respect as the steady professor in poke bonnet, as a civilized nation with some international tact and diplomatic skill.

Notes

1. Norris Yates, *The American Humorist* (New York, 1965), p. 244.
2. Ralph Curry, "Robert Benchley and Stephen Leacock: An Acknowledged Literary Debt," *The American Book Collector,* VII (1957), 14.
3. R. E. Watters, "A Special Tang: Stephen Leacock's Canadian Humour," *Canadian Literature,* No. 5 (Summer 1960), 27.
4. See Yates (pp. 61-80), for a complete discussion of Ade's values.
5. George Ade, *The Permanent Ade,* ed. Fred C. Kelly (New York, 1947), p. 129.
6. Yates, p. 24.
7. Stephen Leacock, *Laugh with Leacock* (Toronto, 1930), p. 192.
8. Tiger Dunlop's will includes the following statements: "I leave my sister Jenny my Bible, the property of my great-great-grandmother, Bethua Hamilton of Woodall; and when she knows as much of the spirit of it as she does of the letter, she will be a better Christian than she is," and "I'll give my silver cup, with a Sovereign in it, to my sister Janet Graham Dunlop, because she is an old maid and pious, and therefore will necessarily take to horning." Cited in Earl B. Scarlett, *In Sickness and in Health* (Toronto, 1971), p. 139.
9. Leacock, *Winnowed Wisdom* (1926; rpt. Toronto, 1971), p. viii.
10. Leacock, *Essays and Literary Studies* (1916; rpt. London, 1917), p. 11.
11. Leacock, *Arcadian Adventures with the Idle Rich* (1914; rpt. Toronto, 1969), p. 30.
12. Yates, *Robert Benchley* (New York, 1968), pp. 74-75.
13. Donald Cameron, *Faces of Leacock* (Toronto, 1967), p. 114.
14. Leacock, *Moonbeams from the Larger Lunacy* (1915; rpt. London, 1919), p. 24.
15. See Yates, *Robert Benchley,* p. 80.
16. Leacock, *Frenzied Fiction* (1918; rpt. London, 1919), p. 77.
17. For a discussion of these nature writers see Alex Lucas, "Nature Writers and the Animal Story," *Literary History of Canada,* ed. Carl F. Klinck (Toronto, 1965; rpt. 1966, 1967), p. 367.
18. Roderick Haig-Brown reveals the influence of Walton on his own attitude toward nature in "A Conversation with Roderick Haig-Brown," by Glenys Scow in *Canadian Children's Literature,* I, No. 2 (Summer 1975), 10.
19. Leacock, *Happy Stories* (New York, 1943), p. 62.
20. Leacock, *Winnowed Wisdom,* p. 82.
21. Leacock, *Too Much College* (New York, 1939), p. 207.
22. Leacock, *Frenzied Fiction,* p. 69.
23. Leacock, *Winsome Winnie* (1920; rpt. New York, 1923), p. 54.
24. Leacock, "The Woman Question," *Essays and Literary Studies,* p. 121.
25. Leacock, *Further Foolishness* (1916; rpt. London, 1921), p. 78.
26. Leacock, *Humour: Its Theory and Technique* (London, 1935), pp. 266-67.
27. John D. Robbins and Margaret O. Day, *A Book of Canadian Humour* (Toronto, 1934), p. xi.
28. Robertson Davies, *Samuel Marchbanks' Almanak* (Toronto, 1967), p. 17.
29. Robert Thomas Allen, *A Treasury of Canadian Humour* (Toronto, 1967), p. 17.
30. Leacock, *Behind the Beyond* (1916; rpt. Toronto, 1969), p. 81.
31. Davies, *A Voice from the Attic* (New York, 1960; rpt. 1972), pp. 1-38.
32. Stow Persons, *The Decline of American Gentility* (New York, 1973), p. 112.
33. Yates explains that the American literary critics, Bernard de Voto and Walter Blair, have made this claim (*Robert Benchley,* p. 61).
34. Leacock, *The Greatest Pages of American Humor* (1936; rpt. London, 1937), p. 230.
35. Constance Rourke, *American Humor* (New York, 1931), p. 297.
36. Hugh MacLennan, *Cross-Country* (Edmonton, 1949; rpt. 1962), p. 5.

Francis Zichy (essay date 1987)

SOURCE: "The Narrator, the Reader, and the Mariposa: The Cost of Preserving the Status Quo in *Sunshine*

Sketches of a Little Town," in *Journal of Canadian Studies,* Vol. 22, No. 1 Spring, 1987, pp. 51-65.

[*In the following essay, Zichy argues that a "special kind of equivocation" on the part of the narrator rules in* Sunshine Sketches of a Little Town, *and that the work's purpose is not to satirize the town of Mariposa but to convince the narrator himself that the town, with all its faults, is the best world after all.*]

Since the first signs of a considered criticism of Leacock's comic writing in the late 1950s, much of the discussion of ***Sunshine Sketches of a Little Town*** has focussed on the narrator's relation to his subject and his somewhat equivocal tone in presenting it. Some readers have judged ***Sunshine Sketches*** to be a satire, a telling exposé of the folly and even the corruption of small town life; others have described it as a work of genial humour by a writer who, in the words of Malcolm Ross, "loves what he hates."[1] The uncertainty in the telling is paralleled by an uncertainty about the character and position of the narrator, vis-à-vis Mariposa, which has also been widely noticed: at times, he appears to be sophisticated and well-informed about the great world; at other times, he speaks as if he shared the limited vision of the Mariposans. Some critics have therefore found the treatment evasive, and regretted the signs of what they have taken to be an affected naiveté in the narrator, "a spurious naiveté, which is even more depressing than spurious sophistication."[2] This is a serious charge, which must be faced if we are to believe that in ***Sunshine Sketches*** Leacock is more than a casual and none too ingenuous humourist. I will argue here that the equivocation in the telling of ***Sunshine Sketches*** is not merely evasive, nor a sign that the author has simply refused to "take the moral measure of his world,"[3] but that this equivocation is rooted in the nature of the subject as the narrator sees it, and therefore must be reflected in his treatment. I am as interested, also, in the purpose of this equivocation, as it can be registered in the tale, as I am in judging whether the equivocation is a sign of good or bad art, for I think we can show that the presentation is neither feeble-minded nor intentionally and unnecessarily misleading. I will argue that the narrator's equivocation has a purpose—a purpose which is a response to his subject as he sees it—which is not to satirize Mariposa by comparison with some external standard (although that possibility is raised), but over the long run to convince himself and the reader, a former inhabitant of Mariposa who may feel the utility and persuasiveness of this argument, that with all its faults the world of Mariposa is, or was, the best world after all (for our final view of Mariposa is retrospective, suggesting that the narrator has been looking back from the first). By a skillful use of comic equivocation the narrator attempts to rescue the reader (and of course, himself) from the disadvantages of a more "consistent" (D. J. Dooley's word) satiric treatment, though he must surrender the possible advantages of such a treatment. The advantage to be surrendered is that in telling us how silly Mariposa is, satire will tell us that there is a place where life is more serious and consequential than in Mariposa. The disadvantage, which weighs more heavily for the narrator as a former Mariposan, is that satire must also tell us that we might aspire to that place hopelessly, as Myra Thorpe aspires to take up dancing in New York city before she learns to be a true Mariposan and love her job with the telephone company. Worst of all, we might arrive in that serious, grown-up place after all, and dislike it when we get there, perhaps because of something in Mariposa and in ourselves we have not been able to surrender. From this fate the Mariposans are preserved, but we realize at the conclusion that this is the position of the narrator and the reader who has followed his meaning. For this disillusionment, in the chairs of the Mausoleum Club, an equivocally comic portrait of Mariposa may be a last-ditch consolation, which cannot entirely save us from a knowledge of our losses (ambiguously, the loss of something we may be perfectly able to see through), and of how little we have gained to make up for them.

In this connection, it has always seemed to me that one of the most characteristic and telling episodes in ***Sunshine Sketches*** is the account of the rescue of Peter Pupkin (himself the would-be rescuer of his latest lady friend) and the passengers on board the Mariposa Belle in **"The Marine Excursion of the Knights of Pythias."** In the celebration of the rescue of Pupkin, "Saved! Saved!" (53) a major theme is raised, and the narrator's characteristic tone and pressure can be registered, if we trace the development of this episode and explore its resonances.

Working back, then, from the rescue of Pupkin from his own efforts, and the bringing into its berth of the Mariposa Belle, we can see that these comically dubious feats have been prepared by a confounding of the reader's bearings, in the extended comparison of what it means to sink on Lake Wissanotti in the Mariposa Belle, and what it means to sink in a great ocean liner in mid-Atlantic. Right after we are told that the Mariposa Belle is really going down (a first "surprise" which has been repeatedly hinted at from the beginning), a second surprise, this time a happy one, is sprung when the narrator reveals that "I don't suppose that in this stretch of [Lake Wissanotti] . . . you could find six feet of water . . . if you tried." But our complacency is quickly undercut with yet a further consideration: "Safe! I'm not sure now that I come to think of it that it isn't worse than sinking in the Atlantic" (49, 50). This second reversal leaves us disoriented and needing to be rescued ourselves, by "one of the smartest pieces of rescue work ever seen on the lake" (52), or seen in comic writing, that steers between the rock of satire and the soft place of sentimentality. It is the narrator who rescues us, after he has nearly sunk us with his equivocating reversals and made it impossible for us to derive any definite satiric conclusion from a clear orientation of our bearings. By now we cannot say whether life in Mariposa is serious and dangerous, or merely as sheltered and foolish as it appears to be. Like Peter Pupkin, we are exhausted by our unsuccessful efforts to make out the reality of the situation, and we need to be saved, and we are saved, because in this episode as in all others the Mariposa status quo is preserved in spite of the illusion of significant action which the narrator's comic frenzy creates. So too Jeff Thorpe is back in the barber shop after his flirtation with high finance, and glad to be there, as the narrator assures us; so the Whirlwind Campaign ends with not a cent of money changing hands (save the hundred dollars of Mullins, the exception that only proves the rule), though hundreds of thousands have been promised; and so the new church is mercifully burned to the ground, and the town saved from the fire by the ultimate piece of rescue work in the story. Peter Pupkin is saved from the possibility that he might have completed some effectual action, and thus lost his ineffable innocence. But he is saved at a price, since his rescue makes his utter ineffectualness clear, though not to Pupkin himself. Thus this price, though indicated, is not paid by Pupkin—he is rescued by the narrator as well as by the men on the Mariposa Belle. And even the reader has been finally saved from satire, if he is reading as he is encouraged to do by the happy ending of the episode. It is fundamental to the narrator's method that equivocation prevails, in the piling of reversal upon reversal, preventing a clear satiric thrust, a conclusive comparison of life in Mariposa with another standard, implicit or explicit. In Mariposa every force is cancelled by an equal opposite force, just as in the narrator's telling every consideration is met by an equal opposite one, so that satire is both allowed and then stymied, and we may feel moved to conclude that all is for the best in the end. Thus Peter Pupkin rows out into the middle of the lake and is rescued (or stymied) by a reciprocal effort launched from the steamer; two shots are exchanged in the robbery of the Mariposa bank, both miss, and the sum is zero: no money has been lost, no robbery has taken place, and the snooping detectives return to the big city, their hands empty, convinced perhaps of the nullity and ridiculousness of Mariposa life—convinced, with the same partial correctness as those who would read ***Sunshine Sketches*** as a satire, or as a satire manqué. This zero result is the "mystery" of life in Mariposa (as in the chapter title, **"The Mariposa Bank Mystery"**). As for change or effectual action, "that kind of thing never happens on Lake Wissanotti" (49), and the narrator's story demonstrates that it never happens in Mariposa at large. The repeated recourse to facetious humour expresses the underlying message that it is no use invoking another standard, though such an invocation may be unavoidable, that this is how it is and must be in Mariposa: "there's no use describing it; you need to see rescue work of this kind by lifeboats to understand it" (53). Yes, but what does this understanding amount to? The reader who follows this narrator must perform a special mental operation, even while he is never let off the hook of comic equivocation, if the rescue is to work for him—not the rescue of Pupkin (we can see through that) but the rescue of the narrator and the reader from the consequences of having seen through the rescue of Pupkin. Initially, of course, we are tempted to make the comparison with another standard, with rescue work in the Atlantic (which the narrator himself insistently invokes, suggesting that if this is not a satire, it is not unintentionally so), and making that comparison we might conclude that this is no rescue at all. More fully, we may understand that this is the only "real," the only appropriate rescue in this "real" world and "real danger, a line of thinking that may finally convince us that things are very well in Mariposa, that this is the real world after all (now with inverted commas removed). To suggest this understanding and acceptance of the mystery of Mariposa may be the canny purpose behind the narrator's facetious foolery.

These investigations bring us, then, to a consideration of Smith's pivotal role in the action of ***Sunshine Sketches*** and in the life of Mariposa. His importance is evident from his mere prominence in the story and from the way in which his exploits provide a beginning and a conclusion to its episodes. More essentially, Smith plays a central role as the cunning, knowing (within limits) preserver of the ineffable Mariposa status quo.[4] Thus Smith does from within Mariposa, as an actor in the story, what the narrator does by his special way of telling the story, and what the reader is invited to do by assenting to it as told; he preserves it as it is.

It is not necessary to argue, then, as some readers have done, that as an outsider with superior knowledge Smith preys on and manipulates the Mariposans, or that his *modus operandi* is very different from theirs, for we find that the story has dealt with and discounted that possibility.[5] When he first arrives from the great North, Smith appears indeed to be a potentially disruptive force and is viewed with suspicion. His character as an outsider is of course essential to his role and significance, but it only confirms, as all things in the story do, the final triumph of the Mariposa standard and way of life. As an outsider with "superior" knowledge (he knows about the long distance telephone, but cannot read or write) Smith is the exception that proves the Mariposa rule, though as we read on we see that his differences are more apparent than real (Pupkin, the other outsider, proves the rule rather differently by turning out to be more naturally equipped for life in Mariposa than anyone ever born there). Smith repeatedly uses his limited but real knowledge of the world precisely to maintain the immunity of the sheltered world of Mariposa: that he also benefits by this only confirms his participation in that world, and of course he has plenty of help (as in the burning of the new church) from the Mariposans themselves, who have everything to gain as well. By the end of the story the outsider has become the town figurehead, its "representative man" (the phrase used of his defeated opponent in the election). It could be argued that Smith's citizenship in Mariposa is finally confirmed precisely by his departure—for four years at least—to Ottawa, an event that is so completely nominal as to suggest forcibly that in this instance, as always, things in Mariposa are never more the same than when they give the appearance of changing: nowhere will Smith be more a Mariposan than in Ottawa (we shall see, when we look at **"L'Envoi,"** that this is also true of the narrator and the reader).

It is worth tracing the career of Smith in more detail, to clarify the process by which he is both absorbed by the town and becomes its leader, an active force in keeping it as it is. The key to Smith's relations with the town is complicity, and complicity of a special kind, a left-handed complicity which does not entirely know itself for what it is and which is essential as well to the whole life of the town. Smith's role is to highlight the operation of this complicity, since he comes from elsewhere and by his successful adaptation makes clear how complicity in Mariposa works. By observing Smith the reader may become conscious of something which the townspeople unthinkingly accept as natural. For instance, when we see Smith break the unwritten law of complicity and close his hotel bar on time, locking Judge Pepperleigh and the prosecuting attorney out, the sanctions of the official law (which is normally flouted in favour of an unspoken understanding) are suddenly brought down on him.[6] Such a situation can best be expressed by facetious humour, for the whole episode is predicated on a double inversion, the upsetting of the law that normally rules Mariposa, which is itself a subversion of the official law. Smith understands the customary law of Mariposa perfectly, although as an outsider (and a help to the reader) he trips once in acting on that understanding: "on this point Mr. Smith's moral code was simplicity itself—do what is right and take the consequences. So the bar stayed open" (13).[7]

The narrator's facetiousness is entirely to the point; this low humour is the right means for presenting the process whereby complicity operates to invert the official law, just as circumstances conspire to ensure that there is never more than six feet of water in Lake Wissanotti. The narrator's facetious humour is the tip-off that this is only shadow-boxing and that all will be resolved in the end by a cancelling of forces that brings everything back to the safe status quo. So after the success of Smith's elaborate, and potentially transforming, campaign to regain his licence the real innovations silently disappear from his hotel, and if he keeps the "caff" it's because it costs him nothing now and because of the possibility of a Conservative candidacy for its owner, a reminder of the on-going complicity between the town and its prominent citizen. The town is claiming him as its own, and he can enjoy it as a preserve for exercising a pre-eminence based on (and limited by) the politics of "I'll scratch your back if you scratch mine."

Equally interesting is Smith's role in burning the new church and then saving Mariposa from the menacing fire that results. It is surely significant that the vexatious troubles over the financing of the new church are brought upon the town by the aspirations of one of its most innocent members, Dean Drone. In the very bosom of Mariposan innocence lurk ambitions which come near to entangling the town in a network of liabilities to the great world outside, represented by the bank that holds the mortgage and the insurance company and its agents who investigate the fire (compare Jeff Thorpe's unfortunate dealings with New York land brokers). There is a parable in these events (confirming Smith's importance to, and affiliation with, Mariposa) whereby the innocent Dean must be saved, and his innocence and its privileges preserved, by the operations of the cunning but entirely assimilated Smith. It was the Dean's new church which made necessary the Whirlwind Campaign, that bright idea from the great world outside, imported in all innocence and enthusiasm by the banker Mullins, which somehow did not quite work out in Mariposa. Yet here the assessment of events and results becomes problematic in a way typical of life in Mariposa and of the narrator's presentation of it. For the narrator's account raises the question whether it would have been worse, not better, if the Whirlwind Campaign had succeeded, as success is judged in the city. There are plenty of hints that its failure was due to a collective cunning at work in Mariposa, which might not entirely know or acknowledge itself, but which operates all the more effectively for that (in Mariposa, innocence and a kind of cunning are entirely compatible). On the simplest comic level (and we are always free to consider this level in this story which is, after all, a work of humour in spite of what criticism may feel empowered or compelled to make of it), those worthy citizens who pledged money contingent on the accumulation of impossible sums may have known very well what they were doing. They were making it highly unlikely that they would ever have to part with any cash. And collectively the town also may have had an important purpose, its self-preservation as it is, even in correction of its own impulse to ape the big city. This half-knowledge cannot be articulated in Mariposa or it would cease to function; so too it must be relayed by implication in the narrator's account of the progress of the campaign, replete with hints for the receptive reader, a former inhabitant of Mariposa who has eyes to see and ears to hear. From within Mariposa, this instinct for self-preservation gets a decisive helping hand from Smith who, in his appreciation of the realities of the Mariposa situation, stands somewhere between the people of Mariposa and the narrator.

Some of the hints as to these realities are both pointed and, as is typical, oblique. Thus we are told that in the city the success of the Whirlwind Campaign was attested to by the tears of the deans and professors of the colleges which were to benefit (70). These tears, like the refusal to give money unconditionally in Mariposa, are simple things on one level. In the city, it is not possible to evade the claims of Whirlwind Campaigns, and the deans and professors are regretting their own contributions, which may even have made up most of the sum raised. The contrast with what happens in Mariposa could not be more complete though its meaning is equivocal, making success of failure and failure of success. Just as Mariposa can be defined (only partly to its cost) as the place where the Whirlwind Campaign will fail, so the city is the place where such projects succeed. But what price success? (This perhaps is the subject of ***Arcadian Adventures With the Idle Rich.***) Here are the alternatives the narrator presents with his equivocating vision, which is not the defining vision of satire. We begin to see how much is conveyed by the deceptively folksy and simple observation that "perhaps there are differences between Mariposa and the larger cities that one doesn't appreciate at first sight" (71).

Before returning to the conclusion of the failed (and therefore successful) Whirlwind Campaign, in Mr. Smith's saving of Mariposa from the fire he set to save the town from a greater evil, we can look more closely at the narrator's deployment of this sense of the differences between Mariposa and the larger cities, for this contrast is of course central to the comedy and the moral argument. Nowhere is the equivocating vision of these differences more aptly expressed than in that early passage where the narrator goes the whole distance and compares Mariposa to New York City, the inevitable final point of reference (as the sign outside Biggar, Saskatchewan has it, "New York is big, but this town is Biggar"):

> Of course if you come to the place fresh from New York, you are deceived. Your standard of vision is all astray. You do think the place is quiet. You do imagine that Mr. Smith is asleep merely because he closes his eyes as he stands. But live in Mariposa for six months or a year and then you will begin to understand it better; the buildings get higher and higher; the Mariposa House grows more and more luxurious; McCarthy's Block towers to the sky; the buses roar and hum to the station; the trains shriek; the traffic multiplies.
>
> (3)

When you have lived in Mariposa a while "you will begin to understand it better." Yes, but what does this understanding amount to? As always, the narrator seems on one level to be making a simple satiric joke, to the effect that someone who thinks that Mariposa is a "mere mad round of gaiety" (3) is quite obviously deceived, with a standard of vision gone comically astray. But perhaps a former inhabitant of Mariposa, the proper audience for a story like this, will see more in the joke, without of course missing the joke. What have we forgotten, and what have we learned, during our education—or reeducation—in the "realities" of Mariposa? It was Leacock's brilliant comic ploy, which was not fundamentally a ploy at all (and so this book is his most memorable and lasting) but the natural outgrowth of his experience of the indeterminacies of small-town life, to pose this question without answering it. He answered it only as he felt it had to be answered, equivocally and by implication, leaving his readers unable to resolve the question whether his book is a satire or a tribute, but also leaving them with a rich fund of widely suggestive humour to be enjoyed, and pondered too, if approached in the right spirit, with the right background of experience. The simple and repetitious devices of Leacock's comic method are marshalled to a more than simple purpose, to frame an image of Mariposa in all its resistant, special reality. The highest level of implication is not always sustained: some of the treatment consists of unsubtle though often pointed jokes, as when the narrator remarks with mock-hickish insistence that the streets of Mariposa are so much wider than Wall Street and Piccadilly—because, of course, there is nothing in them. Yet the varied and lively responses of readers and critics suggest that Leacock took hold of the larger possibilities by seeing Mariposa as it really is, and not only possibilities for giveaway jokes and "exploded clichés," but also for a kind of validating comedy pitched at just the right level for the revelation and appreciation of its particular subject.

A good example of this equivocating yet often curiously validating presentation of the Mariposa reality (again with the focus on Smith) arises when, in what looks like a straightforward satiric thrust, a comic righting of our vision, the narrator tells us that "Mr. Smith was on the eve of one of the most brilliant and daring strokes ever effected in the history of licensed liquor," or when he asserts in the same connection that "the utter hopelessness of knowing what Mr. Smith is thinking by merely looking at his features gets on your mind and makes the Mona Lisa seem an open book and the ordinary human countenance as superficial as a puddle in the sunlight" (8, 6). It may be that in Mariposa the history of licensed liquor is indeed important (this is, after all, a Canadian story!), once we have adjusted our vision, like the visitor from New York, and the narrative may be meant to encourage us to make this adjustment. The image of the puddle in the sunlight echoes the title of the book and suggests some of its implications. Sunlight will make the puddle appear shallow and opaque (as a "sunny" treatment of a subject may do); this surface, however, may conceal untold depths (and so might an apparently friendly, superficial treatment). Then again, what if the surface only betokens real shallowness? A "sunshine" vision may be either revealing or forgiving, or both; in the sunlight, things may stand out clearly, but they may also be masked by the brilliance of the surface. There is no clear satiric message to be garnered from this passage, or others like it, except if we put ourselves at cross-purposes with the tone and movement of mind throughout this story. Instead, the narrator involves us in a circle of equivocation which causes him also to throw up his hands at moments (although over the long haul he steers us home, like Smith, to a less than completely safe berth in Mariposa, a haven which can only be enjoyed retrospectively as a dream in the armchairs of the Mausoleum Club): "then the utter hopelessness of knowing what Mr. Smith is thinking by merely looking at his features gets on your mind." Here both the satiric home thrust (it's impossible to know what's on his mind because there is nothing on his mind, and so appearance and reality are in simple consonance) and the deeper equivocation are retained. Mr. Smith, we are told, is "one of the greatest minds in the hotel business," an apparently fine satiric line that seems to cut Smith down to size, yet the next paragraph tells us about Smith's real effectiveness in Mariposa, partly due to the mere fact of his size—"two hundred and eighty pounds as tested on Netley's scales" (6). Smith is the only hotel keeper in the town's history who eschewed "such feeble names as the Royal Hotel and the Queen's and the Alexandria," and "simply put up the sign with 'JOS. SMITH, PROP.,' and then stood underneath in the sunshine as living proof that a man who weighs nearly three hundred pounds is the natural king of the hotel business" (6). Here the Mariposa standard triumphs over any satire derived from our big-city experience; it is in the equivocal Mariposa sunshine—all revealing yet all forgiving—that Smith's "size" speaks for itself and the "natural" triumphs over any possibility that there may be another standard of measurement than Netley's scales and another way of evaluating a hotel keeper than by his weight and common sense in choosing a sign. To repeat, perhaps in Mariposa it is the history of licensed liquor that really counts, and this point is being made not only satirically, but as a matter of fact and plain common sense. It is to this special common sense, derived from our intimacy with Mariposa, with "the inner life and movement of it" (5), that the narrator is appealing, as much as to our satiric sense (derived from our experience of places other than Mariposa) of the absurdity of Mariposa standards. This means, as will be seen more fully in **"L'Envoi,"** that the narrator's tale can only be addressed to a reader like himself, a former resident of Mariposa who has seen the rest of the world (Piccadilly and Wall Street) but cannot, or will not, overcome his affinity with Mariposa life. Perhaps the mixed reception ***Sunshine Sketches*** received in Orillia confirms that it was not meant for actual residents of Mariposa.[8]

The problematics of definition in Mariposa are once again comically, sharply raised in the thematically central passage explaining that in Mariposa "practically everybody belongs to the Knights of Pythias just as they do to everything else." The result is a special kind of solidarity obtained at the cost of a blurring of lines of distinction, for if "everybody is in everything" (37) then nobody is anybody in particular.[9] At the conclusion of the passage describing how Mariposans celebrate their affinity with all nations (a further wrinkle in the matter of Mariposa's connectedness with, and preservation from, the great world), the narrator focuses the issue of definition more sharply than usual, as if he were telling us something especially important:

> The Mariposa Belle always seems to me to have some of those strange properties that distinguish Mariposa itself. I mean, her size seems to vary so. . . . In the summer time, especially after you've *been* in Mariposa for a month or two . . . she gets taller and taller . . . till you see no difference between the Mariposa Belle and the Lusitania. Each one is a big steamer and that's all you can say.
>
> (39)

Is this offered as a satiric confirmation of an unfortunate fact, that to adjust oneself to the Mariposa standard is to lose all sense of the real proportions of things? Or is this an invitation to join in a folksy, radical skepticism, a questioning of all distinctions and scales of value? As we know by now, the narrator will not say; although low facetiousness (the exploded or inverted cliché) is always his way out of the problems he poses (of the Mariposa Belle as a second Lusitania, he comments, "Harland and Wolff didn't build her. They couldn't have," leading the reader to wonder—because she is not good enough, or too good?), there is more than facetiousness in his purposes. To anticipate, **"L'Envoi"** complements facetiousness with sentiment, revealing the goal of this foolery and equivocation, which is to soften the effects of that loss of an external standard and the ability to discriminate, or perhaps to console us for what this ability must continue to tell us about Mariposa and ourselves, and finally to reconcile us to our own Mariposa, our own diminished version of the Lusitania.

The narrator's attitude, and the attitude the reader is encouraged to adopt, is curious and special. All is given away that is needed to make a satirist's case against the town, and if this case is not made it may be because of the narrator's own complicity with these cunning innocents, which presumably serves him in some way. He is rescuing the subject by a sleight of hand that is very much like Smith's skulduggery in burning the church, and he would like to get away with it as Smith has done. Thus, he invites the reader to conspire with him, or dares him to be so churlish and obtuse as to refuse.

This recourse to comic sleight of hand constantly produces tensions, as in the conclusion to the story of Dean Drone which in striking an unusual note of disillusionment offers a foretaste of ***Arcadian Adventures.*** Here the narrator's facetiousness, usually so genial and resourceful, has an insistent, defensive edge: "Dean Drone? Did he get well again? Why, what makes you ask? You mean, was his head at all affected after the stroke? No, it was not. Absolutely not" (86). And the placing of Dean Drone in his right context (as when the narrator asks about Smith, "Can he take her in?") is surely less good-humoured and tolerant than usual; indeed, it is almost possible for once to derive a clear satiric judgment, not just of the hapless Dean but of the incompetent Mariposan innocence that he embodies: "And, as for audiences, for intelligence, for attention—well, if I want listeners who can hear and understand about the great spaces of Lake Huron, let me tell of it, every time face to face with the blue eyes of the Infant Class, fresh from the infinity of spaces greater still" (86).

This rough-edged sarcasm (very much the note of ***Arcadian Adventures***) is an extension of the normal tone, but not completely out of keeping with it, and expansions are possible. Like the Dean's, the narrator's tone and approach are perhaps appropriate to his subject and to his audience, former Mariposans who may have reason to wish to think well of their old town (we note the insistence above on the narrator himself as a possible teller of stories). The difference is that the narrator (and perhaps his audience) has not been able to surrender his intelligence, in spite of the sleights of hand that he practises; in fact, the comic game only sharpens the wits for the appreciation of what is at stake. Here the narrator is a disillusioned former Mariposan, addressing others who know the town as he does and sharing this knowledge in the way the subject deserves and requires, through the filter of an equivocal facetiousness that has become sarcastic under the strain. The narrator has revealed more than ever before what it costs to preserve the status quo in Mariposa, the cost for the Mariposans (who pay by being what they are, if not by consciousness of what they are), but more interestingly the cost for the narrator who has tried, not quite successfully, to prevent his left hand from knowing what his right hand is doing. But then, perhaps, this lack of success in fooling oneself is precisely what we are meant to see.

There is evidence that good humour is also tested in the account of the election that concludes ***Sunshine Sketches,*** yet it is possible to see the outcome as a final twist in the equivocal process whereby Mariposa is saved from the dangers and advantages of becoming more or other than itself. As before, the town is saved partly by Smith's manipulations and partly by its own complicity with Smith as its representative citizen. Mariposa elects Smith, for good and ill, as much as he works on Mariposa to get elected. The true state of Mariposa politics is conveyed with the usual ineffable, untranslatable equivocation when the narrator explains that "everybody in Mariposa is either a Liberal or a Conservative or else is both." The corollary is that "the one thing that nobody is allowed to do in Mariposa is to have no politics" (125). This conclusion is of course deceptive, for here is an affirmation of concerted political activity which is really a denial of any meaningful politics, when coupled with the quip that goes before. The demarcations that signal a vigorous political life are affirmed in such a way as to deny all possibility of meaningful differences, and this is the key to everything that happens in the election, in which one rascal is replaced by another who is merely better at the same game of evading all real issues, to the delight of the representative four little girls in white who once adorned the Liberal campaign but who hand the bouquet of victory to Mr. Smith, "for it turned out they were all Conservatives" (146).

As the election campaign heats up, the actions and strategy of the candidates can be seen as expressive of the plot of the status quo preserved at a certain cost, by the cancelling of opposing forces and potential differences. The incumbent Bagshaw's difficulty is that for once the Liberal party has chosen a substantive issue, the lowering of the tariff on U.S. goods, on which to fight the election. Bagshaw would prefer to "fight it merely on the question of graft. . . . Why not have fought the thing out on whether I spent too much money on the town wharf or the post-office? What better issues could a man want? Let them claim that I am crooked, and let me claim that I'm not" (131). The point of course is that in such an exchange of assertion and counter-assertion no appeal to any real issue needs to be made; in fact, it is plainly discouraged. Bagshaw wins whether he is believed or not—he manages both the innocent and the cunning—because even if people are reminded of his corruption they will also be perceptive enough to realize that this corruption has served them very well, and so the appeal to complicity which underlies Mariposa life will be made. It is because Smith makes this appeal more effectively, and because he is not hampered in his freedom of movement by having to take a stand on a real issue, that he can beat Bagshaw at his own Mariposa game and become the new representative man. Smith concocts the perfect Mariposa program: just as Bagshaw the bagman would like to run on honesty in office, so Smith the hotel keeper and barman will run on "temperance and total prohibition" (133). The cunning of this platform (for—this is the suggestion, to be taken advisedly—it would not work in the big city, where people are more educated and honest) is that it will be understood for what it is. It's like Smith's "honourable" behaviour in keeping the bar open whenever Judge Pepperleigh and the prosecutor have not yet arrived, or like the promise to give money for the Whirlwind Campaign, contingent on the fund reaching impossible sums. There is an instructive hitch in Smith's campaign, precipitated by the bringing in of an outsider who really takes prohibition seriously, and exhorts an audience of Mariposa Conservatives by reminding them of unspeakable iniquities at a Liberal meeting, where "seventeen bottles of whiskey [are] hidden in between the blackboard and the wall." This information clears the hall, and Smith shows the usual Mariposa flexibility with issues when "after that the total prohibition plank was changed and the committee substituted a declaration in favour of such a form of restrictive license as should promote temperance while encouraging the manufacture of spiritous liquors" (141).

There are further indications of how widely an all-conquering and all-cancelling complicity rules in Mariposa when, after the first returns put Edward Drone the "independent" (in Mariposa!) candidate in the lead, everyone is delighted, and "already three or four [townspeople] had taken Drone aside and explained that what was needed in the town was a straight, clean, non-partisan post-office, built on a piece of ground of a strictly non-partisan character" (143). It is clear that even if Drone had won, nothing would have changed; but of course Drone's role is to illustrate what it takes to win by being the one who cannot win (this is how he is true to the dictum that "the one thing that nobody is allowed to do in Mariposa is to have no politics"). The Conservative victory and election of Smith reinforces the fact that in Mariposa everybody is in everything, and also makes clear the cost of this solidarity, though as usual the narrative may be asking us to view this cost as a benefit. There is no change, no turning point here, as the Mariposans rediscover their identity, such as it is: "it turned out that there wasn't really a Liberal in the whole town and that there never had been" (145). To say at this point that there are no Liberals in Mariposa amounts to saying that there are no Conservatives either, as Mariposans may discover in the next election. The triumph of Smith is significant for what hasn't happened, for the way in which apparently opposing forces have merely cancelled each other out—a fitting conclusion to a story that includes Jeff's lucky rise and fortunate fall, the bank "mystery" in which the mystery is that there is no mystery, and the "entanglement" (a key word, like "mystery" and "rescue," all used equivocally to signify non-events or only apparent difficulties) of Mr. Pupkin, in which it is discovered that Zena Pepperleigh can put up with a rich man after all, and that Pupkin is just such a rich man, though in good Mariposa fashion utterly disguised by his innocence and incompetence. The narrator's humourous presentation of all this is not exactly satiric, but perhaps it is even more widely destructive than satire and cuts even deeper, for it endorses the very thing it has so brilliantly shown up and forcefully suggests that no alternative is preferable.

It is this special sort of disillusionment, this state of being caught between exploded innocence and unachieved experience, that may account for the understated wash of sentiment in the final chapter, **"L'Envoi. The Train to Mariposa."** In the conclusion to this story the narrator himself appears to swallow the bitter-sweet pill of the Mariposa status quo in the hope that it will be substantial nourishment. Yet, in line with the ruling equivocation of the telling, even that possibility is undercut when Mariposa is relegated to a terminus on a forgotten railway, a dream that can only be dreamed in the big city by former Mariposans like the narrator and the reader, who are left stranded at the end, "sitting here again in the leather chairs of the Mausoleum Club, talking of the little Town in the Sunshine that once we knew" (153). Yes, but knew it as what? We are left unsure as to what we knew, or now know, although we cannot avoid the suggestion that the dream of Mariposa offered in **"L'Envoi"** is only a sentimental illusion. But equivocation, not clarifying satire, rules at the end, so we cannot know what is real and what is delusion, and this presumably is the confirmation of our own on-going citizenship in Mariposa, even in the chairs of the Mausoleum Club.

In his interesting essay on Leacock, which I cited at the outset of this paper, D. J. Dooley has judged that there are "inconsistencies" in ***Sunshine Sketches*** that make it "something less than the masterpiece it might have been."[10] I hope my discussion has shown that these inconsistencies are essential to the subject and the author's vision of it and that, to risk paradox, the book presents an equivocal and therefore meaningful account of the indeterminacies of small-town life in Canada. The equivocation of this presentation is, by this argument which flirts with the "fallacy of imitative form," part of the message, a means for rendering the subject faithfully as it is and rendering the view taken of that subject. Whether we agree with this description or not, it is clear that something in his subject and his relation to it made it impossible for Leacock, over the long haul, to adopt the method of straightforward satire in ***Sunshine Sketches*** (as, for instance, Robertson Davies can be said to have done in his "Salterton Trilogy," where the main yalues espoused lie outside the small Canadian town). And what may appear to a student of satire to be evasiveness, a failure to "take the moral measure of his world" (in Dooley's phrase), may really be another vision of life less determinate than the satiric one; and yet it is also my argument that for Leacock this vision too had its cost, and its tensions which could not be resolved. In a wise and perceptive essay that was also one of the first serious contributions to Leacock criticism, Reginald Watters sought to define the special quality of Leacock's vision and humour by indicating their roots in the conditions of Canadian life. The Canadian position in North America has always been precarious, Watters observes, and

> . . . as a people bent on self-preservation Canadians have had to forego two luxuries; that of forgetting themselves in gay abandon and that of losing their tempers in righteous wrath. Yet there is a kind of humour that combines full understanding of the contending forces with a wry recognition of one's ineffectiveness in controlling them—a humour in which one sees himself as others see him but without any admission that this outer man is a truer portrait than the inner [see the Mariposans' opinion of the Federal census!]—a humour based on the incongruity between the real and the ideal, in which the ideal is repeatedly thwarted by the real but never quite annihilated. Such humour is Canadian.[11]

This seems to me to go a long way towards really explaining what has puzzled and disappointed some of Leacock's critics. I would add, however, that a price is paid for this position, too, and that this price is to be seen at the conclusion of ***Sunshine Sketches.*** The comic equivocations of ***Sunshine Sketches,*** I think we may safely say, are not merely signs of caginess or softheadedness; they are both a reflection of the special nature of the subject and a means for drawing a portrait of that subject for the right reader, anyone who has lived in Mariposa and survived to tell the tale or listen to it comprehendingly. Finally, however, the equivocations are both an attempt at a consolatory argument, couched in deceptively comic terms, and a simultaneous admission of the narrator's failure to console even himself. Thus, in its conclusion this classic Canadian comedy becomes quite unfunny, while making its final plea for the preservation of the Mariposa status quo as the best thing we have, even as it reveals that the Mariposa game, which may never have been worth playing, has at any rate been lost long ago. But this "lostness"—the lost world and the game of preserving its status quo at the cost of suppressing our best knowledge (is this a winning or a losing game?)—is finally, probably admittedly, of the essence of Mariposa's appeal. Now we have reached the point where failure is a kind of success, both for the Mariposans and, more complexly, for the narrator, and with that recognition our investigation must end, just at the point where Leacock also left it.

Notes

1. "Editor's Preface" to *Sunshine Sketches of a Little Town* (Toronto: McClelland and Stewart, 1960), p. ix. Further references to *Sunshine Sketches* will be by page number to this edition. Among those writers who conclude that *Sunshine Sketches* is mainly satiric are Vincent Sharman, "Satire of Stephen Leacock's *Sunshine Sketches,*" *Queen's Quarterly,* 78 (Summer 1971), pp. 261-67; and Robertson Davies, "Stephen Leacock," in *Our Living Tradition,* First Series, ed. Claude Bissell (Toronto: University of Toronto Press, 1957). For another view, that Leacock is neither a satirist nor a humourist, but an

ironist, see D. A. Cameron, *Faces of Leacock* (Toronto: Ryerson, 1967).

2. D. J. Dooley, *Moral Vision in the Canadian Novel* (Toronto: Clarke, Irwin, 1979), p. 4. Dooley is paraphrasing a remark by Robertson Davies.
3. Dooley, p. 6.
4. See Douglas Spettigue, "A Partisan Reading of Leacock," *The Literary Half-Yearly,* 13 (July 1972), p. 174: "Smith is the presiding genius of the town and an essential part of Leacock's vision, for his efforts are directed not only to his own profit but to keeping Mariposa the way it is."
5. See especially Gerald Lynch, "*Sunshine Sketches*: Mariposa versus Mr. Smith," *Studies in Canadian Literature,* 9, No. 2 (1984), p. 170.
6. Earlier, Smith was in trouble for being caught playing the game of complicity, when Judge Pepperleigh discovered that he had contributed to both the Liberals and Conservatives. This shows that in Mariposa complicity operates best when it is unacknowledged—in fact, such operation is part of the definition of Mariposa complicity.
7. This is good example of Leacock called the "exploded cliche": "words and phrases are rushed forward into a significance they won't bear on closer inspection; in fact the significance involves a complete impossibility" (Leacock, *Humor. Its Theory and Technique,* p. 35, as cited by W. H. Magee, "Genial Humour in Stephen Leacock," *Dalhousie Review,* 56 [Summer 1976], p. 269).
8. See Ralph L. Curry, *Stephen Leacock* (New York: Doubleday, 1959), p. 98.
9. As evidence of the narrator's long-term equivocation, even in his most categorical statements, we may remember his earlier remark that "that's the trouble with people in Mariposa; they're all so separate and different—not a bit like people in the cities" (30). The two statements, each backed up by solid evidence, cancel each other out, yet both must stand.
10. Dooley, p. 4.
11. Reginald Watters, "A Special Tang: Stephen Leacock's Canadian Humour," *Canadian Literature,* No. 5 (Summer 1960), p. 26.

FURTHER READING

Bibliography

Spadoni, Carl. *Stephen Leacock: A Bibliography.* Toronto: ECW Press, 1998. 622 p.

Detailed record of all of Leacock's published work, including details on their publication history, plus a listing of secondary sources.

Biography

Davies, Robertson. *Stephen Leacock.* Toronto: McClelland and Stewart, 1970. 63 p.

Short appraisal of Leacock's life and work by a well-known Canadian fiction writer.

Criticism

Lynch, Gerald. *Stephen Leacock: Humour and Humanity,* Montreal: McGill's-Queen's University Press, 1988, 211 p.

Considers Leacock's satire to be the result of a combination of two traditions—toryism and humanism—and examines the relation between his theory of humor and his view of the world in *Sunshine Sketches* and *Arcadian Adventures of the Idle Rich.*

———. "Sunshine Sketches: Mariposa versus Mr. Smith." *Studies in Canadian Literature* 9, No. 2, 1984, pp. 169-205.

Intensive analysis of the opposition between Mariposa and the individualist Josh Smith.

Moritz, Albert. "Return to Mariposa." *Southwest Review* 77, Nos. 2 & 3, Spring/Summer, 1992, pp. 309-404.

Reflections on Leacock's work and influences by a critic who visits Leacock's house.

Additional coverage of Leacock's life and career is contained in the following sources published by the Gale Group:*Contemporary Authors,* Vols. 104, 141; *DISCovering Authors: Canadian; DISCovering Authors Modules: and Most-studied Authors; Dictionary of Literary Biography,* Vol. 92; *Major 20th-Century Writers,* Vol. 2; *Twentieth-Century Literary Criticism,* Vol. 2.

Patrick White
1912–1990

(Full name Patrick Victor Martindale White; also wrote under the pseudonym P. V. M.). English-born Australian novelist, short story writer, playwright, memoirist, and poet.

INTRODUCTION

A notable voice in Australian literature, White is known for his stylistically complex novels and short fiction that feature eccentric characters, harsh environments, and satirical portrayals of Australian society. White's frequent use of isolation as a theme stemmed from his personal feelings of alienation and nonacceptance by his fellow countrymen. White's work has never captured a large audience, but critical understanding and appreciation of White's work has increased over time.

BIOGRAPHICAL INFORMATION

White was born in London, the oldest child of a wealthy Australian couple. At an early age, White began writing plays and attended Australian schools. When he was thirteen years old, his parents sent him to Cheltenham College, a boarding school near Gloucester, England. Following graduation in 1929, White returned to Australia and worked as a jackeroo, or ranch hand. During this time, he published a thin volume of poetry and began writing novels. In 1932 White returned to England to attend Cambridge University, where he studied French and German. After graduating in 1935, White remained in London but took a trip to the United States and Europe. White returned to Australia following service in the Royal Air Force as an intelligence officer in the Middle East. His literary career spanned nearly a half century, producing twelve novels, several plays, three volumes of poetry, and three short story collections. White's work established him as an authentic voice of Australia, winning him the 1973 Nobel Prize for Literature. White died in 1990.

MAJOR WORKS OF SHORT FICTION

White once remarked that the present is "a tireless dance," and is always "a variation of the same theme." During an interview with *The New York Times Book Review,* White told the interviewer that his "dominant obsession" was the search for "meaning and design" in what he described as "the tragic farce of life—to find reason in apparent unreason, and how to accept a supernatural force which on the one hand blesses and on the other destroys." His comments during that interview reflect many of the themes that recur in his short fiction. White's three short story collections—*The Burnt Ones, The Cockatoos,* and *Three Uneasy Pieces*—feature many of the same themes, including isolation, the interplay between illusion and reality, and past events and memories intruding into the present. Employing techniques such as stream-of-consciousness narratives, complex flashbacks, use of unusual syntax, and the exploration of dreams and states of madness, White's short fiction delves into human psychology, spirituality, and man's search for meaning. Characters portrayed in White's first collection, *The Burnt Ones,* are haunted by feelings of isolation, intense self-examination, and an acute awareness of how they are different from others. Loneliness as a theme is present in White's second short story collection as well. In *The Cockatoos,* characters in many of the stories are bourgeois older couples, who in their remaining years, make various attempts to escape feelings of isolation within their marriages. In "A Woman's Hand," Evelyn Fazackley's invasive matchmaking leads to the marriage of two acquaintances. The union, however, leads to the mental collapse of one partner and the death of the other. In "The Cockatoos," the title story of the collection, Mrs. Davoren and her husband are alienated from each other and have not spoken for years until the unusual arrival of cockatoos in their yard. The birds provide the couple a topic for conversation as well as a connection long absent from their marriage. But the connection is short-lived after a neighbor shoots two of the birds and Mr. Davoren is killed in his attempt to wrest the gun from him. *Three Uneasy Pieces,* White's last published book and short story collection, differs from the previous two collections in that most of the stories are confessional and written in first person.

CRITICAL RECEPTION

White's literary reputation rests primarily on his novels and plays; since his death, the majority of critical commentary has focused on his longer fictional works. White's short stories, which mimic many of the same themes and literary techniques found in his novels and plays, are similarly criticized for their multiplicity of symbols, myths, and allegories. Some critics have remarked that his writing is "unreadable" and convoluted, while others have praised White's use of language and imagery. Despite criticism of the language White used to write his stories, many have noted that his short stories and longer fiction provide insight into the mystery of the human psyche and the collective unconscious through psychological exploration of his characters. "In describing the pathos of a slow crumbling of suburban souls, his stories evoke a sense of tragedy—a tragedy not so much of an individual, but of a civilization, of a whole way of life," said critic Hameeda Hossain. Scholar William Walsh has described White as a "richly gifted, original and highly significant writer whose powers are remarkable and whose achievement is large. His art is dense, poetic, and image-ridden. . . . At its finest it is one which goes beyond an art of mere appearances to one of mysterious actuality."

PRINCIPAL WORKS

Short Fiction

The Burnt Ones 1964
The Cockatoos 1975
Three Uneasy Pieces 1988
Patrick White: Selected Writings (short stories, poetry, drama) 1994

Other Major Works

Thirteen Poems (poetry) 1930
The Ploughman, and Other Poems (poetry) 1935
Happy Valley (novel) 1939
The Living and the Dead (novel) 1941
Return to Abyssinia (drama) 1947
The Aunt's Story (novel) 1948
The Tree of Man (novel) 1955
Voss (novel) 1957
The Ham Funeral (drama) 1961
Riders in the Chariot (novel) 1961
The Season at Sarsaparilla (drama) 1962
A Cheery Soul (drama) 1963
A Night on Bald Mountain (drama) 1964
The Solid Mandala (novel) 1966
The Vivisector (novel) 1970
The Eye of the Storm (novel) 1973
Poems (poetry) 1974
A Fringe of Leaves (novel) 1976
Big Toys (drama) 1977
The Twyborn Affair (novel) 1980
Flaws in the Glass: A Self-Portrait (autobiography) 1981
Netherwood (drama) 1983
Signal Driver (drama) 1983
Shepherd on the Rocks (drama) 1987
Patrick White Speaks (speeches) 1989

CRITICISM

The Times Literary Supplement (review date 1964)

SOURCE: "Sparks from a Burning Wheel," in *The Times Literary Supplement,* October 22, 1964, p. 953.

[*In this review of* The Burnt Ones, *the critic provides a negative assessment of the short fiction collection.*]

In Mr. White's more recent novels a centrifugal tendency has been increasingly apparent: things do not fall apart—Mr. White has too much control to permit that—but they do tug apart. In *Voss* the centre holds only by a dream communion between Voss and Laura Trevelyan which intensifies and tightens as the physical distance between them increases. In *Riders in the Chariot* even Mr. White's technical ingenuity is hard put to it to keep the reins of his quadriga; and the real unity of the novel depends less on its structure than on the burning vision which informs it. Now, in this collection of stories, sparks from his anvil rather than chips from the axe which shaped that holy rood, the most unified of his novels, *The Tree of Man,* he seems to have accepted a further fragmentation.

If a reviewer confesses to a gratitude tempered by disappointment for ***The Burnt Ones,*** this cannot be attributed to any failure in his technique. The skill is as pervasive as ever and the flaws too minor. For there are flaws: certain characteristic devices seem to recur because they have become a mannerism rather than because they have a specific function. This is particularly true of his elliptical trick of beginning a sentence with a conjunction and dropping the subject pronoun:

> Nora could have been beautiful, Eileen thought. And suddenly felt old, she who had stripped once or twice at amusing parties.

And there are times when he allows the device to intrude into dialogue and become dramatically damaging: we realize it is Mr. White writing, not the character speaking.

Of the eleven stories four are set in Greece, seven in Australia. They are not separately grouped and it is difficult to penetrate the significance of the actual arrangement, though Mr. White does nothing without a reason. And his reasons for taking modern Greece as his second milieu can only be guessed at. Merely because he has lived and felt and worked there? Because of the challenge—successfully accepted—in the difficulty of being inward with people of an alien race? Because he sees something common, besides humanity, to the inhabitants of these two sun-scorched countries? Or for the pleasure he takes in the contrast between an ancient culture and the one, brash and jejune, which bred and angers his own fastidious sensibility?

The title at least, ***The Burnt Ones,*** belongs to the whole book and must imply that the chief characters, Greek or Australian, are alike unfortunates, burnt by life, or seared by experience. Yet the tragedy which such a title seems to bespeak is seldom matched by the characters themselves. Anthea Scudamore of **"Dead Roses"**, for example, is far below the tragic scale: she is not burnt by life; she fails to live it. Tragedy is missing also from **"Willy-Wagtails by Moonlight"**. This story savagely develops the theme which Katherine Mansfield handled so beautifully in "Bliss". But in her denouement we feel with the heroine. In Mr. White's we grant the situation established but no character in the story alleviates our sense of being uncomfortably present at a squalid mess created by commonplace people.

In fact, as one reads story after story, admiring the accuracy of Mr. White's observation, his economy, his ear for dialogue, his resource of language and resourcefulness of technique, his tight-lipped comedy, one begins to feel that the common misfortune of these unfortunates is that they have been seen by Mr. White and it is his vision which has burnt them. There remains the unsatisfying sense that the short story has not only caged the eagle and confined his epic scope (this was inevitable) but has contracted the range of his sympathy. His ear receives and records, nothing escapes his eye, but his heart rejects. One misses the major characters who would give scale to the weaker brethren of Smyrna or Sarsaparilla: the mystics, the visionaries, the artists and the mad, who in the major novels incurred his love.

A scale of values is implied, of course. We know that these mean, or at most minor, people are being chastised for their failures in imagination, generosity, magnanimity, love, and in the grander qualities for which Mr. White conveys by implication a proper and passionate regard. But that regard is expressed too often by negation, left to be inferred from the sardonic and severe portrayal of those who fall short and are ignoble. It is too seldom embodied, incarnate and breathing, in the characters themselves. Love of life is not incompatible with a disgust for the way we live. But too much disgust puts us out of love with the art that shows it, if not with life. Mr. White's admirers are left in trepidation. Will burning indignation dominate and dehydrate his talent, and the moral satirist take over from the universal novelist? We think of Tolstoy and the way that led from *Anna Karenina* to *The Kreutzer Sonata.* At least if he is heading for Jerusalem, however, it is no rough beast we need fear.

Robert L. Stilwell (review date 1964)

SOURCE: "A Dangerous Spark of Life," in *Saturday Review,* Vol. XLVII, No. 44, October 31, 1964, p. 54.

[*In this negative review of* The Burnt Ones, *Stilwell sharply criticizes the style of White's writing, arguing that many reviewers have overpraised his writing talent and accomplishments.*]

It may seem perverse to suggest that the Australian Patrick White is among the more difficult practitioners of fiction now living and working. At first glance—and often at twentieth glance—his pages are likely to look shallow, ungainly, homemade, even simple-minded. You might suspect that, far from being masterful exploitations of language and experience, they were scribbled on rough-grained boards by a novice writer wielding a carpenter's pencil. Yet much of White's difficulty arises precisely from this unpromising "surface." For before you can decide whether really profound matters are going forward within his work, you need a constantly reasserted act of faith to believe that such writing could be worth bothering with at all.

Once you achieve this act of faith, what then? Does Patrick White deserve, and repay, a reading in depth? I think he may, at least partially. There can be little doubt that far too many critics and reviewers have overpraised his gifts, his accomplishments. At the same time, however, there can be little doubt that his voice is incomparably the most commanding yet raised within the dialogue of Australian literature. Until recently a sort of prophet without honor in his own country, he has devoted himself, across the past fifteen years or so, to shaping a distinctive tone, an inner vision, a rugged moral fervor. His novels *The Tree of Man* (1955), *Voss* (1957), and *Riders in the Chariot* (1961) were ponderous, earnest creations, preoccupied with the largest issues of good and evil and with the sheer burden of existence. And for those who itch to rank writers there is perhaps nothing wrong with placing White beside the good lesser-lights—the Alan Patons and Brian Moores, for instance—of our day.

The present volume rakes together eleven stories, two of which grope toward novella length, completed since 1961; and many admirers of White's big novels will probably obtain from it their initial acquaintance with what he can do in shorter forms. (Although most of the pieces in ***The Burnt Ones***—not "some of them," as the dustjacket equivocates—have been given to Australian and English magazines, none has hitherto seen publication in the United States). The book's title represents a literal translation of the phrase *hoi kaumenoi,* which the Greeks euphemized to "the poor unfortunates" but which originally meant something like "those who are burned." It makes an apt title, too; for the people in each of White's stories, as in his novels, are men and women who somehow have gotten scorched or charred by their lives, like brambles left in a blackened field.

Several of the stories are set against the backdrop of White's native Australia; others take place in Athens and the Near East, both of which he came to know as an RAF intelligence officer during World War II. What concerns him most, however, is not so much landscape as the soulscape of his characters; and at his best he can illuminate that soulscape in a particularly merciless way. To read the slighter pieces here—such as **"The Evening at Sissy Kamara's," "The Letters,"** or the contrived **"Willy-Wagtails by Moonlight"**—is rather like sipping tepid water from a broken pop bottle. The stronger stories, though, generate a kind of cumulative and hard-to-deny power. **"A Cheery Soul"** grotesquely inverts Flaubert's "A Simple Heart." **"Clay"** presses the terrifying whole of a psychotic lifetime into twenty pages, and **"Dead Roses"** provides a slow, careful study of a woman's withdrawal from reality. **"A Glass of Tea"** explores sexuality and disaster, as do **"Miss Slattery and Her Demon Lover"** and **"Being Kind to Titina"** (both replete with footnotes). And I thought **"Down at the Dump"** a competent seriocomic story, despite the triteness of its title and despite a sugared, ain't-everybody-wonderful ending that might cause even William Saroyan to blush.

Let me mention one aspect of White's style that distracted my respect for *The Tree of Man*, *Voss*, and *Riders in the Chariot* and that I found nearly intolerable throughout the present gathering of stories. It would seem immutable fact that the sovereign writers, to paraphrase Goethe, are those with whom no grammar text can possibly keep pace. Nevertheless, I don't for the life of me understand White's compulsion to litter his exposition with ugly fragments of sentences. Lumpy bits of sentences. Just chunks. Exactly similar to these. Hundreds of them. If this pidgin syntax possessed some rationale of art and truth, if it helped to hone the sledgehammer gracelessness of its author's prose, it could of course be perfectly justified. As things stand, however, I can't agree that it does. Instead, it rather reminds me of a Remedial Composition theme.

Robert Kiely (review date 1964)

SOURCE: "Patrick White: The Short Story Pinches," in *The Christian Science Monitor,* Vol. 56, No. 297, November 12, 1964, p. 11.

[*In his unfavorable review of* The Burnt Ones, *Kiely maintains that the "exceedingly gifted writer may be dabbling in the wrong form" by penning short stories.*]

Most Americans are not quite sure how to take Australia. The vast stretches of land, the rough living and ranch humor appeal to us and remind us of what we once were and would sometimes still like to be. But the little pockets of provincial snobbery and British respectability disturb our frontier ideal. They not only alter the vistas of open spaces and natural living, they stand right up and block the view, making it strange, incomprehensible, and unreal. The seven Australian tales in Patrick White's collection of eleven stories entitled ***The Burnt Ones*** are effective explorations of this problem, told not from an American but from an Australian point of view.

None of the stories takes place in the great "outback," but rather in the smallish cities and suburbs fringing the continent's rim, suspended between the deep interior and the sea. The fellow countrymen whose lives Mr. White explores huddle at the edges of these desolate and immense regions cultivating their rose gardens or picking through their rubbish piles in a variety of pathetic and bitterly comic efforts to guard against the intolerable emptiness of their lives. As an evoker of this atmosphere and its osmotic effect on the human psyche, Mr. White is a master. The Australian stories in this collection could have been written by no one but an Australian. The use of the English language, in both diction and cadence, is unmistakably not American nor British; and this is as true of the descriptive passages as it is of dialogue.

But the very authenticity or, more than that, the truth of the Australian stories makes the four tales set in Greece and Egypt appear artificially contrived. Even the Greek names and idiomatic phrases fall heavily and self-consciously from the author's tongue, which fact would be less objectionable had Mr. White been willing to adopt the narrative voice of an outsider. He doesn't do this, however; he wants his Greeks to be exotic and strange and yet, at the same time, he wants to see them from the inside. Of course, he cannot have it both ways. Athens and Alexandria simply do not seem as bizarre to Athenians and Alexandrians as they seem to Mr. White.

The longest of the Greek stories does, in part, show Athenians as they may appear to outsiders, in this case, a prosperous Greek-American couple returning to the old country for a visit. The narrative centers on several encounters between the unintellectual "Americanized" Hajistavrous with Kikitsa Alexiou, who has an obsession for cats, and her flabbily contemplative husband, Aleko, who is not a cat but almost. Yet **"The Woman Who Wasn't Allowed to Keep Cats"** is one of Mr. White's least convincing stories partly because the "joke" is told as a knowingly inside one at the expense of the predictably *nouveau monde* outsiders. Actually, both couples are vaguely grotesque caricatures which appear to be equidistant from the author's sympathies and comprehension.

The Australian stories are a different matter altogether. However much Mr. White's narrative devices tax our credulity and occasionally our patience, the created presence of the lives he probes remains undeniable. The themes are remarkably unvaried: a good-natured futility and the consequences of moral vacancy are examined under slightly different conditions. The white sun and metallic sea—two of Mr. White's favorite images—cancel out or absorb most attempts at self-definition with their own blank permanence. We are shown youth without hope, old age without respect, marriage without love, sex without pleasure, friendship without affection, and wealth without comfort.

The characters who symbolize and personify this hollow state of affairs are also themselves very much alike from one story to another. The domineering and vain women, the passive, silent, slightly insane husbands and sons could move from story to story without even being noticed as intruders from another world. Indeed, they wouldn't really be intruders at all because the world they inhabit, though presented in segments, is all of a piece.

And this is probably the clue to Mr. White's success as a writer of fiction generally and his limitation as a writer of the short story. Many of his tales read like chapters from the same novel which somehow got mixed up and out of proper sequence. And two of the longer and more successful stories, **"Dead Roses,"** which is the first in the book, and **"Down in the Dump,"** which is the last, seem like curiously condensed summaries of much longer works.

Mr. White often likes to cram the events of several years and occasionally of a lifetime into the pages of his stories. This is an interesting ambition, but it places particular stress on the artist's skills with transition and endings, neither of which appears to be Mr. White's forte. He resorts to chance meetings in unlikely places ten years (more or less) after previous significant encounters and with reckless abandon, precipitates his characters into sudden sex, death, or madness. There is an unavoidable sensationalism in the abruptness with which obsessions, hallucinations, masochistic tendencies, and other assorted oddments are pulled out of the hat. In one story there is a silly and unlikely exposure, by means of a tape recorder, of a supposedly "steady" husband's extramarital love life in the bush. In another, called **"Letters,"** a man reveals startling Oedipal desires after fifty years of dotty but peaceful repression.

The trouble is not that the reader cannot believe these things may happen but that we sense Mr. White invented them to get on with the story or, more accurately, to get it over with. He makes himself apply the brakes of short fiction to material with the texture and breadth normally associated with the novel. If we wince to see him do this, it is because we suspect now and then that an exceedingly gifted writer may be dabbling in the wrong form.

George Greene (review date 1964)

SOURCE: "Taking the Measure of the Terror of Isolation," in *Commonweal,* Vol. 81, No. 8, November 13, 1964, p. 241-42.

[*In the following positive review, Greene discusses the common themes that tie together the stories in* The Burnt Ones.]

Every living short story, as Elizabeth Bowen reminds us, demands a measure of experiment. Today, what narrows the range of some practitioners is that they pit technical bravery against their need to document a lost paradise. In this contest, invention too often becomes the first casualty. Most of us have read quite enough narratives with a "My Days as an Unlicensed Dentist in Detroit" format. Such nostalgia Mr. White vigorously dismisses. Seven of these stories occur in his own Australia; the rest introduce people who live in the Mediterranean world. Initially, perhaps, one frets about the identity of the wallaby, and what is signified by the ugly word "fridge," but this man's imagination by-passes more than geographical boundaries. Mr. White commands attention even when he leaps—lapses is too weak to characterize diction so alive, if hieroglyphic—toward the inexpressible.

As one reads one recalls another melancholy searcher, Sherwood Anderson. Just as for his less sophisticated American brother, Mr. White's adversary is the terror of isolation. In **"Dead Roses"** a hefty Australian girl rejects the advances of a young physicist. She marries a stingy older man, who eventually dies. As his heir, Anthea travels widely. In Greece she meets the scientist, and his easygoing wife gives her a rose. Anthea pins the flower with a brooch, accidentally drawing attention to her diamonds. Returning to her hotel, she feels sure that a molester is tracking her. Forlorn, inhibited, she lies on her bed as in a tomb.

In **"Being Kind to Titina"** a Greek lad chances upon a girl he had known in the strict, hieratic security of childhood. Titina has become a striking young woman and the mistress of a Frenchman. In a futile gesture of reconstruction, the young people go swimming. Caught by the allure of her new world, Titina insists that she must remain with her older friend. The narrator knows better than to protest. ". . . I had begun to understand that such remarks are idiocy."

Thwarted widows and ingénues who fall from virtue are as common as slugs in a public telephone. What carries the day is that Mr. White frequently unearths paradoxes which are less fuzzy than unfathomable. One is not certain how much of his power depends on technique and how much on temperament. This is one of those rare cases where puzzlement, tantalizing because it is honest, constitutes an author's best card.

In **"A Cheery Soul"** Miss Docker trumpets her urge to do good. She takes pride in her fondness for metaphysical debate—she has read *Manong Lescoat.* Dutifully she admonishes the choir, at length sabotaging it. She alienates all benefactors, causing the collapse of her own pastor. She becomes the scourge of the Sundown Home for the aged. At the close, still preaching, she entreats a dog to keep her company. The animal lifts one leg and urinates on her.

What saves Mr. White from the leer that erudite connoisseurs of the grotesque commonly affect is the height from which he watches his misfits. Mr. Szabo, the Hungarian refugee who has an affair with an athletic Australian girl, begs to be struck with a whip. What fascinates him about love, as he chooses to define it, is that it causes rot. But even Mr. Szabo never disintegrates from human wreck into cinematic ogre. In Mr. White's world the blackest sin is inattention, even if there is nothing one may do to alter cases. "They had continued to live," we are told about a married couple, "in the one envelope, as it were, which nobody had bothered to tear, because no one was sufficiently interested."

Whatever insights nature provides depend on explosion rather than illumination. With their complexions like that of a moth, these wanderers pay a high price for their rare "bursts of sun, and a bashing of wind, and the blaze of ripe barley." Only through assault, apparently, can such strays touch the world as well as one another. The August heat smoulders "garnet-red." Old men's hands are like "purple bird's claws," and there is a lingering smell of mould in all of the summerhouses. "'So grotesque,'" a Greek wife condemns her own behavior. "'But then one is, in almost all situations where reality intrudes.'"

If there is any road out of this international Sahara, Mr. White does not encourage us about our chances of finding it. In **"Down at the Dump,"** the last story, a girl, Meg, whose aunt is being buried in an adjoining cemetery meets the son of the shiftless family next-door. As they kiss, her enraged mother discovers them. The mother laments the passing of her sister, yet she is furtively relieved because of Maisie's reputation for being loose. Trapped, Meg does not want to run the risk of anger. "Since joy had laid her open, she had forgotten how to defend herself." Transfiguration limits one's range of choices even more than daily wariness. The girl tries to picture her aunt, whom she loved, but finds it impossible to do so. "Yet, each time she failed, the landscape leaped lovingly."

One should not accent this major chord: it is as rare as it is sudden. At best Mr. White's people aspire to a dusty beatitude, the physical projection of which is Greece, "a poor landscape, splendid, too, in its own way, of perfectly fulfilled austerity." One understands this bond between the son of a new country and that land where tragedy is as durable as its stunted pines and its whitewashed walls.

If Mr. White's "burnt ones" are damned—his title translates freely a Greek phrase—they disappear while still scrambling to reason, or barter, or even bribe their way to some harbor. One woman inquires about the number of times a human being is buried alive. The frequency of this nightmare may well be what Mr. White wishes to underline. Even as dirt tumbles into their eyes, nonetheless, his moths make noises of protest.

With both gratitude and pique one realizes that existence in the Land Down Under isn't so unconditioned. We have all entered those liver-colored brick houses where girls develop voices like blotting paper, and where roses burn to a malodorous brown under the brutal sun. Mr. White shuts yet another door through which one had peered in quest of fresh fantasies, new ways of defying a known world, only to find oneself staring back from the front hall mirror.

One wonders about Antarctica.

Jack Lindsay (essay date 1964)

SOURCE: "The Stories of Patrick White," in *Meanjin Quarterly,* Vol. XXIII, No. 4, December, 1964, pp. 372-76.

[*In the following essay, Lindsay praises* The Burnt Ones, *saying White's work "shows some important advances and makes clearer than ever the need to grapple with his work in full critical seriousness."*]

It is a tribute to the work of Patrick White that one is forced to judge it by the highest standards: even a qualified praise of its achievement means far more than easy superlatives evoked by writing which carries on in the closed circle of more conventionalised methods. His latest book, ***The Burnt Ones,*** shows some important advances and makes clearer than ever the need to grapple with his work in full critical seriousness. The eleven tales vary in length and value, but at their best they rank high. **'Dead Roses'**, **'The Woman Who Wasn't Allowed to Keep Cats'**, and **'Down at the Dump'** show his literary method, his aesthetic vision, gaining a new clarity and compactness, with nothing of the self-indulgence that can be urged against certain aspects of the novels. Indeed it is by a consideration of the sparer and more intellectually controlled form of such stories that one can bring out what was cloudy and weak in the larger canvases; what was there fabricated to suggest a grand and penetrative view of life rather than springing directly from the material and White's understanding of it.

In saying that one is forced to judge White's work by the highest standards, one does not mean that one seeks to compare it with some synthetic notion of the Great Novel compounded of all the significant works from Petronius to Lawrence. The novel is a form hard to define, and any statement of its limits is sure to break down when tested in practice. What I mean is that White forces us to reconsider the nature of the novel, its relation to social process and individual experience, its ways of exploring new dimensions of consciousness; and this involves in turn a reconsideration of the nature of man himself and of just what is happening to people in the modern world—what are the forces to which they are subjected, how they are changing, and in what direction. The modern, or modernist, age began around 1900 and had posed its main problems by 1914, problems with which we are still grappling aesthetically as well as politically. Many critics chafe at the idea that we must still go back to Cézanne or Joyce in order to come round with full effect to today's issues; but I think they are wrong. We must begin at the beginning or we shall see the later events in a distorted focus, a cramped perspective; and this is so, however complicated the working out has become.

What then are the issues in art or in literature that came with the new century and are still with us? There was a jolt, a break, that was more decisive than previous efforts to gain a new start. All existing methods of construction became suspect as based on generalisations no longer valid. The relation of individual to society became suddenly more complex, not just in a quantitative way, with more strands to unravel, but with the intrusion of quite new factors of dislocation. Something unutterably baffling had arrived with the highly centralised State: something that Kafka managed to distil in its essence. The inner division of the individual reached a new intensity; one's 'real life' was less and less the life one lived. To express this deepening alienation the Bergsonian formulation was found the most useful, and through Joyce and Proust it has passed into general circulation in endlessly modified forms: the opposition of clocktime (habit, the workaday world, the abstracting intellect, all that divides, oppresses, and reflects the fragmentation of man in a mechanistic world) to inner time, the intuition of the timeless moment of concrete experience. With the revolt against the clock-world and its habitual (false) constructions, the old forms of characterisation and narrative lost their virtues and appeared as forms for deadening and disguising human reality. The novelist (poet, artist, etc.), faced with such a disintegrated and delusive world, felt the need for new methods capable of grasping the concrete moment in its fullness and of breaking down the false appearances.

These comments are highly generalised, but they state briefly what have been the preoccupations of serious art for the last couple of generations. (Socialist writing has in general so far failed to solve the problems because it has assumed that the restoration of social purpose makes it possible to carry on with pre-1900 forms and ignore all that has since been done; it attempts a contemporary art without a contemporary sensibility.) White's work insists on being judged as a part of the development I have sketched; the only question is how far he contributes something new, and the ways in which he does it. He has a deep and pervasive sense that something has gone wrong with people; his theme is always the process of alienation. But his intellectual powers have not so far been equal to his emotional comprehensions. Hence his efforts to impose a mystique upon his material in order to escape from sheer pessimism and the picture of life as a dull repetitive *huit clos* (as *The Tree of Man* tends to be). It seems to me that he has turned to the tale in a sustained struggle to overcome his weaknesses and to learn how to develop the more positive aspects of his outlook. The concentrated form enables him to sharpen his judgments, to incarnate his values more directly in human beings without recourse to mystique.

He consistently realises what I should call the unprecedented falsity of modern life—the widening gap between reality and what people think of themselves, between 'real life' and the everyday round of habitual reactions in which the stereotypes imposed from without by ceaseless manipulations grow ever more dominant. He feels all the while the need to reject this falsity and break through to the lost or imprisoned human being; and he therefore knows that the old methods of characterisation cannot help. He seeks to understand the rôle of fantasy in this situation, where it expresses both the aimless loss of self and the struggle to break through the rational (mad) world into the sphere of true human need and impulse; and he knows that this fantasy-life of the individual, destructive and yet owning the sole clue to the truth, must be more than material for the writer. It must also supply essential aspects of form in his struggle to renew the novel.

Where he is weak is in his intellectual framework. Once the old systems have been jettisoned, the novelist has to build up his own world-system, his own large scale reorganisation of tradition, philosophic as well as technical. Hence the great importance of Joyce and Proust, who most fully succeeded in merging the new sensibility with comprehensive structures of thought. White has the capacity to evolve his own system; for in the best of his tales he shows that he is securely finding his own method of defining time. (Time, in a sense, is the hidden hero, or villain, of the modernist novel.) Joyce used his inner-dialogue (apart from Marion's reverie) in what he called a series of epiphanies—momentary fusions of inner and outer in a significant or revelatory unity; the method is thus always at root dramatic and has nothing to do with a rambling drift of associations. White uses his alternation of inner and outer for dynamic effect, a radiation-out of the individual into his environment and back again. A person is thus made organically a part of his world. The tension is always sustained, the physical presence of the main actors is always felt, and this above all is what marks White out as an important writer.

As a result ***The Burnt Ones*** shows much variety of mood and attitude. There is a considerable growth in the capacity for humour; and this means a growth in human sympathy—for instance in **'A Cheery Soul'**, **'Miss Slattery and Her Demon Lover'**, and indeed in several others as an undercurrent. A tale like **'Clay'**, which is more simply subjective, I find less interesting; it is built on the sado-masochistic mood which is White's main danger. It is instructive to look back at a tale like **'The Twitching Colonel'**, published in the *London Mercury* of April, 1937. Far more than White's first novel, it shows his characteristic powers. Invertebrate in comparison with the present tales, it attempts to find dynamic ways of merging a character with the imagery of the forces that have made him; of surrounding him with a sort of crackling field-of-force. India has got inside the colonel for all his British imperviousness, and its unrealised but shattering energies are what twitch in his body and finally disintegrate him into the smoke of the consuming fire. The ideas under the imagery are vague, thin, uncertain; yet looking back at the tale from the present perspective, we can see the seeds of the poetic method that is now maturing.

How far can one define the position now reached by Patrick White? The solid base appears as something of a D. H. Lawrence attitude: those who accept the flow of life are opposed to those arrested on points of property and convention. **'Dead Roses'** powerfully achieves this contrast; and in more complex ways so does **'The Woman Who Wasn't Allowed to Keep Cats'**, which is perhaps the finest thing White has done. (Yet here is an odd point of callous lack of sympathy and imagination. 'She accepted curfews, and travel permits, not to mention his forced absence on the Island. Not even when Alexiou payed the Official Visit together with other chosen members, was Kyria Alexious more than incidentally put out.' The Island can only be Ai Stratis. Either White does not know of the horrors endured by the prisoners there, or he is insensitive to sufferings brought about by moral and political conviction. In either case, his claim to understand the Greeks in the postwar setting is compromised. Yet his experience of the Greeks has certainly done much to help him through to a positive humanity.) He is moving to the point where he can find human values in others than the lost, humiliated, and down-and-out: thus avoiding the danger of Steinbeckian sentimentality or Beat nihilism. There are rich elements of humour and lyricism that refuse to be chilled out by adolescent sado-masochistic bitterness (such as threatens the excellent story, **'Being Kind to Titina'**) or to be flattened by the imposition of fabricated mystiques. The D.H.L. oppositions need to be extended and rooted in a fuller understanding of alienation, and strengthened by relevant intellectual constructions—not repetitions of Joycean or Proustian systems, but whatever corresponds to such systems in terms of White's sensibility. Then we shall see Patrick White's insights and skills liberated into their full scope, his vision given a true force of universality.

J. F. Burrows (essay date 1964)

SOURCE: "The Short Stories of Patrick White," in *Southerly,* Vol. 24, No. 2, 1964, pp. 116-25.

[*In the following essay, Burrows illustrates how White uses observations and anecdotes about Australian society in his fiction as a form of social satire.*]

At her first appearance in *Happy Valley* (1939), the loneliness and discontent of poor Vic Moriarty are epitomised in her absurd day-dream of being mentioned in the social pages of the *Herald* as having played bridge at David Jones. She pictures herself wearing a powder-blue dress (p. 37). At her final appearance in *Riders in the Chariot* (1961), Mrs. Chalmers-Robinson, socially rehabilitated at last, actually does lunch at a smart Sydney restaurant. She is wearing a powder-blue dress (p. 544).

Out of innumerable trifles like this, many of them similarly recurrent, there is made up one of the most striking, even obtrusive, characteristics of the work of Patrick White. It ranges from this flicker of bored but perhaps mildly compulsive distaste for a social cliché to a fascinated loathing for contemporary Australian society in certain of its aspects.

For illustration we can turn to a passage from *Riders in the Chariot* which seems at first sight to provide a notable exception. At the end of the novel, Mrs. Godbold—"the rock of love", "the infinite quiver" full of "the arrows of desire"—walks up the hill where Xanadu had stood. Her outflowing of love for all she sees—children, houses, a row of young cauliflowers, an unknown woman in a dressing-gown—leads her on to a culminating vision of the Chariot. But even though this universal loving-kindness seems to be offered for our endorsement, it constitutes a programme for the Godbolds rather than an actuality for the Whites. Immediately before Mrs. Godbold's setting out on this walk, the omniscient narrator had described those very houses and those very people in language much more familiar to White's readers:

> When Xanadu had been shaved right down to a bald, red, rudimentary hill, they began to erect the fibro homes. Two or three days, or so it seemed, and there were the combs of homes clinging to the bare earth. The rotary clothes-lines had risen, together with the iceland poppies, and after them the glads. The privies were never so private that it was not possible to listen to the drone of someone else's blowflies. The wafer-walls of the new homes would rub together at night, and sleepers might have been encouraged to enter into one another's dreams, if these had not been similar. Sometimes the rats of anxiety could be heard gnawing already at bakelite, or plastic, or recalcitrant maidenhead. So that, in the circumstances, it was not unusual for people to run outside and jump into their cars. . . . They would drive and look for something to look at.
>
> (p. 546)

The automatic gestures of contempt in such passages as this point to more typical and, I believe, more significant aspects of White's work than does the slightly strained *vox humana* of Mrs. Godbold.

As Vic Moriarty's dress suggests, this antipathy to our society, or to certain things about it, has been apparent in White's work from the beginning. At first it manifested itself chiefly in characters of only moderate importance, like Vic Moriarty herself, Fanny Parrott in *The Aunt's Story* (1948) and Thelma Parker in *The Tree of Man* (1956). In *Voss* (1957), the Bonners and the Pringles are, among other things, the wealthy ancestors of this repulsive progeny.

Yet it was only with White's discovery and creation, presumably in the late 1950's, of that most desirable suburb, Sarsaparilla, that this antipathy came to be given heavy emphasis in his work. Whatever its meaning and whether that meaning is complex or only nebulous, it is true that Sarsaparilla plays an important part in *Riders in the Chariot* (1961) and in *The Season at Sarsaparilla* (1962). It is also true, though perhaps less widely-known, that during this "Sarsaparillan period", White has published eight short stories,[1] three of them set in Sarsaparilla itself and three in pre-Sarsaparillas or in suburbs none too remote. (The remaining two stories are set in modern Athens and in modern Alexandria.) In addition to their intrinsic interest, these stories afford a useful way of reconnoitring an aspect of White's work that is much easier to distinguish than to define or assess.

The rapidity with which White's stories have been published suggests that the order of publication is not necessarily that of their composition. Internal evidence nevertheless indicates that **"Willy-Wagtails by Moonlight"** is one of the earliest. Certainly it contains many of the seeds of others of White's stories, and, for this reason, it warrants a closer examination than its own slightness might otherwise recommend.

The anecdote from which the story evolves concerns a tape-recording of bird-song, in the middle of which the willy-wagtails give place to a love-scene between a married man and his secretary. No one knows of this insertion until a couple named Wheeler, visiting the unfaithful husband and his devoted wife but for the time being in the room by themselves, hear the tape. At first maliciously amused by the situation and then shocked out of their amusement, the Wheelers tacitly resolve to say nothing at all. And there the story ends.

The Wheelers are stock figures—the malicious "North Shore" matron and the pompous executive—presented sharply enough but possessed of, and needing, no great depth. So, too, are Arch Mackenzie, the bird-watcher gone astray, and his secretary, Miss Cullen. It is in Nora Mackenzie that the real possibilities and the eventual failure of the story appear: the possibilities arise when Nora promises to be complex; the failure occurs when the complexity proves only to be confusion and inconsistency.

The most obvious of the three faces of Nora is that of a discreetly status-seeking hypocrite, hardly less an object of satire than her husband and her so-called friends. Her house is "what is known as a Lovely Old Home—colonial style—among some carefully natural-looking gums." Its furnishings, insipidly ostentatious, are "period" pieces in a string-and-beige coloured setting. Despite her courses in French cookery and the like, Nora is an abominable cook, a muddling housekeeper, and an ungenerous hostess. There is even a suggestion that she became a bird-watcher only in pursuit of bigger (if not nobler) game. Such a Nora would have served well in a story, after de Maupassant, of the biter bit. The difficulty is that this Nora is contradicted out of existence by other aspects of her behaviour. (It is not possible to argue that all this is Nora as seen by the malicious Eileen Wheeler: the hypothesis about her bird-watching may be Eileen's; but most of Nora's other unpleasantness is remarked by the omniscient narrator.)

The second Nora is a Freudian figure whose single dominant motive is a frustrated urge for motherhood. Her spinsterish self-consciousness, her motherly devotion to Arch, her altruistic concern for his employees, even Miss Cullen, and her passionate absorption in bird-watching ("The children she had never had . . .") are all advanced as sublimations of the one central drive. The alliance of husband, employee, and even birds in her betrayal, the hints that she is half-conscious of Arch's infidelity, and the way in which, even when the story ends, the betrayal has yet to reach daylight, all serve to give this version a somewhat Chekhovian air. Of the three stories that are here confused, this one is the most fully evolved. If it were not for the distractions of its competitors, it would make its comic-pathetic point very effectively.

The last Nora appears only briefly and is, therefore, a threat to the integrity of her sisters rather than a figure in her own right. Yet even though, in the glimpses we are given, she is blurred by self-pity, she is recognizable as a member—and perhaps the prototype—of that little band of renegade individuals, aloof from and invulnerable to the assaults of a contemptible society, who dominate some of the other stories. In her imagination,

> Nora Mackenzie was standing alone amongst the inexorable moonlit gums. She thought perhaps she had always felt alone, even with Arch, while grateful even for her loneliness.

The clashes between these different aspects of the story emerge clearly from an examination of any of a number of passages. Thus:

> Nora said they'd be more comfortable drinking their coffee in the lounge.
>
> Where Arch fetched the tape-recorder. He set it up on the Queen Anne walnut piecrust. It certainly was an impressive machine.

Presumably this passage is ironical and not mere reportage. If so, the most obvious irony seems to be directed at those (the Wheelers?) whose shoddy "modern" values lead them to be more impressed by a tape-recorder than by such a table as this. But then, we wonder, just what sort of table *is* this? Nothing else in the Mackenzies' home would lead us to expect that their table would be "Queen Anne" in the strict sense. If it is so only in the looser sense in which the term is used by Vulgar Australians, then presumably it is Nora's values as well as (or rather than?) the Wheelers' that are White's target of the moment.[2] Depending in part but not entirely upon the answer to this question, we are left in doubt whether Arch's treatment of the table is to be seen as mere vandalism or as an expression of a superbly natural ability to *use* an object, whatever its snob-value, for an immediate purpose. Even the innocent-looking first sentence raises a further problem. Is it offered as the casual and sensible remark of any hostess? Or is it to be seen as the satiric rendering of a cliché, directed at Nora and given force by the word "lounge", a common Australianism which, by English standards, is distinctly non-U when it is used at all? Questions like these ought, of course, to be answerable from the text itself. That they are not is due to a blurring of satiric focus, a radical uncertainty of purpose. Here and elsewhere White is often so anxious to score off everybody at once that he does not really score off anybody at all.

The kind of social satire which depends upon the registering of a multitude of socio-aesthetic signs and which is most dominant in the first of "my" versions of **"Willy-Wagtails by Moonlight"** persists, in one form or another, in all the other stories. It is at its most direct in **"Miss Slattery and Her Demon Lover"** and **"The Woman Who Wasn't Allowed to Keep Cats"**. The former, an uproarious farce, consists essentially in a clash of values between migrant male and Australian female. The latter is a rambling and portentous tale of lesbians, marital troubles, and cat-worship, too much of which is given over to cheap contrasts between Greek Greeks and Americanised Greeks. Because of the damning fact that, broken English apart, the Australians of the former story are virtually indistinguishable from the "Americans" of the latter, the former can, for the present, do double duty.

When Miss Slattery, a "market researcher", encounters Tibor Szabo, a wealthy Hungarian migrant, she is almost instantaneously seduced. For a time she remains alike overwhelmed by his lavish supply of imported luxuries—Jaguars, mink bedspreads—and by his bland assumption that she, being Australian, exists only for him to exploit. On his side, a complacent acceptance of her physical charms overrules a profound contempt for her inertness and conventionality, especially on the subject of Love. Then, at a party, she begins cracking a stock-whip, arousing nostalgic memories in them both: in her, of an older Australia of dust, cattle, and sweaty leather; in him, of the masochistic delights of being flogged. Thereafter he finds her unique and indispensable while she, nostalgic only for a moment and bored from the first by this strange new sport, gains a complete ascendancy. Tibby has been assimilated by a vast inertness, much as a sleepy leviathan might engulf a lively shrimp or as Sarsaparilla seeks to engulf the Charioteers.

At the level of farce the story is admirably sustained. The clash of opposing manners is central and lucid and the manners themselves are registered with all White's verbal wit. That the subtler possibilities of this conflict go largely ignored is manifest not only in White's willingness to record manners as such rather than to explore the attitudes that they signify, but also in an apparently naive preference for all things imported even though they, too, are only *objets de bourgeois.*

A second group of stories—**"The Letters"**, **"Clay"**, and **"Being Kind to Titina"**—is concerned with frustrations and sublimations akin to those of the second Nora Mackenzie. Widely as they differ in appearance, each is virtually a textbook instance of one or another of the classic manifestations of the Oedipus complex. And in all three stories, the broader social setting, though at times obtrusive, is really incidental. **"The Letters"**, where an adult son fears for a moment that his eyes will be gouged out by his mother's brooch, shows this Freudian pattern at its simplest. Mrs. Polkinghorn babies Charles all his life—"Sometimes the mother almost expected to see a pulse still beating in her child's head"—until, on his fiftieth birthday, he betters the instruction by assaulting her in an attempt at suckling. The setting, like its mistress, is Sarsaparilla-Olde-Englyshe, and it provides the occasion for touches of satire which are neat enough in themselves but which lack any fully-imagined connection with the central action. The one moment of real poignancy comes when, from the depths of Charles's memories of university, there floats up an unidentified French tag. It is a line from Racine's *Phèdre,* spoken when Phèdre is about to explode into confessing to Oenone her love for Hippolyte: *"De l'amour j'ai toutes les fureurs".*

In **"Clay"**, a feeble but "poetic" son is driven from a mother whom he loves and hates, both passionately, to a wife who is her replica in everyday behaviour but whose emotional life hardly exists. His dreams of freedom from his mother's tyranny turn, after her death, to orgies of imagined incest. The mother-figure of these affairs, whom he calls Lova, bedevils him increasingly until the story ends in a manner no less erotic and even more melodramatic than the ending of **"The Letters"**. As a whole, the story displays White's "fine writing" at its worst. It is a painfully-wrought labyrinth of chain-images and balanced and contrasted situations, all on the best Freudian models:

> One night Clay wrote: 'I have never observed a flower-pot intimately until now its hole is fascinating the little down of green moss it is of greater significance than what is within though you can fill it if you decide to if you concentrate long enough.'

The real felicities of this story are comparatively small and spontaneous: the utterly lifeless speech of the wife; the dead and crumbling house; or the mother's Delilah-like insistence, when Clay unwarily recounts one of his dreams, on having his hair shorn to the scalp.

The other major variant of Freud's mother-son relationship gives point to **"Being Kind to Titina"**. Here a Graeco-Alexandrian youth of the present day is so fortunate as to experience in real life what amounts to an erotic daydream of Ceres in all her bounty. This nervous youth (whose name is Dionysios!) is positively showered with maternal gold: ices, fruits glacés, "vissinada", swimming à deux, and a gentle and expert induction in the art of love. The story varies the textbook formula in another way also: for Titina, the serene patroness, is not the boy's mother at all but a mother-substitute in the person of a little whore, younger than himself, whose patron and father-substitute *he* had been, in their childhood. This oddly pleasant and amusing tale is marred by the half-relevant clichés of its setting. Irritating as it can be in the original, D. H. Lawrence's sentimental primitivism about the "organic" community and the "organic" family is even more so in a tourist version. In Alexandria, it seems, even the camels are on the side of life:

> I believe we were at our happiest in the evenings of those days. Though somebody might open a door, threatening to dash the light from the candles on our aunt's piano, the flames soon recovered their shape. Silences were silenter. In those days it was not uncommon to hear the sound of a camel, treading past, through the dust. There was the smell of camel on the evening air.
>
> Oh yes, we were at our happiest.

Notwithstanding their minor merits, these three stories are damaged by the mechanical working-out of a preordained idea and by a unity of action and setting that is contrived rather than imagined. Apart from those gestures which are designed as Freudian symbols, the "manners" of these stories are, on the whole, neither closely observed nor very rich in meanings.

Although they differ radically in their degree both of unity and complexity, the remaining two stories are alike in treating clashes between social renegades and the society of Sarsaparilla. Daise Morrow, the renegade of **"Down at the Dump"**, has lately died and those Sarsaparillans who must are attending her funeral. Since her rebellion had consisted essentially in extreme sexual generosity—neither Mrs. Lusty nor Nola Boyle can approach her—the tone of the story is mainly reminiscent. All the obvious attitudes are represented, from the envious frustration of her brother-in-law to the pathetic gratitude of her last lover, from the puritanical intolerance of her sister to the promise of re-incarnation in the sister's daughter. To round it all off there is a sententious contrast between Daise's charitable carnality and Mum Whalley's egocentric lust.

A great deal of the naiveté, over-simplification, and sentimental dishonesty that usually vitiate White's portrayal of Sarsaparilla emerges if we briefly join him in his study of Freud. Although **"Down at the Dump"** is thickly studded with Freudian symbols, its central conflict looks shallow and schematic and its approval of Daise is seen to be faked when the story is considered in the light of Freud's own discussions of the very subtle, complex, and far-reaching relationships between society and the individual libido.[3] No simple antithesis (Two-backs good: one back bad) constitutes an adequate comment on such complex relationships as these. And the situation is not much remedied by the presence of such qualifications as Mum Whalley affords.

Leaving **"A Cheery Soul"** out of account for a little longer, we can now attempt to establish a meaningful relationship between White's treatment of "manners" and the success or failure of his stories. Whereas it is obvious that manners can consist in *any* kind of small gesture pointing to *any* of the deeper workings of a personality, White seems to find significance in only two kinds of gesture: those which act as socio-aesthetic signs of class or nationality, and those which are patently Freudian.

Since they need to be—and are—comprehensible to the lay reader, White's Freudian symbols are rather simple, unequivocal, and even heavy-handed. As a result, those stories where relationships between individuals *qua* individuals are of central importance tend to reduce, as Freud himself never did, the subtle range of human behaviour to a few rather stereotyped gestures. In these Freudian stories, as we have seen, manners of the socio-aesthetic kind merely provide ready-made but rather incidental settings.

In those stories where the characters are above all social—or anti-social—beings, it is, of course, the socio-aesthetic gestures that predominate. Although they are not very common and certainly never sustained in the stories so far considered, there are moments of very acute and penetrating observation. There is, again, the sustained but rather limited conflict of manners in **"Miss Slattery and Her Demon Lover"**. On the other hand, there are many occasions when the demands of that stage-villain, Sarsaparilla, distract White's attention—and a well-imagined character momentarily dies on our hands. Worst of all, there are times when White becomes the mere slave of his loathing for Sarsaparilla. It is then that the Mackenzies's "carefully natural-looking gums", Mrs. Polkinghorn's exotic shrubs, and the "bald, red, rudimentary hill", clad only in Iceland poppies and gladioli, to which Xanadu is reduced all stand as signs of the one Australian Ugliness. It is then that, as in the passage cited from *Riders in the Chariot,* a term so vague and all-embracing as "plastic" comes to be used by a serious writer as an adequate symbol for a shoddiness in our society.

The force of all these strictures is borne out, by sheer contrast, in **"A Cheery Soul"**, to which none of them have any serious application. It is as if Mr. White awoke one morning and saw his world with fresh eyes. In this story alone he sees virtue in Sarsaparilla and vice in the rebellious individual. Yet this is no mere reversal: appalling as she is, Miss Docker has her side of the argument and must share in the pity that we more willingly bestow on her victims. And yet, again, her individuality lies in the nature of her tyranny, for her sin is universal benevolence. Her victims know, as Charles Dickens never learnt, what it is to be at the mercy of John Jarndyce.

Of her earlier life we are told little except that, like any other cuckoo-chicken, she has had to fend for herself since infancy. Her amiable confidence that other people are merely replicas of herself and that, being imperfect replicas, their vocation is to serve her has the air of something congenital, something confirmed rather than created when she learns of Manon Lescaut. Sharing Manon's attitudes but lacking her particular gifts, Miss Docker has to seek a little further for her one unique vocation. The revelation comes finally from the natural source of revelations:

> 'I once read the Bible from cover to cover. That was when I was at the end of me tether. A whole fortnight it took me. I lay in bed, and read, and read. It was raining cats and dogs. Never stopped. Before that I was pagan. But suddenly I saw.'
>
> 'What did you see?'
>
> Ted Custance was looking at her now.
>
> 'Don't be silly!' she said. 'You can't say what you see. But *see,* See?'

Even though she cannot say what she saw, there is no doubt at all that Miss Docker saw it. And we come to see it, too. It is the simple but magnificent notion of employing Christian attitudes, such as charity and loving-kindness, as weapons in her fight with a society whose lip-service to Christianity renders it completely vulnerable to her. Since she is neither superficial nor inconsistent in her display of these attitudes, she is able to win from the halt and lame the upkeep and the gratitude that are her chief social satisfactions. Since it is her specialty to act as unpaid nurse-housekeeper in households where the husband is weak or ailing, she is able to gain vicarious sexual satisfactions. And since she is no mere hypocrite, but a person absolutely self-persuaded, she is even able to solace her soul.

When she meets resistance and "ingratitude", Miss Docker pityingly but bravely moves elsewhere. At last she overreaches herself. But Society's victory comes not through direct resistance but through a tacit conspiracy to ignore, even to deny, her existence. Thus an Old People's Home rapidly depopulates itself and the congregation of the local church disappears almost overnight. One sees their point. And yet, as she trudges along the empty street at the end, one neither fully believes nor even wholly wishes her downfall to be permanent.

As a natural consequence of this awareness that, even in Sarsaparilla, Society is made up of people and that a Rebellious Individual is not always or necessarily admirable, White's portrayal of manners takes on, almost without exception, a depth and subtlety that are lacking elsewhere. Whether she is begging the shrewdly obstinate Ted Custance to use her Christian name, plastering a woman newly-widowed with lipstick, entertaining old people with photographs of herself, or choosing the hymns that she, as sole survivor of the choir, will sing, Miss Docker is unique and lovingly-observed. And the Sarsaparillans who are her victims are also observed in a spirit of satire rather than one of contempt.

If the loving-kindness of Mrs. Godbold is over-strained not only by the way in which the woman herself is presented but also by White's doctrinaire insistence on the worthlessness of most of its recipients, that of Miss Docker is a quite spontaneous overflow of powerful feelings on her part, springing from a rare tranquility of observation and organisation on the part of White himself.

Notes

1. These stories are: "Willy-Wagtails by Moonlight", *Australian Letters,* IV, iii (1962), 35-43; "The Letters", *Quadrant* 22 (1962), 5-17; "Being Kind to Titina", *Meanjin,* XXI (1962), 5-19; "The Woman Who Wasn't Allowed to Keep Cats", *Australian Letters,* V, ii (1962), 30-57; "A Cheery Soul", *The London Magazine,* II, vi (1962), 6-36; "Clay", *Overland* 26 (1963), 5-13; "Miss Slattery and Her Demon Lover", *Australian Letters,* V, iii (1963), 27-37, reprinted in *The London Magazine* in November 1963; and "Down at the Dump", *Meanjin,* XXII (1963), 153-179.
2. These uncertainties are not relieved by the circumstance that the "piecrust" style post-dates the death of Queen Anne. If this contradiction is deliberate, White's satiric point recedes into an even wider landscape of possibilities.
3. Cf. Sigmund Freud, *A General Introduction to Psycho-Analysis* (New York, 1943), pp. 23-4.

Andrew Taylor (essay date 1965)

SOURCE: "White's Short Stories," in *Overland,* No. 31, March, 1965, pp. 17-19.

[*In the following essay, Taylor discusses the shortcomings and the success of White's short stories in* The Burnt Ones, *maintaining that the stories are "fine, penetrating, courageous and illuminating in their economy."*]

Patrick White is central to Australian literature just in so far as he chooses to remain at odds with its society. To say that he is one of our sharpest and best social critics is stating a commonplace. The "suburban" world of Sarsaparilla and Barranugli receive about as much sympathy as they offer love. But one of his strengths is the ability not only to make us feel strongly about the mess we have created, but also to make us feel that it's worth feeling strongly about. For barren, ugly, or sweet and sickly though it may be, it is still the breeding ground of human lives. And where human lives are being bred, there are always some who will, perhaps even only part-consciously, grope towards the fullness of living that can be sensed among a mass of flowers and foliage.

In this volume of short stories, ***The Burnt Ones***, White, as in **"The Aunt's Story"** and **"Riders in the Chariot,"** can turn his attention to Europe without diverting it from Australia. Four of the eleven stories here reprinted are set in the Greek Mediterranean. There is, it is true, a Greece of pines and temples on headlands, but there are also Hasselblads, and aunts who are professors in Paris, and new apartments and tinned dolmadakia. Romantic though he is, for White the Greek Mediterranean is just another place he happens to know well, where he can see taking place the same basic conflict that is taking place in Australia.

Still, it is hard to feel happy about the end of that otherwise fine **"Being Kind to Titina"**. It is not for nothing that the girl, the pines, the Saronic Gulf and "the man with the accordian . . . playing his five or six notes, as gentle and persuasive as wood-pigeons" are seen through the eyes of an adolescent. But one wonders if they are seen sufficiently through any other eyes as well. What kind of self-realisation is it that expresses itself in these terms: "As I leant out of the window, and held up my throat to receive the knife, nothing happened . . . and I realised that my own extended throat was itself a stiff sword"?

But the main contrast in one of the best stories, **"The Woman Who Wasn't Allowed to Keep Cats,"** set in Athens, is not between the Greeks and their Americanised visitors, but between an indulgent and smothering sensuality that bores, tires or irritates, and the sharp feline sexuality that succeeds it. The Americans don't escape White's characteristic censure ("'Some people are like animals!' she gasped; it was too hateful"). But it is not just Cadillacs and cameras that smother vitality. White would probably agree that good sensuality is good for one, but not all sensuality is good.

The funniest story in the collection is one in which this is seen in an intensely comic light. **"Miss Slattery and her Demon Lover"** is a satirical delight. It is Miss Slattery, usual and Aussie, who becomes the demon, and Tibby, that monstrous Hungarian, bewitched by her dexterity with the stockwhip, becomes, despite his feline name, a spaniel to his own perversion. Tibby, rather than qualifying for sympathy as one of the burnt ones of the title, comes in for a little humorous roasting.

But White does not always find life so amusing, nor is he always so kind to it. The majority of these stories have that odd mixture of luxuriance and grimness that we now expect of him. Among the rich smell of leaves and decay there is the shrill cry of the neighbor and the bony pricking of brooches. Unwanted relatives have to be buried out of sight, businesses run and acquaintances kept going. We live in a suburban society, and it has to be kept up because it keeps us up. Consequently, there are always little bits left over that, if they can't be thrown out, can at best be ignored, at worst shunned with contempt. These are the "burnt ones" of the title.

To call these oddities outcasts, rejects or outsiders is inaccurate. They are none of these. They are rather misfits, often struggling almost tragically to retain sheer normality. Some don't even realise their difference. Their difference is that they accept suffering, rather than pretend to ignore its existence. This itself sets them apart from the world of washing machines and neighbors in which normal humanity shuts itself. And, White implies, if a soul shuts itself from suffering, it must also shut itself from love. One recalls the dying Voss, and Theodora Goodman and Mrs. Godbold. But what White means by love is no simple thing. There is something of charity, and self-denial, but there is also sensuality and self-fulfilment, and a sensuous apprehension of objects by which love can and ought to extend itself to the inanimate or non-human. White's language is almost bumpy in its concreteness, and Meg Hogben, feeling "the furry darkness, as the semitrailer roared and bucked, its skeleton of coloured lights," (**"Down at the Dump"**) is on the same road as Miss Hare crawling through her friendly jungle.

It is in **"Clay,"** in my opinion the best here, and in **"The Letters,"** both very fine stories, that White examines most closely the basic problems he diagnoses. Clay himself is a pathetic, unplaced creature who withdraws increasingly from the suburban world which has inappropriately claimed him. He fashions a reality of his own, finally christening her Lova. She is the love and fulfilment he has never experienced and can only amateurishly copy, after the models he has. He is a seer with nothing outside himself to see. He creates Lova in total isolation, and as isolated women tend to do, she becomes bitchy. Instead of providing the white bridal boat in which he can sail to Avalon, she ends by beating him to death with a stiletto heel. Despite the acute satirical surface and Clay's near ludicrous patheticness ("At last my ryvita has turned to velveeta life is no longer a toastrack") White succeeds in amalgamating an astonishing variety. Clay's unpunctuated mother, both responsible and incapable, is a masterpiece of minor tragedescence.

If **"Clay"** is uncompromising, almost affronting, **"The Letters"** appears even bleaker, stripped as it is of much of the comedy. Here the satire is harsher; Mrs. Polkinghorn, the mother, responsible and not incapable, gets no sympathy. Her son Charles, like Clay, is "in withdrawal". But whereas Clay has withdrawn to look, Charles is in retreat, hiding from threat. Among poultry catalogues he is safe; the letters locked in the box cannot threaten him. It is his sudden desire to be finally rid of threat that impels him to release the letters. And in doing so, he also releases fear: "packages contain the worst dangers, threatening the lives of politicians, diplomats . . ." There is only one refuge, and he is hurled from that with elderly middle-class disgust. Charles has locked himself into hell with the same key with which he opened his Pandora's box and faced fear. For he did not shut it in time to keep Hope with him.

In both of these stories, as in **"The Aunt's Story"** and **"Riders,"** White takes us over the edge of madness in an unmistakably sane manner. He makes us face a kind of morality of injustice; he makes us see that certain states of madness are in fact a state of truth and exposure that just can't cope with its own reality. The victims of this state don't become saints or heroes; their martyrdom is only partly, almost negligibly imposed on them by society, which prefers on the whole to leave them alone. It is imposed by their own condition. They are part burning bush, lights for us, and part minor and unintentional Ulysses, turned, as in Dante, into flame and suffering 'e dentro dalla lor flamma si geme.'

None the less, White seldom ceases his muscular attack on contemporary society. Some of it is very funny. Most of it is accurate. His devastating utilisation of the phraseology and rhythms of Australian speech and inarticulateness carries his attack into the heart of the enemy, and modulates without strain into the most personal dialogue. But his satire sometimes penetrates to the point of indiscriminacy or sheer destructiveness. It's such accurate observations as his that makes his targets more than mere targets. Yet the unmitigated attack that observation furnishes leaves me with the feeling that White himself sometimes lacks the charity he is condemning them for lacking. He evaluates his "heroes" by their subjective experience. Yet condemns the hypocrisy of the majority while seeming frightened to allow his sympathy to look too closely into their own subjective life. Could they all be found to be burnt ones?

These strictures apply mostly to the poorer stories in the volume. The stories are, like any collection, a mixed bag, and the worst of them, **"Willy-Wagtails by Moonlight"** is very slight, and creakily engineered. Some display the chronic weaknesses of the short story and White—obviousness, facile symbolism, crudeness of conception—which the expansive novels tend to eliminate. But at their best, these stories are fine, penetrating, courageous and illuminating in their economy.

Hameeda Hossain (review date 1965)

SOURCE: A review of *The Burnt Ones*, in *The Australian Quarterly,* Vol. VII, No. 4, December, 1965, pp. 120-23.

[*In the following review, Hossain discusses how the stories in* The Burnt Ones *mirror themes in White's novels and act as commentary on Australian society and the human condition.*]

Patrick White was introduced to me as one of the best Australian writers of today. On reading ***The Burnt Ones,*** a collection of his short stories, which led me to read two of his more recent novels, *The Aunt's Story* and *Riders in the Chariot,* it seemed evident that he is outstanding among contemporary fiction writers outside Australia as well.

As with most good writing it is possible to approach Patrick White's work on several levels. First for its regional connotations as having something to say about Australian society. Although one gets glimpses of the concerns and values of middle-class Australian society, such as a consciousness of money, class and status, and a striving to attain at least one if not all of these; an involvement with objects (also important symbolically) and a suggestion of intellectual emptiness—it would be presumptuous as a foreigner to appraise it on this level. His work, however, transcends this environment, as Patrick White's ultimate concern is the basic human condition as it unfolds in the portrayal of the inner lives and the tragic predicament of persons who just miss being "ordinary". In this collection of short stories, published in different literary journals over a number of years, Patrick White is versatile, not only in his selection of the setting which moves from Australia to Greece, but there is also a distinct variation of mood. Nevertheless, there is an underlying link which fits into the larger pattern worked out in his novels, giving them a certain unity.

His incisive and penetrating characterization of the outsider depicts a contemporary tragedy, a theme that is relevant to our times. The repressions of modern man in an Anglo-Saxon world haunted by an efficient machine-like existence, and a fear of war and extinction make him emotionally dwarfed and he feels caged in by these pressures. A profound sense of isolation—mystical in *Riders in the Chariot,* and painfully compelling in *The Aunt's Story,* pervades his short stories. In most of them the author is also concerned with the inter-play of illusion and reality, of the past over-lapping the present.

Patrick White's "burnt ones" are charged by a futile knowledge of their differentness. If they had remained oblivious of this characteristic they would have merged into the world of normal, ordinary people. But, born with inward looking eyes, they bear the stamp of their alienation. They feel caged in by their fear of the condescending scorn and pity to which they feel doomed. Yearning for experience and yet shirking from it within themselves, there is a complete failure of communication between the inner world of ordinary conventionalities. They touch each other marginally but slip away before any meaningful contact is established.

Anthea Scudamore, around whom the story develops in **"Dead Roses"**, is dominated by her mother, tries but just stops short, almost frightened of any contact either with her mother, or her father, or even when she marries Mr. Mortlock, an ageing friend of her father's, "a substantial man", but one who is not alive in any positive sense. We find her "opening the drawers of other people's lives", but like Theodora Goodman, in *The Aunt's Story* unable to "discover the secret of unlocking other people for she herself had never opened". Incommunicative, these painfully silent people withdraw from life—Anthea, eager to find "experience" in marriage is left only with the husk of a marital relationship; in **"Clay"**, the lonely "different" boy, dominated by his mother prolongs the apparent continuity of his life by marrying a girl very much like her even down to her prosaic concern for kitchen sinks, while he recedes further within himself. In *The Letters* this isolation is carried still further into the realm of insanity. Here the impact of a fast-moving competitive society is most poignantly shown in the predicament of the son, Charles, a shy, retiring and reserved person who is torn away from his idyllic, academic life by his father's sudden death. The demands of his father's business now devolve upon him, but he feels completely inadequate to cope with men or machines. His domineering mother then accepts his awkwardness as "insanity". His godmother, the only person who understands him is far away and dying. Thus Charles withdraws. In the last powerful scene, he tries to go back in time to assert his childhood relationship of at least, physical communication with his mother. But she fails to understand him and in recoiling sets a seal on his withdrawal.

Patrick White's "outsiders" burn inwardly with a patient endurance, for there is no redemption only an escape, often beyond the pale of reality into an illusory world of their own creation. Clay's childhood interest in his mother's wedding photograph, which develops into a strange fascination for her white wedding shoe becomes symbolical of the human need for love. Its denial leads to a withdrawal into a completely make-belief world where the imaginary Love answers his need for love and understanding, until even the reader is lost in these shifting sands. In **"A Glass of Tea"**, the old man's memory, as he recounts the story of his life to his visitor, seems to waver between the real and the unreal and to create a mystical aura around the Russian fortune-teller who gives him the glasses of his destiny, and the unfolding of his wife's personality, "a passionate, a difficult woman, but worth the suffering involved". The mystical unfolding of the story builds up to an anticipation of a meeting with his wife. As the interest of the visitor, and, for that matter, of the reader, is aroused and the curiosity to see his wife reaches its peak, there is a sudden drop to reality, and we realize that we had been carried unknowingly on the waves of illusion.

Isolated as the outsider may seem, the "ordinary" people are not capable of anything more than a superficially conventional relationship. In their world which abounds with self-assured domineering women, overprotective towards cowed and quiet men there is an emphasis on the ghostly unreality of the human relationship. Marriage, even when it is not entered into for a purely selfish purpose, provides little meaningful contact; there is a clinging and dependence, but not out of love or understanding.

The contrast between these two worlds is brought out most successfully in **"Down at the Dump"**, undoubtedly the best story in this collection not only aesthetically but even more for its assertion of certain positive values. There is a brilliant depiction of opposite worlds, a meeting of opposing states of mind: the conventionally respectable and the social outcast; the old and the young; the inside and the outside of people; the encroachment of the past over the present. The world of the poor Walleys is bright with disordered abandon. Their neighbours, Councillor Hogben and his wife, tied as they are in conventional lifelessness, preside over the last formalities of her sister's death. Mr. Hogben, "whose shape suggested she had been made of several scones joined together in the baking", grieves not so much for her sister's death as for the unconventional life she led. Grotesquely involved with the possession of objects, Mrs. Hogben's other nature—acquisitive, resentful, grasping and cruel—lurks not very far from her superficially conventional stance of the dutiful wife and mother and a responsible member of society. In contrast her dead sister Daisy Morrow, genuinely kind, warm and understanding is misunderstood and scorned only because she has defied social conventions. As such Daisy Morrow remains positive in life. And her death is an affirmation—a symbolic affirmation which gives to this story a deeply religious significance. For although the bored, apathetic mourners—the pall-bearers of life, get ready to bury Daisy, she evokes terror and hope as she by her very unconcern for society seems to proclaim:

> Listen to me all you successful no-hopers, all you who wake in the night, jittery because something may be escaping you, or terrified to think that there may never have been anything to find. Come to me you sour women, public servants, anxious children and old scabby, desperate men. . . . Truly we needn't experience tortures, unless we build chambers in our minds to house instruments of hatred in. Don't you know, my darling creatures, that death isn't death until it is the death of love? Love should be the greatest explosion it is reasonable to expect which sends us whirling, spinning, creating millions of other worlds. Never destroying.

Daisy Morrow is indeed dumped, unheard and disbelieved. But when Meg Hogben and Lummy Walley the two teenage children can transcend their parents prejudices and their own fears, they reaffirm Daisy Morrow's symbolic resurrection.

Added to this is a profoundly comic vision, startling in **"A Cheery Soul"**, and in the ironic story of **"Miss Slattery and Her Demon Lover"**, which is reflected in all his stories: in the sad humour of **"Being Kind to Titina"**, and in the caricatured description of the affluent American Greek couple visiting their land or the intellectual, a Party member who makes good writing biographies of famous men, and moves up the social scale in **"The Woman Who Wasn't Allowed to Keep Cats."**

None of Patrick White's characters are great, nor is the impact of their lives eloquent. Yet in weaving a meaning into the smouldering of lives seemingly detached and wasted, the author expresses a deep compassion for these introspective human beings. In describing the pathos of a slow crumbling of suburban souls, his stories evoke a sense of tragedy—a tragedy not so much of an individual, but of a civilization, of a whole way of life.

H. P. Heseltine (review date 1965)

SOURCE: "Writer and Reader," in *Southerly,* Vol. 25, No. 1, 1965, pp. 69-71.

[*In the following review, Heseltine asserts that* The Burnt Ones *is "an essentially uneven book," but that through the unevenness "shines one of our great creative spirits."*]

"Dead Roses", the story which Patrick White has placed at the beginning of ***The Burnt Ones,*** is long, previously unpublished, and resumes the chief features of the ten which follow it. It is largely concerned, for instance, with the influence on Anthea Scudamore of her dreadful, domineering mother. It is a theme which has already engaged Patrick White in his novels; but he has imagined no more hatefully satirical version of it than those scenes in **"Dead Roses"** where poor Anthea has to make long-distance telephone conversations to Mummy in the delighted presence of some holidaying friends. Yet it is not even in **"Dead Roses"** that White vents his hatred of Australian matrons with the most passionate intensity. He reaches the height of his hate in **"Clay"** and **"The Letters"**. In both stories, a son suffers at the hands of an over-possessive mother; in both, the son takes refuge in total psychotic collapse. In both, the pattern of the prose seems to be woven less from satiric comment than obsessive emotional need; in both, the almost hysterical tone spreads out so far beyond the necessary requirements of dramatization as to endanger the balance of the whole performance.

While on her brief holiday from Mother, Anthea Scudamore has a brush with the untrammelled life of the senses in an attempted seduction by a physicist, Barry Flegg. Her rejection of such experience, however, does not represent White's only or final valuation of his theme. In a number of other stories he registers further attitudes towards a life of passionate sensuality. **"Miss Slattery and Her Demon Lover"** is a grotesquely funny tale about an Australian girl who becomes entangled with a Hungarian migrant who has a penchant for stockwhips and mirrors on the ceiling. One Bohemian party, in particular, reads like a scene from a Coward comedy to be performed in a chamber of horrors. A vein of grotesquerie, indeed, runs through many of the stories wherein White investigates passionate relationships. It swamps most of the other elements of **"Willy-Wagtails by Moonlight"** in bizarre comedy. In the climax of **"The Woman Who Wasn't Allowed to Keep Cats"** it shines through with genuine brilliance. In **"Dead Roses"** it less successfully motivates the image of Anthea, yoked to a two-man harness, helping her ageing husband to drag a barrowload of manure up a hill.

For Anthea Scudamore does marry—not Barry Flegg, but a middle-aged, respectable, atrocious businessman. Hessell Mortlock translates Anthea to a now familiar corner of White country, Sarsaparilla. Several other stories in ***The Burnt Ones*** also contribute to our knowledge of this mythical Sydney suburb. The Polkinghorns (mother and son), of **"The Letters,"** live there, in isolated splendour and psychological decay. The main scene of **"Down at the Dump"** takes place at Sarsaparilla cemetery and the adjacent rubbish tip. The Sarsaparilla Sundown Home for Old People is the focal point for much of **"A Cheery Soul"**. The map of this region is filled in with each new action that White places within its boundaries; it is a Hell where evil masquerades as middle-class respectability, decency is too easily destroyed, and grandiose designs run to seed.

The fullest study of Sarsaparilla vice disguised as virtue is, of course, Miss Docker in **"A Cheery Soul"**. The hypocritical destructiveness of her cloying sweetness is exposed mercilessly and totally. The Custances, protected by their simplicity and a streak of toughness, escape before disaster overtakes them; but in Mr. Wakeman, the Anglican parson of Sarsaparilla, Miss Docker finds a victim altogether worthy of her talents. Mrs. Wakeman's anguished cry over her husband's dead body is one of the great moments of ***The Burnt Ones***: "Miss Docker, you have killed my saint. Only time will show whether you have killed my God as well". After that, one can only regret that White allows himself the petty revenge of a dog urinating on Miss Docker's leg. Even her realization that "dog . . . is God turned round" cannot, it seems to me, save the ending of **"A Cheery Soul"** from the sense of a major imaginative achievement unnecessarily cheapened.

So long, indeed, as White remains in Sarsaparilla, one has the uneasy feeling that a number of his victories are tactical rather than strategic. The satire, with its almost revue-like labelling, can be pointed rather than penetrating; the characterization a little too one-sided (straw men don't put up much of an argument). It is for this reason that I find the Greek stories in ***The Burnt Ones*** especially interesting. They are not to be cherished for any travelogue revelation of exotic places and people but because, for whatever reason, in them White has drawn on deeper springs of understanding and technique. **"A Glass of Tea," "Being Kind to Titina," "The Woman Who Wasn't Allowed to Keep Cats," "The Evening at Sissy Kamara's"** all seem to me to embody a more complex and truthful (because less partisan?) view of individual human beings than most of the Australian stories. The relationship between Dionysios (the narrator of **"Being Kind to Titina"**), for instance, and Titina becomes a beautifully judged vehicle for all the boy's childhood and adolescent awareness of the world. Or the flashback technique of **"A Glass of Tea"** allows past and present to fuse in a vision of the nature of married love and the imagination of the solitary artist.

Concern for the varieties of love runs all through the Greek stories, as does an equal concern for the varieties of suffering. The destruction of Smyrna by the Turks casts over some of their most important pages the light of purgative flames which will be readily recognizable by any experienced reader of Patrick White. The very title of the book, ***The Burnt Ones*** (or ***The Unfortunate Ones***), indicates that suffering is to be one of its leading themes. Three main kinds can be detected: suffering which results in a genuine purification of life (mainly in the Greek stories); suffering which, hardening rather than refining, becomes a mask for hypocrisy and evil (located centrally in

Sarsaparilla); and a kind of limited suffering which causes the individual, his fingers singed by the world to withdraw from it. Of this last class, Anthea Scudamore-Mortlock is the prime example. But even Anthea has her moment of truth. With Mr Mortlock conveniently removed by death, she can at last enjoy his fortune—mainly in foreign travel. One day in Greece she encounters the same Barry Flegg who had once tried to seduce her, now married and with three children. Then, and only then, does a vision of her own emptiness come to Anthea.

The concluding scene of **"Dead Roses"** is, in itself, very powerfully done; not quite so powerfully, however, as to blot out all doubts about the coincidental nature of the meeting. Again, one is just a little too aware of White the technician rigging his effects to suit his prejudged ends. The whole of **"Dead Roses,"** in fact, has a strangely diagrammatic structure; it is a blueprint of how Anthea Scudamore turns into her mother. In other stories, any arbitrariness of plotting may be absorbed into intensity of emotional tone (**"Clay"**); richly rendered psychological and physical detail (**"Being Kind to Titina"**); the comic possibilities of situation (**"Willy-Wagtails by Moonlight"**). But one of the most impressive means White has found for animating his fictional diagrams is a complex counterpointing of theme and motif. It can be detected in **"The Evening at Sissy Kamara's," "A Glass of Tea,"** and **"The Woman Who Wasn't Allowed to Keep Cats"**. But it is used nowhere more triumphantly than in the Sarsaparilla story, **"Down at the Dump"**. The short-term victories of the other Sarsaparilla tales could probably be abstracted from **"Down at the Dump"**; even the vulgarity of the episode which mars the end of **"A Cheery Soul"**. But any such abstraction would be critically invalid; in **"Down at the Dump"** theme, character, incident are woven into an organic and inseparable unity. It is the co-operating wholeness of all its parts rather than any lushness of texture which has, I suspect, led other reviewers to identify a "poetic" quality in this story. Its prose, indeed, is remarkable for its detached and ironic poise, but it is capable of containing what ultimately emerges as an oddly affirmative vision.

I have to confess that when **"Down at the Dump"** first appeared in *Meanjin* I did not admire it as I do now. Perhaps time and further re-reading will demand a corresponding adjustment in my attitude towards some of the other stories. I am sure, however, that no amount of reconsideration will alter my opinion that ***The Burnt Ones*** is an essentially uneven book. Its best stories are among the most imaginative ever written by an Australian; its worst sacrifice control to intensity, understanding to aphorism. Through all the unevenness, of course, shines one of our great creative spirits. Yet for all its rewards, ***The Burnt Ones*** does not convince me that that spirit is as fully and richly at home in the shorter reaches of fiction as in the full-length novel.

Barry Argyle (essay date 1967)

SOURCE: "Short Stories," in *Patrick White,* Oliver and Boyd LTD, 1967, pp.66–89.

[*In the following excerpt, Argyle points out that while White is primarily known as a novelist, his short stories show the same "intelligence" and "wealth of experience" that mark the author's longer fiction.*]

When in the early sixties White began publishing those stories which he has since collected, with two additions, under the title of ***The Burnt Ones,*** many of his recent English readers were surprised that a novelist who dealt in great themes at great length should bother with an art-form used mainly by beginners. It had also become an axiom among many professional English readers of novels that the short-story was dead. Had they not, they felt, helped to kill it, assisted by a dearth of magazines and a surfeit of television and Somerset Maugham? With its roots in Scotland and its greatest modern practitioners in Ireland and America, the short-story, belonging to a wide tradition, did not fit easily into the Great Tradition. But in publishing ***The Burnt Ones,*** White was returning to a form he had first used nearly thirty years before, when he wrote **"The Twitching Colonel,"** which appeared in the *London Mercury* of April 1937, and **"Cocotte,"** which *Horizon* printed in 1940.

Neither shares the quality that so distinguishes his later stories, and their main interest now can only be in what they anticipate. The first, possibly an early draft of the fire incident in *The Aunt's Story,* is an old, alcoholic, Indian Army colonel's stream-of-consciousness playing over a distant past, which, superficially boring, has had its moments of excitement in battle and passion and the surrounding exoticism of Hindu civilisation to which, politically, he has been required to oppose that of the Raj. The colonel is alone in the tattered splendours of London's Pimlico, his only companion a landlady who values him for his antecedents, his medals, and his stories of India. In reliving his similar glories, he is a younger Sokolnikov, like him melancholic from age, a dead passion, and ennui. He dies in a fire which mingles with, even becomes, his memories of India. The story ends with a heavy finger pointing the heavier moral difference between us, the spectators, and the colonel: "We creep away. It is something we do not understand. We are afraid." It is a young man's story in which a good fire removes any technical difficulties. The heavily-punctuated moral is the justification for the earlier, and the fashionable, verbal pyrotechnics.

"Cocotte" is a very much shorter impression, this time the stream of consciousness become the flood of conversation. The story takes the seemingly formless form of a Frenchwoman on a bench talking to an English sailor about her husband, who is in Marseilles, and the dog which is with her. It is in fact a very clever and funny *montage* of French and Gallic-English, in which the dog Cocotte—a delightfully ambiguous name—plays with Maman as Maman plays with the sailor. It ends lightly with her "good-bye, Monsieur. J'èspere. . . ." The breathless but purposeful sallying back and forth of the woman's monologue already shows the mark of White's mordant accuracy in selecting in order to appear to record words actually spoken.

Their French and London settings, with overtones of the Indian Empire and weekend trips across the Channel, suggest these stories could have been written by any one of a number of faintly critical pre-war ex-public schoolboys, as indeed a glance at the magazines in which they appeared quickly confirms.

White, however, is an Australian, who since the war has decided, with many misgivings, to live in Australia. Although this has clearly influenced his choice of themes and his attitude towards them in at least some of his short stories, it has had a much greater influence on his decision to return to the writing of short stories. In Australia there is a long and still very lively tradition of short-story writing, and there are many more magazines there to publish them than exist in England. Of the eleven stories in ***The Burnt Ones,*** seven were first published in four Australian magazines; two of these seven, with two others, have also appeared in *The London Magazine,* the only present English publication at all comparable with *Australian Letters*, *Meanjin*, *Quadrant* and *Overland.* As the reasons for Australia's relative good fortune are discussed in John Tregenza's useful book, *Australian Little Magazines,* it is necessary here only to suggest the possibility that English writers, by inflating to the proportions of novels what are really short-stories, have conspired with publishers to starve if not to kill the goose that used in England to lay an occasional golden egg. One is led to this conclusion by the immediacy with which one recognises the broader range of intelligence and concern in White's novels when they are compared with those of his English contemporaries, and by the intelligence with which in the best of the short-stories a wealth of experience and sympathy is shaped into an intense art.

Of the eleven, seven are set in Australia, four among Greeks. Except in one of the finest, **"Down at the Dump,"** there is no reference to myth or legend, nor anywhere that verbal puissance so readily discernible in the best of the novels. The stories in the main cannot be read as Lawrence's are, as a closer examination of themes found in the novels; nor as Faulkner's, an extension of the world the novels deal with in which even the same characters are found. Although four of them, **"Dead Roses," "A Cheery Soul," "The Letters,"** and **"Down at the Dump"** are set either wholly or in part in Sarsparilla, in only **"The Letters"** is there a character mentioned in the novels—Mrs. Sugden, the postmistress, who briefly introduces *Riders in the Chariot*—and her appearance in the story is even briefer. In **"A Cheery Soul,"** we learn, perhaps in anticipation of a future novel, that Sarsparilla's history goes back to the convict era. But that is all; and it is not important. We have instead social comment directed at Australian and Greek suburban life, not because it is suburban, but because it conforms to the mean standards set by American suburban life, which appear in the story called **"The Woman Who Wasn't Allowed to Keep Cats."** On the whole, however, such comment is incidental to the main theme of generous fulfilment and its reverse, the deprivation suburban life enforces by hoisting up conformity as an ideal. The theme often takes the form of a comparison, within the timelessness memory allows, of childhood and adulthood, of past and present; but unlike the novels, in which the child is father of the man, the stories show the man as not of the same flesh, so that many of the characters echo the Young Man of *The Ham Funeral:* "You may even find . . . you have begun to feed . . . on memory."[1] So starved is the present of each, that each becomes his own Chronos. Their ironic fate, which sustains many of the stories, is in their inability to digest what they so greedily devour. This difference between an idyllic past and a suburban present also introduces into the stories an element absent from most of the novels, namely marriage. Like having a two-car garage, or hot-and-cold in the main bedroom, suburbs exist to prove that trouble shared is trouble halved. An object of White's concern is to show how often it is trouble doubled, that hot and cold produce tepid water, and two cars a muttering immobility in the front drive.

"The Evening at Sissy Kamara's," for instance, is a story wholly about marriage. It employs the "box" form, the past entirely framed by the present. Mrs. Pantzopoulos is at the dentist's and while having her tooth drilled, recalls "incidents of no significance," one of which is a visit she and husband Basil paid Sissy Louloudis, born Kamara, and her husband Sotos. The cause and much of the substance of the visit are of the distant past, the two women having known each other as children in Smyrna, about which they reminisce. They also share a feeling of being exiled among mainland Greeks, Basil being unwilling to let them forget their provincial origins, though overlooking "his original grain of Piraeus sand." Their common colonial origins and experiences allow the two women momentarily to overcome their differences of personality—Sissy, an unread poetess, collector of unknown artists, and a poor cook; Poppy Pantzopoulos, her always attentive because admiring opposite.

The pastness of the past is similarly indulgent towards their original social differences, which Poppy's marriage to a city bank manager and Sissy's to an anonymous clerk have emphasised. The link between frame and object is established via Poppy's willingness to have her tooth drilled without an injection and Kitty's theory, which annoys Basil the "true" Greek, that all Greeks are sadomasochists. The irony is that only a colonial is imaginative enough, because pressed by necessity, to formulate a theory to explain a metropolitan society she cannot otherwise understand, the further irony being that the theory explains rather more about colonials who try to live as metropolitans. The situation, though in the context of different societies, is one into which White was of course born.

In the two marriages the story includes, there is an added irony. Whereas Poppy loves her husband despite his infidelities, he merely tolerates her for the wealth she brought him; while Kitty ignores Sotos and is loved in return. Although this is also a variation on the theme of the Greeks' sado-masochism, the story also suggests that Kitty and Basil would find each other more agreeable than they find their spouses; so too would Poppy and Sotos. Neither Basil nor Kitty has married for that love which foreigners, and even some Greeks like Kitty, imagine as a heritage of passion from a more heroic age, a passion which marriage is elsewhere assumed to make permanent. Economic greed or necessity has played its part, leaving Poppy and Sotos, its contented victims, free to recognise in each what the other has never had. The final irony, evident in the sexual imagery of the passage describing the dentist drilling her tooth, is that Poppy at least would have been afraid to welcome it. She prefers to keep her bad tooth, somehow repaired, rather than have it removed.

At first reading a casually slight story, at second subtle and complex, **"The Evening at Sissy Kamara's"** still seems, because of its shape, to have a fustian air about it, which is perhaps to say more about readers nurtured on naturalism than about the story. There remain however two objections to White's use here of the "box" form. Where such a form succeeds, as in Twain's "The Notorious Jumping Frog of Calaveras County," both theme and style are also fustian, so that the story presents a satisfying unity; but in White's story, theme and style conflict with the form. Secondly, the two additional ironies which are the result of the box form seem insufficiently important to justify its use, if the first objection to it is granted. The life of the story is in the evening visit to Sissy Kamara's, not in the two sticks which unnecessarily prop it up.

"The Woman Who Wasn't Allowed to Keep Cats" uses a comparable situation at much greater length but, despite the absence of what might be called contrivance, less successfully. The Hajistavri, rich American Greeks, visit the Alexious in Athens just after the war. Again, it is the wives who have known each other as children, the love which was only slightly suggested in the previous story here having been fiercely experienced. The Alexious live in what to their guests seems squalor, the woman, surrounded by cats, seems to dote on her husband; the man, an occasional journalist and a member of the Communist Party, tolerates her excessive amiability. The visit is not a success; the past is not strong enough to overcome the present; yet it is repeated years later, by which time Aleko Alexiou has achieved fame and fortune as a chronicler of Party history, so that they now live at a good address, which his wife has chosen, and without cats, which he has decided. The Hajistavri, whose marriage is a union of his money and her name, find them on the second visit making love in the middle of the afternoon, and leave, Mrs. Hajistavrou appalled by what she has learnt, yet enviously aware of what she has never experienced. She felt herself "submitted to Greece as never before. But she would not, would not allow herself to disintegrate. She closed her eyes against present and past. How glad she was, really, to be in a position to look forward to America."[2]

As in *Riders in the Chariot,* the difficulties of those whose roots have atrophied or been severed is a major theme: the Hajistavri in America feel themselves to be Greeks, and in Greece are made to feel themselves Americans to the extent of responding as Americans are traditionally supposed to respond when confronted publicly by Europe's private passions. That it so easily follows such conventions weakens the story, particularly when the crasser manifestations of American materialism are also lampooned: such social comment is less than new; but the final response is only seemingly American. What apparently is the last comment on the social theme is actually the conclusion of the lesbian theme, which generates the story's occasional intensity against the torpid background of late Athenian summer. The past on which Mrs. Hajistavrou closes her eyes includes her girlish love for Kikitsa Alexou, the moments of "softest cat-flesh bundled together in the sun."[3] The disappearance of Kikitsa's cats is the result of her husband's decision to impose his own brand of normality on their relationship, which previously his wife has been content to consider a happy twinning of souls. A modest fame and fortune requires sexual conformity.

Although White twines a deal of feline imagery around the story, lest it collapse from the strain of so much journeying on foot, and by car and ship, the story still exhausts itself from trying to do too much. Ancient, prewar, and post-war Greece are all included, as well as the 1948 revolution; and because it is Greek history, it entangles the other themes, which are numerous. Occasionally in a passage like the following White relaxes from the effort to compel a novel within a short-story:

> The heat had lifted from Attica. Autumn hung a swag of gold from the poles of the horizon. If the car had pulled up, all knew that the silence would have been too much for them, the ground too hard under the olive trees. So they drove on, and nostalgia grated on their minds, like a withered olive grating and turning between the cheek and an earthy pillow.[4]

The briefly heightened prose stresses the prevalence of the story's hectic chatter, to which are fastened adjectives of convenience to signpost the dazed reader across oceans of history and significance.

"Being Kind to Titina" is very different, its single theme helped by the story being told in the first person by a young man, Dionysius, transparent by nature and his first experience of love. He is a colonial, an Alexandrian Greek of a large and rich family cared for in the absence of parents by aunts from Smyrna and tutors and maids from France, Germany and Lesbos. In its fruitful mixing of European nationalities, it is a typically overseas Greek household, with its as typical closeness and snobbery a defence against the Arab world on which it lives. The children meet a neighbour's child, Titina, who is altogether pathetic, and because she is of poor family as well, the acquaintanceship lapses. Dionysius and family, of which he is a supposedly unimaginative and therefore odd part, move to Athens, where, because they are impoverished by refugee-relatives from Smyrna and their aunt's old-fashioned colonial insistence on insuring the future by extending charity to the present, Dionysius begins work in an uncle's bank. By chance he meets Titina again, now beautiful, rich, experienced, altogether desirable, with whom he goes to the beach where briefly he loves her. The next day she is to leave for Paris and her protector. Later that evening the boy's aunt, a professor from Paris, arrives and in the course of her mainly aridly abstract conversation, mentions that she has seen Titina, who is, she says, a whore. Dionysius concludes: "As I leaned out of the window, and held up my throat to receive the knife, nothing happened. Only my Aunt Thalia continued playing Schumann, and I realised that my extended throat was itself a stiff sword."[5]

Despite its Alexandrian Greek opening, the story makes no mention of the exile theme. One sees instead a restless household being rude in an enlightened way to those obliged to be polite; one is merely left to infer it, encouraged by the commonsensical Dionysius's narration, to which his ingenuousness gives a sparkle of humour. His character, more civilised than anything around him, establishes and controls the story's single theme. He can confer distinction on a shoddy event, as when he says, "Titina Stavridi withdrew from our lives, to a distance of windows, or balconies."[6] As he tells of his friends already at brothels while he is still chalking "I love" on empty walls before going home to an empty bed, when "The nights were never stained with answers,"[7] we recognise language embodying the interaction between the possible and the actual. We also recognise the truthfulness of response such linguistic discrimination in White's characters always proposes. It is this occasional distinction that prepares us for the final brief intensity of the concluding image, of knife and sword, which serves the same honest purpose as the imagery of resilience in **"Down at the Dump."** That a whore can love, is not an original discovery, but to the man who recognises it for the first time, it is. The atmosphere of discovery, of innocence confirmed by experience, which White communicates so well and characteristically, makes the story valuable in a way his novels are. A thin sharp line is drawn between charity and charitableness, a character created by means of an acute moral perceptiveness.

"A Glass of Tea" is a similar story in that a slightly older but no less commonsensical Alexandrian Greek is faced by an original experience. Unlike Dionysius, Malliakas is aware that he possesses an imagination, but until the ancient Philippides tells him *his* story, he is without even an experience of love on which to exercise it. In other words, Malliakas, like Alf Dubbo in *Riders in the Chariot* is "Neither the actor, nor the spectator, he was that most miserable of human beings, the artist."[8] **"A Glass of Tea"** is White's story of Malliakas's story of Philippides' story of his experience. Whereas Dionysius recognises the worth of his experience by means of moral rectitude, Malliakas recognises the worth of his by means of that imagination Dionysius is said to lack.

In Geneva on business, Malliakas visits Philippides, the older friend of an old friend, and finds him on a summer day in his garden-house drinking tea from a glass. His wife, he explains, is out; he then begins the story of his love for his wife, Constantia. In the course of their lives in Greece and the Levant, a gipsy has foretold that he will die when the last of twelve glasses he owns is broken. Despite their travels and being in Smyrna in 1922 during the Turkish attack, they manage with the help of a peasant maid, Aglaia, to keep some of the glasses. Finally only two remain from which Philippides and his wife are drinking one evening after he has returned from bridge, a game for which Constantia does not care because of the intimacies it encourages. Her passion for her husband develops into a jealousy that suspects not only his bridge partners but her maid, Aglaia. In a temper that is perhaps madness she smashes one of the two remaining glasses, and at least in her husband's narration appears to faint, while feeling, in smashing the glass, that she has killed herself. At this point in the story, Madame Philippides enters the garden in time only to show Malliakas out, who has heard what he thinks the whole story. As she is obviously not the woman Philippides described, he is encouraged to ask about Constantia's death, the second Madame Philippides having told him she has guessed the subject of the old man's conversation. He learns that, on breaking the glass, Constantia jumped from the balcony; and that the present wife is Aglaia, whose one anxiety is for the remaining glass from which her husband has been drinking while telling the story: for if it breaks, she will have nothing left.

One of the finest short-stories in English, despite the injustice any summary is bound to inflict on it, **"A Glass of Tea"** is remarkable in many ways. White moves inside a culture foreign to his language, at the same time using that language to convince us of the foreignness of the culture. Although the frequent ease with which he achieves this becomes familiar, the achievement here is more involuted than on most other occasions. Chios, Smyrna, Athens, Alexandria and Geneva are involved, the differences pointed by a habit, the shape of a house, or the punctuality of a bus, the deft economy reminiscent of *The Aunt's Story.* The same novel comes to mind in the change of personality, or confusion, attributed here to Philippides' failing memory, which strengthens the reader's conviction of the mutualness of the couple's love. Love is also presented in Philippides at least, as an expansive affair of literally a world's extent, its intensity and constancy undiminished by the need for mistresses, or the wife's need for a girl's love of a woman. Nor is it lessened by the wife's careful preparedness to die for a love which only his serenity can threaten.

While the psychology White employs is enormously subtle, the form in which he conveys the story's modernity is correspondingly old. Not only is it a story-within-a-story, its being told at all depends on the prompting of a listener who virtually asks the aged teller, "What happened next?" That it is told in a peaceful garden, by a rich man living frugally in a pastoral atmosphere of sun, lake and mountains, recalls Boccaccio's original short-story, as the glass itself and its related imagery recalls Boccaccio's so-called "Falkenmotiv." The setting throws into relief the violence of a drama which the obviousness of the form insists on containing within the pastness of the past. As Constantia says in an early letter to her absent husband, one "is able to re-live the past without any of the interferences—none of those jagged incidents which continue to strew the present! You may say: What about the jagged incidents of the past? Well, one is no longer cut by them."[9] This compelling orderliness of the past, the logic with which hindsight endows it, is reiterated even in the past's future when the gipsy prophesies that death will follow the breaking of the last glass. That White is aware of the resources he is using to etch even a love story with his own vision is most evident in the prophecy's cadence and repetition: "First you must pull a hair from your chest, and I shall take it, and dance, bare in front and bare behind, amongst the rocks at Ayia Moni."[10]

Although **"A Glass of Tea"** is one of those few perfect short-stories, the existence of which most writers admit as at least a possibility, **"Clay,"** despite its comparable opaque quality, fails to convince the reader of the significance of the experience with which it confronts him. Clay himself, whose name surprisingly puzzles both him and his friends, is moulded by the able hands of his Australian Mum into the shape of the dutiful son, whose father died apparently in escaping such treatment but whose spirit his wife still invokes in her frequent moments of distress. Shortly before his mother's death, Clay is set to work in Her Majesty's Customs and Excise Offices, where he becomes a credit to the institution. After his mother's death, he gratefully marries Marj, who is made in her image. Eventually and diffidently, he rebels by growing his hair long, his mother having always insisted on it being short in an accentuated form of the Australian fashion. Slowly he neglects to notice that he is neglecting his wife, and begins to write, creating out of his mother's wedding photograph and his own dreams a woman called Lova, to attend to whom becomes more important than work or wife. Marj eventually finds him dead in his own room, clutching a wedding-shoe his mother had kept with so much else of a past more interesting than the present. When Marj says she can't believe what has happened, White slides the reader out of dreamland by concluding, "Because everyone knows that what isn't isn't, even when it is."[11]

In part dedicated to Barry Humphries, whose country of Moonee Ponds it covers in many ways, the story begins as a comment on that place's weird matriarchal society; but with Mrs. Flack and Mrs. Jolley in mind, the reader accepts Clay's Mum as at least possible. It is when the story shifts to Clay that if falters. His childhood dreams of the neighbouring sea and its uterine attractions are real, but as they take over his adult life, converting the story itself into fantasy, we lose the reference to those values with which White encouraged us to measure Clay's family and his acceptance of it. Neither, however, does White allow us to take the fantasy seriously. On Marj's announcement to her husband, who is by now dead, that tea is getting cold, the author's laconic comment, so "traditionally" Australian that it recalls Clay's Mum, "That is the way of things", produces a giggled response; but not at Marj's expense. Fantasy, as Kafka showed, need not always be a comic release; but here, where Clay's dreams suggest a similar rejection of a mad world, fantasy is confused with whimsy, a riddle which the oracular wisdom of the last line does not resolve. It is White's most unsatisfactory story, possibly because it suggests a parody of his best.

Another much longer but finally unsatisfactory story is the previously unpublished **"Dead Roses,"** the first story in the collection. It opens for no very obvious reason at a house-party on what is probably Kangaroo Island, off the South Australian coast. There the Tullochs, amiable, fecund, and nonchalantly rich enough to withstand, perhaps to need, the occasional rigour of holiday-shack life, entertain their university colleagues and friends, among whom is an acquaintance, Anthea Scudamore. She is a young Adelaide girl who is clearly, and possibly intended to be, ill-at-ease amidst so much amiability, fecundity, and nonchalance. Telephoning her social-climbing mother each evening and by day fending off the not altogether unwelcome attentions of the braw and single Doctor Flegg, she returns home dutifully and thankfully when her mother conveniently injures herself. By design she meets her ineffectual father's gay but elderly friend of former years, Hessell Mortlock, of Sarsparilla, whom she marries. Despite the indications of his name, she is as surprised as the reader to find him a mean, deadening capitalist, quite unlike the Tullochs, whose wealth came with their wit. She battles on courageously for years, symbolically trudging up hills harnessed to a barrow-load of horse-dung, her husband driving, as it were. Suddenly learning of a second wife who left him as precipitately as the first, she returns to her mother, by this time the widow of a suicide; and as suddenly, she learns that her husband, on his way to alter his will in another's favour, has died, leaving her sole legatee. After some heart-search alone in the Tulloch's island shack—for by chance she has met the wife, who is as she ever was—she decides to contest her shadowy sister-in-law's claims on the Mortlock millions. She wins the case, and with the money begins her travels. In Greece she by chance meets the amiable, fecund but impoverished academic, Doctor Flegg, surrounded by his children and garish ex-beauty-queen wife. She refers to her times on the island, and embarrasses him, so she leaves to walk along the beach, where she is approached by a young Greek whose intentions she suspects, and panics, outrunning him utterly. She then decides to return home.

The point of the story is posed by the Tullochs: what does Anthea Scudamore want from life? does she know? will she get it? Academic opinion is that she will. The reader notices that she is a fearful, frigid woman to whom riches are love's tepid substitute, which she acquires through coincidence rather than courage. As with Waldo Brown in *The Solid Mandala,* White is interested in her predicament, but unsympathetic towards her, first making her young and silly, and then older, so that her predicament remains as unchanged as she. There is no tension, of possibility tugging against probability. The shape of the story is dictated by coincidence which resolves the gentle complications of the prosaic world she inhabits. The passage of time is suggested only by the story's length: the Tullochs are unchangeable, so is Anthea.

The second story in the collection, **"Willy-Wagtails by Moonlight,"** does not attempt to raise or answer problems, but briefly and simply surprises the reader into acknowledging that there is more in a dull character than meets the eye even of his friends. The Wheelers visit the Mackenzies, who are newly rich and still embarrassed about it. They are in time to see Mackenzie's dowdy secretary leaving the house, where she has been helping her boss, whose firm she is said to run. As a mark of their having moved from colour-slides to Sydney's North Shore, the Mackenzies entertain their guests with tape-recordings of birdsongs they have heard. During the dull evening, which in the story is established by the sharper Wheelers' comments to one another, Arch Mackenzie cuts his hand on a lamp-globe his wife has asked him to change and calls her to attend to it. Correctly sociable in a North Shore way, she plays her guests a tape she does not know of Willy-wagtails singing at night, while she is out of the room. As well as the bird-song, it has recorded the drunken revelries of Arch Mackenzie seducing his compliant secretary. The Mackenzies return to the room in time to hear the concluding beauties of the bird song, which is enough to indicate to Mackenzie at least that his guests have heard more than they should have done. An offer of drinks re-establishes the level of polite dullness on which the Mackenzies normally live, by choice it would seem, but in fact from necessity.

In order that the surprise should work, the story depends on the coincidence of Arch Mackenzie's absence and his wife's choosing just this tape to play; yet it arises naturally out of the two characters themselves. She is a harmless, helpless woman, frightened of sex as a girl, Mrs Wheeler recalls, unadventurous as a cook, and daunted by the material manifestations of her husband's happy stumbling on experience. As the young girl flickers to life in her friend's memory, she grows into the woman who would await her husband's convenience to tell him a lamp needs replacing, and bandage him when he bled from grasping too hard an experience too hot to hold. Nor would she forget to entertain guests with his hobby, which, as one of them guesses, she has learnt to love out of a sense of duty.

Besides its quality of being psychologically intact, the story exhibits a structural irony. Mrs Mackenzie's characteristically pacifying remark, "A little alcohol releases the vitality," which she makes on her guest's early joke with her husband about the need to have a drink while the host finishes showering, is not only in itself ironic: a "little" is all she has offered them, and her vitality is not strong enough ever to need release; it as well comments on the later boozy seduction scene the tape has recorded, and on everyone's final lame struggle against embarrassment.

Because the setting is Sydney North Shore and the comment on suburbia's new-rich so agreeably exact, **"Willy-Wagtails by Moonlight"** suggests one of the limitations of Sarsparilla as a microcosm of modern Australia. While an Australian country town turned suburb, such as we know Sarsparilla to be, can plausibly include almost all manner of characters, it seems too small to have what estate-agents call desirable and most-desirable residential areas. Social comment that depends on this difference must move, like the large social group to which the Mackenzies belong, into the city, as for instance happened in *Riders in the Chariot*: the Rosetrees are North Shore people. The inference is that White will in future extend his fictional locale to proportions resembling those of Faulkner's Yoknapatawpha County, in order to comment on that major social group which, unlike George Brown in *The Solid Mandala,* is actually given Head Office and distinguishes its members one from another by their addresses. Sarsparilla, so far as we know it, is the kind of place to which people go to die, with whatever measure of grace is in them. It is not an address to excite envious friends.

The splendidly-titled **"Miss Slattery and her Demon Lover,"** for instance, is a story dealing with two members of that society to which Australia House most often brings out a Briton. Miss Slattery, a door-to-door pollster for Better Sales Pty. Ltd., in the course of business, meets Tibor Szabo, or Szabo Tibor as he explains it would be in his native Hungary. He enjoys a sybaritic opulence to which, in the course of the interview, he adds Miss Slattery, without ever making her feel he considers her a match for it. In Australia, he tells her, "zere is nossing," and despite her claim that Australia in 1961 is at least civilised, promises, or threatens to teach her what civilisation really means. The distinction is seminal to the story. Loving his ardour as much as his possessions—a Jaguar car, marble floors, a mink bedspread, the so-important view of Sydney harbour, and a mirror on the ceiling above the bed below—she wonders, sometimes in his hearing, about marriage, while he sets aside two evenings a week for her. As a token of that civilisation to which he has raised her, she takes him to what he anticipates is an "Australian-bohemian-proveenshul" party given by a lady who sculpted *Hypotenuse of Angst.* Suddenly Miss Slattery finds herself freed from her love for him by the lucidity it has given her. She borrows a stockwhip from "'the crummiest crack'" of a grazier, and recalling her outback childhood, plays it across Tibor. During the rest of the story he responds to the crack of a whip with that love he has previously withheld, which she no longer wants, or needs.

She is able, as she says, to leave the little fat man and his civilisation for that of thin Australians and washing-machines.

The story is a variation on White's theme of character-exchange, transferred experience bringing about a transfer of independence. The situation is taut with the irony of two civilisations, half in conflict, a thrifty version of Australia's post-war relations with her immigrants, and through them with the outside world. White does not take sides in this disputatious love. He is content to hint at the pathos in the situation, slowly evolving through the development of the characters as they tangle with experience, the irony tautened by the comments of Miss Slattery's friends and her own increasingly astringent response. When for instance Miss Whimble remarks at the party that "there are two men locked in the lavatory together. One is a teddy, but they haven't worked out who the other can be," she briefly suggests he is a social-realist. The result of the cumulative irony and the underlying pathos is that at the centre of the story the previously comic *Hypotenuse of Angst* sparkles with possible associations, so that it becomes the symbol its pretentious creator thought it was.

Though without such physical presence, *Angst* is the theme of **"The Letters,"** set in Sarsparilla, "the friendly suburb" as it is called in **"A Cheery Soul,"** to which retire many of White's characters who are elderly by years or inclination. Mrs Polkinghorn, widowed, lives there with her son, Charles, whose fiftieth birthday she is proposing to celebrate. After a comparatively successful Cambridge career, he has returned to Australia at his mother's motherly prompting to prepare to take over the family firm. Instead, over the years, despite his godmother's friendship, his paranoia increases until, hearing of his godmother's likely death, he is comforted by his mother, which releases the spring that has held him back from a complete return to infantilism. As he nuzzles her breast in search of the original darkness of the babyhood she has always tried to perpetuate in him, she throws off what she calls her "unnatural child."

While the irony of her final refusal confirms the irony of the situation, in which the mother feels herself to be in many ways younger than her ageing son, as in **"Miss Slattery and Her Demon Lover," "The Letters"** is most immediately impressive for its spare but compelling evocation of the paranoia of fear. Charles' terror of Time coalesces round letters he refuses to open, for as a child he had been told not to open letters, because of what he might learn to his discomfort; but the letters in adulthood are not only reminders of a childhood experience as well as the responsibilities of manhood. They also demand replies and epitomise Time's progression; and in their enclosedness they become the externalisation of his fear. Which is to say, they are a true symbol, the nexus of both cause and effect, shaping the story and our response.

"Down at the Dump" is about the other two-thirds of Sarsparilla society, the Whalley family who scavenge rubbish-tips for odds and ends that only require a change of owner to become useful again; and the Hogbens, who, like Mrs. Flack and Mrs. Jolley, disapprove of all who do not conform to their own faith in being seen to conform. Linking the two is Mrs Hogben's recently dead sister, Daise Morrow, to the Hogbens a whore, and to those who knew her well a woman of sustaining love. Their names indicate White's attitude to them—the whale-of-a-time, Whalleys, the hogpen Hogbens, and the day's morrow or morning.

They are brought more or less together by Daise's funeral, to which Councillor Hogben is accompanying his wife and daughter Meg. Their neighbours, the Whalleys, including their eldest son Lum, are scavenging the Sarsparilla dump next to the cemetery. While his feckless parents drink, quarrel and make love, Lum Whalley wanders into the surrounding scrub where he meets Meg Hogben. She has similarly wandered away from her parents, who contrive to be both dutifully bereaved at Daise's enforced absence and characteristically grieved at Ossie Coogan's unnecessary presence, Ossie being the dead-beat to whom Daise extended her last kindness. Against this background of parental hypocrisy and anarchic honesty, the two adolescents tentatively explore each other's dreams, which their parents have hitherto kept bleakly apart. Lum hopes to become a long-distance lorry-driver and leave Sarsparilla; Meg hopes to write a poem in memory of her favourite aunt, who has already left. As experience marks him, Lum's hopes of a manly mateship with his hero, Darkie, aspire to a seemly domesticity which Meg for him incarnates. She, influenced by her aunt's memory, sees herself as the loving companion to his roaming. As they kiss, they are interrupted by their parents, who drag them back into their severed worlds which, White is saying, are without tenderness and therefore merely approximate to the inviting dreams of adulthood the two children have formed round each other. What he calls "the warm core of certainty" Daise and Ossie experienced, is as briefly theirs.

Like the early parts of *The Tree of Man,* the story encompasses great compassion and earthy comedy, as well as the incisive comment of *Riders in the Chariot* and *The Solid Mandala* on those spiritually dead. Organised round the symbols of cemetery and dump, it resembles a *collage,* in which the dead and useless is enforced to contribute to life's constantly renewed permanence. Even in that Australia whose austere beauty man has often dirtied, the process goes on:

> Here and there it appeared as though trash might win. The onslaught of metal was pushing the scrub into the gulley. But in many secret, steamy pockets, a rout was in progress: seeds had been sown in the lumps of grey, disintegrating kapok and the laps of burst chairs, the coils of springs, locked in the spirals of wirier vines, had surrendered to superior resilience. Somewhere on the edge of the whole shambles a human ally, before retiring, had lit a fire, which by now the green had almost choked, leaving a stench of smoke to compete with the sicklier one of slow corruption.[12]

Placed centrally, the passage not only confirms the assertion of life the rest of the story propounds through character, it also illustrates by means of a variation of tempo and constancy of imagery the way in which a junk-heap can miniature the wider war between nature and human nature. The mention of nature's "human ally" refers us to this metallic but ungolden age in which the gods themselves stand again in need of Promethean help. The reference immediately enhances the pastoral quality of Meg and Lum's first discovery of love. Meg, garlanded with memories of her aunt's carnations, becomes Euterpe herself, and Lum, who "walked with a grace of which he had himself never been aware," momentarily a young god. The protégées of Daise Morrow and Darkie flood the story with a compelling light to establish it as one of White's finest achievements.

The story, however, by which he is best known, because it has been seen as a play on stage and television, is **"A Cheery Soul."** Its locale is again Sarsparilla, its main character and most of its minor characters elderly, its setting an old people's home, Sundown Home, a name sufficiently near "sundowner" to indicate White's view of the attitude of those who put old people there. Miss Docker stays first with the Custances, who invite her as a challenge to their kindness. Exhausting them, she moves to the home where Mrs Brown of *The Solid Mandala* ended her days. Taunting their present with photographs of her past, she sets out to entertain the inmates, not entirely without success. One with whom she fails, the aristocratic Mrs Lillie, is a former acquaintance whose husband Miss Docker nursed—to death, his wife believes. In a flashback, we see Miss Docker politely angled out of her place in Mr Lillie's funeral cortège by the impoverished widow and her well-connected friends. At Sundown Home Miss Docker returns Mrs Lillie the humiliation by means of photographs and the insinuation that she, Miss Docker, was Mr Lillie's favourite. White then compounds the atmosphere of cruelty—which is only partially presented as the result of Miss Docker's Christian selflessness; we are aware from his comments of the element of spite in her—by taking up the story of the Reverend Wakeman, who conducted Mr Lillie's burial service. Miss Docker is almost the only remaining pillar of his church. She attempts to correct this fact by telling him his faults as a preacher, thereby also explaining it. These faults he only too keenly recognises; though through his wife he suspects he is not entirely to blame. In an almost empty church, he tries to preach, pointedly, on the sin of goodness, becomes tied in his own rhetoric, and finds himself arguing with Miss Docker. The strain of his life, of which only his wife knows, is finally too much for him; he collapses in the pulpit. His wife's cry, "Miss Docker, you have killed my saint. Only time will show whether you have killed my God as well"[13] is the harrowing equivalent of Mrs Lillie's wordless distress. Miss Docker leaves for home, on the way trying to make friends with a dog, which wets her. Her conclusion, and that of the story, is that she saw for the first time that dog is God spelt backwards, a realisation she will never share because, as she says, she is "not the kind to spread despondency, encourage grief."

Described on the dust-cover of ***The Burnt Ones*** as "straightforwardly funny," **"A Cheery Soul"** is not straightforward in any way. Its comedy is certainly repetitive, as it arises from Miss Docker's directness and misplaced goodness. Only when showing her photographs to Mrs Lillie does she seem more than a one-dimensional humour. The distress her spite causes, when juxtaposed with Mrs Lillie's recollection of her own love for her husband, produces a plangent sadness, which Mrs Wakeman's cry echoes. Mrs Wakeman's response, however, is occasioned by Miss Docker's directness, so that its effect is weakened by its association with the story's prevailing comicality, itself the result of that same cause. The Reverend Wakeman himself, martyr that he is to his own ineffectuality, does appear a "stuttering stage clergyman"[14] because of this same comedy of humours Miss Docker represents, despite White's urgent instruction in the play that he should not. Mr and Mrs Custance, whose embarrassment occupies the first of the story's three parts, disappear as soon as their usefulness as butts is exhausted. Similarly Mrs Lillie and her nameless friends leave without a trace when the story moves into the church. The conclusion, whose facetiousness might have amused Samuel Butler, is here at once so hoary and inconsequentially neat and earnest as to bemuse the reader as much as it enlightens Miss Docker. In the play of this story, White removes some of the difficulties, but in doing so unfortunately introduces as many more.

Notes

1. F.P., p.15
2. *B.O.*, p. 282.
3. *B.O.*, p. 273.
4. *B.O.*, p. 260.
5. *B.O.*, p. 205.
6. *B.O.*, p. 196.
7. *B.O.*, p. 197.
8. *R.C.*, p. 407.
9. *B.O.*, p. 103.
10. *B.O.*, p. 92.
11. *B.O.*, p. 133.
12. *B.O.*, p. 295.
13. *B.O.*, p. 185.
14. *F.P.*, p. 211.

Eudora Welty (review date 1975)

SOURCE: A review of *The Cockatoos*, in *The New York Times Book Review*, January 19, 1975, pp. 4, 37.

[*In the following review, Welty discusses how the six short stories in* The Cockatoos *have similar themes involving characters who "come to a point of discovery" by confronting their problems.*]

These [the stories in ***The Cockatoos***] are six stories (a few are short novels) to do with lives often driven or hopeless, but what they are ultimately about is what might have been. They bring together the possibilities and the impossibilities of human relationships. They happen in Australia, Egypt, Sicily, Greece, where they go off like cannons fired over some popular, scenic river—depth charges to bring up the drowned bodies. Accidentally set free by some catastrophe, general or personal—war, starvation, or nothing more than a husband's toothache—Patrick White's characters come to a point of discovery. It might be, for instance, that in overcoming repugnancies they are actually yielding to some far deeper attraction; the possibilities of a life have been those very things once felt as its dangers. Or they may learn, in confronting moral weakness in others, some flaw in themselves they've never suspected, still more terrifying.

The common barriers of sex, age, class, nationality *can* in uncommon hands operate as gates, which open (for White's characters) to experience beyond anything yet traveled, hope of which may have beckoned from earliest years and gone ignored, only haunting dreams and spoiling the day at hand. Passing us through these barriers is what Mr. White is doing in his writing.

All these stories are studies of ambiguities, of which the greatest is sex. In **"A Woman's Hand,"** a long-married couple, traveling after the husband's retirement find themselves rather peculiarly put back in touch with two old friends out of their respective pasts—a man for him, a woman for her—representing to each a different turn than had offered itself to their young lives. The wife's wifely solution is simple and disastrous (her bothersome guilt for her own inadequacy is set at rest if she can rearrange other people's lives): instead of letting these two make things awkward, why not marry the misfits off to each other?

This is the longest (86 pages) and in some ways the most sinister of Mr. White's stories treating of the realities and the unrealities of developing human relationships. It is highly symbolic, presided over by peacocks. (According to fable, a peacock's flesh is incorruptible, which made it a symbol of the Resurrection; here it assumes the meaning of liberation from captivity.) In this story, too, the irony lies most clearly in the fact that the true and guiding relationships of our lives—for whatever inhibiting reasons—may never achieve the reality credited the ones that are acknowledged and binding but remain superficial and daunting.

"The Full Belly," a short novel laid in Athens during the German Occupation, takes us deep into the humiliations and terrible intimacies of starving to death as a family: the excruciating pressures of competing unselfishness, the demanding self-sacrifice. Aunt Pronoë radiates a "kind of hectic gaiety" as they dine off boiled dandelions. Aunt Maro takes to her bed, declining ever to eat or drink again: "Remember the children. Who am I to deny them food?" The young boy in question is a musical prodigy, with his ticket to Paris still at the bottom of his handkerchief drawer; he goes on practicing ("play to me, Costika," says the determined martyr, "music is more nourishing than food") and sees everything "with a vividness which only sickness or hunger kindles." Away from the house, there are the temptations coming out of doorways and the cautionary sights lying in the gutters: one old woman greedy for a boy's hand in her bosom—she'd give him a fresh egg; the next old woman lying dead in her decent dress with her emptied purse beside her and her shoes already taken from her feet.

Hunger and shame merge into a single monster. A terrible scene in front of Aunt Maro on her dying day spoils her victory for her: the boy and Aunt Pronoë come to desperate grappling over the plate of sacrificial rice lying untouchable before the icon, struggling together, smashing the plate and losing it all; then Costa is down on the carpet. "If only the few surviving grains. Sometimes fluff got in. Or a coarse thread. He licked the grains. He sucked them up. The splinters of porcelain cutting his lips. The good goo. The blood running. Even blood was nourishment."

"Five-Twenty" is the time a certain car passes in the traffic line every afternoon. The scene is a front porch where sits an aging and childless married couple, a man, now an invalid in a wheel chair and imperious as ever, and his wife, a plain woman whose marriage has been one long deprivation of love, which she has taught herself to handle as best she can; she finds it easier now, being a nurse. She fastens on the 5:20 car as something to watch for and point out: it makes her day. Inevitably, the strands converge. It happens down on the garden path, after the husband leaves her a widow. A flower garden like hers, that's been overtended, and a love like hers, that's gone unnourished too long, may burst out alike into the overwhelming and monstrous.

The characters in most of these stories are men and women whose predicaments are rooted in their pasts, to whom fresh pressure is put by the predicaments of growing old. In **"The Night the Prowler,"** we are plunged into the world of a 17-year-old girl whose state of being has everything to do with today. When Felicity is raped, she hadn't been afraid; she'd even hoped something real and revealing might be going to occur, but the rapist is a failure and pathetic. She sees that her conventional parents, in the shock of what's happened, think mostly of themselves and that the conventional boy she's been about to marry is relieved to get his ring back, and enters into a secret life of her own. Beginning by breaking in and wreaking havoc on a house near hers and like hers, she goes on the loose into the city night with its derelicts, drunks and hoods. She remains alone, roaming the park kicking at lovers, accusing and punishing all the world, shouting up at God "for holding out on me," calling out only to others like herself for guidance, so they can give each other "the strength to face ugliness in any form," which might offer some kind of revelation. She herself becomes the night the prowler. As we see her "whirling in the air above her head a bicycle chain she had won from a mob of leather-jackets," she is like some saint-to-be of the Troubled Young. This story, with all the rawness of today in it, is not without its old progenitors. Felicity's progress through the scarifying world of Sydney nightlife is also a path of self-mortification. She is divested of that pride too; when she comes in the final scene to an abandoned house and finds there a naked, diseased, dirty, solitary old man lying on a mattress at point of death, she has her revelation. It is a stunning story.

A middle-aged Australian couple is on holiday, in **"Sicilian Vespers,"** when the husband gets stuck in their hotel with toothache. Ivy would will herself to feel the pain for him; she believes in the efficacy of love, but suspecting her husband (with his "honest un-Sicilian eyes") believes in it only theoretically. She doesn't confess it to him: "She did not want to damage his affection for her: it was too precious." She is held back in her life, too, by a ghost out of her girlhood riding with her still—father. There seems nothing for it but a deliberate act of adultery with a repugnant American (another hotel guest). In the Cathedral of San Fabrizio, she drags him from the crowd into a side chapel and down onto the marble floor.

If nearly all the stories do end up on the floor, it is, after all, the natural place for humiliation, degradation, lust, despair and hunger to reach their limit. **"The Cockatoos"** does not—it ends with a smell of cake.

A flock of wild cockatoos makes a descent upon a residential neighborhood, alighting first at one house, then another, arousing jealousies, coveting, intent to murder, and other things, even causing a husband and wife who haven't spoken for years in the same house to break silence—"trapped into comforting each other," they fall into bed "with laughing mouth on mouth." The characters are wayward, rather than driven. Passions fly thick and fast but in a neighborhood level, like the cockatoos themselves, selecting the house they'd like to visit and making their choice of feeding places, setting up no more than a neighborhood commotion.

"The Cockatoos," the only story here that's a comedy, is also the only one in which the sexual aggressor is a man. As Mick (the husband who doesn't speak to his wife) sits straddling the lady who lives down the street (it's Busby LeCornu, who waits for him every day leaning on her gate, and the only time he puts on a hat is to walk through it), they exchange these words—the subject of course, is the cockatoos:

> "See here Busby . . . I didn't tell you about me birds to have you seduce um away from me."
>
> She sighed from within the crook of her arm. "I don't see why we can't share what doesn't belong to either of us."
>
> He was already getting back into his clothes. "The wife would be disappointed," he said.

Sheldon Frank (review date 1975)

SOURCE: "Nobelity Without Authenticity," in *The National Observer,* Vol. 14, No. 4, January 25, 1975, p. 21.

[*In the following negative assessment of White's fiction, Frank deems White's short stories "disappointing," arguing that while they exhibit a "verbal richness" and "psychological acumen," they feature characters who never seem real and plots that "verge on melodrama."*]

The Nobel Prize for Literature has often been a suspect award. Writers have frequently been honored not for their literary greatness, but for their moral courage (Pasternak, Solzhenitsyn) or for their good fortune in coming from a country that had not yet had a winner in this most famous of literary sweepstakes.

No one can deny that in their desire to honor literature, morality, *and* nationalism, the Nobel committee has at times immortalized some deservedly neglected authors. (Remember that of the six Americans to receive the prize, three were Sinclair Lewis, John Steinbeck, and Pearl Buck.) On the other hand, though, in recent years truly great writers like Samuel Beckett and Pablo Neruda have also been singled out by the sages of Stockholm. Which all means that you never know with the Nobel Prize; maybe the winner is the genuine article, maybe another dud.

Patrick White is the Australian who won the prize in 1973. Few people I knew had ever heard of White; fewer still had ever read him. Was he being honored merely for being Australian, or was he in fact a great novelist carelessly neglected by our provincial selves? History, of course, will render the final judgment, but for now it appears to me that nationalism, not literature, was being honored. While White is no mere chronicler of convicts, kangaroos, and koala bears, neither is he a modern master. He is a serious novelist with serious limitations.

No Astonishment

White was awarded the Nobel for his immense novels about Australia, cited for his "epic and psychological narrative art . . . and a wrestling with the language in order to extract all its power." And, indeed, the novels are difficult, even exhausting to read. The prose is verbally dense and complex; each paragraph, each sentence demands careful attention. The characters are described with a rare degree of psychological detail. But where the Nobel committee discerns epic power, I find only highly skilful, often ponderous melodrama. For this reader, White's complexity seems willed and unnecessary; his sculpted prose turns turgid; and his characters, however well-portrayed, remain case studies. Despite all the obvious intelligence and sophisticated craft in his novels, they never convince or astonish.

White's short stories are equally disappointing. ***The Cockatoos*** is a collection of six recent ones, ranging from the novella-length **"A Woman's Hand"** to the 20-page **"The Full Belly."** Again one finds a verbal richness and psychological acumen, but they are still coupled with characters that never seem quite real or alive and plots that verge on melodrama. White has learned all the lessons of the modern short-story masters except how to make his fiction come to life.

A typical Patrick White story involves the unusual or the unexpected in the course of an ordinary life. A retired couple meet a long-forgotten friend, with consequences that shake their apparently settled lives. Another married couple, vacationing in Sicily, have their lives disturbed by the husband's toothache, leaving the wife available for a bizarre sexual escapade. In the title story, a group of beautiful cockatoos settle on a family's lawn, and around their appearance and disappearance a number of lives are altered or rearranged. In all of these stories something out-of-the-ordinary disrupts the customary routines of living; the characters are flooded with memories of past pains and disappointments; old wounds are reopened. In the end the unexpected event has either destroyed, changed, or merely redirected the characters' accustomed ways, quotidian reality regains its power, and the characters continue to muddle through.

The Unordinary Ordinary

White has a superb eye and ear for the social conventions that give coherence to our lives, especially for the half-truths and unspoken proprieties that make marriage endurable. And he is equally sensitive to the private terror and confusion hidden behind these public decencies. He knows that ordinary people are never really ordinary: They may live conventional lives, but they still seethe because life has delivered so much less than it promised.

If White has such manifest talents for understanding our reluctant compromises with growing up and growing old, why is ***The Cockatoos*** so unsatisfying? Well, a great psychiatrist is not necessarily a great writer of fiction, and White's characters are simply never engaging enough. Despite the wealth of psychological detail lavished upon them, they remain mere manikins onto which his insights are draped, locked into plots that are strained and arbitrary, leading lives that offer the appearance of authenticity but not the substance of it.

John Alfred Avant (review date 1975)

SOURCE: A review of *The Cockatoos*, in *The New Republic,* Vol. 172, No. 12, 1975, pp. 23-4.

[*In the following review, Avant maintains that the short story form "demands immediate rapport between artist and audience; and White, the most austere of modern novelists, isn't an intimate writer."*]

White is a master of the novel. At his best he draws us in, but only so far: the vise that grips the reader is carefully distanced, and that distance can provide an oracular power. But the short story is a form that demands immediate rapport between artist and audience; and White, the most austere of modern novelists, isn't an intimate writer. The stories in his early collection ***The Burnt Ones*** are either whimsical, with O. Henry twists and lovable Greeks talking in English except for occasional italicized Greek words, or portentous without delivering. ***The Cockatoos,*** a new collection of novellas and stories, shows White trying to shape the short form to his own special gifts rather than degrading those gifts by trying to be cozy. The title story and two others, **"Sicilian Vespers"** and **"Five-Twenty,"** are too attenuated to hold much interest; but the rest, although one doesn't necessarily *like* them, command attention.

"The Night the Prowler" rings changes on that hoary motif, the victim who is actually the victimizer. Felicity, the proper daughter of proper parents and engaged to a proper diplomat, longs to be mastered by brute male strength. When prowler tries to rape her, he turns out to be a slimy weakling whom she forces to submit to her ravenous desires. After staging a rape as an out from her dull engagement, she goes on orgies of destruction. If she can't find a man who is up to her, she'll vent her anger on the possessions that the respectable hide behind. She becomes a housebreaker, not to rob but to destroy, and achieves a garish release in disfiguring expensive chairs, mounting them as though they were centaurs: "Riding their thick thighs, still slashing, sawing at the mouth which held the bit, she was to some extent vindicated, if guiltily racked by the terrible spasms which took possession of her." White completes Felicity's appalling liberation by taking her through a capsule version of the ages of man; and if he strips her of some humanity by making her a device, he rounds his grotesque fable into a bearably comic one.

"The Full Belly," about a family of starving Greek aristocrats during the German occupation, isn't quite bearable. Although White's prose has never been more razor-sharp, he uses it to slice his characters to bits. When hunger is unsatisfied, the spirit corrodes, and these Greeks turn into vipers. They are the reverse of Voss, whose spirit expands as his flesh falls away. I think that White intended us to sense our own atavistic potentiality in the family's dehumanization, but what we sense is that the author loathes his characters. White has compressed his grimmest personal vision into 20 pages—a feat of storytelling, but the compulsive read seems an eternity.

The opening novella, **"A Woman's Hand,"** is less accessible and, perhaps for that reason, not nearly so repellent. I shuddered at the central figure a frigid busybody wife who brings about a marriage that leads to insanity and death. She appears throughout White's work in one form or another, and he clearly despises her. Although I'm not sure what **"A Woman's Hand"** is supposed to be about and don't understand the motivations, and although I suspect that White shares my uncertainties, the novella is riveting. White has gone further with one of his stylistic specialties: prose rhythms that provide equivalents for the characters' hang-ups and eruptions into madness, eruptions that the reader can only partially intuit. The madness in **"A Woman's Hand"** is never clarified; it's suggested by the insane friend's perception of ocean sunsets as blazing peacocks, emblems of a voluptuous redemption that is unattainable. White has taken the most lucid passages of madness from *The Aunt's Story* into pure impressionism. He almost succeeds, because his subliminally erotic imagery, tinged with religious elements, pulls one in although the imagery has nothing coherent behind it.

It's a measure of White's artistry that ***The Cockatoos,*** flawed and disturbing as it is, makes one eager to see what he will do next. But the short form is not, and probably never will be, the best showcase for his genius. Since White is now a Nobel winner, many readers are eager to encounter his work for the first time and may imagine that a new story collection is a good introduction. ***The Cockatoos,*** although it should be read, isn't the ideal starting point. It will tantalize some; others need to respond to the breadth of vision in the major, novels before they approach these strange but impressive minor works.

Patrick White's procession of novels is majestic; no other living novelist in English is so consistently audacious or writes on such a large scale. In America only pulp novelists like Michener are interested in full-dress productions. White, a serious artist, has given us *Voss,* a historical epic of Tolstoyan proportions; and his work ranges from the spacious epic to the fiercely introverted writhings of his new book, ***The Cockatoos.*** We are drawn to White's heroic writing even when he puts us off. His satiric dialogue can be overly vicious, as in *Riders in the Chariot*; and his schematized conceptions cripple a poor novel like *The Living and the Dead* and mar one of his best, *The Solid Mandala.* His hatred of his characters reaches a culmination in ***The Cockatoos.*** But White is full of surprises. He follows his worst novel, *The Vivisector,* which loads an overheated Passion Play tone onto a standard tortured-artist story of the Irving Stone variety, with *The Eye of the Storm,* a serenely visionary work in which his prose reaches new heights.

In the seven-year hiatus between his false starts (*Happy Valley* and *The Living and the Dead*) and the appearance of *The Aunt's Story,* White began developing his prose, a mixture of the tangy, lazy rhythms of Australian diction and glittering bursts of imagery that sometimes emerge from the text with a beautiful naturalness, sometimes with a shock that is like a slap in the reader's face—a prose style both precise and flexible. Speaking voices overlap into description; and points of view can be separated by slight modulations in one brief scene, even in one paragraph. Pitch is heightened by minor chord changes from sentence to sentence, from phrase to phrase. The prose daringly calls attention to itself in such passages as the German housekeeper's cabaret act before her painted death-doll mistress in *The Eye of the Storm,* or the aged Waldo's preening in his dead mother's ball gown in *The Solid Mandala.* These scenes are incomparable pieces of stage direction, but White provides everything—actors and props aren't needed. (Oddly, his plays are hopelessly "literary" and derivative, while his fiction is miraculously scenic.)

In *The Aunt's Story* White rearranges the pieces of an Australian spinster's mind as though they were chips in a mosaic. Although he doesn't entirely control his effects, parts of the novel even today read like a breakthrough. Unfortunately the middle section is a stiffly self-conscious nightmare-reverie, possibly modeled after "Nighttown" in *Ulysses,* in which Theodora is supposed to be crossing over into madness. White records the tiny alterations in Theodora's perceptions of reality without resorting to conventional explanations and metaphors for insanity.

The Tree of Man, unlike *The Aunt's Story,* has no obvious experimentation. It's an Australian farm saga told, for White, as simply as possible. A basic fallacy creeps in: because of the Parkers' poverty, White grants them a wholeness he denies his more affluent characters. But this epic of the soil avoids most Pearl Buck overtones by the power of the images; the fire and flood are White's first great descriptive scenes. Another important factor in White's growth as an imaginative artist first appears: the view of Australia as a primordially unshaped, almost mythic continent. The transportation of the first convicts is like Lucifer cast into hell; and the natural disasters in *The Tree of Man* are plagues, manifestations of divine wrath at those who would try to shape the wilderness.

The great part of Australia is still unshaped today; in the last century the land outside the few settled areas held untold terrors. White's 19th-century explorer Johann Voss, the epic figure of his next novel, meets the divine wrath head on in the hinterland, with its aborigines and their sacred death rituals in which civilized man is the natural sacrifice. What White does in *Voss* is immense: the cross-cutting between the disintegrating expedition and Sydney's balls and picnics, the sensual evocation of colonial life in the 1840s, the supple dialogue that flashes into epigrams, the suffering of Voss, the love between him and Laura Trevelyan (one of the strongest woman characters in modern fiction)—a love that is cerebral and spiritual rather than sexual, a love that is Voss' salvation and lifts the novel out of despair into celebration. *Voss* is one of those rare novels that pulls the reader up successive peaks of intensity until he emerges, purged, at the top. The book is completely achieved, despite a typical last White touch: a trivializing epilogue that neatly wraps up all the narrative threads that might better have been left free.

Voss is the last of White's straight narratives. The later novels, except for *The Vivisector,* form a trilogy of symbolic works. Instead of archetypal characters, like Voss and the Parkers, White gives us characters who are extensions of another kind of archetype—a risky attempt for a novelist, but White has never been one to avoid risks. Each novel's title is the governing metaphor. *Riders in the Chariot,* the least successful, presents four characters, various examples of the earth's wretched, who will finally ride in triumph in the apocalyptic chariot of fire. The riders are joined by tenuous plot linkages, and White uses them questionably. One is a tubercular black painter, another is a Jew crucified by working-class louts (the religious symbolism tries one's patience). The oppressed will be victors by virtue of their oppression; and, although White wastes no sympathy on the oppressors, the novel seems erotically attracted to them. Does White really like his miserable creatures, or does he only think he should? *Riders in the Chariot* is split down the middle; but it has powerful scenes, such as the Jew's recollection of the death camps (with White's characteristic connections between violent death and sex, connections that increase the horror), and curious exchanges, that suggest Jane Bowles, between bizarrely matched couples drawn together by mutual freakishness.

White, whose fiction is rarely far from the feel of flesh, can't get his winged chariot to soar. He does much better with earthbound symbols: the storm's eye, and the mandala, which is an ordering of chaos, not a transcendence of it. *The Solid Mandala* is a glass marble, a child's toy, with twin strands of color that in different lights twist and untwist in colors that blind and illuminate. The "solid mandalas" are named by Arthur Brown, the "deficient" twin, the man of "spirit," to the derision of his twin Waldo, the desperate intellectual, the man of "reason." White clearly wants to be on Arthur's side; and this spirit/reason duality, this division of the whole man into warring twins, creates suspicions that the novel harbors an intellectual self-hatred. But White carries this duality to visionary status. The Browns' story is told first from Waldo's view, in terse, stifled prose that gradually burns with an insane rage. It is then retold from Arthur's view, and here the rhythms uncoil and our recognition of the horrible release that must follow comes full circle. Symbol and character are fused; we and the Browns and the mandala are one. The twin lives that wind together in torture loosen in beauty. One thinks of Bernard's speech to Susan in *The Waves*: "Words, moving darkly, in the depths of your mind will break up this knot of hardness, screwed in your pocket-handkerchief."

The Solid Mandala probes further beneath the surface of human frailty than any other White novel. *The Eye of the Storm*—about a dying woman, once a great beauty and sexual monster, and those who wait for her to die is a panoramic view, suggesting what is underneath by resonant language and juxtaposition of shifting time and place. The themes are highly charged: the helplessness with which we anticipate death, the shame of old age and the body's ugly tyranny (the imagery, as George Steiner notes, is largely fecal), the ways that recollections of sex and sexual failure and continuing desires push us into collision with others, who are pursued by their own demons. This is the most highly plotted of White's works, and some of the subplots are embarrassments; but the plotting advances the action only slightly. The plots principally serve as supporting metaphors to the central scene: the dying woman's memory of being trapped in the eye of a hurricane. The savage beauty of destruction as seen from that small area of calm brings back her entire life, the past recaptured in that one instant of revelation. The novel is structured around the storm scene, like ripples spreading in a pool. White seems to be writing from the storm's eye, from that lucidity that is reached only after tortuous mazes have been traveled.

Anthony J. Hassall (review date 1975)

SOURCE: "Patrick White's 'The Cockatoos,'" in *Southerly,* Vol. 35, No. 1, March, 1975, pp. 3-13.

[*In the following review, Hassall praises White, contending that the author's writing shows he is "clear-eyed," compassionate, and "can tell a good old-fashioned story extremely well."*]

Most of the six shorter novels and stories in Patrick White's second collection begin, like *The Eye of the Storm* and *The Solid Mandala,* at the end of life. They are about retired couples, living out their last years together. Though three of the stories have previously been published separately,[1] the collection is a comparatively unified one, held together by the characters' common predicament—loneliness—and by their common, often violent, attempts to break out of it. It is a little surprising to find as the protagonists of these stories some of the ordinary, dun-coloured inhabitants of suburbia, people incapable of the magnificent isolation of an Elizabeth Hunter, but tough enough to withstand the helpless alienation which overwhelmed their counterparts in ***The Burnt Ones.*** Most of them have made peace, of a kind, with life, settling for what they have got as best they can. But if they are ostensibly better adjusted than some of White's earlier characters, they have not escaped from the more intimate rigours of marriage, nor from the hunger of the heart for a human companionship which might assuage the loneliness which haunts them all. Patrick White brings to their depiction his customary merciless eye for the petty squalors and deceptions of life, and a newly enlarged compassion for run-of-the-mill humanity, struggling with its own inadequacies. The result is a profound, and at times dazzlingly acute insight into otherwise humble and unremarkable lives.

Of the afflictions endemic to the latter part of life, loneliness is most emphasized in these stories, though not to the complete exclusion of poverty and sickness. The Makridis family of **"The Full Belly"**, for example, are poor, surviving on boiled dandelions in an Athens occupied by the

Germans in the Second World War, though the younger members of the family can still sell their talents, or themselves, for food. And Royal Natwick in **"Five-Twenty"** is confined to a wheelchair by a combination of hernia, heart and "artheritis", though his wife's remorseless care ensures that that is the least of his problems. In general, however, the people in these stories are wealthy enough, and healthy enough. Their loneliness is another matter. It is not the loneliness of White's elect who, however they may suffer at the hands of Blue and his boozy mates, instinctively recognize one another, and take comfort from their shared private vision. Such characters do appear briefly in these stories, but as minor figures, whose insights are not shared, and who therefore attempt violent remedies to overcome their isolation. Clem Dowson, for example, in **"A Woman's Hand"** gives up his lifelong self-sufficiency to marry, late in life, a woman chosen for him by Evelyn Fazackerley, a thin-blooded, genteel descendant of Mrs Flack. They come together over a discussion of how to make cumquat jam, from which it is clear that Clem, supposedly in need of a woman's touch, is in fact the better cook, though Nesta Pine, his wife-to-be, has cooked for the best families. Clem and Nesta have too much in common to need one another, and their marriage is a disaster which kills Clem and drives Nesta mad. Harold Fazackerley, who has understood something of his wife's destruction of his friend, does make a feeble protest, scattering the pearls of her treasured necklace in an uncharacteristic outburst of violence. But they are "such mates", her concern for his comfort is so professional, their relationship is too comfortable and his awareness of its sterility too blunted, for the protest to be more than a passing flicker of life. Harold is not burnt, he is killed with kindness. His wife takes him on a tour of the Dead Heart of Australia.

Felicity Bannister, the much younger protagonist of **"The Night the Prowler"**, protests more fiercely, as one would expect from someone in whom the full tide of life has just begun to run. The conventional, over-protected daughter of a heavy-handed middle-class family, Felicity is released from her carefully schooled frustration by a prowler who breaks into the house and "rapes" her. Unfortunately when she gives every indication of willingly cooperating in the assault, the prowler turns out to be as impotent as Faulkner's Popeye, though without the latter's resourcefulness in finding a substitute weapon. A pathetic little man with bad teeth, he has to be forced by Felicity to drink some of her father's brandy so it will look as if he has ransacked the house as well as its daughter. Felicity's supposed violation enables her to discard the passionless diplomat to whom she is engaged, and she embarks on a quest for a real experience which will, in Addie Bundren's phrase, "violate her aloneness".[2] She drops her mousy, twin-set stereotype, and takes up black leather, working in a boutique called "Pot Luck", and breaking into neighbours' houses to assault their ponderous and ugly complacency. She haunts the park by night, seeking some ultimate experience, and finding only gangs of bikies who back off like the prowler, leaving her brandishing their captured bike-chains while they flee from a desire to which their petty lusts are no answer. Failed by man, Felicity turns on God: "I fuck you, God, for holding out on me".[3] Her ultimate revelation, if that is what it is, is one of total, Beckettian nihilism. It comes from a dying down-and-out in a derelict house: "I can honestly say I never believed in or expected anything of anyone. I never loved, not even myself—which is more than can be said of most people. . . . I always saw myself as a shit. I am nothing. I believe in nothing. And Nothing's noble faith. Nobody can hurt nothing. So you've no reason for being afraid". (pp. 166-167) Cold comfort for a young girl urgently seeking some real contact with life.

If her demon lover were one day to materialize, like Miss Slattery's in ***The Burnt Ones,*** and if they were to marry and grow old, Felicity would eventually find herself in the same situation as her parents, and most of the protagonists of these stories. The main focus of ***The Cockatoos*** is not on isolated loneliness, but on the special kind of loneliness which exists within long and ostensibly successful marriages, a theme White has not really attempted since *The Tree of Man.* In the title-story Mick and Olive Davoren have not spoken to one another for seven years, since he let her budgie die while she was away at her sister's funeral. They exchange essential information by writing notes on a pad in the kitchen. It becomes apparent that they do not have much to say to one another anyway. Mick has taken to sometimes having tea with Busby Le Cornu, a spinster up the road, and once in a while their relations have been more intimate, though Mick shows as little enthusiasm for love as he does for talk, and Miss Le Cornu does not seem to mind too much. The women in this triangle share an interest in music—Olive used to play the violin and Miss Le Cornu is partial to a velvety mezzo-soprano—but they never succeed in talking about it. The catalyst which introduces life, and death, into this long-standing deadlock is the arrival of a flock of brilliant, wild cockatoos. Olive and Mick take turns to feed them, and their shared enthusiasm for the birds leads them to exchange words, and even inarticulate love, for the first time in many years. Mick is shot trying to protect the cockatoos from a neighbour with a shotgun, and the women join hands supporting his dying body. Despite this violent, almost melodramatic ending the story is understated. White's observation is as superb as ever, and his sympathy, sometimes vitiated by a patrician contempt for the herd, is here allowed full scope. There is the sureness of touch of his best work in the spare, compassionate, unsentimental view he takes of his three central characters. Listening to a favourite aria in her backyard, Miss Le Cornu "was crouching over what might have been her own lament for a real passion she had never quite experienced". (p. 287) This elegiac note pervades the story, and indeed the whole collection. As the unravished Felicity complains to her passionless stick of a fiancé, "how can love be 'engaged'? . . . and how can an engagement be 'broken'? Anything big enough ought to be '*shattered*'!" (p. 143) But nothing big enough comes to the people in these stories. They must make do with the altogether more mundane realities of marriage. Love is something else.

They do not give in, however, without a struggle, often a surprisingly violent struggle, to snatch something closer to their aspirations, and further from their fate. The couple in **"Sicilian Vespers"** are superficially more than content with their lot. "Prudence was a virtue normally present in both of them. What had made their marriage such an exceptionally happy one was its balance." (p. 198) Not exactly stirring stuff, but comfortable. Dr. Charles Simpson has retired from practice, and with his wife Ivy is touring Europe. Like so many of White's couples they are childless, and their retirement, and travelling, have thrown them entirely on their own, and one another's resources. Just what those resources are is relentlessly exposed in the following pages. The doctor comes down with a toothache, and meditates on the difference between his public self, responsible, reassuring, healing the sick, and the true self inside the image: "What if all the patients who had brought him their forebodings as well as their actual cancers—what if *Ivy* were to realize that inside the responsible man there had always lurked this diffident, whimpering boy?" (p. 199) Inside Ivy there lurks the plain daughter of a flamboyant artist who was greatly disappointed by her lack of *ton* and told her so. She has pursued his withheld approval all her life—without success. In Sicily she has one last try to escape from the irreproachably comfortable world she has made for herself, into the imagined bohemian splendour of her father's. Her partner is Clark Shacklock, an American staying at their hotel. Leaving his wife and her husband at the hotel, they visit the duomo of San Fabrizio in time for Vespers one evening. Ivy overwhelms Clark and they make love on the "particularly fine" Cosmati paving, watched over by "a very beautiful Passion", while the service continues in the almost dark church. The splendid comedy of the scene—they are locked in, and Ivy immediately worries about getting home for Charles's dinner—is flanked on one side by the casual squalor of the adultery, and on the other by Ivy's long-suppressed religious yearning to "learn . . . how to climb a ladder of prayer". (p. 139) She seeks both these extremes deliberately, if guiltily, as escapes from the prison of her marriage, which is no less a prison for being filled with sweetness and light. In the unlovely moment of her coupling with Clark, she looks down on "the box in which He my Dearly Beloved Husband has thrown off the sheet is rising from amongst the limp grey wrinkles on the yellow bed offering Himself afresh for sacrifice under the extinct acryllic object". (p. 243) Ivy betrays her escape in a farewell letter to Clark the next morning, only to find that he has already fled the hotel and what she had called her "bizarre Sicilian reactions". (p. 252) The quiet desperation underlying lives of steady and useful purpose has seldom been more expertly revealed. Once again the distance from the characters is just right. We can laugh at the beautifully observed surfaces of the Simpsons, their petty snobberies, their pseudo-matiness, the sterile clichés of their relationship, without losing sympathy for the haunting insecurities which have driven them to seek this refuge, which time and habit have metamorphosed into a prison from which they are losing the will to try to escape.

Ella Natwick in **"Five-Twenty"** delays her protest against the kiss of death represented by her marriage until after her husband has passed on. The Natwicks, like the Fazackerleys, are "such mates", but only because Ella has worked hard and self-effacingly at keeping her grocer husband Royal conscious of his Englishness, his good nose, and the Natwick family home in Kent. Childless, they sit on the verandah of their retirement home on the Parramatta Road and watch the traffic, and in particular the man in the Holden who goes past every day at five-twenty. When he asks one day to use her phone to ring the N.R.M.A., the newly liberated Ella begins to love him. But when he comes back the next night he is ill, and dies at Ella's feet, a victim, as it seems to her, of the fierce intensity of her guilty passion for him. The point of view remains Ella's throughout this finely controlled story. The author makes no comment on the meagreness of her world, her subservience to her "Royal God Almighty" husband, her limited awareness. The result is an evenness of tone unusual in White. The pathos is restrained by Ella's lack of awareness that her situation deserves pity, and it is uninterrupted by the author's ironic or satiric voice. An inhabitant of the ageing inner suburbs, she attracts neither White's loathing for the bourgeois pretensions of the North Shore, nor his distaste for the easy vulgarity of such denizens of the outer suburbs as the Whalleys of **"Down at the Dump"**. Instead there is a strong but discreet sympathy devoid of any but the most gentle mockery.

All of the stories are concerned, in one way or another, with violent betrayals caused by the irruption of basic human cravings into a world which either ignores them, or builds to contain them institutions like marriage which are pitifully inadequate to the task. In **"A Full Belly"**, the least obviously interrelated of the stories, hunger drives Costa Iordanu and his elderly aunt Pronoë to violate both religious belief and aristocratic family decorum by fighting over a plate of rice left as a ritual offering before the family ikon. Their city has been desrated by the invading Germans, and the Greeks are driven to desecrate their own most cherished traditions in the fight for survival. In the title story nine-year-old Tim Goodenough, another of White's lonely, prescient children, despairs, like Felicity Bannister, of making contact with his parents, and spends a night in the park in a similarly fruitless pursuit of a vaguely imagined fulfilment. On his way home in the morning he kills an old cockatoo, one of the Laurentian life-symbols of the story, hoping perhaps that the violent destruction of life will enable him somehow to touch its essence. Desecrations and betrayals of this kind recur in the stories, and in the degradation which follows them it is possible, though by no means certain, that the characters will rediscover their lost humanity. Though some of the characters involved in this process are young, like Costa, Tim and Felicity, it happens most often to the old who, though they still have yearnings which the solipsistic young and the smug middle-aged might deny them, have even less chance of realizing those yearnings than the rest of us. Their attempts, and failures, chronicled with insight and compassion, make up the bulk of this volume.

An exception to the generally high level of authorial sympathy is the first story, **"A Woman's Hand"**, first published in 1966, when the author was fresh from his battles with the cultural establishment over the production of his plays, and when his revulsion from "Sarsaparilla" was at its height. The subtitle of ***The Cockatoos*** is "Shorter Novels and Stories", and this, the longest piece in the collection, clearly falls into the first category. It opens in White's tartest satirical manner:

> What must originally have appeared an austere landscape, one long rush of rock and scrub towards the sea, was prevented from wearing its natural expression by the parasite houses clinging to it as obstinately as wax on diseased orange branches. Not that the houses weren't, nearly all of them, technically desirable, some of them even Lovely Homes worth breaking into. Although the owners of the latter were surely aware of this, they had almost completely exposed their possessions behind unbroken plate-glass. To view the view might have been their confessable intention, but they had ended, seemingly, overwhelmed by it. Or bored. The owners of the lovely seaside homes sat in their worldly cells playing bridge, licking the chocolate off their fingers, in one case copulating, on pink chenille, on the master bed.
>
> (p. 9)

This assault on the crass materialism, the philistine stupor of the Australian scene will not surprise readers familiar with White's other work about this time. He surveys the surface of this life with a caricaturist's eye for the vulgarity of the lamb chop and tomato sauce consuming ordinary Ocker. It is a vein that has been worked hard in recent years by Barry Humphries and David Williamson as well as White, and it has more mud than gold left in it by now. Perhaps we can look forward to more writers like Randolph Stow who, when they go out into the cold world of the outsider, remember, with sorrow as well as anger, the warmth they leave behind.

Strolling through the blasted landscape of Bandana Beach we find the Fazackerleys, comfortably off and retired. Evelyn Fazackerley's response to the scene is almost as repulsive as the author's description of it: "how vulgar they all are . . . there are certain standards the ones who know can't afford to drop". (p. 10) After such a beginning, one cannot but wonder how White is going to fill a nouvelle-length story unless he introduces some real people to ballast these Dickensian grotesques. The Fazackerleys live, we discover, in a cosy and tasteful unit very like a prison cell from which they constantly escape by going on tours. But they never escape from themselves and one another, nor from the author's meticulous observation of their posturings and mannerisms, one of the best touches of which is the way they communicate, like Walter and Toby Shandy, quite independently of the actual words which pass between them.

The two characters introduced to this hermetically sealed marriage are, as we have seen, Clem Dowson and Nesta Pine, school-friends of Harold and Evelyn. Though they do not make a great impact on the Fazackerleys' anaesthetized self-sufficiency, Clem does stir vague, poetic longings in Harold, and Evelyn is able to relieve some of her boredom by arranging the poisonous marriage between them. The trouble with the story is that we see the interesting characters, Clem and Nesta, only through the eyes of the "normal" Harold and Evelyn. Thus we get external, old-maidish details about Clem, his automatic egg-remover and his three garbage cans for his three classes of garbage, but we see nothing of his inner life, nothing of the motivation for his extraordinary decision to marry Nesta. Nesta is even more shadowy, and this makes the brilliant, disturbing letter she writes to Evelyn (pp. 69-70) a rather clumsy authorial insertion. Evelyn, it seems, is to be forcibly confronted with an account of redemption to ensure that her own damnation is wilful and complete. Writing *Hamlet* from the point of view of Rosencrantz and Guildenstern is all very well, but it is difficult not to hanker after what gets lost in the process. White has written about his outsiders with such perception and sensitivity elsewhere that it is hard to accept the mere outlines they present to the limited vision of an Evelyn Fazackerley as a truth of much value. The angle is simply too narrow. And the slightly rancid, Kingsley Amis humour of the opening does not readily modulate into what should become the tragic view of Clem and Nesta, or the ultimate pathos of the Fazackerleys trapped, like the dead souls in Joyce's *Dubliners,* in their own nothingness.

The Cockatoos, in which White is more concerned with the paralysed normalcy of Australian society than with its unfortunate victims, the burnt ones of the earlier collection, has a good deal in common with *Dubliners*.[4] As well as a hate/love attitude towards their homelands, Joyce and White share a fine sense of irony, and a deflating awareness of the restrictions of the physical. Both find life in their native countries deadening, and the people in need of spiritual liberation. Both hold up a mirror in which the victims may see the unpalatable truth about themselves, and if they are not sanguine enough to hope, like Gulliver, for the immediate reform of the country, they do lend moral support to those characters like Harold Fazackerley or Maria in Joyce's "Clay" who make their protest, however feebly, against the stifling of their human needs. There are, however, important differences. Joyce's epic work was ahead of him when he wrote *Dubliners,* and he was to become one of the great innovators of modern fiction. Patrick White has already written a major body of epic work, and is a self-confessedly old-fashioned novelist. As he says in a recent interview, "I feel my novels are quite old-fashioned and traditional—almost Nineteenth Century. I've never thought of myself as an innovator".[5] Almost alone among major twentieth-century novelists he has not created a markedly individual form to embody his own distinctive vision, though he has certainly put the capacious potential of the Victorian novel to precise and specialized use.

Unlike the novel, the short story has not undergone radical development in the twentieth century, and it is therefore a congenial form for a traditionally-minded writer. As **"A Glass of Tea"** from ***The Burnt Ones*** indicates, Patrick White can tell a good old-fashioned story extremely well. The brevity of the short story encourages the use of a single narrative stance, and its impersonality discourages an underdistanced authorial relation to the subject. It also comfortably accommodates the grand, central symbol of which White, like Ibsen and Lawrence, is fond. The shorter of the stories in this volume certainly gain from the inherent restrictions on the author's varying of stance and mode of narration. They have a freshness and crispness which Dorothy Green, for one, found lacking in White's last novel, *The Eye of the Storm.*[6] One might be tempted to argue that White, like Faulkner, is essentially a short-story writer, and not a novelist at all, and that he makes his novels, as Faulkner does, by putting together a series of units conceived and executed as stories. His collections, particularly this one, do explore particular thematic preoccupations in the manner of *Go Down, Moses,* and many of his novels are composed of disparate segments juxtaposed in the Faulkner manner. The similarity between the four person structure of *Riders in the Chariot* and that of *The Sound and the Fury,* in both of which the ritual of Easter is a central symbol, is the most obvious, but by no means the only example. His novels, like Faulkner's, sometimes grow out of stories—*The Eye of the Storm* clearly had its beginnings in **"Dead Roses"**—and the author has said that he finds writing stories a useful way of breaking a writing drought, and of limbering up for a new novel.

On the other hand both authors have larger ambitions that the modern novel, with its careful scrutiny of a small and sharply defined segment of time or human character, comfortably contains. There is an epic magnitude in the conception of *Voss,* as there is in *Absalom, Absalom,* that belongs at the other end of the fictional spectrum to the short story, with the massive European novels of the nineteenth century. These two works attempt in Virgilian manner to capture the quintessential nature of the civilizations which produced them, and whose formative history they explore. Faulkner's ambition on this scale was twofold: the single, epic novel like *Absalom, Absalom,* and a lifetime's work recreating the South in the multi-faceted fictional world of Yoknapatawpha. It is becoming increasingly clear that Patrick White has all along been working towards a similar goal, not merely introducing a new continent into literature, as the Nobel Prize citation stated, but attempting the truly epic task of fictionalizing a lifetime's observation of the Australian experience. The attempt, like Voss's, is doomed by the very magnitude of its ambition: Voss failed, though he also succeeded. Within this grand plan ***The Cockatoos*** occupies a modest, though by no means undistinguished place. From Theodora Goodman on, a number of White's characters have been driven mad, like Gulliver, by discovering their inescapable similarity to the Yahoo, an animal first encountered in this part of the world. And like Swift he has not lacked readers ready to identify the character's madness with the author's imbalance. If any refutation were necessary in Patrick White's case, it certainly comes in this book, in which he is as clear-eyed, as unillusioned about his fellows as ever, and yet which is dominated by an insistent compassion for those growing old, desperate and unlovely, the fringe-dwellers of an empty continent of unfulfilment.

Notes

1. The stories previously published are: "A Woman's Hand", *Australian Letters* 7 No. 3 (August 1966), 13-40; "The Full Belly", *Coast to Coast: Australian Short Stories, 1965-66,* ed. Clement Semmler (Sydney Angus and Robertson, 1966), 225-242; and "Five-Twenty", *Southerly,* XXVIII (1968), 3-25.
2. William Faulkner, *As I Lay Dying* (London: Chatto & Windus, 1958), p. 160.
3. *The Cockatoos* (London: Jonathan Cape, 1974), p. 164. Subsequent page numbers refer to this edition.
4. Both *Dubliners* and *The Burnt Ones* include a story entitled "Clay". It is possible that White intended a direct reference, and it certainly suggests a familiarity with Joyce's work, a suggestion reinforced by the title of Waldo Brown's destroyed literary work, "Tiresias a Youngish Man". Some of the similarities between *A Portrait of the Artist as a Young Man* and *The Tree of Man* are described in Bernard Hickey, *James Joyce and Patrick White: A Study in Correspondences* (Roma: Tip. Zampini, 1971).
5. "A Conversation with Patrick White", *Southerly* III (1973), p. 139.
6. "Queen Lear or Cleopatra Rediviva? Patrick White's *The Eye of the Storm*", *Meanjin Quarterly,* II (1973), 395-405.

Rose Marie Beston (essay date 1975)

SOURCE: "More Burnt Ones: Patrick White's 'The Cockatoos,'" in *World Literature Written in English,* Vol. 14, No. 2, 1975, pp. 520-24.

[In the following essay, Beston asserts that the short story form "does not offer White the space he needs for his greatest strength," which is the portrayal of his characters' fantasies.]

In ***The Cockatoos,*** Patrick White's latest collection of stories, there are only six stories against the eleven in ***The Burnt Ones*** (1964), his last collection. Two of the stories are of novella length (**"A Woman's Hand"** and **"Sicilian Vespers"**), and another two could also be considered novellas (**"The Night the Prowler"** and **"The Cockatoos"**). Nevertheless, White's concept of the novella is no different from his concept of the short story, so that one can validly refer to all the stories as short stories.

The short story as a form does not offer White the space he needs for his greatest strength, the portrayal of a character's fantasy. It is in her fantasies that Theodora Goodman comes most to life in his masterpiece, *The Aunt's Story*; to White, a character's fantasies represent his most real and vital self. But in order that the reader can interpret the significance of a fantasy, the author has to provide a background of fact and experience from which the character's fantasy can emerge. Even in a full length novel like *The Aunt's Story*, White is normally sparing with this background; and in these short stories he is too sparing entirely. In **"Sicilian Vespers,"** for instance, we know only enough of Ivy Simpson's relationship with her father to understand her general makeup, not enough to interpret her dream or fantasy life. Likewise, we see Felicity in **"The Night the Prowler"** acting out vandalizing fantasies in what we can recognize as angry retaliation against restrictive and asexual parents; but White fails to differentiate these parents from the parents of other characters whose reaction is less extreme. We remain aghast at the bizarreness of Felicity's behavior rather than saddened by its inevitability. Except in the title story, **"The Cockatoos,"** White is too eager to leap into the fantasy life of his characters, failing to lay the foundation that would explain how the fantasies originate and what they tell us of the inner life of the character.

For some reason, the short story brings out all that is most negative in White's thinking. There are, for instance, no illuminates in these short stories—and the illuminates of the novels represent his major concession to positive thinking. One would have to describe ***The Cockatoos*** as a negative collection. The main themes that run through the stories are the sterility of marriage, the lack of communication between people, and the vindication of aloneness. White does appear to be making his point especially of Australian marriages and of the Australian inability to relate to other people (he opposes the Shacklocks to the Simpsons in **"Sicilian Vespers"** to the Americans' credit), but he is not exempting other countries from his sweep.

All the marriages portrayed in this collection are sterile. Most of them are childless; the two couples with a child, the Bannisters in **"The Night the Prowler"** and the Goodenoughs in **"The Cockatoos,"** are no less sterile than the childless couples. In fact, as a result of their own problems, they destroy their child's hope of a healthy adulthood.

The marriages cover a range of social classes, from lower middle class (the Natwicks in **"Five-Twenty"**) to professional (the Simpsons in **"Sicilian Vespers"**). The Goodenoughs and the Davorens in **"The Cockatoos"** fall somewhere in between. White makes some very acute, if malicious observations on the kinds of behavior that are characteristic of couples at the various social levels. Against the Natwicks, fairly average Australians, he directs a satiric scorn: their lives are filled with consumer goods and the contemplation of life at one remove, the traffic that crowds Parramatta Road in Sydney. In accordance with her social class, Ella Natwick spends her life within the four walls of her house, leaving it only to shop. She is sexually frigid, but compensates by strange fantasies, involving some aspect of rape or murder. Ivy Simpson is married to a doctor, but differs from Ella more in degree than in kind. Ivy is less afraid of social contacts than Ella, but her dealings with people are hardly expansive. Her social and economic class enables her to deal with people at a first meeting, but she shrinks from a second, which demands more from her than the superficialities she has exchanged at the first meeting. She is terrified when she meets the Shacklocks at the elevator on the day after she has made an outing with them.

All the marriages in these stories are shown as asexual. White implies strongly that sex has become an embarrassment for the couples and so is either abandoned or is a ritual exercise to be performed at prescribed intervals (every two weeks for the Simpsons). The most "successful" marriages depicted are those in which the couple are able to maintain the illusion of being good friends, to cover the essential emptiness of their relationship. In fact they do not communicate with one another in any meaningful way. Even the accumulation of shared experiences over the years does not bring them any closer together.

White has never presented marriage favorably. His most detailed study of a marriage, that of Stan and Amy Parker in *The Tree of Man*, shows the relationship as a deteriorating one: conversation becomes an exchange of question and answer, and habit comes to substitute for love. In the marriages portrayed in ***The Cockatoos***, the people simply do not communicate with one another. At the most literal level, that is true in the title story of the Davorens, who communicate only by writing on a pad of paper. But it is true also of the Goodenoughs in the same story, who do at least speak to one another. When young Tim Goodenough overhears his parents discussing the Davorens, he is not surprised:

> "Lots of people don't speak," said the boy. . . .
>
> "I never heard of anybody, Tim. Not when they live together." The mother was more concerned about the contents of her pan.
>
> "Lots," said Tim. "They speak, but don't say."

It is by portraying the lives of a small community, a street in a Sydney suburb, that White presents his most depressing picture since *Happy Valley* of Australians' inability to relate to others and their lack of any community sense. The characters in **"The Cockatoos"** are alone and resent any effort to make them less alone. Clyde Goodenough's door knock for the Heart Foundation is his substitute for neighborliness and community spirit (while also enabling him to pry a little into lives otherwise closed to him), but after the patter that accompanies his extraction of a donation, he is quick to make his getaway before the conversation can make any personal demands. Two women of the neighborhood, Miss Le Cornu and Mrs. Davoren, undergo a deeply moving experience together, but retreat from it into their isolation. When next they meet,

> "Lovely day, Mrs. Davoren," Miss Le Cornu said; after all, why not celebrate the fact that you are neighbours? Mrs. Davoren admitted that it was, indeed, a lovely day. To meet Miss Le Cornu in the flesh as opposed to conversing together in her thoughts was unnerving Mrs. Davoren. She had often thought that if she did come face to face with Her she would introduce the subject of music, and now this idea came into her head, but fortunately she saved herself in time.
>
> "It'll warm up later, though." Mrs. Davoren was quite firm about it. . . .
>
> "Well," Mrs. Davoren said, "I'm off to the city. Thought I'd start early. Walk. Look round the shops while they're still empty. . . ."
>
> "Have a good time," Miss Le Cornu recommended.
>
> Mrs. Davoren left on accepting this advice.

Likewise, when the Fazackerleys in **"A Woman's Hand"** meet an old friend after some years, they stop and talk, but at their departure, no one bothers to exchange addresses.

For the most part, the stories in this collection are conceived in a lack of compassion for the characters and narrated in a tone of derision. The derision appears in the names of the characters (Fazackerley, Nesta Pine, Natwick, Goodenough), the jabs at aspects of Australian life (the unimaginative cooking, the lavender Kleenex, and Onkaparinka blankets), and a certain enjoyment of the characters' distress. As said, White is more negative in his short stories than in his novels. **"The Night the Prowler,"** for instance, recounts a situation very similar to the Sidney Furlow story in *Happy Valley*, but with a stress on negative aspects. Felicity is angrier and more violent than Sidney Furlow, thereby deflecting our sympathy; her parents are more ludicrous than Sidney's; her fiancé is more ineffectual than Sidney's suitor; and her would be rapist is pathetic against Sidney's would-be lover Clem Hagan. **"Five-Twenty,"** too, recounts a situation similar to the Leo episode in *The Tree of Man*, again given a negative twist. Whereas Amy's meeting with Leo represents a pathetic attempt to experience romantic passion, Ella's encounter with the man in the Holden grows into a disburbing fantasy.

Although few of these short stories are outstanding as examples of their genre, some are important in throwing light on aspects of White's novels. **"Five-Twenty,"** for instance, through its references to the cinerarias growing in the shade of the house gives the clue needed to interpret the fuchsias around the house in *The Tree of Man*. The color range of cinerarias and fuchsias is the same: both have the colors of flesh with blood pulsing beneath the skin. Fuchsias and cinerarias alike, growing in the shade, would appear to stand for a repressed sexuality. And the conversation between Evelyn Fazackerley and Clem Dowson in the Egyptian Delta (**"A Woman's Hand"**) makes clearer the emotional implications of the similar scene between Laura and Voss in the Bonners' garden. Both conversations show a woman essentially violating a man's soul in an effort to gain ascendancy over him. This point is especially important for Voss, since the Voss-Laura relationship is often mistakenly read as a kind of spiritual love affair.

The best story in the collection, and White's best short story altogether, is the title story, **"The Cockatoos."** The elements of derision in the other stories are softened here by the sympathetic portrait of the boy Tim, the potential artist. In general White's sympathy flows most freely for the artist child born of sterile or destructive parents. The story is further lightened by the poetic symbol of the cockatoos, representing such things as freedom and aspiration, pride of sexuality, and a sense of togetherness.

The advent of the band of cockatoos in the lives of the non-communicating community serves as a reminder to them of what their lives could contain, and so evokes strong reactions in them for or against the cockatoos. It is naturally the undertaker who is most opposed to the cockatoos; the note-writing Davorens on the other hand are brought into verbal communication again by the presence of the cockatoos. For young Tim the cockatoos represent the world of adulthood in its finest promise, a world however that his own experiences and observations make appear increasingly warped and restricted. After his night spent in the park opposite, a sort of puberty rite, he comes upon a crippled old cockatoo, which he kills and scalps (circumcises?) in a symbolic angry rejection of the adult world that he will never accept. The story has similarities to the 1970 English movie Kes, which also treats the possibility of a boy's growth to an expanding adulthood, frustrated by the killing of his kestrel.

This most recent work by Australia's most distinguished prose writer is a strong anti-marriage tract. Australia's most distinguished poet, Judith Wright, reaches her greatest heights when she sings of love and marriage. How ironical that Patrick White and Judith Wright are distantly related—by marriage!

Ingmar Björksten (essay date 1976)

SOURCE: "Short Stories and Plays," in *Patrick White: A General Introduction,* translated by Stanley Gerson, University of Queensland Press, 1976, pp. 75-8.

[*In the following excerpt, Björksten states that the short story is "not Patrick White's best medium of expression" during his discussion of* The Burnt Ones.]

The Burnt Ones

After *Riders in the Chariot* Patrick White wrote eleven short stories, which were published in 1964 in his first collection of short stories. He named the collection after the Greek *hoi kaumenoi*—the burnt ones, the poor unfortunates. The title characterizes all White's "elect", those inhabitants of his created world who have been burnt by society and by existence. However, even if one recognizes the characters in the short stories, they are not representative of the whole of White's portrait gallery. They reflect features of some of the figures in his novels, placed in a familiar setting—Sarsaparilla and the Australian emptiness—as well as a Greek, particularly a Smyrniot Greek, background which White sometimes makes use of as a parallel. The social satire directed at a "dead" materialism and against hostility to nonconformists, with its touches of indignation, has the tendency, however, to make a trite caricature of the satire. Clearly enough, Patrick White has since realized that a biting and bitter tone, while it facilitates a statement of the case, is less capable of illuminating it. After this collection of stories (indeed in the last of the stories) he has more and more directed attention to the existence of the "dead" and to why they are dead.

Three of the stories in ***The Burnt Ones*** deal with the figure which is further developed in Elizabeth Hunter in his latest novel *The Eye of the Storm,* and which occurs in White even in his earlier work: the figure of the mother, the person who leaves so strong an impression on her offspring that he or she becomes ill-equipped for life without her. In these stories, the sympathy is always on the side of those who are the victims—on the side of Anthea Scudamore, who in **"Dead Roses"** is so moulded by her mother that finally she is changed into a barren reflection of her; on the side of Clay Skerritt who "was born with inward-looking eyes" and who in the story **"Clay"** embarrasses his mother through behaving differently: "You will suffer in life if you start talking queer remember it doesn't pay to be different and no one is different without they have something wrong with them." And White's sympathies are also with Charles Polkinghorn, the fifty-year-old son who is never allowed to grow up and who in **"The Letters"** lives with his aunt Maud as a substitute for his mother. After her death he reverts completely to his childhood and looks for his mother's withered breasts to suckle.

The women in White's novels who are not presented as mothers of the typical White kind don't have an easier time of it; their lives too become a matter of keeping their heads above water. What threatens to drown them is their sexual nature. Life with husbands or lovers never becomes what their imaginations, wishes, or romantic literature has filled them full of hopes of. This becomes a path to degradation. Thus it turns out for Nora Mackenzie, the respectable upper-class housewife in **"Willy-Wagtails by Moonlight"** who together with her husband invites some close friends to dinner and lets them listen to tapes of interesting bird songs, tapes which, as it happens, also contain evidence of her husband's infidelity. Thus it turns out for the Australian Miss Slattery, who in **"Miss Slattery and Her Demon Lover"** is aroused to a height of sexual passion by the immigrant Tibby Szabo which she never believed herself to possess, but the price of which she finally refuses to pay. Sexual passion is not one of the human drives that Patrick White thinks of as a useful gift in life; it seldom happens in his novels that two individuals are united, enrich one another's lives, and become inseparable through *eros.* He has greater faith in spiritual love. This sets limitations on his vision, and makes it in some way a rejection of life.

In White's novels marriage is not based on a harmonious sexual life. People marry for reasons such as in **"The Woman Who Wasn't Allowed to Keep Cats"**, one of the four short stories in the collection that are connected with Greece: "Different in habit and variety they relied upon each other for support; he for the thorny traditions of her class which she brought to bear on daily life, she for the succulence on which her parasitic nature fed." Therefore these people fill their lives with ersatz experiences behind which they try to conceal their emptiness and the feeling of icy monotony. The males withdraw into an inaccessible world of silence, the females devote themselves to their desire for property, their neurotic craving to rule.

The greater the experience Patrick White has of life as it is lived, the more has his understanding increased not only of its victims but also of those who shape it. The spirit of reconciliation he presents in his works seems also to have coloured his own attitude to life. The somewhat venomous, bitter conception of Australia has matured, and thus that theme appears which is fundamental to White: What happens to man in the world he calls modern, civilized, materially secure, what are the values that get lost, and what is the price we pay for their loss? In the short stories he speaks without metaphysical overtones. He hardly adds anything to what his novels have already communicated concerning his attitudes. But particularly in **"Down at the Dump"** one feels an optimism, a cause for hope in spite of everything. It begins with an acceptance of life as it is. And what that life is need not necessarily be in Australia, even if the story is set in Sarsaparilla. There the Whalley family are engaged in the same occupation as Hurtle Duffield's parents: they collect refuse. Myrtle Hogben has married herself to a brick house, status and security; her sister Daise has broken away from her background and has lived out her life according to what she was born to do. Now she is dead. The person who is dead as far as present existence is concerned survives the one who is still living, for she has instilled her attitude to life in her niece Meg. Meg makes friends with Lum Whalley. At the funeral of Daise Morrow it becomes evident to what extent everybody looks to himself. It is what those present at the funeral remember of the social outcast that reveals their own natures. But White does not lash the "dead" for their shortcomings. He begins to feel compassion for them, and suggests the possibility that the young pair, Meg and Lum, will become different.

The short story is not Patrick White's best medium of expression. His vision needs more space to unfold itself, the whole existence of man to give itself justice. But the short stories clarify certain points overshadowed by the huge structure of the epic. At the same time they demand concentration in characterization, in composition, in language. The reader can achieve little more than absorption of White's point of view, can achieve only the passing impressions before it is all over, when in retrospect he can examine it and his reactions to it. This is not all advantageous to White. Themes treated in the form of an *etude* become emasculated. The broad symphonic style, the great carefully planned canvases rather than the sketch are better suited to express White's visionary insights. But the short stories serve as an introduction to and a harbinger of his world.

R. B. J. Wilson (essay date 1976)

SOURCE: "The Rhetoric of Patrick White's 'Down at the Dump'," in *Bards, Bohemians, and Bookmen,* edited by Leon Cantrell, University of Queensland Press, 1976, pp. 281-88.

[*In the following essay, Wilson praises White's short story "Down at the Dump," asserting that it "demonstrates the superb adroitness with which White can modulate his discourse among many functions—satiric, compassionate, speculative—and give it a dimension that is metaphysical, even religious, in its range."*]

This typical and very effective example of White's prose is a reminder of how fully he has exploited the resources of language to create his literature and how well he has assimilated some of those more successful technical experiments that have given to the prose of Joyce and of Faulkner such extreme flexibility and intensity, and how White has in fact produced a mode of discourse that generates a distinctly new rhetoric. The elements comprising it have undergone further sophistication; the new mix is full of surprises, sudden switches of kind and of key and of pace. Interestingly, the prevailing tone produced by all this variety and flux most often resembles low-keyed, casual chat. Next to it, the remarkable closing paragraphs of *The Dead* and the equally remarkable eloquence of "Barn Burning" seem to have achieved their effects by means much more familiar and obvious. All three writers are concerned with moments of self-awareness: Gabriel Conroy and Sarty Snopes and the two youngsters Lum and Meg have their confrontation with selfhood; and there is in White's rendering of this experience a protean quality that derives from stylistic subtleties representing an important advance in the art of fiction.

White tells of the funeral of Daise Morrow, a woman of abundant compassion for those who have been rejected by the Philistine middle-class suburban society of the small Australian town. While Daise's relatives make their hypocritical self-centred visit to the graveside, the town rubbish-dump next door to it is visited by the Whalleys, a rough and earthy family whose directness and humanity White obviously prefers. He presents the story in nineteen sections, marshalled to throw into significant relationship the various human values involved—especially the relationship of all these people to the dead woman. He alternates our attention between on the one hand such figures as Daise's limited, mean-minded, and mercenary sister Myrtle, whose boorish husband Les, a corrupt town-councillor, was only sensually aware of Daise, and on the other hand figures such as the dead-beat Ossie and Daise's niece Meg, who have recognized and been fortified by Daise's great capacity for loving-kindness. White juxtaposes a section on Meg's sadly superficial parents, Myrtle and Les Hogben, with one on the vitally alive Whalleys, the neighbours who so shock their pretensions and pretences. He follows a section on citizens such as the Hogbens and the like-minded Lasts, imprisoned in loveless marriages, with one on Meg and young Lum Whalley drawn to each other as they explore their private adolescent fantasies. The method affords mobility and speed. Implicit ironies and poignancies are made swiftly and variously clear, and eventually White is ready to resurrect Daise in a section to which I now devote closer attention.

It embodies in microcosm a dynamic and fluid illustration of the idea developed in the story as a whole. White darts from description to comment, from one character to another, from irony to admiration, from one kind of narrative voice or tone to another—whether satiric, compassionate, or philosophical—working always in sentences free in syntax and often fragmentary in form. He begins the scene by the graveside thus: "Even if their rage, grief, contempt, boredom, apathy, and sense of injustice had not occupied the mourners, it is doubtful whether they would have realized the dead woman was standing amongst them."[1] The sentence is part of the frankly omniscient manner that allows him from time to time to distance his people: even Daise is for him at this point so treated; she is "the dead woman". He then touches briefly, sceptically, on the religious notion of resurrection which he soon uses figuratively. "The risen dead—that was something which happened, or didn't happen, in the Bible". And this is immediately followed by the ironic: "Fanfares of light did not blare for a loose woman in floral cotton."—with its quick synaesthetic linking of the sublime and the mundane. From these concrete images, he moves to speculation: "Those who had known her remembered her by now only fitfully in some of the wooden attitudes of life. How could they have heard, let alone believed in, her affirmation?" So to the directness of the dramatic mode: he gives voice to her spirit. "Yet Daise Morrow continued to proclaim".

The affirmative proclamation that follows, revealing her insights and her understanding and her urgent gesture of salvation, moves us away from White's authorial conducting of the story and gives us Daise's own racy idiom.

> Listen, all of you, I'm not leaving, except those who want to be left, and even those aren't so sure—they might be parting with a bit of themselves. Listen to me, all you successful no-hopers, all of you who wake in the night, jittery because something may be escaping you, or terrified to think there may never have been anything to find. Come to me, you sour women, public servants, anxious children, and old scabby, desperate men. . . .

It is daring of White to have risked such an explicit statement of his theme, and he makes provisions for guarding this higher-pitched rhetoric from too naked a didacticism: one is the context provided by the preceding narrative with its sharp realism and astringent ironies; another is the way this hypothetical statement—the words she might have used if she could have spoken—are characterized by Daise's own attractive humanity; a further precaution is the tempering of this passionate altruistic plea by having it include also her candid impatience; and finally White, who has had to use words to evoke his idea of a someone whose medium was not words, resumes thus: "Physically small, words had seemed too big for her. She would push back her hair in exasperation. And take refuge in acts." We are reminded of his feeling for Miss Hare and Mrs. Godbold when he continues: "Because her feet had been planted in the earth, she would have been the last to resent its pressure now, while her always rather hoarse voice continued to exhort in borrowed syllables of dust." And an old idiomatic dead-metaphor gains from this phrasing and this context a new force.

The exhortation switches us back to the immediacy of her own voice:

> Truly, we needn't experience tortures, unless we build chambers in our minds to house instruments of hatred in. Don't you know, my darling creatures, that death isn't death, unless it's the death of love? Love should be the greatest explosion it is reasonable to expect. Which sends us whirling, spinning, creating millions of other worlds. Never destroying.

In sustaining the figurative language just noted in White's own preceding intrusion, this passage raises the pitch of her peroration one step even higher, and, as is usual at such points in his prose, the ensuing language becomes commensurately complex: able to bear the emotional intensities he seeks with it, and also able to express with clarity and force the metaphysical notion of an all-embracing, all-redeeming love, so central to this story and indeed so fundamental in most of White. "From the fresh mound which they had formed unimaginatively in the shape of her earthly body, she persisted in appealing to them." Immediately after this he gives us on a separate line three sentences printed in the italics that have hitherto been reserved for the utterances of the clergyman as he reads the burial service. "*I will comfort you. If you will let me. Do you understand?*" The formal religious idea of divine succour and compassion is thus translated into the human love and understanding that the voice of the dead woman is offering to those about her.

For obvious reasons of emphasis, the fragmentary nature of the prose is continued by three similarly isolated lines. The first, in roman typeface again, gives White's rejoinder: "But nobody did, being only human." The rancorous satire of his earlier comments on most of the spectators of Daise's life and burial is thus replaced by a new acceptance and forgiveness. He instantly underlines this by reverting to italics for another line from her in the liturgical mode: "*For ever and ever. And ever.*" And the next, the last, of these carefully isolated elements of prose that are introduced at this climatic stage in the narrative, shows us White rendering the story in a manner even more indirect; by taking the storytelling away from even the vocal spirit of the dead woman and by inserting a single line of scenic description that expresses the woman's benedictory words in symbolic terms which, in the immediate context, are unmistakably clear, and in the general context of the whole antecedent narrative, intensely potent: "Leaves quivered lifted in the first suggestion of a breeze." The grammar and the lack of commas make the word "lifted" ambiguous, but both of the allowable functions of the word reinforce the same meaning: the leaves did lift and the leaves were lifted, and each interpretation continues the idea of a living, quivering energy returning to all things.

These crucial isolated lines work like verse, and White is here using the poet's device at the novelist's leisure. Or, again, they have the impact of lines delivered in a well-acted drama where the protagonist and chorus time their pauses and then break the stillness and quietness with words that reverberate portentously. They shift the discourse from the naturalistic and humorous one with its photographic snapshots of the human scene, to one concerned with abstractions, with ideas and spiritual qualities. The movement is from spectatorship to contemplation and it is achieved by means just as subtle and fluent as the move back to a note of wry affectionate irony which now follows: "So the aspirations of Daise Morrow were laid alongside her small-boned wrists, smooth thighs and pretty ankles. She surrendered at last to the formal crumbling which, it was hoped, would make an honest woman of her." To be followed by the single quiet: "But had not altogether died."

With which White turns from Daise to young Meg who, in her fresh faith and sensibility, has always felt awe for this woman's command of life. "Meg Hogben had never exactly succeeded in interpreting her aunt's messages, nor could she have witnessed the last moments of the burial, because the sun was dazzling her." It is her next sentence, the final one in this whole section, which rewards the closest attention. "She did experience, however, along with a shiver of recollected joy, the down laid against her cheek, the little breeze trickling through the moist roots of her hair, as she got inside the car, and waited for whatever next." Its principal clause, linking her with the breeze that "lifted" and "quivered" the leaves, links her too with the redeeming and energizing spirit of which White has made it symbolic; and its final clause insists on the forward-looking, hope-sustaining nature of this force by which Meg will be equipped to face with good faith her future. It is a sentence that balances finely between what is felt and thought and what is seen and heard; it shows the outward while still keeping central to our attention the inward. It demonstrates in particular terms what Daise's hypothetical exhortation can mean. The whole story, with its diversity of human types and reactions and its general ramifications is resolved into a meaningful unity by the girl's dim, excited but certain apprehending or "interpreting" of "her aunt's message".

The interesting *difference* of this rhetoric is quickly seen when comparison is made with sentences from peaks of significance in the *The Dead*and "Barn Burning". Here are the famous concluding words in Joyce's account of Gabriel Conroy's epiphany: "His soul swooned slowly as he heard the snow falling faintly through the universe and faintly falling, like the descent of their last end, upon all the living and the dead."[2] And here is the Faulkner sentence in which Sarty Snopes first glimpses the southern mansion that his vicious father may threaten, a sentence that moves from the boy's own words ("Hit's big as a courthouse") to hypothetical language attributed to him and then returns to the familiar Faulknerian manner:

> People whose lives are part of this peace and dignity are beyond his touch, he no more to them than a buzzing wasp: capable of stinging for a little moment but that's all; the spell of this peace and dignity rendering even the barns and stables and cribs which belong to it impervious to the puny flames he might contrive . . . this, the peace and joy, ebbing for an instant as he looked again at the stiff black back, the stiff and implacable limp of the figure which was not dwarfed by the house, for the reason that it had never looked big anywhere and which now, against the serene columned back-drop, had more than ever that impervious quality of something cut ruthlessly from tin, depthless, as though, sideways to the sun, it would cast no shadow.[3]

As might be expected in declamatory prose, the vocabulary and diction in these passages are abstract. We find in key positions in the Joyce, "soul", "descent", "end", the "living" and the "dead", and in the given context, even the material fact of the "universe" loses most of its concreteness. Similarly, in the Faulkner, except for the strong particularity of the "wasp" and the "flames", the really operative positions are occupied by "peace" and "dignity"—both of them repeated—and by "spell". All the other nouns itemized are robbed of a considerable degree of their concreteness by being cast in the plural and by the emphasis thus being placed on their representative qualities: "barns", "cribs", "people", "lives". Both these writers derive a considerable rhetorical force from the connotative values of words generally renowned for being highly charged with emotional overtones. White, on the other hand, seems concerned with casual conversation even with the mundane, and he appears to take pains to qualify each of the essential abstract quantities by a phrasing that emphasizes a very concrete and physical manifestation. So: the "recollected joy" is experienced by Meg with a "shiver"; this "joy" she felt with Lum is embodied in "the down" of the adolescent's incipient beard that he laid against her cheek; "the little breeze" that, in the context of the prose, connotes the spirit of loving-kindness central to Daise's gospel, is described as "trickling through the moist roots of her hair" and is thus made part of her physical response to the boy's expression of his feelings. The rendering of this crucial incident appears almost off-hand; the more familiar agencies of rhetoric have been eschewed. The fervour is there but it is all the girl's, and it is generated without the use of the more standard devices of persuasion.

The same is true of the use of rhythm. The Joyce sentence makes immense music with its alliterative, almost fugal, account of the snowfall and moves to its conclusions with majestic solemnity. The Faulkner one is frankly hortatory, calculated to make a direct appeal to the ear; it is high in pitch and elaborate in cadence, almost frenetic in its mass appeal. The White one is by comparison designed for familiar discourse; even for subdued yarning. The seven distinct parts into which it falls have been selected by him to meet the needs of analysis and arranged for the achievement of clarity, and as each comma checks our progress through it, we ponder the various ideas it contains and those relationships among them that White offers for appreciation. These are: the whole tender question of young Meg's experience; the impact upon her of her first encounter with physical love; her dim but very relevant awareness of what her aunt's life and death may mean; her obedience to her present immediate circumstances in which parents bid her to enter a car and be driven home; and her frankly eager anticipation of her future, for which her experiences with the aunt and the boy have now prepared her. This is the rhythm not of the onward rush but of deliberation, and the impact of the whole sentence is derived not from elements in it that are intrinsic to conventional rhetoric but from the context provided by the antecedent narrative, to which it deftly makes indirect allusion and reference. The ramifications of the girl's excited awareness are all the more penetrating for having been signalled by such quiet means.

As a piece of shorter fiction, ever grateful for prose of great economy, **"Down at the Dump"** demonstrates the superb adroitness with which White can modulate his discourse among many functions—satiric, compassionate, speculative—and give it a dimension that is metaphysical, even religious, in its range. Only the later E. M. Forster has achieved such breadth of reference with so little overt apparatus and with such throwaway eloquence. White's dramatic modes prove his ear for the mimetic to be fully as faithful, for idioms and tones, as is Joyce's, and his technical adventurousness is every bit as bold as Faulkner's. His important difference lies in his undercutting of the strident to a point where passages that are in fact declamatory in function come through as almost laconic. His is indeed chameleon prose; or, to change the figure, experimenters in fiction during the earlier years of this century have provided him with a loom on which he now weaves a fabric of lustrous texture which is not necessarily "better" but is certainly important in its kind, for it suggests one more way in which even art that has the most manifold effects can conceal its means; and one more way in which an arresting treatment of particulars in time and place can be released from the particularity of that time and of that place.

Notes

1. All references are to the first book publication of this story in Patrick White, *The Burnt Ones* (London: Eyre & Spottiswoode, 1964), pp. 283–314. Section occupies pp. 309–10.
2. James Joyce, *Dubliners,* (London: Jonathan Cape, 1956), p. 256.
3. *The Collected Stories of William Faulkner,* Vol. 3 (London: Chatto & Windus, 1958), p. 16.

William Walsh (essay date 1977)

SOURCE: "Other Work," in *Patrick White's Fiction,* Rowman and Littlefield, 1977, pp. 67-84.

[*In the following essay, Walsh discusses the common aspects of White's short stories, plays, and novels.*]

The scope of the eleven stories in ***The Burnt Ones*** (1964) is naturally more confined than in the novels, but the shape and proportions are the same. There is a similar sense of the depth of human nature and the same strikingly individual sensibility, giving off a mixed odour of sweat and spirituality. The people in the Australian group of stories may be ordinary (**"Dead Roses"**, **"Willy-Wagtails by Moonlight"**) or drab (**"Clay"**, **"Down at the Dump"**), the events few and unspectacular, the context conventional or down at heel, the air wretched or melancholy, and yet from these unpromising constituents Patrick White constructs a celebration of human possibility which is at once lyrical and quite unsentimental. White has an eye which is gluttonous for detail. Each passage is firm from the presence of discriminated actuality. But all the solid, objective existence, convincing in surface, sure in implication, is submissive to the initiative of the writer. It is as much the result of reflection as observation, and it is composed of detail which is both authentic in its own right and quick at every point with the highly individual quality of the author's mind. This is particularly evident in the pace with which details follow one another. They tumble out with unforced vivacity, products of an endless energy. And they exhibit the peculiar violence of White's imagination which is capable of informing the mildest symptom of character or the most delicate indication of place with a strange intensity.

Not all the stories, naturally, are on the same level. The best are **"Down at the Dump"**, **"The Woman Who Wasn't Allowed to Keep Cats"**, **"A Cheery Soul"**. **"Willy-Wagtails by Moonlight"**, designed to exhibit with an almost Somerset Maugham kind of cynicism that people are not always what they appear to be, is altogether too neat and deficient in White's characteristic resonance and seriousness. **"Miss Slattery and Her Demon Lover"** is a fine, flourishing cartoon of a story with a conventionally eccentric Hungarian, an ordinary loose Australian girl, and a context of a somewhat dandruffed Bohemia. **"Dead Roses"** and **"Clay"**, one about an unawakened and emotionally oppressed girl, the other about what one can only call in an unkind but appropriate way, a compulsive loony, seem designed as comments on D. H. Lawrence's motto in his posthumous essay 'Education of the People',[1] 'down with mothers'. They convey a kind of personal distrelish and they seem to attribute to the mother in each case, a malformation of the subject's nature and brutality in dealing with it on the part of the parent as a kind of effect and cause instead of, perhaps, as cause and effect. Each of these two, the beefy, Betjeman-type Anthea Scudamore and the poor, deluded obsessionist Clay, are altogether too passive and malleable to engage the reader's interest in anything more than a mildly observant way. They are specimens rather than subjects, and while the two worlds in which they live are depicted with characteristic energy and significance, the one distinctly upper, the other lower class, the central figures are altogether too weak and limp. Each story appears to have a vacancy at a point where it should pulse with life.

Perhaps I could illustrate from these stories two unattractive defects which are more obtrusive in the short stories, where they cannot be lost in a longer, more complex movement. Here, for example, from **"Dead Roses"**, are a few lines which illustrate White rubbing gratingly on the reader's sensibility and calling his attention to the effect in an altogether too ostentatious way:

> It was only the receptacle of which she was in desperate need, in which her uncommunicative nature might spill itself, if silently. So she was hungrily grateful for this stone cell, for the sound of the bent tea-tree as it sawed at iron and silence. And sawed.
>
> (p. 19)

That 'And sawed' is a calamitous application of a device White sometimes uses with success in the novels; and so is the apparent precision of the concluding phrase in the following lines, which are clearly intended to pin down and refine the meandering course of Clay's illusion:

> Then she came towards him, and he saw that she herself might sink in the waters of time she spread before him cunningly the nets of water smelling of nutmeg over junket the steamy mornings and the rather shivery afternoons.
>
> (p. 132)

'And sawed' and 'the rather shivery afternoons' are White at his more relaxed and careless.

A more impressive Australian story, **"The Letters"**, is the tale of a dim, dry creature, Charles Polkinghorn, who slips more and more away from the roughness of life into some terrifying remoteness. Charles's life, and the influence on it of his self-entranced mother, both indicated with tactful economy, are most intimately and subtly displayed. Her grandeur is that of the self-deifying; her possessions, including her son, are exquisite and cared for because they are hers, perhaps because they are her. The withdrawal of

Charles from family, work and life is most convincingly insinuated in the quietest, mildest manner, which makes the horrifying conclusion when the fifty-year-old man is reduced to nuzzling his horrified mother's breasts, more acceptable and inevitable than the equally horrifying conclusion of **"Clay"**, which has about it something gratuitous and ostentatious.

Most of these stories deal, as do some of the major novels, with afflicted human nature, with the wound in the mind or the burn in the soul. But whereas in the novels the deprivation, or wretchedness, or imperfection becomes a means towards another and deeper reality, in most of the short stories the malady or calamity is part of a self-enclosed system. Neither in **"Clay"** nor **"Dead Roses"**, nor **"The Letters"**, nor **"A Cheery Soul"** do we have that drama of dialectic we find in the novels. The effect in most of these is, however complex, essentially single in its impact, and the only value released appears to be a quality of intensity for its own sake. This is true even of so fine a story as **"A Cheery Soul"**. Miss Docker is one whose goodness is a disease. Her sickness is doing good to others. She is indeed a monster, and her monstrosity is made all the more appalling by the accuracy, sometimes the savage accuracy, with which her surroundings are conveyed: the little suburban house where she goes to live with the taciturn Ted Custance and his generous wife, the old people's home where she goes to continue her devastation after being turned out finally by the worn-out Custances, and the church where she succeeds in destroying a clergyman. Here, for example, are some lines which combine clinical accuracy and disgust:

> The whole of Sarsaparilla knew something of Miss Docker's present circumstances: how, since old Miss Baskerville died, and the niece had decided *Lyme Regis* must be sold, there was Miss Docker, soon to find herself without a roof. Almost everyone had been the object of the poor woman's thoughtfulness. One need only mention the Christmas presents she could not afford. Miss Docker was a gift to the gift-shops: all those little ash-trays with gumnuts in relief, the shepherdesses of dusty lace, the miniature boomerangs, with the holes to hold the toothpicks, to spear the chipolatas with. Everybody knew, but almost everybody forgot. It was more convenient to remember she had her pension and her health.
>
> (p. 151)

Miss Docker in her relations with the Custances provides a comedy of desperation:

> 'For some time,' Miss Docker said, 'I have wondered why, amongst good friends, there seems to be a ban on Christian names.'
>
> Ted Custance could have been warding it off.
>
> 'I was christened Gertrude,' Miss Docker told. 'But everybody calls me Gee. Gee would feel she really was your friend to hear her name occasionally.'
>
> Mrs Custance hung her head.
>
> 'I expect we are not that kind,' she confessed. 'We are not exactly cold people, not formal in any way, but stiff'—here she made the greatest effort—'yes, I suppose, too, we are shy.'
>
> 'A name is friendship's sweetener,' Miss Docker coaxed.
>
> Mr Custance was sweating.
>
> 'I'm buggered if I will!' he said, very quiet, and quickly went outside.
>
> (pp. 160-1)

In the old people's home the play of desperation becomes a farce of destructive cruelty. In the church the comedy becomes one of discrepancy carried to a violent extreme, and in fact the comic is quite absorbed in the horror of destruction. But Miss Docker remains at the end what she began as, a monster without insight, a hero of destruction and a kind of martyr to negation.

Good as **"A Cheery Soul"** is, an even better achievement is the group of Greek stories, **"A Glass of Tea"**, **"The Evening at Sissy Kamara's"**, **"Being Kind to Titina"** and **"The Woman Who Wasn't Allowed to Keep Cats"**. I do not know any modern writer who has been more successful in illuminating the opacity of the Mediterranean world, at least in its Greek aspects. It is a world scored by lines of discrepancy and incomprehension; the men divided from the women, the children from the parents, the visitor from the inhabitant. Never were Greeks so unclassical as these, altogether lacking, as they are, in coolness, coherence and austerity. They are either fractious and nervy, or indolent and abstracted, or blithely, self-centredly crazy. Europe in them seems to be shading into some remoter terrain. Malliakas in **"A Glass of Tea"** finds, for example, 'that every Swiss seemed to have achieved a balance, while he, the Greek, could only oppose his undemonstrable inner life and a certain soft elegance' (p. 89). The comparatively calm, commonsensical young man who tells the story in the beautifully organised tale **"Being Kind to Titina"** is transformed into 'the awkward thing of flesh' (p. 199) which his childhood acquaintance Titina Stavridi, now an accomplished *putain,* had once been, changing, among shouting uncles and neurotic aunts, into something as tense and feverish as they.

> Outside, the lilac-bushes were turned solid in the moonlight. The white music of that dusty night was frozen in the parks and gardens. As I leaned out of the window, and held up my throat to receive the knife, nothing happened. Only my Aunt Thalia continued playing Schumann, and I realized that my extended throat was itself a stiff sword.
>
> (p. 205)

These characters show a glittering surface and a tremblingly vulnerable centre. They cannot bear to be ordinary. '"Average!" screeched Sissy Kamara, with an expression of triumph and a gold bridge. "Who is average?"' (p. 143). The women have a hectic, feverish air; the men are remote or passive; each kind is a stranger to the other except for love: 'Often Poppy Pantzopoulos refused to forgive her husband's still perfect profile until she found it on her pillow' (p. 135). The air is melancholy, reminiscent, the memories dominated by Smyrna and the Catastrophe, things dusted with nostalgia assume a vaguely religious aspect: 'Poppy Pantzopoulos had remembered the drawing-room on Frankish Street, the summer stealing through iron shutters, by stealth of light and grace of jasmine, to flirt with the neo-Byzantine plate' (p. 140).

Perhaps the finest of these Greek stories is **"The Woman Who Wasn't Allowed to Keep Cats"**, in which Mr and Mrs Spiro Hajistavros, the owners of restaurants and Cadillacs in the United States, are reduced on their return to Greece to being simply 'Maro and Spiro, a couple of Greeks' come to visit Mrs Hajistavros's childhood friend, now Mrs Alexiou. This story brilliantly evokes the intense and disappointed memories of the two women, Mrs Alexiou's roof flat with its permanent smell of cat, her ludicrously intellectual husband, and the poor, rich Greek-American husband who 'would have liked to live at peace with all men, but was continually brought to a halt on the edge of a hostile country, partly obscure, partly lambent, which he would end by recognising as the human mind' (p. 248). With what clinical nicety the indolent intellectual is evoked:

> Aleko Alexiou was staring out to sea. He had allowed wind and sunlight to prepare his head for sacrifice.
>
> 'Take nature,' Alexiou said.
>
> His hand was helping him extract, or mould, a painfully refractory object.
>
> 'Nature is so—so—*un*-co*op*erative, ultimately so *unreal!*'
>
> Then his hand fell, and with it his failure, while the illusory light continued to cascade into a spurious sea.
>
> (pp. 263-4)

This middle-class Mediterranean world of poverty and pretension, of natures both exquisite and brutal, of aspiration which wholly ignores reality, is conveyed with an extraordinary inwardness and conviction. Its melancholy, its bared human nerves, its direct and powerful tradition, its truth of resistance to the modern world: all these are conveyed with an amazing and creative accuracy.

The finest story in ***The Burnt Ones*** is **"Down at the Dump"**, a complex lyrical piece, engaging much that is best and most authentic in White's talent, and a triumph of sensibility which, as Henry James says, 'Takes to itself the faintest hints of life [and] converts the very pulses of the air into revelation'. The story is set in Sarsaparilla between a 'red brick propriety' on the one side, occupied by Councillor and Mrs Hogben and their daughter Meg who had 'the eyes of a mopey cat', and the gray, unpainted weatherboard of the Whalleys who were in the bits-and-pieces trade. Everything associated with these people is astonishingly eloquent of character and ethos. The Hogbens' liver-coloured brick house had not a single damp mark on the ceiling, nor, one is sure, is there a mark of any kind on the washing machine, the septic, the TV, the cream Holden Special, or the telephone, kept swabbed with Breath-o'-Pine. And Wal Whalley had a better eye than anyone for the things a person really needs: '. . . dead batteries and musical bedsteads, a carpet you wouldn't notice was stained, wire, and again wire, clocks only waiting to jump back into the race of time' (p. 284). If the Whalleys (Wal is still a fairly appetising male, the children had inherited their mother's colour, 'and when they stood together, golden-skinned, tossing back their unmanageable hair, you would have said a mob of taffy brumbies') stand for the richness, health and grossness of life and the Hogbens for meanness and deprivation, skinny young Meg in her cramped school uniform and surly Lum Whalley with his dreams of driving through the night in his own truck, or at least a semi-trailer, represent possibilities of renewal. Lum and Meg's first awkward interrogation of each other takes place at the Sarsaparilla dump, separated from Sarsaparilla cemetery only by a few strands of barbed wire, while the interment of Mrs Whalley's sister Daise is proceeding. The dump itself heaves with a strange, sprawling life:

> Here and there it appeared as though trash might win. The onslaught of metal was pushing the scrub into the gully. But in many secret, steamy pockets, a rout was in progress: seeds had been sown in the lumps of grey, disintegrating kapok and the laps of burst chairs, the coils of springs, locked in the spirals of wirier vines, had surrendered to superior resilience.
>
> (p. 295)

Another and purer stage of existence is implied in the vividly summoned life of Daise, the dead woman whose morals may have been loose but whose feelings were generous and tender, whether for the man who kept her or for the repulsive, deadbeat Ossie whom she wheeled home from the dump in a wheel barrow one night and nourished with food, sex and Franciscan compassion.

Not, I hasten to add, that **"Down at the Dump"** is in any way marked by a banal and static symbolism. Wal is really a dustman, Councillor Hogben a creepy politician, Meg a genuine schoolgirl. It is just that the things, the people, the location, all the items and gear of the fiction, carry a spontaneous, flowing significance. Moreover, the radically disjunctive consciousness, the intuition of grace and life, frequently succumbing to or only occasionally resisting the calculated, discursive and Benthamite mentality, which makes for an absolute division in some of the work, operates here in a subtler, altogether more poetically concrete way.

This story, like the best of White's achievement, springs from a pure sense of existence, which stretches in its sympathy from the dense and dirty embodiments of existence in the haphazard gear of the rubbish dump, through every kind of modulation of life up to a level of experience which is spiritual in its candour and fineness. I have called Patrick White a traditional artist. But this is not to declare that in discriminating grades of existence he freezes them into any falsely static posture. He is not in that sense a hierarchical writer. On the contrary, there is a constant touching of different worlds, a Lawrentian sort of mobility and flow. A point of contrast becomes a point of connection. The rubbish dump in **"Down at the Dump"** runs into the cemetery. The voice of goodness from the grave calls out to the devious town councillor. It is among the heaving rubbish of the dump that the young lovers make their first tender inquiries of one another. The mystery of existence, the mystery of self, the mutuality of experience and self—this 'metaphysical' theme, no more than hinted at here—rolls like a profound current all through Patrick White's work. This depth of preoccupation is the animating presence which quickens the multiplying details and orders the vast range of material in the fiction (but also, and not infrequently, which clouds the clues the artist offers to what he is about with too large and unmanageable a significance).

Just as **"Down at the Dump"**, simple and brief as it is, involves in undertone and suggestion Patrick White's preoccupation with being, so too it is constantly in touch, at least in hint and intimation, with the other sustaining theme of his fiction—the exploration of self. His precise interest in this short story is one that a distinction of Coleridge lights up: '. . . self—i.e. the image or complex cycle of imagination . . . which is the perpetual representative of our Individuum . . .'[2]. Patrick White is concerned in miniature in **"Down at the Dump"**, *in extenso* in the novels, with all the subtleties of relationship between individuality and the self.

The six *novellas* and short stories in ***The Cockatoos*** (1975), varying in location from Sicily to Sydney, show Patrick White, if not absolutely at the pitch of his powers—since this would require a richer orchestration of theme and a larger area to manoeuvre in—certainly as possessed as ever of a ferocity of communicating skill, and as capable of constructing from common and dandruffed material a world which is rhapsodic and realistic. There is the same flow of creative capacity that one sees in the major novels, which can find, in situations of a seedy simplicity and characters of conventional mediocrity, subjects and themes of depth and urgency. The manner combines the more nearly abstinent idiom developed about the period of *The Solid Mandala* with the endless, burrowing, spiritual inquisitiveness so characteristic of the mature work. The stories are told with a straighter narrative, a more regular syntax, and a much less drowning torrent of metaphor. But there is still the accustomed ease and flow of imaginative energy.

There is, indeed, one positive advantage in these stories in that they head off White's occasional inability to resist gratuitous and unnecessary symbolism, of the kind, for example, which marred significant junctures in *Voss* and *Riders in the Chariot*. In the short stories, or in most of them, the movement between idea and material is vital and unbroken, the theme as intimate with the material as soul with body.

When I spoke of a celebration both lyrical and terrifying, I had in mind once again the binomial or rather, since one feels something tearing and intense in the artist's reaction, the Manichaean nature of Patrick White's sensibility. On one side is the flow of love and grace brilliantly exemplified in the clouds of birds glittering in the neglected suburban gardens in **"The Cockatoos"**, or the sudden, Franciscan flood of pity and love felt by the brutally delinquent Felicity for the dying derelict in **"The Night the Prowler"**, or the similar surge of devotion which the elderly, widowed Mrs Natwick feels for her cocky little friend in **"Five-Twenty"**, or the subdued saintliness of Dowson in **"A Woman's Hand"**. On the other, there is the dialectic of loathing expressed in the appalling horrors of the flesh, like the loathsome sex in **"Sicilian Vespers"**: 'Like two landed fish, they were lunging together, snout bruising snout, on the rucked-up Cosmati paving' (p. 243).

Part of the same idiom is the constant reference, both expressed and metaphorical, to what is raw, ugly, or offensive. Patrick White has always made great play in his work with such elements in Australian provincial life, which often serves as a baseline against which the reader is to measure simplicity and goodness. But where these things once filled him with mockery or bitterness, they now suffuse him wth disgust and despair. Stench, slime, mucus, excrement, decay, the ruined body—these are notes very often touched on in these stories. Even a meal in a restaurant assumes an appearance of horrors: 'There were some splinters of fish done in sawdust. She refused to wrestle with her cartilage of mutton. Over their helpings of marshmallow and tinned pineapple-ring the honeymoon couples were beginning to uncoil' (p. 83); and when a candle burns in church in the Greek war story **"The Full Belly"**, it is anaemic 'amongst the grubby pellets, the sickly stalactites, of last year's wax' (p. 115).

White in these shorter works, as in the major novels, shows himself not greatly concerned with originality in situation or character. The situation in most of these stories is orthodox, even traditional. An officious wife tries to arrange a marriage for her husband's friend, a Greek family looks for food under the German occupation, a young woman experiences an unsuccessful rape, birds visit and then invade a neighbourhood and the lives of the neighbours, a widow's new friend is killed by a car, two married couples meet as tourists in Sicily, a teenage girl turns to violence.

For most novelists these are circumstances and people which would pretty firmly limit treatment and development, but Patrick White's extraordinary skill allows them to become—I put it like this because his treatment, once seen, seems inevitable—monstrous and illuminating. Like the pianist with his piano in **"The Full Belly"** he turns this 'furniture into instrument'. One cannot too highly praise, for example, his power of representation, the conviction of his surfaces, textures, implied depths. At the same time, his incessant interrogation of every form of existence gives to the dense reality of things and persons an intellectual and imaginative buoyancy. Everything moves, there is no arrest in personality, existence glides and turns and flows. What we see in these stories is the process of *becoming.* White's art is at the other extreme from the static, his universe—like the relations of his characters—melting and modulating at every point.

The stories in ***The Cockatoos*** are the product of a powerful and singular literary personality. At its centre is a vision of the violence of existence, of the intensity of being itself; and it is rendered with an astonishing energy of realisation. I have perhaps stressed unduly the separation in his vision, the divorce of grace and horror. It might be added that it shows itself in a more than usual share of the current awareness of the nastiness of certain spheres of experience, particularly in matters of sex, and a fierce disdain of the middling and the commonplace—aristocratic characteristics that White shares with Eliot. This argues, I think, a certain failure or distortion in the range of his sympathy for human nature and experience. Perhaps it is a deficiency in our civilisation forcing itself into the artist's work and revealing itself in deficiencies of tact and grasp, as well as in a certain lack of tenderness toward the language.

But at its most mature (as in *Voss* some of these stories come close to belonging to that category, particularly **"Sicilian Vespers"**, **"The Cockatoos"**, **"The Full Belly"**, and **"Five-Twenty"**), White's art is quickened and unified by the most powerful and creative quarter of his sensibility, namely a concept of goodness which depends upon an unspoiled wholeness of the person. Such goodness, although it may be striven for, cannot be deserved. It is a stroke of providence or a form of genius, but in any case a gift, a grace, and one most likely to be found in the possession of those commonly regarded as blemished or eccentric or hateful, like Voss, or Theodora Goodman, or Arthur Brown in *The Solid Mandala.* In Patrick White's eyes the supreme gift of man, existing in a context of surliness, ugliness and cruelty, is precisely this clarified consciousness. It is something which belongs above all to those he called 'the poor unfortunates' in the epigraph of his other book of short stories, ***The Burnt Ones.*** There is a sufficient presence of the burnt ones, the poor unfortunate ones, in ***The Cockatoos*** to justify, to put into place, the monstrous horrors of human living, of which this sumptuous and tortured talent is harshly conscious.

So much of the action in Patrick White's novels is internally generated, so many distinctive idioms are managed so successfully, so often the vivid surface detail connects naturally with serious and even profound themes, that one might well have expected—apart from his known personal predilection for the theatre, as I pointed out before—had he lived in a country and at a time when the institution of drama thrived, that he would have devoted considerably more of his mind and art to the drama. In fact, four of his plays have been produced in Australia and appeared in print in 1965 (a very early one, *Return to Abyssinia,* of which no copy survives, was put on in London in 1947 and called by *The Times* 'a disarmingly ingenuous little play'). The most dramatically effective of them, at least so far as one can tell from the printed page, is *The Ham Funeral* which was written in 1947 before his novelist's gift had fully formed, and produced in Australia in 1961. In this play White has been more successful than in the others in subordinating the natural intrusiveness of the novelist, particularly one with so peremptory and overwhelming a talent as his own. Nevertheless, one can see from the stage directions the bias of the novelist, which is to make himself more actively present than as a dramatist he should. Here are two short excerpts from the stage directions in *The Ham Funeral:*

> Before the CURTAIN rises, the YOUNG MAN appears, and speaks the following prologue. He is dressed informally, in a fashion which could be about 1919. He is rather pale. His attitude throughout the play is a mixture of the intent and the absent, aggressiveness and diffidence.
>
> The LANDLORD is seated on one of the deal chairs beside the kitchen table. He sits with his legs apart, facing the audience. He is a vast man, swollen, dressed from neck to ankle in woollen underclothes, of a greyish colour, and in carpet slippers. His face is pallid, flushing to strawberry in the nose, and in a wen on one cheek. He wears a thick, drooping moustache, and is smoking a short, black pipe. The LANDLADY is also seated at the kitchen table, with a saucepan, peeling potatoes. She is a large woman in the dangerous forties, ripe and bursting. Her hair, still black, is swept up untidily in a vaguely Edwardian coiffure. She is wearing a shabby white satin blouse, dark skirt, and an old pair of pink mules. LANDLADY continues to peel potatoes, but with mounting boredom and distaste.

These passages themselves seem to me to demonstrate the novelist's passion to be seen mastering the material and ordering each step and shade in the action. And, indeed, all the plays suggest a certain lack of confidence on the part of the dramatist in his actors and partners. Drama as a collaboration is something very hard for the novelist to accept.

White as dramatist, then, asks for a very exact and even finicky correspondence with his intentions. He also avails himself of the poetic and technical devices reintroduced into the theatrical repertoire by the German Expressionists. Now, of course, one finds them perfectly acceptable and even conventional, although one feels, particularly in *A Cheery Soul* and *The Season at Sarsaparilla,* a degree of discomfort in the passage from the allegorical to the representational manner. In *The Ham Funeral,* however, there is a much more natural flow between the two sides. The play is set in some vaguely London scene—really, simply in a place—in a crummy boarding house kept by Alma Lusty (even the names are somewhat obviously made to work for the theme), who is driven by an uncomprehended rage for life, and her reticent husband, Will, whose death is the main event in the play.

One of the lodgers is the young man, whose progress from fastidious, willed detachment to a more naturally and exclusive implication provides the dramatic mobility of the piece. The other side of the young man's self, his anima, or image as Coleridge puts it, is projected on to a dreary fellow lodger, Phyllis Pither. As the anima, the girl is romantic and reminiscent of the figure in Eliot's 'Marina' (indeed, there are several hints of Eliot in the play as one would expect from the period); as Phyllis she is a limp creature with a cold. Will, an ex-wrestler, philosopher, and finally silent contemplator of reality, dies—we do not know why, although explanations are offered during the ham tea, one even being that Mrs Lusty is responsible. The young man rejects the advances of the writhing Alma, although this is not proposed as any final rejection of life but rather as a stage of his journey towards maturity and completeness. The romantic ideal represented by the young woman, who leaves a sprig of lilac as an earnest of her reality, is a trifle thin and Rossetti-like. But there is also some superb comedy in the play, particularly a splendid scene in which the young man on his way to inform Will's relatives of his death, discovers two old ladies rummaging in the dust bins in search of bits and pieces which we realise are very much more than what they seem. And the ham tea itself after the funeral has a positively Chaucerian vitality and thrust.

The Ham Funeral seems to me an economically organised and highly actable play, both theatrically and dramatically effective, and managed both with instinct and skill. Its deficiency, which is one rarely associated with White's major work, is a certain attenuated and misty quality in the central experience, reminiscent of *The Living and the Dead.* That is certainly not a charge that could be levelled at *The Season at Sarsaparilla,* which is described as 'A Charade of Suburbia in Two Acts'. This is a robust and energetic play, but to me it is strangely lacking in those skills of dramatic management evident in *The Ham Funeral.* The half dozen principal characters are, in this context, not only orthodox but conventional. Even the little girl, Pippy Pogson, whom White describes in his novelist's way in the stage directions as 'a forthright and astute small girl', is more of a camera eye than a living person. (Compare her, for example, in respect of complexity and conviction with Maisie in Henry James's *What Maisie Knew.* How thin, and merely perky she is!) The males, whether of the office or the manual kind, and the women, whether refined or earthy, are generalised in their ordinariness. The two dim young men, one decent and one romantic, again are gestures towards personalities. The point of the contrast between a natural, breathing vitality and the clichés of suburbia are hammered home with a repetitive and unsubtle emphasis. The pack of dogs in pursuit of a bitch in heat, howling intermittently through the play, which so much engages Pippy Pogson, who was beginning to sniff at the facts of life, are a raucous and somewhat too obvious device.

The set of contrasts which constitute the substance of the play, between suburbia and life, between the artistic and the commonplace, between man and his man-made wilderness, between the Australian pastoral myth and its huddled actuality, between mateship and lust, are not articulated with White's customary mastery but lie lumpily side by side. Nor has the language that resonance and evocative power which it so often has in the novels. Here is a characteristic passage in which Nola Boyle, the unfaithful wife of Ernie the sanitary man, expresses her kind of self-indulgent and slouching sensuality:

> Nola (*strolling, picking at this and that in the garden, smelling here and there at a flower, soliloquising*) This is the best time of all. Before the men come. (*However, she looks at her watch*) Even in summer, at the end of the day, when you feel you could have been spat out, when the hair is stuck to your forehead, it is best, best. A time to loiter. The flowers are lolling. The roses are biggest. (*Stoops to smell*) The big, lovely roses, falling with one touch . . . (*Laughs*) I could eat the roses! Dawdling in the back yard. If there was none of these busybodies around (*glancing at the Pogson home*)—thin, prissy, operated women—I'd take off me clothes, and sit amongst the falling roses. I've never felt the touch of roses on my body. (*Examining her bare arm*) Green in the shade. Green for shade. Splotchy. You can imagine the petals, trickling, trickling, better than water, because solid. . . . (*She looks again at her watch, irritation rising*) But the men don't come! They gotta come! When you expect them. Now, or then, it's the same. They gotta come. The men. Standing in bars, with arms round one another's shoulders, faces running together, to tell a bluer story. . . . Men are dirty buggers! But they oughta come. They're expected.
>
> (pp. 125-6)

The combination of realistic and non-realistic techniques works uncomfortably in the suburban scene, which seems much more naturally made for a more caustic kind of realism. The play is episodic rather than organic in its development, and the themes a set of abstract convictions applied to rather than drawn out of the situation.

In two of the most intelligent treatments of White's plays, that by Barry Argyle[3] and that by R. F. Brissenden,[4] a similar point is made. Here is the shorter and clearer version of it given by Brissenden:

> At the risk of gross oversimplification one can, I think, isolate these two centres of interest in White's plays: on the one hand the individual, struggling to come to terms with himself and with the universe in which he lives—a universe in which inanimate objects and the world of nature can be as important as other human beings; and on the other the cyclic processes of living, impersonal, inscrutable, and inescapable. Dramatic tensions and interests are generated in his work not only out of the relationship of the characters with each other (as in the case of most plays) but also out of their involvement with these larger biological and physical forces.

This seems to me an admirable expression of White's dramatic intentions, more fully realised in *The Ham Fu-*

neral, less adequately substantiated in the other three plays. In the drama more than any other literary form, ideas and themes must be, in Coleridge's word, 'impersonated'. The season in the title and the howling pack of dogs after the bitch in heat in the play *The Season at Sarsaparilla,* not to speak of other theatrical devices like the gauzily, filmy back-presence of Mrs Lillie's youth in *A Cheery Soul,* are wholly insufficient substitutes for actual, dramatic embodiment. They tend, rather, to give the impression of a novelist desperately seeking to reproduce on the stage the wider and subtler effects that his words are capable of suggesting in the novel.

The dramatised version of *A Cheery Soul* illustrates this employment of inappropriate techniques and irrelevant kinds of subtlety. In *A Cheery Soul* the necessary element of conflict exists theoretically between Miss Docker's insensitive passion to help her neighbours and some more balanced concept of neighbourliness. She illustrates one side of the opposition, but nothing 'impersonates' the other. Moreover, Miss Docker is a cartoon rather than a character, limited and one-dimensional. *A Cheery Soul* certainly contains some vigorous and pointed scenes but they are in a strict sense farcical rather than comic or tragic. As this play illustrates, White has a brilliant sense for the dramatic situation or moment. The scene in the church between the inarticulate and virtuous clergyman and the bullying goodwill of Miss Docker combines ridicule and pathos in an original and telling way. But such things are momentary and the rest of the play appears simply as an arrangement or context in which dramatic functions may appear, not the irresistible ground for them. The last scene in the play in which a dog urinates on the frustrated Miss Docker's leg, is, like the chorus of howling dogs in *The Season at Sarsaparilla,* another example of willed imagery which cannot support the weight put on it.

The burden of critical opinion on *Night on Bald Mountain* seems to be that it is an impressive but failed tragedy. By tragedy people usually have in mind here the Greek form, a disposition enforced by the pretty exact observance of the unities, the choric function performed by the splendid Miss Quodling, the hints of incest or its surrogate psychological form, the intensity of guilt and the sacrifice of the victim. I find this account of it not so much inadequate as irrelevant. No amount of the application of Greek modes can transform the material of what is essentially a melodrama. Indeed, it seems to me a spirited and fascinating one. The characters are not particularly original but they are individually seized and displayed, the varieties of their suffering are conventionally demonstrated, and above all the language of the play and the idiom of each character are both lively and well fitted. Several critics have noticed how passive the central experience is. Hugo Sword, the Professor of English, is tortured by his own frustrations both scholarly and personal; his wife, the alcoholic Miriam, is tortured by him, and by herself, and by her addiction; Stella Summerhayes, the pretty virgin nurse, is tortured by both. The minor characters, Cantwell a grocer, and the rather dim lecturer Denis Craig, add a touch of realism and imply the existence of another world and other values, but not with sufficient force to make the experience embodied in the Swords's house and family more than an obsessively negative and solipsistic one.

The one vital thing in the play seems to me to be the language, and the most moving and potent form of it is that of Miss Quodling, whose crackling, racily active speech generates whatever is positive in the play. Too much attention has been paid to its symbolic content and shading. What is splendid about it is its force, raciness and sharpness. Here is her hymn of praise to the morning, with which the play begins:

> Mornun . . . I love it even when it skins yer! Oh, yes, it can hurt! . . . When the ice crackles underfoot . . . and the scrub tears the scabs off yer knuckles . . . and the spiders' webs are spun again . . . first of all . . . out of dew . . . it's to remind that life begins at dawn. Bald Mountain! I wasn't born here. Oh, no! But know it, how I know it! I've learnt to understand the silences of rocks. Only the barren can understand the barren. I came, because I couldn't help it. I tasted the little, runty apples . . . and sour apricots . . . that somebody planted before they died. On Bald Mountain, nobody else has survived. Nobody else. I've lived here so long, I've forgotten now. (*Pause*) I don't go down . . . (*pointing behind her*) . . . not down there . . . though I watch the lights . . . at night . . . that glitter too much to be trusted. In the end, you can't trust anythun but goats and silence. Oh, yes, I know now! I've seen the mountain from a distance, too . . . moisture glist'nun on its bald patch . . . on bare rock. Sun on rock . . . that's the kiss that never betrays . . . because it doesn't promise nothun . . .
>
> (p. 272)

The truth is that as a dramatist Patrick White is a casualty of the times and of the theatrical tradition in his own country. The living drama of his work is to be found in the novels.

Notes

1. D. H. Lawrence, 'Education of the People', *Phoenix,* ed. E. D. McDonald (London, 1936).
2. Kathleen Coburn (ed.), op. cit., p. 68.
3. Barry Argyle, op. cit., pp. 90-107.
4. R. F. Brissenden, op. cit., pp. 41-2.

David Myers (essay 1978)

SOURCE: "Narrative Techniques in the Shorter Prose Fiction," in *The Peacocks and the Bourgeoisie,* Adelaide University Union Press, 1978, pp. 173-90.

[*In the following excerpt, Myers observes that White's more successful short stories mimic the intensity, tension, and density of imagery in his novels.*]

In an interview with Craig McGregor that took place some years after the publication of ***The Burnt Ones*** and some years before ***The Cockatoos*** appeared, Patrick White had the following to say about his short stories:

> Short stories? I don't really like writing them so much—though I have nearly got enough for another volume. All my effects are cumulative, and one doesn't really have the time to get the effects you want. The novella is more satisfactory; you can put more into it. Sometimes if I become very depressed while writing a novel and I get an idea for a short story I get that down, and afterward I feel as though I have been liberated somehow.

It is not uncommon for writers of fiction to compose stories or novellas as off-shoots of their major works, composed while this is in progress, and embodying a theme or an incident which doesn't quite fit within the framework of the novel. Thomas Mann, for example, composed *Death in Venice* as a companion piece on death to his great epic *The Magic Mountain.* But authors' intentions about whether an idea will grow under artistic treatment to a story, a novella, or a novel are unreliable, because Thomas Mann informs us that he had intended *The Magic Mountain* to be a brief, comic story as an antidote to the tragic-lyric form of *Death in Venice.*

If we accept this connection between short story and novel, we will expect to find certain bonds of theme and imagery between the shorter and the longer works of Patrick White's prose fiction. Although, as I have affirmed in the introduction to this monograph, the short stories and novellas can stand alone on their own merits, susceptible to interpretation as independent works of art, it is equally true that their themes and images are enriched when read in conjunction with the novels. For example, in the short story **"Clay"** there is a brief and mildly puzzling reference to Clay as a child being terrified by the antics of clowns at a circus and burying his head in his Aunt Maud's bosom. In the novel *Riders in the Chariot,* where White has the space to develop the omitted scene at length, he provides a detailed description of presumably these same clowns enacting a farcical-macabre scenario of a public hanging, in which a clown is required to spin at the end of a hanging rope and to feign death, and one of the grannies in the audience screams "They will kill the silly bugger yet!"[1] The amplifying of this incident in the novel is more satisfying aesthetically, but the story **"Clay"** stands as an independent narrative entity because the focus of our interest there is not on the clowns, but on Clay's hysterical reaction to any mildly scary incident and on his instinctive reaction to dive for the cover of the nearest mature female's bosom for protection, a reaction that he repeats in insanity with his mother at the end of the story.

To take another example: in *The Tree of Man* Mr. Parker senior is said to be a drunkard who once "answered a question in a sermon."[2] This incident is amplified in *A Cheery Soul* to form a theologically farcical climax. Further, at the end of this story a decrepit old cattle dog pisses on Miss Docker, and we are given to understand this is the sentence of God upon her because dog "is God turned round."[3] But at the conclusion of the novel *The Solid Mandala* Waldo Brown's corpse is eaten by his own dogs as a fitting punishment because as a proud rationalist he had denied God and religion all his life. White's implied judgement in the story is farcical with overtones of pathos for a woman now irrevocably condemned to loneliness, whereas his judgement in the novel is harsh and unrelenting. Nevertheless, the common pun or word-play on which they depend confirms our hypothesis about White's religious sense of humour. We have already noted this inclination to religious puns in connection with the word "stroked" at the climactic epiphany of *The Vivisector,* and with the word-plays on "blessés" and "remumber" at the climax of **"The Letters"**, and with the pun on the word "floods" at the end of *The Night the Prowler.*

Obviously there are many other connecting links between White's stories and novels, but to trace them all is not the purpose of this work. It is rather the function of this section to characterize the narrative and structural techniques of the stories, and to decide to what extent these differ from the techniques of the novels.

Many critics have now attempted to define the short story and in so doing to differentiate it from the anecdote, the sketch, the novella and the novel. I have no original words of wisdom to offer on these theoretical definitions, except perhaps to observe that none of the definitions works for the myriad of stories written in this century, but many of them work for some of these stories. White himself says, as we have noted in the initial quotation of this section, that he prefers to write novellas to short stories, but perhaps what he means by this is that he prefers to write longer stories to shorter stories. Are there hard and fast rules distinguishing a short story from a novella? Do we for example postulate that any story in excess of 6000-8000 words is a novella rather than a story? Or that any story that meaningfully illuminates the lives of more than say two characters separately is so complex as to make it a novella rather than a short story? Or that any story that does not limit itself to the representation of a single crisis or turning-point in the life of one central character, but instead creates capsule biographies of three or four characters through a complex network of flashbacks, constitutes a novella? Or where the thematic intentions of the author within the one story are not limited to the creation of a single effect but where instead there are clearly sub-themes and a number of effects ranging from the farcical to the tragic, that here the border from short story to novella is clearly crossed? The last two questions seem to point towards useful distinctions between short story and novella, particularly as they are written by Patrick White, but are certainly not sufficient justification for the literary theoretician to insist on drawing a dogmatic line between the two closely related forms.

I now propose to take what seem to me to be some of the more perceptive generalisations about the rhetorical and structural techniques pertinent to the short story and the novella, and investigate the measure of their relevance to White's stories.

These generalisations raise the following issues: the search for the overriding point of view and the hidden narrator; the art of an author making indirect comment and implied value judgments without reducing his characters to manipulated puppets; the startling metamorphosis of apparently simple and mundane events into disturbing spiritual problems; the analogy with film techniques in cutting abruptly from one scene to another and thus relying on themes and leitmotifs to establish a continuum rather than on the chronological sequence and the causality of the traditional plot; the selection of a single crisis in the life of the main character as an illustration of the crucial turning-point in his life and hinting at a climactic epiphany for this character, or for the reader of the story; the structural relationship of beginning, middle and end; endings which feature a twist in the tail or a dramatic shock as opposed to open endings which leave the reader puzzled and disturbed; the increasing significance attached to inanimate objects and their often symbolic influence on the characters; the tendency of the contemporary short story to evolve a new kind of open-ended parable; the moral task of the short story to celebrate the uniqueness of the individual as a counterbalance to the conveyor-belt uniformity of modern mass society (in this sense perhaps the short story is making a virtue out of a necessity, because its very conciseness forces it to limit its perspective to one or two main characters); the tendency of modern short stories to the grotesque and the absurd as another way of emphasizing the moral contrast between the way of life of the often strange outsider-protagonist and conventional society and therefore the close relation of the short story to theatre of the absurd and to epic theatre, both of which aim to shock rather than to lull, to trouble rather than to console; the notion that the novella is especially suitable to render "degenerative or pathetic tragedy"; the uniqueness of the novella as consisting in the "double effect of intensity with expansion"; the achievement of a compressive quality in the novella "by an unwavering thematic focus and an accumulation of structural parallels."[4]

Structurally considered, Patrick White's stories almost inevitably rise, often from paradoxically inappropriate, mundane or farcical levels, to a passionate climax. This climax is either set in the concluding scene, or if in the penultimate scene, it is in order to create a deliberately ironic anticlimax in the end. This climax often coincides with some decisive event such as death or insanity, but the climax itself is not external, but internal. It almost invariably takes the form of an epiphany, either for the main character, or often, for the reader.

Reid defines epiphanies as "sudden momentous intuitions . . . when an individual is most alert or most alone."[5] Patrick White favours an especially elevated kind of epiphany which he features as a characteristic climax for so many of his stories. In the stories collected in ***The Cockatoos*** the intuition of the epiphany is often related to the search of the outsider for an ecstatic insight into the underlying principle of all being in the cosmos, a fleeting moment of understanding of the workings of a hidden God in our earthly world, or a tragic triumph over petty egoism and possessiveness, which White sees as the evil of our world, through the medium of inspired love. This moment of transcendence of earthly preoccupations and of death and of the tormenting fact of individuation is characteristically gained by an isolated, unconventional individual, a romantic revolutionary against conventional society.[6] Even where the medium of the character's *unio mystica* is love, it is not the intimacy of two lovers that White stresses, but the panerotic or universal qualities of this love. The medium for these epiphanies can be solitary meditation on infinity as with Clem Dowson, aesthetic delight in the beauty of nature with Christian overtones as with Nesta Pine, or a vision uniting the dualistic principle of all being as with Harold Fazackerley, all within the one novella, **"A Woman's Hand."** In **"The Full Belly"** Iordanou seeks for God through the medium of music and confused erotic worship of the ascetic Panayia. In **"The Night the Prowler"** Felicity Bannister finds harmony with the ways of a hidden God through the unconventional practice of *caritas.* In **"Five-Twenty," "Sicilian Vespers"** and **"The Cockatoos"** there are what I would call negative sexual epiphanies, in which a character yearns for sexual union rather than mystic union and is either farcically or grotesquely taught the imperfections of this goal. The main characters in these three stories do not show sufficient understanding to grasp what they are being taught, and it is we the readers who experience a decisive insight into their failure. Mrs. Natwick in **"Five-Twenty"** farcically loses the object of her lust in the moment preceding its consummation. The grotesque inadequacy of Ivy Simpson's blasphemous and tasteless copulation is brought out by contrast with both the praying congregation and with the tear in the eye of Christ Pantocrator. The praying congregation has found spiritual serenity whereas she has gained only a temporary respite from the tormenting mundanity of her rationalistic and atheistic, and therefore pointless existence. The cockatoos inspire flowing passion in the inhibited Mick Davoren and the frigid Busby Le Cornu, but Mick cannot overcome the sin of his possessiveness and presumably for this reason he is punished by being grotesquely murdered. Olive Davoren is accorded an ironic heightening of her artistic sensitivity and her erotic love for her husband. But she drops away from her inspiration to a trivial widowhood, and Busby sinks back to isolation and despair. Although all three of them, and Tim Goodenough too in his own way, spontaneously feel religious awe of the cockatoos, they never do understand the transformation this vision should make to their lives. It is the reader who comprehends the tragic inevitability of their failure and experiences in this sense a negative epiphany. In "Fête Galante," by way of contrast, Thekla herself understands all too well the dual nature of her sexual failure. In lusting for the Olympians she has committed the sin of hybris, and in her lust she has betrayed her ascetic Panayia, just as hunger had driven Iordanou to betray his Panayia in **"The Full Belly."** Like Ivy Simpson in **"Sicilian Vespers"** she is grotesquely transformed by her lust into a monstrous fish with the sly face of a woman. In **"The Eye of the Storm"** we find yet another reference by White to this strange monster.[7]

It is fascinating to note how many of the climactic epiphanies in ***The Burnt Ones*** are negative and sexual in character. When Mrs. Mortlock's breath goes "crrkk in her throat" in the last lines of **"Dead Roses,"** she is annihilated by her awareness of her sexual envy of Cherie Flegg and of having wasted her life because of her sexual inhibitions and her social pretentiousness. In **"Willy-Wagtails by Moonlight"** there is a climactic revelation from the tape recorder, but no character gains real insight because of this revelation. Instead Nora stands isolated in her purity and her humility, and it is we the readers who are hit by the decisive insight into her moral superiority over the other characters' average corruption and deceitfulness. Constantia Phillipides experiences a tragic epiphany at the conclusion of **"A Glass of Tea"**; she says, as she rises for "a moment above the mounting tide of blood: 'I am the one, you see, who broke!"[8]

She has taken her life because of her jealousy for her husband. But more than this she rises above her jealousy at this moment, because now in the self-sacrifice of her death, she is concerned only with guaranteeing her husband's future happiness. It is of course ironic that it is herself rather than the glasses who breaks and that she dies knowing that Aglaia will not break under the strain of becoming Phillipides' second wife, and that her sacrifice has not been in vain. In **"Clay"** the main character's ecstatic sexual suicide is only instinctive self-gratification and it is once again the reader who is given a climactic detail of his clinging to the white wedding shoe in death. In the two concluding scenes of **"The Evening at Sissy Kamara's"** it is once again not the main character, Poppy Pantzopoulos, who comes to an intuitive understanding of her life's dilemma, but the reader. Because White has startlingly juxtaposed the tragic with the trivial, the reader intuitively grasps, without any comment from the author, the true nature of heroic self-sacrifice as opposed to Poppy's nervous, self-belittling flirtation with the idea. Similarly at the conclusion of **"A Cheery Soul"** Miss Docker continues on her falsely cheerful path, unaware that God has passed judgement on her through both Mr. Wakeman's sermon and the dog, but we the readers have comprehended the failure of her life and her way. But if **"A Cheery Soul"** features a negative, farcical religious climax, **"Down at the Dump"** compensates with the spiritual realisation by Daise Morrow of the love that transcends death and the partial comprehension of her gospel by Meg Hogben. The ensuing anti-climactic coda of four pages in fact rises out of its triviality and sordidness to a renewal of the climactic epiphany in White's representation of Meg's spiritual meditation and the resultant "warm core of certainty."[9] The remaining four stories in ***The Burnt Ones*** all feature climaxes involving sexual suffering. In **"Being Kind to Titina"** Dionysaki feels with full bitterness the irony that he has come to love Titina too late because she has now become a whore. But when he offers up his throat for self-sacrifice in expiation of earlier sin against her, he is forced to comprehend a further irony, namely that his "extended throat was itself a stiff sword."[10] White will not allow him to escape from his sin into the comfortingly passive pose of martyrdom; he must continue to accept the responsibility for further acts of aggression, as these are symbolically indicated by his 'sword.' The suffering awareness that Tibby Szabo gains from sexual disappointment remains, by way of contrast with Dionysaki, strictly farcical and Andrew Taylor is justified when he wittily points out that Tibby is not so much 'a burnt one' as he is 'roasted.'[11] In **"The Letters"** Charles Polkinghorn is allowed only one moment of tragic lucidity as he understands that all three of them, himself, his mother and his aunt, are fatefully "blessés." But his epiphany is, apart from Maud's letter, set in a context that is grotesque and farcical, and his moment of brief dignity is quickly lost in the ensuing parody of the Oedipus-myth. **"The Woman Who Wasn't Allowed to Keep Cats"** constitutes a rare exception among White's stories, because here the main character Kikitsa is allowed to transform herself and her way of life as the result of her suffering when she is deprived of her cats and as a result of her epiphanous understanding of sexual psychology. "It was simply that Kikitsa's face had undergone a change, the way faces will, by joy, or suffering."[12] This is the only one of White's stories with a climax that is both sexual in nature and also happy, indeed farcically so; the concluding anticlimax of Maro Hajistavrou's hatred and envy only serves by way of contrast to highlight Kikitsa's sexual joy.

We have noted that the climactic epiphany in White's stories is often followed by an ironic anticlimax. When the anticlimax is extended sufficiently, it tends to form a coda with a structural importance in its own right. We have also noted how in **"Down at the Dump"** the coda actually presented a renewal of the epiphany. This structural feature has particular relevance to **"A Woman's Hand,"** where in a lengthy coda whose artistic justification had been difficult to perceive until this moment, Harold Fazackerley perceives the healing union of the world's dualistic poles and merges himself in ecstatic unity with nature:

> He was the black water trickling, trickling at the bottom of it (a great gorge). He was the cliffside pocked with hidden caves. He was the deformed elbows of stalwart trees.[13]

The earlier epiphanies of Clem and Nesta here reach not just a renewal but a new and high er peak of spiritual understanding. But inevitably this peak too is followed by an anticlimax of trivia as the Fazackerleys wait uncomprehendingly to die. **"Sicilian Vespers"** and **"The Cockatoos"** also feature extended codas. The function of the coda in **"Sicilian Vespers"** is to allow us to understand through a flashback to Ivy's childhood why she was driven to her sexual-religious blasphemy in San Fabrizio. We understand, but Ivy doesn't, that her confusion has been caused by her having sexually adored her father who had scorned her and who had also drummed into her that religious exaltation is only hocus-pocus. For her adulthood she has learnt from his rationalism and atheism, but in so doing she has had to drain out her instinctive religious fervour, leaving her an empty but tough shell. The coda in **"The Cockatoos"** is less well integrated, and Tim Goodenough's story is really a separate one, tenuously linked by the cockatoos. The inadequacy and brutality of Tim's response to the cockatoos are not excused by his justifiable fear of forever being tied to his mother's apron strings, and the reader, as so often in the other stories, is left to come to his own understanding during the extended anticlimax of the coda, of the spiritual and moral failure of all four major characters in this novella.

White's stories tend to have a surface of social trivia and a tension emanating from a hidden, psychological or spiritual truth towards which White's few elect protagonists struggle. White prefers on the whole to replace chronological plot development with a complex network of flashbacks designed to allow the story to comment on itself by the careful juxtaposition of these flashbacks with the present, and to give depth to the characterisation to the extent that the structural movement might be said to resemble a whirlpool spiral into the past and into the subconsciousness of the present with the moment of greatest suffering and highest awareness coinciding at the bottom of the spiral. White's characters tend to fall into two distinct groups in their attitudes to this whirlpool. The larger group are the satirized bourgeoisie who pretend that the whirlpool is simply not there, and who construct fortress-homes and fortress-conventions to protect themselves from it. The alleged positivity of their gospel of happiness and their commitment to order and respectability are undercut by their sour denial of love and their fear of the mysterious and the unknown. The smaller group of seers is not happier, but is often blessed with the instant of epiphanous transfiguration we have discussed above. These seers have given themselves up to the whirlpool, sometimes involuntarily because they bear the mark of fate, and sometimes as a sign of their romantic revolt against the conformist majority. They are more open to such emotions as religious awe, humility, serenity, affinity with nature and generosity in love. They are also more prone in the moments of highest pressure to depths of agony, insanity, violence or death.

We have already noted that the moods in White's stories vary enormously and often abruptly within the one story from farce and satire to tragic pathos. The key to these variations is inevitably to be found in White's many styles which range from the ridiculing mimicry of Australian slang to the lyric positivity and startling power of his serious imagery. One has the feeling that the intensity and the sensitivity of the style and the character-psychology are such that White is sometimes obliged to let off steam in these stories either through outbursts of incoherent passion or through an explosion of ribald farce that can be glaringly out of harmony with the rest of the story. For the most part, however, White remains austere, ironic and elusively aloof from his material. These words denote the essentials of White's overriding point of view in most of his stories. Michael Wilding, in commenting on the story **"Five-Twenty,"** notes

> a somewhat patrician note of the superior anthropologist in denoting the minutiae with a rather distasteful objectivity. It's a narrow line between deep sympathy and contempt. White presents a terrifying picture of the urban industrial world, redeemed by no possibilities, no hopes; it is a powerful nihilism whose gestures and attempts towards mystical communions and epiphanies only confirm the hopelessness.[14]

It may be true of **"Five-Twenty,"** and of certain others of White's stories that feature what I have called negative sexual epiphanies, that the attempts at "mystical communions" are unsuccessful. But this does not justify Wilding in claiming that the stories are informed by "a powerful nihilism." Failure and suffering are for White necessary paths to religious experience and "true knowledge comes only from torture in the country of the mind."[15] The depressing ordinariness of his characters' lives is redeemed, but not so much by erotic ecstasy, as by a flash of intuitive vision into the hidden harmony of creation or by a spiritual acceptance of the necessity of suffering.

Even in the inevitability of failure, White's characters are saved from nihilism because what appears to be the triviality of their lives opens up to show hidden depths of repressed intensity. At their climaxes these only apparently humdrum characters fairly explode with emotional intensity and thereby prove their human individuality. R. Hinton Thomas claims that it is

> the task of contemporary literature, in the mass-society of this scientific age, . . . 'die menschliche Substanz in einer Welt zu zeigen, die allen poetischen Reizes entbehrt,' 'die Behauptung des Menschen im Alltag und in der Uniformität'[16] ('to show the essence of being human in a world that lacks all poetic allure,' 'the assertion of what is human in everyday life and in the midst of uniformity'). This is a task which the short story can be particularly well fitted to perform, whether by the special interest it may show in 'konkrete, oft nebensächliche oder unscheinbare Vorgänge' ('concrete, often trivial or insignificant events') . . . or by preoccupation with the frankly absurd.[17]

These generalisations about the contemporary German short story seem particularly pertinent to White, who is expert in stirring apparently absurd mixes of the trivial and the mystic, the mundane and the Dionysian, the materialistic-rationalistic and the religious-miraculous. These prodigious and abrupt leaps in mood and meaning give White's stories a kinship with the shock effect emanating from theatre of the absurd. Ionesco's "The Rhinoceros" for example, aims, like White's stories, to reveal through an exploration of the absurd, the incongruous and the surreal, the vital differences between the social conformism of the bourgeoisie and the potentially volcanic tremors of the individual soul.

There is another form of modern theatre that White's stories resemble, and that is epic theatre. R. Hinton Thomas perceptively establishes the relationship between epic theatre and many short stories when he says:

> We are here concerned with a feature of many a short story that might be spoken of as a 'Verfremdungseffekt' ('distancing device') and this establishes a point of contact with epic theatre, which, renouncing the conventional structural unity of a play and allowing it to consist of a series of more or less loosely connected scenes, aims not at creating the sense of illusion, but at putting the audience in a critical state of mind, at creating 'epische Distanze' ('epic distance') at lifting 'alltägliche Dinge . . . aus dem Bereich des Selbstverständlichen'[18] ('everyday phenomena out of the realm of the self-evident').[19]

There are two major points here. The first is the structural point about the "series of more or less loosely connected scenes." The second is the aesthetic effect on the readers or the audience, namely to give them critical distance from the characters and to estrange them from what has always appeared obvious, thus jolting them into reviewing the familiar with new eyes.

Taking the structural point first: it is dubious whether the sequence of scenes in epic theatre is quite as loose as is generally assumed. The sequence in White's stories is certainly not loose. I would suggest that Brecht, and White too, substitute another pattern of order for the old one of linear chronology and rising emotions, namely the order of a network of juxtapositions that are determined by such intellectual considerations as illumination of contrasting themes and dialectical paradoxes in characterisation. Indirect comment, often satirical, is created by this network of juxtapositions. But here the comparison between Brecht and White must be abruptly halted. For in all other respects they are at the opposite end of the literary poles. It was Brecht's intention to alienate the audience from the familiar environment in order to provoke them into demanding social change towards what he saw as the political rationalism of communism, whereas White forces his readers to review the familiar from a new spiritual awareness that is entirely anarchistic, irrational and private. Brecht optimistically celebrates man as a social creature rationally and historically working towards a utopian political organisation. White pessimistically celebrates man as a religious creature doomed to a suffering remoteness from God and obsessed in his loneliness with a spiritual transcendence of his inevitable agony. With unembarrassed obviousness Brecht pushes his audience didactically towards his simple, political message, whereas White as narrator prefers to remain elusive, remote, complex, non-political and even obscure.

A brief comparison between the narrative stance and the structural technique of juxtaposition in the fiction of James Joyce and Patrick White brings us far closer to understanding the functions of relative distancing between author and characters, and characters and readers. In a statement on the narrative stance of James Joyce that he claims "has now become a commonplace of modern fiction," Richard Ellmann says that this stance seeks

> a presentation so sharp that comment by the author would be an interference. It leaves off the veneer of gracious intimacy with the reader, of concern that he should be taken into the author's confidence, and instead makes the reader feel uneasy and culpable if he misses the intended but always unstated meaning, as if he were being arraigned rather than entertained. The artist detaches himself from his material so as to push the reader into it.[20]

We do indeed feel uneasy at the end of such stories by White as **"A Cheery Soul"** or **"The Cockatoos,"** as we search for a meaning that will integrate the many puzzling jigsaw-pieces. Instead of coolly debating the morality of characters as Brecht intended us to, we find ourselves at the conclusions of the above two stories sympathizing in surprising intimacy with Miss Docker, Busby Le Cornu and Tim Goodenough as they confront the insoluble dilemmas of their lives. These insoluble dilemmas are caused by the inevitability, the unchangeability of their characters. Almost none of White's characters is allowed to develop meaningfully in the course of the stories. They are trapped tragically or farcically in the conformist and usually puritanical prisons or their class or in the haunting traumas of their alienated childhood. There is no escape for them, but there is for the reader through his liberating understanding of the reasons for their limitations.

There are a few notable exceptions to this law of immutability of character in White's shorter prose fiction. They are Kikitsa Alexiou in **"The Woman Who Wasn't Allowed to Keep Cats,"** Meg Hogben in **"Down at the Dump"** and Felicity Bannister in **"The Night the Prowler."** Meg and Felicity do not so much develop gradually and naturally as they are transformed potentially by an intimation of the spiritual transcendence for which they have been seeking. Kikitsa acts out her transformation in her new sensual serenity towards nature and her own body, and also towards the awakened sexuality of her husband. Undoubtedly the time-jumps and the general compression of White's novellas contribute to this impression of abrupt change rather than gradual development, but it is also true that White wishes to depict above all the unpredictable abruptness and isolation of the moment of grace and the full illogicality and often grotesque negativity of the epiphanous transfiguration.

The question of compression in White's stories brings us to the issue whether his stories might not be more usefully classified as novellas. Even in such a comparatively uncomplicated story as **"Five-Twenty,"** White tends to reach back through the flashback into extensive evocation of the past and to tell the story of the malformation of Royal Natwick's character as much as the story of Ella Natwick's insane, erotic expectations of the gentleman in the pink Holden. **"The Letters"** too shows the germ of White's inclination to reach back into the past and relate impressionist, capsule biographies, instead of illuminating one crucial turning-point in time and leaving the before and the after to be hinted at or filled in by the reader. But **"The Letters"** is vigorously unified by White's device of quoting the letters themselves and thus thematically and stylistically integrating the extended chronology. The only stories that are unambiguously short stories, it seems to me, are **"Willy-Wagtails by Moonlight." "Miss Slattery and Her Demon Lover," "The Letters," "The Full Belly"** and **"Five-Twenty."** These stories tend to restrict themselves to a single incident, a single theme, or a single confrontation.

But I am undoubtedly being very conservative in speaking of the short story in these terms. Ian Reid tells us that it was in the first two decades of this century that critics insisted that a short story had to have

> three related qualities: it makes a single impression on the reader, it does so by concentrating on a crisis, and it makes that crisis pivotal in a controlled plot.[21]

It is clear that White's stories make complex impressions on the reader, that they are often almost plotless, predominantly low-key and slow to build up pressure, and that the protagonists are often suffering a permanent crisis of quiet desperation throughout their lives and the stories. It is also clear that most of White's stories have no definitive beginnings, are almost all middle, and have open endings that show the suffering as often as not going on uniformly after the conclusion of the story. Most of the stories, it is true, reach a climactic epiphany of one kind or another, but in the anticlimaxes that follow, the inexorable, low-key rhythm of quiet anguish seems to stretch out like an unending desert into the future. In this respect White's stories fit very well into William James' characterisation of his brother's complex shorter prose fiction as giving

> an impression like that we often get of people in life: their orbits come out of space and lay themselves for a short time along ours, and then off they whirl again into the unknown, leaving us with little more than an impression of their reality and a feeling of baffled curiosity as to the mystery of the beginning and of their being.[22]

Many of White's stories can be usefully interpreted as novellas if we agree that "the novella's medial scope enables it to render with especial force the 'degenerative or pathetic' kind of tragedy, as Springer calls it, in which the protagonist's fate is neither heroic nor petty." Springer further claims that the "relentlessness and the depth of the misery (in the tragic novella) expand it beyond the single episode which often characterizes the short story." Leibowitz advances the theory that the novella has the "double effect of intensity with expansion." Reid adds that the "compressive quality is achieved by an unwavering thematic focus and an accumulation of structural parallels."[23] Let us attempt to relate these generalizations to the medium-length story, **"Clay."** Certainly the main figure of the story, Clay, is not heroic, not even in his transfigurations at the end. He is often petty, until he begins to realise himself in insanity, but we might best ascribe this pettiness to an inevitable inheritance from his mother and his environment, which he outgrows at the same time as he remains faithful to them, in a spiritually heightened state, as his continuum. This raises the paradoxical question of whether his tragedy is degenerative. True, he does lapse into insanity, presumably from the pressure of his unfulfilled dream on his unbearably dreary reality. But how gloriously visionary, and also how hilarious this insanity is, when compared with the flat nothingness of his painfully learnt conformism. So he does not just degenerate into insanity, he rises at the same time to a spiritual self-realisation in insanity and despair, like so many of White's central figures in the novels and the stories. Nevertheless, the ambiguous direction of his fate allows him to be compared quite well with the heroic antihero of that classical tragic novella, *Death in Venice,* Gustav Aschenbach. Aschenbach degenerates from dignified artist respected by the conventional middle classes to a leering, cosmetically adorned pedophile who is trapped by his lust into a fatal passivity towards the ravages of disease in Venice. But Aschenbach is compensated for his tragic fall by a visionary insight into the daemonic relationship of the artist to life whence he draws inspiration and to the artistic form which he reveres. The ambiguity of Aschenbach's degenerative tragedy is parallel to that of Clay, except that Clay's drama unfolds on an incomparably more pedestrian and trivial plane. But then that is explicable because White, as we have already noted, is committed to "discovering the extraordinary behind the ordinary." In a way White's artistic task is much harder than Thomas Mann's, because White is aiming to express a spiritual revelation in the unpromising host of a simpleton and bureaucrat, whilst Thomas Mann had a sophisticated artist as his medium. The visions accorded to Aschenbach and Clay are therefore on planes as different as the sublime and the grotesque. The parallel nevertheless is an illuminating one, because in both cases ecstasy is achieved at the cost of rationality, and in both cases the inspiration floods from the Dionysian impulse, from the repressed libido, and overwhelms a lifetime based on Apollonian order and the self-restraint called for by convention. To summarise then: the structural movement of degenerative tragedy is to compensate the central character spiritually for what he has suffered in his fall.

To return to the other aspects of the novella's structure present in **"Clay"**: chronologically the story takes us from Clay at five years old being tormented because he was different, through his equally tormented adolescence, his first and only job as a civil servant, the death of his mother, his marriage, and further through attainment of his true self in insanity, his compulsive attempts at art and his erotic daydreaming, to death by suicide. White does not mark off the chronological segments one from the other in his usual fashion of inserting abrupt blanks of silence. Instead he glues the various segments together with generalisations about Clay's character that cover the years in between. The resultant impression is of a parodied epitome of a

"Bildungsroman," or novel of apprenticeship, in that the main character is educated to mature years, but instead of taking a responsible place in middle class society he turns compulsively inward to dreams and insanity. In any case the focus is unwaveringly on his misery, and it is the intensity of this focus which expands **"Clay"** as a novella from the single episode. These episodes gather accumulative impetus and force as they rush towards his fall into insanity, and a feeling of growing intensification is created as the style becomes more laconic in the dialogue-parodies and more and more frenetic, abstracted and obscure in the surreal prose of Clay's interior monologue. This feeling of intensification is also created by the repetition of a few key images or leitmotifs, such as the wedding picture and the bridal shoe, by the increasingly dense colour symbolism, and by what Patrick White in *The Tree of Man* calls a "mysticism of objects."

We have briefly noted in the previous section Heseltine's discovery that certain objects in White's fiction "console and soothe by the solidity of their presence" and thus gain a more than ordinarily symbolic significance. Heseltine quotes from *The Aunt's Story,* "There is perhaps no more complete a reality than a chair and a table" and claims that these two objects are made into "two of the major unifying symbols of the entire novel."[24] In **"Clay,"** when the titular antihero first begins to write, he is obsessed with the apparent permanence of a table, and in general with "objects, the mysterious life which inanimacy contains."[25] In my specific analysis of **"Clay"** I have shown in detail how White traces the increasing insanity of the main character with a prose that is feverishly surreal, and how objects like the table or the white wedding shoe acquire from Clay's point of view an eerie, independent life of their own. Objects play similarly eerie and supernatural roles in others of White's stories. Herbert Heckmann claims that objects have acquired a vital new significance in modern literature generally:

> There is in modern literature something like an uprising of objects against the falsifying sovereignty of the subject. This is particularly noticeable in Franz Kafka's *Description of a Struggle,* to take just one example. Here objects escape the orderly control of a respectable, bourgeois world: they themselves become active and defend themselves against the thoughtless clutches of man. They thereby acquire a new fascination, which transports the observer into orgies of discoveries. This requires, however, a virtually phantasmagoric alertness, a dreamlike sacrificing-up of the self to objects.[26]

This theory clearly has general validity for White's fiction. Think of the supernatural significance of the glasses in **"A Glass of Tea,"** of the primitive, magical power invested in his talisman of the cockatoo's sulphur crest by Tim Goodenough in **"The Cockatoos,"** of the "blaze of pumpkins" at the conclusion of **"A Cheery Soul,"** of the miraculous glass eye of Christ Pantocrator in **"Sicilian Vespers,"** of the role of Clem Dowson's hutch in **"A Woman's Hand,"** of Harvey's raped mausoleum in **"The Night the Prowler,"** and on the more farcical level of the vengeful declaration of independence by the tape-recorder in **"Willy-Wagtails by Moonlight,"** and the "disembowelled mattress" in **"Down at the Dump."**[27]

The spiritually heightened significance of things is of course just as widespread in White's novels as it is in the stories. But then this is true of most of the rhetorical and structural techniques that we have analysed in White's shorter prose fiction, whether we are talking about searching for the overriding point of view, about beginnings, middles and ends, epiphanies, or open-ended parables. I would therefore suggest that the conclusions I have reached about White's stories are in general valid for his novels and that the only real differences between his stories and his novels are the effects of compression, of sustained intensity and tension, and of a lyric density of imagery that we find in the stories. Indeed the more successful works of Patrick White's shorter prose fiction resemble nothing quite so much as climatic compressions of his own novels.

Notes

1. *Riders in the Chariot,* Penguin, pp. 453-5.
2. *Tree of Man,* Penguin, p. 11.
3. *The Burnt Ones,* Viking, N.Y. 1964, p. 180.
4. Ian Reid, *The Short Story: The Critical Idiom,* Methuen, 1977, pp. 43-47, and pp. 54-65. An admirably succinct summary of a myriad of theoretical definitions of short story and novella is to be found in these pages.
5. Ian Reid, *ibid.,* p. 28. Cf. the definition of epiphany by Richard Ellmann which I quote in the preceding section of this work.
6. Cf. Frank O'Connor's claim that the short story is "by its very nature remote from the community—romantic, individualistic and intransigent" (*The Lonely Voice,* p. 21).
7. In a work by Odilon Redon, Elizabeth Hunter finds her spiritual semblance in "the artist's image of what he called a skiapod." "Unlike most of the other monsters in the book, this half-fish half-woman appeared neither allied to, nor threatened by, death: too elusive in weaving through deep waters, her expression a practically effaced mystery; or was it one of dishonesty, of cunning?" (*The Eye of the Storm,* Penguin, p. 194).
8. *The Burnt Ones,* p. 104.
9. *ibid.,* p. 308.
10. *ibid.,* p. 198.
11. Andrew Taylor, "White's Short Stories," in *Overland,* No. 31, March 1965, p. 18.
12. *The Burnt Ones,* p. 268.
13. *The Cockatoos,* Viking, N.Y., 1975, p. 91.
14. Michael Wilding, "Short Story Chronicle," in *Meanjin Quarterly,* June 1971, p. 259.

15. *Voss,* Penguin, p. 475.

16. W. Jens, *Literatur und Politik,* Verlag Günter Neske, Pfullingen, 1963, p. 20. As quoted by R. Hinton Thomas, see reference 17.

17. R. Hinton Thomas, Introduction to *Seventeen German Stories,* O.U.P., 1968, p. 28.

18. B. Brecht, *Schriften zum Theater,* Suhrkamp, Frankfurt, 1957, p. 76.

19. R. Hinton Thomas, *op. cit.,* p. 30.

20. Richard Ellmann, *James Joyce,* N.Y., 1959, p. 88.

21. Ian Reid, *op. cit.,* p. 54.

22. As quoted by Ian Reid, *op. cit.,* p. 65.

23. As quoted by Ian Reid, *op. cit.,* p. 46. Reid names his sources as Judith Leibowitz, *Narrative Purpose in the Novella,* The Hague, 1974, and Mary Doyle Springer, *Forms of the Modern Novella,* Chicago, 1975.

24. Harry Heseltine, "Patrick White's Style," in *Quadrant,* VII, 1963, p. 67.

25. *The Burnt Ones,* p. 117.

26. Herbert Heckmann, "Aufstand der Dinge," in *Die Welt der Literatur,* 17, September 1964.

27. *The Burnt Ones,* p. 290 and p. 305.

David Myers (essay date 1978)

SOURCE: "The Cockatoos," in *The Peacocks and the Bourgeoisie,* Adelaide University Union Press, 1978, pp. 131-37.

[*In the following excerpt, Myers examines the title story of* The Cockatoos, *asserting that it "is not a short story but a remarkably compressed novella" that integrates complex narrative methods and variations in mood.*]

This is a story about very ordinary people's suffering from lovelessness and crippling inhibitions, and about their tormented yearning for the release of passion. It is also a story about both the brutal cruelty and the kindness of which humans are capable; about the perversion of sexual love into smothering possessiveness or into neurotic fear of intimacy and the reaction to such perversion in the quest for freedom and the courage to bear this freedom. The story vibrates with intensity of vision into the paradoxes of human misery and successfully probes the inner truths of four major characters, Mick and Olive Davoren, Busby Le Cornu and Tim Goodenough. In the scope of its characterisation, the rich development of the titular image, the unflinching representation of life's and people's loathsomeness as well as their joy, and in the integration of complex narrative methods and variations in mood, this is not a short story but a remarkably compressed novella.

Structurally, **"The Cockatoos"** is a non-sequence of isolated scenes, with absolutely no transition from scene to scene, each being a compressed representation of suburban life-styles within the privacy of neighbouring but unneighbourly houses. It is White's aim to reveal that beneath the conventional surface of suburban respectability there are latent lives that are intensely irrational, compulsive, frightened or zany. It is the terrifying secrets of these latent lives from which normal people hide and which the cockatoos function as catalysts to release. White shows his characters suffering from their repressed traumas with techniques ranging from cool irony to farce. Miss Le Cornu does not cry in her loneliness, she blubbers, "heaving and glugging, it sounded" (p. 273). This style is similar to the distancing devices of epic theatre. Or more farcically, when Miss Le Cornu gets up after unenjoyable coitus with Mick Davoren, she says, "Next time it will be better. I'll frizzle it up" (p. 275). She is of course referring obliquely to the steak she had cooked for him.

White does similar mining operations on the subconsciousness of Olive Davoren and Tim Goodenough. Olive Davoren's adult life has been a series of sad disillusionments. As a girl she had been Dadda's spoilt darling, but now her aspirations to be a violinist have ended in humiliating failure, and the consequence of her headstrong "craving for love or hurt" (p. 263) is a bitter non-marriage. Her resentful over-reaction to the death of her pet budgie is shown by a juxtaposed flashback of interior monologue to stem really from the death of her stillborn child. But as usual, White does not allow us the slightest opportunity to misread sentimentality into this misfortune. The passage is typical of White's technique and is worth quoting in full:

> She had told him, 'You let it die on purpose. Because I was gone. You knew I loved the bird. You was jealous—that was it!' Her grief made her forget the grammar she had always been respectful of.
>
> 'It was sick,' he said. 'Anyone could see. A person only had to look at its toenails.'
>
> 'I should have cut his claws,' she admitted. 'But was afraid. He was too frail and small.'
>
> (She had asked to see what they had taken from her—you couldn't have called it a child. She had even touched it. And wouldn't ever let herself remember. He certainly wouldn't be one to remind her of it.)
>
> (pp. 264-5)

Most of the words are devoted to trivial squabbling about the cause of the budgerigar's death. There is also incidental satire on her snobbish worrying about grammatical niceties. The real meaning of the passage is only hinted at in bracketed parentheses. And immediately after this the passage concludes in a farcical jest about the bird's name. The pathos of Olive Davoren's failure in life is thus sandwiched between dry satire and anticlimactic farce.

Tim Goodenough is a persecuted child-outsider like Clay in **"The Burnt Ones,"** but he is less a loony and more an adventurer struggling not just against his mother's domination, but against the conformist suburban dread of his satirized parents that he will become an artistic poof (p. 267). To sustain himself in his battle for independence and courage he maintains a private museum of "mystic" objects (p. 269) which have personal, supernatural significance as talismans. This hidden museum is the externalisation of his inner terror that corresponds to the hidden suffering of the Davorens and Miss Le Cornu.

As in many of White's stories, there is in **"The Cockatoos"** virtually no plot. Instead, mainly through flashbacks of interior monologue, the misery of four different lives is revealed in a stasis that is paradoxically tense with frustrated emotions. Only the birds of the title can break this deadlock and re-enthuse the drooping spirits of the characters with a brief but exhilarating rebirth of ecstasy and passion. It is an essential part of White's artistic honesty that the participant must pay for this brief splendour with death, grief and a return to the dragging isolation that is worse than it was before because it is haunted by a vague memory of the vision of grace.

The cockatoos are strange symbols of this grace[1] as they move mysteriously like drunken flowers through the magnolia tree (pp. 277, 286, 290). They are unknowable, worshipped messengers of nature's visionary beauty; their phallic, knife-like crests cut through the resentments, the fears, and the twisted passivity of the four main characters and draw them into a strangely compelling dance of dynamic passion. Not that the cockatoos are misused aesthetically to represent an ethereal and remote vision. On the contrary. White has observed them with meticulous care and insight, and has made of them symbols of human potential in heightened intensity. In their different moods they express a universality of human emotions. They are like the Greek Olympian Gods who are in every respect human in their passions, their rages and their weaknesses, but somehow incomparably more magnificent and dazzling in their naive expression of these emotions. Alternatively, one could see them in a more negative light as the equivalent of the officials in Kafka's castle. As inhabitants of the other, the spiritual world, they reflect in a cruel mirror-image the contrariness of human behaviour. The only transcendence they have to offer is to act as catalysts in releasing the potential of the human irrational from its bondage to rational, social norms and the appearances of civilized intercourse. True to their mirror-image reality, the cockatoos are different things to different people at different times. They can be "striding and stamping" in anger, or quiet in wisdom (pp. 261, 264, 266, 281); heartless slashers in their vicious conformist persecution of the outsider (p. 281) or have "kind eyes" (pp. 275, 282, 286); their crests are often threateningly phallic (pp. 261, 265, 281, 288), but on one occasion are seen affectionately as ladies' gently opening fans (p. 282); at times the cockatoos are a gaggle of gossiping adults (p. 282), at others, they provide a nightmare of overobvious Freudian symbolism for Olive Davoren when they pick with their beaks at her childless womb and the big clamshell (p. 279), and at other times again they inspire unexpected, uncontrollable passion. Sometimes their passion is healthily animal as an antidote to repression and to fear of sexual intimacy (p. 285). At other times the cockatoos provoke a grotesque competition to win their love and possess them (pp. 280, 281), but tend to transcend this grotesqueness in Busby Le Cornu's plea for freedom and sharing (p. 286). In this way the deadening habit of bourgeois marital possessiveness is gloriously broken, if only for a moment. The transcendence of ecstasy is there, but it is fleeting. Because the character must return to a world where "time passes: nothing better can be said of it" (p. 295).

In a slapstick farce that contrasts strangely with the preceding ecstasy, some of the cockatoos are murdered by that Victorian villain and Freudianly perverted nark, Figgis the undertaker. The remaining cockatoos then lose their god-like magnificence. They turn "a nasty grey colour, more like hens which have been fluffing themselves on an ash-heap" (p. 294). There follows an anti-vision of loathsomeness in the story's coda, featuring White's usual collection of "alkies and freaks and pervs and old women with stockings half down and scabs on their faces." The last cockatoo undergoes a correspondingly loathsome martyrdom. It is aged and seems to offer itself for the boy Tim Goodenough's ritual slaughter in order to provide an irrational talisman guaranteeing him courage and independence from his Oedipal mother's suffocating love. The quest for manly independence comes through brutal slaughter of one of nature's wild creatures. Man's inevitable brutality, primitivity and irrationality stand tragically exposed at the story's conclusion as the necessary correlatives of freedom, independence and even love in its true form. For Olive Davoren to rid herself of sulking resentment, for Mick Davoren to rid himself of narcissistic indifference to sexual love and falsely romantic adulation of war and death, for Busby Le Cornu to overcome her neurotic terror of intimacy and for Tim Goodenough to seek courage, the inspiration of the cockatoos in one form or another is necessary. The cockatoos are a vehicle for externalisation of hidden, inner life, a ritual cleansing of inhibitions and perversions, a purification through catharsis and a tormenting enrichment of subsequent mundane life through memory of ecstasy.

The visit of the cockatoos to the society of human beings attains its ecstatic climax not in the release of physical passion but in their mysterious revelation in the magnolia tree. Here they are revealed in transfigured glory "like big white drunken flowers in motion" (pp. 277, cf. p. 286). It is a Dionysian revelation of the repressed irrational, of pre-civilized passion and barbarism and the magic tokens of superstition. It is a renewal of emotional vitality that has been sapped, in White's Nietzschean and Freudian terms, by the conformist mediocrity and deadening repressions of middle-class suburban mundanity.

Corresponding to their visual transfiguration in the magnolia tree is the magical ability of the cockatoos to provide transcendence through the spirit of music. Olive Davoren expresses her devotional worship of them with the "thin and angular" tones of her long disused violin. It seemed that "the composer was collaborating with her. And cockatoos" (p. 287) and thus she produces "moments of exaltation in what must otherwise have been a horrible travesty of the Partita" (p. 287). Olive has produced music under the influence of her love for the cockatoos so that while it remains empirically and sensually horrid, it is in another religious world where the intentions rather than the notes are heard, and this is an act of inspired grace. Interestingly enough, this provides a very close parallel to the situation in Grillparzer's 19th century story, *The Poor Minstrel.* The minstrel is mocked and deceived by all and seeks consolation in his violin from which he produces the most excruciating noise, off-key, off-tempo, in fact unrecognizable renderings of the classical greats which he offers up in praise to the greater glory of God. It is implied by Grillparzer that God, like White's cockatoos, accepts this devotion with inscrutable good-will and no evidence of earache. The essential difference between Grillparzer's nineteenth century tale and White's ironical study of a more zany epiphany is that Grillparzer, appropriate to his Romantic epoch, sentimentalizes his inauspicious antihero into a saint of heroism and moral self-sacrifice to coincide with his acts of musical worship, but Patrick White remains grimly naturalistic in his characterization, confronting his very ordinary characters with an environment that is often loathsome as they sink back into the greyish morass from which they had sprung for the one epiphany of their lives. Olive Davoren, for example, becomes a puzzled widow in a sealskin coat whose "weight is a comfort—even if hot" (p. 305) because it reminds her of her husband's weight on her during sexual intercourse.

Like Olive, Busby Le Cornu experiences a similar rise to ecstasy and fall into disenchantment. Her ecstasy is also not just one of physical passion, but stems from her communing with the cockatoos via Mozart's *Don Giovanni.* She crouches over an aria of betrayed and abandoned love which is "her own lament for a real passion she had never quite experienced" (p. 287). But out of suffering she soars against reason (p. 288) and is rejoined by those symbols of grace, the cockatoos, "in vindicating spirals, white to sun-splashed" (p. 288). The sensation of being awash in light is one of White's favourite images to express grace. White concludes this experience with a puzzling sentence which is doubtless an intentionally obscure joke: "she could not have faced the moonlit statue by daylight: a pity, because the Commendatore might have appealed to cockatoos" (p. 288). In *Don Giovanni* the Commendatore is the just avenger who comes back from the grave to exact justice from the unrepentant Don. Do the cockatoos exact a somewhat more farcical and decidedly less melodramatic punishment upon the mortals who have dared to look upon them and court their favour? Figgis ends up in the insane asylum, Mick Davoren in the morgue. Mrs. Dalhunty retreats from the farcical killing to "Our Lady of the Snows, Ashfield" (p. 294). Olive Davoren alone in her bed strains her ears in vain to hear "Him bumping around in the next room" (p. 299). Busby Le Cornu cries for the one "habit" in her unstable life, Mick Davoren (p. 304). She returns to the loneliness of her house, taking all of her stimulants in an unsuccessful bid at suicide. She is not comforted by a surreal phantasy of lesbian love with Olive and prefers her isolation to the banalities of suburban chit-chat about the weather. Tim Goodenough returns guilty but triumphant from his self-inflicted initiation into manhood, but is squashed into blubbering babyhood by his mother: "any vision he may have imagined having, ever, was splodged into one, great, white blur, at the centre of it a smear of sulphur" (p. 307). That is, the vision of the liberating cockatoos is merged with and lost in his mother's suffocating apron. And as for Mick Davoren, his false romanticising of the brutality of war is avenged by the cockatoos thus: they wheel in the sky to chase and kill an outsider and he is reminded with unspeakable terror of his own aeroplane being shot down in the mid-East in the second world war. He becomes aware of the darker side of the cockatoos, of their brutality and their stench as they bash at each other with their beaks (p. 289). He withdraws in a nightmare of waking terror "an old, frightened man" (p. 289). Shortly after, he is accidentally killed by Figgis, not so much as a noble martyr defending the cockatoos as an insignificant participant in a suburban farce.

Are all of these grim endings the stern punishments of the cockatoos on human beings or simply the grotesque coincidences of life? White's elaborate parallels between cockatoo and human behaviour suggest the more romantic, supernatural explanation. That is, human beings have shown themselves to be too morally flawed to sustain the pure vision of the cockatoos in the magnolia tree. Their experiences of joy, beauty, love and courage are correspondingly blurred and imperfect, and they must pay for their brief ecstasy with an inexorable return to the dull incomprehension of their daily routine.

Note

1. Cockatoos are of course not the only birds in White's fiction to bear the symbolic import of grace and transcendence. Cf. Harry Heseltine: "the number of birds which sweep through the pages of White's books is quite remarkable. It is not often that they are there for their own sake. The advent of wings almost invariably coincides with scenes in which human beings aspire to a state of existence beyond the normal" ("Patrick White's Style" in *Quadrant,* VII, 1963, p. 65). Cf. Sylvia Gzell: "The white bird of the soul occurs in both *Voss* and *Riders in the Chariot* to suggest the possibility of a freedom which allows transcendent experience and is part of it. The image is frequently linked with description of awkward movement to imply the difficulty of achieving this freedom" ("Themes and Imager in *Voss* and *Riders in the Chariot*" in Clement Semmler (ed), *Twentieth Century Australian Literary Criticism,* O.U.P., Melbourne, 1967, p. 256). Cf. the birds which Sister de Santis feeds in a ritual ceremony at the conclusion of *The Eye of the Storm* and which brings her a moment of transcendent joy: "She could feel claws snatching for a hold in her

hair. She ducked, to escape from this prism of dew and light. This tumult of wings and her own unmanageable joy. Once she raised an arm to brush aside a blue wedge of pigeon's feathers. The light she could not ward off: it was by now too solid, too possessive; herself possessed." (Penguin, p. 589)

Ron Shepherd (essay date 1978)

SOURCE: "An Indian Story: 'The Twitching Colonel,'" in *Patrick White: A Critical Symposium,* edited by R. Shepherd & K. Singh, Centre for Research in the New Literatures in English, 1978, pp. 28-33.

[*In the following essay, Shepherd views "The Twitching Colonel," one of White's earliest short stories, as a harbinger of themes that surface later in the author's fiction.*]

I wish to look at an early short story by Patrick White, **"The Twitching Colonel,"** which appeared for the first (and only) time in *London Mercury* in 1937 two years before *Happy Valley* in 1939. This story is of special interest for several reasons. It is a very early piece and quite unlike anything in the early novels, though, thematically, it anticipates the whole corpus of White's fiction concerning the nature of "reality." My present interest lies with the special oddness of this story, its aura of Indian-ness in the way it reflects something of the essential philosophy and symbolism of classical India. I personally approach White's fiction with some familiarity of India and its cultural traditions. Reading White I am always impressed by what strikes me as his similarity with a modern Indian metaphysical novelist, Raja Rao, especially in the treatment of ideas concerning illusion and reality, the psychological and physical, the spiritual and material.

"The Twitching Colonel" is indeed an Indian story rather than a story about India, not only in the way the narrative point of view centres around a goal of transcendence but also in the way many distinctly Indian symbols and intricate symbolic meanings are incorporated into the text. White creates a reality of inner and outer meanings where a veil of appearances thinly conceals a deeper and more cogent layer of reality. Technically, he employs a structural dualism representing the realities of surface and depth, and this *schema* serves to interconnect other dialectical fragments—ideas about good and evil, the absolute and the relative, the subsconscious and the ego, and so on.

The story's plot can be summed up in a few sentences. It is about an aged and ailing retired British army officer who looks back over his experiences of India from the distance of his London flat and old age. Like Forster's Mrs. Moore in *A Passage to India* the Colonel has undergone a rather remarkable conversion as a result of his Indian experience. For so long the typical army man, he is now struck by a quite different sort of awareness and one which reverses most of his former attitudes. The British mentality he now equates with ignorance and illusion, "the illusion of greatness that lies in patriotic songs, British supremacy, and the Stiff Upper Lip" (p. 604)[1]. India, on the other hand, remains in his mind as something more subtly compelling and is described (perhaps in memory of Forster) as "the blue echo of recaptured thought" (p. 603). India is a state of mind or a way of seeing, corresponding with the view of Indian novelist Raja Rao that India is "an idea, a metaphysic."[2] India and England lose their geographic referentials to become a part of the narrator's broader dialectic. England stands for "the effigies of . . . pomp" (p. 605), India for a deeper reality comparable in White's later works with the lands of Abyssinia, Ethiopia, Greece, and so on. The story merely registers this dawning realisation in the mind of the single central character, and ends when the Indian rope-trick (an Oriental version of Jacob's ladder) allows the Colonel spiritual release in a puff of fire and smoke.

This is the extent of the plot. But already in this early story White can be seen experimenting with prose-style and with narrative-technique. The tone of the narrative is quite unlike the simpler style of *Happy Valley,* though it shares the spikey and tough quality of *The Living and the Dead* (1941). White's approach in this story really bears closer resemblance to the Indianisms of Raja Rao than to his own methods in other stories. In both writers one finds the following combination of features: a structural mixture of concrete detail and spiritual abstraction, a certain mantra-like narrative voice, and a deliberate esoteric symbolism redolent of the Upanishads. Technically they correspond on further points: an ambiguous manner of story-telling such that author and *persona* merge in the same voice, a use of words such that ordinary meanings elude one's certain grasp and such that lexographical considerations become less important than the spirit in which the utterance is made, and a use of formal elements to emphasise the connections between ideas.

In **"The Twitching Colonel"** the Indian notion of *Maya* is shown to be the key to man's dualist dilemma, and hence the answer to the question about the nature of reality central in White's fiction. All of White's stories centre around this same problem, the apparent dualism between mind and body, spirit and matter. The physical world and bodily existence is a facade which must be pierced by the deeper mind in order to arrive at a better understanding.

> Only in dissolution is salvation from illusion, in dream perhaps that is shadow of death, or decomposition of substance, the frail symbol of reality which man clutches, holding himself by the throat, strangling himself through fear while denying suicide, that is man, this is also Maya, this imperfection that is man denying his shadow as day lengthens, as mind is restless with striving yet afraid of sleep.
>
> (p. 607)

The meaning of this passage relies on a number of special assumptions: that all physical life is illusion or *Maya,* that man's physical nature is imperfect and that it would deny its deeper self and yet remain afraid and uncertain, that sleep is virtually synonymous with the deeper reality which man fears to recognise, that dissolution of the flesh is the only way past the flesh. These assumptions, some of which are familiar to Christianity, belong to a Hindu view of the world which says that the world does not really exist, only appears to. Man's job in life is therefore to acquire the penetration necessary to understand this particular point of view.

The mental world of Colonel Trevellick during the last days of his life hovers at this threshhold. The story's impetus springs from White's ability to play ambivalently at separate levels with the symbols of surface and depth, illusion and reality. The only "event" in the story is the house-fire towards the end. But as so often in White's stories, an "event" stands somewhat uncertainly in terms of any actual temporal and spatial context. That the fire is an actual occurrence is suggested by further circumstantial detail: the fire-alarms, the smoke, the crowd of sightseers watching from below. But White thickens his textures and complicates the shapes on his canvas by the intermingling of a different sort of imagery, an Indian imagery of Hindu conjurers, rope-tricks, ceremonial elephants, and illusory facades. The result is a sort of psycho-expressionism where fragments of the real and the unreal, the actual and the imagined, fuse together in a state of psychic trance. This is the point of psychic break-through celebrated by Hindus and surrealists alike:

> The smoke suspends curtains of revealing gauze but not suspense of faces demanding explanation, the whiteness and fear of upturned faces that do not realize realization in smoke, only pavement, stone, the feet planted in custom that cannot accept coralline trees whose branches substanceless, and sometimes deceptive, the deceptive hands of the Hindu producing doves from the air, and the white doves and the white faces flicker with surprise. But beyond the gauze the world is memory and non-existent, no obelisk to regret, no memorial to Trevellick, as climbing rope to window opens, I am climbing rope or smoke and the flame smiles with the warmth of smiles that welcome, no longer the half-guessed significance of smiles, of wave, of rope, of the brown eye of jewelled elephants, as slipping effortless and without elegy the world dissolves. . . .
>
> (p. 609)

The story ends thus with the Colonel's disappearance in fire and smoke, a fire as real and unreal as the other fires in *The Aunt's Story* (1948) and *The Tree of Man* (1955). In this story the fire becomes an apocalyptic symbol of release, a metaphor illustrating a particular idea. The connection between inner and outer meanings is made explicit in a further metaphor describing the significance of the fire to the Colonel and to mankind more generally: ". . . this is what we have lived for, to lose control, secretly longing to toss a match into our desires" (p. 608). White celebrates the vitality of the soul trapped within the human flesh, which translated into an Indian context becomes a recognition of one's inner essential nature. He celebrates also the lone individual, the person who seeks a personal solution to the problem of living within an inert society.

Apart from its Indian-ness **"The Twitching Colonel"** anticipates another curious though characteristic feature of White's later writing. I have discussed one kind of ambivalence which tends to undermine the reader's certainty regarding the actuality of an event. There are further ambivalences, however, which cumulatively point towards ambiguity. For example, we are often uncertain how to distinguish between authorial and other voices in his fiction. It is extraordinarily difficult at times to pin White down to a single authorial position or to a single voice. The whole problem of uncertainty is compounded by White's linguistic obliqueness, by the way he will use verbal texture like a belly-dancer's veil to reveal and conceal at one and the same time. His further penchant for certain devices—such as the use of "perhaps," or his disregard for the punctuation which conventionally distinguishes *oratio recta* from *obliqua*—permit his stories to drift free of referential moorings on a symbolic Jungian surface.

In **"The Twitching Colonel"** White ambiguously associates with, and dissociates from, the Colonel depending whether the world is regarded through the Colonel's or the author's eyes. Moreover, the Colonel's mystic vision is ironically undercut by the story's structural organisation. I have described the way "actual" and "imaginative" realities merge together in Colonel Trevellick's mind. This transcendent moment is given a lighter touch by the comic interruptions of the Colonel's landlady, Mrs. Whale. His exotic dream of brown faces, rope-acts, ceremonial elephants, and the like is pierced by the staccato crudity of Mrs. Whale's voice: "Those niggers . . . [are] not to be trusted an inch, they'd stick a knife in your back like winking" (p. 606). The total effect here is ludicrous; any overt affirmation of metaphysical idealism is qualified by the landlady's insistent banalities. Generally speaking, the central characters in White's stories are immune from the author's own satiric thrusts, but not always. Although we do not get to know the Colonel very well there is something Falstaffian in the mixture of serious and comic elements which make up his character. But this comparison is not quite accurate either, since the unique blend here is a blend of comedy and of metaphysics which is rather un-Shakespearean. White is fond of giving surprises, and he often seems to employ a technique of unusual forms and combinations in order to catch the reader unprepared. This kind of metaphysical comedy is yet another aspect of White's characteristic eclecticism.

These matters lead me to two conclusions. Because of the way White deliberately confuses "point of view" and authorial voice with other views and voices, and because of the way metaphysical affirmation in this story is to some degree contradicted by a comic and satiric perspective, the reader is left with a feeling of uncertainty as to where precisely the author stands and what precisely his attitude is towards the circumstances of the story. And this, I believe, is a characteristic of White's writing more generally, in which most apparently overt and undisguised statements are on closer examination hedged around and qualified by some carefully assembled technical device. The seriousness of the Colonel's transcendence is in some way qualified by the other more local details involving his relationship with his housekeeper, though qualified in a way which is not immediately obvious. There appears to be deliberate mystification in White such that whenever the author's commitment to some particular idea threatens to become too apparent he will deliberately resort to a rhetoric of uncertainty in order to vitiate any glib conclusion. Either this is mystification for its own sake, or for art's sake; or else it is mystification for the purpose of commenting on the problems involved in human communication—that while man must continue to communicate in words which are bound by the limiting conditions of space and time human certainty must remain partly doubtful.

But I want to suggest that there remains another possible explanation for this apparent uncertainty, an explanation which follows from my discussion of White's Indian-ness in this story, and this is my second conclusion. I have called**"The Twitching Colonel"** a metaphysical comedy because of the unusual combination of comic and metaphysical elements. Actually, the words are not mine but were used by Raja Rao to describe the special nature of his Indian metaphysical novel *The Cat and Shakespeare.* This is a novel (and also species of Indian literature) in which the usual formula for comedy does not strictly apply: instead of the usual comic resolution consisting of happy ending and reinstatement of the hero, the metaphysical comedy involves a moment of supreme individual recognition and subsequent clarification from the understanding he has acquired; it also involves the supervention of some metaphysical agency in the more usual processes of cause and effect. At the end of a metaphysical comedy the world is seen in its true colours as *Maya* and as a game (*lila*). A recognition of this larger reality vitiates all worldly truths, all solemnity and all overseriousness; life in its physical and temporal context is seen to be absurd and also trivial. Most of these qualities are, I think, reflected in this early story by Patrick White. This Indian view of things helps explain the place of uncertainty in White's fiction, for not only is the world *Maya* but all worldly differences and distinctions are seen to be insignificant in view of a deeper undifferentiated "essence" beneath appearances. Hence at the deeper levels of his fiction author and *personae,* direct and indirect speech, metaphor and actuality merge together in the one essence. Nor does the "comedy" undercut the "metaphysic" in this species of writing but rather defines the specific quality of the comedy. Actually, this second conclusion and Indian explanation comes fairly close to my first conclusion regarding White's linguistic and structural mystification. From the Indian point of view all attempts to communicate with words and all attempts to arrive at certainty must result in failure, contradiction or paradox.

Life is absurd, grotesque. So the Colonel twitches. So he proceeds to disintegrate. And so, finally, he disappears in a ball of smoke, ending with neither a bang nor whimper, but rather in the spirit of absurdist drama, with a sound more like the well-known raspberry.

Notes

1. *The London Mercury,* 35, 210, April 1937, pp. 602-609. All subsequent page references are to this edition.
2. Raja Rao, *The Serpent and the Rope* (London: John Murray, 1960), p. 380.

Brian Kiernan (excerpt date 1980)

SOURCE: "The 1960s," in *Patrick White,* The Macmillan Press, 1980, pp. 83-7.

[*In the following excerpt, Kiernan observes that* The Burnt Ones *is marked by abrupt contrasts in setting, mode, and tone among the stories in the collection.*]

Although it is as a novelist that Patrick White has established his reputation, his shorter fiction and drama have their own intrinsic merits, as well as interest in relation to his novels. The stories and plays written in the period framed by *Riders in the Chariot* and *The Solid Mandala* can surprise the reader, by revealing unexpected attitudes and departures from what for many came to be seen as the 'typical' characteristics of White's work. The range of modes and moods in the stories and plays suggest an element of self-conscious literary play that needs to be balanced against presumptions of too direct an expression of the writer's attitudes, or his presentation of rigidly preconceived ideas, in the novels.

In 1964, short stories which had appeared in Australian and English magazines over the previous couple of years were collected, with two previously unpublished stories, under the title ***The Burnt Ones.*** The 'burnt ones' refers, though ironically on occasions, to those who are seen in each story as having encountered life in its vital and ambiguous manifestations. This theme common to the stories, of the natural life of the instincts and the imagination breaking through the repressive social surface, runs throughout the novels also. Yet, what is most immediately apparent with ***The Burnt Ones*** is not the thematic connection, but the abrupt contrasts in setting, mode and tone between the stories. The most obvious division is between those with Australian settings, in which a range of satiric tones predominate, and others set in Greece which with a virtuoso flourish, suggest an intimate acquaintance with the complexities and subtleties of another culture. Formally, the stories range from a one-act comedy, **'Willy Wagtails by Moonlight'**, or a revue sketch, **'Miss Slat-**

tery and Her Demon Lover', which although presented fictionally could be readily translated to the stage, to extended psychological studies like **'Dead Roses'** or **'The Evening at Sissy Kamaras'**. These latter enable the reader to observe how, in the more extended forms of his novels, White works through similarly compressed sequences of scenes, and, as here, equips each character with a complete personality, or psychology, of his own through vivid and symbolic details from his past. One story, **'A Glass of Tea'** adopts the conventions of the nineteenth century tale, the story of a story one character tells another, replete with mysterious possibilities and a surprise revelation at the end. Another, **'Clay'** is a surreal fable, a parody of the sensitive biographical study of the imaginative youth at odds with his society.

'Clay' anticipates a more general shift in the contemporary short story, away from realistic fictions towards fantasy, parody and elliptical fable, and the exploitation of possibilities for imaginative and linguistic play. Critical agreement seems to be that White is at his best in the short story form in his longer pieces, which approach novella length, because, in these his ability to create characters finds room to display itself. Yet there is something circular about the expression of this preference. The critics prefer the stories which most nearly approach the novels because they really prefer the novels, and their no longer tenable conception of 'the short story form' is of conventional novels in miniature. **'Clay'** plays zanily with the conventions of the *Bildungsroman,* or story of the development of a sensitive and imaginative young man (in this respect it seems a first sketch of the 'Waldo' section in *The Solid Mandala*) and with the language and habits of the society he is at odds with. For Clay is imaginative, in a way that parodies the seers in White's novels: 'He did, in fact, wonder a great deal, particularly while picking the bark off trees, or stripping a flower down to its core of mystery' and he is fascinated by his mother's wedding shoe: 'Sometimes its great boat would float out from the shore of frozen time into the waters of his imagination, rocking his cargo of almost transparent thoughts' (p. 115). In the context of his inner fantasy life, the social satiric observations have their own surreality, as when his mother has his hair shorn by the barber to cure Clay of speaking nonsense (at the time the story was written a belief in the moral efficaciousness of short hair was general in the community). The linguistic parodies of his mother's speech, or the officialese in the letter from a family acquaintance who finds Clay a Public Service job, are wildly funny. Yet the direction, and point, of the story might very well worry the reader, as surely it is meant to. The heavily Oedipal 'clues' to Clay's bizarre and grotesque fantasies suggest, falsely, a key to the absurdity; and the conventional expectation that Clay, the seer, will provide a revelation in his final moments of madness leads only to the 'moral' that 'everyone knows that what isn't isn't, even when it is' (p. 135). It is a story that plays with, and against, expectations and deliberately cultivates a disorienting uncertainty in the reader.

Although the view that the longer and psychologically realistic stories are superior, and represent better White's characteristics as a novelist is open to question, it would be difficult to dispute the general agreement that the long concluding story **'Down at the Dump'** is the most memorable in the collection. The funeral of Sarsaparilla's loose woman brings together a range of characters, some exhibiting grief, others relief, others again indifference. It shows how the venial sins of pride in respectability and hypocrisy are more destructive of life than the 'mortal' sin of sexual licence, and how the natural and instinctual processes of life are denied by social existence, which attempts to regulate these forces and impose its own false or inessential needs in place of what is vital and spontaneous. It is, though, the comic presentation of this romantic theme, the mingling of farce and pathos with the funeral, the satire of suburban respectability, and the sub-plot of life renewing itself down at the dump, amid 'the bags and iron' of Australian life that give the story its rich tonal effect. It opens at the Whalleys' place, where 'easy was policy' (p. 285), with Mrs Whalley's wood chopping interrupted by her husband's suggestion that they 'pick up a coupla cold bottles' (p. 286) and spend the Sunday morning at the Sarsaparilla dump, fossicking. The Whalleys with their tumbledown weatherboard house, and old utility for fossicking on the dumps (but a Customline on hire purchase), with their concern for sensual satisfactions but disregard for respectability contrast with their neighbours opposite, the Hogbens. Mum Whalley is a variation on a stereotype that turns up frequently in the novels and plays, the 'essential woman' untrammelled by social conventions and possessions, a passionate earth mother, except that she has not always had children as she has wanted. Mum Whalley has, however, and all her kids 'had inherited their mother's colour, and when they stood together, golden-skinned, tossing back their unmanageable hair, you would have said a mob of taffy brumbies' (p. 289). In contrast with this image of natural vitality the life of the Hogbens is controlled, and denied, by material possessions 'the liver-coloured brick home . . . the washing machine, the septic, the TV, and the cream Holden Special' (p. 291).

The social gulf between the Whalleys and the Hogbens is bridged by their children Lum and Meg who, while the funeral is in progress, meet and are innocently attracted to each other in the dump next to the cemetery (which is only another kind of dump). Both feel the call of life and imagine a shared future, in which they rush together through the night in a semi-trailer. Meg dreams of her few possessions, including the pad on which she would write a poem if they ever stopped, and Lum of swaggering back to the cabin at a service station to take possession of his property. Between their shared but separate day dreams, are old Ossie Coogan's memories at the funeral of Daise Morrow having taken him into her bed:

> Then the lad Ossie Coogan rode again down from the mountain, the sound of the snaffle in the blue air, the smell of sweat from under the saddle-cloth, towards the great, flowing river. He rocked and flowed with the

> motion of the strong, never-ending river, burying his mouth in brown cool water, to drown would have been worth it.
>
> (p. 304)

The story opens to reveal these dreams, memories and desires—the world of the imagination. Ossie is the burnt one in this story, the one who experiences suffering. He is the only one to cry at Daise's funeral, much to Councillor Hogben's embarrassed disgust at his behaviour, and his relationship with his sister-in-law. Ossie's memories of youth, virility and movement meet Lum and Meg's sexual dreams, which promise that life will go on, that the new generation will escape mere social existence, at least temporarily. The story ends on an open note as the Hogbens and the Whalleys, children included, drive off in their different directions, and driving becomes an image of the continuity and restless energy of life for Lum and Meg.

> The warm core of certainty settled stiller as driving faster the wind paid out the telephone wires the fences the flattened heads of grey grass always raising themselves again again again.
>
> (p. 316)

Brian Kiernan (excerpt date 1980)

SOURCE: "The 1970s," in *Patrick White,* The Macmillan Press, 1980, pp. 123-24.

[*In the following excerpt, Kiernan shows that the short stories in* The Cockatoos *mimic the "satiric charicature" and the "poetic intensity" of White's novel* Riders in the Chariot *as well as the author's work during the 1960s.*]

A second collection of stories, ***The Cockatoos,*** appeared in 1974. Some of the six 'Short Novels and Stories' it contained had appeared in periodicals and anthologies as far back as 1966 and, overall, the tone of the collection harmonises more closely with White's work of the sixties than with that of the previous decade. All but one of the stories have Australian settings, or characters, and the shifts in them from satiric caricature to poetic intensity recall something of the strained combination of modes in *Riders in the Chariot.* As in ***The Burnt Ones*** there is a pervasive theme of the frustration of lonely lives within bourgeois society, and especially within the institution of marriage, yet there is less here of the spirit of playfulness that marked the earlier collection. The pattern of sexual passion erupting into drab, repressed lives in story after story seems too neat, the attitude towards the characters too insistently ironic for the wit and the play with various modes to dispel an impression that these stories are schematic and lacking in the complicating dramatic qualification of the novels.

In **'A Woman's Hand'**, the longest story or 'short novel', Evelyn Fazackley's meddlesome matchmaking leads to the marriage of two of her self-sufficient acquaintances, but shortly afterwards to the death of one and the mental collapse of the other. **'The Night the Prowler'**, in which a disappointed rape victim of stockbroker respectability and a dominating mother, sets about raping society in revenge for her repressed upbringing, and discovers the true nature of life, both sordid and vital, on the other side of the Park railings, begins as satiric farce and wildly Freudian fantasy but ends in absurdist solemnity. In **'Sicilian Vespers'**, the wife of an Australian doctor holidaying in Sicily, a situation which allows for an amusing play with the comedy of manners, is disturbed by a confusion of sexual and religious impulses in an ancient basilica. Finally, in the title story, as in *The Season at Sarsaparilla,* the deadening routines of suburban life are disturbed by the intrusion of natural energies, this time none too thinly disguised as native birds.

The sense of a somewhat schematic presentation of already familiar assumptions about 'Life' and society's withdrawal from it would seem to confirm judgements that White, as essentially a novelist, needs an ampler form in which to develop characters and situations. This would be plausible were it not that the two shortest pieces, indisputably short stories, are the most memorable in the collection. **'Five-Twenty'** in which an elderly couple retired from the country sit outside their suburban house to watch the peak hour traffic on the Parramatta Road, until death and repressed sexuality destroy them surreally, is a disturbing reverberant black comedy untouched by the tendentiousness apparent in the longer stories. The only story in this collection set in Greece, and also the shortest, relates indirectly to the common theme of conflict between the banality, even sordidity of existence and the revelation of transcendent life. During the German occupation, the adolescent Costa who aspires to be a concert pianist discovers how much his higher faculties are at the mercy of his primitive drives. The extremes recognised here in **'The Full Belly'**, and convincingly established through character and situation, seem however to be forced into the satiric Australian settings of the longer stories, with the result that there is not the 'middle range' of experience offered in the novels that appeared immediately before and after this collection.

Timothy G. A. Nelson (review date 1981)

SOURCE: "Proserpina and Pluto, Ariadne and Bacchus: Myth in Patrick White's 'Dead Roses,'" in *Australian Literary Studies,* Vol. 10, No. 1, May, 1981, pp. 111-14.

[*In the following review, Nelson asserts that "Dead Roses" is one of the best works in* The Burnt Ones *and shows how White uses myth to add comedy to the story.*]

'Dead Roses,' the longest and one of the best stories in Patrick White's collection ***The Burnt Ones,*** is saturated in classical myth. The central figure, Anthea Scudamore, is a goddess *manquée* who, faded and suburban as she is, seems in her finer moments to have 'strayed out of some other category, of divinities and statues' (p. 68).[1] When Anthea arrives for the first time at the Tullochs' island retreat she appears to the watching Flegg as 'a regular Juno', monumental, over-dressed, and forbidding (p. 18). But on her second, solitary visit she is metamorphosed into Venus wading in the foam:

> So deserted was her desert beach that she took off her clothes once, without even looking over her shoulder, and walked into the milky sea. Exquisite skirts of foam clung to her ankles, and began to soothe her thighs . . .
>
> (p. 64)

This latter theophany is a little pathetic, since there is nobody around to see it. Anthea herself evidently senses that it has been wasted, since she later tries to evoke it for Flegg:

> "I went across to the Island, Barry, not so very long before I left. I was alone. I lived on eggs. And bread. I tramped about the bush. I was pretty miserable at the time. I swam."
>
> She was surprised at the directness, the candid softness of her own voice. Did she, perhaps, hope he might watch her rising from the sea?
>
> (p. 73)

But if Flegg does momentarily visualize Anthea as Venus rather than Juno, he refuses to admit it; he merely laughs an embarrassed laugh, and the last meeting between the two of them ends as inconclusively as the first.

White moves, with Olympian casualness, from myth to myth. Fleetingly, he will transform Anthea into an unnoticed Venus or all-too-conspicuous Juno, but his favourite characterization of her is as an ashen parody of Proserpina, goddess of spring. At the beginning of the story she is offered a chance to blossom, which she fails to take: elsewhere there are many signs that she 'was meant to swell, and ripen and burst',[2] but somehow she never does so. The critical action of her life is her acceptance of a proposal of marriage from Hessell Mortlock: Mortlock's name, like his riches, his miserliness, his dead roses, and his morgue-like house, is irresistibly suggestive of Pluto, god of the dead, who carried Proserpina off to hell.[3] Even Pluto's chariot has its counterpart in Mortlock's elegant but old-fashioned car. But Anthea, unlike Proserpina, is not carried off by force: she goes of her own accord. She is an accomplice in the death of spring. Likewise Mrs Scudamore, though outwardly as fond and possessive a mother as Ceres in the ancient story, resigns herself remarkably easily to the loss of her daughter. In a letter written shortly after Anthea's marriage (and dotted, incidentally with discreet allusions to the myth), Mrs Scudamore announces that she cannot yet manage a visit: '. . . Perhaps when it is spring, Anthea dear . . . I do not feel it is altogether right for a mother to intrude . . . I cannot help feeling you have changed towards me since Hessell Mortlock carried you off . . .' (pp. 45-46). Far from searching tirelessly through the world for her lost child, Mrs Scudamore allows almost five years to elapse before flying to Adelaide to visit her daughter.

I have said that White moves freely, when it suits him, from myth to myth. If Mortlock, whom Anthea chooses, is Pluto, the central character in a myth of death, then Flegg, whom Anthea rejects, is Bacchus, the protagonist in a myth of life. In the early encounter on the beach Flegg offers Anthea the part of Ariadne,[4] she turns it down, but it continues to fascinate her, so much so that when she hears Flegg has got someone else to play it she finds herself overcome in church with dionysian visions:

> Once Mrs. Mortlock, from behind her Gothic hands, was horrified to receive a vision of the bodies of Barry Flegg and Cherie Smith lashed together by ropes of hair. Lashed and lashing. She was so horrified with herself, she felt faint. . . . All she could do was bow her head and suffer the blasphemy which had been thrust upon her . . .
>
> (pp. 47-48)

Just as Mortlock is endowed by White with Pluto's chariot in the shape of a bottlegreen Riley, so Flegg is equipped with Bacchus'chariot in the shape of a minibus with an attached tent. In Titian's painting of Bacchus and Ariadne, as in Keats' poems 'Endymion' and 'Ode to a Nightingale', Bacchus' chariot is drawn by leopards, and this attribute of the god is reflected in the leopard-skin pants of Flegg's wife.[5] These pants disturb Anthea because they represent a part of her being with which she has never come to terms: subconsciously, she would like to wear such pants herself. In the penultimate paragraph of the story, after the meeting with the Fleggs, Anthea rouses herself from a troubled sleep and begins 'with slow distaste, to accept that she [has] been dreaming of Cherie Flegg, of her stained leopard-skin matador pants.'

White uses myth; he does not let myth use him. Just as Mrs Scudamore and Anthea are in many ways unlikely castings for Ceres and Proserpina, so Flegg is an unexpectedly tawdry Bacchus (his hairiness makes him almost a Silenus) and Mortlock a too-prepossessing Pluto. That is the point. There is a spring goddess latent in Anthea, but she allows this part of her personality to be appeased rather than fulfilled. And it is appeased by something in Mortlock that is delusively suggestive of life and growth. Mortlock's car is green, he has a passion for roses, and he even turns out (a less dignified touch) to nurse acquisitive feelings about horse-dung. He also drinks wine, though he seems pleased that Anthea does not normally 'tipple' (p. 35). But the roses Anthea finds on arrival at Pluto's palace are dead roses, and Mortlock's wine-drinking has nothing Bacchic about it: in an Australian context, both wine and roses are irredeemably respectable and safe. On the paradisal island holiday Anthea daringly drinks gin, and at the mock-heroic banquet around the minibus she is offered 'a drop of that ouzo stuff' (which is at least Greek) as an alternative to 'an authentic Australian cuppa tea' (p. 70). She accepts the tea.

Inevitably it is the titular roses that epitomize Anthea's confusion over the respective attributes of Mortlock and Flegg. Before the marriage Mortlock comes in 'on a hot morning bringing Anthea Scudamore the largest bunch of crimson roses', roses 'of the overpowering kind' (p. 37). Anthea is duly overwhelmed, even though the cleaning woman reminds her that there is a glut of roses, so that Mortlock may not have paid much for his impressive bunch. The appeasement of the fertility-goddess latent in Anthea is never more obvious than in her joy over the flowers: 'She liked to look up and catch sight of herself in the glass. She remembered a photo she had seen, of a film star, her bust brushing a bowlful of enormous roses' (p. 38). Mortlock's gift helps Anthea persuade herself to associate Mortlock with lushness, even ecstasy: the moment when he holds her hand in front of the arranged roses is 'one of the serious moments in life, which the scent of the roses attempted to intoxicate' (p. 38). Yet the Mortlock family's usual way with roses is to imprison them in metal and glass, amongst funeral furniture, as Anthea finds when she first enters her husband's house:

> . . . All that brooding furniture. And the roses. The neglected roses. For somebody had filled the rooms with silver vases and cut-glass bowls of roses. There they were, the brown roses, in some cases almost turned to metal, to bronze. The petals of the dead roses creaked as she passed.
>
> (pp. 42-43)

As she falls asleep on her wedding night this scene struggles for mastery in her dreams with images of her encounter with Flegg on the beach: 'And soon the gulls were lashing at the metal petals of Egyptian roses. While she was sunk in safety. The creaking of roses, their knife-edged wings, grew silenter for distance' (p. 44).

Finally, too late, Anthea is allowed to see that roses are properly an attribute of the bacchic Flegg, not the stygian Mortlock. The insight comes as she sits, momentarily goddess-like again, 'enthroned on the camp stool' beside Flegg's car:

> So, she was preparing to leave, when the old Greek came along the path with the bunches of roses, the crimson-purply, country bunches. Because he was asked, Doctor Flegg bought a bunch, giving too much, Mrs Mortlock saw—she was quick to master the currency of any country she visited—and tossed the roses into his wife's leopard-skin lap.
>
> (p. 72)

Mrs Flegg protests and tells her husband to give the roses to 'Mrs Scudamore.' But Anthea is no longer Scudamore, she is Mortlock, encrusted with jewels and preoccupied with the prices of things. She accepts just one flower:

> And pinned the rose with a brooch, which seemed, rather, to draw attention to the diamonds, though she had not intended it that way.
>
> "Flowers die on me," she apologized, "very quickly."

White's use of myth in **'Dead Roses'** is organic, not casual or accidental. Not the least of its merits is that it helps to buoy up the comedy of the story, which might so easily have become submerged in the prevailing atmosphere of melancholy and pathos. Yet, like most other successful essays in mock heroic, it dignifies its subject matter at the same time as it ridicules it. The mythic level of reference helps White to establish in the reader's mind an image of the scintillating Anthea who might have stood alongside the image of the tarnished Anthea who actually exists.

Notes

1. Page references are to the first edition of *The Burnt Ones* (London: Eyre and Spottiswoode, 1964). I am grateful to my colleague Michael Cotter for constructive criticism and advice.
2. cf. Patrick White, *The Aunt's Story* (London: Routledge, 1948), p. 33.
3. See Robert Graves, *The Greek Myths* (Harmondsworth: Penguin Books, 1955), Vol. I, Sections 25 c, f—k. Graves normally gives only the Greek names for the divinities, whereas I have used the more familiar Roman ones. The equivalences are: Hades/Pluto; Demeter/Ceres; Core-Persephone/Proserpina; Dionysus/Bacchus; Zeus/Jupiter; Hera/Juno; Aphrodite/Venus.
4. For Ariadne see Graves, *Greek Myths,* I, sections 98 n, o. Bacchus and Ariadne meet on the seashore. White uses this detail but not much else. (See, however, note 6 below).
5. See John Keats, *The Poems,* ed Miriam Allott (London: Longman, 1970), pp. 255-57. The note on 'Endymion', IV, 241, points out that the leopards are a post-classical addition. A deliberate, impish misreading of IV. 240-42.

   > And, save when Bacchus kept his ivy tent,
   > Onward the tiger and the leopard pants,
   > With Asian elephants.

   may have been the starting point for White's description of Flegg's minibus with tent attached, and of his cat-like concubine with 'leopard-skin matador pants' (*The Burnt Ones,* pp. 70-71).

Veronica Brady (essay date 1983)

SOURCE: "'Down at the Dump' And Lacan's Mirror Stage," in *Australian Literary Studies,* Vol. 11, No. 2, October, 1983, pp. 233-37.

[*In the following essay, Brady praises White's story "Down at the Dump," calling it one of the author's most interesting stories "for the insight it offers into people and society."*]

'Down at the Dump' is one of White's most interesting stories, not merely for the insight it offers into people and society but also for the structures underlying it, structures which deepen our understanding not only of White and his art but also of his relations with his culture as a whole.

By now, of course, it is a truism to say that White's art is not mimetic, not concerned to reproduce surface appearances, but expressive, concerned with inwardness, with the writer's sense of himself and the world. This story, like nearly all of his work, relates primarily to psychic archetypes and only secondarily to social realities. But it is also an attempt at self-portraiture, at putting on stage 'the cast of contradictory characters of which I am composed'.[1] Paradoxically this attempt leads beyond the self. As in psychoanalysis the psyche becomes a myth among myths, part of a fully fledged mythology, and the need to become aware of one's situation in inner space leads to a reorientation in the outer world. Whatever might be the case elsewhere, as far as Australian culture is concerned, this makes White something of a radical. Not only does his work attack the accepted paradigms of behaviour; more disturbingly, he implies that the ego is not an adaptive or synthesizing power but something that rises up and interrogates these paradigms in general and, most disturbingly, language in particular. **'Down at the Dump'** calls for a transfer of allegiance from the comfortable commonsense world of Mrs Hogben to that of Daise, which is both disreputable and occult. The goal of this story, like most of his novels, is thus something out of this world to the extent that it exceeds the current boundaries of social discourse and points to what 'you do not know, but know'. Unlike most of his novels, however, this story is presented in such a way that it becomes clear that this knowledge is not transcendent, much less mystical, but is in effect knowledge of an aspect of the self in a particular stage, Lacan's 'mirror stage' in which the developing self longs for a permanent image of the equivalent of what it sees in a mirror.

This becomes evident in the first place from a consideration of the story's structure, a series of binary oppositions between characters and situations. The two sisters, Daise and Mrs Hogben are antithetically opposed. Mrs Hogben reflects on the difference:

> It was Daise who had said: I'm going to enjoy the good things of life—and died in that pikey little hut, with only a cotton frock to her back. While [she] had the liver-coloured brick home—not a single dampmark on the ceiling—she had the washing machine, the septic, the TV, and the cream Holden Special, not to forget her husband, Les Hogben, the councillor. A builder into the bargain.
>
> (p. 291)

Mrs Hogben puts her trust in things and fears everything that she is unable to possess. Hence she is always busy, 'bunched up tight' protecting herself from thought and feeling. Daise is the opposite, abundant, sensuous, and life-giving, prodigal of herself and of the little she owns.

Mrs Hogben is also contrasted with her daughter Meg who is drawn to the warmth and spontaneity of her aunt, and with Ossie Coogan, the 'deadbeat', who disgusts her but whom Daise has loved and comforted. The final and perhaps overriding contrast is between Mrs Hogben and the Whalleys, vulgar but disreputably vital. In contrast with these antipathies, there is also a system of sympathies, between Daise and Ossie, Meg and Lum, Mr and Mrs Whalley and, to a lesser extent, between Daise and Harrie Last, Mr Hogben's friend, and Daise and Mr Hogben himself.

From this analysis it is clear that Daise and Mrs Hogben constitute the modal points, the centre of attraction on the one hand and repulsion on the other, of reconciliation and antagonism, and of centripetal and centrifugal movement. This binary system is continued in the spatial antithesis between body (associated with the gross and disgusting) and spirit (associated with flow and light and freedom) but most of all between the dump and the cemetery, the opposition which provides the key to the story. According to Lacan,[2] the formation of the ego is often symbolized in dreams by a fortress or stadium surrounded on the one hand by marshes or lawns, places where everything is smooth and ordered—as the cemetery is in White's story—, and on the other by rubbish tips where nature is in decay. The self must not merely pass between but also contest these two opposed areas in its quest for the lofty, remote inner fastness. This quest not only engages the young people, Meg and Lum in this story but, implicitly White himself. *Flaws in the Glass* opens with the image of the fourteen year old boy gazing at his reflection in the mirror. The failure of maternal love leaves a Narcissistic wound, the sense of mourning which prevails in **'Down at the Dump'**, and elsewhere in White's work of course. In this sense, the figure of Ossie Coogan may therefore be closest to the story's origin. Expelled prematurely from the womb and weak and vulnerable ever since, he 'finds' himself only in Daise's bed:

> Then the lad Ossie Coogan rode again down from the mountain, the sound of the snaffle in the blue air, the smell of sweat from under the saddle-cloth, towards the great, flowing river. He rocked and flowed with the motion of the strong, never-ending river, burying his mouth in cool brown water, to drown would have been worth it.
>
> (p. 304)

While the mirror stage in the formation of the self, arising between six and eighteen months when the child, still lacking motor coordination, begins to perceive an image of itself, anticipates future mastery, the mirror stage can also be a permanent state. Then, as here with Ossie, personal identity comes to depend on maintaining a dialogue between the self and its reflection, its desired image.

But it is in the image of Daise, however, that one senses the author leaning forward most strongly, holding in his gaze not an image of weakness (as in the creation of Ossie) but of triumphant unity and then, jubilantly, assuming this image. The illusion of verisimilitude, strained anyway in the exaggerations of character and their presentation, gives way as the story draws to its conclusion and Daise returns from the dead, a suburban and feminine Christ figure calling to the 'sour woman, public servants, anxious children and old, scabby desperate men' (p. 311) with a message of love and comfort, countering all that Mrs Hogben stands for in her refusal to assume the armour of a social identity that is alienating, destructive to self and to others:

> Truly, we needn't experience tortures, unless we build chambers in our minds to house instruments of hatred in. Don't you know my darling creatures, that death isn't death, unless it's the death of love? Love should be the greatest explosion it is reasonable to expect, which sends us whirling, spinning, creating millions of other worlds. Never destroying.
>
> (p. 311)

The beatitude she speaks of here leaves behind the question of identity. Instead, with her creator she is absorbed into the presence of the holy, some state forbidden to profane experience. As the pressure on the language suggests, this is a state difficult, if not impossible, to put into words; Narcissus has drowned in the pool of self-reflection, has withdrawn from the world of common experience and therefore of language. The omniscient narrator is the only one who sees Daise and hears what she is saying:

> Even if their rage, grief, contempt, boredom, apathy, and sense of injustice had not occupied the mourners, it is doubtful whether they would have realized the dead woman was standing amongst them. The risen dead—that was something which happened, or didn't happen, in the Bible. Fanfares of light didn't blare for a loose woman in floral cotton. Those who had known her remembered her by now only fitfully in some of the wooden attitudes of life. How could they have heard, let alone believed in, her affirmation?
>
> (p. 311)

Her message is not merely threatening to people like Mrs Hogben, custodian of commonsense and common morals, to them it is also wicked. Yet Meg, Mrs Hogben's daughter, begins to understand. Even though she had never exactly succeeded in interpreting her aunt's message, she is stirred by something she senses at this moment in herself and in the natural world:

> She did experience, however, along with a shiver of recollected joy, the down [of Lum's face] laid against her cheek, a little breeze trickling through the moist roots of her hair, as she got inside the car, and waited for whatever next.
>
> (p. 312)

In Daise's words about love, she has glimpsed an image of her own possibility, an image that is both formative and erogenic. So the story concludes with a promise that she and Lum are moving in the direction in which Daise's life has pointed them, the mysterious renewal of life figured in 'the flattened heads of grey grass always raising themselves again again again' (p. 316). Providing for them an image of completeness, Daise has made it possible to grow beyond the limits imposed on them by society and family.[3]

In contrast, Mr and Mrs Hogben and Horrie Last, to a greater or lesser extent, find Daise a threatening figure, since she reminds them of the self that might have been and of their failure to recognize it, their misconstruction of reality.[4] Thus as the story concludes they seem condemned to perpetual restless movement—in contrast with Lum and Meg settled in a 'warm core of certainty' (p. 316): 'driving and driving, in long, lovely bursts, and at the corners, in semi-circular swirls' (p. 314). They represent mere desire, not appetite but hunger in Marx's sense which is the product of inner need rather than of longing for something outside the self and is thus forever insatiable and eccentric. They drive for the sake of driving, self-enclosed unable to make contact with anyone or anything else, whereas Meg's existence is dialectical:

> The landscape leaped lovingly . . . she could have translated any message into the language of peace . . . the wooden houses stuck beside the road, the trunks of willows standing round the brown saucer of a dam. Her too candid, grey eyes seemed to have deepened, as though to accommodate all she still had to see, feel.
>
> (p. 315)

The Whalleys, also 'driving . . . driving', are different again, aware at least of their bodiliness and delighting in it but aware of little else. In them, the antithesis between body and spirit, dump and cemetery, reveals its significance. As Lacan points out, the ego which constitutes itself as a unity in fact constantly needs to defend that unity, swinging between two affective poles of jubilance and paranoia. The Whalleys exemplify this swing, now exulting in their bodies, now quarrelling with them, aggressively on defence against a society they affect to ignore. 'Mucking around' in the dump, the place where nature shows its power in decay,[5] they are in effect laying claim to an image of themselves unified with nature—in contrast to the Hogbens who belong in the smooth abstractions of the cemetery. But, the story suggests, this unity is not theirs, nature is in control, not they. So the last image we see of them is discontented, Mrs Whalley is grumbling, ostensibly at Lum but actually at her existence:

> It was not strictly Lum, not if you was honest. It was nothing. Or everything. The grog. You was never ever gunna touch it no more. Until you did, and that bloody Lummy, what with the Caesar and all, you was never ever going again with a man.
>
> (p. 314)

Normally this rivalry between the two sides of the self is controlled and diminished by the introduction of a third regulatory term, a socially assumed image of the self. But this the Whalleys are unable to achieve, while, at the other extreme, the Hogbens remain imprisoned, unable to come to terms with the physical world and their own bodiliness.

In this sense the goal of unity implicit in the story remains unachieved. Daise may be a triumphant figure, but the integrity she represents is out of this world, the completion of the life in which she refused to assume a social identity, living independent of her sister and society in general. So too with Meg and Lum with whom the story ends: the 'warm core of certainty' they experience is as undefined as what they have seen, now know and wish 'to cherish' (p. 316). What is implied here is either sentimental, 'working off in words and feelings [they] haven't really got' (D. H. Lawrence) or cannot be believed to have or, what is worse in the terms the story sets up, social—that is, that they will one day marry and live happily ever after. This inability in White to ground his ideal in social reality points to the crucial problem, the sense of defilement, the nauseating and nauseated consciousness of physical and social reality evident here in the descriptions of sagging bodies, decaying teeth, 'liver coloured' houses, smelling sinks, rubbish dumps and so on. Meg's relationship with Lum begins, for example, on the day 'he threw dog poo at her' (p. 289), and White goes on to detail her disgusted reactions, as if delighting in them. So too with descriptions of social and personal relations, which also suggest an inability to establish a connection between the self and its physical environment. The violence in the relationships between the sexes, between parents and children and between the sisters Daise and Mrs Hogben, suggests that it is impossible to trust, much less believe in social appearances or values. This distrust is intensified by the melodramatic intensity of the language which forces what might seem indifferent to take its place in what is ultimately a moral schema. Mrs Whalley's eyes are not merely blue, for example, but 'blazing' blue, and their attractiveness has to be qualified by the 'something' which happens when she smiles, 'her mouth opening on watery sockets and the jags of brown, rotting stumps' (p. 285). Similarly, Mrs Hogben is not merely seen as cold and superficial but punished for it, made to whimper, 'very faintly, for everything you have to suffer, and death on top of it all' (p. 288).

From one point of view, as Sartre argues, a nauseating consciousness of reality of this kind can be a means to freedom, protecting the self from surrendering to the immediate and contingent, pressing it to go further—as White's imagination does here in the figure of Daise and to a lesser extent, in Meg and Lum. But from another point of view, from where most readers stand, the urgent question rises: where, if anywhere, can they exist? As we have said, although Daise is meant to represent the 'real', existence as it should be, she does not belong in the world of commonsense and what she represents is not verifiable in its terms. More crucially, although she gives life to others, the ecstatic goal of her life is the loss of self, the undifferentiated identification with all that is which is characteristic of Eastern mysticism. Moreover this identification is with nature, with the image of 'grass always raising itself again again again' (p. 316) with which the story concludes, as much as with human beings. But, as the pervading images of decay insist, this endless return of the natural world mocks human beings with their desire for immortality, the desire to which White pays tribute in bringing Daise back from the dead. If nature is the equivalent to the City of God in the contemporary imagination, Mary Douglas has commented, it is a city of silence since it has no human citizenship.[6] Elsewhere, White equates nature with the physical necessity which makes human existence tragic—unless, of course, one believes in an after life. Yet here, even though there is a suggestion of this in Daise's return, there is no real belief in immortality. The narrator may hear her promise: '"I will comfort you. If you will let me. Do you understand?" . . . Nobody [else] did, as they were only human' (p. 311). We are left, then, with the conclusion that the transformation has not occurred, the writer has not been able to assume the image he has created.

Nonetheless, this story offers some important insights into White's project as a writer, his attempt at the reconstruction of reality which involves the expression of what 'you do not know, but know', an experience which is neither symbolic nor imaginary but something in between, an experience foreclosed to analytic experience, to the rational language and ordering of the culture he lives in which still relies on the promises of the Enlightenment. As I have said, the strain of this attempt is most evident in the language, in the melodramatic pressures upon it in the lexical and syntactical distortions and violations as well as in the concreteness of description—of 'the saliva of bitterness' (p. 291), for instance—and anthropomorphism—the Whalley's house 'was threatening to give in to them' 'because they were in the bits and pieces trade' (p. 286). Finally, the writer's uncertainty, the lack of commonality which leads to the autocratic individuality, appears even in his narrative method. The story is discontinuous, does not develop according to a logic of its own but depends on the will and intention of its teller who transfers us suddenly and without reason between the different worlds and most suddenly of all produces the figure of Daise risen from the dead. While aesthetically there may be problems with these tensions and discontinuities, they throw light on his concern as a writer not so much with things as they are but as they may be, what James calls the 'possible other case'.

Notes

Editors' Note: A different interpretation of 'Down at the Dump' may be found in David Myers, *The Peacocks and the Bourgeoisie* (Adelaide: Adelaide University Press, 1978).

1. Patrick White, *Flaws in the Glass* (London: Cape, 1981), p. 20.
2. Jacques Lacan, *Ecrits* (Paris, Editions du Seuil, 1966), 'le Stade du Miroir comme Formateur de la fonction du Je), pp. 89-101. Lacan gives an example from observation. It is a necessary condition for the maturation of the gonad in the female pigeon that it sees another member of its own species, of either sex.
3. Lacan's 'Méconnaissance', Lacan, 96.
4. In Lévi-Strauss' scheme, nothing is the state in which nature shows its power most clearly, Edmund

Leach, *Lévi-Strauss* (London: Fontana/Collins, 1973), pp. 30 ff. In *Flaws in the Glass,* White connects the 'private mysteries of his childhood with corners of the garden where things seemed to be rotting, a rich mattress of slater-infested humus' (p. 16).

5. Mary Douglas, *Natural Symbols, Explorations in Cosmology* (Harmondsworth: Penguin, 1973), Chapter 10.
6. 'Down at the Dump' appeared in Patrick White, *The Burnt Ones* (Ringwood: Penguin, 1972), pp. 285-316.

John A. Weigel (excerpt date 1983)

SOURCE: "Epiphanies in Tables and Goats: *The Burnt Ones*, *The Cockatoos*, and *Four Plays*," in *Patrick White,* Twayne Publishers, 1983, pp. 87-103.

[*In the following excerpt, Weigel surveys the critical reception of White's short story collections and points out that White's short stories "employ diverse techniques for a wide range of effects like the author's novels."*]

Most of Patrick White's short stories have been collected and published in two volumes, ***The Burnt Ones*** (1964) and ***The Cockatoos*** (1975). Four of his early plays, originally produced in Australia, have been published in one volume in 1965. For many admirers of Patrick White, his shorter fiction and his plays are epiphenomena. That is, although White's reputation as a significant writer may be reinforced by them, they are not essential. Like his novels, they do, however, bear witness to the author's cosmopolitanism and his ambivalence about Australia. The stories in particular, which vary in length from extended sketches to novellas, employ diverse techniques for a wide range of effects.

When White returned to Australia after years abroad as a student, a soldier, and a wanderer, he brought with him memories of his sojourns in exotic places, material which he used in his short fiction. He was unsympathetic with the Australian literary nationalism that had emerged during the 1930s.[1] The writings of Joseph Furphy and Henry Lawson were always cited as examples of what the home folks could do. Both Furphy and Lawson were masters of the anecdotal style and their stories are easy to understand. Their homespun quality contrasts with the literary sophistication of White and Richardson, who could not conceal, even if they had chosen, their interest in the experiments of British and Continental dramatists and storytellers.

Patriots such as Nettie Palmer continued to prefer the home-made stories of Henry Lawson, for example, praising their "loose, easy look."[2] At the same time, others began to break away from the old ways. Hal Porter, for one, took a new look at familiar places and people. G. A. Wilkes was one of the critics who understood what Porter was trying to do, and he tried to explain it: "The world of Porter's stories is the familiar world seen as slightly askew, the personalities sometimes neurotic, the events sometimes macabre." Human beings are perceived as "enigmatic and astonishing."[3] Just as Virginia Woolf in England had rejected gig-lamps for the personal reality of luminous halos, Christina Stead and Randolph Stow in Australia—as well as White and Porter—began to express impressions rather than report. White's short stories, in particular, led the way.

The Burnt Ones

Patrick White's first collection, which he called ***The Burnt Ones,*** contains eleven stories. Nine of them originally appeared in periodicals such as *Meanjin*, *Australian Letters*, and *London Magazine*.[4] Several of the stories are Greek in setting and characters. One mixes modalities by transporting an Australian woman to Greece for its moment of truth. One is set in the neutral city of Geneva, while others are highlighted by the plastic suburbia near Sydney which White calls Sarsaparilla. All of them, however, investigate concerns familiar to White's readers: suffering, loneliness, and frustration as constants in the human equation, an equation in which the variables may contain humor and irony but seldom high tragedy.

White found ideas and characters compatible with his themes—unfortunates burned by life—while living in post-war Greece where he met and sympathized with the victims and exiles whose quest for salvation had been secularized by wartime hardships. God seemed remote and improbable, often even a mockery after the "Catastrophe" at Smyrna, where many Greeks were slaughtered by the Turks and others fled with their lives only. Also, severe shortages following World War II, particularly in Athens, where aristocrats were forced to forage for food, intensified passions and escalated issues.

In **"The Woman Who Wasn't Allowed to Keep Cats"** White contrasts two rich, Americanized Greeks, proud owners of a Cadillac, with a married couple struggling to adjust to life in Athens. The local Greeks seem eccentric. The man is a left-wing writer, the woman a cat-lover. The "authentic" Greek woman blames her compatriots for not loving cats. Greeks, she says, are "too egotistical, quarrelsome, lazy, and gluttonous to understand the force of love" (257). The visitors find the cat-lover mad, and when they return two years later to visit their friends again, they discover that the cat-lover has given up her cats because the formerly liberal husband has forbidden them now that he is a prosperous, right-wing writer. The Americanized Greeks get the impression that the cat-lover has been transformed into a cat. They are glad to return to New York. No one has escaped deterioration.

In another of the Greek stories, **"The Evening at Sissy Kamara's,"** memories of Smyrna are the pedal point in a contrapuntal conversation between two couples. The hostess, Sissy, once had intellectual pretensions. She has published some poems, but "so privately nobody has read them." Once she declaimed an epic poem—"On a theme nobody can remember," says Basil Patzopoulos upon being informed by Poppy, his wife, that she has accepted an invitation to spend an evening at Sissy's. Of Sissy's declamation he adds: "On a mountain side. To a group of women, most of them by now dead" (128-29).

In the course of the evening the hosts and guests share a small balcony. As Sissy serves indifferent food, her husband breaks Sissy's last good dish from Smyrna. In a confusion of emotions Sissy laughs as she cries, then philosophizes: "Almost my last possession of importance . . . when one had hoped with age to grow less attached when age itself is the arch-disappointer a final orgy of possessiveness of of of [*sic*] a gathering of minor vanities" (139). Sissy also "explains" Greeks to her guests: "We are a brutal, detestable race," she pontificates. "If we care to admit, we are little better than Turks turned back to front" (136). Although Basil and Poppy Patzopoulos disagree with Sissy, they suppress possible rejoinders and depart with feelings of guilt. There is no resolution.

"Being Kind to Titina" begins in Alexandria where a "good" Greek family and a "bad" Greek family are neighbors; then the story moves on to Athens for an ironic conclusion. There the Greek boy-man from the good family has his first sexual experience with an amoral but happy whore. The woman turns out to be the formerly plain Titina from the bad Greek family, whom he had once been forced to treat politely when they were childhood neighbors. The upgrading of Titina is contrasted with the disillusionment of the good boy. Again, however, there is no resolution.

In **"A Glass of Tea"** White utilizes Geneva as a neutral setting for a conversation between two casual acquaintances, both Greeks of different histories and generations. Malliakas, a middle-aged bachelor, a writer *manqué* in search of a story and in Geneva on business, finally decides to present a letter of introduction to Philippides, an elderly Greek now living in Switzerland. During his short visit Malliakas finds his story. It is based on what the old man tells him of his first wife, Constantia, emended by what the old man's second wife, Aglaia, tells him about the first wife and a set of tea glasses. A gypsy had once prophesied that the old man would live until the last of the glasses was broken, but it was his first wife who broke instead. At the time of the visit there is just one glass left unbroken. It will not last long, however, Malliakas knows, as he sadly leaves.

In **"Dead Roses"** White combines the decadence of Greece with the sterility of respectable Australia. Anthea Scudmore, a forerunner of Theodora Goodman of *The Aunt's Story,* is a wealthy Australian widow traveling in Greece. There she is eventually rebuffed by a former admirer also visiting Greece. She is also insulted and threatened by a beautiful young Athenian. That night the Australian woman, who is so sterile that most flowers die on her, dreams neither of the young Greek nor of her former admirer but rather of the latter's wife, who had been wearing "stained leopard-skin matador pants" (66). The story is heavy with Freudian symbols and itself ends in a dying fall—as dead as the dead roses Anthea had found in the home of her impotent husband on her wedding night.

The Australian stories in the collection often satirize generalizations that begin "We Australians," but with a difference from the "We Greeks" philosophers. There is less poignancy in the Australians, with whom White is less patient than he is with babbling Greeks. In **"Miss Slattery and Her Demon Lover"** an Australian lady objects strenuously when she hears her country reduced to "nossing" by her Hungarian lover. She counters at once with "we Australians are not all that uncivilized. Not in 1961" (200). Miss Slattery, however, is not taken very seriously by Tibby Szabo, her masochistic, rich, and fat Hungarian lover, until she threatens to leave him. When Szabo asks her if she is "ze Defel perheps?" she answers: "We Australians are not all that unnatural" (215).

In **"A Cheery Soul"** a self-righteous husband and wife argue themselves into sharing their home with an unfortunate woman, a Miss Docker. When the arrangement soon turns into a domestic disaster, the "cheery soul" is transferred to a respectable institution for impecunious aged men and women. There her cheeriness moves from nuisance to menace when she challenges the minister in church, destroying his sermon and literally striking him down so that the minister's wife accuses her of having killed not only her husband but perhaps also her God. The effect of such blasphemy is devastating, as White well knew, and he later developed this story into a drama.

Reasonable people often insist on being considered both civilized and normal and are easily satirized because no one is ever quite reasonable except in his own opinion. When the hero of the story **"Clay"** asks his mother why she named him Clay, he receives a reasonable answer: his mother had been interested in making pottery. There is little else in the sketch, but it makes a sharp point economically. In another short piece, **"The Letters,"** a mother-dominated son finally tries to make love to his mother. White suggests that the son's violent behavior was programmed by his mother's devotion to him. The incest episode yields to an anticlimax. Instructed as a child never to read other people's letters, the son finally stops reading even those addressed to him!

In the most ambitious story in the collection, **"Down at the Dump,"** a boy-man and girl-woman meet at the line between the dump and the cemetery, having been brought to the dump and the cemetery respectively by their parents. The boy's family are "doing the dump"—which means scavenging. The girl's parents are burying a relative, Daise, a woman of easy virtue. It is clear that she is also one of the *illuminati* when at the cemetery her spirit speaks of love.

Although the meeting between the youths is contrived, the effect crescendoes before the quiet ending as the potential lovers return home with their respective parents, passing one another on the road: "They lowered their eyes, as if they had seen enough for the present, and wished to cherish what they knew" (308).

Big questions are asked of Destiny and Accident in the story called **"Willy-Wagtails by Moonlight"** via a slip in the making of a tape of the song of a bird. A respectable husband, while recording the Willy-Wagtail, also inadvertently records the sounds of his adultery with his secretary. Only a visiting couple, however, hear that part of the tape, the unfaithful husband and the betrayed wife being destined accidentally to be out of the room. This trivial and bitter story is characteristic of the "black in White." Accidents are the only miracles.

The Cockatoos

The Cockatoos, White's second collection of stories, appeared in 1975.[5] It contains six substantial pieces of short fiction which testify to the writer's growing maturity. Less gimmicky than several of the stories in ***The Burnt Ones,*** these later narratives reflect the author's concern for ways in which desperate human beings confront the odds against them. Here a few of them are allowed to find a kind of salvation outside churches, or even in the improper use of a church as a place of assignation. White's secular offerings include a cup of coffee, a handful of rice, a glimpse of cockatoos or peacocks, sunsets, and an old man's urine.

In **"The Night the Prowler"** an old man, far into his dying, explains to a young woman that there are only two goods: to piss easily and to shit smoothly. And so when he urinates over himself as the woman holds his hand, the woman feels a momentary grace as "she continued up the hill to report the death of an old man she had discovered a few moments before, but knew as intimately as she knew herself, in solitariness, in desolation, as well as in what would seem to be the dizzy course of perpetual becoming" (168).

Evelyn Bannister, the recipient of this unusual grace, is just nineteen years old on the eventful night in which she encounters a prowler in her home. The assumption that she is raped and otherwise mistreated by the prowler is the invention of her parents and neighbors, who need to be protected from the truth that Evelyn frightens the prowler more than he frightens her. After drinking and smoking in his presence, she sends him away, disgusted by his unimaginative timidity.

Soon thereafter, using her "rape" as an excuse, Evelyn cancels her engagement to a nice young man, who is relieved. Evelyn then begins to break into houses in the neighborhood herself, not to steal or rape but to extend her freedom. In the final, good-Samaritan scene she embraces a repulsive derelict. He dies in her arms while offering her his urine.

In **"Sicilian Vespers"** White again challenges convention and Christian morality. The piece is a carefully dramatized tale about a failure of faith between persons who rely too heavily on rationalism and humanism. Ivy and Charles Simpson represent those Australians who accept being Australian without either glorifying colonialism or hating other colonials, such as Americans. The Simpsons are genuinely kind, honest, intelligent, and well enough off to travel. Abroad, they tolerate foreign eccentricities they would not dream of accepting at home. In Sicily their planned itinerary becomes an empty time because of Charles's almost incapacitating toothache.

During the pause the Simpsons make friends with the Clark Shacklocks, a rich American couple who seem a bit vulgar but kind. Clark *may* be Roman Catholic but the Simpsons are not sure. His wife Imelda certainly seems to be a Christian Scientist. As the relationship between the couples begins to get complicated, Ivy Simpson suddenly, against her better judgment, allows herself to be possessed one evening by Clark in the Duomo at San Fabrizio during vespers. Imelda and Charles, meanwhile, wait patiently for their respective spouses in the lobby of the hotel. Imelda is reading an ironically appropriate Italian novel: *I Promessi Sposi.*

Upon her return, Ivy Simpson remains cool and lies. She later realizes she is still hungry for a religious experience, or rather, she tells herself, at least for religious words. She had always respected the word "*Godhead*: as a mere word leaping at her from off the printed page, it made her turn over quickly, to escape something far beyond what Charles and she had agreed to find acceptable" (230).

In **"A Woman's Hand"** Clem Dowson tries to explain to his friend, Harold Fazackerly, why he and his wife have separated:

> "My God," Dowson was gasping and mouthing, "one day, Harold, when we meet—in different circumstances—I must try to tell you all I've experienced." He was speaking from behind closed eyes. "That was the trouble between us. Between myself and that woman. We had lived at the same level. It was too great a shock to discover there was someone who could read your thoughts."
>
> (76)

There is no chance, however, for the two men to meet "in different circumstances," for that night Clem is killed by a bus whose wheels he makes no attempt to avoid. Harold is left friendless and confused, realizing he has missed something. His need, however, has not been defined so there is no way of satisfying it. Also, Harold's wife, despite her good intentions, cannot understand either her husband's need or that of his friend. It was she who was originally responsible for adding "a woman's hand" to bachelor Clem's house overlooking the sea. The woman she paired with Clem, however, ends in a psychiatric hospital: she had heard the sunset shriek "with the throats of peacocks" (70). The moral is a bitter one: it is dangerous to hear the sunset shriek.

In the title story of the collection, **"The Cockatoos,"** a Mrs. Davoren and her husband are as alienated from one another as possible until the cockatoos arrive. They have not exchanged spoken words for years. When necessary, they communicate via pencil and pad. But when they see the spectacular cockatoos, the Davorens begin to speak to one another again—about the birds, of course—and even celebrate their reunion in bed. Their joy is short-lived, however. One day a neighbor shoots two of the birds, and in the ensuing struggle for the gun Mr. Davoren is killed. But that is not all that happens. When a neighbor boy, Tim Goodenough, finds the last of the cockatoos, a cripple, he kills it and cuts off the bird's crest as a trophy to mark his victory. Cockatoos can bring joy to those who love them but the price is high.

The two most ambitious stories in the collection are **"Five-Twenty"** and **"The Full Belly,"** each of which celebrates a secular communion and its terrifying inadequacy: a cup of coffee that is never served and a handful of rice that degrades decent people. In the former story a childless, elderly couple spend their days sitting on a porch watching the traffic pass on the highway. Royal and Ellen Natwick are dependent on the regularity in the lives of others, particularly upon a man in a Holden who drives by at five-twenty every evening. He is a flat-headed, unusual looking fellow. They have found him memorable and essential. If he occasionally misses his "five-twenty" passing, the Natwicks are upset. Their clock has betrayed them: the universe is not orderly after all.

When Royal Natwick dies quietly, Ella is left "with his hand, already set, in her own. They hadn't spoken except about whether she had put out the garbage" (184). Ella accepts widowhood and takes the pills the doctor prescribes. As far as she can, she begins to relate to her "things," among which the man in the Holden is still real. Then one day he stops and asks to use the phone.

Excited, unable to speak clearly, she babbles in a "new language." He is not upset. He holds her in his arms. She responds, watching "the world of his mouth"—he has a hare lip—"struggling to open." At this moment of recognition Ella kisses him "as though she might never succeed in healing all the wounds they had ever suffered" (190). He promises to return the next day for a cup of coffee. In the meantime Ella learns how to make coffee, having had previous experience with tea only. This communion cup will contain a brew new to her.

When five-twenty comes and passes without him, Ella fears the worst. There is a bad wreck up the road. Has he perhaps been killed? He finally appears: he is late because he is ill. The symptoms indicate angina, with pains up and down his left arm. Ella vows to save him. In fact, however, in her eagerness she embraces him too forcefully and kills him "by loving too deep, and too adulterously" (196). The author's verdict is ruthless: Ella's worldly reward for all that patient watching was only a chance at adultery, no more and no less than a chance, and she lost. The coffee was never served.

The rice becomes moot in the story **"The Full Belly,"** which returns to the Athenian scene. During the occupation of Greece, Athenians were severely tested not only by hunger but also by a patriotism that required strict resistance to collaboration. Two proud and elderly spinster sisters, Maro and Pronoë, have long ago bartered away all their valuable possessions for food but still refuse to collaborate with the prosperous Germans who occupy the city. The older sister, Maro, begins to starve herself to death in order to save food for others in the family. Her nephew, Costa, who is a talented music student and the orphaned son of a former President of Greece, decides to sell himself for food.

Costa first refuses the advances of a neighbor woman who would pay him in eggs. He then encounters a German soldier in one of the side streets of Athens who offers him meat in exchange for what Costa knows he has already done but this time chooses to refuse. Not much later, driven by hunger for meat, he changes his mind and searches for the soldier, who, however, has disappeared. Rushing home because he remembers a dish of rice left next to dying Aunt Maro's bedside, he finds Aunt Pronoë already there and gorging herself on the few grains of rice. They struggle for the food, breaking the dish in the contest. After Pronoë leaves in disgust, Costa kneels and picks up bits of rice mixed with bits of carpet and stuffs them into his mouth. When his dying aunt sees him, she says: "Eat, poor souls. . . . Fill your stomachs, children." Then she adds, before she dies: "I only pray you'll know how to forgive each other" (118). After such knowledge, what forgiveness?

Secular Sacraments

The extent to which one can accept White's specifications for and significance of the "course of perpetual becoming," which for him is obviously a good—if not the only good—in living, correlates with the degrees of praise allowed these stories. The alleged epiphanies are often blurred. Grace is neither easily won nor freely bestowed by either writer or reader. Characters behaving decently in a godless universe are sometimes seen as foolish. What price courage if there is no reward here or in an afterlife? Certainly White allows little probability of judgment days that will rectify and punish fairly.

The Cockatoos is condemned as "a strong anti-marriage tract" by a woman obviously upset about the failure of marital bonds in the stories to restrain immorality. The same critic prefers White's novels, concluding that "the short story does not offer White the space he needs for his greatest strength, the portrayal of a character's fantasy."[6] Eudora Welty, however, praises White's stories, noting that "they go off like cannons fired over some popular, scenic river—depth charges to bring up the drowned bodies."[7] Brian Kiernan compares White's stories favorably with those of Hal Porter, finding that "White's style has become more muted over the years, more an instrument than a self-regarding end." Unlike Porter, however, "White is concerned to engage life, and in the better stories, this takes the form of his emphatically imagining how life might be experienced by others."[8]

White's shorter fiction has recently been honored by a book-length study in which David Myers explores the many "dualities" in the stories: ". . . not only the tragic irreconcilability of such antitheses as grace and horror, epiphany and sanity, caritative love and bourgeois conventions. . . . There is also the dual vision of his irony which incessantly modifies both the bitterness and the bliss of his protagonists." Because there is less room to manipulate these dualities in a short story, the pieces are not all equally successful. Furthermore, what Myers calls "White's grotesque sense of humour" seems harsher in the short stories, and Myers notes that White has confessed that he does not like writing shorter fiction as much as he does a novel. "All my effects are cumulative," White has said, "and one doesn't really have the time to get the effects you want."[9]

Notes

1. See Vincent Buckley, "Towards an Australian Literature," in *Twentieth Century Australian Literary Criticism,* pp. 75-85. Buckley, in 1958, was daring enough to advocate the teaching of "Australian Literature" at the university level.
2. A. A. Phillips, *Henry Lawson* (New York: Twayne Publishers, 1970), p. 138.
3. G. A. Wilkes and J. C. Reid, *The Literatures of the British Commonwealth: Australia and New Zealand,* ed. A. L. McLeod (University Park, 1970), p. 120.
4. All references here are to *The Burnt Ones* (New York, 1964); page references cited in the text in parentheses.
5. All references here are to *The Cockatoos* (New York, 1975); page references cited in the text in parentheses.
6. Rose Marie Beston, "More Burnt Ones: Patrick White's *The Cockatoos,*" *World Literature Written in English* 14, no. 2 (1975): 520.
7. Eudora Welty, "Patrick White's *The Cockatoos,*" in *The Eye of the Story* (New York: Random, 1978), p. 264.
8. Brian Kiernan, "Short Story Chronicle," *Meanjin Quarterly* 34, no. 1 (1975): 37.
9. David Myers, *The Peacocks and the Bourgeoise* (Adelaide, 1978), pp. 1, 173.

Lorna Sage (review date 1988)

SOURCE: "Potato Peel," in *Observer Review,* October 30, 1988, p. 44.

[*In the following laudatory review of* Three Uneasy Pieces, *Sage praises White's short story collection, calling it "a marvelously cunning raid on the inarticulate."*]

Patrick White's new book isn't slim, it's emaciated. If his last one, *Memoirs of Many in One,* was about role-playing and multiplying yourself, then ***Three Uneasy Pieces*** is pared down with a vengeance to 59 pages. He's trying out a new route in his cranky, self-consuming search for illumination—not so much reviewing his repertoire as puzzling about what he has left out.

The negative way (in mystic's jargon): and though if you followed this paradox to its conclusion you would find yourself contemplating a blank page, ***Three Uneasy Pieces*** is good value in every sense, a marvellously cunning raid on the inarticulate that pulls off the hardest trick, simplicity.

This makes paraphrase more embarrassing than usual. The pieces come in ascending order of explicitness. The first, **'The Screaming Potato'**, takes a kitchen sink dilemma ('wondering whether to gouge the eyes . . . a certain amount of flesh would disappear with the gouging') as a metaphor for cruelties inflicted 'in the name of morality and justice'. The second, **'Dancing with Both Feet on the Ground'**, is a *danse macabre* featuring 'the Contessa del Castelmarino, alias Gladys (Baby) Horsfall of Gundy, New South Wales' taking a senile pratfall on the brink of eternity. 'When the draughts started blowing down her cleavage, she knew she needed a faith': but needing is not finding.

The third and longest piece, **'The Age of a Wart'**, comes closest to spelling out the unwisdom old age can bring. It starts as a vivid reminiscence of Bluey Platt, the alien boy at school with warts (and poverty, and kindness): 'he lurches against me . . . holds a fist against one of my knuckles, and mumbles "Twins!" as he grinds his wart into mine.' Bluey leaves school early, drifts off to visit the Abos, is heard of over the years in Blitzed London, a Japanese POW camp, Hiroshima, and is never found again. And gradually the story converts itself into a vision of the alternative life you didn't live, that stays with you like an invisible excrescence, the long-lost wart, the (impossible) identification with human suffering, the twin.

The narrator finds at the last that all his self-gougings in search of perfection have served only to bring him to this realisation of his spiritual emptiness, the beginning of wisdom. Patrick White, a Gemini, contemptuous of his name and Nobel fame and always convinced he was ugly yet fully human inside ('this black, bubbling pool'), has here found a triumphant metaphor for his twin nature, his heritage of doubleness. He may look forward to silence and dismiss 'carefully chosen words and the studied sentences of literature', but only his own words on the page (down there in black and white) can get him there.

D. J. Enright (review date 1988)

SOURCE: "Warts and All," in *The Times Literary Supplement,* No. 4470, December 2-8, 1988, p. 1350.

[*In the following mixed review of* Three Uneasy Pieces, *Enright contends that while there are "brilliant passages" throughout the collection, the "book's chief uneasiness lies in the reader's fear of having missed the point."*]

On the first leaf of this slim triptych Patrick White suggests that we do indeed grow wiser with age, just as long as we disbelieve the myth about growing wiser with age. Sterility and decay are the primary themes here; and guilt: even vegans must feel guilty as they hear "the whimper of a frivolous lettuce, the hoarse-voiced protest of slivered parsnip".

In the third and most substantial story, **"The Age of a Wart"**, the narrator, born into a wealthy Sydney family and now a famous writer, "a stuffed turkey at banquets", broods on his vanity and false ambition. He compares himself with his schoolfellow, a poor boy called Bluey, who has since lived with Aborigines and taught them carpentry, helped to drag out bodies in Bethnal Green during the Blitz, kept up the spirits of prisoners of the Japanese ("'E was the best mate a man ever'ad'", says a survivor), and ministered to A-bomb victims in Hiroshima.

This almost excessively exemplary history, underscoring "the distance between life and literature", heightens the narrator's sense that he has always been trapped inside his own inadequacy. Bluey, he says, "is the part of me I've always aspired to. My unlikely twin, who got away." He cannot call his house a home: it is crammed with his books, translated into "every inaccessible language", and he is so often away from it, making speeches on behalf of literature and ethics or collecting honorary degrees. "Being famous is such a solemn and consuming occupation, I have to laugh sometimes. If only I could share my laughter with someone who would see the point." Bluey is never available, he has always moved on.

In the closing sentence, as the hypodermic takes effect, the old, weary, desolate "I" turns into "we":

> It is *we* who hold the secret of existence *we* who control the world WE.

Otherwise—or notwithstanding, for the apparent implication is that only with death does the evil in us die—the story is pretty cheerless, a grim, self-punishing illustration of the lines in "Little Gidding" on "the rending pain of reenactment" and other gifts reserved for age.

"O Lord", the first piece asks, "dispel our dreams, of murders we did not commit—or did we?" Warts, whose lifetime is said to last two years, link Bluey and the narrator, and may be thought to symbolize their twinship or possibly the evil that dies in due course. But the transition from gouging out the eyes of potatoes and slicing parsnips to the cruelties we inflict on other people isn't especially convincing. The book's chief uneasiness lies in the reader's fear of having missed the point, for distinguished authors must surely mean something distinct, and Nobel Prize winners are likely to mean nobly or at least largely. There are brilliant passages: for example, in the second piece, "the skitter of drums" in the ballroom of a ghastly Alpine hotel, and the resident priest who will administer either extreme unction or an enema; the bare-bones dialogue is adroitly mimetic; and the indignities of geriatric hospitals are succinctly conveyed. It wouldn't be right to say the Emperor has no clothes, but he is scantily clad on this appearance, and perhaps rather uneasy about showing himself in public.

Carolyn Bliss (review date 1988)

SOURCE: "Crusades Against Hoopla and Pain," in *Critical Essays on Patrick White,* edited by Peter Wolfe, G. K. Hall & Co., 1990, pp. 65-7.

[*In the following review, originally published in* Antipodes: A Journal of Australian Literature *in 1988, Bliss maintains that the stories in* Three Uneasy Pieces *"lack the convincing density and scope of the major novels and even of much of White's short fiction."*]

Patrick White's ***Three Uneasy Pieces*** is a slender, 10,000-word short story collection, which makes a sharp and caustic statement in its timing, an intriguingly antiphonal suggestion in its prose. Published in December of 1987, it was rushed into production before 1988 in order to avoid any appearance on White's part of having validated Australia's Bicentennial by issuing a celebratory volume. So anxious was White to disassociate himself from the Bicentennial hoopla that he snatched the manuscript from its original Melbourne publisher, when that house was unable to meet his December 31 deadline, and handed it over to astonished and delighted Pascoe Publishing, a small firm whose head man, Bruce Pascoe, admits that the book's acquisition is "more of a windfall than a coup." Taking full advantage of its windfall, Pascoe had the book typeset in a matter of days, took White's corrections on the proofs by telephone, and reportedly "camped" at the printer's until the first run of bound copies was delivered. The volume's triumphant copyright date is 1987.

Judgmental, preemptory, irascible: White's censure of the Bicentennial seems of a piece with his recent public persona. But his book collects "uneasy pieces," works which shed a very different light on Australia's only Nobel Laureate in literature, an indisputable master of his art and one of the twentieth century's greatest novelists. This new light is a gentle and subdued one: mellow, conciliatory, finally almost serene. All three of the volume's pieces are written in the first person and adopt a voice which begins in reflection and moves toward confession. Thus, while the book sounds again the note of penitential self-exposure that has counterpointed White's fiction at least since *The Vivisector,* it settles at last for a kind of shriven self-acceptance that expands in the direction of a wider reconciliation.

The first "uneasy piece," entitled **"The Screaming Potato,"** is a scant two pages long. Within this meager space, however, it manages to develop an image of excised potato eyes into a comment on the inevitably cruel and murderous exigencies of living. Like Heriot in Randolph Stow's *To the Islands,* the elderly narrator of **"The Screaming Potato"** is forced to equate life itself with preying and to offer up the prayer to be either absolved or disabused of his deep sense of guilt. In this story, even lettuce, parsnips, and potatoes whimper or scream as we prepare them for our nourishment, and all our acts are marked and marred by "a fair bit of gouging" and "the chopping to be done."

The narrator of **"Dancing with Both Feet on the Ground"** is also an old man, one who has learned that life must be celebrated only "cautiously." In its opening image of careful, arthritic dancing in a kitchen—"Over spilt milk. through lettuce leaves and potato peelings. Bloodstains too . . ."—**"Dancing"** echoes the volume's opening piece, as it also does in the rest of the story's prevalent food imagery, which pictures sustenance as always inadequate, saccharine, or accusatory. The story's other controlling image is that of dancing, whether in a solitary moment of unreason and abandon which "M" might term "senility," or in the ballroom of a winter-locked European hotel remembered from the days of youth. As the story not so much unfolds as dilates, the act of dancing begins to suggest the teleological nature of time, which drives over those it fells or will fell. These include the pretentious, widowed Contessa whose feet of Australian clay paddle the air when she slips on the hotel dance floor, and the still upright narrator who shuffles toward an uncertain future and shares with the sham Contessa a need for faith aroused by the icy draughts of approaching mortality. As in White's novel *Voss,* life in this story is like a river which runs over "upturned faces," but also a river whose light and motion mirror "figures of the timeless dance."

The center of the book's interlocking pieces is the last and longest story, **"The Age of a Wart."** Here we find again the White who notes the extramundane dimensions inherent in the humblest, most disgusting physicalities. In *A Fringe of Leaves,* a boil became "spiritual matter"; here it's a wart. Wart and boil are put to similar thematic purposes: to link characters of spiritual affinity, in this case the narrator and his afflicted schoolmate Bluey Platt. As youngsters, both the boys grow matching warts on their right hands, and the narrator is sure he caught his from his classmate. Bluey, whose real name is Tancred, after the Christian Crusader of history and Rossini's opera, resembles the narrator in other ways as well. Both will be artists, one working in lives and substances and the other in words; both could be mystics; and they are, as Bluey claims and the narrator later acknowledges, "twins." Yet the latter initially chafes at this identification with someone of indifferent academic achievement and an address on the "Wrong Side." Accordingly, he cures himself of his emblematic wart through, as it eventuates, an act of deliberate will. Soon he also loses proximity to his friend, as Bluey's sojourn with western Aboriginals and the narrator's schooling in England separate them.

Following his formal education, the narrator and his bad chest sit out the subsequent War in a Scottish hotel, where he begins to write the novels which will bring him fame, honors, degrees, and self-contempt. He describes them as works which only "pretended to search for truth, reality, in carefully chosen words and the studied sentences of literature." Suspecting that Bluey, whose wart must have survived to "praise . . . the ugliness of life," could admit him to a reality he circles unsteadily and desperately craves, the narrator mounts an instinctive crusade to reclaim him.

Tancred, meanwhile, carries his own crusade against suffering through the worst of the War and its aftermath, leaving signs to surface everywhere for the narrator. Still, he remains beyond reach of his friend. The search for Tancred thus becomes a pilgrimage whose stages are signaled by relics and testimony, but only intermittent and unsatisfactory epiphany. True revelation must await the reappearance of the wart, which seems to the now dying narrator a melanoma whose darkness may engulf the world. His extremity summons twin Tancred, who rejoins him in a reconciling vision in which evil dies, a brotherhood of suffering and survival is affirmed, man's potency is proclaimed, and the story closes.

The "three uneasy pieces" of White's latest book thus ultimately yield the ease of resolution. Yet a caveat is called for. White could be tempting us to make too much of this resolution, something the style may be warning us against. These stories lack the convincing density and scope of the major novels and even of much of White's short fiction. Instead of proceeding by means of a rich proliferation of ambiguous, evocative, but finally consonant detail, they merely gesture toward implication through a shorthand predicated on suggestive imagery.

Nonetheless, transcribed in the reader's heart or soul, which, as always in White, receive more credence than the intellect, the signs of this shorthand constitute a prayer much like that of Le Mesurier in *Voss*: a petition that the spirit come to rest "in true love of all men and in you, O God, at last." It is a wrenching prayer to raise, one founded in a humility which White's fiction insists must be forever and painfully repossessed. These stories, too, trace that repetitive process. But they also hint that if White shuns the chauvinism of the Bicentennial, the volume which heralds this renunciation simultaneously reaches toward the family of man. As a member of the family, I welcome him amongst us.

Lee Spinks (essay date 1995)

SOURCE: "Patrick White's 'Five-Twenty,'" in *Westerly,* Vol. 40, No. 1, Autumn, 1995, pp. 39-44.

[*In the following essay, Spinks praises White's short story, "Five-Twenty," for its "austerity" and insight into human character.*]

The pages of ***The Cockatoos,*** Patrick White's second collection of short stories, are littered with ruined epiphanies. In the title story each character interprets the migratory birds as a symbol for an experience of transcendence they neither expect nor feel they deserve. Compelled by years of lovelessness into a bitter and silent marriage, Mick and Olive Davoren begin to develop a new language of tenderness in the presence of their mysterious visitors. The cockatoos appear to offer a glimpse into a world of harmony, order and beauty; but their departure leaves death, silence and aching loneliness in its wake. Meanwhile **"The Full Belly"** depicts the horror of Greece under German occupation, where villagers make faltering attempts to spiritualise their physical distress through religion, sex, and music. The spiritual isolation enforced upon the individual trapped in a world devoid of grace or redemption is perfectly expressed in the character of Costa Iordanou, the young musician, who is alive to the "austerities" of Bach but unable to grasp the "epiphanies"[1] that Bach's music promises to reveal. The mundane and supramundane worlds touch for a moment and then diverge; denied the aesthetic resolution of a musical epiphany Costa is compelled to find sustenance in his own fantasies of change and renewal.

With its stubborn refusal to resolve the tension between existential austerity and the desire for a transcendent release from the rigours of the human condition, Costa's story functions as a hermeneutic rubric for the collection as a whole. Ensnared by the constrictions of history and language, individuals struggle towards a moment of revelation that will infuse their lives with meaning, only to collapse back amidst the ruins of their dreams. White consistently resists these moments of epiphanic resolution because he wishes to explore the dreamscapes, narrative projections and compensatory fantasies that his characters develop in the absence of a redemptive moment of secular transcendence. Nowhere is the space between austerity and epiphany more tellingly articulated than in **"Five-Twenty,"** a story that charts Ella Natwick's faltering passage from the arid monotonies of a fading marriage towards the possibility of erotic release in the arms of a fantasy lover. Forced to care for Royal, her invalid husband, in his declining years, Ella beguiles the time watching the commuters drive home on the Parramatta Road. Gradually her attention is monopolised by one man, the driver of a Holden, and White's tale describes her growing interest in this unremarkable individual, the two visits he pays to her home in the wake of Royal's death, and the tragedy that destroys her domestic idyll and exposes her once more to evanescence and loss. Recounted in these terms, **"Five-Twenty"** risks approximation to minor suburban drama; but it is rescued from banality by White's deliberate erosion of the boundaries between fantasy and reality. We are not told the source of Ella's attraction to the unnamed driver, and his figure is only tentatively sketched; but as his image mutates in Ella's mind she is left to confront a lifetime of repressed memories and forgotten dreams. This synthesis of dream and reality is then repeated in the melancholy confusion of Ella's twilight reveries, where desire and the repression of desire combine to produce her unstable and contradictory narrative.

White's subtle exploration in **"Five-Twenty"** of Ella's mutilated fantasies is assisted by his use of free indirect style to create a mode of address indifferently positioned between first and third person narrative positions. Free indirect style is a technique widely employed by Modernist writers because it places the truth-claims of narrative fiction within parentheses, and, in the epistemological gap so produced, enables the writer to focus upon the difficulty of communicating knowledge between minds. In the hands of a writer like Joyce it is used to describe the effects that linguistic incompetence has upon the perception of the phenomenal world. The axiom upon which both *Dubliners* and **"Five-Twenty"** turn is that our ability to transform our existence is determined by our ability to describe and reimagine our experience. Existential paralysis is therefore, for both writers, an effect of *linguistic* paralysis. **"Five-Twenty"** describes precisely this tortured relationship between word and world in Ella's doomed attempt to articulate her fantasies and take the first steps into a new life.

By gently refracting the story through Ella's consciousness, White quickly reveals her inability to negotiate the abyss between thought and expression. The opening paragraph, which introduces us to the Natwick's ritual observance of the evening traffic along the Parramatta Road, notes that the stream of cars slowly thickened until it sometimes jammed "solid-like" (169). With this casual phrase, a term of equivalence that threatens to become a simile but lacks any final comparative term, we enter Ella's world. "Like what?," we want to ask. White's point is economically made: the story is about experiences or states of mind for which its witnesses can find no adequate verbal expression. The bestowal of narratorial responsibility upon a character for whom language is an opaque medium gradually opens the text up to multiple ironies. Thus the syntactic confusion of Ella's deference to Royal, "on account of he was more educated", makes an ironic point about the power of education to confer the linguistic competency she sorely lacks. A similar note is struck by her disinclination to rebuke Royal for spitting "because he'd only create if she did" (171), where the stultification engendered by their daily routine is implied by a verb that evokes an effortless spontaneity. Through Ella's verbal infelicities White continually reminds us of the limitations of the account that we are reading; it is apparent in her reference to her "arthritis" and her casual admission that "[i]t was all very well for men, they could manage more of the hard words" (172). Even in these early moments of the story, White is careful to underline his principle theme: Ella's difficulty in translating experience into language precludes her from the redemptive movement of grace. This becomes grimly apparent in the scene that describes the death of the Chevy driver outside the Natwick's house, an episode which prefigures the collapse of Ella's mysterious visitor at the end of the story. The young man is crushed and unable to speak; his fate is to die within the confines of Ella's narrative, where his last words are buried beneath the typographic monstrosity of "Extreme Unkshun" (171).

Ella's inarticulacy is the dominant theme of the story's opening pages. Even in those moments when she is overcome by an incipient lyricism she manages to keep the feeling at arm's length. Disgusted with her impractical desire to kiss and bite Royal's nose in the moonlight, she proceeds "solidly" (176) to sleep. One assumes she would appreciate the unfussiness of the adjective that governs her rest. Her own explanation for her mental dullness is contradictory: she "hadn't the imagination" to articulate the "thoughts" that swarmed in her mind; but since Royal rebuked her for her "foolishness" in having thoughts at all she concedes they "couldn't have been her own" but must have been "put into her" by some mysterious outside force. The chasm that opens here between intention and denunciation enables White to concentrate our attention upon the theme of repression that gradually dominates the rest of the story and which he uses to interrogate the fantasies Ella constructs to reliever her inner turmoil. This focus upon repression is unavoidable because Ella's personality is constituted by the denial of the libidinal play of the desiring self. It is her refusal to acknowledge the force of the dreams, desires and fantasies that define our modern subjectivity which leaves her damaged and unable to take effective control of her life. We do not need to be reminded of Lacan's dictum that the unconscious is structured like a language to recognise that Ella's inarticulacy and her repression of the economy of desire share a common origin. White underscores this recognition by showing, even in those moments later in the story when Ella begins to elaborate her dream of release, that her fantasies crumble at the point of articulation, relapse into fragmentation when confronted with the conscious demands of narrative coherence.

The twin themes of wordlessness and repressed desire recur in the symbol of the hare-lip "badly sewn, opening and closing" (177) that sends Ella into paroxysms of fear and the images of rebirth that punctuate the text. The most important of these images is, of course, the driver of the Holden, whose daily journey home is absorbed into a fantasy narrative which offers Ella some measure of compensation for a life of fragments and discontinuities. He is only "half" (179) a joke to her: comical because slightly unreal; serious because seriously desired. The Holden driver is in part a creation, a figure who takes on a new identity in her mind, without reason or design. His status as a projection of Ella's unconscious desire is reinforced by her insistence that he reappear in her vision at exactly twenty minutes past five every evening. Against the flow of time, subtly suggested by the chaotic movement of the traffic along the Parramatta Road, the Holden signifies to her a mode of constancy capable of redeeming her hopes and aspirations from the randomness of history. The growing discrepancy in Ella's mind between reality and fantasy is indicated by the "guilt" (181) that sends her scuttling back from her reveries to Royal's sickbed. But her fantasies cannot be so easily assuaged: they reappear in her dream of a man on the path alongside the cinerarias, a vision which recurs like the return of the repressed to such deadly effect at the conclusion of the story.

Ella's dreams of metamorphoses are also suggested in less overt terms. White's confidence in developing his main theme by indirection rather than narrative explication is demonstrated by his short detours into pastoral, such as the scenes in which Ella escapes from a lifetime of scrupulous devotion to lose herself in the sensuous riot of her garden:

> She loved her garden.
>
> The shady side was where she kept her staghorn ferns, and fishbones, and the pots of maidenhair. The water lay sparkling on the maidenhair even in the middle of the day. In the blaze of summer the light at either end of the tunnel was like you were looking through a sheet of yellow cellophane, but as the day shortened, the light developed to a cold, tingling green, which might have made a person nervous who didn't know the tunnel by heart.
>
> (180)

The garden in **"Five-Twenty"** has a similar function to the forest in *A Midsummer Night's Dream*: it denotes a marginal world, closely linked to the unconscious, in which the normal rules and structures of civil society are temporarily suspended. In this new imaginative domain each value encounters its opposite: water, with its plural association of flux, process and regeneration, sparkles on the "maidenhair," which symbolises innocence and self-enclosure. Ella inhabits the interstate between these two conditions, dreaming of a metamorphosis for which a child is the most visible symbol, while addicted to a life composed of rituals, routines and minor prohibitions. Adrift between the compensations of fantasy and the safety of self-restraint she gazes at life through "a sheet of cellophane", secure within a "tunnel" whose exits have long since been forgotten.

Royal's death releases Ella into a benign narcotic freedom. This release announces itself, appropriately enough, in her riotous desecration of the garden. In an afternoon of Dionysian excess, she dresses herself up in flowers, a suburban Ophelia, and visits the latent violence of her "thoughtless" unconscious upon the visible world:

> She couldn't blame anybody, probably only herself. Everything depended on yourself. Take the garden. It was a shambles. She would have liked to protest, but began to cough from running her head against some powdery mildew. She could only blunder at first, like a cow, or runty starved heifer, on breaking into a garden. She had lost her old wiriness. She shambled, snapping dead stems, uprooting. Along the bleached palings there was a fretwork of hollyhock, the brown fur of rotting sunflower. She rushed at a praying mantis, a big pale one, and deliberately broke its back, and was sorry afterwards for what was done so easy and so thoughtless.
>
> (185-86)

It is also in Ella's garden, where she has constructed an imaginary world to rival the real, that the "two objects" (187) central to her fantasy converge. By insinuating himself into the tunnel that marks the separation between fantasy and reality, the Holden driver enters Ella's privileged interior space. White is quick to emphasise the correspondence between the realisation of Ella's fantasy existence, implicit in the sexual metaphor of his unexpected entry into her secret "tunnel", and the death of her former self, signified by her conviction that his wish to use her telephone was "a way to afterwards murder you" (187). Her unconscious yearning for a definitive break with her repressive isolation then erupts for a moment into language as she connects "telephone" with "bed" (188) and begins to utter her nameless desires.

But as White repeatedly demonstrates in his fiction, the reality of repression cannot be so easily evaded. Ella's desire to escape from the constriction of her former life is thwarted by the loss of a language in which desire can be articulated. Brought to a point of crisis at which she must choose between two versions of herself, Ella is overcome by the sheer force of language and the promise of redefinition that it extends. As she wanders with her visitor among the cinerarias, flowers that have become imbued in her mind with eroticism and unrestraint, "[h]er throat became a long palpitating funnel through which the words she expected to use were poured out in a steam of almost formless agonised sound" (190). White's touch is mercilessly exact here: the "funnel" of formless sound that denotes her collapse recalls, through the savage ironies of language, the exitless "tunnel" of her married life with Royal. The entire story turns upon this moment when the slip *out* of language is reconstituted as a linguistic pun. Ella's sudden lurch into the "new language" (190) of tactility cannot therefore be interpreted as a liberating gesture precisely because White relentlessly intertwines the whole question of desire with narrative and story.

The return of Ella's "lover" to her secret garden underlines the inevitable failure of her attempts at metamorphosis. The episode is at once poignant and ironic: poignant because his reappearance, accompanied by the snapping of the "heavily loaded" cinerarias, dramatises her need to break the chains of the bounded self; ironic because the response demanded from her by his gradual slide towards death merely illustrates the abyss that exists within her between desire and expression:

> "More air!" she cried. "What you need is air!" hacking at one or two cinerarias which remained erect.
>
> Their sap was stifling, their bristling columns callous.
>
> "Oh! Oh!" she panted. "Oh God! Dear love!" comforting with hands and hair and words.
>
> Words.
>
> While all he could say was, "It's all right."
>
> Or not that at last. He folded his lips into a white seam. His eyes were swimming out of reach. "Eh? Dear-dearest-darl-darling-darling love-*love*-LOVE?" All the new words still stiff in her mouth, that she had heard so far only from the mouths of actors.
>
> (196)

At moments like these White reveals how deeply he has absorbed the lessons of Modernist writers: the struggle of the conscious mind to order its repressed desires into coherence finds expression in a narrative of rigorous delimitations and displacements that has its antecedents in Joyce and Stein. It is fitting that **"Five-Twenty"** ends, as it began, with paralysis and suspended judgements because the text describes a closed circle within which characters are doomed to repeat the same experiences into a nameless future.

Lives in this twilight world are dominated by repetition and compulsion; they move in the same narrow groove as the "rubber tyred wheels" (179) of Royal's wheelchair. The only escape from repression is fantasy; but fantasy brings with it self-consciousness and the terrifying knowledge of existential isolation. Interviewed in 1973, at a time when the stories collected in ***The Cockatoos*** were being written, White declared that "everything I write has to be dredged up from the unconscious—which is what makes it such an exhausting and perhaps finally, destructive process. . . . My first draft of a novel is the work of intuition and it is a chaos nobody but myself could resolve".[2] His achievement in **"Five-Twenty"** is to discover, in the tortured figure of Ella Natwick, a character who conveys the destructive force of the unconscious unable to translate its desires into expressive form, as she waits for a vision of transcendence beside a pot of communion coffee that is never served.

Notes

1. Patrick White, *The Cockatoos* (London: Jonathan Cape, 1974), 99. All further page references refer to this edition of White's text.
2. Thelma Herring and G A Wilkes, "A Conversation with Patrick White", *Southerly* 33, (2) 1973, 139.

FURTHER READING

Criticism

Barnes, John. "New Tracks to Travel: The Stories of White, Porter, and Cowan." *Meanjin Quarterly.* XXV, No. 2 (June 1966): 154-70.

Compares the short stories written by Australian writers Patrick White, Hal Porter, and Peter Cowan.

Bliss, Carolyn. "Transpositions: Patrick White's Most Recent Fiction." *Westerly* 34, No. 3 (September 1989): 77-82.

Discusses White's short story collection, *Three Uneasy Pieces,* as well as some of the author's other works.

Brissenden, R. F.. *Patrick White,*London: Longmans, Green & Co. LTD, 1966, pp.3-49.

Explores White's background and development as a writer.

Gowda, H. H. Anniah. "R. K. Narayan and Patrick White as Short-Story Tellers," in *R. K. Narayan: Critical Perspectives*. New Delhi: Sterling Publishers Private Limited, 1994, pp. 53–65.

Explicates the stylistic and thematic differences between short stories written by Narayan and White.

Additional coverage of White's life and career is contained in the following sources published by the Gale Group: *Contemporary Literary Criticism,* Vols. 3-5, 7, 9, 18, 65, 69; *Contemporary Authors,* Vols. 81-84, 132; *Contemporary Authors New Revision Series,* Vol. 43; and *Major 20th-Century Writers,* Vol. 1.

How to Use This Index

The main references

Calvino, Italo 1923-1985 .... **CLC 5, 8, 11, 22, 33, 39, 73; SSC 3**

list all author entries in the following Gale Literary Criticism series:

BLC = *Black Literature Criticism*
CLC = *Contemporary Literary Criticism*
CLR = *Children's Literature Review*
CMLC = *Classical and Medieval Literature Criticism*
DA = *DISCovering Authors*
DAB = *DISCovering Authors: British*
DAC = *DISCovering Authors: Canadian*
DAM = *DISCovering Authors: Modules*
DRAM: *Dramatists Module;* ***MST:*** *Most-Studied Authors Module;*
MULT: *Multicultural Authors Module;* ***NOV:*** *Novelists Module;*
POET: *Poets Module;* ***POP:*** *Popular Fiction and Genre Authors Module*
DC = *Drama Criticism*
HLC = *Hispanic Literature Criticism*
LC = *Literature Criticism from 1400 to 1800*
NNAL = *Native North American Literature*
NCLC = *Nineteenth-Century Literature Criticism*
PC = *Poetry Criticism*
SSC = *Short Story Criticism*
TCLC = *Twentieth-Century Literary Criticism*
WLC = *World Literature Criticism, 1500 to the Present*

The cross-references

See also CANR 23; CA 85-88; obituary CA116

list all author entries in the following Gale biographical and literary sources:

AAYA = *Authors & Artists for Young Adults*
AITN = *Authors in the News*
BEST = *Bestsellers*
BW = *Black Writers*
CA = *Contemporary Authors*
CAAS = *Contemporary Authors Autobiography Series*
CABS = *Contemporary Authors Bibliographical Series*
CANR = *Contemporary Authors New Revision Series*
CAP = *Contemporary Authors Permanent Series*
CDALB = *Concise Dictionary of American Literary Biography*
CDBLB = *Concise Dictionary of British Literary Biography*
DLB = *Dictionary of Literary Biography*
DLBD = *Dictionary of Literary Biography Documentary Series*
DLBY = *Dictionary of Literary Biography Yearbook*
HW = *Hispanic Writers*
JRDA = *Junior DISCovering Authors*
MAICYA = *Major Authors and Illustrators for Children and Young Adults*
MTCW = *Major 20th-Century Writers*
SAAS = *Something about the Author Autobiography Series*
SATA = *Something about the Author*
YABC = *Yesterday's Authors of Books for Children*

Literary Criticism Series Cumulative Author Index

Author Index

Author Index

Author Index

SSC Cumulative Nationality Index

SSC Cumulative Title Index

Title Index

Title Index

Title Index

Title Index

Title Index

Title Index

Title Index

Title Index

Title Index

Title Index

Title Index

Title Index

Title Index

Title Index

Title Index

Title Index

Title Index

Title Index

Title Index

Title Index

ISBN 0-7876-3275-9
9 780787 632754
90000